Section One
Introduction

I Overview

1   Few causes promoted by the United Nations have generated more intense and widespread support than the campaign to promote and protect the equal rights of women. Fifty years after the Charter of the United Nations became the first international agreement to proclaim gender equality as a fundamental human right, the Organization has helped create a historic legacy of internationally agreed strategies, standards, programmes and goals to advance the status of women worldwide.

2   Then as now, the Charter pointed the way, affirming the equal rights of men and women and declaring that the work of the Organization must be conducted without distinction as to race, sex, language or religion.[1] But the Charter's words are not self-enforcing. Decades of struggle were needed to elevate the human rights of women to a prominent place on the international agenda. Beginning with the codification of women's legal and civil rights, the campaign for the advancement of women has stirred widespread recognition of their indispensable role in addressing the critical issues facing the world in the late twentieth century: poverty; unemployment; social disintegration; unchecked population growth; human rights abuses; environmental degradation; militarism. Throughout this process, the United Nations has played a unique role: as a catalyst for change, as a global standard setter for the eradication of gender discrimination; as a forum for debate; and as an unparalleled source of balanced, comprehensive data on the status of women worldwide.

1/ Document 1
See page 103

3   Although the international women's movement began at the grass-roots level many years before the founding of the United Nations, the Organization moved quickly to affirm that the advancement of women was central to its work. Half a century later, four progressive phases are discernible in the evolution of these efforts.

4   In the first period, from 1945 to 1962, the United Nations worked to secure women's legal equality. The United Nations was born at a time when women in most regions faced numerous obstacles in law and in fact. These included inequalities in laws and customs concerning marriage and the family. In education, they were denied the same opportunities as men and boys. Entering the workforce in rapidly growing numbers, they found barriers in both employment and pay. In politics, women were often denied the right to vote, to hold office or otherwise to participate in political life.

5   Stirred by the determined efforts of Member States' female delegates and by the collective energy of non-governmental organiza-

tions (NGOs), the United Nations moved to address these symptoms of discrimination on a worldwide basis. With the creation of the Commission on Human Rights and the Commission on the Status of Women in 1946, and the adoption of the Universal Declaration of Human Rights in 1948, the Organization began its work on behalf of women with a drive to establish the legal basis for the promotion of their equal rights.[2]

2/ Document 6
See page 112;
Document 14
See page 125

6   But this was no simple task. It was one thing to reaffirm the Charter's mandate to uphold faith in fundamental human rights, in the dignity and worth of all people and in the equal rights of men and women. It was quite another to put these principles into practice on a universal scale.

7   The Commission on the Status of Women recognized that the process of codifying the legal rights of women had to begin with factual information about the extent to which discrimination against women existed in law and in practice. The United Nations thus embarked on a vast research and polling effort to assess the status of women worldwide.

8   Subsequent United Nations fact-finding efforts produced a detailed, country-by-country picture of the political and legal status of women, cataloguing the gains and identifying the remaining obstacles. Over time, these findings became the basis for global standards that were incorporated into international law through a series of treaties and conventions. In drafting these human rights instruments, close working relationships began to develop between the Commission on the Status of Women and other United Nations bodies such as the International Labour Organization (ILO) and the United Nations Educational, Scientific and Cultural Organization (UNESCO), as well as other intergovernmental organizations such as the Inter-American Commission of Women. At the national level, Governments were asked to develop laws and programmes to deal with such imperatives as women's political and legal rights; women's access to education and training; women's employment; and combating violence against women.

9   During the second period, from 1963 to 1975, more and more Governments responded to the United Nations by adopting laws and programmes to protect women's rights. Impetus for this came in 1967 when the General Assembly adopted the Declaration on the Elimination of Discrimination against Women.[3] The Organization's focus broadened from codification of equality of rights under the law to encompass the economic and social realities of women's daily lives. Such matters as policy formulation, attitude change, political commitment and institution-building came to the forefront, particularly as they affected women in developing countries. Recognition grew among the international community that development was essential if women were to achieve equal-

3/ Document 36
See page 175

ity, and the United Nations increasingly structured its development assistance programmes to meet this challenge.

10   The campaign for women's advancement gathered momentum with the proclamation of 1975 as International Women's Year and the convening, that same year, of the first major conference on the status of women. Held in Mexico City, the World Conference of the International Women's Year helped mobilize women around the world, expanded the working relationship between the United Nations and NGOs and led to the elucidation of a three-part theme—equality, development and peace—which became the basis for the Organization's work for women in the years to follow.[4]

11   The third phase, from 1976 to 1985, coincided with the United Nations Decade for Women, a period which saw the international community undergo an important transformation in its understanding of the role of women. Whereas previous thinking had regarded women almost exclusively in terms of their development needs, the Decade augmented and updated this viewpoint by recognizing women as essential contributors to the entire development process. This new awareness was borne out by statistics collected and published by the United Nations which dramatized the fact that women's equality and rights, far from being isolated issues, were important factors in the well-being of societies everywhere. The undervaluation of women was identified as both a cause and an effect of underdevelopment, closely linked to such global problems as poverty, overpopulation, illiteracy, food shortages, malnutrition and poor health conditions.

12   The impact of these findings—and of the global consciousness-raising that the Decade helped promote—cannot be overestimated. One direct result was an increased momentum towards the adoption by the General Assembly of a landmark treaty in the struggle for women's rights: the 1979 Convention on the Elimination of All Forms of Discrimination against Women, which constitutes an international bill of human rights for women.[5] The Decade also generated a series of action programmes that recognized the importance of women's role in development and the need to expand United Nations assistance to women in developing countries. And it energized global efforts to promote the equality of men and women; to acknowledge women's contributions to development at all levels; and to recognize their role in charting a route to disarmament and lasting peace.

13   Another watershed was reached in 1985 with a world conference on women in Nairobi, held to mark the end of the Decade for Women and assess its achievements. As in Mexico City in 1975 and again in Copenhagen in 1980, women from widely varying political and cultural backgrounds gathered to review progress made in their struggle for advancement. Delegates at Nairobi adopted the Nairobi Forward-

4/ Document 45
See page 187

5/ Document 69
See page 244

6/ Document 84
See page 310

looking Strategies for the Advancement of Women to the Year 2000, a blueprint for women's future in all realms of life and another milestone on the path to equality.[6]

14   In the fourth and current phase, from 1986 to the present, the work of the United Nations for women's rights has been closely tied to the dramatic changes that have occurred in world affairs. The post-cold-war era has allowed the Organization to redouble its efforts in many areas of long-standing concern, among them the advancement of the status of women. United Nations institutions and mechanisms have been strengthened, and support for women has been woven into the mainstream efforts of all the Organization's agencies and bodies.

15   Within this new climate, a continuum of United Nations conferences and summit meetings has served as a cohesive vehicle through which the international community has been able to address the advancement of women across a broad yet interlocking spectrum of issues and concerns. The 1990 World Summit for Children set goals for health, education and nutrition for women and their children. The 1992 Earth Summit called for the full integration of women in the task of solving environmental problems and promoting sustainable development. The 1993 World Conference on Human Rights affirmed women's rights as a central element in the overall global human rights agenda, and stressed the importance of confronting the specific problem of violence against women. The 1994 International Conference on Population and Development produced agreement on the connection between demographic issues and the advancement of women through education, health and nutrition. The 1995 World Summit for Social Development synthesized these achievements, recognizing the pivotal role of women in eradicating poverty and mending the social fabric. It was followed six months later, by the Fourth World Conference on Women, which set a new global agenda for achieving gender equality. The preparatory work for the final conference in the series, the 1996 United Nations Conference on Human Settlements (Habitat II), has stressed that women's expertise, needs and perspective should form an integral part of policy formulation on housing and the development of settlements in both rural and urban areas.

16   But for women, the culmination of these international efforts was undeniably the 1995 Fourth World Conference on Women and parallel NGO Forum. The largest conference in the history of the United Nations, the meeting unanimously adopted a new global blueprint for women's empowerment, spelt out in a five-year Platform for Action and a Beijing Declaration.

17   All of these events have focused the world's attention on a central organizing principle of the work of the United Nations: that no enduring solution to society's most threatening social, economic and

political problems can be found without the full participation, and the full empowerment, of the world's women. Thanks to the efforts of the United Nations, the encouragement of Governments and the tireless work of NGOs, public acceptance and awareness of the rights of women have never been so widespread. Millions of women, especially in developing countries and newly independent States, have begun moving towards self-realization and self-sufficiency.

18   Nevertheless, much remains to be done. The world's 2.8 billion women remain humanity's largest marginalized group. Women outnumber men in the one fifth of humanity living in absolute poverty. In developed and developing countries alike, they suffer a disproportionate share of the effects of social disintegration, unemployment, environmental degradation and war. And in many countries there is a vast gap between women's rights on paper, according to law and policy, and their actual experience.

19   This Introduction traces the history of the United Nations campaign to confront these problems and to promote and attain the advancement of women. Part II chronicles the Organization's early efforts to secure the legal foundations of women's rights, a process that began with the creation of institutions and mechanisms to ensure that women's issues remained prominent on the global human rights agenda. Part III examines the next stage of the Organization's work, which began with recognition of the indispensable role of women in development and of the chasm between the existence of women's rights in law and the exercise of those rights in fact. Parts IV and V examine how the years of codification and implementation have given way to an era of new and more complex challenges, in which the political and economic empowerment of women is seen increasingly as the key not only to ending gender discrimination, but to eradicating poverty, enhancing productive employment, ending social disintegration and building just and democratic societies. Part VI presents some concluding remarks on the strategies and issues that will figure most prominently in the Organization's next half-century of work in improving opportunities for women and eliminating gender-based discrimination once and for all.

20   The collection of documents reproduced on pages 103-823 in Section Two represents a selection of the many thousands of documents on women published by the United Nations which form a comprehensive record of the involvement of the Organization in the campaign to promote women's rights. Included are the complete texts of the major conventions, treaties and declarations, selected resolutions of the General Assembly and other United Nations bodies, reports and other relevant material.

II   Securing the legal foundations of equality, 1945-1962

21   The long, devastating Second World War saw numerous barriers to women fall as a natural consequence of the war effort. In many countries, men and women worked, fought and suffered together as equals. Many hoped the end of the conflict would yield a peacetime world energized by the same spirit, a world in which women could enjoy the same freedoms and status as men. Within months, the framers of the United Nations Charter, prodded by women's groups and delegates, succeeded in weaving this vision into the fabric of the Organization's founding document.

22   The United Nations involvement in women's issues marked the beginning of a historic change in political discourse, in which issues once thought of as strictly private, domestic matters steeped in custom and tradition—such as the status of women as wives, home-makers and mothers—would come to be openly debated in a global context. It triggered the first phase of the Organization's activities on behalf of women: the codification in law of women's rights and the collection of data documenting the situation of women in many parts of the world. Such surveys were a vital first step in the central United Nations goal of setting standards for the international community.

23   Early United Nations surveys showed that discrimination against women was prevalent in nearly every region of the world. In most societies, women were not free to do such things as attend the same schools as men, own property or receive equal pay for equal work. Discrimination in political and civil life was particularly widespread. In 1945, only 30 of the original 51 United Nations Member States allowed women equal voting rights with men or permitted them to hold public office. Just a handful of women were involved in the founding of the United Nations.

24   The United Nations built upon the early work of other intergovernmental bodies, establishing international treaties and acting as a catalyst for the promotion of laws asserting the equal rights of women. These efforts required the creation of new institutional capabilities, including the creation of the United Nations Commission on the Status of Women. The Commission helped ensure that provisions on women's equality were included in the Universal Declaration of Human Rights, adopted by the General Assembly in 1948, and used the principles of the Declaration as the basis for its work.[7] The early years of United Nations support for women focused upon establishing women's legal equality in

7/ Document 14

See page 125

such areas as political participation, work, education, nationality and marriage.

Building momentum for women's rights

25   International efforts to address problems involving the status of women began at the turn of the century, as the women's suffrage movement—whose roots went back to the 1860s—gathered momentum. In 1902, Governments meeting in The Hague, the Netherlands, adopted a series of conventions aimed at setting international standards for marriage, divorce and the custody of minor children. Soon after, comparable measures were adopted concerning the abolition of trafficking in women and children.

26   Much of the conceptual groundwork for the Charter's language on women's rights grew out of the pioneering efforts of the Pan American Union (the precursor to the Organization of American States) and the League of Nations. Meeting in 1923 in Santiago, the Pan American Union agreed to address the question of how to eliminate legal and constitutional impediments to the exercise of women's political and civil rights. By 1928, delegates gathered in Havana had decided to create the Inter-American Commission of Women, whose mandate was to examine the status of women in Latin America as a first step towards achieving equality for women in civil and political fields. The Inter-American Commission's work led to the adoption, in 1933, of the Montevideo Convention on the Nationality of Married Women, the first international treaty to proclaim the equality of the sexes in regard to nationality.

27   In 1935, the League of Nations endorsed the Montevideo Convention on the Nationality of Married Women as worthy of ratification by all of its members. The League took several other steps on behalf of women, beginning with the adoption of its Covenant on 28 April 1919, which declared that member countries should work to guarantee fair and humane working conditions for men, women and children, and to discourage trafficking in women and children. It also decreed that membership in the League Secretariat would be open to women.

28   The issue of trafficking in women—a central focus of antislavery efforts early in the century—was also a concern of the League of Nations. The League's work helped prepare the way for the United Nations General Assembly's adoption of a treaty outlawing exploitation of prostitution. This agreement, the 1949 Convention for the Suppression of the Traffic in Persons and of the Exploitation of the Prostitution of Others, was approved by the General Assembly on 2 December 1949 and came into force on 25 July 1951.[8] It helped establish the principle

8/ Document 18
See page 130

that to countenance the treatment of women as commodities—dehumanized objects that could be bought and sold—helped perpetuate women's low status in many societies.

29   Pressed by non-governmental organizations and female delegates, the League began a survey of the state of women's rights as a preparatory step in drawing up new international agreements. Information was gathered on matters such as voting rights, administration of property and earnings, guardianship of children and the right to work. The data revealed wide differences among countries.

30   In 1937, the League undertook a more ambitious project: a study of the legal status of women worldwide. The study, aimed at assessing the effects of public, private and penal law, was to be carried out by several scientific institutions and overseen by an expert committee empowered to consult regularly with women's groups. However, shortly after one of the three sections was completed—on the status of women under private law—the Second World War erupted in Europe. The survey was never completed.

The Charter of the United Nations

9/ Document 1
See page 103

31   The Charter of the United Nations, signed on 26 June 1945, set out three main goals for the new Organization: to prevent future wars by fostering peace and security; to promote social and economic progress; and to define and protect the rights and freedoms of every human being regardless of race, sex, language or religion.[9] The Preamble begins: "We the peoples of the United Nations", and reaffirms not only "faith in fundamental human rights" and the "dignity and worth of the human person", but also "the equal rights of men and women". The equality of rights is also explicitly asserted in three Articles of the Charter.

32   Earlier drafts of the Charter did not start out that way. The passages outlawing discrimination on the basis of sex were introduced later, at the insistence of women delegates and representatives of the 42 NGOs accredited to the founding Conference.

33   For the women present at the birth of the United Nations, the Charter's provisions on women's equality offered a clear and compelling basis for the assertion of international law to advance the political and legal status of women. Although international and intergovernmental bodies had begun working to advance the status of women long before 1945, no previous legal document had so forcefully affirmed the equality of all human beings, or specifically outlawed sex as a basis for discrimination.

The first General Assembly convenes

34　In 1946, during the inaugural meetings of the United Nations General Assembly in London, the issue of women's rights reappeared as a prominent item on the international agenda for the first time since the beginning of the Second World War. Mrs. Eleanor Roosevelt, a United Nations delegate representing the United States of America, appeared before the General Assembly and read an open letter addressed to "the women of the world" that she and 16 other women attending the session had prepared.[10]

10/ Document 2
See page 103

35　The open letter, dated 12 February 1946, hailed the coming of peace to a democratic world—and the vital role that women had played in making victory possible. "This new chance for peace", the letter pointed out, "was won through the joint efforts of men and women working for the common ideals of human freedom at a time when need for united effort broke down barriers of race, creed and sex". The five-paragraph letter expressed the hope that women's involvement in the United Nations "may grow and may increase in insight and skill". It called on Governments "to encourage women everywhere to take a more active part in national and international affairs". Several delegations spoke strongly in support of these views, urging that the Organization bring more women into its work.[11]

11/ Document 2
See page 103

36　The founding delegates were well aware that shaping a postwar world dedicated to the ideals of the Charter of the United Nations would take far more than good intentions. For one thing, the United Nations bodies dedicated to ensuring equality of rights for men and women had to work within the context of Article 2, paragraph 7, of the Charter, which affirms that the Organization has no authority to intervene in matters that are essentially within the domestic jurisdiction of any State. There was a widespread opinion in the early years of the United Nations that this principle extended to the question of human rights.

37　Moreover, it was clear that years of preparatory work would be needed to pave the way for the international instruments that would be necessary to promote equality of rights between men and women. The international community had to agree on a definition of these rights and on what was necessary to ensure that they were enjoyed by everyone. This would require comprehensive surveys and studies of the extent to which women were discriminated against in law and in practice. Fact-finding and standard-setting thus became the main preoccupations of the United Nations in its early efforts to secure the legal foundations of women's equality.

Subcommission on the Status of Women

38　The Charter of the United Nations specified that the Economic and Social Council—one of the six main organs of the United Nations—

should have responsibility for promoting human rights, including women's rights. The Council was authorized to establish commissions in economic and social fields and for the promotion of human rights. Its chief operational arm in this field is the Commission on Human Rights, which was established in February 1946 under Article 68 of the Charter. The first seven members appointed to the projected 18-member body consisted of six men and Mrs. Roosevelt as Chair.[12]

12/ Document 3
See page 109

39   After considerable debate, the Council concluded that the Commission on Human Rights would require "special advice" on problems relating to the status of women, and that this would necessitate creating a special body.[13] Many female delegates and representatives of non-governmental organizations had strongly advocated that the United Nations establish a body specifically dedicated to women's issues. They did this not because they viewed women's rights as somehow distinct from human rights, but out of concern that the Commission on Human Rights would be so preoccupied with carrying out its other mandates that eliminating discrimination against women would not be a priority.

13/ Document 3
See page 109

40   In February 1946, the Council voted to create the Subcommission on the Status of Women, a separate, subsidiary body to the Commission on Human Rights. The Subcommission's overall mandate, the Council said, would be to "submit proposals, recommendations and reports to the Commission on Human Rights regarding the status of women".[14]

14/ Document 3
See page 109

41   The first seven members of the Subcommission were women, but three persons were to be appointed *ex officio* to ensure that it was not composed of women only.[15] The Subcommission first met from 29 April to 13 May 1946 at the Bronx campus of Hunter College in New York (now Lehman College) to draw up a programme of work. The recommendations made by the Subcommission to the Council included proposals for a United Nations women's conference to discuss the aims of the Subcommission; a worldwide survey of laws affecting women; the compilation of records on matters pertaining to women; polling efforts to sound out public opinion; a forum to hear the views of experts; and the launching of a worldwide campaign to inform the public about women's issues with the help of the United Nations Department of Public Information.[16]

15/ Document 3
See page 109;
Document 4
See page 110

16/ Document 5
See page 111

42   The Subcommission decided it was especially important that improvements for women be brought about in the political, civil, education, social and economic fields, and that these would be addressed simultaneously in cooperation with organizations affiliated with the United Nations, such as the United Nations Educational, Scientific and Cultural Organization (UNESCO) and the International Labour Organization (ILO). The Subcommission also proposed a universal survey of laws pertaining to the status of women. A comparable survey by the League of Nations was considered outdated and somewhat limited in

scope. More importantly, the League study had dealt with laws only, and had not investigated their application.[17]

43   The Subcommission had a broad mandate, but it was not nearly as daunting as that of the Commission on Human Rights, to which it reported. Among other things, the Commission on Human Rights had been asked by the Economic and Social Council to begin working on an international bill of rights; to prepare proposals for treaties concerning such issues as civil liberties, the status of women and freedom of information; and to begin working to halt discrimination on grounds of race, sex, language or religion.

44   The Subcommission Chair told the Council at its second session in May 1946 that she and her colleagues understood why the Subcommission had been placed "under the wing" of the Commission on Human Rights. But she said they felt strongly that the Subcommission should not "be dependent on another commission". The ideal solution, she said, would be to make the Subcommission a fully fledged commission, a counterpart of the Commission on Human Rights.[18]

Commission on the Status of Women

45   The Economic and Social Council agreed to establish a separate commission, and on 21 June 1946 the four-month-old Subcommission on the Status of Women was abolished and replaced by the Commission on the Status of Women.[19] The new Commission was to report directly to the Economic and Social Council and through the Council to the General Assembly. The Commission, which began with 15 members, grew in several stages to its current size of 45 members. Its membership increased as the number of United Nations Member States swelled, with the allocation of seats based on a formula designed to ensure balanced geographical representation. Its members are appointed by Governments.

46   In its June 1946 resolution, the Council determined that the Commission on the Status of Women would have two basic functions: to "prepare recommendations and reports to the Economic and Social Council on promoting women's rights in political, economic, civil, social and educational fields", and to make recommendations "on urgent problems requiring immediate attention in the field of women's rights".[20] The Commission's mandate remained essentially the same, until it was expanded, in 1987, to include such activities as the advocacy of equality, development and peace; monitoring the implementation of internationally agreed measures for the advancement of women; and reviewing and appraising progress at the national, subregional, regional, sectoral and global levels.[21]

47   The Commission on the Status of Women had its inaugural meeting from 10 to 24 February 1947 at Lake Success, New York. It decided to work "to raise the status of women, irrespective of national-

17/ Document 5
See page 111

18/ Document 5
See page 111

19/ Document 6
See page 112

20/ Document 6
See page 112

21/ Document 89
See page 372

ity, race, language or religion", to promote "equality with men in all fields of human enterprise, and to eliminate all discrimination against women in the provisions of statutory law, in legal maxims or rules, or in interpretations of customary law".[22]

22/ Document 8
See page 113

48   "Freedom and equality are essential to human development", the Commission declared in its 1947 statement of principles, and "since woman is as much a human being as man, she is entitled to share these attributes with him". Beyond that, the Commission maintained, "woman has . . . a definite role to play in the building of a free, healthy, prosperous and moral society, and she can fulfil that obligation only as a free and responsible member".

49   At that first meeting a consensus emerged that the Commission needed to be involved in all United Nations discussions of issues relevant to women. In particular, it was recognized as vital that the Commission have a voice in upcoming discussions on the international bill of rights.[23] The importance of this request was not lost on the Economic and Social Council, and it formalized arrangements for the Commission on the Status of Women to be represented in deliberations by other United Nations bodies, beginning with the Commission on Human Rights meetings on the international bill of human rights.[24] Comparable arrangements were made for the Commission to be represented during relevant deliberations of the Subcommission on Prevention of Discrimination and Protection of Minorities, an arm of the Commission on Human Rights. Despite some initial resistance, the Commission on the Status of Women also won agreement from the Council to be allowed to hold annual sessions, like the Commission on Human Rights.

23/ Document 8
See page 113

24/ Document 9
See page 120

50   At their first sessions in 1947, both the Commission on the Status of Women and the Commission on Human Rights considered the sensitive issue of how to deal with allegations of rights violations reported by individuals, groups and NGOs. The Economic and Social Council eventually resolved, in August 1947, that although the commissions were free to review such complaints in private, they had no power to take any action.[25] The Commission on the Status of Women was never given the mandate to investigate individual claims of rights violations, a power later granted to the Commission on Human Rights by the Council and by parties to the Optional Protocol to the International Covenant on Civil and Political Rights. The Commission on the Status of Women did not have the power to investigate specific cases of discrimination, nor was it authorized to take measures to ensure compliance with United Nations standards. Instead, it has served to set standards of women's rights, supported educational efforts, encouraged Governments to bring laws into conformity with international conventions and fostered global awareness of women's rights and the obstacles women face.

25/ Document 10
See page 122

51   The institutional capabilities of the Commission on the Status of Women were augmented by various bodies in the United Nations system as well as by collaboration with NGOs. Close working relationships developed between the Commission and such United Nations bodies as the Social Commission, later known as the Commission for Social Development, and the Trusteeship Council; United Nations agencies such as the ILO, UNESCO, the World Health Organization (WHO) and the Food and Agriculture Organization of the United Nations (FAO); and various non-governmental and intergovernmental organizations, such as the Inter-American Commission of Women.

Secretariat institutions

52   The work of the Commission on the Status of Women was supported by a unit within the United Nations Secretariat dealing with the status of women. The role of the Secretariat was crucial because of its many responsibilities, which included preparing reports, providing services for meetings and conferences, helping to formulate policy, creating follow-up mechanisms and shepherding budgets through the approval process.

53   A Section on the Status of Women was set up in 1946 within the Human Rights Division of the United Nations Department of Social Affairs. Staff of the Section played a key role in advising and supporting members of the Commission on the Status of Women.

54   Despite a number of organizational moves over the years, overall management of the Secretariat apparatus for women remained part of the Human Rights Division until 1972, when the first woman appointed to the post of Assistant Secretary-General was made head of the newly created Centre for Social Development and Humanitarian Affairs, which included responsibility for women's affairs. At the same time, the Section on the Status of Women was upgraded to a Branch within the Centre; it was called the Branch for the Promotion of Equality of Men and Women. After 1978, it was renamed the Branch for the Advancement of Women, and in 1988 it was further upgraded to a Division.

Universal Declaration of Human Rights

55   The Commission on the Status of Women helped shape the language of the Universal Declaration of Human Rights, and used the principles of the Declaration as the basis for its agenda. The adoption by the United Nations General Assembly of the Universal Declaration of Human Rights—the first of three components in the International Bill of Human Rights—at a meeting in Paris on 10 December 1948, was at

26/ Document 14
See page 125

once a triumph and a defining moment for the Commission on the Status of Women.[26] During the drafting process, the Commission had successfully sought to include language that explicitly set forth the equality of women. Commission members also argued against the inclusion of what they saw as gender-insensitive language, such as references to "men" as a synonym for humanity and phrases like "all men are brothers". Many of these references were eventually changed after the Commission on the Status of Women offered substitute drafts.[27]

27/ Document 12
See page 123

56   Later the Commission used the Declaration as a basis for action to promote the cause of equal rights and freedoms. For example, article 16 of the Declaration, which specifies that men and women have "equal rights as to marriage, during marriage and at its dissolution", became the basis for a detailed study, conducted by the Secretariat at the Commission's request, of discriminatory practices pertaining to marriage.

57   The Declaration, elaborating on the principles set out three years earlier in the Charter, proclaims that all human rights and freedoms are to be enjoyed equally by women and men "without distinction of any kind, such as race, colour, sex, language, religion, political or other opinion, national or social origin, property, birth or other status".[28] The Declaration adds that "no distinction shall be made on the basis of the political, jurisdictional or international status of the country or territory to which a person belongs, whether it be independent, trust, non-self-governing or under any other limitation of sovereignty". The Declaration offered what the General Assembly called "a common standard of achievement for all peoples and all nations".

28/ Document 14
See page 125

29/ Document 35
See page 174

58   It would take nearly two decades to complete the other components of the bill of rights: the International Covenant on Civil and Political Rights and the International Covenant on Economic, Social and Cultural Rights.[29] These Covenants, which came into force in 1976, provide the ethical and legal basis for the human rights work of the United Nations. Like the Declaration, both Covenants include provisions specifying that the rights therein apply equally to men and women. This emphasis was added after the Commission on the Status of Women presented the Commission on Human Rights with suggested amendments to the drafts of the Covenants.

Fact-finding

59   The Economic and Social Council advised the Commission on the Status of Women that if it was going to frame proposals for action speedily, it needed to devise a concrete future programme of work. It was agreed that a first step was to adopt the proposal, which had been made by the Chair of the Subcommission on the Status of Women, to

conduct a global survey of the status of women's rights. In effect, the Commission took up where the League of Nations had left off nearly a decade before. The survey would focus on the extent to which law and custom were blocking women's political, civil, social and economic rights and educational opportunities.

60   At its first session in 1947, the Commission on the Status of Women recommended to the Economic and Social Council that Governments assist the Secretariat in the survey by completing annually a form known as the Questionnaire on the Legal Status and Treatment of Women. The responses received, subsequently presented in regular reports by the Secretary-General and by other offices of the Secretariat, offered an unprecedented wealth of detailed information on the status of women in nearly every region of the world. The success of the questionnaire approach ensured its future use as a tool in surveys on women's issues.

61   One of the first such Secretariat reports, dated 16 December 1947, revealed that of 74 sovereign States responding, 25 had not granted full political rights to their female citizens, including the right to vote or hold public office. The report also concluded that in countries where women were denied equal access to educational opportunities these practices were most often based on custom and religion, not legislation. Subsequent reports over the next two years offered compelling evidence that illiteracy was more widespread among women worldwide than men. It also found correlations between the inadequacy of women's education and each country's economic status. And in 1949 and 1950, a series of Secretariat memoranda and analyses from 60 countries throughout the world documented the existence of numerous conflicts among nationality laws pertaining to married women.

62   These and many other reports, compiled by the Secretariat from questionnaire responses by Governments and NGOs, as well as private research, were used as the factual underpinning for resolutions of the Commission on the Status of Women which highlighted inequalities in law and requested Governments to change discriminatory legislation. Subsequently, they were also used as justification for drafting international treaties on the equal rights of men and women in a number of areas, including political rights.

Forging a political rights convention

63   The Convention on the Political Rights of Women, adopted by the General Assembly in 1952, is the first instrument of international law aimed at recognizing and protecting the political rights of women

30/ Document 26
See page 164

everywhere.[30] It provides that women, on an equal basis with men, are entitled to vote in any election, run for election to any office, and hold any public office or exercise any public function under national law.

64   The General Assembly helped to generate momentum for this treaty beginning on 11 December 1946, when it unanimously adopted a resolution recommending that Member States that had not yet done so should "fulfil the purposes and aims of the Charter" by "granting to women the same political rights as to men".[31] The Assembly's action was inspired by reports on the extent to which women were denied political rights, compiled from responses to questionnaires circulated by the Secretariat. At its 1948 session, the Economic and Social Council called upon the Secretary-General to update the survey each year until the point was reached at which all women were accorded the same political rights as men.

31/ Document 7
See page 113

65   At its third session, held in Beirut from 21 March to 4 April 1949, the Commission on the Status of Women discussed the approval, by the Organization of American States in May 1948, of the Inter-American Convention on the Granting of Political Rights to Women. The Commission asked the Secretary-General to examine the possibility of a convention sponsored by the United Nations. The Secretary-General reported back in 1950 that there were no technical barriers to a treaty guaranteeing the political rights of women. More importantly, he concluded that a convention would accomplish two goals: it would help enfranchise women who had not yet won the right to vote and it would prevent the disenfranchisement of women who already had it.[32] Data published by the Secretariat that year showed that in 22 countries women still did not have equal rights to vote or hold political office. And in some countries women had never voted or held political office, even though there were no laws denying those rights.[33] These reports convinced the Commission on the Status of Women that the time was right for a convention guaranteeing the political rights of women.

32/ Document 21
See page 141

33/ Document 19
See page 134

66   However, many States opposed parts of the Convention drafted by the Commission, especially the provisions of article III, which provides that women may hold public office and exercise all public functions established by national law. After an extended debate, the Convention was adopted by the General Assembly on 20 December 1952 by 46 votes in favour and none against, with 11 abstentions. It came into force on 7 July 1954. But in ratifying the Convention, more than 40 States parties said they would reserve the right not to abide by some provisions. The outcome illuminated the resistance yet to be overcome to women's legal equality.

67   Even in States that did not deny women their political rights, women were still far from exercising them on a uniformly equal basis with men. The Commission on the Status of Women thus increased its

efforts to develop civic and political education programmes and other measures to encourage women to take an active part in public life.

Equality in work and education

68   In the late 1940s, the Commission on the Status of Women began its first collaborative study with the International Labour Organization on women's economic rights, including employment and pay. It suggested ways to build on the right-to-work provisions of article 23 of the Universal Declaration of Human Rights, which specified that "everyone, without any discrimination, has the right to equal pay for equal work".[34] The Commission on the Status of Women offered numerous recommendations to the ILO on the subject.

34/ Document 14
See page 125

69   On 10 March 1948, the Economic and Social Council formally approved the principle of equal remuneration for work of equal value, and called on Member States to implement it "in every way, irrespective of nationality, race, language and religion".[35] The following year, on 18 February 1949, the Economic and Social Council endorsed the ILO's work with the Commission on the Status of Women, and invited the organization to present a report on how best to promote the principle.[36] In 1951, the ILO, responding to recommendations by the Commission, approved the 1951 Convention on Equal Remuneration, which enshrined the principle and practice of equal pay for work of equal value.

35/ Document 13
See page 125

36/ Document 15
See page 128

70   The Commission and UNESCO collaborated on developing programmes of basic education without distinction as to sex, race or creed. Driven by article 26 of the Universal Declaration, on the right of all people to education, UNESCO reported to the Commission in 1950 on the extent to which women were discriminated against in education.[37] This comprehensive review formed much of the basis of the Commission's later recommendations on the importance of education to women's advancement. These recommendations included efforts to convince Governments to move decisively to deal with the problem of illiteracy among women, starting with programmes to provide girls and women with educational opportunities equal to those of boys and men.

37/ Document 22
See page 145

Legal issues for married women

71   The question of women's rights of nationality in marriage was a major focus of the Commission on the Status of Women from its first session in 1947 onward.[38] The 1948 Universal Declaration of Human Rights had affirmed every individual's right to a nationality and marked

38/ Document 17
See page 129

39/ Document 14
See page 125;
Document 17
See page 129

a path for the Commission's efforts to set a legal standard to protect that right for all women.[39]

72   Reports of the Secretary-General, using questionnaires and other survey data from various Governments, revealed that discrimination against women was frequently a consequence of conflicts between laws relating to nationality, domicile, marriage and divorce. In most countries, nationality laws were based on the time-honoured assumption that women who marry should automatically take their husband's nationality. This view, largely unchallenged until the end of the nineteenth century, was based on the notion that the wife must defer to the primacy of the husband as family leader.

73   Laws governing nationality reflect one of the most fundamental legal relationships between the individual and the State: the protection and rights of citizenship are extended to those who profess loyalty to the State. There was a strong feeling in the Commission that, because nationality was so basic a right, it should be enjoyed by women as well as men on a non-discriminatory basis. The Commission found, however, that, as a result of conflicting laws in many countries, a woman who married a man of a different nationality could find herself deprived of her own nationality without her consent. In some cases, she could even find herself stateless, especially in the event of a divorce.

74   By 1955, the Commission on the Status of Women had completed a draft treaty on the nationality rights of married women for submission to the General Assembly. Called the Convention on the Nationality of Married Women, the proposed agreement was aimed at protecting the right of a woman to retain her nationality if she wished, even if it differed from her husband's. The agreement was also intended to eliminate conflicts of law involving the nationality of women who were married or divorced, or whose husbands had changed their nationality.

75   Nevertheless, the idea that a nation's sovereign interests could be overridden by the international human rights principle of non-discrimination was opposed by some delegations. After several weeks of debate in the General Assembly, it became clear that some Governments would not abandon their resistance to certain treaty provisions and the final days of discussion focused on the format in which countries would express reservations to the Convention. The Convention was approved by the General Assembly on 29 January 1957, with 47 votes in favour and 2 against; there were 24 abstentions, a strikingly large number. The treaty came into force the following year, on 11 August 1958.[40]

40/ Document 29
See page 167

76   There was wide agreement that the adoption of the Convention was a historic step, on a par with the Convention on the Political Rights of Women. However, the reservations raised by various countries made it clear that a long road lay ahead to achieving the full exercise of these rights.

Marriage and the question of consent

77   Following the adoption of the Convention on the Nationality of Married Women, the Commission on the Status of Women turned its attention to complex problems involving marriage itself. The Commission focused upon the right of free consent to marriage and the related issues of child marriage and the age of consent.

78   In addition to the right of nationality, the 1948 Universal Declaration of Human Rights had enshrined two other interrelated principles pertaining to marriage: that men and women, without any limitations due to race, nationality or religion, have the right to marry and start a family; and that they are entitled to "equal rights as to marriage, during marriage and at its dissolution."[41] The basic premise of the marriage-rights provisions of the Universal Declaration is that a marriage can be entered into only with the "free and full consent" of "men and women of full age".

41/ Document 14
See page 125

79   The Commission on the Status of Women found that the practice of giving girls away in marriage between the ages of 11 and 13 was widespread. In 1956, the General Assembly approved an international treaty to prevent such practices: the Supplementary Convention on the Abolition of Slavery, the Slave Trade, and Institutions and Practices Similar to Slavery. The Convention covered abuses considered analogous to slavery, including the sale of women into marriage without their consent.

80   However, States that were parties to the Convention proposed that the United Nations consider stronger measures on forced marriage. At the same United Nations Conference that drew up the Convention, those Governments recommended that the Economic and Social Council look into the desirability of establishing the principle of free consent of both parties to a marriage and consider setting a minimum age for marriage, preferably not less than 14 years. In April 1957, three months after the adoption of the Convention on the Nationality of Married Women, the Economic and Social Council authorized the Commission to examine these questions.

81   In 1959, the Commission on the Status of Women urged the Economic and Social Council to press for an international instrument carrying great authority that would cover the minimum age for marriage, free consent and registration of marriages. The Council accepted the proposal on 14 July 1959, and asked the Secretary-General to draft both a convention and a recommendation on the subject.

82   The addition of a non-binding recommendation, Council members said, would serve as a guideline for Governments unable to ratify the Convention. The result was two separate instruments, sometimes referred to collectively as the Convention and Recommendation on Consent to Marriage, Minimum Age for Marriage and Registration of Marriages. The Convention itself, which was adopted by the General Assembly on

42/ Document 31
See page 170

7 November 1962 and entered into force on 9 December 1964, decrees that no marriage may occur without the full and free consent of both parties.[42] It sets specific conditions under which the consent is to be given. However, the Convention leaves it up to Governments to decide for themselves on an appropriate minimum age for marriage. The Recommendation on marriage, which the General Assembly approved as a formal resolution on 1 November 1965, is a non-binding restatement of the legally binding Convention, except for one new element: it recommends a specific minimum age for marriage of 15 years.[43]

43/ Document 34
See page 173

83   Together, these measures represent the only international agreements on women's rights relating to marriage adopted by the United Nations, apart from portions of the 1967 Declaration on the Elimination of Discrimination against Women and the 1979 Convention on the Elimination of All Forms of Discrimination against Women, which incorporated provisions of all the early Conventions.[44] Subsequent discussions held under United Nations auspices have come to the conclusion that additional measures are needed to address the rights of women in civil law.

44/ Document 36
See page 175;
Document 69
See page 244

Traditional practices

84   Early in the 1950s, the Commission on the Status of Women and other United Nations bodies also began to focus on the problem of customs, ancient laws and practices that were harmful to the health and well-being of women and girls. The prevalence of these customs had first been brought to the attention of the United Nations by administrative authorities in the Trust and Non-Self-Governing Territories, whose annual reports were regularly reviewed by the Commission and the General Assembly, among other bodies.

85   Such practices still prevail today in many societies under customary law. They include female genital mutilation, early childhood marriage, virginity tests, violence related to dowry, widow burning and other inhumane practices. A consensus emerged that many of these practices were wholly inconsistent with universal human rights principles. However, to question the very existence of such practices—many ingrained in the tradition, culture and power structures of societies—was a delicate undertaking that invariably aroused resistance.

86   In May 1952, the Economic and Social Council, acting on the recommendation of the Commission on the Status of Women, called upon all Member States, including those with responsibility for the Trust and Non-Self-Governing Territories, to "take immediately all necessary measures with a view to abolishing progressively . . . all customs which violate the physical integrity of women, and which thereby violate the dignity and worth of the human person as proclaimed in the Charter and

in the Universal Declaration of Human Rights".[45] A similar resolution was adopted by the Council in 1954, after the Commission on the Status of Women had begun collecting data in preparation for discussions of the rights of women in family law in the context of the Charter and the Universal Declaration of Human Rights.

45/ Document 25
See page 164

87   In the General Assembly, there was wide agreement that practices that harmed women and girls should be abolished, but no consensus on how this should be done. Some delegations argued that the elimination of customs deeply rooted in culture and religion would come about only as a result of education and other preparatory steps, and that it was necessarily a gradual process. Others cautioned that urging the abolition of traditional practices would raise questions about the possible violation of the provision in the Charter of the United Nations that forbids interference in the domestic affairs of Member States.

88   Despite the disagreements, on 17 December 1954, the General Assembly approved a resolution urging all Member States and Non-Self-Governing and Trust Territories to take all appropriate measures to abolish practices that violated human rights. The resolution was adopted by a vote of 43 to 0, with one abstention. The resolution included no specific references to such practices as genital mutilation. But it cited such issues as ensuring freedom of choice in choosing a spouse; eliminating child marriages and the betrothal of young girls before puberty; abolishing the practice of the bride-price, or dowries; and guaranteeing widows custody of their children as well as the right to remarry.[46]

46/ Document 28
See page 167

89   Concerning the issue of traditional practices affecting young girls, at the Commission's urging, the Economic and Social Council asked the World Health Organization to undertake a study that could be presented to the Commission on the Status of Women at its 1961 session. WHO responded that the ritual operations in question involved social and cultural elements whose study was beyond its sphere of competence. Following a United Nations seminar held in Addis Ababa in 1961, at which African women had clearly and firmly expressed the wish that such operations be abolished, the Commission asked the Council once again to request medical information from WHO on the practices. However, WHO reiterated that it would not carry out such an inquiry because it would require detailed and specific references to socio-economic and cultural factors that were beyond its competence.

90   At that point, there seemed little likelihood of any strong international action to eliminate practices such as female genital mutilation. The matter was put aside for what turned out to be nearly two decades. It did not surface again as a focus of international discussion at the United Nations until a World Health Assembly held in 1975, the International Women's Year. In 1979, the World Health Organization

convened a seminar in Khartoum on "Traditional Practices Affecting the Health of Women and Children".

91   Even then, there was still no consensus as to whether the question of traditional practices harmful to women and girls should have a prominent place on the international human rights agenda. It was not until the mid-1980s and later that research by the Subcommission on Prevention of Discrimination and Protection of Minorities, the World Health Organization and other United Nations bodies made a strong case that genital mutilation and other such traditional practices were a form of violence against women and a human rights issue that could not be justified on the grounds of tradition, culture or social conformity.

Women in the United Nations system

92   From its earliest sessions, the Commission on the Status of Women addressed the issue of discrimination against women within the United Nations system. The Commission expressed concern about the low status of women at the United Nations, requesting that statistics on the number and rank of women in the Secretariat be provided regularly for its review.[47] As early as 1947, it urged the Secretary-General to appoint a woman as head of the Section on the Status of Women of the Human Rights Division.[48]

93   Despite the clear intent of Article 8 of the Charter—that there must be "no restrictions" on the eligibility of men and women to participate in the Organization "in any capacity and under conditions of equality"—women were poorly represented not only in the top tiers of United Nations management, but within the professional ranks.[49] There were relatively few women in national delegations as well. The Commission, in its third-session report to the Economic and Social Council, also drew attention to the desirability of greater participation by women in delegations. On the other hand, Council members said that this was a problem that should properly be left to the discretion of Governments.

94   Secretary-General Dag Hammarskjöld, in personal appearances before the Commission in 1954 and 1955, assured the members that there would be no discrimination against women during his administration. The small number of women in policy-making and professional-level posts in the Secretariat was a phenomenon mirrored in the public life of all nations, he explained, and was a natural consequence of the fact that "women's emancipation" was a relatively recent phenomenon. The Secretary-General said he was confident the situation would change as time went on and the pool of qualified women gradually expanded. He held that all United Nations personnel matters should be dealt with by the appropriate arm of the General Assembly, the Fifth Committee.[50]

47/ Document 16
See page 128

48/ Document 8
See page 113

49/ Document 1
See page 103;
Document 16
See page 128;
Document 20
See page 136;
Document 24
See page 161

50/ Document 27
See page 166

95 Beginning in the late 1960s, women in the Secretariat, encouraged by the efforts on their behalf by the Commission on the Status of Women and by women's NGOs, began organizing a support network to focus on improving the status of women at the United Nations. Despite General Assembly resolutions, women's representation in the United Nations system, including the Secretariat, had remained low.[51] It was not until later that the Secretariat began to make significant progress towards the equitable participation of women, including women in positions of high authority.

51/ Document 40
See page 182

III   Recognizing women's role in development, 1963-1975

96   Despite progress made in codifying women's rights in law, it was becoming apparent that laws were not enough to assure the equal rights of women. There also had to be efforts to ensure that women could actually exercise these rights. Moreover, it became clear during the 1960s that the legal status of women was only one element of a larger theme: the advancement of women within a broader social and economic context. There was a growing recognition that the central role of women in the overall economic and social progress of society had been vastly underestimated.

97   The 1960s and 1970s were a time of profound change within the United Nations, whose membership had begun to expand dramatically with the emergence of more and more newly independent nations, many of them former colonies in their economic infancy. As the ranks of these developing countries swelled, the Organization began widening its focus to include the problems of what was then commonly referred to as the third world. The role of economic relations between developed and developing nations, which directly and indirectly affected the lives of women, increasingly overshadowed debates over women's legal equality. Because early action on women's issues was oriented primarily by the concerns of women from Western Europe and the Americas, some delegations were concerned that the problems of women in developing countries and rural areas would be neglected. As a result, United Nations efforts towards the advancement of women increasingly focused on the role of women in development, both as beneficiaries and as agents of change.

98   To meet this challenge, the United Nations responded by redirecting and enhancing its technical assistance programmes in order specifically to support women in developing countries. At the same time, efforts continued to be made to establish women's legal equality with the consolidation of women's rights provisions in the Declaration on the Elimination of Discrimination against Women, adopted in 1967. By 1975, the International Women's Year, the role of women in achieving peace and disarmament had emerged as a third crucial issue—along with equality and development—that would be forged into a comprehensive programme during the United Nations Decade for Women, 1976-1985.

Technical assistance

99   Many development theorists had originally believed that industrialization and economic growth would benefit women by opening up employment opportunities, hastening their attainment of equal rights with men. Since 1947, the Commission on the Status of Women had been a strong supporter of technical assistance for women on these grounds.

100   But evidence began to accumulate during the 1960s that women were affected disproportionately by poverty, and that inequality with men—including barriers to women's ownership of land and access to credit—perpetuated their low status in many regions. The work of the Commission on the Status of Women in the 1960s and 1970s thus began to take it beyond the negotiating tables in New York and Geneva and into the fields and rice paddies of the developing world. Such issues as women's needs in community and rural development, agricultural work, family planning and the impact of scientific and technological advances on women became increasingly prominent in the Commission's work. This was the first step in a growing perception among United Nations bodies concerned with development that the Charter's promise to "promote social progress and better standards of life in larger freedom" could not be met without the full participation of women in society.

101   By 1962, the Commission on the Status of Women, the Economic and Social Council and the General Assembly were already actively debating the question of whether—and how—the United Nations could further the advancement of women, especially in developing countries. The Council and the Commission were in general agreement that the United Nations already had sufficient resources to help, in both its regular and expanded programmes of technical assistance.[52] On 16 July 1962, the Council, acting on the Commission's recommendation, urged Governments to avail themselves of the Organization's assistance programmes.[53] In its resolution the Council also called upon United Nations bodies such as the United Nations Children's Fund (UNICEF) to expand and strengthen their efforts to assist women in developing countries.

102   In addition, the Secretary-General's help was sought in efforts to generate public interest by continuing a Secretariat-sponsored seminar series on the status of women, and by offering human rights fellowships and scholarships to women in developing countries. This outreach effort was the result of the United Nations Human Rights Advisory Services Programme, which the General Assembly had approved in 1956. Financed under the regular United Nations budget, the programme was for many years the only one of its kind specifically concerned with the advancement of women. The regional seminars afforded women the opportunity to share experiences and discuss common problems at a

52/ Document 23
See page 154

53/ Document 30
See page 169

time when many regional commissions were devoting little, if any, time to women's issues. The Economic and Social Council also called on women's non-governmental organizations to help supplement United Nations efforts by sponsoring regional, national, local and, if possible, international seminars.[54]

54/ Document 30
See page 169

103   The General Assembly welcomed these steps, adopting a resolution on 7 December 1962 that called upon the Secretary-General to study "the possibility of providing and developing new resources aimed especially at the initiation and implementation of a unified long-term United Nations programme for the advancement of women".[55] The study, the Assembly said, should assess whether the advancement of women in developing countries could be furthered through the expansion of existing United Nations technical assistance and advisory services programmes in human rights and social welfare. The Assembly's request to the Secretary-General included a proposal that the Secretariat study the feasibility of "expanding the assistance which can be rendered, through seminars, fellowships and the services of experts, for the advancement of women in developing countries".

55/ Document 32
See page 172

104   In 1966, the Economic and Social Council recommended that Governments and non-governmental organizations be polled on the role of women in the economic and social development of their countries. Responses to the questionnaire indicated that women were faring so poorly at the national level that they would need special assistance for indefinite periods. The Council also addressed a request to other bodies in the United Nations system, including UNICEF and the United Nations Development Programme (UNDP), to assist in developing a unified long-term programme for the advancement of women. As a result, United Nations bodies concerned with development issues began to emphasize programmes that promoted economic and social development, including the expansion of assistance to women in developing countries.

105   The Secretary-General was asked to look into the possibility of establishing a special fund that could be used to help Governments implement national programmes. The Economic and Social Council suggested that industrial and business concerns, non-governmental organizations, foundations and individuals might be invited to contribute. The idea was to culminate with the creation, in 1976, of the Voluntary Fund for the United Nations Decade for Women which grew out of the Voluntary Fund for the International Women's Year.[56]

56/ Document 56
See page 231;
Document 80
See page 303

106   In 1970, the advancement of women and their role in development received new impetus when the General Assembly unveiled a comprehensive plan for better economic and social conditions for all— the International Development Strategy for the Second United Nations Development Decade. The measure was the first such initiative to mention women explicitly, endorsing the full integration of women in the total development effort.

107   In a resolution adopted later that year, the General Assembly called for a programme of concerted international action for the advancement of women.[57] It recommended that a series of regional and international conferences be convened with Governments, experts and NGOs to consider ways and means of promoting the status of women within the framework of overall development. The resolution offered a list of "minimum targets to be achieved during the Second United Nations Development Decade". These included such steps as the progressive elimination of illiteracy; universal acceptance of the principle of equal pay for equal work; health and maternity protection, including the ready availability of family planning information; and a "substantial increase in the number of women participating in public and government life" at all levels.

57/ Document 39
See page 179

Declaration on the Elimination of Discrimination

108   With women's concerns increasingly bound up in discussions of development strategy, the Commission on the Status of Women emphasized that discrimination could take many forms—legal or factual, public or private, direct or indirect—and that it could affect anyone: asylum-seekers, displaced farmers, the disabled, women of diverse races or nationalities, or the well-to-do.

109   In 1963, in an effort to solidify earlier gains, members of the General Assembly's Third Committee argued that the cause of equal rights would gain immeasurably if the United Nations approved a declaration that consolidated, in one document, all of the standards on women's rights that had been developed since 1945. With the Commission on the Status of Women not scheduled to meet for two years, it fell to the General Assembly to take the first formal step towards bringing that idea to life.

110   On 5 December 1963, the General Assembly requested the Commission on the Status of Women to begin work on a draft declaration on the elimination of discrimination against women. The Assembly noted that while there had been measurable progress in achieving equal rights, "in various fields there still remains, in fact if not in law, considerable discrimination against women".[58]

58/ Document 33
See page 173

111   When the Commission on the Status of Women commenced work on drafting the text of the Declaration, a lack of consensus quickly became apparent in a number of areas. Although much of the non-binding Declaration dealt with issues already covered in earlier instruments and

resolutions, there were disagreements in connection with the provisions on marriage and the family and on employment. The draft Declaration was not accepted by the General Assembly, which sent it back to the Commission for revision.

112   Early in 1967, the Commission submitted a revised draft to the General Assembly through the Economic and Social Council. Sixty-six amendments were proposed, many of them in the disputed areas of equal rights in employment, marriage and family law. Eleven of the amendments were finally agreed to, and on 7 November 1967 the General Assembly unanimously adopted the Declaration on the Elimination of Discrimination against Women.[59]

59/ Document 36
See page 175

113   Although the Declaration was a non-binding instrument, it was an important step in securing the legal foundation of women's equality. It brought together in a single document a concise listing of the areas in which equality of men and women had to be asserted as a matter of law and practice. The Declaration proclaimed that discrimination against women was fundamentally unjust and constituted an offence against human dignity. It also called gender discrimination a practice incompatible with the welfare of the family and of society. New laws would have to be written—and old laws, customs, regulations and practices abolished—in order to end discrimination against women under the law, and in political, economic and social life.

114   The Declaration advanced the movement for women's rights, but its effects in practice were limited. The reporting procedures for the Declaration's implementation were voluntary, and the level of responses by Governments was low. The need for a legally binding Convention defining women's rights—which was ultimately to be adopted in 1979—largely grew out of the perception that attempts to implement the Declaration had been limited.

The Tehran Human Rights Conference

115   In 1963, the General Assembly moved to increase United Nations human rights activities by designating 1968 as the International Year for Human Rights. The date was chosen to coincide with the twentieth anniversary of the adoption of the Universal Declaration of Human Rights. The Assembly declared that Member States should devote the Year to activities, ceremonies and observances, with special emphasis on rights and freedoms in connection with which they had faced special problems.

116   In a December 1965 resolution the General Assembly urged Member States to use the International Year to hasten the ratification of

pending human rights accords, including the 1952 Convention on the Political Rights of Women; the 1965 International Convention on the Elimination of All Forms of Racial Discrimination; and the 1966 International Covenants on Civil and Political Rights and on Economic, Social and Cultural Rights.

117   The General Assembly's resolution included an annex that stressed the importance of educational programmes to teach citizens about fundamental human rights and freedoms. It said there should be a world-wide educational programme on human rights that would mobilize schools, colleges and universities as well as NGOs. This was in line with recommendations by the Commission on the Status of Women. From its earliest sessions, the Commission had stressed the importance of disseminating information on the advancement of women's rights..

118   The major event of 1968 was the International Conference on Human Rights, held in Tehran in April and May. The topic of women's rights in the modern world, in addition to being a major theme of the International Year of Human Rights, was also an agenda item of the Tehran Conference. The Conference adopted 29 resolutions on a wide variety of human rights questions, including one endorsing the objectives of a "unified long-term programme for the advancement of women suggested by the Secretary-General".[60] In the resolution, Conference members expressed the concern that despite existing international instruments "there continues to exist considerable discrimination against women in the political, legal, economic, social and educational fields". They also expressed the conviction that "any advancement in the status of women depends to a very large degree on changes in traditional attitudes, customs and laws based on the idea of the inferiority of women".

60/ Document 37
See page 177

119   Education was vital to eliminating discrimination, according to the delegates, and Governments could hasten the advancement of women by ensuring that all their citizens received at least an elementary education, one that emphasized the importance of equal rights and the elimination of all discrimination.

120   The Tehran resolutions—as well as subsequent discussions by the Commission on the Status of Women, the Economic and Social Council and the General Assembly—emphasized that an expansion of technical assistance to women in developing countries was an important element in any unified long-term plan. The advancement of women, these discussions stressed, was dependent upon international cooperation under the auspices of the United Nations.

Linking development, equality and peace

121 In June 1972, the Secretary-General convened a meeting of experts from various regions to discuss development and the role of women. The gathering, under the auspices of the Commission on the Status of Women and the Commission for Social Development, was the first such expert meeting on the subject.

122 Among their recommendations were proposals for programmes to create jobs for women, as well as opportunities for job training and vocational guidance. The experts group also stressed the importance of regional commissions such as the United Nations Economic Commission for Africa—the first such body to begin a coordinated effort to help African women. The experts' findings helped buttress a growing perception at the United Nations and elsewhere that the low status of women, especially in developing countries, was a major factor in such increasingly globalized problems as poverty, rapid population growth, illiteracy, malnutrition, migration and forced urbanization, and poor health conditions. These views were reinforced at high-level United Nations gatherings such as the 1974 World Population Conference, held in Bucharest; its Plan of Action affirmed the central importance of women in population policies. The World Food Conference, held the same year in Rome, endorsed the view that improvement in the global food situation could not occur without the full participation of women.

123 The protection of women and children in armed conflicts and emergencies was another area of concern for the Commission on the Status of Women. In 1969, the issue had touched off a strong debate, with some Commission members arguing that women and children were not entitled to any more protection than any other civilians caught in dangerous situations. It was also pointed out that in many armed conflicts women were themselves combatants. Nevertheless, the Commission decided that women and children should be considered the most vulnerable members of the population, who were too often the victims of inhuman acts.

61/ **Document 44**
See page 185

124 In a resolution adopted on 14 December 1974, the General Assembly urged Governments to do everything possible "to spare women and children from the ravages of war".[61] It reminded them of their obligations under the 1925 Geneva Protocol and the 1949 Geneva Conventions, and affirmed that all forms of repression and cruel and inhuman treatment of women and children were criminal acts.

International Women's Year

125 The year 1972 marked 25 years since the first meeting of the Commission on the Status of Women. The Commission that year recommended to the Economic and Social Council and the General Assembly that 1975 be designated International Women's Year. Its observance, according to the Commission, would serve to remind the international community that discrimination against women, entrenched in law and deeply rooted cultural beliefs, was a persistent problem in much of the world—and that Governments, NGOs and individuals needed to increase their efforts not only to promote equality between men and women, but to acknowledge women's vital role in national and international development efforts.

126   The General Assembly endorsed the Commission's recommendation on International Women's Year and added a third theme to those of equality and development: the recognition of the importance of women's increasing contribution to the strengthening of world peace.[62] The addition had been suggested by the delegations of Greece and Guatemala, whose members argued that women, as much as men, should be encouraged to join in the search for solutions to two of the most urgent issues of the period, peace and disarmament.

62/ Document 41
See page 183

127   The campaign for the advancement of women had begun as a struggle for equality and gradually evolved to encompass the role of women in society and especially in development. Now, with the General Assembly adding peace, the theme of a three-part agenda for the advancement of women had clearly emerged.

The Mexico City Conference

128   Meeting in January 1974, the Commission on the Status of Women decided that it was important to convene a major conference to coincide with International Women's Year. Members agreed that such an international women's conference should have four principal aims: to assess how successfully the United Nations system had implemented Commission recommendations to end discrimination against women; to consider new ways to promote the full participation of women, with special attention to women in rural areas, in the total development effort; to develop a plan of action to increase women's contribution to the goals of the Second United Nations Development Decade; and to recognize the role of women in achieving world peace.

129   On 10 December 1974, the General Assembly approved the programme for International Women's Year and formally requested that the Secretary-General move ahead with preparations for the Conference to be held in Mexico City.[63] The Assembly called for an international action programme, including short-term and long-term measures for achieving the integration of women as full and equal partners with men in the total development effort and steps to eliminate gender-based discrimination and to achieve the widest involvement of women in

63/ Document 42
See page 184

efforts to strengthen international peace and eradicate racism and racial discrimination.

64/ Document 43
See page 184

130   The General Assembly also authorized the creation of a 23-nation Consultative Committee with a limited mandate to offer advice on the draft outcome of the Conference.[64] A voluntary fund was also established for contributions to finance activities during International Women's Year. With the General Assembly's formal permission to proceed in December 1974, the organizers of the two-week Conference had only six months to prepare, but proceeded quickly, including drafting the Conference document.

131   On 8 March 1975, the United Nations observed International Women's Day for the first time—and three months later, the Organization convened the first global conference on women's issues. Opening the Conference on 19 June 1975, the Secretary-General said the gathering in Mexico City was the first major step in a worldwide attempt to achieve equality between men and women and to end separation of the sexes in matters of education, opportunities and economic priorities.

132   Delegations from 133 Member States attended the Conference, 113 of them headed by women. Of the 2,000 delegates, 73 per cent were female. There were also representatives of 15 United Nations bodies and specialized agencies; 9 offices/departments of the Secretariat; 7 national liberation movements; the Commission on Human Rights; 8 intergovernmental organizations—and 114 non-governmental organizations in consultative status with the Economic and Social Council.

133   An estimated 6,000 NGO representatives were involved in a parallel gathering called the International Women's Year Tribune. There had been similar NGO meetings at the 1972 World Conference on the Human Environment in Stockholm and at the 1974 Bucharest Population Conference. But the scope and intensity of the Mexico City Tribune were unique; many participants later called it history's largest consciousness-raising session.

134   The Tribune's stated purpose was to bring together men and women from all geographical areas and varied backgrounds to exchange information and opinions on the position of women in economic and social life. In hundreds of panel discussions and workshops as well as countless informal gatherings, women from countries in vastly different stages of development met to share experiences and perspectives on a wide range of topics. For many women, the NGO gathering was a transforming experience. It brought home the realization that their problems, far from being unique, were shared by women all over the world—and that the key to meeting the needs of ordinary women everywhere was through international cooperation.

135   By 2 July 1975, when the Conference came to a close, delegates had adopted a World Plan of Action; the Declaration of Mexico on the Equality of Women and Their Contribution to Development and Peace; a set of regional follow-up plans for Africa, and Asia and the Pacific—and 35 separate resolutions and decisions on a wide-ranging set of issues relevant to women.[65]

136 The Declaration, reflecting current international political concerns and the pervasive effects of cold-war tensions prevalent at the time, included references to zionism and a number of other controversial issues. This led to objections from some delegations. The Declaration was ultimately adopted by the Conference in an 89-to-3 vote, with 18 abstentions.

137 In the Declaration, Governments pledged to abide by 30 separate principles, including the elimination of all obstacles standing in the way of women's full integration into national development and peace. It stressed the important role that women had to play not only in the achievement and maintenance of international peace, but in "peace in all spheres of life: in the family, the community, the nation and the world". In the words of the Declaration: "Women must participate equally with men in the decision-making processes which help to promote peace at all levels".

The Plan of Action

138 The Plan of Action has proved to be the most enduring legacy of the Conference. The document, formally known as the World Plan of Action for the Implementation of the Objectives of the International Women's Year, offered a comprehensive set of guidelines for the advancement of women until 1985. In line with the General Assembly resolution establishing International Women's Year, its overall objective was threefold: to promote equality between men and women; to ensure the integration of women in the total development effort; and to increase the contribution of women to the strengthening of world peace. Delegates stressed the interrelatedness of the objectives; without progress in each, they said, there could be no success for any.

139 The Plan included minimum targets to be met by 1980, the mid-point of the Decade. These included equal access for women to every level of education and training; the enactment of legislation guaranteeing the political participation of women; increased employment opportunities; and improvements in health services, sanitation, housing, nutrition and family planning. The targets also included action on a host of other social issues, including the problems of migrant women, female prisoners and rehabilitation of offenders, and measures to combat forced prostitution and trafficking in women. "Each country", the Plan declared, "should decide upon its own national strategy and identify its own targets and priorities".[66]

65/ Document 45
See page 187

66/ Document 45
See page 187

140 The Plan of Action also included a provision on ways to improve data collection and analysis—both essential in United Nations assessments of the situation of women in various countries. It also urged that more attention be paid to the influence of the mass media in shaping popular perceptions about the role of women in society. It proposed that the General Assembly establish mechanisms for regular review of its recommendations.

141 The Mexico City Conference called for the United Nations to press for a binding convention on the elimination of discrimination against women with effective procedures for its implementation—one that would codify the anti-discrimination principles of the 1967 Declaration on the Elimination of Discrimination against Women.[67] The delegates agreed that the convention should ensure that women enjoyed equal rights with men in every area, including political activities, employment, education, health services, civil and legal relations, and social security and the family.

67/ Document 36
See page 175

142 To ensure that national and international action to advance the status of women was sustained, the Conference urged that the United Nations proclaim the period from 1976 to 1985 as the United Nations Decade for Women and Development, and recommended that another world conference on women be held in 1980.

143 With the conclusion of the Conference in 1975, a long-sought process of change had been set in motion. The Commission on the Status of Women was now in a position to help sustain the momentum of this process while continuing its regular appraisals of progress towards achieving equal rights for women in all fields.

IV   The United Nations Decade for Women, 1976-1985

144   Five months after the Mexico City Conference, the General Assembly proclaimed the period from 1976 to 1985 as the United Nations Decade for Women: Equality, Development and Peace.[68] The very existence of the United Nations Decade for Women served to promote and legitimize the international women's movement. Its various activities at the national, regional and international levels helped to bring women's issues to the forefront of world attention.

68/ Document 49
See page 214

145   The Decade for Women is remembered for its historic events, such as the Copenhagen and Nairobi Conferences, and its important legal and policy achievements, such as the 1979 Convention on the Elimination of All Forms of Discrimination against Women.[69] The Decade's major world conferences offered a forum in which women's organizations had a voice in shaping the work of the United Nations. Non-governmental organizations broadened women's participation in the Organization's work of protecting human rights, fostering development and securing peace. These groups helped Governments to recognize that these fundamental goals were impossible to achieve and secure without the participation and advancement of women.

69/ Document 69
See page 244

146   The most fundamental transformation during the Decade involved the shift from a belief that development served to advance women to a new consensus that development was not possible without the full participation of women. United Nations statistics, for the first time, dramatized the fact that women's equality and rights, far from being isolated issues, were important factors in the well-being of all people. The undervaluation of women was identified as both a cause and an effect of underdevelopment, closely linked to such global problems as poverty, overpopulation, illiteracy, food shortages, malnutrition and poor health conditions. Studies conducted throughout the world showed that declines in infant mortality, improved nutrition and medical care as well as lower fertility rates were functions of a mother's level of education.

147   Over the course of the Decade, there was agreement on the need for pragmatic measures to improve women's lives. New institutions were created to provide technical assistance, and regional commissions of the United Nations began developing their own programmes as part of a broad effort to strengthen the drive for the advancement of women and to support grass-roots organizations.

Encouraging broader participation

148   The Decade contributed to a fundamental transformation of the United Nations itself from an Organization in which Governments set policies and agendas to one in which policy and direction were also generated from the grass-roots level and by NGOs. NGOs brought the voices of women suffering from discrimination, poverty and oppression to the attention of the United Nations.

149   Although even in 1945 the NGOs of the women's movement were assisting the United Nations in defining women's rights, the influence of NGOs, as well as their number, grew dramatically during the Decade. At Mexico City, 6,000 NGO representatives had participated in the official Conference or in the related NGO Tribune; 10 years later in Nairobi some 15,000 were present.

150   At the national level, many NGOs worked to implement United Nations policies enhancing the human rights of women and helping to lift them out of poverty. NGOs helped in generating support for the idea of an international women's conference in Mexico City, establishing the United Nations Decade for Women, establishing government programmes and legal reforms and winning adoption of the 1979 Convention. They also created research and policy centres as well as countless programmes empowering women through grass-roots organizing and micro-enterprise development. As this global "civil society" emerged, the voices and concerns of women in developing countries, particularly in rural areas, increasingly shaped United Nations assistance programmes.

151   In a resolution adopted on 15 December 1975, the General Assembly declared that the Decade would be devoted to the implementation of the Mexico City initiatives, and called on all concerned—Governments, organizations of the United Nations system, intergovernmental organizations, NGOs—to join in the broad array of new activities to strengthen international commitments to improve the status of

70/ Document 49
See page 214

women.[70] The 1976-1985 period was to be devoted to "effective and sustained national, regional and international action to implement the World Plan of Action and related resolutions" of the 1975 Conference, particularly the goals of equality and the full integration of women in the development process and in the promotion of world peace.

152   In the same resolution, the General Assembly called for a series of concrete steps to begin bringing women into the development process, starting with an inter-agency programme to assist Governments with technical cooperation projects. It also urged all financial institutions, including all international, regional and subregional development banks and bilateral funding agencies, to give priority to development projects that would promote the full involvement of women, especially

in rural areas. It further suggested that NGOs take all possible measures to implement the goals of the Mexico City Conference.

INSTRAW and UNIFEM

153　In 1975, the General Assembly also recommended that the Secretary-General create a new, autonomous United Nations–affiliated institution, the International Research and Training Institute for the Advancement of Women (INSTRAW), and requested that an expert group make proposals for its establishment.[71] INSTRAW's establishment had been recommended by the Mexico City Conference, which had noted the need for improvements in research and training, especially in issues related to women and development.

154　"The Institute should direct its activities with special attention to the needs of women in developing countries", the Economic and Social Council declared in a resolution on 12 May 1976.[72] The General Assembly, in approving the Council's recommendation, said it was convinced that the promotion of development objectives and the solution of crucial world economic and social problems should contribute significantly to the improvement of the situation of women, in particular that of women in rural areas and low-income groups. In 1983 the Secretary-General reported to the General Assembly on the programme of work being undertaken by the Institute, now functioning from its headquarters in the Dominican Republic. He noted that its work programme was related to "practical and specific objectives" which paid special attention "to those activities which would lead to increased technical cooperation for development benefiting women".[73] The following year the General Assembly approved the Institute's programme of activities and Statute. Its principal functions were listed as conducting action-oriented research and studies, with particular attention paid to problems facing women in developing countries; establishing training programmes, including a fellowship programme and advisory services, to raise awareness on issues concerning women and development and to increase opportunities for women to acquire new skills; and establishing an information system on women.[74]

155　Regional commissions began developing their own women-oriented programmes, while bodies such as the United Nations Development Programme began focusing more and more on the inclusion of women in their projects. Seed money for some of these undertakings came from the Voluntary Fund for the United Nations Decade, which provided direct, practical assistance to women in developing countries.[75] Programmes included such activities as helping women start their own

71/ Document 49
See page 214

72/ Document 54
See page 221

73/ Document 76
See page 292

74/ Document 78
See page 299;
Document 79
See page 302

75/ Document 56
See page 231

businesses, or easing their daily labour by drilling water wells close to households.

156   In 1984, the General Assembly renamed the Fund the United Nations Development Fund for Women (UNIFEM) and authorized it as a permanent, autonomous body.[76] In the countries where it assists women, UNIFEM often trains and works with NGOs and government groups as part of an effort to enhance cooperation between citizens' organizations and Governments. It helps improve the living standards of women in developing countries by addressing their concerns through the provision of technical and financial support and by promoting the inclusion of women in the decision-making process of mainstream development programmes. By the end of the Decade, UNIFEM had financed over 400 projects totalling more than US$ 24 million.

76/ Document 80
See page 303

The 1979 Convention

157   The Commission on the Status of Women had two major tasks when it gathered for its 1976 session: the elaboration of a programme of action for the United Nations Decade for Women, and the drafting of the Convention on the Elimination of All Forms of Discrimination against Women.[77]

77/ Document 55
See page 222

158   The Commission had already agreed, in 1972, to press for an anti-discrimination convention. However, it left open the question of whether such an agreement should take the form of one instrument, or more than one. At the Commission's next session, in 1974, members opted for a single, comprehensive treaty, and a drafting group began working on the Convention.

159   However, it became apparent that achieving a consensus on the wording of the Convention would be difficult. For this reason the Commission on the Status of Women agreed that, rather than vote on each substantive issue, the drafting group would incorporate proposed alternative texts, recommendations and reservations into the document as the work proceeded. This was to become the accepted method of operation as the draft Convention made its way through the Commission, on to the Economic and Social Council and finally to the General Assembly.

160   The draft document that developed from the Commission's 1974 discussions included a preamble; general provisions (one of which defined discrimination against women); and three substantive sections on political, social, economic, civil and family rights. It was widely circulated for comment, and the response was voluminous: suggestions for changes were submitted by 40 Governments, 4 specialized agencies and 10 non-governmental organizations.

161   The Commission adopted the draft Convention without a vote on 17 December 1976 and forwarded it, through the Economic and Social Council, for the approval of the General Assembly. A complex and lengthy debate began early the following year in the Third Committee of the Assembly. A working group established to negotiate the text adjourned after 12 meetings, having failed to complete work on a large number of paragraphs. The lack of consensus was a reflection of the many remaining obstacles to women's advancement. These involved such issues as the elimination of discrimination against women in law; rights in marriage and family, and in education, employment, and rural development; and health-care services and bank loans and credit. The language of most of these provisions was worked out by a second General Assembly negotiating group in 1978.

162   But by late 1979, strong differences still remained over provisions for implementing the Convention; for expressing reservations to it; and over parts of the preamble, which affirmed policies and principles to promote social progress and contribute to the attainment of full equality between men and women. These remaining issues were addressed at protracted meetings of the Third Committee on 6 and 7 December 1979. Some delegations, concerned by the continuing lack of consensus, suggested that the differences over the document would require even more time to resolve. Proposals were made that the draft Convention should be recirculated for comments, and there was a formal proposal that any move to adopt the Convention should be put off until 1980.

163   On 18 December 1979, the General Assembly finally adopted the Convention on the Elimination of All Forms of Discrimination against Women, by a vote of 130 to none, with 11 abstentions.[78] However, it was clear that the overwhelming vote in favour did not reflect general satisfaction with the agreement. The balloting had been preceded by separate votes on several of the controversial paragraphs—and nearly 40 countries had expressed reservations on specific provisions.

78/ Document 69
See page 244

164   The Convention brings together, in a comprehensive, legally binding form, internationally accepted principles on the rights of women—and makes clear that they are applicable to all women in all societies. It commits Governments to take all appropriate measures, including legislation, to ensure the full development and advancement of women and to guarantee them the exercise and enjoyment of human rights and fundamental freedoms on a basis of equality with men. The Convention makes it clear that the passage of laws is not enough, and that Governments must ensure that women are actually permitted to exercise the rights that the laws are designed to protect.

165   The Convention was the first international legal instrument to define discrimination against women, which it described as "any distinction, exclusion or restriction made on the basis of sex which has the effect or purpose of impairing or nullifying the recognition, enjoyment or exercise by women, irrespective of their marital status, on a basis of equality of men and women, of human rights and fundamental freedoms in the political, economic, social, cultural, civil or any other field".[79]

79/ Document 69
See page 244

166   A basic premise of the Convention is that women must be as free as men to make choices not only in the political and legal sphere, but also in such areas as marriage, the home and family life generally. What made the Convention unique is its requirement that Governments work to eliminate discrimination against women not only in the public sphere, but in private life as well.

167   At the same time, the Convention affirms the importance of education—on an equal basis with men—in empowering women and creating an enlightened public. It also calls for the elimination of all restrictions on women's full and equal participation in political and public life; in the workplace; in health services; and in all civil and legal matters. Moreover, it directs Governments to make an additional effort to address the problems of women in rural areas, and especially to "ensure, on a basis of equality of men and women, that they participate in and benefit from rural development".[80]

80/ Document 69
See page 244

168   The formal signing of the Convention took place on 17 July 1980, on the third day of the two-week World Conference of the United Nations Decade for Women held in Copenhagen. Sixty-four Member States signed the Convention at that time, and two submitted instruments of ratification. The Convention went into effect on 3 September 1981 after 20 instruments of ratification were received. At the time, it was the swiftest entry into force of any human rights instrument.

169   As of 15 March 1996, 152 of the 185 United Nations Member States have become parties to the Convention. The Convention provides for reservations to allow States to become party to it even before their laws are fully in compliance with it. More than 40 States have accompanied their ratifications of the treaty with formal reservations involving 11 different articles. While the largest number of reservations refer to the role of the International Court of Justice in arbitrating disputes, the largest number of substantive reservations—from close to 20 countries—concern the provisions on the elimination of discrimination in marriage and the family (article 16).

170   Other reservations involve the provisions on the definition of discrimination (article 1); the commitment to eradicate discrimination (article 2); temporary measures to accelerate de facto equality (article 4); measures to eliminate prejudices and stereotyping (article 5); elimination of discrimination in political and public life (article 7); equal citizenship rights (article 9); elimination of discrimination in education (article 10); elimination of discrimination in employment (article 11); equal labour

rights (article 11); equal access to financial credit (article 13); and full legal capacity (article 15).

171   The Convention leads other human rights conventions in the number of States parties that have withdrawn their reservations. But a significant number of Governments are still not fully committed to some of its most basic principles.[81]

172   The General Assembly directed that an independent group of experts be formed to oversee compliance with the 1979 Convention. This group, the Committee on the Elimination of Discrimination against Women (CEDAW), first met in 1982. The Committee's main task, as described in article 18 of the Convention, is to consider reports submitted by Governments concerning "legislative, judicial, administrative or other measures which they have adopted" to comply with the Convention, and to submit reports that "may indicate factors and difficulties affecting the degree of fulfilment of obligations".[82]

81/ Document 139
See page 793

82/ Document 69
See page 244

The Copenhagen Conference

173   In addition to reaffirming the importance of the Convention on the Elimination of All Forms of Discrimination against Women, the 1980 Copenhagen Conference had two additional objectives: to review the progress in implementing the goals of the Mexico City Conference at the midpoint of the United Nations Decade for Women and to update the 1975 World Plan of Action adopted at the earlier Conference.[83]

174   The Conference's theme pinpointed three areas of especially urgent concern for women: employment, health and education. These issues came to the fore out of a sense that the broad goals of equality, development and peace enumerated at the Mexico City Conference could not be achieved unless they were refined into specific, highly focused objectives for women.[84]

175   The Secretary-General opened the Conference by expressing the hope that the delegates could make a realistic appraisal of what had been achieved since the Mexico City Conference. He noted that there was an increased recognition by Governments and other international institutions that women's participation was critical to the achievement of their goals of progress. However, at the same time, he said there were gaps between law and practice which could only be closed by sustained social action, resource allocation and political will.

176   There was general agreement among the 145 delegations that, over the five years since Mexico City, there had been significant accomplishments. The impetus generated by the United Nations Decade for Women was credited with having accelerated the adoption of the Con-

83/ Document 62
See page 238;

Document 63
See page 239

84/ Document 62
See page 238

vention on the Elimination of All Forms of Discrimination against Women, as well as having encouraged Governments to begin launching national anti-discrimination programmes. The United Nations had expanded and refined its data-collection process, creating an invaluable store of fresh information.

177   At the same time, issues of relevance to women were being discussed on a wider scale within the United Nations, not only at other conferences and in resolutions of the specialized agencies, but in the General Assembly itself. Debates on women's issues, once confined largely to the Assembly's Third Committee (Social, Humanitarian and Cultural Affairs), were increasingly heard in other forums, such as the Second Committee (Economic and Financial).

Programme of Action

178   The Conference's Programme of Action and 48 resolutions included calls for stronger national measures to ensure women's ownership and control of property, as well as improvements in women's rights to inheritance, child custody and loss of nationality. The Conference delegates urged an end to stereotyped attitudes toward women. They also recommended that future data collection be broken down in terms of gender and age, arguing that this was especially important in assessing the situation of rural women, the unemployed, migrants, the young and elderly, and single mothers.[85]

85/ Document 70
See page 250

179   Controversy among delegations erupted during deliberations over certain political aspects of the Programme of Action. These debates were conducted against a backdrop of political tensions, some of them carried over from the Mexico City Conference five years earlier.

180   The Conference ultimately adopted the Programme of Action, but not by consensus, as had occurred with the World Plan of Action in Mexico City. Instead, the document was agreed to by a roll-call vote of 94 in favour and 4 against, with 22 delegations abstaining. Some participants said later that the failure to produce a consensus document made follow-up efforts more difficult.

181   The Copenhagen recommendations amplified the findings of the Commission on the Status of Women, which in March 1980 had reported on the problems of implementing the goals of the Mexico City Conference. A variety of factors were cited, including lack of sufficient involvement of men in improving women's role in society; lack of political will to improve women's status in many countries; non-constructive attitudes on the part of both men and women in many countries; lack of recognition of the value of women's contributions to society; lack of attention to the particular needs of women in planning;

too few women in decision-making positions; insufficient services to support the role of women in national life, such as cooperatives, day-care centres and credit facilities; overall lack of necessary financial resources; lack of communication between policy makers and women in the greatest need; and ignorance among women about opportunities available for their development.

182 In a report issued through the Economic and Social Council, the Commission said that during the second half of the Decade for Women special efforts were needed to improve the situation of the most vulnerable women, including the disabled, rural women, female migrant workers and the wives of migrant workers. Despite these needs, in the 1980s, development efforts began to shrink with the global economic retrenchment, and frustration mounted as prospects for women's advancement slowed and even appeared to regress.

183 Among its recommendations, the Copenhagen Conference urged that the General Assembly authorize a third global women's conference in 1985, one that would assess the accomplishments of the United Nations Decade for Women and prepare a new set of guidelines for the 15 years leading up to the twenty-first century.

184 At the end of 1980, the General Assembly endorsed the Copenhagen Conference's Programme of Action, and asked the Secretary-General to submit proposals for implementing it to the Economic and Social Council. These were to take into account "the need for the speedy establishment of the new international economic order and the implementation of the goals and objectives of the International Development Strategy for the Third United Nations Development Decade, which are indispensable for the advancement of women".[86]

86/ Document 71
See page 284

185 Several days earlier, in a resolution adopted on 5 December 1980, the General Assembly requested the Secretary-General to prepare a report surveying the role of women in development. The report was to focus on women's role in agriculture, industry, trade, money and finance, science and technology, the use and conservation of energy resources, and women's self-reliance and integration in the development process. This report, first issued in 1985 as the *World Survey on the Role of Women in Development* and updated every five years, has become a major source of statistical and analytical data on women in the global economy. The *World Survey* documented two specific findings: although both men and women benefit from development, women benefit less; and while women make a major contribution to economic development, their work—mostly in informal sectors, chiefly agriculture and trade—is rarely reflected in national statistics.[87]

87/ Document 86
See page 366

The Nairobi Conference

186 The *World Survey on the Role of Women in Development* and other reports prepared by the Secretariat during 1984 helped lay the groundwork for the third global conference on women, held the following year in Nairobi. The reports revealed that improvements in the status of women and reductions in discrimination had benefited only a small minority of women. They also showed that improvements in the situation of women in the developing world had been marginal at best.

88/ Document 74
See page 289;
Document 82
See page 307

187 The Commission on the Status of Women was designated as the preparatory body for the Nairobi Conference.[88] At a major planning session in Vienna early in 1984, the Commission began its work amid general agreement that the objectives of the second half of the United Nations Decade for Women had not been met, and that an intensified drive towards equal treatment of women and their integration into development would be required well beyond 1985.

188 The World Conference to Review and Appraise the Achievements of the United Nations Decade for Women: Equality, Development and Peace opened in Nairobi on 15 July 1985 with a mandate to establish concrete measures to overcome the obstacles to achieving the Decade's goals. These obstacles included the persistence of underdevelopment and mass poverty, major factors in the enduring inequality of women and *de jure* and *de facto* discrimination against them; the continuation of women's subordinate roles in development, a consequence of physiological, social and cultural biases; and ongoing threats to international peace, resulting in an arms race, armed conflicts, human rights violations, terrorism and other obstacles to overall progress, especially the advancement of women. Participants in the Conference included delegations from 157 Member States and representatives of the United Nations Secretariat, regional commissions, 8 specialized agencies, 17 intergovernmental organizations, 4 national liberation movements and 163 NGOs.

Forward-looking Strategies

189 The centre-piece document of the two-week Conference, the 372-paragraph Nairobi Forward-looking Strategies for the Advancement of Women, was debated at length, with four paragraphs approved in separate votes. A number of delegations made it known that they had reservations about the document. But by the final day of the Conference, 26 July 1985, Governments had agreed to adopt the Forward-looking Strategies by consensus—thus avoiding what had occurred five years earlier at the second global women's conference in Copenhagen.[89]

89/ Document 84
See page 310

190 The Forward-looking Strategies were nothing less than an updated blueprint for the future of women to the end of the century. The heart of the document was a series of measures for implementing equality at the national level. "Since countries are at various stages of development", the Strategies explained, "they should have the option to set their own priorities based on their own development policies and resource capabilities". There were three basic categories: constitutional and legal steps; equality in social participation; and equality in political participation and decision-making. Specific measures were recommended in many key areas, especially employment; health; education; food, water and agriculture; industry, trade and commercial services; science and technology; communications; housing, settlement and community development and transport; energy; environment; and social services.

191   The document offered guidelines for national measures to promote women's participation in efforts to promote peace, and education for peace. These included references to the situation of women and children under apartheid, Palestinian women and children, and women in areas afflicted by foreign intervention, armed conflicts and other threats to peace. Violence against women in the family was also included, for the first time, as an issue related to peace.

192   The Forward-looking Strategies also singled out for special concern the need for measures to help women in special situations of distress, such as those affected by drought; the urban poor and the elderly; young women; abused and destitute women; victims of trafficking and forced prostitution; women deprived of their traditional means of livelihood; women who are their families' sole source of support; physically and mentally disabled women; women in detention and those subject to penal law; refugees and displaced women and children; migrant women; and minority and indigenous women.

193   The General Assembly responded to the results of the Nairobi Conference in a resolution of 13 December 1985 in which it urged Governments "to establish collaborative arrangements and to develop approaches" in their national programmes to implement the Nairobi Forward-looking Strategies. It also asked the Secretary-General and all others in the United Nations system "to establish, where they do not already exist, focal points on women's issues in all sectors of the work of the organizations of the United Nations system".[90] At the same time, the Assembly assigned the Commission on the Status of Women the task of overseeing implementation of the Nairobi Forward-looking Strategies —and urged that all organizations of the United Nations system cooperate in this task.

90/ Document 85
See page 363

V Towards equality, development and peace, 1986-1996

194 By the mid-1980s, it was becoming increasingly apparent that despite the energy and optimism which had launched the United Nations Decade for Women, the campaign had fallen short of achieving significant and sustained progress for many women. Major United Nations studies showed that there had been virtually no improvement in the three priority areas of the Decade: employment, health and education. And although the worldwide economic, social and political changes which came about in the 1990s created new opportunities for women, they also posed new obstacles to their economic and social advancement.

195 A series of world conferences and summit meetings sponsored by the United Nations since 1990 has helped to forge a consensus on actions to be taken in support of the advancement of women as part of comprehensive United Nations goals on development issues. These include the 1990 World Summit for Children, the 1992 United Nations Conference on Environment and Development, the 1993 World Conference on Human Rights, the 1994 International Conference on Population and Development, the 1995 World Summit for Social Development, the 1995 Fourth World Conference on Women and the 1996 United Nations Conference on Human Settlements.

196 Beginning in the 1980s, the United Nations also refocused its attention on violence against women. Addressing the situation of women working within the United Nations itself, the Organization began implementing a plan of action to attain gender equality by the end of the century.

Assessing progress

197 Five years after the Nairobi Conference, a review of progress made by the Secretary-General to the Commission on the Status of Women at its 1990 session painted a discouraging picture of the general progress of development worldwide, and especially the effects this had on women in developing countries. Echoing the earlier sombre assessment given in the 1989 *World Survey on the Role of Women in Development*, it pointed out that despite economic progress measured in growth rates, there had been virtually no improvement in the three priority areas highlighted by the Nairobi Conference: women's employment, education and health. As the report indicated, "for the average woman today—poor, lacking equal opportunities for education, subject to work for a lesser remuneration, often unable to control her own fertility, increasingly more often the head of the family—development has been an illusion".[91]

91/ Document 92
See page 378

198   The seventeenth annual United Nations observance of International Women's Day on 8 March 1992 was an occasion to reflect on the progress that had been made in eliminating discrimination against women. It was a moment to recognize that while the world had moved forward in ensuring greater respect for human rights and greater freedoms, the rate of progress in the advancement of women had slowed—and the gap between equality before the law and equality in practice was still apparent.

199   The evolving role of women in development in the transformed economic environment of the early 1990s was explored at length in the 1994 *World Survey on the Role of Women in Development*, which examined the implications of 10-year trends in poverty, unemployment and economic development. Although it has become clear that "economic change is not gender-neutral", the study said, there is little evidence that policy makers "have considered gender as a key variable in their policy-making".[92]

92/ Document 109
See page 481

200   The study recommended a series of steps to address poverty, which, as it noted, affects women disproportionately. Chief among those steps was to give women equal access to employment opportunities and to bring them fully into the economic decision-making process. The latter was deemed pivotal, for "unless policies and programmes increase women's participation in economic decision-making, opportunities to address poverty and improve the working world are unlikely to develop".

201   In January 1995, with preparations for the Fourth World Conference on Women well under way, the second five-year report on progress towards implementing the Nairobi Forward-looking Strategies, a major agenda item at the Beijing Conference, was issued. The report documented a major shift in perceptions of the role of women in development.[93]

93/ Document 120
See page 591

202   In the 1960s and 1970s, women had been viewed as potential beneficiaries of development, their interests heavily bound up in such basic public-health and population issues as family planning, child rearing and nutrition. Their economic contributions, principally through the informal sector, had barely been acknowledged, let alone quantified, in national development assessments. But the most recent report revealed that sweeping economic, social and political changes in the decade following the 1985 Nairobi Conference—all reflective of the growing interdependence of the world economy in the aftermath of the

cold war—had altered the development process, creating both new opportunities and further obstacles for women.

203   The report stated that democratization in developing and transitional economies had opened up whole new avenues of opportunity for women, freeing them to participate equally with men in the social, economic and political life of their societies. Women were "now recognized as agents of change, as an economic force in themselves and as a valuable resource without which progress in development would be limited".

204   Yet the increasing globalization of the world economy rendered countries more vulnerable to economic and political upheavals, which tend to affect women disproportionately. The overall opening up of economies sharpened the competition for increasingly scarce economic resources—in which women and other marginalized groups are normally at a natural disadvantage in developing and developed countries alike. Among the hardest-hit groups, according to the report, were women in developing countries, particularly in Africa and other regions where structural adjustment programmes were in place, and women in Eastern Europe and the countries of the former Soviet Union. There, as elsewhere, growing unemployment among men, lack of child-care facilities because of budgetary pressures and privatization, and rising social tensions have precipitated a return to traditional attitudes towards the role of women. In the industrialized nations, on the other hand, women's unemployment rates are generally no worse than men's, except in five European countries, where there are significantly larger numbers of jobless women.

205   In many regions, the new economic landscape and the increased participation of women in the labour force have brought no real improvements even for women fortunate enough to have jobs. With wages increasingly tied to gains in productivity, many women—who are concentrated in the services sector—have seen their wage-bargaining power erode. As the report pointed out, "national reports show that women's earnings are lower than men's in most of the reporting countries". The increasing number of women working at part-time jobs has brought about greater inequalities in economic rewards, salaries and benefits, a problem which has been further worsened by the perpetuation of low-paying "feminized" job categories such as cashier, telephone operator and secretary.[94]

94/ Document 120

See page 591

206   Given these findings, many academics and development practitioners now recognize the need to consider gender as a variable in the design of economic policies if their implementation is to produce an outcome that is both efficient and socially desirable. The 1995 report on the integration of women in development notes that it is questionable "whether current economic models that underpin national and interna-

tional economic policy fully factor in this critical variable". That report, the fourth of a series of biennial reports to the General Assembly on the subject, focused on gender issues in entrepreneurship, macroeconomic policy-making and development planning.[95]

207   The situation of rural women also continues to be an area of concern. Rural women form the backbone of the agricultural labour force across much of the developing world and produce an estimated 35 to 45 per cent of the gross domestic product and well over half of the developing world's food. Yet more than half a billion rural women are poor and lack access to resources and markets. Nevertheless, the importance of rural women in the next century will rest more on their impact on the economy and society than on their numbers. It will be related to their contribution to food security and to economic growth, as well as to the maintenance of social cohesion, the report observes.[96]

208   Another major report that year, *The World's Women 1995*, issued as an official document of the Fourth World Conference on Women, further elaborated on current trends affecting women's economic, social and political status.[97]

209   The study notes that education is one of the areas where women have made significant gains over the past 20 years, though there are marked regional contrasts. According to *The World's Women*, literacy rates for women have increased to at least 75 per cent in most countries of Latin America and the Caribbean as well as in those of East and South-East Asia. However, high rates of illiteracy among women still prevail in much of Africa and in parts of Asia. More women are also working in paid employment in all regions except sub-Saharan Africa and East Asia. By contrast, men's economic activity rates have declined everywhere except in Central Asia.

210   Women's increased access to education, employment and contraception have contributed to the nearly worldwide decline in fertility. However, country data recorded in the report reveal great differences among regions: the number of children women bear in developed regions is now 1.9, or slightly below population replacement levels, while African women still have an average of six children each. Life expectancy for women has also increased everywhere, with the greatest gains in northern Africa, Eastern and Western Asia and Central America. The smallest gains are seen in Eastern Europe.

211   Despite their educational advances, the report notes, women still face major obstacles to assuming top decision-making positions in their societies. Women at the highest levels of government are the exception in all regions. At the end of 1994, only 10 women were heads of State or Government, and there were few women at the ministerial and sub-ministerial levels. Likewise, women rarely account for more than 1 or 2 per cent of top executive business positions. In many

95/ Document 125
See page 622

96/ Document 126
See page 640

97/ Document 119
See page 584

countries women are well represented in the health and education professions, but most still work at the bottom levels of the status and wage hierarchy.

98/Document 120

See page 591

212   "Much therefore remains to be done before the world can claim that the objectives of the Nairobi Forward-looking Strategies have been achieved", stated the second review and appraisal on the implementation of the Nairobi Forward-looking Strategies.[98] A third and final review of progress since Nairobi will be made in the year 2000. The Economic and Social Council, in a 1987 decision, recommended holding an international meeting at that time to assess the results and actions taken.

Strengthening the Commission on the Status of Women

213   As the scope of United Nations assistance to advance the status of women expanded during the Decade for Women and increasingly became an element of mainstream United Nations programmes, the Commission on the Status of Women became less influential. The Commission's lack of influence is attributable to the fact that from 1970 to 1986 it had only met biennially—and then just for a few weeks. Also the Commission had not been charged with the preparations for the Mexico City or Copenhagen Conferences and the reporting and implementation mechanisms established for the Decade had been diffused throughout the United Nations system. The Commission exercised little review over the development assistance that increasingly had become the focus of United Nations support for women. Some States had even proposed the abolition of the Commission in 1980, and argued for transferring its functions to the Economic and Social Council.

99/ Document 89

See page 372;

Document 90

See page 374

214   However, the fact that the Commission was given full responsibility for the preparations for the Nairobi Conference led the General Assembly to establish a new mandate for it in 1987: to monitor the global implementation of the Nairobi Forward-looking Strategies.[99] As a result, the Commission's focus shifted from its earlier efforts to promote women's equality to the problems of women in broader contexts. The themes dealt with by the Commission cut across traditional lines and include matters related to economic development, human rights, political conditions and cultural issues, as well as social policy questions. Its approach was now to deal with women's issues as part of the mainstream rather than in isolation.

215   After the Nairobi Conference, the Commission on the Status of Women expanded its role as a catalyst for women's issues at all levels,

working to develop action-oriented proposals to help Governments devise national programmes to overcome structural, systemic and pervasive discrimination against women. The Commission devoted its 1987 session to reformulating its work plans in the light of the Nairobi Forward-looking Strategies. "The role of the Commission as the principal technical body in its field is to provide dynamic, creative and catalytic policy input to the work of the Economic and Social Council and the General Assembly", the Commission said in the report of its 1988 session.

216   Despite the Commission's efforts to prepare for the task ahead, it was becoming apparent that the full implementation of the Nairobi Strategies by the target year of 2000 would be difficult. "After five years of implementation of the Nairobi Forward-looking Strategies for the Advancement of Women, and one third of the time set for achieving the objectives has elapsed, obstacles remain", the Economic and Social Council concluded in 1990. Although the continued efforts of women throughout the world to achieve equality, development and peace had begun to have an effect at the grass-roots level, their efforts had yet to be translated into improvements in the daily lives of most women.[100]

100/ Document 98
See page 444

217   The Commission also served as the preparatory body for the 1995 Fourth World Conference on Women. Following the Conference, the General Assembly mandated the Commission to integrate into its work programme a follow-up process to the Conference, in which the Commission would play a catalytic role, regularly reviewing the critical areas of concern in the Platform for Action. At its 1996 session, the Commission addressed these increased responsibilities in the formulation of its multi-year work programme for 1996-2000.

Monitoring the 1979 Convention

218   Under article 18 of the Convention on the Elimination of All Forms of Discrimination against Women, States which are parties to the Convention are obligated to report within one year of ratification, and subsequently every four years, on the steps they have taken and the obstacles they face in implementing the Convention.[101]

101/ Document 69
See page 244

219   These reports are submitted to the Committee on the Elimination of Discrimination against Women, the multinational expert panel empowered to meet annually to monitor the implementation of the Convention. The Committee examines the government reports in public meetings at which government representatives are present to answer questions put by Committee members. It also requests information from United Nations agencies and NGOs to help its members assess the

government reports. Members of the Committee have emphasized the importance of information provided by NGOs in their task of assessing the status of women in the countries under review.

220   The Committee issues general recommendations that provide detailed guidance to States parties on different articles of the Convention, and the steps necessary to comply with them. These recommendations, although non-binding interpretations of the Convention, help to influence Governments to take steps towards coming into compliance. General recommendations adopted by the Committee since 1986 cover such issues as women's economic position, the impact of structural adjustment programmes, maternity leave, measures taken to allow women to combine child-bearing with employment, violence against women, the dissemination of the Convention and its provisions, and the extent to which NGOs have been incorporated into the process of preparing national reports on the implementation of the Convention.

221   Like the Commission on the Status of Women, the Committee is concerned with general trends and patterns and is not charged with investigating individual cases of violations of women's rights. In 1995, the Commission on the Status of Women recommended to the Economic and Social Council that it begin work on an optional protocol to the 1979 Convention that would allow the right of petition in individual cases.[102] In response, the Council adopted a resolution, requesting the Secretary-General to invite Governments, intergovernmental organizations and NGOs to submit their views on the question. Work on drafting an optional protocol began at the 1996 session of the Commission on the Status of Women.[103] At present, individual women can bring complaints under the various procedures of the Commission on Human Rights. These include country-specific complaints as well as those on specific themes, such as violence against women, torture or degrading treatment or punishment, freedom of expression and others. Individuals can also bring complaints before the Human Rights Committee against any of the 87 States that are parties to the first Optional Protocol to the International Covenant on Civil and Political Rights. Only a handful of cases concerning the rights of women have been successfully brought before the Human Rights Committee. The Committee has stated that complaints which claim violations of the 1979 Convention may be brought against parties to the Optional Protocol.

222   In 1994, the General Assembly expressed concern that many Governments that have ratified the Convention have done so with reservations. Although the Convention is among the international human rights agreements with the largest number of ratifications (152 as of 15 March 1996), it also has had appended to it one of the largest bodies of reservations of any human rights instrument. A 1994 report of the Secretary-General noted that no reservations had been withdrawn

102/ Document 121
See page 609

103/ Document 138
See page 777

that year, despite the General Assembly's view that many ran "contrary to the object and purpose of the Convention".[104] In 1995, two countries withdrew reservations, but additional reservations were made by two more countries.

104/ Document 139
See page 793

223   In 1994 the General Assembly also said it was troubled by the inadequacy of the time and resources that had been allocated to CEDAW, which had resulted in a backlog of reports awaiting review. Under the terms of the Convention, the Committee was authorized to meet only two weeks a year to review such reports. By comparison, other human rights treaty bodies have longer and more flexible meeting schedules.[105]

105/ Document 111
See page 495

224   In 1994, the General Assembly proposed that the States parties address the Committee's insufficient meeting time by formally amending the Convention. It also strongly supported the Committee's request that the Secretary-General "accord higher priority, within existing resources, to strengthening technical and substantive support for the Committee".[106] In May 1995, States parties to the Convention agreed to amend article 20 of the Convention to allow the length of the Committee's annual meetings to be determined by a meeting of the States parties. The amendment will enter into force when two thirds of the States parties ratify it.[107]

106/ Document 118
See page 581

107/ Document 123
See page 612

Targeting violence against women

225   Violence against women takes many forms, which are now recognized as major impediments to the right of women to participate fully in society. This represents a major shift in perception since 1979, when the Convention on the Elimination of All Forms of Discrimination against Women was adopted. The Convention contains no specific provision on gender-based violence, despite the fact that the issue is fundamental to its provisions, as the Commission on the Status of Women and, later, the Committee on the Elimination of Discrimination against Women made clear.

226   In earlier decades, international discussions in the Commission on the Status of Women and other forums did not address the issue of violence as an all-encompassing human rights problem requiring specific government response. Instead, the problem was framed in terms of domestic violence and violence involving specific categories of women, such as refugees and migrant workers. Many in the international community regarded violence against women as a private matter between individuals, not a public human rights issue requiring government or international action. However, after many years of work by women's organizations and other NGOs, a view began to take hold among Governments that all forms of violence against women, including domestic abuse, are a matter of major concern to the international community.

227 The 1985 Nairobi Forward-looking Strategies had acknowledged that "violence against women exists in various forms in everyday life in all societies", and urged Governments to adopt legal measures "to prevent violence and to assist women victims". It called such abuses as beatings, mutilations, burnings, sexual abuse and rape a major obstacle to peace for which "preventive policies should be elaborated, and institutionalized forms of assistance to women victims provided". But it did not explicitly categorize violence against women as a specific human rights abuse covered by the 1979 Convention.[108] In 1986, the Economic and Social Council declared that violence in the family was a grave violation of the rights of women, and in 1991 the Commission on the Status of Women recommended the convening of an expert group meeting to determine what international instrument might be needed to confront the problem.

108/ Document 84
See page 310

228 In January 1992, the Committee on the Elimination of Discrimination against Women adopted a general recommendation in which it affirmed that under the Convention, violence against women was indeed a form of gender discrimination. The Committee held that the Convention obliged Governments to eliminate gender discrimination by any person, organization or enterprise. It was clear that discrimination on the basis of gender included "violence which is directed against a woman because she is a woman or which affects women disproportionately".[109] This included acts which inflicted physical, mental or sexual harm or suffering, threats of such acts, coercion or other deprivations of liberty. The Committee also noted that "States may also be responsible for private acts (of violence) if they fail to act with due diligence to prevent violations of rights, or to investigate and punish acts of violence, and to provide compensation".

109/ Document 115
See page 528

229 In August 1992 an inter-sessional working group of the Commission on the Status of Women, the first in many years, completed the draft of a declaration on violence against women. The Declaration on the Elimination of Violence against Women was adopted by the General Assembly on 20 December 1993.

230 "States should condemn violence against women", the Declaration said, "and should not invoke any custom, tradition or religious consideration to avoid their obligations with respect to its elimination."[110] The General Assembly recognized that violence against women was "a manifestation of historically unequal power relations between men and women" to which certain women were "especially vulnerable"—members of indigenous and minority groups, refugees, the disabled, the elderly, the destitute and those caught in armed conflicts. "Violence against women is an obstacle to the achievement of equality, development and peace", the Assembly added, expressing alarm that opportunities for women to achieve legal, social, political and economic equality in society were limited by continuing and endemic violence.

110/ Document 107
See page 474

A Special Rapporteur on violence

231   A new phase in the United Nations commitment to the growing campaign against violence began in March 1994, when the Commission on Human Rights welcomed the General Assembly's adoption of the Declaration on the Elimination of Violence against Women, and announced that it had decided to appoint a Special Rapporteur to collect the most comprehensive data, and to recommend measures at the "national, regional and international level" to eliminate violence against women and its causes.[111] The impetus for this action came from the World Conference on Human Rights, held the previous year, which had declared that violence against women was a fundamental human rights issue and called for the appointment of a Special Rapporteur on violence against women.

111/ Document 110
See page 492

232   The Commission on Human Rights said it was deeply concerned at evidence of "continuing and endemic violence against women". It expressed alarm at the "marked increase in acts of sexual violence" against women and children as described in the Final Declaration of the International Conference for the Protection of War Victims, held in Geneva in 1993.

233   In November 1994, the Special Rapporteur on violence against women submitted a preliminary report to the Commission on Human Rights proposing "the formulation of an optional protocol" to the 1979 Convention that would allow individuals victimized by violence the right of petition once local remedies had been exhausted. "This will ensure", she said, "that women victims of violence have a final recourse under an international human rights instrument to have their rights established and vindicated".[112] The proposal was endorsed by the Commission on the Status of Women in a 1995 resolution.

112/ Document 115
See page 528

234   Of special concern was violence perpetrated against certain groups of women, including women migrant workers. Presenting in some detail the dimensions of the problem, the Special Rapporteur noted that violence against women migrant workers ranged from inhumane working conditions, such as long working hours, no days off and non-payment of wages, to starvation, beatings and rape. In her 1994 preliminary report, the Special Rapporteur suggested that international instruments should be used to reinforce the duty of sending countries to apprise citizens of their rights and of receiving countries to ensure protection for the human rights of all people within its borders.

235   The first report of the Secretary-General to the General Assembly on this issue, in 1994, indicated that the problem of violence against women migrant workers had been increasing as part of a growth in international migration and a shift in its nature toward temporary migration for the purpose of work.[113] The methods of recruitment of women migrant workers and the types of work they performed made

113/ Document 112
See page 506

them vulnerable to violence. In 1995, the General Assembly urged Member States to enact and reinforce penal, civil, labour and administrative sanctions in domestic legislation to punish and redress the wrongs done to women who were subjected to any form of violence, whether in the home, the workplace, the community or society as a whole. The Assembly reiterated the need for sending and receiving States to conduct regular consultations for the purpose of identifying and addressing problems in promoting and protecting the rights of women migrant workers.[114]

114/ Document 133
See page 766

236   In a related issue, the General Assembly noted with concern the increasing number of women and girls from developing countries and from some countries with economies in transition who were being victimized by traffickers.[115] As reported in 1995, trafficking has become a highly organized worldwide phenomenon.[116] As a result, the focus of attention has increasingly shifted to the international dimensions of the problem and away from the issue as a purely domestic concern. "The effective suppression of trafficking in women and girls for the sex trade is a matter of pressing concern", the General Assembly stated, and there is an "urgent need" to adopt effective measures to protect them from this nefarious traffic. The Assembly declared all forms of sexual violence and sexual trafficking to be violations of the human rights of women and girls, and invited Governments to consider the development of standard minimum rules for the humanitarian treatment of trafficked persons, consistent with internationally recognized human rights standards. In addition, it urged concerned Governments to support comprehensive, practical approaches to assist women and children victimized by international trafficking to return home.

115/ Document 132
See page 764

116/ Document 124
See page 614

237   Violence against children, in particular against girls, was of particular concern to the General Assembly in 1995 when it adopted its first-ever resolution on the girl child.[117] Noting that discrimination against girls and the violation of their rights had been identified as a critical area of concern at the Beijing Conference (see paragraph 264), the General Assembly urged Member States to eliminate such discrimination, including negative cultural attitudes and practices, as well as all forms of violence against children, especially girls.

117/ Document 130
See page 762

238   In areas of continuing conflict, violence against women has escalated. Women in the former Yugoslavia have been subjected to systematic rape, a war crime under the Geneva Conventions of 1949 and the Additional Protocols of 1977. Both the Security Council and the General Assembly have strongly condemned these acts of extreme brutality. In 1994, the Commission on the Status of Women adopted a resolution encouraging the International Tribunal for the former Yugoslavia to give priority to the consideration of such heinous crimes as rape. In 1995, the General Assembly reaffirmed that rape in the conduct

of armed conflict constitutes a war crime and, under certain circumstances, is a crime against humanity and an act of genocide as defined in the Convention on the Prevention and Punishment of the Crime of Genocide. Women and children must be protected from such acts and the perpetrators brought to justice, the Assembly declared.[118]

118/ Document 134
See page 767

239   There is also a growing recognition that refugee women and girls need special protection against human rights abuses. Eighty per cent of refugees and displaced persons are women and children. A legal instrument, the Convention relating to the Status of Refugees, had been adopted in 1951, and Guidelines on the Protection of Refugee Women had been drawn up by the Office of the United Nations High Commissioner for Refugees (UNHCR) in 1991. In 1995, UNHCR issued new guidelines on preventing and responding to sexual violence against refugees. Later in 1995, the General Assembly asked that States develop and implement criteria and guidelines on responding to the persecution of refugee women, including persecution through sexual violence and other gender-related persecution.

240   In my message marking International Women's Day on 7 March 1995, I declared that it was time for Member States to consider putting the Declaration on the Elimination of Violence against Women into legally binding form.

A continuum of conferences

241   The 1990s saw the emergence of a joint effort by the United Nations Secretariat, Member States, non-governmental organizations and other representatives of civil society to create an integrated global agenda for development. As part of this undertaking, the United Nations has led a drive for greater international cooperation. The cornerstone of that drive is a series of global conferences and summit meetings on various aspects of development in the years leading up to the twenty-first century. They are designed not only to achieve concrete programmes of action, but also to open the world's eyes to the reality that the issues they address—the environment, human rights, population, social development—are interconnected. The goals they seek are all dependent upon the advancement of women.

Conference on Environment and Development

242   The 1992 United Nations Conference on Environment and Development (UNCED), or Earth Summit, drew an estimated 30,000 delegates and non-governmental representatives to Rio de Janeiro, including 108 heads of State or Government. UNCED reflected a global consensus on the vital role of women in promoting sustainable development. It also marked the international community's formal recognition

of the importance of strengthening women's expertise in environment and development issues while enhancing their legal and administrative capacities to be managers and decision makers.

243   "Women have a vital role in environmental management and development", world leaders affirmed in the Rio Declaration on Environment and Development. "Their full participation is therefore essential to achieve sustainable development." Agenda 21, a set of guidelines for sustainable development into the twenty-first century that resulted from UNCED, declared that the effort to develop sustainably, using the resources of the planet in a way that perpetuates them for future generations, cannot succeed unless it involves the full participation of women—and reflects women's interests, needs and perspectives.

244   In the Agenda 21 chapter entitled "Global action for women towards sustainable and equitable development", the leaders called for clear government policies and national guidelines, strategies and plans for the achievement of equality in all aspects of society. This included "the promotion of women's literacy, education, training, nutrition and health, and their participation in key decision-making positions and in the management of the environment".[119]

119/ Document 104
See page 467

The World Conference on Human Rights

245   The ongoing United Nations effort to build on the principles of the Charter of the United Nations and the Universal Declaration of Human Rights continued in June 1993 at the World Conference on Human Rights held in Vienna. That meeting—which drew representatives from 171 Member States—provided the impetus for the ongoing international campaign for the implementation, promotion and protection of the human rights of women. In response to calls from women's organizations around the world, the issue of women's rights was a major theme of the Conference. The Vienna Declaration and Programme of Action adopted by the Conference urged that Governments and the United Nations ensure the "full and equal enjoyment by women of all human rights"; underlined the importance of the integration and full participation of women "as both agents and beneficiaries" of development; and reiterated the importance of achieving the goals for women set forth in the Rio Declaration and Agenda 21.[120]

120/ Document 106
See page 472

246   At the related NGO Forum, a Global Tribunal on Violations of Women's Rights attended by some 1,000 people heard dramatic testimony from many parts of the world on the violations of women's rights and demonstrated that existing human rights mechanisms are inadequate to protect women.

247   The Vienna Conference recommended that measures to assure "the equal status of women and the human rights of women" be integrated into the mainstream of the United Nations system, with

increased cooperation between the Commission on the Status of Women, the Commission on Human Rights, the Committee on the Elimination of Discrimination against Women, the United Nations Development Fund for Women, the United Nations Development Programme and other United Nations bodies. It also concluded that steps should be taken by the Division for the Advancement of Women to ensure that human rights activities of the United Nations regularly address women's human rights, including gender-specific abuse.

248   In the Vienna Declaration and Programme of Action, delegates stressed the importance of working towards the elimination of violence against women in public and private life; the elimination of all forms of sexual harassment, exploitation and trafficking in women; the elimination of gender bias in the administration of justice; and the eradication of "any conflicts which may arise between the rights of women and the harmful effects of certain traditional or customary practices, cultural prejudices and religious extremism".

249   The Conference found that violations of women's rights in situations of armed conflict—together with murder, systematic rape, sexual slavery and forced pregnancy—were all affronts to the most fundamental principles of internationally recognized human rights and humanitarian law.

International Conference on Population and Development

250   The International Conference on Population and Development, held in Cairo in September 1994, affirmed that there are four requirements for any programme of population and development: gender equality and equity; the empowerment of women; the ability of women to control their own fertility; and the elimination of all violence against women.[121]

251   The empowerment of women and the elevation of their status are both important ends in themselves, the Conference declared in its Programme of Action, and are essential if sustainable development is to succeed. To achieve those ends, the Conference made three basic recommendations: that mechanisms be established for women's equal participation and equitable representation at all levels of the political process and public life; that efforts be made to promote women's education, employment and skills development; and that all discriminatory practices be eliminated, including those in the workplace and those affecting access to credit, control of property and social security.

252   The Conference also singled out for special attention the problem of discrimination against female children. Noting that in all societies discrimination on the basis of gender often starts at the earliest stages of life, the Conference called on Governments and leaders at all levels of society to speak out strongly and take effective action against

121/ Document 113
See page 515

gender discrimination within the family based on preference for sons. It also urged special education and public information efforts to promote equal treatment of boys and girls in matters involving nutrition, health, education and social, economic and political activity, as well as equitable systems of inheritance. Governments were urged to prohibit female genital mutilation and to prevent infanticide, prenatal sex selection, trafficking in female children and the use of young women in prostitution and pornography. In addition, the Conference endorsed integrated national programmes to protect the social health of girls and young women, including the strict enforcement of laws to ensure that marriage is entered into only with the free and full consent of the intended spouses.

253   In a chapter of the Programme of Action entitled "Male responsibilities and participation", the Cairo Conference called upon Governments to promote the "equal participation of women and men in all areas of family and household responsibilities, including family planning, child rearing and housework". Men, the Conference declared, have a vital role to play in ensuring gender equality because, in most societies, they exercise preponderant power in nearly every sphere of life.[122]

122/ Document 113
See page 515

The World Summit for Social Development

254   The central role of women in fighting poverty, creating productive jobs and strengthening the social fabric was proclaimed in the international agreement adopted at the World Summit for Social Development in March 1995 in Copenhagen. One hundred seventeen world leaders attended the Summit, which eclipsed the 1992 Rio Conference as history's largest conference of heads of State or Government.

255   The Copenhagen Declaration, built around 10 commitments for achieving social development, included an acknowledgement by the world leaders that more women than men live in absolute poverty and that they carry a disproportionate share of the problems of coping with poverty, social disintegration, unemployment, environmental degradation and the effects of war. "We acknowledge that social and economic development cannot be secured in a sustainable way without the full participation of women", the leaders said in the Copenhagen Declaration. Moreover, they stated, "equality and equity between women and men is a priority for the international community and, as such, must be the centre of economic and social development".

256   There was a recognition at the Copenhagen Summit that, with the end of the cold war, the concept of security had changed profoundly. As the threat of direct aggression by one State against another decreased, people's security in their daily lives—in their homes, their jobs, their communities, their environment—became a new imperative. A vital element in this campaign, the world leaders reaffirmed, was the recogni-

tion and enhancement of the role of women—in development, and at all levels of political, civil, economic, social and cultural life.

257   "The world has embraced the market economy with its boundless potential", I told the Summit on 11 March 1995, but "there has come a recognition that the very poorest countries cannot follow that model until they possess foundations that can only be built with help from others." The Copenhagen Summit was the international community's most forthright acknowledgement that the problems faced by women lie at the heart of the global agenda.

258   Commitment Five of the Copenhagen Declaration—a pledge to promote "full respect for human dignity" and to achieve "equality and equity between men and women"—includes promises to promote a series of goals at the national level. These include pledges to promote the participation of women—both urban and rural women, as well as women with disabilities—in social, economic and political life; to broaden women's roles in decision-making at all levels, with special emphasis on indigenous women, those at the grass-roots level and the poor; to promote women's full access to literacy, education and training; and to remove all obstacles to women's acquisition of credit and to their equal right to buy, hold and sell land and property.[123]

259   The heads of State or Government also agreed to ensure women's equal right to work; to assure the status, welfare and opportunity of female children, especially in regard to health, nutrition, literacy and education; to promote the equal partnership of women and men in family and community life and society; to eliminate all forms of discrimination, exploitation, abuse and violence against women and female children; and to ensure women's full and equal enjoyment of all human rights and fundamental freedoms.

260   The Declaration also affirmed the importance of the Social Summit as a bridge to the Beijing Women's Conference. World leaders pledged to "give specific attention to the preparations for the Fourth World Conference on Women", and to the "implementation and follow-up of the conclusions" of the women's gathering.[124]

Fourth World Conference on Women

261   The 1995 Fourth World Conference on Women, held in Beijing from 4 to 15 September during the fiftieth anniversary year of the United Nations, moved the global agenda for the advancement of women into the twenty-first century and beyond. The Beijing Declaration and the Platform for Action, adopted unanimously by 189 countries, consolidated five decades of legal advances aimed at securing the equality of women and men in law and in fact. They built on political agreements reached at the three previous global conferences on women to establish 12 priority areas for action by the international community over the next

123/ Document 122
See page 611

124/ Document 122
See page 611

five years. With over 47,000 people attending the intergovernmental meeting and its parallel NGO Forum in Huairou, the Beijing Conference was the largest gathering ever held of government and NGO representatives.

262   The Conference was preceded by a preparatory process that was perhaps more participatory and inclusive than any in history. Between June and November 1994, five regional preparatory meetings were held under the auspices of the United Nations regional commissions. Each regional meeting either coincided with or was preceded by NGO preparatory meetings and consultations with youth delegations. In addition, National Committees, set up by Governments and NGOs, reviewed the status of women in their respective countries, analysed the draft Platform and forwarded their own recommendations to the Commission on the Status of Women, the preparatory body for the Beijing Conference. Reports submitted by 170 countries formed the basis of the Second Review and Appraisal of the Nairobi Forward-looking Strategies for the Advancement of Women to the Year 2000, which in turn served as a basis for the recommendations made in the Platform for Action.

263   However, by its very nature the preparatory process revealed diverging views which made consensus difficult. Five months before the Conference, in April 1995, the Commission on the Status of Women concluded negotiations on the draft Platform for Action and recommended that the document be transmitted to Beijing for adoption by the Conference. The Commission members, gathered in New York, had reached general agreement on 12 critical areas of concern to women and on a broad strategy for overcoming them. But there was no consensus on about one third of the proposed actions. These included such issues as sexual and reproductive health and rights and the definition of the word "gender". Central to the Commission's debate were issues that had defined the Population Conference in 1994: gender equality and equity; the empowerment of women; women's reproductive rights; and the elimination of violence against women.

Beijing Platform for Action

264   The Platform identified 12 critical areas of concern considered to represent the main obstacles to women's advancement since the Nairobi Conference and which required concrete action by Governments and civil society over the next five years.[125] They included the burden of poverty on women; unequal access to education and training; unequal access to health care and related services; violence against women; the effects of armed or other kinds of conflict on women; inequality in economic structures and policies, in all forms of productive activities and in access to resources; inequality in the sharing of power and decision-making; insufficient mechanisms to promote the advancement of

125/ Document 127
See page 647

women; inadequate protection and promotion of women's human rights; stereotyping of women and inequality in women's access to and participation in all communication systems, especially in the media; gender inequalities in the management of natural resources and in safeguarding the environment; and persistent discrimination against girls and violations of their rights.

265   In proposing strategic objectives and multi-tiered actions for removing existing obstacles to women's advancement, the Platform's drafters were guided by developments since the Nairobi conference on women a decade before. Important progress had been made towards achieving gender equality in the areas of education, health, employment and human rights. A worldwide movement towards democratization had opened up the political process in many nations, giving women a greater voice.

266   At the same time, in no country in the world did women and men enjoy complete equality of rights and opportunities. Decisions that affected all people's lives were still being made mostly by men, and political instability, economic recession, structural adjustment programmes and environmental degradation continued to have a disproportionately negative impact on women. Facing flagrant as well as subtle discrimination and marginalization, women often were unable to share equally in the fruits of their own labour. The Platform for Action proposed a new course of action which, if implemented, would reverse this trend and make a difference in women's status.

Broadening women's rights through consensus

267   The draft Platform, as it was sent to Beijing from the final preparatory meeting, contained 468 bracketed passages—each delineating an area of disagreement that needed further negotiations. After 12 days of intense discussions, the delegates at the Conference finally agreed on a consensus document that would greatly enhance women's rights and set new benchmarks for the advancement of women and the achievement of gender equality.

268   Among other things, the Conference reiterated women's right to have control over and decide freely and responsibly on matters related to their sexuality, including sexual and reproductive health, free of coercion, discrimination and violence. Governments agreed to provide women with accessible and affordable health-care services, including sexual and family planning information and services.

269   Agreement was also reached on strategic objectives and actions to combat poverty, beginning with absolute poverty, which affects well over 1 billion people, the majority of them women. Building on commitments made at the World Summit for Social Development held six months earlier, Governments agreed to review, adopt and maintain

macroeconomic policies and development strategies that addressed the needs and efforts of poor women. They also pledged to revise laws and administrative practices aimed at ensuring women's equal rights and access to economic resources.

270   The Platform for Action called upon Governments to take steps to abolish traditional practices harmful to girls, including female infanticide, prenatal sex selection, genital mutilation, sexual abuse and sexual exploitation, as well as early marriage and discrimination against girls in food allocation. They were also asked to enact laws that would ensure that marriage is entered into only with free and full consent.

271   Consensus was also reached on the need to recognize women's unremunerated household work and contribution to food production, both of which are undervalued and under-recorded. The Platform for Action called for measuring, in quantitative terms, unremunerated work that is outside current national accounting systems.

272   In areas of health and education, the Platform set time-specific targets. It committed Governments to ensure universal access to basic education and the completion of primary education by at least 80 per cent of primary-school-age children, to close the gender gap in primary- and secondary-school education by the year 2005 and to provide universal primary education in all countries before 2015. It also asked Governments to reduce maternal mortality by at least 50 per cent of 1990 levels by the year 2000 and by another 50 per cent by the year 2015.

273   The Conference reiterated that women's rights were human rights. Governments were asked to limit reservations to the 1979 Convention on the Elimination of All Forms of Discrimination against Women and to withdraw reservations that were contrary to the purpose of the Convention. They were urged to adopt and implement legislation to end violence against women and work actively to ratify and implement all international agreements related to violence against women.

274   On power-sharing, the Platform recommended actions by Governments to ensure women's equal access to and full participation in power structures and decision-making in governmental bodies and public administration entities. It also recommended creating or strengthening national machineries and other governmental bodies and bringing gender perspectives to legislation, public policy programmes and projects. The Platform asked Governments to involve women actively in environmental decision-making at all levels and to strengthen or establish mechanisms at the national, regional and international levels to assess the impact of development and environmental policies on women.

275   Similarly, the Platform called for increasing women's participation in the media. Governments should aim at gender balance through the appointment of women and men to all advisory, management, regulatory or monitoring bodies. The media were asked to

develop professional guidelines, codes of conduct and other forms of self-regulation to promote the presentation of non-stereotyped images of women, consistent with freedom of expression.

276   In a section that linked peace with development and equality, the three sub-themes of the Conference, the Platform recognized that women are affected in many ways during war or armed conflicts. Though women often do not have any role in the decisions leading to such conflicts and seldom are combatants themselves, they are left to maintain families as the sole parent and as managers of the household, caretakers of elderly relatives and caregivers for injured combatants. The Platform acknowledged that women and girls particularly suffer the consequences of armed conflict because of their status in society and their gender. Parties to conflict often rape women with impunity, sometimes using rape as a tactic of war and terrorism.

277   To address the situation, the Platform called for increasing the participation of women in conflict resolution at decision-making levels. It also called for, as appropriate and subject to national security considerations, reducing excessive military expenditures and converting military resources and related industries to development and peaceful purposes. Mindful of the fact that the overwhelming majority of the world's millions of refugees are women and children, the Platform urged Governments, intergovernmental bodies and NGOs to provide protection, assistance and training to refugee women.

278   In another significant decision relating to peace, the Platform recognized that women and children are particularly affected by the indiscriminate use of anti-personnel mines. It called for the universal ratification by the year 2000 of international instruments that prohibit or restrict the use of land-mines, and urged the strengthening of the 1981 Convention on Prohibitions or Restrictions on the Use of Certain Conventional Weapons Which May Be Deemed to Be Excessively Injurious or to Have Indiscriminate Effects.

279   Differences became apparent in discussions on such issues as inheritance rights, the role of culture and religion, and the role of the family. For example, some delegates who felt that traditional legal structures often discriminated against women in land rights supported "equal inheritance". Others argued that their religious inheritance laws, based on the principle of equity, mandated a distribution of assets that gave a woman half the amount that her brother inherited. Informal consultations produced a compromise that placed emphasis on the injustice and discrimination faced by women and girls and upheld their equal right to inheritance. The formulation agreed upon in the Platform called for "enacting, as appropriate, and enforcing legislation that guarantees equal right to succession and ensures equal right to inherit, regardless of the sex of the child".

280   Some of the longest and most intense debates concerned a draft text in the Platform dealing with health, which called for "full respect for the various religious and ethical values and cultural backgrounds". The text was finally incorporated in the Global Framework chapter of the Platform, which recognized the "significance of and full respect for various religious and cultural backgrounds and philosophical convictions of individuals and their communities" in achieving equality, development and peace. It also described the implementation of the Platform as "the sovereign responsibility of each State, in conformity with all human rights and fundamental freedoms".

281   On the role of the family, the delegates agreed to recognize it as the basic unit of society and acknowledged the "social significance" of maternity, motherhood and the role of parents in the family and in the upbringing of children. The Platform for Action also emphasized that maternity must not be a basis for discrimination or restrict the full participation of women in society. On parental responsibility, the Platform recognized the rights and duties of parents and legal guardians to provide guidance in the exercise of the rights of young people, but it also upheld rights of young people to information, privacy, confidentiality and informed consent on matters related to sexuality and reproduction.

282   The 189 Governments attending the Beijing Conference also unanimously adopted the Beijing Declaration, in which they declared their commitment to the full implementation of the Platform and pledged to intensify efforts to ensure equal enjoyment of human rights and fundamental freedoms for women and girls.[126] Governments recognized the need to take priority action for the advancement of women and to ensure a gender perspective in their policies and programmes. The Beijing Declaration and the Platform for Action are the two fundamental documents to guide women's advancement into the twenty-first century, Governments declared.

126/ **Document 127**
See page 647

Implementation, follow-up and monitoring

283   Governments are identified by the Platform for Action as having primary responsibility for the implementation of the proposed actions. They are called upon to begin, as soon as possible, to develop implementation strategies for the Platform, with a view to their completion by the end of 1996. National planning should be broad-based and participatory, comprehensive, time-bound, and should include proposals for allocating or reallocating resources for implementation. However, the success of the new five-year plan will depend on various national, regional and international institutions. To ensure its implementation, the Platform calls for committing adequate financial resources from all sources and across all sectors.

284   The General Assembly, in a resolution adopted in December 1995, endorsed the Beijing Declaration and the Platform for Action and called upon all States and bodies of the United Nations system and other international organizations, as well as NGOs, to take action to implement them.[127] The Assembly decided to review progress in implementing the Platform for Action on a regular basis, starting in 1996 and culminating in the year 2000 with a review of both the Nairobi Forward-looking Strategies and the Platform for Action "in an appropriate forum".

127/ Document 135
See page 769

285   The Platform accords the United Nations system in general, and the Secretary-General in particular, a key role in the implementation and monitoring of the Platform. The United Nations system is asked to integrate a gender perspective into all its policies and programmes. United Nations bodies, including the General Assembly and the Economic and Social Council, are asked to include follow-up to the Conference as part of their continuing work on the advancement of women. The Council, for example, is asked to devote at least one high-level segment before the year 2000 to considering the advancement of women. The Platform also calls for strengthening the Commission on the Status of Women and the Committee on the Elimination of Discrimination against Women and providing both with necessary financial support through the allocation of resources from within the regular United Nations budget.

286   As Secretary-General of the Organization, I am firmly committed to carrying out the tasks entrusted to me by the Platform for Action. As I told the delegates in Beijing, these responsibilities pose a challenge to the capacity and commitment of the United Nations. I accept that challenge. To this end, as stated in my 1995 report to the General Assembly on the outcome of the Beijing Conference, I have proposed the establishment of an inter-agency committee on the empowerment and advancement of women.[128] Work is being completed on a revised system-wide medium-term plan for the advancement of women for the period 1996-2000. In response to a recommendation by the Beijing Conference, I have designated a senior member of my office as my adviser on gender issues. This Special Adviser will facilitate coordination and will assist me in ensuring that the gender perspective is integrated into overall policy-making and programming, and in furthering the Organization's linkages with civil society.

128/ Document 129
See page 748

Advancing women's status in the United Nations system

287   I have also taken measures to implement the mandate from the Beijing Conference to improve the status of women in the United Nations Secretariat, which has been an ongoing process. The General Assembly,

first in a 1986 resolution, asked the Secretary-General and the heads of the specialized agencies and other United Nations bodies to establish five-year targets for raising the percentage of women in professional and decision-making positions in the United Nations system.[129] Later, in 1990, the Assembly established targets for the percentage of women in professional jobs, saying that by year's end the Secretariat staff should be at least 30 per cent female in posts subject to geographical distribution. This figure was to increase to 35 per cent by 1995—and to 25 per cent for women in senior management positions.[130] The Secretary-General was also asked to develop an action programme for the advancement of women in the Secretariat for the period 1991-1995; and to produce "a comprehensive evaluation and analysis" of the main obstacles to improving women's status at the United Nations.

288 My Strategic Plan of Action for the Improvement of the Status of Women in the Secretariat (1995-2000), which was endorsed by the General Assembly in 1994, sets out three targets: to achieve an overall female staff representation of 35 per cent by the end of 1995; to have women in 25 per cent of all senior positions before 1997; and to reach complete gender equality in the Secretariat (50 per cent women) by the end of the century.[131] These are more than numbers. The 1995 Strategic Plan is part of a comprehensive approach, requiring major changes in the United Nations management culture, in the system of staff appraisal and accountability and in the recruitment and promotion process. I have established a new Planning and Development Service to develop overall human-resources planning strategies by projecting vacancies, determining the staff function requirements of organizational units, inventorying the skills of current staff and developing strategies to match the two. A new performance appraisal system has been introduced with measures built into it to hold managers accountable for how they deal with gender-related issues. Consolidated guidelines on the achievement of gender equality have been issued and I have reiterated to the staff my commitment to achieving this target.[132]

289 As I reported to the General Assembly in 1995, improvements have been made in appointing and promoting qualified women.[133] For example, the percentage of women in posts subject to geographical distribution had increased to 34.6 per cent at the end of 1995, just below the 35 per cent target established by the General Assembly. The percentage of women in senior management was 17 per cent, still well below the 25 per cent target. But during 1995, a higher proportion of women than men were promoted (51.2 per cent), 29.2 per cent to senior management levels. I am also pleased to report that one department, the Department of Public Information, reached gender equality for professional posts at the end of 1995. I expect more departments to follow, in line with the recommendations of the Beijing Plat-

129/ Document 95
See page 440

130/ Document 101
See page 455

131/ Document 114
See page 519

132/ Document 136
See page 773;

Document 137
See page 776

133/ Document 128
See page 735

form for Action that overall gender equality, particularly at the professional level and above, be achieved by the year 2000.

A growing partnership with civil society

290　The United Nations has always been part of a broad, global movement for gender equality, and the most visible and active forces behind this drive have been the non-governmental organizations. Ever since an NGO Forum was organized in Mexico City at the first world conference on women, this parallel event has emerged as an integral part of all United Nations conferences on women. The growth of the NGO Forum has been impressive. In Mexico City, less than 5,000 non-governmental representatives attended the Conference and the Forum. Ten years later, in Nairobi, at the third world conference on women, the number of NGO participants had risen to over 15,000. In Beijing, almost 30,000 NGO representatives were drawn to the Forum.

291　The Beijing NGO Forum, held in Huairou, about 65 kilometres outside Beijing, had two goals: to influence the content of the Platform for Action and to hold a substantive and celebratory gathering highlighting women's vision and strategy for the world in the twenty-first century. With over 3,000 workshops and collaborative events included in the 10-day programme, the Forum provided women from all over the world with a venue to meet together, renewing a sense of global solidarity. NGOs, which were also very active in lobbying at the inter-governmental conference, helped craft new wordings for sections of the Platform for Action dealing with women's human rights, environment and development, disarmament and unpaid work.

292　The NGOs that attended the Beijing Conference will also play an important role in follow-up, especially at the national level. The formal commitments made in speeches to the Conference by over 100 Governments on concrete actions they would take as follow-up to the Conference were quickly compiled by NGO groups and circulated. They vowed to keep their national leaders reminded of the promises made in Beijing.

293　These and thousands of other NGOs are important allies for the United Nations. Their influence, passion and intellectual conviction have helped define the gender agenda of the United Nations. In a fitting tribute, the Beijing Conference acknowledged in the Platform for Action the crucial role civil society plays in mobilizing public opinion in support of the proposed actions for gender equality and the advancement of women's status.

VI Conclusion

294 Throughout the first half-century of its existence, the United Nations has served as a catalyst for the advancement of women, working to promote the principles of gender equality and non-discrimination enshrined in the Charter. From the 1945 founding Conference in San Francisco to the 1995 Fourth World Conference on Women in Beijing, the Organization has been instrumental in elevating the cause of women's rights to the very centre of the global agenda. As today's international community grapples with a vast array of problems whose magnitude and complexity are, in many ways, greater than those faced by the original signatories to the Charter, few would now deny that the advancement of all women—young and old, rich and poor, urban and rural, educated and illiterate—is a prerequisite for progress.

295 The United Nations began its work at a time when women's civil and political rights existed in only a handful of countries. Working through the Commission on the Status of Women and other bodies, the Organization led the way in codifying the legal basis of equality for women. This effort, based on rigorous fact-finding and analysis, produced a series of ground-breaking conventions, declarations and other instruments designed to promote and protect women's political and civil rights in fact as well as in law.

296 Through a campaign that combined diplomacy, public consciousness-raising and technical-assistance programmes and other forms of development aid, the United Nations has also played a central role in expanding the concept of equality beyond politics, marriage and the family to encompass such human rights as equal access to education, job opportunities and health care. These principles found their ultimate expression in a landmark agreement, the 1979 Convention on the Elimination of All Forms of Discrimination against Women. It must be noted, however, that the number of reservations expressed by Governments in adopting the Convention was the highest for any human rights instrument negotiated under the auspices of the United Nations—providing just one indication of the considerable obstacles women face on the road to full equality.

297 In 1975, the World Conference of the International Women's Year adopted a Plan of Action that led to the proclamation by the General Assembly of the United Nations Decade for Women and its goals of equality, development and peace. At the end of the period, in 1985, the Nairobi Forward-looking Strategies for the Advancement of Women to the Year 2000 detailed obstacles still to be overcome and set

forth a comprehensive new framework for action, emphasizing the need for women's equal involvement and participation at all levels of decision-making.

298   With the end of the cold war, the international community began to focus on a range of long-neglected global problems, especially the deepening crises of poverty, unemployment and social unrest and the degradation of the physical environment. In an unprecedented series of interrelated conferences and summit meetings beginning in 1990, the United Nations brought together Governments and increasing numbers of non-governmental organizations—always a potent force in shaping United Nations efforts in support of women—and other elements of civil society in the search for a shared vision of development, one that is human-centred, equitable and environmentally and socially sustainable.

299   This was demonstrated at the 1995 Fourth World Conference on Women. The Platform for Action stands as a milestone for the advancement of women into the twenty-first century. The Beijing gathering, the most heavily attended United Nations conference in history, refocused strategic objectives and set new priorities to enhance the role of women as equal partners in the drive for the betterment of society. It strengthened the consensus that the advancement of women is central to every dimension of development. The 189 Governments represented in Beijing unanimously affirmed that the advancement of women and the achievement of equality with men are matters of fundamental human rights—and therefore a prerequisite for social justice.

300   Yet the Beijing Platform for Action is only a tool in the struggle for the empowerment of women. No true social transformation can occur until every society learns to adopt new values, forging relationships between women and men based on equality, equal responsibility and mutual respect.

301   Although there is formal recognition of women's rights and a legal acceptance of women's equality with men, extensive data gathered by the United Nations show that women continue to face discrimination and marginalization. There is still a gap between what should be, according to law and policy, and what is. The United Nations, its Member States and their partners in civil society must now focus as never before on how to accelerate the practical implementation of programmes aimed at improving women's daily lives and consolidating their status as equals with men.

302   This effort is inextricably linked to the overarching goals of the Charter: the maintenance of international peace and security, the protection of human rights, the creation of an environment of respect for international law and the promotion of economic and social well-being for all people. It is an effort that must overcome stubborn, long-standing barriers as well as new manifestations of discrimination and abuse. And

it is an effort that will demand new forms of international cooperation—and new and powerful expressions of political will. It will challenge traditional approaches to global action and development. But its success will mean a better world for all humanity, for the cause of women's advancement unites us all.

BOUTROS BOUTROS-GHALI

Section Two
Chronology and Documents

I Chronology of events

26 June 1945
The Charter of the United Nations is signed in San Francisco, setting out three objectives for the new Organization: to foster international peace and security, to promote social and economic progress and to define and protect the rights and freedoms of every individual regardless of race, sex, language or religion.
See Document 1, page 103

12 February 1946
During the inaugural session of the United Nations General Assembly in London, Eleanor Roosevelt, wife of the former President of the United States of America and United Nations delegate, reads an "open letter to the women of the world" calling for their increased involvement in national and international affairs.
See Document 2, page 103

16-18 February 1946
The Economic and Social Council (ECOSOC) establishes the Commission on Human Rights, chaired by Mrs. Roosevelt, with a Subcommission on the Status of Women. A Section on the Status of Women is established within the Human Rights Division of the United Nations Secretariat's Department of Social Affairs.
See Document 3, page 109; and Document 4, page 110

29 April–25 May 1946
The Subcommission on the Status of Women, with Bodil Begtrup (Denmark) as Chair, holds its first meeting at the Bronx campus of Hunter College in New York.

21 June 1946
In its resolution 2/11, ECOSOC states that the Subcommission on the Status of Women shall henceforth be known as the Commission on the Status of Women (CSW) — an elevation in the body's status, making it a counterpart of the Commission on Human Rights.
See Document 5, page 111; and Document 6, page 112

11 December 1946
The General Assembly unanimously adopts resolution 56 (I), recommending that all Member States which have not already done so grant women political rights equal to those granted to men and that, in this connection, States adopt measures necessary to fulfil the purposes and aims of the Charter.
See Document 7, page 113

10-24 February 1947
The CSW holds its first session at Lake Success in New York State.
See Document 8, page 113

29 March 1947
On the basis of recommendations made by the CSW at its February session, ECOSOC, in its resolution 48 (IV), formalizes arrangements for the Commission to be represented in the deliberations of other United Nations bodies and to meet annually.
See Document 9, page 120

2 May 1948
The Inter-American Commission of Women adopts the Inter-American Convention on the Granting of Political Rights to Women. The Convention subsequently serves as the model for the 1952 United Nations–sponsored Convention on the Political Rights of Women.

10 December 1948
The General Assembly adopts, in resolution 217 A (III), the Universal Declaration of Human Rights, which sets forth the civil, political, economic, social and cultural rights to which every individual is entitled. The Declaration is the first of three components of an International Bill of Human Rights and includes the proclamation that all human rights and freedoms are to be enjoyed equally by women and men without distinction of any kind.
See Document 14, page 125

2 December 1949
The General Assembly adopts the Convention for the Suppression of the Traffic in Persons and of the Exploitation of the Prostitution of Others, calling for the punishment of those who would procure others, with or without their consent, for the purposes of prostitution.
See Document 18, page 130

29 June 1951
The International Labour Organization (ILO) adopts the Convention on Equal Remuneration, incorporating the principle of equal pay for men and women workers for work of equal value and calling for rates of remuneration to be established without discrimination based on sex.

28 June 1952
The ILO adopts the Maternity Protection Convention, entitling all women workers to maternity leave with cash and medical benefits.

20 December 1952
The Convention on the Political Rights of Women, one of the first legally binding rights agreements negotiated under the auspices of the United Nations, is adopted by the General Assembly. The Convention, under which Member States commit themselves to allowing women to vote, stand for election and hold public office on equal terms with men and without discrimination, comes into force on **7 July 1954**.
See Document 26, page 164

8 April 1954
The Secretary-General addresses the Commission on the Status of Women. This is the first occasion a Secretary-General has done so.
See Document 27, page 166

29 January 1957
The General Assembly adopts the Convention on the Nationality of Married Women, aimed at protecting the right of a married woman to retain her nationality and at eliminating conflicts of law involving the nationality of women who are married, divorced or whose husbands have changed their nationality. The Convention comes into force on **11 August 1958**.
See Document 29, page 167

25 January 1958
The ILO adopts the Discrimination (Employment and Occupation) Convention, whereby member States would adopt national policies to eliminate discrimination in employment on the basis of race, colour, sex, religion, political opinion, national extraction or social origin.

10 July 1958
ECOSOC, by its resolution 680 B II (XXVI), invites the World Health Organization to undertake a study of the persistence of customs which subject girls to ritual operations and of the measures adopted or planned for putting a stop to such practices.

16 July 1962
ECOSOC, by its resolution 884 E (XXXIV), recommends that Governments of Member States make full use of the United Nations technical assistance programme, advisory services programme in human rights and advisory services programme in social welfare serv-

ices for the purpose of promoting and advancing the status of women in developing countries.
See Document 30, page 169

7 November 1962
The General Assembly adopts the Convention on Consent to Marriage, Minimum Age for Marriage and Registration of Marriages, decreeing that no marriage may occur without the consent of both parties. The Convention comes into force on **9 December 1964**.
See Document 31, page 170

7 December 1962
By its resolution 1777 (XVII), the General Assembly requests the Secretary-General to study means of providing and developing new resources aimed especially at the initiation and implementation of a unified long-term United Nations programme for the advancement of women and of expanding assistance for the advancement of women in developing countries.
See Document 32, page 172

5 December 1963
By its resolution 1921 (XVIII), the General Assembly asks the Commission on the Status of Women to begin work on a draft declaration on the elimination of discrimination against women.
See Document 33, page 173

12 December 1963
The General Assembly designates 1968 as the International Year for Human Rights and the occasion for an International Conference on Human Rights to be held in Tehran. The Assembly urges Member States to use the Year — the twentieth anniversary of the adoption of the Universal Declaration of Human Rights — as a deadline for ratifying pending human rights accords, including the 1952 Convention on the Political Rights of Women.

1 November 1965
The General Assembly adopts the Recommendation on Consent to Marriage, Minimum Age for Marriage and Registration of Marriages, which, though non-binding, adds a specific minimum age of 15 years to the 1962 Convention on Consent to Marriage.
See Document 34, page 173

16 December 1966
The General Assembly adopts the International Covenant on Civil and Political Rights and the International Covenant on Economic, Social and Cultural Rights, which, together with the 1948 Universal Declaration of Human Rights, form the International Bill of Human Rights. Both Covenants contain provisions specifying

that all the rights therein apply equally to men and women.
See Document 35, page 174

7 November 1967
The General Assembly unanimously approves the Declaration on the Elimination of Discrimination against Women. The Declaration, consisting of 11 articles, proclaims that discrimination against women is fundamentally unjust and incompatible with the welfare of the family and society, calls for new laws to end discrimination against women and resolves that all women must have full protection under the law.
See Document 36, page 175

22 April–13 May 1968
The International Conference on Human Rights in Tehran adopts 29 resolutions, including one concerning the promotion of women's rights that elaborates the need for a unified long-term programme for the advancement of women. The resolution stresses, among other things, that advancement in the status of women depends upon changes in those traditional attitudes, customs and laws which are based on the idea of the inferiority of women, that education is vital to eliminating discrimination and that technical assistance to women in developing countries should be expanded.
See Document 37, page 177

20 October 1970
The General Assembly, in its resolution 2626 (XXV), adopts the International Development Strategy for the Second United Nations Development Decade (1970-1979), which calls for the full integration of women in the total development effort.

6 April 1971
The Ad Hoc Group on Equal Rights for Women in the United Nations holds its first formal meeting. The Group aims to improve the status of women employed in the Organization.

18 December 1972
The General Assembly designates 1975 as International Women's Year, with a three-part theme: equality, development and peace.
See Document 41, page 183

19-30 August 1974
The United Nations World Population Conference is held in Bucharest; its Plan of Action affirms the central importance of women in population policies.

5-16 November 1974
The World Food Conference, held in Rome, adopts the Universal Declaration on the Eradication of Hunger and Malnutrition, which calls for the recognition by all States of the key role of women in agricultural production and the rural economy and for the availability of appropriate education, extension programmes and financial assistance to women on equal terms with men.

10 December 1974
The General Assembly endorses the ECOSOC decision to convene during International Women's Year a world conference to examine the extent to which United Nations organizations have implemented recommendations for the elimination of discrimination against women made by the CSW since its establishment and to launch an international action programme aimed at achieving the integration of women as full and equal partners with men in the total development effort.
See Document 42, page 184; and Document 43, page 184

14 December 1974
The General Assembly adopts the Declaration on the Protection of Women and Children in Emergency and Armed Conflict, affirming that all forms of repression and cruel and inhuman treatment of women and children are criminal acts and that Governments should do everything to spare women and children from the ravages of war.
See Document 44, page 185

1975
International Women's Year, with a three-part theme: equality, development and peace, as established by General Assembly resolution 3010 of 1972.
See Document 41, page 183

7 March 1975
The United Nations first observes International Women's Day (8 March).

19 June–2 July 1975
The World Conference of the International Women's Year in Mexico City is the first global conference to be held on women's issues, with 133 Governments represented. The Conference adopts a World Plan of Action for the Advancement of Women for the coming decade. Helvi Sippila (Finland), the first woman Assistant Secretary-General of the United Nations (appointed in 1972 to head the Centre for Social Development and Humanitarian Affairs), is the Secretary-General of the Conference. Some 6,000 representatives of non-governmental organizations (NGOs) attend the related International Women's Year Tribune.
See Document 45, page 187

15 December 1975
The General Assembly, by its resolution 3520 (XXX), proclaims **1976-1985 the United Nations Decade for Women: Equality, Development and Peace,** to be devoted to effective and sustained national and international action to implement the World Plan of Action of the 1975 Conference. By the same resolution, the Assembly calls for the establishment of an International Research and Training Institute for the Advancement of Women (INSTRAW).
See Document 49, page 214

1976-1985
United Nations Decade for Women: Equality, Development and Peace, as established by General Assembly resolution 3520 of 15 December 1975.
See Document 49, page 214

12 May 1976
ECOSOC decides to establish INSTRAW as an autonomous body under the auspices of the United Nations, funded through voluntary contributions. The Institute is directed to focus its activities on the needs of women in developing countries. INSTRAW begins operation in **January 1980.**
See Document 54, page 221

8 November 1977
At the first Pledging Conference for the United Nations Decade for Women, pledges of more than $3 million are received for the Voluntary Fund for the United Nations Decade for Women and more than $500,000 for INSTRAW.
See Document 56, page 231; and Document 59, page 235

18 December 1979
The General Assembly adopts the Convention on the Elimination of All Forms of Discrimination against Women, first drafted and approved by the Commission on the Status of Women in 1976. The 30-article women's bill of rights is the first international legal instrument to stipulate what constitutes discrimination against women. The Convention comes into force on **3 September 1981.**
See Document 69, page 244

14-30 July 1980
The World Conference of the United Nations Decade for Women takes place in Copenhagen with delegations from 145 Member States. Sixty-four Member States sign the Convention on the Elimination of All Forms of Discrimination against Women. The Programme of Action for the Second Half of the United Nations Decade for Women, adopted by the Conference, calls for

special emphasis on improving women's employment, health and education. Lucille Mair (Jamaica), the first woman Under-Secretary-General of the United Nations is Secretary-General of the Conference. About 7,000 NGO representatives attend the related NGO forum.
See Document 70, page 250

11 December 1980
The General Assembly, by its resolution 35/136, decides to convene in 1985 a World Conference to Review and Appraise the Achievements of the United Nations Decade for Women.
See Document 71, page 284

23 June 1981
The ILO adopts the Workers with Family Responsibilities Convention calling for equal opportunities and equal treatment for men and women workers with family responsibilities and for action by States to eliminate discrimination in employment for those with family responsibilities.

14 December 1981
The General Assembly, by its resolution 36/129, extends the activities of the Voluntary Fund for the United Nations Decade for Women, which includes funding for 68 new development projects, beyond the end of the Decade.
See Document 73, page 288

16 April 1982
At the first meeting of the States parties to the Convention on the Elimination of All Forms of Discrimination against Women, the Committee on the Elimination of Discrimination against Women (CEDAW), an expert panel to monitor compliance with the 1979 Convention, is established. The Committee holds its inaugural session from 18 to 22 October 1982 in Vienna.

3 December 1982
The General Assembly adopts the Declaration on the Participation of Women in Promoting International Peace and Cooperation, which states that since women and men have an equal interest in contributing to international peace and cooperation, women must be enabled to participate equally with men in economic, social, cultural, civil and political affairs.
See Document 75, page 290

1-12 August 1983
The Declaration and Programme of Action adopted by the Second World Conference to Combat Racism and Racial Discrimination, held in Geneva, states that whenever there is racial discrimination, women are

subjected to a second layer of discrimination, and calls for detailed legislative and educational measures to combat all forms of discrimination.

11 August 1983
INSTRAW inaugurates its permanent headquarters in Santo Domingo, Dominican Republic.
See Document 76, page 292

11 December 1984
The first *World Survey on the Role of Women in Development* is issued. Updated every five years, the *World Survey* is a major source of statistical and analytical data on women in the global economy.
See Document 86, page 366

14 December 1984
The Voluntary Fund for the United Nations Decade for Women is renamed the United Nations Development Fund for Women (UNIFEM) and is made a separate entity in association with the United Nations Development Programme. In 1984, the Fund provides assistance totalling $24 million to almost 400 projects.
See Document 80, page 303

26 February 1985
The Secretary-General appoints a Coordinator for the Improvement of the Status of Women in the Secretariat, Mercedez Pulido de Briceño (Venezuela), at the Assistant Secretary-General level. The Secretary-General also establishes a Steering Committee for the Improvement of the Status of Women in the Secretariat.

15-26 July 1985
The third global women's conference, the World Conference to Review and Appraise the Achievements of the United Nations Decade for Women: Equality, Development and Peace, takes place in Nairobi, with delegations from 157 Member States present. The final document, the Nairobi Forward-looking Strategies for the Advancement of Women, is a blueprint for measures to improve the status of women by the end of the century. Leticia Shahani (Philippines), United Nations Assistant Secretary-General, is Secretary-General of the Conference. Some 15,000 NGO representatives attend the related NGO forum.
See Document 84, page 310

20 April 1987
Nafis Sadik (Pakistan) is appointed Director of the United Nations Population Fund — the first woman to head a major United Nations programme.

26 May 1987
ECOSOC adopts the long-term work programme proposed by the CSW, prioritizing implementation of the Nairobi Forward-looking Strategies.
See Document 89, page 372

May 1988
The Section on the Status of Women in the United Nations Secretariat, which in 1972 was renamed and upgraded to the Branch for the Promotion of Equality between Men and Women, and in 1979 renamed as the Branch for the Advancement of Women, is further upgraded to become the Division for the Advancement of Women. In 1993 the Division moves from Vienna to New York to become part of the newly created Department for Policy Coordination and Sustainable Development.

25 February–5 March 1990
The CSW completes the first review and appraisal of the implementation of the Nairobi Forward-looking Strategies and adopts 21 recommendations for eliminating obstacles to their implementation. The Commission recommends the convening of a world conference on women in 1995.
See Document 92, page 378

5-9 March 1990
The World Conference on Education for All: Meeting Basic Learning Needs, held in Jomtien, Thailand, calls for a universal reduction of the disparities which exist in the education of girls and boys.

29-30 September 1990
The World Summit for Children, held at United Nations Headquarters in New York, discusses the global status of children and emphasizes the disadvantages faced by girls as compared to boys. The World Declaration on the Survival, Protection and Development of Children states that improving the status of children depends greatly upon ensuring the equal rights of women.

14 December 1990
The General Assembly, by its resolution 45/129, decides to hold a fourth world conference on women in 1995.
See Document 99, page 451

21 December 1990
The General Assembly adopts resolution 45/239 establishing targets for the employment of women in the Secretariat of 35 per cent women in professional posts subject to geographical distribution by 1995 and 25 per cent women in senior posts.
See Document 100, page 452

18 June 1991
The United Nations publishes *The World's Women 1970-1990: Trends and Statistics.*
See Document 101, page 455

22 July 1991
The United Nations High Commissioner for Refugees issues Guidelines on the Protection of Refugee Women, which call for special protection for refugee women and girls. In **March 1995**, the High Commissioner issues Guidelines on Prevention and Response to Sexual Violence against Refugees.

31 January 1992
CEDAW adopts General Recommendation 19 on Violence against Women, stating that the issue of violence against women is covered by most of the articles of the Convention on the Elimination of All Forms of Discrimination against Women.
See Document 115, page 528

7 February 1992
The Secretary-General appoints Margaret Joan Anstee (United Kingdom) as his Special Representative for Angola (UNAVEM II), the first woman to be in charge of a United Nations peace-keeping mission and the first woman to be appointed as a Special Representative of a Secretary-General.

25-26 February 1992
The Summit on the Economic Advancement of Rural Women is held in Geneva under the auspices of the International Fund for Agricultural Development. The Summit participants — the wives of heads of State or Government — adopt the Geneva Declaration for Rural Women in which they express solidarity with rural women of the world and proclaim their determination to raise awareness of conditions affecting rural women among decision makers at the national, regional and international levels.

8 March 1992
On the occasion of the seventeenth annual United Nations observance of International Women's Day, the Secretary-General announces a Strategic Plan of Action for the Improvement of the Status of Women in the Secretariat from 1995 until the year 2000.
See Document 114, page 519

18 March 1992
The CSW accepts the invitation of the Government of China to hold the Fourth World Conference on Women in Beijing.

3-14 June 1992
The United Nations Conference on Environment and Development in Rio de Janeiro adopts the Rio Declaration on Environment and Development, which proclaims that women have a vital role to play in environmental management and development and that their full participation is essential to the achievement of sustainable development. The Conference also adopts Agenda 21, a far-reaching blueprint for sustainable development into the twenty-first century, which calls for the full representation of women and their interests, needs and perspective in sustainable development.
See Document 103, page 464

14-25 June 1993
The World Conference on Human Rights in Vienna adopts the Vienna Declaration and Programme of Action, which urges Governments and the United Nations to ensure equal rights for women and stresses the importance of working towards the elimination of violence against women.
See Document 106, page 472

27 July 1993
ECOSOC, in its resolution E/1993/235, agrees to the recommendation of a United Nations task force that INSTRAW and UNIFEM be merged into a unified programme.

20 December 1993
The General Assembly, in its resolution 48/104, adopts the Declaration on the Elimination of Violence against Women, which condemns any act causing physical, sexual or psychological harm or suffering to women in the family or the community or by the State and urges States not to invoke custom, tradition or religious consideration to avoid their obligations with respect to the elimination of violence against women.
See Document 107, page 474

4 February 1994
CEDAW adopts General Recommendation 21 on equality in marriage and family relations, which indicates that the Convention on the Elimination of All Forms of Discrimination against Women prohibits any discrimination in family law.
See Document 115, page 528

11 March 1994
The United Nations Commission on Human Rights appoints a Special Rapporteur to collect information on acts of gender-based violence and to recommend measures at the national, regional and international levels for its elimination.
See Document 111, page 495; and Document 116, page 577

5-13 September 1994
The International Conference on Population and Development in Cairo affirms that there are four requirements for any programme of population and development: gender equality; the empowerment of women; the ability of women to control their own fertility; and the elimination of violence against women.
See Document 113, page 515

6-12 March 1995
The World Summit for Social Development in Copenhagen, the largest gathering in history of heads of State or Government, proclaims the central role of women in fighting poverty, creating productive employment and strengthening the social fabric. The Copenhagen Declaration includes a commitment by world leaders to make equality and equity of women and men a priority.
See Document 126, page 640

8 March 1995
On the occasion of International Women's Day, the Secretary-General calls on Member States to consider putting the Declaration on the Elimination of Violence against Women into legally binding form.

15 March–7 April 1995
The CSW undertakes a second review and appraisal of the Nairobi Forward-looking Strategies and holds the final preparatory meeting for the Fourth World Conference on Women.
See Document 124, page 614

11 April 1995
The Secretary-General appoints Carol Bellamy (United States of America) as the Executive Director of UNICEF, one of five women to head United Nations programmes. The others are the High Commissioner for Refugees, Sadako Ogata (Japan); the Executive Director of the United Nations Environment Programme, Elizabeth Dowdeswell (Canada); the Executive Director of the World Food Programme, Catherine Bertini (USA), and the Executive Director of the United Nations Population Fund, Nafis Sadik (Pakistan).

12 July 1995
The Security Council and the General Assembly elect Rosalyn Higgins (United Kingdom) to the International Court of Justice, the first woman to sit on the Court.

4-15 September 1995
The Fourth World Conference on Women is held in Beijing, with delegations from 189 countries. The largest United Nations Conference ever, it adopts by consensus the Beijing Declaration and a five-year Platform for Action which identifies 12 critical areas of concern. Ms. Gertrude Mongella (United Republic of Tanzania), United Nations Assistant Secretary-General, is Secretary-General of the Conference. Some 30,000 NGO representatives attend the related NGO Forum at Huairou.
See Document 127, page 649

28 December 1995
In response to a recommendation from the Fourth World Conference on Women, the Secretary-General designates Assistant Secretary-General Rosario Green (Mexico) as his Senior Adviser on gender issues, to help ensure the system-wide implementation of the Platform for Action.

10 January 1996
The Secretary-General issues a report on the elaboration of an optional protocol to the Convention on the Elimination of All Forms of Discrimination against Women.
See Document 137, page 776

29 February 1996
The Security Council appoints Justice Louise Arbour (Canada) as Prosecutor of the International Tribunal for the Prosecution of Persons Responsible for Serious Violations of International Humanitarian Law Committed in the Territory of the Former Yugoslavia and the International Tribunal for Rwanda.

II Chronology of United Nations conferences and seminars

The following chronology of selected United Nations conferences and seminars includes international meetings convened to support the work of the Commission on the Status of Women and other intergovernmental bodies and preparatory and follow-up meetings for the world conferences on women. The symbols following the entries represent United Nations reports and publications relevant to the proceedings. These documents can be found at the Dag Hammarskjöld Library at United Nations Headquarters in New York, at other libraries in the United Nations system or at libraries around the world which have been designated as depository libraries for United Nations documents.

5-16 August 1957
Seminar on the Civic Responsibilities and Increased Participation of Asian Women in Public Life, Bangkok.
ST/TAA/HR/1 (57.IV.10)

18-29 May 1959
Seminar on Participation of Women in Public Life, Bogotá.
ST/TAO/HR/5

12-23 December 1960
Seminar on Participation of Women in Public Life, Addis Ababa.
ST/TAO/HR/9 and Corr.1

19 June–3 July 1961
Seminar on the Status of Women in Family Law, Bucharest.
ST/TAO/HR/11

8-21 May 1962
Seminar on the Status of Women in Family Law, Tokyo.
ST/TAO/HR/14

3-16 December 1963
Seminar on the Status of Women in Family Law, Bogotá.
ST/TAO/HR/18

18-31 August 1964
Seminar on the Status of Women in Family Law, Lomé, Togo.
ST/TAO/HR/22

3-17 August 1965
Seminar on the Participation of Women in Public Life, Ulan Bator, Mongolia.
ST/TAO/HR/24

6-19 December 1966
Seminar on Measures Required for the Advancement of Women with Special Reference to the Establishment of a Long-term Programme, Manila.
ST/TAO/HR/28

1-14 August 1967
Seminar on Civic and Political Education of Women, Helsinki.
ST/TAO/HR/30

19 November–2 December 1968
Seminar on Civic and Political Education of Women, Accra, Ghana.
ST/TAO/HR/35

5-18 August 1969
Seminar on the Effects of Scientific and Technological Developments on the Status of Women, Iasi, Romania.
ST/TAO/HR/37

8-21 September 1970
Seminar on the Participation of Women in the Economic Life of Their Countries (with reference to the implementation of article 10 of the Declaration on the Elimination of Discrimination against Women), Moscow.
ST/TAO/HR/41

27 July–9 August 1971
Seminar on the Participation of Women in Economic Life (with reference to the implementation of article 10 of the Declaration on the Elimination of Discrimination against Women and of General Assembly resolution 2716 (XXV)), Libreville, Gabon.
ST/TAO/HR/43

19-28 June 1972
Interregional Meeting of Experts on the Integration of Women in Development, New York.
ST/SOA/120 (73.IV.12)

25 February–1 March 1974
International Forum on the Role of Women in Development, New York.
ST/ESA/SDHA/AC.5/6/Add.1

13-17 May 1974
Regional Consultation for Asia and the Far East on the Integration of Women in Development with Special Reference to Population Factors (in preparation for the World Conference of the International Women's Year), Bangkok.
E/CONF.66/34; ST/ESA/SER.B/5/Add.1; E/CONF.66/BP.2

3-7 June 1974
Regional Seminar for Africa on the Integration of Women in Development with Special Reference to Population Factors (in preparation for the World Conference of the International Women's Year), Addis Ababa.
E/CONF.66/34; ST/ESA/SER.B/6/Add.1; E/CONF.66/BP.3

4-17 September 1974
Interregional Seminar on National Machinery to Accelerate the Integration of Women in Development and to Eliminate Discrimination on Grounds of Sex, Ottawa.
ST/ESA/SER.B/7; E/CONF.66/BP.4

28 April–2 May 1975
Regional Seminar for Latin America on the Integration of Women in Development with Special Reference to Population Factors, Caracas.
ST/ESA/SER.B/7/Rev.2-E/CEPAL/1006/Rev.2

26 November–10 December 1975
United Nations Interregional Seminar on Women, the Media and the Arts, Sydney, Australia.

17-23 February 1976
Group of Experts on the Establishment of an International Research and Training Institute for the Advancement of Women, New York.
E/5772

22-30 March 1976
Regional Seminar on Women's Participation in Economic, Social and Political Development, Buenos Aires.
ST/ESA/SER.B/9

15-22 February 1977
Regional Seminar on the Participation of Women in Political, Economic and Social Development with Special Emphasis on Machinery to Accelerate the Integration of Women in Development, Kathmandu, Nepal.
ST/ESA/SER.B/10

28 March–5 April 1977
Seminar on the Changing Roles of Men and Women in Modern Society: Functions, Rights and Responsibilities, Groningen, the Netherlands.
SOA/ESDP/1977/2 and Add.1

13-17 June 1977
First Regional Conference on the Integration of Women in the Economic and Social Development of Latin America, Havana.
E/CEPAL/1042/Rev.1

13-16 July 1977
United Nations Institute for Training and Research (UNITAR) Colloquium on Women and Decision-making in the United Nations, Hernstein, Austria.
UNITAR/CR/10 (78.XV.CR/10)

27 September–2 October 1977
Regional Conference on the Implementation of National, Regional and World Plans of Action for the Integration of Women in Development, Nouakchott, Mauritania.
E/CN.14/714

29 May–4 June 1978
Regional Conference for the Integration of Women in Development, Amman.
E/ECWA/SDHS/CONF.2/9

19-30 June 1978
First session of the Preparatory Committee for the World Conference of the United Nations Decade for Women: Equality, Development and Peace, Vienna.
A/CONF.94/PC/4

6-10 November 1978
Preparatory Meeting for the World Conference of the United Nations Decade for Women on the Role of Women in Industrialization in Developing Countries, Vienna.
A/CONF.94/BP.1

10-15 February 1979
World Health Organization (WHO) Seminar on Traditional Practices Affecting the Health of Women and Children: Female Circumcision, Childhood Marriage, Nutritional Taboos, Khartoum.
A/CONF.94/BP.9/Rev.1

6-13 May 1979
Conference of Non-Aligned and Other Developing Countries on the Role of Women in Development, Baghdad.
A/34/321

9-12 July 1979
Seminar on the Participation of Women in the Economic Evolution of the Economic Commission for Europe (ECE) Region, Paris.
A/CONF.94/14

27 August–8 September 1979
Second session of the Preparatory Committee for the World Conference of the United Nations Decade for Women: Equality, Development and Peace, New York.
A/CONF.94/PC/12

5-9 November 1979
Regional Preparatory Meeting for Asia and the Pacific for the World Conference of the United Nations Decade for Women, New Delhi.
A/CONF.94/15

12-16 November 1979
Regional Preparatory Meeting for Latin America for the World Conference of the United Nations Decade for Women, Macuto, Venezuela.
A/CONF.94/16

3-7 December 1979
Regional Preparatory Meeting for Africa for the World Conference of the United Nations Decade for Women and Second Regional Conference on the Integration of Women in Development, Lusaka.
A/CONF.94/17 and Corr.1

10-13 December 1979
Regional Preparatory Meeting for Western Asia for the World Conference of the United Nations Decade for Women, Damascus.
A/CONF.94/4; A/CONF.94/18 and Corr.1; A/CONF.94/21 and Corr.1

7-18 April 1980
Third session of the Preparatory Committee for the World Conference of the United Nations Decade for Women: Equality, Development and Peace, New York.
A/CONF.94/23

9-11 May 1980
Hemispheric Seminar on Women under Apartheid, Montreal, Canada.
A/CONF.94/BP.17

19-22 May 1980
International Seminar on Women and Apartheid, Helsinki.
A/CONF.94/BP.17; A/AC.115/L.528

20-23 May 1980
International Seminar on Women and the Media, New York.
A/CONF.94/BP.10

24-27 November 1981
Expert Group Meeting on Women and the Media, Vienna.
ST/IESA/SDHA/AWB/EGM/1981/1

17-19 May 1982
International Conference on Women and Apartheid, Brussels.
A/AC.115/L.571 and Corr.1

23 February–4 March 1983
First session of the Commission on the Status of Women acting as the Preparatory Body for the World Conference to Review and Appraise the Achievements of the United Nations Decade for Women, Vienna.
A/CONF.116/PC/9 and Corr.1 and Add.1

11-15 April 1983
Expert Group on Improving Statistics and Indicators on the Situation of Women, New York.
ST/ESA/STAT/AC.17/9-INSTRAW/AC.1/9

8-10 August 1983
Third Regional Conference on the Integration of Women into the Economic and Social Development of Latin America and the Caribbean, Mexico City.
E/CEPAL/G.1265-E/CEPAL/CRM.3/L.8

27 February–7 March 1984
Second session of the Commission on the Status of Women acting as the Preparatory Body for the World Conference to Review and Appraise the Achievements of the United Nations Decade for Women, Vienna.
A/CONF.116/PC/19 and Corr.1 and Add.1 and Corr.1

12-16 March 1984
Interregional Seminar on Women and the International Drinking Water Supply and Sanitation Decade, Cairo.
INSTRAW/BT/1985/CRP.1

26-30 March 1984
Regional Intergovernmental Preparatory Meeting for Asia and the Pacific for the World Conference to Review and Appraise the Achievements of the United Nations Decade for Women, Tokyo.
A/CONF.116/9

17-28 September 1984
Interregional Seminar on National Experience relating to the Improvement of the Situation of Women in Rural Areas, Vienna.
A/40/239

8-12 October 1984
Regional Intergovernmental Preparatory Meeting for Africa for the World Conference to Review and Appraise the Achievements of the United Nations Decade for Women, Arusha, United Republic of Tanzania.
A/CONF.116/9 and Corr.1

15-19 October 1984
Seminar on the Economic Role of Women in the ECE Region, Vienna.
A/CONF.116/9 and Corr.1

19-23 November 1984
Regional Preparatory Meeting for Latin America and the Caribbean for the World Conference to Review and Appraise the Achievements of the United Nations Decade for Women, Havana.
A/CONF.116/9 and Corr.1

3-6 December 1984
Regional Preparatory Meeting for Western Asia for the World Conference to Review and Appraise the Achievements of the United Nations Decade for Women, Baghdad.
A/CONF.116/9 and Corr.1

4-13 March 1985
Third session of the Commission on the Status of Women acting as the Preparatory Body for the World Conference to Review and Appraise the Achievements of the United Nations Decade for Women, Vienna.
A/CONF.116/PC/25

10-11 April 1985
Ministerial Conference of Non-Aligned and Other Developing Countries on the Role of Women in Development, New Delhi.
A/40/365

29 April–7 May 1985
Resumed third session of the Commission on the Status of Women acting as the Preparatory Body for the World Conference to Review and Appraise the Achievements of the United Nations Decade for Women, New York.
A/CONF.116/25/Add.1-3 and A/CONF.116/12

7-11 May 1985
International Conference on Women and Children under Apartheid, Arusha, United Republic of Tanzania.
A/AC.115/L.623

1-3 October 1985
Consultative High-level Expert Meeting on the Role of Women in International Economic Relations, Geneva.
INSTRAW/BT/1986/CRP.2

13-17 October 1986
Expert Group on Measurement of Women's Income and Their Participation and Production in the Informal Sector, Santo Domingo.
ESA/STAT/AC.29/8-INSTRAW/AC.3/8

8-12 December 1986
Expert Group Meeting on Violence in the Family with Special Emphasis on Its Effects on Women, Vienna.
E/AC.57/1988/12

10-13 February 1987
International Safe Motherhood Conference, Nairobi.
Report: Preventing the Tragedy of Maternal Deaths, Kenya, 1987

25-29 January 1988
Seminar on Information Systems for National Machineries for the Advancement of Women, Vienna.
United Nations Press Release WOM/415

27-30 September 1988
Fourth Regional Conference on the Integration of Women into the Economic and Social Development of Latin America and the Caribbean, Guatemala City.
LC/G.1539(CRM.4/13)

3-7 October 1988
Interregional Seminar on Women and the Economic Crisis, Vienna.
United Nations Press Release WOM/467

14-18 November 1988
Expert Group Meeting on Social Support Measures for the Advancement of Women, Vienna.
E/CN.6/1989/6

22-26 May 1989
International Seminar on Women and Rural Development Programmes and Projects, Vienna.
A/44/516

18-24 September 1989
Expert Group on Equality in Political Participation and Decision-making, Vienna.
E/CN.6/1990/2

2-6 October 1989
Regional Seminar for Latin America and the Caribbean on the Implementation of the Convention on the Elimination of All Forms of Discrimination against Women, Guatemala City.
E/CN.6/1991/CRP.2

6-10 November 1989
Regional Conference on the Integration of Women in Development and on the Implementation of the Arusha Strategies for the Advancement of Women in Africa, Abuja, Nigeria.

29-31 January 1990
Meeting of High-level Experts on the Role of Women in the Development of Least Developed Countries, Niamey, Niger.
A/CONF.147/UNCLDC II/5

2-6 July 1990
Expert Group Meeting on Refugee and Displaced Women and Children, Vienna.
E/CN.6/1991/4

20-24 August 1990
Seminar on Disabled Women, Vienna.
E/CN.6/1991/CRP.1

2-12 September 1990
Commemorative Seminar on the Convention on the Elimination of All Forms of Discrimination against Women, Kiev.
E/CN.6/1991/CRP.2

24-28 September 1990
Expert Group Meeting on Women and HIV/AIDS and the Role of National Machinery for the Advancement of Women, Vienna.
E/CN.6/1991/CRP.2

19-24 November 1990
Second Conference of the Inter-African Committee on Traditional Practices Affecting the Health of Women and Children, Addis Ababa.

26-30 November 1990
Expert Group Meeting on Vulnerable Women, Vienna.
E/CN.6/1991/2

8-12 April 1991
Regional Seminar on the Impact of Economic and Political Reform on the Status of Women in Eastern Europe and the Union of Soviet Socialist Republics: The Role of National Machinery, Vienna.
ST/CSDHA/19 (92.IV.4)

29 April–3 May 1991
United Nations Seminar on Traditional Practices Affecting the Health of Women and Children, Ouagadougou, Burkina Faso.
E/CN.4/Sub.2/1991/48

21-24 May 1991
Expert Group on the Role of Women in Public Life, Vienna.
E/CN.6/1992/10

27-30 May 1991
Women and Children First: Symposium on Poverty and Environmental Degradation, Geneva.
A/CONF.151/PC/114

16-19 September 1991
Fifth Regional Conference on the Integration of Women into the Economic and Social Development of Latin America and the Caribbean, Curaçao, Netherlands Antilles.
LC/G.1684(CRM.5/6)

7-11 October 1991
Expert Group Meeting on the Integration of Ageing and Elderly Women into Development, Vienna.
E/CN.6/1992/8, annex II

22-25 October 1991
United Nations Expert Meeting on the Feminization of Internal Migration, Aguascalientes, Mexico.
ST/ESA/SER.R/127 (94.XIII.3)

4-8 November 1991
Global Assembly of Women and the Environment: "Partners in Life", Miami, United States of America.
E/CN.6/1992/9; A/CONF.151/PC/114

11-15 November 1991
Expert Group Meeting on Violence against Women, Vienna.
E/CN.6/1992/4

9-11 December 1991
Seminar on the Integration of Women in Development, Vienna.
E/CN.6/1992/8

11-20 March 1992
First session of the Commission on the Status of Women acting as the Preparatory Body for the Fourth World Conference on Women, Vienna.
E/1992/24 and Add.1-2

18-22 May 1992
Expert Group Meeting on Increased Awareness by Women of Their Rights, including Legal Literacy, Bratislava, Slovakia.
E/CN.6/1992/3

31 August–4 September 1992
Working Group on Violence against Women, Vienna.
E/CN.6/1993/12

9-15 September 1992
Interregional Workshop on the Role of Women in Environmentally Sound and Sustainable Development, Beijing.
INSTRAW/SER.A/37

9-12 November 1992
Seminar on Women in Extreme Poverty; Integration of Women's Concerns in National Development Planning, Vienna.
E/CN.6/1993/3

17-26 March 1993
Second session of the Commission on the Status of Women acting as the Preparatory Body for the Fourth World Conference on Women, Vienna.
E/1993/27 and Corr.1

4-8 October 1993
Expert Group Meeting on Measures to Eradicate Violence against Women, New Brunswick, United States.
E/CN.6/1994/4

10-14 January 1994
Inter-sessional Working Group of the Commission on the Status of Women acting as the Preparatory Body for the Fourth World Conference on Women, New York.
E/CN.6/1994/12

7-18 March 1994
Third session of the Commission on the Status of Women acting as the Preparatory Body for the Fourth World Conference on Women, New York.
E/1994/27 and Add.1

7-14 June 1994
Regional Preparatory Meeting for Asia and the Pacific for the Fourth World Conference on Women, Jakarta.
E/CN.6/1995/5/Add.1

4-8 July 1994
Second United Nations Regional Seminar on Traditional Practices Affecting the Health of Women and Children, Colombo, Sri Lanka.
E/CN.4/Sub.2/1994/10

25-29 September 1994
Regional Preparatory Meeting for Latin America and the Caribbean for the Fourth World Conference on Women, Mar del Plata, Argentina.
E/CN.6/1995/5/Add.2

10-14 October 1994
Expert Group Meeting on Gender, Education and Training, Turin, Italy.
E/CN.6/1995/11

17-21 October 1994
Regional Preparatory Meeting for Europe for the Fourth World Conference on Women, Vienna.
E/CN.6/1995/5/Add.3

6-10 November 1994
Regional Preparatory Meeting for Western Asia for the Fourth World Conference on Women, Amman.
E/CN.6/1995/5/Add.4

16-23 November 1994
Regional Preparatory Meeting for Africa for the Fourth World Conference on Women, Dakar.
E/CN.6/1995/5/Add.5

15 March–7 April 1995
Fourth session of the Commission on the Status of Women acting as the Preparatory Body for the Fourth World Conference on Women, New York.
E/1995/26

III List of reproduced documents

The documents reproduced on pages 103-823 include resolutions of the General Assembly and the Economic and Social Council, texts of international conventions, reports of the World Conferences on Women, reports of the Commission on the Status of Women, reports by the Secretary-General and other materials.

Document 1

Charter of the United Nations, signed 26 June 1945 (extract).
See page 103

Document 2

"Open Letter to the women of the world", read by Eleanor Roosevelt, representative of the delegation of the United States of America, to the first session of the General Assembly; and statements made by representatives on the participation of women in the work of the United Nations and the creation of a committee on the status of women (extract).
A/PV.29, 12 February 1946
See page 103

Document 3

Economic and Social Council (ECOSOC) resolution establishing the Commission on Human Rights and the Subcommission on the Status of Women.
E/RES/5 (I), 16 February 1946
See page 109

Document 4

Statements made at the first session of ECOSOC regarding the composition of the Subcommission on the Status of Women (extract).
E/SR.14, 18 February 1946
See page 110

Document 5

Statement made by the Chair of the Subcommission on the Status of Women to ECOSOC recommending that the status of the Subcommission be raised to full commission (extract).
E/PV.4, 28 May 1946
See page 111

Document 6

ECOSOC resolution establishing the Commission on the Status of Women (CSW).
E/RES/2/11, 21 June 1946
See page 112

Document 7

General Assembly resolution calling on Member States to adopt measures necessary to fulfil the aims of the Charter of the United Nations in granting women the same political rights as men.
A/RES/56 (I), 11 December 1946
See page 113

Document 8

Report of the CSW to ECOSOC on the first session of the Commission, held at Lake Success, New York, from 10 to 24 February 1947.
E/281/Rev.1, 25 February 1947
See page 113

Document 9

ECOSOC resolution defining the functions of the CSW and requesting Member States to provide the Commission with data on the legal status and treatment of women in their countries.
E/RES/48 (IV), 29 March 1947
See page 120

Document 10

ECOSOC resolution requesting the Secretary-General to provide the CSW with communications received concerning the status of women.
E/RES/76 (V), 5 August 1947
See page 122

Document 11

ECOSOC resolution requesting Member States to adopt measures to ensure women the same rights as men in regard to employment and remuneration.
E/RES/122 G (VI), 1 March 1948
See page 123

Document 12

ECOSOC resolution transmitting the suggestions of the CSW for amendments to the draft Universal Declaration of Human Rights and requesting Member States to provide information on political rights and educational opportunities for women.
E/RES/120 (VI), 3 March 1948
See page 123

Document 13
ECOSOC resolution calling on Member States to implement the principle of equal pay for work of equal value for men and women workers, irrespective of nationality, race, language or religion.
E/RES/121 (VI), 10 March 1948
See page 125

Document 14
The Universal Declaration of Human Rights, adopted by the General Assembly in its resolution 217 A (III) of 10 December 1948.
ST/HR/1/Rev.4 (Vol. 1/Part 1)
See page 125

Document 15
ECOSOC resolution calling for cooperation between the International Labour Organization (ILO) and the CSW on the issue of equal pay for work of equal value.
E/RES/196 (VIII), 18 February 1949
See page 128

Document 16
Report of the CSW to ECOSOC on the Commission's third session regarding the participation of women in the work of the United Nations (extract).
E/1316, Chapter IV, 19 April 1949
See page 128

Document 17
ECOSOC resolution calling for the preparation of a convention on the nationality of married women.
E/RES/242 C (IX), 1 August 1949
See page 129

Document 18
Convention for the Suppression of the Traffic in Persons and of the Exploitation of the Prostitution of Others, adopted by the General Assembly on 2 December 1949.
UN Treaty Series, vol. 96, No. 1342, p. 271
See page 130

Document 19
Report of the Secretary-General to the CSW on discrimination against women in the field of political rights.
E/CN.6/131, 15 March 1950
See page 134

Document 20
Report of the Secretary-General to the CSW on the participation of women in the work of the United Nations.
E/CN.6/132, 16 March 1950
See page 136

Document 21
Report of the Secretary-General to the CSW on the possibility of proposing a convention on the political rights of women.
E/CN.6/143, 28 April 1950
See page 141

Document 22
Report of the Secretary-General to the CSW on the United Nations Educational, Scientific and Cultural Organization study of educational opportunities for women.
E/CN.6/146, 9 May 1950
See page 145

Document 23
Report of the Secretary-General to the CSW on the United Nations Technical Assistance Programme in relation to the status of women.
E/CN.6/145, 12 May 1950
See page 154

Document 24
Memorandum by the Secretary-General to the CSW on the participation of women in the work of the United Nations.
E/CN.6/167, 19 March 1951
See page 161

Document 25
ECOSOC resolution concerning the deprivation of the essential human rights of women in Trust and Non-Self-Governing Territories.
E/RES/445 C (XIV), 28 May 1952
See page 164

Document 26
Convention on the Political Rights of Women, adopted by the General Assembly on 20 December 1952.
UN Treaty Series, vol. 193, No. 2613, p. 135
See page 164

Document 27
Summary of the statement made by Secretary-General Dag Hammarskjöld to the eighth session of the CSW on, among other things, the participation of women in the work of the United Nations.
E/CN.6/SR.149, 8 April 1954
See page 166

Document 28
General Assembly resolution calling on Member States to eliminate customs, ancient laws and practices affecting the human dignity of women.
A/RES/843 (IX), 17 December 1954
See page 167

Document 29

Convention on the Nationality of Married Women, adopted by the General Assembly on 29 January 1957.
UN Treaty Series, vol. 309, No. 4468, p. 65
See page 167

Document 30

ECOSOC resolution recommending that Member States make full use of the United Nations technical assistance and human rights advisory services programmes for the purpose of advancing the status of women in developing countries.
E/RES/884 E (XXXIV), 16 July 1962
See page 169

Document 31

Convention on Consent to Marriage, Minimum Age for Marriage and Registration of Marriages, adopted by the General Assembly on 7 November 1962.
UN Treaty Series, vol. 521, No. 7525, p. 231
See page 170

Document 32

General Assembly resolution requesting that the Secretary-General study the possibility of providing resources aimed especially at the initiation and implementation of a unified long-term United Nations programme for the advancement of women.
A/RES/1777 (XVII), 7 December 1962
See page 172

Document 33

General Assembly resolution requesting ECOSOC and the CSW to prepare a draft declaration on the elimination of discrimination against women.
A/RES/1921 (XVIII), 5 December 1963
See page 173

Document 34

General Assembly resolution adopting the Recommendation on Consent to Marriage, Minimum Age for Marriage and Registration of Marriages.
A/RES/2018 (XX), 1 November 1965
See page 173

Document 35

Article 3 of the International Covenant on Civil and Political Rights and article 3 of the International Covenant on Economic, Social and Cultural Rights, both adopted by the General Assembly on 16 December 1966 (extract).
UN Treaty Series, vol. 999, p. 171, and vol. 993, p. 3
See page 174

Document 36

General Assembly resolution adopting the Declaration on the Elimination of Discrimination against Women.
A/RES/2263 (XXII), 7 November 1967
See page 175

Document 37

Resolution IX adopted by the International Conference on Human Rights in Teheran on measures to promote women's rights in the modern world and endorsing the Secretary-General's proposal for a unified long-term United Nations programme for the advancement of women.
A/CONF.32/41, 12 May 1968
See page 177

Document 38

General Assembly resolution calling for the employment of qualified women in senior and other professional positions by the secretariats of organizations in the United Nations system.
A/RES/2715 (XXV), 15 December 1970
See page 179

Document 39

General Assembly resolution outlining a programme of concerted international action for the advancement of women.
A/RES/2716 (XXV), 15 December 1970
See page 179

Document 40

General Assembly resolution reiterating that organizations in the United Nations system take measures to ensure equal opportunities for the employment of qualified women at the senior and professional levels and in policy-making positions.
A/RES/3009 (XXVII), 18 December 1972
See page 182

Document 41

General Assembly resolution proclaiming 1975 International Women's Year.
A/RES/3010 (XXVII), 18 December 1972
See page 183

Document 42

General Assembly resolution inviting all States to participate in the Conference of the International Women's Year.
A/RES/3276 (XXIX), 10 December 1974
See page 184

Document 43

General Assembly resolution establishing a Consultative Committee for the Conference of the International Women's Year.
A/RES/3277 (XXIX), 10 December 1974
See page 184

Document 44

General Assembly resolution adopting the Declaration on the Protection of Women and Children in Emergency and Armed Conflict.
A/RES/3318 (XXIX), 14 December 1974
See page 185

Document 45

Report of the World Conference of the International Women's Year, held in Mexico City from 19 June to 2 July 1975; including the Agenda, the World Plan of Action for the Implementation of the Objectives of the International Women's Year, the Declaration of Mexico on the Equality of Women and Their Contribution to Development and Peace, and resolutions and decisions adopted by the Conference (extract).
E/CONF.66/34, 1976
See page 187

Document 46

General Assembly resolution on implementation of the World Plan of Action adopted by the World Conference of the International Women's Year.
A/RES/3490 (XXX), 12 December 1975
See page 211

Document 47

General Assembly resolution calling for the integration of women in the development process.
A/RES/3505 (XXX), 15 December 1975
See page 212

Document 48

General Assembly resolution on women's participation in the strengthening of international peace and security and in the struggle against colonialism, racism, racial discrimination, foreign aggression and occupation and all forms of foreign domination.
A/RES/3519 (XXX), 15 December 1975
See page 213

Document 49

General Assembly resolution proclaiming the period from 1976 to 1985 the United Nations Decade for Women: Equality, Development and Peace, establishing an International Research and Training Institute for the Advancement of Women (INSTRAW) and deciding to convene in 1980 a world conference to review and evaluate the progress made in implementing the objectives of the International Women's Year.
A/RES/3520 (XXX), 15 December 1975
See page 214

Document 50

General Assembly resolution calling on States to ratify international conventions and other instruments concerning the protection of women's rights and the elimination of discrimination against women and requesting the CSW to complete the draft convention on the elimination of discrimination against women.
A/RES/3521 (XXX), 15 December 1975
See page 217

Document 51

General Assembly resolution calling on Governments to enable women at the lowest level in rural and urban areas to obtain credit and loans to improve their economic activities and integration in national development.
A/RES/3522 (XXX), 15 December 1975
See page 218

Document 52

General Assembly resolution on improving the status of women in rural and low-income areas.
A/RES/3523 (XXX), 15 December 1975
See page 219

Document 53

General Assembly resolution calling for increased United Nations assistance for the integration of women in development.
A/RES/3524 (XXX), 15 December 1975
See page 220

Document 54

ECOSOC resolution establishing INSTRAW as an autonomous body funded through voluntary contributions, and setting guidelines for its work, including, among other things, that the Institute should direct its activities with special attention to the needs of women in developing countries and their integration in the development process.
E/RES/1998 (LX), 12 May 1976
See page 221

Document 55

Programme for the United Nations Decade for Women: Equality, Development and Peace, 1976-1985, adopted by the CSW.
E/5894, 14 October 1976
See page 222

Document 56

General Assembly resolution adopting the criteria for the management of the Voluntary Fund for the United Nations Decade for Women.

A/RES/31/133, 16 December 1976

See page 231

Document 57

General Assembly resolution calling on States to improve the status and role of women in education and to take all possible measures to eliminate illiteracy among women.

A/RES/31/134, 16 December 1976

See page 233

Document 58

General Assembly resolution approving the Programme for the United Nations Decade for Women and calling on Governments and United Nations bodies to prioritize the Programme's goals for the Decade.

A/RES/31/136, 16 December 1976

See page 234

Document 59

General Assembly resolution calling for a pledging conference for contributions to the Voluntary Fund for the United Nations Decade for Women.

A/RES/31/137, 16 December 1976

See page 235

Document 60

General Assembly resolution establishing the Preparatory Committee for the World Conference of the United Nations Decade for Women: Equality, Development and Peace.

A/RES/32/140, 16 December 1977

See page 236

Document 61

General Assembly resolution requesting the CSW to draft a declaration on women's participation in the strengthening of international peace and security.

A/RES/32/142, 16 December 1977

See page 237

Document 62

General Assembly resolution on preparations for the World Conference of the United Nations Decade for Women: Equality, Development and Peace, including the adoption of the subtheme "Employment, Health and Education".

A/RES/33/185, 29 January 1979

See page 238

Document 63

General Assembly resolution adopting the agenda for the World Conference of the United Nations Decade for Women: Equality, Development and Peace.

A/RES/33/189, 29 January 1979

See page 239

Document 64

General Assembly resolution deciding on Copenhagen as the venue for the World Conference of the United Nations Decade for Women.

A/RES/33/191, 29 January 1979

See page 241

Document 65

General Assembly resolution on the importance of improving the status and role of women in education and in the economic and social fields for the achievement of the equality of women with men.

A/RES/34/159, 17 December 1979

See page 242

Document 66

General Assembly resolution adding an item on Palestinian women to the provisional agenda for the World Conference of the United Nations Decade for Women.

A/RES/34/160, 17 December 1979

See page 242

Document 67

General Assembly resolution adding an item on the situation of women refugees throughout the world to the provisional agenda for the World Conference of the United Nations Decade for Women.

A/RES/34/161, 17 December 1979

See page 243

Document 68

General Assembly resolution approving the recommendations of the Preparatory Committee for the World Conference of the United Nations Decade for Women and requesting the Secretary-General to provide the necessary financial appropriations.

A/RES/34/162, 17 December 1979

See page 243

Document 69

Convention on the Elimination of All Forms of Discrimination against Women, adopted by General Assembly on 18 December 1979.

UN Treaty Series, vol. 1249, No. 20378, p. 13

See page 244

Document 70

Report of the World Conference of the United Nations Decade for Women: Equality, Development and Peace, held in Copenhagen from 14 to 30 July 1980; including the Agenda, Programme of Action for the Second Half of the United Nations Decade for Women and resolutions adopted by the Conference (extract).
A/CONF.94/35
See page 250

Document 71

General Assembly resolution endorsing the outcome of the World Conference of the United Nations Decade for Women.
A/RES/35/136, 11 December 1980
See page 284

Document 72

General Assembly resolution on implementation of the Programme of Action for the Second Half of the United Nations Decade for Women.
A/RES/36/126, 14 December 1981
See page 286

Document 73

General Assembly resolution extending the activities of the Voluntary Fund beyond the end of the United Nations Decade for Women.
A/RES/36/129, 14 December 1981
See page 288

Document 74

General Assembly resolution on preparations for a World Conference to Review and Appraise the Achievements of the United Nations Decade for Women.
A/RES/37/60, 3 December 1982
See page 289

Document 75

General Assembly resolution adopting the Declaration on the Participation of Women in Promoting International Peace and Cooperation.
A/RES/37/63, 3 December 1982
See page 290

Document 76

Report of INSTRAW on its programme activities.
A/38/406, 21 October 1983
See page 292

Document 77

General Assembly resolution deciding on Nairobi as the venue for the World Conference to Review and Appraise the Achievements of the United Nations Decade for Women, considering the recommendation that particular attention be paid to the problem of women in Territories under racist colonial rule and in Territories under foreign occupation and welcoming the decision of ECOSOC to invite non-governmental organizations to participate in preparations for the Conference.
A/RES/38/108, 16 December 1983
See page 298

Document 78

Statute of INSTRAW adopted by the General Assembly on 26 September 1984.
E/1984/41, 28 March 1984
See page 299

Document 79

General Assembly resolution approving the programme of activities of INSTRAW.
A/RES/39/122, 14 December 1984
See page 302

Document 80

General Assembly resolution establishing the Voluntary Fund for the United Nations Decade for Women as a separate entity in autonomous association with the United Nations Development Programme (UNDP) and renaming the fund the United Nations Development Fund for Women (UNIFEM).
A/RES/39/125, 14 December 1984
See page 303

Document 81

General Assembly resolution calling on all bodies of the United Nations system to implement comprehensive policies for the integration of women in all aspects of development.
A/RES/39/128, 14 December 1984
See page 306

Document 82

General Assembly resolution endorsing the recommendations of the CSW acting as the preparatory body for the World Conference to Review and Appraise the Achievements of the United Nations Decade for Women.
A/RES/39/129, 14 December 1984
See page 307

Document 83

General Assembly resolution on the appointment of a Coordinator for the Improvement of the Status of Women in the Secretariat of the United Nations (extract).
A/RES/39/245 I, 18 December 1984
See page 309

Document 84

Report of the World Conference to Review and Appraise the Achievements of the United Nations Decade for Women: Equality, Development and Peace, held in Nairobi from 15 to 26 July 1985; including the Agenda and the Nairobi Forward-looking Strategies for the Advancement of Women (extract).

A/CONF.116/28/Rev.1, 1986

See page 310

Document 85

General Assembly resolution endorsing the Nairobi Forward-looking Strategies for the Advancement of Women and calling on Governments to take measures towards their implementation.

A/RES/40/108, 13 December 1985

See page 363

Document 86

"Overview of the role of women in development", from the *World Survey on the Role of Women in Development* (extract).

A/CONF.116/4/Rev.1-ST/ESA/180, 1986

See page 366

Document 87

General Assembly resolution on the role of women in society, calling on Governments, among other things, to encourage such support as paid maternity, parental and child-care leave, and to provide women with job security with a view to allowing them to fulfil their roles as mothers without prejudice to their professional and public activities.

A/RES/41/110, 4 December 1986

See page 370

Document 88

General Assembly resolution emphasizing the need for immediate and full implementation of the Nairobi Forward-looking Strategies and the importance of the total integration of women in the development process, having in mind the specific and urgent needs of the developing countries.

A/RES/41/111, 4 December 1986

See page 371

Document 89

ECOSOC resolution adopting the long-term programme of work of the CSW to the year 2000.

E/RES/1987/24, 26 May 1987

See page 372

Document 90

General Assembly resolution emphasizing, among other things, the need to give urgent attention to redressing socio-economic inequities at the national and international levels as a necessary step towards the full realization of the goals and objectives of the Forward-looking Strategies.

A/RES/42/62, 30 November 1987

See page 374

Document 91

General Assembly resolution reiterating the need for the Forward-looking Strategies to be translated immediately into concrete action by Governments, as determined by overall national priorities, as well as by the organizations of the United Nations system, the specialized agencies and the intergovernmental and non-governmental organizations.

A/RES/43/101, 8 December 1988

See page 376

Document 92

"Overview of the role of women in development", from the 1989 *World Survey on the Role of Women in Development* (extract).

ST/CSDHA/6, 1989

See page 378

Document 93

Report of the Secretary-General to the CSW on the first review and appraisal of the implementation of the Nairobi Forward-looking Strategies, assessing progress at the national, regional and international levels.

E/CN.6/1990/5, 22 November 1989

See page 385

Document 94

General Assembly resolution on the occasion of the tenth anniversary of the adoption of the Convention on the Elimination of All Forms of Discrimination against Women, urging States that have not yet done so to ratify the Convention.

A/RES/44/73, 8 December 1989

See page 438

Document 95

General Assembly resolution emphasizing the priority of implementation, monitoring, review and appraisal of the Nairobi Forward-looking Strategies for the Advancement of Women and calling on Member States to give priority to policies and programmes relating to employment, health and education.

A/RES/44/77, 8 December 1989

See page 440

Document 96
General Assembly resolution calling for improvement of the situation of women in rural areas.
A/RES/44/78, 8 December 1989
See page 442

Document 97
ECOSOC resolution recommending that a world conference on women be held in 1995 and requesting the CSW to act as preparatory body.
E/RES/1990/12, 24 May 1990
See page 443

Document 98
ECOSOC resolution adopting the recommendations and conclusions arising from the first review and appraisal of the implementation of the Nairobi Forward-looking Strategies for the Advancement of Women to the year 2000 and urging Governments to implement the recommendations.
E/RES/1990/15, 24 May 1990
See page 444

Document 99
General Assembly resolution calling for efforts to increase the literacy of women.
A/RES/45/126, 14 December 1990
See page 451

Document 100
General Assembly resolution endorsing the ECOSOC recommendation that a world conference on women be held in 1995.
A/RES/45/129, 14 December 1990
See page 452

Document 101
General Assembly resolution calling for improvement in the status of women in the United Nations Secretariat.
A/RES/45/239 C, 21 December 1990
See page 455

Document 102
"Overview of the world's women", from *The World's Women: Trends and Statistics, 1970-1990* (extract).
ST/ESA/STAT/SER.K/8, 1991
See page 456

Document 103
General Assembly resolution on implementation of the Nairobi Forward-looking Strategies and requesting the CSW to give special attention to women in developing countries.
A/RES/46/98, 16 December 1991
See page 464

Document 104
Agenda 21, adopted by the United Nations Conference on Environment and Development, held in Rio de Janeiro from 3 to 14 June 1992—Chapter 24: Global action for women towards sustainable and equitable development (extract).
A/CONF.151/26/Rev.1 (Vol. 1), 1992
See page 467

Document 105
General Assembly resolution on implementation of the Nairobi Forward-looking Strategies and requesting the CSW to complete work on a declaration on the elimination of violence against women.
A/RES/47/95, 16 December 1992
See page 470

Document 106
Vienna Declaration and Programme of Action, adopted by the World Conference on Human Rights, held in Vienna from 14 to 25 June 1993—Section II.A.3: The equal status and human rights of women (extract).
A/CONF.157/24 (Part I), 13 October 1993
See page 472

Document 107
General Assembly resolution adopting the Declaration on the Elimination of Violence against Women.
A/RES/48/104, 20 December 1993
See page 474

Document 108
General Assembly resolution on implementation of the Nairobi Forward-looking Strategies and on the participation of non-governmental organizations in the Fourth World Conference on Women.
A/RES/48/108, 20 December 1993
See page 477

Document 109
Executive summary of the 1994 *World Survey on the Role of Women in Development* (extract).
ST/ESA/241, 1995
See page 481

Document 110
Commission on Human Rights resolution appointing a Special Rapporteur on violence against women.
Commission on Human Rights resolution 1994/45 (ESCOR, 1994, Suppl. No. 4, p. 140), 11 March 1994
See page 492

Document 111

Report of the Secretary-General to the General Assembly on the status of the Convention on the Elimination of All Forms of Discrimination against Women (extract).
A/49/308, 12 August 1994
See page 495

Document 112

Report of the Secretary-General to the General Assembly on violence against women migrant workers.
A/49/354, 1 September 1994
See page 506

Document 113

Programme of Action, adopted by the International Conference on Population and Development, held in Cairo from 5 to 13 September 1994—Chapter IV and Principle 4: Gender equality, equity and empowerment of women (extract).
A/CONF.171/13, 18 October 1994
See page 515

Document 114

Report of the Secretary-General to the General Assembly on the improvement of the status of women in the Secretariat.
A/49/587, 1 November 1994
See page 519

Document 115

Preliminary report of the Special Rapporteur on violence against women to the Commission on Human Rights.
E/CN.4/1995/42, 22 November 1994
See page 528

Document 116

General Assembly resolution on implementation of the Nairobi Forward-looking Strategies.
A/RES/49/161, 23 December 1994
See page 577

Document 117

General Assembly resolution calling attention to the concerns of older women in development policies and requesting that special attention be paid to discrimination against older women in the implementation of the Convention on the Elimination of All Forms of Discrimination against Women.
A/RES/49/162, 23 December 1994
See page 580

Document 118

General Assembly resolution calling on States to ratify the Convention on the Elimination of All Forms of Discrimination against Women and urging compliance with the Convention.
A/RES/49/164, 23 December 1994
See page 581

Document 119

"Overview of the world's women in 1995", from *The World's Women 1995: Trends and Statistics* (extract).
ST/ESA/STAT/SER.K/12, 1995
See page 584

Document 120

Overview of the report of the Secretary-General to the CSW on the second review and appraisal of the implementation of the Nairobi Forward-looking Strategies for the Advancement of Women (extract).
E/CN.6/1995/3, 10 January 1995, and E/CN.6/1995/3/Add.1, 24 February 1995
See page 591

Document 121

Annex II (on an optional protocol to the Convention) to the report of the fourteenth session of CEDAW (extract).
E/CN.6/1995/CRP.1, 3 February 1995
See page 609

Document 122

Copenhagen Declaration on Social Development, adopted by the World Summit for Social Development, held in Copenhagen from 6 to 12 March 1995—Commitment 5, on the achievement of equality and equity between women and men (extract).
A/CONF.166/9, 1995
See page 611

Document 123

Report of the Secretary-General to the General Assembly on the Convention on the Elimination of All Forms of Discrimination against Women, including the text of the proposed amendment to article 20 of the Convention (extract).
A/50/346, 11 August 1995
See page 612

Document 124

Report of the Secretary-General to the General Assembly on traffic in women and girls.
A/50/369, 24 August 1995
See page 614

Document 125

Report of the Secretary-General to the General Assembly on the effective mobilization and integration of women in development: gender issues in macroeconomic policy-making and development planning.
A/50/399, 22 September 1995
See page 622

Document 126

Report of the Secretary-General to the General Assembly on the improvement of the situation of women in rural areas.
A/50/257/Rev.1, 28 September 1995
See page 640

Document 127

Report of the Fourth World Conference on Women, held in Beijing from 4 to 15 September 1995; including the Agenda, the Beijing Declaration and the Platform for Action (extract).
A/CONF.177/20, 17 October 1995
See page 649

Document 128

Report of the Secretary-General to the General Assembly on improvement of the status of women in the Secretariat.
A/50/691, 27 October 1995
See page 735

Document 129

Report of the Secretary-General to the General Assembly on implementation of the outcome of the Fourth World Conference on Women: Equality, Development and Peace.
A/50/744, 10 November 1995
See page 748

Document 130

General Assembly resolution on the girl child.
A/RES/50/154, 21 December 1995
See page 762

Document 131

General Assembly resolution calling for the improvement of the situation of women in rural areas.
A/RES/50/165, 22 December 1995
See page 763

Document 132

General Assembly resolution on traffic in women and girls.
A/RES/50/167, 22 December 1995
See page 764

Document 133

General Assembly resolution on violence against women migrant workers.
A/RES/50/168, 22 December 1995
See page 766

Document 134

General Assembly resolution on rape and abuse of women in the areas of armed conflict in the former Yugoslavia.
A/RES/50/192, 22 December 1995
See page 767

Document 135

General Assembly resolution on follow-up to the Fourth World Conference on Women and full implementation of the Beijing Declaration and Platform for Action.
A/RES/50/203, 22 December 1995
See page 769

Document 136

Memorandum to United Nations staff consolidating special measures introduced over the years for the achievement of gender equality (extract).
ST/AI/412, 5 January 1996
See page 773

Document 137

Memorandum from the Secretary-General to United Nations staff on policies to achieve gender equality in the United Nations.
ST/SGB/282, 5 January 1996
See page 776

Document 138

Report of the Secretary-General to the CSW on the elaboration of an optional protocol to the Convention on the Elimination of All Forms of Discrimination against Women.
E/CN.6/1996/10, 10 January 1996, E/CN.6/1996/10/Add.1, 9 February 1996, and E/CN.6/1996/10/Add.2, 29 February 1996
See page 777

Document 139

Declarations, reservations, objections and notifications of withdrawal of reservations relating to the Convention on the Elimination of All Forms of Discrimination against Women.
CEDAW/SP/1996/2, 8 February 1996
See page 793

The following is a breakdown, by category, of the documents reproduced in this book.

Charter of the United Nations
Document 1

The Universal Declaration of Human Rights
Document 14

International conventions
Documents 18, 26, 29, 31, 35, 69

Resolutions of the General Assembly
Documents 7, 28, 32, 33, 34, 36, 38, 39, 40, 41, 42, 43, 44, 46, 47, 48, 49, 50, 51, 52, 53, 56, 57, 58, 59, 60, 61, 62, 63, 64, 65, 66, 67, 68, 71, 72, 73, 74, 75, 77, 79, 80, 81, 82, 83, 85, 87, 88, 90, 91, 94, 95, 96, 99, 100, 101, 103, 105, 107, 108, 116, 117, 118, 130, 131, 132, 133, 134, 135

Resolutions of the Economic and Social Council
Documents 3, 6, 9, 10, 11, 12, 13, 15, 17, 25, 30, 54, 89, 97, 98

Resolution of the Commission on Human Rights
Document 110

Reports of the Secretary-General to the General Assembly
Documents 111, 112, 114, 123, 124, 125, 126, 128, 129

Reports of the Secretary-General to the Commission on the Status of Women
Documents 19, 20, 21, 22, 23, 24, 93, 120, 138

Statement by the Secretary-General to the Commission on the Status of Women
Document 27

Reports of the Commission on the Status of Women to the Economic and Social Council
Documents 8, 16

Report of the Special Rapporteur on violence against women to the Commission on Human Rights
Document 115

Materials relating to World Conferences
Documents 37, 45, 70, 84, 104, 106, 113, 122, 127

Statute of the International Research and Training Institute for the Advancement of Women (INSTRAW)
Document 78

Report of the International Research and Training Institute for the Advancement of Women (INSTRAW) to the General Assembly
Document 76

Extracts from editions of the *World Survey of the Role of Women in Development*
Documents 86, 92, 109

Extracts from *The World's Women: Trends and Statistics, 1970-1990* and *The World's Women 1995: Trends and Statistics*
Documents 102, 119

Other
Documents 2, 4, 5, 55, 121, 136, 137, 139

IV Texts of documents

The texts of the 139 documents listed on the preceding pages are reproduced below. The appearance of ellipses (. . .) in the text indicates that portions of the document have been omitted. A subject index to the documents appears on page 824.

Document 1

Charter of the United Nations, signed 26 June 1945 (extract)

Preamble

WE THE PEOPLES
OF THE UNITED NATIONS
DETERMINED

to save succeeding generations from the scourge of war, which twice in our lifetime has brought untold sorrow to mankind, and

to reaffirm faith in fundamental human rights, in the dignity and worth of the human person, in the equal rights of men and women and of nations large and small,

...

Article 1

The Purposes of the United Nations are:

...

3. To achieve international co-operation in solving international problems of an economic, social, cultural or humanitarian character, and in promoting and encouraging respect for human rights and for fundamental freedoms for all without distinction as to race, sex, language or religion;

...

Article 8

The United Nations shall place no restrictions on the eligibility of men and women to participate in any capacity and under conditions of equality in its principal and subsidiary organs.

...

Article 101

...

3. The paramount consideration in the employment of the staff and in the determination of the conditions of service shall be the necessity of securing the highest standards of efficiency, competence, and integrity. Due regard shall be paid to the importance of recruiting the staff on as wide a geographical basis as possible.

Document 2

"Open Letter to the women of the world", read by Eleanor Roosevelt, representative of the delegation of the United States of America, to the first session of the General Assembly; and statements made by representatives on the participation of women in the work of the United Nations and the creation of a committee on the status of women (extract)

A/PV.29, 12 February 1946

MRS. ROOSEVELT (United States of America): I have only a short statement to make and I will take up very little of your time. As you know, a number of women have been present in the various delegations either as delegates or alternates or advisers. We met together and we prepared a statement which we addressed to "the women of our various countries". We are very happy to have the opportunity—I am speaking for my colleagues—to present this statement to the delegates here and ask your cooperation when you go home, in relation to your Governments and to the various ways in which this statement may be given publicity, because we feel that the women of all our countries should have an opportunity to receive this letter.

"An Open Letter to the women of the world from the women delegates and advisers at the first Assembly of the United Nations:

"This first Assembly of the United Nations marks the second attempt of the peoples of the world to live peacefully in a democratic world community. This new chance for peace was won through the joint efforts of men and women working for common ideals of human freedom at a time when the need for united effort broke down barriers of race, creed and sex.

"In view of the variety of tasks which women performed so notably and valiantly during the war, we are gratified that seventeen women representatives and advisers, representatives of eleven Member States, are taking part at the beginning of this new phase of international effort. We hope their participation in the work of the United Nations Organization may grow and may increase in insight and in skill. To this end we call on the Governments of the world to encourage women everywhere to take a more active part in national and international affairs, and on women who are conscious of their opportunities to come forward and share in the work of peace and reconstruction as they did in war and resistance.

"We recognize that women in various parts of the world are at different stages of participation in the life of their community, that some of them are prevented by law from assuming full rights of citizenship, and that they therefore may see their immediate problems somewhat differently.

"Finding ourselves in agreement on these points, we wish as a group to advise the women of all our countries of our strong belief that an important opportunity and responsibility confront the women of the United Nations: first, to recognize the progress women have made during the war and to participate actively in the effort to improve the standards of life in their own countries and in the pressing work of reconstruction, so that there will be qualified women ready to accept responsibility when new opportunities arise; second, to train their children, boys and girls alike, to understand world problems and the need for international cooperation, as well as the problems of their own countries; third, not to permit themselves to be misled by anti-democratic movements now or in the future; fourth, to recognize that the goal of full participation in the life and responsibilities of their countries and of the world community is a common objective toward which the women of the world should assist one another."

Every woman here present signed that letter, and we only ask for the cooperation of every delegate here.

In closing, I want to thank the General Assembly for giving me the opportunity of presenting this letter here, and to say that I have been grateful for the opportunity to be here with you to see the work which has been accomplished and that in the end I hope none of us will go home without remembering that we have a great responsibility to carry to our peoples the feeling that this can be an instrument, if we give to it as much work as we have given in the past to winning the war, an instrument to win the peace.

THE PRESIDENT (*Translation from the French*): I call upon Miss Bernardino, representative of the Dominican Republic.

MISS BERNARDINO (Dominican Republic): As a representative of my country, the Dominican Republic, to the first General Assembly of the United Nations, and especially as Chairman of the Inter-American Commission of Women, an official organization composed of twenty-one members appointed by the Governments of the Americas to study and report on the status of women, I would like to give the strongest support to the letter read by the delegate for the United States of America, my distinguished colleague, Mrs. Franklin D. Roosevelt, and to the declaration of the French delegation that "feminine participation should occupy a more important place in the various delegations to the next Conference of the United Nations".

I wonder if, in the history of the world, women have ever been confronted with graver responsibilities, have ever enjoyed greater opportunities than those which are theirs today?

I do not mean exclusively women who have official, high ranking positions; nor necessarily those who are gifted through talent and training with superb gifts of leadership which enable them to clear the way and set the example for others to follow; nor do I mean only those delegated by their Governments to attend international parleys. Rather, I refer to the wife; the mother in the home; the teacher in the school; the church-worker; the missionary; the social service worker, who goes from door to door helping to set weary feet back on the beaten path; the nurse, who at this moment in hospitals throughout the world is taxing her strength to aid the restoration of sick and wounded to health and normality.

In short, women everywhere, who have turned their minds and hearts to the problems of humanity, and to the even more formidable undertaking of re-educating, re-adjusting and enlightening the recalcitrant peoples of the conquered countries.

The work which is ours must be carried on quickly, definitely, with sympathy, discernment and judgement. It must have the benefit of every effort of experience on the part of women; but we cannot forget that women in many parts of the world are still handicapped by the lack of right to play any role in the discussions of peace and international affairs. We still find women in some parts of the world who have graduated from law schools but are prevented from practicing their profession because of strict prohibition in their countries' laws.

The fact that in the preamble to the Charter of the United Nations there is an affirmation of faith in the principle of equal rights of men and women and the fact that Article 8 of the Charter establishes "that the United Nations shall place no restrictions on the eligibility of men and women to participate in any capacity and under conditions of equality in its principal and subsidiary organs" are powerful reasons for women to demand the fulfilment of those principles.

That is why the creation of a committee, under the Commission on Human Rights, to study and work for the status of women is so important, as it will contribute to the abolition of any existing discrimination by reason of sex, which retards the prosperity and the intellectual, social and political development of the nations of the world.

In the name of the women of my country, who for many years have been enjoying the same rights and privileges that men enjoy, and in the name of the women of Latin America, and especially those from countries that still walk in obscurity, without the inherent rights to which the dignity of their sex, and their responsibilities as mothers of the race, should entitle them, I salute all the delegations here present for the full support they have given to our appeal.

I hope that in future assemblies, as my outstanding colleague from France, Mrs. Lefaucheaux, proposed, we shall have more women delegates to cooperate with men to the end that all peoples may enjoy the essential human freedoms proclaimed in 1941 by that great world leader of all time, President Franklin D. Roosevelt.

THE PRESIDENT (*Translation from the French*): I call upon Mrs. Dalen, representative of Norway.

MRS. DALEN (Norway): I shall be very brief; but I feel that I must say how very grateful I am to the French delegation for moving this declaration. On behalf of the Norwegian delegation I heartily support it.

During the war, women in all countries participated and worked in the armed forces, in factories and in the resistance movement in a way never before thought of. During the war, women's experience, insight and strength were highly appreciated and welcomed. When the nation was in danger the women were called upon and they came, did their jobs, sacrificed and suffered. Now, when the war is over and the United Nations are trying to build a new world, trying to lay the foundations of peace and freedom for humanity, the world cannot afford to do so without using the rich resources that women's experience and capacity for work, women's insight and equipment mean for the various nations of the world. All human beings have to cooperate in dignity and unity and fidelity. Then we shall succeed in building up a happy, peaceful and harmonious world.

THE PRESIDENT (*Translation from the French*): I call upon Mrs. Verwey, representative of the Netherlands.

MRS. VERWEY (Netherlands): Might I, to begin with, express my gratitude to those male members of this General Assembly who have so warmly supported this motion? We know that we, who represent here the women of our countries, have many friends in this Assembly, and that they will always help us to express our views and those of other women not represented here. But I should like to add that I have missed something, and that is an opposing voice to this motion. No one has so far said that he does not want the women of his country to speak and to act here. I am afraid that they have abstained, not because they agree with the purpose of this motion, but because they think that it does not concern them. They might be of the opinion that women in their countries are just faithful wives and mothers, that they do not want to be members of delegations, that they are not qualified for it and take no interest in it. To them I want to say a few words.

There is no one in this General Assembly who supposes that a recommendation like this would result in a future Assembly with as many women as there are men. There are very strong reasons why, in public life, women will always be in a minority. There are biological, socio-logical and psychological reasons; biological reasons because, after all, the first essential woman's right is the right to be a mother, and also the opportunity to enjoy that right to the full. This means that we would never agree to a world in which social conditions resulted in a situation in which married women should be perma-nently obliged to work in the factories and on the farms and to neglect their families; but this does not mean that we should for ever compel all women to confine themselves to the home. There are women whom nature and man have denied the right to have children and some women think that they can do some good public work apart from their domestic life; it is very essential that they should have all the opportunities they want.

There may be social reasons against feminine participation as well. In most societies women seem to be marked out for special jobs, for the school and the office, rather than for the meeting-room. But we should not be too eager to draw our conclusions from facts like that.

A hundred years ago, before Miss Florence Nightingale started her campaign, there was no question of training women to be nurses. Ten years ago there were many doubts, even I think in this country, about women's services. Some views about jobs fit for women are inclined to be changed rather rapidly.

Then, in the third place, some people might quote psychological reasons. They might point out that this is still a man-built world and that women feel strangers as soon as they venture into it. This is true in a way. I must say that men have built this world quite impressively and that we feel duly impressed at first. After a certain time, however, some of us feel inclined to say: Is that all? All this pomp and all these intricate sentences can be translated into quite simple relations and words; and from that moment we feel quite capable of playing our part.

What I should like to emphasize is this: there may seem to be very strong reasons why no woman of your country can participate in international work. But are you sure? Is there no woman somewhere hidden away in a corner, no teacher, no woman professor, no woman doctor, no one who would be a credit to your delegation and who would be extremely glad to have this opportunity to meet men and women in an international sphere? It is on their behalf and on behalf of the women they represent that we make this recommendation.

THE PRESIDENT (*Translation from the French*): I call upon Mr. Paul-Boncour, representative of France.

MR. PAUL-BONCOUR (France) (*Translation from the French*): The General Assembly will, I feel sure, have understood why I did not accept the President's invitation to speak just now, and why I wished to leave the honour of opening this discussion—which will I hope be no discussion, but only an act of homage and gratitude—to a woman whose presence amongst us has given to our debates a distinction which derives not only from a universally great name and one, I hope, that will be for ever loved and respected, but from one whose wide, vivid, warm-hearted and understanding contributions have given these debates an added value.

The intention of the French delegation, in bringing forward the declaration which I will read from this rostrum, is to perform not an act of chivalry, but an act

of justice. The horrors of the war we have just lived through and the after-effects which we are, unhappily, still feeling, have put women at once on an equal footing with men on the world's stage. In every country the necessities of defence led to the mobilization of women. Almost everywhere a law, for which I was responsible in my own country nearly twenty years ago, was put into force: auxiliary services in great numbers and many armed services sprang into being. Then, there was the part played by women in the Resistance movement, which not only saved the honour of the conquered countries, but paved the way for later revenge and for that landing by which we were set free.

Furthermore, besides those who fought in the armed services, served in the auxiliary services or took an active and splendid part in the Resistance, there were the countless women who helped to relieve the difficulties of the food situation, even though, alas, they could not save us from them altogether. In France, eighty percent of the work on the land was done by women during the war.

It is these qualities, and the outstanding part played by women in their respective countries, that the Charter has set out to honour in several of its provisions. It has laid down the principle of complete equality without distinction as to age, sex or religion, and the presence of women delegates in our midst and the activity that they have displayed in the Committees show that the Charter was right in the confidence it reposed in them.

For this reason, the French delegation, on the initiative of our colleague Mrs. Lefaucheaux, whose absence, I regret to state, prevents her from taking my place at the rostrum, has proposed, not indeed any share in the composition of the delegations, which should be left entirely to the discretion of the countries concerned, but an offer of friendly advice and encouragement, so that each of us, on our return to our own country, may help still further to develop the letter and spirit of the Charter and see that women are given a fuller part to play in the work of the various delegations to the United Nations.

This is the declaration which I make in the name of the French delegation:

"Considering the desirability of recognizing the part played by women during the war and their participation in the work of the Resistance movements and the Armed Forces, and the desirability of interesting all the women of the world more directly in the efforts of the United Nations Organization as well as in the maintenance of peace and in social progress;

"Considering the desirability of applying both the letter and the spirit of paragraph (c) of Article 55 of the Charter, which lays down that the principal aim of the Economic and Social Council is to promote universal respect for and observance of human rights and fundamental freedoms for all, without distinction as to race, sex, language or religion;

"The French delegation considers that feminine participation should occupy a more important place in the various delegations to the next conference of the United Nations."

THE PRESIDENT (*Translation from the French*): I call upon Mr. Fraser, representative of New Zealand.

MR. FRASER (New Zealand): I join in the expression of regret from all those who have spoken of the absence of Mrs. Lefaucheaux, who brought forward the proposal which has been moved in a general way by Mrs. Roosevelt and supported by Miss Bernardino, by Mr. Paul-Boncour and others.

There is no need to stress the necessity for pushing on the practical work in connection with the parts of our Charter which have emphasized the equality of women. The intellectual battle has been won after a very considerable time. The political battle in practically every country has also been won, and I would suggest that, if there are any countries where the women are not politically equal (and none spring to my mind at the moment) and politically active also, then the sooner these countries bring their women up politically to what is the normal standard in all democratic countries, the better for the world and for the United Nations.

But there is something more than the intellectual battle and something more than winning a political victory in the various countries, and that is the economic status and the social status of women. Here, I know, it is easier to state the problems than to solve them, but the question of solving them is an obligation upon the United Nations, and during the course of this General Assembly meeting and the meetings of the Committees the women delegates have been very busy in endeavouring to see what was the best way in which the questions of economic and social equality in respect to women could be pushed ahead.

At San Francisco I supported them also in regard to a committee or commission composed of women exclusively, not in an exclusive way, but to let women do the preliminary work. That was agreed to. I do not think that is material at all, but when some delegates said they did not think a committee of women could do the job, well, I simply had to say that they could, and that was all. From my experience, I could prove that a committee of women is very practical when they are practical women; there are unpractical women just as there are unpractical men.

I want to say, however, that my experience at this General Assembly with the women delegates on the Committee (I think all of them were on the Committee of which I was Chairman) has shown me that to talk about their equality would be patronizing. It is just there, a self-evident fact, at least to most of us. I can say that, in their grip of the problems, in their intuition, in their application to the work, in their clarity of thought and diction—I believe they were equal to any there. So there is no question any more about the equality or the capacity of women who are sent to these international assemblies, and if they are not up to the normal standard they ought not to be sent any more than men ought to be; that is the sound attitude to take in regard to sex equality.

I have been particularly interested in knowing what progress has been made, because otherwise a resolution would have had to be introduced (in fact, it was prepared) into our Committee, but the matter was taken up very, very speedily by the Economic and Social Council. I would just like to recount briefly what progress has been made, so that when delegates go away they will understand what the Economic and Social Council has done. I endeavoured to get Sir Ramaswami Mudaliar, the Chairman of the Council, to attend this meeting, but it was not possible for him to come. But the explanation I have been able to gather is as follows:

"The Economic and Social Council has been keenly aware of the importance of establishing a Sub-Commission on the status of women.

"The Committee of the Economic and Social Council on the organization of the Council has instructed its Drafting Sub-Committee to submit a draft providing for the establishment by the Economic and Social Council of a Sub-Commission of the Commission on Human Rights to deal with the question of the status of women. This Drafting Sub-Committee is now preparing a draft on this subject, incorporating the recommendations made by the Committee of the Council.

"It is proposed that the Sub-Commission on the status of women be established by the Council at its present session, and that it initially consist only of a nucleus of a few members. This initially constituted Sub-Commission would, among other things, be called upon to make recommendations to the Council concerning the definitive composition of the Sub-Commission and its terms of reference."

This shows that the Economic and Social Council is dealing with this problem in a very practical way, and in what I believe will be a very effective way. There are problems that cut across custom, problems that, in some instances, may even impinge upon religion. There are many difficult problems, and we do want patience and we do want tolerance. While never lowering our flag in regard to equality we still have to take into consideration the circumstances in the various countries and get the support and the sympathy of the various Governments and organizations, so that the women of the world will march forward to progress and a better society, hand in hand and side by side with the men and so that they will help to bring in, as the women delegates and Mr. Paul-Boncour so elegantly stated, a world of peace and human brotherhood and a world of social justice and equality.

THE PRESIDENT (*Translation from the French*): I call upon Mr. Fusco, representative of Uruguay.

MR. FUSCO (Uruguay) (*Translation from the French*): I was so deeply moved by Mrs. Roosevelt's appeal from this platform that I am prompted to speak in a language I have not quite mastered. The women of this General Assembly could not have found a better exponent of their aspirations than the lady they have chosen. Throughout the war years, everybody regarded Mrs. Roosevelt as the most charming representative of her sex, seeing in her the companion whose strength and affection sustained the great fighter who embodied the hopes of all mankind.

The delegation of Uruguay will be the most faithful protagonist of the ideas voiced by Mrs. Roosevelt; but it will have little action to take in this field, since my country has already achieved the results to which the women of all the countries in the world aspire. In Uruguay, women have the same rights as men. We have women Members of Parliament and women Senators, freely elected by the people. We even had a woman delegate at the San Francisco Conference, where the Charter of the United Nations was born.

Travelling in Europe before the General Assembly began its session, I had the good fortune—if such it can be called—to see how women's effort in the struggle for freedom has equalled that of men. Women fought, suffered and died in the same way as men.

I have been able to observe in the course of the General Assembly's work how women, because of their insight, rivalled and sometimes outdid the men.

We are proud to be able to say that we have anticipated the wishes expressed by the women of the world, and more particularly by the most authoritative among them, Mrs. Roosevelt.

THE PRESIDENT (*Translation from the French*): I call upon Mr. Noel-Baker, representative of the United Kingdom.

MR. NOEL-BAKER (United Kingdom): I am reluctant that the voice of the United Kingdom should not be heard in this debate, if only for the reason that it was in our country forty years ago that the first struggle for the political rights of women took place. I have not, however, risen simply to express my adherence to the proposed declaration or to the cause of the rights of women. I have risen in order to draw the attention of the Secretary-General, very respectfully, to two practical points: first, that there ought to be representation of women in responsible posts in the Secretariat itself; and, secondly, that the services of the Information Section of the Secretariat ought to keep in close contact with the great women's organizations throughout the world. I think, in those ways, the views of Mrs. Roosevelt, and her colleagues, so eloquently expressed, could well be served.

THE PRESIDENT (*Translation from the French*): The general discussion is closed. There is no formal proposal to submit to the vote, but I think I can safely tell Mrs. Roosevelt and those who supported her intervention, that the manner in which it was received by the General Assembly leads us to hope that it will be taken into very serious consideration.

Document 3

Economic and Social Council (ECOSOC) resolution establishing the Commission on Human Rights and the Subcommission on the Status of Women

E/RES/5(I), 16 February 1946

Section A

1. The Economic and Social Council, being charged under the Charter with the responsibility of promoting universal respect for, and observance of, human rights and fundamental freedoms for all without distinction as to race, sex, language or religion, and requiring advice and assistance to enable it to discharge this responsibility,

ESTABLISHES A COMMISSION ON
HUMAN RIGHTS.

2. The work of the Commission shall be directed towards submitting proposals, recommendations and reports to the Council regarding:

(a) an international bill of rights;

(b) international declarations or conventions on civil liberties, the status of women, freedom of information and similar matters;

(c) the protection of minorities;

(d) the prevention of discrimination on grounds of race, sex, language or religion.

3. The Commission shall make studies and recommendations and provide information and other services at the request of the Economic and Social Council.

4. The Commission may propose to the Council any changes in its terms of reference.

5. The Commission may make recommendations to the Council concerning any subcommission which it considers should be established.

6. Initially, the Commission shall consist of a nucleus of nine members appointed in their individual capacity for a term of office expiring on 31 March 1947. They are eligible for re-appointment. In addition to exercising the functions enumerated in paragraphs 2, 3 and 4, the Commission thus constituted shall make recommendation on the definitive composition of the Commission to the second session of the Council.

7. The Council hereby appoints the following persons as initial members of the Commission:

Mr. Paal Berg	(Norway)
Professor René Cassin	(France)
Mr. Fernand Dehousse	(Belgium)
Mr. Victor Paul Haya de la Torre	(Peru)
Mr. K. C. Neogi	(India)
Mrs. Franklin D. Roosevelt	(United States of America)
Dr. John C. H. Wu 1/	(China)

and, in addition, persons whose names will be transmitted to the Secretary-General not later than 31 March 1946 by the members of the Council for the USSR and Yugoslavia. 2/

Section B

1. The Economic and Social Council, considering that the Commission on Human Rights will require special advice on problems relating to the status of women,

ESTABLISHES A SUBCOMMISSION ON
THE STATUS OF WOMEN.

2. The subcommission shall submit proposals, recommendations, and reports to the Commission on Human Rights regarding the status of women.

3. The subcommission may submit proposals to the Council, through the Commission on Human Rights, regarding its terms of reference.

4. Initially, the subcommission shall consist of a nucleus of nine members appointed in their individual capacity for a term of office expiring on 31 March 1947. They are eligible for re-appointment. In addition to exercising the functions enumerated in paragraphs 2 and 3, the subcommission thus constituted shall make recommendation on the definitive composition of the subcommission to the second session of the Council through the Commission on Human Rights.

5. The Council hereby appoints the following persons as initial members of this subcommission:

Mrs. Bodil Begtrup	(Denmark)
Miss Minerva Bernadino	(Dominican Republic)
Miss Angela Jurdak	(Lebanon)

1/ In accordance with the procedure laid down by the Economic and Social Council, Dr. C. L. Hsia has since been nominated in place of Dr. John C. H. Wu.

2/ Dr. Jerko Radmilovic has since been nominated by the member of the Council for Yugoslavia.

Rani Amrit Kaur	(India)
Miss Mistral	(Chile)
Mrs. Viénot 3/	(France)
Miss Wu Yi-Fang 3/	(China)

and, in addition, the names of one national each from Poland and the USSR to be transmitted to the Secretary-General, not later than 31 March 1946, by the member of the Council for the Union of Soviet Socialist Republics,

and three members appointed by the Commission on Human Rights to serve as *ex officio* members of this subcommission.

3/ In accordance with the procedure laid down by the Economic and Social Council, Madame Lefaucheux has since been nominated in place of Madame Viénot. Similarly, Mrs. W. S. New has been nominated in place of Miss Wu Yi-Fang.

Document 4

Statements made at the first session of ECOSOC regarding the composition of the Subcommission on the Status of Women (extract)

E/SR.14, 18 February 1946

President: Sir Ramaswami MUDALIAR (India)

49.   Report of the Sub-Committee on the Composition of the Commissions (document E/26)

Sub-Commission on the Status of Women

Mr. VERGARA (Chile) pointed out that "Miss Mistral" was the pen name used by the Chilean representative, and it was decided that it would be more appropriate to maintain this pseudonym in view of the fact that she was so well known for her literary ability under this name.

The PRESIDENT informed the Council that, on the recommendation of the Sub-Committee, Turkey had been included in the list of those countries which would transmit names to the Secretary-General before 31 March 1946, but it had since been brought to his attention that Lebanon was not represented on any of the commissions. On the suggestion of the representative of Lebanon, the President proposed that the name of Miss Angela Jurdak be added and expressed the hope that Turkey might become a member of the full commission at a later date.

The last phrase relating to this Sub-Commission should read as follows:

"and, in addition, the names of one national each from Poland and the Union of Soviet Socialist Republics to be transmitted to the Secretary-General, not later than 31 March 1946, by the member of the Council for the Union of Soviet Socialist Republics and three members appointed by the Commission on Human Rights to serve as *ex officio* members of this Sub-Commission."

The PRESIDENT pointed out that all nominations must be made through a member of the Council even when they emanated from Members of the United Nations not represented on the Council. He further stated with regard to the Sub-Commission on the Status of Women that three persons were to be appointed as *ex officio* members which would ensure that the Sub-Commission was not composed of women only.

Decision: *The composition of the Sub-Commission, with these modifications, was approved.*

Document 5

Statement made by the Chair of the Subcommission on the Status of Women to ECOSOC recommending that the status of the Subcommission be raised to full Commission (extract)

E/PV.4, 28 May 1946

I want, first of all, to thank the Members of the Economic and Social Council for the wisdom and foresight they have shown in taking up the question of the status of women at such an early stage of their work. It shows a deep understanding of the importance attached to the very fundamental social and economic inequalities which lies in the different status of men and women.

The nuclear sub-commission on the Status of Women, set up the 16th and 18th of February, by the Economic and Social Council, held its first meeting the 29th of April at Hunter College, and after a fortnight of concentrated and harmonious teamwork, the report presented to this Council by the Chairman of the Commission for Human Rights was ready. The work has shown us that the purpose of the Commission was to make proposals about how to raise the status of women to equality with men in all fields of human enterprise. They felt that it was necessary, as a background for their practical suggestion, about how to achieve this aim, to make a broad outline of the main fields in which progress was needed. These were (a) political, which is desirable to have; equal participation in governments and possibility to express all the rights and assume all the duties of citizens, (b) civil rights; marriage, guardianship, nationality and property—equal rights to hold and acquire, administer and inherit property. (c) social and economic: full possibility of taking equal part in social life, which implies full opportunity of fulfilling our duties towards society. (d) education: equal participation in education and means for education for men and women.

As a means to achieve these aims, the sub-commission proposes: that world opinion be stimulated in favor of raising the status of women as an instrument to further human rights and peace.

We suggest that the United Nations Information Service should give special consideration—perhaps have a special person to see to that—which can be done through the means of press, radio, free lectures and so on.

We think that it is of the utmost importance to have a United Nations Office of Women's Affairs in the framework of the Secretariat, run by a highly competent woman. This office should be the planning center for the work and clearing house for information about the status of women and women's activities. It would give the women all over the world a feeling of satisfaction to have a special office at the Headquarters of the United Nations.

The third point is that the United Nations makes a worldwide, up-to-date, reliable and valid survey of laws pertaining to the status of women, their application and the actual status of women.

The Sub-Commission has investigated in the work started and partly done by the League of Nations in this field. We found that, due to the changes brought about by the war, it was already out-of-date, and it only covered a limited field and it only dealt with laws and not application, which we think is fundamental. The Commission therefore proposes that this new survey should be completed in the different countries themselves, in collaboration with governments, specialized agencies, women's organizations, trade unions, academic institutes and others. However, to be able to compare the material, the work would have to follow plans laid by the Secretariat by experts in research planning. When this knowledge is acquired, we suggest to call a United Nations Conference on the Status of Women, where government delegates and representatives of women's organizations could discuss the problems and the further aims of the Sub-Commission.

As the political rights and development are fundamental, the Sub-Commission on the Status of Women earnestly requests the Economic and Social Council to direct an appeal to the governments of the United Nations that have not yet accorded suffrage to the women, to take such action at the earliest date possible within their frame of government in order that all the terms of the Charter of the United Nations shall be put into effect.

About the Constitution of the full sub-commission, we have proposed that it should consist of twelve ordinary members elected in their individual capacity with regard to expert knowledge in the field of the status of women. We think it is of importance that they represent different regions of the world and different stages of social development; that a sound system of rotation should take place, but we also think that perhaps the group having started this work should be allowed a few years to work together in the period of initiation.

I want to stress, as a matter of fact, that it is the wish of the Sub-Commission that both men and women can be elected members of this Commission and that both men and women could work in the office in the Secretariat.

I want also to stress that in this field mentioned here, the work is to be done by different specialized agencies of the United Nations and not by just this Commission. We have to work closely together and many of the things will have to be carried on between these various specialized agencies, such as UNESCO, the ILO and others, and other sub-commission perhaps themselves.

We understand well why the Economic and Social Council placed this question of the status of women under the wing of the Commission of Human Rights. Plans for development towards full equality certainly is a work for essential human rights. But I am asked, by my Commission, to propose to the Economic and Social Council that this Sub-Commission should be made a full Commission. The reasons for this would be that in view of the importance of this worldwide social scheme which covers, in fact, the condition of half the population of the world, the work ought to have the best possible working conditions and not be dependent upon another Commission, and that it would give this work more weight in the social field if it was done by a full Commission.

It has been said also, in these days, that women's problems should not be separate from those of men. But however idealistic, this point of view is purely unrealistic and academic. The practice shows that the Economic and Social Council has special problems that are connected with the status of women.

These problems have now for the first time in history to be studied internationally as such and to be given the social importance they ought to have. And it would be, in the opinion of this Sub-Commission of experts in this field, a tragedy to spoil this unique opportunity by confusing the wish and the facts. Some situations can be changed by laws, education, and public opinion, and the time seems to have come for happy changes in conditions of women all over the world, first due to the fact that the attitude of men toward women has changed tremendously during the war in the countries having taken part in the war, because of the comradeship in the resistance movement and in the war activities, and in having signed the Charter all the Governments of the United Nations have pledged themselves, have shown an interest in working for equality between men and women. And finally, this interest shown by the United Nations in the conditions of women has aroused hope and interest among women all over the world in this new world. The feeling that this big body, this United Nations, with all the social and political difficulties before it, still has time to take an interest in the daily life and in raising the status of women has aroused an enormous interest, and I can assure you that the women all over the world will give all their heart, mind and will to serve in the work of peace entrusted to the United Nations.

PRESIDENT: Thank you, Mrs. Begtrup. The Council is certainly carefully considering the recommendations that your Sub-Commission has made, including the recommendation that your Sub-Commission may be raised to the status of a Commission. Thank you.

Document 6

ECOSOC resolution establishing the Commission on the Status of Women (CSW)

E/RES/2/11, 21 June 1946

The Economic and Social Council, having considered the report of the nuclear Commission on Human Rights and of the nuclear Sub-Commission on the Status of Women of 21 May 1946 (document E/38/Rev.1),

Decides to confer upon the Sub-Commission the status of a full commission to be known as the Commission on the Status of Women.

1. Functions

The functions of the Commission shall be to prepare recommendations and reports to the Economic and Social Council on promoting women's rights in political, economic, social and educational fields. The Commission shall also make recommendations to the Council on urgent problems requiring immediate attention in the field of women's rights.

The Commission may submit proposals to the Council regarding its terms of reference.

2. Composition

(a) The Commission on the Status of Women shall consist of one representative from each of fifteen Members of the United Nations selected by the Council.

(b) With a view to securing a balanced representation in the various fields covered by the Commission, the Secretary-General shall consult with the Governments so selected before the representatives are finally nominated by these Governments and confirmed by the Council.

(c) Except for the initial period, the term of office shall be for three years. For the initial period, one-third of the members shall serve for two years, one-third for three years, and one-third for four years, the term of each member to be determined by lot.

(d) Retiring members shall be eligible for re-election.

(e) In the event that a member of the Commission is unable to serve for the full three-year term, the vacancy thus arising shall be filled by a representative designated by the Member Government, subject to the provisions of paragraph (b) above.

3. Policy and programme

Sections I and II of the report of the Sub-Commission, concerning policy and programme, shall be referred for study to the Commission on the Status of Women.

4. Documentation

In order to assist the Commission on the Status of Women, the Secretary-General is requested to make arrangements for a complete and detailed study of the legislation concerning the status of women and the practical application of such legislation.

Document 7

General Assembly resolution calling on Member States to adopt measures necessary to fulfil the aims of the Charter of the United Nations in granting women the same political rights as men

A/RES/56 (I), 11 December 1946

The General Assembly,

Whereas,

In the Preamble of the Charter the peoples of the United Nations have reaffirmed faith in the equal rights of men and women, and in Article 1 it is stated that the purposes of the United Nations are, among others, to achieve international cooperation in promoting and encouraging respect for human rights and for fundamental freedoms for all without distinction as to sex, and to be a centre for harmonizing the actions of nations in the attainment of these common ends,

Whereas,

Certain Member States have not yet granted to women, political rights equal to those granted to men,

Therefore:

(a) *Recommends* that all Member States, which have not already done so, adopt measures necessary to fulfil the purposes and aims of the Charter in this respect by granting to women the same political rights as to men;

(b) *Invites* the Secretary-General to communicate this recommendation to the Governments of all Member States.

Document 8

Report of the CSW to ECOSOC on the first session of the Commission, held at Lake Success, New York, from 10 to 24 February 1947

E/281/Rev.1, 25 February 1947

Chapter I
Introduction

1. The Commission on the Status of Women held its first session from 10 February to 24 February 1947. The following members were present:

Mrs. Jessie Street, Australia

Mrs. E. Uralova, Byelorussian Soviet Socialist Republic

Mrs. W. S. New, China

Mrs. G. de Echeverria, Costa Rica

Mrs. B. Begtrup, Denmark

Mrs. M. Lefaucheux, France

Miss S. Basterrechea, Guatemala

Begum Hamid Ali, India

Mrs. A. de Castillo Ledon, Mexico

Mrs. A. Cosma, Syria

Mrs. Mihri Pektas, Turkey

Mrs. E. Popova, Union of Soviet Socialist Republics

Miss M. Sutherland, United Kingdom

Miss D. Kenyon, United States of America

Mrs. I. Urdaneta, Venezuela

2. Miss E. Aguirre represented Mexico until the arrival of the regular member.

3. The specialized agencies were represented at the Commission by the following:

International Labour Organization, Mrs. E. Rowe

United Nations Educational Scientific and Cultural Organization, Miss J. Maass

4. The following consultants were present:

American Federation of Labor, Miss T. Sender

International Co-operative Alliance,
   Mrs. H. Fuhrmann

World Federation of Trade Unions, Miss L. Spiegel

5. The secretary of the Commission was Miss Elsie Bowerman.

6. The Commission elected the following officers:

Mrs. B. Begtrup (Denmark), Chairman

Mrs. J. Street (Australia), Vice-Chairman

Mrs. E. Uralova (Byelorussian SSR), Rapporteur

7. The Commission decided to adopt for the first session the provisional rules of procedure as laid down in document E/CN.6/W.2 and to postpone consideration and amendment of those rules until the second session.

8. The Commission expressed the desire that its next session should be held in 1947 at Geneva shortly before the session of the Commission on Human Rights.

Chapter II
Terms of reference

9. The Commission decided to recommend to the Economic and Social Council that its terms of reference, as stated in document E/90, 1/ be amended to read as follows:

"(a) *Functions*

"The function of the Commission shall be to prepare recommendations and reports to the Economic and Social Council on promoting women's rights in political, economic, civil, social and educational fields with the object of implementing the principle that men and women shall have equal rights, and to work out proposals to give effect to such recommendations. The Commission shall also make recommendations to the Council on urgent problems requiring immediate attention in defence of women's rights. The Commission may submit proposals to the Council regarding its terms of reference."

Chapter III
Communications

10. The Commission appointed a sub-committee, consisting of the representatives of China, Guatemala, and the United States, to consider communications already received and the question of how the Commission should deal with communications received in the future.

11. The sub-committee presented a report (document E/CN.6/19) in which it made recommendations to the Commission as to the manner of dealing with communications, and drew the attention of the Commission to the communication from the Inter-American Commission of Women.

12. As regards communications received in the future, the Commission decided to make the following recommendations to the Economic and Social Council:

(a) That the Secretary-General be requested to compile a confidential list of communications received concerning the status of women, before each session of the Commission;

(b) That this confidential list, which would also specify the contents of the communications, and give the names of the organizations from which they were received, be forwarded to the members of the Commission at least fourteen days before the opening of each session;

(c) That the members of the Commission, at their request, have the right to consult the originals of these communications;

(d) That the Secretary-General be requested to inform the authors of all such communications that they will be brought to the attention of the Commission on the Status of Women.

13. With respect to the communication from the Inter-American Commission of Women, the Commission decided to include consideration of the question among the items on the agenda.

Chapter IV
Relations with non-governmental organizations

14. Article 71 of the Charter of the United Nations reads as follows:

"The Economic and Social Council may make suitable arrangements for consultation with non-governmental organizations which are concerned with matters within its competence. Such arrangements may be made with international organizations and, where appropriate, with national organizations after consultation with the Member of the United Nations concerned."

1/ Resolution adopted 21 June 1946; see *Official Records of the Economic and Social Council*, First Year, Second Session, page 405.

The Commission took note of this article and decided, in view of the fact that the Economic and Social Council had already set up a Committee on Arrangements for Consultation with Non-Governmental Organizations, that all requests for consultative status from women's organizations should be referred to that Committee, and that whatever decisions the Committee might take should be discussed by the Commission on the Status of Women at its next session. This shall not affect the principle of recognizing national coordinating agencies. 2/

15. The Commission expressed its desire that the Economic and Social Council should recommend that unless such agencies were already in existence, the Member States encourage the establishment within their respective countries of coordinating agencies of non-governmental organizations to which any organization dealing with the political, economic, social, educational and other problems relating to the status of women would be entitled to belong. The Commission further recommended that when such agencies were formed, their applications for consultative status should be duly considered.

16. The Commission decided to hear representatives of the following international women's organizations, which had made application to be heard:

The Women's International Democratic Federation

The Associated Countrywomen of the World

The International Alliance of Women

The International Co-operative Women's Guild

The International Federation of University Women

The Women's International League for Peace and Freedom

The International Union of Catholic Women's Leagues

The World Young Women's Christian Association

The International Federation of Business and Professional Women

The International Council of Women

The Pan-Pacific Women's Association

The World Women's Party

After hearing the representatives of these international women's organizations, the Chairman thanked them and expressed satisfaction that a first contact between the Commission and the international organizations had thus been established. 3/

17. The Commission specially signified its desire to collaborate with the World Federation of Trade Unions, the American Federation of Labor, and the International Co-operative Alliance, and stated that it wished to make use of their experience in working out its decisions.

Chapter V
Relations with specialized agencies

18. The Commission took note of the agreements concluded between the United Nations and the specialized agencies, and the facilities they provided for consultation and cooperation between these agencies and the commissions of the United Nations.

19. The Commission asked the Economic and Social Council to request the Secretary-General to send all appropriate literature to all members of the Commission before its next session so that they might study the work relating to the principles of the Commission accomplished by the International Labour Organization.

20. The Commission wholeheartedly supported the statement contained in the International Labour Organization's Declaration of Philadelphia adopted on 17 May 1944, to the effect that "all human beings, irrespective of race, creed or sex, have the right to pursue both their material well-being and spiritual development in conditions of freedom and of economic security and equal opportunity."

2/ In view of the fact that two proposals were submitted regarding the question of cooperation with women's national organizations, the Commission decided to establish a drafting sub-committee, consisting of the Chairman of the Commission and the representatives of Australia and the Byelorussian SSR. As a result of the work of the drafting sub-committee, two draft resolutions were presented for consideration by the Commission. The Australian proposal as explained in paragraph 14 was adopted. The proposal of the representative of the Byelorussian SSR read as follows:

"The Commission expresses the desire that the Economic and Social Council recommend to the Member Governments to encourage in their countries the establishment of coordinating democratic non-governmental organizations, which would cooperate in the political, economic, social, educational, and other fields connected with the status of women, and the fight for the full elimination of the remnants of fascism, and the establishment of a democratic peace among peoples.

"The Commission recommends that on the establishment of such organizations, these should be able to turn to the Economic and Social Council with the request to provide them with consultative status and that such request should be considered in accordance with Article 71 of the Charter of the United Nations."

3/ At this point the representatives of Australia, the Byelorussian SSR, France and the USSR wished to add the following statement:

"The representative of the USSR submitted a proposal recommending that the Economic and Social Council grant consultative status under category A to the Women's International Democratic Federation. The representative of Australia, supporting the proposal of the representative of the USSR, also proposed to recommend to the Economic and Social Council the granting of consultative status to the Liaison Committee of International Women's Organizations. The Commission decided not to consider this question, since earlier (see paragraph 14 of this report) it had decided to refer such questions for consideration by the Committee on Arrangements for Consultation with Non-Governmental Organizations."

21. The Commission welcomed with satisfaction the chance to cooperate in carrying out the programme of UNESCO, and wished to draw to the attention of that specialized agency the section on education in the Commission's programme.

22. The Commission took note of the programme adopted by UNESCO in the field of basic education, and decided to recommend to the Economic and Social Council:

(a) That the Secretary-General should consult with UNESCO on plans for developing the programme of basic education without distinction of sex, race or creed, and that he should be invited to report to the next session of the Commission on its progress and any assistance which the Commission might be able to render in this connection;

(b) That it should be suggested to UNESCO that in its education programme it should devote particular attention to those regions where women have as yet no voice in political affairs or to those regions where women have already been granted the franchise, but do not yet enjoy full political rights; furthermore, that it should take steps to promote an effective programme of basic education for women and communicate with the Commission periodically on the progress made in carrying out that programme;

(c) That the Secretary-General should request the Member States to reply without delay to the questions in Part I, paragraph D, relating to education, of the Questionnaire on the Legal Status and Treatment of Women in order to provide the Commission with data which could permit early consideration of measures for advancing the rights of women in the educational field.

Chapter VI
Relations with Trusteeship Council and information from Non-Self-Governing Territories

23. The Commission decided to recommend that the Economic and Social Council call the attention of the Trusteeship Council to the importance attached by the Commission to the inclusion, in the questionnaires required by Article 88 of the Charter, of questions relating to the status of women, to the nature and form of such questions, and to the methods whereby the rights of women in political, economic, social and educational fields might be promoted in the Trust Territories.

24. The Commission decided to request the Economic and Social Council to make arrangements for consultation and collaboration between the Trusteeship Council, once it has been established, and the Commission.

25. The Commission took note of the resolution of the General Assembly regarding the convocation of conferences of representatives of Non-Self-Governing Territories by the Member States responsible for the administration of such territories, 4/ and expressed the hope that women who were leaders in the movement for obtaining equal rights for women would be included as representatives at such conferences.

Chapter VII
Implementation of the General Assembly resolution on the political rights of women

26. The Commission decided:

(a) To recommend to the Economic and Social Council that the Secretary-General be requested to urge each Member Government to complete and transmit to him by 1 June 1947, if possible, the following sections of the Questionnaire on the Legal Status and Treatment of Women—Part I, Public Law: section A, Franchise; and section B, Eligibility to hold public office—and to indicate, as far as possible, any changes in law or practice concerning these matters since the General Assembly resolution was passed; 5/

(b) To recommend to the Economic and Social Council that the Secretariat be requested to make by 1 September 1947 or before the next session, a preliminary report on the political rights of women, based on the replies of Member Governments to the above-mentioned sections of the Questionnaire, and on such information as may be available from other authoritative sources, for presentation to the next session of the Commission on the Status of Women;

(c) To appoint the representatives of Mexico, Syria, the United States of America and the Union of Soviet Socialist Republics to plan the preparation of this preliminary report, review its findings, and make recommendations with respect to it to the next session of the Commission;

(d) To recommend that such a report be submitted to the Economic and Social Council every year with the request that it be transmitted to the General Assembly.

27. The Commission decided to recommend to the Economic and Social Council:

(a) That the Secretariat be instructed to act as a clearing-house for the collection and dissemination of information and publications on the use of the franchise for the benefit of women who have recently acquired the right to vote;

(b) That the Secretariat be instructed to prepare a preliminary report based on accounts of pertinent experience from countries where effective programmes have

4/ See Resolutions adopted by the General Assembly during the second part of its first session, resolution 67 (I), page 126.

5/ See Resolutions adopted by the General Assembly during the second part of its first session, resolution No. 56 (I), page 90.

already been undertaken in this field, and to submit this report to the Commission at its next meeting.

28. The Commission decided to express its gratification at the inclusion in the Peace Treaties with Rumania, Italy, Hungary, Bulgaria, and Finland of provisions demanding that there should be no discrimination by the Governments of those countries on grounds of sex, in the exercise of human rights.

29. The Commission recommended to the Economic and Social Council that the Secretary-General be requested to expedite the preparation of a questionnaire on the economic rights of women and to circulate it to Member Governments with requests for answers as rapidly as possible.

30. The Commission expressed the desire that the Economic and Social Council should recommend that the General Assembly consider means of attaining complete adult suffrage as rapidly as possible in countries where there is no adult suffrage, or where the franchise of women is limited or curtailed.

Chapter VIII
Consideration and study of sections I and II of the report of the Sub-Commission on the Status of Women

31. Having considered sections I and II of the report of the Sub-Commission on the Status of Women (document E/38/Rev.1), 6/ the Commission decided to express its satisfaction with that report and, in accordance with its fundamental principles, to use it as a basis for its future work.

Chapter IX
Coordination with other commissions

32. *Commission on Human Rights*

The Commission decided:

(a) To request the Economic and Social Council to arrange that the Commission on the Status of Women be represented by its officers (the Chairman, Vice-Chairman and Rapporteur) at the sessions of the Commission on Human Rights devoted to consideration of the draft international bill of human rights;

(b) To ask that the drafting group of the Commission on Human Rights circulate copies of the preliminary draft of the international bill of human rights to members of the Commission on the Status of Women at the same time as it is made available to members of the Commission on Human Rights.

33. *Social Commission*

The Commission decided:

(a) To support the resolution of the Social Commission relating to town planning and housing, in view of the fact that the bad state and lack of housing constitutes a major obstacle to the betterment of the condition of women;

(b) To request that if the Economic and Social Council arranged for the establishment of a service of housing and town planning as proposed in the Social Commission's resolution, the Council should be asked to arrange for effective collaboration between that service and the Commission on the Status of Women;

(c) To request the Economic and Social Council to communicate to the Social Commission the desire of the Commission on the Status of Women that provision be made for community centres and facilities for the care of children and the equipment of homes with labour-saving devices to enable housewives to take an active part in public and civil affairs.

34. *Sub-Commission on the Prevention of Discrimination and the Protection of Minorities*

(a) The Commission decided to recommend that the Economic and Social Council call the attention of the Sub-Commission on the Prevention of Discrimination and the Protection of Minorities to the importance attached by the Commission on the Status of Women to the work of that Sub-Commission;

(b) The Commission wished to be informed of the constitution, and of the efforts made by the aforementioned Sub-Commission for promoting the rights of women belonging to the various minority groups in the political, economic, social and cultural fields;

(c) The Commission suggested that the best means of cooperation between the two organs would be the effective participation of a representative of the Commission on the Status of Women in the work of the Sub-Commission on the Prevention of Discrimination and the Protection of Minorities.

Chapter X
Programme of future work

35. The Commission decided by eight votes to two to adopt the following guiding principles and aims in its future work:

I. *Principles*

Freedom and equality are essential to human development; since woman is as much a human being as man, she is entitled to share these attributes with him.

The well-being and progress of society depend on the extent to which both men and women are able to develop their personalities and are cognizant of their responsibilities to themselves and to each other.

Woman has thus a definite role to play in the building of a free, healthy, prosperous and moral society,

6/ This document was published under document symbol E/HR/18/Rev.1. See *Official Records of the Economic and Social Council*, First Year, Second Session, pages 235 ff.

and she can fulfil that obligation only as a free and responsible member of that society.

Women must take an active part in the struggle for the total elimination of the fascist ideology and for international cooperation directed towards the establishment of a democratic peace among the peoples of the world and the prevention of further aggression.

In order to achieve this goal, the Commission intends to raise the status of women, irrespective of nationality, race, language or religion, to equality with men in all fields of human enterprise, and to eliminate all discrimination against women in the provisions of statutory law, in legal maxims or rules, or in interpretations of customary law.

II. *Aims*

Therefore, the Commission recommends that its aims shall be as follows:

A. *Political*

Equal participation of women in government and the possibility of exercising all the rights of citizenship, irrespective of race, language, or religion, and of assuming all the duties of a citizen, which comprise:

1. Universal adult suffrage
2. Equal right to vote
3. Equal right to be elected
4. Equal right to hold public office

B. *Civil*

Full equality for women to exercise all civil rights, irrespective of nationality, race, language, or religion, including among others:

1. *Marriage.* Freedom of choice, dignity of the wife, monogamy, equal right to dissolution of marriage.
2. *Guardianship.* Equal right to guardianship of her own and other children.
3. *Nationality.* Right to retain her own nationality, and for her children, the right to choose the nationality of the mother upon attaining their majority.
4. *Legal capacity.* Equal right to enter into contracts and to acquire, dispose of and inherit property.
5. *Domicile.* A married woman to have the same right to establish her domicile as a man or a single woman.

C. *Social and economic*

Full opportunity for women to take equal part in social life, which implies full opportunity of fulfilling their duties towards society.

1. To prevent discrimination against women in social and economic status and customs, irrespective of nationality, race, language or religion. Women should be given equal rights with men with respect to labour, wages, holidays, and other economic and social rights.

2. To abolish prostitution.

3. Not only should no limitation be applied to women because of their sex, in regard to the enjoyment of full equality in the exercise of social rights and the assumption of labour duties, but consideration on grounds of health should be given equally to men and women, and special consideration to women on grounds of motherhood. With that aim in view, the Commission shall try to obtain, among other benefits, State protection of the interests of the mother and child by providing holidays with pay for the mother before and after childbirth; by arranging leave of absence during working hours for nursing mothers, without deductions for such time from wages; by the establishment of special rooms for nursing the children; and by the organization of a wide network of nursing homes and medical consultation centres, *crèches* and kindergartens, and other facilities.

4. There should be an effective system of health and social insurance legislation providing equal preventive and remedial opportunities for women and including special provisions for maternal and child welfare.

D. *Education*

Equal opportunity for compulsory, free and full education, equal opportunity in all specialized fields and the right to enjoy scientific discoveries applied to human growth and development.

To achieve these aims, the Commission proposes:

1. That world public opinion be stimulated in favour of raising the status of women as an instrument for promoting human rights and peace. In view of the fact that in signing the Charter the Governments of all the Members of the United Nations recognized that one of its principal aims, as stated in the Preamble, was "to reaffirm faith in fundamental human rights, in the dignity and worth of the human person, in the equal rights of men and women and of nations large and small", the Commission on the Status of Women expects the full collaboration and support of the Governments of all Member States of the United Nations in their endeavours to raise the status of women throughout the world. At the same time, the Commission earnestly desires to render all possible assistance to those Governments in the application of the principle of equal rights for men and women.

2. To collaborate with United Nations organs, Governments, specialized agencies, non-governmental organizations and any experts it shall deem necessary.

Chapter XI
Urgent problems

36. The Commission expressed the wish that the Economic and Social Council should recommend to the General Assembly that the laws of all countries be codified in order to enforce equal rights impartially for all citizens, or, where necessary, that each country be requested to codify all its laws, political, economic, civil and social, in order to confer complete equality of rights on all women.

37. The Commission decided that in view of the importance of carrying out its work effectively, and of keeping in touch with women all over the world, it was urgently necessary that the Secretary-General should as soon as possible appoint a competent woman who had taken an active part in the work to improve the status of women, as head of the Status of Women section of the Division of Human Rights.

Chapter XII
Other questions

38. The Commission decided

(a) To establish relations with a view to cooperation and coordination of work with the Inter-American Women's Commission, in order to make use of the experience and the valuable studies of that organization regarding the status of women in the Americas;

(b) To request the Inter-American Women's Commission to send an observer to the meetings of the Commission on the Status of Women to act in an advisory and informative capacity;

(c) To recommend to the Economic and Social Council that it consider ways and means of implementing the terms of this resolution, and that it recognize that the Inter-American Women's Commission is an intergovernmental regional organization dealing with the same problems as the Commission on the Status of Women. 7/

39. The Commission decided to recommend to the Economic and Social Council that, in order to make known and stimulate interest in the work of the Commission and to assist in compiling the information required, the Secretariat should be instructed to arrange with Member States for one or more members of the Commission to visit Member States.

40. The Commission recommends that the Economic and Social Council should investigate the question of convening regional conferences, the first of which might be arranged during 1948, and should request the Secretariat to work out detailed alternatives with regard to place, programme, budgets, management, and potential attendance, for consideration at the next session of the Commission.

Appendix 8/

Summary of financial implications of resolutions contained in the report of the Commission on the Status of Women submitted to the fourth session of the Economic and Social Council (document E/281/Add.1)

The Commission on the Status of Women, in its report to the fourth session of the Economic and Social Council, made proposals involving certain work by members of the Commission in the invervals between sessions of the Commission. This would entail expenditure on travelling and subsistence allowances.

1. *Report on the Questionnaire on the Legal Status and Treatment of Women*

The Commission recommended that four members (representing the United States, the USSR, Syria, and Mexico) should plan the organization of a preliminary report on the political rights of women, based on the replies to part I of the Questionnaire on the Legal Status and Treatment of Women. If these members are to assist the Secretariat as suggested, they will be obliged to spend some time (about a fortnight) at Lake Success prior to the

7/ The representatives of the USSR and of the Byelorussian SSR stated that they had abstained from voting because the question of the Inter-American Commission called for further study. Such presentation of this question as had been made at the meeting of the Commission was premature, especially in view of the fact that it had so far not taken any decision in regard to the real international mass organization (the Women's International Democratic Federation); this latter question had not been submitted for consideration by the Committee on Arrangements for Consultation with Non-Governmental Organizations, and the Commission had not considered the substance of the matter.

The representative of Mexico desired that the following statement be incorporated in the record:

"The Inter-American Commission of Women is an official organization composed of one representative from each of the Governments of the American Republics. Its purpose is to study the status of women in the Western Hemisphere, and to report on the problems concerning women to the conferences of American States. The Inter-American Commission is similar to our Commission on the Status of Women. Its work and status cannot be confused with those of any other non-governmental or voluntary organization in any part of the world. This organization is neither a specialized nor a non-governmental agency. Because it is a regional body, it has a special status, which should be recognized by the Economic and Social Council. I insist that to establish a working relationship and to ask the Inter-American Commission of Women to send an observer to our session is not a departure from the Charter. On the contrary, it is of the utmost importance that we have friendly relations with a body that for eighteen consecutive years has been doing for the women of the Western Hemisphere what our Commission on the Status of Women intends to do for the women of the world."

8/ This appendix, although not forming part of the original report, is added for the convenience of readers.

next session of the Commission on the Status of Women. Their subsistence allowances during that period, estimated at $1,500, must be paid by the United Nations.

2. Coordination with the Commission on Human Rights

The Commission expressed the wish to be kept in close touch with the work of the Commission on Human Rights, particularly in connection with the proposed draft international bill of human rights. The Commission decided that the Economic and Social Council should be asked to arrange for the three officers of the Commission to attend the meetings of the Commission on Human Rights.

This would involve the travel expenses of these three officers from Copenhagen, Sydney and Moscow respectively, and their subsistence allowances during the session of the Commission on Human Rights which is to be held in June 1947.

The estimated cost of such travel and subsistence allowances for a fortnight is $5,400.

3. Visits of members of the Commission to Member States

The representative of Syria proposed that, in order to make known and stimulate interest in the work of the Commission and to assist in compiling the information required, the Commission recommend that the Secretariat arrange for one or more members of the Commission to visit Member States.

As no particular areas are mentioned in the resolution, it is only possible to estimate the cost of such visits on the basis of average travel and subsistence allowances for a given number of persons. Assuming that three members travel for six months in the Near East, the Pacific Islands or South and East Africa, for example, at an average cost of $40 per person per day for travel and subsistence, the estimated total cost would be $21,600.

4. Regional conferences

The Commission recommended to the Economic and Social Council a tentative plan for regional conferences, the first of which might be held in 1948; it also recommended that the Secretariat be requested to outline detailed alternatives as to place, programme, budgets, leadership, and potential attendance, for consideration at the next session of the Commission. In view of the Commission's intention to study the question at its next meeting, no estimate of the cost involved is included at this stage.

5. The estimates mentioned in paragraphs 1, 2, and 3 above total $28,500 and are not contained in those listed in the summary of financial implications of resolutions already submitted to the Council (document E/312) . 9/

9/ Resolutions involving expenditures from United Nations funds.

Document 9

ECOSOC resolution defining the functions of the CSW and requesting Member States to provide the Commission with data on the legal status and treatment of women in their countries

E/RES/48(IV), 29 March 1947

The Economic and Social Council

Takes note of the report of the Commission on the Status of Women (document E/281/Rev.1), and

A. Resolves

1. That the functions of the Commission on the Status of Women shall be defined as follows: "The functions of the Commission shall be to prepare recommendations and reports to the Economic and Social Council on promoting women's rights in political, economic, civil, social and educational fields. The Commission shall also make recommendations to the Council on urgent problems requiring immediate attention in the field of

women's rights with the object of implementing the principle that men and women shall have equal rights, and to develop proposals to give effect to such recommendations";

2. That the consideration of chapter III of the report of the Commission on the Status of Women concerning the handling of communications be deferred until its fifth session;

3. That the Commission on the Status of Women be represented by its officers, the Chairman, Vice-Chairman and Rapporteur, at the sessions of the Commission on Human Rights when sections of the draft of the international bill of human rights concerning the particu-

lar rights of women are under consideration, to participate, without vote, in the deliberations thereon;

4. That the preliminary draft of the international bill of human rights be circulated to the members of the Commission on the Status of Women at the same time as it is made available to the members of the Commission on Human Rights;

5. That the Sub-Commission on the Prevention of Discrimination and the Protection of Minorities be requested to invite the Commission on the Status of Women to send a representative to participate in its deliberations when items relating to discrimination based on sex are to be discussed;

6. That the Commission on the Status of Women be requested at its next session to take as its immediate programme of work the examination of existing legal and customary disabilities of women as regards political and social rights, and (subject to consultation with the International Labour Organization) economic rights and also educational opportunities, with a view to framing proposals for action;

7. (a) To approve the declaration of principles in part I of chapter 10 of the report,

(b) To reaffirm that it is the fundamental purpose of the Commission to develop proposals for promoting equal rights for women and eliminating discrimination on grounds of sex in the legal, political, economic, social and educational fields,

(c) To recognize that it is desirable for such proposals to be developed on the basis of all relevant information with as little delay as possible.

B. *Requests* the Secretary-General

1. To consult with the United Nations Educational, Scientific and Cultural Organization on plans for developing the programme of basic education without distinction of sex, race, or creed and to report to the next session of the Commission on its progress and any assistance which the Commission may be able to render in the development of the programme;

2. To invite Member States to reply as early as possible to the questions in part I, paragraph D (relating to education) of the questionnaire on the legal status and treatment of women in order to provide the Commission with data which will enable it to give early consideration to recommendations for possible action to advance the rights of women in the educational field;

3. To invite each Member Government to complete and transmit to him by 1 July 1947, if possible, replies to the following sections of the questionnaire on the legal status and treatment of women: part I, Public Law: (section A, Franchise, and section B, Eligibility to hold public office), to indicate as far as possible any changes in law or practice concerning these matters since the passage of resolution No. 56 (I) of the General Assembly of 11 December 1946; 1/

4. To make a preliminary report on the political rights of women by 1 September 1947 based on the replies of Member Governments to part I of the questionnaire on the legal status and treatment of women and on such information as may be available from other authoritative sources;

5. To prepare a preliminary report to the Commission on the Status of Women based on accounts of pertinent experience from countries where effective programmes have already been undertaken in the field of information on use of the franchise, for the benefit of women who have recently acquired the right to vote, and to report on methods by which the Secretariat might act as a centre for the collection of publications in this field and making them available to the Members of the United Nations;

6. To issue part II of the questionnaire on the legal status and treatment of women, and to expedite the preparation of such further questionnaires on the economic rights of women as may be considered necessary, after consultation with the International Labour Organization;

7. To make arrangements for the presence of observers from regional intergovernmental organizations in the field of women's rights at sessions of the Commission on the Status of Women to act in an advisory and informative capacity, and to arrange for the exchange of information between the Commission and these organizations on subjects relating to the status of women;

8. To consider the appointment of a competent woman as Head of the Status of Women Section of the Division of Human Rights as soon as possible.

C. *Recommends*

1. That UNESCO consider the desirability of paying special attention in its educational, social programme to those countries and regions where women have no voice in political affairs, and to those countries and regions where women have the franchise but have not been granted full political rights; and further, to consider the steps to be taken to promote an effective programme of basic education for women in such countries and regions and to send reports on the progress of such a programme to the Economic and Social Council for transmission to the Commission on the Status of Women;

2. That the Trusteeship Council be invited to take note of the importance attached by the Council to the inclusion in the questionnaire required by Article 88 of

1/ See *Resolutions adopted by the General Assembly* during the second part of its first session, page 90.

the Charter of questions relating to the status of women, to the nature and form of such questions and to the methods whereby the rights of women in political, economic, social and educational fields may be promoted in the Trust Territories;

3. That the Commission on the Status of Women give further consideration to the recommendations in paragraphs 38 and 39 of chapter XII of its report relating respectively to visits of members of the Commission to Member States and to the summoning of regional conferences.

Document 10

ECOSOC resolution requesting the Secretary-General to provide the CSW with communications received concerning the status of women

E/RES/76(V), 5 August 1947 1/

The Economic and Social Council,

Having considered chapter III of the report of the first session of the Commission on the Status of Women concerning communications (document E/281/Rev.1),

Recognizes that, as in the case of the Commission on Human Rights, the Commission on the Status of Women has no power to take any action in regard to any complaints concerning the status of women;

Requests the Secretary-General

(a) To compile a confidential list of communications received concerning the status of women, before each session of the commission, with a brief indication of the substance of each;

(b) To furnish this confidential list to the Commission, in private meeting, without divulging the identity of the authors of the communications;

(c) To enable the members of the Commission, upon request, to consult the originals of communications dealing with the principles relating to the promotion of women's rights in political, economic, civil, social and educational fields;

(d) To inform the writers of all communications concerning the status of women, however addressed, that

their communications have been received and duly noted for consideration in accordance with the procedure laid down by the United Nations. Where necessary, the Secretary-General should indicate that the Commission has no power to take any action in regard to any complaint concerning the status of women;

(e) To furnish each Member State not represented on the Commission with a brief indication of the substance of any communication concerning the status of women which refers explicitly to that State or to territories under its jurisdiction, without divulging the identity of the author;

Suggests to the Commission on the Status of Women that it should at each session appoint an ad hoc committee to meet shortly before its next session for the purpose of reviewing the confidential list of communications prepared by the Secretary-General under paragraph (a) above and of recommending which of these communications, in original, should in accordance with paragraph (c) above, be made available to members of the Commission on request.

1/ See document E/521.

Document 11

ECOSOC resolution requesting Member States to adopt measures to ensure women the same rights as men in regard to employment and remuneration

E/RES/122 G (VI), 1 March 1948

G

The Economic and Social Council,

Recognizing that restrictions with regard to the equality of rights of men and women constitute an infringement of the fundamental rights of the human person and are incompatible with the obligations assumed by the States Members of the United Nations under the terms of the United Nations Charter,

Noting that there exist, in a certain number of countries, discriminatory practices with regard to the economic and social condition of women, which are not compatible with the dignity of woman and which make it more difficult for her to participate in the economic life of such countries,

Invites the States Members of the United Nations to adopt the necessary measures so that:

(a) Whatever their nationality, their race, their language or their religion, women shall benefit by the same rights as men in regard to employment and remuneration therefore, as provided for in Council resolution 121 (VI), leisure, social insurance and professional training; and

(b) In each country there should be legal safeguards for the rights of mothers and children;

Draws attention to divergencies in various local systems in this field, some of them restricting the right of married women to act as guardians, to control property and earnings, and to undertake independent business ventures, and to engage in various other activities.

Document 12

ECOSOC resolution transmitting the suggestions of the CSW for amendments to the draft Universal Declaration of Human Rights and requesting Member States to provide information on political rights and educational opportunities for women

E/RES/120 (VI), 3 March 1948 1/

A

POLITICAL RIGHTS OF WOMEN

The Economic and Social Council

Requests the Secretary-General:

(i) To bring up to date, including reference to action taken by Governments since the signing of the Charter, the memorandum supplementing his preliminary report on the political rights of women and their eligibility for public office, 2/ and present it to the third regular session of the General Assembly, in line with the resolution submitted by Denmark to the first regular session of the General Assembly on the political rights of women; 3/ and

(ii) To circulate similar material annually to Members of the United Nations until all women throughout the world have the same political rights as men.

B

EDUCATIONAL OPPORTUNITIES FOR WOMEN

The Economic and Social Council

Requests the Secretary-General:

(i) To invite Governments that have not already done so to reply to Part I, section D (Educational opportunities) of the Questionnaire on the Legal Status and Treatment of Women by 1 June 1948;

1/ The resolution of the Commission on the Status of Women on equal pay contained in the report of its second session (document E/615) was considered by the Council together with the item on the principle of equal pay for equal work for men and women workers; see resolution 121 (VI).

2/ See document E/CN.6/30.

3/ See *Resolutions adopted by the General Assembly* during the second part of its first session, resolution 56 (I), page 90.

(ii) To prepare, on the basis of these replies, supplemented where necessary by other available material, and for circulation not later than six weeks before the third session of the Commission, a detailed comparative report, arranged by subject, showing the existing disabilities of women in the field covered by the said section of the Questionnaire; and

(iii) To make these replies available to UNESCO, with the consent of the Governments concerned, in order to facilitate its work in areas where women and girls suffer disabilities in the field of education.

C

INTERNATIONAL BILL OF HUMAN RIGHTS

The Economic and Social Council

Transmits to the Commission on Human Rights and its Drafting Committee on an International Bill of Human Rights the following suggestions of the Commission on the Status of Women for amendments to the Draft International Declaration of Human Rights:

Article I

"All people are born free and equal in dignity and rights. They are endowed by nature with reason and conscience, and should act towards one another in the spirit of brotherhood".

Article 13

"Men and women shall have equal rights to contract or dissolve marriage in accordance with the law."

D

PLACE OF MEETING OF THE THIRD SESSION OF THE COMMISSION ON THE STATUS OF WOMEN

The Economic and Social Council,

Having regard to the invitation of the Government of Lebanon that the Commission on the Status of Women should hold its session of 1949 in that country,

Requests the Secretary-General to make suitable arrangements for holding the 1949 session of the Commission in Lebanon, to last not more than three weeks, provided that he should further consult the Council at its seventh session if the arrangements are found to involve substantial extra costs to the United Nations over those of a meeting at Headquarters;

Takes note with satisfaction of the suggestion of the Commission that official agencies, non-governmental organizations and others in the region develop a conference on the status of women to be held at the same time, the promotion, direction and expense of which will be the responsibility of the local agencies and not of the United Nations, and in which conference individual members of delegations to the Commission can participate.

E

QUESTIONNAIRE

The Economic and Social Council

Requests the Secretary-General to invite Member Governments which have not yet done so to reply to Part I of the Questionnaire regarding political rights of women before the following dates:

Sections A and B, Political Rights	1 June 1948
Section D, Education Opportunities	1 June 1948
Section C, Nationality	1 July 1948
Remaining sections	1 December 1948

Document 13

ECOSOC resolution calling on Member States to implement the principle of equal pay for work of equal value for men and women workers, irrespective of nationality, race, language or religion

E/RES/121 (VI), 10 March 1948

The Economic and Social Council,

Having considered the question of the application of the principle of equal pay for equal work for men and women workers placed on its agenda at the request of the World Federation of Trade Unions, and the memorandum submitted on the subject by the Federation,

Having considered the recommendation on equal pay adopted by the Commission on the Status of Women,

Reaffirms the principle of equal rights of men and women laid down in the Preamble of the United Nations Charter and approves the principle of equal remuneration for work of equal value for men and women workers;

Calls upon the States Members of the United Nations to implement the latter principle in every way, irrespective of nationality, race, language and religion;

Decides to transmit the memorandum of the World Federation of Trade Unions to the International Labour Organization, inviting the latter to proceed as rapidly as possible with the further consideration of this subject and to report to the Council on the action which it has taken;

Further resolves to transmit the memorandum of the World Federation of Trade Unions to the Commission on the Status of Women for its consideration and for any suggestions it may wish to make to the Council; and

Invites non-governmental organizations in category A concerned to present their views on the subject to the ILO and to the Council.

Document 14

The Universal Declaration of Human Rights, adopted by the General Assembly in its resolution 217 A (III) of 10 December 1948

ST/HR/1/Rev.4 (Vol. 1/Part 1)

Preamble

Whereas recognition of the inherent dignity and of the equal and inalienable rights of all members of the human family is the foundation of freedom, justice and peace in the world,

Whereas disregard and contempt for human rights have resulted in barbarous acts which have outraged the conscience of mankind, and the advent of a world in which human beings shall enjoy freedom of speech and belief and freedom from fear and want has been proclaimed as the highest aspiration of the common people,

Whereas it is essential, if man is not to be compelled to have recourse, as a last resort, to rebellion against tyranny and oppression, that human rights should be protected by the rule of law,

Whereas it is essential to promote the development of friendly relations between nations,

Whereas the peoples of the United Nations have in the Charter reaffirmed their faith in fundamental human rights, in the dignity and worth of the human person and in the equal rights of men and women and have determined to promote social progress and better standards of life in larger freedom,

Whereas Member States have pledged themselves to achieve, in cooperation with the United Nations, the promotion of universal respect for and observance of human rights and fundamental freedoms

Whereas a common understanding of these rights and freedoms is of the greatest importance for the full realization of this pledge,

Now, therefore,

THE GENERAL ASSEMBLY

proclaims

THIS UNIVERSAL DECLARATION OF HUMAN RIGHTS

as a common standard of achievement for all peoples and all nations, to the end that every individual and every organ of society, keeping this Declaration constantly in mind, shall strive by teaching and education to promote respect for these rights and freedoms and by progressive measures, national and international, to secure their universal and effective recognition and observance, both among the peoples of Member States themselves and among the peoples of territories under their jurisdiction.

Article 1

All human beings are born free and equal in dignity and rights. They are endowed with reason and conscience and should act towards one another in a spirit of brotherhood.

Article 2

Everyone is entitled to all the rights and freedoms set forth in this Declaration, without distinction of any kind, such as race, colour, sex, language, religion, political or other opinion, national or social origin, property, birth or other status. Furthermore, no distinction shall be made on the basis of the political, jurisdictional or international status of the country or territory to which a person belongs, whether it be independent, trust, non-self-governing or under any other limitation of sovereignty.

Article 3

Everyone has the right to life, liberty and security of person.

Article 4

No one shall be held in slavery or servitude; slavery and the slave trade shall be prohibited in all their forms.

Article 5

No one shall be subjected to torture or to cruel, inhuman or degrading treatment or punishment.

Article 6

Everyone has the right to recognition everywhere as a person before the law.

Article 7

All are equal before the law and are entitled without any discrimination to equal protection of the law. All are entitled to equal protection against any discrimination in violation of this Declaration and against any incitement to such discrimination.

Article 8

Everyone has the right to an effective remedy by the competent national tribunals for acts violating the fundamental rights granted him by the constitution or by law.

Article 9

No one shall be subjected to arbitrary arrest, detention or exile.

Article 10

Everyone is entitled in full equality to a fair and public hearing by an independent and impartial tribunal, in the determination of his rights and obligations and of any criminal charge against him.

Article 11

1. Everyone charged with a penal offence has the right to be presumed innocent until proved guilty according to law in a public trial at which he has had all the guarantees necessary for his defence.

2. No one shall be held guilty of any penal offence on account of any act or omission which did not constitute a penal offence, under national or international law, at the time when it was committed. Nor shall a heavier penalty be imposed than the one that was applicable at the time the penal offence was committed.

Article 12

No one shall be subjected to arbitrary interference with his privacy, family, home or correspondence, nor to attacks upon his honour and reputation. Everyone has the right to the protection of the law against such interference or attacks.

Article 13

1. Everyone has the right to freedom of movement and residence within the borders of each State.

2. Everyone has the right to leave any country, including his own, and to return to his country.

Article 14

1. Everyone has the right to seek and to enjoy in other countries asylum from persecution.

2. This right may not be invoked in the case of prosecutions genuinely arising from non-political crimes or from acts contrary to the purposes and principles of the United Nations.

Article 15

1. Everyone has the right to a nationality.

2. No one shall be arbitrarily deprived of his nationality nor denied the right to change his nationality.

Article 16

1. Men and women of full age, without any limitation due to race, nationality or religion, have the right to marry and to found a family. They are entitled to equal rights as to marriage, during marriage and at its dissolution.

2. Marriage shall be entered into only with the free and full consent of the intending spouses.

3. The family is the natural and fundamental group unit of society and is entitled to protection by society and the State.

Article 17

1. Everyone has the right to own property alone as well as in association with others.

2. No one shall be arbitrarily deprived of his property.

Article 18

Everyone has the right to freedom of thought, conscience and religion; this right includes freedom to change his religion or belief, and freedom, either alone or in community with others and in public or private, to manifest his religion or belief in teaching, practice, worship and observance.

Article 19

Everyone has the right to freedom of opinion and expression; this right includes freedom to hold opinions without interference and to seek, receive and impart information and ideas through any media and regardless of frontiers.

Article 20

1. Everyone has the right to freedom of peaceful assembly and association.

2. No one may be compelled to belong to an association.

Article 21

1. Everyone has the right to take part in the government of his country, directly or through freely chosen representatives.

2. Everyone has the right of equal access to public service in his country.

3. The will of the people shall be the basis of the authority of government; this will shall be expressed in periodic and genuine elections which shall be by universal and equal suffrage and shall be held by secret vote or by equivalent free voting procedures.

Article 22

Everyone, as a member of society, has the right to social security and is entitled to realization, through national effort and international cooperation and in accordance with the organization and resources of each State, of the economic, social and cultural rights indispensable for his dignity and the free development of his personality.

Article 23

1. Everyone has the right to work, to free choice of employment, to just and favourable conditions of work and to protection against unemployment.

2. Everyone, without any discrimination, has the right to equal pay for equal work.

3. Everyone who works has the right to just and favourable remuneration ensuring for himself and his family an existence worthy of human dignity, and supplemented, if necessary, by other means of social protection.

4. Everyone has the right to form and to join trade unions for the protection of his interests.

Article 24

Everyone has the right to rest and leisure, including reasonable limitation of working hours and periodic holidays with pay.

Article 25

1. Everyone has the right to a standard of living adequate for the health and well-being of himself and of his family, including food, clothing, housing and medical care and necessary social services, and the right to security in the event of unemployment, sickness, disability, widowhood, old age or other lack of livelihood in circumstances beyond his control.

2. Motherhood and childhood are entitled to special care and assistance. All children, whether born in or out of wedlock, shall enjoy the same social protection.

Article 26

1. Everyone has the right to education. Education shall be free, at least in the elementary and fundamental stages. Elementary education shall be compulsory. Technical and professional education shall be made generally available and higher education shall be equally accessible to all on the basis of merit.

2. Education shall be directed to the full development of the human personality and to the strengthening of respect for human rights and fundamental freedoms. It shall promote understanding, tolerance and friendship among all nations, racial or religious groups, and shall further the activities of the United Nations for the maintenance of peace.

3. Parents have a prior right to choose the kind of education that shall be given to their children.

Article 27

1. Everyone has the right freely to participate in the cultural life of the community, to enjoy the arts and to share in scientific advancement and its benefits.

2. Everyone has the right to the protection of the moral and material interests resulting from any scientific, literary or artistic production of which he is the author.

Article 28

Everyone is entitled to a social and international order in which the rights and freedoms set forth in this Declaration can be fully realized.

Article 29

1. Everyone has duties to the community in which alone the free and full development of his personality is possible.

2. In the exercise of his rights and freedoms, everyone shall be subject only to such limitations as are determined by law solely for the purpose of securing due recognition and respect for the rights and freedoms of others and of meeting the just requirements of morality, public order and the general welfare in a democratic society.

3. These rights and freedoms may in no case be exercised contrary to the purposes and principles of the United Nations.

Article 30

Nothing in this Declaration may be interpreted as implying for any State, group or person any right to engage in any activity or to perform any act aimed at the destruction of any of the rights and freedoms set forth herein.

Document 15

ECOSOC resolution calling for cooperation between the International Labour Organization (ILO) and the CSW on the issue of equal pay for work of equal value

E/RES/196 (VIII), 18 February 1949

The Economic and Social Council,

In view of the terms of its resolution 121(VI) of 10 March 1948, and more particularly of the fourth paragraph of that resolution,

Notes with satisfaction the action of the International Labour Organization at its thirty-first session as set forth in its resolution of 7 July 1948 entitled: Resolution concerning equal remuneration for work of equal value,

Notes that the ILO, as the recognized specialized agency in the field, is making further studies and inquiries with a view to the development of one or more international conventions and recommendations;

Invites the ILO to report specifically on this subject to the Economic and Social Council after the first discussion of the proposed conventions and recommendations at the thirty-third session of the International Labour Conference;

Refers the entire documentation on equal pay to the Commission on the Status of Women with the recommendations that the Commission:

(a) Make available to the ILO any relevant material in its possession; and

b) In its own deliberations, examine all relevant documents.

Document 16

Report of the CSW to ECOSOC on the Commission's third session regarding the participation of women in the work of the United Nations (extract)

E/1316, Chapter IV, 19 April 1949

Chapter IV
Participation of women in the work
of the United Nations

19. In the course of the discussion on item 4 of the agenda, political rights of women, the representative of the United States quoted from a report which indicated that while a limited number of women had been appointed to high posts in the Secretariat of the United Nations, the majority of women employed by the Secretary-General were engaged in minor administrative du-

ties, rather than in work of a policy-making nature. She submitted to the Committee on Resolutions a proposal that the Secretary-General be asked to make a study of the number and the grades of women at present holding positions in the Secretariat and in the various delegations of Member States to the United Nations, so that information on these points could be placed before the Commission at its next session (E/CN.6/SR.41).

20. After a general debate, the Committee on Resolutions formulated the following resolution on the par-

ticipation of women in the work of the United Nations (E/CN.6/94), which the Commission subsequently adopted by 10 votes for and none against, with 3 abstentions (E/CN.6/SR.44):

"PARTICIPATION OF WOMEN IN THE WORK OF THE UNITED NATIONS

"*The Commission on the Status of Women,*

"*Considering* that Article 8 of the Charter, which states that 'the United Nations shall place no restrictions on the eligibility of men and women to participate in any capacity and under conditions of equality in its principal and subsidiary organs', should be progressively implemented,

"*Notes* that the Secretary-General has appointed women to certain additional posts in the Secretariat;

"*Requests* the Secretary-General to prepare a report on the nature and proportion of posts in the Secretariat occupied by women for the consideration of the Commission at its next session;

"*Notes* that the Economic and Social Council, at its seventh session, recommended that Member Governments consider women equally with men when appointing their delegations to organs and agencies of the United Nations; and accordingly

"*Requests* the Secretary-General to indicate also in his report the extent to which the Member Governments have included women in their delegations to organs and agencies of the United Nations."

Document 17

ECOSOC resolution calling for the preparation of a convention on the nationality of married women

E/RES/242 C (IX), 1 August 1949

C
NATIONALITY OF MARRIED WOMEN

The Economic and Social Council,

Noting the conflicts in law and in practice relating to the nationality of married women which are apparent from the replies of Governments to part I, section G, of the questionnaire on the legal status and treatment of women as summarized in the Secretary-General's report on this subject, 1/

Noting that article 15 of the Universal Declaration of Human Rights states that:

1. "Everyone has the right to a nationality",
2. "No one shall be arbitrarily deprived of his nationality nor denied the right to change his nationality",

Considering that a convention on the nationality of married women, which would assure women equality with men in the exercise of these rights and especially prevent a women from becoming stateless or otherwise suffering hardships arising out of these conflicts in law, should be prepared as promptly as possible,

Invites Member States to transmit to the Secretary-General by November 1949 their replies to the supplementary list of questions on nationality and domicile as they affect the status of married persons, 2/

Requests the Secretary-General to prepare and circulate to Member States an analysis of the conflicts in law demonstrated in documents E/CN.6/82, E/CN.6/82/Add.1 and 2 and E/CN.6/81/Rev.1 and in any further replies received from Governments;

Invites Member States to transmit to the Secretary-General by 1 April 1950, on the basis of this analysis, their comments and suggestions as to the resolution of these conflicts; and

Requests the Secretary-General to provide the Commission on the Status of Women, at its fourth session, with a summary of the replies received from Governments and suggestions as to alternative articles which might be incorporated into such a convention, with a view to the final drafting of a convention at an early date.

1/ See documents E/CN.6/82 and E/CN.6/82/Add.1 and 2.
2/ See document E/CN.6/81/Rev.1.

Document 18

Convention for the Suppression of the Traffic in Persons and of the Exploitation of the Prostitution of Others, adopted by the General Assembly on 2 December 1949

UN Treaty Series, vol. 96, No. 1342, p. 271

Preamble

Whereas prostitution and the accompanying evil of the traffic in persons for the purpose of prostitution are incompatible with the dignity and worth of the human person and endanger the welfare of the individual, the family and the community,

Whereas, with respect to the suppression of the traffic in women and children, the following international instruments are in force:

1. International Agreement of 18 May 1904 for the Suppression of the White Slave Traffic, as amended by the Protocol approved by the General Assembly of the United Nations on 3 December 1948,

2. International Convention of 4 May 1910 for the Suppression of the White Slave Traffic, as amended by the above-mentioned Protocol,

3. International Convention of 30 September 1921 for the Suppression of the Traffic in Women and Children, as amended by the Protocol approved by the General Assembly of the United Nations on 20 October 1947,

4. International Convention of 11 October 1933 for the Suppression of the Traffic in Women of Full Age, as amended by the aforesaid Protocol,

Whereas the League of Nations in 1937 prepared a draft Convention extending the scope of the above-mentioned instruments, and

Whereas developments since 1937 make feasible the conclusion of a convention consolidating the above-mentioned instruments and embodying the substance of the 1937 draft Convention as well as desirable alterations therein;

Now therefore
The Contracting Parties
Hereby agree as hereinafter provided:

Article 1

The Parties to the present Convention agree to punish any person who, to gratify the passions of another:

1. Procures, entices or leads away, for purposes of prostitution, another person, even with the consent of that person;

2. Exploits the prostitution of another person, even with the consent of that person.

Article 2

The Parties to the present Convention further agree to punish any person who:

1. Keeps or manages, or knowingly finances or takes part in the financing of a brothel;

2. Knowingly lets or rents a building or other place or any part thereof for the purpose of the prostitution of others.

Article 3

To the extent permitted by domestic law, attempts to commit any of the offences referred to in articles 1 and 2, and acts preparatory to the commission thereof, shall also be punished.

Article 4

To the extent permitted by domestic law, intentional participation in the acts referred to in articles 1 and 2 above shall also be punishable.

To the extent permitted by domestic law, acts of participation shall be treated as separate offences whenever this is necessary to prevent impunity.

Article 5

In cases where injured persons are entitled under domestic law to be parties to proceedings in respect of any of the offences referred to in the present Convention, aliens shall be so entitled upon the same terms as nationals.

Article 6

Each Party to the present Convention agrees to take all the necessary measures to repeal or abolish any existing law, regulation or administrative provision by virtue of which persons who engage in or are suspected of engaging in prostitution are subject either to special registration or to the possession of a special document or to any exceptional requirements for supervision or notification.

Article 7

Previous convictions pronounced in foreign States for offences referred to in the present Convention shall, to the extent permitted by domestic law, be taken into account for the purpose of:

1. Establishing recidivism;

2. Disqualifying the offender from the exercise of civil rights.

Article 8

The offences referred to in articles 1 and 2 of the present Convention shall be regarded as extraditable offences in any extradition treaty which has been or may hereafter be concluded between any of the Parties to this Convention.

The Parties to the present Convention which do not make extradition conditional on the existence of a treaty shall henceforward recognize the offences referred to in articles 1 and 2 of the present Convention as cases for extradition between themselves.

Extradition shall be granted in accordance with the law of the State to which the request is made.

Article 9

In States where the extradition of nationals is not permitted by law, nationals who have returned to their own State after the commission abroad of any of the offences referred to in articles 1 and 2 of the present Convention shall be prosecuted in and punished by the courts of their own State.

This provision shall not apply if, in a similar case between the Parties to the present Convention, the extradition of an alien cannot be granted.

Article 10

The provisions of article 9 shall not apply when the person charged with the offence has been tried in a foreign State and, if convicted, has served his sentence or had it remitted or reduced in conformity with the laws of that foreign State.

Article 11

Nothing in the present Convention shall be interpreted as determining the attitude of a Party towards the general question of the limits of criminal jurisdiction under international law.

Article 12

The present Convention does not affect the principle that the offences to which it refers shall in each State be defined, prosecuted and punished in conformity with its domestic law.

Article 13

The Parties to the present Convention shall be bound to execute letters of request relating to offences referred to in the Convention in accordance with their domestic law and practice.

The transmission of letters of request shall be effected:

1. By direct communication between the judicial authorities; or

2. By direct communication between the Ministers of Justice of the two States, or by direct communication from another competent authority of the State making the request to the Minister of Justice of the State to which the request is made; or

3. Through the diplomatic or consular representative of the State making the request in the State to which the request is made; this representative shall send the letters of request direct to the competent judicial authority or to the authority indicated by the Government of the State to which the request is made, and shall receive direct from such authority the papers constituting the execution of the letters of request.

In cases 1 and 3 a copy of the letters of request shall always be sent to the superior authority of the State to which application is made.

Unless otherwise agreed, the letters of request shall be drawn up in the language of the authority making the request, provided always that the State to which the request is made may require a translation in its own language, certified correct by the authority making the request.

Each Party to the present Convention shall notify to each of the other Parties to the Convention the method or methods of transmission mentioned above which it will recognize for the letters of request of the latter State.

Until such notification is made by a State, its existing procedure in regard to letters of request shall remain in force.

Execution of letters of request shall not give rise to a claim for reimbursement of charges or expenses of any nature whatever other than expenses of experts.

Nothing in the present article shall be construed as an undertaking on the part of the Parties to the present Convention to adopt in criminal matters any form or methods of proof contrary to their own domestic laws.

Article 14

Each Party to the present Convention shall establish or maintain a service charged with the coordination and centralization of the results of the investigation of offences referred to in the present Convention.

Such services should compile all information calculated to facilitate the prevention and punishment of the offences referred to in the present Convention and should be in close contact with the corresponding services in other States.

Article 15

To the extent permitted by domestic law and to the extent to which the authorities responsible for the services referred to in article 14 may judge desirable, they shall furnish to the authorities responsible for the corresponding services in other States the following information:

1. Particulars of any offence referred to in the present Convention or any attempt to commit such offence;

2. Particulars of any search for and any prosecution, arrest, conviction, refusal of admission or expulsion of persons guilty of any of the offences referred to in the present Convention, the movements of such persons and any other useful information with regard to them.

The information so furnished shall include descriptions of the offenders, their fingerprints, photographs, methods of operation, police records and records of conviction.

Article 16

The Parties to the present Convention agree to take or to encourage, through their public and private educational, health, social, economic and other related services, measures for the prevention of prostitution and for the rehabilitation and social adjustment of the victims of prostitution and of the offences referred to in the present Convention.

Article 17

The Parties to the present Convention undertake, in connection with immigration and emigration, to adopt or maintain such measures as are required in terms of their obligations under the present Convention, to check the traffic in persons of either sex for the purpose of prostitution.

In particular they undertake:

1. To make such regulations as are necessary for the protection of immigrants or emigrants, and in particular, women and children, both at the place of arrival and departure and while *en route*;

2. To arrange for appropriate publicity warning the public of the dangers of the aforesaid traffic;

3. To take appropriate measures to ensure supervision of railway stations, airports, seaports and *en route*, and of other public places, in order to prevent international traffic in persons for the purpose of prostitution;

4. To take appropriate measures in order that the appropriate authorities be informed of the arrival of persons who appear, *prima facie*, to be the principals and accomplices in or victims of such traffic.

Article 18

The Parties to the present Convention undertake, in accordance with the conditions laid down by domestic law, to have declarations taken from aliens who are prostitutes, in order to establish their identity and civil status and to discover who has caused them to leave their State. The information obtained shall be communicated to the authorities of the State of origin of the said persons with a view to their eventual repatriation.

Article 19

The Parties to the present Convention undertake, in accordance with the conditions laid down by domestic law and without prejudice to prosecution or other action for violations thereunder and so far as possible:

1. Pending the completion of arrangements for the repatriation of destitute victims of international traffic in persons for the purpose of prostitution, to make suitable provisions for their temporary care and maintenance;

2. To repatriate persons referred to in article 18 who desire to be repatriated or who may be claimed by persons exercising authority over them or whose expulsion is ordered in conformity with the law. Repatriation shall take place only after agreement is reached with the State of destination as to identity and nationality as well as to the place and date of arrival at frontiers. Each Party to the present Convention shall facilitate the passage of such persons through its territory.

Where the persons referred to in the preceding paragraph cannot themselves repay the cost of repatriation and have neither spouse, relatives nor guardian to pay for them, the cost of repatriation as far as the nearest frontier or port of embarkation or airport in the direction of the State of origin shall be borne by the State where they are in residence, and the cost of the remainder of the journey shall be borne by the State of origin.

Article 20

The Parties to the present Convention shall, if they have not already done so, take the necessary measures for the supervision of employment agencies in order to prevent persons seeking employment, in particular women and children, from being exposed to the danger of prostitution.

Article 21

The Parties to the present Convention shall communicate to the Secretary-General of the United Nations such laws and regulations as have already been promulgated in their States, and thereafter annually such laws and regulations as may be promulgated, relating to the subjects of the present Convention, as well as all measures taken by them concerning the application of the Convention. The information received shall be published periodically by the Secretary-General and sent to all Members of the United Nations and to non-member States to which the present Convention is officially communicated in accordance with article 23.

Article 22

If any dispute shall arise between the Parties to the present Convention relating to its interpretation or application and if such dispute cannot be settled by other means, the dispute shall, at the request of any one of the Parties to the dispute, be referred to the International Court of Justice.

Article 23

The present Convention shall be open for signature on behalf of any Member of the United Nations and also on behalf of any other State to which an invitation has been addressed by the Economic and Social Council.

The present Convention shall be ratified and the instruments of ratification shall be deposited with the Secretary-General of the United Nations.

The States mentioned in the first paragraph which have not signed the Convention may accede to it.

Accession shall be effected by deposit of an instrument of accession with the Secretary-General of the United Nations.

For the purpose of the present Convention the word "State" shall include all the colonies and Trust Territories of a State signatory or acceding to the Convention and all territories for which such State is internationally responsible.

Article 24

The present Convention shall come into force on the ninetieth day following the date of deposit of the second instrument of ratification or accession.

For each State ratifying or acceding to the Convention after the deposit of the second instrument of ratification or accession, the Convention shall enter into force ninety days after the deposit by such State of its instrument of ratification or accession.

Article 25

After the expiration of five years from the entry into force of the present Convention, any Party to the Convention may denounce it by a written notification addressed to the Secretary-General of the United Nations.

Such denunciation shall take effect for the Party making it one year from the date upon which it is received by the Secretary-General of the United Nations.

Article 26

The Secretary-General of the United Nations shall inform all Members of the United Nations and non-member States referred to in article 23:

(a) Of signatures, ratifications and accessions received in accordance with article 23;

(b) Of the date on which the present Convention will come into force in accordance with article 24;

(c) Of denunciations received in accordance with article 25.

Article 27

Each Party to the present Convention undertakes to adopt, in accordance with its Constitution, the legislative or other measures necessary to ensure the application of the Convention.

Article 28

The provisions of the present Convention shall supersede in the relations between the Parties thereto the provisions of the international instruments referred to in sub-paragraphs 1, 2, 3 and 4 of the second paragraph of the Preamble, each of which shall be deemed to be terminated when all the Parties thereto shall have become Parties to the present Convention.

IN FAITH WHEREOF the undersigned, being duly authorized thereto by their respective Governments, have signed the present Convention, opened for signature at Lake Success, New York, on the twenty-first day of March, one thousand nine hundred and fifty, a certified true copy of which shall be transmitted by the Secretary-General to all the Members of the United Nations and to the non-member States referred to in article 23.

Document 19

Report of the Secretary-General to the CSW on discrimination against women in the field of political rights

E/CN.6/131, 15 March 1950

Introduction

1. At its third session, the Commission on the Status of Women adopted the following resolution: 1/

"*The Commission on the Status of Women,*

"*Noting* that the memorandum on the political rights of women (A/619, A/619/Corr.1, A/619/Add.1 and 2) circulated to the General Assembly in 1948, does not indicate whether women have equal political rights with men, in particular in regard to the right to vote and the right to be elected to public office in the seventy-four countries listed,

"*Noting* further that replies to the letter circulated to Member States by the Secretary-General on 17 May 1948 show only thirty-five countries where women enjoy the same political rights as men,

"*Requests* the Secretary-General to prepare a further report, based on information received from governments, and other relevant information, to show whether there is discrimination based on sex, in law or in practice, with respect to the right to vote and the right to be elected to public office in elections of all kinds."

Part I: Situation in Law

2. The memorandum on political rights of women (A/619) referred to in the resolution quoted above, which is to be brought up to date and circulated annually "to Members of the United Nations until all women throughout the world have the same political rights as men" 2/ was revised and circulated to Member Governments as document A/1163 on 30 November 1949. This document, which is based on constitutional or other legal provisions regulating women's right to vote and to be elected to public office, shows the extent to which women enjoy legal equality with men in this field as far as it has been possible for the Secretary-General to ascertain.

3. According to the information compiled in the above-mentioned document, women have equal legal rights with men in the political field, and consequently possess the right to vote and to be elected to public office on equal terms with men, in fifty-two countries. These are the following:

Albania, Argentina, Australia, Austria, Belgium, Brazil, Bulgaria, Burma, Byelorussian Soviet Social-ist Republic, Canada, Ceylon, Chile, China, Cuba, Czechoslovakia, Denmark, Dominican Republic, Ecuador, 3/ Finland, France, Federal Republic of Germany, Hungary, Iceland, India, Ireland, Israel, Italy, Japan, Korea, Liberia, Luxembourg, Mongolian People's Republic, Netherlands, New Zealand, Norway, Pakistan, Panama, Philippines, Poland, Romania, Saarland, Sweden, Thailand, Turkey, Ukrainian Soviet Socialist Republic, Union of South Africa, Union of Soviet Socialist Republics, United Kingdom of Great Britain and Northern Ireland, United States of America, Uruguay, Venezuela and Yugoslavia.

4. Twenty-two countries have legislation which does not provide equality as between men and women in the field of political rights. They can be divided into the following groups:

(a) Countries where women have in law equal political rights with men, subject to the fulfilment of certain educational or property qualifications not required of men. In this group there are four countries:

Guatemala: Women must be literate. Voting is compulsory and secret for literate men; optional and secret for women who have the required qualifications; and optional and public for illiterate men.

Portugal: Women are subject to higher educational requirements or, when fulfilling the same tax qualifications as those prescribed for men, must be heads of families in order to have the right to vote.

El Salvador: Women must prove that they are 25 years of age and have passed the third school grade.

Syria: Women must have an elementary school certificate, a condition not required for men.

(b) Countries where women have the right to vote and to be elected in municipal elections only. In the case of some of these countries, the right is subject to the fulfilment of certain qualifications not required of men.

1/ See document E/1316, paragraph 18, resolution 4.
2/ Resolution 120 (VI) of the Economic and Social Council.
3/ Voting is compulsory for men, voluntary for women.

In this group there are five countries: Bolivia, Greece, 4/ Mexico, Monaco and Peru. 5/

(c)   Countries where by law women are not permitted to vote or to hold elective office. In this group, there are thirteen countries: 6/ Colombia, Liechtenstein, Nicaragua, and Switzerland.

Part II: Situation in Practice

5.   The replies from Governments to the Questionnaire on the Legal Status and Treatment of Women 7/ contain no material which establishes that women have been denied the right to vote and to be elected where they are not legally debarred from these rights. It does appear from information available to the Secretary-General that, in at least two countries, 8/ women have in fact never voted or been elected to public office, although there are no laws denying such rights to women.

6.   Ten Governments in their replies to the Questionnaire on the Legal Status and Treatment of Women gave data concerning the number of women in their legislative assemblies. Two of these Governments, those of Poland and Sweden, also commented on this subject as follows:

Poland: "The actual situation of women does not correspond yet fully with the legal position. The percentage of women holding office in legislative departments, in State and local governments in still low. There is however a considerable improvement as compared to the pre-war period."

Sweden: "As it will appear from the statistical data given ... the legal equality does not imply that women are actually holding public offices proportionally to the same extent as men." 9/

7.   In Sweden women constitute 6.6 per cent of the Riksdag (legislative assembly). In Poland they constitute 7.5 per cent.

8.   The same situation exists in most of the other countries. Only exceptionally does the percentage of women in any legislative assembly exceed ten, even though women in most cases total approximately 50 per cent of the electorate.

9.   The following is a table showing the number and percentage of women in the legislative assemblies of various countries on which information is available to the Secretary-General. Members of the Commission will realize, however, that many factors other than possible discrimination against women are reflected in these statistics.

4/ Until 1953, women are subject to higher age requirements: 25 years for women as against 21 years for men.
5/ Women are subject to higher age requirements: 21 years for women against 18 years for men.
6/ No elections are held in the following three countries: Ethiopia, Saudi Arabia and Yemen.
7/ The following thirty-nine Governments have replied so far: Afghanistan, Argentina, Australia, Belgium, Brazil, Burma, Canada, Chile, China, Cuba, Czechoslovakia, Denmark, Dominican Republic, Ecuador, Egypt, El Salvador, France, Greece, Guatemala, Iceland, India, Luxembourg, Mexico, Netherlands, New Zealand, Norway, Pakistan, Philippines, Poland, Siam, Sweden, Turkey, Union of South Africa, Union of Soviet Socialist Republics, United Kingdom of Great Britain and Northern Ireland, United States of America, Uruguay, Venezuela and Yugoslavia.
8/ These two countries are Afghanistan and Paraguay. Regarding Afghanistan, reference is made to document A/1163. Regarding Paraguay, reference is made to the report of the Inter-American Commission of Women to the Eighth International Conference of American States on the Political and Civil Rights of Women, page 73, and to Informe de la Comision Interamericana de Mujeres a la Novena Conferencia International Americana sobre Derechos Civiles y Politicos de la Mujer, pages 26 and 70.
9/ The reply continues:
"As to political activity of women in Sweden, the following figures may be quoted which show the proportion of men and women that voted in the general elections to the Second Chamber of the Riksdag in 1944:
74.8 per cent out of 2,111,989 men entitled to vote
69.2 per cent out of 2,198,252 women entitled to vote."

Country	Year	Number of members of the legislative assemblies	Number of women	Percentage of women
Australia	1950	112	5	4.5
Belgium	1949	369	13	3.5
Canada	1947	333	3	1
China	1947	1,691	84	5
Cuba	1949	190	6	3.2
Denmark	1947	225	20	9
Dominican Republic	1949	59	0	0
El Salvador	1949	42	0	0

Country	Year	Number of members of the legislative assemblies	Number of women	Percentage of women
Finland	1947	200	24	12
France	1949	939	51	5.4
Guatemala	1949	68	0	0
India	1950	328	11	3.3
Israel	1949	120	12	10
Japan	1949	716	23	3.2
New Zealand	1950	80	3	3.75
Norway	1950	150	6	4
Panama	1949	42	1	2.4
Philippines	1947	122	1	0.8
Poland	1947	442	33	7.5
Sweden	1947	380	25	6.6
Union of South Africa	1949	196	2	1
Union of Soviet Socialist Republics	1948	1,339	277	20.7
United Kingdom of Great Britain and Northern Ireland	1950	625	20	3.2
United States of America Senate		96	1	1
House of Representatives		435	8	1.8
Uruguay	1947	129	4	3
Yugoslavia	1947	575	20	3.5

Document 20

Report of the Secretary-General to the CSW on the participation of women in the work of the United Nations

E/CN.6/132, 16 March 1950

Summary

This report describes the nature and proportion of positions occupied by women in the United Nations Secretariat, and furnishes some information on the conditions of employment of women in the Secretariat. The report also provides information on the extent to which Member Governments have included women in their delegations to meetings of United Nations bodies and conferences of the specialized agencies.

Introduction

1. At its third session, the Commission on the Status of Women requested 1/ the Secretary-General to prepare a report on the nature and proportion of positions occupied by women in the Secretariat of the United Nations and also to indicate in the report the extent to which Member Governments have included women in their delegations to organs and agencies of the United Nations. In resolution 242 A(IX), the Economic and Social Council took note of the Commission's report and the recommendations contained therein.

2. Accordingly, the Secretary-General has the honour to present herewith information on the nature and proportion of positions occupied by women in the Secretariat (Part I), and information concerning the extent to which Member Governments have included women in their delegations to organs and agencies of the United Nations (Part II).

1/ See document E/1316, paragraph 20.

Part I

Nature and proportion of positions occupied by women in the Secretariat

A. Distribution of personnel with regard to grades and sex

3. On 30 November 1949, the total staff of the United Nations Secretariat at Headquarters, at the Geneva Office and the Information Centres, including consultants and personnel paid at hourly rates, consisted of 3,916 persons of whom 2,179 were men and 1,737 were women. The distribution of the personnel with regard to grades and sex was as follows:

Grades	Totals	Male	Female
23	9	9	-
21	15	14	1
19	26	26	-
18	46	46	-
17	84	82	2
16	168	160	8
15	169	155	14
14	196	168	28
13	213	170	43
12	225	154	71
11	144	102	42
10	103	64	39
9	164	80	84
8	116	55	61
7	231	62	169
6	447	76	371
5	634	170	464
4	274	131	143
3	207	117	90
2	49	30	19
1	49	35	14
	3,569	1,906	1,663
Personnel paid at hourly rates	256	184	72
Consultants	91	89	2
Totals	3,916	2,179	1,737

Note: The above figures do not include persons on General Assembly or short-term appointments.

4. In the above table, grade 23 designates Assistant Secretaries-General; grade 21, principal or "top-ranking" directors; grade 19, directors; grades 16 to 18, senior officials; grades 12 to 15, intermediate officials; grades 8 to 11, junior officials. The remaining grades are those of secretarial, clerical and non-professional personnel.

B. Conditions of employment for women

5. The Secretary-General feels that the Commission may wish to have before it some information concerning the conditions of employment of women in the Secretariat with regard to those aspects which are of particular interest in the light of the terms of reference of the Commission. He therefore presents to the Commission information concerning dependency benefits and conditions of home leave.

6. Under the staff rules, certain allowances and the cost-of-living adjustment are paid, or paid at an increased rate, to staff members who have dependants. Staff Rule 29 (a) provides that these higher payments are made "to a staff member who has a wife or who, as the head of a family, has one or more of the following dependent upon him or her for full and continuing support: husband, son, daughter, parent, brother or sister".

7. In the administrative Manual, Volume 2, page 125, the term "head of family" used in Staff Rule 29 (a) is defined as follows:

"The following categories of staff shall be considered as heads of families for purposes of receiving allowances and cost of living adjustment at dependency rates:

"- a married man;

"- a married woman whose husband is incapacitated and dependent upon her for full and continuing support;

"- a single, widowed, or divorced staff member who has a member of the immediate family dependent upon him or her for full and continuing support."

8. The Commission will note that a distinction is being made between men and women in that a married man ("a staff member who has a wife") is automatically entitled to the payment of all allowances and the cost-of-living adjustment at dependency rates, while a married woman comes under the notion of "head of family" and within the category of staff members entitled to payment of allowances and the cost-of-living adjustment at dependency rates only if her husband is incapacitated and dependent upon her for full and continued support. A single, widowed or divorced staff member of either sex who has a member of the immediate family dependent upon him or her for full and continued support is considered "head of family".

9. The rule set forth and interpreted in the preceding paragraphs (6-8) governs, in particular, whether a staff member is entitled to:

(a) The children's allowance ($200 per annum) and the education grant ($200 per annum). (Staff rules 35 and 36; Administrative Manual, volume 2, pages 150, 151 and 154).

(b) The expatriation allowance at a higher rate ($500 per annum) as against $250 per annum. (Staff Rule 33; Administrative Manual, Volume 2, page 141).

(c) The rental allowance at a higher rate (Staff Rule 34). The schedule of rates is to be found on page 148 of the Administrative Manual, Volume 2.

(d) The installation allowance at a higher rate (Staff Rule 31). The rates and conditions are to be found on pages 135 and 136 of the Administrative Manual, Volume 2.

(e) The installation grant at a higher rate ($200 as against $125). (Staff Rule 32; Administrative Manual, Volume 2, page 138).

(f) The dependency credit under the Staff Assessment Plan (Staff Rule 38; Administrative Manual, Volume 2, pages 166 and 167).

10. A staff member whose home is outside the country of his official duty station is entitled, in addition to annual leave, to home leave consisting of two working weeks every two years plus actual travel time not to exceed 30 days (Staff Rule 80 (a)). A similar provision is made for a non-locally recruited staff member whose home is in the country of his official duty station. For purposes of home leave, a staff member is entitled to the payment of travelling expenses for himself, his wife and dependent children. (Staff Rule 83).

11. In so far as the home leave of the staff member is concerned, no distinction is made between men and women. As an administrative practice, the Secretariat allows a woman staff member whose husband is also on the staff to accompany the latter on his home leave. The same right is not accorded to the husband.

12. The question of travel expenses of a staff member's dependants in connection with home leave is regulated by Staff Regulation 25 adopted by the General Assembly. It authorized the payment of such transportation costs only in the case of wives and dependent children (Annex II of General Assembly resolution 13 (I) on the organization of the Secretariat).

13. In this connection, the term "dependent children" has been defined as including only children for whom the children's allowance is payable under the provisions referred to above. (Staff Rule 124, Administrative Manual, Volume 2, pages 377 and 378).

14. Following upon a decision taken by the General Assembly on 11 December 1948, a comprehensive review of the salary and allowance system was to be undertaken by the Secretary-General for consideration at the fourth regular session of the General Assembly and a working-party of three experts appointed to assist in the review (A/798, paragraph 8). In their report to the Secretary-General (A/C.5/331, paragraph 94), the experts suggested that the children's allowance should be paid equally to male and female staff members who certify that a child is "dependent" and furnish a birth certificate or other documentary evidence. The experts, while of the opinion that this proposal would admit a number of claims which would scarcely meet any strict test of dependency, expressed the belief that, since the number of individual allowances that would need to be paid was understood not to exceed seventy, the extra expense would be compensated by savings in administrative costs and the avoidance of any feeling of discriminatory treatment.

15. In his memorandum on the report of the Committee of Experts, the Secretary-General stated that he was in full agreement with the suggested liberalization of the conditions of eligibility for children's allowances and education grants. He accordingly proposed appropriate changes in the Staff Regulations (A/C.5/331/Add.1, paragraph 16 and annex I).

16. Action on the report on the Salary, Allowance and Leave Systems was postponed by the Fifth Committee, and the matter was referred to the Advisory Committee on Administrative and Budgetary Questions with the request that it submit its conclusions and recommendations to the General Assembly at its fifth session. The Fifth Committee in its report reaffirmed the view that its decision to postpone action should not be interpreted as diminishing in any way the authority vested in the Secretary-General by the Charter to effect those improvements in the United Nations system of personnel administration which are consistent with the staff regulations and within the limits of existing budgetary appropriations (A/1232, paragraphs 45 and 45 (a)).

17. In keeping with this opinion, the Secretary-General decided that certain recommendations of the Committee of Experts should be implemented in 1950, including the recommendation that children's allowances should be paid equally to any staff member with dependent children in the proper age bracket.

Part II

Information concerning the extent to which member Governments have included women in their delegations to organs and agencies of the United Nations

A. *General Assembly*

18. A study of the composition of the membership of the four regular and two special sessions of the General Assembly reveals no significant trend in the proportion of women to men delegates.

19. Five hundred and eighty-eight representatives, alternates and advisers from fifty-nine Member States attended the fourth regular session of the General Assembly. This number included four women representatives,

one each from Canada, Chile, India and the United States of America; nine women alternate representatives, two from Sweden and one each from Belgium, Denmark, Mexico, Netherlands, Norway, the United Kingdom of Great Britain and Northern Ireland, and the United States, eleven women advisers, experts and consultants, two each from Australia, Iraq and the Netherlands, and one each from China, France, Israel, the Philippines and Poland.

20. The following figures relating to the officers of the fourth regular session of the General Assembly may be noted:

Officers of the General Assembly	Total	Men	Women
President	1	1	-
Vice-Presidents	7	7	-
Chairmen of Main Committees	6	6	-
Chairman of the Ad Hoc Committee	1	1	-
Vice-Chairman of Committees	7	6	1
Rapporteurs	7	6	1

21. Besides the six Main Committees and the Ad Hoc Committee—all committees of the whole closely associated with the work of the Assembly—certain other committees and commissions are usually elected by the Assembly to perform certain specified functions. The following table concerns representation on these committees and commissions:

Committees and commissions of the General Assembly

	Total members	Men	Women
Credentials Committee	9	8	1
Advisory Committee on Administrative and Budgetary Matters	9	9	-
Committee on Contributions	10	9	1
Board of Auditors	3	3	-
Investments Committee	3	3	-
Staff Pension Committee			
Members elected by the General Assembly	6	5	1
Members appointed by the Secretary-General	6	5	1
Members elected by participants in the Pension Fund	6	6	-
International Law Commission	15	15	-

22. In addition to the committees and commissions listed above, there are certain United Nations commissions that have been named for special assignments in connection with the peaceful settlement of disputes and other matters. Among these may be noted the Special Committee on the Balkans, the Commission on Korea, and the Conciliation Commission for Palestine. To none of these commissions have women been appointed to serve as representatives.

23. In 1949, fifty-three countries sent a total of ninety-one representatives and alternates, and thirty-nine advisers to the Interim Committee of the General Assembly. (The Byelorussian Soviet Socialist Republic, Czechoslovakia, Poland, the Ukrainian Soviet Socialist Republic, and the Union of Soviet Socialist Republics were not represented.) The Netherlands sent one women as an alternate representative; Denmark and Costa Rica each had one women among their advisers.

B. Security Council

24. The Security Council is composed of eleven member States, each represented by an accredited representative. So far, there have been no women representatives on the Council.

25. Of the committees and commissions of the Security Council, the Military Staff Committee is made up of representatives of the five permanent members; the Atomic Energy Commission includes all members of the Council plus Canada; and the Commission for Conventional Armaments, the Committee of Experts, and the Committee on the Admission of New Members include all members of the Council. On none of these committees or commissions have women acted as representatives.

C. Economic and Social Council

26. During the last three sessions of the Economic and Social Council (eighth, ninth and tenth), no woman was chief representative of any of the eighteen countries that comprise the Council. Women, however, were included in delegations as alternate representatives and advisers, as the following table shows:

Session	Total alternates and advisers	Women
Eighth	96	6
Ninth	123	11
Tenth	82	9

27. The following table deals with the membership of functional commissions and sub-commissions of the Economic and Social Council during 1949:

Commission or sub-commission	Members	Men	Women
Economic and Employment Commission	15	15	-
Sub-Commission on Employment and Stability	7	7	-
Sub-Commission on Economic Development	7	7	-
Transport and Communications Commission	15	15	-
Fiscal Commission	15	15	-
Statistical Commission	12	10 2/	-
Sub-Commission on Statistical Sampling	5	5	-
Population Commission	12	12	-
Social Commission			
May	18	16	2
December	18	15	3
Commission on Narcotic Drugs	15	15	-
Commission on Human Rights	18	15	3 3/
Sub-Commission on Freedom of Information and of the Press	12	12	-
Sub-Commission on Prevention of Discrimination and Protection of Minorities	12	11	1
Commission on the Status of Women	15	-	15 4/

28. The following table deals with the membership of regional commissions of the Economic and Social Council during 1949:

Commission	Members	Men	Women
Economic Commission for Europe	18	17	1
Economic Commission for Asia and the Far East	13 Members 7 Associates	20	-
Economic Commission for Latin America	24	24	-
Economic Commission for the Middle East	11	11	-

D. Trusteeship Council

29. The Trusteeship Council has twelve members. Each Member State has one representative and such alternates and advisers as may be required. No women have so far served in the capacity of representatives. At the fifth session of the Trusteeship Council, held in June 1949, among thirty-six representatives, alternates, and advisers, there were two women listed as advisers. At the sixth session, held in January 1950, among thirty-eight representatives, alternates and advisers, one woman was listed as an adviser.

E. International Court of Justice

30. The International Court of Justice is composed of fifteen members, elected for nine-year terms by the General Assembly and the Security Council voting separately. Up to the present, no woman has been elected to the Court.

F. Specialized agencies

31. The following paragraphs deal with the composition of delegations to the main conference held during 1949 by the United Nations specialized agencies. Delegations are usually made up of representatives and alternates. In the case of the International Labour Organization, a different system of representation prevails.

32. Each member State of the International Labour Organisation has the right to be represented at the International Labour Conference by four representatives, two of whom are Government delegates and the other two are delegates representing respectively the employers and the workers of each country. Each delegate may be accompanied by advisers not to exceed two for any particular item on the agenda of the meeting. When questions specially affecting women are to be considered by the Conference, at least one of the advisers has to be a woman. States responsible for the international relations of non-metropolitan territories may appoint additional advisers under certain conditions.

33. At the 32nd session of the International Labour Conference, held in Geneva in 1949, fifty countries were represented. Out of a total of 543 persons attending the Conference, Government representatives, including alternates and advisers, totalled 244, of whom seventeen were women; of the 143 employers' representatives, only one was a woman; and of the 156 workers' representatives, four were women.

34. At the fifth session of the Food and Agriculture Organization, held in Washington in November 1949,

2/ Two countries sent no representatives.
3/ A woman was chairman.
4/ A woman was chairman.

fifty-nine member countries were represented by 109 representatives and alternates, 189 associates and advisers. Among them were five women: one representative from Hungary, one associate from Denmark and three advisers from the United States of America.

35. At the Fourth Conference of the United Nations Educational, Scientific and Cultural Organization in Paris in September 1949, forty-seven member States were represented by 185 representatives and alternates; of these, three were women.

36. The World Health Organization held its last Assembly in Rome, in June 1949. Fifty-three out of the fifty-eight member Governments were represented by a total of 230 representatives, alternates and advisers. Of these, nine were women, two being principal representatives.

37. With respect to the other specialized agencies which held conferences in 1949—the International Civil Aviation Organization, the International Bank for Reconstruction and Development, the International Monetary Fund, the Universal Postal Union, the International Refugee Organization, the International Telecommunication Union—no women were listed on any of the delegations.

Document 21

Report of the Secretary-General to the CSW on the possibility of proposing a convention on the political rights of women

E/CN.6/143, 28 April 1950

1. At its third session, in Beirut, in March 1949, the Commission on the Status of Women adopted the following resolution: 1/

"*The Commission on the Status of Women*

"*Noting* the Inter-American Convention on the Granting of Political Rights to Women, signed at Bogota in May 1948, by fourteen of the American Republics, as a proposal helpful to countries which have not yet removed existing discrimination against women in this field,

"*Requests* the Secretary-General to examine the possibility of proposing a similar convention to assist countries which have not granted women equal political rights, and to submit the result of his examination to the next session of the Commission".

2. In considering the operative part of this resolution, it may be pointed out that no information is available as to what countries would eventually become parties to such a convention. The present report is therefore restricted to a consideration of the following topics:

A. The technical possibility of drafting the convention;

B. The force of a convention drawn up under the auspices of the United Nations;

C. Countries in which women are still without full political rights;

D. The Inter-American Convention on the Granting of Political Rights to Women, its signatories, ratification and effect;

E. Resolution 56 (I) of the General Assembly on political rights of women;

F. The Universal Declaration of Human Rights and the draft International Covenant on Human Rights;

G. Conclusions.

A. **The technical possibility**

3. It seems unlikely that the mere drafting of a convention would create any problems different from those encountered in the drafting of other conventions under the auspices of the United Nations.

4. The authority to prepare conventions is vested in the Economic and Social Council by Article 62 of the Charter, paragraphs (3) and (4) of which read as follows:

"3. It [the Economic and Social Council] may prepare draft conventions for submission to the General Assembly, with respect to matters falling within its competence.

"4. It may call, in accordance with the rules prescribed by the United Nations, international conferences on matters falling within its competence."

5. Under paragraph 4 of Article 62 the Council may call an international conference with authority to draft a convention for signature. The Council may call such a conference, however, only if "after consultation with the Secretary-General and the appropriate specialized agencies, it is satisfied that the work to be done by

1/ See report of the Third Session of the Commission on the Status of Women, document E/1316, paragraph 18 (1).

the conference cannot be done satisfactorily by any other organ of the United Nations or by any specialized agency". 2/

B. The force of a Convention drawn up under the auspices of the United Nations

6. Although the Commission in its resolution obviously envisages such a convention primarily as a means of enfranchising women not yet enfranchised, this aspect does not exhaust the possible legal force of the convention. It might also prevent states, parties to it, from abrogating existing provisions of their internal law in a way which would be contrary to the provisions of the convention.

7. While no information is available as to what countries would become parties to the convention, it may be pointed out, that the adoption of a convention by the General Assembly is usually supplemented by a recommendation to Member States to adhere to it. In this connection it should be noted that the General Assembly by its resolution 119 (II) called upon "all Member States to carry out all recommendations of the General Assembly passed on economic and social matters" and recommended that "in fulfilment of Article 64 of the Charter of the United Nations the Secretary-General report annually to the Economic and Social Council and that the latter report to the General Assembly on steps taken by the Member Governments to give effect to the recommendations of the Economic and Social Council as well as to the recommendations made by the General Assembly on matters falling within the Council's competence." 3/

8. As a consequence of this resolution the Economic and Social Council by resolution 255 (IX) established an *Ad Hoc* Committee on Implementation of Recommendations on Economic and Social Matters, *inter alia*, to recommend "means whereby the Council and the Secretary-General can improve the procedure so that more effective action is taken as a result of Council and Assembly recommendations." 4/

9. The report of the *Ad Hoc* Committee which was adopted unanimously by the Council at its Tenth Session 5/ states in the chapter: Request for information from Governments:

"In regard to treaties, conventions, and protocols on economic and social matters the Secretary-General should ask those Members of the United Nations which have not ratified or adhered to them what steps they have taken to do so." 6/

10. The report further states in the chapter: Form of Secretary-General's report:

"The Committee considered that a separate section of the report should be devoted to treaties, conventions and protocols; and also that a separate section should contain a list of requests for specific information made during the two years under review and should indicate those countries which had or had not supplied the desired material." 7/

C. Countries in which women are still without full political rights

11. Twenty-one countries have legislation which does not provide equality as between men and women in the field of political rights. They can be divided into the following groups:

(a) Countries where women have in law equal political rights with men, subject to the fulfilment of certain educational or property qualifications not required of men. In this group, there are four countries:

Guatemala: Women must be literate. Voting is compulsory and secret for literate men, optional and secret for women who have the required qualifications and optional and public for illiterate men.

Portugal: Women are subject to higher educational requirements or when fulfilling the same tax qualifications as those prescribed for men must be heads of families in order to have the right to vote.

El Salvador: Women must prove that they are 25 years of age and have passed the third school grade.

Syria: Women must have an elementary school certificate, a condition not required for men.

(b) Countries where women have the right to vote and to be elected in municipal elections only. In the case of some of these countries the right is subject to the fulfilment of certain qualifications not required of men. In this group there are five countries: Bolivia, Greece, 8/ Mexico, Monaco and Peru. 9/

(c) Countries where by law women are not permitted to vote or to hold elective office. In this group, there are twelve countries: 10/ Colombia, Costa Rica, Egypt,

---

2/ Rule 1 of "Rules for the calling of international conferences of States". General Assembly resolution 366 (IV).

3/ Official Records of the Second Session of the General Assembly Resolutions, 16 September–29 November 1947 (document A/519), page 24.

4/ Economic and Social Council Official Records: Fourth Year, Ninth Session, 5 July–15 August 1949 resolutions (document E/1553) page 63.

5/ Resolution 283 (X) (document E/1624) of the Economic and Social Council.

6/ Document E/1585, paragraph 17.

7/ Document E/1585, paragraph 19.

8/ Until 1953, women are subject to higher age requirements: 25 years for women as against 21 years for men.

9/ Women are subject to higher age requirements: 21 years for women against 18 years for men.

10/ No elections are held in the following three countries: Ethiopia, Saudi Arabia and Yemen.

Haiti, Honduras, Iran, Iraq, Jordan, Lebanon, Liechtenstein, Nicaragua, and Switzerland.

12. In two countries, Afghanistan and Paraguay, women have, in fact, never voted or been elected to public office although there are no laws denying such rights to women.

13. Five of these countries are non-Member States: Jordan, Liechtenstein, Monaco, Portugal and Switzerland.

D. The Inter-American Convention on the Granting of Political Rights to Women

14. Eleven of the countries where women's political rights are restricted—Bolivia, Colombia, Costa Rica, El Salvador, Guatemala, Haiti, Honduras, Mexico, Nicaragua, Paraguay and Peru—are members of the Organization of American States, an intergovernmental organization, under whose auspices the Convention which was signed at Bogota in May 1948 and which is referred to in the resolution quoted in paragraph 1 above (the only existing intergovernmental convention of this kind) was drawn up.

15. Article 1 of this Convention reads as follows: 11/

"The High Contracting Parties agree that the right to vote and to be elected shall not be denied or abridged by reason of sex."

16. The Convention was signed by the following countries: Argentina, Brazil, Chile, Colombia, Costa Rica, Cuba, Dominican Republic, Ecuador, Guatemala, Panama, Peru, United States of America, Uruguay and Venezuela.

17. As of 15 January 1950, the Convention has been ratified by the following three countries: Cuba, Ecuador and Dominican Republic.

18. As will be noticed, only four of the countries that have signed the Convention have not as yet given full political rights to women, namely Colombia, Costa Rica, Guatemala and Peru, of which Guatemala already recognizes the principle of political rights for women. 12/

19. Since the signing of the Convention, one member of the Organization of American States, Chile, has given political rights to women. 13/ This country, however, has not as yet ratified the Convention.

E. Resolution 56 (I) of the General Assembly on Political Rights of Women

20. The concern of the United Nations in the field of political rights of women has been repeatedly expressed by the Economic and Social Council and by the General Assembly, the most important relevant occasion being that of the unanimous adoption by the General Assembly on 11 December 1946 of the following resolution: 14/

"The General Assembly

"Whereas

"In the Preamble of the Charter the peoples of the United Nations have reaffirmed faith in the equal rights of men and women, and in Article I it is stated that the purposes of the United Nations are, among others, to achieve international cooperation in promoting and encouraging respect for human rights and for fundamental freedoms for all without distinction as to sex, and to be a centre for harmonizing the actions of nations in the attainment of these common ends,

"Whereas

"Certain Member States have not yet granted to women political rights equal to those granted to men,

"Therefore:

"(a) Recommends that all Member States, which have not already done so, adopt measures necessary to fulfil the purposes and aims of the Charter in this respect by granting to women the same political rights as to men;

"(b) Invites the Secretary-General to communicate this recommendation to the Governments of all Member States."

F. The International Bill of Human Rights

21. The members of the Commission on the Status of Women are aware that the Commission on Human Rights is at present engaged in the preparation of an International Bill of Human Rights, the first part of which, the Universal Declaration of Human Rights, was adopted by the General Assembly on 10 December 1948, with 48 votes for, 0 against and 8 abstentions.

22. Article 21 of the Universal Declaration reads as follows:

"1. Everyone has the right to take part in the government of his country, directly or through freely chosen representatives;

"2. Everyone has the right of equal access to public service in his country;

"3. The will of the people shall be the basis of the authority of government; this will shall be expressed in periodic and genuine elections which shall be by universal and equal suffrage and shall be held by secret vote or by equivalent free voting procedures".

11/ The complete text of the Convention is given in the Annex to the present report.
12/ See document A/1163, page 27.
13/ See document A/1163, page 30.
14/ Resolution 56(I). See Resolutions adopted by the General Assembly during 2nd Part of its 1st Session, page 90.

23. The second part of the International Bill of Human Rights will be the International Covenant of Human Rights. This Covenant will be drafted in the form of a treaty and will be legally binding upon those Member States which become parties to it.

24. No article of the draft Covenant as tentatively agreed upon by the Commission on Human Rights at its Fifth Session deals with political rights as defined in Article 21 of the Universal Declaration of Human Rights. 15/

25. During the various stages of the drafting of the Covenant, proposals have been advanced to the effect that an article should be included in it providing for the right to participate in the government of one's country, the most recent one being the following article proposed at the fifth session of the Commission on Human Rights by the representative of the Government of the USSR: 16/

"Every citizen, irrespective of race, colour, nationality, social position, property status, social origin, language, religion or sex shall be guaranteed by the State an opportunity to take part in the government of the State, to elect and be elected to all organs of authority on the basis of universal, equal and direct suffrage with secret ballot, and to occupy any State or public office. Property, educational or other qualifications restricting the participation of citizens in voting at elections to representative organs shall be abolished".

26. Upon the request of the Commission on Human Rights, the Secretary-General invited Member Governments to comment on, *inter alia*, the Draft International Covenant on Human Rights, and on all proposals for new articles on economic and social rights as given in the Report of the fifth session of the Commission on Human Rights.

27. As of 10 April 1950, eleven Governments have transmitted their comments, and these are set out in documents E/CN.4/353 and addenda 1-10.

28. As stated above, the right of participation in the government of one's country is not included in the present text of the draft Covenant. Article 20 (1) of the draft Covenant provides, however, that all are equal before the law and shall be accorded equal protection of the law. This article, if adopted, might affect the status of women with regard also to political rights in such States as will become parties to the Covenant.

G. Conclusions

29. The conclusions to be drawn from the information given above are the following:

(a) The convention may, if adopted, serve a dual purpose:

    i. it may enfranchise women not yet enfranchised, and

    ii. it may prevent the disenfranchisement of women already enfranchised;

(b) Technically there should be no unsurmountable difficulties involved in drawing up a convention;

(c) There are twenty-three countries which have not as yet given full political rights to women, eighteen of which are Members of the United Nations;

(d) Eleven of these 18 Member States are also members of the Organization of American States under whose auspices the regional convention on the granting of political rights to women was drawn up: this convention has been signed by three of these Members but ratified by none of them;

(e) The General Assembly has already adopted the Universal Declaration of Human Rights, according to which everyone has the right to take part in the government of his country, directly or through freely chosen representatives, without distinction of any kind, which includes distinction as to sex;

(f) The draft International Covenant on Human Rights provides that all are equal before the law and shall be accorded equal protection of the law. The right to participate in the government of one's country is not, however, specifically included in the draft Covenant, although its inclusion therein has been suggested.

Annex

Inter-American Convention on the Granting of Political Rights to Women, Signed 2 May 1948

The Governments represented at the Ninth International Conference of American States,

CONSIDERING: That the majority of the American Republics, inspired by lofty principles of justice, have granted political rights to women;

That it has been a constant aspiration of the American community of nations to equalize the status of men and women in the enjoyment and exercise of political rights;

That Resolution XX of the Eighth International Conference of American States expressly declares:

"That women have the right to political treatment on the basis of equality with men";

That long before the women of America demanded their rights they were able to carry out nobly all their responsibilities side by side with men;

15/ Report of the fifth session of the Commission on Human Rights, document E/1371, Annex I.

16/ Report of the fifth session of the Commission on Human Rights, document E/1371, Annex I, page 29.

That the principle of equality of human rights for men and women is contained in the Charter of the United Nations,

HAVE RESOLVED:

To authorize their respective Representatives, whose Full Powers have been found to be in good and due form, to sign the following articles:

Article 1. The High Contracting Parties agree that the right to vote and to be elected to national office shall not be denied or abridged by reason of sex.

Article 2. The present Convention shall be open for signature by the American States and shall be ratified in accordance with their respective constitutional procedures. The original instrument, the English, French, Portuguese and Spanish texts of which are equally authentic, shall be deposited with the General Secretariat of the Organization of American States, which shall transmit certified copies to the Governments for the purpose of ratification. The instruments of ratification shall be deposited with the General Secretariat of the Organization of American States, which shall notify the signatory Governments of the said deposit. Such notification shall serve as an exchange of ratification.

Document 22

Report of the Secretary-General to the CSW on the United Nations Educational, Scientific and Cultural Organization (UNESCO) study of educational opportunities for women

E/CN.6/146, 9 May 1950

1. The Economic and Social Council at its ninth session passed a resolution (242 B (IX)) which *inter alia* decided that the study of the legal position should be completed by an investigation into the actual conditions in the field of women's education, and suggested that the investigation should aim at ascertaining not only the existence of discrimination but also the causes of such discrimination.

2. The Secretary-General was requested to collaborate with the United Nations Educational, Scientific and Cultural Organization in planning and carrying out a study along these lines in cooperation with Governments, and to report to the fourth session of the Commission on the Status of Women.

3. Pursuant to this resolution, UNESCO undertook to prepare the documentation on this subject which the Secretary-General herewith has the honour to present to the Commission.

Educational opportunities for women

A. *Sources of the present document*

The Universal Declaration of Human Rights proclaimed equality of rights without distinction of sex and the right of everyone to education, to participate in the cultural life of the community, to enjoy the arts and to share in scientific advancement and its benefits (Articles 26 and 27).

The United Nations sent their Member States a questionnaire (E/CN.6/W.1) *inter alia* concerning opportunities for women to obtain education and practice professions and, in January 1949, published the results of this enquiry in respect of the thirty-two countries which sent replies (document E/CN.6/78, Corr.1 and Add.1).

At its ninth session, the Economic and Social Council recommended a complementary inquiry (resolution 242 B (IX)) to show how far the conditions for women's education were actually realized. This inquiry was to be completed by a study of the nature and causes of the obstacles hindering full equality of educational opportunities for women.

The United Nations Educational, Scientific and Cultural Organization, whose General Conference had considered the question of women's education at each of its annual sessions, offered to collaborate with the Commission on the Status of Women in the following tasks:

(1) Communication to the Economic and Social Council of the statistics furnished by UNESCO's member States in reply to the Form (Unesco/Educ/67) prepared by the secretariat on educational organization and statistics;

(2) Study of the obstacles in the way of educational equality between the sexes.

The statistics in the annexed table, derived mainly from official sources and partly from private sources, relate to the years between 1938 and 1947. They give a provisional estimate of the educational situation throughout the world, pending the Secretariat's publication of the whole of the replies by Governments to the questionnaire sent out to the seventy States early in January 1950. 1/

1/ By 1 May 1950, only the Union of South Africa and France had sent replies.

It has not been possible to secure figures for the comparative school attendance of boys and girls in the USSR.

Non-statistical information was supplied by direct consultation with non-governmental and intergovernmental organizations and by the Committee of Experts which met at UNESCO House from 5 to 7 December 1949 to examine the obstacles to equality of educational opportunities. This Committee included representatives of eighteen international non-governmental organizations (women's associations and associations of educators and social workers) as well as representatives of the Inter-American Commission of Women and the Moslem-Arab League. It had instructions to draw up a general report on the basis of the replies received from the participating organizations to a questionnaire framed by the secretariat (Ed /Conf.8/3 and Ed/Conf.8/4).

The purpose of the present document is to present to the fourth session of the Commission on the Status of Women the statistics so far collected and the results of consultation with competent international organizations.

B. Statistical comments

1. Fundamental education and illiteracy

From two different data it is possible to estimate the respective position of boys and girls as regards fundamental education. These are:

(a) *The percentage of illiteracy among men and women.* There are no later data about illiteracy than those furnished by the national censuses of the different countries. Some of this information goes some way back and calls for certain preliminary observations. It will need correcting as time goes on and we learn the results of literacy campaigns. Secondly, some countries have made education compulsory since the date of their last census, and illiteracy must have been very substantially reduced, particularly among children of school age.

In the light of these remarks, it will be found that, except for Canada, Finland, Sweden and the United States, the percentage of illiterates is everywhere higher among females than among males, whether the law imposes compulsory education or not.

(b) *Registrations, divided into sexes, in primary schools* in the following countries: Albania, Algeria, Argentina, Belgium, Brazil, Bulgaria, Canada, Ceylon, Chile, Colombia, Czechoslovakia, Dominican Republic, Ecuador, Egypt, Finland, France, Gold Coast, Greece, Guatemala, Hong Kong, India, Iraq, Ireland, Japan, Lebanon, Luxembourg, Madagascar, Mexico, Netherlands, New Zealand, Panama, Peru, Poland, Portugal, Salvador, Singapore, Spain, Sweden, Switzerland, Syria, Turkey, United Kingdom and the United States of America.

Percentage of male and female registrations in primary schools
(in relation to the general population, per thousand inhabitants)

A. *Countries in which the percentage of male registrations is at least double that of female:*

Country	Per 1,000 boys	Per 1,000 girls
Albania	34	17
Algeria	21	7
Gold Coast	39	11
India	27	10
Iraq	23	8
Syria	33	14

B. *Countries where the difference in percentage is more than 10 in favour of boys:*

Country	Per 1,000 boys	Per 1,000 girls
Ceylon	87	66
Peru	62	38
Portugal	42	31
Singapore	43	25
Turkey	45	26

C. *Countries in which the percentage difference in favour of boys is less than 10:*

Country	Per 1,000 boys	Per 1,000 girls
Belgium	58	57
Brazil	37	35
Chile	62	57
Colombia	36	35
Dominican Republic	28	27
Ecuador	48	41
Egypt	30	24
Finland	59	56
France	62	53
Guatemala	30	22
Luxembourg	52	49
Netherlands	68	65
New Zealand	58	53
Panama	66	62
Poland	71	67
Switzerland	48	47
United Kingdom	39	37
United States	70	66

D. *Countries in which the percentage of female registrations exceeds that of males:*

Country	Per 1,000 boys	Per 1,000 girls
Canada	82	85
Ireland	63	64
Spain	48	49

The total proportion of male and female registrations in primary schools in the forty-two countries for which there are figures for each sex, differs appreciably from the almost equal ratio of boys and girls of school age, viz. 809 girls to 1,000 boys. It will be noticed that many countries are not mentioned in this study, either because they have not yet furnished figures or because their data do not distinguish between girls and boys.

2. *Secondary education*

Our information, with mention of the number of boys and girls, relates to the secondary schools of thirty-six countries: Albania, Algeria, Argentina, Belgium, Brazil, Bulgaria, Canada, Chile, Colombia, Czechoslovakia, Dominican Republic, Egypt, Finland, France, Gold Coast, Greece, India, Iraq, Ireland, Italy, Japan, Luxembourg, New Zealand, Norway, Panama, Peru, Poland, Portugal, Singapore, Spain, Sweden, Switzerland, Syria, Turkey, United Kingdom and United States of America.

Countries in which boy pupils outnumber girl pupils by at least 50 per cent

Country	Proportion of total population per thousand inhabitants Boys	Girls
Algeria	1.1	0.5
Argentina	2.6	1.1
Egypt	3	0.5
Gold Coast	0.9	0.1
Greece	8	4
India	6	2
Iraq	4	0.8
Peru	3	1
Singapore	6	1
Spain	0.45	0.22
Syria	3	1
Turkey	2	1

The other countries, although the difference is smaller, have fewer girls than boys in their secondary schools, except Denmark, Finland, New Zealand and Panama, where girl pupils form the majority.

The total ratio of girls to boys in the secondary schools is 775 to 1,000.

3. *Technical studies*

The annexed table shows that there is little information about the technical training of girls and boys. The data refer to the following countries: Argentina, Australia, Belgium, Bulgaria, Ceylon, Colombia, Czechoslovakia, Denmark, Dominican Republic, Egypt, France, Greece, India, Iraq, Italy, Japan, Lebanon, Luxembourg, Madagascar, Netherlands, Peru, Portugal, Spain, Turkey, United Kingdom, United States of America.

It should be mentioned that, although many countries provide technical education for girls, they classify as "technical" schools both those which prepare pupils for a trade or profession outside the family, and those which train only for domestic and household occupations.

Countries in which technical schools are attended by more girls than boys

Country	Boys	Girls
Argentina	3.4	5.8
Belgium	0.4	0.6
Colombia	0.8	1.1
Panama	4	7
Peru	0.7	0.7

Countries where the ratio of girls to boys in the technical schools is lowest

India	1	0.1
Iraq	0.3	0.09
Madagascar	0.7	0.1
Spain	4	0.9
Turkey	2	0.5

The total ratio of girls to boys in the technical schools is 508 to 1,000.

4. *University studies*

The university figures show matriculations for the following countries: Algeria, Australia, Belgium, Brazil, Bulgaria, Canada, Chile, Colombia, Czechoslovakia, Denmark, Dominican Republic, Ecuador, Egypt, Finland, France, Greece, Hong Kong, India, Iraq, Japan, Lebanon, Netherlands, New Zealand, Norway, Panama, Peru, Poland, Portugal, Singapore, Spain, Sweden, Switzerland, Turkey, United Kingdom, United States of America.

The United States universities, which in this table show seven male to five female students, did not maintain this sex ratio in 1948. Owing to the return of servicemen to their studies, we find by then 1,712,283 male to 695,966 female students. 2/ Whether this last figure or the figure for 1945/46 is counted in the general ratio, the

2/ Source: U.S. Office of Information, Fall Enrollment in Higher Educational Institutions, 1948.

total ratio of male to female students shows a considerable change (494 females to 1,000 males according to the figures given in the table, and 343 females to 1,000 males according to the 1948 figures).

Leaving out the United States, where owing to the Second World War the number of students is affected by the variations just mentioned, the ratio of female to male students is 176 to 1,000. Seeing that Canada, France, Finland and the United Kingdom have approximately two male students to every female student, this shows what a very small proportion of women attend universities in most of the countries considered.

It should be added, however, that women university students are on the increase and this increase is more rapid in countries that have organized or reorganized their educational system during the last forty years, whether as the result of a complete change in their political structure or because they have acquired national independence.

Approximate ratio of girls and boys attending educational establishments of all kinds

(according to estimates given in the annexed table and account being taken of the fact that the figures do not all refer to the same year and that the war and post-war years have affected the ratio)

	Girls per 1,000 boys
Primary schools	809
Secondary schools	75
Technical institutions	506
Universities (including the United States of America)	494
Universities (excluding the United States ofAmerica)	176

It should be noted that the information is hardly comparable from country to country because primary, technical and higher education varies considerably from country to country. Moreover the point here in question is only the proportion of female to male students.

C. *Limitations imposed on women's education in various countries*

The information, given in the statistical tables above, on the quantitative aspect of the inequality of educational opportunities for women, is supplemented by information on the scope and causes of such inequality, supplied by the answers of non-governmental associations of women educators and social workers to the questionnaire that was sent out in preparation for the Meeting of Experts. Here a summary of the answers is given, listed by countries that replied.

The questionnaire dealt mainly with the following two points:

1. Where in fact is there educational inequality between men and women (schools, attendance, curriculum)?

2. To what causes can such inequality be attributed?

Argentina

1. Technical schools, other than those training for women's occupations and family duties, are not attended by women.

In the universities, few women attend the faculties of law, medicine and sciences.

2. The tardy admission of women to participation in the political life of the country (1947), and the force of tradition, which outside the home left but a small number of professions open to women (education, business, art), are responsible for these conditions.

Australia

1. The only point on which there is legal inequality is the disability of married women to engage in the teaching profession.

Belgium

1. In technical education, certain special schools do not admit girls, and ordinary technical schools have different curricula for boys and girls.

2. Family life continues to be the main preoccupation of the Belgian woman. The custom of employing men in preference to women is firmly established and influences the studies pursued by women. The overpopulation of the country and the threat of unemployment contribute to the maintenance of this custom.

Brazil

1. The number of women attending universities is limited.

2. The situation is accounted for by the number of early marriages, which concentrate the activities of the young woman on the home.

Burma

1. After puberty, girls are not admitted to the monastic schools in underdeveloped regions, and there are no other schools available. There are no boarding facilities for girls.

2. Religious customs, complete economic disorganization due to the war, and the desire to ensure that boys' needs are met first, since they will be called upon to contribute to the support of the family, are responsible for these unfavourable conditions of women's education in Burma.

Canada

1. Catholic theological schools and colleges, and professional mining schools in Ontario are closed to women.

2. The traditions of the Catholic Church and legislation excluding women from work in the mines are the causes of these two restrictions. The social customs of the Province of Quebec give pride of place to woman's activities in the home, which accounts for the fact that in this province women avail themselves less of educational facilities than they do elsewhere.

Ceylon

1. In certain communities, few girls go to school and they leave at the age of thirteen. Girls do not take advantage of adult education (evening classes).

2. Overpopulation and poverty result in the education of boys—who later on will have to support a family—being regarded as more important than that of the girls. Owing to the Moslem and Hindu custom of early marriage, studies are soon given up. Local custom, which in practice prohibits girls from going out after dusk, prevents them from attending evening classes.

The budget for women's education is too small and accounts for the shortage of teachers and the complete lack of boarding facilities for girls in rural districts.

Chile

1. Technical schools that admit girls give instruction only in dressmaking, laundering, hairdressing, drawing and housekeeping.

2. Custom results in a marked preference being given to preparation for domestic occupations.

Colombia

1. Girls leave secondary schools earlier than boys. The number of State schools for girls is small, particularly in technical education.

2. The prevailing prejudice that in employment men are superior to women means that the latter are given only unimportant jobs that require no training. Tradition restricts the activities of girls and women to the home.

Cuba

1. The curricula of technical colleges for women are restricted to instruction for professions that are followed only by women; other technical schools are attended by only a small number of women.

Denmark

1. No school in Denmark is closed to women.

2. The small number of female students is accounted for by the practical difficulties encountered by married female students and the tendency of parents to give priority to the university education of their sons.

Ecuador

1. Girls have only limited opportunities for technical training.

2. Tradition, which in numerous professions does not favour women, is responsible for the small number of women attending universities. Until recently married women were not allowed to be teachers.

Egypt

1. Military schools, the Mohammedan University "Al Azhar" and other religious colleges do not admit women.

The number of girls attending schools is smaller than that of boys; girls attend for shorter periods; their attendance is less strictly supervised.

2. Tradition, which for a long time kept girls and women at home, and early marriages are in part responsible for the backwardness of women's education.

The general standard of living is low, and fees for secondary schools or universities cannot be met. If there is any money that might be expended on a daughter, it is set aside for her dowry.

School equipment is still inadequate, in particular in girls' schools.

Finland

The only limitation imposed on women's education is the Mining School, to which they are not admitted, as attendance at the School involves work underground, prohibited for women by law.

France

1. Catholic theological colleges and faculties, military academies and civil and mining engineering schools are closed to women.

Certain professional schools that in theory are open to women are attended by only very few: agricultural engineering, veterinary and industrial institutes.

2. Other limitations, affecting above all professional education, are due to public opinion, and to the difficulties involved in exercising a profession and at the same time keeping house, in a country where amenities in the home leave much to be desired and the principle of women working half-time has not yet been admitted.

Greece

1. Fewer girls than boys attend school and the former finish their schooling earlier.

2. Traditionally the education of boys is regarded as more important, as the part they will be called upon

to play in civic and economic life is considered superior to that of women.

The dire poverty found in rural districts accounts for the fact that girls have frequently to help their mothers in the house or in the fields, or are sent at an early age to work as domestic servants in the towns.

Damage caused by the war has considerably worsened the conditions under which girls' schools have to work.

Honduras

1. Theoretically no limitations are imposed on the education of women.

2. The progress of women's education has been slow, for by tradition the home is the woman's sphere.

Hungary

De jure and *de facto*, educational opportunities for men and women are equal.

India

1. Girls leave school earlier than boys—either a law making school attendance compulsory does not yet exist, or it does not apply equally to the two sexes, or, if school attendance is compulsory, the law is not strictly enforced as far as girls are concerned.

Science and mathematics do not figure on the curricula of girls' schools.

2. Purdah imposes the seclusion of the daughters of orthodox Muslim families. The customary early marriage brings school attendance by girls to a close. There is a prejudice against girls taking up work.

Parents see to the education of their sons, who will have to support a family later on, and set aside for the dowry any money that is available for the daughters.

Family resources are generally insufficient to ensure the education of the daughters and at the same time to provide for all the other members for whom the head of the family is responsible—young children, old men and widows. Means at present available in India preclude the speedy establishment and equipment of schools necessary for ensuring the widespread education of women.

Iraq

1. School attendance is not compulsory and, as yet, the number of girls going to school is very small.

The curricula of boys' and girls' schools differ greatly. In the latter, stress is laid above all on domestic training.

2. The custom of secluding the women still obtains or at any rate influences manners and education.

In the family the need for girls' schools is not felt.

Iceland

1. The only inequality noted is that the number of young men pursuing academic studies exceeds that of young women.

2. The cause of this difference is to be found in the greater facility with which young men are able to find work in the summer which will pay for their studies during the winter.

Italy

1. The number of boys attending school is greater than that of girls. There are few vocational schools for girls.

2. The Latin tradition is still strong, the man is the head of the family and has to support it—the woman's foremost duty is to keep house.

Due to overpopulation and disturbed economic conditions, men are liable to be unemployed and the employment of women, even if they are professionally trained, is not encouraged.

Japan

1. Vocational schools for girls are few in number and provide instruction only for specifically feminine occupations. The number of women entering universities is very small and is restricted to those who have attained the requisite level of knowledge.

2. The neglect of women's education is due to the old tradition of sacrificing a woman's life in the interest of the family, to present economic difficulties and to destruction caused by the war.

Luxembourg

Trade schools are reserved for boys; girls' technical schools train nurses and housekeepers.

Netherlands

1. There are two legal restrictions: women are not admitted to the tax inspectors' school and the degree of mining engineer may not be conferred on them. A small number of women attend the universities.

2. The influence of family traditions, the density of the population and the fact that certain careers are closed to married women account for the general conditions of women's education in the Netherlands.

New Zealand

There are no restrictions of educational opportunity for women.

Difference in interests is the only factor determining the choice of professional training.

Norway

The only distinction is that the timetable for girls is adapted to provide for needlework and housekeeping (compulsory subjects for girls, optional for boys), the time being subtracted from that normally devoted to some other subject, this subject being a different one each year.

Sweden

1. The only educational establishments not open to women are military academies.

2. Although the Government encourages women to work in industry and encourages employers to engage them, the traditional tendency of employing men still persists.

Switzerland

1. Switzerland places no restrictions on the education of girls, but endeavours to provide them with a special type of education, the principal aim of which is the maintenance of family life. The special timetables for girls include such subjects as practical housekeeping; the time set aside for science is restricted. Courses for young women having left school also aim at developing domestic science.

2. The status of citizen being enjoyed only by men, woman's lack of interest in public life, the high standard of living and the large population are factors that restrict the professional education of women for a specific task.

Turkey

1. Girls leave schools at an early age. Girls' vocational schools dispense training for strictly feminine occupations: dressmaking, fine sewing, dress-designing, hairdressing, child-rearing and housekeeping.

2. Religion and the custom of early marriage account for these conditions. Furthermore, young girls help their mothers in the home or, by going to work, make a contribution to the family budget.

United Kingdom

1. Only military colleges do not admit women; a quota of women doctors are admissible to the hospital schools in London.

Education in science is frequently less highly developed in girls' schools than in boys' schools.

2. What remains of the traditional hostility to women's education is gradually disappearing.

United States of America

1. Some privates academic institutions (such as Princeton University) are exclusively reserved for men.

The admission quotas to medical examinations are unfavourable to women. Establishments for instruction in domestic economy (secondary and higher degree) are reserved for girls.

In general, women give up their academic studies sooner than men.

2. Social tradition and economic factors limit the participation of women in higher education. Parents give priority to the education of their sons. Parents and daughters hesitate before deciding in favour of continued study, for marriage remains the girl's principal interest and, with the high standard of living, the house can be kept on only the husband's salary.

From these indications the following conclusions can be drawn as to the extent of *de facto* inequality between male and female education.

1. *Types of schools*

(a) A certain number of schools remain officially closed to women: schools preparing for a career in the armed forces on land, on the sea or in the air; police schools (except in so far as training is given for women's posts presenting a purely administrative or social character); theological colleges and institutes (except faculties of Protestant theology); schools and institutes preparing for the profession of magistrate or notary in certain countries that have not yet granted women their full civil, juridical and political rights.

(b) Though legally open to girls, since no restriction has ever been officially pronounced, certain schools are attended by girls only as an exception, owing to the persistence of tradition: schools preparing for a career in the mines, or for active employment in transport by sea, road or rail, or in forest administration, etc.

(c) Technical schools open to women or reserved for women are not numerous; in general they prepare girls for occupations that are regarded as being particularly suitable to the feminine temperament.

2. *General curricula for girls*

Though schools dispensing a general education at the primary and secondary levels are open to girls in nearly all the countries that have been considered, it must be pointed out that, in countries where co-education is not the rule, the curricula and timetables are not always the same for boys and girls.

The following points are to be noted:

(a) Restricted science curriculum for girls.

(b) Additional subjects for girls: needlework, housekeeping, child-rearing.

(c) A reduced number of hours for science classes, the time saved being allotted to subjects that are assumed to be specifically feminine.

3. Examinations

In countries where girls are given quite a different education from boys, different examinations are set, the examinations for girls being generally of smaller scope. Yet even in countries that have adopted the principle of educational equality, it sometimes still happens that candidates are marked differently according to whether they are boys and girls.

Such differences, however, are disappearing—there is a strong tendency to combine examinations for boys and girls, and to assess candidates from the sole point of view of intellectual merit.

4. School attendance

It is smaller in the case of girls as they drop their education earlier and interrupt their education more frequently.

D. Study of obstacles to equality of educational opportunities for women

Before putting to use the variety of information here outlined, the Committee of Experts convened by UNESCO had one preliminary observation to make: if women do not possess the same educational facilities as men, it is not for any psychological or pedagogic reason that could justify the existing qualitative and quantitative difference between the opportunities offered to boys and to girls.

The only established differences in intellectual aptitudes are differences between individuals and not differences as between the sexes.

The factors that have delayed or prevented the educational advancement of women, already referred to in the replies to the questionnaire preceding the meeting of experts, were methodically listed, after discussion, in the final report of the Committee, whose main conclusions are here recapitulated.

1. Social factors

Persistence of the traditional view of the respective social roles of man and woman

This view has assigned to men a sphere of activity outside the family circle, while attributing to women the whole responsibility for the home.

In spite of substantial changes in living conditions, which for the most part no longer call for exclusive care of the home, the constant protection of children against physical dangers or the production of all consumption goods inside the home, it is still held that education should enable a boy to perform his part as citizen and productive member of society, while giving girls only such knowledge as is necessary for the material and moral management of the family.

For many centuries this essential knowledge was taught practically by the mother to her daughters. The need for developing a woman's intellectual gifts appeared, with very few exceptions, much later, and in no society has it prevailed altogether over the original conception of female education.

Persistence of the idea that marriage, as the primary purpose of a woman's life, brings her education to an end.

A woman's education is supposed to end with marriage and motherhood. Both impose upon her definite duties and in most cases interrupt all intellectual study. Since marriage usually occurs between the ages of 14 and 25, according to the country or community, it marks the end of a girl's schooling. For boys, on the other hand, it carries the obligation of more intensive professional training for the responsibilities of maintaining a family.

Belief that continued intellectual development is an obstacle to the natural goal of marriage.

In a modern society, in which women are offered comparatively large educational possibilities, parents do not want their daughters to continue their studies beyond the elementary stage, lest a girl's interest in these studies and the concentration they call for should distract her attention from her main purpose, which is marriage. Any attempt to attain a degree of knowledge which does not exclusively serve the needs of the home is considered a dangerous idiosyncrasy. It invites ridicule and censure, arouses suspicion and may ruin a young girl's normal hope of founding a family.

In this way tradition tends to limit girls' education.

Persistence of habits of life based upon the idea of protecting women.

(a) The idea of the physical weakness of women is still at the root of certain restrictions upon equality of educational opportunities for the two sexes. Study is thought to be more tiring for girls than for boys, and it is considered that the former should have a lighter syllabus. Hence, of course, a difficulty is obtaining access to higher studies common to men and women. This is a problem linked with access to the professions, where the same arguments are often used.

(b) Another result of this notion of feminine frailty is that which, in an age when physical safety in peace time is practically assured, fosters the fear of allowing girls to attend schools situated far away from their homes.

(c) In some parts of the world, it is still the custom to seclude girls and, even where these habits have officially disappeared, tradition in Eastern countries has failed to keep pace with changes in the law.

These conceptions of the personality and role of women explain the partial or total resistance to efforts made to enable everyone without distinction of sex to develop their potential gifts by education. The results of this resistance have been:

(i) Legislation has been mainly concerned with the education of boys;

(ii) The establishment of girls' schools has lagged behind;

(iii) There is less close supervision over girls' attendance at school;

(iv) Schools and syllabuses are directed towards different aims;

(v) Resistance by the legislator and by public opinion to the abandonment of these traditional and almost universal views of the social role of man and woman, even when such views have no longer any foundation in contemporary social facts;

(vi) Acceptance of these views by most women, an acceptance which prevents them from making the most of the educational facilities now offered them.

All these social conceptions and practices are factors from which it is exceedingly difficult to escape and which weigh upon both sexes even when the laws have granted women civil equality, the vote and theoretically equal educational opportunities.

2. *Economic factors*

If economic conditions in the different countries have helped to restrict the educational opportunities of women, it is because they are strongly influenced by the social factors mentioned above.

Financial considerations lead families to subordinate the education of girls to other requirements:

(a) A young girl of school age is used to help or replace her mother at home;

(b) Girls' schooling is prematurely suspended—without regard for their intellectual gifts—for the sake of the education and professional training of boys;

(c) A young girl is taken away from school and put into shop or factory where her wages help in industrialized countries to swell the family income;

(d) Girls help in producing consumer goods in non-industrialized countries;

(e) The family resources available for girls are used to build up her dowry or trousseau instead of for educational purposes.

The economic conditions of the country, if these are bad, also react unfavourably upon female education;

(a) Governments influenced by tradition tend to see in women's education (especially professional training) an unprofitable investment, since a woman who is trained for a profession nearly always leaves it on getting married;

(b) Employers, who prefer male labour because it is supposed to be more stable and regular than female labour, do not give to qualified women the posts to which they are entitled and thus discourage women's ambition to enter the professions and their training for them;

(c) Public opinion in thickly-populated countries, where jobs are keenly competed for, resents the competition of qualified women and, *a priori*, any new development in professional female education.

Thus, for the same reasons, both families and Governments are primarily concerned to develop in boys all those qualities which will allow them to work for the economic enrichment of the family and the country. They first improve the conditions of boys' education and are slow to establish the same conditions for girls.

3. *Obstacles due to the organization of family life*

While long-standing tradition, and economic factors working concurrently with them, react upon the conditions governing women's access to education by limiting their period of schooling, it is also certain that the organization of family life, for which in all communities the woman is responsible, constitutes an obstacle to the educational progress of adult women.

(a) *Material obstacles*

The domestic work of women has to provide all the family with the necessary conditions of feeding, lodging and clothing, and all this, as a rule, takes a lot of time. In economically less developed societies, it is the woman's industry which created these conditions and, however elementary they may be, they do not leave time over for other occupations, especially for cultivation of the mind.

In more developed societies, the requirements of civilization have created fresh needs as production of consumer-goods outside the family has released women from some of their duties. These have been replaced by fresh burdens.

The idea of rationalizing domestic work is of very recent date and has only progressed to the extent that paid work for women outside the home is permitted. This rationalization itself encounters resistance, even from women, who still cling to their unique housekeeping function.

Costly labour-saving devices remain available for the well-to-do, and in most countries no serious effort has been made to organize domestic work on a communal basis.

(b) Obstacles due to lack of collective social services

Accidental complications in family life may compel women to meet new emergencies; care of sick and of aged parents prevents them from performing other duties.

This is rightly regarded as one of the main reasons for absenteeism among women in all occupations. They have to sacrifice their professional duty to family obligations. These almost unpredictable obligations also underlie the intellectual apathy of women in all matters that do not affect the family circle. This apathy, like professional absenteeism, has its roots in the lack of collective social services and in the survival of the view of the family as a homogeneous and self-sufficient social unit.

(c) Psychological and social obstacles

Without question, every society rests upon the work of the housewife, and no educational system can contemplate either any change in the natural laws and complementary biological functions of the sexes or the destruction of the natural family fabric.

Nevertheless, two new conceptions of the role of women are becoming more and more important in the modern world: the idea of the individual's inviolable right to choose the education and work by which his potential gifts will best develop and the idea of the importance of women as productive elements in society.

Caught between tradition and the new course of things, woman is not yet able to grasp the full implications of the problem, lacking the precise information to be supplied by psychologists, sociologists and educators.

There is an absence of scientifically proven data as to the length of time for which the mother should exercise direct and continuous influence over the child if it is not to suffer either physical neglect or a feeling of frustration that may have an injurious effect upon its behaviour and moral growth.

Trustworthy information on these essential matters would be of the very greatest service to women and, by releasing mothers from the dilemma of choosing between the family and the profession, would encourage girls to aspire to both study and wedlock.

Nor has any serious attempt been made to diffuse the idea that the responsibilities of the home rest, not upon one person, but upon all its adult members, and neither teaching in the home nor teaching at school has as yet tried to train children and adults alike for these responsibilities.

Lastly, the complete separation between the school and the family, which has led to an exaggeration of the school's importance to males and of the importance of the home to females, is an educational formula which, arbitrary though it is, still obtains, and it competes with the more balanced conception of a full education that aims at developing every individual gift and at abolishing barriers between the school and the family.

Such are the obstacles which appear most often to oppose women's educational opportunities in the majority of countries.

The study of these obstacles needs to be pursued with care and precision, for we are dealing with fundamental problems in human life, with very long-standing traditions as well as with practical difficulties.

Systematic study should be devoted to the obstacles which hamper certain countries where tradition and slow economic development make women's educational opportunities fewer than in countries where much has been done gradually to reduce inequality between the sexes.

Finally, this quest for information should be supplemented by recommendations and methods which will help women, the general public and Governments to establish a trend of opinion and legislation in favour of equal educational opportunities for men and women.

Document 23

Report of the Secretary-General to the CSW on the United Nations Technical Assistance Programme in relation to the status of women

E/CN.6/145, 12 May 1950

I. Introduction

1. The Commission on the Status of Women at its third session, being cognizant of resolutions 198 (III) and 200 (III) of the General Assembly dealing with economic development of underdeveloped countries, Economic and Social Council resolution 180 (VIII) on technical assistance for economic development and the Secretary-General's report on technical assistance activities (document no. E/1174), adopted the following resolution: 1/

1/ Document E/1316, Chapter XII, paragraph 42.

"*The Commission on the Status of Women,*

"*Considering* the need (a) for better technical assistance in the organization of household tasks and (b) for increased professional training to enable women to qualify for promotion to executive posts in commerce, trade, industry, and government,

"*Requests* the Secretary-General to take these needs into account in his proposals and plans for expert and technical assistance, including the provision of necessary funds and for the cooperation of appropriate specialized agencies."

2. Subsequently, the Economic and Social Council, at its ninth session, adopted the following resolution. 2/

"*The Economic and Social Council,*

"*Noting* the request of the Commission on the Status of Women for expert assistance to women in certain fields,

"*Invites* the Commission at its next session to give further consideration to the questions of technical assistance in these fields and to make further proposals on this subject for the consideration of the Secretary-General in formulating further plans for technical assistance."

3. In the course of the discussion in the ninth session of the Council, it was suggested that the Secretary-General be asked to supply the Commission with background information on the subject in order that the Commission would be better able to make specific suggestions.

II. Relevant Actions of the General Assembly and the Economic and Social Council

A. *Technical assistance in the social field*

4. Even before the General Assembly authorized the programme of technical assistance for economic development at its 3rd session, the United Nations Secretariat was engaged in a similar type of activity with reference to social welfare problems, that is, the Advisory Social Welfare Services Programme. This work still continues under General Assembly resolution 58 (I) which was adopted in December 1946. It involves the sending of experts and consultants on social welfare problems to various countries, the granting of fellowships, the provision of pilot projects and training material (demonstration equipment, technical social welfare literature and films), and the organization of seminars. The services are carried out upon the request of governments. Among the topics with regard to which social advisory welfare services may be procured through the United Nations are the following: training of social workers; housing and community development; cooperative organizations; delinquency; problems of family welfare, child welfare, children's day care, welfare of youths and welfare of mothers. 3/

At its fourth regular session the General Assembly voted to place the advisory social welfare programme on a continuing basis within the regular budget of the United Nations. 4/

B. *Current programme of technical assistance for economic development*

5. In August 1948, the Economic and Social Council authorized the Secretary-General to organize teams of experts, upon request, to advise governments in their economic development programmes. 5/ At its third session the General Assembly adopted the resolution under which the present United Nations programme of technical assistance for economic development of underdeveloped countries is carried out. 6/ In that resolution the Assembly decided to appropriate funds necessary to enable the Secretary-General to provide underdeveloped countries, at their request, with services in the form of advisory teams, fellowships, local training, seminars, exchange of information, etc.

6. The Secretary-General submitted to the Economic and Social Council, at its eighth, ninth, and tenth sessions, reports on the measures which had been taken to carry out the programme recommended by the General Assembly. 7/ The report at the ninth session was accompanied by a recommendation that the appropriation for this work in 1950 be increased in order to permit carrying out the programme on a larger scale, and that the work be placed on a continuing basis by making annual provision for it within the regular budget of the United Nations. These measures were recommended by the Council to the General Assembly, which adopted a resolution to that effect at its fourth session. 8/

C. *Expanded programme of technical assistance for economic development*

7. The Economic and Social Council at its eighth session 9/ requested the Secretary-General, in consultation with the Specialized Agencies, to prepare a report for consideration at the ninth session of the Council contain-

2/ Resolution 242 (IX) E.
3/ For recent reports of activities under Resolution 58 (I), see documents E/CN.5/109, E/CN.5/109/Corr.1, E/CN.5/109/Add.1, A/C.3/521, E/CN.5/193, E/CN.5/193/Add.1, E/828, and E/828/Add.1.
4/ GA res. 316 (IV).
5/ Resolution 139 A (VII).
6/ Resolution 200 (III) of 4 December 1948.
7/ Documents E/1174, E/1335, E/1335/Add.1, E/1335/Add.2/Annex, E/1335/Add.3, and E/1576.
8/ General Assembly resolution 305 (IV) "Technical Assistance for Economic Development under General Assembly Resolution 200 (III)."
9/ Resolution 180 (VIII), 4 March 1949.

ing a comprehensive plan for an expanded cooperative programme of technical assistance for economic development, paying due attention to questions of a social nature which directly condition economic development. The report submitted by the Secretary-General in response to this request 10/ contained statements of the objectives and nature of the proposed programme, the forms of technical assistance which might be offered and the fields in which it could be given, and proposed methods of organizing and financing the work. It also contained detailed proposals with regard to specific types of technical assistance to be offered by the United Nations and each specialized agency concerned.

8. At its ninth session, the Council adopted a resolution 11/ concerning the organization of the expanded programme of technical assistance, the administrative machinery for coordination of projects to be undertaken by the United Nations and specialized agencies, the financing of the programme and the guiding principles for carrying it out. At its fourth session the General Assembly unanimously adopted a resolution approving the action of the Council, authorizing the Secretary-General to proceed with the work, and inviting all Governments to make as large contributions as possible to the technical assistance fund. 12/

D. *Other means of promoting economic development*

9. The Council also has under consideration and review other measures for advancing economic development of underdeveloped countries, including the stimulation of the international flow of capital for this purpose and measures relating to the domestic financing of economic development. 13/

10. The General Assembly, at its fourth session, 14/ took note of the arrangements made by the Council for the consideration of such measures, and recommended that the Economic and Social Council, *inter alia*:

"(a) Continue to give urgent attention to the problems of economic development of underdeveloped countries, giving due consideration to questions of a social nature which directly condition economic development;

"(b) Stimulate its commissions and the specialized agencies to give similar urgent attention to these problems..."

III. Basic Principles of the Technical Assistance Programme

11. Special attention is called to the guiding principles for the expanded programme of technical assistance which are set forth in Annex I of Resolution 222 (IX). These principles, for the most part, are the same as those guiding the regular programmes of technical assistance.

(a) *General principles*

Following is the statement of the general principles that will guide the expanded programme of technical assistance for economic development:

The participating organizations should, in extending technical assistance for economic development of underdeveloped countries:

1. Regard it as a primary objective to help those countries to strengthen their national economies through the development of their industries and agriculture, with a view to promoting their economic and political independence in the spirit of the Charter of the United Nations; and to ensure the attainment of higher levels of economic and social welfare for their entire populations;

2. Observe the following general principles laid down in General Assembly resolution 200 (III):

(a) Technical assistance for economic development of underdeveloped countries shall be rendered by the participating organizations only in agreement with the Governments concerned and on the basis of requests received from them;

(b) The kinds of services to be rendered to each country shall be decided by the Government concerned;

(c) The countries desiring assistance should perform, in advance, as much of the work as possible in order to define the nature and scope of the problem involved;

(d) The technical assistance furnished shall:

(i) Not be a means of foreign economic and political interference in the internal affairs of the country concerned and not be accompanied by any considerations of a political nature;

(ii) Be given only to or through Governments;

(iii) Be designed to meet the needs of the country concerned; and

(iv) Be provided as far as possible in the form which that country desires;

3. Avoid distinctions arising from the political structure of the country requesting assistance, or from the race or religion of its population.

(b) Attention is called also to the following paragraph, concerned with the social aspects of technical

10/ Document E/1327/Add.1, "Technical Assistance for Economic Development."

11/ Resolution 222 (IX) A, 15 August 1949.

12/ General Assembly resolution 304 (IV), "Expanded Programme of Technical Assistance for Economic Development of Under-Developed Countries."

13/ See Council resolution 222 (IX) D, 14 August 1949.

14/ General Assembly resolution 306 (IV), "Economic Development of Under-Developed Countries."

assistance, in the section of Annex I entitled "Selection of Projects."

The participating organizations, in deciding on a request for assistance, should be guided solely by the Charter of the United Nations, by the principles of the United Nations programme for technical assistance and by appropriate resolutions of the General Assembly and of the Economic and Social Council. The services envisaged should aim at increased productivity of material and human resources and a wide and equitable distribution of the benefits of such increased productivity, so as to contribute to the realization of higher standards of living for the entire populations. Due attention and respect should be paid to the national sovereignty and national legislation of the underdeveloped countries and to the social conditions which directly affect their economic development. Requests for technical assistance may therefore be approved which will help Governments to take account of the probable consequences of proposed projects for economic development in terms of the welfare of the population as a whole, including the promotion of full employment, and also to take account of those social conditions, customs and values in a given area which would directly influence the kinds of economic development that may be feasible and desirable. Similarly, requests may also be approved for technical assistance to Governments desiring to undertake the specific social improvements that are necessary to permit effective economic development and to mitigate the social problems—particularly problems of dislocation of family and community life—that may arise as a concomitant of economic change. As in any national programme for economic development any increased services undertaken by the Government can be maintained, in the long run, only out of national production, special attention should be given in timing and emphasis to activities tending to bring an early increase in national productivity of material and human resources.

IV. Forms of Technical Assistance

12. The Secretary-General, in his statement of plans for the expanded programme of technical assistance presented to the ninth session of the Economic and Social Council, 15/ pointed out that such assistance might take a wide variety of forms, including advisory missions, comprehensive surveys of natural and human resources, training of personnel, pilot projects and demonstrations of modern techniques, dissemination of technical information and research activities. He also indicated that the facilities already offered by the United Nations and the specialized agencies for assistance to Governments in the formulation of general policies and legislative and technical standards and in publication of technical reports could be expanded, if the requests of Governments made this necessary.

V. Fields of Technical Assistance

13. The proposals of the United Nations and the Specialized Agencies for the expanded programme of technical assistance offer services in a large number of different fields, 16/ it being understood, however, that the assistance rendered must be directly related to economic development. In such broad fields as agriculture, food and nutrition, industry, labour, cooperatives and handicrafts, education, public administration, finance, health and hygiene, social welfare, and housing and community development, the programme is not specifically directed toward the separate problems and needs of either men or women, but is designed to promote the welfare of the total population. There is within the framework of the programme, however, opportunity for underdeveloped countries to request assistance specifically with regard to problems and needs of women when these problems and needs are directly related to the economic development of the countries concerned. Various occasions for such requests may be envisaged. For example:

(a) As the report of the Special Working Party on Technical Assistance for Economic Development at the Fifth Session of the FAO pointed out, "in many cases faulty social customs and the traditional division of duties between men and women put obstacles in the way of agricultural improvement and improvement in condiitions of life, particularly those of women as home-makers. Technical assistance experts must therefore be qualified to formulate recommendations both on the improvements of social customs and on the means of securing such improvement." 17/

(b) The problem of the working conditions of women in industrial and agricultural enterprises, particularly the exploitation of women as a source of cheap labour, has been and is today in many areas a serious obstacle to economic and social progress. The exploitation of women as a source of cheap labour may create a vicious circle by depressing male wages below minimum standards for maintaining families, with the result that, whether they wish it or not, wives and mothers find themselves obliged to work outside the home for meagre wages.

(c) Women's functions of child-bearing and child-raising create special employment problems that require protective measures, as well as special health and welfare problems.

15/ Document E/1327/Add.1, "Technical Assistance for Economic Development," Chapter 4.
16/ Cf. Chapter 3 and Chapters 7-16 of E/1327/Add.1
17/ FAO document C/49/II/TA/5, page 7.

(d) Certain kinds of development projects can most effectively be carried out through advice to women, because of the traditional responsibilities of women in the home. For example, technical assistance concerned with home economics, household techniques, budgeting and family buying, diet, home sanitation, child-rearing practices, and family and household adjustments to new environments and changing economies, can in many areas be most effectively rendered through demonstration projects and extension work among women.

(e) Various education and training projects may particularly concern women, either because the training is for occupations especially associated with women (e.g., nursing) or because the greatest deficiencies and needs lie in the field of training and education of women.

14. The attention of the Commission on the Status of Women is called to the excerpts in the following Annex which have been taken from the proposals of the United Nations and specialized agencies for the expanded programme of technical assistance.

Annex

Excerpts Illustrating Technical Assistance Proposals of the United Nations and Specialized Agencies Explicitly Directed Towards Problems of Women

(A) *United Nations*

"*Problems of women.* In many areas, traditional divisions of duties between men and women, and related differences in status and rights, put obstacles in the way of economic improvement and raising of the standards of living. Expert advice may also be desired to deal with the problems of women who enter an entirely new environment and mode of life, as a result of economic development projects, and who must learn the techniques of managing households in the new environment. Similar problems confront women who enter industry and must at the same time raise children." 18/

(B) *ILO*

Enforcement of labour legislation including labour inspection

"...*Technical advisory missions*

"It is proposed to constitute teams of experts for Asia, Latin America and the Near and Middle East who would visit the countries concerned and advise the national inspection services on their organization and technical problems. The missions would comprise an expert in general problems of organization of inspection services and, as necessary, experts in industrial safety, industrial hygiene and special questions such as those relating to

women and children or to particular branches of industry or industrial processes." 19/

"...*Inspection manual*

"It is proposed to compile and publish in appropriate languages a basic manual for the use and guidance of labour inspection officials. This manual, based on the best inspection methods and procedures developed in national services with long experience, would include material dealing with administrative instructions and practices, inspection procedures in respect of safety, health, hours, wages, the employment of women and young persons, etc., and the maintenance of employment records. The manual would also include sets of sample poster and record and administrative forms." 20/

Employment problems of women and young workers

General nature of the programme

"In areas in which a substantial number of women are employed on a wage or salary earning basis or in homework, special problems arise in connection with their vocational guidance and training, their placement, their protection against conditions of employment prejudicial to their health, well-being and efficiency (e.g., excessive hours of work, night work and work during periods immediately preceding or following child-birth) and their general welfare. While the general measures contemplated in the other projects outlined in this chapter would cover women as well as men, special provisions will be needed in most of these areas if women's skill and capacity are to be developed and utilized effectively...

Relation to economic development

"Many of the women now employed in underdeveloped countries are either engaged in heavy or unskilled labour or are struggling to perform semi-skilled or skilled tasks with inadequate preparation. Technical training is urgently required if these women are to make their full contribution to increased production and so achieve higher standards of life. Moreover, as economic development progresses an increasing number of women are likely to be employed in agricultural, industrial or commercial undertakings and also in home trades. The increased employment of women and the improvement of their technical qualifications can make an important contribution both to economic development and to better living standards, provided the necessary measures are taken to safeguard their welfare...

18/ Document E/CN.5/209, page 11, paragraph 15 (c).
19/ Document E/1327/Add.1, page 103.
20/ Document E/1327/Add.1, page 104.

Regions concerned

"The special services provided for in this programme will be required in practically all of the underdeveloped countries. Both the nature of the problem and the services required will, however, vary in different cases.

"In Asia, for example, greater emphasis must be placed upon special services for the vocational training, counselling and employment of women in India and Pakistan, than in Burma and China where women are traditionally employed in more skilled occupations. Special services for women will be particularly necessary in the countries of the Middle East where segregation of women has been most highly developed and persistent, but again, differences, both in the degree of industrialization and in religious and social traditions, will affect the character and extent of the services needed. Even in Latin America, where the problem of utilizing the potential capacity of women workers is in large part, though not entirely, related to the degree of industrialization, special attention to the needs of women for technical and vocational training and for skilled guidance and placement are called for...

Analysis of projects

(1) Women workers

"Technical advice and assistance would be given both in adapting general legislation and administrative arrangements to the needs of women workers and in designing such special provisions and services as may be necessary. The fields covered would include:

(i) Vocational training, counselling and placement

"The general objective would be to develop services adapted to the special needs of women workers rather than to set up separate services, except as these latter prove to be essential. Special attention would be given to the inclusion of women in all training programmes and in meetings of experts.

(ii) Wage determination

"Advice and assistance would be given in the extension to women workers of machinery for the determination of minimum wage rates and in the adaptation to women's work of systems of remuneration calculated to contribute to increased efficiency.

(iii) Industrial safety and occupational health

"Assistance would be given in establishing the special programmes of research or investigation and the special clinics or facilities for prevention and treatment which will frequently be required for women workers. In areas, especially in sections of the Middle East and Latin America, where traditional attitudes of protection for women tend to lead to general restrictions upon their employment, rather than to investigation and reduction of particular occupational hazards, special attention would be given to the safety measures required to make possible the more extensive employment of women as industrial development proceeds.

(iv) Enforcement of labour legislation and labour inspection

"While it must not be assumed that labour laws can be applied effectively to women workers only by women inspectors and administrators, it remains true that women are an essential part of all inspection and enforcement agencies in the industrially advanced countries and that a lack of qualified and experienced women officials in such services is a serious handicap in most of the industrially less advanced countries. Special attention would therefore be paid in all training programmes, meetings of experts, and other forms of technical assistance in this field to the character and qualifications of personnel required to deal with the particular needs of women workers.

(v) Social security

"One of the outstanding needs of women workers in all the less advanced countries where low standards of living prevail, and the employment of women is therefore closely related to the poverty of the masses of the people, is for adequate systems of maternity protection, with maternity leave and maternity benefits so organized as to reach the working women requiring such protection. Attempts in many countries to make such services a charge upon employers have led to the discharge or avoidance of employment of the women concerned; and experience has shown conclusively that such protection is in fact effective only if organized under broad schemes of health insurance or medical care financed from public funds. Special attention would therefore be given to this subject in developing schemes of social security appropriate to the needs of the underdeveloped countries.

(vi) Cooperation and handicrafts

"Throughout the less developed areas of the world, especially in the countries of Asia, the Middle East and Latin America, the part played by women in the handicraft and cottage industries is very great. Women, moreover, are frequently employed as industrial home workers, often under exploitative conditions of work and wages. Special measures are required for the protection of women workers in such industries, not only in the interests of the women concerned, but also for the maintenance of standards in factory employment, and for the retention on an economically sound basis of such handicrafts as the countries concerned may wish to preserve. Assistance would therefore be given in the devising of such measures.

(vii) *Agriculture*

"Special measures will also be required in many cases for the training, employment and protection of women workers in plantations and in other forms of commercialized or semi-commercialized agriculture; and also for women employed under a system of family contract and therefore not listed as individual employees, or falling outside existing systems of labour law...

Experience of the International Labour Organization in this field

"The ILO has ever since its inception been concerned with the preparation of International Labour Conventions dealing with the protection of women workers and has prepared a number of reports and extensive studies covering legislation and practice in these matters and discussing the problems involved. Technical advice and assistance in dealing with problems of women's employment have been provided to many countries, in recent years particularly to underdeveloped countries. The ILO is therefore well prepared to undertake an expanded programme of technical assistance to Governments in this field...

Proposed cooperation and coordination with the United Nations and specialized agencies

"This field of activity falls primarily within the competence of the ILO. Close cooperation would, however, be maintained with the United Nations, particularly as regards child and family welfare programmes and the general status of women, with UNESCO as regards the educational basis for technical and vocational education, with FAO as regards conditions of employment in rural areas and with WHO in relation to health matters, in particular maternity protection." ... 21/

(C) *FAO*

Extension and related educational services

"Bridging the gap between the knowledge possessed by scientists and technicians and the practices of producers requires efficient extension or advisory services and related educational activities. The work is important not only in agriculture but also in forestry and fisheries. Since efficiency in production is influenced by living conditions, successful extension work always includes programmes for the education of farm women in home management, nutrition, child rearing and other home problems"... 22/

(D) *WHO*

Maternal and child health

"...it will be the purpose of WHO to give high priority to providing assistance to countries and to areas within countries where programmes [of maternal and child health] are underdeveloped and undeveloped, especially where high infant mortality rates indicate greatest need, and to attempt to meet the wants of any country for assistance in special aspects of the total programme.

"The programme will be one of active field service, including longer-term field demonstrations and shorter-term visits by consultants.

"In accordance with the requests of Governments, this assistance may be in the form of:

(1) Demonstrations of health services for mothers and children, preferably in conjunction with demonstrations of general health services or of some other type of special programme, such as malaria or tuberculosis control;

(2) The assignment of visiting consultants to advise on special aspects of the programme, including maternity care, care of newborn infants, health services to infants, pre-school and school age children, immunization programmes, nutrition, school meals, mental health and child guidance, and so forth.

(3) The dissemination of information on all aspects of maternal and child health and welfare to territories requesting information;

(4) A training programme to increase substantially the supply of qualified personnel for the maternal and child health field, both administrative and field workers in the medical, nursing and related auxiliary fields. 23/"...

Venereal diseases

"The realization of the general need for wider availability of penicillin is to some extent the basis for the preventive-syphilis projects for pregnant women and for children which are financed by UNICEF. Responsibility for their technical aspects rests with the Joint WHO/UNICEF Committee on Health Policy and with WHO. During 1950 such programmes and similar ones should be initiated in additional countries. Under the overall allocation already made for such schemes by UNICEF, WHO should contribute to the expansion of such projects, in terms of organization, personnel, penicillin and supplies needed for the adult population" 24/...

Nutrition

"... *Methods*

"... (6) Training in nutrition of maternal and infant specialists, of dieticians, of personnel for nutrition surveys and others;

21/ Document E/1327/Add.1, pages 105-110.
22/ Document E/1327/Add.1, page 190.
23/ Document E/1327/Add.1, pages 260-262.
24/ Document E/1327/Add.1, pages 278-279.

"(7) Advice on the nutrition of mothers and children."... 25/

Technical training of medical and auxiliary personnel

"In underdeveloped regions, even the existing health facilities with a small number of doctors could give much wider and better service if well-trained auxiliary personnel could be provided. It is very probable that the main bulk of health work in underdeveloped areas and, particularly in maternal and child health, will be carried out by nurses, midwives, medical assistants, etc. There, the greatest need is for simple instruction, simple treatment and leadership. The question of the training, employment and supervision of various grades of auxiliary personnel is of the most urgent importance.

"For these reasons, the greatest care and effort should be devoted to the development of educational resources for this type of personnel. WHO should give as great assistance as possible to individual countries in the establishment and development of schools for nurses, midwives, medical assistants, sanitary inspectors and other auxiliary personnel."... 26/

25/ Document E/1327/Add.1, pages 287-288.
26/ Document E/1327/Add.1, pages 296-297.

Document 24

Memorandum by the Secretary-General to the CSW on the participation of women in the work of the United Nations

E/CN.6/167, 19 March 1951

Introductory note

1. In accordance with a request of the Commission on the Status of Women made at its third session, 1/ the Secretary-General prepared for the fourth session of the Commission a report on the nature and proportion of positions occupied by women in the Secretariat of the United Nations, and the extent to which Member Governments included women in their delegations to organs and agencies of the United Nations. 2/

2. Having studied the Secretary-General's report, the Commission at its fourth session adopted a resolution 3/ noting that "women have been engaged mainly in subordinate positions in the Secretariat, and that very few women have been appointed as members of delegations", and requesting the Secretary-General to examine the reasons why women have not yet been able to take up more important positions in the Secretariat, and report thereon; in this resolution, the Commission also invited the Secretary-General "to take the necessary steps to give promotion to qualified women staff members and to appoint more women to higher posts which they are competent to fill in order to secure equality between the sexes in the Secretariat and thereby assure more fully the participation of women in all capacities in United Nations organs".

3. The Commission in the same resolution suggested that the Economic and Social Council should draw the attention of Member States to the desirability of greater participation of women in delegations. When the Economic and Social Council discussed this item at its eleventh session, 4/ several members expressed the view that the resolution of the Commission raised questions which fell within the discretion of Member States, on the one hand, and of the Secretary-General under the terms of the Charter, on the other. The Council decided to take no action on the recommendation of the Commission, but to transmit the summary record of the discussion to Governments of Member States and to the Advisory Committee on Administrative and Budgetary Questions.

4. The Secretary-General has the honour to submit herewith information on the nature and proportion of positions occupied by women in the Secretariat in the year 1950: a statement on policy with respect to appointments to, and promotions in, the Secretariat; and information with respect to changes in the Staff Rules removing previous inequalities between women and men staff members.

A. Nature and proportion of positions occupied by women in the Secretariat

5. On 31 December 1950, the staff of the United Nations Secretariat at Headquarters, including consultants and personnel paid at hourly rates, consisted of 3,320 persons of whom 1,969 were men and 1,531 were women. The distribution of the personnel with regard to grades and sex was as follows:

1/ E/1316, paragraph 20.
2/ E/CN.6/132.
3/ E/1712, paragraph 48.
4/ E/AC.7/SR.134, pp. 9-11.

Grades	Female	Male	Total
A.S.G.	-	9	9
T.R.D	1	14	15
19	-	28	28
18	-	36	36
17	3	68	71
16	8	128	136
15	11	133	144
14	36	150	186
13	33	157	190
12	66	130	196
11	37	87	124
10	28	41	69
9	73	74	147
8	53	52	105
7	134	59	193
6	325	75	400
5	375	155	530
4	97	122	219
3	52	93	145
2	-	109	109
1	3	44	47
Totals	1335	1764	3099
Hourly staff	8	139	147
Consultants	8	66	74
	1351	1969	3320

(The above figures do not include persons on short-term appointments.)

6. The following tables show the appointments to headquarters staff and the promotions of headquarters staff during 1950, respectively, for Grades 8 and above:

APPOINTMENTS:

Grades	Female	Male	Total
A.S.G	-	2	2
T.R.D.	-	1	1
19	-	4	4
18	-	3	3
17	-	4	4
16	1	7	8
15	1	6	7
14	4	9	13
13	-	4	4
12	1	7	8
11	1	8	9
10	2	8	10
9	3	11	14
8	6	11	17
	19	85	104

PROMOTIONS

Grades	Female	Male	Total
A.S.G.	-	-	-
T.R.D	-	-	-
19	-	4	4
18	-	5	5
17	2	10	12
16	1	12	13
15	2	23	25
14	10	19	29
13	2	33	35
12	7	37	44
11	4	14	18
10	6	15	21
9	13	15	28
8	13	13	26
	60	200	260

B. Policy with respect to appointments to and promotions in the Secretariat

7. There is no bar against women as such for appointment to any post in the Secretariat and women are occupying or have occupied very high and responsible positions such as Top Ranking Director, Director of Division, Chief of Division and Chief of Secion. Whenever a vacancy occurs to which a new staff member has to be appointed, the aim is to get the best candidate irrespective of sex and there has been, to the Secretary-General's knowledge, no case where a person was rejected because of sex.

8. Similarly on the matter of promotion, the policy is that the most deserving candidate receives it irrespective of sex. A number of women staff members have been promoted in pursuance of this policy and the Secretary-General is not aware of any instance where a staff member has been prejudiced by sex from getting due promotion.

C. Conditions of employment for women

9. Implementing the resolution adopted by the Fifth Session of the General Assembly at its 326th plenary meeting on Salary, Allowance and Leave System of the United Nations, 5/ providing for simplification of the organization and classification of the staff in accordance with the principles set forth by the Committee of Experts on Salary, Allowance and Leave System, 6/ the Secretary-General has revised the Staff Rules to conform with the resolution of the General Assembly. The revised Staff Rules 7/ became effective as from 1 January 1951 and superseded the staff rules in force before that date.

5/ A/1761.
6/ A/C.5/331.
7/ ST/AFS/SGB/81/Rev.2.

10. The new Staff Rules provide some changes in the conditions of employment for women. Under the former Staff Rules, 8/ Staff Rule 29 (a) provided for payment of all allowances, and the cost of living adjustment, at dependency rates only to a staff member who had a wife or who as the head of the family, had one or more of the following dependent upon him or her for full and continuing support: husband, son, daughter, parent, brother or sister. In the Administrative Manual, Volume 2, page 125, the term "head of the family" was defined either as "a married man", "a married woman whose husband is incapacitated and dependent upon her for full and continuing support", or "a single, widowed or divorced staff member who has a member of the immediate family dependent upon him or her for full and continuing support". The new Staff Rules no longer use the term "head of the family"; former Staff Rule 2 is cancelled.

11. The distinction between male and female staff members indicated in document E/CN.6/132, paragraph 8 is eliminated in the new Staff Rules so far as the children's allowance, education grant, and rental allowance or subsidy are concerned. It is noted that expatriation allowance, installation allowance and installation grant have been abolished. There is no dependency factor in the new non-resident's allowance or language allowance.

Staff Rule 35 now provides that "a staff member shall receive a children's allowance of $200. (U.S.) per annum in respect of each of his children who is dependent upon him for main and continuing support and who is under the age of eighteen years..." and Rule 36 (a) gives to "each staff member whose official duty station is outside his own country and who is entitled to a children's allowance..." an education grant of $200. (U.S.) per annum "for each child in full time attendance at a school or a university (or similar educational institution) in his country...". The test in all cases is whether the staff member (female or male) provides main and continuing support of the dependent.

12. The new Staff Rule 80 9/ governing the terms and conditions for eligibility to home leave does not alter the situation in its applicability to women staff members. The conditions relating specifically to women reported in paragraphs 10-13 in document E/CN.6/132 remain substantially unchanged. Whereas in the former Staff Rule 80 (a) 10/ no distinction is made between men and women staff members, the distinction was made in former Staff Rule 83. 11/ In the new Staff Rules, the distinction is maintained. 12/

13. Former Staff Rule 83 is incorporated into Rule 80 (f) which reads: "subject to the rules of Chapter 7, and the 30-day limitation specified in (e), the United Nations shall pay the travel expenses of the staff member, his wife and dependent children for purposes of home leave. Travel of the dependents shall be in conjunction with the approved home leave of the staff member, provided that exceptions may be granted if the exigencies of the service or other special circumstances prevent the staff member and his dependents from travelling together on home leave".

14 A male staff member is therefore entitled to payment of travel expenses for his wife and dependent children, accompanying him on home leave, while the right for the female staff member extends to her dependent children only. This is in accordance with the General Assembly's Provisional Staff Regulation 25. 13/

15. With regard to home leave for staff members who are husband and wife, the administrative practice, mentioned in paragraph 11 of document E/CN.6/132, has become part of Rule 80. Rule 80 (g) states: "If both husband and wife are staff members eligible for home leave, the wife shall have the choice of taking her own home leave or accompanying her husband on his home leave, but not both. If the wife accompanies her husband, she shall be entitled to the allowances and accommodations provided for wives under the rules of Chapter 7, but shall be allowed travelling time not to exceed that which would have been authorized had she taken her own home leave."

16. It is noted that the staff rules on travel are the same in the case of appointment, separation and change of official duty station as they are for home leave, and that in all cases they are based on the General Assembly's Provisional Staff Regulation 25.

8/ SGB/81 and ST/AFS/SGB/81/Rev.1

9/ ST/AFS/SGB/81/Rev.2/Add.1.

10/ SGB/81, Staff Rule 80 (a): A staff member whose home is outside the country of his official station shall receive, in addition to annual leave, home leave consisting of two working weeks every two years, plus travelling time not to exceed thirty days, by an approved route and type of transport to and from the place established as his home. Rule 212: In these rules, terms referring to persons and staff members in the masculine gender shall apply also to women, except where the contrary intention is evident from the context.

11/ SGB/81, Staff Rule 83: For the purpose of home leave, a staff member shall receive payment of travel expenses for himself, his wife and dependent children in accordance with the conditions prescribed in Chapter 7.

12/ ST/AFS/SGB/81/Rev.2: rule 212 referred to in 10/ is retained as Rule 222.

13/ See document A/64 XII, Resolutions adopted on the Reports of the Fifth Committee, Annex II, page 19.

Document 25

ECOSOC resolution concerning the deprivation of the essential human rights of women in Trust and Non-Self-Governing Territories

E/RES/445 C (XIV), 28 May 1952

The Economic and Social Council,

Considering that one of the purposes of the United Nations is to promote and encourage respect for human rights and for fundamental freedoms for all without distinction as to race, sex, language or religion,

Considering that there are areas of the world, including certain Trust and Non-Self-Governing Territories, where women are deprived of certain essential human rights, including the right to their physical integrity and moral dignity,

1. *Invites* all States, including States which have or assume responsibility for the administration of Non-Self-Governing Territories, to take immediately all necessary measures with a view to abolishing progressively in the countries and territories under their administration all customs which violate the physical integrity of women, and which thereby violate the dignity and worth of the human person as proclaimed in the Charter and the Universal Declaration of Human Rights;

2. *Invites* the Trusteeship Council, in collaboration with the Administering Authorities, to take immediately all appropriate measures to promote the progressive abolition of such customs in Trust Territories, and to consider the inclusion of the necessary questions in the questionnaires provided for in Article 88 of the Charter as well as the inclusion of the pertinent information received from Administering Authorities in its annual report to the General Assembly;

3. *Invites* the General Assembly to request the Committee on Information from Non-Self-Governing Territories to take paragraph 1 above into account in its examination of the information transmitted under heading C of part III of the Standard Form for the guidance of Members in the preparation of information to be transmitted under Article 73 e of the Charter adopted by the General Assembly on 7 December 1951 under resolution 551 (VI).

Document 26

Convention on the Political Rights of Women, adopted by the General Assembly on 20 December 1952

UN Treaty Series, vol. 193, No. 2613, p. 135

The Contracting Parties,

Desiring to implement the principle of equality of rights for men and women contained in the Charter of the United Nations,

Recognizing that everyone has the right to take part in the government of his country, directly or indirectly through freely chosen representatives, and has the right to equal access to public service in his country, and desiring to equalize the status of men and women in the enjoyment and exercise of political rights, in accordance with the provisions of the Charter of the United Nations and of the Universal Declaration of Human Rights.

Having resolved to conclude a Convention for this purpose,

Hereby agree as hereinafter provided:

Article I

Women shall be entitled to vote in all elections on equal terms with men, without any discrimination.

Article II

Women shall be eligible for election to all publicly elected bodies, established by national law, on equal terms with men, without any discrimination.

Article III

Women shall be entitled to hold public office and to exercise all public functions, established by national law, on equal terms with men, without any discrimination.

Article IV

1. This Convention shall be open for signature on behalf of any Member of the United Nations and also on

behalf of any other State to which an invitation has been addressed by the General Assembly.

2. This Convention shall be ratified and the instruments of ratification shall be deposited with the Secretary-General of the United Nations.

Article V

1. This Convention shall be open for accession to all States referred to in paragraph 1 of article IV.

2. Accession shall be effected by the deposit of an instrument of accession with the Secretary-General of the United Nations.

Article VI

1. This Convention shall come into force on the ninetieth day following the date of deposit of the sixth instrument of ratification or accession.

2. For each State ratifying or acceding to the Convention after the deposit of the sixth instrument of ratification or accession the Convention shall enter into force on the ninetieth day after deposit by such State of its instrument of ratification or accession.

Article VII

In the event that any State submits a reservation to any of the articles of this Convention at the time of signature, ratification or accession, the Secretary-General shall communicate the text of the reservation to all States which are or may become parties to this Convention. Any State which objects to the reservation may, within a period of ninety days from the date of the said communication (or upon the date of its becoming a party to the Convention), notify the Secretary-General that it does not accept it. In such case, the Convention shall not enter into force as between such State and the State making the reservation.

Article VIII

1. Any State may denounce this Convention by written notification to the Secretary-General of the United Nations. Denunciation shall take effect one year after the date of receipt of the notification by the Secretary-General.

2. This Convention shall cease to be in force as from the date when the denunciation which reduces the number of parties to less than six becomes effective.

Article IX

Any dispute which may arise between any two or more Contracting States concerning the interpretation or application of this Convention which is not settled by negotiation, shall at the request of any one of the parties to the dispute be referred to the International Court of Justice for decision, unless they agree to another mode of settlement.

Article X

The Secretary-General of the United Nations shall notify all Members of the United Nations and the non-member States contemplated in paragraph 1 of article IV of this Convention of the following:

(a) Signatures and instruments of ratifications received in accordance with article IV;

(b) Instruments of accession received in accordance with article V;

(c) The date upon which this Convention enters into force in accordance with article VI;

(d) Communications and notifications received in accordance with article VII;

(e) Notifications of denunciation received in accordance with paragraph 1 of article VIII;

(f) Abrogation in accordance with paragraph 2 of article VIII.

Article XI

1. This Convention, of which the Chinese, English, French, Russian and Spanish texts shall be equally authentic, shall be deposited in the archives of the United Nations.

2. The Secretary-General of the United Nations shall transmit a certified copy to all Members of the United Nations and to the non-member States contemplated in paragraph 1 of article IV.

IN FAITH WHEREOF the undersigned, being duly authorized thereto by their respective Governments, have signed the present Convention, opened for signature at New York, on the thirty-first day of March, one thousand nine hundred and fifty-three.

Document 27

Summary of the statement made by Secretary-General Dag Hammarskjöld to the eighth session of the CSW on, among other things, the participation of women in the work of the United Nations

E/CN.6/SR.149, 8 April 1954

The ACTING CHAIRMAN declared open the eighth session of the Commission on the Status of Women and welcomed new representatives.

Much progress in the advancement of women's rights had been made since the close of the seventh session. The election of Mrs. Pandit as President of the General Assembly was a significant milestone and the women who had attended the eighth session of the General Assembly as representative of their countries had demonstrated that they were fully capable of fulfilling the same functions as men.

The General Assembly had adopted a number of resolutions proposed by the Commission which would significantly alter the status of women in many fields. It had adopted a resolution on the development and safeguarding of women's rights in connection with the technical assistance programme and had urged governments to take all necessary measures to promote the development of political rights for women in the Member States and in the Trust and Non-Self-Governing Territories. It had also invited governments to sign and ratify the Convention on Political Rights of Women. The Commission, which has already achieved much, would continue its work until all women enjoyed equal rights with men.

The SECRETARY-GENERAL (Dag Hammarskjöld) wished the Commission every success in its work. The provisional agenda for the Commission's eighth session showed that it was faithfully seeking to carry out its mandate. The Commission could note with pride that as a result of its activities, the United Nations, under the authority of the General Assembly, had sponsored the opening of an international Convention on Political Rights of Women under which women would have the right to vote, to be elected, to hold all public offices and to discharge all public functions. Thirty-five countries had signed the Convention and instruments of ratifica-

tion had been deposited by three countries, the first being the Dominican Republic.

Among the many important matters on the Commission's agenda, he was particularly interested in the item relating to the participation of women in the work of the United Nations. Although the number of women in higher posts of the United Nations and the specialized agencies were few, that did not prove that women were subject to discrimination. Women's emancipation was so recent that highly qualified women had not yet been trained in anything like the same numbers as men, who had long enjoyed all the advantages of specialized education and training. In addition, instead of entering public life many women who were highly qualified chose other equally important roles in the community. As a result there were few women, compared with men, in high posts in the public life of all countries and the United Nations naturally reflected that situation. It was logical to think that as the proportion of trained women in national life increased, the change would be reflected in the staffs of the international organizations.

He assured the Commission, however, that under his administration there would be no discrimination on the ground of sex; the best person available for a post would be given the post regardless of race, sex, colour or creed. In that connection he suggested that in the interests of good and effective administration questions regarding personnel should be channeled through the appropriate body, the Fifth Committee, to which the Secretary-General must report on all personnel matters and from which, therefore, all requests for information on personnel administration should normally come.

In conclusion, he paid tribute to women's contributions to civilization and reiterated his belief that they would make a still greater contribution in future when men and women working together in partnership might succeed in creating a better and more peaceful world.

Document 28

General Assembly resolution calling on Member States to eliminate customs, ancient laws and practices affecting the human dignity of women

A/RES/843 (IX), 17 December 1954

The General Assembly,

Recalling the principles set forth in the United Nations Charter and in the Universal Declaration of Human Rights,

Considering that, in certain areas of the world, women are subject to customs, ancient laws and practices relating to marriage and the family which are inconsistent with these principles,

Believing that the elimination of such customs, ancient laws and practices would tend to the recognition of the human dignity of women and contribute to the benefit of the family as an institution,

Having considered Economic and Social Council resolution 547 H (XVIII) of 12 July 1954,

1. *Urges* all States, including States which have or assume responsibility for the administration of Non-Self-Governing and Trust Territories, to take all appropriate measures in the countries and Territories under their jurisdiction with a view to abolishing such customs, ancient laws and practices by ensuring complete freedom in the choice of a spouse; abolishing the practice of the bride-price; guaranteeing the right of widows to the custody of their children and their freedom as to remarriage; eliminating completely child marriages and the betrothal of young girls before the age of puberty and establishing appropriate penalties where necessary; establishing a civil or other register in which all marriages and divorces will be recorded; ensuring that all cases involving personal rights be tried before a competent judicial body; ensuring also that family allowances, where these are provided, be administered in such a way as to benefit directly the mother and child;

2. *Recommends* that special efforts be made through fundamental education, in both private and public schools, and through various media of communication, to inform public opinion in all areas mentioned in the second paragraph of the preamble above concerning the Universal Declaration of Human Rights and existing decrees and legislation which affect the status of women.

Document 29

Convention on the Nationality of Married Women, adopted by the General Assembly on 29 January 1957

UN Treaty Series, vol. 309, No. 4468, p. 65

The Contracting States,

Recognizing that conflicts in law and in practice with reference to nationality arise as a result of provisions concerning the loss or acquisition of nationality by women as a result of marriage, of its dissolution, or of the change of nationality by the husband during marriage,

Recognizing that, in article 15 of the Universal Declaration of Human Rights, the General Assembly of the United Nations has proclaimed that "everyone has the right to a nationality" and that "no one shall be arbitrarily deprived of his nationality nor denied the right to change his nationality",

Desiring to cooperate with the United Nations in promoting universal respect for, and observance of, human rights and fundamental freedoms for all without distinction as to sex,

Hereby agree as hereinafter provided:

Article 1

Each Contracting State agrees that neither the celebration nor the dissolution of a marriage between one of its nationals and an alien, nor the change of nationality by the husband during marriage, shall automatically affect the nationality of the wife.

Article 2

Each Contracting State agrees that neither the voluntary acquisition of the nationality of another State nor the renunciation of its nationality by one of its nationals shall prevent the retention of its nationality by the wife of such national.

Article 3

1. Each Contracting State agrees that the alien wife of one of its nationals may, at her request, acquire the nationality of her husband through specially privileged naturalization procedures; the grant of such nationality may be subject to such limitations as may be imposed in the interests of national security or public policy.

2. Each Contracting State agrees that the present Convention shall not be construed as affecting any legislation or judicial practice by which the alien wife of one of its nationals may, at her request, acquire her husband's nationality as a matter of right.

Article 4

1. The present Convention shall be open for signature and ratification on behalf of any State Member of the United Nations and also on behalf of any other State which is or hereafter becomes a member of any specialized agency of the United Nations, or which is or hereafter becomes a Party to the Statute of the International Court of Justice, or any other State to which an invitation has been addressed by the General Assembly of the United Nations.

2. The present Convention shall be ratified and the instruments of ratification shall be deposited with the Secretary-General of the United Nations.

Article 5

1. The present Convention shall be open for accession to all States referred to in paragraph 1 of article 4.

2. Accession shall be effected by the deposit of an instrument of accession with the Secretary-General of the United Nations.

Article 6

1. The present Convention shall come into force on the ninetieth day following the date of deposit of the sixth instrument of ratification or accession.

2. For each State ratifying or acceding to the Convention after the deposit of the sixth instrument of ratification or accession, the Convention shall enter into force on the ninetieth day after deposit by such State of its instrument of ratification or accession.

Article 7

1. The present Convention shall apply to all non-self-governing, trust, colonial and other non-metropolitan territories for the international relations of which any Contracting State is responsible; the Contracting State concerned shall, subject to the provisions of paragraph 2 of the present article, at the time of signature, ratification or accession, declare the non-metropolitan territory or

territories to which the Convention shall apply *ipso facto* as a result of such signature, ratification or accession.

2. In any case in which, for the purpose of nationality, a non-metropolitan territory is not treated as one with the metropolitan territory, or in any case in which the previous consent of a non-metropolitan territory is required by the constitutional laws or practices of the Contracting State or of the non-metropolitan territory for the application of the Convention to that territory, that Contracting State shall endeavour to secure the needed consent of the non-metropolitan territory within the period of twelve months from the date of signature of the Convention by that Contracting State, and when such consent has been obtained the Contracting State shall notify the Secretary-General of the United Nations. The present Convention shall apply to the territory or territories named in such notification from the date of its receipt by the Secretary-General.

3. After the expiry of the twelve-month period mentioned in paragraph 2 of the present article, the Contracting States concerned shall inform the Secretary-General of the results of the consultations with those non-metropolitan territories for whose international relations they are responsible and whose consent to the application of the present Convention may have been withheld.

Article 8

1. At the time of signature, ratification or accession, any State may make reservations to any article of the present Convention other than articles 1 and 2.

2. If any State makes a reservation in accordance with paragraph 1 of the present article, the Convention, with the exception of those provisions to which the reservation relates, shall have effect as between the reserving State and the other Parties. The Secretary-General of the United Nations shall communicate the text of the reservation to all States which are or may become Parties to the Convention. Any State Party to the Convention or which thereafter becomes a Party may notify the Secretary-General that it does not agree to consider itself bound by the Convention with respect to the State making the reservation. This notification must be made, in the case of a State already a Party, within ninety days from the date of the communication by the Secretary-General; and, in the case of a State subsequently becoming a Party, within ninety days from the date when the instrument of ratification or accession is deposited. In the event that such a notification is made, the Convention shall not be deemed to be in effect as between the State making the notification and the State making the reservation.

3. Any State making a reservation in accordance with paragraph 1 of the present article may at any time

withdraw the reservation, in whole or in part, after it has been accepted, by a notification to this effect addressed to the Secretary-General of the United Nations. Such notification shall take effect on the date on which it is received.

Article 9

1. Any Contracting State may denounce the present Convention by written notification to the Secretary-General of the United Nations. Denunciation shall take effect one year after the date or receipt of the notification by the Secretary-General.

2. The present Convention shall cease to be in force as from the date when the denunciation which reduces the number of Parties to less than six becomes effective.

Article 10

Any dispute which may arise between any two or more Contracting States concerning the interpretation or application of the present Convention, which is not settled by negotiation, shall, at the request of any one of the Parties to the dispute, be referred to the International Court of Justice for decision, unless the Parties agree to another mode of settlement.

Article 11

The Secretary-General of the United Nations shall notify all States Members of the United Nations and the non-member States contemplated in paragraph 1 of article 4 of the present Convention of the following:

(a) Signatures and instruments of ratification received in accordance with article 4;

(b) Instruments of accession received in accordance with rticle 5;

(c) The date upon which the present Convention enters into force in accordance with article 6;

(d) Communications and notifications received in accordance with article 8;

(e) Notifications of denunciation received in accordance with paragraph 1 of article 9;

(f) Abrogation in accordance with paragraph 2 of article 9.

Article 12

1. The present Convention, of which the Chinese, English, French, Russian and Spanish texts shall be equally authentic, shall be deposited in the archives of the United Nations.

2. The Secretary-General of the United Nations shall transmit a certified copy of the Convention to all States Members of the United Nations and to the non-member States contemplated in paragraph 1 of article 4.

IN FAITH WHEREOF the undersigned, being duly authorized thereto by their respective Governments, have signed the present Convention, opened for signature at New York, on the 20th day of February, one thousand nine hundred and fifty-seven.

Document 30

ECOSOC resolution recommending that Member States make full use of the United Nations technical assistance and human rights advisory services programmes for the purpose of advancing the status of women in developing countries

E/RES/884 E (XXXIV), 16 July 1962

E

United Nations Assistance for the Advancement of Women in Developing Countries

The Economic and Social Council,

Having considered the reports by the Secretary-General on United Nations assistance for the advancement of women in developing countries 1/ prepared in accordance with its resolution 771 H (XXX) of 25 July 1960, and the views expressed in the Commission on the Status of Women at its sixteenth session, 2/

Recalling General Assembly resolution 1509 (XV) of 12 December 1960, in which the Commission on the Status of Women and the Council were invited to pursue their efforts in advancing the status of women in developing countries and to take appropriate measures that would lead to special assistance by the United Nations and the specialized agencies in this regard,

1/ *Official Records of the Economic and Social Council, Thirty-fourth Session, Annexes*, agenda item 10, documents E/3493,E/3566 and Add.1.
2/ Ibid., *Supplement No. 7*, E/3606/Rev.1, paras. 115 to 124.

Noting with satisfaction General Assembly resolution 1679 (XVI) of 18 December 1961 in which the Assembly decided to increase the resources of the advisory services programme in human rights in order to permit the provision of a number of human rights fellowships each year, in addition to the seminars,

Considering that under the United Nations Development Decade it is now appropriate to develop and coordinate the various programmes of the United Nations, of the specialized agencies and of the United Nations Children's Fund designed to advance the status of women in developing countries,

Believing that, in order to achieve this goal, the cooperation of the Governments, the specialized agencies and the United Nations Children's Fund, and of non-governmental organizations in consultative status is indispensable,

1. *Recommends* to Governments of States Members of the United Nations and members of the specialized agencies that they make full use, for the purpose of promoting and advancing the status of women in developing countries, of the services presently available under the regular programme and the Expanded Programme of Technical Assistance, as well as of the advisory services programme in human rights and the advisory social welfare services, by requesting the advisory services of experts, by promoting the attendance at seminars and other meetings, and by taking advantage of the availability of fellowships and scholarships;

2. *Invites* the International Labour Organization, the United Nations Educational, Scientific and Cultural Organization, the Food and Agriculture Organization of the United Nations, the World Health Organization and the United Nations Children's Fund, in cooperation with the United Nations, to strengthen and to expand their programmes designed to meet the needs of women in developing countries, and to seek new methods to achieve this purpose;

3. *Requests* the Secretary-General:

(a) To direct his attention, when planning the various United Nations programmes of assistance, to the needs of women in developing countries and to include in these programmes projects especially directed to meet such needs;

(b) To continue to utilize the available resources of the United Nations to advance the condition of women in the developing countries, by holding seminars dealing with the status of women, by providing experts on women's rights at the request of Governments and by offering human rights fellowships and scholarships to persons concerned with the status of women, and to make available to Governments, specialized agencies and non-governmental organizations in consultative status all information concerning the facilities available for the advancement of women;

4. *Urges* women's non-governmental organizations in consultative status to cooperate with the Secretary-General, by stimulating public opinion with regard to the programmes of the United Nations which contribute to the advancement of women and by supplementing the efforts of the United Nations on the international and national levels through the holding of regional, national or local seminars, including if possible in the future an international seminar, the provision of fellowships, scholarships and expert advice, and other related activities.

Document 31

Convention on Consent to Marriage, Minimum Age for Marriage and Registration of Marriages, adopted by the General Assembly on 7 November 1962

UN Treaty Series, vol. 521, No. 7525, p. 231

Preamble

The Contracting States,

Desiring, in conformity with the Charter of the United Nations, to promote universal respect for, and observance of, human rights and fundamental freedoms for all, without distinction as to race, sex, language or religion,

Recalling that article 16 of the Universal Declaration of Human Rights 1/ states that:

"(1) Men and women of full age, without any limitation due to race, nationality or religion, have the right to marry and to found a family. They are entitled to equal rights as to marriage, during marriage and at its dissolution.

"(2) Marriage shall be entered into only with the free and full consent of the intending spouses.",

1/ United Nations, *Official Records of the General Assembly, Third Session, Part I, Resolutions* (A/810), p. 71.

Recalling further that the General Assembly of the United Nations declared, by resolution 843(IX) of 17 December 1954, 2/ that certain customs, ancient laws and practices relating to marriage and the family were inconsistent with the principles set forth in the Charter of the United Nations and in the Universal Declaration of Human Rights,

Reaffirming that all States, including those which have or assume responsibility for the administration of Non-Self-Governing and Trust Territories until their achievement of independence, should take all appropriate measures with a view to abolishing such customs, ancient laws and practices by ensuring, *inter alia*, complete freedom in the choice of a spouse, eliminating completely child marriages and the betrothal of young girls before the age of puberty, establishing appropriate penalties where necessary and establishing a civil or other register in which all marriages will be recorded,

Hereby agree as hereinafter provided:

Article 1

(1) No marriage shall be legally entered into without the full and free consent of both parties, such consent to be expressed by them in person after due publicity and in the presence of the authority competent to solemnize the marriage and of witnesses, as prescribed by law.

(2) Notwithstanding anything in paragraph 1 above, it shall not be necessary for one of the parties to be present when the competent authority is satisfied that the circumstances are exceptional and that the party has, before a competent authority and in such manner as may be prescribed by law, expressed and not withdrawn consent.

Article 2

States parties to the present Convention shall take legislative action to specify a minimum age for marriage. No marriage shall be legally entered into by any person under this age, except where a competent authority has granted a dispensation as to age, for serious reasons, in the interest of the intending spouses.

Article 3

All marriages shall be registered in an appropriate official register by the competent authority.

Article 4

(1) The present Convention shall, until 31 December 1963, be open for signature on behalf of all States Members of the United Nations or members of any of the specialized agencies, and of any other State invited by the General Assembly of the United Nations to become party to the Convention.

(2) The present Convention is subject to ratifica-

tion. The instruments of ratification shall be deposited with the Secretary-General of the United Nations.

Article 5

(1) The present Convention shall be open for accession to all States referred to in article 4, paragraph 1.

(2) Accession shall be effected by the deposit of an instrument of accession with the Secretary-General of the United Nations.

Article 6

(1) The present Convention shall come into force on the ninetieth day following the date of deposit of the eighth instrument of ratification or accession.

(2) For each State ratifying or acceding to the Convention after the deposit of the eighth instrument of ratification or accession, the Convention shall enter into force on the ninetieth day after deposit by such State of its instrument of ratification or accession.

Article 7

(1) Any Contracting State may denounce the present Convention by written notification to the Secretary-General of the United Nations. Denunciation shall take effect one year after the date of receipt of the notification by the Secretary-General.

(2) The present Convention shall cease to be in force as from the date when the denunciation which reduces the number of parties to less than eight becomes effective.

Article 8

Any dispute which may arise between any two or more Contracting States concerning the interpretation or application of the present Convention which is not settled by negotiation shall, at the request of all parties to the dispute, be referred to the International Court of Justice for decision, unless the parties agree to another mode of settlement.

Article 9

The Secretary-General of the United Nations shall notify all States Members of the United Nations and the non-member States contemplated in article 4, paragraph 1, of the present Convention of the following:

(a) Signatures and instruments of ratification received in accordance with article 4;

(b) Instruments of accession received in accordance with article 5;

(c) The date upon which the Convention enters into force in accordance with article 6;

2/ United Nations, *Official Records of the General Assembly, Ninth Session, Supplement No. 21* (A/2890), p. 23.

(d) Notifications of denunciation received in accordance with article 7, paragraph 1;

(e) Abrogation in accordance with article 7, paragraph 2.

Article 10

(1) The present Convention, of which the Chinese, English, French, Russian and Spanish texts shall be equally authentic, shall be deposited in the archives of the United Nations.

(2) The Secretary-General of the United Nations shall transmit a certified copy of the Convention to all States Members of the United Nations and to the non-member States contemplated in article 4, paragraph 1.

IN FAITH WHEREOF the undersigned, being duly authorized, have signed on behalf of their respective Governments, the present Convention which was opened for signature at the Headquarters of the United Nations, New York, on the tenth day of December, one thousand nine hundred and sixty-two.

Document 32

General Assembly resolution requesting that the Secretary-General study the possibility of providing resources aimed especially at the initiation and implementation of a unified long-term United Nations programme for the advancement of women

A/RES/1777 (XVII), 7 December 1962

The General Assembly,

Recalling Economic and Social Council resolution 771 H (XXX) of 25 July 1960 and General Assembly resolution 1509 (XV) of 12 December 1960 concerning special assistance by the United Nations and the specialized agencies for the advancement of women in developing countries,

Having considered the reports prepared by the Secretary-General in accordance with the above-mentioned resolutions, 1/

Reaffirming Economic and Social Council resolution 884 E (XXXIV) of 16 July 1962, by which the Council recognized the necessity to develop and coordinate the various programmes of the United Nations, the specialized agencies and the United Nations Children's Fund which are designed to promote the advancement of women in developing countries,

Recognizing the importance of the work accomplished by the Commission on the Status of Women,

Believing that the coordination and development of these various programmes should be implemented through a unified, long-term United Nations programme for the advancement of women,

Recognizing that new resources required for this purpose may be provided by the contributions of Member States, especially of the advanced countries, and by those non-governmental organizations whose aims are to advance the welfare of women everywhere,

Recognizing that it is appropriate to draw the attention of world public opinion to the importance of this problem,

1. *Welcomes* Economic and Social Council resolution 884 E (XXXIV) by which the Council, *inter alia*, invites the International Labour Organisation, the United Nations Educational, Scientific and Cultural Organization, the Food and Agriculture Organization of the United Nations, the World Health Organization and the United Nations Children's Fund, in cooperation with the United Nations, to strengthen and expand their programmes designed to meet the needs of women in developing countries and to seek new methods to achieve this purpose;

2. *Requests* the Secretary-General to study, in co-operation with the Member States, the specialized agencies, the United Nations Children's Fund and appropriate non-governmental organizations, the possibility of providing and developing new resources aimed especially at the initiation and implementation of a unified long-term United Nations programme for the advancement of women;

3. *Requests* the Secretary-General, within the scope of the programme of advisory services in the field of human rights and the advisory social welfare services programme, to study especially the possibility of expanding the assistance which can be rendered, through seminars, fellowships and the services of experts, for the advancement of women in developing countries;

4. *Invites* the Commission on the Status of Women to cooperate with the Secretary-General to these ends;

5. *Further requests* the Secretary-General to report

1/ *Official Records of the Economic and Social Council, Thirty-fourth Session, Annexes,* agenda item 19, documents E/3493, E/3566 and Add.1.

to the Economic and Social Council and to the General Assembly on developments in this respect, especially with regard to the possibility of establishing the above-mentioned programme.

Document 33

General Assembly resolution requesting ECOSOC and the CSW to prepare a draft declaration on the elimination of discrimination against women

A/RES/1921 (XVIII), 5 December 1963

The General Assembly,

Desirous of implementing the provisions of the Charter of the United Nations and the principles of the Universal Declaration of Human Rights in which are affirmed the equal rights of all human beings regardless of sex,

Noting with satisfaction the increasing part played by women in society and the progress made in the field of equal rights,

Noting also with satisfaction the efforts made by the United Nations and the specialized agencies in achieving that progress,

Noting however that in various fields there still remains, in fact if not in law, considerable discrimination against women,

1. *Requests* the Economic and Social Council to invite the Commission on the Status of Women to prepare a draft declaration on the elimination of discrimination against women, with a view to its consideration by the General Assembly, if possible at its twentieth session;

2. *Invites* Governments of Member States, the specialized agencies and appropriate non-governmental organizations to send to the Secretary-General their comments and proposals relating to the principles that might be incorporated in the draft declaration, with a view to their being brought to the attention of the Commission on the Status of Women.

Document 34

General Assembly resolution adopting the Recommendation on Consent to Marriage, Minimum Age for Marriage and Registration of Marriages

A/RES/2018 (XX), 1 November 1965

The General Assembly,

Recognizing that the family group should be strengthened because it is the basic unit of every society, and that men and women of full age have the right to marry and to found a family, that they are entitled to equal rights as to marriage and that marriage shall be entered into only with the free and full consent of the intending spouses, in accordance with the provisions of article 16 of the Universal Declaration of Human Rights,

Recalling its resolution 843(IX) of 17 December 1954,

Recalling further article 2 of the Supplementary Convention on the Abolition of Slavery, the Slave Trade, and Institutions and Practices Similar to Slavery of 1956, 1/ which makes certain provisions concerning the age of marriage, consent to marriage and registration of marriages,

Recalling also that Article 13, paragraph 1 b, of the Charter of the United Nations provides that the General Assembly shall make recommendations for the purpose of assisting in the realization of human rights and fundamental freedoms for all without distinction as to race, sex, language or religion,

Recalling likewise that, under Article 64 of the Charter, the Economic and Social Council may make arrangements with the Members of the United Nations to obtain reports on the steps taken to give effect to its own recommendations and to recommendations on matters falling within its competence made by the General Assembly,

1. *Recommends* that, where not already provided by existing legislative or other measures, each Member

1/ United Nations publication, Sales No. 57.XIV.2.

State should take the necessary steps, in accordance with its constitutional processes and its traditional and religious practices, to adopt such legislative or other measures as may be appropriate to give effect to the following principles:

Principle I

(a) No marriage shall be legally entered into without the full and free consent of both parties, such consent to be expressed by them in person, after due publicity and in the presence of the authority competent to solemnize the marriage and of witnesses, as prescribed by law.

(b) Marriage by proxy shall be permitted only when the competent authorities are satisfied that each party has, before a competent authority and in such manner as may be prescribed by law, fully and freely expressed consent before witnesses and not withdrawn such consent.

Principle II

Member States shall take legislative action to specify a minimum age for marriage, which in any case shall not be less than fifteen years of age; no marriage shall be legally entered into by any person under this age, except where a competent authority has granted a dispensation as to age, for serious reasons, in the interest of the intending spouses.

Principle III

All marriages shall be registered in an appropriate official register by the competent authority.

2. *Recommends* that each Member State should bring the Recommendation on Consent to Marriage, Minimum Age for Marriage and Registration of Marriages contained in the present resolution before the authorities competent to enact legislation or to take other action at the earliest practicable moment and, if possible, no later than eighteen months after the adoption of the Recommendation;

3. *Recommends* that Member States should inform the Secretary-General, as soon as possible after the action referred to in paragraph 2 above, of the measures taken under the present Recommendation to bring it before the competent authority or authorities, with particulars regarding the authority or authorities considered as competent;

4. *Recommends further* that Member States should report to the Secretary-General at the end of three years, and thereafter at intervals of five years, on their law and practice with regard to the matters dealt with in the present Recommendation, showing the extent to which effect has been given or is proposed to be given to the provisions of the Recommendation and such modifications as have been found or may be found necessary in adapting or applying it;

5. *Requests* the Secretary-General to prepare for the Commission on the Status of Women a document containing the reports received from Governments concerning methods of implementing the three basic principles of the present Recommendation;

6. *Invites* the Commission on the Status of Women to examine the reports received from Member States pursuant to the present Recommendation and to report thereon to the Economic and Social Council with such recommendations as it may deem fitting.

Document 35

Article 3 of the International Covenant on Civil and Political Rights and article 3 of the International Covenant on Economic, Social and Cultural Rights, both adopted by the General Assembly on 16 December 1966 (extract)

UN Treaty Series, vol. 999, page 171, and vol. 993, page 3

International Covenant on Civil and Political Rights

Article 3

The States Parties to the present Covenant undertake to ensure the equal right of men and women to the enjoyment of all civil and political rights set forth in the present Covenant.

International Covenant on Economic, Social and Cultural Rights

Article 3

The States Parties to the present Covenant undertake to ensure the equal right of men and women to the enjoyment of all economic, social and cultural rights set forth in the present Covenant.

Document 36

General Assembly resolution adopting the Declaration on the Elimination of Discrimination against Women

A/RES/2263 (XXII), 7 November 1967

The General Assembly,

Considering that the peoples of the United Nations have, in the Charter, reaffirmed their faith in fundamental human rights, in the dignity and worth of the human person and in the equal rights of men and women,

Considering that the Universal Declaration on Human Rights asserts the principle of non-discrimination and proclaims that all human beings are born free and equal in dignity and rights and that everyone is entitled to all the rights and freedoms set forth therein, without distinction of any kind, including any distinction as to sex,

Taking into account the resolutions, declarations, conventions and recommendations of the United Nations and the specialized agencies designed to eliminate all forms of discrimination and to promote equal rights for men and women,

Concerned that, despite the Charter of the United Nations, the Universal Declaration of Human Rights, the International Covenants on Human Rights and other instruments of the United Nations and the specialized agencies and despite the progress made in the matter of equality of rights, there continues to exist considerable discrimination against women,

Considering that discrimination against women is incompatible with human dignity and with the welfare of the family and of society, prevents their participation, on equal terms with men, in the political, social, economic and cultural life of their countries and is an obstacle to the full development of the potentialities of women in the service of their countries and of humanity,

Bearing in mind the great contribution made by women to social, political, economic and cultural life and the part they play in the family and particularly in the rearing of children,

Convinced that the full and complete development of a country, the welfare of the world and the cause of peace require the maximum participation of women as well as men in all fields,

Considering that it is necessary to ensure the universal recognition in law and in fact of the principle of equality of men and women,

Solemnly proclaims this Declaration:

Article 1

Discrimination against women, denying or limiting as it does their equality of rights with men, is fundamentally unjust and constitutes an offence against human dignity.

Article 2

All appropriate measures shall be taken to abolish existing laws, customs, regulations and practices which are discriminatory against women, and to establish adequate legal protection for equal rights of men and women, in particular:

(a) The principle of equality of rights shall be embodied in the constitution or otherwise guaranteed by law;

(b) The international instruments of the United Nations and the specialized agencies relating to the elimination of discrimination against women shall be ratified or acceded to and fully implemented as soon as practicable.

Article 3

All appropriate measures shall be taken to educate public opinion and to direct national aspirations towards the eradication of prejudice and the abolition of customary and all other practices which are based on the idea of the inferiority of women.

Article 4

All appropriate measures shall be taken to ensure to women on equal terms with men, without any discrimination:

(a) The right to vote in all elections and be eligible for election to all publicly elected bodies;

(b) The right to vote in all public referenda;

(c) The right to hold public office and to exercise all public functions.

Such rights shall be guaranteed by legislation.

Article 5

Women shall have the same rights as men to acquire, change or retain their nationality. Marriage to an alien shall not automatically affect the nationality of the wife either by rendering her stateless or by forcing upon her the nationality of her husband.

Article 6

1. Without prejudice to the safeguarding of the unity and the harmony of the family, which remains the basic unit of any society, all appropriate measures, particularly legislative measures, shall be taken to ensure to women, married or unmarried, equal rights with men in the field of civil law, and in particular:

(a) The right to acquire, administer, enjoy, dispose of and inherit property, including property acquired during marriage;

(b) The right to equality in legal capacity and the exercise thereof;

(c) The same rights as men with regard to the law on the movement of persons.

2. All appropriate measures shall be taken to ensure the principle of equality of status of the husband and wife, and in particular:

(a) Women shall have the same right as men to free choice of a spouse and to enter into marriage only with their free and full consent;

(b) Women shall have equal rights with men during marriage and at its dissolution. In all cases the interest of the children shall be paramount;

(c) Parents shall have equal rights and duties in matters relating to their children. In all cases the interest of the children shall be paramount.

3. Child marriage and the betrothal of young girls before puberty shall be prohibited, and effective action, including legislation, shall be taken to specify a minimum age for marriage and to make the registration of marriages in an official registry compulsory.

Article 7

All provisions of penal codes which constitute discrimination against women shall be repealed.

Article 8

All appropriate measures, including legislation, shall be taken to combat all forms of traffic in women and exploitation of prostitution of women.

Article 9

All appropriate measures shall be taken to ensure to girls and women, married or unmarried, equal rights with men in education at all levels, and in particular:

(a) Equal conditions of access to, and study in, educational institutions of all types, including universities and vocational, technical and professional schools;

(b) The same choice of curricula, the same examinations, teaching staff with qualifications of the same standard, and school premises and equipment of the same quality, whether the institutions are co-educational or not;

(c) Equal opportunities to benefit from scholarships and other study grants;

(d) Equal opportunities for access to programmes of continuing education, including adult literacy programmes;

(e) Access to educational information to help in ensuring the health and well-being of families.

Article 10

1. All appropriate measures shall be taken to ensure to women, married or unmarried, equal rights with men in the field of economic and social life, and in particular:

(a) The right, without discrimination on grounds of marital status or any other grounds, to receive vocational training, to work, to free choice of profession and employment, and to professional and vocational advancement;

(b) The right to equal remuneration with men and to equality of treatment in respect of work of equal value;

(c) The right to leave with pay, retirement privileges and provision for security in respect of unemployment, sickness, old age or other incapacity to work;

(d) The right to receive family allowances on equal terms with men.

2. In order to prevent discrimination against women on account of marriage or maternity and to ensure their effective right to work, measures shall be taken to prevent their dismissal in the event of marriage or maternity and to provide paid maternity leave, with the guarantee of returning to former employment, and to provide the necessary social services, including child-care facilities.

3. Measures taken to protect women in certain types of work, for reasons inherent in their physical nature, shall not be regarded as discriminatory.

Article 11

1. The principle of equality of rights of men and women demands implementation in all States in accordance with the principles of the Charter of the United Nations and of the Universal Declaration of Human Rights.

2. Governments, non-governmental organizations and individuals are urged, therefore, to do all in their power to promote the implementation of the principles contained in this Declaration.

Document 37

Resolution IX adopted by the International Conference on Human Rights in Teheran on measures to promote women's rights in the modern world and endorsing the Secretary-General's proposal for a unified long-term United Nations programme for the advancement of women

A/CONF.32/41, 12 May 1968

The International Conference on Human Rights,

Considering that the peoples of the United Nations have, in the Charter, reaffirmed their faith in fundamental human rights, in the dignity and worth of the human person and in the equal rights of men and women,

Considering that, in accordance with the United Nations Charter and the Universal Declaration of Human Rights, women should be recognized as having a right to the development of their full potentialities in the family, in work and in public life,

Concerned that, despite the Charter of the United Nations, the Universal Declaration of Human Rights, the International Covenants on Human Rights and other instruments of the United Nations and the specialized agencies and despite the progress made in the matter of equality of rights, there continues to exist considerable discrimination against women in the political, legal, economic, social and educational fields and that the Conventions adopted by the United Nations in these fields have not been ratified by many Member States,

Noting that the Declaration on the Elimination of Discrimination against Women proclaims that discrimination against women, leading to the denial or limitation of equal rights between men and women, is fundamentally unjust and constitutes an offence against human dignity,

Convinced that satisfactory progress for humanity as a whole depends on more rapid progress in respect of the status of women and that the full and complete development of a country, the welfare of the world and the cause of peace require the maximum participation of women as well as men in all fields,

Believing that for more effective social and economic development the formulation and execution of national development plans needs the active participation of women at every level,

Considering that discrimination against women is incompatible with human dignity and with the welfare of the family and of society, prevents their participation, on equal terms with men, in the political, social, economic and cultural life of their countries and is an obstacle to the full development of the potentialities of women in the service of their countries and of humanity,

Considering that colonialism, apartheid and racialism in regions where they continue to exist aggravate the injustice from which women suffer,

Bearing in mind the great contribution made by women to social, political, economic and cultural life and the part they play in the family, particularly in the rearing of children,

Considering that it is necessary to ensure the universal recognition in law and in fact of the principle of equality of men and women,

Convinced that any advancement in the status of women depends to a very large degree on changes in traditional attitude, customs and laws based on the idea of the inferiority of women:

1. *Endorses* the basic objectives of a unified long-term programme for the advancement of women suggested by the Secretary-General of the United Nations (E/CN.6/467, page 67), namely:

"(a) To promote the universal recognition of the dignity and worth of the human person and of the equal rights of men and women in accordance with the Charter of the United Nations and the Universal Declaration of Human Rights;

"(b) To enable women to participate fully in the development of society in order that society may benefit from the contribution of all its members;

"(c) To stimulate an awareness among both men and women of women's full potential and of the importance of their contribution to the development of society";

2. *Urges* the States Members of the United Nations and of the specialized agencies and their peoples to take immediate and effective measures to conform to the Charter and the Universal Declaration of Human Rights in order to ensure the equality of men and women and to eliminate discrimination against women in accordance with the Declaration on the Elimination of Discrimination against Women;

3. *Invites* Governments of States Members of the United Nations and of the specialized agencies to draw up and execute, in cooperation with national commissions on the status of women or similar bodies and

appropriate voluntary organizations, long-term programmes for the advancement of women within the context of national development plans where they exist;

4. *Recommends* that, to the ends indicated in operative paragraphs 1, 2 and 3 above, every effort be made:

(a) To ratify as soon as possible the following Conventions adopted under the auspices of the United Nations and of the specialized agencies:

   (i) Convention for the Suppression of the Traffic in Persons and of the Exploitation of the Prostitution of Others, 1949;

   (ii) Convention on the Political Rights of Women, 1952;

   (iii) Convention on the Nationality of Married Women, 1957;

   (iv) Convention on Consent to Marriage, Minimum Age for Marriage and Registration of Marriages, 1962;

   (v) ILO Convention on Equal Remuneration for Men and Women Workers for Work of Equal Value, 1951;

   (vi) ILO Convention on Discrimination (Employment and Occupation), 1958;

   (vii) UNESCO Convention Against Discrimination in Education, 1960;

   (viii) International Convention on the Elimination of all Forms of Racial Discrimination, 1965;

(b) To amend or add to constitutions and other national laws so as to bring them into harmony with the United Nations Charter, the Universal Declaration of Human Rights, the International Covenants on Human Rights, the Declaration on the Elimination of Discrimination Against Women, the conventions of the United Nations and the specialized agencies, and their resolutions and recommendations on the status of women;

(c) To intensify efforts to ensure the implementation of these various instruments especially by making at least elementary education compulsory for all, by adopting educational methods and programmes eliminating all discrimination between the sexes and promoting understanding of the equality of all human beings, by providing, in economic development plans, for optimal utilization of woman power and the social infrastructure on which it depends;

(d) To establish in accordance with Economic and Social Council resolution 961 F (XXXVI) national commissions on the status of women or appropriate bodies;

(e) To establish programmes for the utilization and development of human resources and community services through which women can contribute to national development;

(f) To create a Women's Social Service;

(g) To encourage educational programmes with special provisions, where required, to assure full attendance by girls and women, taking into account existing literacy and other needs, and using all methods of communication, including mass media, as appropriate;

(h) To promote vocational guidance programmes and means to facilitate vocational and professional training at all levels for the full participation of women in the economic life of their countries;

(i) To ensure the equality of men and women in the field of social and economic rights, including the right to work, the right to equal pay, the right to rest, the right to social security and the right to health protection;

(j) To ensure the equality of men and women in the field of civil and family rights;

(k) To establish educational programmes for boys and girls, as well as men and women, to prepare them to meet the responsibilities of family life;

(l) To give opportunities and to promote the access of women to public office and other responsible posts at all levels including the exercise of all public functions;

5. *Invites* Member States, specialized agencies and UNICEF and intergovernmental and non-governmental organizations to give the widest publicity to all the instruments of the United Nations and the specialized agencies concerning the status of women and, in particular, to the Declaration on the Elimination of Discrimination against Women and to take all appropriate measures to give effect to their implementation;

6. *Invites* non-governmental organizations to intensify their efforts to inform and educate women all over the world;

7. *Requests* the General Assembly to invite Governments of Member States to transmit their national long-term programmes for the advancement of women to the Commission on the Status of Women for study and exchange of experiences, and to report each year on the progress made;

8. *Requests* the United Nations bodies and the specialized agencies concerned to:

(a) Contribute, through appropriate technical assistance, to national long-term programmes for the advancement of women;

(b) Establish or review their budgetary priorities, as appropriate, with a view to meeting the requirements of national long-term programmes for the advancement of women, particularly in developing countries;

(c) Recommend to the Commission on the Status of Women to accord priority in its work programme to the examination of problems concerning the education of women and their contribution to the economic and social development of their countries;

(d) Recommend to the Commission on the Status of Women to consider drafting conventions on the status of women in family law and in other fields of private law, and in all other fields where discrimination exists and where conventions are still missing;

(e) Recommend to the Commission on the Status of Women to reconsider and to adapt its programme and methods of work to meet the needs of women in the contemporary world;

(f) Encourage studies to be made by experts regarding attitudes and values in different societies which affect the advancement of women and the promotion of their equal rights with men as well as the implementation of these rights.

Document 38

General Assembly resolution calling for the employment of qualified women in senior and other professional positions by the secretariats of organizations in the United Nations system

A/RES/2715 (XXV), 15 December 1970

The General Assembly,

Recalling Article 101 of the Charter of the United Nations,

Recalling the Universal Declaration of Human Rights,

Recalling further the Declaration on the Elimination of Discrimination against Women,

1. *Expresses the hope* that the United Nations, including its special bodies and all intergovernmental agencies in the United Nations system of organizations, will set an example with regard to the opportunities they afford for the employment of women at senior and other professional levels;

2. *Urges* the United Nations, including its special bodies and all intergovernmental agencies in the United Nations system of organizations, to take or continue to take appropriate measures to ensure equal opportunities for the employment of qualified women in senior and other professional positions;

3. *Requests* the Secretary-General to include in his report to the General Assembly on the composition of the Secretariat data on the employment of women at senior and other professional levels by the secretariats of the above-mentioned bodies, including their numbers and the positions they occupy.

Document 39

General Assembly resolution outlining a programme of concerted international action for the advancement of women

A/RES/2716 (XXV), 15 December 1970

The General Assembly,

Recalling its resolution 1777 (XVII) of 7 December 1962 initiating the study of a unified, long-term United Nations programme for the advancement of women,

Recalling also the Declaration on the Elimination of Discrimination against Women, adopted on 7 November 1967, and the Declaration on Social Progress and Development, adopted on 11 December 1969,

Noting resolution IX of the International Conference on Human Rights held at Teheran in 1968, 1/ on measures to promote women's rights in the modern world, including a unified, long-term United Nations programme for the advancement of women, which established guidelines for such a programme,

Noting also that, in accordance with General Assembly resolution 2571 (XXIV) of 13 December 1969 and with paragraph 79 of Assembly resolution 2626 (XXV) of 24 October 1970, concerning the International Development Strategy for the Second United Nations Development Decade, arrangements should be made to keep under systematic scrutiny the progress towards achieving the goals and objectives of the Decade, to

1/ *Final Act of the International Conference on Human Rights* (United Nations publication, Sales No. E.68.XIV.2), p. 10.

identify shortfalls in their achievement and the policies that are not consistent with the attainment of those objectives and to recommend positive measures, including new goals and policies as needed,

Expressing the hope that general and complete disarmament under effective international control will allow for the use of resources released progressively for purposes of economic and social progress of all peoples, including the elaboration of programmes designed to advance the status of women,

Believing that a programme of concerted international action, planned on a long-term basis, will advance the status of women and increase their effective participation in all sectors,

Considering that the success of such a programme will require intensified action on the part of Member States, at the national and regional levels, as well as maximum use of the methods and techniques available through the United Nations system of organizations,

Believing that an important step in the further development of such a programme would be the establishment of concrete objectives and minimum targets,

1. *Recommends* that the objectives and targets set forth in the annex to the present resolution should be achieved as widely as possible during the Second United Nations Development Decade;

2. *Invites* States Members of the United Nations or members of specialized agencies and all organs and agencies within the United Nations system to cooperate in achieving these objectives and targets, and hopes that adequate staff and resources will be made available for this purpose;

3. *Recommends* that concerted efforts should be made to increase the resources available for technical cooperation projects which advance the status of women and that consideration be given to allocating a specific percentage of the available funds for this purpose;

4. *Requests* the Secretary-General to make available to the Commission on the Status of Women, if possible at its twenty-fourth session, information on the extent to which women are participating in, and benefiting from, technical cooperation projects;

5. *Recommends* that conferences, seminars and similar meetings at the regional and international levels should be organized with the participation, wherever possible, of ministers, high government officials and specialists concerned with problems of development, and of representatives of non-governmental organizations concerned with this problem, to consider ways and means of promoting the status of women within the framework of overall development;

6. *Draws attention* to the important role that may also be played in this respect by the regional training and research centres for social development to be established pursuant to Economic and Social Council resolution 1406 (XLVI) of 5 June 1969;

7. *Suggests* that the continuous education of adults be encouraged with a view to changing in particular their attitude of mind towards the roles to be played by men and women in order to help them to assume their responsibilities in society;

8. *Notes*, notwithstanding the provisions of all the preceding paragraphs, that the family, as the corner-stone of society, must be protected.

Annex

I. *General objectives*

1. The ratification of, or accession to, the relevant international conventions relating to the status of women.

2. The enactment of legislation to bring national laws into conformity with international instruments relating to the status of women, including in particular the Declaration on the Elimination of Discrimination against Women.

3. The taking of effective legal and other measures to ensure the full implementation of these instruments.

4. The development of effective large-scale educational and informational programmes using all mass media and other available means to make all sectors of the population in rural as well as urban areas fully aware of the norms established by the United Nations and the specialized agencies in the conventions, recommendations, declarations and resolutions adopted under their auspices, and to educate public opinion and enlist its support for all measures aimed at achieving the realization of the standards set forth.

5. The assessment and evaluation of the contribution of women to the various economic and social sectors in relation to the country's overall development plans and programmes, with a view to establishing specific objectives and minimum targets which might realistically be achieved by 1980 to increase the effective contribution of women to the various sectors.

6. The study of the positive and negative effects of scientific and technological change on the status of women with a view to ensuring continuous progress, especially as regards the education and training as well as the living conditions and employment of women.

7. The elaboration of short-term and long-term programmes to achieve these specific objectives and minimum targets, where possible within the framework of overall national development plans or programmes, and the provision of adequate funds for programmes which advance the status of women.

8. The establishment of machinery and procedures to make possible the continuous review and evaluation of women's integration into all sectors of economic and social life and their contribution to development.

9. The full utilization of the desire and readiness of women to devote their energies, talents and abilities to the benefit of society.

II. *Minimum targets to be achieved during the Second United Nations Development Decade*

A. *Education*

1. The progressive elimination of illiteracy, ensuring equality in literacy between the sexes, especially among the younger generation.

2. Equal access of boys and girls to education at the primary and secondary levels and at educational institutions of all types, including universities and vocational, technical and professional schools.

3. Decisive progress in achieving free and compulsory education at the primary level and in achieving free education at all levels.

4. The establishment of the same choice of curricula for boys and girls, the same examinations, equally qualified teaching staff, and the same quality of school premises and equipment, whether the institutions are co-educational or not, and equal opportunities to receive scholarships and grants.

5. The achievement of equality in the percentage of boys and girls receiving primary education and of a substantial increase in the number of girls at all educational levels, in particular in the field of technical and professional education.

6. The establishment of educational policies that take account of employment needs and opportunities and of scientific and technological change.

B. *Training and employment*

1. Provision of the same vocational advice and guidance to members of both sexes.

2. Equal access of girls and women to vocational training and retraining at all levels, with a view to achieving their full participation in the economic and social life of their countries.

3. Universal acceptance of the principle of equal pay for equal work and the adoption of effective measures to implement it.

4. Full acceptance of the policy of non-discrimination in relation to the employment and treatment of women, and measures to give effect to that policy on a progressive basis.

5. A substantial increase in the numbers of qualified women employed in skilled and technical work, and at all higher levels of economic life and in posts of responsibility.

6. A substantial increase in the opportunities for involvement of women in all facets of agricultural development and agricultural services.

C. *Health and maternity protection*

1. The progressive extension of measures to ensure maternity protection, with a view to ensuring paid maternity leave with the guarantee of returning to former or equivalent employment.

2. The development and extension of adequate child care and other facilities to assist parents with family responsibilities.

3. The adoption of measures for the creation and development of a wide network of special medical establishments for the protection of the health of the mother and child.

4. Making available to all persons who so desire the necessary information and advice to enable them to decide freely and responsibly on the number and spacing of their children and to prepare them for responsible parenthood, including information on the ways in which women can benefit from family planning. Such information and advice should be based on valid and proven scientific expertise, with due regard to the risks that may be involved.

D. *Administration and public life*

1. A substantial increase in the number of women participating in public and government life at the local, national and international levels. Special attention might be paid to training women for such participation, especially in middle-level and higher posts.

2. A substantial increase in the number of qualified women holding responsible posts at the executive and policy-making levels, including those related to overall development planning.

Document 40

General Assembly resolution reiterating that organizations in the United Nations system take measures to ensure equal opportunities for the employment of qualified women at the senior and professional levels and in policy-making positions

A/RES/3009 (XXVII), 18 December 1972

The General Assembly,

Recalling the declarations and instruments adopted by the United Nations acknowledging the equality of status of men and women — *inter alia*, the Charter of the United Nations, the Universal Declaration of Human Rights, the International Covenant on Economic, Social and Cultural Rights, 1/ the International Covenant on Civil and Political Rights 1/ and the Declaration on the Elimination of Discrimination against Women 2/ — and also relevant instruments of the International Labour Organisation and the United Nations Educational, Scientific and Cultural Organization,

Recalling its resolution 2715 (XXV) of 15 December 1970, in which it requested the Secretary-General to include in his report to the General Assembly on the composition of the Secretariat data on the employment of women at senior and other professional levels, including their numbers and the positions they occupy,

Noting with appreciation that the report of the Secretary-General on the composition of the Secretariat submitted to the General Assembly at its twenty-sixth session 3/ included for the first time some information on the employment of women, showing the number of women and the level at which they were employed in senior and professional positions within the secretariats of organizations in the United Nations system, and that a further report has been submitted to the General Assembly at its twenty-seventh session 4/ which likewise includes data on the employment of women,

Noting that, as at 30 June 1972, no women were employed within the United Nations Secretariat at the Under-Secretary-General or Assistant-Secretary-General level, that only three of the total of 59 employed at the D-2 level were women, and that only four of the total of 181 employed at the D-1 level were women,

Further noting that in the less senior and professional ranks of the Secretariat the percentage of women is in inverse proportion to the level of the position, ranging from 6.2 per cent of the staff at the P-5 level to 40.4 per cent at the P-1 level in posts subject to geographical distribution, and from 7.3 per cent at the P-5 level to 39.8 per cent at the P-1 level for the Secretariat as a whole,

Noting as well that in all the other organizations in the United Nations common system there are no women at the highest levels, only on woman employed at the D-2 level and only 10 women at the D-1 level,

1. *Notes with satisfaction* the recent appointment by the Secretary-General of a woman to the rank of Assistant Secretary-General and hopes that more women will be appointed to positions at high levels of the United Nations Secretariat;

2. *Requests* the Secretary-General to include in his annual report to the General Assembly on the composition of the Secretariat more comprehensive data on the employment of women in the secretariats of the organizations in the United Nations system, so as to show the nature of posts and types of duties performed by women at the professional and policy-making levels;

3. *Urges once again* the organizations in the United Nations system to take or continue to take appropriate measures, including more extensive publicizing of the right of individuals personally to apply for vacant positions, in order to ensure equal opportunities for the employment of qualified women at the senior and professional levels and in policy-making positions;

4. *Calls upon* Member States, when proposing nationals for appointment to the senior and professional positions in the secretariats of the organizations in the United Nations system, to give full consideration to submitting the candidatures of qualified women for all positions, particularly at the policy-making level.

1/ See resolution 2200 A (XXI), annex.
2/ Resolution 2263 (XXII).
3/ A/8483.
4/ A/8831 and Corr.1 and Add.1.

Document 41

General Assembly resolution proclaiming 1975 International Women's Year

A/RES/3010 (XXVII), 18 December 1972

The General Assembly,

Considering that twenty-five years have elapsed since the first session of the Commission on the Status of Women was held at Lake Success, New York, from 10 to 24 February 1947, and that this is a period which makes it possible to take stock of the positive results obtained,

Bearing in mind the aims and principles of the Declaration on the Elimination of Discrimination against Women, adopted by the General Assembly in resolution 2263 (XXII) of 7 November 1967,

Recognizing the effectiveness of the work done by the Commission on the Status of Women in the twenty-five years since its establishment, and the important contribution which women have made to the social, political, economic and cultural life of their countries,

Considering that it is necessary to strengthen universal recognition of the principle of the equality of men and women, *de jure* and *de facto*, and that both legal and social measures have to be taken by Member States which have not yet done so to ensure the implementation of women's rights,

Recalling that its resolution 2626 (XXV) of 24 October 1970, containing the International Development Strategy for the Second United Nations Development Decade, includes among the goals and objectives of the Decade the encouragement of the full integration of women in the total development effort,

Drawing attention to the general objectives and minimum targets to be attained in the course of the Second United Nations Development Decade, as defined by the Commission on the Status of Women and adopted by the General Assembly in its resolution 2716 (XXV) of 15 December 1970,

Considering that, with those ends in view, the proclamation of an international women's year would serve to intensify the action required to advance the status of women,

1. *Proclaims* the year 1975 International Women's Year;

2. *Decides* to devote this year to intensified action:

(a) To promote equality between men and women;

(b) To ensure the full integration of women in the total development effort, especially by emphasizing women's responsibility and important role in economic, social and cultural development at the national, regional and international levels, particularly during the Second United Nations Development Decade;

(c) To recognize the importance of women's increasing contribution to the development of friendly relations and cooperation among States and to the strengthening of world peace;

3. *Invites* all Member States and all interested organizations to take steps to ensure the full realization of the rights of women and their advancement on the basis of the Declaration on the Elimination of Discrimination against Women;

4. *Invites* Governments that have not yet done so to ratify as soon as possible the Convention concerning Equal Remuneration for Men and Women Workers for Work of Equal Value, 1951, 1/ adopted by the International Labour Conference at its thirty-fourth session;

5. *Requests* the Secretary-General to prepare, in consultation with Member States, specialized agencies and interested non-governmental organizations, within the limits of existing resources, a draft programme for the International Women's Year and to submit it to the Commission on the Status of Women at its twenty-fifth session in 1974.

1/ International Labour Organization, *Conventions and Recommendations, 1919-1966* (Geneva, 1966), Convention No. 100, p. 795.

Document 42

General Assembly resolution inviting all States to participate in the Conference of the International Women's Year

A/RES/3276 (XXIX), 10 December 1974 1/

The General Assembly,

Recalling its resolution 3010 (XXVII) of 18 December 1972 in which it proclaimed the year 1975 International Women's Year,

Noting that the Economic and Social Council in its resolution 1851 (LVI) of 16 May 1974 requested the Secretary-General to convene in 1975, in consultation with Member States, specialized agencies and interested non-governmental organizations in consultative status with the Council, an international conference during the International Women's Year to examine to what extent the organizations of the United Nations system have implemented the recommendations for the elimination of discrimination against women made by the Commission on the Status of Women since its establishment, and to launch an international action programme including short-term and long-term measures aimed at achieving the integration of women as full and equal partners with men in the total development effort and eliminating discrimination on grounds of sex, and at achieving the widest involvement of women in strengthening international peace and eliminating racism and racial discrimination,

Noting further that in the same resolution the Economic and Social Council recommended that a separate item entitled "International Women's Year", including the proposals and recommendations of the Conference of the International Women's Year, should be examined by the General Assembly at its thirtieth session,

Noting further that the Economic and Social Council, in resolution 1849 (LVI) of 16 May 1974, approved the Programme for the International Women's Year,

1. *Decides* to invite all States to participate in the Conference of the International Women's Year;

2. *Decides* to invite also the national liberation movements recognized by the Organization of African Unity and/or by the League of Arab States in their respective regions to participate in the Conference as observers, in accordance with the practice of the United Nations;

3. *Requests* the Conference to submit, if possible, such proposals and recommendations as it deems appropriate to the General Assembly at its special session to be held in September 1975;

4. *Decides* to consider at its thirtieth session an item entitled "International Women's Year, including the proposals and recommendations of the Conference of the International Women's Year" and an item entitled "Status and role of women in society, with special reference to the need for achieving equal rights for women and to women's contribution to the attainment of the goals of the Second United Nations Development Decade, to the struggle against colonialism, racism and racial discrimination and to the strengthening of international peace and of cooperation between States".

1/ At its 1938th plenary meeting, on 15 January 1975, the Economic and Social Council decided that the Conference to be held during the International Women's Year should be entitled "World Conference of the International Women's Year" (Council decision 67 (ORG-75)).

Document 43

General Assembly resolution establishing a Consultative Committee for the Conference of the International Women's Year

A/RES/3277 (XXIX), 10 December 1974

The General Assembly,

Noting Economic and Social Council resolution 1851 (LVI) of 16 May 1974, in which the Secretary-General was requested to convene, in consultation with Member States, specialized agencies and interested non-governmental organizations in consultative status with the Council, an international conference during the International Women's Year, in 1975,

Realizing the importance of consultations, at the highest possible level, for the preparation of the Conference of the International Women's Year,

1. *Expresses the hope* that the preparation of the

Conference of the International Women's Year will be given the full attention which it warrants, having regard to the importance of the question;

2. *Decides* to establish a Consultative Committee for the Conference of the International Women's Year composed of not more than twenty-three Member States designated by the Chairman of the Third Committee after consultation with the different regional groups, on the basis of equitable geographical distribution;

3. *Expresses the hope* that the Consultative Committee will be comprised of highly qualified individuals designated by their respective Governments;

4. *Requests* the Secretary-General to convene the Consultative Committee not later than March 1975 at United Nations Headquarters, for a period not exceeding ten working days, to advise him on the preparation of an international plan of action to be finalized by the Conference;

5. *Decides* that all the costs of convening the Consultative Committee, including the travel expenses of its members, will be met from the fund for voluntary contributions for the International Women's Year established under Economic and Social Council resolution 1850 (LVI) of 16 May 1974;

6. *Appeals* to Member States to make, in so far as it lies within their power, voluntary contributions to the above-mentioned fund in order to meet the necessary financial implications for the convening of the Consultative Committee;

7. *Requests* the Secretary-General to prepare a draft international plan of action in time to be considered by the Consultative Committee and to submit a progress report on the preparation of the Conference to the organizational session of the Economic and Social Council in January 1975.

* * *

At the 2311th plenary meeting, on 10 December 1974, the President of the General Assembly announced that the Chairman of the Third Committee, in pursuance of paragraph 2 of the above resolution, had designated the members of the Consultative Committee for the Conference of the International Women's Year.

As a result the Consultative Committee is composed of the following Member States: AUSTRALIA, BELGIUM, BRAZIL, FRANCE, GERMAN DEMOCRATIC REPUBLIC, INDIA, IRAN, JAMAICA, JAPAN, JORDAN, MEXICO, NIGER, PHILIPPINES, ROMANIA, RWANDA, SENEGAL, SIERRA LEONE, SWEDEN, TUNISIA, UNION OF SOVIET SOCIALIST REPUBLICS, UNITED KINGDOM OF GREAT BRITAIN AND NORTHERN IRELAND, UNITED STATES OF AMERICA *and* VENEZUELA.

Document 44

General Assembly resolution adopting the Declaration on the Protection of Women and Children in Emergency and Armed Conflict

A/RES/3318 (XXIX), 14 December 1974

The General Assembly,

Having considered the recommendation of the Economic and Social Council contained in its resolution 1861 (LVI) of 16 May 1974,

Expressing its deep concern over the sufferings of women and children belonging to the civilian population who in periods of emergency and armed conflict in the struggle for peace, self-determination, national liberation and independence are too often the victims of inhuman acts and consequently suffer serious harm,

Aware of the suffering of women and children in many areas of the world, especially in those areas subject to suppression, aggression, colonialism, racism, alien domination and foreign subjugation,

Deeply concerned by the fact that, despite general and unequivocal condemnation, colonialism, racism and alien and foreign domination continue to subject many peoples under their yoke, cruelly suppressing the national liberation movements and inflicting heavy losses and incalculable sufferings on the populations under their domination, including women and children,

Deploring the fact that grave attacks are still being made on fundamental freedoms and the dignity of the human person and that colonial and racist foreign domination Powers continue to violate international humanitarian law,

Recalling the relevant provisions contained in the instruments of international humanitarian law relative to the protection of women and children in time of peace and war,

Recalling, among other important documents, its resolutions 2444 (XXIII) of 19 December 1968, 2597 (XXIV) of 16 December 1969 and 2674 (XXV) and 2675 (XXV) of 9 December 1970, on respect for human rights and on basic principles for the protection of civilian populations in armed conflicts, as well as Economic and Social Council resolution 1515 (XLVIII) of 28 May 1970 in which the Council requested the General Assembly to consider the possibility of drafting a declaration on the protection of women and children in emergency or wartime,

Conscious of its responsibility for the destiny of the rising generation and for the destiny of mothers, who play an important role in society, in the family and particularly in the upbringing of children,

Bearing in mind the need to provide special protection of women and children belonging to the civilian population,

Solemnly proclaims this Declaration on the Protection of Women and Children in Emergency and Armed Conflict and calls for the strict observance of the Declaration by all Member States:

1. Attacks and bombings on the civilian population, inflicting incalculable suffering, especially on women and children, who are the most vulnerable members of the population, shall be prohibited, and such acts shall be condemned.

2. The use of chemical and bacteriological weapons in the course of military operations constitutes one of the most flagrant violations of the Geneva Protocol of 1925, 1/ the Geneva Conventions of 1949 2/ and the principles of international humanitarian law and inflicts heavy losses on civilian populations, including defenceless women and children, and shall be severely condemned.

3. All States shall abide fully by their obligations under the Geneva Protocol of 1925 and the Geneva Conventions of 1949, as well as other instruments of international law relative to respect for human rights in armed conflicts, which offer important guarantees for the protection of women and children.

4. All efforts shall be made by States involved in armed conflicts, military operations in foreign territories or military operations in territories still under colonial domination to spare women and children from the ravages of war. All the necessary steps shall be taken to ensure the prohibition of measures such as persecution, torture, punitive measures, degrading treatment and violence, particularly against that part of the civilian population that consists of women and children.

5. All forms of repression and cruel and inhuman treatment of women and children, including imprisonment, torture, shooting, mass arrests, collective punishment, destruction of dwellings and forcible eviction, committed by belligerents in the course of military operations or in occupied territories shall be considered criminal.

6. Women and children belonging to the civilian population and finding themselves in circumstances of emergency and armed conflict in the struggle for peace, self-determination, national liberation and independence, or who live in occupied territories, shall not be deprived of shelter, food, medical aid or other inalienable rights, in accordance with the provisions of the Universal Declaration of Human Rights, the International Covenant on Civil and Political Rights, 3/ the International Covenant on Economic, Social and Cultural Rights, 3/ the Declaration of the Rights of the Child 4/ or other instruments of international law.

1/ League of Nations, *Treaty Series,* vol. XCIV, No. 2138, p. 65.

2/ United Nations, *Treaty Series*, vol. 75, Nos. 970-973.

3/ Resolution 2200 A (XXI), annex.

4/ Resolution 1386 (XIV).

Document 45

Report of the World Conference of the International Women's Year, held in Mexico City from 19 June to 2 July 1975; including the Agenda, the World Plan of Action for the Implementation of the Objectives of the International Women's Year, the Declaration of Mexico on the Equality of Women and Their Contribution to Development and Peace, and resolutions and decisions adopted by the Conference (extract)

E/CONF.66/34, 1976

...

Agenda

...

1. Opening of the Conference and election of the President

2. Adoption of the rules of procedure

3. Adoption of the agenda

4. Establishment of committees and organization of work

5. Election of officers other than the President

6. Credentials of representatives to the Conference

    (a) Appointment of the Credentials Committee

    (b) Report of the Credentials Committee

7. The objectives and goals of International Women's Year: Present policies and programmes

8. The involvement of women in strengthening international peace and eliminating racism, apartheid, racial discrimination, colonialism, alien domination and acquisition of territories by force

9. Current trends and changes in the status and roles of women and men, and major obstacles to be overcome in the achievement of equal rights, opportunities and responsibilities

10. The integration of women in the development process as equal partners with men

11. World Plan of Action

12. Adoption of the report of the Conference

Introduction

1. In subscribing to the Charter, the peoples of the United Nations undertook specific commitments: "to save succeeding generations from the scourge of war..., to reaffirm faith in fundamental human rights, in the dignity and worth of the human person, in the equal rights of men and women and of nations large and small, and ... to promote social progress and better standards of life in larger freedom".

2. The greatest and most significant achievement during recent decades has been the liberation of a large number of peoples and nations from alien colonial domination, which has permitted them to become members of the community of free peoples. Technological progress has also been achieved in all spheres of economic activity during the past three decades, thus offering substantial possibilities for improving the well-being of all peoples. However, the last vestiges of alien and colonial domination, foreign occupation, racial discrimination, apartheid and neo-colonialism in all its forms are still among the greatest obstacles to the full emancipation and progress of developing countries and of all the peoples concerned. The benefits of technological progress are not shared equitably by all members of the international community. The developing countries, which account for 70 per cent of the population of the world, receive only 30 per cent of world income. It has proved impossible to achieve uniform and balanced development of the international community under the present economic order, and, for this reason, it is urgent to implement a new international economic order in accordance with General Assembly resolution 3201 (S-VI of 1 May 1974).

3. Conventions, declarations, formal recommendations and other instruments have been adopted since the Charter came into force, 1/ with a view to reinforcing, elaborating and implementing these fundamental principles and objectives. Some of them seek to safeguard and promote the human rights and fundamental freedoms of all persons without discrimination of any kind. Others deal with the promotion of economic and social progress and development and the need to eliminate all forms of alien domination, dependence, neo-colonialism, and include international strategies, programmes and plans of action. Some have the more specific purpose of eliminating discrimination on the ground of sex and promoting the equal rights of men and women. These documents reflect the ever increasing awareness in the international community of the uneven development of peoples, and of the tragedy of all forms of discrimination, be it on the ground of race, sex or any other ground, and the evident

1/ See Appendix (below).

will to promote progress and development in conditions of peace, equity and justice.

4. In these various instruments the international community has proclaimed that the full and complete development of a country, the welfare of the world and the cause of peace require the maximum participation of women as well as men in all fields. It has declared that all human beings without distinction have the right to enjoy the fruits of social and economic progress and should, on their part, contribute to it. It has condemned sex discrimination as fundamentally unjust, an offence against human dignity and an infringement of human rights. It has included the full integration of women in the total development effort as a stated objective of the International Development Strategy for the decade of the 1970s. 2/

5. Despite these solemn pronouncements and notwithstanding the work accomplished in particular by the United Nations Commission on the Status of Women and the specialized agencies concerned, progress in translating these principles into practical reality is proving slow and uneven. The difficulties encountered in the preparation and implementation of these many instruments are attributable to the complexities created by the considerable differences between countries, regions, etc.

6. History has attested to the active role which women played, together with men, in accelerating the material and spiritual progress of peoples and in the process of the progressive renewal of society; in our times, women's role will increasingly emerge as a powerful revolutionary social force.

7. There are significant differences in the status of women in different countries and regions of the world which are rooted in the political, economic and social structure, the cultural framework and the level of development of each country, and in the social category of women within a given country. However, basic similarities unite women to fight differences wherever they exist in the legal, economic, social, political and cultural status of women and men.

8. As a result of the uneven development that prevails in the international economic relations, three quarters of humanity is faced with urgent and pressing social and economic problems. The women among them are even more affected by such problems and the new measures taken to improve their situation as well as their role in the process of development must be an integral part of the global project for the establishment of a new economic order.

9. In many countries women form a large part of the agricultural work force. Because of this and because of their important role in agricultural production and in the preparation, processing and marketing of food, they constitute a substantial economic resource. Nevertheless, if the rural worker's lack of technical equipment, education and training is taken into account, it will be seen that in many countries the status of women in this sector is doubly disadvantaged.

10. While industrialization provides jobs for women and constitutes one of the main means for the integration of women in the process of development, women workers are disadvantaged in many respects because of the fact that the technological structure of production in general has been oriented towards man and his requirements. Therefore special attention must be paid to the situation of the woman worker in industry and in services. Women workers feel painfully the effects of the present economic crisis, the growth of unemployment, inflation, mass poverty, lack of resources for education and medical care, unexpected and unwanted side-effects of urbanization and other migration, etc.

11. Scientific and technological developments have had both positive and negative repercussions on the situation of women in many countries. Political, economic and social factors are important in overcoming any adverse effects of such developments.

12. During the last decades women's movements and millions of women together with other progressive forces acting in many countries have focused public opinion at the national and international levels on all these problems.

13. However, that public opinion often overlooks the many women of regions under alien domination, particularly those subjected to apartheid who experience daily the terror of repression and who struggle tirelessly for the recovery of the most elementary rights of the human person.

14. The reality of the problems which women still meet in their daily life in many countries of the world in their efforts to participate in the economic and social activities, in the decision-making process and the political administration of their countries, and the loss represented by the under-utilization of the potentialities of approximately 50 per cent of world's adult population, have prompted the United Nations to proclaim 1975 as International Women's Year, and to call for intensified action to ensure the full international cooperation and the strengthening of world peace on the basis of equal rights, opportunities and responsibilities of women and men. The objective of International Women's Year is to define a society in which women participate in a real and full sense in economic, social and political life and to devise strategies whereby such societies could develop.

15. This Plan of Action is intended to strengthen

2/ General Assembly resolution 2626 (XXV) of 24 October 1970.

the implementation of the instruments and programmes which have been adopted concerning the status of women, and to broaden and place them in a more timely context. Its purpose is mainly to stimulate national and international action to solve the problems of underdevelopment and of the socio-economic structure which places women in an inferior position, in order to achieve the goals of International Women's Year.

16. The achievement of equality between men and women implies that they should have equal rights, opportunities and responsibilities to enable them to develop their talents and capabilities for their own personal fulfilment and the benefit of society. To that end, a reassessment of the functions and roles traditionally allotted to each sex within the family and the community at large is essential. The necessity of a change in the traditional role of men as well as of women must be recognized. In order to allow for women's equal (fuller) participation in all societal activities, socially organized services should be established and maintained to lighten household chores and, especially, services for children should be provided. All efforts should be made to change social attitudes—based mainly on education—in order to bring about the acceptance of shared responsibilities for home and children by both men and women.

17. In order to promote equality between women and men, Governments should ensure for both women and men equality before the law, the provision of facilities for equality of educational opportunities and training, equality in conditions of employment, including remuneration, and adequate social security. Governments should recognize and undertake measures to implement men's and women's right to employment on equal conditions, regardless of marital status and their access to the whole range of economic activities. The State has also the responsibility to create conditions that promote the implementation of legal norms providing for equality of men and women and in particular the opportunity for all individuals to receive free general and primary education, and eventually compulsory general secondary education, equality in conditions of employment, and maternity protection.

18. Governments should strive to ameliorate the hard working conditions and unreasonably heavy work load, especially those that fall upon large groups of women in many countries and particularly among underprivileged social groups. Governments should ensure improved access to health services, better nutrition and other social services that are essential to the improvement of the condition of women and their full participation in development on an equal basis with men.

19. Individuals and couples have the right freely and responsibly to determine the number and spacing of their children and to have the information and the means to do so. The exercise of this right is basic to the attainment of any real equality between the sexes and without its achievement women are disadvantaged in their attempt to benefit from other reforms.

20. Child-care centres and other child-minding facilities are means to supplement the training and care that the children get at home. At the same time they are of vital importance in promoting equality between men and women. Governments have, therefore, a responsibility to see to it that such centres and facilities are available in the first place for those children whose parents or parent are employed in self-employment and particularly in agriculture for rural women, in training or in education or wish to take up employment, training or education.

21. The primary objective of development being to bring about sustained improvement in the well-being of the individual and of society and to bestow benefits on all, development should be seen not only as a desirable goal in itself but also as the most important means of furthering equality of the sexes and the maintenance of peace.

22. The integration of women in development will necessitate widening their activities to embrace all aspects of social, economic, political and cultural life. They must be provided with the necessary technical training to make their contribution more effective in terms of production, and to ensure their greater participation in decision-making and in the planning and implementation of all programmes and projects. Full integration also implies that women receive their fair share of the benefits of development, thereby helping to ensure a more equitable distribution of income among all sectors of the population.

23. The promotion and protection of human rights for all is one of the fundamental principles of the Charter of the United Nations, the achievement of which is the goal of all people. An essential element for securing the protection of human rights and full equality between men and women throughout the world is sustained international cooperation based on peace, justice and equity for all and the elimination of all sources of conflict. True international cooperation must be based, in accordance with the Charter of the United Nations, on fully equal rights, the observance of national independence and sovereignty including sovereignty over natural resources and the right of their exploitation, non-interference in internal affairs, the right of peoples to defend their territorial integrity, and the inadmissibility of acquisition or attempts to acquire territory by force, mutual advantage, the avoidance of the use or the threat of force, and the promotion and maintenance of a new just world economic order, which is the basic purpose of the Charter of

Economic Rights and Duties of States. 3/ International cooperation and peace require national liberation and political and economic independence, and the elimination of colonialism and neo-colonialism, fascism and other similar ideologies, foreign occupation and apartheid, racism and discrimination in all its forms as well as recognition of the dignity of the individual and appreciation of the human person and his or her self-determination. To this end, the Plan calls for the full participation of women in all efforts to promote and maintain peace. True peace cannot be achieved unless women share with men the responsibility for establishing a new international economic order.

24. It is the aim of the Plan to ensure that the original and multidimensional contribution—both actual and potential—of women is not overlooked in existing concepts for development action programmes and an improved world economic equilibrium. Recommendations for national and international action are proposed with the aim of accelerating the necessary changes in all areas, and particularly in those where women have been especially disadvantaged.

25. Since the integral development of the personality of the women as a human being is directly connected with her participation in the development process as mother, worker and citizen, policies should be developed to promote the coordination of these different roles of the woman so as to give the most favourable conditions for the harmonious development of her personality—an aim which is equally relevant to the development of man.

I. National action

26. This Plan provides guidelines for national action over the 10-year period from 1975 to 1985 as part of a sustained, long-term effort to achieve the objectives of the International Women's Year. The recommendations are not exhaustive, and should be considered in addition to the other existing international instruments and resolutions of the United Nations bodies which deal with the condition of women and the quality of life. They constitute rather the main areas for priority action within the decade.

27. The recommendations for national action in this Plan are addressed primarily to Governments, and to all public and private institutions, women's and youth organizations, employers, trade unions, mass communications media, non-governmental organizations, political parties and other groups.

28. Since there are wide divergencies in the situation of women in various societies, cultures and regions, reflected in differing needs and problems, each country should decide upon its own national strategy, and identify its own targets and priorities within the present World Plan. Given the changing conditions of society today, an operative mechanism for assessment should be established and targets should be linked to those set out in, in particular, in the International Development Strategy for the Second United Nations Development Decade, 2/ and in the World Population Plan of Action. 4/

29. Changes in social and economic structures should be promoted which would make possible the full equality of women and their free access to all types of development, without discrimination of any kind, and to all types of education and employment.

30. There should be a clear commitment at all levels of government to take appropriate action to implement these targets and priorities. Commitment on the part of Governments to the ideals of equality and integration of women in society cannot be fully effective outside the larger context of commitment to transform fundamental relationships within a society in order to ensure a system that excludes the possibility of exploitation.

31. In elaborating national strategies and development plans in which women should participate, measures should be adopted to ensure that the set targets and priorities should take fully into account women's interests and needs, and make adequate provision to improve their situation and increase their contribution to the development process. There should be equitable representation of women at all levels of policy- and decision-making. Appropriate national machinery and procedures should be established if they do not already exist.

32. National plans and strategies for the implementation of this Plan should be sensitive to the needs and problems of different categories of women and of women of different age groups. However, Governments should pay special attention to improving the situation of women in areas where they have been most disadvantaged and especially of women in rural and urban areas.

33. While integrated programmes for the benefit of all members of society should be the basis for action in implementing this Plan, special measures on behalf of women whose status is the result of particularly discriminatory attitudes will be necessary.

34. The establishment of interdisciplinary and multisectoral machinery within government, such as national commissions, women's bureaux and other bodies, with adequate staff and budget, can be an effective transitional

3/ During the World Conference of the International Women's Year some representatives stated that reference to the Charter of Economic Rights and Duties of States should not be interpreted as indicating a change in the positions of delegations on the Charter as stated at the twenty-ninth session of the General Assembly.
4/ See *Report of the United Nations World Population Conference, 1974* (United Nations publication, Sales No. E.75.XIII.3), part one, chap. I.

measure for accelerating the achievement of equal opportunity for women and their full integration in national life. The membership of such bodies should include both women and men, representative of all groups of society responsible for making and implementing policy decisions in the public sector. Government ministries and departments (especially those responsible for education, health, labour, justice, communication and information, culture, industry, trade, agriculture, rural development, social welfare, finance and planning), as well as appropriate private and public agencies, should be represented on them.

35. Such bodies should investigate the situation of women in all fields and at all levels and make recommendations for needed legislation, policies and programmes establishing priorities. Follow-up programmes should be maintained to monitor and evaluate the progress achieved within the country to assess the implementation of the present Plan in national plans.

36. These national bodies should also cooperate in the coordination of similar regional and international activities, as well as those undertaken by non-governmental organizations, and self-help programmes devised by women themselves.

37. Constitutional and legislative guarantees of the principle of non-discrimination on the ground of sex and of equal rights and responsibilities of women and men are essential. Therefore, general acceptance of the principles embodied in such legislation and a change of attitude with regard to them should be encouraged. It is also essential to ensure that the adoption and enforcement of such legislation can in itself be a significant means of influencing and changing public and private attitudes and values.

38. Governments should review their legislation affecting the status of women in the light of human rights principles and internationally accepted standards. Wherever necessary, legislation should be enacted or updated to bring national laws into conformity with the relevant international instruments. Adequate provision should also be made for the enforcement of such legislation, especially in each of the areas dealt with in chapter II of the Plan. Where they have not already done so, Governments should take steps to ratify the relevant international conventions and fully implement their provisions. It should be noted that there are States whose national legislation guarantees women certain rights which go beyond those embodied in the relevant international instruments.

39. Appropriate bodies should be specifically entrusted with the responsibility of modernizing, changing or repealing outdated national laws and regulations, keeping them under constant review, and ensuring that their provisions are applied without discrimination.

These bodies could include, for example, law commissions, human rights commissions, civil liberties unions, appeals boards, legal advisory boards and the office of *ombudsman*. Such bodies should have full governmental support to enable them to carry out their functions effectively. Non-governmental organizations could also play an important role in ensuring that relevant legislation is adequate, up to date and applied without discrimination.

40. Appropriate measures should be taken to inform and advise women of their rights and to provide them with every other type of assistance. Accordingly, the awareness of the mass communication media should be heightened so that they may offer their broad cooperation through public education programmes. Non-governmental organizations can and should be encouraged to play similar roles with regard to women. In this context, special attention should be paid to the women of rural areas, whose problem is most acute.

41. Efforts to widen opportunities for women to participate in development and to eliminate discrimination against them will require a variety of measures and action by society at large through its governmental machinery and other institutions.

42. While some of the measures suggested could be carried out at minimum cost, implementation of this Plan will require a redefinition of certain priorities and a change in the pattern of government expenditure. In order to ensure adequate allocation of funds, Governments should explore all available sources of support which are acceptable to Governments and in accordance with Governments' goals.

43. Special measures should also be envisaged to assist Governments whose resources are limited in carrying out specific projects or programmes. The Fund for International Women's Year established under Economic and Social Council resolution 1851 (LVI) of 16 May 1974, in addition to multilateral and bilateral assistance, which is vital for the purpose, should be extended provisionally pending further consideration as to its ultimate disposition in order to assist Governments whose resources are limited in carrying out specific programmes or projects. Women in countries holding special financial responsibilities entrusted by the United Nations and its specialized agencies with a view to assisting developing countries are called upon to make their contribution to the implementation of the goals set in connection with the governmental assistance earmarked for improving the status of women, especially of those in the underdeveloped States.

44. It is recognized that some of the objectives of this Plan have already been achieved in some countries, while in others they may only be accomplished progressively. Moreover, some measures by their very nature will

take longer to implement than others. Governments are therefore urged to establish short-, medium- and long-term targets and objectives to implement the Plan.

45. On the basis of this World Plan of Action, the United Nations Secretariat should elaborate a two-year plan of its own, containing several most important objectives, directed towards the implementation of the World Plan of Action under the current control of the Commission on the Status of Women and the overall control of the General Assembly.

46. The achievement of the following should be envisaged as a minimum by the end of the first five-year period (1975-1980):

(a) Marked increase in literacy and civic education of women, especially in rural areas;

(b) The extension of co-educational technical and vocational training in basic skills to women and men in the industrial and agricultural sectors;

(c) Equal access at every level of education, compulsory primary school education and the measures necessary to prevent school drop-outs;

(d) Increased employment opportunities for women, reduction of unemployment and increased efforts to eliminate discrimination in the terms and conditions of employment;

(e) The establishment and increase of the infrastructural services required in both rural and urban areas;

(f) The enactment of legislation on voting and eligibility for election on equal terms with men, equal opportunity and conditions of employment including remuneration, and on equality in legal capacity and the exercise thereof;

(g) Encouragement of a greater participation of women in policy-making positions at the local, national and international levels;

(h) Increased provision for comprehensive measures for health education and services, sanitation, nutrition, family education, family planning and other welfare services;

(i) Provision for parity in the exercise of civil, social and political rights such as those pertaining to marriage, citizenship and commerce;

(j) Recognition of the economic value of women's work in the home in domestic food production and marketing and voluntary activities not remunerated;

(k) The direction of formal, non-formal and life-long education towards the re-evaluation of the man and woman, in order to ensure their full realization as an individual in the family and in society;

(l) The promotion of women's organizations as an interim measure within worker's organizations and educational, economic and professional institutions;

(m) The development of modern rural technology, cottage industry, pre-school day centres, time-and-energy-saving devices so as to help reduce the heavy work load of women, particularly those living in rural sectors and for the urban poor and thus facilitate the full participation of women in community, national and international affairs;

(n) The establishment of interdisciplinary and multisectoral machinery within the government for accelerating the achievement of equal opportunities for women and their full integration into national life.

47. These minimum objectives should be developed in more specific terms in regional plans of action.

48. The active involvement of non-governmental women's organizations in the achievement of the goals of the 10-year World Plan of Action at every level especially by the effective utilization of volunteer experts and in the setting and running of institutions and projects for the welfare of women and in the dissemination of information for their advancement.

II. Specific areas for national action

49. The specific areas included in this chapter of the Plan have been selected because they are considered to be key areas for national action. They should not be viewed in isolation, however, as they are all closely interrelated and the guidelines proposed should be implemented within the framework of integrated strategies and programmes.

A. International cooperation and the strengthening of international peace

50. An essential condition for the maintenance and strengthening of international cooperation and peace is the promotion and protection of human rights for all in conditions of equity among and within nations. In order to involve more women in the promotion of international cooperation, the development of friendly relations among nations, in the strengthening of international peace and disarmament, and the combating of colonialism, neo-colonialism, foreign domination and alien subjugation, apartheid and racial discrimination, the peace efforts of women as individuals and in groups, and in national and international organizations should be recognized and encouraged.

51. Women of all countries of the world should proclaim their solidarity in support of the elimination of gross violations of human rights condemned by the United Nations and contrary to its principles involving acts against the moral and physical integrity of individuals or groups of individuals for political or ideological reasons.

52. The efforts of intergovernmental and non-governmental organizations having as their aim the

strengthening of international security and peace and the development of friendly relations among nations and the promotion of active cooperation among States should be supported, and women should be given every encouragement to participate actively in the endeavours of those organizations.

53. The United Nations should proclaim a special day to be devoted to international peace and celebrated every year, nationally and internationally. Meetings and seminars should be organized for this purpose by interested individuals and groups, with wide coverage in the press and other communications media. Women should lend their full support to these objectives and explore, as co-equals with men, ways to overcome existing obstacles to international cooperation, the development of friendly relations among nations, and the strengthening of international peace. However, it must be emphasized that peace is a matter for constant vigilance and not only for a one-day observance.

54. The free flow of information and ideas among countries should be facilitated, with due regard for national sovereignty and the principles of international law; the exchange of visits between women of different countries to study common problems should be promoted. Educational, cultural, scientific and other exchange programmes should be expanded and new forms developed in order to facilitate mutual understanding among peoples, particularly the young, and develop friendly relations and active cooperation among States. For these purposes the mass communications media should be utilized fully.

55. Women and men should be encouraged to instill in their children the values of mutual respect and understanding for all nations and all peoples, racial equality, sexual equality, the right of every nation to self- determination and the desire to maintain international cooperation, peace and security in the world.

56. Women should have equal opportunity with men to represent their countries in all international forums where the above questions are discussed, and in particular at meetings of the organizations of the United Nations system, including the Security Council and all conferences on disarmament and international peace, and other regional bodies.

B. Political participation

57. Despite the fact that, numerically, women constitute half the population of the world, in the vast majority of countries only a small percentage of them are in positions of leadership in the various branches of government. Consequently, women are not involved in the decision-making and their views and needs are often overlooked in planning for development. As the majority of women do not participate in the formulation of development plans and programmes, they are frequently unaware of their implications and less inclined to support their implementation and the changes the programmes seek to bring about. Many women also lack the education, training, civic awareness and self-confidence to participate effectively in political life.

58. A major objective of this Plan is to ensure that women shall have, in law and in fact, equal rights and opportunities with men to vote and to participate in public and political life at the national, local and community levels, and that they shall be made aware of their responsibilities as citizens and of the problems affecting society and affecting them directly as women.

59. Participation in political life implies participation as voters, lobbyists, elected representatives, trade-unionists and public officials in the various branches of government, including the judiciary.

60. Where legislation does not exist guaranteeing women the right to vote, to be eligible for election and to hold all public offices and exercise public functions on equal terms with men, every effort should be made to enact it by 1978.

61. Where special qualifications for holding public office are required, they should apply to both sexes equally and should relate only to the expertise necessary for performing the specific functions of the office.

62. Governments should establish goals, strategies and timetables for increasing within the decade 1975-1985 the number of women in elective and appointive public offices and public functions at all levels.

63. Special efforts to achieve these objectives could include:

(a) The reaffirmation of, and wide publicity for, the official policy concerning the equal political participation of women;

(b) The issuance of special governmental instructions for achieving an equitable representation of women in public office, and the compilation of periodic reports on the number of women in the public service, and levels of responsibility in the areas of their work;

(c) The organization of studies to establish the levels of economic, social and political competence of the female compared to the male population for recruitment, nomination and promotion;

(d) The undertaking of special activities for the recruitment, nomination and promotion of women, especially to fill important positions, until equitable representation of the sexes is achieved.

64. Special efforts and campaigns should be initiated to enlighten the female electorate on political issues and on the need for their active participation in public

affairs, including parties and other political organizations such as pressure groups.

65. Educational and informational activities should also be undertaken to enlighten the public at large on the indispensable role of women in the political processes, and on the need to promote their greater political participation and leadership.

66. Special drives should be undertaken to encourage the increased participation of women and girls in rural, community and youth development programmes, and in political activities, and to facilitate their access to training for leadership in such programmes.

C. *Education and training*

67. Access to education and training in not only a basic human right recognized in many international instruments, it is also a key factor for social progress and in reducing the gaps between socio-economic groups and between the sexes. In many countries girls and women are at a marked disadvantage. This not only constitutes a serious initial handicap for them as individuals and for their future position in society; it also seriously impedes the effectiveness of their contribution to development programmes and the development process itself.

68. Illiteracy and lack of education and training in basic skills are some of the causes of the vicious circle of underdevelopment, low productivity and poor conditions of health and welfare. In a great many countries illiteracy is much more widespread among women than among men, and the rates are generally higher in rural than in urban areas.

69. In most countries female enrolment at all levels of education is considerably below that of men. Girls tend to drop out of school earlier than boys. Boys are given precedence over girls when parents have to make a choice if education is not free. There is often discrimination in the nature and content of the education provided and in the options offered. Girls' choices of areas of study are dominated by conventional attitudes, concepts and notions concerning the respective roles of men and women in society.

70. As long as women remain illiterate and are subject to discrimination in education and training, the motivation for change so badly needed to improve the quality of life for all will fail, for in most societies it is the mother who is responsible for the training of her children during the formative years of their lives.

71. Governments should provide equal opportunities for both sexes at all levels of education and training within the context of lifelong education, and on a formal and non-formal basis, according to national needs.

72. The measures taken should conform to the existing international standards and, in particular, to the Convention and Recommendation against Discrimination in Education, 1960, and to the revised Recommendation concerning Technical and Vocational Education, 1974, of the United Nations Educational, Scientific and Cultural Organization.

73. Educational, training and employment strategies should be coordinated and based on population projections. The content and structure of education should be such as to ensure its relevance to the present and future needs of the communities concerned, taking into account their own culture and the advances made through technical and scientific developments. It should also seek to prepare the individual adequately for an active civic and family life and for responsible parenthood.

74. Target dates should be established for the eradication of illiteracy, and high priority given to programmes for women and girls between the ages of 16 and 25 years.

75. The acquisition of literacy should be promoted as an integral part of other kinds of learning activities of direct interest and value to the daily lives of the people. Parallel with the efforts of Governments, all social institutions, such as cooperatives, voluntary organizations and enterprises, should be fully utilized to overcome illiteracy.

76. Voluntary task forces, especially of young persons, could be established to teach literacy, numbers, nutrition and methods of food preservation during vacations or periods of national service. Such task forces should include both women and men with expertise in the skills needed. The volunteers could also train local personnel to become trainers, thus expanding the available task forces.

77. Integrated or special training programmes should be developed for girls and women in rural areas to enable them to participate fully and productively in economic and social development and to take advantage of technological advances and thereby reduce the drudgery of their daily lives. Such programmes should include training in modern methods of agriculture and use of equipment, cooperatives, entrepreneurship, commerce marketing, animal husbandry and fisheries, and in health, nutrition, family planning and education.

78. Free and compulsory primary education for girls and boys without discrimination should be provided and effectively enforced as quickly as possible. Every effort should also be made to provide textbooks, school lunches transport and other essentials, wherever possible free of charge.

79. In order to assist in overcoming high drop-out rates among school-age girls and to enable women to participate in literacy and basic skills, programmes, inexpensive child-care and other arrangements should

be organized to coincide with school or training hours to free women and girls from confining domestic work.

80. Special programmes for continuing education on a part-time basis should be arranged to ensure retention of what has been learned at school and to assist women in their family, vocational and professional activities.

81. Programmes, curricula and standards of education and training should be the same for males and females. Courses for both sexes, in addition to general subjects, should include industrial and agricultural technology, politics, economics, current problems of society, responsible parenthood, family life, nutrition and health.

82. Textbooks and other teaching materials should be re-evaluated and, where necessary, rewritten to ensure that they reflect an image of women in positive and participatory roles in society. Teaching methods should be revised, wherever necessary, to make sure that they are adapted to national needs and to promote changes in discriminatory attitudes.

83. Research activities should be promoted to identify discriminatory practices in education and training and to ensure educational equality. New teaching techniques should be encouraged, especially audio-visual techniques.

84. Co-education and mixed training groups should be actively encouraged and should provide special guidance to both sexes in orienting them towards new occupations and changing roles.

85. Widely diversified existing and new vocational programmes of all types should be equally accessible to both sexes, enabling girls and boys to have a wide choice of employment opportunities, including those which require higher skills, and to match national needs with job opportunities. Both sexes should have equal opportunities to receive scholarships and study grants. Special measures should be developed to assist women who wish to return to work after a comparatively long absence, owing in particular to family responsibilities. Multipurpose training centres could be established in rural and urban areas to provide education and training in various techniques and disciplines and to encourage a self-reliant approach to life.

86. Girls and boys alike should be encouraged through vocational and career guidance programmes to choose a career according to their real aptitudes and abilities rather than on the basis of deeply ingrained sex stereotypes. They should also be made aware of the education and training required to take full advantage of the employment opportunities available.

87. Informational and formal and non-formal educational programmes should be launched to make the general public, parents, teachers, counsellors and others aware of the need to provide girls with a solid initial education and adequate training for occupational life and ample opportunities for further education and training. Maximum use should be made of the mass communications media, both as a tool for education and as a means for effecting changes in community attitudes.

D. *Employment and related economic roles*

88. This Plan seeks to achieve equality of opportunity and treatment for women workers and their integration in the labour force in accordance with the accepted international standards recognizing the right to work, to equal pay for equal work, to equal conditions of work and to advancement.

89. Available data show that women constitute more than a third of the world's economically active population and approximately 46 per cent of women of working age (15 to 64 years) are in the labour force. Of these, an estimated 65 per cent are to be found in the developing countries and 35 per cent in the more developed regions. These data, together with the many economic activities of women that are not now included in the official statistics (see chap. III, below*) demonstrate that women's contribution to the national economy and development is substantial and has not been fully recognized. Further, the occupations in which most women workers are concentrated are not the same as those in which most men are employed. The vast majority of women are concentrated in a limited number of occupations at lower levels of skill, responsibility and remuneration. Women frequently experience discrimination in pay, promotion, working conditions and hiring practices. Cultural constraints and family responsibilities further restrict their employment opportunities. Where job opportunities are severely limited and widespread unemployment exists, women's chances of obtaining wage-earning employment are in practice further reduced, even where policies of non-discrimination have been laid down.

90. Governments should formulate policies and action programmes expressly directed towards equality of opportunity and treatment for women workers and the guarantee of their right to equal pay for equal work. Such policies and programmes should be in conformity with the standards elaborated by the United Nations and the International Labour Organisation. They should include legislation stipulating the principle of non-discrimination on the grounds of sex or marital status, guidelines for implementing the principles, appeals procedures, and effective targets and machinery for implementation.

91. Special efforts should be made to foster positive attitudes towards the employment of women, irrespective

*[Editor's note: Not reproduced here.]

of marital status, among employers and workers and among women and men in society at large, and to eliminate obstacles based on sex-typed divisions of labour.

92. In attempting to achieve gainful employment for women and to deal with problems of unemployment and underemployment, special efforts should be made to create a variety of economic roles and to encourage and support self-employment and self-help activities, especially in rural areas. Existing self-help activities should be encouraged and strengthened through the participation of women.

93. Governments should seek new sources of self-help activities, such as training programmes in community development and entrepreneurial skills, which should be open on an equal basis to both sexes.

94. In order to extend women's range of economic roles, cooperatives and small-scale industries could be developed and encouraged with the necessary help and support of government. Where cooperatives already exist, women should be encouraged to take an active part in them. New cooperatives and, where appropriate, women's cooperatives should be organized, especially in areas where women play a major role, such as food production, marketing, housing, nutrition and health. cooperatives may also be the most appropriate and feasible arrangement for child-care and could also provide employment opportunities.

95. Essential to the effective implementation of such programmes is the provision of adequate training in cooperatives and entrepreneurial skills, access to credit and necessary seed capital for improved tools, assistance with marketing, the provision of adequate rural social services and amenities, decentralized development of towns in rural areas and basic infrastructural arrangements, such as child-care arrangement, transportation and conveniently situated water supplies.

96. Special efforts should be made to increase the participation of rural women in the formulation of national plans for integrated rural development. Policies and programmes for rural development should take into account the creation of employment opportunities along with other essential related components, such as projects for diversification, import substitution and expansion of rural activities for farming, forestry, fisheries, animal husbandry and agro-industries.

97. Specific target dates should be established for achieving a substantial increase in the number of qualified women employed in skilled and technical work.

98. Special efforts should also be made to increase the number of women in management and policy-making in commerce, industry and trade.

99. Access to skills and the provision of institutional and on-the-job training should be open to women

in the same way and on the same conditions as to men so as to make them equally eligible for promotion.

100. Governments, employers and trade unions should ensure to all women workers the right to maternity protection, including maternity leave with a guarantee of returning to their former employment, and to nursing breaks, in keeping with the principles laid down in the International Labour Organisation Convention concerning maternity protection (revised) and Recommendation, 1952. Provisions relating to maternity protection should not be regarded as unequal treatment of the sexes.

101. Special attention should be given to the need for multilateral approaches to facilitate the combination of family and work responsibilities. These could include: a general reduction and/or staggering of working hours; flexible working hours; part-time work for women and men; child-care facilities and child-care leave systems to assist parents to take care of their children; communal kitchens; and various kinds of facilities to help them discharge household tasks more easily. Governments and trade unions should ensure that the economic and social rights of part-time workers are fully protected.

102. Protective legislation applying to women only should be reviewed in the light of scientific and technological knowledge, and should be revised, repealed or extended to all workers as necessary.

103. Minimum wages, which play an important role in the improvement of working conditions of women, should be enforced and made applicable to cottage industries and domestic work.

104. Special measures should also be taken to eliminate the exploitation of female labour, in particular that of young girls, wherever it exists.

105. Discriminatory treatment of women in national social security schemes should be eliminated to the maximum extent. Women workers should be covered equally with men by all aspects of such schemes.

106. Governments should encourage and stimulate concerted efforts, in particular on the part of employers' and workers' organizations, to bring about a marked improvement in the position of women in employment and should cooperate with all voluntary organizations concerned with the status of women workers in economic life and in society as a whole.

107. Trade unions should adopt policies to increase the participation of women in their work at every level, including the higher echelons. They should have special programmes to promote equality of opportunity for jobs and training for women workers and leadership training for women. They should play a leading role in developing new and constructive approaches to problems faced by workers, paying special attention to the problems of women workers.

E. *Health and nutrition*

108. While everyone has an undeniable right to health, conditions in many countries, and especially in rural areas, have often precluded the actual enjoyment by women of this right equally with men. The situation becomes more accentuated in societies with considerable shortages of health personnel and facilities and constitutes a high cost to the family, society and development by impairing the productivity of women. Women also need special care during pregnancy, delivery and lactation.

109. Adequate nutrition is of fundamental importance for the full physical and mental development of the individual, and women have a vital role to play in this area in the production, preparation, processing and consumption of food. When food is scarce women often experience a greater degree of malnutrition than men, either because they deprive themselves for the sake of their families or because society places a lesser value on women.

110. Improved access to health, nutrition and other social services is essential to the full participation of women in development activities, to the strengthening of family life, and to a general improvement in the quality of life. To be fully effective, these services should be integrated into overall development programmes with priority being given to rural areas.

111. Governments should ensure adequate investments in public health programmes, especially in rural areas.

112. Comprehensive simple community health services could be developed in which the community identifies its own health needs, takes part in decisions on delivery of health care in different socio-economic contexts, and develops primary health care services that are easily accessible to every member of the community. Women themselves, especially in rural areas, should be encouraged, through adequate training programmes, to provide such health care services to their communities. Provision should be made to ensure that women shall have the same access to that care as men. Travelling clinics and medical teams should make periodic visits to all communities.

113. Within the context of general health services, Governments should pay particular attention to women's special health needs by provision of: pre-natal and post-natal and delivery services; gynaecological and family planning services during the reproductive years; comprehensive and continuous health services directed to all infants, pre-school children and school children, without prejudice on grounds of sex; specific care for pre-adolescent and adolescent girls and for the post-reproductive years and old age, and research into the special health problems of women. Basic health services should be reinforced by the use of qualified medical and paramedical personnel.

114. Programmes should be formulated for the reduction of infant, child and maternal mortality by means of improved nutrition, sanitation, maternal and child health care and maternal education.

115. Education programmes should be developed to overcome prejudices, taboos and superstitions that prevent women from using existing health facilities. Special efforts should be made to inform the urban poor and rural women about existing medical facilities.

116. Within the context of a massive programme of health education and services, courses in health education, maternal and child care could be organized in rural and urban neighbourhoods, and women should be actively encouraged to participate. These classes should be advertised by the communication media and by all existing social networks. They should include information about what medical facilities are available, and how to reach them. Physicians should periodically conduct physical examinations of the participants in as many of these classes as possible.

117. In view of the importance of women not only as users but as providers of health care, steps should be taken to incorporate them as fully informed and active participants in the health-planning and decision-making process at all levels and in all phases. Efforts should be made to encourage women to participate actively in community efforts to provide primary health care and improve coverage. Women should also be trained as paramedics and encouraged to organize health cooperatives and self-help programmes. Recruitment and training should be undertaken at the village level to prepare villagers as health workers to provide basic health services for their community.

118. Women should have the same right of access as men to any training establishment course for any health profession and to continue to the highest levels. Practices which exclude women from certain health professions on traditional, religious or cultural grounds should be abolished.

119. Improved, easily accessible, safe water supplies (including wells, dams, catch-piping etc.), sewage disposal and other sanitation measures should be provided both to improve health conditions of families and to reduce the burden of carrying water which falls mainly on women and children.

120. In national food and nutrition policies Governments should give priority to the consumption by the most vulnerable groups in the population (adolescent girls, pregnant and lactating women, and young children)

of certain types of food produce, such as milk and milk products, and especially nutritious foods. The practice of breast feeding and good feeding practices for the weaning period should be encouraged. Supplementary food programmes for mothers and children at imminent risk of manultrition should be introduced. Nutritional deficiencies should be prevented through fortification of staples or other widely consumed foods or by direct distribution of the deficient nutrients.

121. Techniques and equipment for food processing, preservation and conservation at the local village level should be improved and made available to rural women. Cooperatives for the production, quality improvement and distribution of food should be organized to give impetus to this effort and, where appropriate, campaigns to educate the consumer should be organized.

122. Opportunities should be created for women to contribute more efficiently to the production of proper types of food through vegetable gardens in rural and urban areas and through the provision of better tools, seeds and fertilizer. Girls and boys should also be encouraged to grow food in school gardens to supplement daily school meal programmes.

123. Campaigns on nutrition education should be launched through the communications media to explore the most effective techniques for introducing previously unacceptable nutritious foods into the daily diets of people. These campaigns should also inform women how to use the family income most economically towards the purchase of more nutritious foods and to eliminate wastage of food. The exchange of experience on effective nutrition programmes through seminars, informal visits and publications should be arranged.

F. *The family in modern society*

124. The institution of the family, which is changing in its economic, social and cultural functions, should ensure the dignity, equality and security of each of its members, and provide conditions conducive to the balanced development of the child as an individual and as a social being.

125. In the total development process the role of women, along with men, needs to be considered in terms of their contribution to the family as well as to society and the national economy. Higher status for this role in the home—as a parent, spouse and homemaker—can only enhance the personal dignity of a man and a woman. Household activities that are necessary for family life have generally been perceived as having a low economic and social prestige. All societies should, however, place a higher value on these activities if they wish the family group to be maintained and to fulfil its basic functions of the procreation and education of children.

126. The family is also an important agent of social, political and cultural change. If women are to enjoy equal rights, opportunities and responsibilities, and contribute on equal terms with men to the development process, the functions and roles traditionally allotted to each sex within the family will require continual re-examination and reassessment in the light of changing conditions.

127. The rights of women in all the various forms of the family, including the nuclear family, the extended family, consensual union and the single-parent family, should be protected by appropriate legislation and policy.

128. Legislation relating to marriage should be in conformity with international standards. In particular it should ensure that women and men shall have the same right to free choice of a spouse and to enter into marriage only with their free and full consent. A minimum age for marriage should be fixed by law and be such as to provide a sufficient period of education for girls and boys, but particularly girls, to enable them to complete their education and develop their potentialities prior to marriage. Official registration of marriages should be made compulsory.

129. All institutions and practices which infringe these rights should be abolished, in particular, child marriage and the inheritance of widows.

130. Legislative and other measures should be taken to ensure that men and women shall enjoy full legal capacity and the exercise thereof relating to their personal and property rights, including the right to acquire, administer, enjoy, dispose of and inherit property (including property acquired during marriage). Limitations, where such exist, should apply to both partners alike. During marriage the principle of equal rights and responsibilities would mean that both partners should perform an active role in the home, taking into account the importance of combining home and work responsibilities, and share jointly decision-making on matters affecting the family and children. At the dissolution of marriage, this principle would imply that procedures and grounds of dissolution of marriage should be liberalized and apply equally to both spouses; assets acquired during marriage should be shared on an equitable basis; appropriate provisions should be made for the social security and pension coverage of the work contributed by the homemaker; and decisions relating to the custody of children should be taken in consideration of their best interests.

131. In order to assist in the solution of conflicts arising among members of the family, adequate family counselling services should be set up wherever possible and the establishment of family courts staffed with personnel, including women, trained in law as well as in various other relevant disciplines should be considered.

132. Programmes of education for personal rela-

tionships, marriage and family life, health, including psycho-sexual development, should be integrated into all school curricula at appropriate levels and into programmes for out-of-school education, to prepare young people of both sexes for responsible marriage and parenthood. These programmes should be based on the ideals of mutual respect and shared rights and responsibilities in the family and in society. Child-rearing practices within each society should be examined with a view to eliminating customs that encourage and perpetuate ideas about superiority or inferiority on the basis of sex.

133. In recognition of the growing number of single-parent families, additional assistance and benefits, wherever possible, should be provided for them. The unmarried mother should be granted full-fledged status as a parent, and children born out of wedlock should have the same rights and obligations as children born in wedlock. Special nursing homes and hostels should be established for married and unmarried mothers, before and after delivery.

134. Social security programmes should, to the maximum extent, include children and family allowances in order to strengthen the economic stability of family members. Cross-cultural studies might be undertaken of the influence upon the condition of women in the family and in society of family and children's allowances and benefits, motherhood awards and similar measures.

G. *Population*

135. Social, economic and demographic factors are closely interrelated, and change in one or more invariably involves changes in others. The status of women is both a determinant and a consequence of these various factors. It is inextricably linked with both the development process and the various components of demographic change: fertility, mortality and migration (international and internal and the latter's concomitant, urbanization).

136. The status of women and, in particular, their educational level, whether or not they are gainfully employed, the nature of their employment, and their position within the family are all factors that have been found to influence family size. Conversely, the right of women to decide freely and responsibly on the number and spacing of their children and to have access to the information and means to enable them to exercise that right has a decisive impact on their ability to take advantage of educational and employment opportunities and to participate fully in community life as responsible citizens.

137. The exercise of this right and the full participation of women in all aspects of national life are closely interrelated with such crucial demographic variables as age at marriage, age at birth of first child, the length of interval between births, age at termination of child-bearing, and total number of children born.

138. The hazards of child-bearing, characterized by too many pregnancies, pregnancies at too early or too late an age and at too close intervals, inadequate pre-natal, delivery and postnatal care and resort to illegally induced abortions, result in high rates of maternal mortality and maternity-related morbidity. Where levels of infant and early childhood mortality as well as of foetal mortality are high, their reduction—a desirable end in itself—may also be a prerequisite of the limitation of the number of pregnancies that the average women will experience, and of the society's adoption of a smaller ideal family size where this is a desired goal. Fewer pregnancies may be more easily achieved when there is a reasonable expectation that children born will survive to adulthood.

139. In some parts of the world, urbanization involves mainly a migration of young men; in other parts, young women constitute the major component in the rural-to-urban migratory stream. Such situations partly reflect differences in women's opportunities to work in either urban or rural occupations, and these are related to cultural variations in the acceptance of women in diverse roles. While differences in women's social status are among the causes of diverse sex selections in the migration to cities and towns, the consequences of such selective migration are to be found in resulting sex imbalances, in both the urban and the rural population. These population imbalances can be detrimental to individual and family welfare and to the stability of either urban or rural residence. Just over half of the total female population of the world currently resides in rural areas of developing countries. In the light of the particular demographic, economic and social problems of rural communities in these regions, special development efforts are required.

140. This Plan endorses the recommendations of the World Population Plan of Action, especially those relating to the status of women.

141. In the elaboration and execution of population policies and programmes, within the framework of overall development, Governments are urged to pay particular attention to measures designed to improve the situation of women, especially with regard to their educational and employment opportunities, conditions of work, and the establishment and enforcement of an appropriately high minimum age at marriage.

142. While States have a sovereign right to determine their own population policies, individuals and couples should have access, through an institutionalized system, to the information and means that will enable them to determine freely and responsibly the number and spacing of their children and to overcome sterility. All

legal, social or financial obstacles to the dissemination of family planning knowledge, means and services should be removed. Every effort should be made to improve knowledge and identification of the causes of involuntary sterility, subfecundity and congenital birth defects and to secure their reduction.

143. Family planning programmes should direct communication and recruitment efforts towards women and men equally, since successful fertility regulation requires their mutual understanding and cooperation. This policy would enable women to exercise equally with men their right to decide how many children they will bear and the timing of the births. Attainment of these goals requires the development of means of contraception and birth control that will be both efficient and compatible with cultural values prevailing in different societies. Family planning programmes should be integrated and coordinated with health, nutrition and other services designed to raise the quality of family life.

144. Governments should make concerted efforts systematically to ameliorate conditions of mortality and morbidity as part of the development process, and pay particular attention to the reduction of those risks that especially affect the health of women.

145. Policies and programmes to improve the status of women and to enable them to contribute fully to social and economic development must take into account migration and the ways in which it affects the family and working lives of women.

146. Both the causes and the consequences of varied modes of urbanization should be examined carefully, so as to yield the information needed to devise appropriate social policies, especially those designed to meet the varying needs of women.

147. Rural development programmes including the creation of suitable industrial and employment opportunities, should be initiated or expanded to reduce the migration to urban areas and its attendant problems. Decentralization of education and health facilities to rural areas should also be promoted, as an aid to lowering rural rates of illiteracy, mortality and fertility, which have traditionally been higher than those in urban communities. These measures would bring rural women into greater contact with the mainstream of national life and release opportunities for their contribution to the progress and prosperity of their country.

H. *Housing and related facilities*

148. The majority of women still spend more of their time in and around the house than do men; this, the improvement of the house, its related facilities and its neighbourhood will bring about a direct improvement in their daily lives. In addition to the consideration of health and comfort, well-designed and suitably furnished houses and related facilities, as well as neighbourhoods, offer comparative relief from monotony and drudgery, making easier the pursuit of other interests and activities, and bringing women's lives closer to the demands of human dignity.

149. Legislative and other measures should be taken to guarantee that the views and needs of women are taken into account in the planning and design of urban and housing development as well as human settlements.

150. The design of the house should take into account the needs of the entire family, especially the women and children. Use of the following should be encouraged: (a) building materials that require minimal or no maintenance; (b) equipment and appliances that do not present safety hazards; (c) labour-saving interior finishes and surfaces conducive to comfort and hygiene; (d) furniture that is movable, storable and easily replaceable; and (e) where feasible and appropriate, an area for women to undertake activities such as reading, sewing and weaving (in some societies this may be a communal space to increase social cohesion).

151. In the projection of the house into a neighbourhood, designs should provide for services and utilities and neighbourhood facilities that respond, *inter alia*, to the expressed needs of women, and reduce labour as well as travel for vital needs such as water, food, fuel and other necessities.

152. In the design of a network of neighbourhoods, consideration should be given to accessibility of neighbourhood centres for the women and children.

153. Training and orientation courses should be organized in the use of new facilities made available to women, as well as in various aspects of home ownership and maintenance.

I. *Other social questions*

154. Social services play a crucial role in anticipating social problems deriving from rapid modernization and industrialization and in reducing the need for remedial measures at a later stage. Women are usually affected by these social problems to a greater extent than men, especially in the initial stages of the development process.

155. Governments should therefore encourage the development of social services as a useful tool in mobilizing human and technical resources for the benefit of all marginal and social groups, bearing in mind the contribution that non-governmental organizations can offer.

156. Special efforts should be made to provide for the needs of migrant women whether from rural areas or from abroad, and for women workers and their families who live in urban slums and squatter settlements. Training, job counselling, child-care facilities, financial aid

and, where necessary, language training and other forms of assistance should be provided.

157. Special attention should also be given to the needs of elderly women, who frequently receive less protection and assistance than men. They predominate numerically in the age group of 50 years and over, and many are indigent and in need of special care.

158. In the area of the prevention of crime and treatment of offenders, special attention should be paid to female criminality, which is increasing in many parts of the world, and to the rehabilitation of female offenders, including juvenile delinquents and recidivists. Research in this field should include study of the relationship between female criminality and other social problems brought about by rapid social change.

159. Specific legislative and other measures should be taken to combat prostitution and the illicit traffic in women, especially young girls. Special programmes, including pilot projects, should be developed in cooperation with international bodies and non-governmental organizations to prevent such practices and rehabilitate the victims.

160. Government which have not already done so should ratify or accede to the United Nations Convention for the Suppression of the Traffic in Persons and of the Exploitation of the Prostitution of Others. 5/

III. Research, data collection and analysis

161. This Plan gives high priority to national, regional and international research activities, and to data collection and analysis on all aspects of the situation of women, since adequate data and information are essential in formulating policies and evaluating progress and in effecting attitudinal and basic social and economic change.

162. A major difficulty in assessing the economic contribution of women at the present time is lack of or incomplete data and indicators to measure their situation as it affects the process of development and is in turn affected by it.

163. Many women are automatically excluded from the economically active population in national statistics because they are homemakers only and homemaking is nowhere considered to be an economic activity. Another large group of women are erroneously classified as homemakers only because it is assumed that women have no economic activity and their status is therefore not carefully investigated. This occurs particularly in relation to women who, in addition to their homemaking activities, are also self-employed handicraft and other home industry workers or unpaid family workers in subsistence agriculture. Further, statistics on unemployment often present an inaccurate picture of the situation because they omit women who are not recognized as part of the economically active population (e.g., women classified as homemakers or housewives). They may, however, in fact be in need of and available for employment.

164. Among other data biased by preconceptions are those on heads of households or families, when it is assumed that a women can be the head only in the absence of a man. Many households actually headed by women are therefore erroneously classified as having male heads.

165. Differences in these and other national statistical practices also make cross-country comparisons of data very difficult. In the non-market sector, for example, the distinction between economic and non-economic activities is seldom clear and the criteria used are often arbitrary and vary from country to country.

166. A scientific and reliable data base should be established and suitable economic and social indicators urgently developed which are sensitive to the particular situation and needs of women as an integral part of national and international programmes of statistics.

167. All census and survey data relating to characteristics of individuals (e.g., urban/rural residence, age, marital status, including consensual unions, literacy, education, income, level of skills and participation in both modern and traditional economic activities) and to household and family composition should be reported and analysed by sex.

168. In the collection of such data special efforts should be made to measure:

(a) The participation of women in local and national planning and policy-making in all sectors of national life;

(b) The extent of women's activities in food production (cash crop and subsistence agriculture), in water and fuel supply, in marketing, and in transportation;

(c) The economic and social contribution of housework and other domestic chores, handicrafts and other home-based economic activities;

(d) The effect on the national economy of women's activities as consumers of goods and services;

(e) The relative time spent on economic and household activities and on leisure by girls and women compared to boys and men;

(f) The quality of life (e.g., job satisfaction, income situation, family characteristics and use of leisure time).

169. The United Nations system should extend the scope of its standards for data collection, tabulation and analysis to take the above recommendations into account. National statistical offices should adhere to the standards established by the United Nations and its specialized agencies.

170. The United Nations should prepare an inven-

5/ General Assembly resolution 317 (IV) of 2 December 1949.

tory of social and economic indicators relevant to the analysis of the status of women as soon as possible and not later than 1980, in cooperation with the interested specialized agencies, the United Nations Research Institute for Social Development, the regional commissions and other relevant bodies.

171. This Plan gives high priority also to cross-cultural studies, especially of the causes of discriminatory customs, practices, attitudes and beliefs, which impede women's contribution to the development process, and of the mechanisms of change.

172. Research oriented towards specific country and regional problems should be made by competent women and men acquainted with specific national and regional conditions.

173. The wide exchange of information and research findings should be promoted and maximum use made of existing national and regional research institutes and universities, including the United Nations University, the United Nations Institute for Training and Research, the United Nations Research Institute for Social Development and the United Nations Social Defence Institute. A network of such institutes and universities should be built up to facilitate the regular exchange of information and knowledge in cooperation with the United Nations.

IV. Mass communication media

174. A major obstacle in improving the status of women lies in public attitudes and values regarding women's roles in society. The mass communication media have great potential as a vehicle for social change and could exercise a significant influence in helping to remove prejudices and stereotypes, accelerating the acceptance of women's new and expanding roles in society, and promoting their integration into the development process as equal partners.

175. At the present time, the media tend to reinforce traditional attitudes, often portraying an image of women that is degrading and humiliating, and fail to reflect the changing roles of the sexes. They may also have harmful effects in imposing alien cultures upon different societies.

176. Mass communication media should be understood as encompassing not only radio, television, cinema, press (newspapers, periodicals, comic strips and cartoons), advertising, and public meetings and similar forums but also traditional types of entertainment such as drama, story telling, songs and puppet shows, which are essential for reaching the rural areas of many countries.

177. Governmental and non-governmental organizations should encourage and support national, regional and international research to determine the image of women and men portrayed by the media; and the negative and positive influences exercised by them in their various roles as conveyors of information, entertainers, educators and advertisers.

178. Governmental and non-governmental organizations should also take steps to ensure that information shall be provided on the current situation of women in various countries, with particular emphasis on the changing roles of both sexes.

179. Those in control of the media should seek to raise public consciousness with respect to these changing roles, and the serious concern that both women and men have about important issues that affect their families, communities and society at large. They should be urged to project a more dynamic image of women (as well as of men) and to take into account the diversity of women's roles and their actual and potential contribution to society.

180. They should depict the roles and achievements of women from all walks of life throughout history, including women in the rural areas and women of minority groups. They should also seek to develop in women confidence in themselves and in other women, and a sense of their own value and importance as human beings.

181. Women should be appointed in greater numbers in media management decision-making and other capacities, as editors, columnists, reporters, producers and the like, and should encourage the critical review, within the media, of the image of women projected.

V. International and regional action

A. *Global action*

182. The United Nations should proclaim the decade 1975-1985 as the United Nations Decade for Women and Development in order to ensure that national and international action shall be sustained throughout the period.

183. The decade and this Plan of Action call for a clear commitment on the part of the international community to accord importance and priority to measures to improve the situation of women, both as a means of achieving the goals of social progress and development and as an end in itself. The plan envisages that all organizations of the United Nations system should take separated and joint action to implement its recommendations, including the relevant United Nations organs and bodies, especially the regional commissions, the United Nations Children's Fund, the United Nations Development Programme, the United Nations Fund for Population Activities, the United Nations Industrial Development Organization, the United Nations Conference on Trade and Development, the United Nations Institute for Training and Research, and the specialized agencies. Their activities should be properly coordinated

through the existing machinery, especially the Economic and Social Council and the Administrative Committee on Co-ordination. Each organization should evaluate what it has done to improve the status of women and enhance their contribution to development and identify the measures needed to implement this Plan.

184. International and regional intergovernmental organizations outside the United Nations system are also urged to develop programmes to implement this Plan and achieve the objectives of International Women's Year during the proposed decade.

185. International non-governmental organizations and their national affiliates should also act jointly and separately, within their particular spheres of interest, to give effect to the recommendations of the Plan within the 10-year period.

186. The Plan endorses programmes and strategies setting forth similar or related objectives; in particular, the International Development Strategy for the Second United Nations Development Decade, the Programme of Concerted International Action for the Advancement of Women, the Programme for the Decade for Action to Combat Racism and Racial Discrimination, the World Population Plan of Action, the recommendations of the World Food Conference, and the regional plans of action for the integration of women in development, adopted in 1974 for the regions of the Economic and Social Commission for Asia and the Pacific and the Economic Commission for Africa. 6/

187. Women should be fully involved in policy-making at the international level as well as the national level. Governments should make sure that they are equitably represented among the principal delegates to all international bodies, conferences and committees, including those dealing with political and legal questions, economic and social development, disarmament, planning, administration and finance, science and technology, the environment and population. The secretariats of the international organizations should set an example by eliminating any provisions or practices in their employment policies that may be discriminatory against women. They should also take all necessary measures to ensure that an equitable balance between men and women staff members shall be achieved before the end of the Second United Nations Development Decade, and establish goals, strategies and timetables to achieve this end. The equitable balance should apply to all substantive areas, and to field posts where operational programmes are initiated and carried out.

188. International organizations should review the implications of the Plan in the context of their own existing and new programmes, and should make appropriate recommendations to their governing bodies on any revisions of their financial and administrative arrangements that may be required to implement the Plan.

189. International action should support existing programmes and expand their scope in the following main areas: (a) research, data collection and analysis (see chap. III above); (b) technical cooperation, training and advisory services, including coordination with national and regional activities of organizations within the United Nations system; (c) elaboration and ongoing review of international standards; (d) dissemination and exchange of information and liaison with non-governmental organizations and other groups; (e) review and appraisal, including monitoring of progress made in achieving the aims and objectives of the Plan; and (f) executive and management functions including overall coordination with all the organizations of the United Nations system, and with the national and regional machinery referred to in the Plan.

1. *Operational activities for technical cooperation*

190. The United Nations Development Programme, the United Nations Fund for Population Activities, the United Nations Environment Programme, the United Nations specialized agencies, including the International Bank for Reconstruction and Development and the International Monetary Fund, the regional commissions, intergovernmental organizations, bilateral assistance agencies and foundations, and international and regional development banks and other international financial institutions, all carry out their work through projects that are highly specific in terms of the objectives to be reached, the resources to be employed, and the target areas and populations for which they are intended. Given the scope and diversity of the world-wide system of assistance agencies, action can be initiated in a large number of areas without delay once the needs are understood and diffused throughout the United Nations system.

191. A deliberate and large-scale effort should therefore be made to ensure that high priority and attention shall be given by Governments and the international community to programmes, projects and activities that give women the skills, training and opportunities necessary to improve their situation and enable them to participate fully and effectively in the total development effort.

192. Field surveys should be undertaken in each region to assist Governments and the international community by establishing the necessary data base to develop projects that will implement the objectives of the Plan.

193. All existing plans and projects should be scrutinized with a view to extending their sphere of activities

6/ For the regional plans of action, see sect. B below.

to include women. New and innovative projects should also be developed to include women.

194. The following areas are of special importance:

(a) Integrated rural development. Special attention should be given to women's role as producers, processors and vendors of food, stressing the need for training women and girls. Training is especially needed in modern methods of framing, marketing purchasing and sales techniques; basic accounting and organizational methods; fundamentals of hygiene and nutrition; training in crafts and cooperatives;

(b) Health, reproduction and growth and development, including family health and child health, family planning, nutrition and health education;

(c) Education and training at all levels and in all sectors related to the creation of employment opportunities so that women can play an economic role;

(d) Youth projects, which should be examined to make sure that they include adequate emphasis on the participation of young women;

(e) Public administration, with the aim of preparing women to participate in development planning and policy-making, especially in middle- and higher-level posts.

195. The resident representatives of the United Nations Development Programme (UNDP) should play a key role in helping Governments to formulate requests for such assistance within the framework of country programming. Advisory services provided by the specialized agencies in the form of special consultants or task forces could also render assistance in the formulation of project requests. Periodic reviews should be initiated to suggest crucial areas where special support might be needed. Projects should be constantly reviewed and evaluated to determine their impact and success in improving the position of women.

196. Women should participate fully in planning and implementing UNDP country programmes and regional, interregional and global projects under the auspices of the United Nations and other international agencies. Governments should bear in mind the importance of including, in national planning organizations and other bodies responsible for public policy-making and management, persons with special competence in the subject of women's integration in development.

2. *Formulation and implementation of international standards*

197. The preparation of international conventions, declarations and formal recommendations, and the development of reporting systems and other procedures for their implementation are important elements of international programmes and should be continued.

198. High priority should be given to the preparation and adoption of the convention on the elimination of discrimination against women, with effective procedures for its implementation.

199. Studies should be undertaken by the appropriate organizations of the effectiveness of the implementation of existing instruments and periodic reviews made to determine their adequacy in the light of changing conditions in the modern world, and of experience gained since their adoption.

200. The need for the development of new standards in new fields of concern to women should be kept constantly under review in relation to the implementation of the present Plan. Appropriate research and studies should be undertaken to determine the need for such new standards.

3. *Exchange of information and experience*

201. The exchange of information and experience at the international level is an effective means of stimulating progress and encouraging the adoption of measures to eliminate discrimination against women and encourage their wider participation in all sectors of national life. Countries with different political, economic and social systems and cultures and at differing stages of development have benefited from the common knowledge of problems, difficulties and achievements and from solutions worked out jointly.

202. Effective international machinery should be established or existing bodies, such as the Commission on the Status of Women, utilized to afford women in all regions of the world the opportunity to support one another in mutual understanding of their national and local problems and fight for the elimination of all forms of discrimination and oppression.

203. Meetings and seminars, including those organized under the United Nations technical cooperation programme, which have proved to be most valuable in providing a regional and international exchange of information and experience, should be continued.

204. Educational and informational programmes supported by the international community should be developed and extended to make all sectors of the population aware of the international norms established, the goals and objectives of this Plan of Action, and the findings of research and data envisaged under the relevant chapter of the Plan.

205. Material documenting the situation of women in specific countries of the world should also be prepared and widely distributed. It should be issued in the form of a yearbook or almanac containing facts which should be maintained and kept up to date. Material should also be prepared and widely publicized on methods and techniques that have proved useful in promoting

the status of women and integrating them into the process of development.

206. International organizations, both governmental and non-governmental, should strengthen their efforts to distribute information on women and related matters. This could be done through periodic publications on the situation of women, their changing roles and their integration into the development effort through the planning and implementation of policies, as well as through the utilization of communication media and aids, and the wide distribution of newsletters, pamphlets, visual charts and similar material on women.

B. *Regional action*

207. The regional commissions for Africa, Asia and the Pacific, Europe, Latin America and Western Asia should stimulate interest in the Plan and provide national Governments and non-governmental organizations with the technical and informational support they require to develop and implement effective strategies to further the objectives of the Plan in the regions. Where they have not already done so, the regional commissions should establish appropriate machinery for the purpose. This might include a regional standing committee of experts from countries of the region to advise the commission on its activities directed towards the integration of women in development in relation to those of Governments and other agencies in the region. The committee's functions could include the following:

(a) To initiate country studies and assist national institutions to identify the types of information needed for a proper understanding of the situation of women and the factors facilitating or limiting their advancement;

(b) To assist with the design and implementation of surveys for the collection of data and other information;

(c) To give leadership in the methods of reporting on the situation of women and in the development of indicators for assessing the progress made towards the goals of this Plan in conjunction with regional statistical bodies and international efforts to this end;

(d) To provide a clearing-house for the exchange of information which would facilitate coordination and mutual support between programmes for the advancement of women at various levels, and for the sharing of relevant experience among the countries of the region.

208. States members of the regional commissions, in requesting technical and financial assistance, should endeavour to raise the priority accorded to projects to enhance opportunities for women and increase recognition of the importance of these projects for overall development in consultation with regional offices of the United Nations Development Programme.

209. The regional commissions should provide assistance to governmental and non-governmental organizations to identify needed action, develop policies, strategies and programmes for strengthening women's role in national development, and formulate requests for technical and financial assistance for such programmes. They should encourage training institutions in the region to expand their curricula to encompass topics related to the integration of women in development, and assist in the development of training programmes, particularly those whose initial aim is to increase women's potential for leadership and develop the cadres for formulating the programmes and implementing the activities indicated by this Plan.

210. The regional commissions should also promote technical cooperation between the countries of the region, utilizing the existing talent available. Trained women could, for example, offer short-term assistance to women in countries other than their own on a voluntary basis, or as part of a special task force. Special advisers should be attached to the regional field offices in order to strengthen the regional field structure and carry out more effectively the functions and aims described above. They could also seek to stimulate increased contributions of funds for financing programmes for the advancement of women from existing sources of multilateral and bilateral assistance, and to secure new sources of funds, including the establishment of revolving funds at the national and local levels.

211. In the implementation of the Plan, special efforts should be made by the commissions and other United Nations bodies having regional offices to coordinate their programmes with those of existing United Nations and other regional centres whose fields of competence relate to the aims of the Plan, such as centres for research and training in development planning, literacy, social welfare, social defence, employment, health and nutrition and community development.

212. Regional development banks such as the African Development Bank, the Asian Development Bank and the Inter-American Development Bank as well as subregional banks, such as the Central American Bank for Economic Integration and the East African Development Bank, and bilateral funding agencies should be urged to accord high priority in their development assistance to projects that include the integration of women into the development effort and the achievement of equality. Such assistance would stimulate national support for innovative national and local programmes, including self-help activities.

VI. Review and appraisal

213. A comprehensive and thorough review and appraisal of progress made in meeting the goals of this

Plan should be undertaken at regular intervals by the United Nations system. Such an exercise should be part of the procedures for the review and appraisal of progress made under the International Development Strategy for the Second United Nations Development Decade, and closely coordinated with any new international development strategic that may be formulated.

214. The General Assembly has already made provision in its resolution 3276 (XXIX) of 10 December 1974 to consider relevant recommendations of the World Conference of the International Women's Year at its seventh special session and at its thirtieth session in 1975. The Plan should also be considered at the sixtieth session of the Economic and Social Council in the spring of 1976. The Secretary-General should be invited to make appropriate arrangements for the first biennial review of progress in 1978, in cooperation with Governments and taking into account the existing structure and resources of the United Nations system. The Economic and Social Council should review the findings of such a systematic evaluation with the object of making, whenever necessary, appropriate modifications in the goals and recommendations of the Plan.

215. The monitoring of trends and policies relating to women and relevant to this Plan of Action should be undertaken continuously as a specialized activity of the United Nations. They should be reviewed biennially by the appropriate bodies of the United Nations system, beginning in 1978. Because of the shortness of the intervals, such monitoring would necessarily be selective and focus mainly on new and emerging trends and policies.

216. The Plan of Action should also be considered by the regional commissions, the United Nations Development Programme, the United Nations Children's Fund, the United Nations Industrial Development Organization, the relevant specialized agencies and other intergovernmental and non-governmental organizations at their meetings following the World Conference. The discussions and decisions of these bodies concerning the Plan should be submitted to the Economic and Social Council and its relevant functional commissions and advisory bodies (the Commission on the Status of Women, the Commission for Social Development, the Population Commission, the Statistical Commission, the Committee for Development Planning, and the Committee on Review and Appraisal) at their sessions in 1976 and 1977. An item on action on the implementation of the Plan should be included in the agenda of the sessions of all these bodies at intervals of no longer than two years.

217. At the regional level, the regional commissions should assume responsibility for monitoring progress towards the greater and more effective participation of women in all aspects of development efforts. Such monitoring should be carried out within the framework of the review and appraisal of the International Development Strategy for the Second United Nations Development Decade. The commissions should include information on the integration of women in development in their reports to the Economic and Social Council on the social and economic situation in the regions. They should also discuss at appropriate intervals (such as every two years) the progress made towards achieving the aims of this Plan of Action. They should encourage Governments to provide equal opportunities for women to be represented on their delegations to the sessions of the commissions and to other relevant meetings.

218. At the national level, Governments are encouraged to undertake their own regular review and appraisal of progress made to achieve the goals and objectives of the Plan and to report on its implementation to the Economic and Social Council in conjunction, where necessary, with other existing reporting systems (e.g., those of the International Development Strategy for the Second United Nations Development Decade, the World Population Plan of Action, the recommendations of the World Food Conference, and the implementation of the Declaration on the Elimination of Discrimination against Women, and of the Programme of Concerted International Action for the Advancement of Women).

219. Governments should, in the context of their own development plans, evaluate the implications of this Plan and make any necessary financial and administrative arrangements for its implementation.

Appendix

Relevant international instruments

A. *United Nations instruments*

1. *General instruments*

Charter of the United Nations

Universal Declaration of Human Rights (1948)

International Covenant on Economic, Social and Cultural Rights (1966)

International Covenant on Civil and Political Rights and Optional Protocol (1966)

Convention for the Suppression of the Traffic in Persons and of the Exploitation of the Prostitution of Others (1949)

Supplementary Convention on the Abolition of Slavery, the Slave Trade, and Institutions and Practices Similar to Slavery (1956)

International Convention on the Elimination of All Forms of Racial Discrimination (1965)

Declaration on Social Progress and Development (1969)

International Development Strategy for the Second United Nations Development Decade (1970)

World Population Plan of Action (1974)

Programme of Action on the Establishment of a New International Economic Order (1974)

Charter of Economic Rights and Duties of States (1974)

2. *Instruments relating specifically to the status of women*

Convention on the Political Rights of Women (1952)

Convention on the Nationality of Married Women (1957)

Convention and Recommendation on Consent to Marriage, Minimum Age for Marriage and Registration of Marriages (1962 and 1965)

Declaration on the Elimination of Discrimination against Women (1967)

Programme of concerted international action for the advancement of women (1970)

B. *Specialized agency instruments*

1. *International Labour Organisation*

Convention concerning the employment of women on underground work in mines of all kinds, No. 45, 1935

Convention concerning night work of women employed in industry (revised), No. 89, 1948

Convention concerning equal remuneration for men and women workers for work of equal value, No. 100, 1951; and Recommendation No. 90, 1951

Convention concerning minimum standards of social security, No. 102, 1952

Convention concerning maternity protection (revised), No. 103, 1952; and Recommendation No. 95, 1952

Convention concerning discrimination in respect of employment and occupation, No. 111, 1958; and Recommendation No. 111, 1958

Convention concerning employment policy, No. 122, 1964; and Recommendation No. 122, 1964

Recommendation concerning vocational training, No. 117, 1962

Recommendation concerning the employment of women with family responsibilities, No. 123, 1965

2. *United Nations Educational, Scientific and Cultural Organization*

Convention against Discrimination in Education (1960)

Protocol instituting a Conciliation and Good Offices Commission to be responsible for seeking a settlement of any disputes which may arise between States Parties to the Convention against Discrimination in Education (1962)

Declaration of Mexico on the Equality of Women and Their Contribution to Development and Peace, 1975

The World Conference of the International Women's Year,

Aware that the problems of women, who constitute half of the world's population, are the problems of society as a whole, and that changes in the present economic, political and social situation of women must become an integral part of efforts to transform the structures and attitudes that hinder the genuine satisfaction of their needs,

Recognizing that international cooperation based on the principles of the Charter of the United Nations should be developed and strengthened in order to find solutions to world problems and to build an international community based on equity and justice,

Recalling that in subscribing to the Charter, the peoples of the United Nations undertook specific commitments: "to save succeeding generations from the scourge of war ..., to reaffirm faith in fundamental human rights, in the dignity and worth of the human person, in the equal rights of men and women and of nations large and small, and to promote social progress and better standards of life in larger freedom",

Taking note of the fact that since the creation of the United Nations very important instruments have been adopted, among which the following constitute landmarks: the Universal Declaration of Human Rights, the Declaration on the Granting of Independence to Colonial Countries and Peoples, the International Development Strategy for the Second United Nations Development Decade, and the Declaration and Programme of Action for the Establishment of a New International Economic Order based on the Charter of Economic Rights and Duties of States,

Taking into account that the United Nations Declaration on the Elimination of Discrimination against Women considers that: "discrimination against women is incompatible with human dignity and with the welfare of the family and of society, prevents their participation, on equal terms with men, in the political, social, economic and cultural life of their countries and is an obstacle to the full development of the potentialities of women in the service of their countries and of humanity",

Recalling that the General Assembly, in its resolution 3010 (XXVII) of 18 December 1972, proclaimed 1975 as International Women's Year and that the Year was to be devoted to intensified action with a view to: promoting equality between men and women, ensuring the integration of women in the total development effort, and increasing the contribution of women to the strengthening of world peace,

Recalling further that the Economic and Social Council, in its resolution 1849 (LVI) of 16 May 1974, adopted the Programme for International Women's Year, and that the General Assembly, in its resolution 3275 (XXIX) of 10 December 1974, called for full implementation of the Programme,

Taking into account the role played by women in the history of humanity, especially in the struggle for national liberation, the strengthening of international peace, and the elimination of imperialism, colonialism, neo-colonialism, foreign occupation, zionism, alien domination, racism and apartheid,

Stressing that greater and equal participation of women at all levels of decision-making shall decisively contribute to accelerating the pace of development and the maintenance of peace,

Stressing also that women and men of all countries should have equal rights and duties and that it is the task of all States to create the necessary conditions for the attainment and the exercise thereof,

Recognizing that women of the entire world, whatever differences exist between them, share the painful experience of receiving or having received unequal treatment, and that as their awareness of this phenomenon increases they will become natural allies in the struggle against any form of oppression, such as is practised under colonialism, neo-colonialism, zionism, racial discrimination and apartheid, thereby constituting an enormous revolutionary potential for economic and social change in the world today,

Recognizing that changes in the social and economic structure of societies, even though they are among the prerequisites, cannot of themselves ensure an immediate improvement in the status of a group which has long been disadvantaged, and that urgent consideration must therefore be given to the full, immediate and early integration of women into national and international life,

Emphasizing that under-development imposes upon women a double burden of exploitation, which must be rapidly eliminated, and that full implementation of national development policies designed to fulfil this objective is seriously hindered by the existing inequitable system of international economic relations,

Aware that the role of women in child-bearing should not be the cause of inequality and discrimination, and that child-bearing demands shared responsibilities among women, men and society as a whole,

Recognizing also the urgency of improving the status of women and finding more effective methods and strategies which will enable them to have the same opportunities as men to participate actively in the development of their countries and to contribute to the attainment of world peace,

Convinced that women must play an important role in the promotion, achievement and maintenance of international peace, and that it is necessary to encourage their efforts towards peace, through their full participation in the national and international organizations that exist for this purpose,

Considering that it is necessary to promote national, regional and international action, in which the implementation of the World Plan of Action adopted by the World Conference of the International Women's Year should make a significant contribution, for the attainment of equality, development and peace,

Decides to promulgate the following principles:

1. Equality between women and men means equality in their dignity and worth as human beings as well as equality in their rights, opportunities and responsibilities.

2. All obstacles that stand in the way of enjoyment by women of equal status with men must be eliminated in order to ensure their full integration into national development and their participation in securing and in maintaining international peace.

3. It is the responsibility of the State to create the necessary facilities so that women may be integrated into society while their children receive adequate care.

4. National non-governmental organizations should contribute to the advancement of women by assisting women to take advantage of their opportunities, by promoting education and information about women's rights, and by cooperating with their respective Governments.

5. Women and men have equal rights and responsibilities in the family and in society. Equality between women and men should be guaranteed in the family, which is the basic unit of society and where human relations are nurtured. Men should participate more actively, creatively and responsibly in family life for its sound development in order to enable women to be more intensively involved in the activities of their communities and with a view to combining effectively home and work possibilities of both partners.

6. Women, like men, require opportunities for developing their intellectual potential to the maximum. National policies and programmes should therefore provide them with full and equal access to education and training at all levels, while ensuring that such programmes and policies consciously orient them towards

new occupations and new roles consistent with their need for self-fulfilment and the needs of national development.

7. The right of women to work, to receive equal pay for work of equal value, to be provided with equal conditions and opportunities for advancement in work, and all other women's rights to full and satisfying economic activity are strongly reaffirmed. Review of these principles for their effective implementation is now urgently needed, considering the necessity of restructuring world economic relationships. This restructuring offers greater possibilities for women to be integrated into the stream of national economic, social, political and cultural life.

8. All means of communication and information as well as all cultural media should regard as a high priority their responsibility for helping to remove the attitudinal and cultural factors that still inhibit the development of women and for projecting in positive terms the value to society of the assumption by women of changing and expanding roles.

9. Necessary resources should be made available in order that women may be able to participate in the political life of their countries and of the international community since their active participation in national and world affairs at decision-making and other levels in the political field is a prerequisite of women's full exercise of equal rights as well as of their further development and of the national well-being.

10. Equality of rights carries with it corresponding responsibilities; it is therefore a duty of women to make full use of opportunities available to them and to perform their duties to the family, the country and humanity.

11. It should be one of the principal aims of social education to teach respect for physical integrity and its rightful place in human life. The human body, whether that of woman or man, is inviolable and respect for it is a fundamental element of human dignity and freedom.

12. Every couple and every individual has the right to decide freely and responsibly whether or not to have children as well as to determine their number and spacing, and to have information, education and means to do so.

13. Respect for human dignity encompasses the right of every woman to decide freely for herself whether or not to contract matrimony.

14. The issue of inequality, as it affects the vast majority of the women of the world, is closely linked with the problem of under-development, which exists as a result not only of unsuitable internal structures but also of a profoundly unjust world economic system.

15. The full and complete development of any country requires the maximum participation of women as well as of men in all fields: the underutilization of the potential of approximately half of the world's population is a serious obstacle to social and economic development.

16. The ultimate end of development is to achieve a better quality of life for all, which means not only the development of economic and other material resources but also the physical, moral, intellectual and cultural growth of the human person.

17. In order to integrate women into development, States should undertake the necessary changes in their economic and social policies because women have the right to participate and contribute to the total development effort.

18. The present state of international economic relations poses serious obstacles to a more efficient utilization of all human and material potential for accelerated development and for the improvement of living standards in developing countries aimed at the elimination of hunger, child mortality, unemployment, illiteracy, ignorance and backwardness, which concern all of humanity and women in particular. It is therefore essential to establish and implement with urgency the New International Economic Order, of which the Charter of Economics Rights and Duties of States constitutes a basic element, founded on equity, sovereign equality, interdependence, common interest, cooperation among all States irrespective of their social and economic systems, on the principles of peaceful coexistence and on the promotion by the entire international community of economic and social progress of all countries, especially developing countries, and on the progress of States comprising the international community.

19. The principle of the full and permanent sovereignty of every State over its natural resources, wealth and all economic activities, and its inalienable right of nationalization as an expression of this sovereignty constitute fundamental prerequisites in the process of economic and social development.

20. The attainment of economic and social goals, so basic to the realization of the rights of women, does not, however, of itself bring about the full integration of women in development on a basis of equality with men unless specific measures are undertaken for the elimination of all forms of discrimination against them. It is therefore important to formulate and implement models of development that will promote the participation and advancement of women in all fields of work and provide them with equal educational opportunities and such services as would facilitate housework.

21. Modernization of the agricultural sector of vast areas of the world is an indispensable element for progress, particularly as it creates opportunities for millions of rural women to participate in development. Governments, the United Nations, its specialized agencies and other competent regional and international organizations

should support projects designed to utilize the maximum potential and develop the self-reliance of rural women.

22. It must be emphasized that, given the required economic, social and legal conditions as well as the appropriate attitudes conducive to the full and equal participation of women in society, efforts and measures aimed at a more intensified integration of women in development can be successfully implemented only if made an integral part of overall social and economic growth. Full participation of women in the various economic, social, political and cultural sectors is an important indication of the dynamic progress of peoples and their development. Individual human rights can be realized only within the framework of total development.

23. The objectives considered in this Declaration can be achieved only in a world in which the relations between States are governed, *inter alia*, by the following principles: the sovereign equality of States, the free self-determination of peoples, the unacceptability of acquisition or attempted acquisition of territories by force and the prohibition of recognition of such acquisition, territorial integrity, and the right to defend it, and non-interference in the domestic affairs of States, in the same manner as relations between human beings should be governed by the supreme principle of the equality of rights of women and men.

24. International cooperation and peace require the achievement of national liberation and independence, the elimination of colonialism and neo-colonialism, foreign occupation, zionism, apartheid, and racial discrimination in all its forms as well as the recognition of the dignity of peoples and their right to self-determination.

25. Women have a vital role to play in the promotion of peace in all spheres of life: in the family, the community, the nation and the world. Women must participate equally with men in the decision-making processes which help to promote peace at all levels.

26. Women and men together should eliminate colonialism, neo-colonialism, imperialism, foreign domination and occupation, zionism, apartheid, racial discrimination, the acquisition of land by force and the recognition of such acquisition, since such practices inflict incalculable suffering on women, men and children.

27. The solidarity of women in all countries of the world should be supported in their protest against violations of human rights condemned by the United Nations. All forms of repression and inhuman treatment of women, men and children, including imprisonment, torture, massacres, collective punishment, destruction of homes, forced eviction and arbitrary restriction of movement shall be considered crimes against humanity and in violation of the Universal Declaration of Human Rights and other international instruments.

28. Women all over the world should unite to eliminate violations of human rights committed against women and girls such as: rape, prostitution, physical assault, mental cruelty, child marriage, forced marriage and marriage as a commercial transaction.

29. Peace requires that women as well as men should reject any type of intervention in the domestic affairs of States, whether it be openly or covertly carried on by other States or by transnational corporations. Peace also requires that women as well as men should also promote respect for the sovereign right of a State to establish its own economic, social and political system without undergoing political and economic pressures or coercion of any type.

30. Women as well as men should promote real, general and complete disarmament under effective international control, starting with nuclear disarmament. Until genuine disarmament is achieved, women and men throughout the world must maintain their vigilance and do their utmost to achieve and maintain international peace.

Wherefore,

The World Conference of the International Women's Year

1. *Affirms* its faith in the objectives of the International Women's Year, which are equality, development and peace;

2. *Proclaims* its commitment to the achievement of such objectives;

3. *Strongly urges* Governments, the entire United Nations system, regional and international intergovernmental organizations and the international community as a whole to dedicate themselves to the creation of a just society where women, men and children can live in dignity, freedom, justice and prosperity.

Resolutions and decision adopted by the Conference

1. Research and training for the advancement of women in Africa

2. International cooperation under projects designed to achieve the objectives of the World Plan of Action

3. The status of women in South Africa, Namibia and Southern Rhodesia

4. Role of the United Nations system in implementing the World Plan of Action

5. Women and health

6. Participation of women in the seventh special session of the United Nations General Assembly and in other meetings of the various bodies of the United Nations

7. Prevention of the exploitation of women and girls

Document 46

General Assembly resolution on implementation of the World Plan of Action adopted by the World Conference of the International Women's Year

A/RES/3490 (XXX), 12 December 1975

The General Assembly,

Recalling the World Plan of Action for the Implementation of the Objectives of the International Women's Year, adopted by the World Conference of the International Women's Year 1/, held at Mexico city from 19 June to 2 July 1975,

Convinced that a comprehensive and thorough review and appraisal of progress made in meeting the goals of the World Plan of Action is of crucial importance for the success of the Plan and should be undertaken at regular intervals by organizations of the United Nations system,

Recognizing that the results of the exercise of the

implementation of the World Plan of Action will contribute to the consideration of the review and appraisal of the International Development Strategy for the Second United Nations Development Decade and will consequently promote the role of women in the development process,

1. *Calls upon* the governing bodies of the United Nations Development Programme, the United Nations Children's Fund, the United Nations Industrial Development Organization, the relevant specialized agencies and

1/ *Report of the World Conference of the International Women's Year* (United Nations publication, Sales No. E.76.IV.1), chap.II, sect.A.

the regional commissions to review annually the activities they have undertaken in accordance with the World Plan of Action for the Implementation of the Objectives of the International Women's Year and to integrate such reviews into the reports submitted to the Economic and Social Council;

2. *Affirms* that a system-wide review and appraisal of the implementation of the World Plan of Action should be undertaken, in the years of the biennial review and appraisal of the International Development Strategy for the Second United Nations Development Decade, as an input to the process of review and appraisal of progress made under the Strategy;

3. *Urges* all States and the relevant organs of the United Nations to report to the Secretary-General on measures they have taken for implementing the World Plan of Action and to include relevant information about the integration of women in development;

4. *Requests* the Commission on the Status of Women to consider reports submitted on measures undertaken in implementation of the World Plan of Action, in accordance with the International Development Strategy, and to report its findings and conclusions on major trends and policies with regard to the status of women, particularly the integration of women in development, to the Economic and Social Council through the Committee for Development Planning and the Committee on Review and Appraisal;

5. *Urges* the Committee for Development Planning, the Committee on Review and Appraisal and the Economic and Social Council to pay special attention to the question of the status of women in the review and appraisal of the International Development Strategy;

6. *Invites* the Secretary-General to make appropriate arrangements for the first review and appraisal of the implementation of the World Plan of Action.

Document 47

General Assembly resolution calling for the integration of women in the development process

A/RES/3505 (XXX), 15 December 1975

The General Assembly,

Recalling its resolution 3010 (XXVII) of 18 December 1972 in which it proclaimed the year 1975 International Women's Year,

Recalling its resolutions 3201 (S-VI) and 3202 (S-VI) of 1 May 1974 containing the Declaration and the Programme of Action on the Establishment of a New International Economic Order,

Recalling also its resolution 3281 (XXIX) of 12 December 1974 containing the Charter of Economic Rights and Duties of States,

Recalling further its resolution 3362 (S-VII) of 16 September 1975 on development and international economic cooperation,

Bearing in mind its resolution 3276 (XXIX) of 10 December 1974 on the World Conference of the International Women's Year and 3342 (XXIX) of 17 December 1974 on women and development, and also Economic and Social Council resolution 1959 (LIX) of 28 July 1975 on the World Conference of the International Women's Year,

Taking note of the principles of the Declaration of Mexico on the Equality of Women and their Contribution to Development and Peace, 1975, 1/ and the World Plan of Action for the Implementation of the Objectives

of the International Women's Year, 2/ adopted by the World Conference of the International Women's Year, held at Mexico City from 19 June to 2 July 1975, and also the resolutions of the Conference relating to the full integration of women in development, 3/

Recognizing that the results of the World Conference of the International Women's Year, in particular the World Plan of Action, indicate that the role of women in the development process must be made an integral part of the establishment of the new international economic order,

Recalling Economic and Social Council resolution 1855 (LVI) of 16 May 1974 on the significance of the full integration of women in development,

Aware that the economic value of the substantial contribution of women to overall development has not been widely recognized,

Recognizing that women, owing to the unequal treatment they have endured, constitute a vast potential force in the process of economic and social change, as well as in the struggle against all forms of exploitation and oppression,

1/ Report of the World Conference of the International Women's Year (United Nations publication, Sales No. E.76.IV.1), chap. I.
2/ Ibid., chap. II, sect. A.
3/ Ibid., chap. III.

Emphasizing that accelerated development requires the real and effective participation of men and women in all areas of national activity and the creation of the necessary conditions for equality of rights, opportunities and responsibilities for men and women,

1. *Recognizes* that the World Conference of the International Women's Year has established that improvement of the status of women constitutes a basic element in any development process;

2. *Urges* all States to undertake the necessary changes, as appropriate, in their economic and social structures in order to ensure the participation of women, on an equal basis with men, in the development process;

3. *Invites* the relevant organizations within the United Nations system, particularly the United Nations Conference on Trade and Development, the United Nations Industrial Development Organization, the United Nations Development Programme and the Food and Agricultural Organization of the United Nations, to pay special attention to development programmes relating to women, *inter alia*, in the fields of agriculture, industry, trade and science and technology;

4. *Requests* the Secretary-General to prepare, on the basis of information received from Governments and relevant organizations of the United Nations system, as well as on the basis of existing studies, a preliminary report, for the consideration of the General Assembly at its thirty-first session, on the extent to which women participate in fields such as agriculture, industry, trade and science and technology, with a view to making recommendations on ways and means of increasing and upgrading the participation of women therein;

5. *Urges* all Governments to give special attention to the inclusion of the question of the integration of women in the development process in United Nations conferences and meetings on matters which have an impact on the participation of women in development;

6. *Requests* the Secretary-General to report to the General Assembly at its thirty-first session on the implementation of the present resolution.

Document 48

General Assembly resolution on women's participation in the strengthening of international peace and security and in the struggle against colonialism, racism, racial discrimination, foreign aggression and occupation and all forms of foreign domination

A/RES/3519 (XXX), 15 December 1975

The General Assembly,

Recalling its resolution 3276 (XXIX) of 10 December 1974,

Considering the report of the World Conference of the International Women's Year, 1/ held at Mexico City from 19 June to 2 July 1975, in particular the Declaration of Mexico on the Equality of Women and Their Contribution to Development and Peace, 1975, 2/ the World Plan of Action for the Implementation of the Objectives of the International Women's Year 3/ and the resolutions contained in the report of the Conference, 4/

Appreciating that the Conference emphasized the important role women must play in the strengthening of international peace and security and in the expansion of cooperation among States, irrespective of their social and economic systems, based on the principles of peaceful coexistence in accordance with the Charter of the United Nations,

Endorsing the statement of the Conference that international cooperation and peace require the achievement of national liberation and independence, the preservation of sovereignty and territorial integrity, the elimination of colonialism and neo-colonialism, foreign aggression and occupation, apartheid and racial discrimination in all its forms, as well as the recognition of the dignity of peoples and their right to self-determination,

Noting with satisfaction the opinion expressed by the Conference that peace requires that women as well as men should reject any type of intervention in the domestic affairs of States, openly or covertly carried out by other States or by transnational corporations, and that women as well as men should also promote respect for the sovereign right of a State to establish its own economic, social and political system without political and economic pressures or coercion of any type,

Taking into account the view of the Conference that the Charter of Economic Rights and Duties of States 5/

1/ United Nations publication, Sales No. E.76.IV.1.
2/ Ibid., chap. I.
3/ Ibid., chap. II, sect. A
4/ Ibid., chap. III.
5/ Resolution 3281 (XXIX).

confirms, *inter alia,* the obligation of all States to promote the implementation of general and complete disarmament, to use the funds thus saved for economic and social development and to provide part of these funds for the needs of the developing countries,

Noting with satisfaction the positive changes which have taken place during the last few years in international relations, such as the elimination of the dangerous sources of war in Viet-Nam and the results of the Conference on Security and Co-operation in Europe, and noting also the importance of deepening the process of international détente and strengthening an international just peace based on full respect for the Charter of the United Nations and the interests of all States, large and small,

Emphasizing the grave concern that in some regions of the world colonialism, apartheid, racial discrimination and foreign aggression continue to exist and territories are still occupied, which represents a most serious infringement of the principles of the Charter of the United Nations and of human rights of both men and women, and of the people's right to self-determination,

1. *Reaffirms* the principles promulgated in the Declaration of Mexico on the Equality of Women and Their Contribution to Development and Peace, 1975;

2. *Reaffirms* that the strengthening of international peace and security, cooperation among all States irrespective of their social and economic systems, based on the principle of peaceful coexistence, and the elimination of the remaining vestiges of colonialism, neo-colonialism, apartheid, all forms of racism and racial discrimination, alien domination and foreign aggression and occupation are indispensable for the safeguarding of the fundamental human rights of both men and women;

3. *Calls upon* all Governments, intergovernmental and non-governmental organizations, particularly women's organizations and women's groups, to intensify their efforts to strengthen peace, to expand and deepen the process of international détente and make it irreversible, to eliminate completely and definitely all forms of colonialism and to put an end to the policy and practice of apartheid, all forms of racism, racial discrimination, aggression, occupation and foreign domination;

4. *Urges* all Governments to take effective measures towards bringing about general and complete disarmament and convening the World Disarmament Conference as soon as possible;

5. *Expresses* its solidarity with and its assistance for women who contribute towards the struggle of the peoples for their national liberation;

6. *Invites* the Secretary-General to submit to the General Assembly at its thirty-second session a comprehensive report on the implementation of the present resolution.

Document 49

General Assembly resolution proclaiming the period from 1976 to 1985 the United Nations Decade for Women: Equality, Development and Peace, establishing an International Research and Training Institute for the Advancement of Women (INSTRAW) and deciding to convene in 1980 a world conference to review and evaluate the progress made in implementing the objectives of the International Women's Year

A/RES/3520 (XXX), 15 December 1975

The General Assembly,

Recalling its resolution 3010 (XXVII) of 18 December 1972 in which it proclaimed the year 1975 International Women's Year,

Recalling also Economic and Social Council resolutions 1849 (LVI) and 1851 (LVI) of 16 May 1974 on the convening of an international conference during the International Women's Year as a focal point of the international observance of the Year,

Recalling further its resolutions 3276 (XXIX) and 3277 (XXIX) of 10 December 1974 as well as Economic and Social Council resolution 1959 (LIX) of 28 July 1975 concerning the World Conference of the International Women's Year,

Recalling the importance of the participation of women in the implementation of the decisions of the General Assembly at its sixth 1/ and seventh 2/ special sessions as well as in the implementation of the Programme of Action on the Establishment of a New International Economic Order, 3/

Having considered the report of the World Conference of the International Women's Year, 4/ held at Mexico City from 19 June to 2 July 1975,

Having considered also the note by the Secretary-General on the establishment of an international research and training institute for the advancement of women, 5/

Convinced that the Conference, through the adoption of the Declaration of Mexico on the Equality of Women and Their Contribution to Development and Peace, 1975, 6/ the World Plan of Action for the Implementation of the Objectives of the International Women's Year 7/ and related resolutions, 8/ has made a valuable and constructive contribution towards the achievement of the threefold objectives of the Year, namely, to promote equality between men and women, to ensure the full integration of women in the total development effort and to promote women's contribution to the development of friendly relations and cooperation among States and to the strengthening of world peace,

Considering the valuable and constructive contributions towards the implementation of the threefold objectives of the International Women's Year made by conferences and seminars held during the Year,

Convinced also that the promotion of development objectives and the solution of crucial world economic and social problems should contribute significantly to the improvement of the situation of women, in particular that of women in rural areas and in low-income groups,

Convinced further that women must play an important role in the promotion, achievement and maintenance of international peace,

Considering that the decisions and recommendations of the Conference should be translated into concrete action without delay by States, organizations of the United Nations system and intergovernmental and non-governmental organizations,

Recalling that the Conference stressed the important role of regional commissions in the implementation of the World Plan of Action and related resolutions of the Conference,

Convinced that periodic and comprehensive reviews and appraisals of the progress made in meeting the goals of the World Plan of Action and related resolutions endorsed by the Conference are of crucial importance for their effective implementation and should be undertaken at regular intervals by Governments and by the organizations of the United Nations system within an agreed time-frame,

Noting that the Conference recommended the continuing operation of the Commission on the Status of Women or some other representative body, within the structure of the United Nations, designed specifically to deal with matters relating to the status of women, so as to ensure the implementation of ongoing projects designed to carry out the programmes set forth in the World Plan of Action, 9/

1. *Takes note* of the report of the World Conference of the International Women's Year, including the Declaration of Mexico on the Equality of Women and Their Contribution to Development and Peace, 1975, the World Plan of Action for the Implementation of the Objectives of the International Women's Year, the regional plans of action and the resolutions and other recommendations adopted by the Conference, and endorses the action proposals contained in these documents;

2. *Proclaims* the period from 1976 to 1985 United Nations Decade for Women: Equality, Development and Peace, to be devoted to effective and sustained national, regional and international action to implement the World Plan of Action and related resolutions of the Conference;

3. *Calls upon* Governments, as a matter of urgency, to examine the recommendations contained in the World Plan of Action and related resolutions of the Conference including action to be taken at the national level, such as:

(a) The establishment of short-term, medium-term and long-term targets, and priorities to this end, taking into account the guidelines set forth in sections I and II of the World Plan of Action, including the minimum objectives recommended for achievement by 1980; 10/

(b) The adoption of national strategies, plans and programmes for the implementation of the recommendations within the framework of overall development plans, policies and programmes;

(c) The undertaking of regular reviews and appraisals of progress made at the national and local levels in

1/ See *Official Records of the General Assembly, Sixth Special Session, Supplement No. 1* (A/9559).
2/ Ibid., *Seventh Special Session, Supplement No. 1* (A/10301).
3/ Resolution 3202 (S-VI).
4/ United Nations publication, Sales No. E.76.IV.1.
5/ A/10340.
6/ *Report of the World Conference of the International Women's Year* (United Nations publication, Sales No. E.76.IV.1), chap. I.
7/ Ibid., chap. II, sect. A.
8/ Ibid., chap. III.
9/ Ibid., chap. III, resolution 4.
10/ Ibid., chap. II, sect. A, para. 46.

achieving the goals and objectives of the World Plan of Action within the framework of overall development plans, policies and programmes;

4. Requests the Secretary-General to transmit to the relevant organs of the United Nations and to the organizations of the United Nations system the decisions and recommendations of the Conference;

5. Invites all relevant organizations of the United Nations system concerned:

(a) To submit, within the framework of the Administrative Committee on Co-ordination, to the Economic and Social Council at its sixty-second session their proposals and suggestions for implementing the World Plan of Action and related resolutions of the Conference during the United Nations Decade for Women: Equality, Development and Peace;

(b) To develop and implement, during the first half of the Decade, under the auspices of the Administrative Committee on Co-ordination, a joint interagency medium-term programme for the integration of women in development, which should coordinate and integrate activities undertaken in accordance with subparagraph (a) above, with special emphasis on technical cooperation in programmes relating to women and development;

(c) To render, in accordance with requests of Governments, sustained assistance in the formulation, design, implementation and evaluation of projects and programmes which would enable women to be integrated in national and international development;

6. *Calls upon* the regional commissions to develop and implement, as a matter of priority, effective strategies to further the objectives of the World Plan of Action at the regional and subregional levels, bearing in mind their respective regional plans of action;

7. *Urges* all financial institutions and all international, regional and subregional development banks and bilateral funding agencies to accord high priority in their development assistance, in accordance with requests of Governments, to projects that would promote the integration of women in the development process, in particular women in the rural areas, as well as the achievement of the equality of women and men, priority being given to countries with limited financial means;

8. *Urges* non-governmental organizations, at the national and international levels, to take all possible measures to assist in the implementation of the World Plan of Action and related resolutions of the Conference within their particular areas of interest and competence;

9. *Decides* in principle, in accordance with resolution 26 8/ adopted by the Conference, to establish, under the auspices of the United Nations, an International Research and Training Institute for the Advance-

ment of Women, which would be financed through voluntary contributions and would collaborate with appropriate national, regional and international economic and social research institutes;

10. *Invites* the Secretary-General therefore to appoint, with due consideration to the principle of equitable geographical distribution, a Group of Experts on the Establishment of an International Research and Training Institute for the Advancement of Women, consisting of five to ten experts, to draw up, in consultation with the representatives of existing regional centres and/or institutes for research and training which have similar objectives and goals, the terms of reference and structural organization of the Institute, giving special consideration to the needs of women of developing countries, and requests the Secretary-General to report to the Economic and Social Council at its sixtieth session on the basis of the recommendations of the Group of Experts;

11. *Affirms* that a system-wide review and appraisal of the World Plan of Action should be undertaken biennially, and that such reviews and appraisals should constitute an input to the process of review and appraisal of progress made under the International Development Strategy for the Second United Nations Development Decade, 11/ taking into account the Programme of Action on the Establishment of a New International Economic Order and the decisions resulting from the sixth and seventh special sessions of the General Assembly;

12. *Affirms* that the General Assembly and other relevant bodies should also consider biennially the progress achieved in the promotion of the full equality of women with men in all spheres of life in accordance with international standards and, in particular, the participation of women in political life and in international co-operation and the strengthening of international peace;

13. *Expresses the hope* that the Ad Hoc Committee on the Restructuring of the Economic and Social Sectors of the United Nations System, which will consider the report of the Group of Experts on the Structure of the United Nations System entitled *A New United Nations Structure for Global Economic Co-operation*, 12/ will take full account of the need to implement the World Plan of Action and related resolutions of the Conference, as well as the requirements of the United Nations Decade for Women: Equality, Development and Peace, and appeals to the Ad Hoc Committee to ensure that the machinery designed to deal with questions relating to women should be strengthened, taking into account, in particular, the role of the Commission on the Status of

11/ Resolution 2626 (XXV).
12/ E/AC.62/9 (United Nations publication, Sales No. E.75.II.A.7).

Women and the procedures established for the system-wide review and appraisal of the World Plan of Action;

14. *Decides* to include in the provisional agenda of its thirty-first session an item entitled "United Nations Decade for Women: Equality, Development and Peace";

15. *Invites* the Secretary-General to submit a progress report to the General Assembly at its thirty-first session on the measures taken to implement the World Plan of Action and related resolutions of the Conference, and on the progress achieved in initiating the procedures for the Plan's review and appraisal by Member States, the United Nations organs, the regional commissions, the specialized agencies and other intergovernmental organizations concerned;

16. *Requests* the Secretary-General to ensure, if possible within existing resources, that the Secretariat unit responsible for women's questions possesses adequate personnel and budgetary resources in order to discharge its functions under the World Plan of Action in cooperation with all organizations of the United Nations system;

17. *Further requests* the Secretary-General, in the light of paragraph 16 above, to take into account the requirements of the World Plan of Action and related resolutions of the Conference in preparing revised estimates for 1977 and the medium-term plan for 1978-1981 and to report thereon to the General Assembly at its thirty-first session, in accordance with established procedures;

18. *Urges* all States, the organizations of the United Nations system and intergovernmental and non-governmental organizations concerned, as well as the mass communications media, to give widespread publicity to the achievements and significance of the Conference at the national, regional and international levels;

19. *Requests* the Secretary-General, as a matter of high priority, to issue within existing resources, in the official languages of the United Nations, a simplified version of the World Plan of Action as a booklet, which would highlight the targets, goals and main recommendations for action by Governments, the United Nations system and non-governmental organizations and which would explain the relevance of the implementation of the Plan to the daily lives of men and women throughout the world;

20. *Decides* to convene in 1980, at the mid-term of the United Nations Decade for Women: Equality, Development and Peace, a world conference of all States to review and evaluate the progress made in implementing the objectives of the International Women's Year as recommended by the World Conference of the International Women's Year and, where necessary, to readjust existing programmes in the light of new data and research available.

Document 50

General Assembly resolution calling on States to ratify international conventions and other instruments concerning the protection of women's rights and the elimination of discrimination against women and requesting the CSW to complete the draft convention on the elimination of discrimination against women

A/RES/3521 (XXX), 15 December 1975

The General Assembly,

Welcoming the results of the World Conference of the International Women's Year, 1/ held at Mexico City from 19 June to 2 July 1975,

Recalling the provisions of the Charter of the United Nations which, *inter alia*, emphasize the importance of respect for human rights and fundamental freedoms for all without distinction as to race, sex, language or religion and for the equality of men and women,

Firmly convinced that discrimination against women is incompatible with human dignity and prevents social progress and the achievement of the goals of development,

Mindful that the continuation of armed conflicts, the arms race, colonialism, foreign occupation, racism, racial discrimination and apartheid hinders the effective realization of equal rights for women and prevents the improvement of the situation of women and their wider participation in all spheres of life,

1/ See *Report of the World Conference of the International Women's Year* (United Nations publication, Sales No. E.76.IV.1).

Noting conventions and recommendations concerning the rights of women adopted under the aegis and within the framework of the United Nations and its specialized agencies and the progress achieved in their implementation,

Noting that all States are not yet parties to relevant conventions and other instruments elaborated by the United Nations, the International Labour Organization, the United Nations Educational, Scientific and Cultural Organization and other United Nations bodies,

Expressing concern in connection with continuing discrimination in many countries against women in many fields, in particular in labour relations and general and professional education and training,

Aware that women, enjoying fully the rights provided for in the relevant international instruments, should play an equal role with men in all spheres of life, including the ensuring of peace and the strengthening of international security, and should fully participate in political life,

Confident that the relaxation of international tension contributes to the development and implementation of standards in all fields of concern to women,

1. *Calls upon* all States that have not done so to ratify the international conventions and other instruments concerning the protection of women's rights and the elimination of discrimination against women and to implement effectively the provisions of these conventions and other instruments, including declarations of the United Nations and recommendations of the International Labour Organization and the United Nations Educational, Scientific and Cultural Organization;

2. *Requests* the Commission on the Status of Women to complete, in 1976, the elaboration of the draft Convention on the Elimination of Discrimination against Women;

3. *Calls upon* all States to promote vigorously wider participation of women in the strengthening of international peace and in extending the relaxation of international tension, on the basis of full respect for the Charter of the United Nations as well as for United Nations resolutions, in settling the problems of disarmament, in the elimination of colonialism, foreign occupation, racism, racial discrimination and apartheid and in all other forms of political life, contributing in this way to the creation of the most favourable conditions for the complete elimination of discrimination against women.

Document 51

General Assembly resolution calling on Governments to enable women at the lowest level in rural and urban areas to obtain credit and loans to improve their economic activities and integration in national development

A/RES/3522 (XXX), 15 December 1975

The General Assembly,

Recognizing that many women in low-income countries are engaged in various economic activities on a self-reliant basis not normally taken into account when considering the gross national product,

Convinced that the contribution of such economic activities by women to the overall national economic development is substantial,

Further convinced that credit facilities are a necessary prerequisite for the improvement of economic activities of women engaged in self-reliance projects,

Recognizing the continued benefits that can accrue from access to even moderate financial resources, when such become available,

Concerned that many lending and financial institutions continue to practice discrimination against women, considering them poor credit risks, and that local and national practices and customs in many parts of the world bar women from engaging in responsible financial transactions,

Reaffirming resolution 10, entitled "Access of women to financial assistance", 1/ adopted by the World Conference of the International Women's Year, held at Mexico City from 19 June to 2 July 1975,

1. *Urges* Governments and governmental and non-governmental organizations to support more vigorously official and private efforts to extend to women the facilities now being offered only to men by financial and lending institutions;

2. *Requests* Governments to encourage all efforts by women's organizations, cooperatives and lending in-

1/ See *Report of the World Conference of the International Women's Year* (United Nations publication, Sales No. E.76.IV.1), chap. III.

stitutions which will enable women at the lowest level in rural and urban areas to obtain credit and loans to improve their economic activities and integration in national development;

3. *Urges* Governments and the organizations of the United Nations and development system, including specialized agencies and non-governmental organizations, to incorporate, in their training programmes, workshops and seminars, courses designed to improve the efficiency of women in business and financial management.

Document 52

General Assembly resolution on improving the status of women in rural and low-income areas

A/RES/3523 (XXX), 15 December 1975

The General Assembly,

Recalling its resolution 3276 (XXIX) of 10 December 1974, in which it decided to consider at its thirtieth session an item entitled "International Women's Year, including the proposals and recommendations of the Conference of the International Women's Year",

Taking into account resolution 21 1/ adopted by the World Conference of the International Women's Year, held at Mexico City from 19 June to 2 July 1975, the principles contained in the Declaration of Mexico on the Equality of Women and Their Contribution to Development and Peace, 1975, 2/ the World Plan of Action for the Implementation of the Objectives of the International Women's Year 3/ and the relevant resolutions bearing on the contribution of women to equality, peace and development,

Realizing the importance of adherence to the recommendations of the World Plan of Action, especially those related to women in rural and low-income areas,

Considering the vital role rural women play, not only within the family unit but also in the process of national development, through agricultural and particularly through food production and distribution,

Bearing in mind that in many parts of the world illiteracy, lack of education and training, inadequate distribution of human and economic resources, and severe unemployment problems for women have hindered them from contributing fully to national development efforts,

Convinced that the struggle for development is a primary responsibility of all peoples and Governments, taking into account the principles of the Charter of Economic Rights and Duties of States 4/ and the Declaration and the Programme of Action on the Establishment of a New International Economic Order, 5/

Noting the need for both quantitative and qualitative data on the position of women and their role in all rural activities,

Noting also the activities relating to rural women undertaken to date by the United Nations bodies and specialized agencies concerned,

Noting further the need for coordinated and systematic examination of the situation of rural women and their role in all rural activities,

1. *Urges* all Governments to accord, within their respective plans, higher priorities for:

(a) Gathering relevant date on the status and role of women in rural and low-income areas;

(b) Achieving socio-economic conditions based on the realization of the full and equal partnership of men and women in the development of society, both in law and in fact;

(c) Promoting agricultural productivity, agro-based industries and integrated rural development programmes;

2. *Requests* the Secretary-General to prepare and submit, through the Economic and Social Council, on the basis of the views of relevant United Nations bodies and specialized agencies as well as those of Governments, guidelines for non-formal educational programmes designed to enable rural women to use fully their capabilities and to contribute to the development of society;

3. *Urges* United Nations Organizations, specialized agencies, regional commissions and international financial institutions to accord special attention to government programmes and projects aimed at the full integration of rural women in development;

1/ See *Report of the World Conference of the International Women's Year* (United Nations publication, Sales No. E.76.IV.1), chap. III.
2/ Ibid., chap. I.
3/ Ibid., chap. II, sect. A.
4/ Resolution 3281 (XXIX).
5/ Resolutions 3201 (S-VI) and 3202 (S-VI).

4. *Urges* all Governments to develop extensive training programmes relevant to women and to make full use of all existing and proposed research institutes and centres, particularly the regional and international institutes and centres for the advancement of women in rural areas;

5. *Requests* the Secretary-General, in consultation with Member States and the specialized agencies and organizations of the United Nations system, to report to the General Assembly biennially on the progress achieved in connection with the work referred to in the previous paragraphs.

Document 53

General Assembly resolution calling for increased United Nations assistance for the integration of women in development

A/RES/3524 (XXX), 15 December 1975

The General Assembly,

Recalling its resolution 3010 (XXVII) of 18 December 1972 in which it proclaimed the year 1975 International Women's Year,

Recalling also its resolution 3505 (XXX) of 15 December 1975, adopted on the recommendation of the Second Committee,

Having considered the report of the World Conference of the International Women's Year, 1/ held at Mexico City from 19 June to 2 July 1975, which contains the resolutions adopted by the Conference 2/ and the World Plan of Action for the Implementation of the Objectives of the International Women's Year, 3/

Noting that the World Plan of Action set forth guidance on action programmes for the integration of women in development,

Recalling its resolution 2626 (XXV) of 24 October 1970 containing the International Development Strategy for the Second United Nations Development Decade, in which the General Assembly included among the Objectives of the Strategy the full integration of women in the total development effort, and recalling also that the majority of the specialized agencies, other United Nations bodies and Member States have already advocated similar action, as have individual donor agencies,

Recalling that, in its resolution 3342 (XXIX) of 17 December 1974, it invited the United Nations system to provide increased assistance to those programmes, projects and activities that will encourage and promote the further integration of women in national, regional and interregional economic development activities,

Recommends that all organs of the United Nations development system, including the United Nations Development Programme and the specialized agencies, and other international technical and financial assistance programmes and agencies should:

(a) Give sustained attention to the integration of women in the formulation, design and implementation of development projects and programmes;

(b) Assist Governments that so request to incorporate in their development plans, their programme and sector analyses and their development programme and project documents an impact statement of how such proposed programmes will affect women as participants and beneficiaries.

1/ United Nations publication, Sales No. E.76.IV.1.
2/ Ibid., chap. III.
3/ Ibid., chap. II, sect. A.

Document 54

ECOSOC resolution establishing INSTRAW as an autonomous body funded through voluntary contributions, and setting guidelines for its work, including, among other things, that the Institute should direct its activities with special attention to the needs of women in developing countries and their integration in the development process

E/RES/1998 (LX), 12 May 1976

The Economic and Social Council,

Recalling the research and training needs indicated in several of the resolutions 1/ and in the World Plan of Action for the Implementation of the Objectives of the International Women's Year, 2/ adopted by the World Conference of the International Women's Year,

Recalling also General Assembly resolution 3520 (XXX) of 15 December 1975,

Taking note of the report of the Secretary-General 3/ based on the recommendations of the Group of Experts on the Establishment of an International Research and Training Institute for the Advancement of Women,

1. *Welcomes* the recommendations of the Group of Experts on the Establishment of an International Research and Training Institute for the Advancement of Women; 4/

2. *Decides* to establish not later than 1977, providing the necessary financial provisions are made, an International Research and Training Institute for the Advancement of Women as an autonomous body under the auspices of the United Nations, funded through voluntary contributions;

3. *Decides also* on the following guidelines for the International Research and Training Institute for the Advancement of Women:

(a) The Institute should work in close collaboration with all relevant organizations within the United Nations system, including the United Nations Educational, Scientific and Cultural Organization, the Food and Agriculture Organization of the United Nations, the World Health Organization, the International Labour Organization, the United Nations Institute for Training and Research, the United Nations University, the United Nations Research Institute for Social Development, and national and regional centres and institutes which have similar objectives;

(b) The Institute should, taking fully into account the activities of the above-mentioned bodies as inputs to its work, coordinate its activities with theirs;

(c) The Institute should direct its activities with special attention to the needs of women in developing countries and their integration in the development process;

(d) The Institute should maintain close cooperation with the Commission on the Status of Women;

4. *Decides further* that the International Research and Training Institute for the Advancement of Women should develop its activities in stages, starting by building on the collection of already existing data on ongoing research and training needs;

5. *Requests* the Secretary-General, in order to establish the International Research and Training Institute for the Advancement of Women as soon as possible:

(a) To prepare a timetable and undertake all other necessary administrative steps for the establishment of the Institute, if possible by 1977, the cost of which may be charged, as an interim measure, against the Voluntary Fund for the United Nations Decade for Women;

(b) To assign staff to undertake the substantive preparation for the establishment of the Institute, to make a survey of existing data and information prepared by United Nations organizations and other international, regional and national institutes;

(c) To seek actively financial and technical support from Member States, the United Nations Development Programme, the United Nations Technical Assistance Programme, the specialized agencies, as well as from philanthropic and academic institutes, individuals and other possible sources;

6. *Takes note with appreciation* of the offer of the Government of Iran to act as host to the International Research and Training Institute for the Advancement of Women;

7. *Requests* the Secretary-General to continue to seek the most suitable location for the International Research and Training Institute for the Advancement of Women, taking into account accessibility, the availability of adequate accommodation, supportive institutions, personnel, and other services, and to report to the General Assembly at its thirty-first session on the progress achieved towards the establishment of the Institute.

1/ See E/CONF.66/34 (United Nations publication, Sales No. E.76.IV.1), chap. III.
2/ Ibid., chap. II, sect. A.
3/ E/5772.
4/ Ibid., paras. 4-23.

Document 55

Programme for the United Nations Decade for Women: Equality, Development and Peace, 1976-1985, adopted by the CSW

E/5894, 14 October 1976

I. United Nations Decade for Women: policies, principles and mandates

1. The policies, principles and mandates for the Programme for the United Nations Decade for Women: Equality, Development and Peace are set forth in a number of international documents, 1 / including in particular:

(a) The Declaration of Mexico on the Equality of Women and their contribution to Development and Peace, the World Plan of Action for the implementation of the objectives of the International Women's Year, the regional plans of action for Asia and the Pacific and for Africa and related resolutions of the Conference, endorsed by the General Assembly in its resolution 3520 (XXX);

(b) General Assembly resolutions 3490 (XXX), 3505 (XXX), 3518 (XXX), 3519 (XXX), 3520 (XXX), 3521 (XXX), 3522 (XXX), 3523 (XXX), 3524 (XXX) and 3416 (XXX) of December 1975;

(c) Economic and Social Council resolutions 1998 (LX), 1999 (LX) and 2005 (LX) of May 1976.

These international documents, and especially the World Plan of Action, stress the importance of *national action*, supported by action at the *regional and global levels*, involving all organizations in the United Nations system. The World Plan and the regional plans provide detailed guidelines for such action.

2. In addition to the above-mentioned texts, a number of resolutions and declarations have been adopted during International Women's Year by the specialized agencies. These resolutions and declarations request action by these agencies in various technical subjects which are included in the Programme for the Decade and for which they should, according to the mandate given to them in the United Nations system, continue to have the technical responsibility.

3. At the same time the World Plan provides that "each country should decide upon its *own national strategy and identify its own targets and priorities* within the present "World Plan". It also stipulates that by 1980 the achievement of the following should be envisaged and that these minimum objectives should be developed in more specific terms in regional plans of action.

"(a) Marked increase in literacy and civic education of women, especially in rural areas;

"(b) The extension of co-educational technical and vocational training in basic skills to women and men in the industrial and agricultural sectors;

"(c) Equal access at every level of education, compulsory primary school education and the measures necessary to prevent school drop-outs;

"(d) Increased employment opportunities for women, reduction of unemployment and increased efforts to eliminate discrimination in the terms and conditions of employment;

"(e) The establishment and increase of the infrastructural services required in both rural and urban areas;

"(f) The enactment of legislation on voting and eligibility for election on equal terms with men and equal opportunity and conditions of employment including remuneration, and on equality in legal capacity and the exercise thereof;

"(g) To encourage a greater participation of women in policy-making positions at the local, national and international levels;

"(h) Increased provision for comprehensive measures for health education and services, sanitation, nutrition, family education, family planning and other welfare services;

"(i) Provision for parity in the exercise of civil, social and political rights such as those pertaining to marriage, citizenship and commerce;

"(j) Recognition of the economic value of women's work in the home in domestic food production and marketing and voluntary activities not traditionally remunerated;

"(k) To direct formal, non-formal and life-long education towards the re-evaluation of the man and woman, in order to ensure their full realization as individuals in the family and in society;

"(l) The promotion of women's organizations as an interim measure within workers' organizations and educational, economic and professional institutions;

1/ "The inclusion of this paragraph should not be interpreted as indicating a change in the positions taken by certain delegations when the documents and resolutions referred to in the paragraph were adopted."

"(m) The development of modern rural technology, cottage industry, pre-school day centres, time and energy saving devices so as to help reduce the heavy workload of women, particularly those living in rural sectors and for the urban poor and thus facilitate the full participation of women in community, national and international affairs;

"(n) The establishment of an interdisciplinary and multisectoral machinery within the Government for accelerating the achievement of equal opportunities for women and their full integration into national life." (World Plan of Action, article 46.)

4. The General Assembly, in proclaiming the United Nations Decade for Women: Equality, Development and Peace, called upon Governments as a matter of urgency to examine the recommendations contained in the World Plan of Action and related resolutions of the Conference including action to be taken at the national level, such as:

"(a) The establishment of short-term, medium-term and long-term targets, and priorities to this end, taking into account the guidelines set forth in sections I and II of the World Plan of Action, including the minimum objectives recommended for achievement by 1980;

"(b) The adoption of national strategies, plans and programmes for the implementation of the recommendations within the framework of overall development plans, policies and programmes;

"(c) The undertaking of regular reviews and appraisals of progress made at the national and local levels in achieving the goals and objectives of the World Plan of Action within the framework of overall development plans, policies and programmes."

5. The Assembly also called for the cooperation of the entire United Nations system in implementing the World Plan, and the development and implementation within the framework of the Administrative Co-ordination Committee of a joint interagency programme for the integration of women in development. This joint programme now has the title: "Joint Inter-Organizational Programme for the United Nations Decade for Women: Equality, Development and Peace".

6. The Assembly also urged non-governmental organizations to assist in implementing the World Plan and related recommendations of the Conference within their particular areas of interest and competence.

7. It is proposed to implement the Programme for the Decade in two phases 1976-1980—the year of the World Conference, and the period 1981-1985 constituting the second half of the Decade.

8. The programme outlined below focuses on the *first half of the Decade 1976-1980.*

9. In order to ensure the effective integrated implementation of the Programme it is essential to strengthen the organizational structures responsible for the overall coordination, development of programmes, public information and evaluation of the Decade for Women, at all levels, international, regional and national. Such structures should be basically responsive to the realistic needs of women at country level, in urban and rural areas.

10. The Programme, if it is to achieve its objectives will require resources, both within the regular budgets of organizations in the United Nations system and through bilateral and multilateral extrabudgetary funds, including the Voluntary Fund for the Decade for Women.

11. It is recommended that adequate resources from the Regular Budget both for staffing for Headquarters and for the secretariats of regional commissions be provided as they are essential to ensure the continuity in the infrastructure required for the satisfactory implementation of the Programme for the Decade at the international and regional levels.

II. Specific areas for action to attain the threefold objectives of the decade

A. *Formulation and implementation of international and national standards to eliminate discrimination against women*

INTERNATIONAL AND REGIONAL ACTION 1976-1980

1. *Adoption and entry into force of the Convention on the Elimination of Discrimination against Women with effective measures for its implementation*

Adoption of the Convention by the General Assembly and entry into force of the Convention and application of its implementation measures as soon as possible.

2. *Implementation of existing international instruments relating to the status of women*

(a) Biennial review by the Commission on the Status of Women of the implementation of the Declaration on the Elimination of Discrimination against Women and other international instruments with related provisions (Economic and Social Council resolution 1677 (LII)).

(b) Review of the implementation of Convention on the Elimination of Discrimination against Women when it has been adopted, in accordance with the implementation provisions laid down in it.

(c) Biennial review by the General Assembly and other relevant bodies of progress achieved in the promotion of full equality with men in all spheres of life in accordance with international standards and in particular the participation of women in political life and in international cooperation and the strengthening of international peace (General Assembly resolution 3520 (XXX), para. 12) (Cf. also sect. C below)).

(d) Review of existing instruments by relevant international organizations including the United Nations specialized agencies, to ensure that they do not contain obstacles to the full integration, utilization and participation of women in development with a view to amending them where necessary.

3. *Studies in specific areas with a view to the elaboration of new instruments (conventions, declarations, recommendations)*

The objective is to broaden the field of studies and preparation of international standards in specific areas, so as to seek and find the best way of introducing new definitions of family functions in terms of rights and responsibilities, with a view to improving the status of women by changing the present patterns of behaviour.

(a) Comparative studies on different aspects of civil and family law to be submitted to the Commission on the Status of Women in accordance with ECOSOC resolution 1849 (LVI).

Such studies should cover legislation, regulations and customs relating to age of marriage, legal capacity, rights and responsibilities on entering marriage, during marriage and at its dissolution, laws on inheritance and taxation, rights and responsibilities of parents *vis-à-vis* their children.

(b) Studies relating to the sharing of family responsibilities to be submitted to the Commission on the Status of Women (in accordance with the Commission on the Status of Women resolution 2 (XXIII)).

These studies should take into account the need to reform school curricula to do away with traditional stereotypes of men and women and to renew in the best possible way the picture generally given to boys and girls of the respective roles and of the sharing of the tasks in the family and in the society.

(c) The ILO should study the application of Recommendation No. 123 of 1965 and the elaboration of a convention on the employment of women with family responsibilities.

4. *Activities to increase knowledge and awareness of international standards*

United Nations regional commissions and regional centres and other concerned international organs as well as competent regional intergovernmental organizations;

(a) Should take all appropriate measures to disseminate information on all the United Nations instru-

ments dealing with the status of women and to assist and encourage the governments in their respective regions to ratify and implement these instruments;

(b) Promote studies in and between countries to assess the effects of existing legislation and determine further legislative needs; and technical seminars, workshops or similar meetings to discuss these matters at national and intercountry levels.

5. *Appropriate public information activities*, designed to ensure that men and women in urban and rural areas are made aware of their rights and responsibilities under international instruments (e.g. pamphlets, publications, audio-visual means, seminars, meetings, non-governmental activities etc.).

NATIONAL ACTION 1976-1980

(a) The principle of eliminating discrimination on grounds of sex should be secured through constitutional and legislative and/or other appropriate measures;

(b) Enactment of legislation to bring national laws into conformity with international instruments and review of national legislation in order to ensure equality between men and women;

(c) Ratification of or accession to relevant international conventions;

(d) Adoption of measures to inform and advise women with the assistance of non-governmental organizations of their rights and responsibilities and to assist them in securing their implementation.

B. *Integration of women in development*

In elaborating programmes promoting the integration of women in development, international, regional and national bodies and organizations may, as an initial step, establish *separate programmes* exclusively for women where their status is particularly low and where discriminatory attitudes towards them are strong. The aim of programmes for the advancement of women, however, is ultimately to integrate their activities with those of men in all sectors so that women do not remain isolated in their activities. Separate programmes for the integration of women in development should therefore be appropriately phased out as women gain more confidence in themselves and as men accept more readily the role of women as equal partners in development.

Priority should be given to the elaboration of programmes which tend towards the implementation of the new international economic order in order to help eliminate situations in which any human being may be exploited or left out of society and to emphasize that inadequate conditions of the population, including the female population, are closely linked to the inadequate internal structures of countries. Programmes of the integration of women in the process of development must be periodically revised in the light of the socio-economic progress of the countries.

INTERNATIONAL AND REGIONAL ACTION 1976-1980

1. *Structural organization*

(a) All organizations in the United Nations system should participate in implementing the Programme for the Decade.

(b) At the regional level, the United Nations Regional Commissions and existing intergovernmental commissions should play an important role in stimulating national action through the development of regional programmes for the Decade.

   (i) Where they have not yet done so, the regional commissions should create appropriate machinery such as regional standing committees, following the guidelines of the World Plan of Action, article 207.

   (ii) Regional bureaux and/or regional research and training centres should also be established in each region. 2/

(c) Establishment of the International Institute for Research and Training for the Advancement of Women in 1977 in accordance with Economic and Social Council resolution 1998 (LX).

(d) In accordance with ECOSOC resolution 1998 (LX) the International Institute for Research and Training for the Advancement of Women should work in close collaboration with all relevant organizations within the United Nations system. In particular, it should coordinate its activities with those of the regional centres and regional economic commissions and other regional intergovernmental organizations.

(e) The activities of the International Research and Training Institute for the Advancement of Women should not be restricted to research but should be a part of general methodological and research process in order that the International Institute will be of major assistance in programming aimed at the integration of women in development. It should:

   (i) Constitute one of the key elements for assisting in the implementation of the programme for the Decade for Women: Equality, Development and Peace, 1976-1985, in accordance with the goals of the World Conference on the International Women's Year;

   (ii) Make a substantial contribution to the preparation of the World Conference of 1980.

2. *Improvement of the database and information necessary for drawing up programmes and policies*

(a) *General research and methodologies*

   (i) Collection and analysis, by sex, of all census and survey data relating to such factors as urban/ rural residence, age, marital status, including consentual unions, literacy, education, income, levels of skill and participation in both modern and traditional economic activities and to household and family composition.

   (ii) Special efforts should be made to measure:
   —the extent of women's activities in food production (cash crop and subsistence agriculture), in water and fuel supply, in marketing and in transportation;
   —the economic and social contribution of housework and other domestic chores, handicrafts and other home-based economic activities.

   (iii) The development of social and economic indicators, sensitive to the situation and needs of women, in particular, regional and subregional indicators to enable better and more realistic evaluation of progress to be made, and to assist governments in using relevant data to increase the contribution of women to development.

   (iv) Development of methodologies required to measure the total human resource needs of countries.

(b) *Studies in specific areas*

The studies mentioned in this section all have specific mandates as indicated. Priorities will have to be established among all the studies requested in the light of the survey undertaken under paragraph (i) below. Some of the studies may ultimately be undertaken by the Institute and where appropriate, by interested agencies, within the framework of the joint interorganizational programme for the Decade.

   (i) Survey by 1977 of existing data and information available in United Nations organizations and other international, regional and national institutes;

   (ii) Study on the extent to which women participate in agriculture, industry, trade, science and technology, with recommendations for increasing and upgrading their participation (General Assembly resolution 3505 (XXX));

2/ The African Training and Research Centre for Women already exists in Addis Ababa. The Asian Institute for Research and Training will shortly be established in Tehran.

(iii) Preparation of guidelines for non-formal education programmes for rural women, and biennial review by the General Assembly of progress achieved in developing programmes and projects aimed at the full integration of rural women in development (General Assembly resolution 3523 (XXX));

(iv) Studies on the interrelationship of the role of women, population change and development (Economic and Social Council resolution 1854 (LVI); World Plan of Action, paras. 142 and 146; Conference resolution 11);

(v) Study on the impact of scientific and technological developments on the status of women and their contribution to development (Economic and Social Council resolution 1849 (LVI));

(vi) Study of questions relating to prostitution and the traffic in women (World Plan of Action, paras. 159 and 160; Conference resolution 7);

(vii) Cross-cultural study of the causes of discriminatory customs, practices and attitudes which impede women's contribution to the development process and mechanisms of change (World Plan of Action, para. 171);

(viii) Cross-cultural study of the influence on the condition of women in the family and in society of family and children's allowances and benefits, motherhood awards and similar measures (ibid., para. 134);

(ix) Study on the needs of women at different life cycles: youth, adult and elderly;

(x) Studies in the field of health and nutrition, including the special health problems of women and the improvement of maternal and child health and family planning (ibid., para. 113; Conference resolutions 5 and 9);

(xi) Review of the International Standard Classification of Occupations with a view to redefining current classifications (Conference resolution 23);

(xii) Study on the impact of foreign economic interests on the condition of women (World Plan of Action, para. 8).

3. *Regional and global programmes for the integration of women in development*

(a) *Elaboration and implementation of a joint interorganizational programme for the Decade for Women*

(i) The joint interorganizational programme is based on a synthesis of organizations' activities in relation to nine agreed principal objectives and a number of specific objectives relating to:
—national development plans and programmes; political life and international co-operation, social welfare and peace and policy-making; economic life; education and training; culture and leisure time activities; attitude and practices; health, nutrition and social well-being; family and community life; situations of armed conflict and emergency.

(ii) The synthesis of activities will be updated every two years;

(iii) Areas identified by organizations with the United Nations system for concentrated joint interorganizational action in assisting countries for the period 1976-1980 are:
—National development planning and evaluation of progress;
—Participation in political life and decision-making;
—Participation in economic life;
—Education and training;
—Maternal and child health, family planning, nutrition and health and social services.

The United Nations organizations have decided that:

(i) Priority will be given to country level activities, particularly in the least developed and the most seriously affected countries with special attention to the poorest areas and most vulnerable groups;

(ii) Public information and communication support activities should be developed as integral inputs of programmes;

(iii) Mechanisms for evaluation and monitoring should be a built-in part of all projects.

(b) *Development of regional and subregional programmes to promote the integration of women in development*

(i) Adoption by 1977 of regional plans of action for those regions which have not yet adopted them;

(ii) Incorporation by 1977 in regional action plans of the minimum objectives set forth in article 46 of the World Plan of Action;

(iii) Regional commissions and interregional commissions in collaboration with the United Nations system should in particular:

—Provide governments which so request and non-governmental organizations with the technical support and information they require to formulate and implement effective strategies to further the objectives of the World Plan of Action;

—Assist governments when they ask in the preparation of development projects designed to improve opportunities for women and engage in continuous consultation with UNDP regional officers for that purpose;

—Assist governments and non-governmental organizations to develop policies, strategies and programmes to strengthen the role of women in national development especially in rural areas and to formulate requests for technical and financial assistance;

—Promote technical cooperation among developing countries in the region, making use of available knowledge and expertise and encouraging existing sources of bilateral and multilateral assistance to make greater contributions of funds for the financing of programmes for the advancement of women and seeking new sources of funds, including the establishment of revolving funds at national and local levels;

c) *Coordination of activities with United Nations Headquarters, between regional commissions, and with interested regional intergovernmental organizations outside the United Nations system*

(i) A network system should be established between United Nations Headquarters, the United Nations system, the regional commissions, regional intergovernmental commissions and offices of the specialized agencies to facilitate the exchange of information concerning projects and programmes, and mutual assistance to strengthen the integration of women in development on a world-wide basis;

(ii) Regional commissions should establish links with existing and future United Nations centres, including the International Institute for Research and Training for the Advancement of Women and other regional and national centres working in related fields.

(d) *Expansion of technical cooperation activities to support the integration of women in development*

(i) Special attention should be given to the development of programmes in the following areas:

—Integrated rural development, special attention should be given to women's role as producers, processors and vendors of food, stressing the need for training women and girls. Training is especially needed in modern methods of farming: marketing, purchasing and sales techniques; basic accounting and organizational methods; fundamentals of hygiene and nutrition; training in crafts and cooperatives;

—Technological assistance for women including full participation in community and extension services particularly in the rural areas; including access to loans, credit facilities and cooperatives on the same basis as men;

—Health, reproduction and growth and development, including family health and child health, family planning, nutrition and health education;

—Education and training at all levels and in all sectors including on-the-job training in production centres related to the creation of employment opportunities so that women can play an economic, social and political role which corresponds to their training in the interest of their society as a whole;

—Youth projects, which should be examined to make sure that they include adequate emphasis on the participation of young women;

—Public administration, with the aim of preparing women to participate in development planning and policy-making, especially in middle- and higher-level posts;

(ii) Resident Representatives of the United Nations Development Programme (UNDP) should collaborate with Governments in formulating requests for technical assistance as part of country programming, at the same time providing for periodic review of the programmes to suggest crucial areas where special support might be needed and to assess their influence and success in improving the position of women;

(iii) Women should participate fully in planning and implementing UNDP country programmes and regional, interregional and global projects under the auspices of the United Nations and other international agencies;

(iv) Organizations of the United Nations system especially UNDP and national Governments should give better opportunity for women to participate as technical experts in providing assistance among developing countries;

(v) Special attention should be paid to the provision of employment opportunities for women in the developing countries. Short-term training courses should be set up at the rural and smaller urban levels for training nursery school teachers and day-care personnel. Production centres should also be established where on-the-job teaching can continue with provision of marketing facilities for the production centres so that the whole scheme can be made self-supporting. This integrated approach of training, production and marketing should be followed at all levels, starting from the villages right up to the big cities;

(vi) The United Nations specialized agencies, national Governments, non-governmental organizations in cooperation with regional commissions should give attention within their existing consultative services to the need for creating a corps of experts to provide guidance to countries on request in the adaptation and implementation of the World Plan of Action in accordance with specific country needs. These experts should have the necessary qualifications to assist intergovernmental organizations, non-governmental organizations, regional commissions and national machinery in the following areas:

—Designing of projects adapted from the World Plan of Action and relevant to national needs and priorities;

—The techniques for creating an awareness among women's groups in order to get their full support for such projects;

—The strengthening of national machinery for the effective implementation of the World Plan of Action during the Decade for Women.

NATIONAL ACTION 1976-1980

At the national level, efforts to widen opportunities for women to participate in development will require action by the society at large through its governmental machinery, non-governmental organizations and other groups and individuals, all of which may be supported by international and regional organizations. To this end, appropriate machinery and administrative procedures are essential.

The following objectives should be taken into account when national programmes are being drawn up:

—that equality between men and women means equality of dignity and value as human beings, as well as equality of rights, opportunities and duties;

—the removal of all obstacles to women's enjoyment of equal status with men, with a view to ensuring the full participation of women in the social and economic development of their countries;

—the achievement of full participation by women in the task of maintaining international peace and security.

National machinery and mechanisms

1. National machinery and mechanisms (national commissions, women's bureaux, information and documentation centres) should have mandates and resources sufficient to ensure the inclusion of women in planning and other activities for development, and to propose special programmes for women as necessary, based on the World Plan of Action, the regional plans and relevant General Assembly resolutions.

National bodies would be entrusted with the responsibility of maintaining under constant review national laws and regulations and to report to Governments on the result achieved every second year with the aim to ensure that the objects of the Decade are secured on a national basis.

In the elaboration of the programme to implement the World Plan of Action, the national mechanism will take into account the opinion of the interested sectors concerned with the integration of women in development.

2. Inclusion in the overall national development plans of programmes to integrate women in development, based on the World Plan of Action, the regional plans and relevant General Assembly resolutions.

3. All national plans and programmes for economic development should include positive policies and targets for increasing the employment of women in both the public and private sectors, so as to achieve equality with men.

4. Establishment of programmes with concrete targets and measures including financial allocations, as well as a system of in-built evaluation to monitor progress in the implementation of the programme.

5. Adoption of measures to ensure participation of women in development planning and policy making.

C. Increased involvement of women in political life and in international cooperation and the maintenance of peace

INTERNATIONAL AND REGIONAL ACTION 1976-1980

1. *Review of the nature and extent of women's participation in political life and in international cooperation and the maintenance of peace*

(a) Periodic collection and publication of reports containing data and other relevant information concerning women's participation in public and political life at the national, regional and international levels, including their participation in efforts to achieve general and complete disarmament under strict and effective international controls, international cooperation and peace.

(b) Study, under the terms of General Assembly resolution 3519 (XXX), on women's participation in the strengthening of international peace and security and in the struggle against colonialism, racism, racial discrimination, foreign aggression, occupation and all forms of foreign domination.

2. *Development of programmes to increase women's involvement in international cooperation and the maintenance of peace*

(a) Development of and training programmes for women, especially in the areas of public administration and management and international politics, mediation, peacemaking and peace-building.

Particular attention should be paid to the institutions which endeavour to stimulate greater participation by women in political activities and processes, urban and rural development programmes and communal and youth programmes and to facilitate their access to training for the direction of such programmes.

(b) Establishment in consultation with Governments and in cooperation, as appropriate, with non-governmental organizations of rosters of women qualified to participate in decision-making relating to international cooperation and the maintenance of peace.

(c) Organization, in consultation with Governments and in cooperation, as appropriate, with non-governmental organizations, of panel discussions, seminars, conferences and similar meetings to create greater awareness among women of national and international issues.

(d) Organization of courses, seminars, lectures and similar activities to encourage the participation of women in the promotion of friendship between the peoples and the effort to achieve general and complete disarmament under strict and effective international control.

3. *Measures to alleviate the condition of women and children in particular situations of hardship, emergency and armed conflict*

(a) Studies (to be carried out every four years) for the Commission on the Status of Women on the condition of women and children in emergency and armed conflict, in the struggle for peace, self-determination, national liberation and independence and elaboration and/or implementation of international conventions, declarations and similar instruments in this field (Economic and Social Council resolution 1687 (LII)).

(b) Development of measures for the implementation of the Declaration on the Protection of Women in

Situations of Emergency and Armed Conflict as set forth in General Assembly resolution 3318 (XXIX).

(c) Study on the effects of apartheid on the condition of women and on their role in the struggle against apartheid. Submission of a report by the Secretary-General to the Commission on the Status of Women at its twenty-seventh session and to the Special Committee against Apartheid on the effects of apartheid in South Africa (Conf. resolution 3 as endorsed by General Assembly resolution 3505 (XXX)).

NATIONAL ACTION 1976-1980

1. Increase the participation of women in political life and decision-making at all levels—local, national and international;

2. Establish specific goals, strategies and timetable to achieve the above end;

3. Measures to encourage women to take part on an equal footing with men, in all international meetings on political and legal subjects, on economic development, on planning, administration and financing, on science and technology, on the environment, on human settlements and on population.

III. **Informational and educational activities for the Decade for Women**

INTERNATIONAL AND REGIONAL ACTION 1976-1980

1. *Dissemination of information*

(a) Development and maintenance of channels of communication at the national, regional and international levels (e.g. liaison officers, national correspondents, national and regional machinery, non-governmental organizations, universities and academic institutions).

(b) Use of the IWY symbol to promote the Decade.

(c) Publication of the Programme for the Decade, in pamphlet form.

(d) Publicity for the Decade by means of radio, television, films and audio-visual programmes for all socio-economic categories of men and women.

(e) Issuance of pamphlets, posters, etc.

(f) Commemorative postage stamps.

(g) Commemorative publications, etc.

(h) Publication of a Decade bulletin (at least twice a year), calendar of forthcoming United Nations events, and special supplements to the Development Forum.

(i) Dissemination of information on the situation of women in every country through the preparation of a publication such as a yearbook.

(j) Development of programmes with non-governmental organizations to reach women at the grass-roots level.

2. Exchange of information and experience

Organization of international and regional symposia, seminars, workshops or other types of meetings and briefings.

(i) For planners and policy makers of relevant Government departments, educational authorities and opinion leaders.

(ii) Organization of seminars for writers, journalists, film and broadcasting producers on treatment of news relating to and production of programmes on women.

(iii) Provision of technical assistance and consultative advice for information programmes, mass media campaigns etc.

3. Establishment of information networks

(a) The establishment of information research centres to serve as key repositories of relevant documentation for all the United Nations bodies, specialized agencies, regional commissions etc. and of audio-visual material, films, recorded radio and television programmes.

(b) The creation of information feedback systems relating to women.

4. Educational activities

(a) Encouragement of the inclusion in the school curricula of teaching about the principles of the United Nations, of human rights, and non-discrimination on grounds of sex, the history of the United Nations Commission on the Status of Women, International Women's Year, the Conference of Mexico and the United Nations Programme for the Decade for Women: Equality, Development and Peace.

(b) Encourage the elimination, from school textbooks, of stereotypes about "masculine" and "feminine" roles and occupations.

(c) Undertake research and develop guidelines for media on images of women projected by the media and publish studies on women and the media.

(d) Study of the use of the mass communication media as a vehicle to enhance the status of women and encourage the use of the media in accelerating the acceptance of women's new and expanding roles in society (World Plan of Action, para. 174).

(e) Organize training activities for qualified women in journalism and in all aspects of the media—programming, production, management, etc.

(f) Use of radio and television for educational purposes in addition to their informational role.

NATIONAL ACTION 1976-1980

All the informational and educational activities listed under international and regional levels should be carried out and developed at the national levels by governments, the schools systems, the media authorities, the non-governmental organizations, etc. as appropriate.

IV. Review and appraisal of progress made in relation to the threefold theme of the United Nations Decade for Women: Equality, Development and Peace

INTERNATIONAL AND REGIONAL ACTION 1976-1980

1. *Development of procedures* in accordance with General Assembly resolutions 3490 (XXX) and 3520 (XXX) paragraph 11 for a system-wide biennial review and appraisal of the implementation of the World Plan of Action as an input to the process review and appraisal of the International Development Strategy for the Second United Nations Development Decade, taking into account the Programme of Action on the Establishment of a New International Economic Order;

Such procedures should begin in 1976 and ensure that items on the implementation of the World Plan of Action are included in the agenda of the sessions of the Economic and Social Council and its relevant functional commissions and advisory bodies at two-year intervals.

2. *Biennial review of material received from Governments, United Nations organizations and non-governmental organizations concerning the implementation of the World Plan of Action and the International Development Strategy and determination of major trends and policies with regard to the status of women and their integration in development.*

Under General Assembly resolution 3490 (XXX) the Commission on the Status of Women is requested to report its findings and conclusions on major trends and policies with regard to the status of women particularly their integration in development to the Economic and Social Council through the Committee for Development Planning and the Committee on Review and Appraisal.

The review and appraisal of progress made should also include:

(i) assessment of current development programmes and projects, and evaluation as to their relevance for women, the adequacy of current financial support, and whether they meet the objectives and goals of the World Plan of Action;

(ii) evaluation of women's voluntary organization projects to determine whether or not they should be strengthened through support from technical assistance agencies and national governments, particularly as they relate to the goals of development and the priority needs of women.

1. Establish appropriate machinery and mechanisms to undertake regular biennial reviews and appraisals of progress made in implementing the World Plan of Action and the regional plans at the local and national levels.

2. Such reviews should be carried out within the framework of overall development plans, policies and programmes.

3. All United Nations organizations and national governments should be urged to make all efforts for the achievement by 1980 of the minimum objectives set forth in article 46 of the World Plan of Action.

Document 56

General Assembly resolution adopting the criteria for the management of the Voluntary Fund for the United Nations Decade for Women

A/RES/31/133, 16 December 1976

The General Assembly,

Recalling its resolution 3520 (XXX) of 15 December 1975, in which it proclaimed the period from 1976 to 1985 United Nations Decade for Women: Equality, Development and Peace,

Recalling also that it decided at its thirtieth session that the voluntary fund for the International Women's Year, established by Economic and Social Council resolution 1850 (LVI) of 16 May 1974, should be extended to cover the period of the Decade, 1/

Aware that some countries, particularly the least developed ones, have limited financial resources for carrying out their national plans and programmes for the advancement of women and for the implementation of the World Plan of Action for the Implementation of the Objectives of the International Women's Year 2/ adopted by the World Conference of the International Women's Year, held at Mexico City from 19 June to 2 July 1975,

Recognizing the necessity for continuing financial and technical support for these programmes,

Having considered the report of the Secretary-General on the Voluntary Fund for the Decade, 3/

1. *Adopts* the following criteria and arrangements for the management of the Voluntary Fund for the United Nations Decade for Women:

(a) Criteria:

The resources of the Fund should be utilized to supplement activities in the following areas designed to implement the goals of the United Nations Decade for Women: Equality, Development and Peace, priority being given to the related programmes and projects of the least developed, land-locked and island countries among developing countries:

(i) Technical cooperation activities;

(ii) Development and/or strengthening of regional and international programmes;

(iii) Development and implementation of joint inter-organizational programmes;

(iv) Research, data collection and analysis, relevant to (i), (ii) and (iii) above;

(v) Communication support and public information activities designed to promote the goals of the Decade and, in particular, the activities undertaken under (i), (ii) and (iii) above;

(vi) In the selection of projects and programmes, special consideration should be given to those which benefit rural women, poor women in urban areas and other marginal groups of women, especially the disadvantaged;

(b) Arrangements:

The General Assembly endorses the arrangements for the future management of the Fund contained in the annex to the present resolution;

2. *Requests* the Secretary-General to consult the Administrator of the United Nations Development Programme on the use of the Fund for technical cooperation activities;

3. *Requests* the President of the General Assembly to select, with due regard to regional distribution, in the first instance for a period of three years, five Member States, each of which should appoint a representative to serve on the Consultative Committee on the Voluntary Fund for the United Nations Decade for Women to advise the Secretary-General on the application to the use of the Fund of the criteria set forth in paragraph 1 above;

1/ See *Official Records of the General Assembly, Thirtieth Session, Supplement No. 34* (A/10034), p. 100, items 75 and 76.
2/ *Report of the World Conference of the International Women's Year* (United Nations publication, Sales No. E.76.IV.1), chap. II, sect. A.
3/ E/5773.

4. *Requests* the Secretary-General to report annually to the General Assembly on the management of the Fund.

Annex

Arrangements for the management of the Voluntary Fund for the United Nations Decade for Women

1. The Secretary-General shall apply the following arrangements for the management of the Voluntary Fund for the United Nations Decade for Women:

I. *Solicitation and acknowledgement of pledges and the collection of contributions*

2. The Controller, in consultations with the Under-Secretary-General for Economic and Social Affairs and the Assistant Secretary-General for Social Development and Humanitarian Affairs, shall determine the responsibility and procedures for soliciting voluntary contributions to the Fund.

3. Any prospective donor desiring to make a voluntary contribution to the Fund shall submit a written proposal to the Secretary-General; the request for acceptance should contain all relevant information, including the amount of the proposed contribution, the currency and the timing of payments, and may indicate the purposes and any action expected of the United Nations.

4. The proposal, with the comments, *inter alia*, of the Under-Secretary-General for Economic and Social Affairs and the Assistant Secretary-General for Social Development and Humanitarian Affairs, shall be forwarded to the Controller, who shall determine whether or not any proposed gift or donation might directly or indirectly involve additional financial liability for the Organization. Before acceptance of any gift or donation involving such liability, the Controller shall request and obtain the approval of the General Assembly through the Advisory Committee on Administrative and Budgetary Questions.

5. The Controller shall acknowledge all pledges and shall determine the bank account or accounts in which contributions to the Fund should be deposited; he shall be responsible for collecting contributions and following up on payments of contributions pledged.

6. The Controller may accept contributions in any national currency donated for the purpose of the Fund.

II. *Operations and control*

7. The Controller shall ensure that the operation and control of the Fund shall be in accordance with the Financial Regulations and Rules of the United Nations; he may delegate responsibility for the operation and administration of the Fund to the heads of departments or offices designated by the Secretary-General to execute activities financed by the Fund; only officials so designated may authorize the execution of specific activities to be financed by the Fund.

8. Subject to the criteria for disbursements from the Fund endorsed by the General Assembly, the Controller may, after consultation with the Department of Economic and Social Affairs, allocate resources of the Fund to a specialized agency or another United Nations body for the execution of projects financed by the Fund; in such an event, the administrative procedures of the executing body would apply, subject to such provisions for periodic reporting as the Controller may specify. Before making disbursements for technical cooperation activities, the Controller should consult the Administrator of the United Nations Development Programme.

9. In respect of activities conducted by the United Nations, requests for allotments of funds shall be submitted to the Controller by the Department of Economic and Social Affairs, accompanied by such supporting information as the Controller may require. After review, allotments to provide for expenditures of the funds received shall be issued by the Director of the Budget Division, and certifying officers for the Fund shall be designated by the Controller in accordance with established procedures.

10. The Controller shall be responsible for the reporting of all financial transactions concerning the Fund and shall issue quarterly statements of assets, liabilities and unencumbered Fund balance, income and expenditure.

11. The Fund shall be audited by both the Internal Audit Service and the Board of Auditors, in accordance with the Financial Regulations and Rules of the United Nations.

III. *Reporting*

12. An annual report showing funds available, pledges and payments received and the expenditures made from the Fund shall be prepared by the Controller and submitted to the General Assembly and, as appropriate, to the Commission on the Status of Women.

* * *

The President of the General Assembly subsequently informed the Secretary-General 4/ that, in accordance with paragraph 3 of the above resolution, he had selected the following States as members of the Consultative Committee on the Voluntary Fund for the United Nations Decade for Women: GERMAN DEMOCRATIC REPUBLIC, JAMAICA, NIGERIA, PHILIPPINES *and* UNITED KINGDOM OF GREAT BRITAIN AND NORTHERN IRELAND.

4/ A/31/477.

Document 57

General Assembly resolution calling on States to improve the status and role of women in education and to take all possible measures to eliminate illiteracy among women

A/RES/31/134, 16 December 1976

The General Assembly,

Recalling that the Declaration on the Elimination of Discrimination against Women emphasizes the need to take all appropriate measures to ensure to women equal rights with men in education at all levels,

Recalling further its resolutions 3520 (XXX), 3521 (XXX), 3522 (XXX), 3523 (XXX) and 3524 (XXX) of 15 December 1975,

Recognizing that the full and complete development of a country requires the maximum participation of women on equal terms with men in all fields,

Recognizing also the necessity for women to have equal rights, opportunities and obligations with men, particularly in the fields of education and professional and vocational training, to enable their full participation in the process of development,

Recognizing further the importance of promoting the education of women and its impact on the rearing of the young generation,

Noting that, despite the world-wide progress in reducing illiteracy, the illiteracy rate for women far exceeds that of men and, in some cases, continues to rise,

Recognizing the importance of exchange of experience in the elimination of illiteracy and improvement of the educational standard of women at the national, regional and international levels,

1. *Appeals* to all States which have not yet done so to become parties to the Convention against Discrimination in Education, 1960, 1/ elaborated by the United Nations Educational, Scientific and Cultural Organization, and to the Discrimination (Employment and Occupation) Convention, 1958 2/ and the Human Resources Development Convention, 1975, 3/ elaborated by the International Labour Organization;

2. *Calls upon* States to undertake, whenever necessary, in their economic, social and cultural programmes, specific short-term and long-term measures aimed at improving the status and role of women in education, bearing in mind the following:

(a) The provisions of the Declaration on the Elimination of Discrimination against Women;

(b) The provisions of the World Plan of Action for the Implementation of the Objectives of the International Women's Year 4/ concerning education and training,

particularly with respect to an increase in literacy and equal access of women at every level of education, as well as the provisions of the Convention and Recommendation against Discrimination in Education, 1960 and the appropriate recommendation concerning technical and vocational education of the United Nations Educational, Social and Cultural Organization, and the provisions of the Discrimination (Employment and Occupation) Convention, 1958, the Human Resources Development Convention, 1975 and the appropriate recommendations concerning discrimination (employment and occupation), employment (women with family responsibilities) and human resources development of the International Labour Organization;

3. *Calls upon* States, whenever necessary, to undertake all possible measures to eliminate illiteracy among women, especially during the United Nations Decade for Women;

4. *Calls upon* States which not yet done so to consider undertaking all appropriate measures:

(a) To introduce free and compulsory education at the elementary level and, where possible, free education at all levels, including professional, vocational and technical education, which should be accessible to women without discrimination;

(b) To promote co-education;

(c) To ensure that men and women have access on a footing of equality to scholarships and other study grants when these are provided nationally or are made available to States under bilateral or multilateral agreements;

5. *Recommends* that States should introduce measures to expand the exchange of experience on issues concerning the improvement of the status and role of women in education, particularly through courses, seminars and symposiums organized at the national, regional and international levels;

1/ United Nations, *Treaty Series*, vol. 429, p. 93.

2/ International Labour Organization, *Conventions and Recommendations, 1919-1966* (Geneva, 1966), Convention No. III,

3/ International Labour Office, *Official Bulletin*, vol. LVIII, 1975, Series A, No. 1, Convention No. 142.

4/ *Report of the World Conference of the International Women's Year* (United Nations publication, Sales No. E.76.IV.1), chap. II, sect. A.

6. *Invites* Member States, as well as the United Nations Educational, Scientific and Cultural Organization, the International Labour Organization and other organizations of the United Nations system, including regional commissions, and interested intergovernmental organizations and non-governmental organizations having consultative status with the Economic and Social Council, to submit to the Secretary-General their observations concerning the improvement of the status and role of women in education;

7. *Requests* the Secretary-General, in collaboration with the Directors-General of the United Nations Educational, Scientific and Cultural Organization and the International Labour Organization and taking into account the comments and observations received under paragraph 6 above, to submit to the General Assembly at its thirty-third session a report on the status and role of women in education;

8. *Decides* to consider the report of the Secretary-General at its thirty-third session.

Document 58

General Assembly resolution approving the Programme for the United Nations Decade for Women and calling on Governments and United Nations bodies to prioritize the Programme's goals for the Decade

A/RES/31/136, 16 December 1976

The General Assembly,

Considering that in its resolution 3520 (XXX) of 15 December 1975 it proclaimed the period from 1976 to 1985 United Nations Decade for Women: Equality, Development and Peace, to be devoted to effective and sustained national, regional and international action to implement the World Plan of Action for the Implementation of the Objectives of the International Women's Year, 1/ and related resolutions 2/ adopted by the World Conference of the International Women's Year, held at Mexico City from 19 June to 2 July 1975,

Aware of the importance of developing and implementing without delay a programme of concrete action for the Decade,

Considering further its decision to convene in 1980 a world conference to review and evaluate progress made and, where necessary, readjust existing programmes in the light of new data and research available,

Noting with satisfaction the Programme for the United Nations Decade for Women as adopted by the Commission on the Status of Women at its twenty-sixth session and transmitted to the General Assembly by the Economic and Social Council at its resumed sixty-first session, 3/

1. *Approves* the Programme for the United Nations Decade for Women, which focuses on the first half of the Decade, 1976 to 1980;

2. *Urges* Governments and United Nations bodies to take all necessary steps to give effect to the Programme for the Decade and to give it priority in view of the real need to attain the goals of the Decade;

3. *Calls upon* Governments to take measures to ensure equal and effective participation of women in political, economic, social and cultural life and in policy-making at local, national, regional and international levels, thereby increasing their role in international cooperation and in the strengthening of peace;

4. *Recommends* that Governments should establish machinery, where appropriate, which could include governmental and non-governmental agencies, bureaux and commissions, in order to ensure the effective implementation and evaluation of the World Plan of Action and of the Programme for the Decade within the framework of national development plans and regional policies;

5. *Recommends further* that Governments, in cooperation with the Secretary-General, the specialized agencies, the regional commissions, appropriate regional and international research centres and institutes as well as appropriate intergovernmental bodies, should undertake the organization of training courses and seminars whereby officials responsible for the formulation and implementation of national development plans would study multidisciplinary techniques and methods which can be utilized in effectively integrating women in development;

6. *Invites*, as a matter of priority, Governments and organizations and bodies of the United Nations system as well as all governmental and non-governmental organizations concerned and the mass media to undertake

1/ *Report of the World Conference of the International Women's Year* (United Nations publication, Sales No. E.76.IV.1), chap. II, sect. A.

2/ Ibid., chap. II.

3/ E/5894.

massive public information programmes with a view to making all sectors of the population aware of the need to implement fully the Programme for the Decade;

7. *Requests* the Secretary-General to take fully into account the financial and staff needs required to implement effectively the World Plan of Action and the Programme for the Decade;

8. *Requests* the Secretary-General to prepare, for the consideration of the General Assembly at its thirty-second session, a report on the measures taken to implement the present resolution, in particular paragraphs 4, 5 and 6 above, as well as a progress report on other measures taken to implement the World Plan of Action and the Programme for the Decade.

Document 59

General Assembly resolution calling for a pledging conference for contributions to the Voluntary Fund for the United Nations Decade for Women

A/RES/31/137, 16 December 1976

The General Assembly,

Recalling its resolution 3520 (XXX) of 15 December 1975, in which it proclaimed the period from 1976 to 1985 United Nations Decade for Women: Equality, Development and Peace,

Recalling further that in its resolution 31/136 of 16 December 1976 it endorsed the Programme for the United Nations Decade for Women,

Noting that it decided at its thirtieth session that the voluntary fund for the International Women's Year, established by Economic and Social Council resolution 1850 (LVI) of 16 May 1974, should be extended to cover the period of the Decade,

Aware that in its resolution 31/133 of 16 December 1976 it adopted the criteria and arrangements for the management of the Voluntary Fund for the United Nations Decade for Women,

Conscious that, in its resolution 31/135 of 16 December 1976 concerning the establishment of the International Research and Training Institute for the Advancement of Women, it requested the Secretary-General to seek actively financial and technical support for the Institute,

1. *Reaffirms* its support for the implementation of the World Plan of Action for the Implementation of the Objectives of the International Women's Year, 1/ adopted by the World Conference of the International Women's Year, held at Mexico City from 19 June to 2 July 1975, as well as the Programme for the United Nations Decade for Women;

2. *Requests* the Secretary-General to convene during the thirty-second session of the General Assembly, in 1977, a pledging conference for voluntary contributions to be made to the Voluntary Fund for the United Nations Decade for Women, for the purpose of financing programmes under the World Plan of Action and the Programme for the Decade, and to the International Research and Training Institute for the Advancement of Women;

3. *Appeals* to Governments to extend their full cooperation to help make this pledging conference a success.

1/ *Report of the World Conference of the International Women's Year* (United Nations Publications, Sales No. E.76.IV.1), chap. II, sect. A.

Document 60

General Assembly resolution establishing the Preparatory Committee for the World Conference of the United Nations Decade for Women: Equality, Development and Peace

A/RES/32/140, 16 December 1977

The General Assembly,

Recalling its resolution 3520 (XXX) of 15 December 1975, in paragraph 20 of which it decided to convene at the mid-term of the United Nations Decade for Women a world conference to review and evaluate the progress made in implementing the objectives of the International Women's Year as recommended by the World Conference of the International Women's Year and, where necessary, to readjust existing programmes in the light of new data and research available,

Recalling that the Economic and Social Council, in its resolution 1999 (LX) of 12 May 1966, requested the Commission on the Status of Women at its twenty-sixth session to consider different aspects of the preparatory work for the World Conference of the United Nations Decade for Women, including its agenda, and also decided to consider at its sixty-fourth session, in the spring of 1978, the preparatory work for the Conference,

Recalling also that, in accordance with the request of the Economic and Social Council, the Commission on the Status of Women has considered various aspects of the material preparations and the organization of the Conference as well as the implications of the Conference for the programme budget, bearing in mind a note by the Secretary-General, 1/

Recalling further that the Economic and Social Council, at its sixty-second session, adopted resolution 2062 (LXII) of 12 May 1976, in which it:

(a) Requested the Commission on the Status of Women at its twenty-seventh session to give the highest priority to the consideration of the preparatory work for the World Conference of the United Nations Decade for Women,

(b) Requested the Secretary-General to prepare for the consideration of the Commission on the Status of Women at its twenty-seventh session a report outlining a programme of concrete action for the second half of the Decade,

(c) Decided to establish, not later than June 1978, a preparatory committee to make recommendations concerning the substantive and organizational arrangements for the Conference,

(d) Invited the regional commissions to consider ways and means of contributing effectively to the Conference,

Noting that preliminary exchanges of views on the preparatory work for the Conference have also taken place in the Administrative Committee on Co-ordination at the two special interagency meetings held in September 1976 and July 1977, which were brought to the attention of the Commission on the Status of Women at its twenty-sixth session and will be brought to its attention at its twenty-seventh session,

1. *Accepts* the offer of the Government of Iran to act as host to the World Conference of the United Nations Decade for Women;

2. *Notes* that the Conference will in principle be held at Teheran in May 1980 for a period of two weeks;

3. *Decides* that the first session of the Preparatory Committee for the World Conference of the United Nations Decade for Women, to be convened pursuant to Economic and Social Council resolution 2062 (LXII), shall be held at the Headquarters of the United Nations in June 1978;

4. *Notes* the efforts made thus far by the Secretary-General and the Commission on the Status of Women with a view to undertaking the preparatory work for the Conference;

5. *Requests* the Secretary-General to report to the General Assembly at its thirty-third session, through the Economic and Social Council, on the work of the Preparatory Committee during its first session.

1/ E/CN.6/600.

Document 61

General Assembly resolution requesting the CSW to draft a declaration on women's participation in the strengthening of international peace and security

A/RES/32/142, 16 December 1977

The General Assembly,

Recalling its resolutions 3519 (XXX), 3520 (XXX) and 3521 (XXX) of 15 December 1975 and 31/136 of 16 December 1976,

Taking into account that secure peace and social progress, the establishment of the new international economic order as well as the full enjoyment of human rights and fundamental freedoms require the active participation of women, their equality and development,

Appreciating the contribution of women to the strengthening of international peace and security and to the struggle against colonialism, racism, racial discrimination, foreign aggression and occupation and all forms of foreign domination,

Emphasizing its grave concern that in some regions of the world colonialism, apartheid, racial discrimination and aggression continue to exist and territories are still occupied, which represents a most serious infringement of the principles of the Charter of the United Nations and of human rights of both women and men, and of the peoples' right to self-determination,

Reaffirming the objectives of the United Nations Decade for Women, the Declaration of Mexico on the Equality of Women and Their Contribution to Development and Peace, 1975 1/ and the World Plan of Action for the Implementation of the Objectives of the International Women's Year, 2/

1. *Takes note* of the report of the Secretary-General on the implementation of General Assembly resolution 3519 (XXX); 3/

2. *Calls upon* all States to continue to make their contribution to creating favourable conditions for the elimination of discrimination against women and for their full and equal participation in the social development process and to encourage broad participation of women in the effort to strengthen international peace, extend the process of international détente, curb the arms race and take measures for disarmament;

3. *Seizes the occasion* of the International Anti-Apartheid Year to be observed in 1978 to invite all States fully to support women exposed to colonialism, racism and apartheid in their just struggle against the racist régimes in southern Africa;

4. *Invites* all States to proclaim, in accordance with their historical and national traditions and customs, any day of the year as United Nations Day for Women's Rights and International Peace and to inform the Secretary-General thereon;

5. *Requests* the Commission on the Status of Women to consider, as a contribution to the preparation of the World Conference of the United Nations Decade for Women, to be held in 1980, the elaboration of a draft declaration on the participation of women in the struggle for the strengthening of international peace and security and against colonialism, racism, racial discrimination, foreign aggression and occupation and all forms of foreign domination and to report thereon to the Economic and Social Council at its sixty-fourth session;

6. *Invites* the Secretary-General to submit to the General Assembly at its thirty-fourth session a progress report on the implementation of resolution 3519 (XXX);

7. *Decides* to include in the provisional agenda of its thirty-fourth session, under the item "United Nations Decade for Women: Equality, Development and Peace", a subitem entitled "Implementation of General Assembly resolution 3519 (XXX): report of the Secretary-General".

1/ *Report of the World Conference of the International Women's Year* (United Nations publication, Sales No. E.76.IV.1), chap. I.
2/ Ibid., chap. II, sect. A.
3/ A/32/211.

Document 62

General Assembly resolution on preparations for the World Conference of the United Nations Decade for Women: Equality, Development and Peace, including the adoption of the subtheme "Employment, Health and Education"

A/RES/33/185, 29 January 1979

The General Assembly,

Recalling its resolutions 3520 (XXX) of 15 December 1975, in which it decided to convene a world conference in 1980, and 33/189 of 29 January 1979, in which it, *inter alia,* emphasized the subtheme "Employment, Health and Education" for the Programme of Action for the second half of the United Nations Decade for Women: Equality, Development and Peace, and requested the Secretary-General to invite the regional commissions to convene preparatory meetings and seminars,

Recalling also Economic and Social Council resolution 1978/32 of 5 May 1978, in which the Council recommended the subtheme "Employment, Health and Education" for the World Conference of the United Nations Decade for Women: Equality, Development and Peace, and invited Member States to submit reports on national experience, which would include specific information on projects related to these three fields,

Bearing in mind that women will not be able to play an equal and effective role in the process of development unless they have equal opportunities for education and employment and have the health care facilities and social atmosphere necessary for the utilization of these opportunities,

Considering that the equal participation of women in the development process and in political life will contribute to the achievement of international peace,

Recognizing that intensification of international cooperation for accelerated economic and social progress in developing countries, through the establishment of the new international economic order, is an essential means for the progressive integration of women in the development process,

1. *Decides* upon the subtheme "Employment, Health and Education" for the World Conference of the United Nations Decade for Women: Equality, Development and Peace, whose purpose will continue to be to review and evaluate the progress made in the first half of the Decade and to recommend a programme of action, with necessary changes and readjustments in the World Plan of Action for the Implementation of the Objectives of the International Women's Year, 1/ for the second half of the Decade, in order to attain its objectives of equality, development and peace;

2. *Recommends,* therefore, that the Conference should place emphasis on elaborating action-oriented plans for integrating women in the development process, particularly by promoting economic activities and employment opportunities on an equal footing with men through, *inter alia,* the provision of adequate health and educational facilities, and that the preparatory work for the Conference should take this into account;

3. *Invites* the regional commissions, the International Labour Organization, the World Health Organization, the Food and Agriculture Organization of the United Nations, the United Nations Children's Fund, the United Nations Development Programme, the United Nations Educational, Scientific and Cultural Organization, the United Nations Industrial Development Organization, the World Food Programme, the United Nations Relief and Works Agency for Palestine Refugees in the Near East, the United Nations Fund for Population Activities and any other United Nations agency concerned to review progress made as well as constraints and specific problems encountered in their technical and operational areas in the achievement of the aims and objectives of the Decade, and to suggest appropriate programmes for the second half of the Decade, with special emphasis on the subtheme "Employment, Health and Education", in cooperation with each other wherever feasible, to the regional preparatory meetings, if possible, or to the Conference;

4. *Requests* regional preparatory meetings to suggest appropriate programmes for the second half of the Decade, through a review and evaluation of the progress made and obstacles encountered in the first half of the Decade, with special emphasis on the subtheme "Employment, Health and Education", taking into account the following broad approaches:

(a) Technical cooperation;

(b) Research, data collection and analysis, including the strengthening of existing arrangements at the regional level to collect qualitative and quantitative data

1/ *Report of the World Conference of the International Women's Year, Mexico, 19 June-2 July 1975* (United Nations publication, Sales No. E.76.IV.1), chap.II, sect.A.

on the conditions and problems of women, especially relating to their employment and educational status;

(c) Dissemination of information to eliminate stereotyped concepts of masculine and feminine roles and exchange of information about projects related to the objectives of the Decade;

5. *Requests* the Secretary-General:

(a) To prepare a report for the Conference on the problems encountered, and the status and future role of both urban and rural women in the areas of employment and participation in economic life, especially at the policy-making level, education and technical and other kinds of training, and health, nutrition and family planning, basing it on the information received in response to his questionnaire on review and evaluation of progress in the first half of the Decade and on any other information available to him, including that received from Member Status in response to Economic and Social Council resolution 1978/32;

(b) To take the above-mentioned information as well as the recommendations of regional preparatory meetings, the regional commissions and United Nations agencies into account in preparing documents related to item 9 of the provisional agenda for the Conference; 2/

(c) To draw the attention of Member States to the present resolution, and to circulate it also to the regional commissions and relevant United Nations agencies and non-governmental organizations having consultative status with the Economic and Social Council, and to regional preparatory meetings and seminars held to prepare for the Conference.

2/ Resolution 3/189, annex.

Document 63

General Assembly resolution adopting the agenda for the World Conference of the United Nations Decade for Women: Equality, Development and Peace

A/RES/33/189, 29 January 1979

The General Assembly,

Recalling its resolution 3520 (XXX) of 15 December 1975, in which it decided to convene a world conference in 1980, at the mid-term of the United Nations Decade for Women: Equality, Development and Peace,

Recalling also Economic and Social Council resolution 2062 (LXII) of 12 May 1977, in which the Council decided to establish a preparatory committee to make recommendations concerning the substantive and organizational arrangements for the Conference,

Recalling further all the relevant resolutions and decisions of the United Nations on substantive and administrative aspects of the preparatory work for the Conference,

1. *Decides* that the provisional agenda for the World Conference of the United Nations Decade for Women: Equality, Development and Peace shall be as set out in the annex to the present resolution;

2. *Further decides* on the following organization of work for the Conference:

(a) Thirteen working days shall be allocated for the Conference;

(b) In addition to the plenary, there shall be two main committees, for which interpretation shall be provided in six languages;

(c) The general debate, to be held in plenary, shall be limited to fifteen minutes per speaker;

(d) The number of working groups required shall be decided upon by the Conference, on the understanding that one working group will be provided with interpretation;

3. *Requests* the Secretary-General to ensure that the documentation for the Conference will be made available and distributed six weeks before the Conference is convened, in accordance with United Nations practice;

4. *Authorizes* the Secretary-General, in preparing the substantive documentation for the Conference, to make use, as necessary, of the expertise of consultants;

5. *Recommends* to the executive heads of the specialized agencies concerned and other relevant parts of the United Nations system to prepare in a coordinated manner reports evaluating progress in substantive areas relating to the United Nations Decade for Women: Equality, Development and Peace;

6. *Requests* the Secretary-General to ensure that

due account is taken of the recommendations on the rationalization of methods in the preparation of the questionnaire on the implementation of the World Plan of Action for the Implementation of the Objectives of the International Women's Year, 1/ in compliance with Economic and Social Council resolution 2060 (LXII) of 12 May 1977, and of the findings and conclusions emanating from all preparatory work for the Conference;

7. *Requests* the Secretary-General to ensure that the Conference will have at its disposal the documentation referred to in his note of 2 March 1978 on the preparatory work for the Conference 2/ as well as in the relevant resolutions of the United Nations;

8. *Requests* the Secretary-General to invite:

(a) All States to participate in the Conference;

(b) Representatives of organizations that have received a standing invitation from the General Assembly to participate in the sessions and the work of all international conferences convened under its auspices in the capacity of observers to participate in the Conference in that capacity in accordance with Assembly resolution 3237 (XXIX) of 22 November 1974;

(c) Representatives of the national liberation movements recognized in its region by the Organization of African Unity to participate in the Conference in the capacity of observers in accordance with General Assembly resolution 3280 (XXIX) of 10 December 1974;

(d) The United Nations Council for Namibia to participate in the Conference in its capacity as the Administering Authority for Namibia;

(e) The specialized agencies and the International Atomic Energy Agency, as well as interested organs of the United Nations, to be represented at the Conference;

(f) Interested intergovernmental organizations to be represented by observers at the Conference;

(g) Interested non-governmental organizations in consultative status with the Economic and Social Council to be represented by observers at the Conference who will have the right to submit written statements, in which connection the Secretary-General of the Conference will provide a list of the non-governmental organizations which may address the Conference, for approval by the Preparatory Committee at its second session, on the understanding that the number will be limited and the duration of the speeches will be in accordance with the rules of procedure of the Conference;

9. Requests the Secretary-General:

(a) To appoint as soon as possible a Secretary-General of the Conference, at the level of Assistant Secretary-General;

(b) To appoint the Secretary-General from out-side the United Nations system and from a developing country;

(c) To ensure that the secretariat of the Conference, which shall be located at United Nations Headquarters, will be composed of a full-time Secretary-General, as well as the appropriate members of the Advancement of Women Branch of the Center for Social Development and Humanitarian Affairs of the Secretariat and the necessary additional staff for the preparation of the Conference, the secretariat to work in close cooperation with the Centre as a whole, which is the focal point of the activities of the Decade;

10. *Also requests* the Secretary-General to prepare draft rules of procedure for the Conference for submission to the Preparatory Committee at its second session, on the basis of the standard rules of procedure for United Nations conferences, taking into account the procedure adopted by the World Conference of the International Women's Year, held at Mexico City from 19 June to 2 July 1975, with respect to the composition of the Bureau;

11. *Requests* the Secretary-General to invite the regional commissions to convene as early as possible in 1979 preparatory meetings and seminars in support of the aims and objectives of the Conference;

12. *Further requests* the Secretary-General to invite the specialized agencies and other relevant parts of the United Nations system to convene sectoral meetings, as appropriate, and to participate actively in the preparation of the regional meetings;

13. *Invites* the regional intergovernmental organizations and non-governmental organizations to contribute to the preparations for the regional meetings and to participate in those meetings wherever possible;

14. *Authorizes* the Secretary-General, with the prior concurrence of the Advisory Committee on Administrative and Budgetary Questions and subject to the Financial Regulations of the United Nations, to enter into commitments which, in accordance with General Assembly resolution 31/93 of 14 December 1976, it has determined are of a pressing and unforeseeable nature, arising out of extraordinary expenses for the Conference resulting from the decisions in paragraphs 2 to 8 above and based on preliminary estimates appearing in annex IV of the report of the Preparatory Committee for the Conference; 3/

15. *Decides* that adequate financial resources shall be made available to ensure the successful prepara-

1/ *Report of the World Conference of the International Women's Year, Mexico, 19 June-2 July 1975* (United Nations publication, Sales No. E.76.IV.1), chap.II, sect.A.
2/ E/CN.6/610.
3/ A/CONF.94/PC/4.

tion of the Conference for the last part of the biennium 1978-1979 and for the first part of the biennium 1980-1981 in order to provide necessary resources as soon as possible.

Annex

Provisional agenda for the World Conference of the United Nations Decade for Women: Equality, Development and Peace

1. Opening of the Conference.
2. Election of the President and members of the Bureau of the Conference.
3. Adoption of the rules of procedure.
4. Adoption of the agenda.
5. Establishment of main committees and organization of work.
6. Credentials of representatives to the Conference:
   (a) Appointment of the members of the Credentials Committee;
   (b) Report of the Credentials Committee.
7. Effects of apartheid on women in southern Africa:
   (a) Review of the situation;
   (b) Special measures for assistance to women in southern Africa.
8. Review and evaluation of the progress made and obstacles encountered in attaining the objectives of the United Nations Decade for Women: Equality, Development and Peace, at the national, regional and international levels, from 1975 to 1980, in keeping with the World Plan of Action for the Implementation of the Objectives of the International Women's Year:
   (a) Review and evaluation of progress made and obstacles encountered at the national level in attaining the minimum objectives set forth in paragraph 46 of the World Plan of Action;
   (b) Review and evaluation of regional and global programmes of the United Nations system of organizations aimed at promoting the objectives of the Decade.
9. Programme of Action for the second half of the United Nations Decade for Women: Equality, Development and Peace, 1981-1985, designed to implement the World Plan of Action:
   (a) National targets and strategies for women's integration and participation in economic and social development with special emphasis on the subtheme "Employment, Health and Education"
      (i) Planning and monitoring;
      (ii) National machineries;
   (b) Regional and international targets and strategies, taking into account the subtheme "Employment, Health and Education".
10. Adoption of the report of the Conference.

Document 64

General Assembly resolution deciding on Copenhagen as the venue for the World Conference of the United Nations Decade for Women

A/RES/33/191, 29 January 1979

The General Assembly,

Recalling its resolution 3520 (XXX) of 15 December 1975, in paragraph 20 of which it decided to convene at the mid-term of the United Nations Decade for Women: Equality, Development and Peace a world conference to review and evaluate the progress made in implementing the objectives of the International Women's Year as recommended by the World Conference of the International Women's Year and, where necessary, to readjust existing programmes in the light of new data and research available,

Noting with appreciation that the Government of Denmark has offered to act as host for the Conference, 1/

Noting also with appreciation the offer of the Government of Costa Rica to act as host to the Conference, 2/

Decides, after being informed of the friendly and cordial understanding between the two countries offering to act as host to the World Conference of the United Nations Decade for Women: Equality, Development and Peace:

(a) To accept, with thanks, the offer of the Government of Denmark to act as host to the Conference;

(b) To hold the Conference in Copenhagen in 1980.

1/ A/C.3/33/5.
2/ A/C.3/33/4.

Document 65

General Assembly resolution on the importance of improving the status and role of women in education and in the economic and social fields for the achievement of the equality of women with men

A/RES/34/159, 17 December 1979

The General Assembly,

Recalling its resolution 3520 (XXX) of 15 December 1975, in which it proclaimed the period from 1976 to 1985 the United Nations Decade for Women: Equality, Development and Peace,

Recalling also its resolutions 31/134 of 16 December 1976 and 33/184, 33/185 and 33/189 of 29 January 1979,

Recognizing the urgent need to improve the status and role of women in education and in the economic and social fields for the achievement of the equality of women and men,

Recognizing also the importance of the exchange of experience in these matters among States,

Taking note of the analytical report of the Secretary-General on the status and role of women in education and in the economic and social fields, 1/

1. *Urges* States to take necessary measures to promote full equality of women with men in education and in the economic and social fields;

2. *Recommends* that States should envisage in their policies all appropriate measures to create necessary conditions which will enable women to participate in work on an equal footing with men;

3. *Recommends further* that States should take measures to expand the exchange of experience in matters concerning the improvement of the status and role of women in education and in the economic and social fields for the achievement of the equality of women and men;

4. *Requests* the Secretary-General to circulate his analytical report on the status and role of women in education and in the economic and social fields as a background document for the World Conference of the United Nations Decade for Women: Equality, Development and Peace, under item 8 of its provisional agenda; 2/

5. *Invites* the Conference to give due attention to the question of the improvement of the status and role of women in education and in the economic and social fields for the achievement of the equality of women with men.

1/ A/34/577 and Add.1
2/ See resolution 33/189, annex.

Document 66

General Assembly resolution adding an item on Palestinian women to the provisional agenda for the World Conference of the United Nations Decade for Women

A/RES/34/160, 17 December 1979

The General Assembly,

Recalling its resolutions 3520 (XXX) of 15 December 1975, in which it decided to convene a world conference in 1980, and 33/189 of 29 January 1979, in which it emphasized the subtheme "Employment, Health and Education" for the programme of action for the second half of the United Nations Decade for Women: Equality, Development and Peace,

Recalling also its resolution 33/185 of 29 January 1979, entitled "Preparations for the World Conference of the United Nations Decade for Women: Equality,

Development and Peace, including the adoption of the subtheme 'Employment, Health and Education'",

Taking note with interest and appreciation of the reports of the Preparatory Committee for the World Conference of the United Nations Decade for Women 1/ and of the provisional agenda for the Conference adopted by the General Assembly at its thirty-third session, 2/

Decides to include in the provisional agenda for the World Conference of the United Nations Decade for

1/ A/CONF.94/PC/12, A/34/657 and Add.1.
2/ Resolution 33/189, annex.

Women: Equality, Development and Peace an item on Palestinian women, entitled:

"Effects of Israeli occupation on Palestinian women inside and outside the occupied territories:

"(a) Review of the social and economic needs of Palestinian women;

"(b) Special measures for assistance to Palestinian women inside and outside the occupied territories".

Document 67

General Assembly resolution adding an item on the situation of women refugees throughout the world to the provisional agenda for the World Conference of the United Nations Decade for Women

A/RES/34/161, 17 December 1979

The General Assembly,

Recalling its resolutions 34/60, 34/61 and 34/62, adopted by consensus on 29 November 1979 under agenda item 83, on the Office of the United Nations High Commissioner for Refugees,

Recognizing the urgent needs and problems of women refugees the world over,

Conscious that the situation of women refugees has not yet been systematically studied,

1. *Decides* that the situation of women refugees the world over should be included in the provisional agenda for the World Conference of the United Nations Decade for Women: Equality, Development and Peace 1/ as a subitem under agenda item 9, on the programme of action for the second half of the United Nations Decade for Women;

2. *Requests* the Office of the United Nations High Commissioner for Refugees to prepare a draft report to be submitted to the Preparatory Committee for the World Conference of the United Nations Decade for Women at its third session and a final report to be submitted to the Conference, which would:

(a) Review the situation of women refugees the world over within the framework of the overall problem with which the Office is seized;

(b) Make recommendations concerning measures which could be undertaken by Member States, the United Nations system and non-governmental organizations to assist women refugees, taking into account the requirements of the regions concerned.

1/ Resolution 33/189, annex.

Document 68

General Assembly resolution approving the recommendations of the Preparatory Committee for the World Conference of the United Nations Decade for Women and requesting the Secretary-General to provide the necessary financial appropriations

A/RES/34/162, 17 December 1979

The General Assembly,

Recalling its resolution 33/189 of 29 January 1979, concerning substantive and organizational arrangements for the World Conference of the United Nations Decade for Women: Equality, Development and Peace,

Recalling also its resolution 33/185 of 29 January 1979, in which it adopted the subtheme "Employment, Health and Education",

Convinced of the need to ensure the most effective

preparation of the Conference, its success and the effectiveness of follow-up activities,

Noting that regional preparatory meetings have taken place in Paris, New Delhi and Caracas and that two more are scheduled to take place at Lusaka and Damascus,

Having considered the report of the Preparatory Committee for the World Conference of the United Nations Decade for Women on its second session, 1/

1/ A/CONF.94/PC.12.

Having also considered the detailed proposals for the Conference contained in the note by the Secretary-General, 2/

1. *Approves* the recommendations contained in the report of the Preparatory Committee for the World Conference of the United Nations Decade for Women concerning the activities related to the preparation of the Conference, 3/

2. *Requests* the Secretary-General to provide the necessary budgetary appropriations specified in his note in respect of the areas listed below:

(a) To ensure the participation in the Conference of one representative of each of the least developed countries;

(b) To ensure the satisfactory preparation of the documentation for the Conference;

(c) To allow adequate preparation for the presentation of the report of the Conference to the General Assembly at its thirty-fifth session;

(d) In relation to measures proposed by the Department of Public Information of the Secretariat, to strengthen the relevant activities planned for the period prior to and during the Conference;

(e) To make the appropriate arrangements to ensure the success of the preparatory seminars and meetings for the Conference;

(f) To provide the secretariat of the Conference with the appropriate staff, including staff to carry out information activities after the Conference, and with the resources necessary for the travel of the Secretary-General of the Conference;

(g) To hold a third session of the Preparatory Committee in 1980;

3. *Also requests* the Secretary-General to seek extra-budgetary funds to ensure the participation in the Conference of one representative from each of the island and land-locked developing countries;

4. *Further requests* the Secretary-General to endeavour to find extrabudgetary funds to provide for the information activities proposed for the period after the Conference;

5. *Takes note* of the provisional rules of procedure formulated by the Preparatory Committee at its second session; 4/

6. *Notes with appreciation* the statement of the representative of Denmark concerning steps which the Government of Denmark, in line with General Assembly resolution 33/189, has taken regarding the practical organization of the work of the Conference; 5/

7. *Strongly urges* Member States to ensure their adequate preparation for the Conference, including the presentation of studies of development projects and programmes which have been successful in improving the condition of women and in promoting their participation in economic and social development, as required by Economic and Social Council resolution 1978/32 of 5 May 1978;

8. *Calls upon* Member States, the competent organs of the United Nations and the specialized agencies to take all necessary measures, including the use of their information resources, to mobilize public opinion in support of the Conference and its objectives.

2/ A/34/657 and Add.1.
3/ See also sect. X.B.1, decision 34/434.
4/ A/CONF.94/PC.12, chap.II, sect.A.
5/ *Official Records of the General Assembly, Thirty-fourth Session, Third Committee*, 53rd meeting, paras. 27-30; and ibid., *Third Committee, Sessional Fascicle*, corrigendum.

Document 69

Convention on the Elimination of All Forms of Discrimination against Women, adopted by General Assembly on 18 December 1979

UN Treaty Series, vol. 1249, No. 20378, p. 13

The States Parties to the present Convention,

Noting that the Charter of the United Nations re-affirms faith in fundamental human rights, in the dignity and worth of the human person and in the equal rights of men and women,

Noting that the Universal Declaration of Human Rights affirms the principle of the inadmissibility of discrimination and proclaims that all human beings are born free and equal in dignity and rights and that everyone is entitled to all the rights and freedoms set forth therein, without distinction of any kind, including distinction based on sex,

Noting that the States Parties to the International Covenants on Human Rights have the obligation to ensure the equal right of men and women to enjoy all economic, social, cultural, civil and political rights,

Considering the international conventions concluded under the auspices of the United Nations and the specialized agencies promoting equality of rights of men and women,

Noting also the resolutions, declarations and recommendations adopted by the United Nations and the specialized agencies promoting equality of rights of men and women,

Concerned, however, that despite these various instruments extensive discrimination against women continues to exist,

Recalling that discrimination against women violates the principles of equality of rights and respect for human dignity, is an obstacle to the participation of women, on equal terms with men, in the political, social, economic and cultural life of their countries, hampers the growth of the prosperity of society and the family and makes more difficult the full development of the potentialities of women in the service of their countries and of humanity,

Concerned that in situations of poverty women have the least access to food, health, education, training and opportunities for employment and other needs,

Convinced that the establishment of the new international economic order based on equity and justice will contribute significantly towards the promotion of equality between men and women,

Emphasizing that the eradication of apartheid, of all forms of racism, racial discrimination, colonialism, neocolonialism, aggression, foreign occupation and domination and interference in the internal affairs of States is essential to the full enjoyment of the rights of men and women,

Affirming that the strengthening of international peace and security, relaxation of international tension, mutual cooperation among all States irrespective of their social and economic systems, general and complete disarmament, and in particular nuclear disarmament under strict and effective international control, the affirmation of the principles of justice, equality and mutual benefit in relations among countries and the realization of the right of peoples under alien and colonial domination and foreign occupation to self-determination and independence, as well as respect for national sovereignty and territorial integrity, will promote social progress and development and as a consequence will contribute to the attainment of full equality between men and women,

Convinced that the full and complete development of a country, the welfare of the world and the cause of peace require the maximum participation of women on equal terms with men in all fields,

Bearing in mind the great contribution of women to the welfare of the family and to the development of society, so far not fully recognized, the social significance of maternity and the role of both parents in the family and in the upbringing of children, and aware that the role of women in procreation should not be a basis for discrimination but that the upbringing of children requires a sharing of responsibility between men and women and society as a whole,

Aware that a change in the traditional role of men as well as the role of women in society and in the family is needed to achieve full equality between men and women,

Determined to implement the principles set forth in the Declaration on the Elimination of Discrimination against Women and, for that purpose, to adopt the measures required for the elimination of such discrimination in all its forms and manifestations,

Have agreed on the following:

Part I

Article 1. For the purposes of the present Convention, the term "discrimination against women" shall mean any distinction, exclusion or restriction made on the basis of sex which has the effect or purpose of impairing or nullifying the recognition, enjoyment or exercise by women irrespective of their marital status, on a basis of equality of men and women, of human rights and fundamental freedoms in the political, economic, social, cultural, civil or any other field.

Article 2. States Parties condemn discrimination against women in all its forms, agree to pursue by all appropriate means and without delay a policy of eliminating discrimination against women and, to this end, undertake:

(a) To embody the principle of the equality of men and women in their national constitutions or other appropriate legislation if not yet incorporated therein and to ensure, through law and other appropriate means, the practical realization of this principle;

(b) To adopt appropriate legislative and other measures, including sanctions where appropriate, prohibiting all discrimination against women;

(c) To establish legal protection of the rights of women on an equal basis with men and to ensure through competent national tribunals and other public institutions the effective protection of women against any act of discrimination;

(d) To refrain from engaging in any act or practice of discrimination against women and to ensure that public authorities and institutions shall act in conformity with this obligation;

(e) To take all appropriate measures to eliminate

discrimination against women by any person, organization or enterprise;

(f) To take all appropriate measures, including legislation, to modify or abolish existing laws, regulations, customs and practices which constitute discrimination against women;

(g) To repeal all national penal provisions which constitute discrimination against women.

Article 3. States Parties shall take in all fields, in particular in the political, social, economic and cultural fields, all appropriate measures, including legislation, to ensure the full development and advancement of women, for the purpose of guaranteeing them the exercise and enjoyment of human rights and fundamental freedoms on a basis of equality with men.

Article 4. 1. Adoption by States Parties of temporary special measures aimed at accelerating *de facto* equality between men and women shall not be considered discrimination as defined in the present Convention, but shall in no way entail as a consequence the maintenance of unequal or separate standards; these measures shall be discontinued when the objectives of equality of opportunity and treatment have been achieved.

2. Adoption by States Parties of special measures, including those measures contained in the present Convention, aimed at protecting maternity shall not be considered discriminatory.

Article 5. States Parties shall take all appropriate measures:

(a) To modify the social and cultural patterns of conduct of men and women, with a view to achieving the elimination of prejudices and customary and all other practices which are based on the idea of the inferiority or the superiority of either of the sexes or on stereotyped roles for men and women;

(b) To ensure that family education includes a proper understanding of maternity as a social function and the recognition of the common responsibility of men and women in the upbringing and development of their children, it being understood that the interest of the children is the primordial consideration in all cases.

Article 6. States Parties shall take all appropriate measures, including legislation, to suppress all forms of traffic in women and exploitation of prostitution of women.

Part II

Article 7. States Parties shall take all appropriate measures to eliminate discrimination against women in the political and public life of the country and, in particular, shall ensure to women, on equal terms with men, the right:

(a) To vote in all elections and public referenda and to be eligible for election to all publicly elected bodies;

(b) To participate in the formulation of government policy and the implementation thereof and to hold public office and perform all public functions at all levels of government;

(c) To participate in non-governmental organizations and associations concerned with the public and political life of the country.

Article 8. States Parties shall take all appropriate measures to ensure to women, on equal terms with men and without any discrimination, the opportunity to represent their Governments at the international level and to participate in the work of international organizations.

Article 9. 1. States Parties shall grant women equal rights with men to acquire, change or retain their nationality. They shall ensure in particular that neither marriage to an alien nor change of nationality by the husband during marriage shall automatically change the nationality of the wife, render her stateless or force upon her the nationality of the husband.

2. States Parties shall grant women equal rights with men with respect to the nationality of their children.

Part III

Article 10. States Parties shall take all appropriate measures to eliminate discrimination against women in order to ensure to them equal rights with men in the field of education and in particular to ensure, on a basis of equality of men and women:

(a) The same conditions for career and vocational guidance, for access to studies and for the achievement of diplomas in educational establishments of all categories in rural as well as in urban areas; this equality shall be ensured in preschool, general, technical, professional and higher technical education, as well as in all types of vocational training;

(b) Access to the same curricula, the same examinations, teaching staff with qualifications of the same standard and school premises and equipment of the same quality;

(c) The elimination of any stereotyped concept of the roles of men and women at all levels and in all forms of education by encouraging coeducation and other types of education which will help to achieve this aim and, in particular, by the revision of textbooks and school programmes and the adaptation of teaching methods;

(d) The same opportunities to benefit from scholarships and other study grants;

(e) The same opportunities for access to programmes of continuing education, including adult and functional literacy programmes, particularly those aimed at reducing, at the earliest possible time, any gap in education existing between men and women;

(f) The reduction of female student drop-out rates and the organization of programmes for girls and women who have left school prematurely;

(g) The same opportunities to participate actively in sports and physical education;

(h) Access to specific educational information to help to ensure the health and well-being of families, including information and advice on family planning.

Article 11. 1. States Parties shall take all appropriate measures to eliminate discrimination against women in the field of employment in order to ensure, on a basis of equality of men and women, the same rights, in particular:

(a) The right to work as an inalienable right of all human beings;

(b) The right to the same employment opportunities, including the application of the same criteria for selection in matters of employment;

(c) The right to free choice of profession and employment, the right to promotion, job security and all benefits and conditions of service and the right to receive vocational training and retraining, including apprenticeships, advanced vocational training and recurrent training;

(d) The right to equal remuneration, including benefits, and to equal treatment in respect of work of equal value, as well as equality of treatment in the evaluation of the quality of work;

(e) The right to social security, particularly in cases of retirement, unemployment, sickness, invalidity and old age and other incapacity to work, as well as the right to paid leave;

(f) The right to protection of health and to safety in working conditions, including the safeguarding of the function of reproduction.

2. In order to prevent discrimination against women on the grounds of marriage or maternity and to ensure their effective right to work, States Parties shall take appropriate measures:

(a) To prohibit, subject to the imposition of sanctions, dismissal on the grounds of pregnancy or of maternity leave and discrimination in dismissals on the basis of marital status;

(b) To introduce maternity leave with pay or with comparable social benefits without loss of former employment, seniority or social allowances;

(c) To encourage the provision of the necessary supporting social services to enable parents to combine family obligations with work responsibilities and participation in public life, in particular through promoting the establishment and development of a network of child-care facilities;

(d) To provide special protection to women during pregnancy in types of work proved to be harmful to them.

3. Protective legislation relating to matters covered in this article shall be reviewed periodically in the light of scientific and technological knowledge and shall be revised, repealed or extended as necessary.

Article 12. 1. States Parties shall take all appropriate measures to eliminate discrimination against women in the field of health care in order to ensure, on a basis of equality of men and women, access to health care services, including those related to family planning.

2. Notwithstanding the provisions of paragraph 1 of this article, States Parties shall ensure to women appropriate services in connection with pregnancy, confinement and the post-natal period, granting free services where necessary, as well as adequate nutrition during pregnancy and lactation.

Article 13. States Parties shall take all appropriate measures to eliminate discrimination against women in other areas of economic and social life in order to ensure, on a basis of equality of men and women, the same rights, in particular:

(a) The right to family benefits;

(b) The right to bank loans, mortgages and other forms of financial credit;

(c) The right to participate in recreational activities, sports and all aspects of cultural life.

Article 14. 1. States Parties shall take into account the particular problems faced by rural women and the significant roles which rural women play in the economic survival of their families, including their work in the non-monetized sectors of the economy, and shall take all appropriate measures to ensure the application of the provisions of this Convention to women in rural areas.

2. States Parties shall take all appropriate measures to eliminate discrimination against women in rural areas in order to ensure, on a basis of equality of men and women, that they participate in and benefit from rural development and, in particular, shall ensure to such women the right:

(a) To participate in the elaboration and implementation of development planning at all levels;

(b) To have access to adequate health care facilities, including information, counselling and services in family planning;

(c) To benefit directly from social security programmes;

(d) To obtain all types of training and education, formal and non-formal, including that relating to functional literacy, as well as, *inter alia*, the benefit of all community and extension services, in order to increase their technical proficiency;

(e) To organize self-help groups and cooperatives in order to obtain equal access to economic opportunities through employment or self-employment;

(f) To participate in all community activities;

(g) To have access to agricultural credit and loans, marketing facilities, appropriate technology and equal treatment in land and agrarian reform as well as in land resettlement schemes;

(h) To enjoy adequate living conditions, particularly in relation to housing, sanitation, electricity and water supply, transport and communications.

Part IV

Article 15. 1. States Parties shall accord to women equality with men before the law.

2. States Parties shall accord to women, in civil matters, a legal capacity identical to that of men and the same opportunities to exercise that capacity. In particular, they shall give women equal rights to conclude contracts and to administer property and shall treat them equally in all stages of procedure in courts and tribunals.

3. States Parties agree that all contracts and all other private instruments of any kind with a legal effect which is directed at restricting the legal capacity of women shall be deemed null and void.

4. States Parties shall accord to men and women the same rights with regard to the law relating to the movement of persons and the freedom to choose their residence and domicile.

Article 16. 1. States Parties shall take all appropriate measures to eliminate discrimination against women in all matters relating to marriage and family relations and in particular shall ensure, on a basis of equality of men and women:

(a) The same right to enter into marriage;

(b) The same right freely to choose a spouse and to enter into marriage only with their free and full consent;

(c) The same rights and responsibilities during marriage and at its dissolution;

(d) The same rights and responsibilities as parents, irrespective of their marital status, in matters relating to their children; in all cases the interests of the children shall be paramount;

(e) The same rights to decide freely and responsibly on the number and spacing of their children and to have access to the information, education and means to enable them to exercise these rights;

(f) The same rights and responsibilities with regard to guardianship, wardship, trusteeship and adoption of children, or similar institutions where these concepts exist

in national legislation; in all cases the interests of the children shall be paramount;

(g) The same personal rights as husband and wife, including the right to choose a family name, a profession and an occupation;

(h) The same rights for both spouses in respect of the ownership, acquisition, management, administration, enjoyment and disposition of property, whether free of charge or for a valuable consideration.

2. The betrothal and the marriage of a child shall have no legal effect, and all necessary action, including legislation, shall be taken to specify a minimum age for marriage and to make the registration of marriages in an official registry compulsory.

Part V

Article 17. 1. For the purpose of considering the progress made in the implementation of the present Convention, there shall be established a Committee on the Elimination of Discrimination against Women (hereinafter referred to as the Committee) consisting, at the time of entry into force of the Convention, of eighteen and, after ratification of or accession to the Convention by the thirty-fifth State Party, of twenty-three experts of high moral standing and competence in the field covered by the Convention. The experts shall be elected by States Parties from among their nationals and shall serve in their personal capacity, consideration being given to equitable geographical distribution and to the representation of the different forms of civilization as well as the principal legal systems.

2. The members of the Committee shall be elected by secret ballot from a list of persons nominated by States Parties. Each State Party may nominate one person from among its own nationals.

3. The initial election shall be held six months after the date of the entry into force of the present Convention. At least three months before the date of each election the Secretary-General of the United Nations shall address a letter to the States Parties inviting them to submit their nominations within two months. The Secretary-General shall prepare a list in alphabetical order of all persons thus nominated, indicating the States Parties which have nominated them, and shall submit it to the States Parties.

4. Elections of the members of the Committee shall be held at a meeting of States Parties convened by the Secretary-General at United Nations Headquarters. At that meeting, for which two thirds of the States Parties shall constitute a quorum, the persons elected to the Committee shall be those nominees who obtain the largest number of votes and an absolute majority of the votes of the representatives of States Parties present and voting.

5. The members of the Committee shall be elected

for a term of four years. However, the terms of nine of the members elected at the first election shall expire at the end of two years; immediately after the first election the names of these nine members shall be chosen by lot by the Chairman of the Committee.

6. The election of the five additional members of the Committee shall be held in accordance with the provisions of paragraphs 2, 3 and 4 of this article, following the thirty-fifth ratification or accession. The terms of two of the additional members elected on this occasion shall expire at the end of two years, the names of these two members having been chosen by lot by the Chairman of the Committee.

7. For the filling of casual vacancies, the State Party whose expert has ceased to function as a member of the Committee shall appoint another expert from among its nationals, subject to the approval of the Committee.

8. The members of the Committee shall, with the approval of the General Assembly, receive emoluments from United Nations resources on such terms and conditions as the Assembly may decide, having regard to the importance of the Committee's responsibilities.

9. The Secretary-General of the United Nations shall provide the necessary staff and facilities for the effective performance of the functions of the Committee under the present Convention.

Article 18. 1. States Parties undertake to submit to the Secretary-General of the United Nations, for consideration by the Committee, a report on the legislative, judicial, administrative or other measures which they have adopted to give effect to the provisions of the present Convention and on the progress made in this respect:

(a) Within one year after the entry into force for the State concerned; and

(b) Thereafter at least every four years and further whenever the Committee so requests.

2. Reports may indicate factors and difficulties affecting the degree of fulfilment of obligations under the present Convention.

Article 19. 1. The Committee shall adopt its own rules of procedure.

2. The Committee shall elect its officers for a term of two years.

Article 20. 1. The Committee shall normally meet for a period of not more than two weeks annually in order to consider the reports submitted in accordance with article 18 of the present Convention.

2. The meetings of the Committee shall normally be held at United Nations Headquarters or at any other convenient place as determined by the Committee.

Article 21. 1. The Committee shall, through the Economic and Social Council, report annually to the General Assembly of the United Nations on its activities and may make suggestions and general recommendations based on the examination of reports and information received from the States Parties. Such suggestions and general recommendations shall be included in the report of the Committee together with comments, if any, from States Parties.

2. The Secretary-General shall transmit the reports of the Committee to the Commission on the Status of Women for its information.

Article 22. The specialized agencies shall be entitled to be represented at the consideration of the implementation of such provisions of the present Convention as fall within the scope of their activities. The Committee may invite the specialized agencies to submit reports on the implementation of the Convention in areas falling within the scope of their activities.

Part VI

Article 23. Nothing in this Convention shall affect any provisions that are more conducive to the achievement of equality between men and women which may be contained:

(a) In the legislation of a State Party; or

(b) In any other international convention, treaty or agreement in force for that State.

Article 24. States Parties undertake to adopt all necessary measures at the national level aimed at achieving the full realization of the rights recognized in the present Convention.

Article 25. 1. The present Convention shall be open for signature by all States.

2. The Secretary-General of the United Nations is designated as the depositary of the present Convention.

3. The present Convention is subject to ratification. Instruments of ratification shall be deposited with the Secretary-General of the United Nations.

4. The present Convention shall be open to accession by all States. Accession shall be effected by the deposit of an instrument of accession with the Secretary-General of the United Nations.

Article 26. 1. A request for the revision of the present Convention may be made at any time by any State Party by means of a notification in writing addressed to the Secretary-General of the United Nations.

2. The General Assembly of the United Nations shall decide upon the steps, if any, to be taken in respect of such a request.

Article 27. 1. The present Convention shall enter into force on the thirtieth day after the date of deposit with the Secretary-General of the United Nations of the twentieth instrument of ratification or accession.

2. For each State ratifying the present Convention or acceding to it after the deposit of the twentieth instrument of ratification or accession, the Convention shall enter into force on the thirtieth day after the date of the deposit of its own instrument of ratification or accession.

Article 28. 1. The Secretary-General of the United Nations shall receive and circulate to all States the text of reservations made by States at the time of ratification or accession.

2. A reservation incompatible with the object and purpose of the present Convention shall not be permitted.

3. Reservations may be withdrawn at any time by notification to this effect addressed to the Secretary-General of the United Nations, who shall then inform all States thereof. Such notification shall take effect on the date on which it is received.

Article 29. 1. Any dispute between two or more States Parties concerning the interpretation or application of the present Convention which is not settled by negotiation shall, at the request of one of them, be submitted to arbitration. If within six months from the date of the request for arbitration the parties are unable to agree on the organization of the arbitration, any one of those parties may refer the dispute to the International Court of Justice by request in conformity with the Statute of the Court.

2. Each State Party may at the time of signature or ratification of this Convention or accession thereto declare that it does not consider itself bound by paragraph 1 of this article. The other States Parties shall not be bound by that paragraph with respect to any State Party which has made such a reservation.

3. Any State Party which has made a reservation in accordance with paragraph 2 of this article may at any time withdraw that reservation by notification to the Secretary-General of the United Nations.

Article 30. The present Convention, the Arabic, Chinese, English, French, Russian and Spanish texts of which are equally authentic, shall be deposited with the Secretary-General of the United Nations.

IN WITNESS WHEREOF the undersigned, duly authorized, have signed the present Convention.

Document 70

Report of the World Conference of the United Nations Decade for Women: Equality, Development and Peace, held in Copenhagen from 14 to 30 July 1980; including the Agenda, Programme of Action for the Second Half of the United Nations Decade for Women and resolutions adopted by the Conference (extract)

A/CONF.94/35

...

Agenda

...

1. Opening of the Conference
2. Election of the President
3. Adoption of the rules of procedure
4. Adoption of the agenda
5. Election of officers other than the President
6. Other organizational matters
    (a) Allocation of items to the Main Committees and organization of work
    (b) Credentials of representatives of the Conference
        (i) Appointment of the members of the Credentials Committee
        (ii) Report of the Credentials Committee

7. Effects of apartheid on women in southern Africa
    (a) Review of the situation
    (b) Special measures for assistance to women in southern Africa

8. Review and evaluation of the progress made and obstacles encountered in attaining the objectives of the United Nations Decade for Women: Equality, Development and Peace, at the national, regional and international levels, from 1975 to 1980, in keeping with the World Plan of Action for the Implementation of the Objectives of the International Women's Year:
    (a) Review and evaluation of progress made and obstacles encountered at the national level in attaining the minimum objectives set forth in paragraph 46 of the World Plan of Action

(b) Review and evaluation of regional and global programmes of the United Nations system of organizations aimed at promoting the objectives of the Decade

9. Programme of Action for the second half of the United Nations Decade for Women: Equality, Development and Peace, 1981-1985, designed to implement the World Plan of Action

(a) National targets and strategies for women's integration and participation in economic and social development, with special emphasis on the subtheme "Employment, Health and Education"

   (i) Planning and monitoring

   (ii) National machineries

(b) Regional and international targets and strategies, taking into account the subtheme "Employment, Health and Education"

(c) The situation of women refugees the world over

10. Effects of Israeli occupation on Palestinian women inside and outside the occupied territories

(a) A review of the social and economic needs of the Palestinian women

(b) Special measures for assistance to Palestinian women inside and outside the occupied territories

11. Adoption of the report of the Conference

PART ONE: BACKGROUND AND FRAMEWORK

Introduction

A. *Legislative mandates*

1. The mandates for the Programme of Action for the Second Half of the United Nations Decade for Women: Equality, Development and Peace are as follows:

(a) General Assembly resolution 3520 (XXX) of 15 December 1975, in which the Assembly decided that in 1980, at the mid-point of the Decade, a world conference would be convened to review and evaluate progress made in implementing the recommendations of the World Conference of the International Women's Year, held in 1975 and to readjust programmes for the second half of the Decade in the light of new data and research;

(b) Economic and Social Council resolution 2062 (LXII) of 12 May 1977, in which the Council requested the Secretary-General to prepare for the consideration of the Commission on the Status of Women, at its twenty-eighth session, a report outlining a programme of concrete action for the second half of the United Nations Decade for Women: Equality, Development and Peace;

(c) General Assembly resolution 33/185 of 29 January 1979, in which the Assembly decided upon the subtheme, "Employment, Health and Education", for the World Conference and recommended that the Conference should place emphasis on elaborating action-oriented plans for integrating women into the developmental process, particularly by promoting economic activities and employment opportunities on an equal footing with men, through, *inter alia*, the provision of adequate health and educational facilities;

(d) General Assembly resolution 33/191 of 29 January 1979 by which it was decided that the World Conference of the United Nations Decade for Women: Equality, Development and Peace would be held in Copenhagen.

B. *Objectives of the United Nations Decade for Women: Equality, Development and Peace*

2. In 1975, International Women's Year, a World Conference was held in Mexico City which adopted the World Plan of Action for the United Nations Decade for Women: Equality, Development and Peace, 1976-1985, and the Declaration on the Equality of Women and their Contribution to Development and Peace. The principles and objectives proclaimed at the Mexico City Conference for the Decade for Women: Equality, Development and Peace are still relevant today and constitute the basis of action for the Decade. They were further reaffirmed by a number of United Nations regional, sectoral and international meetings as well as by the social and economic recommendations of the Conference of Non-Aligned and Developing Countries on the Role of Women in Development held in Baghdad in May 1979, which were endorsed by the sixth summit of Heads of State and Government of Non-Aligned Countries.

3. Equality is here interpreted as meaning not only legal equality, the elimination of *de jure* discrimination, but also equality of rights, responsibilities and opportunities for the participation of women in development, both as beneficiaries and as active agents. The issue of inequality as it affects the vast majority of women of the world is closely related to the problem of underdevelopment which exists mainly as a result of unjust international economic relations. The attainment of equality pre-supposes equality of access to resources and the power to participate equally and effectively in their allocation and in decision-making at various levels. Accordingly, it should be recognized that the attainment of equality by women long disadvantaged may demand compensatory activities to correct accumulated injustices. The joint responsibility of men and women for the wel-

fare of the family in general and the care of their children in particular should be reaffirmed.

4. Development is here interpreted to mean total development, including development in the political, economic, social, cultural and other dimensions of human life, as also the development of economic and other material resources and also the physical, moral, intellectual and cultural growth of the human person. The improvement of the status of women requires action at the national and local levels and within the family. It also requires a change in the attitudes and roles of both men and women. Women's development should not only be viewed as an issue in social development but should be seen as an essential component in every dimension of development. To improve the status of women and their role in the process of development, such development should be an integral part of the global project for the establishment of a New International Economic Order based on equity, sovereign equality, interdependence, common interest and cooperation among all States.

5. Without peace and stability there can be no development. Peace is thus a prerequisite to development. Moreover, peace will not be lasting without development and the elimination of inequalities and discrimination at all levels. Equality of participation in the development of friendly relations and cooperation among States will contribute to the strengthening of peace, to the development of women themselves and to equality of rights at all levels and in all spheres of life, as well as to the struggle to eliminate imperialism, colonialism, neo-colonialism, zionism, racism, racial discrimination, apartheid, hegemonism, and foreign occupation, domination and oppression as well as full respect for the dignity of the peoples and their right to self-determination and independence without foreign interference or intervention and to promote guarantees of fundamental freedoms and human rights.

C. *Nature and scope of the Programme of Action*

6. In compliance with the mandates given above, the present Programme of Action has been drawn up for the second half of the Decade, 1980-1985, to promote the attainment of the three objectives of equality, development and peace, with special emphasis on the sub-theme—namely, employment, health and education—as significant components of development, taking into account that human resources cannot achieve their full potential without integrated socio-economic development. The Programme aims at strengthening comprehensive and effective strategies to remove obstacles and constraints on women's full and equal participation in development, including actions to solve the problems of underdevelopment and of the socio-economic structure which places women in an inferior position and to increase their contribution to the strengthening of world peace.

7. The following Programme of Action, formulated at the mid-point of the Decade, recognizes that considerable efforts have been made by the majority of countries in furtherance of the objectives of the Decade, but that progress has been insufficient to bring about the desired quantitative or qualitative improvements in the status of women. On the assumption that the three main objectives of the Decade—Equality, Development and Peace—are closely interlinked with one another, the purpose of this Programme of Action is to refine and strengthen practical measures for advancing the status of women, and to ensure that women's concerns are taken into account in the formulation and implementation of the International Development Strategy for the Third United Nations Development Decade.

8. The present Programme focuses on ensuring women's increased participation in the realization of the objectives of the World Plan of Action. The recommendations seek to indicate the interrelated nature of actions that need to be taken simultaneously on several fronts such as those related to world economic issues for the International Development Strategies for the Third United Nations Development Decade and the implementation of the Programme of Action for the Establishment of the New International Economic Order thus elaborating the approach adopted in the World Plan of Action. In particular, the World Plan of Action gives high priority to improving the conditions of the most disadvantaged groups of women—especially the rural and urban poor and the vast group of women workers in the tertiary sector. This programme gives high priority to improving the conditions of the most disadvantaged groups of women, particularly those disadvantaged because of socio-economic and historic conditions, with emphasis on rural and urban poor and on the subtheme: employment, education and health. An attempt has also been made to recommend practical measures to be incorporated in all aspects of the development of society.

9. Although the World Plan of Action for the Implementation of the Objectives of the International Women's Year 1/ already contains a comprehensive list of measures necessary to achieve those objectives, it is evident, and has been further borne out by the review of progress made over the past five years, that they cannot be achieved in such a short span of time and that periodic reviews are needed to strengthen the strategies and objectives of the Plan in line with major world developments.

1/ See *Report of the World Conference on International Women's Year, Mexico City, 19 June-2 July 1975*, United Nations publication, Sales No. E.76.IV.1, document E/CONF.66/34, chap. II, sect. A.

Therefore, the possibility of a second decade could be envisaged for the period 1985-1995. The recommendation to hold another conference in 1985 has already been made by two of the regional preparatory meetings—those of the Economic Commission for Western Asia and the Economic and Social Commission for Asia and the Pacific.

I. Historical perspective

A. *The roots of inequality of women: the problems of development and equality of participation of women and men in development*

10. The causes of the inequality between women and men are directly linked with a complex historical process. The inequality also derives from political, economic, social and cultural factors. The form in which this inequality manifests itself is as varied as the economic, social and cultural conditions of the world community.

11. Throughout history and in many societies women have been sharing similar experiences. One of the basic factors causing the unequal share of women in development relates to the division of labour between the sexes. This division of labour has been justified on the basis of the childbearing function of women, which is inherent in womanhood. Consequently, the distribution of tasks and responsibilities of women and men in society has mainly restricted women to the domestic sphere and has unduly burdened them. As a result, women have often been regarded and treated as inferior and unequal in their activities outside the domestic sphere and have suffered violations of their human rights. They have been given only limited access to resources and participation in all spheres of life, notably in decision-making, and in many instances institutionalized inequality in the status of women and men has also resulted.

12. The inequality of women in most countries stems to a very large extent from mass poverty and general backwardness of the majority of the world's population caused by underdevelopment which is a product of imperialism, colonialism, neo-colonialism and also of unjust international economic relations. The unfavourable status of women is aggravated in many countries, developed and underdeveloped, by de facto discrimination on the grounds of sex. 2/

13. It can be argued that the predominant economic analyses of labour and capital insufficiently trace the linkages between production systems in world economics and women's work as producers and reproducers; nor is the subjection, exploitation, oppression and domination of women by men, sufficiently explained in history. Women are not simply discriminated against by the productive systems, but subject to the discrimination that arises by virtue of being the reproductive force.

14. While women's childbearing function and their traditional nurturing roles are respected, in many countries there has been little recognition of women's actual or potential contribution to economic activity. The role of women within the family, combined with a high level of unemployment and underemployment of the population in general, often results in priority being given to the employment of men in economic activities outside the family household.

15. These cumulative processes of discrimination within and outside the family characterize the dual oppression that women suffer on the basis of their sex and social class. Poverty and underdevelopment have sharpened and continue to sharpen these inequities.

16. The effects of these long-term cumulative processes of discrimination have been accentuated by underdevelopment and are strikingly apparent in the present world profile of women: while they represent 50 per cent of the world adult population and one third of the official labour force, they perform nearly two thirds of all working hours, receive only one tenth of the world income and own less than 1 per cent of world property.

B. *Review of progress achieved in the first half of the Decade: lessons for the future*

17. The review and appraisal of progress achieved during the past five years indicates that the integration of women into development has been formally accepted by most Governments as a desirable planning objective. Many countries have made significant efforts, undertaken a number of activities and measures and established institutional and administrative mechanisms to integrate women in development.

18. The accomplishments of the first half of the Decade include sensitizing planners and decision-makers to women's needs and problems, conducting research and building a database on women, and promoting legislation safeguarding women's rights. However, with the general exception of the countries with advanced social services, serious problems, such as inadequate allocation of financial resources, lack of skilled personnel, and so on, continue to exist in many countries. This constraint is to a considerable extent—especially in developing countries—due to the general economic problems, such as scarcity of resources and/or under-utilization of existing resources. In many cases it reflects the priority Governments accord to issues concerning women. Another major constraint facing such mechanisms is their limited mandates. Thus, several existing mechanisms do not have

2/ Which in a group of countries is called sexism.

strong executive and implementing authority. Similarly, the terms of reference given to such mechanisms tend to restrict them to welfare activities traditionally associated with women and thereby reinforcing stereotyping of women's roles and attitudinal prejudices. The sensitizing task of these special mechanisms has, as yet, insufficiently resulted in an actual integration into policy planning and implementation by Governments and international organizations of the question of sharing all responsibilities between the sexes.

19. The review of legislative enactments and provisions reveals that a significant number of Governments reported new constitutional and legislative provisions which guarantee or promote equal rights of women and men. However, legislative provisions are not always matched by adequate enforcement measures and machinery. In many countries specific measures have been taken to redress past discrimination and to promote equal opportunities for women, especially in the fields of education and employment.

20. In the developed market-economy countries significant progress has been made in establishing national machineries, while achievements in the subtheme areas of education, health and employment are impressive. In many countries, new legislation has ensured the legal rights of women in social, economic and political aspects of national life. The percentage of women in positions of policy formulation has increased significantly. Women have joined the labour force in increasing numbers, enrolments have achieved parity in secondary, university and graduate education in many nations, and expansion of primary health care has reached most rural areas of the various market-economy countries. Current studies on work of comparable value, occupational segregation and valuation of household work are positive signs of further progress in the second half of the Decade. Acknowledgement of the double burden has enabled women and men to move forward to challenge existing stereotypes and to develop social programmes aimed at effecting full equality of women and men.

21. In the developing countries, despite their resource constraints and the adverse effect of the world economic structure and the world economic situation, initiatives have been taken for integrating women into development, including the establishment of national machineries and legislative enactments and efforts to overcome prejudices against women. The economic contribution of rural women to agriculture and national development is increasingly being recognized in national and rural development plans and policies. Research and studies have been undertaken to identify the critical needs of women and to formulate and implement programmes and projects for them. In many developing countries

efforts have been made in the public sector to increase the participation of women and representation at the decision-making levels. There has been an increase in the enrolment of girls in educational institutions at different levels, an increase in the availability of health care to women and efforts have been made to improve the work conditions and the employment needs of women.

22. In the countries with centrally planned economies a further advancement of women took place in various fields. Women in those countries actively participated in social and economic development and in all other fields of public life of their countries, including the active struggle for peace, disarmament, détente and international cooperation. A high level of employment, health, education and political participation of women was achieved in countries with centrally planned economies, in which national mechanisms are already in existence with adequate financial allocations and sufficient skilled personnel.

23. Women in all countries love peace and women all over the world have conducted active struggles for peace, disarmament, détente and international cooperation against foreign aggression and all forms of foreign domination and hegemony. Women have played and can play an active role at the national and international level to strive for détente and to make it a continuing and universal process of an all-embracing scope so that the goals of the Decade might be achieved.

24. The review and appraisal of progress achieved during the past five years indicates that in many countries the situation of women in the so-called "backward" sectors has worsened. In particular, it has worsened with respect to the conditions of employment and education for women in the rural and the so-called marginal urban sectors. In many countries the actual number of female illiterates is increasing. In fact, illiteracy rates for the female population appear to have increased and are projected to increase in several countries. In terms of the percentage of enrolment that women constitute of the total enrolment, at the first, second and third levels of education, progress in the participation of women has been made in most countries; however, declines have been reported by several in female participation at the second level. It appears that, in many countries, only in the higher and middle socio-economic strata did women gain some significant increases in educational opportunities. However, this improvement has not been followed by a parallel increase in levels of employment, even in certain developed countries and in those developing countries with higher industrialization rates. In employment, there is evidence of increasing numbers of women being forced into unemployment or being transferred outside the formal sectors of the economy into the peripheral labour

market in the developed countries and into the informal sectors of subsistence agriculture, handicrafts, and so on. This move from the formal to the informal market is evidenced by estimates of the International Labour Organization and projections for overall activity rates in the economies of the developing countries.

25. In many instances, transfer of inappropriate technology has worsened the employment and health conditions of women; displacement of labour occurs, and foreign models of consumption accompany such transfer. In certain large industries, some of them operated by transnational corporations, new discriminatory labour practices have appeared in both rural and urban areas, while in the urban areas increases in the employment of women have been largely the result of an increase in the exploitation of cheap, semi-skilled labour of young and unmarried women, related to increases in the migration of young women to the cities.

26. In many countries, women have not been integrated into national development plans. Where special programmes have existed, they have failed for the most part in achieving significant results, owing to their narrow focus on stereotyped sex roles which have further increased segregation based on sex.

27. Finally, the current world economic crisis has contributed to the worsening of the situation of women in general. Women's employment in industries which have high levels of female labour has been negatively affected by protectionist measures. In developing countries the negative impact on women is even greater than in developed countries.

28. There have been some significant achievements in the implementation of a number of recommendations of the World Plan of Action both at the regional and at global levels in the first half of the Decade. Of particular significance was the establishment of the Voluntary Fund for the Decade for Women and the preparatory work leading to the establishment of the International Research and Training Institute for the Advancement of Women. A joint interagency programme for the advancement of women was prepared and regional programmes were implemented in accordance with the regional plans of action adopted in Mexico. Several United Nations organizations were involved in these activities, including the United Nations, regional commissions, UNICEF, UNDP, UNCTAD, UNIDO, UNFPA, ILO, FAO, UNESCO and WHO. It is apparent that such programmes can be strengthened and that greater efforts could be made to introduce a more multidisciplinary approach in these programmes. In a number of conferences held under the auspices of the United Nations system, linkages were established between women's status and the priority areas of concern, including population, food, water, primary health care, education, rural development and agrarian reform, employment, industrialization and overall development.

29. The review of implementation of the objectives of the second United Nations Development Decade as well as of the progress of negotiations on the establishment of the New International Economic Order shows that hopes and expectations in connection with the International Development Strategy and establishment of the New International Economic Order have not been fulfilled. Instead of a gradual resolution of the world economic situation and encouragement of accelerated economic development of developing countries, the crisis in the world economy has become more acute. This has affected developing countries in particular and, because of the real economic and social situation in these countries, it is women who are most adversely affected. The international development conditions have deteriorated and become an even more limiting factor for the development of developing countries, specially restricting the implementation of the objectives of the World Plan of Action.

30. The lessons for the future to be learnt from this review are many. First, it proves that any measures for women isolated from the major priorities, strategies and sectors of development cannot result in any substantial progress toward attaining the goals of the Decade. Second, legislative and developmental action, unless accompanied by positive and concerted action to change attitudes and prejudices, cannot be fully effective. Third, mere provision of equal rights, development services and opportunities will not, by themselves, help women to benefit from them without simultaneous special supportive measures, e.g. legal aid, earmarking of benefits, information and knowledge, institutional innovation etc.

31. The three main objectives of the United Nations Decade for Women—equality, development and peace—are closely interlinked with one another. Progress towards any one of these has a beneficial effect on the others. In turn, failure in one sphere has a negative impact on the others. Since the primary objective of development is to bring about a sustained improvement in the well-being of the individual and of society and to bestow benefits on all, development should be seen not only as a desirable goal in itself but also as a most important means of maintaining peace and of furthering equality of the sexes. However, the present world is by no means tranquil and there exist factors detrimental to peace. Women in some countries are still suffering from wars of aggression.

32. Thus, the universal strengthening of world peace and international security, struggle against foreign

interference, aggression and military occupation, respect for national independence and sovereignty, curbing of the arms race, the achievement of the goals of general and complete disarmament and a reduction of military budgets, the achievement of détente, the establishment of the New International Economic Order and increased cooperation among States, on the basis of equality, will advance the economic, social and cultural development of countries and the situation of women, while still recognizing their special vulnerability. Consequently, it is only under conditions of peace that it is possible to move forward to the full implementation of the other two objectives of the Decade.

33. In accordance with their obligations under the Charter to maintain peace and security and to achieve international cooperation in promoting and encouraging respect for human rights and fundamental freedoms, bearing in mind, in this respect, the right to live in peace, States should help women to participate in promoting international cooperation for the sake of the preparation of societies for a life in peace.

34. Similarly, a close relation exists between the world economic situation, development and the strengthening of international peace and security, disarmament and a relaxation of international tension. It is imperative that resources released as a result of disarmament be used for promoting the well-being of all nations and contribute to bridging the gap between developed and developing countries, thus increasing favourable conditions for improving the situation of all members of society. In this context particular attention should be give to the advancement of women and the protection of mother and child.

35. The lack of progress in the establishment of the New International Economic Order has had a direct effect on the socio-economic situation of women. Recent studies on the impact of international economic problems on the employment and working conditions of women show that in fact the adverse effects on the wage levels and job stability of women are more extensive than on those of men. For example, women are the first to lose their jobs on plantations that produce crops for export and in the textile, clothing and electronics industries, which are more sensitive to price fluctuations and to protectionist measures recently introduced by some developed countries.

36. The realization of all the aims mentioned above would provide new possibilities for a more intensive promotion of the status of women. An improvement in the status of women is of overall national importance, and responsibility for this rests upon the State and all sectors of society. Such an improvement can be realized only if it is carried out in accordance with the national

needs and conditions, as a sovereign right of each country, without any country imposing its own model.

37. In the traditional and agricultural sectors, the effects of such factors, when associated with rapid displacement and changes in women's basic tertiary activities and a lack of appropriate compensatory measures and especially with the lack of corresponding efforts for the integrated development, are even more detrimental. In other words, the lack of access to land, credit and financial and technological resources worsens the impact of rapid displacements in the work activities of women.

38. On the one hand, the recent expansion of capital- and technology-intensive and large-scale agricultural estates, often operated by transnational corporations, adversely affects women's work in basic tertiary activities, such as those related to small-scale urban, semi-rural and agricultural trade, which are crucial income-generating activities and are essential for community self-reliance. Indeed, in many cases this process has actually jeopardized food production and the distribution of food and basic subsistence goods. On the other hand, in the modern sectors of developing economies, although the expansion of industries operated by transnational corporations has in certain cases increased employment opportunities for women, it has nevertheless also brought new problems both for women and for overall development. Care should be taken so that the redeployment of industry in the developing countries is not used as a means of providing a cheap labour force, especially women, or that the redeployment of obsolete and "dirty" industries is not carried out in the developing countries. Industrialization should be carried out in accordance with the overall national aims, priorities and aspirations of the developing countries, as part of a process which will contribute to the transfer of technology to the developing countries. Women's right to participate in and benefit from the industrialization process on equal terms with men must be secured.

39. In fact, there has been some concern about future trends in export oriented industries and their impact on employment in developing countries. Such industries are said to be more sensitive to the needs of the international market than to those of the host countries. Although important for creating employment and providing foreign exchange earnings, in other respects their impact on the domestic economy is minimal, since virtually all their input is imported and all their output exported. The Governments of host countries seem to view such enterprises, for the most part, as short-run solutions to the problem of generating employment, but for development in the long term Governments prefer industries that will engage highly skilled workers. If such long-term

plans are actually realized, the employment of women in labour-intensive manufacturing might only be a temporary phase in the industrialization of developing countries.

40. As part of the industrialization and development process, activities of indigenous companies and corporations also have an impact on women and their employment options. Although, in some cases, cottage industries and other forms of small industry are replaced or absorbed by larger entities, these corporations often have a multiplier effect on female employment. Under some circumstances the employment options of women are narrowed by corporate development, while in other instances women thus displaced are eventually absorbed into the newly established larger industries.

41. The processes described above demonstrate that, while traditions, customs and practices greatly hinder the advancement of women, some serious constraints to the economic participation of women in national development are international in nature and derive from the pattern of relationships between developing and developed countries.

42. In many countries, at the national level, a comparison of the performances of men and women in every sector of economic and social development shows that the wide gap between the economic opportunities available to men and those open to women has not been reduced in proportion to the increases achieved in overall economic growth, regardless of the levels of development, which vary from country to country, the intensity of the world economic crisis increasingly affecting working people in general. Even in countries where significant increases in general wage employment were obtained, women have failed to share equally in this increase, while men, due to greater job security, have developed opportunities for sustained employment in the labour force, learned skills and increased their relative wages. Women constitute a substantial and growing proportion of the unemployed sector of the population, especially in the area of intermediary services and activities of the so-called tertiary and informal sectors. In those sectors women workers, like men workers, are often underpaid and receive for the most part extremely low wages; they are also subjected to a high degree of job instability and have, in most countries, no legislative protection, and existing labour organizations do not always pay sufficient attention to their needs and demands. Moreover, in most countries, new incentives designed to improve their commitment to the labour force, such as occupational mobility, education or training and infrastructure assistance in the areas of credit and finance, have been inadequate.

II. Conceptual framework

A. *The need to include new data and strategies concerning the participation of women in development in the Third United Nations Development Decade*

43. The sharpening of the world economic crisis in many countries during the latter half of the Second United Nations Development Decade requires an in-depth reassessment of established strategies and imposes the need for undertaking additional and comprehensive measures, at national and international levels, with a view to the strategy for the Third United Nations Development Decade. The shortfalls of the Second United Nations Development Decade have been linked to major problems related to external debts, insufficient increases in food production (a factor that has also affected industrialization) and inadequate levels and patterns of industrialization. Those failures were said to be further intensified by the low capacity of many countries, particularly developing countries, for absorbing their constantly increasing unemployment. Moreover, the major failures in productivity have been linked not only to key international factors but also to inadequate and/or non-existent national policies aimed at maximizing the training and utilization of human resources. In this respect, the need for an in-depth reassessment of strategies concerning the mobilization of women (approximately 50 per cent of the adult world population) has been consistently emphasized in recent studies and policy-oriented analyses, particularly at the regional and local levels. The discussion of women's issues at a recent conference on an area of priority in the new international economic order—namely, the World Conference on Agrarian Reform and Rural Development—has forged a new consensus and action proposals in this area.

44. These new developments are of particular relevance in overcoming the alarming shortfalls in the agricultural sector, where women constitute a large proportion of labour force. In order to promote integrated rural development, to improve productivity in the food and other agricultural commodity sectors, the wages, conditions of employment and training of women, as well as their access to credit, land and infrastructural technology in rural areas, should be significantly improved; technologies adapted to the needs of rural areas should be developed and made accessible to women. Conditions where internal migration is the only possibility for employment could be eliminated by generating productive employment and development through more uniform geographical distribution of economic projects and social services. To this end, such adverse effects of technology transfer to rural women as may exist and such

effects of migration as are adverse to women should be diminished.

45. The International Development Strategy for the Third United Nations Development Decade should formulate goals, objectives and policy measures which would contribute to the solution of international economic problems and sustained global economic development, including the accelerated development of developing countries and the reduction of the existing gap between developing and developed countries. It is therefore necessary to expedite the establishment of the New International Economic Order. This goal cannot be achieved unless the inequality between men and women is eliminated. In the formulation and review of strategy for the Third United Nations Development Decade, full consideration should be given to the conceptualization and review presented in the present Programme of Action as well as in the background documents before the World Conference. Furthermore, this new strategy should also include ways and means of developing new data that can more adequately measure the participation of women in the development process in every sector and at every level in order to provide a systematic and effective basis for the establishment of new national, regional and international policies to maximize and evaluate the utilization of the resources of women and the involvement of women as equal participants in social life and economic development—this being a pre-condition for the successful development of each and every country.

B. *The interrelationship of the objectives of the United Nations Decade for Women and the subtheme of the World Conference: "Employment, Health and Education"*

46. The experience of the Decade has clearly revealed that the objectives of equality and peace cannot be realized without an unequivocal commitment at national, regional and global levels to women's integration in all aspects of development. The objective of development, which incorporates the principle of socio-economic and political equality, is closely related to stability and peace, which is more than an absence of violence within or between countries. In selecting the subtheme of the World Conference: employment, health and education, it was recognized that these interrelated aspects of development are of crucial concern to the advancement of women. The principles of the right of women to work, to receive equal pay for work of equal value, to be provided with equal opportunities for training and education were clearly stated in the World Plan of Action. It was also stressed that the full participation of women in development required that they should be given adequate and equitable access to health, nutrition and other social services including family planning and child care facilities. In all countries there is need for continuing attention to the implementation of these principles. For the remainder of the Decade, they should be given a high priority in Governments' planning and programmes. The level of development depends upon international conditions and national efforts towards integrated development particularly in the fields of employment, health and education, these being fields of exceptional significance for the underdeveloped sectors, of which women constitute the major segment. In fact, the sectors of employment, health and education, especially for women workers in the agricultural and industrial sectors of the economy, offer a stark index of the levels and quality of development in any given country. As reproducers of the labour force, women's socio-economic and health conditions are crucial determinants of the prospects for development. Their employment and educational opportunities not only reflect the extent to which a given society offers women the possibility to develop their full potential and eliminates inequalities but also the extent to which countries are maximizing their endogenous technical and economic resources, especially in times of acute economic crisis which threaten world stability. The strengthening of regional commissions by adequate institutional arrangements which would also ensure intersectoral programming and coordination of activities for women is essential. The improvement of linkages among the organizations of the United Nations system with a view to coordinating implementation where there are separate programmes is also essential.

PART TWO: THE PROGRAMME OF ACTION AT THE NATIONAL LEVEL

III. **National targets and strategies for the full participation of women in economic and social development**

A. *National strategies for accelerating the full participation of women in economic and social development*

47. The improvement of the status of women requires action at the national, local and family levels. It also requires a change of men's and women's attitudes towards their roles and responsibilities in society. The joint responsibility of men and women for the welfare of the family in general and the care of their children in particular should be reaffirmed.

48. Governments should explicitly state their firm commitment to accord high priority to legislative and other measures for accelerating the equal and full participation of women in economic and social development

with a view to eliminating the existing inequalities between men and women in all sectors.

49. National strategies should as a matter of urgency integrate women into their efforts towards the New International Economic Order and a new international development strategy for the Third United Nations Development Decade by:

(a) Studying and identifying new areas for national projects that would accelerate socio-economic growth and at the same time enhance the socio-economic participation of women by fostering economic and technical cooperation among countries;

(b) Providing advisory services for accelerating national self-reliance in cooperation with United Nations organizations; also ensuring that women assist in determining that technology transfer has a positive impact on the socio-economic situation and health of women, as well as on their working conditions;

(c) Providing women in the most disadvantaged sectors of the population with the ways and means of increasing their access to infrastructure, basic services and appropriate technology in order to alleviate the heavy workload imposed by the basic requirements and demands of their families and communities, women should also be provided with opportunities to gain new skills and with job opportunities in the construction and maintenance of the above-mentioned services, as well as in other sectors;

(d) Adopting measures to make equal opportunities for development and services available to women in rural areas and to women in urban areas by reversing processes of unequal economic growth, implementing special investment and incentive programmes in disadvantaged sectors, controlling mechanisms for the transfer of resources from one sector to another and, where possible, preventing the rural sector from being impoverished to the advantage of the urban sector.

50. Governments should, where appropriate, design certain special transitional strategies and establish compensatory mechanisms aimed at achieving equality of opportunity in education, employment and health as a means of overcoming existing inequalities in national administration, the educational system, employment, health services and the like, it being clearly understood that the special strategies are designed to correct imbalances and discrimination and will be phased out when such imbalances and discrimination no longer exist.

1. *National development plans and policies*

51. Governments should undertake the following:

(a) The establishment of qualitative and quantitative targets for the second half of the United Nations Decade for Women: Equality, Development and Peace;

projections for the planning cycles of 1985-1995 should be made where appropriate, and reviews conducted in 1985 and 1990. These should especially seek to remove the gap between the attainments of men and women, between rural and urban women and between all women in underprivileged population groups, and other women in all sectors and particularly in the fields of employment, health and education;

(b) Systematic and sustained linking of efforts to integrate women into national development planning and policies, particularly in the sectors of employment, education and health, and in the allocation of adequate material, technical and personnel resources within each sector of national development;

(c) The establishment of appropriate arrangements for monitoring and evaluating the extent to which women participate in and benefit from both general and sectoral development programmes. Reliable data should be collected and technical services provided for periodic reviews of the progress made at all levels of society in every major sector of the national development programmes; targets should be established along with the allocation of physical and financial resources in every development programme, in order to ensure a more just distribution of benefits to women;

(d) The development and improvement of infrastructural technology, basic services and incentives, particularly for the rural sectors of the population and the urban poor; women should be given equal rights of land ownership, equal access to credit and financing, basic sanitation, safe water and energy resources, and the skills to maintain and build community self-reliance. Special attention and additional services should be given to women in the area of health;

(e) Initiate where necessary, as a result of socio-economic conditions, processes of integral agrarian reform, which will subsequently make it possible to implement measures for promoting the development of women in rural areas:

(i) To mobilize women, particularly poor women, in rural and urban areas;

(ii) To organize learning and productive activity and access to needed developmental services and inputs (e.g., education, primary health and child care, skill development, credit and marketing facilities);

(iii) To organize working women, including those in the unorganized sectors, for protection against exploitation, for socio-occupational mobility through education and training and necessary supportive services for children;

(f) Systematic efforts to promote and assist grass-roots level organizations as one of the instruments of development;

(g) The establishment of incentives and concrete programmes for increasing the participation of women in decision-making processes at all levels and in all spheres of national development;

(h) Wherever possible timetables should be established for the achievement of particular objectives;

(i) Where appropriate, initiate consultations between government and employer and employee organizations as well as community groups to examine and improve conditions for women workers.

2. National machinery

52. Where it does not exist, national machinery preferably at the highest level of government, where appropriate, should be established. By national machinery should be understood not only the establishment of central institutions at the national level but furthermore, where appropriate, the establishment of a comprehensive network of extensions in the form of commissions, offices or posts at different levels, including the local administrative level because of its better capacity for dealing with specific local situations, as well as working units in the relevant branches of administration, in order to ensure the effective implementation of action programmes ensuring the equality of men and women with a view to:

(a) Upgrading its capacity and role in national development plans;

(b) Achieving a more central location within the existing institutional arrangements for the formulation and planning of and strict compliance with policies and programmes and for monitoring their implementation and evaluation;

(c) Conceptualizing women's problems in an integrated manner within each sector of development and at the same time developing effective methodologies, policies and mechanisms for affirmative action, where appropriate, to ensure an integrated approach;

(d) Ensuring the full participation of women in measures taken by government or other agencies.

53. Effective institutional links between national machinery and national planning units as well as national women's organizations, should be established with a view to:

(a) Increasing their decision-making powers;

(b) Increasing their technical, financial and personnel resources;

(c) Advising on new approaches to accelerate the full participation of women in every sector of the development process, according to national priorities;

(d) Drawing up national programmes for women

in the priority areas of employment, health and education so as to make possible their full participation at the national level. These should also aim at intensifying overall efforts to promote technical cooperation among countries and development in the areas of science and technology, water and energy resources among others, in line with the strategy for the Third United Nations Development Decade and the programme of action for the New International Economic Order.

54. Women should be represented on the basis of equality in all bodies and institutions dealing with development so as to be able to influence national policies at their inception—all this with a view to advancing the status of women and their participation in development.

55. The national machinery should increase the participation of grass-roots organizations, such as women's and youth associations, rural workers' organizations, community organizations, religious groups, neighbourhood associations, as well as trade unions, both in decision-making and in the implementation of projects and in this regard should serve as a liaison unit between appropriate government agencies and grass-roots organizations.

56. The national machinery should implement effective programmes aimed at ensuring that women participate in and benefit from the implementation, at the national, regional and international levels, of the relevant recommendations of such major conferences as the World Employment Conference, the World Conference on Agrarian Reform and Rural Development, 3/ the United Nations Conference on Science and Technology for Development, 4/ and the International Conference on Primary Health Care. 5/

57. The national machinery should also provide appropriate channels of communication between women's organizations and other organizations, in order to:

(a) Help women's groups to obtain financial and technical assistance from international and bilateral funding sources;

(b) Provide reliable data on the socio-economic and political participation of women to both governmental and non-governmental organizations, including those that act as formal and non-formal educational agencies, with a view to sensitizing society to the importance of the

3/ See Report of the World Conference on Agrarian Reform and Rural Development (WCAARD/REP), transmitted to the General Assembly by a note by the Secretary-General (A/34/485).

4/ Report of the United Nations Conference on Science and Technology for Development, Vienna, 20-31 August 1979 (United Nations publication, Sales No. E.79.I.21).

5/ Report of the International Conference on Primary Health Care, Alma-Ata, 6-12 September 1978 (UNIDO/IOD.255).

contribution to be made by women to development and informing the public of the obstacles to equality of opportunity.

58. To ensure that the national machinery serves its purpose, it is advisable to carry out studies and interdisciplinary research on the actual status of women, drawing on the experience already acquired in some countries with women's studies programmes.

3. *Legislative measures*

59. All remaining discriminatory legislative provisions in the social, economic and political spheres and in penal and civil codes should be examined with a view to repealing all laws and regulations discriminating against women with regard to rights concerning nationality, inheritance, the ownership and control of property, the freedom of movement of married women, the custody of children and the like, or which inhibit their effective participation in or planning, implementation and evaluation of economic transactions.

60. Governments should develop programmes to inform women of their legal rights and should point out ways in which women can use these rights. Where appropriate, Governments should establish commissions to assess women's legal rights and the establishment of priorities for legislative measures and to identify, specify and classify the necessary legislative measures that have not yet been enacted.

61. In countries where large sections of the population are governed by customary law, Governments should carry out investigations into the degree of protection or oppression and amount of discrimination experienced by women under customary law, in order to deal with or reject such practices by statutory legislation at an appropriate time.

62. Governments should implement the provisions of the Convention on the Elimination of All Forms of Discrimination against Women.

63. Procedures should be provided—or, where they already exist, strengthened—for effectively implementing social legislation, especially that affecting parents.

64. The protection of the social function of parenthood and of maternity should be guaranteed in legislation. Both in the public and in the private sector, the definition of maternity leave should be understood to be the period which is required by expectant mothers for the protection of their health before childbirth and by mothers for the recovery of their health after childbirth. Recognizing that the raising of children is a joint responsibility of parents and the community at large, efforts should be made to provide for parental leave, available to either parent.

65. Legislation should also be enacted and implemented in order to prevent domestic and sexual violence against women. All appropriate measures, including legislative ones, should be taken to allow victims to be fairly treated in all criminal procedures.

66. Educational and informational programmes on the socio-economic implications of laws should be launched among various professional groups, especially the legal and judicial professions, in order to prevent, where possible, the law from being applied inequitably.

67. Programmes of counselling and legal aid should be developed and implemented to enable women, especially those in the disadvantaged sectors, to have effective protection through legislation. Broad programmes to publicize legislation should also be implemented to make women and, in particular, those in the poorest sectors aware of their rights and obligations and of the institutional guarantees therefor.

68. The necessary steps should be taken to ratify or accede to all international instruments of the United Nations and its specialized agencies that deal with women's rights, in particular the Convention on the Elimination of All Forms of Discrimination Against Women. Those affecting the poor, such as those concerning the rights of rural and agricultural women workers, are particularly important.

4. *Participation in the political and other decision-making processes, and participation in efforts to promote international cooperation and strengthen peace*

Participation in the political and other decision-making processes

69. Every effort should be made to enact, before the end of the Decade, legislation guaranteeing women the right to vote, to be eligible for election or appointment to public office and to exercise public functions on equal terms with men, wherever such legislation does not already exist. In particular, political parties should be encouraged to nominate women candidates to positions that give them the possibility equally with men to be elected.

70. Governments and the organizations concerned should foster knowledge of civil and political rights, promote and encourage political organizations which carry out programmes involving the participation of women and implement broad programmes for the training of political officials.

71. Governments and political parties should, where appropriate, establish goals, strategies and timetables and undertake special activities for increasing, by certain percentages, the number of women in elective and appointive public offices and public functions at all

levels, in order that women should be equitably represented.

72. Special governmental instructions should be issued for achieving equitable representation of women in the different branches of Government and in departments at the national, state and local levels. Special activities should be undertaken to increase the recruitment, nomination and promotion of women, especially to decision-making and policy-making positions, by publicizing posts more widely, increasing upward mobility and so on, until equitable representation of women is achieved. Reports should be compiled periodically on the numbers of women in public service and the levels of responsibility in their areas of work.

73. Women should be equitably represented at all levels, especially the senior levels, in delegations to international bodies, conferences and committees dealing with political, economic and legal questions, disarmament and other similar issues. Governments should encourage and support increased employment of women at all levels, technical and professional, in the Secretariat of the United Nations and its subsidiary organs and specialized agencies.

74. Where special qualifications for holding public office are required, they should apply to both sexes equally and should relate only to the expertise necessary for performing the specific functions of the office.

75. Special attention should be given to ensuring that formal or informal practices which result in *de facto* discrimination against women in the selection of candidates for political office or in their exclusion from formal decision-making, particularly in bodies such as public councils, boards or informal committees, should be eliminated.

Participation of women in efforts to promote international cooperation and strengthen peace

76. Women of the entire world should participate in the broadest way in the struggle to strengthen international peace and security, to broaden international cooperation and develop friendly relations among nations, to achieve détente in international relations and disarmament, to establish a new economic order in international relations, to promote guarantees of fundamental freedoms and human rights, and in the struggle against colonialism, neo-colonialism, racism, apartheid, foreign domination, foreign oppression, foreign occupation. High priority should be given to providing training and educational opportunities at all levels. These might include university or college courses, lectures on international affairs, panel discussions, conferences, seminars and other educational activities.

77. Solidarity campaigns with women struggling against colonialism, nco-colonialism, racism, racial discrimination and apartheid and for national independence and liberation should be intensified; such women should receive all possible assistance, including support from agencies of the United Nations system as well as other organizations.

78. The efforts of intergovernmental and non-governmental organizations to strengthen international peace and security should be intensified in every way. The active participation of women in the activities of such organizations should be supported. Exchanges between the national organizations of different countries in favour of international cooperation and the strengthening of peace should be promoted.

79. Intergovernmental and non-governmental organizations should examine more comprehensively the consequences of disarmament for social and economic development in general and for improving the status of women in particular. The results of such studies should be made available to as many women and men as possible and must be given practical effect.

80. In view of the importance of eliminating international inequities, intergovernmental and non-governmental organizations should continue to study the impact of the activities of transnational corporations on the status of women and to make use of the results of such studies in practical programmes.

81. Governments should also be made aware of the results of such studies so that they realize and prevent the negative effects on the status of women which are caused by the activities of transnational corporations, as is the case in South Africa where transnational corporations sustain the system of apartheid by their investments.

82. Support should be provided by all women of the world in proclaiming solidarity with the support for the Palestinian women and people in their struggle for their fundamental rights. Moral and material assistance should be extended by the United Nations system to help Palestinian women. Specific programmes and projects should be carried out to fulfil that aim.

5. *Measures relating to education and the dissemination of information*

83. Independent organizations, including women's organizations at the national, regional and international levels, should study the ways in which the mass communications media, including the news media and advertising, treat the status of women and women's issues. Evidence that women are being treated in a sexist or demeaning way should be brought to the attention of the media concerned for correction.

84. Every effort should be made to encourage the fullest and most active participation of women at all levels

of policy-making and decision-making within media organizations. Governments should use the opportunities they have by way of appointments to regulatory bodies and broadcasting networks to ensure that women are equally represented in senior decision-making.

85. Special efforts, for example, training programmes to sensitize media personnel at all levels, should be made to ensure that women are portrayed as persons in their own right and that the portrayal of women and women's issues reflects women's rights, needs and interests.

86. Educational programmes and campaigns using the media should be instituted in order to eliminate prejudices and traditional attitudes that limit the full participation of women in society. Such campaigns should also inform women and men of their rights and ways of exercising them. Women's organizations and other non-governmental organizations, political parties and trade unions should play an active role in the process of educating women politically in order to increase their capacities for participation in decision-making bodies. Special attention should be given to the role the media can play in reaching the migrant women. Women should also have access to training in the use of various forms of the media, in order to be able to present to as wide a public as possible their own perceptions of their needs, ideas and aspirations.

87. Governments should encourage the mass media to support the increased involvement of women in efforts to strengthen international cooperation and peace and to broadcast programmes that make women more aware of the activities and positions of their Governments in vital questions of international affairs, thus enabling them to fulfil their roles in strengthening international peace and security and in opposing colonialism, racism, racial discrimination, foreign aggression and occupation and all forms of foreign domination.

88. Special campaigns should be undertaken to encourage the increased participation of women and girls in rural community and youth development programmes and in political activities.

89. The mass media should promote the Programme of Action for the Second Half of the United Nations Decade for Women: Equality, Development and Peace, as well as other international, regional and national programmes for women, so that the public is made aware of such programmes and thus participate to a greater extent in their implementation.

90. Bearing in mind the fact that one of the impediments to promoting the status of women lies in social attitudes and the evaluation of women in society, the mass media offer great possibilities as one means of promoting social change. They can help remove prejudices and stereotypes, accelerate the acceptance of the new role of women in society and promote their role as equal partners in the process of development.

91. In all fields of activity, the mass media should become one of the basic means in society of overcoming the contradiction in, on the one hand, the presentation of women as passive, inferior beings having no social significance and, on the other hand, an accurate picture of their increasing role and contribution to society at large. The mass media should also recognize that both parents have equal duties and responsibilities for the training and education of children and for household duties. Governments, as communicators, in preparing communications to or about their countries should ensure that the contents reflect government commitment to status of women issues and concerns.

6. Improvement of the database

92. All data-collecting agencies should give a sex and age breakdown of any information they gather, wherever relevant.

93. Some of the concepts and analytical tools of research, particularly those relating to economic processes—evaluation, labour, work, employment, social productivity, household, family and the like—should be re-examined so as to improve tools for the analysis and conceptualization of the economic and social roles of women within the home and outside.

94. Priority should be given to research concerning those groups of women that have been neglected in social research—namely, rural workers in agriculture and allied activities and working women in the underprivileged sectors of society. These are women who, far from being the dependants they have generally been assumed to be, have always had to perform multiple roles in order to ensure the survival of their families. For better evaluation of development programmes, access to and utilization of data need to be ensured.

95. National and regional indicators should be developed and improved for determining the degree to which women have actually been participating in development, as a means of measuring their actual contribution to the development process. A set of statistical indicators should be established by which progress towards equality between the sexes can be monitored. In establishing such a set of indicators, Government's will need to take into account the current state of their country's statistical development as well as their individual policy priorities. A system should be devised for placing a monetary value on unpaid work, in order to facilitate its reflection in the gross national product.

96. The level of economic growth in general and the sectoral structure of that growth should be established

so as to determine employment openings. Data on the composition of populations (e.g., age structure and the relation between rural and other sectors of a population) should be collected so that the need for employment openings, health services and education can be identified.

97. Current statistical operations and practices should be reviewed to ensure that they are free from sex-based stereotypes.

98. Where appropriate, permanent advisory committees to national statistical authorities should be established to improve the quantity and relevance of data pertaining to the situation of women, their participation in development and equality between the sexes. The work of such advisory committees may be supplemented from time to time by the organization of larger meetings of users and producers of statistics to address specific issues of mutual concern.

99. Research and testing of new or revised concepts and classifications should be designed or expanded to improve the usefulness and relevance of the statistics needed to describe the role and status of women, their participation in the development process and equality between the sexes. Such research and testing, whether carried out by the national statistical services or by university or other research groups, would need to involve both the users and producers of such statistics and would need to encompass both methods and procedures for data collection and those for the analysis and presentation of data.

7. Role of non-governmental organizations

100. There should be mutual cooperation between Governments and non-governmental organizations, women's and youth groups, employers and workers unions, voluntary agencies, community organizations, including religious groups, the mass communication media, political parties and the like, in implementing the Programme of Action for the Second Half of the Decade.

101. Governments should take account of the activities of non-governmental organizations and should support, where appropriate, the efforts of all relevant organizations, institutions and other associations concerned with the welfare and status of women.

102. Governments should recognize the importance of the role of women's organizations, encourage and assist them and provide them with financial and other assistance, particularly at the grass-roots level, to enable them to perform their functions which include activities such as:

(a) The mass mobilization of women and, in particular, poor women in rural and urban areas;

(b) The provision of all development services and facilities (education, health and child care, expansion of credit and marketing capabilities and facilities, information on social, political and economic rights, etc.);

(c) The establishment of organizations for women workers in non-trade-union occupations both in rural and urban areas as a means of protecting them against exploitation and providing the necessary auxiliary child care services.

103. With regard to the follow-up of the World Conference of the United Nations Decade for Women, Governments should:

(a) Make possible the publication and dissemination of the results of the World Conference and of the Forum of non-governmental organizations;

(b) Enable non-governmental groups to become involved in the realization of the Programme of Action for the Second Half of the Decade;

(c) Consider the role and resources of non-governmental groups in the implementation of international, regional and national plans for the improvement of the situation of women;

(d) Consider as a plan for the future, and establish strategies for their implementation, the input and particular recommendations of non-governmental groups;

(e) Give financial resources to non-governmental groups so that these groups can make a contribution towards the implementation of the Programme of Action.

104. Non-governmental organizations should support governmental efforts by:

(a) Investigating the problems of different groups of women;

(b) Assisting and promoting organizations of women at the grass-roots level, especially those established among poor and uneducated women to promote learning and productive and other developmental activities;

(c) Providing liaison services for such groups with educational and other development agencies;

(d) Promoting attitudinal change among men and women;

(e) Promoting solidarity among women's groups;

(f) Influencing and informing the mass media and political groups;

(g) Developing new analytical methodology;

(h) Launching programmes and activities to serve, in particular, rural women;

(i) Promoting public acceptance of family planning, including sex education;

(j) Informing their members of government policies and development plans as well as international standards and programmes for improving the situation of women.

Grass-roots organizations

105. In accordance with the regional plans of action and with a view to implementing the World Plan of Action, Governments and agencies on other levels should, where appropriate, promote the establishment of grass-roots organizations of women as an integral part of their overall development efforts and should provide adequate financial and personnel resources for such efforts to succeed. Such grass-roots organizations of women will serve as forums for women to develop self-reliance and will eventually enable women to obtain real access to resources and power and to shoulder greater socio-economic and political responsibilities within their communities and their societies.

B. *Objectives and priority areas for action taken in connection with the subtheme of the World Conference, "Employment, health and education"*

Introduction

106. The objectives and priority areas of action for improving the employment, health and education status of women in every country should be promoted within the overall context of national planning and development for the whole population. Improvement in the condition of women in these areas is also instrumental in the development of the country. Furthermore, the improvements in any one of these sectors also affect the situation in other sectors. Recognition of this interrelated nature of the programmes is essential if their effectiveness is to be maximized. Socio-cultural values should not suffer as a result of physical economic development. Therefore, integrated and innovative programmes and new methodologies should be explored.

107. The programme should also invariably include measures for building the capacities of women themselves by their training and information programmes and by their organizing themselves, with the assistance of Government and other socio-political forces, to make full use of new opportunities, policies and programmes.

108. Labour policies and action taken in favour of women workers should form part of overall employment policies and measures for the entire working population, men and women alike, with a view to overcoming the problems that affect women only and preventing measures of protection which discriminate against them. Employment policies for underprivileged population groups, such as urban fringe groups, the low-income sector and indigenous population groups, should include references to the specific situation of women workers.

1. *Employment*

Objectives

109. To promote full and equal opportunities and treatment for women in employment, bearing in mind that this requires that both women and men have the possibility to combine paid work with household responsibilities and the caring for children. To ensure that women and men receive equal remuneration for work of equal value and equal educational and training opportunities in both rural and urban areas, so that women may obtain more highly skilled employment and become integrated into the development of their countries with a view to more rapid and balanced growth in agriculture, industry and other non-traditional sectors, with the aim of ensuring better overall working conditions for women, achieving more rapid and balanced growth in both agriculture and industry and integrating women in development.

110. To increase and promote employment opportunities for women as part of national efforts to bring about a more just international economic order, with a view to achieving national self-reliance, increasing economic and technical cooperation among developing countries and the full utilization of the labour force for their own benefit and promoting the socio-economic development of their own countries.

111. To improve the working conditions and occupational mobility of women workers in the lower and middle levels of the sectors in which the majority of women work.

112. To ensure equal rights and opportunities for the gainful employment of rural women both in agricultural and non-agricultural jobs under proper working conditions, improve the capabilities and productivity of rural women workers, increase food production, diminish migration in countries where this is necessary and whose population policies contain explicit provisions to this effect, promote rural development and strengthening of self-reliance programmes; to extend labour and social security legislation to women working in agriculture.

113. To promote effective policies for increasing employment opportunities, to improve existing ones and enable women to obtain jobs involving more skills and responsibility, particularly at the managerial level, in all sectors of the economy, to promote occupational mobility for women, in both rural and urban areas, by encouraging the provision of maternity protection, child-care facilities, technical training and health protection, with a view to achieving the industrialization targets for the third United Nations Development Decade.

114. To facilitate paid employment of women by

encouraging increased involvement of males in sharing domestic and child care responsibilities.

115. To take measures for the implementation of legislation relating to working conditions for women.

116. To formulate and implement national and local training and employment programmes and projects which take particular account of the need to give women access to gainful economic activity and to improve their employment situation in priority areas for the economic and social development of their countries.

117. To adopt measures for ensuring that women's entry into certain sectors of the labour market does not result in lowering the working conditions, remuneration and status of those sectors.

118. To promote technology that will improve the labour productivity of women while decreasing their work time and to guarantee that women workers are the ones who benefit from such an improvement.

119. To review implicit and explicit job evaluation criteria with a view to overcoming difficulties and obstacles to the job advancement and careers of women.

120. To ensure that, in all sectors, the economic returns from women's work accrue directly to them.

Priority areas for action

121. Special action should be taken to institute programmes which would inform women workers of their rights under legislation and other remedial measures. The importance of freedom of association and the protection of the right to organize should be emphasized, this being particularly relevant to the position of women in employment. Special measures should be taken to ratify and implement in national legislation the relevant conventions and recommendations of the International Labour Organization concerning the rights of women as regards access to equal employment opportunities, equal pay for work of equal value, working conditions, job security and maternity protection.

122. Information programming should be instituted aimed at making women, especially those in the rural areas and in socio-economically disadvantaged groups, aware of employment opportunities and of the opportunities for education, training and skill acquisition.

123. Measure should be taken to ensure that development agencies in different sectors of national planning include larger numbers of women in their staff as a matter of policy and, as part of that policy, allocate resources to programmes for women's employment and training, the provision of supporting services and other essential inputs.

124. Legislative and/or other measures should be adopted and implemented which guarantee women protection against any sexually-oriented practice that endangers a woman's access to or maintenance of employment, that undermines her job performance and thus threatens her economic livelihood.

125. Legislation and/or other measures should be adopted and implemented to secure for men and women the same right to work and to unemployment benefits, as well as to prohibit, through *inter alia* the imposition of sanctions, dismissal on the grounds of pregnancy or of maternity leave and discrimination in dismissals on the basis of marital status. Legislative and other measures should be adopted and implemented to facilitate the return to the labour market of women who have left it for family reasons and to guarantee the right of women to return to work after maternity leave.

126. Measures should be taken to ensure on a basis of equality of men and women the right to protection of health and to safety in working conditions, including the safeguarding of the function of reproduction. Special protection should be provided to women during pregnancy in types of work proved to be harmful to them.

127. Measures should be taken to ensure that migrant workers enjoy equal treatment and access to vocational training as nationals of the host country, and to improve the status of women who, in the process of migration, accompany the migrant workers as members of their family.

128. Ways should be investigated in which the unpaid work in the household and in agricultural tasks which women and men perform can be recognized and reflected in official statistical data collections.

129. Urgently needed infrastructure services should be developed and provided, such as adequate housing, safe water, energy and child care centres, for families and poor communities in rural areas and urban slums, in order to alleviate the workload traditionally imposed on women in their performance of tasks essential for the survival of their communities, and to increase their levels of gainful employment and productivity, it being understood that the benefits of higher productivity should accrue to women workers and their families.

130. Where appropriate, flexible formal or informal training programmes should be designed and implemented for women in non-traditional areas in order to widen their employment opportunities and to enable them to generate income through the production of goods and services.

131. The access of women to special technical training programmes should be increased and women so qualified should be helped to obtain jobs suited to their individual skills; legislative measures should be enacted and appropriate legal assistance provided to prevent exploitation based on sex, race, age, marital status or

motherhood in both the traditional and modern sectors. In addition, measures should be taken to ensure that women are introduced, on the same footing as men, to new types of training in the advanced technologies which are now being widely developed.

132. Measures should be taken to provide for part-time workers levels of remuneration and social security benefits which are proportional to those of full-time workers, and the same levels of working conditions and standards of protection.

133. Where necessary, measures should be taken to develop and/or accelerate much-needed changes in policies in the tertiary sector, which includes the informal subsectors of small-scale trading, domestic services and the like in both urban and rural areas, especially by (a) extending the coverage of labour legislation, in particular for domestic services workers; (b) guaranteeing the right to organize trade unions and other appropriate organizations, such as credit and marketing cooperatives controlled by the women concerned; and (c) increasing access to managerial and technical training and to financial resources, credit facilities and other inputs in order to improve the working conditions of women and increase their occupational and educational mobility as well as their productivity and economic returns.

134. Measures should be adopted which guarantee that, when transfers of technology take place, account is taken of the factors of production available in the country to which the transfers are made in order to avoid any labour force disruptions, which usually affect women more severely. Research should be promoted on appropriate endogenous technology which takes account of national characteristics and, in particular, those of developing countries. New programmes and appropriate policies should be developed concerning industrialization and the transfer of technology aimed at maximizing benefits and preventing adverse effects from the transfer of technology on both the employment, training, health and nutrition of women and overall development. Standards should be instituted to ensure that technologies transferred are safe for utilization and recipient countries are alerted to the hazards of particular forms of technology.

135. Studies should be carried out on the policies, programmes of action and expanding operations of transnational corporations to ensure that they offer greater employment opportunities for women and to prevent their negative effects.

136. The access of women workers to recreation and culture should be increased since their double workload prevents them from having enough necessary free time; it is therefore essential that household chores and family care should be shared by men, and special emphasis should be placed on the obligation of couples to share household tasks with a view to facilitating the access of women to gainful employment.

137. Measures should be taken to ensure that in economic recessions the employment market is not less accessible to women than to men. Measures taken under social legislation concerning unemployment should not directly or indirectly lead to inequality between women and men. Retraining facilities should be provided for unemployed women, preferably in growth sectors.

138. To ensure that women and men are able to harmonize their occupational activities with their family life, child-care facilities and amenities for adolescents should be provided, the length of the working day reduced, and flexible working hours introduced.

139. The number of women at the decision-making level in both national and international workers' organizations and advisory bodies should be increased at least until the proportion corresponds to the number of women carrying on an occupation.

140. Equal employment opportunity programmes should be developed to promote the access of women to all levels of management and decision-making positions and effective programmes should be devised that will promote the access of women and girls to non-traditional skilled trades.

2. *Health*

Objectives

141. To improve the physical and mental health of all members of society through:

(a) An improvement in the health status of girls and women, as a necessary aspect of overall socio-economic development;

(b) The formulation of demographic policies;

(c) An improvement in health care for women throughout their life cycles;

(d) The increased participation of women and men, not only as beneficiaries of the promotion of health but also in the formulation and implementation of policy decisions regarding health at community and national levels;

(e) Studies of the causes of diseases, the establishment of clinical and epidemiological research programmes and the organization of services to deal with national problems;

(f) The development of policies and programmes aimed at the elimination of all forms of violence against women and children and the protection of women of all ages from the physical and mental abuse resulting from domestic violence, sexual assault, sexual exploitation and any other form of abuses;

(g) Training human resources for health programmes of the required quantity and quality;

(h) The inclusion of the mental health aspect, as well as programmes for curbing the abuse of alcohol and drugs, in overall health programmes for women.

Priority areas for action

142. Promote primary health care with the participation of the communities as the overriding health priority and as a fundamental vehicle for achieving the health goals and objectives of the World Plan of Action.

143. Give high priority to meeting the health needs of women within primary health care, with particular attention to the special needs of women in rural and depressed urban areas and monitor health programmes in order to secure that women's health needs are properly met.

144. Formulate official policies to involve women in the planning and execution of health programmes at all levels, particularly to increase the participation of women at decision-making levels.

145. Ensure accessibility for all women to maternal health care (including care during pregnancy and childbirth and post-natal care), nutrition (including measures to control nutritional anaemias), family planning, prevention and treatment of infectious diseases— including sexually transmitted and non-communicable diseases—and parasitic diseases, through the establishment of a comprehensive family health, nutrition, and health education network, in order to give women better access to health care.

146. Develop, implement and strengthen child welfare and family planning programmes and family planning information for inclusion also in school curricula for girls and boys on safe and acceptable fertility regulation methods so that both men and women can take the responsibility for family planning, to promote the health, safety and welfare of mothers and infants and to enable women to exercise the right to decide freely and responsibly for the number and spacing of their children. Family planning should be facilitated as one means of reducing maternal and infant mortality where high risk factors prevail, such as high parity, too frequent pregnancies, pregnancies at the extremes of the reproductive age, and the frequency and danger of secretly performed abortions.

147. To promote the physical and mental wellbeing of women, provision should be made for additional research over the next few years to facilitate analysis and assessment of the status of women.

148. Develop programmes to improve the training and utilization of community health workers, especially women, traditional medical practitioners and birth attendants and elderly village women; support women in their contribution to primary health care both within the family and the community, particularly with reference to self-care and self-reliance in health.

149. Draw the attention of doctors and other health professionals to the health needs of women in general, not only in relation to pregnancy and childbirth; emphasize preventive medicine and the need to share responsibility and decision-making with professionals in other disciplines and with women themselves.

150. Establish official incentive policies to give women greater access to training in the medical professions and in health-related research in accordance with local and national needs.

151. Develop simple economic, social and cultural indicators in order to obtain better data on trends in morbidity and mortality among women and their access to and utilization of health services. Establish a national basic health information system to provide up-to-date and reliable indicators of prevailing conditions, future trends and resource productivity.

152. Give high priority to the formulation and implementation of food and nutrition policies based on the needs of women, particularly pregnant and lactating women, and those of women and children of lower socio-economic status in both rural and depressed urban areas; establish educational programmes through vocational schools and community agencies to improve the quality, availability, preparation, preservation, rational use of and distribution of food, especially locally grown food.

153. Protect the health and safety of women and their families from contamination, spoilage and adulteration of foods, harmful additives and preservatives, mislabelling, deceptive packaging and irresponsible promotion of foods of low nutritional value and of breast milk substitutes. High priority should be given to the enactment and enforcement of comprehensive legislation, where appropriate, and the creation of appropriate standards of safety, health, product information and quality, including standards for the preparation, preservation, packaging and labelling of foods and other products sold in the markets. Women and men should be instructed as to the right and hygienic use of such products. Information as to the right to such protection should be widely disseminated through schools, the media, and village and community organizations.

154. Develop explicit programmes at national and local levels to improve hygiene, sanitation and access to safe water supplies and shelter as fundamental bases for good health.

155. Develop policies to ensure a safe working environment both in the home and in the workplace and provide appropriate technology to relieve the workload

of women. Carry out specific studies on labour hygiene and safety, particularly in branches of activity in which the health of women might be affected.

156. Introduce legislation aimed at eliminating occupational health hazards likely to affect reproductive functions, reducing environmental pollution, and controlling disposal of toxic chemicals and radioactive waste.

157. Promote extensive health education programmes, including special efforts to encourage positive traditional practices, especially breastfeeding, and to combat negative practices detrimental to women's health.

158. Formulate specific programmes for the prevention of maternal and infant mortality, giving priority to depressed rural and urban areas and to most vulnerable population groups.

159. Encourage the formulation and implementation of social support measures such as maternity and parental leave, child care, breastfeeding breaks etc. to enable women and men to carry out parental roles in the optimal and healthiest manner.

160. Direct special attention to the needs of elderly women, women living alone and disabled women.

161. Establish programmes giving full medical attention to adolescent women, since adolescence is a critical time in women's biological and psychological development and also involves a change in their relationship to the social environment in which they live.

162. Prevent mutilation practices which damage women's bodies and health.

163. Promote research into the extent and the causes of domestic violence with a view to eliminating it; take measures to eliminate glorification of violence against and sexual exploitation of women in the mass media, literature and advertising; provide effective help for women and children who are victims of violence, e.g. by the establishment of centres for treatment, shelter and counselling victims of violence and sexual assault.

164. Formulate a plan of action for the protection of women against abuse of alcohol, tobacco and drugs and also excessive use of certain medicaments, principally by informing them of the hazards these substances present for them and their children.

3. *Education and training*

Objectives

165. To provide equal access to educational and training opportunities at all levels of all types for girls and women in all sectors of society, thus enabling them fully to develop their personalities and to participate on an equal footing with men in furthering the socio-economic aims of national planning and to achieve self-reliance, family well-being and improve the quality of life.

166. To contribute to a change in attitudes by abolishing traditional stereotypes of men's and women's roles and stimulating the creation of new and more positive images of women's participation in the family, the labour market and in social and public life.

167. To take into consideration in educational programmes and methodologies the special perspective of education for non-violence, mainly with regard to relationships between women and men.

168. Include in educational programmes and methodologies a special emphasis on education against violence, particularly violence in relationships between women and men.

169. To provide for women and girls innovative programmes and methodologies which stimulate creative development, promote the right to freedom and develop the ability to communicate through the eradication of illiteracy, while at the same time upgrading functional skills and basic information about employment and health-related matters as well as their political, economic and social rights.

170. To establish transitional links between school life, apprenticeship and working life, whenever possible, in order to ensure for women and girls better interaction between education, training and employment.

171. Formulate and implement education programmes with final-year courses adapted to the specific needs of the economic and social development of the country, designed to improve and increase the access of women to gainful employment and give them opportunities to take part in non-traditional activities.

172. To increase the opportunities and facilities which promote participation of women in science and technology through education and training in these fields.

173. To devise means of encouraging girls to stay at school longer and to ensure that courses chosen by girls are in a range of fields including the professions, management, economics and the sciences which will enable them to achieve positions of influence in the decision-making process.

Priority areas for action

174. Education, specifically literacy, being a key to national development and a major requisite for improving the status of women, efforts should be made to establish targets for the abolition of differentials in the literacy and educational attainment rates for girls and boys within overall national efforts to increase literacy and education for the whole population.

175. National educational accreditation and equivalency programmes should be designed to encourage the return of women and girls who have dropped out into the formal education system.

176. Promote education programmes for children, particularly those of pre-school age, as well as young people, aimed at strengthening women's contribution to society and at changing the traditional roles assigned by social and cultural norms to women and men.

177. Establish targets for the expansion of educational opportunities and facilities for women, including courses and institutions with adequate personnel and materials, for which resources have been earmarked.

178. Provide new formal and extracurricular education to enable women to combine their household duties with the opportunity to improve their educational level.

179. Encourage, through legislation, free and compulsory education for girls and boys at the primary level, with the provision of assistance to establish co-education when possible. Provide trained teachers of both sexes and, if necessary, transportation and boarding facilities.

180. Increase the enrolment of female students in education courses and, in particular, in science, mathematics and technical courses, and in management training courses in the areas of science and technology, especially by encouraging them to enrol in such courses.

181. Provide for equal access to all levels of general education, vocational education, and training for all types of occupations, including those traditionally accessible to men, and to new training schemes and other facilities such as on-the-job training, scholarships, inexpensive boarding and lodging facilities and accessible child care arrangements, ensuring equal job opportunities after completion of vocational education or training for both entry and re-entry, after a period of absence, into occupational activities.

182. Examine curricula and learning materials with a view to removing sex-bias and the stereotyped portrayal of the roles of girls and women and promote the development of non-sexist resources and curricular materials.

183. Establish targets for the nation-wide implementation of the learning materials developed to optimize the potential of women for countries which have started the work since 1975.

184. Include courses on women's issues in university degree programmes.

185. Develop programmes at the secondary, tertiary and adult education levels to encourage a basic understanding of human rights, including the Universal Declaration of Human Rights and other relevant instruments. Such courses should stress the fundamental importance of the elimination of discrimination on the basis of race and sex.

186. Train guidance counselors and teachers to assist girls and boys in choosing occupations according to their personal capacities and not according to stereotyped sex roles.

187. Design and promote teacher training courses to alert teachers to the stereotyped assumptions which inhibit choice in school subjects and to the need to widen the options available to women and girls in their future training and occupational choices. Provide, whenever possible, counseling services for the benefit of parents, teachers and pupils as well as for workers and employers.

188. Encourage parity of men and women in teaching and administrative positions at all levels of education.

189. Identify the situational constraints on different culturally or socially underprivileged target groups (e.g. girls of school age who are not attending school, illiterate adults or adults who are engaged in home responsibilities and need additional or diversified education, working women of different age groups in rural and urban areas, mature women and immigrant women) and formulate and implement programmes for such groups.

190. Monitor programmes and take measures for improving the data on drop-out rates of girls and women and their causes, and on course content and levels of skills acquired, in order to facilitate the introduction of remedial or accelerated measures and to generate greater commitment to the policy objectives within the system.

191. Where appropriate, provide for particular target groups, giving priority to those needing them most, counseling and supportive services and certain necessities (child care, earning and learning schemes, transport, clothing, books, supplementary nutrition, reading centres, special tuition in basic subjects such as mathematics, scholarships and stipends and the like), on the basis of situational analyses, and include resources for such services as priority items in educational budgets.

192. Provide for education for women in the context of life-long education in all major development sectors, in developed and developing countries, and take specific measures for obtaining the necessary funds and personnel.

193. Promote instruction and interdisciplinary research on women and the implications of the goals of the Decade as an input to the educational process, particularly in institutions of higher and teacher education, in order to draw on the experience acquired in some countries with women's status and to eliminate all attitudinal and conceptual biases and prejudices, especially those relating to class, that hinder understanding of the role and situation of women.

194. Urge Governments to encourage women to enrol in all their technical institutes and to promote,

through every means available to them, the establishment of intermediate technical courses.

C. *Priority areas requiring special attention*

1. *Food*

Objectives

195. To enhance and stimulate the key role performed by women in all phases of the process of food production and their contribution to the economic and social development of their countries, at the same time raising their status.

196. To ensure proper planning of the agricultural production sector so that the agricultural output covers as a matter of priority the supply of products that are socially and nationally necessary for the nutrition and food requirements of women in rural areas.

Priority areas for action

197. Governments should adopt the necessary measures to:

(a) Promote the incorporation of women in all phases of the agricultural productive process, including post-harvesting processing, up to and including the marketing of products;

(b) Provide women with the necessary skills and appropriate technology to enable them to participate better in the process of subsistence food production;

(c) Establish a link between food production and food consumption processes by providing information on the nutrients required for the development of the population and in particular of children and by making rural women aware of the need for proper nourishment. Eliminate inappropriate consumption patterns which have developed as a result of ignorance or manipulation by commercial advertising;

(d) Promote the participation of women, especially in rural areas, in agricultural policy-making, leading to the production of basic foods for family and national consumption;

(e) Ensure access to and use of appropriate technological model of agricultural production for both sexes without distinction;

(f) Stimulate the participation and full voting rights of women in cooperatives and other forms of organization relating to the production, processing, distribution, marketing and consumption of products;

(g) Ensure access for women in conditions of equality with men to financing mechanisms covering all phases of production, up to and including the marketing of food products;

(h) Support forms of marketing of basic foods for family consumption which will be conducive to the opening up of priority markets for the sale of their products.

2. *Rural women*

Objectives

198. Enhance the effective contribution of rural women to the economic and social development of their countries in cases where they are hampered by their inadequate access to appropriate technology, by the inadequate social infrastructures in rural areas and by the double workload they bear through their participation in working the land and their performance of household duties.

199. Improve the living conditions of women in rural areas, and to this end:

(a) Acknowledge the contribution which women make to the economic and social development of their countries, and take steps to ensure that rural women participate equally and effectively in the development process as beneficiaries and as agents for change by affording them participation as policy-makers, organizers and implementers of development programmes;

(b) Give rural women at all levels access to formal and non-formal courses in leadership and decision-making, as well as to programmes that teach skills appropriate to their lifestyle and skills which could be utilized, if necessary, for paid employment;

(c) Provide rural women with basic human needs, including clean water supplies, effective sanitation, adequate food and nutrition, basic health services, shelter and appropriate fuel supplies. They should have access to formal and non-formal education programmes, which should be available at minimum cost and inconvenience to already overburdened women. They should also have assured access to technology at all levels, particularly in relation to food storage and preservation, transport and marketing and labour-saving tools and devices;

(d) Provide rural women with access to improved transport and communication systems, and to all forms of media;

(e) Extend to all rural women free and equal access to credit facilities where these are available;

(f) Aid donor countries and recipient Governments should consult on ways of developing programmes at the village level for involving local women in their planning and implementation. Care should be taken to ensure that development assistance programmes do not exclude women from technological training.

Priority areas for action

200. Governments should adopt the necessary measures to:

(a) Eliminate from legislation on rural development, where necessary, provisions that discriminate against women;

(b) Make rural women aware of their rights so that they can exercise and benefit from them;

(c) Ensure access for rural women to the use, enjoyment and development of land, in conditions of equality with men, by according to women the same practical and legal rights as those of men in access to ownership and the use and management of land, in the production of goods from land by means of agriculture or grazing and in the disposal of any such products or of the land itself;

(d) Allocate sufficient financial resources to carry out research, especially field research, which will provide a sound basis for initiating, expanding and strengthening concrete and integrated actions aimed at promoting the development of rural women and their integration in economic and social activity in rural areas;

(e) Examine carefully the possibility of devising statistics which measure rural women's contribution on an equal basis with men's, including labour in the sphere of agricultural production, unpaid family labour and food production for family consumption, as well as monitor the impact of development so that negative and unforseen consequences, such as increased workload and loss of income earning opportunities, can be identified;

(f) Provide rural women with the appropriate technology and suitable training enabling them to improve and promote their traditional small-scale in-home industries;

(g) Encourage the participation of rural women, in all forms of social organization of labour, with a view to achieving, inter alia, control over their wage levels, participation in the production process and greater equality in working conditions;

(h) Foster the effective participation of rural women in the cultural, political, economic and social activities of the community;

(i) Create and strengthen the necessary infrastructure to lighten the workload of rural women, through, inter alia, the application of appropriate technology but ensuring that such measures do not result in occupational displacement of women;

(j) Design and carry out literacy and training campaigns for specific rural areas, promoting the effective participation of women in such campaigns;

(k) Improve employment opportunities for women in agricultural and non-agricultural jobs in rural areas by providing training and ensuring an adequate allocation of material, technical and financial resources, so as to provide an alternative to migration to urban areas and

ensure a balanced development in the other social services with a view to narrowing the existing development gap between rural and urban sectors, thereby preventing migration and its harmful consequences;

(l) Examine and strengthen rural women's participation and contribution in and benefit from development and diversification of the forest economy;

(m) Establish special schemes to provide basic education for children and adults in remote, sparsely populated or very underprivileged rural areas, for example, by setting up children's hostels which provide board and lodging;

(n) Increase rural women's access to rural services by broadening the range of agricultural training and extension programmes to support women's roles in activities of agricultural production, processing and marketing and by increasing the number of women in the training and extension programmes of development agencies at all levels;

(o) Promote the processing of agricultural products by national, community, State or mixed enterprises; create jobs for rural women and families in the agro-industrial sector; and design and implement national plans for the development of the agro-industrial sector and rural industries.

3. *Child care*

Objectives

201. To develop or extend government-supported early childhood services appropriate to the individual family's needs.

202. Enable women, and especially working women, to discharge their responsibilities with regard to their children, and combine their work outside the home with their responsibilities as mothers. Special efforts should also be made to enable fathers to assume their share of family responsibilities.

Priority areas for action

203. Governments should adopt the necessary measures to:

(a) Include provision of community-based, work-based and work-related child care services, out-of-school hours and holiday care, crisis care and care for those families engaged in shift work;

(b) Improve the existing services by improving the competence of the persons providing them, the quality of the services provided, health conditions and the material aspects of the services;

(c) Create new services suited to the needs and conditions of working women and undertake the necessary studies to determine the real nature of those needs;

(d) Provide the necessary services at the lowest cost so as to match the resources and possibilities of women with limited incomes;

(e) Involve mothers in the planning of those services, and in their provision and assessment on a continuous basis so that they can be developed;

(f) Encourage child care centres in shopping centres to cater for occasional care needs.

4. Migrant women

Objective

204. Migrant women, including wage earners and the family of migrant workers, should have the same access to education, training, employment and support and health services as the national population.

Priority areas for action

205. Governments should adopt the necessary measures to:

(a) Provide language and literacy training facilities in the community and at the workplace. Access to these courses should be facilitated by income maintenance and child care services;

(b) Provide orientation and information programmes, including information on employment and training to all migrant women, in their own languages where necessary, to assist them in settling into the host country;

(c) Establish vocational training and counseling programmes, where necessary, including interpretation services;

(d) Ensure that social support and health services provide interpreters or bilingual workers;

(e) Encourage and assist union and employer organizations to inform migrant women about industrial legislation, procedures and rights;

(f) Provide culturally appropriate child care services to meet the needs of migrant and minority children and their families;

(g) Ensure migrant women, on a basis of equality with the national population, general education and vocational/professional training. Measures should be taken to improve the level of education and training of migrant women through language and literacy courses upon arrival in the host country. Special education and training facilities should be provided for marriageable daughters of migrant workers who are of compulsory school age but who for various reasons do not attend school in the host country. Special attention should be given to reaching migrant women, for instance through the mass media,

notably radio. Supplementary training and special guidance is necessary for social workers and teachers. In most cases these will, of necessity, have to be women;

(h) Ensure, on a basis of equality with the indigenous population, equal health care for migrant women. Measures should be taken to improve the health status of migrant women, paying special attention to stress-related ailments caused by differences in cultural, social and religious conditions. Provide additional training for domestic health care work on the differing cultural and religious attitudes migrant women may have towards health and ill-health.

5. Unemployed women

Objective

206. Governments should take steps to ensure that unemployed women have access to secure employment.

Priority areas for action

207. Governments should adopt the necessary measures to:

(a) Provide formal and non-formal training and retraining to equip unemployed women with marketable employment skills. Such training should include personal and vocational development programmes;

(b) Guarantee to unemployed women social security benefits, adequate accommodation, and medical services on the basis of individual need.

6. Women who alone are responsible for their families

Objective

208. Governments should ensure that women who alone are responsible for their families receive a level of income sufficient to support themselves and their families in dignity and independence.

Priority areas for action

209. Governments should take the necessary measures to:

(a) Provide training and retraining for secure employment through programmes which should include maintenance, child care, parental leave and personal vocational development programmes;

(b) Assist women who alone are responsible for their families to obtain secure appropriate accommodation;

(c) Guarantee favourable access to finance and credit, medical and health services.

7. Young women

Objective

210. Promote specific government policies for the education, health and employment of young women so that, in view of the role they play in revitalizing and carrying on systems of behaviour, attitudes and values, they receive the guidance and support they need, during the time when they are planning their future lives, to act wisely in crucial situations, such as the adoption of values and attitudes; the choice of a husband; the birth and raising of their first child; access to their first job; and election to office.

Priority areas for action

211. Governments should take the necessary measures to:

(a) Give special attention to the education of young women, who are the only human resource with a possibility of bringing about change in the future, with a view to ensuring that they are consciously involved in social and political development; that they enjoy and exercise the right responsibility, deliberately and willingly to found a family; and that they are given more and better opportunities to take part in the process of production;

(b) Give priority attention to young women in matters relating to food and health in general in order to improve the living conditions of present and future generations and to permit the exercise of the right to health.

PART THREE: THE PROGRAMME OF ACTION AT THE INTERNATIONAL AND REGIONAL LEVELS

IV. International targets and strategies

212. International targets and strategies both at the regional and the global levels should be based on a clear recognition that peace, security and national independence are essential prerequisites for an environment wherein the rights, responsibilities and roles of women can be promoted and the three objectives of the Decade—equality, development and peace—can be attained.

213. The perpetuation of global economic inequalities and economic dependence, which are the product of an economic system that is unfair and incompatible with the development of countries, slows down the process of development of all nations, particularly of the developing countries, and inhibits the full utilization of the material and human potentials of those countries, including women. The elaboration of an international development strategy for the third United Nations Development Decade, formulated within the framework of the new international economic order and directed towards the achievement of its objectives is thus of fundamental importance for the achievement of the goals of the United Nations Decade for Women. It is essential to establish goals envisaging the assumption by women of full economic, political, cultural and social responsibility.

214. Progress towards disarmament can greatly contribute to the achievement of an adequate economic, social and cultural environment and enhance the development process through the reallocation of resources, particularly to the developing countries.

215. One of the concerns of the international community has been the need to restructure and reformulate the policies of the economic and social sectors of the United Nations system so that it can help speed up the establishment of the New International Economic Order, the development of developing countries, and the promotion of the goals of the United Nations Decade for Women.

216. The restructuring has taken into account the need for decentralization of certain activities and the strengthening of regional programmes, particularly in the areas of economic and technical cooperation, in advisory services and training and research, data collection and analysis. The past few years have also witnessed the formulation by the regional commissions of regional plans of action for the integration of women into development and programmes aimed at implementation of some of their provisions. Of utmost importance, however, is the need to integrate women at both regional and global levels into the priority areas mentioned above in a programme of concerted and sustained international action for the second half of the Decade and beyond, until the plans to attain women's integration in development are fully implemented.

217. Member States are increasingly looking to the United Nations and to organizations in the United Nations system to take more dynamic international action in promoting women's full and equal partnership in development, both as contributors and beneficiaries. This is evidenced by the increasing number of resolutions, plans and policy declarations. Commensurate with the need for more dynamic programmes and policies is the need for coordination of activities of the various organizations in the United Nations system as well as the appropriate institutional arrangements, within them, involving, wherever necessary, structural transformations. There is also a need for the development of relevant methodologies for integration of women in all their programmes and activities. In line with the integrated nature of the development process itself and with the need to reduce both isolated actions and overlapping of activities, the Programme of Action aims also at greater cohesiveness and coordination of efforts of the various organizations.

218. The Programme seeks to outline essential strategies and broad areas for international action. International action in this context includes regional action. However, some recommendations are addressed specifically to regional commissions and to other organizations concerned in the United Nations system for action at the regional, subregional and national levels in order to assist Governments and supplement national programmes.

V. International policies and programmes

219. All organizations in the United Nations system, in closer cooperation with intergovernmental and non-governmental organizations concerned, should support efforts towards establishing, strengthening and implementing national, regional and global programmes aimed at women's integration in development, revising and redefining, if necessary, development concepts, objectives and policies to achieve it. These programmes at the international level should take into full consideration the essential linkages in the development process at national, subregional and international levels, and with adequate communication between institutions and machineries related to women and major planning units at all these levels.

220. In order to achieve the targets envisaged for the third United Nations Development Decade, all development planning should take due account of the potential contribution and the interests of women. This consideration will lead to more appropriate development programmes which will increase productivity, whilst at the same time guarding against the possibility of any adverse impact which the transfer of technology and the redeployment of industry may have. Development projects should strongly emphasize the indigenous capabilities of the developing countries and enhance their creative capacity.

221. New approaches should be developed for increasing the mobilization of women's resources both for advancing their socio-economic status and increasing productivity. To this end, they should offer, *inter alia*, special incentives to develop cooperative movements, particularly among women of the poorer sectors of society, aimed at developing cooperative technology enterprises for community self-reliance in water, energy, health, sanitation and housing, day care centres, and other basic services.

222. Multilateral and bilateral development and other organizations as well as non-governmental organizations working in the field of development should continue to provide development assistance to programmes and projects of developing countries which promote women's integration and participation in all aspects of the development process, also within the framework of technical cooperation among developing countries. In

this connection efforts should be made to utilize fully locally available expertise in project design and implementation and to ensure greater quality in the project results through, among others, flexible implementation procedures. These programmes and projects should *inter alia* focus on efforts to strengthen developing countries' capabilities to plan and implement programmes for women, including capabilities to develop alternative technology, research and the application of renewable sources of energy.

223. The United Nations Voluntary Fund for the Decade for Women should continue to intensify its efforts to give special support to women most in need, and to encourage consideration of women in development planning. Contributions to the Voluntary Fund will need to be greatly increased during the second half of the Decade if demands now being made on its resources are to be adequately met. Adequate development funds should be available for activities specific to the acceleration of the full participation of women in economic and social development at national, regional and international levels.

224. Studies should be undertaken by the United Nations organizations concerned to identify new ways and means of facilitating the integration of women, especially of the poor sectors of society, into the mainstream of development, including women workers in agriculture and industry. The ILO, in cooperation with bodies such as UNCTAD, UNIDO and FAO, should develop studies to assess the working and employment conditions of rural women with a view to assisting Governments to revise national and international policies concerning wage and labour policies, as well as trade agreements and prices of those commodities where women's and men's wages are adversely affected by and also affect the exchange earnings of the developing countries as obtained from the export of such commodities. UNESCO, in cooperation with other United Nations organs and organizations concerned, should continue to prepare studies and sponsor projects with a view to assisting Governments to assess progress made and obstacles that women face in gaining access to and enjoying primary, secondary and post-secondary educational opportunities and to contribute to the development of research and teaching about women at the university level and in non-formal education. WHO, in cooperation with United Nations organs and organizations concerned should continue to assess progress made and obstacles women face in gaining access to health care, particularly progress in the development of primary health care.

225. The United Nations Secretariat should undertake a comparative compilation of national legislative measures which are aimed at promoting sex equality. Such a compilation would assist in the introduction of

new laws designed to integrate women into all fields of activities by generating ideas and exerting persuasion. The compilation should be issued within the framework of the United Nations Legislative Series.

226. International and regional organizations should provide assistance, if requested, to national machineries for women, for improving their capabilities and resources to accelerate integration of women in the development process and take up programmes and projects for them.

227. In the framework of bilateral development cooperation efforts should be made, in conformity with national priorities, to strengthen national programmes aimed at the full participation and integration of women in all aspects of development, including participation of women at the grass-roots level. In all bilateral development activities women should participate in the preparation and implementation of programmes and projects.

228. The eleventh special session of the General Assembly on economic development should take into full account the women's role in economic development; the forthcoming United Nations Conference on New and Renewable Sources of Energy, the programmes for the International Drinking Water Supply and Sanitation Decade, and other forthcoming international conferences should also take into account issues of particular interest to women.

229. The United Nations and its organizations should, in cooperation with national Governments, develop strategies for increasing women's participation in the social, economic and political life, ensuring full and effective participation of women in all sectors and at all levels of the development process, including planning, decision-making and implementation, and, in keeping with these objectives, seeking to:

(a) Reduce the burden on women of tasks traditionally performed by them in the home and in food production and child care through appropriate technology and a fair division of labour between women and men;

(b) Counteract factors which tend to keep girls and women out of schools and training centres;

(c) Create new employment and occupational mobility opportunities for women;

(d) Increase the economic returns to women for their labour, and implement the principle of equal pay for work of equal value;

(e) Recognize the important contribution of women to economic development, raise the productivity of women's labour for their own benefit and the benefit of their own families, and at the same time undertake appropriate structural changes to prevent women's unemployment;

(f) Recognize the vital role of women in agriculture and guarantee them equitable access to land, technology, water, other natural resources, inputs and services and equal opportunities to develop their skills;

(g) Promote equal participation of women in the industrialization process, counteract possible negative effects of industrialization, and ensure that scientific and technological development will benefit both women and men;

(h) Ensure women's active participation in and access to primary health care, in the light of their specific health needs.

230. International programmes and policies—including regional ones—are grouped into five areas. Each is covered below in a separate section.

A. *Technical cooperation, training and advisory services*

231. Technical cooperation programmes for women should be conceived in the context of overall development and not as welfare programmes.

232. Technical cooperation activities should be directed towards assisting and complementing Governments' efforts aimed at enhancing the development of human resources particularly among the most disadvantaged groups of population with a special emphasis on women.

233. All organizations of the United Nations system, including the regional commissions, should:

(a) Review existing and proposed plans and projects in this area with the aim of integrating the issues of concern to women in all programmes and projects in order to improve the effectiveness of those projects as well as to improve the status of women;

(b) Encourage and support Governments and non-governmental organizations, including research institutions, in elaborating appropriate technology projects and in identifying ways in which women can participate in and contribute to the effectiveness of development projects and improve their own economic and social condition;

(c) Organize seminars and workshops on the issues related to women and development and ensure that the topic of women and development be included in the substantive discussions of international conferences;

(d) Assist Governments in organizing more training courses with the assistance of the International Research and Training Institute for the Advancement of Women (INSTRAW) for improving women's planning, technical and managerial skills in different fields, especially of functionaries implementing programmes and policies for women. Promote fellowships and other special educational and training programmes to increase the capacity of women workers and planners so that they can gain better occupational and social status;

(e) Assist national and regional programmes benefiting women in rural areas. Programmes for women should be viewed as an investment in the process of development and women should be included as active participants in the design, planning and implementation of projects in all sectors and not simply as beneficiaries of services;

(f) Ensure that technical cooperation, training and advisory services by the organizations of the United Nations system are in conformity with national objectives and with policies outlined in the World Plan of Action and the Programme for the Second Half of the Decade.

234. UNDP should intensify its efforts to encourage and assist Governments to find innovative approaches to achieve their development goals through incorporating and benefiting women by:

(a) Instructing resident representatives to advise Governments on issues in country programmes of particular interest to women, and to monitor regularly existing programmes and promote project development, coordination and cooperation among United Nations and other organizations so as to further the achievement of the goals of the Decade;

(b) Continuing to promote regional, subregional and national projects through regional commissions, national machineries for women and research and training centres, especially activities leading to the introduction and development of new programmes in order to achieve the integration of women in development;

(c) Continuing its support for the Voluntary Fund for the Decade for Women.

235. Governments should formulate, as part of their development cooperation policies, guidelines for the implementation of the Programme of Action for the Second Half of the United Nations Decade for Women.

1. Mobilization of human resources

236. Efforts should be intensified within the programmes of organizations of the United Nations system to involve more men in programmes for attitudinal change in all the relevant sectors, particularly employment, health, education, rural development and political participation. Men should be involved in health programmes to ensure that the responsibility for improving the situation of their families and communities is not the sole responsibility of women.

237. The effective participation of women, particularly in the developing countries, in the programmes of organizations in the United Nations system should be encouraged, including their participation in interregional and regional seminars and meetings.

238. Women at all levels, especially those from grass-roots organizations, should be encouraged to play a more effective role at the decision-making level in international organizations.

239. United Nations organizations and Member States are urged to take the necessary measures to increase the proportion of women by nominating and appointing women, particularly from developing countries, for posts in decision-making levels in secretariats and expert bodies. Member States are also urged to increase the proportion of women on their delegations to all United Nations meetings, including meetings of preparatory committees for international conferences and to prepare women to take an active role in such conferences. In this regard, Member States in cooperation with United Nations bodies should make arrangements for the inclusion of items on women's issues in the agenda of such conferences.

240. Measures should be taken to reinforce efforts of Member States, specially developing ones, to develop and strengthen endogenous capabilities and capacities for the elaboration of policies for science and technology and for their application to the solution of problems of development, with special emphasis on the disparities in the access of women to scientific and technical education and training.

2. Assistance to women in southern Africa

241. The recommendations are addressed to United Nations organizations, the specialized agencies, Governments, international and regional intergovernmental organizations, women's and anti-apartheid groups, non-governmental organizations and other groups.

242. The assistance provided will be channelled through the southern African liberation movements recognized by the Organization of African Unity. It is divided into the following categories of assistance:

(a) Legal, humanitarian, moral and political assistance to women inside South Africa and Namibia persecuted under repressive and discriminatory legislation and practices and to their families and to women in refugee camps;

(b) Training and assistance to integrate women into positions of leadership and support within the national liberation movements in the struggle for liberation;

(c) Training and assistance for women to play roles in all areas after liberation in the reconstruction of their respective countries;

(d) International support for and cooperation with the southern African women's struggle;

(e) To disseminate information about apartheid and racism and its effects on women in southern Africa in particular, and to involve all women in efforts to eradicate apartheid and racism and to promote and maintain peace;

(f) To assist in the strengthening of women's sections where they already exist in the national liberation movements and the creation of such sections where they do not currently exist as a means of accelerating the achievement of equal opportunity for women and their full integration in national life. Such women's sections through the national liberation movements should, in consultations with the United Nations organizations, the specialized agencies, intergovernmental and non-governmental organizations, determine and make known their policy and programme priorities.

243. To call on Member States of the United Nations which have not yet done so to ratify the 1973 International Convention on the Suppression and Punishment of the Crime of *Apartheid*.

3. *Assistance to the Palestinian women inside and outside the occupied territories*

244. The United Nations organizations, the specialized agencies, United Nations organs and funds, Governments, international and regional intergovernmental organizations and other groups are called upon to provide assistance in consultation and cooperation with the Palestine Liberation Organization, the representative of the Palestinian people:

(a) To undertake studies and research pertinent to the social and economic conditions of the Palestinian women with a view to identifying their specific needs and to formulate and implement relevant programmes to meet their needs and to develop resources and potentialities of women;

(b) To provide legal, humanitarian and political assistance to Palestinian women in order to allow them to exercise their human rights;

(c) To establish, expand, and diversify educational and training programmes for Palestinian women with particular emphasis on expanding technical and vocational training;

(d) To safeguard and promote the Palestinian heritage and values as the core of the educational context with a view to preserving the Palestinian national identity;

(e) To eliminate all restrictive legal and social measures that hinder Palestinian women from having access to available employment opportunities and equal pay for equal work, and to provide them with equal training and employment opportunities so that they can contribute effectively to the formation of an integrated Palestinian labour force;

(f) To assist materially and technically women's organizations and associations, and to provide support to the General Union of Palestinian Women with a view to develop their institutional capabilities to undertake extension programmes, adult education and literacy programmes for women and child care services;

(g) To formulate and implement integrated health and nutrition programmes; to train Palestinian women in the various medical and paramedical professions and to strengthen existing health services provided by the Palestinian Red Crescent, particularly those related to maternal and child care;

(h) To collect and disseminate information and data about the effect of Israeli occupation on the social and economic conditions of the Palestinian women and their struggle for achieving self-determination, right of return, and right to national independence and sovereignty.

4. *Assistance to women refugees and displaced women the world over*

245. Humanitarian assistance to and resettlement of refugees, regardless of sex, race, religion or national origin, and wherever they may find themselves, is an international responsibility which all nations concerned should help bear. Because the overwhelming proportion of refugees are women, who generally suffer more radical changes in role and status than male refugees, the United Nations and other international organizations are urged to address themselves specifically to the problems and vulnerabilities of women.

246. The following recommendations are addressed to the United Nations High Commissioner for Refugees and, within their competence or special interest, the organizations of the United Nations system, specialized agencies, international, regional and intergovernmental organizations, non-governmental organizations, women's groups and all other relevant institutions, competent associations, and Governments.

247. The United Nations High Commissioner and other bodies mentioned in paragraph 246, as appropriate, in assisting women refugees, are requested to formulate specific programmes relevant to them in all phases of refugee life: relief, local integration, resettlement, and voluntary return to their homes. All Governments concerned are invited to help, thereby easing the burden on countries of first asylum in particular. Third countries should be urged to receive refugees for resettlement without discrimination on the basis of sex or lack of qualifications. There is a particularly urgent need for senior level responsibility for the special needs of refugee women, including monitoring, in the UNHCR and other agencies and organizations involved in refugee relief. These pro-

grammes should also apply to displaced women, wherever appropriate.

248. It should be recognized that in refugee situations and of displaced persons, women and children form the bulk of the refugees and have particular needs. Therefore special efforts are necessary to ensure their survival and well-being, and to prevent their abuse and exploitation. The traditional disadvantages of many women in society are intensified in refugee situations as well as for displaced persons. This must be recognized in formulating any programmes of assistance. The assistance provided through the United Nations High Commissioner for Refugees or through bilateral intergovernmental channels as far as resources permit should include the following categories of assistance:

(a) Legal, humanitarian and moral assistance to women refugees ensuring for them the fullest respect for their human rights in accordance with the principles of the Universal Declaration of Human Rights and the International Covenant on Civil and Political Rights, to prevent exploitation of their ignorance of their rights and of their comparatively weak position;

(b) Special relief efforts directed to refugee women and children, and particularly to handicapped persons, to ensure that available aid reaches them;

(c) Assistance and counselling to women refugees at an early phase of their arrival in the country of asylum, with emphasis on the development of self-reliance;

(d) Special health care measures and health counselling, including family planning services on a nationally acceptable and voluntary basis for women refugees, as well as supplemental feeding programmes for pregnant and lactating women, provided through means relevant to their culture and traditions, and by women medical workers where necessary;

(e) Training and educational programmes, including orientation, language and job training, designed to facilitate the necessary adjustments of women refugees to their new life and the preservation of their cultural links with their country of origin;

(f) Special national and international efforts to facilitate family reunion and support for tracing programmes;

(g) Skill development programmes for refugee women so that they may learn to employ their potential for income-earning activity;

(h) The UNHCR should encourage Governments in whose territory abuses of women refugees take place to bring to justice the perpetrators of such abuses. Host country Governments should be encouraged to allow sufficient international personnel in refugee camps to discourage exploitation or any attacks upon women refugees.

249. Assistance should be provided in strengthening the counselling programme for women refugees, both in rural settlements and urban centres, and the design of special social work programmes to reach women refugees, where such programmes do not at present exist. Special orientation programmes should be provided for women refugees awaiting resettlement in third countries.

250. The role of women refugees in the operation and administration of refugee camps should be substantially expanded, including distribution of food and other supplies, and the design of training and orientation programmes. The UNHCR is urged to develop policies which actively involve refugee women in self-help programmes in an effort to utilize their skills and talents fully.

251. The United Nations system should give high priority in its public information activities to the need to assist refugee women and children the world over.

B. Elaboration and review of international standards

252. Every effort should be made by the United Nations and organizations in the United Nations system to encourage Governments:

(a) To sign and ratify or accede to the Convention on the Elimination of All Forms of Discrimination against Women adopted by the General Assembly in its resolution 34/180, of 18 December 1979, so that it will come into force at an early date within the period of this Programme;

(b) To sign and ratify or accede to, if they have not yet done so, all conventions of the United Nations and specialized agencies which relate to women. 6/

253. The Committee on the Elimination of Discrimination against Women should keep under review the reporting systems under the Convention on the Elimination of All Forms of Discrimination against Women once it comes into force. The Commission on the Status of Women should keep under review the reporting system for the implementation of the World Plan of Action and the implementation of the Programme for the Second Half of the Decade.

254. The United Nations and organizations in the United Nations system should, in the formulation of international standards in areas where they do not exist, take into account the needs of women.

255. The specialized agencies should submit reports on the implementation of the Convention in areas

6/ See, for example, Human Rights: A Compilation of International Instruments, New York, United Nations, 1978; and International Labour Organization, International Labour Conventions and Convention on the Elimination of All Forms of Discrimination against Women, United Nations, New York, 1979; and International Covenant on Civil and Political Rights.

falling within the scope of their activities, when requested to do so, and should attend the meeting of the Committee on the Elimination of Discrimination against Women when invited to do so.

256. Measures should be taken by bodies and organizations in the United Nations system, particularly UNCTAD, UNIDO, the Centre on Transnational Corporations, the International Labour Organization and the Food and Agriculture Organization of the United Nations, to include specific provisions relating to women in the international codes of conduct for transnational corporations and on the transfer of technology aimed at diminishing any adverse effects of redeployment of industry and technology.

C. Research, data collection and analysis

257. The United Nations, the specified agencies, and the regional commissions should give high priority to undertaking multisectoral and interdisciplinary action-oriented research in relevant and important areas where information does not already exist on the ways of integrating women in development, with a view to formulating development objectives, strategies and policy measures responsive to the needs of women and men. Such research should utilize existing institutions such as the International Research and Training Institute for the Advancement of Women as well as more use of joint institutions which deal with questions concerning status of women. The research should be aimed at developing effective methodologies of planning for women's development and at evaluating the participation of women in the informal sectors of the economy; the health status of women; the double burden of working women and data on the degree of absence of women because of maternity, educational opportunities or lack thereof for women, in particular factors contributing to illiteracy, full access of women, including drop-outs among the female population, to all types and all levels of education; the conditions of the female-headed household; the participation in the formal sectors of the economy; political participation and the nature of the contributions of women's organizations. Emphasis should also be given to fuller and more systematic analysis of all the interrelationships between women's roles in development and demographic phenomena. Research should also be conducted on employment opportunities projected for a period of five or ten years after the Decade for Women, and on training/educational programmes that will meet the need for the specific workforce so identified.

258. Taking into consideration that international migration has become an enduring process in the labour market, the special problems of migrant women, as related to their economic functions, legal and social status, difficulties arising from language barriers and the education of the second generation deserve special attention. The ILO, in cooperation with bodies such as UNESCO, FAO and WHO, should continue and develop studies to assess the employment, health and educational conditions of migrant women with a view to assisting Governments in reviewing their national and international policies concerning employment, social security, housing, social welfare policies, and the preservation of the cultural heritage as well as the use of mass media as supportive channels of information for migrant women.

259. The United Nations, in close collaboration with specialized agencies and regional commissions and on the basis of the work done by INSTRAW, should prepare and make available compendiums of statistics on women, containing the most recent data, time-trend analyses where available, as well as national and international measures designed to improve the situation of women. The *Directory of International Statistics*, prepared by the Statistical Office, Department of International Economic and Social Affairs of the United Nations Secretariat, should include a special section indicating where relevant data exist by which progress toward equality between the sexes can be monitored.

260. The Sub-Committee on Statistical Activities of the Administrative Committee on Co-ordination, in agreement with INSTRAW, should, as soon as possible, include in its programme of work consideration of statistics relating to women and develop short- and long-range goals for improving the quality and relevance of data pertaining to the conditions of women. Such discussions should include plans to update data concerning women with a particular emphasis on the development, evaluation and updating of estimates and projections of the participation of women in all areas of national life.

261. The United Nations should, in close collaboration with the specialized agencies, the regional commissions and national Governments encourage statistical operations and practices that are free from sex-based stereotypes and appropriate research methodology that would have relevance to the participation of women in development and equality between the sexes.

262. The United Nations, with the concerned specialized agencies, should pay special attention to the industries in which the overwhelming majority of employees are female, analyse the causes of their existence and the possibilities of new technological patterns leading to deep changes in the respective branches.

263. At the regional level the regional commissions, in collaboration with the specialized agencies, should:

(a) Assist the countries of the region to establish indicators by which progress toward equality between the sexes can be monitored. In establishing such a set of indicators, Governments should be advised to take into account the social and cultural realities of the country, the current state of the country's statistical development as well as their individual policy priorities;

(b) Prepare for each region an inventory of social, economic and demographic indicators relevant to the analysis of the status of women in the region. For a better evaluation of development programmes, the utilization of, and access to, such data should be ensured;

(c) Assist countries in the development of surveys carried out as part of the national household surveys capability programme, including batteries of questions of special relevance to the participation of women in development and equality between the sexes;

(d) Increase their level of investment in long-range fundamental research on women and development, without violation of national priorities, so as to provide a sound scientific base for development planning.

D. *Dissemination of information and experience*

264. The respective specialized agencies of the United Nations, during the second part of this Decade, should give special consideration to the conditions of work of women, including the problems of working hours and working norms for women, and bring their conclusions to the attention of member States.

265. The United Nations and UNESCO should ensure the inclusion of women in the current work undertaken in preparation for the new international information order as both recipients and participants in information systems in which their problems and issues are considered. In the definition of new communication policies the participation of women and their positive and dynamic image must be emphasized.

266. The United Nations system should ensure that women's issues form an integral part of the existing international systems and data banks (such as AGRIS, INRES, INTIB, DIS), particularly the Information System Unit within the Department of International Economic and Social Affairs, in order to facilitate free exchange of experience and knowledge among international organizations and their member States.

267. The Joint United Nations Information Committee in carrying out its responsibilities for programmes of social and economic information should:

(a) Ensure that its annual plans of action take into consideration issues and topics of particular interest to women, matters which particularly affect women, as well as their participation in information activities such as press, publications, radio programmes, film and television projects, reportage of field trips, seminars, etc.;

(b) Advocate that an information component be

built into projects such as those assisted by the Voluntary Fund for the Decade and by other organizations of the United Nations system, and which would be disseminated by the Department of Public Information, specialized agencies etc.;

(c) Ensure that guides and directories of the United Nations Information Centres contain relevant data and information about programmes and activities of the United Nations relating to women.

268. The United Nations and other organizations in the United Nations system such as UNCTAD, UNDP, UNFPA, UNEP, UNIDO, UNICEF, UNITAR, the ILO, FAO, UNESCO, WHO, and WFP, should include in their publications, media support activities, training programmes and seminars etc., specific guidelines on issues and topics of particular interest to women and those in which women could be successfully integrated. In particular, United Nations agencies concerned with development, education, employment, health, population, food production etc., should increase their information output on matters affecting women, especially in developing countries, with emphasis on reaching mass audiences in rural and isolated regions and countries where women tend to be cut off from the main media channels.

269. In its programme on major political, economic and social issues as well as on human interest stories, United Nations radio should include contributions and participation of women in all these areas. The present weekly radio programme on women should be continued through the Decade or longer as the need may be, with adequate provision being made to adapt it in different languages and distribute it more extensively. Co-production agreements between United Nations visual service and local networks to expand the number of films on United Nations topics should include co-production with women producers in developing countries on films related to women's issues.

270. The United Nations should issue booklets, pamphlets and publications with periodic progress reports on Decade activities and encourage the exchange of information and experience between women in Member States through study visits and the distribution of publications. The United Nations Handbook on the New International Economic Order should include data and information on aspects of women's participation. The *Development Forum* and other publications should contain items related to the Decade. The United Nations Information Centres should improve their library materials on women and disseminate information on women more actively, especially in developing countries. Information on women should be on the agenda of meetings of the directors of the Centres throughout the Decade.

271. The United Nations and organizations of the

United Nations system dealing with development should strengthen their information components relating to women in development and highlight the communication component of development projects. Well-documented and built-in communication components should be included in all development programmes or projects for the integration of women in development, and more adequate evaluation of the uses of media in development support to spread knowledge and increase the possibility of transfer. The United Nations and organizations of the United Nations system should collect and disseminate information on training programmes in development communication with special reference to programmes for women.

272. Information including detailed bibliographies of studies and other materials produced by the United Nations and its specialized agencies on women in the development process should be widely distributed to member nations and appropriate private research organizations to facilitate access to such information.

E. *Review and appraisal*

273. The United Nations system should continue to carry out a comprehensive and critical biennial review and appraisal of progress achieved in implementing the provisions of the World Plan of Action and of the Programme for the Second Half of the Decade. The central role in the carrying out of this review and appraisal should be played by the Commission on the Status of Women. The reporting system as well as the measures for dissemination of information should be designed for the effective use of the result of monitoring by all bodies concerned.

274. The Commission on the Status of Women and the Branch for the Advancement of Women should be strengthened by resetting priorities within existing budgetary resources. The integrated reporting system should be improved, as should the Commission's ability to consider communications and the capacity for publicizing its work.

275. With a view to achieving the full integration of women into the overall development planning of the United Nations, the review and appraisal of programmes made in implementing the World Plan of Action and the Programme of Action for the Second Half of the Decade should be part of the procedures for the review and appraisal of progress made in the implementation of international development strategy for the third United Nations Development Decade.

276. The specialized agencies and organizations of the United Nations system as well as other intergovernmental and non-governmental organizations concerned should consider the Programme of Action for the Second Half of the Decade and assist in its implementation.

277. The existing special mechanisms within the United Nations bodies and existing specialized agencies should be strengthened to implement the Programme of Action, to increase the incorporation of women's needs into all their programmes and activities and also to increase women's participation in and benefit from those programmes and activities.

278. The secretariats of all organizations within the United Nations system as well as of intergovernmental and non-governmental organizations concerned should amend their recruitment, training, promotion and remuneration policies as necessary in order to ensure equal treatment and status for men and women employed by the organizations whether as temporary, fixed-term or permanent employees or as consultants. Such organizations should, when requesting data on women's employment from member countries with a view to publication, provide and publish comparable data on the situation as regards women's employment within the organization concerned.

279. Guidelines should be established wherever they do not already exist for the study of programmes and projects in respect of their likely impact on women, and measures should be taken for monitoring and evaluating such programmes with respect to their benefits to women.

280. Co-ordination and cooperation among the specialized agencies and United Nations bodies should be effected by increasing use of the Inter-Agency Programme for the Decade for Women and of the Branch for the Advancement of Women.

281. The regional commissions in their periodic reviews and appraisals submitted to the Economic and Social Council should report fully on specific aspects of the situation of women in every sector of their development programmes on the basis of replies to the questionnaire on the implementation of the World Plan of Action and the Programme of Action for the Second Half of the Decade. These should be supplemented by appraisals of specific sectors undertaken by the regional commissions and specialized agencies, reports of relevant regional meetings of the United Nations and other documents and independent research.

282. Regional commissions should submit reports regularly to the Centre for Social Development and Humanitarian Affairs of the United Nations Secretariat on this Programme as part of the overall review and appraisal of the World Plan of Action. There should be a close coordination of the regional programmes for the advancement of women with United Nations Headquarters to ensure a better use of resources.

283. Regional commissions should ensure that the high-level regional intergovernmental and expert meetings which they periodically convene should include, in

their overall periodic appraisal, an assessment of the situation of women as a fundamental prerequisite for planning action programmes to meet the objectives of the third development decade and the New International Economic Order.

284. Special efforts should be made by the United Nations and regional commissions to assist Governments of Member States which have difficulty in providing resources to complete the questionnaire and submit data required for the review and appraisal.

VI. Regional policies and programmes

285. The international policies and programmes outlined above have clear application at the regional level and should also be regarded as regional priorities. In addition, the regional commissions, in cooperation with the regional offices of the specialized agencies, have specific responsibilities to provide assistance to Governments and non-governmental organizations for developing policies, strategies and programmes for the second half of the Decade in the light of the review and appraisal of progress achieved in the first half.

286. The strengthening of appropriate regional action programmes for women should be based on the development of cooperation between the countries of the region with the aim of promoting the principle of self-reliance. The formulation of regional policies and programmes is a multidimensional process requiring the adoption of action-oriented measures that are both bilateral and multilateral in scope and which require an increase in financial, technical and personnel resources to implement effectively regional programmes and priorities. To this end, regional commissions should adopt the following measures:

(a) Integrate the recommendations of this Programme into the work programme of their respective sectoral units so that its implementation contributes to the development strategy of the third United Nations Development Decade;

(b) Promote fellowship and other special training programmes, particularly in the tertiary sectors which comprise the majority of the female labour force both in rural and urban areas, so that women can improve and/or gain occupational and socio-economic status;

(c) Strengthen the information and data collection systems with a view to providing better analysis of data on the situation and work of women, including, in particular, improved national, regional and subregional reviews of progress achieved in the implementation of this programme of action; and providing a basis for more effective advisory services to Governments regarding programmes for women;

(d) Intensify their activities in promoting adequate national social infrastructure allowing women and men to discharge their dual role in the family and in society;

(e) Undertake "skilled womenpower" inventories at national, subregional and regional levels so that trained women can have equal opportunities to be recruited in jobs related to main areas of the development process at national, regional and international levels.

Institutional arrangements

287. Measures should be taken for:

(a) Strengthening the offices of the regional commissions by recruiting women for posts at a high level of decision-making and responsibility. Such posts should include those of programme officers provided for in regular budgets and not only from extrabudgetary sources, and responsible for implementing the programmes for the second half of the Decade. The regional commissions should establish posts at a high level to coordinate and implement policies and programmes relating specifically to the status of women;

(b) The reinforcement of the regional centres for research and training.

Resolutions and decision adopted by the Conference

1. Family planning
2. Improving the situation of disabled women of all ages
3. Migrant women
4. Elderly women and economic security
5. Battered women and violence in the family
6. Review and evaluation of progress made in the implementation of the World Plan of Action at the national level
7. The role of women in the preparation of societies for life in peace
8. Gathering of data concerning women through census questionnaires
9. Intensification of drought control in the Sahel
10. Assistance to Lebanese women
11. Women's participation in the strengthening of international peace and security and in the struggle against colonialism, racism, racial discrimination, foreign aggression and occupation and all forms of foreign domination
12. The situation of women refugees and displaced women the world over
13. The situation of displaced and refugee women the world over
14. Integrated approach to the health and welfare of women

Document 71

General Assembly resolution endorsing the outcome of the World Conference of the United Nations Decade for Women

A/RES/35/136, 11 December 1980

The General Assembly,

Recalling its resolution 3520 (XXX) of 15 December 1975, in which it proclaimed the period from 1976 to 1985 United Nations Decade for Women: Equality, Development and Peace and decided to convene a world conference at the mid-term of the Decade,

Recalling also its resolution 34/158 of 17 December 1979 on the World Conference of the United Nations Decade for Women,

Recalling further its resolution 34/180 of 18 December 1979, the annex to which contains the text of the Convention on the Elimination of All Forms of Discrimination against Women,

Reaffirming the principles and objectives set forth in the Declaration of Mexico on the Equality of Women and Their Contribution to Development and Peace, 1975, 1/ and in the World Plan of Action for the Implementation of the Objectives of the International Women's Year, 2/

Bearing in mind its resolutions 3201 (S-VI) and

1/ See *Report of the World Conference of the International Women's Year, Mexico City, 19 June-2 July 1975* (United Nations publication, Sales No. E.76.IV.1), chap. I.
2/ Ibid., chap. II, sect. A.

3202 (S-VI) of 1 May 1974, containing the Declaration and the Programme of Action on the Establishment of a New International Economic Order, 3281 (XXIX) of 12 December 1974, containing the Charter of Economic Rights and Duties of States, and 3362 (S-VII) of 16 September 1975 on development and international economic cooperation,

Bearing in mind further the consensus achieved on the text of the International Development Strategy for the Third United Nations Development Decade, 3/ in particular on the implementation of the objectives of the United Nations Decade for Women within the framework of the Strategy,

Having considered the *Report of the World Conference of the United Nations Decade for Women: Equality, Development and Peace, 4/*

Convinced that the Conference, by adopting the Programme of Action for the Second Half of the United Nations Decade for Women and other relevant decisions and resolutions, 5/ has made an important and positive contribution to the attainment of the objectives of the Decade and permitted the maintenance of a policy framework to deal with the concerns of women,

Recognizing the need for the active participation of women in the achievement of a just and lasting peace and social progress, the establishment of the new international economic order, complete respect for human rights and fundamental freedoms and the integration of women into the development process so that the equality of men and women may be affirmed and their situation improved,

Reaffirming that the realization of equal rights for women at all levels and in all areas of life will contribute to the struggle for the elimination of colonialism, neo-colonialism, all forms of racism and racial discrimination and apartheid,

Considering that the recommendations made in the Programme of Action and in other relevant decisions and resolutions adopted by the Conference should immediately be translated into concrete action by States, the organizations of the United Nations system and intergovernmental and non-governmental organizations,

1. *Takes note with satisfaction* of the *Report of the World Conference of the United Nations Decade for Women: Equality, Development and Peace;*

2. *Endorses* the Programme of Action for the Second Half of the United nations Decade for Women, as adopted at the Conference;

3. *Recognizes* that the Conference made an important and constructive contribution by appraising the progress achieved and the obstacles encountered in the implementation of the objectives of the Decade and by

preparing and adopting a programme for the next five years;

4. *Affirms* that the implementation of the Programme of Action should result in the complete integration of women into the development process and the elimination of all forms of inequality between men and women and will guarantee broad participation by women in efforts to strengthen peace and security throughout the world;

5. *Affirms*, in particular, that the implementation of the Programme of Action and of the relevant recommendations, decisions and resolutions of the Conference will contribute to the effective attainment of the objectives of the Decade;

6. *Urges* Governments to take appropriate measures to implement the Programme of Action and other relevant resolutions and decisions at the national, regional and international levels;

7. *Requests*, in particular, Member States when preparing and evaluating the execution of projects, programmes and plans of action at national, regional and international meetings to pay special attention to measures for the involvement and benefit of women;

8. *Calls upon* all Governments, organizations of the United Nations system and intergovernmental and non-governmental organizations to intensify, at regional levels, the dissemination of information and the exchange of experiences on the participation of women in all relevant programmes and information activities with a view to achieving the objectives of the Decade;

9. *Requests* the regional commissions to consider the Programme of Action with a view to formulating appropriate programmes for implementing the recommendations contained therein, including the organizations of seminars, symposia and meetings which will contribute towards furthering the integration of women into the development process and the achievement of the objectives of the Decade;

10. *Urges* the regional commissions to report in full to the Economic and Social Council at its first regular session of 1982 on the specific aspects of the situation of women in all the sectors of their development programmes, in order to strengthen and reorient the reporting methods of those commissions so as to reflect more adequately the regional concerns of women, and thereafter to report on the same subject every two years;

11. *Urges* all the organizations of the United Nations system to take the necessary measures to ensure

3/ See resolution 35/56, annex.
4/ United Nations publication, Sales No. E.80.IV.3 and corrigendum.
5/ Ibid., chap. I.

a concerted and sustained effort for the implementation of the Programme of Action and of other relevant resolutions and decisions of the Conference in the course of the second half of the Decade, with a view to achieving a substantial improvement in the status of women and to ensuring that all their programmes take into account the need for the complete integration of women;

12. *Requests* the Secretary-General to submit to the Economic and Social Council at its first regular session of 1981 proposals for the implementation of the Programme of Action, taking into account the need for the speedy establishment of the new international economic order and the implementation of the goals and objectives of the International Development Strategy for the Third United Nations Development Decade, which are indispensable for the advancement of women;

13. *Also requests* the Secretary-General to consider appropriate measures to enable the Commission on the Status of Women to discharge the functions assigned to it for the implementation of the World Plan of Action for the Implementation of the Objectives of the International Women's Year and the Programmes of Action for the Second Half of the United Nations Decade for Women, and also request him to take immediate action to strengthen the Centre for Social Development and Humanitarian Affairs of the Secretariat at Vienna;

14. *Further requests* the Secretary-General and international organizations to take all the necessary action to establish, where they do not already exist, focal points in all sectors of the organizations of the United Nations system in order to coordinate questions relating to women and integrate them into their work programmes;

15. *Invites* the Secretary-General to circulate the report of the Conference among Member States and intergovernmental and non-governmental organizations in order to ensure that it is publicized and disseminated as widely as possible;

16. *Also invites* the Secretary-General to submit to the General Assembly at its thirty-sixth session a report on the measures taken to implement the present resolution;

17. *Decides* to convene in 1985, at the conclusion of the Decade, a World Conference to Review and Appraise the Achievements of the United Nations Decade for Women;

18. *Decides* to include in the provisional agenda of its thirty-sixth session the item entitled "United Nations Decade for Women: Equality, Development and Peace".

Document 72

General Assembly resolution on implementation of the Programme of Action for the Second Half of the United Nations Decade for Women

A/RES/36/126, 14 December 1981

The General Assembly,

Recalling its resolution 35/136 of 11 December 1980, in which it endorsed the Programme of Action for the Second Half of the United Nations Decade for Women, 1/ and decided to convene in 1985, at the conclusion of the Decade, a World Conference to Review and Appraise the Achievements of the United Nations Decade for Women,

Bearing in mind its resolutions 3201 (S-VI) and 3202 (S-VI) of 1 May 1974, containing the Declaration and the Programme of Action on the Establishment of a New International Economic Order, 3281 (XXIX) of 12 December 1974, containing the Charter of Economic Rights and Duties of States, and 3362 (S-VII) of 16 September 1975 on development and international economic cooperation,

Emphasizing the importance attached in the International Development Strategy for the Third United Nations Development Decade 2/ to the need to improve the status of women and ensure their full participation in the development process as agents and beneficiaries of development,

Taking note of chapter XXV, on the role of women in development, of the New Delhi Declaration, 3/ adopted by the Conference of Ministers for Foreign Affairs of Non-Aligned Countries, held at New Delhi from 9 to 13 February 1981,

Emphasizing that the recommendations made in the Programme of Action for the Second Half of the Decade and in other relevant decisions and resolutions adopted by the World Conference of the United Nations Decade for Women should immediately be translated into con-

1/ See *Report of the World Conference of the United Nations Decade for Women: Equality, Development and Peace, Copenhagen, 14-30 July 1980* (United Nations publication, Sales No. E.80.IV.3 and corrigendum), chap. I, sect. A.
2/ Resolution 35/56, annex.
3/ A/36/116 and Corr.1, annex.

crete action by States, the organizations of the United Nations system and intergovernmental and non-governmental organizations,

Welcoming the entry into force on 3 September 1981 of the Convention on the Elimination of All Forms of Discrimination against Women 4/ and the growing number of States that have ratified it,

Convinced that the International Research and Training Institute for the Advancement of Women must be given the assistance needed to enable it to begin to function as early as possible in the host country,

Noting that the review and appraisal of the progress made by Governments in implementing the Programme of Action will be carried out by the Commission on the Status of Women every two years, beginning with the Commission's twenty-ninth session,

Taking note of the report of the Secretary-General on the World Conference of the United Nations Decade for Women, 5/

1. *Affirms* that the implementation of the Programme of Action for the Second Half of the United Nations Decade for Women and of the relevant recommendations, resolutions and decisions adopted by the World Conference of the United Nations Decade for Women should result in the complete integration of women into the development process and in the effective realization of the objectives of the United Nations Decade for Women: Equality, Development and Peace;

2. *Calls upon* Governments to continue taking the measures necessary for achieving substantial progress in the implementation of the relevant recommendations of the Programme of Action with a view to ensuring equal participation by women as agents and beneficiaries in all sectors and at all levels of the development process;

3. *Calls upon* the organizations of the United Nations system, including the regional commissions, to reserve adequate resources for, and pay increased attention to, the implementation of the Programme of Action, particularly as regards the dissemination of information on the participation of women;

4. *Urges* the regional commissions to report in full to the Economic and Social Council, at its first regular session of 1982, on the evolution of the situation of women in all the sectors of their development programmes, in order to strengthen and reorient the programmes and reporting methods of those commissions, so as to reflect more adequately the regional concerns of women;

5. *Requests* the Economic and Social Council, at its first regular session of 1982, to consider the implementation of the Programme of Action, giving high priority in this regard to the report of the Commission on the Status of Women;

6. *Emphasizes* the role of the Centre for Social Development and Humanitarian Affairs of the Secretariat as the focal point for the organizations of the United Nations system with regard to the implementation of the Programme of Action, in order to achieve the goals and objectives of the Decade, and requests the Secretary-General to give the Centre the assistance required to enable it to carry out its mandate;

7. *Requests* the Commission on the Status of Women at its twenty-ninth session, to be held in February 1982, to give priority to the question of the preparations for the World Conference to Review and Appraise the Achievements of the United Nations Decade for Women, to be held in 1985, which will mark the end of the Decade, with a view to submitting to the General Assembly at its thirty-seventh session, through the Economic and Social Council, specific proposals on that question;

8. *Stresses* the need for close and continued cooperation between the United Nations system and the International Research and Training Institute for the Advancement of Women and requests the Secretary-General to take all necessary measures to allow the Institute to carry out its mandate;

9. *Takes note with satisfaction* of the effective contribution made by the Voluntary Fund for the United Nations Decade for Women to the implementation of the Programme of Action;

10. *Invites* the Secretary-General to submit to the General Assembly, at its thirty-seventh session, a report on the steps taken to implement the present resolution;

11. *Decides* to include in the provisional agenda of its thirty-seventh session the item entitled "United Nations Decade for Women: Equality, Development and Peace".

4/ Resolution 34/180, annex.
5/ A/36/564.

Document 73

General Assembly resolution extending the activities of the Voluntary Fund beyond the end of the United Nations Decade for Women

A/RES/36/129, 14 December 1981

The General Assembly,

Recalling its resolution 3520 (XXX) of 15 December 1975, by which it proclaimed the period from 1976 to 1985 United Nations Decade for Women: Equality, Development and Peace,

Recalling its decision of 15 December 1975 to extend the activities of the Voluntary Fund for the International Women's Year so as to cover the period of the Decade,

Recalling its resolution 31/133 of 16 December 1976, containing the criteria and arrangements for the management of the Fund,

Recalling its resolution 32/138 of 16 December 1977,

Recalling also its resolution 34/156 of 17 December 1979, in which it expressed the desire to see the activities developed by the Fund continued beyond the United Nations Decade for Women and decided to review at its thirty-sixth session the decision regarding the location of the Fund in New York,

Recalling further Economic and Social Council resolution 1980/3 of 16 April 1980,

Bearing in mind its resolution 35/136 of 11 December 1980, in which it endorsed the Programme of Action for the Second Half of the United Nations Decade for Women, 1/

Conscious that the Fund is intended to supplement, through financial and technical support, the activities for implementing the goals for the United Nations Decade for Women: Equality, Development and Peace,

Noting with appreciation the effective management and continuing expansion of the Fund's activities and the cooperation extended by the relevant organs of the United Nations, including the United Nations Development Programme, the United Nations Children's Fund and the regional commissions,

Reaffirming the role of the Centre for Social Development and Humanitarian Affairs of the Secretariat as the focal point for interagency cooperation towards the implementation of the Programme of Action,

Noting with appreciation the support given by the Fund to projects in the developing countries,

Noting also with appreciation the report of the Secretary-General on the future of the Fund, 2/

1. *Notes with satisfaction* the decisions of the Consultative Committee on the Voluntary Fund for the United Nations Decade for Women during its ninth and tenth sessions; 3/

2. *Expresses its appreciation* for the voluntary contributions pledged by Member States and urges them to contribute or increase their contributions to the Fund;

3. *Decides* that the Fund should continue its activities beyond the United Nations Decade for Women;

4. *Stresses* the importance of the contributions of the Fund towards the realization of the goals and objectives of the United Nations Decade for Women;

5. *Stresses also* the interrelationship of the Voluntary Fund with the Advancement of Women Branch of the Centre for Social Development and Humanitarian Affairs of the Secretariat;

6. *Requests* the Secretary-General to invite the views of Member States on how best the Fund can continue its activities beyond the Decade and to submit a report thereon to the General Assembly at its thirty-ninth session;

7. *Requests also* the Secretary-General, taking into account the views expresses by Member States on this matter, to submit to the General Assembly at its thirty-ninth session a report on the substantive and financial implications of, and his proposals for the timing and modalities for, a relocation of the Fund within the Centre for Social Development and Humanitarian Affairs of the Secretariat in order to enable Member States to take a decision in the matter.

1/ *Report of the World Conference of the United Nations Decade for Women: Equality, Development and Peace, Copenhagen, 14-30 1980* (United Nations publication, Sales No. E.80.IV.3 and corrigendum), chap.I, sect. A.
2/ A/36/647 and Corr.1.
3/ Ibid., para. 13.

Document 74

General Assembly resolution on preparations for a World Conference to Review and Appraise the Achievements of the United Nations Decade for Women

A/RES/37/60, 3 December 1982

The General Assembly,

Recalling its resolution 3520 (XXX) of 15 December 1975, in which it endorsed, *inter alia,* the action proposals contained in the World Plan of Action for the Implementation of the Objectives of the International Women's Year, 1/

Recalling its resolution 3490 (XXX) of 12 December 1975, in which it expressed its conviction that a comprehensive and thorough review and appraisal of progress made in meeting the goals of the World Plan of Action was of crucial importance for the success of the Plan and recognized that the results of the implementation of the Plan would contribute to the consideration of the review and appraisal of the International Development Strategy for the Second United Nations Development Decade 2/ and would consequently promote the role of women in the development process,

Recalling also its resolution 35/136 of 11 December 1980, in which it endorsed the Programme of Action for the Second Half of the United Nations Decade for Women 3/ as adopted at the World Conference of the United Nations Decade for Women, and decided to convene in 1985, at the conclusion of the Decade, a World Conference to Review and Appraise the Achievements of the United Nations Decade for Women,

Recalling further that the International Development Strategy for the Third United Nations Development Decade 4/ stressed that the important set of measures to improve the status of women, contained in the World Plan of Action adopted at Mexico City in 1975, 1/ and the important agreed measures relating to the International Development Strategy in the Programme of Action for the Second Half of the United Nations Decade for Women, adopted at Copenhagen in 1980, should be implemented,

Recalling its resolution 36/126 of 14 December 1981, in which it requested the Commission on the Status of Women, at its session to be held in 1982, to give priority to the question of the preparations for the Conference,

Noting that the Economic and Social Council, at its first regular session of 1982, considered the recommendations of the Commission on the Status of Women as set forth in its report 5/ adopted, on 4 May 1982, resolution 1982/26 on the preparations for the Conference,

Bearing in mind all its relevant resolutions and decisions regarding preparations for special conferences, in particular its resolution 33/189 of 29 January 1979,

1. *Endorses* Economic and Social Council resolution 1982/26 on the preparations for the World Conference to Review and Appraise the Achievements of the United Nations Decade for Women, to be held in 1985;

2. *Welcomes* the decision of the Economic and Social Council that the Commission on the Status of Women should be the preparatory body for the Conference and that it should operate on the basis of consensus;

3. *Endorses* the decision of the Economic and Social Council to invite the widest possible participation by States in the preparatory meetings for the Conference and expresses the hope that they will designate representatives who will have the background and experience in the area of women development;

4. *Notes* that the first session of the Commission on the Status of Women as the preparatory body of the Conference is to be held at Vienna from 23 February to 4 March 1983 and that the report on that session will be considered by the Economic and Social Council at its first regular session of 1983;

5. *Requests* the Secretary-General to take into account paragraph 9 of General Assembly resolution 33/189 when appointing the Secretary-General of the Conference;

6. *Decides* to consider at its thirty-eighth session the recommendations of the Economic and Social Council at its first regular session of 1983 based on the report of the first session of the Commission on the Status of Women as the preparatory body for the Conference, together with the observations, if any, of the Secretary-General;

1/ *Report of the World Conference of the International Women's Year, Mexico City, 19 June-July 1975* (United Nations publication, Sales No. E.76.IV.1), chap.II, sect.A.
2/ Resolution 2626 (XXV).
3/ *Report of the World Conference of the United Nations Decade for Women: Equality, Development and Peace, Copenhagen, 14-30 July 1980* (United Nations publication, Sales No. E.80.IV.3 and corrigendum), chap.I, sect.A.
4/ Resolution 35/56, annex.
5/ *Official Records of the Economic and Social Council, 1982,* Supplement No.4 (E/1982/14).

7. *Takes note with appreciation* of the report of the Secretary-General on the progress made in the preparation of a world survey on the role of women in development 6/ and recommends that the survey should be submitted to the Conference;

8. *Decides* to include in the provisional agenda of its thirty-eighth session an item entitled "Preparations for the World Conference to Review and Appraise the Achievements of the United Nations Decade for Women".

6/ A/37/381.

Document 75

General Assembly resolution adopting the Declaration on the Participation of Women in Promoting International Peace and Cooperation

A/RES/37/63, 3 December 1982

The General Assembly,

Considering that the Charter of the United Nations expresses the determination of the peoples of the United Nations to reaffirm faith in the equal rights of men and women and to practise tolerance and live together in peace with one another as good neighbours,

Considering also that the Universal Declaration of Human Rights 1/ proclaims that the inherent dignity and equal and inalienable rights of all members of the human family is the foundation of freedom, justice and peace in the world,

Considering further that the International Covenants on Human Rights 2/ provide for the equal right of men and women to the enjoyment of all economic, social, cultural, civil and political rights,

Reaffirming the objectives of the United Nations Decade for Women: Equality, Development and Peace,

Taking into account the resolutions, declarations, conventions, programmes and recommendations of the United Nations and the specialized agencies and international conferences designed to eliminate all forms of discrimination and to promote equal rights for men and women,

Recalling that the Declaration of Mexico on the Equality of Women and their Contribution to Development and Peace, 1975, 3/ states that women have a vital role to play in the promotion of peace in all spheres of life: in the family, the community, the nation and the world,

Recalling that the Convention on the Elimination of All Forms of Discrimination against Women 4/ declares that discrimination against women violates the principles of equality of rights and respect for human dignity, is an obstacle to the participation of women, on equal terms with men, in the political, social, economic and cultural life of their countries and makes more difficult the full development of the potentialities of women in the service of their countries and of humanity,

Recalling also that the Convention on the Elimination of All Forms of Discrimination against Women affirms that the strengthening of international peace and security, the relaxation of international tension, mutual cooperation among all States irrespective of their social and economic systems, general and complete disarmament, in particular nuclear disarmament under strict and effective international control, the affirmation of the principles of justice, equality and mutual benefit in relations among countries and the realization of the right of peoples under alien and colonial domination and foreign occupation to self-determination and independence, as well as respect for national sovereignty and territorial integrity, will promote social progress and development and as a consequence will contribute to the attainment of full equality between men and women,

Recognizing that the Convention on the Elimination of All Forms of Discrimination against Women obligates States Parties to take all appropriate measures to eliminate discrimination against women in all its forms and in every field of human endeavour, including politics, economic activities, law, employment, education, health care and domestic relations,

Noting that, despite progress towards the achievement of equality between men and women, considerable discrimination against women continues to exist, thereby

1/ Resolution 217 A (III).
2/ Resolution 2200 A (XXI), annex.
3/ *Report of the World Conference of the International Women's Year, Mexico City, 19 June - 2 July 1975* (United Nations publication, Sales No. E.76.IV.1), chap. I.
4/ Resolution 34/180, annex.

impeding the active participation of women in promoting international peace and cooperation,

Welcoming the contribution which women have nevertheless made towards promoting international peace and cooperation, the struggle against colonialism, apartheid, all forms of racism and racial discrimination, foreign aggression and occupation and all forms of alien domination, and towards the unrestricted and effective enjoyment of human rights and fundamental freedoms,

Welcoming also the contribution of women towards a just restructuring of international economic relations and the achievement of a new international economic order,

Convinced that women can play an important and increasing role in these areas,

Solemnly proclaims the Declaration on the Participation of Women in Promoting International Peace and Co-operation set forth in the annex to the present resolution.

Annex

Declaration on the Participation of Women in Promoting International Peace and Cooperation

PART I

Article 1

Women and men have an equal and vital interest in contributing to international peace and cooperation. To this end, women must be enabled to exercise their right to participate in the economic, social, cultural, civil and political affairs of society on an equal footing with men.

Article 2

The full participation of women in the economic, social, cultural, civil and political affairs of society and in the endeavour to promote international peace and cooperation is dependent on a balanced and equitable distribution of roles between men and women in the family and in society as a whole.

Article 3

The increasing participation of women in the economic, social, cultural, civil and political affairs of society will contribute to international peace and cooperation.

Article 4

The full enjoyment of the rights of women and men and the full participation of women in promoting international peace and cooperation will contribute to the eradication of apartheid, of all forms of racism, racial discrimination, colonialism, neo-colonialism, aggression, foreign occupation and domination and interference in the internal affairs of States.

Article 5

Special national and international measures are necessary to increase the level of women's participation in the sphere of international relations so that women can contribute, on an equal basis, with men to national and international efforts to secure world peace and economic and social progress and to promote international cooperation.

PART II

Article 6

All appropriate measures shall be taken to intensify national and international efforts in respect of the participation of women in promoting international peace and cooperation by ensuring the equal participation of women in the economic, social, cultural, civil and political affairs of society through a balanced and equitable distribution of roles between men and women in the domestic sphere and in society as a whole, as well as by providing an equal opportunity for women to participate in the decision-making process.

Article 7

All appropriate measures shall be taken to promote the exchange of experience at the national and international levels for the purpose of furthering the involvement of women in promoting international peace and cooperation and in solving other vital national and international problems.

Article 8

All appropriate measures shall be taken at the national and international levels to give effective publicity to the responsibility and active participation of women in promoting international peace and cooperation and in solving other vital national and international problems.

Article 9

All appropriate measures shall be taken to render solidarity and support to those women who are victims of mass and flagrant violations of human rights such as apartheid, all forms of racism, racial discrimination, colonialism, neo-colonialism, aggression, foreign occupation and domination and of all other violations of human rights.

Article 10

All appropriate measures shall be taken to pay a tribute to the participation of women in promoting international peace and cooperation.

Article 11

All appropriate measures shall be taken to encourage women to participate in non-governmental and intergovernmental organizations concerned with the strengthening of international peace and security, the development of friendly relations among nations and the promotion of cooperation among States and, to that end, freedom of thought, conscience, expression, assembly, association, communication and movement, without distinction as to race, political or religious belief, language or ethnic origin, shall be effectively guaranteed.

Article 12

All appropriate measures shall be taken to provide practical opportunities for the effective participation of women in promoting international peace and cooperation, economic development and social progress including, to that end:

(a) The promotion of an equitable representation of women in governmental and non-governmental functions;

(b) The promotion of equality of opportunities for women to enter diplomatic service;

(c) The appointment or nomination of women, on an equal basis with men, as members of delegations to national, regional or international meetings;

(d) Support for increased employment of women at all levels in the secretariats of the United Nations and the specialized agencies, in conformity with Article 101 of the Charter of the United Nations.

Article 13

All appropriate measures shall be taken to establish adequate legal protection of the rights of women on an equal basis with men in order to ensure effective participation of women in the activities referred to above.

Article 14

Governments, non-governmental and international organizations, including the United Nations and the specialized agencies and individuals, are urged to do all in their power to promote the implementation of the principles contained in the present Declaration.

Document 76

Report of INSTRAW on its programme activities

A/38/406, 21 October 1983

INTERNATIONAL RESEARCH AND
TRAINING INSTITUTE FOR THE
ADVANCEMENT OF WOMEN

Note by the Secretary-General

The General Assembly, in its resolution 37/56 of 3 December 1982, invited the Secretary-General to submit to the Assembly at its thirty-eighth session a report on the programme activities of the International Research and Training Institute for the Advancement of Women. The Secretary-General hereby transmits to the General Assembly the report prepared by the Institute on its programme activities.

Annex

Report of the International Research and Training Institute for the Advancement of Women

. . .

III. Programme of work

26. The initial programme of the Institute for the biennium 1982-1983 is an experimental one geared to exploring the most productive ways and means of securing the incorporation of issues of relevance to women into development efforts at international, regional and national levels in compliance with the Board guidelines which indicated that the INSTRAW work programme should be related to practical and specific objectives. Special attention is being paid to those activities which would lead to increased technical cooperation for development benefiting women, and which would enhance the interdependence of social and economic issues.

A. Improving statistics and indicators on the situation of women

27. One of the first research projects carried out by the Institute was in the field of statistics and indicators, responding to the repeated call for improved statistics and statistical concepts covering the situation of women. The first phase of the Institute's programme on improving statistics and indicators on the situation of women, undertaken jointly with the United Nations Statistical Office, is now completed. Two technical reports on this subject were reviewed by an expert group and are being revised accordingly for publication in 1983.

28. The first document is a state-of-the-art review of existing concepts, data sources and uses for indicators. The report is aimed at providing practical and concrete guidance to producers and users of statistics and indica-

tors on women on their selection, compilation and interpretation, particularly at the national level. The second document is an analysis of conceptual and methodological problems in improving the quality and relevance of data pertaining to the conditions of women over the longer term. It provides a critical review of statistical concepts, methods and analytical interpretations of statistical findings.

29. The Expert Group Meeting on Improving Statistics and Indicators on the Situation of Women was convened by the Institute and the United Nations Statistical Office in New York from 11 to 15 April 1983 to review these two documents. High-level statisticians and analysts from all regions were invited to participate. In addition, representatives from the regional commissions, the specialized agencies and other interested international organizations such as the European Economic Community and the Organization of Economic Development and Co-operation (OECD) were also invited as observers. The group of experts also suggested a number of follow-up activities in the field of statistics and indicators on the situation of women.

30. In the preparation and initial review of these documents, consultations took place with the Food and Agriculture Organization of the United Nations (FAO), the United Nations Educational, Scientific and Cultural Organization (UNESCO), the World Health Organization (WHO), the International Labour Organization (ILO), the Branch for the Advancement of Women of the Centre for Social Development and Humanitarian Affairs (CSDHA/BAW) and the OECD. In this respect, the Institute was also represented at a number of United Nations meetings relevant to this subject.

31. The second phase of the project will be implemented in the biennium 1984-1985. It will focus on follow-up activities as recommended by the Expert Group Meeting. The Institute's intention in this second phase is to concentrate on training programmes and regional needs in the field of statistics and indicators.

B. The incorporation of women into development planning and programming

32. Development planning and programming are the most relevant methods by which the effective integration of women in socio-economic development can be achieved. Bearing this in mind, the Institute has made preparations for an interregional seminar on the incorporation of women into development planning, to be held from 5 to 11 December 1983 at its permanent headquarters in Santo Domingo.

33. On the basis of comparative studies on the efforts carried out so far within and outside the United Nations system, innovative planning methodologies and procedures may be gradually designed which will take into consideration women's role in development.

34. By convening high-level experts in development planning and women's issues from the various regions of the world, the objective of the seminar is twofold: to exchange experience of different countries in the area of planning and programming, to underline the problems encountered and to seek solutions; and to increase the involvement of women in the planning process through raising awareness and determining the most suitable institutional framework, planning and programming mechanisms and techniques.

35. Following the recommendations of the experts in the seminar, the Institute first hopes to issue a publication that would include information and measures for the integration of issues of relevance to women into planning and programming techniques and processes. Next, it plans to initiate training arrangements for officials in charge of the planning process, project and development programme formulation.

C. The role of women in the implementation of the objectives of the International Drinking Water Supply and Sanitation Decade

36. The Institute has a long-term commitment to the objectives of the International Drinking Water Supply and Sanitation Decade (IDWSSD) as approved by the INSTRAW Board of Trustees at its third session, held in January 1983.

37. INSTRAW proposed to the Steering Committee for Co-operative Action of IDWSSD, at its ninth session held in April 1982, the formation of an Inter-Agency Task Force on Women and IDWSSD. This proposal was accepted and it was agreed that INSTRAW and UNICEF would jointly assume the responsibility for the secretariat of the Task Force. INSTRAW, together with UNICEF, is actively engaged in the organizational and substantive preparation required for the various sessions of the Task Force, including the preparation of relevant documents. Moreover, in November 1982, the Steering Committee accepted INSTRAW as a member of the Committee.

38. At the meeting of the Task Force, held in September 1982, it was decided that the Task Force would be an action-oriented body of the Steering Committee geared towards activities that would focus on the needs of women in the question of improving water supply and sanitation, as well as the participation of women in the cooperative programme of the IDWSSD. The Task Force will serve to develop a strategy for enhancing the role of women in IDWSSD; assist in activities to support programmes for the Decade in relation to the role of women; act as a mechanism for collaboration

in the development and implementation of activities at the international and national levels; and monitor, evaluate and report on the implementation of policies and programmes for the Decade to ensure that they adequately reflect the concerns, needs and contributions of women.

39. In accordance with the Institute's mandate as well as its commitment to the objective of IDWSSD, INSTRAW is organizing an interregional seminar on "Women and the International Drinking Water Supply and Sanitation Decade", to be held in March 1984.

40. The purpose of this seminar is to solicit the views of experts, with a national and regional perspective on the problems involved in improving water supply and sanitation particularly as they relate to women and the solutions which have been found or are envisaged. The ultimate objective of the seminar is threefold: to indicate the cause of the major problems confronting women in this domain from a regional viewpoint; to reach a global consensus on the most meaningful approaches to address the problems of women in water supply and sanitation with a view to reaching possible solutions; and to generate interregional and international commitment and momentum within the framework of activities of IDWSSD in support of national efforts to solve the problems.

41. The output of the seminar will be a report incorporating the views expressed by the experts as well as their conclusions and recommendations. In addition, based on the outcome of the seminar, the Institute will establish training guidelines and manuals to assist governmental and non-governmental organizations, institutes and agencies at the national level in developing their training activities for women in the field of water supply and sanitation; publish and disseminate widely information relevant to the subject; and indicate follow-up activities to be carried out in each of the different regions.

42. In addition, INSTRAW is closely following the international and regional debates on this matter and in many cases the Institute has submitted written contributions to meetings and conferences organized to address the problem of water supply and sanitation.

D. *Role of women in international economic relations*

43. According to the Institute's mandate, the focus of its activities is social and economic development with the aim of integrating women into the mainstream development. This requires that the Institute monitor closely the current debate on development and international economic cooperation, and participate in the ongoing search to address the development problems in order to fulfil the objectives of the International Development Strategy for the Third United Nations Development Decade.

44. The current debate highlights a number of trends: (*a*) the ultimate aim of development is the well-being of the people; (*b*) the importance of the population component of development and the full participation of all segments of the population, women and men alike, in the development process; (*c*) development benefits should be shared by all in order to fulfil the call for "growth with equity". Many of these ideas were reflected in the International Development Strategy for the Third United Nations Development Decade, which stated in its preamble that the Development process must promote human dignity.

45. In this respect, a joint UNITAR/INSTRAW proposal on the establishment of an international independent committee on the role of women in the New International Economic Order and the International Development Strategy was considered by the Board of Trustees of UNITAR and INSTRAW in September 1981 and January 1982, respectively.

46. In the course of developing this proposal, INSTRAW undertook numerous activities, including a brain-storming session, which was organized at United Nations Headquarters on 25 July 1982, to solicit views of the specialists on the subject from within and outside the United Nations; consultations with the United Nations Institute for Training and Research (UNITAR), other United Nations bodies and other academic institutions with the view of determining the scope and terms of reference for the project; and a review of United Nations resolutions and decisions relevant to the status of women and their role in development, particularly those adopted by the General Assembly, the Economic and Social Council and the Commission on the Status of Women, in order to determine the areas which need further in-depth study.

47. As a result of surveying the area of women and development, it was found that the aspects to be further developed are: (a) to review and analyse the present model of development and different approaches and concepts so far used in development strategies, with a view to ensuring that women's needs and requirements are integrated in these development strategies; (b) to identify the economic dimension of actual development theories and approaches especially where they merge into the social perception of the work and life of women; (c) to assess the benefits and losses to women that derive from the economic and social changes in present-day society; (d) to examine the linkage between the micro and macro levels of development and the interrelationships between the international and national dimensions, taking into consideration the economic, social and cultural aspects as they relate to women; (e) to examine problems emerging from the world economy and influencing national

economic and social policies which affect the role, status and well-being of women.

48. Having examined the results of this survey, the Board of Trustees, at its third session, decided that the Institute should first conduct a series of research studies on the role of women in international economic relations, concentrating particularly on the analysis of interlinkages between macro and micro economy and their impact on the role and status of women.

49. Collaborating has already been initiated with UNCTAD on the first in the series of these research studies, which deals with the transfer and development of technology, including choice of technology, and their impact on the position and work of women. Moreover, contacts with internationally renowned academic institutions are being actively pursued at present.

E. *Role of women in the implementation of the policy of collective self-reliance of developing countries*

50. The Institute seeks to contribute to the activities which promote individual and collective self-reliance of developing countries and seeks to ensure that women's role is reflected in these cooperative endeavours. In this respect, the Institute is actively developing cooperative arrangements with UNDP Special Unit for Technical Co-operation among Developing Countries and other institutions active in the field.

51. At the High-Level Meeting on Technical Co-operation among Developing Countries in 1980, the important role of women in social and economic development was emphasized. In 1981, the High-Level Meeting invited Governments to enhance the full integration of women in the process of technical cooperation among developing countries and to cooperate closely with women's non-governmental and professional organizations and associations in defining and implementing programmes and projects for technical cooperation among developing countries.

52. In close cooperation with the Special Unit for TCDC, INSTRAW has started a series of publications on women and technical cooperation among developing countries. The initial publication, entitled *Integration of Women in Development through Technical Co-operation among Developing Countries (TCDC)* prepared for the third session of the High-Level Committee, provides an overview of the areas in which the integration of women through TCDC can be implemented. The initial findings indicate that most of the TCDC activities covering women are concentrated in the field of rural development and education. However, other areas should be more fully integrated into the process of TCDC. These include community development, employment, migration, health, industrialization, energy, science and tech-

nology, and use of modern communications for educational purposes. Planning techniques for the inclusion of women into TCDC programmes and projects, which would secure proper use of human resources, could be elaborated through TCDC activities. As the initial experiences have proven, this would contribute to establishing better linkages among national and regional plans and programmes.

53. The High-Level Committee took note of the publication and invited developing countries to strengthen, wherever possible, linkages between their national focal points, as well as other professional institutions; to give due consideration to women's participation and requirements when identifying operational issues which lend themselves to a TCDC approach; and to include specific reference to women in supportive activities for TCDC. The High-Level Committee then requested the Administrator of UNDP to support the incorporation of issues relevant to women in all activities aimed at strengthening technical cooperation among developing countries.

54. INSTRAW is also preparing a contribution on women and developing countries' policy of individual and collective self-reliance for the *World Survey on the Role of Women in Development*, in close cooperation with the Branch for the Advancement of Women of the Centre for Social Development and Humanitarian Affairs, as requested by the General Assembly in its resolution 36/74.

F. *Women and industrial development*

55. In cooperation with UNIDO, guidelines have been developed to secure the incorporation of issues relevant to women in small-scale and rural industry programmes of UNIDO. A study of approaches and methods for mobilizing women in those fields was conducted. Based on the results, recommendations would be made for practical and concrete steps to assist Governments in undertaking corrective measures to overcome obstacles to the full participation of women, as well as to initiate appropriate training programmes. Another project is also under way to enhance the training of women entrepreneurs in industrial activities. To this end, an exploratory mission was sent to the United Republic of Tanzania, and possibilities of joint training programmes between UNIDO and INSTRAW are being further explored.

G. *Strengthening the role of women in food production*

56. The Institute is in the process of developing a framework for policy-oriented research and training on the role of women in agriculture, focusing on food production strategies and post-harvest food preservation. In this regard, the participation of the Institute in an FAO

project related to women and food systems was proposed by FAO after consultations were carried out in Rome in April 1982. Furthermore, a study which examines the role of women in food systems with special reference to Africa is under way.

H. *Energy policies and their relationship to women*

57. Following the 1981 Nairobi Conference on New and Renewable Sources of Energy, the Institute has closely monitored the activities related to energy policies and their relationship to women in order to devise follow-up activities for future programme development in cooperation with other United Nations bodies. A report on the subject is being prepared and will be issued shortly.

I. *Participation in the United Nations University Project on "Household, Gender and Age"*

58. The Institute has participated in the preparation for the United Nations University project on household, gender and age. This is a long-term project which will be closely associated to the major themes of the United Nations University within the medium-term perspective (1982-1987).

59. INSTRAW has participated in two consultative meetings convened by the United Nations University, and has prepared a position paper on "Women and the Hidden Economy". It is expected that the Institute will continue its cooperation in this programme of the University in the near future.

J. *Training activities*

60. The Institute gives training high priority. The training activities and programmes of the Institute are:

(a) Closely aligned to its research programme focusing on women and development;

(b) Implemented by applying the network concept, thus contributing to the establishment of the mode of operation of the Institute. In so doing, the Institute relies on the experience and knowledge of international, regional and national institutions in developing countries;

() Action-oriented, focusing on training of trainers and training *in situ* in developing countries in order to reach the local community and grass-root levels;

(d) Indicative of the catalytic role of the Institute thus ensuring that issues related to women and development are represented more widely in the broad range of ongoing and planned training programmes within and outside the United Nations system.

61. The forms of training activities of the Institute include the following:

(a) Seminars, workshops and expert-group meetings;

(b) Training activities related to planning, evaluation and management of development projects (as previously requested by the General Assembly);

(c) Advisory services to Governments and institutions;

(d) Advocacy activities in raising public awareness of issues on women and development, using printing material and audio-visual aids, computers, etc.;

1. *Training module*

62. As a first step to developing the Institute training programme, a review of the existing training activities within and outside the United Nations system was undertaken in order to be able to build upon existing work and to expedite reference to ongoing training projects. Secondly, cooperation and consultations with regional commissions, the specialized agencies and other United Nations organizations are under way for the preparation of a training module.

63. Acting catalytically, the Institute is following closely the United Nations Staff Training activities. It attended some of the relevant meetings in this regard and is preparing training material to raise awareness on the subject of women and development in staff training activities.

2. *Fellowship programme*

64. The fellowship programme is an important part of the overall training programme of the Institute. It aims at creating opportunities to enable women to increase and acquire new skills in order to meet the rapid changes taking place in today's society. The fields and areas where fellowships are offered coincide with the Institute's programme of work. The type of fellowships offered includes fellowships of both short and long duration, study tours, travel grants and internships.

65. At its third session, the Institute's Board approved $50,000 for the initial stage of the implementation of the fellowship programme on the understanding that this amount would be increased in the future. In accordance with the desire of the Board of Trustees that implementation of the programme be decentralized following the approved network mode of operation, the Institute subsequently implemented this decision in collaboration with the regional commissions and academic institutions. The regional commissions are therefore conducting training in their regions on activities and programmes of particular interest to women. The launching of the Institute fellowship programme was noted by the Economic and Social Council in its resolution 1983/296.

K. *Information, documentation and communication*

66. In its information, documentation and communication activities, the Institute focuses on the estab-

lishment, in stages, of a system for the collection, processng and dissemination of information related to INSTRAW research and training activities. In accordance with the Institute's clearing-house function, it is developing an appropriate collection and retrieval system for data and documentation in order to initiate and strengthen action related to the advancement of women at the national, regional and global levels.

67. Identification of a network of possible contact points at the national, regional and international levels is being developed in order to ensure a constant inflow and feed-back of information on research and training activities being carried out or planned for the future.

68. Following its advocacy role, the Institute delivers numerous lectures at universities, meetings and seminars both within and outside the United Nations system on the role of women in development. It also submits documents to conferences on women's issues as well as INSTRAW's experience in the field with the view of dissemination and exchange of experience. Following its clearing-house functions, it responds regularly to many requests for information and receives information from a variety of sources on the means available for and the institutions involved in the improvement of women's condition world-wide.

69. Much of the Institute's information, documentation and information activities is carried out with non-governmental organizations. In this regard, the Institute has been in contact with hundreds of non-governmental organizations and is constantly receiving correspondence requesting information on United Nations meetings, women's issues, data on particular groups of women, etc.

L. Other activities

70. The mandate of the Institute necessitates its participation in conferences, meetings and seminars which address the issue of the integration of women into the development process. These activities constitute a considerable part of the Institute's work both in terms of attendance and the preparation required for such participation.

71. In addition to attending regular meetings of United Nations organs, namely, those of the General Assembly and the Economic and Social Council, to which the Institute reports, the Institute also participates in meetings sponsored by various United Nations bodies which are relevant to the Institute's work programme.

72. The Institute participates also in numerous conferences and seminars sponsored by academic and non-governmental organizations dealing with women in development issues.

IV. Conclusion

73. The critical formative stage of the Institute has been satisfactorily completed. It implied numerous administrative and substantive efforts being carried out simultaneously with the support of the relevant departments of the United Nations Secretariat. The Institute will expand its activities in the years to come, guided by the results of and experience gained from this initial stage.

74. Having as its prime objective the full integration and the active participation of women in development at all levels as an important step towards the achievement of development directives, the Institute's programme is geared to development problems as they relate to women. Thus, both research and training activities are channelled in this direction.

75. The positive response of the United Nations bodies and regional and national institutions to cooperate with the Institute proves that the network concept for the execution of the programmes of the Institute has started to be implemented successfully.

76. Given the rapid economic, social, technological and cultural changes in today's societies, both research and training activities for the advancement of women are extremely important. However, the world economic situation affecting Member States has a grave impact on the Institute, as it is funded solely by voluntary contributions, whereas a long-term financial commitment by the international community is needed for the successful continuation of INSTRAW programmes.

77. As the Institute is now functioning from its headquarters in Santo Domingo, and in order to ensure the prompt execution of administrative and substantive matters, the Institute needs the continuous support provided by various departments of the United Nations Secretariat at Headquarters and arrangement to ensure continuous contacts with United Nations Headquarters.

Document 77

General Assembly resolution deciding on Nairobi as the venue for the World Conference to Review and Appraise the Achievements of the United Nations Decade for Women, considering the recommendation that particular attention be paid to the problem of women in Territories under racist colonial rule and in Territories under foreign occupation and welcoming the decision of ECOSOC to invite non-governmental organizations to participate in preparations for the Conference

A/RES/38/108, 16 December 1983

The General Assembly,

Recalling its resolution 3520 (XXX) of 15 December 1975, in which it endorsed, *inter alia*, the action proposals contained in the World Plan of Action for the Implementation of the Objectives of the International Women's Year, 1/

Recalling its resolution 3490 (XXX) of 12 December 1975, in which it expressed its conviction that a comprehensive and thorough review and appraisal of progress made in meeting the goals of the World Plan of Action was of crucial importance for the success of the Plan and recognized that the results of the implementation of the Plan would contribute to the consideration of the review and appraisal of the International Development Strategy for the Second United Nations Development Decade 2/ and would consequently promote the role of women in the development process,

Recalling its resolution 35/136 of 11 December 1980, in which it endorsed the Programme of Action for the Second Half of the United Nations Decade for Women 3/ as adopted at the World Conference of the United Nations Decade for Women, and decided to convene in 1985, at the conclusion of the Decade, a World Conference to Review and Appraise the Achievements of the United Nations Decade for Women,

Recalling also that the International Development Strategy for the Third United Nations Development Decade 4/ stressed that the important set of measures to improve the status of women contained in the World Plan of Action adopted at Mexico City in 1975, 1/ and the important agreed measures relating to the International Development Strategy in the Programme of Action for the Second Half of the United Nations Decade for Women, adopted at Copenhagen in 1980, should be implemented,

Recalling further its resolution 37/60 of 3 December 1982, in which it welcomed the decision of the Economic and Social Council that the Commission on the Status of Women should act as the preparatory body for the Conference and noted that the Commission would hold its first session in that capacity at Vienna from 23 February to 4 March 1983,

Taking into consideration Economic and Social Council decision 1983/132 of 26 May 1983 on the recommendations of the Commission on the Status of Women as the preparatory body for the Conference as set forth in its report, 5/ and Council resolution 1983/28 of 26 May 1983 on the participation of non-governmental organizations in the preparations for the Conference,

Bearing in mind all its relevant resolutions and decisions regarding preparations for special conferences,

Having considered the report of the Commission on the Status of Women on the work of its first session as the preparatory body for the Conference, 6/

1. *Decides* to accept with appreciation the offer of the Government of Kenya to act as host at Nairobi, in 1985, to the World Conference to Review and Appraise the Achievements of the United Nations Decade for Women;

2. *Takes note* of the report of the Commission on the Status of Women on the work of its first session as the preparatory body for the Conference;

3. *Endorses* the recommendation contained in the report of the Commission;

4. *Considers* that, within the framework of item 7 of the provisional agenda proposed by the Commission at its first session as the preparatory body for the Confer-

1/ *Report of the World Conference of the International Women's Year, Mexico City, 19 June-2 July 1975* (United Nations publication, Sales No. E.76.IV.1), chap.II, sect.A.
2/ Resolution 2626 (XXV).
3/ *Report of the World Conference of the United Nations Decade for Women: Equality, Development and Peace, Copenhagen, 14-20 July 1980* (United Nations publication, Sales No. E.80.IV.3 and corrigendum), chap.I, sect.A.
4/ Resolution 35/56, annex.
5/ A/CONF.116/PC/9 and Corr.1, chap.I, sect.A.
6/ A/CONF.116/PC/9 and Corr.1 and Add.1, transmitted to the members of the General Assembly by a note by the Secretary-General (A/C.3/38/2 and Add.1).

ence, 7/ particular attention will be paid to the problems of women in Territories under racist colonial rule and in Territories under foreign occupation, on the basis of appropriate documentation from the international conferences on women, held at Mexico City and Copenhagen, with the theme equality, development and peace;

5. *Welcomes* the decision of the Economic and Social Council, in its resolution 1983/28, to invite non-governmental organizations to participate in the preparations for the Conference;

6. *Decides* to include in the provisional agenda of its thirty-ninth session the item entitled "United Nations Decade for Women: Equality, Development and Peace".

7/ See A/CONF.116/PC/9 and Corr.1, chap.I, sect.A, recommendation I.

Document 78

Statute of INSTRAW adopted by the General Assembly on 26 September 1984

E/1984/41, 28 March 1984

Article I

STATUS AND PURPOSES

The United Nations International Research and Training Institute for the Advancement of Women was established by the Economic and Social Council (Council resolution 1998 (LX) of May 1976) in conformity with an earlier decision of the General Assembly (resolution 3520 (XXX) of 15 December 1975), which was based on a recommendation made by the World Conference of the International Women's Year, held at Mexico City from 19 June to 2 July 1975. The Institute is an autonomous institution within the framework of the United Nations established in accordance with the Charter of the United Nations to serve as a vehicle on the international level for the purpose of undertaking research and establishing training programmes to contribute to the integration and mobilization of women in development, to raise awareness of women's issues world-wide and better to assist women to meet new challenges and directions. The Institute, as part of the United Nations, enjoys the status, privileges and immunities provided in Articles 104 and 105 of the Charter of the United Nations and other relevant international agreements and United Nations resolutions relating to the status, privileges and immunities of the Organization.

Article II

OBJECTIVES AND FUNCTIONS

1. The objectives of the Institute are to stimulate and assist, through research, training and the collection and dissemination of information, the advancement of women and their integration in the development process both as participants and as beneficiaries. The Institute is to assist the efforts of intergovernmental, governmental and non-governmental organizations in this regard. Accordingly, the principal functions of the Institute shall be:

(a) To conduct research and studies which would enhance the effective integration and mobilization of women in development; the research and studies programmes of the Institute, including, in particular, action-oriented ones, shall give particular attention to the problems facing women in developing countries and to the integration of women in the formulation, design and implementation of development activities at all levels;

(b) To establish training programmes, including a fellowship programme and advisory services, through which the Institute shall endeavour to raise awareness on issues concerning women and development and shall strive to achieve equal participation of women in all aspects of economic and social development and to increase the opportunities for women to acquire new skills in order to meet the challenges of rapid change in today's society;

(c) To establish and maintain a system of information, documentation and communication so as to enable the Institute to respond to the need for disseminating information world-wide on women's issues.

2. In view of its catalytic role, the Institute shall make every effort to develop and utilize networking, as appropriate, in carrying out its functions. This should be done at the international, regional and national levels.

3. In the pursuit of its objectives the Institute shall carry out its activities in close collaboration and coordination with institutes and other bodies within and outside the United Nations system.

Article III

BOARD OF TRUSTEES

1. The Institute and its work shall be governed by a Board of Trustees (hereinafter referred to as "the Board").

2. The Board shall be composed as follows:

(a) Eleven members nominated by States and appointed by the Economic and Social Council with due regard to the fact that the Institute and its work are funded from voluntary contributions and to the principle of equitable geographical distribution. The members of the Board shall serve in their individual capacities for a term off three years from the date of their appointment. They shall be eligible for reappointment by the Economic and Social Council for one further term. If a casual vacancy occurs in the membership of the Board, the Economic and Social Council shall appoint a new member to serve for the unexpired portion of the term of office of the former member concerned. In nominating candidates for appointment as members of the Board, States should bear in mind the desirability of selecting persons with appropriate qualifications and expertise;

(b) A representative of the Secretary-General, the Director of the Institute, a representative of each of the regional commissions of the Economic and Social Council and a representative of the host country, who shall serve as *ex officio* members of the Board.

3. The Board shall:

(a) Formulate principles, policies and guidelines for the activities of the Institute;

(b) Consider and approve the work programme and the budget proposals of the Institute on the basis of recommendations submitted to it by the Director of the Institute;

(c) Make recommendations necessary or desirable for the operations of the Institute;

(d) Report periodically to the Economic and Social Council and where appropriate to the General Assembly.

4. The Board shall meet at least once a year. It shall elect its own officers, including its President, in accordance with the adopted rules of procedure. It shall take its decisions in the manner provided in its rules of procedure.

5. The Board shall consider methods for enhancing the financial resources of the Institute with a view to ensuring the effectiveness of its future operations, their continuity and the Institute's autonomous character within the framework of the United Nations.

6. Members of the Board in furtherance of the principles and policies of the Institute may be invited to help in achieving the goals of the Institute by attending meetings on behalf of the Institute, raising funds for the Institute's operations and helping to establish national

support teams, if possible, in their respective countries for the attainment of the objectives of the Institute.

7. Organizations of the United Nations system and other institutions may be represented as appropriate at meetings of the Board in respect of activities of interest to them under the conditions outlined in the rules of procedure of the Board.

Article IV

THE DIRECTOR AND THE STAFF

1. The Director shall be appointed by the Secretary-General of the United Nations, after consultation with the Board.

2. The Director shall have overall responsibility for the organization, direction and administration of the Institute in accordance with general directives by the Board and within the terms of the authority delegated to the Director by the Secretary-General. The Director shall, *inter* alia:

(a) Submit the work programmes and the budget estimates of the Institute to the Board for its consideration and adoption;

(b) Oversee the execution of the work programmes and make the expenditures envisaged in the budget of the Institute as adopted by the Board;

(c) Submit to the Board annual and ad hoc reports on the activities of the Institute and the execution of its work programmes;

(d) Submit to the Economic and Social Council or to the General Assembly as appropriate reports approved by the Board;

(e) Appoint and direct the staff of the Institute on behalf of the Secretary-General;

(f) Co-ordinate the work of the Institute with that of other organs and bodies of the United Nations, the specialized agencies and international, regional and national institutions in similar fields;

(g) Negotiate arrangements with Government and intergovernmental organizations as well as non-governmental organizations, academic and philanthropic institutions with a view to offering and receiving services related to the activities of the Institute;

(h) Actively seek appropriate funding for the implementations of the work programme of the Institute;

(i) Accept, subject to the provisions of article VI, paragraph 2, below, voluntary contributions to the Institute;

(j) Make the necessary arrangements for securing established and continuous contact with and support from United Nations Headquarters;

(k) Undertake other assignments or activities as may be determined by the Board or requested by the

Secretary-General, provided that any such requests are consistent with the programme budget approved by the Board.

3. The staff of the Institute shall be appointed by the Director on behalf of the Secretary-General and in accordance with modalities established by the Secretary-General, within the staffing table approved by the Board. Such appointment shall be limited to service with the Institute. The staff shall be responsible to the Director in the exercise of their functions.

4. The staff of the Institute shall be recruited on as wide a geographical basis as possible, full consideration being given to the particular requirements of and qualifications for each post needed by the Institute.

5. The terms and conditions of service of the Director and the staff shall be those provided in the Staff Regulations and Rules of the United Nations, subject to such arrangements for special rules or terms of appointment as may be approved by the Secretary-General. The salaries, allowances and other expenses of the Director and the staff shall be borne by the Trust Fund for the International Research and Training Institute for the Advancement of Women.

6. The Director and the staff of the Institute shall not seek or receive instructions from any Government or from any authority external to the United Nations. They shall refrain from any action which might reflect on their position as international officials responsible only to the Organization.

7. The Director and the staff of the Institute are officials of the United Nations and are therefore covered by Article 105 of the Charter of the United Nations and by other international agreements and United Nations resolutions defining the status of officials of the Organization.

Article V

FELLOWS, CONSULTANTS, CORRESPONDENTS AND FOCAL POINTS

1. The Board may designate as honorary fellows individuals who could contribute substantively to the Institute's objectives.

2. The Director may designate a limited number of especially qualified persons to serve as senior fellows of the Institute, for a period not longer than one year, in accordance with criteria established by the Board and procedures formulated by the Secretary-General. Such persons, who may be invited to participate as lecturers or research scholars, shall be selected on the basis of outstanding contributions they have made in fields germane to the work of the Institute.

3. The Director may also designate junior fellows as part of the Institute's ongoing fellowship programme.

All fellowships will be granted within the financial provisions of the Institute's programme budget.

4. The Director may also arrange for the services of consultants for the purpose of contributing to the analysis and planning of the activities of the Institute or for special assignments in connection with the Institute's programmes. Such consultants shall be engaged in accordance with policies established by the Secretary-General.

5. Correspondents and focal points in countries or regions approved by the Board may be used by the Institute to assist in maintaining contacts with national or regional institutions and in carrying out or advising on studies and research.

6. Honorary, senior or junior fellows, consultants and correspondents shall not be considered to be members of the staff of the Institute.

Article VI

FINANCE

1. The activities of the Institute shall be funded by voluntary contributions from States, intergovernmental and non-governmental organizations, foundations and private sources.

2. Contributions to the Institute may be accepted provided that they are consistent with the purposes and policies of the Institute. Voluntary contributions that are unrestricted or that are designated for the implementation of an activity approved by the Board may be accepted by the Director after obtaining the concurrence of the Controller of the United Nations. Other voluntary contributions may be accepted only with the approval of the Board, which shall take into account the comments of the Secretary-General. Contributions which may directly or indirectly involve an immediate or ultimate financial liability for the United Nations may be accepted only with the approval of the General Assembly.

3. The funds of the Institute derived from voluntary contributions shall be kept in the Trust Fund of the International Research and Training Institute for the Advancement of Women established by the Secretary-General in accordance with the Financial Regulations and Rules of the United Nations.

4. The funds in the Trust Fund of the Institute shall be held and administered solely for the purposes of the Institute. The Controller of the United Nations shall perform all necessary financial and accounting functions for the Institute, including the custody of its funds, and shall prepare and certify the annual accounts of the Institute.

5. The Financial Regulations and Rules of the United Nations and the financial policies and procedures

established by the Secretary-General shall apply to the financial operations of the Institute. Funds of the Institute shall be subject to audit by the United Nations Board of Auditors.

6. The Institute may, in accordance with the Financial Regulations and Rules of the United Nations, enter into contracts with organizations, institutions or firms for the purpose of carrying out its operations. The Institute may acquire or dispose of real and movable property in accordance with the same Regulations and Rules.

Article VII

ADMINISTRATIVE AND OTHER SUPPORT

The Secretary-General of the United Nations shall provide the Institute with appropriate administrative and other support, including financial and personnel services, in accordance with the Financial Regulations and Rules of the United Nations and on conditions determined after consultations between the Secretary-General and the Director of the Institute, it being understood that no extra costs to the regular budget of the United Nations are incurred.

Article VIII

COOPERATION WITH OTHER ORGANIZATIONS AND INSTITUTIONS

1. The Institute shall develop arrangements for active and close cooperation with the specialized and related agencies of the United Nations as well as with other organs, programmes and institutions within the United Nations system.

2. The Institute shall endeavour to develop arrangements for cooperation with other organizations or institutions involved in training and research activities which are relevant to the work of the Institute and which may be of assistance to the Institute in the performance of its functions.

Article IX

LOCATION

The Headquarters of the Institute shall be located in the Dominican Republic at Santo Domingo. The Institute may with the approval of the Board and after consultations with the Secretary-General of the United Nations establish other offices elsewhere.

Article X

AMENDMENTS

1. Amendments to this statute may be made by the Economic and Social Council.

2. The Board may review the provisions of this statute and propose to the Economic and Social Council such amendments as it may consider necessary.

3. The Secretary-General may submit to the Board or, if necessary, to the Economic and Social Council, after consultation with the President of the Board, proposals for the revision of the present statute.

Document 79

General Assembly resolution approving the programme of activities of INSTRAW

A/RES/39/122, 14 December 1984

The General Assembly,

Recalling its resolutions 37/56 of 3 December 1982 and 38/104 of 16 December 1983 on the International Research and Training Institute for the Advancement of Women,

Taking note of the note by the Secretary-General 2/ on recent developments regarding the activities and statute of the Institute,

Recalling Economic and Social Council decision 1984/124 of 24 May 1984 on the statute of the Institute,

Bearing in mind that the entire operation of the Institute depends solely on voluntary contributions,

1. *Welcomes* the statute of the International Research and Training Institute for the Advancement of Women 3/ as approved by the Economic and Social Council in its decision 1984/124;

2. *Takes note with satisfaction* of the programme of activities of the Institute, 4/ which constitutes a valuable contribution to an increased role of women in the development process at all levels and is carried out in cooperation with the organizations of the United Nations system;

3. *Stresses* the relevance of programmes related to women and international economic relations;

1/ See also sect. VIII, resolution 39/249.
2/ A/C.3/39/6.
3/ A/39/511, annex.
4/ See A/C.3/39/6, sect. II.

4. *Requests* the Institute, in preparing its future activities, to take into consideration the trends in research and training relevant to women and development;

5. *Invites* Governments and intergovernmental organizations to contribute to the United Nations Trust Fund for the International Research and Training Institute for the Advancement of Women, in view of the increasing importance of research and training for the advancement of women;

6. *Requests* the Secretary-General to continue to provide support to the Institute, particularly in its fund-raising activities, by encouraging voluntary contributions to the Institute;

7. *Also requests* the Secretary-General to submit to the General Assembly at its fortieth session a report on the activities of the Institute;

8. *Decides* to include in the provisional agenda of its fortieth session a separate item entitled "International Research and Training Institute for the Advancement of Women".

Document 80

General Assembly resolution establishing the Voluntary Fund for the United Nations Decade for Women as a separate entity in autonomous association with the United Nations Development Programme (UNDP) and renaming the fund the United Nations Development Fund for Women (UNIFEM)

A/RES/39/125, 14 December 1984

The General Assembly,

Recalling its resolution 31/133 of 16 December 1976, containing the criteria and arrangements for the management of the Voluntary Fund for the United Nations Decade for Women,

Recalling also its resolution 36/129 of 14 December 1981, in which it decided that the Fund should continue its activities beyond the United Nations Decade for Women: Equality, Development and Peace,

Stressing the urgency of determining at its current session the most effective arrangements for continuing the activities of the Fund beyond the Decade in view of the need for ensuring the long-term stability of the Fund,

Recalling further its resolution 38/106 of 16 December 1983, in which, *inter alia*, it decided that, when considering the reports of the Secretary-General on the future of the Fund, all possible options would be reviewed in depth,

Reaffirming that the Fund has a unique contribution to make to the achievement of the goals of the Third United Nations Development Decade, and even beyond it,

Recognizing the important actual and potential contribution by women to development, as evidenced in the forward-looking assessment of the activities assisted by the Fund and the crucial role of the Fund as a specialized resource base for development cooperation, and the need for continued assistance to activities directly benefiting women,

Considering, accordingly, that it is of paramount importance to establish a future organizational framework that will secure the ability of the Fund to act as a catalytic agent on the main United Nations development cooperation system,

Considering also the innovative and experimental activities of the Fund directed to strengthening both governmental and non-governmental institutional capacities to ensure access for women to development cooperation resources and their full participation at all levels in the development process,

Stressing that general questions of development and access of women to development resources have, as a common objective, to create conditions which will improve the quality of life for all,

Welcoming the completion of the forward-looking assessment of the activities assisted by the Fund and the findings and conclusions with regard to women and development and their implications for technical cooperation agencies and organizations, 1/

Conscious of the highly specialized professional competence of the Fund in the area of development activities for women and the need for strengthening that competence,

Aware of the broad range of linkages of the Fund with national Governments, national women's groups, non-governmental organizations and women's research institutes, besides its close cooperation with United

1/ See A/39/569, sect. II.

Nations development agencies, including the regional commissions,

Taking into consideration the moderate size of the Fund and its continued need to draw on the operational capacity of other agencies and, in this regard, expressing its appreciation to the United Nations Development Programme for its continuing technical and resource assistance to the Fund,

Expressing appreciation to the Department of International Economic and Social Affairs of the Secretariat and its Centre for Social Development and Humanitarian Affairs for their contribution to the work of the Fund during its initial operational years,

Taking note of the reports of the Consultative Committee on the Voluntary Fund for the United Nations Decade for Women on its fifteenth and sixteenth sessions, referred to in the report of the Secretary-General, 2/ prepared in accordance with General Assembly resolution 38/106,

Taking note also of the reports of the Secretary-General on the Fund, 3/

1. *Decides* that the activities of the Voluntary Fund for the United Nations Decade for Women shall be continued through establishment of a separate and identifiable entity in autonomous association with the United Nations Development Programme, which will play an innovative and catalytic role in relation to the United Nations overall system of development cooperation;

2. *Endorses* the modalities for the arrangements between the Fund and the United Nations Development Programme for the future management of the Fund, as contained in the annex to the present resolution, and decides that these arrangements shall enter into force at the latest on 1 January 1986;

3. *Reaffirms* the criteria laid down in its resolution 31/133 on the use of the resources of the Fund and the guidelines established on the advice of the Consultative Committee on the Voluntary Fund for the United Nations Decade for Women, emphasizing the use of these resources for technical cooperation benefiting women;

4. *Requests* the Consultative Committee at its seventeenth session, to be held from 25 to 29 March 1985, to propose an appropriate future title for the Fund;

5. *Stresses* the need for close and continuous working relationships between the Fund and the bodies, organs and organizations of the United Nations system concerned with women's issues and development cooperation, in particular with the Department of International Economic and Social Affairs of the Secretariat and its Centre for Social Development and Humanitarian Affairs;

6. *Expresses its appreciation* for the contributions to the Fund made by Governments and non-governmental organizations, which have a vital role to play in maintaining and increasing the financial viability of the Fund and the effectiveness of its work;

7. *Notes with concern* that contributions to the Fund have not been sufficient to enable it to respond to all the deserving requests for technical assistance that it has received;

8. *Urges*, accordingly, Governments to continue and, where possible, to increase their contributions to the Fund, and calls upon those Governments that have not yet done so to consider contributing to the Fund;

9. *Requests* the Secretary-General, after consultation with the Consultative Committee at its seventeenth session, to report to the General Assembly at its fortieth session on the arrangements he has made with the Administrator of the United Nations Development Programme for the future of the Fund;

10. *Requests* that the Consultative Committee monitor the process of implementing the arrangements for the management of the Fund contained in the annex to the present resolution and that the Committee's views on this matter be reflected fully in the annual report on the Fund to the General Assembly, particularly in its initial years.

Annex

Arrangements for the management of the United Nations Development Fund for Women

1. The United Nations Development Fund for Women (UNIFEM), hereinafter referred to as "the Fund", is hereby established as a separate and identifiable entity in autonomous association with the United Nations Development Programme. The Administrator of the United Nations Development Programme, hereinafter referred to as "the Administrator", shall be accountable for all aspects of the management and operations of the Fund. There shall be a Consultative Committee to advise the Administrator on all policy matters relating to the activities of the Fund in accordance with paragraph 13 below. The following arrangements for the management of the Fund shall apply:

I. *Transfer of existing resources, solicitation and acknowledgement of pledges and collection of contributions*

2. The Voluntary Fund for the United Nations Decade for Women and its subsidiary Supplementary Trust Fund, which was established by a memorandum of understanding between the Secretary-General of the

2/ Ibid., sect. III.
3/ A/39/146 and Corr.1 and Add.1, A/39/569 and Add.1 and A/39/571.

United Nations and the Administrator on 25 June 1980, are hereby liquidated and their assets transferred to the Fund.

3. Governments, intergovernmental and non-governmental organizations and other donors may contribute to the Fund.

4. The Fund shall be included among the programmes for which funds are pledged at the annual United Nations Pledging Conference for Development Activities. The Administrator shall assist with the mobilization of financial resources for the Fund. The contributions to the Fund and the bank accounts into which they are deposited shall be in accordance with the applicable Financial Regulations and Rules of the United Nations Development Programme.

II. *Operations and control*

5. All operations of the Voluntary Fund for the United Nations Decade for Women are hereby transferred to the Fund.

6. The Administrator, in consultation with the Consultative Committee on the Voluntary Fund for the United Nations Decade for Women, shall appoint a Director of the Fund, hereinafter referred to as "the Director", bearing in mind the relevant qualifications and experience with technical cooperation, including those benefiting women. The Administrator shall appoint the staff of the Fund in consultation with the Director, pursuant to the Staff Regulations of the United Nations and the relevant provisions of the Charter of the United Nations.

7. The Administrator shall delegate the management of the Fund and its administration, including responsibility for the mobilization of resources, to the Director, who shall have the authority to conduct all matters related to its mandate and who shall be accountable directly to the Administrator.

8. The operations of the Fund shall be conducted taking into account the innovative and catalytic nature of its development cooperation activities for women and its existing criteria and operational procedures. The present procedures of the Fund, including those governing the identification, formulation, approval, appraisal, execution and evaluation of projects established in accordance with the requirements set out in the criteria adopted by the General Assembly in its resolution 31/133 and on the advice of the Consultative Committee, shall remain in force. Subject to the arrangements for the management of the Fund, the regulations, rules and directives of the United Nations Development Programme shall be applied to the operations of the Fund.

9. The resources of the Fund shall be used mainly within two priority areas: first, to serve as a catalyst, with the goal of ensuring the appropriate involvement of women in mainstream development activities, as often as possible at the pre-investment stages; secondly, to support innovative and experimental activities benefiting women in line with national and regional priorities. Fund resources should be a supplement to and not a substitute for the mandated responsibilities of other United Nations development cooperation organizations and agencies, including the United Nations Development Programme.

10. All the administrative and programme support costs of the Fund shall be met from its own resources.

11. The regional bureaux, other organizational units and field offices of the United Nations Development Programme shall continue to assist the operations of the Fund, *inter alia*, by joint programming missions to ensure the involvement of women in technical cooperation activities financed by the United Nations Development Programme and by supporting the project cycle activities of projects financed by the Fund. For its part, the Fund shall participate in existing machineries for coordination of technical cooperation at headquarters and field levels.

12. The proposed biennial budget for the administrative costs of the Fund shall be reviewed initially by the Consultative Committee prior to its submission by the Administrator for approval by the Governing Council of the United Nations Development Programme.

III. *The Consultative Committee and the relationship of the Fund to other organizations*

13. The President of the General Assembly shall designate, with due regard for the financing of the Fund from voluntary contributions and to equitable geographical distribution, five Member States to serve on the Consultative Committee for a period of three years. Each State member of the Consultative Committee shall designate a person with relevant expertise and experience in development cooperation activities, including those benefiting women, to serve on the Committee. The Committee shall advise the Administrator on all matters of policy affecting the activities of the Fund, including the application of the criteria set forth by the General Assembly in respect of the use of the Fund.

14. The Fund shall establish and maintain close and continuous working relationships with other United Nations organs, in particular the Department of International Economic and Social Affairs of the Secretariat and its Centre for Social Development and Humanitarian Affairs, the regional commissions, the United Nations Children's Fund, the United Nations Fund for Population Activities and the International Research and Training Institute for the Advancement of Women, as well as through the Administrative Committee on Co-ordination with the specialized agencies and other United Nations

entities concerned, in particular the International Fund for Agricultural Development. Co-operation shall also be established for the sharing of information with the Commission on the Status of Women and other relevant global and regional intergovernmental bodies concerned with development and with women. As appropriate, the activities of the Fund may be drawn to the attention of the Committee on the Elimination of Discrimination against Women.

IV. *Reporting and auditing*

15. The Director shall prepare substantive and financial progress reports on the use of the Fund for the Administrator to submit to the Consultative Committee.

16. Taking into account the advice of the Consultative Committee, the Administrator shall submit to the Governing Council of the United Nations Development Programme an annual report on the operations, manage-

ment and budget of the Fund. He shall submit a similar report to the General Assembly, to be referred to the Second Committee for consideration of its technical cooperation aspects and also to the Third Committee.

17. The Commission on the Status of Women shall also be provided with the annual reports referred to in paragraph 16 above.

18. The Administrator shall be responsible for reporting all the financial transactions of the Fund and shall issue annual financial statements in accordance with the Financial Regulations and Rules of the United Nations Development Programme.

19. The Fund shall be subject to the internal and external auditing procedures provided for under the financial regulations, rules and directives of the United Nations Development Programme.

Document 81

General Assembly resolution calling on all bodies of the United Nations system to implement comprehensive policies for the integration of women in all aspects of development

A/RES/39/128, 14 December 1984

The General Assembly,

Recalling its resolution 37/57 of 3 December 1982, as well as Economic and Social Council resolution 1984/12 of 24 May 1984,

Recalling paragraphs 190 to 196 of the World Plan of Action for the Implementation of the Objectives of the International Women's Year, 1/ in which the relevant agencies of the United Nations and intergovernmental, interregional and regional bodies were called upon to scrutinize all existing plans and projects with a view to extending their sphere of activities to include women and to develop new and innovative projects to include women,

Bearing in mind that development is one of the themes of the United Nations Decade for Women: Equality, Development and Peace,

Recalling paragraph 51 of the International Development Strategy for the Third United Nations Development Decade, 2/ which stated that appropriate measures should be taken for profound social and economic changes and for the elimination of the structural imbalances which compound and perpetuate women's disadvantages,

Looking ahead to the World Conference to Review and Appraise the Achievements of the United Nations

Decade for Women: Equality, Development and Peace, to be held at Nairobi from 15 to 26 July 1985, and foreseeing the need to continue such achievements beyond the end of the Decade,

Convinced of the importance of integrating women fully into development in its political, economic, social, cultural and other dimensions, both as agents and as beneficiaries,

Reaffirming the central policy and advisory role of the Commission on the Status of Women within the United Nations in considering matters relating to women, including the achievement of the objectives of the Decade,

Recognizing the efforts made by the specialized agencies to integrate women into their ongoing programmes, especially into the establishment of cross-sectoral mechanisms,

Welcoming Economic and Social Council decision 1984/101 of 10 February 1984, in paragraph 7 of which the Council decided to select the question of women in development for review on a cross-organizational basis at its first regular session of 1985,

1/ *Report of the World Conference of the International Women's Year, Mexico City, 19 June-2 July 1975* (United Nations publication, Sales No. E.76.IV.1), chap. II, sect. A.
2/ Resolution 35/56, annex.

Aware that greater coordination and knowledge of activities in this area within the specialized agencies and the regional commissions and by Member States and non-governmental organizations would facilitate an exchange of experience and concepts and be beneficial to all,

Reaffirming that within the United Nations system the Centre for Social Development and Humanitarian Affairs of the Department of International Economic and Social Affairs of the Secretariat remains the focal point for coordination, consultation, promotion and advice on questions concerning women,

Deeply concerned that international efforts on behalf of women should keep pace with the increasing efforts towards establishing effective national machineries and mobilizing resources to ensure the integration of women into all stages of planning, monitoring and development activities,

Noting that the progress report of the Secretary-General 3/ requested by the General Assembly in its resolution 37/57 was submitted to the Commission on the Status of Women at its thirtieth session,

1. *Urges* the specialized agencies, regional commissions and other organs, bodies and organizations of the United Nations system which have not yet done so to develop and implement comprehensive policies regarding the concerns of women, both as agents and as beneficiaries, in technical cooperation and development activities and to establish effective review measures to ensure that women are an integral part of these policies and activities;

2. *Requests* the specialized agencies, regional commissions and other organs, bodies and organizations of the United Nations system to ensure continued cooperation and coordination with the Commission on the Status of Women beyond the World Conference to Review and Appraise the Achievements of the United Nations Decade for Women, in order fully to achieve the goals of the United Nations Decade for Women: Equality, Development and Peace;

3. *Endorses* the request of the Economic and Social Council in its resolution 1984/12 that the Secretary-General should report to the Commission on the Status of Women at each session on all significant developments pertaining to the advancement of women within the United Nations system that have occurred since the preceding session;

4. *Invites* the Commission on the Status of Women to give greater attention at its future sessions to the reports of the Secretary-General pertaining to the integration of women in development, by continuing to include in its agenda a specific item for that purpose, and to submit its comments on his reports to the Economic and Social Council and, as appropriate, through the Council to the General Assembly;

5. *Reaffirms* its resolution 36/127 of 14 December 1981, which provides for the consideration of issues relating to the integration of women in development in all the relevant organs of the General Assembly.

3/ E/CN.6/1984/4.

Document 82

General Assembly resolution endorsing the recommendations of the CSW acting as the preparatory body for the World Conference to Review and Appraise the Achievements of the United Nations Decade for Women

A/RES/39/129, 14 December 1984 1/

The General Assembly,

Recalling its resolution 3520 (XXX) of 15 December 1975, in which it endorsed, *inter alia*, the action proposals contained in the World Plan of Action for the Implementation of the Objectives of the International Women's Year, 2/

Recalling also its resolution 3490 (XXX) of 12 December 1975, in which it expressed its conviction that a comprehensive and thorough review and appraisal of progress made in meeting the goals of the World Plan of Action was of crucial importance for the success of the Plan of Action and recognized that the results of the implementation of the Plan would contribute to the consideration of the review and appraisal of the International Development Strategy for the Second United Nations Development Decade 3/ and would conse-

1/ See also sect. X.B.1, decision 39/459.
2/ *Report of the World Conference of the International Women's Year, Mexico City, 19 June - 2 July 1975* (United Nations publication, Sales No. E.76.IV.1), chap. II, sect. A.
3/ Resolution 2626 (XXV).

quently promote the role of women in the development process,

Recalling further that the International Development Strategy for the Third United Nations Development Decade 4/ stressed that the important set of measures to improve the status of women contained in the World Plan of Action adopted at Mexico City in 1975, and the important agreed measures relating to the International Development Strategy in the Programme of Action for the Second Half of the United Nations Decade for Women, 5/ should be implemented,

Recalling its resolution 35/136 of 11 December 1980, in which it decided to convene in 1985, at the conclusion of the United Nations Decade for Women: Equality, Development and Peace, a World Conference to Review and Appraise the Achievement of the United Nations Decade for Women,

Reaffirming the objectives of the United Nations Decade for Women: Equality, Development and Peace, with the subtheme "Employment, Health and Education",

Recalling also its resolution 37/60 of 3 December 1982, in which it welcomed the decision of the Economic and Social Council that the Commission on the Status of Women should act as the preparatory body for the Conference,

Recalling further its resolution 38/108 of 16 December 1983,

Having considered the report of the Commission on the Status of Women acting as the preparatory body for the World Conference to Review and Appraise the Achievement of the United Nations Decade for Women: Equality, Development and Peace on its second session, 6/

Taking into consideration Economic and Social Council decision 1984/125 of 24 May 1984,

Bearing in mind the request of the Economic and Social Council in its resolution 1983/28 of 26 May 1983 that the Secretary-General should invite interested non-governmental organizations in consultative status with the Council to submit information to the preparatory body for the Conference, including their views on the progress made and the obstacles still to be overcome towards the attainment of the goals of the Decade, as well as their views on priorities and strategies looking to the year 2000,

Stressing the importance of the World Conference to Review and Appraise the Achievements of the United Nations Decade for Women,

Bearing in mind the important role of the Commission on the Status of Women acting as the preparatory body for the Conference, as well as the need for ensuring the high quality of the documents to be submitted to the Conference,

1. *Reiterates its appreciation* to the Government of Kenya for its offer to act as host to the World Conference to Review and Appraise the Achievements of the United Nations Decade for Women: Equality, Development and Peace at Nairobi from 15 to 26 July 1985;

2. *Urges* all Member States to make all efforts to ensure the success of the Conference;

3. *Takes note* of the report of the Commission on the Status of Women acting as the preparatory body for the Conference on its second session and endorses the recommendations contained therein, as approved by the Economic and Social Council at its first regular session of 1984;

4. *Requests* the Secretary-General to submit to the preparatory body for the Conference at its third session all the recommendations contained in the reports of each of the regional preparatory meetings;

5. *Also requests* the Secretary-General to submit to the preparatory body for the Conference at its third session a report containing information from interested non-governmental organizations in consultative status with the Economic and Social Council, in accordance with Council resolution 1983/28;

6. *Requests* that the preparatory body for the Conference ensure the high quality of the documents to be submitted to the Conference, which should be distributed at least six weeks before the opening of the Conference;

7. *Decides* to include in the provisional agenda of its fortieth session the item entitled "United Nations Decade for Women: Equality, Development and Peace".

4/ Resolution 35/56, annex.

5/ *Report of the World Conference of the United Nations Decade for Women: Equality, Development and Peace, Copenhagen, 14-30 July 1980* (United Nations publication, Sales No. E.80.IV.3 and corrigendum), chap.1, sect.A.

6/ A/CONF.116/PC/19 and Corr.1.

Document 83

General Assembly resolution on the appointment of a Coordinator for the Improvement of the Status of Women in the Secretariat of the United Nations (extract)

A/RES/39/245 I, 18 December 1984

The General Assembly,

I

Recalling its previous resolutions on personnel policy and in particular resolutions 33/143 of 20 December 1978, 35/210 of 17 December 1980, 37/235 of 21 December 1982 and 38/231 of 20 December 1983,

Bearing in mind Article 101, paragraph 3, of the Charter of the United Nations which states that "The paramount consideration in the employment of the staff and in the determination of the conditions of service shall be the necessity of securing the highest standards of efficiency, competence and integrity. Due regard shall be paid to the importance of recruiting the staff on as wide a geographical basis as possible",

Taking note of the reports of the Secretary-General on the composition of the Secretariat, 1/ on personnel policies 2/ and on the status of the linguistic skills of United Nations staff, 3/

Having considered the report of the Joint Inspection Unit on competitive examinations in the United Nations 4/ and the related comments of the Secretary-General, 5/

Concerned by the lack of progress towards meeting the goals and objectives established with respect to:

(a) The situation of unrepresented and underrepresented Member States,

(b) The recruitment, career development and promotion of women,

(c) The achievement of a balanced and equitable geographical distribution of staff throughout the Secretariat,

1. *Reaffirms* the principles embodied in its resolutions 33/143, 35/210, 37/235 and 38/231;

...

5. *Takes note* of the decision of the Secretary-General to designate, on a temporary basis, a senior official with the title of Co-ordinator for the Improvement of the Status of Women in the Secretariat of the United Nations, to review the situation of women in the Secretariat and to make proposals for its improvement, in the framework of the report of the Secretary-General to be submitted to the General Assembly at its fortieth session, requests that the Co-ordinator function within the Office of Personnel Services, requests further that the Office of Personnel Services ensure that the Co-ordinator is provided with all necessary assistance for the effective carrying out of all tasks assigned to the Co-ordinator and notes that the Office of Personnel Services will continue to be responsible for the implementation of General Assembly directives and the Secretary-General's policies in personnel matters, for the formulation and application of personnel policy and for the recruitment and administration of all staff;

...

1/ A/39/453.
2/ A/C.5/39/9.
3/ A/C.5/39/6 and Corr.1.
4/ See A/39/483.
5/ A/39/483/Add.1 and Corr.1, annex.

Document 84

Report of the World Conference to Review and Appraise the Achievements of the United Nations Decade for Women: Equality, Development and Peace, held in Nairobi from 15 to 26 July 1985; including the Agenda and the Nairobi Forward-looking Strategies for the Advancement of Women (extract)

A/CONF.116/28/Rev.1, 1986

...

Agenda

...

1. Opening of the Conference.

2. Election of the President.

3. Adoption of the rules of procedure.

4. Adoption of the agenda.

5. Election of officers other than the President

6. Other organizational matters:

    (a) Allocation of items to the Main Committees and organization of work;

    (b) Credentials of representatives to the Conference:

        (i) Appointment of the members of the Credentials Committee;

        (ii) Report of the Credentials Committee.

7. Critical review and appraisal of progress achieve and obstacles encountered in attaining the goals and objectives of the United Nations Decade for Women: Equality, Development and Peace, and the sub-theme: Employment, Health and Education, bearing in mind the guidelines laid down at the World Conference of the International Women's Year, held at Mexico City, and the World Conference of the United Nations Decade for Women: Equality, Development and Peace, held at Copenhagen:

    (a) Progress achieved and obstacles encountered at national, regional and international levels to attain the goal and objective of equality;

    (b) Progress achieved and obstacles encountered national, regional and international levels to attain the goal and objective of development;

    (c) Progress achieved and obstacles encountered at national, regional and international levels to attain the goal and objective of peace.

8. Forward-looking Strategies of implementation for the advancement of women for the period up to the year 2000, and concrete measures to overcome obstacles to the achievement of the goals and objectives of the United Nations Decade for Women: Equality, Development and Peace, and the sub-theme: Employment, Health and Education, bearing in mind the International Development Strategy for the Third United Nations Development Decade and the establishment of a new international economic order:

    (a) Strategies and measures at the national, regional and international levels to achieve the goal of equality;

    (b) Strategies and measures at the national, regional and international levels to achieve the goal of development;

    (c) Strategies and measures at the national, regional and international levels to achieve the goal of peace.

9. Adoption of the report of the Conference.

    ...

The Nairobi Forward-looking Strategies for the Advancement of Women

INTRODUCTION

A. Historical Background

Paragraph 1

The founding of the United Nations after the victory in the Second World War and the emergence of independent States following decolonization were some of the important events in the political, economic and social liberation of women. The International Women's Year, the World Conferences held at Mexico City in 1975 and Copenhagen in 1980, and the United Nations Decade for Women: Equality, Development and Peace contributed greatly to the process of eliminating obstacles to the improvement of the status of women at the national, regional and international levels. In the early 1970s, efforts to end discrimination against women and to ensure their equal participation in society provided the impetus for most initiatives taken at all of those levels. Those efforts were also inspired by the awareness that women's reproductive and productive roles were closely linked to the political, economic, social, cultural, legal, educational and religious conditions that constrained the advancement of women and that factors intensifying the economic exploitation, marginalization and oppression of women stemmed from chronic inequalities, injustices and exploitative conditions at the family, community, national, subregional, regional and international levels.

Paragraph 2

In 1972, the General Assembly, in its resolution 3010 (XXVII), proclaimed 1975 International Women's Year, to be devoted to intensified action to promote equality between men and women, to ensure the full integration of women in the total development effort and to increase women's contribution to the strengthening of world peace. The World Plan of Action for the Implementation of the Objectives of the International Women's Year, 1/ adopted by the World Conference of the International Women's Year at Mexico City in 1975, was endorsed by the General Assembly in its resolution 3520 (XXX). The General Assembly, in that resolution, proclaimed 1976-1985 the United Nations Decade for Women: Equality, Development and Peace. In its resolution 33/185, the General Assembly decided upon the sub-theme "Employment, Health and Education" for the World Conference of the United Nations Decade for Women: Equality, Development and Peace, to be held at Copenhagen to review and evaluate the progress made in the first half of the Decade.

Paragraph 3

In 1980, at the mid-point of the Decade, the Copenhagen World Conference adopted the Programme of Action for the Second Half of the United Nations Decade for Women: Equality, Development and Peace, 2/ which further elaborated on the existing obstacles and on the existing international consensus on measures to be taken for the advancement of women. The Programme of Action was endorsed by the General Assembly that year in its resolution 35/136.

Paragraph 4

Also in 1980, the General Assembly, in its resolution 35/56, adopted the International Development Strategy for the Third United Nations Development Decade and reaffirmed the recommendations of the Copenhagen World Conference (General Assembly resolution 35/56, annex, para. 51). In the Strategy, the importance of the participation of women in the development process, as both agents and beneficiaries, was stressed. Also, the Strategy called for appropriate measures to be taken in order to bring about profound social and economic changes and to eliminate the structural imbalances that compounded and perpetuated women's disadvantages in society.

Paragraph 5

The strategies contained in the World Plan of Action and in the Programme of Action were important contributions towards enlarging the perspective for the future of women. In most areas, however, further action is required. In this connection the General Assembly confirmed the goals and objectives of the Decade—equality, development and peace—stressed their validity for the future and indicated the need for concrete measures to overcome the obstacles to their achievement during the period 1986-2000.

Paragraph 6

The Forward-looking Strategies for the Advancement of Women during the Period from 1986 to the Year 2000 set forth in the present document present concrete measures to overcome the obstacles to the Decade's goals and objectives for the advancement of women. Building on principles of equality also espoused in the Charter of the United Nations, the Universal Declaration of Human Rights, 3/ the International Covenant on Civil and Political Rights, 4/ the International Covenant on Economic, Social and Cultural Rights, 5/ the Convention on the Elimination of All Forms of Discrimination against Women, 6/ and the Declaration on the Participation of Women in Promoting International Peace and Co-operation, 7/ the Forward-looking Strategies reaffirm the international concern regarding the status of women and provide a framework for renewed commitment by the international community to the advancement of women and the elimination of gender-based discrimination. The efforts for the integration of women in the development process should be strengthened and should take into account the objectives of a new international economic order and the International Development Strategy for the Third United Nations Development Decade.

1/ Report of the World Conference of the International Women's Year, Mexico City, 19 June-2 July 1975 (United Nations publication, Sales No. E.76.IV.1), chap. I, sect. A.
2/ Report of the World Conference of the United Nations Decade for Women: Equality, Development and Peace, Copenhagen, 24-30 July 1980 (United Nations publication, Sales No. E.80.IV.3), chap. I, sect. A.
3/ General Assembly resolution 227 A (III).
4/ General Assembly resolution 2200 A (XXI), annex.
5/ Ibid.
6/ General Assembly resolution 34/180, annex.
7/ General Assembly resolution 37/63, annex.

Paragraph 7

The Nairobi World Conference is taking place at a critical moment for the developing countries. Ten years ago, when the Decade was launched, there was hope that accelerated economic growth, sustained by growing international trade, financial flow and technological developments, would allow the increased participation of women in the economic and social development of those countries. These hopes have been belied owing to the persistence and, in some cases, the aggravation of an economic crisis in the developing countries, which has been an important obstacle that endangers not only the pursuance of new programmes in support of women but also the maintenance of those that were already under way.

Paragraph 8

The critical international economic situation since the end of the 1970s has particularly adversely affected developing countries and, most acutely, the women of those countries. The overall picture for the developing countries, particularly the least developed countries, the drought-stricken and famine-stricken areas of Africa, the debt-ridden countries and the low-income countries, has reached a critical point as a result of structural imbalances and the continuing critical international economic situation. The situation calls for an increased commitment to improving and promoting national policies and multilateral cooperation for development in support of national programmes, bearing in mind that each country is responsible for its own development policy. The gap between the developed and developing countries, particularly the least developed among them, instead of narrowing, is widening further. In order to stem such negative trends and mitigate the current difficulties of the developing countries, which affect women the most, one of the primary tasks of the international community is to pursue with all vigour the efforts directed towards the establishment of a New International Economic Order founded on equity, sovereign equality, interdependence and common interest.

B. Substantive background of the Forward-looking Strategies

Paragraph 9

The three objectives of the Decade—equality, development and peace—are broad, interrelated and mutually reinforcing, so that the achievement of one contributes to the achievement of another.

Paragraph 10

The Copenhagen World Conference interpreted equality as meaning not only legal equality, the elimination of de jure discrimination, but also equality of rights, responsibilities and opportunities for the participation of women in development, both as beneficiaries and as active agents.

Paragraph 11

Equality is both a goal and a means whereby individuals are accorded equal treatment under the law and equal opportunities to enjoy their rights and to develop their potential talents and skills so that they can participate in national political, economic, social and cultural development and can benefit from its results. For women in particular, equality means the realization of rights that have been denied as a result of cultural, institutional, behaviourial and attitudinal discrimination. Equality is important for development and peace because national and global inequities perpetuate themselves and increase tensions of all types.

Paragraph 12

The role of women in development is directly related to the goal of comprehensive social and economic development and is fundamental to the development of all societies. Development means total development, including development in the political, economic, social, cultural and other dimensions of human life, as well as the development of the economic and other material resources and the physical, moral, intellectual and cultural growth of human beings. It should be conducive to providing women, particularly those who are poor or destitute, with the necessary means for increasingly claiming, achieving, enjoying and utilizing equality of opportunity. More directly, the increasingly successful participation of each woman in societal activities as a legally independent agent will contribute to further recognition in practice of her right to equality. Development also requires a moral dimension to ensure that it is just and responsive to the needs and rights of the individual and that science and technology are applied within a social and economic framework that ensures environmental safety for all life forms on our planet.

Paragraph 13

The full and effective promotion of women's rights can best occur in conditions of international peace and security where relations among States are based on the respect for the legitimate rights of all nations, great and small, and peoples to self-determination, independence, sovereignty, territorial integrity and the right to live in peace within their national borders.

Peace depends on the prevention of the use or threat of the use of force, aggression, military occupation, interference in the internal affairs of others, the elimination of domination, discrimination, oppression and exploitation, as well as of gross and mass violation of human rights and fundamental freedoms.

Peace includes not only the absence of war, violence and hostilities at the national and international levels but also the enjoyment of economic and social justice, equality and the entire range of human rights and fundamental freedoms within society. It depends upon respect for the Charter of the United Nations and the Universal Declaration of Human Rights, as well as international covenants and the other relevant international instruments on human rights, upon mutual cooperation and understanding among all States irrespective of their social political and economic systems and upon the effective implementation by States of the fundamental human rights standards to which their citizens are entitled.

It also embraces the whole range of actions reflected in concerns for security and implicit assumptions of trust between nations, social groups and individuals. It represents goodwill toward others and promotes respect for life while protecting freedom, human rights and the dignity of peoples and of individuals. Peace cannot be realized under conditions of economic and sexual inequality, denial of basic human rights and fundamental freedoms, deliberate exploitation of large sectors of the population, unequal development of countries, and exploitative economic relations. Without peace and stability there can be no development. Peace and development are interrelated and mutually reinforcing.

In this respect special attention is drawn to the final document of the tenth special session of the General Assembly, the first special session devoted to disarmament encompassing all measures thought to be advisable in order to ensure that the goal of general and complete disarmament under effective international control is realized. This document describes a comprehensive programme of disarmament, including nuclear disarmament, which is important not only for peace but also for the promotion of the economic and social development of all, particularly in the developing countries, through the constructive use of the enormous amount of material and human resources otherwise expended on the arms race.

Peace is promoted by equality of the sexes, economic equality and the universal enjoyment of basic human rights and fundamental freedoms. Its enjoyment by all requires that women be enabled to exercise their right to participate on an equal footing with men in all spheres of the political, economic and social life of their respective countries, particularly in the decision-making process, while exercising their right to freedom of opinion, expression, information and association in the promotion of international peace and cooperation.

Paragraph 14

The effective participation of women in development and in the strengthening of peace, as well as the promotion of the equality of women and men, require concerted multi-dimensional strategies and measures that should be people-oriented. Such strategies and measures will require continual upgrading and the productive utilization of human resources with a view to promoting equality and producing sustained, endogenous development of societies and groups of individuals.

Paragraph 15

The three goals of the Decade—equality, development and peace—are inextricably linked to the three sub-themes—employment, health and education. They constitute the concrete basis on which equality, development and peace rest. The enhancement of women's equal participation in development and peace requires the development of human resources, recognition by society of the need to improve women's status, and the participation of all in the restructuring of society. It involves, in particular, building a participatory human infrastructure to permit the mobilization of women at all levels, within different spheres and sectors. To achieve optimum development of human and material resources, women's strengths and capabilities, including their great contribution to the welfare of families and to the development of society, must be fully acknowledged and valued. The attainment of the goals and objectives of the Decade requires a sharing of this responsibility by men and women and by society as a whole and requires that women play a central role as intellectuals, policy-makers, decision-makers, planners, and contributors and beneficiaries of development.

Paragraph 16

The need for women's perspective on human development is critical since it is in the interest of human enrichment and progress to introduce and weave into the social fabric women's concept of equality, their choices between alternative development strategies and their approach to peace, in accordance with their aspirations, interests and talents. These things are not only desirable in themselves but are also essential for the attainment of the goals and objectives of the Decade.

Paragraph 17

The review and appraisal of progress achieved and obstacles encountered at the national level in the realization of the goals and objectives of the United Nations Decade for Women: Equality, Development and Peace (see A/CONF.116/5 and Add.1-14) identifies various levels of experience. Despite the considerable progress achieved and the increasing participation of women in society, the Decade has only partially attained its goals and objectives. Although the earlier years of the Decade were characterized by relatively favourable economic conditions in both the developed and developing countries, deteriorating economic conditions have slowed efforts directed towards promoting the equal participation of women in society and have given rise to new problems. With regard to development, there are indications that in some cases, although the participation of women is increasing, their benefits are not increasing proportionately.

Paragraph 18

Many of the obstacles discussed in the Forward-looking Strategies were identified in the review and appraisal (see A/CONF.116/5 and Add.1-14). The overwhelming obstacles to the advancement of women are in practice caused by varying combinations of political and economic as well as social and cultural factors. Furthermore, the social and cultural obstacles are sometimes aggravated by political and economic factors such as the critical international economic situation and the consequent adjustment programmes, which in general entail a high social cost. In this context, the economic constraints due in part to the prevailing macro-economic factors have contributed to the aggravation of economic conditions at the national level. Moreover, the devaluation of women's productive and reproductive roles, as a result of which the status of women continued to be regarded as secondary to that of men, and the low priority assigned to promoting the participation of women in development are historical factors that limit women's access to employment, health and education, as well as to other sectoral resources, and to the effective integration of women in the decision-making process. Regardless of gains, the structural constraints imposed by a socio-economic framework in which women are second-class persons still limit progress. Despite changes in some countries to promote equity in all spheres of life, the "double burden" for women of having the major responsibility for domestic tasks and of participating in the labour force remains. For example, several countries in both the developed and developing world identify as a major obstacle the lack of adequate supportive services for working women.

Paragraph 19

According to responses from the developing countries, particularly the least developed, to the United Nations questionnaire to Governments (see A/CONF.116/5 and Add.1-14), poverty is on the increase in some countries and constitutes another major obstacle to the advancement of women. The exigencies created by

problems of mass poverty, compounded by scarce national resources, have compelled Governments to concentrate on alleviating the poverty of both women and men rather than on equality issues for women. At the same time, because women's secondary position increases their vulnerability to marginalization, those belonging to the lowest socio-economic strata are likely to be the poorest of the poor and should be given priority. Women are an essential productive force in all economies; therefore it is particularly important in times of economic recession that programmes and measures designed to raise the status of women should not be relaxed but rather intensified.

Paragraph 20

To economic problems, with their attendant social and cultural implications, must be added the threat to international peace and security resulting from violations of the principles of the United Nations Charter. This situation, affecting *inter alia* the lives of women, constitutes a most serious obstacle to development and thus hinders the fulfilment of the Forward-looking Strategies.

Paragraph 21

What is now needed is the political will to promote development in such a way that the strategy for the advancement of women seeks first and foremost to alter the current unequal conditions and structures that continue to define women as secondary persons and give women's issues a low priority. Development should now move to another plane in which women's pivotal role in society is recognized and given its true value. That will allow women to assume their legitimate and core positions in the strategies for effecting the changes necessary to promote and sustain development.

C. *Current trends and perspectives to the year 2000*

Paragraph 22

In the absence of major structural changes or technological breakthroughs, it can be predicted that up to the year 2000 recent trends will, for the most part, be extended and adjusted. The situation of women, as it evolves during the period 1986-2000, will also cause other changes, establishing a process of cause and effect of great complexity. Changes in women's material conditions, consciousness and aspirations, as well as societal attitudes towards women, are themselves social and cultural processes having major implications and a profound influence on institutions such as the family. Women's advancement has achieved a certain momentum that will be affected by the social and economic changes of the next 15 years, but it will also continue to exist as a force to be reckoned with. Internal processes will exercise a major influence in the economic sphere, but the state of the global economic system and of the political, social, cultural, demographic and communication processes directly affected by it will invariably have a more profound impact on the advancement of women.

Paragraph 23

At the beginning of the Decade there was an optimistic outlook for development, but during the early 1980s the world economy experienced a widespread recession due, *inter alia*, to sharp inflationary pressures that affected regions and some groups of countries, irrespective of their level of development or economic structure. During the same period, however, the countries with centrally planned economies as a group experienced stable economic growth. The developed market economy countries also experienced growth after the recession.

Despite the recovery in the developed market economy countries which is being felt in the world economy, the immediate outlook for recovery in developing countries, especially in the low-income and the least developed countries, remains bleak, particularly in view of their enormous public and private external debts and the cost of servicing that debt, which are an evident manifestation of this critical situation. This heavy burden has serious political, economic and social consequences for them. No lasting recovery can be achieved without rectifying the structural imbalances in the context of the critical international economic situation and without continued efforts towards the establishment of a new international economic order. The present situation clearly has serious repercussions for the status of women, particularly underprivileged women, and for human resource development.

Women, subject to compound discrimination on the basis of race, colour, ethnicity and national origin, in addition to sex, could be even more adversely affected by deteriorating economic conditions.

Paragraph 24

If current trends continue, the prospects for the developing world, particularly the low-income and least developed countries, will be sombre. The overall growth in the developing countries as currently projected will be lower in the period 1980-2000 than that experienced in the period 1960-1980. In order to redress this outlook and thereby promote the advancement of women, policies should be reoriented and reinforced to promote world trade, in particular so as to promote market access for the exports of developing countries. Similarly, policies should be pursued in other areas which would also promote growth and development in developing countries, for

example, in respect of further lowering interest rates and pursuit of non-inflationary growth policies.

Paragraph 25

It is feared that, if there is slow growth in the world economy, there will inevitably be negative implications for women since, as a result of diminished resources, action to combat women's low position, in particular, their high rates of illiteracy, low levels of education, discrimination in employment, their unrecognized contribution to the economy and their special health needs, may be postponed. A pattern of development promoting just and equitable growth on the basis of justice and equality in international economic relations could make possible the attainment of the goals and objectives of the International Development Strategy, which could make a significant improvement in the status of women while enhancing women's effective contribution to development and peace. Such a pattern of development has its own internal dynamics that would facilitate an equitable distribution of resources and is conducive to promoting sustained, endogenous development, which will reduce dependence.

Paragraph 26

It is very important that the efforts to promote the economic and social status of women should rely in particular on the development strategies that stem from the goals and objectives of the International Development Strategy and the principles of a new international economic order. These principles include, *inter alia*, self-reliance, collective self-reliance, the activation of indigenous human and material resources. The restructuring of the world economy, viewed on a long-term basis, is to the benefit of all people—women and men of all countries.

Paragraph 27

According to estimates and projections of the International Labour Office, women constitute 35 per cent of the world's labour force, and this figure is likely to increase steadily to the year 2000. Unless profound and extensive changes are made, the type of work available to the majority of women, as well as the rewards, will continue to be low. Women's employment is likely to be concentrated in areas requiring lower skills and lower wages and minimum job security. While women's total input of labour in the formal and informal sector will surpass that of men by the year 2000, they will receive an unequal share of the world's assets and income. According to recent estimates, it seems that women have sole responsibility for the economic support of a large number of the world's children, approximately one third and higher in some countries, and the numbers seem to be rising. Forward-looking strategies must be progressive, equitable and designed to support effectively women's roles and responsibilities as they evolve up to the year 2000. It will continue to be necessary to take specific measures to prevent discrimination and exploitation of their economic contribution at national and international levels.

Paragraph 28

During the period from 1986 to the year 2000, changes in the natural environment will be critical for women. One area of change is that of the role of women as intermediaries between the natural environment and society with respect to agro-ecosystems, as well as the provision of safe water and fuel supplies and the closely associated question of sanitation. The problem will continue to be greatest where water resources are limited—in arid and semi-arid areas—and in areas experiencing increasing demographic pressure. In a general manner, an improvement in the situation of women could bring about a reduction in mortality and morbidity as well as better regulation of fertility and hence of population growth, which would be beneficial for the environment and, ultimately, for women, children and men.

Paragraph 29 8/

The issues of fertility rates and population growth should be treated in a context that permits women to exercise effectively their rights in matters pertaining to population concerns, including the basic right to control their own fertility which forms an important basis for the enjoyment of other rights, as stated in the report of the International Population Conference held at Mexico City in 1984. 9/

Paragraph 30

It is expected that the ever-expanding communications network will be better attuned than before to the concerns of women and that planners in this field will provide increasing information on the objectives of the Decade—equality, development and peace—on the Forward-looking Strategies, and on the issues included in the subtheme—employment, health and education. All channels, including computers, formal and non-formal education and the media, as well as traditional mechanisms of communication involving the cultural media of ritual, drama, dialogue, oral literature and music, should be used.

Paragraph 31

Political and governmental factors that are likely to affect prospects for the achievement of progress by women during the period 1986-2000 will depend in large measure upon the existence or absence of peace. If widespread international tensions continue, with threats not only of nuclear catastrophe but also of localized conventional warfare, then the attention of policy-makers will be diverted from tasks directly and indirectly relevant to the advancement of women and men, and vast resources will be further applied to military and related activities. This should be avoided and these resources should be directed to the improvement of humanity.

Paragraph 32

To promote their interests effectively, women must be able to enjoy their right to take part in national and international decision-making processes, including the right to dissent publicly and peacefully from their Government's policies, and to mobilize to increase their participation in the promotion of peace within and between nations.

Paragraph 33

There is no doubt that, unless major measures are taken, numerous obstacles will continue to exist which retard the participation of women in political life, in the formulation of policies that affect them and in the formulation of national women's policies. Success will depend in large measure upon whether or not women can unite to help each other to change their poor material circumstances and secondary status and to obtain the time, energy and experience required to participate in political life. At the same time, improvements in health and educational status, legal and constitutional provisions and networking will increase the effectiveness of the political action taken by women so that they can obtain a much greater share in political decision-making than before.

Paragraph 34

In some countries and in some areas, women have made significant advances, but overall progress has been modest during the Decade, as is evident from the review and appraisal. During this period, women's consciousness and expectations have been raised, and it is important that this momentum should not be lost, regardless of the poor performance of the world economy. The changes occurring in the family, in women's roles and in relationships between women and men may present new challenges requiring new perspectives, strategies and measures. At the same time, it will be necessary to build alliances and solidarity groups across sexual lines in an

8/ The Holy See delegation reserved its position with respect to paragraph 29 because it had not joined in the consensus at the International Conference on Population (Mexico City, 1984) and did not agree with the substance of paragraph 29.

9/ *Report of the International Conference on Population, 1984, Mexico City, 6-14 August 1984* (United Nations publication, Sales No. E.84.XIII.8), chap. I, sect. A, para. 1.

attempt to overcome structural obstacles to the advancement of women.

Paragraph 35 10/

The World Plan of Action for the Implementation of the Objectives of the International Women's Year, 1/ the Declaration of Mexico on the Equality of Women and their Contribution to Development and Peace, 1975, 11/ regional plans of action, the Programme of Action for the Second Half of the United Nations Decade for Women: Equality, Development and Peace, 2/ and the sub-theme—employment, health and education—the Declaration on the Participation of Women in Promoting International Peace and Co-operation 7/ and the Convention on the Elimination of All Forms of Discrimination against Women 6/ remain valid and therefore constitute the basis for the strategies and concrete measures to be pursued up to the year 2000. The continuing relevance of the goals of the United Nations Decade for Women: Equality, Development and Peace—and of its sub-theme—health, education and employment—should be stressed, as should the implementation of the relevant recommendations of the 1975 Plan of Action and the 1980 Programme of Action, so as to ensure the complete integration of women in the development process and the effective realization of the objectives of the Decade. The challenge now is for the international community to ensure that the achievements of the Decade become strong building blocks for development and to promote equality and peace, especially for the sake of future generations of women. The obstacles of the next 15 years must be met through concerted global, regional and national efforts. By the year 2000 illiteracy should have been eliminated, life expectancy for all women increased to at least 65 years of good quality life and opportunities for self-supporting employment made available. Above all, laws guaranteeing equality for women in all spheres of life must by then be fully and comprehensively implemented to ensure a truly equitable socio-economic framework within which real development can take place. Forward-looking Strategies for the advancement of women at the regional level should be based on a clear assessment of demographic trends and development forecasts that provide a realistic context for their implementation.

Paragraph 36

The Forward-looking Strategies and multi-dimensional measures must be pursued within the framework of a just international society in which equitable economic relations will allow the closing of the gap that separates the industrialized countries from the developing countries. In this regard, all countries are called upon to show their commitment as was decided in General Assembly resolution 34/138 and, therefore, to continue informal consultations on the launching of global negotiations, as decided by the General Assembly in decision 39/454.

D. Basic approach to the formulation of the Forward-looking Strategies

Paragraph 37

It is necessary to reiterate the unity, inseparability and interdependence of the objectives of the Decade—equality, development and peace—as regards the advancement of women and their full integration in economic, political, social and cultural development, for which purpose the objectives should remain in effect in the operational strategies for the advancement of women to the year 2000.

Paragraph 38

The Forward-looking Strategies are intended to provide a practical and effective guide for global action on a long-term basis and within the context of the broader goals and objectives of a new international economic order. Measures are designed for immediate action, with monitoring and evaluation occurring every five years, depending on the decision of the General Assembly. Since countries are at various stages of development, they should have the option to set their own priorities based on their own development policies and resource capabilities. What may be possible for immediate action in one country may require more long-range planning in another, and even more so in respect of countries which are still under colonialism, domination and foreign occupation. The exact methods and procedures of implementing measures will depend upon the nature of the political process and the administrative capabilities of each country.

Paragraph 39

Some measures are intended to affect women and others directly and are designed to make the societal context less obstructive and more supportive of their progress. These measures would include the elimination of sex-based stereotyping, which is at the root of continuing discrimination. Measures to improve the situation of women are bound to have a ripple effect in society, since

10/ Reservations to paragraph 35 were formulated by Australia, Belgium, Canada, Denmark, Finland, Germany, Federal Republic of, Iceland, Ireland, Israel, Italy, Luxembourg, Netherlands, New Zealand, Norway, Sweden, Switzerland and United States of America. The United States reserved its position on the reference in paragraph 35 to the Declaration of Mexico on the Equality of Women and their Contribution to Development and Peace, 1975.
11/ Report of the World Conference of the International Women's Year ..., chap. I.

the advancement of women is without doubt a pre-condition for the establishment of a humane and progressive society.

Paragraph 40

The feasibility of policies, programs and projects concerning women will be affected not only by their numbers and socio-economic heterogeneity but also by the different life-styles of women and by the constant changes in their life cycle.

Paragraph 41

The Forward-looking Strategies not only suggest measures for overcoming obstacles that are fundamental and operational, but also identify those that are emerging. Thus, the strategies and measures presented are intended to serve as guidelines for a process of continuous adaptation to diverse and changing national situations at speeds and modes determined by overall national priorities, within which the integration of women in development should rank high. The Forward-looking Strategies, acknowledging existing and potential obstacles, include separate basic strategies for the achievement of equality, development and peace. In line with the recommendations of the commission on the Status of Women, acting as the Preparatory Body for the Conference at its second session, particular attention is given to "especially vulnerable and underprivileged groups of women, such as rural and urban poor women; women in areas affected by armed conflicts, foreign intervention and international threats to peace; elderly women; young women; abused women; destitute women; women victims of trafficking and women in involuntary prostitution; women deprived of their traditional means of livelihood; women who are sole supporters of families; physically and mentally disabled women; women in detention; refugee and displaced women; migrant women; minority women; and indigenous women". 12/

Paragraph 42

Although addressed primarily to Governments, international and regional organizations, and non-governmental organizations, an appeal is made to all women and men in a spirit of solidarity. In particular, it is addressed to those women and men who now enjoy certain improvements in their material circumstances and who have achieved positions where they may influence policy-making, development priorities and public opinion to change the current inferior and exploited condition of the majority of women in order to serve the goals of equality for all women, their full participation in development, and the achievement and strengthening of peace.

I. EQUALITY

A. *Obstacles*

Paragraph 43

One of the objectives of the Decade entails the full observance of the equal rights of women and the elimination of *de jure* and de facto discrimination. This is a critical first step towards human resource development. In developing countries inequality is, to a great extent, the result of underdevelopment and its various manifestations, which in turn are aggravated by the unjust distribution of the benefits of the international economy. The United Nations systems, particularly the Commission on the Status of Women, has worked for four decades to establish international standards and to identify and propose measures to prevent discrimination on the basis of sex. Although much progress has been made in legislation, measures are necessary for effective implementation and enforcement. Legislative enactment is only one element in the struggle for equality, but an essential one as it provides the legitimate basis for action and acts as a catalyst for societal change.

Paragraph 44 13/

The inequality of women in most countries stems to a very large extent from mass poverty and the general backwardness of the majority of the world's population caused by underdevelopment, which is a product of imperialism, colonialism, neo-colonialism, apartheid, racism, racial discrimination and of unjust international economic relations. The unfavourable status of women is aggravated in many countries, developed and underdeveloped, by de facto discrimination on the grounds of sex.

Paragraph 45

One of the fundamental obstacles to women's equality is that de facto discrimination and inequality in the status of women and men derive from larger social, economic, political and cultural factors that have been justified on the basis of physiological differences. Although there is no physiological basis for regarding the household and family as essentially the domain of women, for the devaluation of domestic work and for regarding the capacities of women as inferior to those of men, the belief that such a basis exists perpetuates in-

12/ Report of the Commission on the Status of Women acting as the Preparatory Body for the World Conference to Review and Appraise the Achievements of the United Nations Decade for Women: Equality, Development and Peace on its second session (A/CONF.116/PC/19), chap. I, draft decision I, para. 2 (h).

13/ The United States reserved its position on paragraph 44 because it did not agree that the obstacles listed should be considered the main reasons for the inequality of women in most countries.

equality and inhibits the structural and attitudinal changes necessary to eliminate such inequality.

Paragraph 46

Women, by virtue of their gender, experience discrimination in terms of denial of equal access to the power structure that controls society and determines development issues and peace initiatives. Additional differences, such as race, colour and ethnicity, may have even more serious implications in some countries, since such factors can be used as justification for compound discrimination.

Paragraph 47

Fundamental resistance creates obstacles, which have wide-ranging implications for the objectives of the Decade. Discrimination promotes an uneconomic use of women's talents and wastes the valuable human resources necessary for development and for the strengthening of peace. Ultimately, society is the loser if the talents of women are under-utilized as a result of discrimination.

Paragraph 48

The sharp contrasts between legislative changes and effective implementation of these changes are a major obstacle to the full participation of women in society. De facto and indirect discrimination, particularly by reference to marital or family status, often persists despite legislative action. The law as a recourse does not automatically benefit all women equally, owing to the socio-economic inequalities determining women's knowledge of and access to the law, as well as their ability to exercise their full legal rights without fear of recrimination or intimidation. The lack or inadequacy of the dissemination of information on women's rights and the available recourse to justice has hampered, in many instances, the achievement of expected results.

Paragraph 49

Some legislative changes are made without a thorough understanding of the relationship between existing legal systems. In practice, however, certain aspects of the law—for instance, customary provisions—may be in operation in societies with multiple and conflicting legal systems. Emerging and potential obstacles resulting from possible contradictions should be anticipated so that preventive measures can be taken. When passing new legislation, whatever its subject-matter, all possible care should be taken to ensure that it implies no direct or indirect discrimination so that women's right to equality is fully respected in law.

Paragraph 50

In some countries, discriminatory legislative provisions in the social, economic and political spheres still exist, including civil, penal and commercial codes and certain administrative rules and regulations. Civil codes in some instances have not yet been adequately studied to determine action for repealing those laws that still discriminate against women and for determining, on the basis of equality, the legal capacity and status of women, married women in particular, in terms of nationality, inheritance, ownership and control of property, freedom of movement and the custody and nationality of children. Above all, there is still a deeply rooted resistance on the part of conservative elements in society to the change in attitude necessary for a total ban on discriminatory practices against women at the family, local, national and international levels.

B. Basic strategies

Paragraph 51

The political commitment to establish, modify, expand or enforce a comprehensive legal base for the equality of women and men and on the basis of human dignity must be strengthened. Legislative changes are most effective when made within a supportive framework promoting simultaneous changes in the economic, social, political and cultural spheres, which can help bring about a social transformation. For true equality to become a reality for women, the sharing of power on equal terms with men must be a major strategy.

Paragraph 52

Governments should take the relevant steps to ensure that both men and women enjoy equal rights, opportunities and responsibilities so as to guarantee the development of their individual aptitudes and capacities and enable women to participate as beneficiaries and active agents in development.

Paragraph 53

Changes in social and economic structures should be promoted which would make possible the full equality of women and their free access to all types of development as active agents and beneficiaries, without discrimination of any kind, and to all types of education, training and employment. Special attention should be paid to implementing this right to the maximum extent possible for young women.

Paragraph 54

In order to promote equality of women and men, Governments should ensure, for both women and men, equality before the law, the provision of facilities for equality of educational opportunities and training, health services, equality in conditions and opportunities of employment, including remuneration, and adequate social security. Governments should recognize and undertake measures to implement the right of men and women to employment on equal conditions, regardless of marital status, and their equal access to the whole range of economic activities.

Paragraph 55

Effective institutions and procedures must be established or strengthened to monitor the situation of women comprehensively and identify the causes, both traditional and new, of discrimination and to help formulate new policies and effectively carry out strategies and measures to end discrimination. These arrangements and procedures must be integrated within a coherent policy for development but cannot wait indefinitely for such a policy to be formulated and implemented.

Paragraph 56

The obstacles to the equality of women created by stereotypes, perceptions of and attitudes towards women should be totally removed. Elimination of these obstacles will require, in addition to legislation, education of the population at large through formal and informal channels, including the media, non-governmental organizations, political party platforms and executive action.

Paragraph 57

Appropriate governmental machinery for monitoring and improving the status of women should be established where it is lacking. To be effective, this machinery should be established at a high level of government and should be ensured adequate resources, commitment and authority to advise on the impact on women of all government policies. Such machinery can play a vital role in enhancing the status of women, *inter alia*, through the dissemination of information to women on their rights and entitlements, through collaborative action with various ministries and other government agencies and with non-governmental organizations and indigenous women's societies and groups.

Paragraph 58

Timely and reliable statistics on the situation of women have an important role to play in the elimination of stereotypes and the movement towards full equality. Governments should help collect statistics and make periodic assessment in identifying stereotypes and inequalities, in providing concrete evidence concerning many of the harmful consequences of unequal laws and practices and in measuring progress in the elimination of inequities.

Paragraph 59

The sharing of domestic responsibilities by all members of the family and equal recognition of women's informal and invisible economic contributions in the mainstream of society should be developed as complementary strategies for the elimination of women's secondary status, which has fostered discrimination.

C. Measures for the implementation of the basic strategies at the national level

1. Constitutional and legal

Paragraph 60

Governments that have not yet done so are urged to sign the Convention on the Elimination of All Forms of Discrimination against Women 6/ and to take all the necessary steps to ensure its ratification, or their accession to it. They should consider the possibility of establishing appropriate bodies charged with reviewing the national legislation concerned and with drawing up recommendations thereon to ensure that the provisions of the Convention and of the other international instruments to which they are parties that are relevant to the role, status and material circumstances of women are complied with.

Paragraph 61

Governments that have not yet done so should establish appropriate institutional procedures whereby the application of a revised set of laws and administrative measures may be effectively enforced from the village level up and may be adequately monitored so that individual women may, without obstruction or cost to themselves, seek to have discriminatory treatment redressed. Legislation that concerns women as a group should also be effectively enforced and monitored so that areas of systemic or de facto discrimination against women can be redressed. To this end, positive action policy should be developed.

Paragraph 62

Agrarian reform measures have not always ensured women's rights even in countries where women predominate in the agricultural labour force. Such reforms should guarantee women's constitutional and legal rights in terms of access to land and other means of production and should ensure that women will control the products of their labour and their income, as well as benefits from agricultural inputs, research, training, credits and other infrastructural facilities.

Paragraph 63

National research institutions, both governmental and private, are urged to undertake investigations of the problems associated with the relationship between the law and the role, status and material circumstances of women. These should be integrated into the curricula of relevant educational institutions in an attempt to promote general knowledge and awareness of the law.

Paragraph 64

In the past decade there have been significant advances in the development of statistical concepts and methods for measuring inequality between women and men. The capabilities of national institutions concerned with statistics and women's issues should be improved to implement these concepts and methods in the regular statistical programmes of countries and to make effective use of these statistics in the policy-planning process. Training for producers and users of statistics on women should play a key role in this process.

Paragraph 65

In-depth research should be undertaken to determine instances when customary law may be discriminatory or protective of women's rights and the extent to which the interfaces between customary and statutory law may retard progress in the implementation of new legislative measures. Particular attention should be paid to double standards in every aspect of life, with a view to abolishing them.

Paragraph 66

Law-reform committees with equal representation of women and men from Governments and from non-governmental organizations should be set up to review all laws, not only as a monitoring device but also with a view to determining research-related activities, amendments and new legislative measures.

Paragraph 67

Employment legislation should ensure equity and provide benefits for women not only in the conventional and formal labour force but also in the informal sector, particularly with regard to migrant and service workers, by providing minimum wage standards, insurance benefits, safe working conditions and the right to organize. Opportunities for similar guarantees and benefits should also be extended to women making vital economic contributions in activities involving food production and processing, fisheries and food distribution through trade. These benefits should also pertain to women working in family enterprises and, if possible, to other self-employed women in an effort to give due recognition to the vital contribution of all these informal and invisible economic activities to the development of human resources.

Paragraph 68

Civil codes, particularly those pertaining to family law, should be revised to eliminate discriminatory practices where these exist and wherever women are considered minors. The legal capacity of married women should be reviewed in order to grant them equal rights and duties.

Paragraph 69 14/

Such social and economic development should be encouraged as would secure the participation of women as equal partners with men in all fields of work, equal access to all positions of employment, equal pay for work of equal value and equal opportunities for education and vocational training, and would coordinate the legislation on the protection of women at work with the need for women to work and be highly productive producers and managers of all political, economic and social affairs and would develop branches of the social services to make domestic duties easier for women and men.

Paragraph 70

Measures for the implementation of legislation relating to working conditions for women must be taken.

Paragraph 71

Legislative and/or other measures should be adopted and implemented to secure for men and women the same right to work and to unemployment benefits, as well as to prohibit, through, inter alia, the imposition of sanctions, dismissal on the grounds of pregnancy or of maternity leave and discrimination in dismissals on the grounds of marital status. Legislative and other measures should be adopted and implemented to facilitate the return to the labour market of women who have left it for family reasons and to guarantee the right of women to return to work after maternity leave.

Paragraph 72

Governments should continue to take special action to institute programmes that would inform women workers of their rights under legislation and other remedial measures. The importance of freedom of association and the protection of the right to organize should be emphasized, this being particularly relevant to the position of women in employment. Special measures should be taken to ratify and implement in national legislation the relevant conventions and recommendations of the International Labour Organization concerning the rights of women as regards access to equal employment opportu-

14/ The United States reserved its position on paragraphs 69, 72 and 137 specifically because it did not agree with the concept of "equal pay for work of equal value—and maintained the principle of "equal pay for equal work".

nities, equal pay for work of equal value, equal working conditions, job security and maternity protection.

Paragraph 73

Marriage agreements should be based on mutual understanding, respect and freedom of choice. Careful attention should be paid to the equal participation and valuation of both partners so that the value of housework is considered equivalent of financial contributions.

Paragraph 74

The right of all women, in particular married women, to own, administer, sell or buy property independently should be guaranteed as an aspect of their equality and freedom under the law. The right to divorce should be granted equally to both partners under the same conditions, and custody of children decided in a non-discriminatory manner with full awareness of the importance of the input from both parents in the maintenance, rearing and socialization of children. Women should not forfeit their right to custody of their children or to any other benefits and freedoms simply because they have initiated a divorce. Without prejudice to the religious and cultural traditions of countries, and taking into account the de facto situations, legal or other appropriate provisions should be made to eliminate discrimination against single mothers and their children.

Paragraph 75

Appropriate action is necessary to ensure that the judiciary and all paralegal personnel are fully aware of the importance of the achievement by women of rights set out in internationally agreed instruments, constitutions and the law. Appropriate forms of in-service training and retraining should be designed and carried out for this purpose, with special attention given to the recruitment and training of women.

Paragraph 76

Special attention should be given in criminology training to the particular situation of women as victims of violent crimes, including crimes that violate women's bodies and result in serious physical and psychological damage. Legislation should be passed and laws enforced in every country to end the degradation of women through sex-related crimes. Guidance should be given to law enforcement and other authorities on the need to deal sensibly and sensitively with the victims of such crimes.

2. Equality in social participation

Paragraph 77

A comprehensive and sustained public campaign should be launched by all Governments, in close collaboration with non-governmental organizations, women's pressure groups, where they exist, and research institutions, as well as the media, educational institutions and traditional institutions of communication, to challenge and abolish all discriminatory perceptions, attitudes and practices by the year 2000. Target groups should include policy-makers and decision-makers, legal technical advisers, bureaucrats, labour and business leaders, business persons, professionals and the general public.

Paragraph 78

By the year 2000, all Governments should have adequate comprehensive and coherent national women's policies to abolish all obstacles to the full and equal participation of women in all spheres of society.

Paragraph 79

Governments should take all appropriate measures to ensure to women, on equal terms with men and without discrimination, the opportunity to represent their Government at all levels on delegations to subregional, regional and international meetings. More women should be appointed as diplomats and to decision-making posts within the United Nations system, including posts in fields relating to peace and development activities. Support services, such as educational facilities and day care, for families of diplomats and other civil servants stationed abroad, of United Nations officials, as well as employment of spouses at the duty station, wherever possible, should be strongly encouraged.

Paragraph 80

As future parents, young people and children should be educated and mobilized to act as stimulators for and monitors of changes in attitudes towards women at all levels of society, particularly with regard to the need for greater flexibility in the assignment of roles between women and men.

Paragraph 81

Research activities should be promoted to identify discriminatory practices in education and training and to ensure quality at those two levels. One priority area for research should be the impact of sexual discrimination on the development of human resources.

Paragraph 82

Governments and private institutions are urged to include in the curricula of all schools, colleges and universities courses and seminars on women's history and roles in society and to incorporate women's issues in the general curriculum and to strengthen research institutions in the area of women's studies by promoting indigenous research activities and collaboration.

Paragraph 83

New teaching methods should be encouraged, especially audio-visual techniques, to demonstrate clearly the equality of the sexes. Programmes, curricula and standards of education and training should be the same for females and males. Textbooks and other teaching materials should be continuously evaluated, updated and, where necessary, redesigned, rewritten to ensure that they reflect positive, dynamic and participatory images of women and to present men actively involved in all aspects of family responsibilities.

Paragraph 84

Governments are urged to encourage the full participation of women in the whole range of occupations, especially in fields previously regarded as male preserves, in order to break down occupational barriers and taboos. Employment equity programmes should be developed to integrate women into all economic activities on an equal basis with men. Special measures designed to redress the imbalance imposed by centuries of discrimination against women should be promoted to accelerate de facto equality between men and women. Those measures should not be considered discriminatory or entail the maintenance of unequal or separate standards. They are to be discontinued when the objectives of equality of opportunity and treatment have been achieved. Governments should ensure that their public service is an exemplary equal opportunity employer.

Paragraph 85

High priority should be given to substantial and continuing improvement in the portrayal of women in the mass media. Every effort should be made to develop attitudes and to produce materials that portray positive aspects of women's roles and status in intellectual and other activities as well as egalitarian relations of sexes. Steps also should be taken to control pornography, other obscene portrayals of women and the portrayal of women as sex objects. In this regard all measures should be taken to ensure that women participate effectively in relevant councils and review bodies regarding mass media, including advertisement, and in the implementation of decisions of these bodies.

3. *Equality in political participation and decision-making*

Paragraph 86

Governments and political parties should intensify efforts to stimulate and ensure equality of participation by women in all national and local legislative bodies and to achieve equity in the appointment, election and promotion of women to high posts in executive, legislative and judiciary branches in these bodies. At the local level, strategies to ensure equality of women in political participation should be pragmatic, should bear a close relationship to issues of concern to women in the locality and should take into account the suitability of the proposed measures to local needs and values.

Paragraph 87

Governments and other employers should devote special attention to the broader and more equitable access and inclusion of women in management in various forms of popular participation, which is a significant factor in the development and realization of all human rights.

Paragraph 88

Governments should effectively secure participation of women in the decision-making processes at a national, state and local level through legislative and administrative measures. It is desirable that governmental departments establish a special office in each of them, headed preferably by a woman, to monitor periodically and accelerate the process of equitable representation of women. Special activities should be undertaken to increase the recruitment, nomination and promotion of women, especially to decision-making and policy-making positions, by publicizing posts more widely, increasing upward mobility and so on, until equitable representation of women is achieved. Reports should be compiled periodically on the numbers of women in public service and on their levels of responsibility in their areas of work.

Paragraph 89

With respect to the increase in the number of couples in which both partners are employed in the public service, especially the foreign service, Governments are urged to consider their special needs, in particular the couple's desire to be assigned to the same duty station, with a view to reconciling family and professional duties.

Paragraph 90

Awareness of women's political rights should be promoted through many channels, including formal and informal education, political education, non-governmental organizations, trade unions, the media and business organizations. Women should be encouraged and motivated and should help each other to exercise their right to vote and to be elected and to participate in the political process at all levels on equal terms with men.

Paragraph 91

Political parties and other organizations such as trade unions should make a deliberate effort to increase and improve women's participation within their ranks. They should institute measures to activate women's constitutional and legal guarantees of the right to be elected and appointed by selecting candidates. Equal access to the political machinery of the organizations and to resources and tools for developing skills in the art and tactics of practical politics, as well as effective leadership capabilities, should be given to women. Women in leadership positions also have a special responsibility to assist in this field.

Paragraph 92

Governments that have not already done so should establish institutional arrangements and procedures whereby individual women, as well as representatives of all types of women's interest groups, including those from the most vulnerable, least privileged and most oppressed groups, may participate actively in all aspects of the formulation, monitoring, review and appraisal of national and local policies, issues and activities.

II. DEVELOPMENT

A. *Obstacles*

Paragraph 93

The United Nations Decade for Women has facilitated the identification and overcoming of obstacles encountered by Member States in integrating women into society effectively and in formulating and implementing solutions to current problems. The continuation of women's stereotyped reproductive and productive roles, justified primarily on physiological, social and cultural grounds, has subordinated them in the general as well as sectoral spheres of development, even where some progress has been achieved.

Paragraph 94 15/

There are coercive measures of an economic, political and other nature that are promoted and adopted by certain developed States and are directed towards exerting pressure on developing countries, with the aim of preventing them from exercising their sovereign rights and of obtaining from them advantages of all kinds, and furthermore affect possibilities for dialogue and negotiation. Such measures, which include trade restrictions, blockades, embargoes and other economic sanctions incompatible with the principles of the United Nations Charter and in violation of multilateral or bilateral commitments, have adverse effects on the economic, political and social development of developing countries and therefore directly affect the integration of women in development, since that is directly related to the objective of general social, economic and political development.

Paragraph 95 16/

One of the main obstacles to the effective integration of women in the process of development is the aggravation of the international situation, resulting in a continuing arms race, which now may spread also to outer space. As a result, immense material and human resources need for development are wasted. Other major obstacles to the implementation of goals and objectives set by the United Nations in the field of the advancement of women include imperialism, colonialism, neo-colonialism, expansionism, apartheid and all other forms of racism and racial discrimination, exploitation, policies of force and all forms of manifestations of foreign occupation, domination and hegemony, and the growing gap between the levels of economic development of developed and developing countries.

Paragraph 96

The efforts of many countries to implement the objectives of the United Nations Decade for Women were undermined by a series of grave economic crises that have had severe repercussions, especially for many developing countries because of their generally greater vulnerability to external economic factors as well as because the main burden of adjustment to the economic crises has been borne by the developing countries, pushing the majority of them towards economic collapse.

Paragraph 97

The worsening of the social situation in many parts of the world, and particularly in Africa, as a result of the disruptive consequences of the economic crisis had a great negative impact on the process of effective and equal integration of women in development. This adverse social situation reflects the lack of implementation of relevant United Nations conventions, declarations and resolutions in the social and economic fields, and of the objectives and overall development goals adopted and reaffirmed in the International Development Strategy for the Third United Nations Development Decade.

Paragraph 98 17/

The lack of political will of certain developed countries to eliminate obstacles to the practical realization of such fundamental documents adopted by the United Nations as the Declaration on Social Progress and Devel-

15/ The United States abstained in the vote on paragraph 94 because of unacceptable language relating to economic measures by developed countries against developing States.
16/ The United States reserved its position on paragraph 95 because it did not agree with the listing of those obstacles categorized as being major impediments to the advancement of women.
17/ The United States requested a vote on paragraph 98 and voted against the paragraph.

opment (General Assembly resolution 2542 (XXIV)), the Charter of Economic Rights and Duties of States (General Assembly resolution 3281 (XXIX)), the Declaration and the Programme of Action on the Establishment of a New International Economic Order (General Assembly resolutions 3201 (S-VI) and 3202 (S-VI), respectively), the International Development Strategy for the Third United Nations Development Decade (General Assembly resolution 35/56, annex), aimed at the restructuring of international economic relations on a just and democratic basis, should be counted among the main reasons for the conservation of the unfavourable and unequal position of women from the point of view of development, especially in the developing countries.

Paragraph 99

The last years of the Decade have witnessed a deterioration of the general economic situation in the developing countries. The financial, economic and social crisis of the developing world has worsened the situation of large sectors of the population, especially women. In particular, the decline in economic activity is having a negative impact on an already unbalanced distribution of income, as well as on the high levels of unemployment, which affect women more than men.

Paragraph 100 18/

Protectionism against developing countries' exports in all its forms, the deterioration in the terms of trade, monetary instability, including high interest rates and the inadequate flow of official development assistance, have aggravated the development problems of the developing countries, and consequently have complicated the difficulties hampering the integration of women in the development process.

One of the principal obstacles now confronting the developing countries is their gigantic public and private external debt, which constitutes a palpable expression of the economic crisis and has serious political, economic and social consequences for these countries. The amount of the external debt obliges the developing countries to devote enormous sums of their already scarce export income to the servicing of the debt, which affects their peoples' lives and possibilities of development, with particular effects on women. In many developing countries there is a growing conviction that the conditions for the payment and servicing of the external debt cause those countries enormous difficulties and that the adjustment policies traditionally imposed are inadequate and lead to a disproportionate social cost.

The negative effects of the present international economic situation on the least developed countries have been particularly grave and have caused serious difficulties in the process of integrating women in development.

The growth prospects of the low-income countries have seriously deteriorated owing to the reduction in international economic cooperation, particularly the inadequate flow of official development assistance and the growing trade protectionism in the developed countries, which restricts the capacity of the low-income countries to attain the objectives of the United Nations Decade for Women.

This situation is even more grave in the developing countries that are afflicted by drought, famine and desertification.

Paragraph 101

Despite significant efforts in many countries to transfer tasks traditionally performed by women to men or to public services, traditional attitudes still continue to persist and in fact have contributed to the increased burden of work placed on women. The complexity and multi-dimensional aspects of changing sex roles and norms and the difficulty of determining the specific structural and organizational requirements of such a change have hindered the formulation of measures to alter sex roles and to develop appropriate perspectives on the image of women in society. Thus, despite gains made by a few women, for the majority subordination in the labour force and in society has continued, though the exploitative conditions under which women often work have become more visible.

Paragraph 102

The effective participation of women in development has also been impeded by the difficult international economic situation, the debt crisis, poverty, continued population growth, rising divorce rates, increasing migration, and the growing incidence of female-headed households. Yet, neither the actual expansion of employment for women nor the recognition that women constitute a significant proportion of producers has been accompanied by social adjustments to ease women's burden of child and household care. The economic recession led to a reduction in investments, particularly in those services that allow greater societal sharing of the social and economic costs of child care and housework.

Paragraph 103

Insufficient awareness and understanding of the complex and multifaceted relationships between development and the advancement of women have continued

18/ The United States reserved its position on paragraph 100 because it did not accept the underlying philosophy of the paragraph as it concerned the economic situation in debtor and developing countries.

to make policy, programme and project formulation difficult. While during the earlier, part of the Decade the belief that economic growth would automatically benefit women was more widely shared, an evaluation of the experience of the Decade has shed considerable doubt on this over-simplified premise. Consequently, the need to understand better the relationship between development and the advancement of women and to gather, analyse and disseminate information for the more effective formulation of policies, programmes and projects has become greater.

Paragraph 104

Although throughout history and in many societies women have been sharing similar experiences, in the developing countries the problems of women, particularly those pertaining to their integration in the development process, are different from the problems women face in the industrialized countries and are often a matter of survival. Failure to recognize these differences leads, *inter alia*, to neglect the adverse effect of the insufficient progress made towards improvement in national policies or programmes and the present international economic situation as well as the interrelationships that exist between the goals and objectives of the International Development Strategy for the Third United Nations Development Decade and the objectives of equality, development and peace.

Paragraph 105

The lack of political will and commitment continued to retard action to promote effective participation by women in development. Exclusion of women from policy-making and decision-making made it difficult for women and women's organizations to include in their preferences and interests the largely male-dominated choices of progress and development. Furthermore, because the issue of women in development has often been perceived as a welfare problem, it has received low priority, viewed simply as a cost to society rather than as a contribution. Thus, the specific formulation of targets, programmes and projects concerning women and development has often received little attention, awaiting the attainment of development rather than being instrumental to it. This, in turn, caused a parallel weakness in the institutional, technical and material resources devoted to the promotion of activities for effective participation by women in development.

Paragraph 106

Appropriate national machinery for the effective integration of women in the development process has been either insufficient or lacking. Where the machinery exists, it often lacks the resources, focus, responsibility and authority to be effective.

B. *Basic strategies*

Paragraph 107

The commitment to remove obstacles to the effective participation of all women in development as intellectuals, policy-makers and decision-makers, planners, contributors and beneficiaries should be strengthened according to the specific problems of women in different regions and countries and the needs of different categories of women in them. That commitment should guide the formulation and implementation of policies, plans, programmes and projects, with the awareness that development prospects will be improved and society advanced through the full and effective participation of women.

Paragraph 108

Different socio-economic and cultural conditions are to be taken into account when identifying the foremost obstacles to the advancement of women. The current economic situation and the imbalances within the world monetary and financial system need adjustment programmes to overcome the difficulties. These programmes should not adversely affect the most vulnerable segments of society among whom women are disproportionately represented.

Paragraph 109

Development, being conceived as a comprehensive process, must be characterized by the search for economic and social objectives and goals that guarantee the effective participation of the entire population, especially women, in the process of development. It is also necessary to work in favour of the structural changes needed for the fulfilment of these aspirations. In line with these concerns, one should endeavour to speed up social and economic development in developing countries; accelerate the development of the scientific and technological capabilities of those countries; promote an equitable distribution of national incomes; and eradicate absolute poverty, experienced disproportionately by women and children, with the shortest possible delay by applying an overall strategy that, on the one hand, eliminates hunger and malnutrition and, on the other, works towards the construction of more just societies, in which women may reach their full development.

Paragraph 110

As the primary objective of development is to bring about sustained improvement in the well-being of the individual and of society and to bestow benefits on all, development should be seen not only as a desirable goal in itself but also as an important means of furthering equality of the sexes and the maintenance of peace.

Paragraph 111

Women should be an integral part of the process of defining the objectives and modes of development, as well as of developing strategies and measures for their implementation. The need for women to participate fully in political processes and to have an equal share of power in guiding development efforts and in benefiting from them should be recognized. Organizational and other means of enabling women to bring their interests and preferences into the evaluation and choice of alternative development objectives and strategies should be identified and supported. This would include special measures designed to enhance women's autonomy, bringing women into the mainstream of the development process on an equal basis with men, or other measures designed to integrate women fully in the total development effort.

Paragraph 112

The actual and potential impact on women of macro-economic processes operating at the international and national levels, as well as of financial spatial and physical development policies, should be assessed and appropriate modifications made to ensure that women are not adversely affected. Initial emphasis should be placed on employment, health and education. Priority should be given to the development of human resources, bearing in mind the need to avoid further increases in the workload of women, particularly when alternative policies are formulated to deal with the economic and debt crisis.

Paragraph 113

With due recognition of the difficulties involved, Governments, international and regional organizations, and non-governmental organizations should intensify their efforts to enhance the self-reliance of women in a viable and sustained fashion. Because economic independence is a necessary pre-condition for self-reliance, such efforts should above all be focused on increasing women's access to gainful activities. Grass-roots participatory processes and planning approaches using local talent, expertise and resources are vital and should be supported and encouraged.

Paragraph 114

The incorporation of women's issues in all areas and sectors and at the local, national, regional and international levels should be institutionalized. To this end, appropriate machinery should be established or strengthened, and further legislative action taken. Sectoral policies and plans should be developed, and the effective participation of women in development should be integrated both in those plans and in the formulation and implementation of mainstream programmes and projects and should not be confined solely to statements of intent within plans or to small-scale, transitory projects relating to women.

Paragraph 115

The gender bias evident in most development programmes should be eliminated and the prejudices hindering the solution of women's problems removed. Particular attention should be given to the restructuring of employment, health and education systems and to ensuring equal access to land, capital and other productive resources. Emphasis should be placed on strategies to assist women in generating and keeping income, including measures designed to improve women's access to credit. Such strategies must focus on the removal of legal, customary and other barriers and on strengthening women's capacity to use existing credit systems.

Paragraph 116

Governments should seek means to increase substantially the number of women who are decision-makers, policy-makers, managers, professionals and technicians in both traditional and non-traditional areas and sectors. Women should be provided with equal opportunities for access to resources, especially education and training, in order to facilitate their equal representation at higher managerial and professional levels.

Paragraph 117

The role of women as a factor of development is in many ways linked to their involvement in various forms and levels of decision-making and management in economic and social structures, such as worker participation in management, industrial democracy, worker self-management, trade unions and cooperatives. The development of these forms of participation, which have an impact on the development and promotion of working and living conditions, and the inclusion of women in these forms of participation on an equal footing with men is of crucial importance.

Paragraph 118

The relationships between development and the advancement of women under specific socio-cultural conditions should be studied locally to permit the effective formulation of policies, programmes and projects designed for stable and equitable growth. The findings should be used to develop social awareness of the need for effective participation of women in development and to create realistic images of women in society.

Paragraph 119

It is vital that the link between the advancement of women and socio-economic and political development be emphasized for the effective mobilization of resources for women.

Paragraph 120

The remunerated and, in particular, the unremunerated contributions of women to all aspects and sectors of development should be recognized, and appropriate efforts should be made to measure and reflect these contributions in national accounts and economic statistics and in the gross national product. Concrete steps should be taken to quantify the unremunerated contribution of women to agriculture, food production, reproduction and household activities.

Paragraph 121

Concerted action should be directed towards the establishment of a system of sharing parental responsibilities by women and men in the family and by society. To this end, priority should be given to the provision of a social infrastructure that will enable society to share these responsibilities with families and, simultaneously, to bring about changes in social attitudes so that new or modified gender roles will be accepted, promoted and become exercisable. Household tasks and parental responsibilities, including decision-making regarding family size and child spacing, should be re-examined with a view to a better sharing of responsibilities between men and women and therefore, be conducive to the attainment of women's and men's self-reliance and to the development of future human resources.

Paragraph 122

Monitoring and evaluation efforts should be strengthened and directed specifically towards women's issues and should be based on a thorough review and extensive development of improved statistics and indicators on the situation of women as compared with men, over time and in all fields.

Paragraph 123

Appropriate national machinery should be established and should be utilized to integrate women effectively in the development process. To be effective, this machinery should be provided with adequate resources, commitment and authority to encourage and enhance development efforts.

Paragraph 124

Regional and international cooperation, within the framework of technical cooperation among developing countries, should be strengthened and extended to promote the effective participation of women in development.

C. Measures for the implementation of the basic strategies at the national level

1. Overall

Paragraph 125

Appropriate machinery with sufficient resources and authority should be established at the highest level of government as a focal point to ensure that the full range of development policies and programmes in all sectors recognizes women's contribution to development and incorporates strategies to include women and to ensure that they receive an equitable share of the benefits of development.

Paragraph 126

To achieve the goal of development, which is inseparably linked to the goals of equality and peace, Governments should institutionalize women's issues by establishing or strengthening appropriate machinery in all areas and sectors of development. In addition, they should direct specific attention to effecting a positive change in the attitudes of male decision-makers. Governments should ensure the establishment and implementation of legislation and administrative policies and mobilize communications and information systems to create social awareness of the legal rights of women to participate in all aspects of development at all levels and at all stages—that is, planning, implementation and evaluation. Governments should stimulate the formation and growth of women's organizations and women's groups and give financial and organizational support to their activities when appropriate.

Paragraph 127

National resources should be directed so as to promote the participation of women at all levels and in all areas and sectors. Governments should establish national and sectoral plans and specific targets for women in development; equip the machinery in charge of women's issues with political, financial and technical resources; strengthen intersectoral coordination in promoting women's participation; and establish institutional mechanisms to address the needs of especially vulnerable groups of women.

Paragraph 128

Governments should recognize the importance of and the need for the full utilization of women's potential for self-reliance and for the attainment of national development goals and should enact legislation to ensure this. Programmes should be formulated and implemented to provide women's organizations, cooperatives, trade unions and professional associations with access to credit and other financial assistance and to training and extension services. Consultative mechanisms through which the views of women may be incorporated in governmental activities should be set up, and supportive ties with women's grass-roots organizations, such as self-help community development and mutual aid societies and non-governmental organizations committed to the cause of women, should be created and maintained to facilitate the integration of women in mainstream development.

Paragraph 129

There should be close coordination between Governments, agencies and other bodies at the national and local level. The effectiveness of national machinery, including the relationship between Governments and non-governmental organizations, should be evaluated and strengthened with a view to improving cooperation. Positive experiences and good models should be widely publicized.

Paragraph 130

Governments should compile gender-specific statistics and information and should develop or reorganize an information system to take decisions and action on the advancement of women. They should also support local research activities and local experts to help identify mechanisms for the advancement of women, focusing on the self-reliant, self-sustaining and self-generating social, economic and political development of women.

Paragraph 131

Governmental mechanisms should be established for monitoring and evaluating the effectiveness of institutional and administrative arrangements and of delivery systems, plans, programmes and projects to promote an equitable participation of women in development.

2. *Areas for specific action*

    EMPLOYMENT

Paragraph 132

Special measures aimed at the advancement of women in all types of employment should be consistent with the economic and social policies promoting full productive and freely chosen employment.

Paragraph 133

Policies should provide the means to mobilize public awareness, political support, and institutional and financial resources to enable women to obtain jobs involving more skills and responsibility, including those at the managerial level, in all sectors of the economy. These measures should include the promotion of women's occupational mobility, especially in the middle and lower levels of the workforce, where the majority of women work.

Paragraph 134

Governments that have not yet done so should ratify and implement the Convention on the Elimination of All Forms of Discrimination against Women and other international instruments relating to the improvement of the condition of women workers.

Paragraph 135

Measures based on legislation and trade union action should be taken to ensure equity in all jobs and avoid exploitative trends in part-time work, as well as the tendency towards the feminization of part-time, temporary and seasonal work.

Paragraph 136

Flexible working hours for all are strongly recommended as a measure tor encouraging the sharing of parental and domestic responsibilities by women and men, provided that such measures are not used against the interests of employees. Re-entry programmes, complete with training and stipends, should be provided for women who have been out of the labour force for some time. Tax structures should be revised so that the tax liability on the combined earnings of married couples does not constitute a disincentive to women's employment.

Paragraph 137

Eliminating all forms of employment discrimination, *inter alia* through legislative measures, especially wage differentials between women and men carrying out work of equal value, is strongly recommended to all parties concerned. Additional programmes should help to overcome still existing disparities in wages between women and men. Differences in the legal conditions of work of women and men should also be eliminated, where there are disadvantages to women, and privileges should be accorded to male and female parents. Occupational desegregation of women and men should be promoted.

Paragraph 138

The public and private sectors should make concerted efforts to diversify and create new employment opportunities for women in the traditional, non-traditional and high productivity areas and sectors in both rural and urban areas through the design and implementation of incentive schemes for both employers and women employees and through widespread dissemination of information. Gender stereotyping in all areas should be avoided and the occupational prospects of women should be enhanced.

Paragraph 139

The working conditions of women should be improved in all formal and informal areas by the public and private sectors. Occupational health and safety and job security should be enhanced and protective measures against work-related health hazards effectively implemented for women and men. Appropriate measures should be taken to prevent sexual harassment on the job or sexual exploitation in specific jobs, such as domestic service. Appropriate measures for redress should be provided by Governments and legislative measures guaranteeing these rights should be enforced. In addition, Governments and the private sector should put in place mechanisms to identify and correct harmful working conditions.

Paragraph 140

National planning should give urgent consideration to the development and strengthening of social security and health schemes and maternity protection schemes in keeping with the principles laid down in the ILO maternity protection convention and maternity protection recommendation and other relevant ILO conventions and recommendations as a prerequisite to the hastening of women's effective participation in production, and all business and trade unions should seek to promote the rights and compensations of working women and to ensure that appropriate infrastructures are provided. Parental leave following the birth of a child should be available to both women and men and preferably shared between them. Provision should be made for accessible child-care facilities for working parents.

Paragraph 141

Governments and non-governmental organizations should recognize the contribution of older women and the importance of their input in those areas that directly affect their well-being. Urgent attention should be paid to the education and training of young women in all fields. Special retraining programmes including technical training should also be developed for young women in both urban and rural sectors, who lack qualifications and are ill-equipped to enter productive employment. Steps should be taken to eliminate exploitative treatment of young women at work, in line with ILO Convention No. 111 concerning discrimination in respect of employment and occupation, 1958, and ILO Convention No. 122 concerning employment policy, 1964.

Paragraph 142

National planning, programmes and projects should launch a twofold attack on poverty and unemployment. To enable women to gain access to equal economic opportunities, Governments should seek to involve and integrate women in all phases of the planning, delivery and evaluation of multisectoral programmes that eliminate discrimination against women, provide required supportive services and emphasize income generation. An increased number of women should be hired in national planning mechanisms. Particular attention should be devoted to the informal sector since it will be the major employment outlet of a considerable number of under-privileged urban and rural women. The cooperative movement could play an indispensable role in this area.

Paragraph 143

Recognition and application should be given to the fact that women and men have equal rights to work and, on the same footing, to acquire a personal income on equal terms and conditions, regardless of the economic situation. They should be given opportunities in accordance with the protective legislation of each country and especially in the labour market, in the context of measures to stimulate economic development and to promote employment growth.

Paragraph 144

In view of the persistence of high unemployment levels in many countries, Governments should endeavour to strengthen the efforts to cope with this issue and provide more job opportunities for women. Given that in many cases women account for a disproportionate share of total unemployment, that their unemployment rates are higher than those of men and that, owing to lower qualifications, geographical mobility and other barriers, women's prospects for alternative jobs are mostly limited, more attention should be given to unemployment as it affects women. Measures should be taken to alleviate the consequences of unemployment for women in declining sectors and occupations. In particular, training measures must be instituted to facilitate the transition.

Paragraph 145

Although general policies designed to reduce unemployment or to create jobs may benefit both men and women, by their nature they are often of greater assistance to men than to women. For this reason, specific measures should be taken to permit women to benefit equally with men from national policies to create jobs.

Paragraph 146

As high unemployment among youth, wherever it exists, is a matter of serious concern, policies designed to deal with this problem should take into account that unemployment rates for young women are often much higher than those for young men. Moreover, measures aimed at mitigating unemployment among youth should not negatively affect the employment of women in other age groups—for example, by lowering minimum wages. Women should not face any impediment to employment opportunities and benefits in cases where their husbands are employed.

Paragraph 147

Governments should also give special attention to women in the peripheral or marginal labour market, such as those in unstable temporary work or unregulated part-time work, as well as to the increasing number of women working in the informal economy.

HEALTH

Paragraph 148

The vital role of women as providers of health care both inside and outside the home should be recognized, taking into account the following: the creation and strengthening of basic services for the delivery of health care, with due regard to levels of fertility and infant and maternal mortality and the needs of the most vulnerable groups and the need to control locally prevalent endemic and epidemic diseases. Governments that have not already done so should undertake, in cooperation with the World Health Organization, the United Nations Children's Fund and the United Nations Fund for Population Activities, plans of action relating to women in health and development in order to identify and reduce risks to women's health and to promote the positive health of women at all stages of life, bearing in mind the productive role of women in society and their responsibilities for bearing and rearing children. Women's participation in the achievement, of Health for All by the Year 2000 should be recognized, since their health knowledge is crucial in their multiple roles as health providers and health brokers for the family and community, and as informed consumers of adequate and appropriate health care.

Paragraph 149

The participation of women in higher professional and managerial positions in health institutions should be increased through appropriate legislations training and supportive action should be taken to increase women's enrolment at higher levels of medical training and training in health-related fields. For effective community involvement to ensure the attainment of the World Health Organization's goal of Health for All by the Year 2000 and responsiveness to women's health needs, women should be represented in national and local health councils and committees. The employment and working conditions of women health personnel and health workers should be expanded and improved at all levels. Female traditional healers and birth attendants should be more fully and constructively integrated in national health planning.

Paragraph 150

Health education should be geared towards changing those attitudes and values and actions that are discriminatory and detrimental to women's and girls' health. Steps should be taken to change the attitudes and health knowledge and composition of health personnel so that there can be an appropriate understanding of women's health needs. A greater sharing by men and women of family and health-care responsibilities should be encouraged. Women must be involved in the formulation and planning of their health education needs. Health education should be available to the entire family not only through the health care system, but also through all appropriate channels and in particular the educational system. To this end, Governments should ensure that information meant to be received by women is relevant to women's health priorities and is suitably presented.

Paragraph 151

Promotive, preventive and curative health measures should be strengthened through combined measures and a supportive health infrastructure which, in accordance with the International Code of Marketing of Breast Milk Substitutes, should be free of commercial pressure. To provide immediate access to water and sanitary facilities for women, Governments should ensure that women are consulted and involved in the planning and implementation of water and sanitation projects, trained in the maintenance of water-supply systems, and consulted with regard to technologies used in water and sanitation projects. In this regard, recommendations arising from the activities generated by the International Drinking Water Supply and Sanitation Decade and other public health programmes should be taken into account.

Paragraph 152

Governments should take measures to vaccinate children and pregnant women against certain endemic local diseases as well as other diseases as recommended by the vaccination schedule of the World Health Organization and to eliminate any differences in coverage between boys and girls (cf. WHO report EB 75/22). In regions where rubella is prevalent, vaccinations should preferably be given to girls before puberty. Governments should ensure that adequate arrangements are made to preserve the quality of vaccines. Governments should ensure the quality of vaccines. Governments should also ensure the full and informed participation of women in programmes to control chronic and communicable diseases.

Paragraph 153

The international community should intensify efforts to eradicate the trafficking, marketing and distribution of unsafe and ineffective drugs and to disseminate information on their ill effects. Those efforts should include educational programmes to promote the proper prescription and informed use of drugs. Efforts should also be strengthened to eliminate all practices detrimental to the health of women and children. Efforts should be made to ensure that all women have access to essential drugs appropriate to their specific needs and as recommended in the WHO List of Essential Drugs as applied in 1978. It is imperative that information on the appropriate use of such drugs is made widely available to all women. When drugs are imported or exported Governments should use the WHO Certification Scheme on the Quality of Pharmaceutical Products Moving in International Commerce.

Paragraph 154

Women should have access to and control over income to provide adequate nutrition for themselves and their children. Also, Governments should foster activities that will increase awareness of the special nutritional needs of women; provide support to ensure sufficient rest in the last trimester of pregnancy and while breast-feeding; and promote interventions to reduce the prevalence of nutritional diseases such as anaemia in women of all ages, particularly young women, and promote the development and use of locally produced weaning food.

Paragraph 155

Appropriate health facilities should be planned, designed, constructed and equipped to be readily accessible and acceptable. Services should be in harmony with the timing and patterns of women's work, as well as with women's needs and perspectives. Maternal and child-care facilities, including family-planning services, should be within easy reach of all women. Governments should also ensure that women have the same access as men to affordable curative, preventive and rehabilitative treatment. Wherever possible, measures should be taken to conduct general screening and treatment of women's common diseases and cancer. In view of the unacceptably high levels of maternal mortality in many developing countries, the reduction of maternal mortality from now to the year 2000 to a minimum level should be a key target for Governments and non-governmental organizations, including professional organizations.

Paragraph 156 19/

The ability of women to control their own fertility forms an important basis for the enjoyment of other rights. As recognized in the World Population Plan of Action 20/ and reaffirmed at the International Conference on Population, 1984, all couples and individuals have the basic human right to decide freely and informedly the number and spacing of their children; maternal and child health and family-planning components of primary health care should be strengthened; and family-planning information should be produced and services created. Access to such services should be encouraged by Governments irrespective of their population policies and should be carried out with the participation of women's organizations to ensure their success.

Paragraph 157 19/

Governments should make available, as a matter of urgency, information, education and the means to assist women and men to take decisions about their desired number of children. To ensure a voluntary and free choice, family-planning information, education and means should include all medically approved and appropriate methods of family planning. Education for responsible parenthood and family-life education should be widely available and should be directed towards both men and women. Non-governmental organizations, particularly women's organizations, should be involved in such programmes because they can be the most effective media for motivating people at that level.

Paragraph 158 19/

Recognizing that pregnancy occurring in adolescent girls, whether married or unmarried, has adverse effects on the morbidity and mortality of both mother and child, Governments are urged to develop policies to encourage delay in the commencement of childbearing. Governments should make efforts to raise the age of entry into marriage in countries in which this age is still quite low. Attention should also be given to ensuring that adolescents, both girls and boys, receive adequate information and education.

Paragraph 159 19/

All Governments should ensure that fertility-control methods and drugs conform to adequate standards of quality, efficiency and safety. This should also apply to

19/ The Holy See delegation reserved its position with respect to paragraphs 156 to 159 because it did not agree with the substance of those paragraphs.

20/ *Report of the United Nations World Population Conference, 1974, Bucharest, 19-30 August 1974* (United Nations publication, Sales No. E.75.XIII.3), chap. I.

organizations responsible for distributing and administering these methods. Information on contraceptives should be made available to women. Programmes of incentives and disincentives should be neither coercive nor discriminatory and should be consistent with internationally recognized human rights, as well as with changing individual and cultural values.

Paragraph 160

Governments should encourage local women's organizations to participate in primary health-care activities including traditional medicine, and should devise ways to support women, especially underprivileged women, in taking responsibility for self-care and in promoting community care, particularly in rural areas. More emphasis should be placed on preventive rather than curative measures.

Paragraph 161

The appropriate gender-specific indicators for monitoring women's health that have been or are being developed by the World Health Organization should be widely applied and utilized by Governments and other interested organizations in order to develop and sustain measures for treating low-grade ill health and for reducing high morbidity rates among women, particularly when illnesses are psychosomatic or social and cultural in nature. Governments that have not yet done so should establish focal points to carry out such monitoring.

Paragraph 162

Occupational health and safety should be enhanced by the public and private sectors. Concern with the occupational health risks should cover female as well as male workers and focus among other things on risks endangering their reproductive capabilities and unborn children. Efforts should equally be directed at the health of pregnant and lactating women, the health impact of new technologies and the harmonization of work and family responsibilities.

EDUCATION

Paragraph 163

Education is the basis for the full promotion and improvement of the status of women. It is the basic tool that should be given to women in order to fulfil their role as full members of society. Governments should strengthen the participation of women at all levels of national educational policy and in formulating and implementing plans, programmes and projects. Special measures should be adopted to revise and adapt women's education to the realities of the developing world. Existing and new services should be directed to women as intellectuals, policy-makers, decision-makers, planners, contributors and beneficiaries, with particular attention to the UNESCO Convention against Discrimination in Education (1960). Special measures should also be adopted to increase equal access to scientific, technical and vocational education, particularly for young women, and evaluate progress made by the poorest women in urban and rural areas.

Paragraph 164

Special measures should be taken by Governments and the international organizations, especially UNESCO, to eliminate the high rate of illiteracy by the year 2000, with the support of the international community. Governments should establish targets and adopt appropriate measures for this purpose. While the elimination of illiteracy is important to all, priority programmes are still required to overcome the special obstacles that have generally led to higher illiteracy rates among women than among men. Efforts should be made to promote functional literacy, with special emphasis on health, nutrition and viable economic skills and opportunities, in order to eradicate illiteracy among women and to produce additional material for the eradication of illiteracy. Programmes for legal literacy in low-income urban and rural areas should be initiated and intensified. Raising the level of education among women is important for the general welfare of society and because of its close link to child survival and child spacing.

Paragraph 165

The causes of high absenteeism and drop-out rates of girls in the educational system must be addressed. Measures must be developed, strengthened and implemented that will, *inter alia*, create the appropriate incentives to ensure that women have an equal opportunity to acquire education at all levels, as well as to apply their education in a work or career context. Such measures should include the strengthening of communication and information systems, the implementation of appropriate legislation and the reorientation of educational personnel. Moreover, Governments should encourage and finance adult education programmes for those women who have never completed their studies or were forced to interrupt their studies, owing to family responsibilities, lack of financial resources or early pregnancies.

Paragraph 166

Efforts should be made to ensure that available scholarships and other forms of support from governmental, non-governmental and private sources are expanded and equitably distributed to girls and boys and that boarding and lodging facilities are equally accessible to them.

Paragraph 167

The curricula of public and private schools should be examined, textbooks and other educational materials reviewed and educational personnel retrained in order to eliminate all discriminatory gender stereotyping in education. Educational institutions should be encouraged to expand their curricula to include studies on women's contribution to all aspects of development.

Paragraph 168

The Decade has witnessed the rise of centres and programmes of women's studies in response to social forces and to the need for developing a new scholarship and a body of knowledge on women's studies from the perspective of women. Women's studies should be developed to reformulate the current models influencing the constitution of knowledge and sustaining a value system that reinforces inequality. The promotion and application of women's studies inside and outside and conventional institutions of learning will help to create a just and equitable society in which men and women enjoy equal partnership.

Paragraph 169

Encouragement and incentives, as well as counselling services, should be provided for girls to study scientific, technical and managerial subjects at all levels, in order to develop and enhance the aptitudes of women for decision-making, management and leadership in these fields.

Paragraph 170

All educational and occupational training should be flexible and accessible to both women and men. It should aim to improve employment possibilities and promotion prospects for women including those areas where technologies are improving rapidly, and vocational training programmes, as well as workers' educational schemes dealing with cooperatives, trade unions and work associations, should stress the importance of equal opportunity for women at all levels of work and work-related activities.

Paragraph 171

Extensive measurers should be taken to diversify women's vocational education and training in order to extend their opportunities for employment in occupations that are non-traditional or are new to women and that are important to development. The present educational system, which in many countries is sharply divided by sex, with girls receiving instruction in home economics and boys in technical subjects, should be altered. Existing vocational training centres should be opened to girls and women instead of continuing a segregated training system.

Paragraph 172

A fully integrated system of training, having direct linkages with employment needs, pertinent to future employment and development trends should be created and implemented in order to avoid wastage of human resources.

Paragraph 173

Educational programmes to enable men to assume as much responsibility as women in the upbringing of children and the maintenance of the household should be introduced at all levels of the educational system.

FOOD, WATER AND AGRICULTURE

Paragraph 174

Women, as key food producers in many regions of the world, play a central role in the development and production of food and agriculture, participating actively in all phases of the production cycle, including the conservation, storage, processing and marketing of food and agricultural products. Women therefore make a vital contribution to economic development, particularly in agriculturally based economies, which must be better recognized and rewarded. Development strategies and programmes, as well as incentive programmes and projects in the field of food and agriculture, need to be designed in a manner that fully integrates women at all levels of planning, implementation, monitoring evaluation in all stages of the development process of a project cycle, so as to facilitate and enhance this key role of women and to ensure that women receive proper benefits and remuneration commensurate with their important contribution in this field. Moreover, women should be fully integrated and involved in the technological research and energy aspects of food and agricultural development.

Paragraph 175

During the Decade, the significant contribution of women to agricultural development has been more widely recognized, particularly their contribution in working hours to agricultural, fishery and forestry production and conservation, and to various parts of the food system. There are indications, however, that poverty and landlessness among rural women will increase significantly by the year 2000. In order to stem this trend, Governments should implement, as a matter of priority, equitable and stable investment and growth policies for rural development to ensure that there is a reallocation of the country's resources which, in many cases, are largely derived from the rural areas but allocated to urban development.

Paragraph 176

Governments should establish multisectoral programmes to promote the productive capacity of rural poor women in food and animal production, create off-farm employment opportunities, reduce their workload, *inter alia*, by supporting the establishment of adequate child-care facilities and that of their children, reverse their pauperization, improve their access to all sources of energy, and provide them with adequate water, health, education, effective extension services and transportation within their region. In this connection it should be noted that the World Conference on Agrarian Reform and Rural Development, held at Rome in 1979, 21/ recognized women's vital role in the socio-economic life in both agricultural and non-agricultural activities as a prerequisite for successful rural development policies, planning and programmes, and proposed specific measures for improving their condition, which are still valid. The Programme of Action for the Second Half of the United Nations Decade for Women also included specific measures to improve the situation of women in food and agriculture, which remain a valid guide for action.

Paragraph 177

The General Assembly, in resolution 39/165 on the critical situation of food production and agriculture in Africa, confirmed the growing concern of the international community at the dramatic deterioration in African food and agricultural production and the resulting alarming increase in the number of people, especially women and children, exposed to hunger, malnutrition and even starvation. Concrete measures and adequate resources for the benefit of African women should be a priority. The international community, particularly donor countries, should be urged to assist African women by continuing and, where possible, by increasing financial assistance to enhance the role of women as food producers, with an emphasis on providing training in food technologies, thereby alleviating the problems of the continent resulting from extended drought and a severe shortage of food. Donor countries should also contribute to the special funds that have been launched by various organizations—for example, the United Nations Development Fund for Women. Emergency assistance should be increased and accelerated to alleviate the suffering of starving and dying women and children under famine conditions in Africa. Furthermore, given the critical food situation in Africa, aggravated *inter alia* by demographic pressures, the international community is urged to give priority to and provide support for the efforts of the African countries to overcome this serious situation. These efforts include the Lagos Plan of Action and the Nairobi Programme of Action, as well as the consultation by African Governments on the role of women in food production and food security.

Paragraph 178

Governments should give priority to supporting effective participation by women in food production and in food security programmes and should develop specific plans of action for this purpose. This would ensure that resources are directed towards women's programmes, that women are integrated in all mainstream rural development projects and that projects are located within technical ministries as well as ministries of social affairs. Governments should promote integrated solutions, such as national food policies, which are diversified according to specific natural regions for the improvement of self-reliance in food production, instead of resorting to palliative or fragmented remedies.

Paragraph 179

Mechanisms should also include monitoring and evaluation and, where necessary, should modify the allocation of resources between women and men in mixed projects; should restructure rural development schemes to respond to women's needs; should assess women's projects in terms of technical and economic viability, as well as on social grounds; and should develop gender-specific statistics and information that reflect accurately women's contribution to food staples. Women's participation in programmes and projects to promote food security should be enhanced by providing them with opportunities to hold official positions, to receive training in leadership, administration and financial management and to organize on a cooperative basis. Research and experimentation should be conducted on food production and storage techniques to improve traditional knowledge and introduce modern technology.

Paragraph 180

Animal husbandry, fishery and forestry programmes should give greater attention to the effective participation of women as contributors and beneficiaries. Similarly, all other off-farm rural production programmes, as well as rural settlement, health, educational and social service programmes, should secure the participation of women as planners, contributors and beneficiaries.

Paragraph 181

Also important are the dissemination of information to rural women through national information campaigns, using all available media and established women's groups;

21/ *Report of the World Conference on Agrarian Reform and Rural Development, Rome, 12-20 July 1979* (WCARRD/REP) (Rome, FAO, 1979), Program of Action, sect. IV.

the exposure of local populations to innovation and creativity through open-air films, talks, visits to areas where needs are similar, and demonstrations of scientific and technological innovations; the participation of women farmers in research and information campaigns; and the involvement of women in technical cooperation among developing countries and the exchange of information.

Paragraph 182

Rural women's access to land, capital, technology, know-how and other productive resources should be secured. Women should be given full and effective rights to land ownership, registration of land titles and allocation of tenancies on irrigation or settlement schemes and should also benefit from land reform. Women's customary land and inheritance rights under conditions of land shortage, land improvement or shifts into cash-cropping should be protected. Implementation of inheritance laws should be modified so that women can inherit a fair share of livestock, agricultural machinery and other property. Women's access to investment finance to increase their productivity and income should be supported by removing legal and institutional restrictions and by promoting women's savings groups and cooperatives and intermediary institutions, as well as training in and assistance with financial management, savings and investments and reallocation of land resources, with priority placed on production, especially of staple foods.

Paragraph 183

Women should be integrated into modern technology programmes that introduce new crops and improved varieties, rotation of crops, mixed farming, mixed and intercropping systems, low-cost soil fertility techniques, soil and water conservation methods and other modern improvements. In this connection, women's involvement in the construction, management and maintenance of irrigation schemes should be promoted.

Paragraph 184

Appropriate food-processing technologies can free women from time- and energy-consuming tasks and thus effect improvements in their health. Appropriate technologies can also increase the productivity and income of women, either directly or by freeing them to engage in other activities. Such technologies should be designed and introduced, however, in a manner that ensures women's access to the new technology and to its benefits and does not displace women from means of livelihood when alternative opportunities are not available. Appropriate labour-saving technologies should utilize local human and material resources and inexpensive sources of energy. The design, testing and dissemination of the technology should be appropriate also to the women who will be the

users. Non-governmental organizations can play a valuable role in this process. Appropriate and affordable food-processing technologies should be made widely available to rural women, along with appropriate and affordable storage, marketing and transportation facilities to reduce post-harvest and income losses. Information on improved methods which have been ecologically confirmed of reducing post-harvest food loss and of preserving and conserving food products should be widely disseminated.

Paragraph 185

Financial, technical, advisory and institutional support should be provided to women's organizations and groups to enhance the self-reliance of rural women. Women's cooperatives should be promoted to operate on a larger scale by improving farm input provisions, primary processing and the wholesale marketing of women's production. Comprehensive support should be given to women's organizations to facilitate the acquisition of farm inputs and information and to facilitate the marketing of produce.

Paragraph 186

Governments should set targets for increased extension contracts with rural women, reorient the training of male extension workers and train adequate numbers of female extension workers. Women should be given access to training programmes at different levels that develop various types of skills to widen the range of methods and technologies used for agricultural production.

Paragraph 187

Governments should involve women in the mobilization and distribution of food aid in countries affected by the drought, as well as in the fight against desertification, through large-scale afforestation campaigns (planting of woodlots, collective farms and seedlings).

Paragraph 188

Governments should pay greater attention to the preservation and the maintenance free from pollution of any kind of sources of water supply for irrigation and domestic consumption, applying special remedial measures to relieve the burden placed on women by the task of fetching water. To this end, they should construct wells, bore-holes, dams and locally made water-catchment devices sufficient for all irrigation and domestic needs, including those of livestock. Women should be included by Governments and agencies in all policy planning, implementation and administration of water supply projects and trained to take responsibility for the management of hydraulic infrastructures and equipment and for its maintenance.

INDUSTRY

Paragraph 189

The problems related to the industrial development of the developing countries reflect the dependent nature of their economies and the need to promote transformation industries based on domestic agricultural production as a fundamental issue of development. Women are an important part of the agricultural workforce; therefore, there should be special interest in the promotion of the technical training of women in this particular field. In this respect, Governments should take into account the following recommendations:

(a) There should be a link between agriculture and industry;

(b) Steps should be taken to eliminate the particular obstacles to industrialization and to the participation of women in industry, such as energy, the limited markets of some developing countries, the rural exodus, poor infrastructure, a lack of technical know-how, the dependence of the industries of some countries and a lack of financial resources;

(c) Steps should also be taken to promote women's equitable and increased participation in industry by enabling them to have equal access to and to participate in adult education and in-service programmes that teach not only literacy but also saleable income-generating skills, and by encouraging women to participate in collective organizations, including trade unions;

(d) Industrial cooperation among developing countries should be promoted by creating subregional industries;

(e) International organizations and developed countries should assist developing countries in their industrialization effort and the integration of women in that process.

Paragraph 190

Governments should ensure that, at all levels of the planning process, women participate both directly in decision-making and indirectly through effective consultation with the potential beneficiaries of programmes and projects. To this end, resources should be allocated to prepare women, through training, vocational guidance and career counselling and through increased incentives and other support measures, for increased participation in policy-making and decision-making roles and to integrate them by means of special measures at all levels.

Paragraph 191

Women should be viewed as users and agents of change in science and technology, and their technological and managerial skills should be enhanced in order to increase national self-reliance in industrial production and to promote innovations in productive design, product adaptation and production techniques. At the same time, industrial technologies should be applied appropriately to the needs and situations of women so as to free them from time- and energy-consuming tasks.

Paragraph 192

The introduction of advanced technologies in industry in particular, must allow women to enter into sectors from which they have been so far excluded.

Paragraph 193

Governments should direct their efforts to expanding women's employment opportunities in the modern, traditional and self-employed sectors of both the rural and urban economy and to avoiding the exploitation of female labour. Efforts to improve the absolute and relative levels of women's earnings and working conditions should be directed simultaneously to all three sectors.

Paragraph 194

In accordance with accepted international labour standards, particularly, though not exclusively, in the field of female employment, appropriate legislation should be adopted and fully implemented at the national level. Specific consideration should be given to the removal of discriminatory practices concerning employment conditions, health and safety, and to guaranteeing provisions for pregnant women and maternity benefits and child care. Social security benefits, including unemployment benefits, should be guaranteed to women on an equal footing with men. Recruitment of female workers in existing or new capital-intensive, high-productivity sectors should be encouraged.

Paragraph 195

Governments should recognize the importance of improving the conditions and structure of the informal sector for national industrial development and the role of women within it. Traditional craft and cottage industries, as well as the small industrial efforts of women, should be supported with credits, training facilities, marketing opportunities and technological guidance. To this end, producers' cooperatives should be supported and women should be encouraged to establish, manage and own small enterprises.

Paragraph 196

Governments should design and promote as well as encourage the design and promotion of programmes and should allocate resources to prepare women to take up traditional and non-traditional industrial activities in organized and small enterprises, as well as in the informal sector, through innovative approaches to training, and should prepare and disseminate training materials and provide training to the trainers. They should support self-employment initiatives and offer guidance and career counselling.

TRADE AND COMMERCIAL SERVICES

Paragraph 197

Governments should recognize the potential impact of short-term economic adjustment policies on women in the areas of trade and commerce. Government policies should promote the full participation and integration of women in these areas. Alternative sources of finance and new markets should be sought to maintain and increase women's participation in these activities. Not only should appropriate measures be taken to ensure that legal and administrative impediments that prevent women from enjoying effective and equal access to finance and credit are removed but in addition positive measures such as loan guarantees, technical advice and marketing development services should be introduced.

Paragraph 198

Governments should also recognize the positive contribution of women traders to local and national economies and should adopt policies to assist and organize these women. The infrastructure and management of markets, transportation and social services should be improved to increase the efficiency, security and income of women traders and to reduce their workload and the hazards to their health, as well as to avoid wastage of marketable produce. Training opportunities in book-keeping, finance, packaging, standardization and processing technology should be provided to women traders. Such training should also aim at opening up employment opportunities to these women in other marketing and credit institutions. Governments should design innovative mechanisms to provide women traders with access to credit and to encourage the establishment and reinforcement of women's trade associations.

Paragraph 199

Efforts should be made to encourage enterprises to train women in economic sectors that traditionally have been closed to them, to promote diversification of women's employment and to eliminate gender bias from labour markets.

SCIENCE AND TECHNOLOGY

Paragraph 200

The full and effective participation of women in the decision-making and implementation process related to science and technology, including planning and setting priorities for research and development, and the choice, acquisition, adaptation, innovation and application of science and technology for development should be enhanced. Governments should reassess their technological capabilities and monitor current processes of change so as to anticipate and ameliorate any adverse impact on women, particularly adverse effects upon the quality of job.

Paragraph 201

The involvement of women in all of the peaceful uses of outer space should be enhanced, and effective measures should be undertaken to integrate women into all levels of decision-making and the implementation of such activities. In all countries special efforts should be made by Governments and non-governmental organizations to provide women and women's organizations with information on the peaceful uses of outer space. Special incentives should be provided to enable women to obtain advanced education and training in areas related to outer space in order to expand their participation in the application of outer space technology for peaceful uses, especially in the high-priority development areas of water, health, energy, food production and nutrition. To achieve these goals, increased opportunities and encouragement should be given to women to study science, mathematics and engineering at the university level and to girls to study mathematics and science at the pre-university level.

Paragraph 202

Women with appropriate skills should be employed at managerial and professional levels and not restricted to service-level jobs. Special measures should be taken to improve working conditions for women in the science and technology fields, to eliminate discriminatory classification of jobs and to protect the right of women to promotion. Efforts should be made to ensure that women obtain their fair share of jobs at all levels in new technology industries.

Paragraph 203

Major efforts should be undertaken and effective incentives created to increase the access of women to both scientific and technological education and training. To achieve these goals, efforts should be made by Governments and women themselves to enhance, where necessary, the change of attitudes towards women's performance in scientific fields.

Paragraph 204

The potential and actual impact of science and technology on the developments that affect women's integration into the various sectors of the economy, as well as on their health, income and status, should be assessed. Relevant findings should be integrated in policy formulation to ensure that women benefit fully from available technologies and that any adverse effects are minimized.

Paragraph 205

Efforts in the design and delivery of appropriate technology to women should be intensified, and attention should be given to the achievement of the best possible standard in such technologies. In particular, the implications of advances in medical technology for women should be carefully examined.

COMMUNICATIONS

Paragraph 206

In view of the critical role of this sector in eliminating stereotyped images of women and providing women with easier access to information, the participation of women at all levels of communications policy and decision-making and in programme design, implementation and monitoring should be given high priority. The media's portrayal of stereotyped images of women and also that of the advertising industry can have a profoundly adverse effect on attitudes towards and among women. Women should be made an integral part of the decision-making concerning the choice and development of alternative forms of communication and should have an equal say in the determination of the content of all public information efforts. The cultural media, involving ritual, drama, dialogue, oral literature and music, should be integrated in all development efforts to enhance communication. Women's own cultural projects aimed at changing the traditional images of women and men should be promoted and woman should have equal access to financial support. In the field of communication, there is ample scope for international cooperation regarding information related to the sharing of experience by women and to projecting activities concerning the role of women in development and peace in order to enhance the awareness of both accomplishments and the tasks that remain to be fulfilled.

Paragraph 207

The enrolment of women in publicly operated mass communication networks and in education and training should be increased. The employment of women within the sector should be promoted and directed towards professional, advisory and decision-making positions.

Paragraph 208

Organizations aimed at promoting the role of women in development as contributors and beneficiaries should be assisted in their efforts to establish effective communications and information networks.

HOUSING, SETTLEMENT, COMMUNITY DEVELOPMENT AND TRANSPORT

Paragraph 209

Governments should integrate women in the formulation of policies, programmes and projects for the provision of basic shelter and infrastructure. To this end, enrolment of women in architectural, engineering and related fields should be encouraged, and qualified women graduates in these fields should be assigned to professional and policy-making and decision-making positions. The shelter and infrastructural needs of women should be assessed and specifically incorporated in housing, community development, and slum and squatter projects.

Paragraph 210

Women and women's groups should be participants in and equal beneficiaries of housing and infrastructure construction projects. They should be consulted in the choice of design and technology of construction and should be involved in the management and maintenance of the facilities. To this end, women should be provided with construction, maintenance and management skills and should be participants in related training and educational programmes. Special attention must be given to the provision of adequate water to all communities, in consultation with women.

Paragraph 211

Housing credit schemes should be reviewed and women's direct access to housing construction and improvement credits secured. In this connection, programmes aimed at increasing the possibilities of sources of income for women should be promoted and existing legislation or administrative practices endangering women's ownership and tenancy rights should be revoked.

Paragraph 212

Government efforts for the International Year of Shelter for the Homeless 22/ should incorporate assessments of the shelter needs of women and encourage the design and implementation of innovative projects that will increase women's access to services and finance. In these efforts special attention should be paid to women who are the sole supporters of their families. Low-cost housing and facilities should be designed for such women.

Paragraph 213

All measures to increase the efficiency of land, water and air transportation should be formulated with due

22/ General Assembly resolution 36/71.

regard to women as producers and consumers. All national and local decisions concerning transportation policies, including subsidies, pricing, choice of technology for construction and maintenance, and means of transport, should consider women's needs and should be based on consideration of the possible impact on the employment, income and health of women.

Paragraph 214

Women's roles as operators and owners of means of transport should be promoted through greater access to credit for women and other appropriate means and equal consideration with regard to the allocation of contracts. This is particularly important for women's groups and collectives, especially in rural areas, that are usually well organized but are cut off from serviceable means of transport and communication.

Paragraph 215

Rural transportation planning in developing countries should aim at reducing the heavy burden on women who carry agricultural produce, water and fuelwood as head-loads. In exploring modes of transportation, efforts should be made to avoid loss of income and employment for women by introducing costs that may be too high for them.

Paragraph 216

In the choice of modes of transportation and the design of transport routes, the increasing ratio of women whose income is essential for family survival should be taken into account.

Paragraph 217

In the design and choice of both commercial and appropriate vehicular technology, the needs of women, especially those with young children, should be taken into consideration. Institutional support to give women access to appropriate vehicles should be provided.

ENERGY

Paragraph 218

Measures developed to rationalize energy consumption and to improve energy systems, especially of hydrocarbons, and to increase technical training should be formulated with a view to women as producers, users and managers of energy sources.

Paragraph 219

In conventional and non-conventional national energy programmes, women should be integrated as contributors and beneficiaries with a view to their needs, as determined by specific socio-cultural factors at local and national levels and in both rural and urban contexts.

Assessment of new energy sources, energy technologies and energy-delivery systems should specifically consider the reduction of the drudgery that constitutes a large part of the work of poor urban and rural women.

Paragraph 220

The grass-roots participation of women in energy-needs assessment, technology and energy conservation, management and maintenance efforts should be supported.

Paragraph 221

Priority should be given to substituting energy for muscle in the performance of the industrial and domestic work of women without loss of their jobs and tasks to men. In view of the high percentage of domestic use in total energy consumption in low-income countries, the implications of increasing energy costs, and the current threats posed by inflation, immediate attention should be directed towards action concerning adapted technologies, fuel conservation and improved or new sources of energy, such as biomass, solar and wind energy, geothermal and nuclear energy, as well as mini-hydroelectric power plants. Improved stoves should be designed and disseminated to reduce the drudgery involved in the collection of fuel by women.

Paragraph 222

In order to prevent depletion of the forest areas on which most rural women rely for much of their energy needs and income, innovative programmes, such as farm woodlot development, should be initiated with the involvement of both women and men. In the commercialization of fuelwood energy, measures should be taken to avoid the loss of women's income to middlemen and urban industries. Development of fuelwood plantations, diffusion of fast-growing varieties of trees and technologies for more efficient production of charcoal should be accelerated with a view to poor rural and urban women being the major beneficiaries. The use of solar energy and biogas should be promoted with due regard to affordability, as well as to use and management by women who are the principal consumers.

Paragraph 223

The involvement of women at all levels of decision-making and implementation of energy-related decisions including peaceful use of nuclear energy should be enhanced. Special efforts should be made by Governments and non-governmental organizations to provide women and women's organizations with information on all sources and uses of energy, including nuclear energy. Special incentives should be provided to enable women to obtain advanced levels of education and training in all energy-related areas in order to expand their participation in decision-making relating to the application of nuclear technology for peaceful uses especially in high priority development areas of water, health, energy, food production and nutrition. To achieve these goals, increased opportunities and encouragement should be given to women to study science, mathematics and engineering at the university level and for girls to study mathematics and science at the pre-university level.

ENVIRONMENT

Paragraph 224

Deprivation of traditional means of livelihood is most often a result of environmental degradation resulting from such natural and man-made disasters as droughts, floods, hurricanes, erosion, desertification, deforestation and inappropriate land use. Such conditions have already pushed great numbers of poor women into marginal environments where critically low levels of water supplies, shortages of fuel, over-utilization of grazing and arable lands and population density have deprived them of their livelihood. Most seriously affected are women in drought-afflicted arid and semi-arid areas and in urban slums and squatter settlements. These women need options for alternative means of livelihood. Women must have the same opportunity as men to participate in the wage-earning labour force in such programmes as irrigation and tree planting and in other programmes needed to upgrade urban and rural environments. Urgent steps need to be taken to strengthen the machinery for international economic cooperation in the exploration of water resources and the control of desertification and other environmental disasters.

Paragraph 225

Efforts to improve sanitary conditions, including drinking water supplies, in all communities should be strengthened, especially in urban slums and squatter settlements and in rural areas, with due regard to relevant environmental factors. These efforts should be extended to include improvements of the home and the work environment and should be effected with the participation of women at all levels in the planning and implementation process.

Paragraph 226

Awareness by individual women and all types of women's organizations of environmental issues and the capacity of women and men to manage their environment and sustain productive resources should be enhanced. All sources of information dissemination should be mobilized to increase the self-help potential of women in conserving and improving their environment. National and international emphasis on ecosystem management and the control of environmental degradation should be strengthened and women should be recognized as active and equal participants in this process.

Paragraph 227

The environmental impact of policies, programmes and projects on women's health and activities, including their source of employment and income, should be assessed and the negative effects eliminated.

SOCIAL SERVICES

Paragraph 228

Governments are urged to give priority to the development of social infrastructure, such as adequate care and education for the children of working parents, whether such work is carried out at home, in the fields or in factories, to reduce the "double burden" of working women in both urban and rural areas. Likewise they are urged to offer incentives to employers to provide adequate child-care services which meet the requirements of parents regarding opening hours. Employers should allow either parent to work flexible hours in order to share the responsibilities of child care. Simultaneously, Governments and non-governmental organizations should mobilize the mass media and other means of communication to ensure public consensus on the need for men and society as a whole to share with women the responsibilities of producing and rearing children, who represent the human resource capabilities of the future.

Paragraph 229

Governments should further establish ways and means of assisting women consumers through the provision of information and the creation of legislation that will increase consumer consciousness and protect consumers from unsafe goods, dangerous drugs, unhealthy foods and unethical and exploitative marketing practices. 23/ Non-governmental organizations should work towards establishing strong and active organizations for consumer protection.

Paragraph 230

Public expenditure directed towards health, education and training and towards providing health-care and child-care services for women should be increased.

Paragraph 231

Governments should undertake effective measures, including mobilizing community resources to identify, prevent and eliminate all violence, including family vio-

23/ The General Assembly adopted guidelines for consumer protection in resolution 39/248 of 9 April 1985.

lence, against women and children and to provide shelter, support and reorientation services for abused women and children. These measures should notably be aimed at making women conscious that maltreatment is not an incurable phenomenon, but a blow to their physical and moral integrity, against which they have the right (and the duty) to fight, whether they are themselves the victims or the witnesses. Beyond these urgent protective measures for maltreated women and children, as well as repressive measures for the authors of this maltreatment, it would be proper to set in motion long-term supportive machineries of aid and guidance for maltreated women and children, as well as the people, often men, who maltreat them.

III. PEACE

A. *Obstacles*

Paragraph 232

The threat to peace resulting from continuing international tension and violations of the United Nations Charter, resulting in the unabated arms race, in particular in the nuclear field, as well as wars, armed conflicts, external domination, foreign occupation, acquisition of land by force, aggression, imperialism, colonialism, neo-colonialism, racism, apartheid, gross violation of human rights, terrorism, repression, the disappearance of persons and discrimination on the basis of sex are major obstacles to human progress, specifically to the advancement of women.

Paragraph 233

Such obstacles, some of which occur with increasing frequency, continually reinforce and are reinforced by historically established hostile attitudes, ignorance and bigotry between countries, ethnic groups, races, sexes, socio-economic groups and by lack of tolerance and respect for different cultures and traditions. Their negative effects are increased by poverty, tensions in international economic and political relations which are often aggravated, as well as by the arms race, both nuclear and conventional. The arms race in particular diverts resources which could be used for developmental and humanitarian purposes, hinders national and international development efforts and further handicaps the well-being of the poorest nations and the most disadvantaged segments of the population.

Paragraph 234

Despite the achievements of the Decade, women's involvement in governmental and non-governmental activities, decision-making processes related to peace, mobilization efforts for peace, education for peace and peace research remains limited. Their participation in the struggle to eradicate colonialism, neo-colonialism, imperialism, totalitarianism including fascism and similar ideologies, alien occupation, foreign domination, aggression, racism, racial discrimination, apartheid and other violations of human rights has often gone unnoticed.

Paragraph 235

Universal and durable peace cannot be attained without the full and equal participation of women in international relations, particularly in decision-making concerning peace, including the processes envisaged for the peaceful settlement of disputes under the Charter of the United Nations nor without overcoming the obstacles mentioned in paragraph 232.

Paragraph 236

Full equality between women and men is severely hampered by the threats to international peace and security, lack of satisfying progress in the field of disarmament, including the spread of the arms race to outer space, violation of the principle of the right of peoples under alien and colonial domination and foreign occupation to self-determination and independence and respect for the national sovereignty and territorial integrity of States as well as justice, equality and mutual benefit in international relations.

Paragraph 237

It is evident that women all over the world have manifested their love for peace and their wish to play a greater role in international cooperation, amity and peace among different nations. All obstacles at national and international levels in the way of women's participation in promoting international peace and cooperation should be removed as soon as possible.

Paragraph 238

It is equally important to increase women's understanding and awareness of constructive negotiations aimed at reaching positive results for international peace and security. Governments should take measures to encourage the full and effective participation of women in negotiations on international peace and security. The rejection of the use of force or of the threat of the use of force and foreign interference and intervention should become widespread.

B. *Basic strategies*

Paragraph 239

The main principles and directions for women's activities aimed at strengthening peace and formulated in the Declaration on the Participation of Women in Promoting International Peace and Co-operation 7/ should be put into practice. The Declaration calls for Governments, the United Nations system, non-governmental organizations, relevant institutions and individuals to strengthen women's participation in this sphere and it provides the overall framework for such activities.

Paragraph 240

Women and men have an equal right and the same vital interest in contributing to international peace and cooperation. Women should participate fully in all efforts to strengthen and maintain international peace and security and to promote international cooperation, diplomacy, the process of détente, disarmament in the nuclear field in particular, and respect for the principles of the Charter of the United Nations, including respect for the sovereign rights of States, guarantees of fundamental freedoms and human rights, such as recognition of the dignity of the individual and self-determination, and freedom of thought, conscience, expression, association, assembly, communication and movement without distinction as to race, sex, political and religious beliefs, language or ethnic origin. The commitment to remove the obstacles to women's participation in the promotion of peace should be strengthened.

Paragraph 241

In view of the fact that women are still very inadequately represented in national and international political processes dealing with peace and conflict settlement, it is essential that women support and encourage each other in their initiatives and action relating either to universal issues, such as disarmament and the development of confidence-building measures between nations and people, or to specific conflict situations between or within States.

Paragraph 242

There exist situations in several regions of the world where the violation of principles of non-use of force, non-intervention, non-interference, non-aggression and the right to self-determination endangers international peace and security and creates massive humanitarian problems which constitute an impediment to the advancement of women and hence to the full implementation of the Forward-looking Strategies. In regard to these situations strict adherence to and respect for the cardinal principles enshrined in the Charter of the United Nations and implementation of relevant resolutions consistent with the principles of the Charter are an imperative requirement with a view to seeking solutions to such problems, thereby ensuring a secure and better future for the people affected, most of whom are invariably women and children.

Paragraph 243

Since women are one of the most vulnerable groups in the regions affected by armed conflicts, special attention has to be drawn to the need to eliminate obstacles to the fulfilment of the objectives of equality, development and peace and the principles of the Charter of the United Nations.

Paragraph 244

One of the important obstacles to achieving international peace is the persistent violation of the principles and objectives of the Charter of the United Nations and the lack of political will of Governments of such countries to promote constructive negotiations aimed at decreasing international tension on the issues that seriously threaten the maintenance of international peace and security. For this reason, the strategies in this field should include the mobilization of women in favour of all acts and actions that tend to promote peace, in particular, the elimination of wars and danger of nuclear war.

Paragraph 245

Immediate and special priority should be given to the promotion and the effective enjoyment of human rights and fundamental freedoms for all without distinction as to sex, the full application of the rights of peoples to self-determination and the elimination of colonialism, neo-colonialism, apartheid, of all forms of racism and racial discrimination, oppression and aggression, foreign occupation, as well as domestic violence and violence against women.

Paragraph 246

In South-West Asia women and children have endured serious suffering owing to the violation of the Charter of the United Nations, leading, among other things, to the vast problem of refugees in neighbouring countries.

Paragraph 247

The situation of violence and destabilization that exists in Central America constitutes the most serious obstacle to the achievement of peace in the region and thus hinders the fulfilment of the Forward-looking Strategies vital to the advancement of women. In this regard and to promote conditions favourable to the objectives of the Strategies, it is important to reiterate the principles of non-intervention and self-determination, as well as the non-use of force or rejection of the threat of use of force in the solution of conflicts in the region. Therefore, the validity of the United Nations resolutions that establish the right of all sovereign states in the area to live in peace, free from all interference in their internal affairs, should be reaffirmed. It is necessary to support the negotiated political solutions and the peace proposals that the Central American States adopt under the auspices of the Contadora Group, as the most viable alternative for the solution of the crisis in Central America for the benefit of their people. In this sense it is important that the five Central American Governments speed up their consultations with the Contadora Group with the aim of bringing to a conclusion the negotiation process with the early signing of the Contadora Act on Peace and Co-operation in Central America (see A/39/562-S/16775, annex).

Paragraph 248

Women have played and continue to play an important role in the self-determination of peoples, including through national liberation, in accordance with the United Nations Charter. Their efforts should be recognized and commended and used as one basis for their full participation in the construction of their countries, and in the creation of humane and just social and political systems. Women's contribution in this area should be ensured by their equal access to political power and their full participation in the decision-making process.

Paragraph 249

Strategies at the national, regional and the global levels should be based on a clear recognition that peace and security, self-determination and national independence are fundamental for the attainment of the three objectives of the Decade: equality, development and peace.

Paragraph 250

Safeguarding world peace and averting a nuclear catastrophe is one of the most important tasks today in which women have an essential role to play, especially by supporting actively the halting of the arms race followed by arms reduction and the attainment of a general and complete disarmament under effective international control, and thus contributing to the improvement of their economic position. Irrespective of their socio-economic system, the States should strive to avoid confrontation and to build friendly relations instead, which should be also supported by women.

Paragraph 251

Peace requires the participation of all members of society, women and men alike, in rejecting any type of intervention in the domestic affairs of States, whether it is openly or covertly carried out by other States or by transnational corporations. Peace also requires that women and men alike should promote respect for the sovereign right of a State to establish its own economic, social and political system without undergoing political and economic pressures or coercion of any type.

Paragraph 252

There exists a relationship between the world economic situation, development and the strengthening of international peace and security, disarmament and the relaxation of international tension. All efforts should be made to reduce global expenditures on armaments and to reach an agreement on the internationally agreed disarmament goals in order to prevent the waste of immense material and human resources, some part of which might otherwise be used for development, especially of the developing countries, as well as for the improvement of standards of living and well-being of people in each country. In this context, particular attention should be given to the advancement of women, including to the participation of women in the promotion of international peace and cooperation and the protection of mothers and children who represent a disproportionate share of the most vulnerable group, the poorest of the poor.

Paragraph 253

Women's equal role in decision-making with respect to peace and related issues should be seen as one of their basic human rights and as such should be enhanced and encouraged at the national, regional and international levels. In accordance with the Convention on the Elimination of All Forms of Discrimination against Women, all existing impediments to the achievement by women of equality with men should be removed. To this end, efforts should be intensified at all levels to overcome prejudices, stereotyped thinking, denial to women of career prospects and appropriate educational possibilities, and resistance by decision-makers to the changes that are necessary to enable equal participation of women with men in the international and diplomatic service.

Paragraph 254

Mankind is confronted with a choice: to halt the arms race and proceed to disarmament or face annihilation. The growing opposition of women to the danger of war, especially a nuclear war, which will lead to a nuclear holocaust, and their support for disarmament must be respected. States should be encouraged to ensure unhindered flow and access to information, including to women, with regard to various aspects of disarmament to avoid dissemination of false and tendentious information concerning armaments and to concentrate on the danger of the escalation of the arms race and on the need for general and complete disarmament under effective international control. The resources released as a result of disarmament measures should be used to help promote the well-being of all peoples and improve the economic and social conditions of the developing countries. Under such conditions, States should pay increased attention to the urgent need to improve the situation of women.

Paragraph 255

Peace education should be established for all members of society, particularly children and young people. Values, such as tolerance, racial and sexual equality, respect for and understanding of others, and good-neighbourliness should be developed, promoted and strengthened.

Paragraph 256

Women of the world, together with men, should, as informal educators and socialization agents, play a special role in the process of bringing up younger generations in an atmosphere of compassion, tolerance, mutual concern and trust, with an awareness that all people belong to the same world community. Such education should be part of all formal and informal educational processes as well as of communications, information and mass-media systems.

Paragraph 257

Further action should be taken at family and neighbourhood levels, as well as at national and international levels, to achieve a peaceful social environment compatible with human dignity. The questions of women and peace and the meaning of peace for women cannot be separated from the broader question of relationships between women and men in all spheres of life and in the family. Discriminatory practices and negative attitudes towards women should be eliminated and traditional gender norms changed to enhance women's participation in peace.

Paragraph 258

Violence against women exists in various forms in everyday life in all societies. Women are beaten, mutilated, burned, sexually abused and raped. Such violence is a major obstacle to the achievement of peace and the other objectives of the Decade and should be given special attention. Women victims of violence should be given particular attention and comprehensive assistance. To this end, legal measures should be formulated to prevent violence and to assist women victims. National machinery should be established in order to deal with the question of violence against women within the family and society. Preventive policies should be elaborated, and institutionalized forms of assistance to women victims provided.

C. *Women and children under apartheid*

Paragraph 259 24/

Women and children under apartheid and other racist minority régimes suffer from direct inhumane practices such as massacres and detention, mass population removal, separation from families and immobilization in reservations. They are subjected to the detrimental implications of the labour migrant system pass laws and of relegation to the homelands where they suffer disproportionately from poverty, poor health and illiteracy. The Programme of Action of the World Conference to Combat Racism and Racial Discrimination (1978) 25/ provides an overall framework for action. Its objective is to eradicate apartheid and to enable black African people in South Africa to enjoy their full sovereign rights in their country. Governments that have not already done so are urged to sign and ratify the International Convention on the Suppression and Punishment of the Crime of Apartheid of 30 November 1973. 26/

Full international assistance should be given to the most oppressed group under apartheid—women and children. The United Nations system, Governments and non-governmental organizations should identify the basic needs of women and children under apartheid and other racist minority régimes, including women in refugee camps in southern Africa, and provide them with adequate legal, humanitarian, medical and material assistance as well as education, training and employment.

Assistance should be given to women's sections in national liberation movements in order to strengthen their work for women's equal opportunities, education and training so as to prepare them to play an important political role in the present struggle and in nation-building after liberation.

The Forward-looking Strategies should take into account the destabilizing effects of apartheid on the economic infrastructure of neighbouring independent African States, which impede the development of the subregion.

Institutionalized apartheid in South Africa and Namibia as realized in the day-to-day political, legal, social and cultural life remains an enormous obstacle and hindrance to advancement, equality and peace in the African region.

The Forward-looking Strategies should aim at the

24/ The United States voted against paragraph 259 because of its opposition to the references in the eighth and ninth subparagraphs to the imposition of sanctions and aid to liberation movements.
25/ *Report of the World Conference to Combat Racism and Racial Discrimination, Geneva, 14-25 August 1978* (United Nations publication, Sales No. E.79.XIV.2), chap. II.
26/ General Assembly resolution 3086 (XXVIII).

speedy and effective implementation of Security Council resolution 435 (1978) concerning the independence of Namibia. The total and unconditional liberation of Namibia should be a major objective of the Forward-looking Strategies, which should also aim at the improvement of the condition of women and children.

The United Nations and the international community must strengthen their resolve to see the abhorrent apartheid system eradicated and Namibia freed from the forces of occupation. Owing to South Africa's position in the international political and economic structure, the international community has the greatest responsibility to ensure that peace and human dignity are restored to southern Africa.

In addition to measures already taken, further effective measures, including sanctions, should be taken to terminate all collaboration with the racist régime of South Africa in the political, military, diplomatic and economic fields with a view to eliminating untold misery and loss of life of the oppressed people, the majority of whom are black women and children.

The international community must insist upon the effective implementation of Security Council resolution 435 (1978) concerning the independence of Namibia and all the United Nations resolutions calling for sanctions against South Africa, its isolation and abandonment of its racist policies. All efforts should be made for the immediate and unconditional withdrawal of South African forces from Angola.

The international community must condemn the direct aggression committed by the armed forces of the racist régime of South Africa against the front-line countries as well as the recruitment, training and financing of mercenaries and of armed bandits who massacre women and children and who are used to overthrow the legitimate Governments of these countries by reason of their support for the people of South Africa and Namibia.

The international community should provide greater moral and material assistance to all the bodies struggling to remove apartheid, especially the national liberation movements—the African National Congress of South Africa, the Pan Africanist Congress of Azania and the South West Africa People's Organization—the African front-line States, the Organization of African Unity, the Movement of Non-Aligned Countries and non-governmental organizations.

Women, together with their Governments, should strengthen their commitment to the eradication of apartheid and support to their struggling sisters in all possible ways. To this end, women and women's organizations should keep themselves constantly informed about the situation of women and children under apartheid, disseminate information widely and build up awareness in their countries about the situation by organizing national solidarity and support committees where these do not yet exist as a means to educate the public about the evils of apartheid and its brutal oppression of women and children in South Africa and Namibia.

D. *Palestinian women and children*

Paragraph 260 27/

For more than three decades, Palestinian women have faced difficult living conditions in camps and outside, struggling for the survival of their families and the survival of the Palestinian people who were deprived of their ancestral lands and denied the inalienable rights to return to their homes and their property, their right to self-determination, national independence and sovereignty (see A/CONF.116/6). Palestinian women are vulnerable to imprisonment, torture, reprisals and other oppressive practices by Israel in the occupied Arab territories. The confiscation of land and the creation of further settlements has affected the lives of Palestinian women and children. Such Israeli measures and practices are a violation of the Geneva Convention. 28/ The Palestinian woman as part of her nation suffers from discrimination in employment, health care and education.

The situation of violence and destabilization which exists in southern Lebanon and the Golan Heights put Arab women and children who are living under Israeli occupation in severe situations. Lebanese women are also suffering from discrimination and detention. Therefore, all relevant United Nations resolutions, in particular Security Council resolutions 497 (1981), 508 (1982) and 509 (1982), should be implemented.

The implementation of the Programme of Action for the Achievement of Palestinian Rights 29/ should be kept under review and coordinated between the United Nations units and agencies concerned, with emphasis on the role of Palestinian women in preserving their national identity, traditions and heritage and in the struggle for sovereignty. Palestinian people must recover their rights to self-determination and the right to establish an independent State in accordance with all relevant United Nations resolutions. The special and immediate needs of Palestinian women and children should be identified and

27/ The United States voted against this paragraph because of its strong objection to the introduction of tendentious and unnecessary elements into the Forward-looking Strategies document which have only a nominal connection with the unique concerns of women.

28/ Geneva Convention relative to the Protection of Civilian Persons in Time of War, of 12 August 1949 (United Nations, *Treaty Series*, vol. 75, No. 973, p. 287).

29/ *Report of the International Conference on the Question of Palestine, Geneva, 29 August-7 September 1983* (United Nations publication, Sales No. E.83.I.21), chap. I, sect. B.

appropriate provision made. United Nations projects should be initiated to help Palestinian women in the fields of health, education, and vocational training. Their living conditions inside and outside the occupied territories should be studied by the appropriate United Nations units and agencies assisted, as appropriate, by specialized research institutes from various regions. The results of these studies should be given broad publicity to promote actions at all levels. The international community should exert all efforts to stop the establishment of new Israeli settlements in the West Bank and the Gaza Strip. Palestinian women should be allowed to enjoy security in a liberated homeland also in accordance with United Nations resolutions.

E. Women in areas affected by armed conflicts, foreign intervention and threats to peace

Paragraph 261

Armed conflicts and emergency situations impose a serious threat to the lives of women and children, causing constant fear, danger of displacement, destruction, devastation, physical abuse, social and family disruption, and abandonment. Sometimes these result in complete denial of access to adequate health and educational services, loss of job opportunities and overall worsening of material conditions.

Paragraph 262

International instruments, ongoing negotiations and international discussions aimed at the limitation of armed conflicts, such as the Fourth Geneva Convention of 1949 and the First Additional Protocol to the Geneva Conventions of 1949, adopted in 1977, provide a general framework for the protection of civilians in times of hostilities and the basis of provisions of humanitarian assistance and protection to women and children. Measures proposed in the 1974 Declaration on the Protection of Women and Children in Emergency and Armed Conflict (General Assembly resolution 3318 (XXIX) should be taken into account by Governments.

F. Measures for the implementation of the basic strategies at the national level

1. Women's participation in efforts for peace

Paragraph 263

Governments should follow the overall framework of action for disarmament as provided by the Final Document of the tenth special session of the General Assembly, which was devoted to disarmament (resolution S-10/2). Women's participation in the World Disarmament Campaign and their contribution to education for disarmament should be supported.

Paragraph 264

Publicity should be given by Governments and non-governmental organizations to the main treaties concluded in the field of arms control and disarmament, and to other relevant documents. More should be done to mobilize women to overcome social apathy and helplessness in relation to disarmament and to generate wide support for the implementation of these agreements. Publicity should also be given to the declaration by the General Assembly of 1986 as the International Year of Peace, 30/ and the participation of women in the programme for the Year should be encouraged.

Paragraph 265

Non-governmental organizations should be encouraged to play an active role in promoting the restoration of peace in areas of conflict, in accordance with United Nations resolutions.

Paragraph 266

Women should be able to participate actively in the decision-making process related to the promotion of international peace and cooperation. Governments should take the necessary measures to facilitate this participation by institutional, educational and organizational means. Emphasis should be given to the grass-roots participation and cooperation of women's organizations with other non-governmental organizations in this process.

Paragraph 267

Governments which have not done so should undertake all appropriate measures to eliminate existing discriminatory practices towards women and to provide them with equal opportunities to join, at all levels, the civil service, to enter the diplomatic service and to represent their countries as members of delegations to national, regional and international meetings, including conferences on peace, conflict resolution, disarmament, and meetings of the Security Council and other United Nations bodies.

Paragraph 268

Women should be encouraged and given financial support to take university courses in government, international relations and diplomacy in order to obtain the necessary professional qualifications for careers in fields relating to peace and international security.

Paragraph 269

Governments should encourage women's participation in the promotion of peace at decision-making levels

30/ General Assembly resolution 37/16.

by providing information on opportunities for such participation in public service and by promoting equitable representation of women in governmental and non-governmental bodies and activities.

Paragraph 270

Non-governmental organizations should provide opportunities for women to learn how to develop self-reliance and leadership capabilities in order to promote peace, disarmament, human rights and international cooperation more effectively. They should emphasize the participation of women from trade unions and organizations in rural areas that have not as yet received sufficient attention and should make periodic assessments of strategies for women's participation in the promotion of peace at all levels, including the highest decision-making levels.

Paragraph 271

National machinery should be established to deal with the question of domestic violence. Preventive policies should be elaborated and institutionalized economic and other forms of assistance and protection for women and child victims should be provided. Legislative measures should be strengthened and legal aid provided.

2. Education for peace

Paragraph 272

Governments, non-governmental organizations, women's groups and the mass media should encourage women to engage in efforts to promote education for peace in the family, neighbourhood and community. Special attention should be given to the contribution of women's grass-roots organizations. The multiple skills and talents of women artists, journalists, writers, educators and civic leaders can contribute to promoting ideas of peace if encouraged, facilitated and supported.

Paragraph 273

Special attention should be given to the education of children for life in peace within an atmosphere of understanding, dialogue and respect for others. In this respect, suitable concrete action should be taken to discourage the provision of children and young persons with games and publications and other media promoting the notion of favouring war, aggression, cruelty, excessive desire for power and other forms of violence, within the broad processes of the reparation of society for life in peace.

Paragraph 274

Governments, educational institutions, professional associations and non-governmental organizations should cooperate to develop a high-quality content for and to achieve widespread dissemination of books and programmes on education for peace. Women should take an active part in the preparation of those materials, which should include case studies of peaceful settlements of disputes, non-violent movements and passive resistance and the recognition of peace-seeking individuals.

Paragraph 275

Governments should create the conditions that would enable women to increase their knowledge of the main problems in contemporary international relations. Information should be widely and freely disseminated among women, thereby contributing to their full understanding of those problems. All existing obstacles and discriminatory practices regarding women's civil and political education should be removed. Opportunities should be provided for women to organize and choose studies, training programmes and seminars related to peace, disarmament, education for peace and the peaceful settlement of disputes.

Paragraph 276

The participation of women in peace research, including research on women and peace, should be encouraged. Existing barriers to women researchers should be removed and appropriate resources provided for peace researchers. Co-operation amongst peace researchers, government officials, non-governmental organizations and activists should be encouraged and fostered.

IV. AREAS OF SPECIAL CONCERN

Paragraph 277

There is an increasing number of categories of women who, because of their special characteristics, are experiencing not only the common problems indicated under the separate themes but also specific difficulties due to their socio-economic and health condition, age, minority status or a combination of these factors. Moreover, in many countries increasing demographic pressure, deteriorating rural conditions, curtailment of subsistence agriculture and difficult political conditions have been exacerbated by the current economic recession, leading to the dislocation of large sections of populations. In this process women experience particular difficulties and are often the more vulnerable because of their traditional lack of access to development opportunities.

Paragraph 278

The special groups of women identified below are extremely diverse, and their problems vary tremendously from one country to another. No single strategy or set of measures can apply adequately to all cases, and the present document is therefore limited to highlighting their special circumstances and the need for each country, as well as the international community, to give these issues the necessary attention. The basic strategy must remain one of fundamentally changing the economic conditions that produce such deprivation and of upgrading women's low status in society, which accounts for their extreme vulnerability to such conditions, especially to poverty. This is aggravated by the increase in drug-dependence, which adversely affects all sectors of society, including women. Building an organizational base for such change is a crucial strategy that can provide a rallying point for solidarity among women. Measures needed to provide immediate emergency assistance should be supplemented by longer-term efforts to enable women to break out of these situations. In many cases, permanent solutions to these issues can only be found through the broader efforts directed towards the reallocation of resources and decision-making power and towards the elimination of inequality and injustice.

Paragraph 279

There is a need to recognize the survival mechanisms already developed by these women as basic strategies in their own right and to build on them. A first priority would be to strengthen their organization capabilities by providing physical, financial and human resources, as well as education and training. Also of extreme importance is the need to revitalize these women's aspirations in order to eliminate the chronic despair that characterizes their daily lives.

Paragraph 280

The economic, social, cultural and political conditions of those groups of women should be improved basically by the implementation of the measures proposed for the attainment of equality, development and peace for women in general. Additional efforts should be directed towards ensuring the gainful and productive inclusion of these women in mainstream development and in political activities. Priority emphasis should be placed upon income-generating opportunities and for the independent and sustained improvement of their condition and by the full integration and active participation of women as agents and beneficiaries of development.

Paragraph 281

Policies, programmes and projects aimed at or incorporating especially vulnerable and underprivileged groups of women should recognize the particular difficulties of removing the multiple obstacles facing such groups and should place equal emphasis on addressing the social, economic and human dimensions of their vulnerability and their underprivileged positions. Measures needed to provide them with immediate assistance should be sup-

plemented by comprehensive long-term plans to achieve lasting solutions to their problems. These will usually necessitate global efforts in resolving the special problems of vulnerable groups, of which women are a significant part.

Paragraph 282

Basic to all efforts to improve the condition of these women should be the identification of their needs and hence the gathering of gender-specific data and economic indicators sensitive to conditions of extreme poverty and oppression. Such data should contain spatial, socio-economic and longitudinal characteristics and should be designed specifically for use in policy, programme and project formulation and implementation. Monitoring efforts at national, subregional, regional and international levels should be intensified.

A. *Women in areas affected by drought*

Paragraph 283

During the Decade, the phenomenon of drought and desertification grew and developed incessantly, no longer affecting merely some localities in a single country but several entire countries. The scale and persistence of drought constitutes a grave threat, particularly for the countries of the Sahel, in which famine and a far-reaching deterioration of the environment set in as a result of the desertification process. Hence, despite the considerable efforts of the international community, the living conditions of the peoples, particularly those of women and children, which were already precarious, have become particularly miserable.

In view of that situation steps should be taken to promote concerted programmes between the countries concerned for combating drought and desertification. Efforts should be intensified for the formulation and implementation of programmes aimed at food security and self-sufficiency, in particular by the optimum control and exploitation of hydro-geological resources.

A distinction should be made between emergency aid and productive activities. Emergency aid should be intensified when necessary and as far as ever possible directed towards development aid.

Measures should be adopted to take into account women's contribution to production, involve them more closely in the design, implementation and evaluation of the programmes envisaged and ensure ample access for them to the means of production and processing and preservation techniques.

B. *Urban poor women*

Paragraph 284

Urbanization has been one of the major socio-economic trends over the past few decades and is expected to continue at an accelerating rate. Although the situation varies considerably from one region to another, it can generally be expected that by the year 2000 close to half the number of women in the world will be living in urban areas. In developing countries, the number of urban women could nearly double by the year 2000, and it is envisaged that there could be a considerable increase in the number of poor women among them.

Paragraph 285

To deal effectively with the issue, Governments should organize multi-sectoral programmes with emphasis on economic activities, elimination of discrimination and the provision of supportive services and, *inter alia*, adequate child-care facilities and, where necessary, workplace canteens to enable women to gain access to economic, social and educational opportunities on an equal basis with men. Particular attention should be devoted to the informal sector, which constitutes a major outlet for employment of a considerable number of urban poor women.

C. *Elderly women*

Paragraph 286

The International Plan of Action on Aging adopted by the World Assembly on Aging in 1982 31/ emphasized both the humanitarian and developmental aspects of aging. The recommendations of the Plan of Action are applicable to women and men with a view to providing them with protection and care, and ensuring their involvement and participation in social life and development. However, the Plan of Action recognizes a number of specific areas of concern for elderly women since their longer life expectancy frequently means an old age aggravated by economic need and isolation for both unmarried women and widows, possibly with little or no prospect of paid employment. This applies particularly to those women whose lifetimes were spent in unpaid and unrecognized work in the home with little or no access to a pension. If women have an income, it is generally lower than men's, partly because their former employment status has in the majority of cases been broken by maternity and family responsibilities. For this reason, the Plan of Action also noted the need for long-term policies directed towards providing social insurance for women in their own right. Governments and non-governmental organizations should, in addition to the measures recommended, explore the possibilities of employing elderly women in productive and creative ways and encouraging their participation in social and recreational activities.

It is also recommended that the care of elderly persons, including women, should go beyond disease orientation and should include their total well-being. Further efforts, in particular primary health care, health services and suitable accommodation and housing as strategies should be directed at enabling elderly women to lead a meaningful life as long as possible, in their own home and family and in the community.

Women should be prepared early in life, both psychologically and socially, to face the consequences of longer life expectancy. Although, while getting older, professional and family roles of women are undergoing fundamental changes, aging, as a stage of development, is a challenge for women. In this period of life, women should be enabled to cope in a creative way with new opportunities. The social consequences arising from the stereotyping of elderly women should be recognized and eliminated. The media should assist by presenting positive images of women, particularly emphasizing the need for respect because of their past and continuing contributions to society.

Attention should be given to studying and treating the health problems of aging, particularly in women. Research should also be directed towards the investigation and slowing down of the process of premature aging due to a lifetime of stress, excessive workload, malnutrition and repeated pregnancy.

D. *Young women*

Paragraph 287

Initiatives begun for the 1985 International Youth Year should be extended and expanded so that young women are protected from abuse and exploitation and assisted to develop their full potential. Girls and boys must be provided with equal access to health, education and employment to equip them for adult life. Both girls and boys should be educated to accept equal responsibilities for parenthood.

Urgent attention should be paid to the educational and vocational training of young women in all fields of occupation, giving particular emphasis to those who are socially and economically disadvantaged. Self-employed young women and girls should be assisted to organize cooperatives and ongoing training programmes to improve their skills in production, marketing and management techniques. Special retraining programmes should also be developed for teenage mothers and girls who have

31/ *Report of the World Assembly on Aging, Vienna, 26 July-6 August 1982* (United Nations publication, Sales No. E.82.I.16), chap. VI, sect. A.

dropped out of school and are ill equipped to enter productive employment.

Steps should be taken to eliminate exploitative treatment of young women at work in line with ILO Convention No. 111 concerning discrimination in respect of employment and occupation, 1958 and ILO Convention No. 122 concerning employment policy, 1964. Legislative measures guaranteeing young women their rights should be enforced.

Governments should recognize and enforce the rights of young women to be free from sexual violence, sexual harassment and sexual exploitation. In particular, Governments should recognize that many young women are victims of incest and sexual abuse in the family, and should take steps to assist the victims and to prevent such abuse by education, by improving the status of women and by appropriate action against offenders. Young women should be educated to assert their rights. Particular attention should also be given to sexual harassment and exploitation in employment, especially those areas of employment such as domestic service, where sexual harassment and exploitation are most prevalent.

Governments must also recognize their obligation to provide housing for young women who because of unemployment and low incomes suffer special problems in obtaining housing. Homeless young women are particularly vulnerable to sexual exploitation.

In the year 2000 women aged 15-24 will constitute over 8 per cent of both rural and urban populations in developing countries. The great majority of these women will be out of school and in search of jobs. For those employed, frequent exploitation, long working hours and stress have serious implications for their health. Low nutritional levels and unplanned and repeated pregnancies are also aggravating factors.

E. Abused women

Paragraph 288

Gender-specific violence is increasing and Governments must affirm the dignity of women, as a priority action.

Governments should therefore intensify efforts to establish or strengthen forms of assistance to victims of such violence through the provision of shelter, support, legal and other services.

In addition to immediate assistance to victims of violence against women in the family and in society, Governments should undertake to increase public awareness of violence against women as a societal problem, establish policies and legislative measures to ascertain its causes and prevent and eliminate such violence in particular by suppressing degrading images and representations of women in society, and finally encourage the development of educational and re-educational measures for offenders.

F. Destitute women

Paragraph 289

Destitution is an extreme form of poverty. It is estimated that its effects on large segments of the population in developing and developed countries are on the increase. Forward-looking Strategies to promote the objectives of the United Nations Decade for Women: Equality, Development and Peace at the national and international levels are the basis for dealing with this problem. In addition strategies already specified for the implementation of the International Development Strategy for the Third United Nations Development Decade and the new international economic order are suggested in these recommendations. Governments should therefore ensure that the special needs and concerns of destitute women are given priority in the above-mentioned strategies. Moreover, efforts being undertaken for the International Year of Shelter for the Homeless (1987) should focus attention on the particular situation of women commensurate with their relative needs.

G. Women victims of trafficking and involuntary prostitution

Paragraph 290

Forced prostitution is a form of slavery imposed on women by procurers. It is, *inter alia*, a result of economic degradation that alienates women's labour through processes of rapid urbanization and migration resulting in underemployment and unemployment. It also stems from women's dependence on men. Social and political pressures produce refugees and missing persons. Often these include vulnerable groups of women who are victimized by procurers. Sex tourism, forced prostitution and pornography reduce women to mere sex objects and marketable commodities.

Paragraph 291

States Parties to the United Nations Convention for the Suppression of the Traffic in Persons and of the Exploitation of the Prostitution of Others should implement the provisions dealing with the exploitation of women as prostitutes. Urgent consideration should also be given to the improvement of international measures to combat trafficking in women for the purposes of prostitution. Resources for the prevention of prostitution and assistance in the professional, personal and social reintegration of prostitutes should be directed towards providing economic opportunities, including training, employment, self-employment and health facilities for women and children. Governments should also endeavour to cooperate with non-governmental organizations to create wider employment possibilities for women. Strict enforcement provisions must also be taken at all levels to stem the rising tide of violence, drug abuse and crime related to prostitution. The complex and serious problems of the exploitation of and violence against women associated with prostitution call for increased and coordinated efforts by police agencies internationally.

H. Women deprived of their traditional means of livelihood

Paragraph 292

The excessive and inappropriate exploitation of land by any party for any purpose, *inter alia*, by transnational corporations, as well as natural and man-made disasters are among the predominant causes of deprivation of traditional means of livelihood. Droughts, floods, hurricanes and other forms of environmental hazards, such as erosion, desertification and deforestation, have already pushed poor women into marginal environments. At present the pressures are greatest in drought-afflicted arid and semi-arid areas. Urban slums and squatter settlements are also seriously affected. Critically low levels of water supplies, shortage of fuel, over-utilization of grazing and arable lands, and population density are all factors that deprive women of their livelihood.

Paragraph 293

National and international emphasis on ecosystem management should be strengthened, environmental degradation should be controlled and options provided for alternative means of livelihood. Measures should be established to draw up national conservation strategies aimed at incorporating women's development programmes, among which are irrigation and tree planting and also orientation in the area of agriculture, with women constituting a substantial part of the wage-earning labour force for those programmes.

I. Women who are the sole supporters of families

Paragraph 294

Recent studies have shown that the number of families in which women are the sole supporters is on the increase. Owing to the particular difficulties (social, economic and legal) which they face, many such women are among the poorest people concentrated in urban informal labour markets and they constitute large numbers of the rural unemployed and marginally employed. Those with very little economic, social and moral support face serious difficulties in supporting themselves as well as in bringing up their children alone. This has serious repercussions for society in terms of the quality, character, productivity and human resource capabilities of its present and future citizenry.

Paragraph 295

The assumptions that underlie a large part of the relevant legislation, regulations and household surveys that confine the role of supporter and head of household to men hinder women's access to credit, loans and material and non-material resources. Changes are needed in these areas to secure for women equal access to resources. There is a need to eliminate terms such as "head of household" and introduce others that are comprehensive enough to reflect women's role appropriately in legal documents and household surveys to guarantee the rights of these women. In the provision of social services, special attention has to be given to the needs of these women. Governments are urged to ensure that women with sole responsibility for their families receive a level of income and social support sufficient to enable them to attain or maintain economic independence and to participate effectively in society. To this end, the assumptions that underlie policies, including research used in policy development, and legislation that confines the role of supporter or head of household to men should be identified and eliminated. Special attention, such as accessible, quality child care, should be given to assisting those women in discharging their domestic responsibilities and to enabling them to participate in and benefit from education, training programmes and employment. The putative father should be made to assist in the maintenance and education of those children born out of wedlock.

J. Women with physical and mental disabilities

Paragraph 296

It is generally accepted that women constitute a significant number of the estimated 500 million people who are disabled as a consequence of mental, physical or sensory impairment. Many factors contribute to the rising numbers of disabled persons, including war and other forms of violence, poverty, hunger, nutritional deficiencies, epidemics and work-related accidents. The recognition of their human dignity and human rights and the full participation by disabled persons in society is still limited, and this presents additional problems for women who may have domestic and other responsibilities. It is recommended that Governments should adopt the Declaration on the Rights of Disabled Persons (1975) and the World Programme of Action concerning Disabled Persons (1982) which provide an overall framework for action and also refer to problems specific to women that have not been fully appreciated by society because they are still not well known or understood. Community-based occupational and social rehabilitation measures, support services to help them with their domestic responsibilities, as well as opportunities for the participation of such women in all aspects of life should be provided. The rights of intellectually disabled women to obtain health information and advice and to consent to or refuse medical treatment should be respected; similarly, the rights of intellectually disabled minors should be respected.

K. *Women in detention and subject to penal law*

Paragraph 297

One of the major areas of current concern in the field of crime prevention and criminal justice is the need for equal treatment of women by the criminal justice system. In the context of changing socio-economic and cultural conditions some improvements have taken place but more need to be made. The number of women in detention has increased over the Decade and this trend is expected to continue. Women deprived of freedom are exposed to various forms of physical violence, sexual and moral harassment. The conditions of their detention are often below acceptable hygienic standards and their children are deprived of maternal care. The recommendations of the Sixth United Nations Congress on the Prevention of Crime and the Treatment of Offenders, held at Caracas, in 1980, 32/ and the principles of the Caracas Declaration with special reference to the "fair and equal treatment of women", should be taken into account in designing and implementing concrete measures at the national and international levels. The proportions of indigenous women imprisoned in some countries is a matter of concern.

L. *Refugee and displaced women and children*

Paragraph 298

The international community recognizes a humanitarian responsibility to protect and assist refugees and displaced persons. In many cases refugee and displaced women are exposed to a variety of difficult situations affecting their physical and legal protection as well as their psychological and material well-being. Problems of physical debility, physical safety, emotional stress and socio-psychological effects of separation or death in the family, as well as changes in women's roles, together with limitations often found in the new environment including lack of adequate food, shelter, health care and social services call for specialized and enlarged assistance. Special attention has to be offered to women with special needs. Furthermore, the potential and capacities of refugee and displaced women should be recognized and enhanced.

Paragraph 299

It is recognized that a lasting solution to the prob-

lems of refugees and displaced women and children should be sought in the elimination of the root causes of the flow of refugees and durable solutions should be found leading to their voluntary return to their homes in conditions of safety and honour and their full integration in the economic, social and cultural life of their country of origin in the immediate future. Until such solutions are achieved, the international community, in an expression of international solidarity and burden-sharing, should continue providing relief assistance and also launching special relief programmes taking into account the specific needs of refugee women and children in countries of first asylum. Similarly, relief assistance and special relief programmes should also continue to be provided to returnees and displaced women and children. Legal, educational, social, humanitarian and moral assistance should be offered as well as opportunities for their voluntary repatriation, return or resettlement. Steps should also be taken to promote accession by Governments to the 1951 Convention relating to the Status of Refugees and to implement, on a basis of equity for all refugees, provisions contained in this Convention and its 1967 Protocol.

M. *Migrant women*

Paragraph 300

The Decade has witnessed the increasing involvement of women in all forms of migration, including rural-rural, rural-urban and international movements of a temporary, seasonal or permanent nature. In addition to their lack of adequate education, skills and resources, migrant women may also face severe adjustment problems due to differences in religion, language, nationality, and socialization as well as separation from their original families. Such problems are often accentuated for international migrants as a result of the openly-expressed prejudices and hostilities, including violation of human rights in host countries. Thus recommendations of the World Population Plan of Action and the Programme of Action for the Second Half of the United Nations Decade for Women pertaining to migrant women should be implemented and expanded in view of the anticipated increase in the scope of the problem. It is also urgent to conclude the elaboration of the draft International Convention on the Protection of the Rights of All Migrant Workers and their Families, as agreed by the General Assembly in the relevant resolutions.

Paragraph 301

The situation of migrant women, who are subject to double discrimination as women and as migrants, should

---

32/ See United Nations publication, Sales No. E.81.IV.4.

be given special attention by the Governments of host countries, particularly with respect to protection and maintenance of family unity, employment opportunities and equal pay, equal conditions of work, health care, benefits to be provided in accordance with the existing social security rights in the host country, and racial and other forms of discrimination. Particular attention should also be given to the second generation of migrant women, especially with regard to education and professional training, to allow them to integrate themselves in their countries of adoption and to work according to their education and skills. In this process, loss of cultural values of their countries of origin should be avoided.

N. Minority and "indigenous" women

Paragraph 302

Some women are oppressed as a result of belonging to minority groups or populations which have historically been subjected to domination and suffered dispossession and dispersal. These women suffer the full burden of discrimination based on race, colour, descent, ethnic and national origin and the majority experienced serious economic deprivation. As women, they are therefore doubly disadvantaged. Measures should be taken by Governments in countries in which there are minority and indigenous populations to respect, preserve and promote all of their human rights, their dignity, ethnic, religious, cultural and linguistic identity and their full participation in societal change.

Paragraph 303

Governments should ensure that the fundamental human rights and freedoms as enshrined in relevant international instruments are fully guaranteed also to women belonging to minority groups and indigenous populations. Governments in countries in which there are indigenous and minority populations should ensure respect for the economic, social and cultural rights of these women and assist them in the fulfilment of their family and parental responsibilities. Specific measures should address dietary deficiencies, high levels of infant and maternal mortality and other health problems, lack of education, housing and child care. Vocational, technical, professional and other training should be provided to enable these women to secure employment or to participate in income-generating activities and projects, and to secure adequate wages, occupational health and safety and their other rights as workers. As far as possible, Governments should ensure that these women have access to all services in their own languages.

Paragraph 304

Women belonging to minority groups or indigenous populations should be fully consulted and should participate in the development and implementation of programmes affecting them. The Governments of countries where minorities and indigenous populations exist should take proper account of the work of bodies such as the Committee on the Elimination of Racial Discrimination and the Sub-Commission on Prevention of Discrimination and Protection of Minorities, in particular its Working Group which is developing a set of international standards to protect the rights of indigenous populations. The General Assembly should consider the advisability of designating an international year of indigenous and traditional cultures in order to promote international understanding and to emphasize the distinctive role of women in sustaining the identity of their people.

V. INTERNATIONAL AND REGIONAL COOPERATION

A. Obstacles

Paragraph 305

Insufficient attention has been devoted during the Decade at the international level and in some regions to the need to advance the status of women in relation to the goals and objectives of the Decade—equality, development and peace. International tensions, arms race, threat of nuclear war, failure to respect human rights and fundamental freedoms and failure to observe the principles of the United Nations Charter as well as global economic recession and other critical situations combined with dissatisfaction due to inadequate progress in multilateral and international cooperation since the Copenhagen World Conference has substantially affected the scope and ability for international and regional cooperation including the role of the United Nations. The progress in the developing world has slackened or in some cases turned negative under conditions of serious indebtedness, economic and monetary instability, resource constraints and unemployment. This has also affected prospects for economic and technical cooperation among developing countries, particularly with regard to women. Nevertheless some progress has been made in terms of achieving equality between women and men, and a greater appreciation of the role of women in development and peace which should also contribute toward effective international cooperation.

Paragraph 306

International and regional organizations have been called upon during the Decade to advance the position of their women staff and to extend hiring practices to include qualified women. The results have been highly uneven and in some cases the situation has actually worsened during the Decade in the face of resource constraints and other limiting criteria, such as geographical distribution and attitudinal barriers. In particular, women are absent from the senior management levels, which seriously limits their influence on decision-making.

Paragraph 307

In order to institutionalize interorganizational exchanges of information and cooperation in relation to women's advancement, several United Nations agencies, non-governmental organizations and regional bodies have designated, in response to pressures applied during the Decade, focal points for women's activities. However, in many cases, insufficient tenure and resources accompanied those actions, thus limiting their long-term effectiveness. Moreover, activities that promote the integration of women in development have often been confined to these focal points and have not been integrated into all organizational planning and programme activities. Progress has also been limited in this area by the inadequate training of many of the staff members of international agencies and organizations with respect to the centrality of women's role in development.

Paragraph 308

International and regional cooperation strategies must be formulated on the premise that effective development requires the full integration of women in the development process as both agents and beneficiaries. Development agencies should take full cognizance of women as a development resource. This requires that all international and regional development institutions adopt explicit policies in this regard and put in place the management systems necessary to ensure the effective implementation and evaluation of these policies in the full range of their programmes and activities. Such policies should incorporate the principles endorsed in the Forward-looking Strategies of Implementation for the Advancement of Women. Strong and visible commitment to and interest in integrating women in the development process should be demonstrated by the senior-level management of development agencies.

B. *Basic strategies*

Paragraph 309

Effective consultative and reporting arrangements are required to collect information on action taken to implement the Forward-looking Strategies and on successful ways and means used to overcome obstacles. Monitoring and evaluation should, therefore, be carried out at international, regional and subregional levels based on national-level monitoring, including input from non-governmental organizations.

Paragraph 310

Technical cooperation, training and advisory services should promote endogenous development and self-reliance with greater emphasis on economic and technical cooperation among developing countries. The special needs of women should be periodically assessed and methods developed to integrate women's concerns into the planning and evaluation of development activities. The participation of women in the formulation of technical cooperation policies and programmes should be ensured.

Paragraph 311

International, regional and subregional institutional coordination should be strengthened, particularly in relation to the exchange of information on the advancement of women and the establishment of collaborative arrangements to undertake activities with interrelated components.

Paragraph 312

Research and policy analysis should focus greater attention on the economic role of women in society, including access to economic resources such as land and capital. Research and policy analysis related to women should be action-oriented without losing sight of key analytical considerations. Further investment in evolving adequate gender-specific data is also required.

Paragraph 313

Steps should be taken to increase the participation of women in international, regional and subregional level activities and decision-making, including those directly or indirectly concerned with the maintenance of peace and security, the role of women in development and the achievement of equality between women and men.

Paragraph 314

Information on progress in achieving the goals of the Decade and on implementing the Forward-looking Strategies should be widely disseminated in the period from 1985 to the year 2000 at international, regional, subregional and national levels, based on experience gained during the Decade. Greater reliance is needed on audio-visual communications and expansion of networks for disseminating information on programmes and activities for women. Discriminatory, stereotyped and degrading images of women must be eliminated in the media.

Paragraph 315

On the basis of the results of the review and appraisal in the United Nations system that indicated the need for continued efforts to ensure the recruitment, promotion and retention of women, all United Nations bodies, the regional commissions and the specialized agencies should take all measures necessary to achieve an equitable balance between women and men staff members at managerial and professional levels in all substantive areas, as well as in field posts, with particular attention to promoting equitable regional representation of women. Women should be appointed to decision-making and management posts within the United Nations system in order to increase their participation in activities at the international and regional levels, including such areas as equality, development and peace.

Paragraph 316

In view of the difficulties of spouses of United Nations officials in securing employment at the various duty stations, the United Nations is urged to make every possible effort to provide the establishment of educational facilities and day care centres for families of officials in order to facilitate the employment of spouses at these duty stations.

C. Measures for the implementation of the basic strategies

1. Monitoring

Paragraph 317

The implementation of the goals and objectives of the Decade—equality, development and peace—and of the Forward-looking Strategies should be monitored during the period 1986 to the year 2000. Monitoring at the international level should be based on reviews, at the regional, subregional and national levels, of action taken, resources allocated and progress achieved. The national reviews should take the form of a response to a regular statistical reporting request from the United Nations Secretariat, which should include indicators of the situation of women. The statistical reporting basis should be developed by the Statistical Commission, in consultation with the Commission on the Status of Women. The United Nations Secretariat should compile the results of such monitoring in consultation with the appropriate bodies of Governments, including national machinery established to monitor and improve the status of women. The action taken and progress achieved at the national level should reflect consultation with non-governmental organizations and integration of their concerns at all levels of government planning, implementation and evaluation, as appropriate.

Paragraph 318

The specialized agencies and other United Nations organizations, including the regional commissions, should establish monitoring capabilities and procedures to analyse the situation of women in their sectoral or geographical areas, and submit their reports regularly to their respective governing bodies and to the Commission on the Status of Women, which is the main intergovernmental body within the United Nations system concerned with women.

Paragraph 319

The Commission on the Status of Women should consider on a regular basis reports on the progress made and concrete measures implemented at national, regional and international levels to advance the status of women in relation to the goals of the Decade—equality, development and peace—and the sub-theme employment health and education—and the strategies and measures to the year 2000. The United Nations system should continue to carry out a comprehensive and critical review of progress achieved in implementing the provisions of the World Plan of Action and of the Programme for the Second Half of the Decade. The central role in carrying out this review and appraisal should be played by the Commission on the Status of Women. The Commission should also monitor progress in the implementation of international standards, codes of conduct, strategies, conventions and covenants as they pertain to women. In view of this important function, high-level expertise and representation on the Commission should be given priority, including officials with substantive policy responsibilities for the advancement of women.

Paragraph 320

The preparation of new instruments and strategies such as the overall strategies for international development, should pay specific, appropriate attention to the advancement of women. Intergovernmental bodies of the United Nations system particularly those concerned with the monitoring, review and appraisal of the existing instruments, strategies, plans and programmes that may be of direct or indirect relevance to women, are urged as a matter of priority to develop explicit policies and reviewable plans of action for the integration of women in their regular work programmes.

Paragraph 321

The methods and procedures employed for collecting information from Governments, regional commissions, non-governmental organizations and other international organizations and bodies should be streamlined and based on guidelines to be discussed by the Commission on the Status of Women.

2. Technical cooperation, training and advisory strategies

Paragraph 322

Measures of technical cooperation, training and advisory services directed towards improving women's status at the international, interregional and regional levels, including cooperation among developing countries, need some impetus. This would require the re-ordering of principles for the allocation of resources as well as targeted financial, material and human resource assistance. Notwithstanding resource constraints, the United Nations should continue the important role of reinforcing these increased benefits for women.

Paragraph 323

Technical cooperation should be approached with a new concept that will break the cycle of dependency, emphasize local needs, and use local materials and resources as well as local creativity and expertise and be based on the full integration of women as agents and beneficiaries in all technical cooperation activities. Local associations and mechanisms should be oriented to play a more active role in planning and policy-making. Emphasis should be given to broader access by women to capital for self-help projects, income-generating activities, enterprise development and projects designed to reduce the drudgery in work performed by women. Innovative demonstration projects, particularly with respect to the integration of women in non-traditional sector activities, should be an essential element in technical cooperation activities.

Paragraph 324

Agencies which do not have specific guidelines or project procedures relating to women in development interlinked with the other aims of the period up to the year 2000 should ensure that they are developed. Such guidelines and procedures should apply to all aspects of the project cycle. Existing guidelines and procedures have to be applied more vigorously and consistently; in particular, each project document should contain a strategy to ensure that the project has a positive impact on the situation of women.

Paragraph 325

Substantive staff training is needed to enhance the ability of staff to recognize and deal with the centrality of women's role in development, and adequate resources must be made available for this purpose. Implementation of policies concerning women is the responsibility of the particular organization as a whole. Responsibility is not merely a matter of personal persuasion. Systems should be developed which allocate responsibility and accountability.

Paragraph 326

Governments should strengthen and improve their institutional arrangements for technical cooperation so that policy is effectively linked to local-level implementing mechanisms, and should promote sustained, endogenous development. In these efforts Governments may wish to make use of the accumulated experience, activities and resources of the whole United Nations system.

Paragraph 327

While technical cooperation should be focused equally on women and men, the incorporation of women's needs and aspirations in the formulation and review of technical cooperation policies and programmes should be ensured and the potential negative effects on women of technical assistance should be minimized. Technical cooperation and women must be linked to overall national development objectives and priorities and technical assistance plans and programmes should be managed so as to ensure the full integration of activities specific to women. As a standard component of technical cooperation policies, women should be full and equal participants in technical cooperation projects and activities. The needs of especially vulnerable and underprivileged groups of women should be addressed in the technical cooperation programmes.

Paragraph 328

Participation of non-governmental organizations as a means to enhance the relevance and impact of technical cooperation activities of benefit to women should be encouraged.

Paragraph 329

In allocating multilateral and bilateral assistance, agencies, in consultation with recipient Governments, should establish measurable and reviewable plans of action, with goals and time frames. They should also give adequate impetus to sustained and real increases in the flow of resources for technical cooperation activities of benefit to women, including greater mobilization of resources from non-governmental sources and the private sector. Bilateral and multilateral aid agencies should give special consideration to assisting the least developed countries in their efforts to integrate women in development. In this regard, particular attention should be given to projects in the fields of health, education and training, and the creation of employment opportunities for women, especially in rural areas.

Paragraph 330

Bilateral and multilateral aid agencies should take a corporate-wide response to the integration of women in development. Bilateral aid agencies' policies for women in development should involve all parts of donors' organizations and programmes, including participation of multilateral and bilateral programmes, training technical assistance and financial aid. Policies for women in development should be incorporated into all applicable aid and agency procedures relating to sectoral and project levels.

Paragraph 331

In order to enable women to define and defend their own interests and needs, the United Nations system and aid agencies should provide assistance for programmes and projects which strengthen women's autonomy, in particular in the integration process.

Paragraph 332

International non-governmental organizations, including such organizations as trade unions, should be encouraged to involve women in their day-to-day work and to increase their attention to women's issues. The capacity of non-governmental organizations at all levels to reach women and women's groups should receive greater recognition and support. The potential role of those non-governmental organizations could be fully utilized by international and governmental agencies involved in development cooperation.

Paragraph 333

Technical and advisory assistance should be provided by the United Nations system at the national level to improve systematically statistical and other forms of gender-specific indicators and information that can help redirect policy and programmes for the more effective integration of women in development as contributors and beneficiaries.

Paragraph 334

Technical cooperation among developing countries should be strengthened in the service of women at all levels and in all sectors of activity, focusing particularly on promoting the exchange of experience, expertise, technology and know-how, as well as on diffusing innovative organizational models suitable for strengthening the self-reliance of women. The urgent need for information flows to facilitate the process of integrating women in development, and the need for relevant, transferable and appropriate information should be a priority of regional cooperation within the framework of technical cooperation among developing countries. Regional cooperation to assist disadvantaged groups of women should also be promoted in this context.

Paragraph 335

Technical assistance should be given by the United Nations system and other international and non-governmental organizations to women involved in the promotion of international peace and cooperation.

Paragraph 336

The United Nations system should continue to strengthen training programmes for women, in particular in the least developed countries, through fellowships and other means of assistance, particularly in the fields of economic planning, public affairs and public administration, business management and accounting, and farming and labour relations, and in scientific, engineering and technical fields. It is necessary to support and expand technical and economic activities for women by means of collaboration with international development assistance agencies. In this respect, the United Nations Development Fund for Women is particularly recognized for its innovative contribution in the area of development and technical assistance for disadvantaged women, and its continuation and expansion beyond the Decade is considered of vital importance to the development needs of women.

Paragraph 337

The participation of women in technical assistance monitoring, planning, programming, evaluation and follow-up missions should be promoted, and guidelines should be developed and applied to assess the relevance and impact of development assistance projects on women. The United Nations funding agencies, such as the United Nations Development Programme, the United Nations Fund for Population Activities, the United Nations Children's Fund and the World Food Programme, as well as the World Bank, should ensure that women benefit from and participate in all projects and programmes funded by them.

3. Institutional coordination

Paragraph 338

System-wide coordination of work on issues relating to women needs to be strengthened. The Economic and Social Council should be encouraged to play a more forceful and dynamic role in reviewing and coordinating all relevant United Nations activities in the field of women's issues. Regular consultations between United Nations agencies and organizations should be institutionalized in conjunction with meetings of the Commission on the Status of Women in order to exchange information on programme activities and coordinate future planning and programming with a view to ensuring adequate resource-allocation that would facilitate action and limit the unnecessary duplication of activities.

Paragraph 339

Future medium-term plans of the United Nations and the specialized agencies should contain intersectoral presentations of the various programmes dealing with issues of concern to women. In order to achieve greater coherence and efficiency of the policies and programmes of the United Nations system related to women and development, the Secretary-General, in his capacity as Chairman of the Administrative Committee on Co-ordination and in conformity with Economic and Social Council resolution 1985/46 of 31 May 1985, should take the initiative in formulating a system-wide medium-term plan for women and development.

Paragraph 340

The Centre for Social Development and Humanitarian Affairs of the Department of International Economic and Social Affairs, in particular the Branch for the Advancement of Women, should continue to serve as the focal point for coordination of, consultation on, promotion of and advice on matters relevant to women in the United Nations system and to coordinate information on system-wide activities related to the future implementation of the goals and objectives of the Decade and the Forward-looking Strategies. In this context, the United Nations system should explore ways and means of developing further collaboration between its organizations including the regional commissions, the International Research and Training Institute for the Advancement of Women and the United Nations Development Fund for women, in particular in connection with the holding of United Nations world conferences on women on a regular basis, if necessary, for example every five years. It is recommended that at least one world conference be held during the period between 1985 and the year 2000, taking into account that the General Assembly will take the decision on the holding of the conference in each case within existing financial resources.

Paragraph 341

Existing sectoral interagency task forces in the United Nations system should always include issues related to the advancement of women in their agenda.

Paragraph 342

Inter-agency coordination should be complemented where possible by networking, particularly in the fields of information, research, training and programme development, in order to facilitate the availability of data and information in these fields and the exchange of experience with national machinery.

Paragraph 343

Resolutions of the United Nations General Assembly, of governing bodies of the specialized agencies and of other organizations which promote the improvement of the status of women should be implemented. All institutions within the United Nations system that have not yet established special internal arrangements and procedures with respect to women's policies are urged to take the necessary measures to do so.

Paragraph 344

International machineries that promote and support education for peace should coordinate their efforts and include the role of women in promoting peace in their curricula. Particular attention should be paid to the Declaration on the Participation of Women in Promoting International Peace and Co-operation adopted by the General Assembly in 1982. The University for Peace should play a leading role in this regard.

4. *Research and policy analysis*

Paragraph 345

Institutes of women's affairs at the regional level should be strengthened or, where they do not exist, their establishment should be considered for the promotion of regional collaboration in undertaking research and analyses on emerging women's issues in order to facilitate and promote regional and international cooperation and understanding in this field.

Paragraph 346

Measures should be taken by the United Nations system to strengthen the capabilities of the United Nations Secretariat to provide assistance to Governments and other international organizations and bodies concerned with integrating women in policy formulation and in assessing the impact of development policies on women. The Branch for the Advancement of Women should act as the focal point for coordinating the exchange of information, providing advice on matters related to the advancement of women and monitoring and evaluating the progress of other bodies in that connection. The United Nations should develop guidelines for this purpose based on comparative analyses of experience world wide.

Paragraph 347

Guidelines should also be developed by the United Nations for action to remove gender-specific discriminatory perceptions, attitudes and behaviour based on models of successful initiatives.

Paragraph 348

The United Nations system should undertake research and prepare guidelines, case studies and practical approaches on integrating women on an equal basis with men into political life. Training programmes for and consultations between women already engaged in political life should be organized.

Paragraph 349

Research should be carried out and a report prepared by the United Nations, in consultation with other organizations and specialized agencies and in cooperation with Governments, on establishing effective institutional arrangements at the national level for the formulation of policies on women, including guidelines and summaries of national case studies.

Paragraph 350

United Nations agencies and, in particular, the Centre for Social Development and Humanitarian Affairs of the United Nations Secretariat, as part of its regular programme of work, should undertake in-depth research on the positive and negative effects of legislative change, the persistence of de facto discrimination and conflicts between customary and statutory laws. In carrying out this research, full use should be made of the work of the Committee on the Elimination of All Forms of Discrimination against Women.

Paragraph 351

In the context of the Third United Nations Development Decade and any subsequent decade, the implications for women of international decisions especially pertaining to international trade and finance, agriculture and technology transfer should be assessed by the United Nations system in consultation with the appropriate international organizations, bodies and research institutes, including the United Nations Research Institute for Social Development, the International Research and Training Institute for the Advancement of Women and any others established by the United Nations University. The lack of reliable data prevents the assessment of relative improvements in women's status in the various sectors. It is therefore essential that the Statistical Commission, the Commission on the Status of Women and the International Research and Training Institute for the advancement of Women should cooperate at the institutional level in the collection, analysis, utilization and dissemination of statistical data on the question of women. The database on women's role in national, regional and international economic activities should be further developed by the United Nations in cooperation with Governments,

specialized agencies and the regional commissions of the United Nations system.

Paragraph 352

The United Nations regional commissions, with a view to integrating women's concerns at all levels in each commission's overall programme of work, should undertake further research on the status of women in their regions to the year 2000 by developing the necessary database and indicators and by drawing upon inputs from the national and local levels, including perspectives on and by women at the grass-roots level. To this end, the regional commissions should include in their annual reports an analysis of changes in the situation of women in their regions.

Paragraph 353

It is also necessary to strengthen the activities of the International Research and Training Institute for the Advancement of Women which performs an important role in the field of research, training, information and communication, and to request States and appropriate organizations, in particular, the organizations of the United Nations system, to continue to collaborate with the Institute in its work for the improvement of the status of women. The Institute should continue its work in appraising and evaluating what has been done by Governments and the United Nations system in promoting the status of women and it should be given increased voluntary financial support.

Paragraph 354

The United Nations should incorporate within its activities related to the World Disarmament Campaign the preparation of a study on the specific consequences of the arms race and modern warfare for women in general, especially aged or pregnant women and young children. Such a study should be given wide publicity in order to mobilize researchers, politicians and non-governmental organizations, as well as women themselves, for the promotion of disarmament.

Paragraph 355

The United Nations system and other intergovernmental, governmental and non-governmental organizations should encourage women, women's organizations and all the appropriate governmental bodies from different countries to discuss and study various aspects of promoting peace and other related issues in order to increase knowledge, facilitate understanding and develop friendly relations between countries and peoples. Exchange visits among women from different countries, and meetings and seminars in which women participate fully should be organized at regional and international levels.

5. Participation of women in activities at the international and regional levels and in decision-making

Paragraph 356

The United Nations system should take all necessary measures to achieve an equitable balance between women and men staff members at managerial and professional levels in all substantive areas, as well as in field posts. Regular reporting to the General Assembly, the governing bodies of the specialized agencies, the regional commissions and the Commission on the Status of Women on the establishment and implementation of targets for the equal representation of women in professional posts should be continued.

Paragraph 357

Women and women's organizations from different countries should be encouraged to discuss and study various aspects of promoting peace and development issues in order to increase knowledge, facilitate understanding and develop friendly relations between countries and peoples. Exchange visits of women from different countries and meetings with full participation by women should be encouraged.

Paragraph 358

In order to ensure that programmes and activities of concern to women are given the necessary attention and priority, it is essential that women should participate actively in the planning and formulation of policies and programmes and in decision-making and appraisal processes in the United Nations. To this end, international, regional and national organizations have been called upon during the Decade to advance the status of their female staff and to increase the number of women recruited. In the absence of overall targets and effective mechanisms for their achievement, however, greater efforts are needed to ensure the recruitment, promotion and career development of women. All bodies and organizations of the United Nations system should therefore take all possible measures to achieve the participation of women on equal terms with men at all levels by the year 2000. To achieve this goal, the secretariats of the United Nations and all the organizations and bodies within the system should take special measures, such as the preparation of a comprehensive affirmative action plan including provisions for setting intermediate targets and for establishing and supporting special mechanisms—for example, coordinators—to improve the status of women staff. Progress made to implement those measures should be reported to the General Assembly, the economic and Social Council and the Commission on the Status of Women on a regular basis.

Paragraph 359

Women should be assured of the opportunity to participate in international, regional and subregional meetings and seminars, including those organized by the United Nations system, particularly those related to equality, development and peace, including peace education, and those directed to promoting the role of women in development through research activities, seminars and conferences to exchange experience and expertise. Similarly, women Parliamentarians should always be included in delegations to inter-parliamentary meetings organized by the Inter-Parliamentary Union and regional inter-parliamentary organizations.

Paragraph 360

The participation of women in promoting peace and in the struggle against the obstacles to peace at the international level should be encouraged. Networking of women at high decision-making levels related to peace and disarmament, including women leaders, peace researchers and educators, should also be encouraged in connection with United Nations system activities such as the International Year of Peace (1986). "Women and peace" should be a separate item in the programme for that Year.

Paragraph 361

In order to provide a firm basis for the integration of issues of concern to women in the overall development process, a greater effort is needed to define such issues and to develop useful models for action in socio-cultural, economic and political contexts. Work in this area can be undertaken in the national and regional research institutions, as well as in the United Nations and other international agencies. In this context, attention should also be given to increasing the planning capabilities of women.

Paragraph 362

Special efforts should be made at both the national and regional levels to ensure that women have equal access to all aspects of modern science and technology, particularly in educational systems. The use of science and technology can be a powerful instrument for the advancement of women. Special research to evolve appropriate technology for rural women should be carried out, and existing and new technology should be disseminated as widely as possible. The coordination of such activities in the regions should be the responsibility of the regional commissions, in cooperation with other intergovernmental bodies and agencies that deal with the status of women and technology.

Paragraph 363

Governments and non-governmental organizations should organize regular training programmes that are aimed at improving the status of women workers and widening women's access to and improving their performance in managerial positions in the sectors of employment or self-employment. In this connection, the United Nations is urged to support programmes on network and exchange of expertise in vocational training being carried out by regional and subregional organizations.

Paragraph 364

Regional and subregional groups have an important role to play in strengthening the roles of women in development. Existing regional and subregional information systems on women should be reinforced. A stronger data and research base on women should be developed in the developing countries and in the regional commissions, in collaboration with the appropriate specialized agencies, and the sharing of information and research data should be encouraged. Information systems at the national level should be strengthened or, where they do not exist, should be established.

Paragraph 365

International, regional, subregional and national organizations should be strengthened through the injection of additional human and financial resources and through the placement of more women at policy- and decision-making levels.

6. Information dissemination

Paragraph 366

International programmes should be designed and resources allocated to support national campaigns to improve public consciousness of the need for equality between women and men and for eliminating discriminatory practices. Special attention should be given to information about the Convention on the Elimination of All Forms of Discrimination against Women.

Paragraph 367

Studies must be carried out by the United Nations system on sex stereotyping in advertising and in the mass media, especially degrading images of women in articles and programmes disseminated world wide. Steps should be taken to promote the elimination or reduction of sex stereotyping in the media.

Paragraph 368

In order to promote peace, social justice and the advancement of women, wide publicity should be given by the United Nations to legal instruments and the United Nations resolutions and reports relating to women and the objectives of the Decade, that is, equality, development and peace. The mass media, including United Nations radio and television, should disseminate information on the role of women in achieving these objectives, particularly in promoting cooperation and understanding among peoples and the maintenance of international peace and security. Cultural mechanisms of communication should also be used to disseminate the importance of the concepts of peace and international understanding for the advancement of women.

Paragraph 369

It is essential that women be trained in the use of audio-visual forms of information dissemination, including visual display units and computers, and participate more actively in developing programmes on the advancement of women and for women at the international, regional, subregional and national levels.

Paragraph 370

The present United Nations weekly radio programme and co-production of films on women should be continued with adequate provision for distributing them in different languages.

Paragraph 371

The Joint United Nations Information Committee should continue to include women's issues in its programmes of social and economic information. Adequate resources should be made available for these activities.

Paragraph 372

Governments and the organizations of the United Nations system, including the regional commissions and the specialized agencies, are urged to give the Forward-looking Strategies the widest publicity possible and to ensure that their content is translated and disseminated in order to make authorities and the public in general, especially women's grass-root organizations, aware of the objectives of this document and of the recommendations contained therein.

Document 85

General Assembly resolution endorsing the Nairobi Forward-looking Strategies for the Advancement of Women and calling on Governments to take measures towards their implementation

A/RES/40/108, 13 December 1985

The General Assembly,

Recalling its resolution 3520 (XXX) of 15 December 1975, in which it proclaimed the period from 1976 to 1985 the United Nations Decade for Women: Equality, Development and Peace,

Bearing in mind the Convention on the Elimination of All Forms of Discrimination against Women, 1/ which was adopted on 18 December 1979 and which came into force on 3 September 1981,

Recalling also the principles and objectives set forth in the Declaration of Mexico on the Equality of Women and Their Contribution to Development and Peace, 1975, 2/ the World Plan of Action for the Implementation of the Objectives of the International Women's Year 3/ and the Programme of Action for the Second Half of the United Nations Decade for Women, 4/

Bearing in mind also its resolutions 3201 (S-VI) and 3202 (S-VI) of 1 May 1974, containing the Declaration and Programme of Action on the Establishment of a New International Economic Order, 3281 (XXIX) of 12 December 1974, containing the Charter of Economic Rights and Duties of States, 3362 (S-VII) of 16 September 1975 on development and international economic cooperation and 2542 (XXIV) of 11 December 1969 proclaiming the Declaration on Social Progress and Development,

Bearing in mind further the consensus achieved in the text of the International Development Strategy for the Third United Nations Development Decade, contained in its resolution 35/56 of 5 December 1980, in particular regarding the implementation of the objectives of the United Nations Decade for Women within the framework of the Strategy,

Recalling also its resolution 37/63 of 3 December 1982, by which it proclaimed the Declaration on the Participation of Women in Promoting International Peace and Co-operation,

Recalling further its resolution 39/29 of 3 December 1984 on the critical economic situation in Africa,

Recalling its resolution 35/136 of 11 December 1980, in which it decided to convene in 1985, at the conclusion of the Decade, a World Conference to Review and Appraise the Achievements of the United Nations Decade for Women,

Conscious of the considerable and constructive contribution made by the Commission on the Status of Women acting as preparatory body for the Conference, the specialized agencies, the regional commissions and other organizations of the United Nations system, Member States and non-governmental organizations in the preparations for the Conference,

Aware of the continued contribution made by the Non-Governmental Organizations Forum to the advancement of women,

Convinced that the full integration of women in all aspects of political, economic and social life, at the international, regional and national levels, is essential if the obstacles to the achievement of the goals and objectives of the Decade are to be overcome,

Having considered the report of the World Conference to Review and Appraise the Achievements of the United Nations Decade for Women: Equality, Development and Peace, 5/

Convinced that the Conference, by adopting the Forward-looking Strategies for the Advancement of Women, 6/ has made an important and positive contribution to the attainment of the objectives of the Decade and provided a policy framework for advancing the status of women to the year 2000,

Further convinced that the Conference has made an important and constructive contribution by appraising the progress achieved and obstacles encountered in the implementation of the objectives of the Decade and by preparing and adopting strategies to advance the status of women for the next fifteen years,

Stressing that during the period 1986-2000 the pri-

1/ Resolution 34/180, annex.
2/ *Report of the World Conference of the International Women's Year, Mexico City, 19 June-2 July 1975* (United Nations publication, Sales No. E.76.IV.1), chap. I.
3/ Ibid., chap. II, sect. A.
4/ *Report of the World Conference on the United Nations Decade for Women: Equality, Development and Peace, Cophenhagen, 14-30 July 1980* (United Nations publication, Sales No. E.80.IV.3 and corrigendum), chap. I, sect. A.
5/ *Report of the World Conference to Review and Appraise the Achievements of the United Nations Decade for Women: Equality, Development and Peace, Nairobi, 15-26 July 1985* (United Nations publication, Sales No. E.85.IV.10).
6/ Ibid., chap. I, sect. A.

mary responsibility for implementing the Forward-looking Strategies rests with individual countries, as they are intended to serve as guidelines for a process of continuous adaptation to diverse and changing situations at speeds and in modes determined by overall national priorities, within which the integration of women in development should rank high,

Reaffirming that the realization of equal rights for women at all levels and in all areas of life will contribute to the achievement of a just and lasting peace, to social progress and to respect for human rights and fundamental freedoms, and that the integration of women in the mainstream of the development process requires not only commitment at the national, regional and international levels, but also continuing financial and technical support, and also requires the establishment of the new international economic order,

Considering that the Forward-looking Strategies should immediately be translated into concrete action by Governments, as determined by overall national priorities, by organizations of the United Nations system, specialized agencies and intergovernmental and non-governmental organizations, including women's organizations,

Persuaded of the importance of taking measures to ensure system-wide coordination within the United Nations in order to develop a comprehensive and integrated approach to the issues which are crucial to the advancement of women,

1. *Takes note with satisfaction* of the report of the World Conference to Review and Appraise the Achievement of the United Nations Decade for Women: Equality, Development and Peace; 5/

2. *Endorses* the Nairobi Forward-looking Strategies for the Advancement of Women; 6/

3. *Affirms* that the implementation of the Forward-looking Strategies should result in the elimination of all forms of inequality between women and men and in the complete integration of women into the development process and that that should guarantee broad participation by women in efforts to strengthen peace and security in the world;

4. *Declares* that the objectives of the United Nations Decade for Women: Equality, Development and Peace, with the sub-theme "Employment, Health and Education", remain valid;

5. *Calls upon* Governments to allocate adequate resources and to take effective appropriate measures to implement the Forward-looking Strategies as a matter of high priority, including the establishment or reinforcement, as appropriate, of national machineries to promote the advancement of women, and to monitor the implementation of these strategies with a view to ensuring the full integration of women in the political, economic, social and cultural life of their countries;

6. *Calls upon* all Governments of Member States to appoint women to decision-making positions, bearing in mind their contribution to national development;

7. *Invites* Governments, when preparing and evaluating national plans and programmes of action, to incorporate measurable targets for overcoming obstacles to the advancement of women and to include measures for the involvement of women in development, both as agents and beneficiaries, on an equal basis with men, and to review the impact of development policies and programmes on women;

8. *Invites* governmental, intergovernmental and non-governmental organizations to give high priority to the implementation of the Forward-looking Strategies and, in particular, to ensure that sectoral policies and programmes for development include strategies to promote the participation of women as agents and beneficiaries on an equal basis with men;

9. *Urges* all Governments to contribute to the strengthening of institutional coordination in their regions and subregions in order to establish collaborative arrangements and to develop approaches for the implementation of the Forward-looking Strategies at those levels;

10. *Urges* all organizations of the United Nations system, including the regional commissions and all specialized agencies, to take the necessary measures to ensure a concerted and sustained effort for the implementation of the provisions of the Forward-looking Strategies with a view to achieving a substantial improvement in the status of women by the year 2000 and to ensure that all projects and programmes take into account the need for the complete integration of women and women's concerns;

11. *Requests* the Secretary-General and the specialized agencies and bodies of the United Nations system to establish, where they do not already exist, focal points on women's issues in all sectors of the work of the organizations of the United Nations system;

12. *Urges* the Administrative Committee on Coordination to review periodically the system-wide implementation of the Forward-looking Strategies and to hold regular interagency meetings on women within the framework of the Administrative Committee on Coordination;

13. *Emphasizes* the central role of the Commission on the Status of Women in matters related to the advancement of the status of women and calls upon it to promote the implementation of the Forward-looking Strategies to the year 2000 based on the goals of the United Nations Decade for Women: Equality, Development and Peace, and the sub-theme "Employment, Health and Educa-

tion", and urges all organizations of the United Nations system to cooperate with the Commission in this task;

14. *Requests* the Secretary-General to ensure that the Commission on the Status of Women receives the support services it requires to fulfil its central role effectively;

15. *Also rrquests* the Secretary-General to invite Governments, organizations of the United Nations system, including regional commissions and specialized agencies, intergovernmental and non-governmental organizations to report periodically through the Commission on the Status of Women to the Economic and Social Council on the activities undertaken at all levels to implement the Forward-looking Strategies;

16. *Further requests* the Secretary-General, in preparing the note on the integrated reporting system for periodic review and appraisal of progress in the advancement of women for submission to the Commission on the Status of Women at its thirty-first session, as called for in Economic and Social Council decision 1984/123 of 24 May 1984, to include proposals for a reporting system to facilitate the monitoring of the implementation of the Forward-looking Strategies as set out in paragraph 15 above, taking into account the experience gained during the Decade, the views of Governments and the need not to duplicate existing reporting obligations, bearing in mind the need to carry out periodical in-depth sectoral reviews of progress achieved and obstacles encountered in implementing the Forward-looking Strategies to the year 2000;

17. *Recommends* that the Secretary-General prepare and submit to the Commission on the Status of Women at its thirty-first session, bearing in mind the remarks and concrete recommendations made during the debate at the fortieth session, in particular the proposals about increasing the number of members and the frequency of meetings of the Commission, a report on alternative measures to strengthen the Commission in the discharge of its functions following the United Nations Decade for Women, and also recommends that the recommendations of the Commission on the matter be reported to the General Assembly at its forty-first session through the Economic and Social Council;

18. *Reaffirms* the role of the Centre for Social Development and Humanitarian Affairs of the Department of International Economic and Social Affairs of the Secretariat, in particular the Branch for the Advancement of Women, as the substantive secretariat of the Commission and as a focal point for matters on women, and requests the Secretariat to collect and disseminate information on system-wide activities related to the implementation of the Forward-looking Strategies;

19. *Takes note with satisfaction* of the appointment of the Co-ordinator for the Improvement of the Status of Women in the Secretariat of the United Nations,

in accordance with General Assembly resolution 39/245 of 18 December 1984, and, in this context, of the fact that the Secretary-General should continue to plan and implement positive actions and programmes to improve the status of women in the Secretariat and to monitor the progress achieved;

20. *Calls upon* the Secretary-General and the heads of the specialized agencies and other United Nations bodies to establish new five-year targets at each level for the percentage of women in Professional and decision-making positions, in accordance with the criteria established by the General Assembly, in particular that of equitable geographical distribution, in order that a definite upward trend in the application of Assembly resolution 33/143 of 20 December 1978 be registered in the number of Professional and decision-making positions held by women by 1990 and to set additional targets every five years;

21. *Welcomes* Economic and Social Council resolution 1985/46 of 31 May 1985 regarding women and development and, noting the particular importance of paragraph 4 of that resolution, recommends that immediate measures be taken to ensure that future medium-term plans of the United Nations and the specialized agencies should contain intersectoral presentations of the various programmes dealing with issues of concern to women and that revisions of current plans should be considered in the light of the results of the World Conference to Review and Appraise the Achievements of the United Nations Decade for Women: Equality, Development and Peace; 5/

22. *Requests* the Secretary-General to take into account the requirements of the Forward-looking Strategies in preparing the programme budget and programme of work for the biennium 1988-1989;

23. *Urges* all financial institutions and all international regional and subregional organizations, institutions, development banks and general funding agencies to ensure that their policies and programmes promote the full participation of women as agents and beneficiaries in the development process;

24. *Invites* the Secretary-General to circulate the report of the Conference among Member States, all organizations of the United Nations system and specialized agencies, intergovernmental and non-governmental organizations in order to ensure that the Forward-looking Strategies are publicized and disseminated as widely as possible, and encourages Governments to translate the Strategies into their national languages;

25. *Requests* the Secretary-General and the heads of all organizations within the United Nations system and of the specialized agencies to continue to give high priority in their public information programmes to dissemi-

nating information concerning women and, in particular, the Forward-looking Strategies and, in the light of the recommendations contained in the Strategies, further requests the Secretary-General to provide in the regular budget for the continuation of the existing weekly radio programmes on women, with adequate provision for distributing them in different languages;

26. *Also requests* the Secretary-General to report to the General Assembly at its forty-first session on measures taken to implement the present resolution;

27. *Decides* to consider these questions further at its forty-first session under an item entitled "Forward-looking strategies for the advancement of women to the year 2000".

Document 86

"*Overview of the role of women in development*", *from the* World Survey on the Role of Women in Development *(extract)*

A/CONF.116/4/Rev.1 - ST/ESA/180, 1986

Background

In its resolution 35/78 of 5 December 1980 on effective mobilization and integration of women in development, the General Assembly requested the Secretary-General to prepare a comprehensive and detailed outline for an interdisciplinary and multisectoral world survey on the role of women in overall development, taking into account the relevant recommendations of the World Conference of the United Nations Decade for Women: Equality, Development and Peace as well as the results of relevant United Nations conferences on development issues.

Pursuant to that resolution, the Secretary-General, in his report on the comprehensive outline of a world survey on the role of women in development (A/36/590), proposed an outline that would include such issues as women in production, distribution and consumption, women in rural and urban development, and women's participation in social and political life. The General Assembly, in its resolution 36/74 of 4 December 1981, took note of that report, emphasized the need for a multisectoral and interdisciplinary survey, and recommended that the survey should analyse the role of women in relation to key developmental issues as envisaged in the International Development Strategy for the Third United Nations Development Decade, focusing in particular on trade, agriculture, industry, energy, money and finance, and science and technology. The Assembly further recommended that the survey should cover: (a) the present role of women as active agents of development in each sector; (b) an assessment of the benefits accruing to women as a result of their participation in development, namely, income, conditions of work and decision-making; (c) ways and means of improving women's role as agents and beneficiaries of development at the national, regional and international levels; and (d) the potential impact of

such improvements on the achievement of overall development goals. The Assembly called upon the Secretary-General to include in the survey an overview analysing interrelationships among key developmental issues with regard to women's current and future roles in development with a view to providing a basis for future action for women's effective mobilization and integration in development. It also requested the Secretary-General to prepare the survey in close collaboration and cooperation with the appropriate organizations of the United Nations system and with contributions from all organs and organizations concerned of the United Nations system, as well as national institutions having expertise on this subject; and to submit a progress report to the Assembly at its thirty-seventh session and to submit the survey in its final form to the Assembly at its thirty-ninth session.

In its resolution 36/127 of 14 December 1981 on consideration within the United Nations of questions concerning the role of women in development, the General Assembly requested the Secretary-General to ensure that the Commission on the Status of Women was consulted in the preparation of the world survey on the role of women in development. After the discussion of the outline of the survey by the Commission on the Status of Women at its twenty-ninth session, a revised outline was prepared reflecting the recommendations of the Assembly in its resolution 36/74.

In its resolution 37/60 of 3 December 1982 on preparations for the World Conference to Review and Appraise the Achievements of the United Nations Decade for Women: Equality, Development and Peace, the General Assembly took note of the report of the Secretary-General on the progress made in the preparation of a world survey on the role of women in development (A/37/381) and recommended that the survey should be submitted to the Conference.

The Commission on the Status of Women Acting as the Preparatory Body for the World Conference to Review and Appraise the Achievements of the United Nations Decade for Women: Equality, Development and Peace at its first session, held from 23 February to 4 March 1983, recommended (see A/CONF.116/PC/9 and Corr.1) that the world survey on the role of women in development should constitute one of the basic documents for the World Conference. That recommendation was endorsed by the Economic and Social Council in its decision 1983/132 of 26 May 1983 and by the General Assembly in its resolution 38/108 of 16 December 1983. A report on the status of preparation of the world survey (A/CONF.116/PC/14) was submitted by the Secretary-General to the Commission on the Status of Women Acting as the Preparatory Body at its second session.

In view of the difficulties encountered in finalizing the survey in time for the General Assembly at its thirty-ninth session, the Secretary-General submitted a report (A/39/566) summarizing the preliminary conclusions that had been reached.

The present Survey, prepared in response to the above recommendations, comprises eight parts: one will present an overview analysing the interrelations between the key developmental issues on the basis of findings presented in the other seven parts, which deal respectively with the role of women in relation to agriculture, industry, money and finance, science and technology, trade, energy, and the concept of self-reliance and the integration of women in development.

Part one was prepared by the Department of International Economic and Social Affairs of the United Nations Secretariat with the exception of chapter I, section A, which was prepared in collaboration with the International Labour Organization; part two was prepared by the Food and Agriculture Organization of the United Nations, part three by the United Nations Industrial Development Organization, parts four, six and seven by the Department of International Economic and Social Affairs, part five by the United Nations Centre for Science and Technology for Development, and part eight by the International Research and Training Institute for the Advancement of Women.

Part One

Overview of the role of women in development

Introduction

The Overview contains three chapters. In the first, the role of women in economic development is assessed by analysing women's participation in the labour force. One of the main conclusions is that the contribution of women to economic development is very significant; one

out of four industrial workers is female, as are four out of ten agricultural and service workers. A section paying particular attention to the role of women in services, has been drafted on the basis of material provided by the International Labour Organization, since this subject was not assigned to a separate sectoral chapter. In the second chapter, some of the absolute and relative benefits accruing to women on account of their participation in development are assessed by drawing on the evidence regarding benefits given in the sectoral chapters and by studying the present situation and medium-term trends in women's occupational segregation. In addition, some of the effects on women of recent economic trends are analysed, mostly on the basis of the statistics available on employment. It has been found that women benefit from development but not as much as men where income (wages and salaries) is concerned. Women have made an inroad in the professional categories, but still fall behind in administration and management. In the third chapter some of the main conclusions emerging from the Survey are presented.

...

III. *Conclusions*

A. *Contribution of women to development*

One of the main generalizations on the role of women in development that emerges from the sectoral chapters of the Survey is that women's contribution to national production activities has been increasing steadily since 1950 and is projected to increase even further to the year 2000. Judging from the data available women represent more than one quarter of the industrial labour force and almost two fifths of the agricultural labour force and of services. Regional variations are significant: in Africa and South Asia, male participation rates will increase at the same speed as those of women up to the year 2000. In all of the others, and especially in Western Europe and North America, female participation rates will increase faster than males.

The contribution of women to economic development is underestimated in national and international statistics. In agriculture, active women are sometimes counted as inactive, and when they are counted as active they are often included in the category of unpaid family labour even though they are performing managerial tasks that should assign them to the category of independent farmers. In industry, women are involved more often than men in the informal economy, so neither their work nor their production is fully recorded in national statistics.

The sectoral distribution of women's labour force is different from men's. Women are disproportionately active in services because employment in services responds to supply pressures more than it does in the other sectors of the economy and because the skills women learn in the household can be transferred to the services sectors more readily than to industry.

B. *Benefits and costs to women*

The second main generalization on the roles of women in development is that women benefit on average less than men from their contribution to national production. In industry, women still belong by and large to the secondary labour force, taking jobs for which men are unavailable or which they are unwilling to take. As a result, their average hourly wages are lower than men's. Women are protected by social legislation less than men, even in countries that have enacted such legislation. Fixed and generally long working hours make it difficult for women's productive and domestic activities to be compatible. In agricultural paid labour, men tend to take higher paying jobs requiring technical skills, while women remain generally confined to lower-paid manual labour. Although, in principle, the productivity of women independent farmers is as high as that of men, the inputs available for their farms are generally lower than for men's farms, and therefore their productivity and the income they generate are lower. Also in the sectors of services, science and technology, financial institutions, insurance, real estate and business, the positions held by women and the benefits accruing to them are lower than men's. Women seldom hold decision-making positions in any of these sectors or in the institutions that determine national policies affecting them.

The lack of reliable data prevents any assessment of relative improvements in women's status in the sectors included in the Survey. It is known that in industry the wage gap between women and men has been shrinking slowly since the 1970s. Little is known, however, of the other components of income, such as social security, pensions, fringe benefits and taxation, and of the other criteria of status such as power and prestige. Also, women in industrial employment constitute a small proportion of economically active women. Relevant global and regional trends in agriculture and services where women are concentrated are impossible to establish.

It is difficult to identify the causes of sexual stratification on the basis of existing data. Stratification is obviously related to the sexual division of labour. Yet in modern societies the social division of labour is more complex than segregation based on sex. The relationship between differentiation and stratification is not automatic. It is also clear that this stratification structure applies to both production and reproduction. Sexual inequality permeates society as a whole and goes beyond the economic sphere. For instance, job segregation in science and technology is preceded by educational seg-

regation of women out of the major science and technology fields. Within the family, men are generally favoured when it comes to applying resources at the disposal of the family in such areas as assigning land for independent farming, and spending the income generated by it. Cultural values and norms on sexual roles seem therefore to have a profound effect on women's inequality and are important variables supporting and reinforcing fundamental inequalities in the economic sphere.

In the short and medium terms the balance of benefits and costs is mixed. In some situations, industrialization can provide women with jobs that are better paid than those they had in agriculture, but it has so far not eliminated the wage gap between the two sexes, and the upward job mobility of women is still an unfulfilled objective. Agricultural modernization has also failed to benefit women as much as men. In some instances women have been asked to contribute more work to modernized farming systems without obtaining greater rewards. In the banking system, women find well-paid employment, but are restricted to the lower layers of the financial institutions. However, these effects cannot be imputed to modernization itself; rather, it is the social conditions in which modernization takes place that cause more of the benefits to accrue to men than to women.

It is also pointed out in the sectoral chapters that, as a result of the pervasiveness of norms of sexual roles and hence status differentials between women and men, the record of public policies on the reduction of such differentials is mixed, in spite of the fact that most Governments express support for equality and have enacted legislation to promote it. The effectiveness of measures designed to improve sexual equality in employment is often reported to have been weakened by the prejudices of employers regarding women's commitment to work. Thus, while the legislation that guarantees equal pay for work of equal value is adopted in an increasing number of countries, women's vertical job segregation has not decreased significantly, and in some countries it is reported to have increased in the last 20 years. The reduction in the wage gap seems to have been more the unintended effect of minimum wage legislation than the effect of legislation on equality. The impact on equality of public intervention in agriculture is also reported to have been weak. Agrarian reforms have seldom assigned land or property to women. Agricultural and rural development policies have generally been targeted to men, or to cash crops that are usually men's crops.

A preliminary analysis of the occupational gap between men and women, which was measured by the share of women in the first two main occupational groups of ISCO-68, namely professional, technical and related workers, and administrative and managerial workers, indicated that this gap is closing in most of the countries studied. It was particularly so in the first occupational group. Women have made a much smaller inroad into the second. Among administrators and managers, they are still a small minority. The direction of change was towards greater equality, but the pace of change was generally slow. In addition, women appear to have increased their share of the least paid and prestigious occupations in the professional category.

Of particular interest is the question of how recent economic trends in international trade and finance and the national policies carried out in response to these trends have affected women. It is not possible to provide a final answer to this question. More research is needed to give account of national differences and of the complexity of this issue. The effects of the international recession of 1973-1975 and especially of the early 1980s on the economic aggregates vary according to the mode of participation of each economy in the international economic system, and the national transmission of these effects on society vary according to the socio-political structures of each country.

The international crisis of the first half of the 1970s is known to have reduced the demand for goods and services of developing countries and worsened their terms of trade and their export earnings. Imports, however, did not drop in equal measure. Foreign credit was brought in to cover the gap. What this meant in developing countries in the face of protracted recession in developed countries and high interest rates is well known. The policies that indebted countries were asked to implement, and often did implement, to reduce the balance-of-payments deficit strengthened the recessive effects of the international crisis. The most important effects were on employment and income. Total employment dropped significantly. In developed countries, unemployment generally increased. In developing countries, under-employment increased and wages tended to decrease.

In terms of direct formal employment women's jobs have probably been less affected than men's jobs by the recession, because the sectors most affected were those in the formal sector and industry, where the majority of employees are men. It is likely, however, that the recovery of the second half of the 1970s has generally bypassed women in the formal sector. Also, the crisis of the early 1980s seems to have affected them particularly, because men began competing with them for low-paid jobs.

Women are likely to have responded to the employment crisis in the formal sector in different ways according to the income level of their households. For fairly prosperous women, what seems to have determined their labour force participation rate is the outcome of the conflict between high consumption demands and the increasing costs of the services that replace domestic work, such as child care and care for dependents in general. For the women in households with a medium to low income, the wives of industrial workers who have been dismissed or are earning less money, the decision is usually to join the labour force. This may push unemployment rates up. Although hard data are not available on a global basis, it can be fairly assumed that the income they receive from their productive activities is low and unstable and that the increase in women's participation rates is likely to have produced a decrease in their average income. For poor women who were already active before the crisis, this has probably meant an even lower income and a heavier workload.

The policies that have generally been carried out in developing countries to counteract the crisis have emphasized promotion of exports instead of import substitution. Although women in the export-oriented sectors might have maintained their jobs, the conditions of work in the industries producing for export are generally worse than in those for the domestic market. The situation of women in free exporting zones has already been outlined. The relatively more protected employment situation of women has been compromised by their decreasing income and worsening working conditions.

The second major mechanism through which the crisis and the monetary and fiscal policies have affected women is in public expenditures. Most countries have been obliged to adopt austerity measures, which in the absence of politically viable measures to improve taxation have generally led to reductions in public expenditures. This has resulted in reducing the support services and other necessary components that are vital to maintaining and promoting women's employment.

Document 87

General Assembly resolution on the role of women in society, calling on Governments, among other things, to encourage such support as paid maternity, parental and child-care leave, and to provide women with job security with a view to allowing them to fulfil their roles as mothers without prejudice to their professional and public activities

A/RES/41/110, 4 December 1986

The General Assembly,

Reaffirming the validity of the objectives of the United Nations Decade for Women: Equality, Development and Peace,

Noting the importance of the documents adopted by the world conferences held during the Decade,

Reaffirming its resolution 40/101 of 13 December 1985, and taking note of Economic and Social Council resolution 1986/27 of 23 May 1986, which reiterated the expression by the Assembly of its awareness of the necessity to enlarge the possibilities for both men and women to combine parental duties and household work with paid employment and social activities, and of its awareness that the role of women in childbearing should not be the cause of inequality and discrimination and that child rearing demands shared responsibilities among women, men and society as a whole,

Convinced of the necessity to secure for all women full and effective enjoyment of the rights embodied in the Charter of the United Nations, the Universal Declaration of Human Rights, 1/ the Convention on the Elimination of All Forms of Discrimination against Women, 2/ the International Covenants on Human Rights 3/ and other pertinent instruments in this field,

Emphasizing that the achievement of equal and full participation of women in all spheres of activity is an integral part of the political, economic, social and cultural development of all countries,

Commending the expanding participation of women in political, economic, social and cultural life and in the promotion of international peace and cooperation,

Convinced that the implementation of the Nairobi Forward-looking Strategies for the Advancement of Women 4/ should be among the developmental and policy priorities of Governments, United Nations organs, specialized agencies and intergovernmental and non-governmental organizations,

Bearing in mind that promotion of the status of women in all its aspects and complete integration of women in society go beyond the problem of legal equality and that deeper structural transformations of society and changes in current economic relations, as well as elimi-

nation of traditional prejudices through education and the dissemination of information, are required to create conditions in which women may develop fully their intellectual and physical capacities and participate actively in the decision-making process related to their political, economic, social and cultural development,

Bearing in mind also that economic inequality, colonialism, racism, racial discrimination in all its forms, apartheid, aggression and interference in the internal affairs of other States, and violation of human rights and fundamental freedoms are obstacles to the active integration of women in all spheres of life,

Bearing in mind the resolution on equal opportunities and equal treatment for men and women in employment, adopted on 27 June 1985 by the International Labour Organization, 5/

1. *Recommends* that all Governments and intergovernmental and non-governmental organizations should pay due attention in their activities to the role of women in society in all its interrelated aspects—as mothers, as participants in the economic development process and as participants in public life;

2. *Reaffirms* that the implementation of the Nairobi Forward-looking Strategies for the Advancement of Women should contribute to the elimination of all forms of inequality between women and men and to the integration of women in the development process, and should ensure the broad participation of women in efforts to strengthen international peace, security and cooperation;

3. *Calls upon* Member States to adopt the necessary effective measures with a view to the implementation of the Forward-looking Strategies as a matter of priority, including the establishment or strengthening of appropri-

1/ Resolution 217 A (III).
2/ Resolution 34/180, annex.
3/ Resolution 2200 A (XXI), annex.
4/ *Report of the World Conference to Review and Appraise the Achievements of the United Nations Decade for Women: Equality, Development and Peace, Nairobi, 15-26 July 1985* (United Nations publications, Sales No. E.85.IV.10), chap. I, sect. A.
5/ International Labour Office, *Official Bulletin,* vol. LXVIII, 1985, Series A, No. 2, p. 85.

ate mechanisms for the advancement of women and for the implementation of the Strategies, in order to ensure the full integration of women in the political, economic, social and cultural life of their countries;

4. *Invites* Member States to encourage such social and economic development as will ensure the equal participation of women in all spheres of work activity, equal pay for work of equal value, and equal opportunities for education and vocational training;

5. *Appeals* to Member States to promote conditions that will enable women to participate as equal partners with men in public and political life, in the decision-making process at all levels and in the management of different spheres of life in society;

6. *Urges* Governments to recognize the special status and social importance of childbearing and child rearing and to take all necessary measures to encourage the support of parenthood, including paid maternity, parental and child-care leave, and to provide women with security for their jobs as long as necessary with a view to allowing them to fulfil their role as mothers without prejudice to their professional and public activities;

7. *Appeals* to Governments to promote the establishment of appropriate facilities for the care and education of children as a means of combining parenthood with economic, political, social, cultural and other activities, and thus to assist women towards full integration in their societies;

8. *Requests* the Secretary-General, when preparing future reports on the world social situation, to pay due attention to the question of the status of women, their role in society and the progress achieved in the implementation of the Forward-looking Strategies;

9. *Requests* the Secretary-General, when preparing surveys on the role of women in development, to pay due attention to all the interrelated aspects of the role of women in society;

10. *Invites* the Commission on the Status of Women to consider the inclusion, in an appropriate form, of the question of the role of women in society in its agenda and programme of work for the implementation of the Nairobi Forward-looking Strategies for the Advancement of Women.

Document 88

General Assembly resolution emphasizing the need for immediate and full implementation of the Nairobi Forward-looking Strategies and the importance of the total integration of women in the development process, having in mind the specific and urgent needs of the developing countries

A/RES/41/111, 4 December 1986

The General Assembly,

Recalling all its relevant resolutions, in particular resolution 40/108 of 13 December 1985, in which, *inter alia,* it endorsed the Nairobi Forward-looking Strategies for the Advancement of Women 1/ for the period up to the year 2000 and set out measures for their immediate implementation and for the overall achievement of the goals and objectives of the United Nations Decade for Women: Equality, Development and Peace,

Taking into consideration Economic and Social Council resolutions 1986/30 of 23 May 1986 and 1986/65 and 1986/71 of 23 July 1986,

Conscious of the considerable constructive contribution to the advancement of the status of women made by the Commission on the Status of Women, the specialized agencies, the regional commissions and other organizations of the United Nations system, Member States and intergovernmental and non-governmental organizations,

Emphasizing the need for the immediate and full implementation of the Forward-looking Strategies and for their evaluation and follow-up,

1. *Takes note* of the reports of the Secretary-General concerning the implementation of the Nairobi Forward-looking Strategies for the Advancement of Women; 2/

2. *Reaffirms* the need for the Forward-looking Strategies to be translated immediately into concrete action by Governments, as determined by overall national priorities, as well as by the organizations of the United Nations system, the specialized agencies and intergovernmental and non-governmental organizations;

3. *Reaffirms also* the central role of the Commission on the Status of Women in matters related to the

1/ *Report of the World Conference to Review and Appraise the Achievements of the United Nations Decade for Women: Equality, Development and Peace, Nairobi, 15-26 July 1985* (United Nations publication, Sales No. E.85.IV.10), chap. I, sect. A.
2/ A/41/623 and A/41/672.

advancement of women and calls upon the Commission to promote the implementation of the Forward-looking Strategies to the year 2000 based on the goals of the United Nations Decade for Women: Equality, Development and Peace and the subtheme "Employment, Health and Education", and urges all organizations of the United Nations system to cooperate with the Commission in this task;

4. *Reaffirms further*, in the implementation of the Forward-looking Strategies, the role of the Centre for Social Development and Humanitarian Affairs of the Department of International Economic and Social Affairs of the Secretariat, in particular the Branch for the Advancement of Women, as the substantive secretariat of the Commission on the Status of Women and as a focal point for matters on women, the catalysing role of the United Nations Development Fund for Women and the role of the International Research and Training Institute for the Advancement of Women in the advancement of women in the context of the participation of women in development;

5. *Endorses* Economic and Social Council resolution 1986/30, in particular the decision by the Council to convene in January 1987 a session of the Commission on the Status of Women for five working days prior to the organizational session of the Council and its decision that the session be held in New York as an exception to the general principle, reaffirmed by the General Assembly in its resolution 40/243 of 18 December 1985, that United Nations bodies shall plan to meet at their respective established headquarters;

6. *Emphasizes*, in the framework of the Forward-looking Strategies, the importance of the total integration of women in the development process, having in mind the specific and urgent needs of the developing countries;

7. *Calls upon* all Member States to establish specific targets at each level in order to increase the percentage of women in professional and decision-making positions in their countries;

8. *Calls upon* the Secretary-General and the heads of the specialized agencies and other United Nations bodies to establish new five-year targets at each level for the percentage of women in Professional and decision-making positions, in accordance with the criteria established by the General Assembly, in particular that of equitable geographical distribution, in order that a definite upward trend in the implementation of Assembly resolution 33/143 of 20 December 1978 be registered in the number of Professional and decision-making positions held by women by 1990, and to set additional targets every five years;

9. *Requests* the Secretary-General to invite Governments, organizations of the United Nations system, including the regional commissions and the specialized agencies, and intergovernmental and non-governmental organizations to report periodically, through the Commission on the Status of Women, to the Economic and Social Council on activities undertaken at all levels to implement the Forward-looking Strategies;

10. *Also requests* the Secretary-General to report to the General Assembly at its forty-second session on measures taken to implement the present resolution;

11. *Decides* to consider these questions further at its forty-second session under the item entitled "Forward-looking strategies for the advancement of women to the year 2000".

Document 89

ECOSOC resolution adopting the long-term programme of work of the CSW to the year 2000

E/RES/1987/24, 26 May 1987

The Economic and Social Council,

Reaffirming the central role of the Commission on the Status of Women in promoting and monitoring the implementation of the Nairobi Forward-looking Strategies for the Advancement of Women, 1/ in accordance with General Assembly resolution 40/108 of 13 December 1985,

Bearing in mind the responsibilities of the Commission as the competent intergovernmental body on matters concerning the status of women, especially with regard to its policy development function,

Aware of the continued importance of the interrelationships between the objectives of the United Nations Decade for Women—equality, development and

1/ *Report of the World Conference to Review and Appraise the Achievements of the United Nations Decade for Women: Equality, Development and Peace, Nairobi, 15-26 July 1985* (United Nations publication, Sales No. E.85.IV.10), chap. I, sect. A.

peace—and the subtheme—employment, health and education,

Mindful of the importance of adopting a coordinated and integrated approach to the implementation of the Forward-looking Strategies by the United Nations system, whereby recommendations of the Commission would take into account the system-wide medium-term plan for women and development and relate to the medium-term plans of the organizations of the United Nations system,

Reaffirming its resolutions 1982/50 of 28 July 1982 on the revitalization of the Economic and Social Council, especially as it relates to the subsidiary bodies of the Council, and particularly paragraph 4 of the annex thereto, in which the Council called for the streamlining of documentation and programmes of work in order to enable its subsidiary bodies to perform effectively the functions entrusted to them,

1. *Endorses* the priority themes for the next five sessions of the Commission on the Status of Women set out in the annex to the present resolution; the themes should be considered at regular sessions of the Commission under an agenda item entitled "Priority themes", notwithstanding world conferences and preparatory meetings or any process of review and appraisal that might take place; the first set of priority themes should be considered by the Commission at its thirty-second session;

2. *Decides* that the work of the Commission in relation to the priority themes should be closely related to the relevant provisions of the Forward-looking Strategies and of other policy documents, the programmes elaborated in the system-side medium-term plan for women and development and the relevant chapters of the *World Survey on the Role of Women in Development*, 2/ with a view to ensuring the effective implementation of the Forward-looking Strategies and lasting improvement in the situation of women; the recommendations of the Commission should be addressed, at the national level, primarily to Governments, but also to non-governmental organizations—in particular women's groups—and research institutions, and, at the regional and international levels, to intergovernmental and non-governmental organizations and research institutions;

3. *Agrees* that in the discussion of the priority themes, appropriate emphasis should be placed on issues of women and development, in recognition of the number and complexity of subject areas addressed in chapter II of the Forward-looking Strategies and in the programmes of the system-wide medium-term plan for women and development;

4. *Recommends*, as part of the regular programme of work of the United Nations Secretariat in areas related to the advancement of women, in particular that of the Centre for Social Development and Humanitarian Affairs, when regular budgetary or extrabudgetary resources are available, the convening of expert group meetings, as required by the Commission, to assist in the preparation of the work of the Commission on priority themes; the expert groups should be composed of an appropriate number of specialists, taking into account equitable geographic distribution and the involvement of non-governmental organizations, in the field or fields of study addressed under specific priority themes in order to prepare an analysis and preliminary proposals to assist the Commission in making informed, practical and action-oriented policy recommendations; each expert group meeting should be structured like the Expert Group Meeting on Violence in the Family, held at Vienna from 8 to 12 December 1986, and should be timed so as to permit the results of the meeting to be made available to Member States in advance of sessions of the Commission;

5. *Recommends* that every effort be made to avoid duplication in the collection of data and production of documentation for expert group meetings and for sessions of the Commission, and that the documentation include, where possible, an indication of the extent of major research undertaken or planned in the fields of study addressed under a particular priority theme;

6. *Invites* the Commission, at each session, when considering the provisional agenda for its next session, to identify and develop the specific work programme required to prepare for the in-depth consideration of the priority themes scheduled for that session.

Annex

Priority themes for the thirty-second to thirty-sixth sessions of the Commission on the Status of Women

At each session, the Commission shall deal with three themes, one under each of the three objectives—equality, development and peace—in the order in which they are listed.

A. *Equality*

1. National machinery for monitoring and improving the status of women

2. Equality in economic and social participation

3. Equality in political participation and decision-making

4. Vulnerable women, including migrant women

5. Elimination of *de jure* and de facto discrimination against women

2/ United Nations publication, Sales No. E.86.IV.3.

B. *Development*

1. Problems of rural women, including food, water resources, agricultural technology, rural employment, transportation and environment

2. Women and education, eradication of illiteracy, employment, health and social services, including population issues and child care

3. Negative effects of the international economic situation on the improvement of the status of women

4. National, regional and international machinery for the effective integration of women in the development process, including non-governmental organizations

5. Integration of women in the process of development

C. *Peace*

1. Access to information, education for peace, and efforts to eradicate violence against women within the family and society

2. Full participation of women in the construction of their countries and in the creation of just social and political systems

3. Women in areas affected by armed conflicts, foreign intervention, alien and colonial domination, foreign occupation and threats to peace

4. Refugee and displaced women and children

5. Equal participation in all efforts to promote international cooperation, peace and disarmament

---

Document 90

General Assembly resolution emphasizing, among other things, the need to give urgent attention to redressing socio-economic inequities at the national and international levels as a necessary step towards the full realization of the goals and objectives of the Forward-looking Strategies

A/RES/42/62, 30 November 1987

The General Assembly,

Recalling all its relevant resolutions, in particular resolutions 40/108 of 13 December 1985 and 41/111 of 4 December 1986, in which, *inter alia*, it endorsed the Nairobi Forward-looking Strategies for the Advancement of Women 1/ for the period up to the year 2000 and set out measures for their immediate implementation and for the overall achievement of the goals and objectives of the United Nations Decade for Women: Equality, Development and Peace,

Taking into consideration Economic and Social Council resolutions 1987/18, 1987/19, 1987/20, 1987/21, 1987/22, 1987/23, 1987/24, 1987/25 and 1987/26 of 26 May 1987,

Taking note of the Guiding Principles for Developmental Social Welfare Policies and Programmes in the Near Future, 2/ adopted by the Interregional Consultation on Developmental Social Welfare Policies and Programmes, held at Vienna from 7 to 15 September 1987,

Noting with concern the serious impact of the world economic situation on the programmes and plans for the advancement of women, especially in the global context,

Conscious of the important and constructive contribution to the advancement of the status of women made by the Commission on the Status of Women, the special-

ized agencies, the regional commissions and other organizations of the United Nations system, Member States and intergovernmental and non-governmental organizations,

Emphasizing once again the priority of the implementation, monitoring, review and appraisal of the Nairobi Forward-looking Strategies,

Welcoming the significant progress made by the Commission on the Status of Women at its special session in 1987 in restructuring its agenda along functional lines, developing a systematic long-term programme of work, strengthening and rationalizing its role and functions and mobilizing the resources of the United Nations system as a whole towards the advancement of women by integrating this objective into the programme planning and budgeting processes of the Organization,

Welcoming also the designation by the Secretary-General of the advancement of women as one of two priorities of the Organization for the next biennium,

Recognizing the need for the Commission on the Status of Women to consider at its regular session the

1/ *Report of the World Conference to Review and Appraise the Achievements of the United Nations Decade for Women: Equality, Development and Peace, Nairobi, 15-26 July 1985* (United Nations publication, Sales No. E.85.IV.10), chap. I, sect. A.
2/ See E/CONF.80/10, chap. III.

priority themes for the next five sessions of the Commission, contained in the annex to Economic and Social Council resolution 1987/24,

1. *Takes note* of the reports of the Secretary-General 3/ concerning the implementation of the Nairobi Forward-looking Strategies for the Advancement of Women;

2. *Takes note also* of resolutions 1,2 and 4 adopted by the Commission on the Status of Women at its special session in 1987, 4/ in particular its recommendation that the implementation of the Nairobi Forward-looking Strategies and the status of women in general should be incorporated as a global priority for the period 1990-1995 in the introduction of the Organization's next medium-term plan;

3. *Reaffirms* the need for the Forward-looking Strategies to be translated immediately into concrete action by Governments, as determined by overall national priorities, as well as by the organizations of the United Nations system, the specialized agencies and intergovernmental and non-governmental organizations;

4. *Reaffirms also* the central role of the Commission on the Status of Women in matters related to the advancement of women and calls upon the Commission to promote the implementation of the Forward-looking Strategies to the year 2000 based on the goals of the United Nations Decade for Women: Equality, Development and Peace and the subtheme "Employment, Health and Education", and urges all organizations of the United Nations system to cooperate with the Commission in this task;

5. *Reaffirms further*, in the implementation of the Forward-looking Strategies, the role of the Centre for Social Development and Humanitarian Affairs of the Secretariat, in particular the Branch for the Advancement of Women, as the substantive secretariat of the Commission on the Status of Women and as a focal point for matters on women, the catalysing role of the United Nations Development Fund for Women and the role of the International Research and Training Institute for the Advancement of Women in the promotion of the role of women in the context of the participation of women in development;

6. *Endorses* Economic and Social Council resolution 1987/21, in which the Council, *inter alia*, decided that the Commission on the Status of Women, commencing with its thirty-second session, should meet annually until the year 2000, with a long-term programme of work that would allow sufficient preparation for each session;

7. *Endorses also* Economic and Social Council resolution 1987/24, in particular the annex thereto containing the priority themes for the next five sessions of the Commission on the Status of Women, which should

be considered at regular sessions of the Commission under an agenda item entitled "Priority themes", notwithstanding world conferences and preparatory meetings or any process of review and appraisal that might take place;

8. *Requests* the relevant United Nations bodies to provide focused and action-oriented input when reporting to the Commission on the priority themes;

9. *Reaffirms* the need for the United Nations to develop an integral reporting system with the Commission on the Status of Women at its centre and, building upon existing information and resources, to monitor the review and appraisal of progress with regard to the advancement of women, based on clear and relevant statistical and other measurable indicators which will assist Member States in identifying problems and in developing remedial measures, at the national, regional and international levels;

10. *Encourages* the Special Commission of the Economic and Social Council on the In-depth Study of the United Nations Intergovernmental Structure and Functions in the Economic and Social Fields to take into consideration the unique multidisciplinary and cross-organizational mandate of the Commission on the Status of Women, which is of particular importance in coordinating the efforts of the United Nations in the economic and social fields towards the advancement of women;

11. *Emphasizes*, in the framework of the Forward-looking Strategies, the importance of the total integration of women in the developing process, bearing in mind the specific and urgent needs of the developing countries, and calls upon Member States to establish specific targets at each level in order to increase the participation of women in professional and decision-making positions in their countries;

12. *Emphasizes also* the need to give urgent attention to redressing socio-economic inequities at the national and international levels as a necessary step towards the full realization of the goals and objectives of the Forward-looking Strategies;

13. *Urges* that particular attention be given by the United Nations and Governments to the situation of disabled women, and that Governments take steps to ensure the equalization of opportunities and social justice for and political participation of disabled women in each sector of society;

14. *Once again calls upon* the Secretary-General and the executive heads of the specialized agencies and other United Nations bodies to establish five-year targets

3/ A/42/516 and A/42/528.
4/ See *Official Records of the Economic and Social Council 1987*, *Supplement No. 2* (E/1987/15), chap. I, sect. C.

at each level for the percentage of women in Professional and decision-making positions, in accordance with the criteria established by the General Assembly, in particular that of equitable geographical distribution, in order that a definite upward trend in the implementation of Assembly resolution 41/206 D of 11 December 1986 be registered in the number of Professional and decision-making positions held by women by 1990, and to set additional targets every five years;

15. *Requests* the Secretary-General to extend the term of office of the Co-ordinator for the Improvement of the Status of Women in the Secretariat of the United Nations for a satisfactory period to ensure that the action programme, 5/ in which, *inter alia*, it is recommended that the situation of women in the Secretariat be improved, will continue to be implemented;

16. *Requests* the Secretary-General to invite Governments, organizations of the United Nations system, including the regional commissions and the specialized agencies, and intergovernmental and non-governmental organizations to report periodically, through the Commission on the Status of Women, to the Economic and Social Council on activities undertaken at all levels to implement the Forward-looking Strategies;

17. *Also requests* the Secretary-General to include

in his report to the General Assembly at its forty-third session on the implementation of the Forward-looking Strategies an assessment of recent developments that are relevant to the priority themes to be considered at the subsequent session of the Commission on the Status of Women and to transmit to the Commission a summary of relevant views expressed by delegations during the Assembly's debate;

18. *Further requests* the Secretary-General to report to the General Assembly at its forty-third session on measures taken to implement the present resolution;

19. *Requests* the Secretary-General to continue to provide for the existing weekly radio programmes on women in the regular budget of the United Nations, with adequate provisions for broadcasts in different languages, and to develop the focal point for issues relating to women in the Department of Public Information of the Secretariat, which, in concert with the Centre for Social Development and Humanitarian Affairs, should provide a more effective public information programme relating to the advancement of women;

20. *Decides* to consider these questions further at its forty-third session under the item entitled "Forward-looking strategies for the advancement of women to the year 2000".

Document 91

General Assembly resolution reiterating the need for the Forward-looking Strategies to be translated immediately into concrete action by Governments, as determined by overall national priorities, as well as by the organizations of the United Nations system, the specialized agencies and the intergovernmental and non-governmental organizations

A/RES/43/101, 8 December 1988

The General Assembly,

Recalling all its relevant resolutions, in particular resolutions 40/108 of 13 December 1985 and 42/62 of 30 November 1987, in which, *inter alia*, it endorsed the Nairobi Forward-looking Strategies for the Advancement of Women 1/ for the period up to the year 2000 and set out measures for their immediate implementation and for the overall achievement of the goals and objectives of the United Nations Decade for Women: Equality, Development and Peace,

Taking into consideration Economic and Social Council resolutions 1987/18, 1987/19, 1987/20, 1987/21, 1987/22, 1987/23, 1987/24, 1987/25 and 1987/26

of 26 May 1987 and 1988/19, 1988/21, 1988/22 and 1988/29 of 26 May 1988,

Recalling the Guiding Principles for Developmental Social Welfare Policies and Programmes in the Near Future, 2/ adopted by the Interregional Consultation on Developmental Social Welfare Policies and Programmes, held at Vienna from 7 to 15 September 1987,

Noting with concern the serious impact of the world

1/ *Report of the World Conference to Review and Appraise the Achievements of the United Nations Decade for Women: Equality, Development and Peace, Nairobi, 15-26 July 1985* (United Nations publication, Sales No. E.85.IV.10), chap. I., sect. A.
2/ See E/CONF.80/10, chap. III.

economic situation on the programmes and plans for the advancement of women, especially in the global context,

Conscious of the important and constructive contribution to the advancement of the status of women made by the Commission on the Status of Women, the specialized agencies, the regional commissions and other organizations of the United Nations system, Member States and intergovernmental and non-governmental organizations,

Emphasizing once again the priority of the implementation, monitoring, review and appraisal of the Forward-looking Strategies,

Welcoming the significant progress made by the Commission at its special session in 1987 in restructuring its agenda along functional lines, developing the systematic long-term programme of work and strengthening its role and functions, and noting the outcome of the thirty-second session of the Commission, held at Vienna from 14 to 23 March 1988 3/ and, in particular, Economic and Social Council resolutions 1988/19, 1988/21, 1988/22 and 1988/29,

Taking note of Economic and Social Council resolutions on issues relating to women,

Welcoming the designation by the Secretary-General of the advancement of women as one of the priorities of the Organization for the biennium 1988-1989,

Recognizing the need for the Commission to consider at its regular sessions the priority themes for its next five sessions, contained in the annex to Economic and Social Council resolution 1987/24,

1. *Takes note* of the report of the Secretary-General 4/ concerning the implementation of the Nairobi Forward-looking Strategies for the Advancement of Women;

2. *Recalls* resolutions 1, 2 and 4 adopted by the Commission on the Status of Women at its special session in 1987, 5/ in particular its recommendation that the implementation of the Forward-looking Strategies and the status of women in general should be incorporated as one of the priorities in the introduction of the Organization's medium-term plan for the period 1992-1997;

3. *Reaffirms* the need for the Forward-looking Strategies to be translated immediately into concrete action by Governments, as determined by overall national priorities, as well as by the organizations of the United Nations system, the specialized agencies and intergovernmental and non-governmental organizations;

4. *Reaffirms also* the central role of the Commission in matters related to the advancement of women and calls upon it to promote the implementation of the Forward-looking Strategies to the year 2000 based on the goals of the United Nations Decade for Women: Equality, Development and Peace and the subtheme "Employment,

Health and Education", and urges all organizations of the United Nations system to cooperate with the Commission in this task;

5. *Endorses* Economic and Social Council resolution 1988/19, in which, *inter alia*, the Council decided that the duration of the thirty-fourth session of the Commission, to be held in 1990, should be extended to ten days;

6. *Reaffirms further*, in the implementation of the Forward-looking Strategies, the role of the Centre for Social Development and Humanitarian Affairs of the Secretariat, in particular the Division for the Advancement of Women, as the substantive secretariat of the Commission and as a focal point for matters on women, the catalysing role of the United Nations Development Fund for Women and the role of the International Research and Training Institute for the Advancement of Women in the promotion of the role of women in the context of the participation of women in development;

7. *Requests* the relevant United Nations bodies to continue to provide focused and action-oriented input when reporting to the Commission on the priority themes;

8. *Endorses* the comprehensive reporting system to monitor, review and appraise the implementation of the Forward-looking Strategies, as outlined in the annex to Economic and Social Council resolution 1988/22, which will assist Member States in identifying problems and in developing remedial measures at the national, regional and international levels, and invites Governments and the organizations of the United Nations system, including the regional commissions and the specialized agencies, to report accordingly, through the Commission, to the Economic and Social Council;

9. *Emphasizes*, in the framework of the Forward-looking Strategies, the importance of the total integration of women in the development process, bearing in mind the specific and urgent needs of the developing countries, and calls upon Member States to establish specific targets at each level in order to increase the participation of women in professional and decision-making positions in their countries;

10. *Emphasizes also* the need to give urgent attention to redressing socio-economic inequities at the national and international levels as a necessary step towards the full realization of the goals and objectives of the Forward-looking Strategies;

11. *Urges* that particular attention be given by the United Nations and Governments to the situation of

3/ E/1988/15.
4/ A/43/638.
5/ See *Official Records of the Economic and Social Council, 1987, Supplement No. 2* (E/1987/15), chap. I, sect. C.

disabled women, and that Governments take steps to ensure the equalization of opportunities and social justice for and political participation of disabled women in each sector of society;

12. *Endorses* Economic and Social Council resolution 1988/29, in which the Council requested the Secretary-General to convene a seminar on women and rural development, using the resources available in the Trust Fund for the Preparatory Activities of the 1985 World Conference to Review and Appraise the Achievements of the United Nations Decade for Women established under Council decision 1983/132;

13. *Endorses also* Economic and Social Council resolution 1988/21, in which the Council recommended that in updating the *World Survey on the Role of Women in Development*, 6/ particular emphasis should be given to those factors that contribute to the deteriorating status of women in developing countries, as well as Economic and Social Council resolution 1988/49 of 26 July 1988, in which the Council called upon the Secretary-General to devote a separate section in the *World Economic Survey* to economic aspects of the situation of women and their contribution to economic development;

14. *Requests* the commission to explore, at its thirty-third session, the possibility of holding, during the period 1990-1991, an interregional consultation on women in public life;

15. *Once again calls upon* the Secretary-General and the executive heads of the specialized agencies and other United Nations bodies to establish five-year targets at each level for the percentage of women in Professional and decision-making positions, in accordance with the criteria established by the General Assembly, in particular that of equitable geographical distribution, in order that a definite upward trend in the implementation of Assembly resolution 41/206D of 11 December 1986 be registered in the number of Professional and decision-

making positions held by women by 1990, and to set additional targets every five years;

16. *Requests* the Secretary-General to invite Governments, organizations of the United Nations system, including the regional commissions and the specialized agencies, and intergovernmental and non-governmental organizations to report periodically to the Economic and Social Council, through the Commission, on activities undertaken at all levels to implement the Forward-looking Strategies;

17. *Also requests* the Secretary-General to include in his report to the General Assembly at its forty-fourth session on the implementation of the Forward-looking Strategies an assessment of recent developments that are relevant to the priority themes to be considered at the following session of the Commission and to transmit to the Commission a summary of relevant views expressed by delegations during the Assembly's debate;

18. *Further requests* the Secretary-General to report to the General Assembly at its forty-fourth session on measures taken to implement the present resolution;

19. *Requests* the Secretary-General to continue to provide for the existing weekly radio programmes on women in the regular budget of the United Nations, with adequate provisions for broadcasts in different languages, and to develop the focal point for issues relating to women in the Department of Public Information of the Secretariat, which, in concert with the Centre for Social Development and Humanitarian Affairs, should provide a more effective public information programme relating to the advancement of women;

20. *Decides* to consider these questions further at its forty-fourth session under the item entitled "Forward-looking strategies for the advancement of women to the year 2000".

6/ E/CN.6/1988/7.

Document 92

"Overview of the role of women in development", from the 1989 World Survey on the Role of Women in Development *(extract)* *

ST/CSDHA/6, 1989

I. **Overview of the role of women in development**

A. *Central theme of the first regular update of the* World Survey on the Role of Women in Development

"The decade of the 1980s has been a period of uneven economic conditions and responses to

them.... While growth continued or was restored in developed countries and a number of developing

*Prepared by the Division for the Advancement of Women, Centre for Social Development and Humanitarian Affairs, United Nations Office at Vienna.

countries in Asia, economic decline prevailed in Africa and Latin America. One major shortcoming of development strategies has been the failure to take into account the role and potential of women. The facts suggest that this shortcoming must be remedied if the development strategies of the 1990s are to succeed."

This statement of the central theme of the *1989 World Survey on the Role of Women in Development* was adopted by an Expert Group Meeting to Review the Final Draft of the First Regular Update of the World Survey on the Role of Women in Development, held at the Vienna International Centre, from 13 to 17 February 1989. The statement continued as follows.

"If the global economic situation in the 1980s is examined in aggregate terms, it has been one of the longest periods of growth ever recorded; but for developing countries, especially in Africa and Latin America, it has meant that development has virtually stopped. The changes in global trade and the problems of external debt have meant that, rather than emphasizing longer term structural transformations of the economic system, policies have emphasized shorter term structural adjustment. There has been an inevitable preoccupation with aggregates of growth, terms of trade and balance of payments.

"Underneath these broad trends, however, has been a change in the distribution of income and opportunities, both within and between countries. Mostly unfavourable, these changes have meant that development, as it has been understood in its broadest sense in international development strategies, has not been occurring. This is particularly true for women. The evidence shows that while some have improved their position through improved access to employment and more remunerated economic sectors, far more have become poor. Ironically, poverty among women has increased, even within the richest countries, resulting in what has become known as the "feminization of poverty".

"If a balance sheet were drawn up for women in the economy, it could be shown that women entered the labour force in large numbers, saw improvements in access to education in most regions, began to appear in sectors where they were previously absent, made up a slightly larger proportion of managerial and technical jobs. But it could also be shown that the rate of improvement in all of these indicators was slower than in the previous decade, that in terms of remuneration and conditions of work no aggregate improvement was registered, that women's unemployment rates tended to be higher and that overall incomes declined. Poverty particularly afflicted families in which women are the sole income earners, a phenomenon that is growing.

"The balance sheet on social conditions of women is similarly mixed. Improvements in legal conditions, in access to goods and services, such as education, have been registered. But increases in maternal and infant mortality in some developing countries have been observed for the first time in decades, as social services have been cut as part of adjustment packages.

"The bottom line shows that, despite economic progress measured in growth rates, at least for the majority of developing countries, economic progress for women has virtually stopped, social progress has slowed, social well-being in many cases has deteriorated and, because of the importance of women's social and economic role, the aspirations for them in current development strategies will not be met.

"Women, however, remain a major force for change. Modification in policies, both to reflect the global norm of equality between men and women, and to enable women to exercise the potential that they have, can have significant effects on the economy. On the one hand, this means ensuring that short- and medium-term policies do not have a negative impact on women, but rather are consistent with long-term objectives of equality. On the other hand, it means seeing long-term structural transformation as a means of accommodating women's increasing economic role for the betterment of society as a whole.

"It also means seeing policies in an integrated way, in which changes in one aspect of women's life can have reinforcing and multiplying positive effects on other aspects. Development for women means development for society. Achieving this means identifying critical points in the economic process where intervention by policies and programmes can have the greatest impact. It means a sharpening of focus on the basic obstacles to women's full participation and on the policies that can address them directly.

"The *1989 World Survey* explores the dimensions of this thesis, by examining the underlying economic and social conditions, the specific economic sectors and some of the key cross-sectoral questions. From this analysis a number of main conclusions and recommendations flow."

The *1989 World Survey* incorporates the recommendations of the experts. This update also makes use of the conclusions of a series of expert groups and seminars convened at Vienna to help in preparing the reports on the priority themes for the Commission on the Status of Women. These include the Seminar on National Machinery for Monitoring and Improving the Status of Women, held from 28 September to 2 October 1987, the Interregional Seminar on Women and the Economic Crisis, held from 3 to 7 October 1988 and the Expert Group Meeting on Social Support Measures for the Advancement of Women, held from 14 to 18 November 1988.

The original *World Survey*, prepared for the World Conference to Review and Appraise the Achievements of the United Nations Decade for Women: Equality, Development and Peace, held at Nairobi, from 15 to 26 July 1985, emphasized material that clearly demonstrated the important role played by women in the world economy. As requested by the General Assembly and the Economic and Social Council, acting on recommendations from the Commission on the Status of Women, the first regular update of the World Survey centres on the more complex questions of how women play their role, the factors that enhance or impede them and the kind of issues that must be addressed if women's full and equal participation in the economy is to be achieved. This approach is more analytical than descriptive, which has been made possible by a dramatic increase of research on economic variables taking the factor of sex into account. Statistical series are now available, and have been used in the report. A small but growing body of micro-level studies are beginning to bring forward reliable information on the dynamics of women's economic role. The reports by States parties to the Convention on the Elimination of All Forms of Discrimination against Women (General Assembly resolution 34/180 of 18 December 1979, annex) are bringing to the international public the results of national appraisals. Finally, the increasing number of units of national machinery for the advancement of women are providing a national impulse for studies on the condition of women and the type of action needed for the improvement of the circumstances in which women live and work.

The five years since the original *World Survey* have been characterized by uneven economic growth that has often aggravated the differences between regions. In the older industrialized States, a period of steady economic growth and slowing population growth, often accompanied by lower energy and food costs, has meant an unprecedented increase in material consumption. In some countries in Asia there has been steady growth through trade and manufacturing that has led to rising levels of prosperity. However, in most developing regions, Africa and Latin America and the Caribbean, economic stagnation or negative growth, continued population increase and the prolonged international debt crisis and adjustment policies designed to deal with this have shaped and constrained the activities of women as individuals, as

carers and providers for families and households, and as participants in the practical development of their countries. The problems of recession and economic restructuring in the face of external debt have led Governments to focus on these, often to the neglect of longer term issues that have a direct bearing on the advancement of women. At the same time, pre-existing conditions of inequality—in health and nutrition, levels of literacy and training, in access to education and economic opportunity, and in participation in decision-making at all levels—between women and men have sometimes been exacerbated both by the crises themselves and by the policies adopted to cope with them. It is this that gives the current economic situation its gender dimension. Yet economic recovery and advancement towards the social and political goals of development require the contribution of all. It is therefore imperative that adjustment programmes be designed to take specific account of women, to ensure their progress is not impeded by existing inequitable burdens and unbalanced structures or by short-sighted policies.

All development will be delayed without economic growth. Without it, the pursuit of equality could become a destructive competition between the sexes for ever-diminishing resources. However, there is no automatic link between economic growth and the advancement of women, even in a limited material sense. Policies to restore and stimulate growth must be accompanied by programmes to eliminate basic inequalities in terms of access to services and opportunities. It is within this context, as outlined in the conclusions of the Expert Group Meeting, that the *1989 World Survey* analyses the current contribution of women and implications for future progress.

The direct economic effects on women of external debt and adjustment policies are examined in chapter 11, looking at reduction in household incomes, rising food prices and the overall impact of the reduced public expenditure that has been a response to the crisis in a number of countries. Wage and recruitment freezes in the public service, a major employer of women in many places, cuts in subsidies for food and staples, and decreased expenditure on education, health and other social services may already be causing a deterioration in living standards. The need to compensate for lowered family income may prevent girls and women from taking advantage of present educational opportunities. Reduced government expenditure in this field, which has been recorded in 60 per cent of Latin American countries and in one third of African and Asian countries in the early 1980s, will continue to affect access to education, with repercussions for equality, access to employment, fertility control and the health and education of families. Chapter II looks at the effect of adjustment policies on health, including malnutrition and maternal and child mortality rates, and also attempts to assess their broader social impact. The world-wide increase in female-headed households has been particularly pronounced during this period. Many social and cultural factors have contributed to this, but responses to more difficult economic conditions, male migration, female participation in the workforce and family breakdown for example, have accelerated the process. Female-headed households tend to be among the poorest in all countries for which data are available, which has grave implications for the present well-being and future advancement of the women involved and their dependents. Women's access to paid employment and recognition and recompense and support for their unpaid economic and societal activities are thus issues for urgent consideration.

The original *World Survey* focused attention on the crucial importance of women's contribution to food and agricultural production. Population pressures and land shortages, environmental depletion and degradation and the emphasis on import substitution by increased local production in most adjustment policies makes facilitating their role an essential ingredient if plans to achieve food security are to be realized. As is pointed out in chapter III, it has been demonstrated that women's involvement in agricultural development leads to increased efficiency and productivity.

This involvement should be stimulated not only by redressing former bias towards women in training, technology and other developmental input, but also by ensuring that women, often the main food producers, are integrated into all agricultural programmes. This means that present constraints on their participation, including obsolete divisions of labour and restricted access to land, capital, credit and training, must be alleviated if production and productivity are to be maximized. In other words, it requires analysis and reassessment of the whole socio-economic environment of rural women, to be followed by policies based on principles and perspectives that ensure their equity and sustainability.

While there has always been a general awareness of women's major role in food production, their increasingly significant participation in the industrial labour force may not be so widely recognized. Yet in 1985 there were already over 166 million women in industry around the world, more than half of them in developing countries where trends indicate that their contribution may in some regions be even greater than in the older centres of industrialization. Joining the industrial work-force has had both positive and negative impacts on women. Chapter IV analyses the economic, industrial and social factors involved and examines issues and policy options in the light of future needs in the context of both effective human resource development and improvement in manufacturing employment. Access to relevant education and training is again a fundamental issue. This is more than a means of liberating women from lower-paid jobs where they may have little security or prospect for betterment; it is a step towards ensuring their equitable sharing of the responsibilities and benefits of all socio-economic activities. Planning to integrate them into industrial development must take structural shifts in the international market and technological advances into account. These and other factors are explored in this chapter, which also presents an in-depth examination of two industrial sectors, textiles and electronics, that are major employers of women in developing countries.

In spite of the importance of industry as a source of employment for women, the service sector absorbs three times more women in Africa and is already the largest employer of women in Asia. High female participation in this sector is also characteristic of developed countries, and chapter V looks at the issues and trends in both. The very reasons for the concentration of women in this area — easy access, low skill requirements, traditional stereotypes directing them into this sector or away from others, and the need for part-time work—are germane to the broader issues of women's ability to participate fully and effectively in all economic activity. Recent studies show that in spite of their significant numbers in the service sector, most women are still clustered at the lowest levels within it, whether in public or private employment, and, in spite of some improvements, there are still marked disparities between male and female pay. New technology and organizational changes will continue to affect women's employment. The role of women as traders and entrepreneurs is also considered in a survey that emphasizes the dynamic and strategic role of the service sector in economic recovery and progress and the achievement of basic development goals.

Not all the women who need income-producing work, however, can be absorbed in agriculture, industry or services. Many of them gravitate to the informal sector. Chapter VI examines the nature, conditions and effect of their participation here. Again, lack of access to credit, skills, technology and other resources hamper their productivity and limit their income. Pre-existing inequalities mean that here, too, factors that constrain both men and women may bear harder upon the latter at the same time as their efforts in this sector represent a direct attempt to overcome problems of increasing unemployment in other sectors, and the effects of recession and poverty on their families by their own resources and effort. Too often these efforts are overlooked when they should be supported. Measures to do this are called for; however, their success will depend on clearer perceptions of the sector and on reliable data. The annex to chapter VI shows that in spite of the difficulties of precise definition, this has already begun.

After these five sectoral analyses, the *1989 World Survey* looks at a number of broader issues that affect all women and at the many-faceted role of women in development. One of these issues is women's access to all forms of paid work. It is indicated in chapter VII that their increasing participation is still impeded by various factors, the application of which in specific sectors has already been seen. Here the question is seen in terms of the fundamental right of all persons to work. Similarly, while the revolutionary effects of technology have been taken into account in specific areas, chapter VIII concentrates on women's preparation for and participation in all aspects of technological change. This must include their involvement in determining its directions so that they have control over its impact on them. Cultural factors will assist in colouring and shaping their response to this challenge. They can sometimes appear to be restrictive and resistant to change. Yet, as is pointed out in chapter IX, culture is itself a dynamic process, part of society's mechanism of adaptation to changing circumstances. If its forms are revived or retained when they may have become irrelevant or ineffective in this process of adjustment, traditional structures and constraints may need to be reassessed in the light of the societal goals and values they originally embodied. They may require revitalization and modification in the light of new ways of achieving these goals and accommodating evolving values.

While all societies have always been dependent on the contribution of both women and men, recognition and appreciation of both differences and similarities of function and potential have varied widely. In recent times, the dominance of value systems that overemphasize renumerated activity have caused some of women's most important roles to be obscured. Chapter X shows how the United Nations is working towards a fuller understanding of women's contribution by the development of statistics and indicators that enable this to be seen more clearly.

As the sectoral studies indicate, this contribution is still held back in all areas of economic endeavour by women's lower access to education and opportunity, in other words, because of inequality. Chapter XI presents equality as perhaps the linchpin in the tripartite relationship between development in its broad sense and the security and well-being of society that can only be guaranteed by peace. Direct and indirect violence are both symptoms of and tools for the perpetuation of inequalities between peoples, genders and individuals. It is concluded in this chapter that education and conditioning to abolish existing stereotypes and structures that reinforce inequalities and inhibit the involvement of women at all levels of decision-making are essential. The current economic crisis should be seen as a challenging opportunity for rethinking and restructuring to enable women to participate as equal partners in development that will provide a sustainable base for lasting peace.

B. *Main trends*

No complete and fully documented estimate can be made of the direct impact of the crisis on the advancement of women. This is due in part to the absence of statistical series sufficiently disaggregated by sex to permit drawing links, in part to the fact that the problems of debt and adjustment in individual countries interact closely with other phenomena. However, the studies that have been made, together with the analysis made of existing indicators, as well as the qualitative experience of women who have lived through the crisis, leave no doubt that there has been a differential effect of the crisis on women. Beyond the obvious effects caused by a reduction in expenditures on public services with its obvious consequences for education and health, and the documented need for more women to enter the labour force in order to maintain acceptable levels of household income, there are less obvious effects on the fabric of women's lives reflected in the increase of female-headed households which, in many countries, are becoming a main factor in increasing poverty in developing and developed countries alike.

The economic crisis colours all aspects of women's role. In agriculture, positive effects such as increases in prices are often offset by the introduction of new technologies primarily to men. In industry, women's employment increased, but often through lower paid labour, and it has not been matched by access to economic decision-making. Even the growth of the service sector, which has proven to be the most resistant to the economic crisis, has not always benefited women. In the informal sector, into which women seem to have retreated, exploitation of women's political and economic weakness has often led to new forms of discrimination. There is growing evidence, presented in detail in chapter II, that there are both direct and indirect effects on the social condition of women. Perhaps most importantly, the economic conditions of the 1980s have contributed to a slowing of progress in advancement, a near stagnation that could threaten the future ability of women to achieve equality.

The analysis of the economic crisis, however, shows that the effects are not always those that might be naively expected, nor are they always negative. Rather, there is a complex interrelationship between economic changes, public economic policy, pre-existing inequalities and advancement of women. What is clear is that, although often unnoticed, women affect and are affected by international and national policies in ways that are only beginning to be understood and that merit further examination. Indeed, examining economic conditions through a "gender lens" is an effective way of incorporating the human dimension into economic planning and policy-making.

Economic changes have to be seen in the context of population growth. The economic slow-down of the 1980s, when coupled with continued growth of population, particularly in developing countries, has meant that what economic growth has occurred in aggregate has not been translated into improvement in per capita terms. In addition, an increasing aging of the world population will in the future become a significant part of social and economic development. The link between population and advancement of women, directly by the reproductive process and indirectly by the caring role women are expected to play in most societies, is now clearly recognized.

One of the consequences of the reduction of public sector programmes, coupled with the slowing of education opportunities for girls, is an increase in teenage pregnancies and a possible reversal of earlier trends indicating a slowing in the growth of population. The close relationship between education, employment opportunities and women's choice to delay parenthood and reduce the number of children means that if these factors are not improved, population expansion can be expected to continue.

The Expert Group Meeting on Social Support Measures for the Advancement of Women, held at Vienna from 14 to 18 November 1988, discussed this issue. Its conclusions (EGM/SSMAW/1988/1) are given below.

Family planning has been recognized on many occasions by the international community as a basic human right; however, due to ignorance and insufficient services vast numbers of women are still unaware of their rights or of the appropriate and safest methods existing to exercise family planning.

Although family planning is a right and essential for the advancement of women, in reality, the practice, services and perceptions surrounding it have frequently transformed it into a political issue. Therefore, the utmost efforts are necessary to upgrade the quality of services and eliminate all forms of abuse that have discredited family planning programmes and effectively deprived women of the possibility of improving their situation. Abortion is not considered as a family planning method, but as a back-up in case of contraceptive failure and as a last resort. There must be relevant education for children and women's groups so that they will be in a position to request exact and appropriate information on methods and risks. Family planning could be introduced as part of other health programmes. This type of integration should be encouraged. Training of health workers to combat erroneous ideas is essential; and programmes should ensure the availability of various methods and high-quality services and products. In this connection, measures are necessary to monitor the safety of the methods provided in order to avoid complications, failures and rejection by the population. The issue of the importation of contraceptives and the need for women's groups and professional associations to monitor the measures needed to be taken in the framework of paragraph 153 of the Nairobi Forward-looking Strategies 1/ on the quality of all drugs provided should be highlighted.

Family planning education should not only cover reproduction, but also sexually transmitted diseases, including the acquired immunodeficiency syndrome (AIDS), which is increasingly a problem for women and motherhood.

It is recognized that in practice no method is 100 per cent safe, but the risks of contraception have to be weighed against those of unwanted pregnancies. Particular risks are infection, utilization of inappropriate methods, inadequate training of medical staff, which results in poor advice and people stopping family planning, and inadequate follow-up of acceptors of family planning. Appropriate training for all categories of health-care workers including auxiliaries who could safely screen for referral to medical doctors is essential.

C. *Emerging issues*

Three issues emerge of particular relevance for future analyses of the role of women in development: women's participation in economic decision-making, the relationship between women's economic role and the support functions provided in the family, and women's involvement in the crucial issue of the environment.

(a) *Participation in economic decision-making*

Women's participation in economic decision-making is currently low, according to most studies. It is particularly low in the formal economic sectors, whether private or public. Few women are to be found in top management positions, in labour unions or in interest associations. At the same time, as women continue to achieve equality in access to education there will be more qualified women available for management positions, and to the extent that affirmative action programmes are applied, they should have increased opportunities to obtain them.

1/ Report of the World Conference to Review and Appraise the Achievements of the United Nations Decade for Women: Equality, Development and Peace. Nairobi, 15-26 July 1985 (United Nations publication, Sales No. E.85.IV.10), chap. I, sect A.

The priority themes, under the rubric of equality in 1990 and peace in 1991, for the Commission on the Status of Women will deal with the participation of women in public decision-making. Information on this, in terms of incidence and factors affecting access, is being acquired, but economic decision-making is not only a matter for the State; in many economic systems it is in the private sector where much economic decision-making takes place. Little is known of the factors that enable or inhibit women's participation in decision-making here. It will have to be decided whether to give priority to the study of this aspect of women's economic role.

(b) *Women's economic role and the family*

In the report of the Secretary-General on the priority themes, under the heading of development (E/CN.6/1989/6, para. 32 and 33) it was stated that:

"The advancement of women is affected by the economic and social changes of the late twentieth century. On the positive side these include the gradual removal of legal barriers to equality between men and women, improved access of women to education and employment and a general narrowing of the differences between women and men, as shown in the report of the Secretary-General on equality in economic and social participation (E/CN.6/1989/5). It is reflected in the increased and recognized role of women in development. On the negative side, the entry of women into the labour force has been largely due to necessity, and conditions under which they work are often inferior to those of men; employment for women is concentrated in the unregulated informal sector and is accompanied by large-scale urbanization or international migration, which has undercut the extended family as an institution. Women's role becomes all the more difficult because of factors already touched on in section I above: the fact that household responsibilities are not shared and the decline in the ability of the extended family or the community to provide the necessary support services to lighten women's double burden.

"Women's further advancement depends in large measure on whether conditions of employment, education, health and other social services are changed so as to provide the necessary support to women's growing economic role."

The consequences of these developments will need to be examined carefully over the next few years.

(c) *Environment*

The question of the environment continues to be critical. The droughts that have affected large segments of the African continent, the possible effects of global climatic change and the problems of pollution and waste make action on these matters imperative. Women's direct involvement in this issue is shown in terms of agriculture and food systems presented in chapter III. It is important to realize that the increasing poverty of women means that the negative effects of environmental change may fall most heavily on them.

D. *The next regular update of the* World Survey

As a result of their review of the first regular update, the Expert Group Meeting on the *World Survey* made specific recommendations on the preparation of the next update, which are given below.

The next regular update of the *World Survey on the Role of Women in Development* should be prepared for consideration in 1994, in order to allow it to provide an input to the quinquennial review and appraisal of the Nairobi Forward-looking Strategies.

In view of the importance of the *World Survey*, which will constitute a basic document for the forthcoming World Conference as a fundamental assessment of progress in the advancement of women, it is necessary that the preparation of the *World Survey* for 1994 be harmonized with the preparation of the *World Economic Survey*, the international development strategies, and the medium-term plan and the system-wide medium-term plan for women and development of the United Nations in order for it to receive sufficient resources and credibility. The process of preparation of the next *World Survey*, which should start at the earliest possible date, should involve the scientific community with the United Nations system synthesizing the results for policy formulation. Care should be taken to standardize methods of work, utilization of data and the balance between the chapters. Efforts should be made to involve national machinery in the process which, if possible, should be assisted to provide similar information at the national level.

Among the issues that should be given more attention in the next regular update are the environment, population (including health), housing and refugee women, in addition to continuing concern with major sectors where women's participation is essential, such as agriculture and industry. Work on the informal sector should be included and an effort made to analyse the problems of urban development as they affect women. It was noted that greater attention should be given to the relationship of international economic policies to women's economic role (as a macro approach) and to a more detailed examination of the micro-economics of the family or household as the smallest economic unit and to women's roles as managers within it.

Appropriate attention should be given to the human dimension, taking into account women's contribution to development. In particular, priority should be given to such problems as family in the development process, poverty, income distribution, quality of life, social sup-

port measures, especially in economic crisis, and violence against women within the family and society.

...

Document 93

Report of the Secretary-General to the CSW on the first review and appraisal of the implementation of the Nairobi Forward-looking Strategies, assessing progress at the national, regional and international levels

E/CN.6/1990/5, 22 November 1989

Summary

The Economic and Social Council, by its resolution 1988/22, established a comprehensive reporting system for the five-yearly review and appraisal of the implementation of the Nairobi Forward-looking Strategies for the advancement of Women, the first of which will take place in 1990. The Council requested a report of the Secretary-General on the review and appraisal based on national reports as well as other information. The review and appraisal presented in this report indicates that there has been progress in some areas since the World Conference to Review and Appraise the Achievements of the United Nations Decade for Women: Equality, Development and Peace, held at Nairobi in 1985, especially in the area of *de jure* equality, but that for a number of reasons, progress in achieving de facto equality, that is, the full integration of women in development or full participation of women in peace has slowed or stopped. The report notes the long-term effects on women of demographic and social factors as well as the consequences of the economic conditions of the late 1980s. It notes national action taken in terms of the Forward-looking Strategies. It points out that a number of steps have been taken by the United Nations system to improve its ability to assist national action in implementing the Strategies

Executive summary

1. More than four years after the adoption of the Nairobi Forward-looking Strategies for the Advancement of Women, 1/ with one third of the time allocated for achieving the goal of equality between women and men elapsed, the principal obstacles to the implementation of the Strategies have become clearer. Despite advances in some areas, the general pattern is one of a loss of dynamism. There is concern that, unless implementation is greatly improved, many of the objectives will not be achieved by the year 2000.

2. The review and appraisal should be based primarily on national reports. By 1 September 1989, only 55 had been received, which may well be an indicator of the difficulties encountered both in implementing the Strategies and in reporting on their implementation.

3. This report is based on statistics and indicators compiled by the Statistical Office of the United Nations, and information from the specialized agencies of the United Nations system, the regional commissions and non-governmental organizations. In addition, the analyses of the priority themes before the Commission on the Status of Women in 1988, 1989 and 1990, 2/ and for the *1989 World Survey on the Role of Women in Development* 3/ were used. These included detailed analyses by expert groups and seminars, as well as data from the national level. They thus draw on the experience gained in all regions and many countries.

4. While progress in the diversity of subjects covered by the Forward-looking Strategies cannot be measured exactly, the reports and statistics show changes that occurred during the United Nations Decade for Women: Equality, Development and Peace (1976-1985), which information was not available at the Nairobi World Conference. National reports also reflect changes that have occurred since 1985. These various sources reveal the obstacles to be overcome and the need to design concrete measures to revitalize progress.

5. In each of the three objectives of the Forward-looking Strategies: equality, development and peace,

1/ *Report of the World Conference to Review and Appraise the Achievements of the United Nations Decade for Women: Equality, Development and Peace, Nairobi, 15-26 July 1985* (United Nations publication, Sales No. E.85.IV.10).

2/ National machinery for the advancement of women; problems of rural women; violence against women in the family and in society and education for peace; 1989: Equality in social and economic participation; education, including eradication of illiteracy, employment, health and other social services including child care and population aspects; full participation of women in the construction of their countries and in the achievement of a just political and economic system; 1990: Equality in political participation and decision-making; negative effects of the world economic situation on the improvement of the status of women; women in situations of armed conflict.

3/ United Nations publication, Sales No. E.89.IV.2.

there are areas in which positive developments have been made and areas in which little progress can be observed. At the national level, the institutional basis for the advancement of women remains weak due to insufficient authority, expertise and resources. At the international level, improvements made in planning and coordination are partially offset by the lack of sufficient resources to ensure implementation.

6. Some countries have advanced further than others, often starting from a stronger base; in others the conditions under which the advancement of women takes place have made progress slow. The applicability of specific provisions of the Strategies in a given country may vary, as many countries have reported. However, there are common factors that can be identified for all countries, concerning both obstacles and measures to be taken.

A. *Equality*

7. In the field of formal legislation, there has been considerable progress in achieving equality. By 1 September 1989, 99 countries had become States party to the Convention on the Elimination of All Forms of Discrimination against Women. An additional 18 Member States had signed the Convention, but not ratified it. Most national reports, as well as the reports of States parties to the Committee on the Elimination of Discrimination against Women (CEDAW) show that national laws are being adjusted to the provisions of the Convention.

8. There is, however, evidence that the elimination of *de jure* discrimination has not been matched by reductions in de facto discrimination. Inequality still exists in access to education, to productive assets and to decision-making, and in conditions of work and remuneration.

9. In most countries women do not seem to be aware of their rights under the Convention, and in many countries, they lack the skills and knowledge to use the legal system to pursue their rights. The lack of what has been termed "legal literacy" constitutes an obstacle to the implementation of the equality objective of the Strategies. Another important obstacles, according to many countries, is the reinforcement of women's lesser status by images in the mass media and advertising, and in the cultural values being transmitted by other means. Many of the obstacles, particularly those of an educational nature, are manifested at the local level in the daily lives of women and men, and can only be removed by policies and programmes at the grass-roots level.

10. As regards equality in economic and social participation, the report of the Secretary-General to the Commission on the Status of Women at its thirty-third session states that: "Where progress has been achieved, it has not been through natural evolutionary processes. It is becoming clear that special efforts are needed to remove the obstacles, both legal and practical, to women's equal participation." (E/CN.6/1989/5, p.4) While a number of countries report policies of affirmative action to overcome, in a short period of time, the effects of past inequality, these policies are still not common and continue to face opposition. They also suffer from the lack of appropriate enforcement machinery. The preference of many countries is to seek long-term achievement of equality by such policies as equal access to education. Such measures may have an effect on young women some time in the twenty-first century, but will not improve the status of women today.

11. This situation is also reflected in women's equality in political participation and decision making. Despite the fact that most countries now use democratic methods of choosing political leaders and making policy choices, and that women make up half of the electorates, relatively few women reach the highest levels of political participation and even fewer become public decision makers. On average, women represent only 10 per cent of members of parliament, and only 3.5 per cent of ministerial-level decision makers. In all forums where policy decisions are proposed and made, but especially those dealing with decisions affecting women's daily lives, at national, international and local levels, women are largely absent. As a result, as was stated in the report of the Expert Group Meeting on Equality in Political Participation and Decision-making, Vienna, 18-22 September 1989: "... women in all countries share a common condition: they are not full participants in the public choices that affect their lives. This must change." (EGM/EPPDM/1989/1, p. 4)

12. Although the factors underlying this situation vary according to the traditions of the country concerned, regardless of region or level of development, a major cause is the absence of women in the leadership of political parties and other organizations, and their consequent absence as candidates for public office. This is coupled with almost invisible barriers to promotion to the highest ranks in the civil service, where women make up a sizeable proportion of the total labour force. Not well-studied at the national level, it is illustrated by the case of women in the international civil service. The few exceptions seem to be in countries where either policies of affirmative action to ensure representation in leadership have been adopted, or where women exercise a "gender interest" in selecting their political leaders and thus help to provide the necessary political will for policies to improve women's status.

B. *Development*

13. The general progress of world development over the past five years has been limited, at best. For

women this means that the conditions of employment, education and health that were meant to be addressed in the implementation of the Strategies continue largely unchanged. For the average woman today—poor, lacking equal opportunities for education, subject to work for a lesser remuneration than men or for no remuneration, often unable to control her own fertility, increasingly more often the head of the family—development has been an illusion. As it was stated in the *1989 World Survey:*

"despite economic progress measured in growth rates, at least for the majority of developing countries, economic progress for women has virtually stopped, social progress has slowed, social well-being in many cases has deteriorated and, because of the importance of women's social and economic role, the aspirations for them in current development strategies will not be met." 4/

14. When measured against 1970 figures, there is evidence that programmes to improve women's access to education have had an effect in many regions, especially for younger women. Equality between women and men in school enrolment has been achieved in several regions, although not in those in which the majority of the world's population is found. In most regions, health services have improved, and infant and maternal mortality have decreased. There is clearly a greater recognition of women's economic role at both national and international levels.

15. At the same time, the differences between women and men in terms of such critical factors as literacy, income and access to services, which were noted in the Strategies, have persisted. Despite a long-term trend suggesting some improvement, this has slowed during the past five years. The economic difficulties faced by most countries in the 1980s due to international economic conditions relating to trade, external debt and general conditions of recession in all countries, but especially by the developing countries, have meant an increase in women's participation in the economy as women have sought to cope with the effects of declining incomes in real terms. This is often not reflected in the official statistics since it occurs in the unregulated and unreported informal sector. In developed countries, despite renewed growth, the proportion of women among the poor has increased. In developing countries, where most women are already poor, it has meant that promised improvements have not occurred.

16. The International Seminar on Women and Rural Development, held at Vienna in 1989, concluded:

"The situation of rural women has been affected by the negative effects of overall development trends and the national and international levels. These trends, given the conditions of discrimination which

are common in the rural areas of many countries, have constituted severe obstacles to the advancement of rural women. They have normally had limited access to the factors of production, particularly land and capital, to technology and to training. This is particularly unfortunate in view of the role that women could perform in a strategy of development that focuses on efficiency as well as equity. As a result of their position as food providers and producers, promoting rural women's agricultural activities would have automatic spin-off effects on social development on nutrition, health and rural housing." (IS/WRD/1989/1)

17. The situation bodes ill. The contrast between the improved access of young women to education and therefore, in principle, their qualifications for better employment and the jobs actually available will constitute a long-term problem unless employment is generated. For adult women, it means an increase in the already heavy double burden of home and remunerated or non-remunerated work. There is, moreover, evidence in the developing countries most affected by external debt and consequent structural adjustment of a slowing in the rate of improvement even in access to education. Lack of improvement in the conditions of rural women is beginning to have an effect on the environment, and will have long-term consequences.

18. A major factor is the reduced availability of public resources. Being among the newest and therefore most vulnerable programmes of Governments, those devoted to women seem to have been among the most affected by cost cutting.

19. At the same time, new needs for social support to women are becoming evident in all societies. This is because of such diverse factors as women's need for remunerated employment, the decline of the extended family as a social support institution, and the increase in the numbers of both the young and the aging in the populations of developing countries. Other factors are the increasing incidence of female-headed households and increasing internal and international migration. There is little evidence of an increase in the sharing of domestic and parental responsibilities between women and men that would provide an alternative means of social support. It is clear that few Governments have been able to provide adequate support and that successful experiences are few and poorly documented.

20. As the Secretary-General in his report on the development priority theme in 1989 stated:

"Any attempt to deal with the problem must involve all components of social support, starting with the

4/ Ibid., p. 6.

family itself, but including the services that are provided for the public good: education and training, health, and family planning. Efforts must also be made to improve conditions in the workplace. The interrelation among the various services and issues needs to be emphasized. Improvements in any of the support services will have a positive effect on the others." (E/CN.6/1989/6, para.8)

21.   The challenge of development is how to provide adequate economic opportunities to women. It is particularly necessary to open their access to technology and the training needed to use it. It is also necessary to ensure the social support needed by women to perform their essential economic activities.

22.   As stated in the report of the United Nations Interregional Seminar on Women and the Economic Crisis held at Vienna, from 3 to 7 October 1988: "The economic crisis, while having a negative impact on women in many respects, could provide an opportunity— indeed force a rethinking of approaches to development. Both solving the negative consequences for women and improving the well-being of men and women can be achieved if the full potential of women to contribute to the development process can be encouraged by the policies adopted by governments. ... it therefore requires a perspective directed towards the future, the year 2000 and beyond." The seminar also recommended that the participation of women in development should be part of the next international development strategy.

C. Peace

23.   Recent years have seen an improvement in global perspectives for peace, as a number of long-standing conflicts have begun to be resolved. Any decrease in conflict benefits women, as any other group in the population. But despite this progress, a large part of the world's women are still subject to the effects of regional conflicts and most of the conflicts to which the Strategies refer are largely unresolved. For example, the progress made in resolving the problems of women in Namibia have yet to be matched by similar improvements in the situation of women in Palestine or living under apartheid in South Africa.

24.   There is also the growing recognition of the pervasiveness of violence against women in the family and in society in all countries, regardless of the level of development, and of the need to do something about it. The phenomenon has begun to be documented since the Nairobi World Conference. As the Expert Group Meeting on Violence in the Family, with Special Emphasis on Women convened in December 1986 concluded:

"The problem is complex and requires careful solutions. At base, the real answers lie within the greater notion of the inherent equality between women and men, and how each society respects that basic equality and ensures and enhances it in all its most fundamental aspects. ... it is essential to provide immediate protection and assistance to women who are physically, emotionally, sexually, economically, or otherwise abused. Such protection must be coordinated and multi-faceted, including legal, health, social service support, and community support. ... [Efforts should] encompass solutions which are short-term and long-term, and which require regional, national and international action." 5/

25.   The review and appraisal, however, shows that the recognition of the problem of violence against women has not been followed by action in many countries, and that violence is a growing problem in the context of the economic, political and social changes affecting societies.

26.   It is significant that, although women have been disproportionately the victims of violence, whether international, national or domestic, they have seldom been involved in the decision-making on combating it. That situation has not changed substantially since 1985.

27.   While the hypothesis that women, because of their experiences, would be less likely to choose conflict than cooperation cannot be tested empirically in the absence of female decision makers, it is a reasonable one based on women's action in other official spheres and in non-governmental organizations. The peace process has also benefited from the work of women outside Government who have worked towards solutions to conflicts. Whether, when these conflicts are resolved, women will be given the recognition and continuing presence in the processes that their contribution merits remains to be seen.

D. Areas of special concern

28.   Many countries have expressed their concern for those women who, because of their situation, are particularly vulnerable to adverse economic and social conditions. Beyond the issue of securing their rights to participate fully in society for special groups of women, such as the elderly, disabled and young, the main issue is one of recognizing and ensuring their contribution to society. The increasing incidence of poverty among women, especially those who become sole heads of household, increases the vulnerability of women. Added to that are women whose situation as refugees or migrants has become worse. For all groups, adequate policies and programmes could enable them to achieve satisfactory

5/ Report of the Expert Group Meeting on Violence in the Family, with Special Emphasis on its Effects on Women, Vienna, 8-12 December 1986, p. 5.

condition. Seen as assets, rather than liabilities, these women could contribute significantly to development.

E. *Means of action*

29. Implementation of the Strategies was anticipated to require the development of institutions, procedures and the mobilization of resources at both national and international levels. In some respects, institutions have begun to develop and procedures have improved. However, mobilization of resources for the advancement of women has not occurred to the extent desired.

30. Successful implementation during the 1990s will require a stronger commitment by Governments to implement the Strategies, both at national and international levels. Fulfilling this commitment in the context of competing policy demands requires an understanding of both the inseparable relationship of the advancement of women to other issues and of the development of institutions that can present it clearly and convincingly.

31. At the international level, there has been some success in equipping the United Nations system to implement its part of the Strategies. A system-wide medium-term plan for women and development has been agreed for the period 1990-1995 and has already affected programmes in the biennium 1988-1989. The network of focal points set up during the Decade for Women, with the Division for the Advancement of Women of the United Nations Secretariat acting as its centre, has continued to grow and has resulted in an increasing level of joint activity. Institutional arrangements dealing with women's concerns have been established in most organizations. At the regional level, the commissions have continued their work based on regionally defined priorities. In organizations concerned with operational activities, there have been efforts to ensure that women are taken into account in mainstream development cooperation projects, and the United Nations Development Fund for Women (UNIFEM) has continued to improve its work in a new organizational setting. The gender-based statistics produced by the Statistical Office of the United Nations, the International Research and Training Institute for the Advancement of Women (INSTRAW) and their partners in the United Nations system should facilitate more serious research at all levels.

32. While the issue of the advancement of women has been more visible at the international level since the Nairobi World Conference, it is proving difficult to maintain. Women are seriously underrepresented at senior management levels in the United Nations system and there is some evidence that the issue is beginning to receive a lower priority in the work of many organizations. Resource levels in real terms for activities related to the advancement of women have not increased, despite the increase in activities at the international level and the increasing requirements of developing countries. Women's programmes have tended to receive the same reductions as other programmes during retrenchment. Much of the work therefore continues to require extra-budgetary funding. Some key activities, such as the updating of the Women's Indicators and Statistics Data Base and the Women's Information System, as well as many activities at the regional level, do not yet have secure funding. Most of the expert groups held on priority themes have been funded from extra-budgetary sources. As a result, at a time in which international programmes have the knowledge and institutional potential to be more active and operational, they may not be able to exercise this potential.

33. At the national level, similar conditions exist in most countries. During the Decade for Women and afterwards, more than two thirds of all countries have established national focal points. Since the Nairobi World Conference this national machinery has continued to receive international attention, and the importance of its role in presenting women's concerns within Government has been underlined at many expert groups and seminars, both regional and interregional, as well as by the Commission on the Status of Women. There have been efforts to support networking between units of national machinery.

34. Most units, however, suffer from a lack of staff and resources. Many are located away from the main sources of decision-making. Yet, if mainstreaming (i.e. integration) women's concerns into development plans and projects is not to mean their disappearance in practical terms, the national machinery has an essential role of advocate, monitor and adviser in national decision-making. The Expert Group Meeting on Equality in Political Participation and Decision-making recommended: "National machinery should be strengthened by enabling it to monitor the incorporation of women's concerns in all government ministries, including their budgets, and be provided with adequate resources to carry out their tasks." (RGM/EPPDM/1989/1, p.5) With a clearly expressed political commitment by government, this should be possible.

35. For this, it is necessary to mobilize information on the status of women in the country and on their comparative position *vis-à-vis* other countries. This in turn requires both technology and resources, neither of which are available for most national machinery, especially in developing countries. It also may require international assistance, both direct and indirect, through the United Nations system at all levels. As the Seminar on National Machinery for Monitoring and Improving the Status of Women, held at Vienna from 28 September to

2 October 1987 put it: "International assistance from both bilateral and multilateral sources was particularly needed in the area of training, especially in monitoring and evaluation methods, project formulation, and appraisal and information management." (E/CN.6/ 1988/3, p.7)

36. Networking, at the national level within Governments and between Governments and non-governmental organizations, has begun to fulfil its expected promise. At the international level, the usefulness of networks among the organizations of the United Nations system, other intergovernmental and non-governmental organizations has been similarly demonstrated. The series of seminars and expert groups undertaken by the United Nations to prepare the priority themes for the Commission on the Status of Women are an example of how the national experience of women can be brought to bear on the elaboration of international policies. This approach merits further explanation.

37. The need to look towards the future, to the critical last decade of this century has been underscored by the Commission. By identifying the most important obstacles that must be dealt with immediately, it should be possible to suggest priorities to be followed internationally, based on national experience, that would permit optimal use of the scarce resources available.

38. Some efforts have already been made to identify issues of immediate concern, such as those by the Expert Group that met at Vienna in February 1989 to review the final draft of the first regular update of the world survey on the role of women in development. It was stated in the report of that meeting: "Environment, population (including health), housing and refugee women, in addition to continuing concern with major sectors where women's participation is essential such as agriculture and industry. Work on the informal sector should be included and an effort made to analyse the problems of urban development as they affect women. ... greater attention should be given to the relationship of international economic policies to women's economic role ... and to a more detailed examination of the microeconomics of the family or household as the smallest economic unit and to women's roles as managers within it. ...Priority should be given to such problems as family in the development process, poverty, income distribution, quality of life, social support services, especially in economic crisis, and violence against women within the family and society." (p. 16)

Introduction

39. By resolution 1988/19, the Economic and Social Council decided that the Commission should meet in 1990 in an extended session to review and appraise the implementation of the Strategies. The Council established a detailed system for this exercise in its resolution 1988/22.

40. The system was to be based on national reports that should address the three objectives: equality, development and peace, and the information collected by a method structured according to the Forward-looking Strategies. The role of the national machinery was emphasized in two Council resolutions: by resolution 1987/18, paragraph 3, Member States were invited to cooperate fully in the review and appraisal and to take into account the needs of the United Nations in this regard when developing their national machinery and reporting systems; by resolution 1988/30, paragraph 10, active participation of the national machinery was urged.

41. Since the review and appraisal was to reflect national action reported by Governments, as in the case of the Nairobi World Conference a questionnaire was chosen as the most appropriate instrument for gathering information. The questionnaire developed for the review and appraisal of the Decade for Women, had covered a wide variety of issues. The result was a document of over 100 pages that Governments found difficult to complete and the United Nations system found difficult to process and analyse.

42. This experience prompted the Commission to insist that the next national questionnaire should be simple. Taking into account the great diversity of national situations and the high rate of non-response to the questions in the Decade review, it was decided to use a short set of open-ended questions for each topic, focusing on major policies and measures, their evaluation and future plans. It was also decided to obtain national perceptions of the relative importance of the issues in national priorities and to determine the perceived level of applicability of the Strategies to the national situation. Finally, an executive summary was requested for each response. These summaries will be made available to Commission members. The draft questionnaire was circulated within the United Nations system for comments before it was finalized.

43. On 28 June 1988, the questionnaire was sent with a *note verbale* to all the countries on the official distribution list (170 countries in June 1988), setting 15 January 1989 as the deadline for the response. A copy was sent to all the national machinery listed in the Directory of National Machinery, 6/ presented to the Commission in 1989 (background paper 2). In order to publicize the exercise and in particular bring it to the attention of non-governmental organizations, an article was published in *Women News*, No. 23 of August 1988. A reminder *note verbale* was sent out on 15 December 1988. By 15 January 1989, only eight Member States (5%) had returned the questionnaire. The Commission,

6/ Directory of National Machinery.

Table 1. *Responses to the questionnaires for the review and appraisal of the Strategies*

Group	Returns, including total, Part II			Total returns	
	Number	(Number)	(%)	(Number)	(%)
Developing countries	132	28	21	34	26
Developed countries	38	17	45	21	55
Total	170	45		55	
Members of the Commission on the Status of Women	32	20	63	21	66

at its thirty-third session discussed the low return rate and recommended a draft resolution, which was adopted by the Economic and Social Council as resolution 1989/32. In compliance with this resolution, the Secretariat immediately contacted the national machinery of the countries that had not responded to the questionnaire. The Secretariat was also requested to use the results of the *1989 World Survey* and to make available to the General Assembly at its forty-fourth session the preliminary results from the review and appraisal.

44. By 31 August 1989, 55 countries or one third of the recipients of the questionnaire, had responded; 7/ of these, 45 Governments complied with the part of the questionnaire requesting detailed substantive information (see table 1). Thus, only one fourth of the respondents provided information for the review and appraisal that could be analysed. 8/

45. The original plan of work had foreseen that bodies of the United Nations system would analyse different sections of the completed questionnaires. This plan was modified by the interagency meeting that was held following the Commission, when specialized agencies and regional commission were requested instead to identify measures and obstacles and to suggest draft recommendations. Those received have been included in this report.

46. In addition to the documentation listed in Council resolution 1988/22, the Secretariat drew information from the case studies prepared for and recommendations of seminars and expert groups organized by the Secretariat since 1985. National reports prepared subsequent to 1985 for the Committee on the Elimination of Discrimination against Women were also used.

47. A parallel survey was conducted on non-governmental organizations as requested in Council resolution 1988/22. A letter dated 10 October 1988 was sent by the Division for the Advancement of Women to the 822 non-governmental organizations in consultative status with the Council, together with a copy of the questionnaire. By June 1989, reports had been received from 39 organizations, 9/ of which 17 dealt with substantive issues. Only 12 organizations completed the questionnaire. The contributions from non-governmental organizations have been inserted in the current text.

48. More developed countries (55%) than developing countries returned either part I or part II of the questionnaire. 10/ The rate for African countries was particularly low (10%).

7/ Argentina,* Austria,* Bangladesh,* Bhutan, Bolivia,* Brazil,* Byelorussian Soviet Socialist Republic,* Cameroon,* Canada,* China,* Colombia, Costa Rica,* Cuba,* Czechoslovakia,* Denmark,* Dominica,* Egypt,* Finland,* France,* Guinea Bissau, Holy See, Hungary, Iraq,* Italy,* Japan,* Jordan,* Kuwait,* Lesotho,* Mali,* Mauritius,* Mexico,* Mongolia, Morocco,* Nepal,* New Zealand,* Niger,* Norway,* Oman, Pakistan,* Paraguay,* Peru,* Philippines,* Poland,* Portugal,* Republic of Korea,* Saint Lucia, Spain,* Sri Lanka,* Sweden,* Switzerland, Turkey,* Union of Soviet Socialist Republics, United Kingdom, Venezuela,* Yugoslavia* (* indicates inclusion of Part II).

8/ Reports received too late to be included in the analyses for this report: Australia, Ethiopia, Gabon, Greece, Mozambique.

9/ American Association of Retired Persons; Associated Country Women of the World; Association of African Universities; Baha'i International; Caritas Internationalis; Centre for Development and Population Activities; European Federation for the Welfare of the Elderly; European Union of Women; Housewives in Dialogue; International Alliance of Women; International Cartographic Association; International Centre for Sociological, Penal and Penitentiary Research and Studies; International Confederation of Free Trade Unions; International Council of Voluntary Agencies; International Federation for Home Economics; International Federation of Associations of the Elderly; International Federation of Business and Professional Women; International Federation of Gynecology and Obstetrics; International Planned Parenthood Federation; International Social Science Council; International Society of City and Regional Planners; International Statistical Institute; International Union of Students; Interparliamentary Union; Muslim World League; National Council of Women and Development; Pan African Institute for Development; Pax Romana; Socialist International Women; Soroptimist International; Sri Aurobindo Society; Women's International Democratic Federation; World Confederation of Labour; World Confederation of Organizations of the Teaching Profession; World Federation of Methodist Women; World Federation of Trade Unions; World Movement of Mothers; World Union of Progressive Judaism; World Young Women's Christian Association; Zonta International.

10/ For the purposes of this report, the category of developed countries includes the industrialized countries of eastern and western Europe, Oceania and North America. Developing countries include countries in Africa, Asia and the Pacific, and Latin America and the Caribbean.

49. There is no clear explanation for the low rate of return. While one explanation might be the questionnaire itself, the high quality of information provided by some countries with very different levels of development indicates that it was possible to provide the information requested.

50. The rate of return is much lower than for the review of the Decade carried out for the Nairobi World Conference. Even though that questionnaire was more difficult, over 120 were completed. For the 1985 review and appraisal, Governments usually set up task forces to gather information in anticipation of the Nairobi World Conference, whereas the review and appraisal of 1990, without a world conference to report to, did not receive the same priority.

PART ONE

GLOBAL AND REGIONAL FACTORS IN THE IMPLEMENTATION OF THE NAIROBI FORWARD-LOOKING STRATEGIES FOR THE ADVANCEMENT OF WOMEN

51. Many of the obstacles to the advancement of women derive from structural and demographic phenomena that change only slowly. Because they are already part of the life history of women, their change has to be reflected in the conditions for younger women. These social and demographic conditions incorporate the pre-existing inequalities that the implementation of the Strategies should eliminate. Primary among these factors are women's life cycle, centring on childbearing, and women's access to education, which factors condition the whole of a woman's life, and thereby her chances for advancement.

52. In addition, for most of the women in the world, the likelihood that they will have jobs, higher income, greater opportunities or programmes designed to meet their needs have been affected by the world economic situation of the 1980s. This situation affected development generally and, for many women, stopped progress in its tracks.

53. Since global and regional factors have shaped events in the first five years of the implementation of the Strategies, they are analysed forthwith. Regional variations are summarized in chapter III.

I. Global demographic and social trends in women's life cycles

54. According to United Nations estimates, of the 5.1 billion global population in mid-1988, 2.5 billion were women and, on the basis of current trends, 46 million females will enter the population annually up to the year 2000.

55. Women have to provide continual care for their children, for the sick when necessary, for the dis-abled in the family and, more frequently nowadays, for aging parents, their own and, often, their husband's.

56. What portion of her life a woman will have to spend in this caring role depends on the number of children she has had, on the extent to which her husband shares these duties and on whether other institutions of the society can provide support. While the concept that this responsibility should be shared within the family has been introduced, studies show that sharing is far from equal in most cases, and is largely impossible in households headed by women, the number of which is increasing. As a result, women have often found themselves having to give priority to their caring role over that of improving their status by remunerated employment. There is a long-term effect on women's advancement when daughters, rather than sons and daughters equally, are expected to provide the same service for the next generation on the same basis as their mother rather than developing their other capacities.

57. Most adult women are already embarked on a life cycle that limits their choices; in that sense, the demographic and social phenomena described below affect them. Changes in many cases can only occur in the next generation for girls not yet adult. Other changes can come about only if the adult women of today change their own circumstances, or when society itself changes its expectations. To clarify this, it is noted that most of the women who will be adults in the year 2000 are already adults. Those who will reach adulthood in 2000 are already in the school system or have not entered it and therefore have mostly lost their educational opportunities.

A. Fertility and child-bearing

58. The reproductive role of women has often been examined, but it is only recently that its implications for women's status has been generally realized. The time women devote to childbearing and the lack of social recognition of this time play a considerable role in their opportunity of participating, and on the mode and degree of their participation, in society (see table 2).

59. In many parts of the world, the ages of puberty and marriage have been traditionally linked. This link has now been broken in many countries, partly because of a younger age at menarche and a higher age at marriage, schooling for girls and the entry of women into the formal labour force.

60. There is now a transitional period between childhood and adulthood during which decisions have a considerable impact: a decision made in 1990 on attending school or getting married at 15 or 16 years of age will affect a woman for the remainder of her life. It will affect her chances of obtaining a job in the year 2010, and her level of pension, if any, well into the twenty-first century.

Table 2. *Demographic indicators for developed and developing countries, mid-1980s*
(Years or number)

Indicator	Developed countries	Developing countries		
		Africa	Asia	Latin America
Age at first marriage	23	17	17	19
Age at birth of first child	23	19	20	20
Interval between first and last birth (years)	7	17	16	16
Number of live births	2	7	7	6
Life expectancy at birth of last child	47	29	36	38

Source: *Data Highlights*, No. 5, February 1989.

Such decisions not only have individual consequences, but also affect society as a whole for decades.

61. In Europe, early fertility, that is between ages 14 and 18, is rare (35 births per 1,000). In Asia, the level is much higher (165 per 1,000); and in Latin America, it is even higher (214 per 1,000). In Africa, nearly one girl out of three has a child before age 18. Many of these girls will spend a life-time struggling to feed and raise children in frequently unfavourable conditions.

62. Generally, a woman who marries at an early age has little opportunity of continuing school or of competing on an equal basis for employment. Furthermore, parents may have less incentive to provide for their daughters' education if they are expected to marry at a very early age. Even if early marriage is not followed by early pregnancy, it is to be expected that the energies of such women will be mostly devoted to household duties. The figures for Africa and Asia speak for themselves, since, by their sixteenth birthday, 25 per cent of the girls are already married. In Latin America and the Caribbean, the rate is significantly lower at 15 per cent.

B. *Female illiteracy and education*

63. As stated in the Strategies "Education is the basis for the full promotion and improvement of the status of women. It is the basic tool that should be given to women in order to fulfil their role as full members of society." [11] There are different levels at which this tool can be available, starting from basic literacy and proceeding through the full range of third-level education. Education levels for today's adult have been dependent on age. Most adult women have already received as much education as they are likely to receive, unless special efforts are made.

1. *Literacy*

64. During the period 1960-1985, the global illiteracy rate for adults (15 years of age and over) of both sexes is estimated to have decreased from 39.3 to 27.7 per cent. However, the total number of illiterates has increased due to the considerable increase in population during the same period. In 1985, an estimated 561 million women were illiterate and constituted nearly two thirds of the 889 million illiterates in the world. Although the female illiteracy rate decreased from 45 per cent to 35 per cent during the same period, nearly half of the adult women in developing countries were still illiterate in 1985 (49%) (see also figure I).

65. While developed countries are close to eradicating illiteracy, developing countries, with the exception of those in Latin America, have some distance to go. The 36 least developed countries have the highest female illiteracy rate, an average of 78 per cent each. More disturbing is that the number of female illiterates is increasing not only in absolute terms but also in relation to males.

66. Although illiteracy rates are expected to continue to decline in the near future, the projected increase in the total adult population would also result in an increase in the total illiterate population. For example, even a drop of 5 percentage points in the world female illiteracy rate between 1985 and 2000 (and it dropped by only 3.5 points between 1960 and 1970) to a level of 29.9 per cent would still mean that the total number of female illiterates would be 637 million, an increase of 76 million over 1985. And the ratio of female to male illiterates would continue to be unfavourable.

2. *Education*

(a) *First-level*

67. Although female enrolment in first-level education has matched the growth of population since 1970, the ratio world-wide of girls to boys in education at the

11/ *Report of the World Conference to Review and Appraise the Achievements ...*, para. 163.

Figure I. Illiteracy rates, 1960-1985

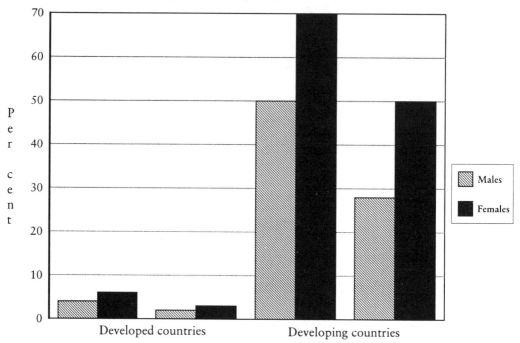

Source: Data Highlights, No. 6, figure 1.

Figure II. Distribution of females in first- and second-level education

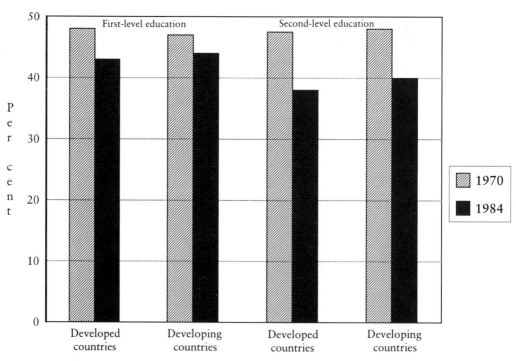

first level has hardly improved: from 80.4 girls to 100 boys in 1970 to 81.6 girls to 100 boys in 1984. To have achieved equality, over 59 million additional girls would have had to be enrolled. In 1984, there were still wide differences between regions, from near parity in the developed regions and in Latin America and the Caribbean to wide differences in Asia and Africa (see figure II).

(b) *Second-level*

68. The increase in absolute numbers for girls in second-level education was large between 1970 and 1984. World-wide, the number of girls in second-level schools increased by 66 per cent during the period. The increase was particularly impressive in developing countries (141%) over the 14-year period.

69 In developed countries, adjusted gross enrolment ratios, which relate the enrolment to the corresponding population age group, have been slightly higher for girls than for boys since 1975. In developing countries, the growth rate of enrolment for girls has been faster than for boys, although largely because of the girls' previously disadvantaged position. The result is that girls represented 38 per cent of the total number of enrolled children in the second level in 1970, and 41 per cent in 1984. However, if girls had had the same adjusted gross enrol-

ment ratio as boys (i.e. 42.7% instead of 29.7%) in developing countries, there would have been approximately 30 million more girls enrolled at the second level. This difference could have important implications for the preparation of future university students or females for the skilled labour force.

70. Besides the inequality observed in the enrolment of girls and boys, the chance for a girl in a developing country to be enrolled at the second level is much lower (29.7%) than that of her sister in a developed country (88.4%).

(c) *Third-level*

71. Third-level education is of particular importance for women as individuals and it largely determines the nature of their contribution to development and society. Furthermore, third-level education determines to a great extent who will be the future managers and decision makers at both the national and international levels. The relative enrolment of women in third-level education for developed and developing countries is shown in figure III.

72. Between 1970 and 1984, the enrolment of women in third-level education nearly doubled in developed countries and almost quadrupled in developing

Figure III. Distribution of women enrolled in third-level education
(Percentage)

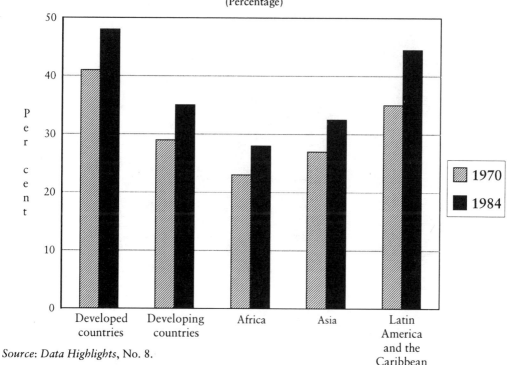

Source: Data Highlights, No. 8.

countries. Thus, the gap between the two groups of countries is closing rapidly although in 1984 developed countries still had only half as many female students as developing countries. There also remain considerable differences between developing regions.

73. It is clear that in developed countries women's enrolment has reached near equality with that of men's. In developing countries, the picture is different: in 1984 just over one third of the students were women and although a rapid increase in the number of women students can be observed, progress in closing the gap has been slow since the number of male students has also increased. In the developing regions, the Latin American and Caribbean countries have almost reached parity of enrolment. This contrasts with countries in the African and Asian regions where, in 1984, less than one third of the students were women, although it represents an improvement over 1970. The changes in the Latin American and the Caribbean countries can be expected to have a profound impact on those discriminatory aspects of culture that have been based on different levels of education for women and men.

74. The World Bank has found (1984) that the cost per student in higher education as a percentage of per capita gross national product (GNP) varies considerably, according to the country's level of development. Cost per student is 3.7 times (370%) the per capita GNP in developing countries in general; and 8 times (800%) the per capita GNP in sub-Saharan Africa, while in industrial countries it represents only 49 per cent of the per capita GNP.

II. Global economic trends affecting progress

75. Participation of women in the economy depends on economic conditions, which affect their opportunities, as well as on their employment history, which defines their experience.

A. *Employment*

76. Despite the improvements in women's access to education noted above, the long-term effects on women's employment in the formal sector have in general not improved. As can be seen from figure IV, in no region has women's participation in the economically active population reached parity with men's and in none has it improved recently.

77. This situation has potentially disturbing consequences, particularly for the prospects of achieving significant improvement by the year 2000. Projections by

Figure IV. Sex ratio in the economically active population, 1970, 1980 and 1985

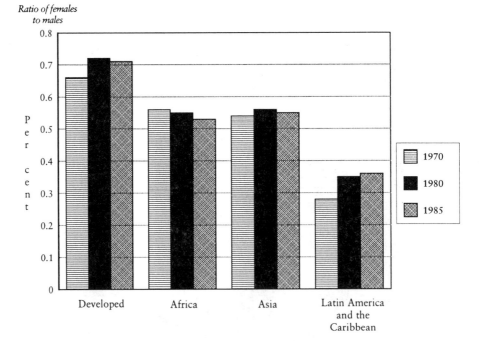

Source: Women's Indicators and Statistics database, compiled by the Statistical Office of the United Nations Secretariat.

Table 3. *Total activity rates in developed and developing countries*
(Percentage of the population)

	1975	1985	1990	2000	2025
Developed countries					
Males	57	58	58	58	54
Females	37	39	39	39	37
Developing countries					
Males	54	56	57	58	59
Females	30	31	30	30	30

Source: International Labour Organization, *Economically Active Population, Estimates and Projections 1950-2025* (Geneva, 1986).

Table 4. *Supplementary jobs that would be necessary for women
if their activity rates were to equal those of men*
(In thousands)

Group of countries	1990	2000	2025
Developed:			
Female active population	361 693	376 144	387 475
Supplementary jobs	118 805	120 971	123 139
Developing:			
Female active population	1 126 827	1 371 825	1 983 429
Supplementary jobs	515 894	649 758	984 590

Source: *1989 World Survey on the Role of Women in Development* (United Nations publication, Sales No. E.89.IV.2), p. 61.

the International Labour Organization (ILO), based on existing trends, suggest no improvement (see table 3). Not only is the activity rate for women unchanged, but also the gap with men is virtually unchanged, although a significant number of the future active population are not yet born or are still small children. One could expect that government policies would be able to modify this situation by the year 2025, especially taking into account the importance given to the employment of women in public policy during the Decade for Women.

78. The magnitude of the task can be seen by estimating the number of supplementary jobs that would be necessary if women had the same activity rates as men in their region, as is shown in table 4. These figures show that in developing countries half a billion more jobs would have to be created immediately, and that deficit is expected to double. The simple quantitative aspect raises questions of the kind of policies necessary or feasible to provide equal job opportunities for men and women. If these jobs are not created, most of the women who need them will find themselves in the informal sector with all the disadvantages that this represents, not only for themselves and

their families but also for the State, which will be faced by mounting demands for social support services.

B. *World economic situation and trends*

79. The economic conditions of the 1980s, by restricting growth and reducing national capacity to mobilize the public sector for social and economic change, have lessened the likelihood of rapid progress towards achieving the objectives of the Forward-looking Strategies.

80. The five years since the first *1989 World Survey* have been characterized by uneven economic growth that has often aggravated the differences between regions. In the older industrialized countries, a period of steady economic growth and slowing population growth, often accompanied by lower energy and food costs, has meant an unprecedented increase in material consumption. In some countries in Asia, there has been steady growth through trade and manufacturing that has led to rising levels of prosperity. In most developing regions, Africa and Latin America and the Caribbean, economic stagnation or negative growth, continued population increase

and the prolonged international debt crisis and adjustment policies designed to deal with this have constrained the activities of women as individuals, as carers and providers for families and households, and as participants in the practical development of their countries.

81. Recession and economic restructuring in the face of external debt have led Governments to focus on these problems, often to the neglect of longer term issues that have a direct bearing on the advancement of women. At the same time, pre-existing conditions of inequality—in health and nutrition, levels of literacy and training, access to education and economic opportunity, and in participation in decision-making at all levels—between women and men have sometimes been exacerbated both by the crises themselves and by the policies adopted to cope with them. It is this that gives the current economic situation its gender dimension. Yet economic recovery and advancement towards the social and political goals of development require the contribution of all.

82. All development will be delayed without economic growth. Without it, the pursuit of equality could become a destructive competition between the sexes for ever-diminishing resources. However, there is no automatic link between economic growth and the advancement of women, even in a limited material sense. The issue is how to accompany policies to restore and stimulate growth with programmes to eliminate basic inequalities in terms of access to services and opportunities.

83. Although both women and men suffer the effects of the crisis, it is more often women who are willing or forced to modify their lives to adjust to the changed economic circumstances of their households. The forms of this adaptation vary, in accordance with the level of development of their countries and their own standards of living.

84. Data on employment and unemployment are inconclusive as to the effects of the crisis and the ensuing adjustment on women's employment conditions. Some of the countries that underwent severe crisis and strict adjustment measures showed that women's employment grew, while in others women's employment declined. It is likely that a first effect of the crisis might have been a withdrawal of women from the labour market, while a further deepening of the crisis forced women back to the labour market, possibly into occupations of lower productivity and income. Unemployment is reported to have grown more for men than for women during the crisis, while it is possible to detect a longer term decline in women's employment in its immediate aftermath. It is possible that women are not the first to be laid off, but they are certainly not the first to be re-hired when the economy picks up again.

85. One effect of the economic situation observed in the *1989 World Survey* was a tendency for improvements in the relative position of girls in school enrolment to stop temporarily. There was a tendency in those countries where adjustment was particularly severe for girls to be withdrawn from school, presumably to help families in economic activity or as substitute carers.

86. The level of nutrition of a population is sensitive to levels of income. Malnutrition is reported to have increased in many of the countries that applied adjustment measures in the 1980s. The decline in the purchasing power of the poor has worsened nutrition. Whether there has been a systematic sex bias in the distribution of food within poor families in favour of their male members is difficult to say because of lack of data.

87. On the basis of research made in several countries on intra-household feeding patterns, which proved that women tended to eat less and also to eat less nutritive food, it is possible to argue that, in periods of declining family incomes, women have suffered malnutrition more than men. Reliable data on maternal mortality, to support this argument, are not available for a sufficient number of countries. Because of the long-term trends towards a reduction in these rates, due for example to better hygiene, wider provision of medical assistance to pregnant women, and better overall health conditions since childhood, the effects of the crisis tend to be absorbed. Also in Latin America, where the debt crisis was felt with greater strength, maternal mortality rates show a constant decline in the 1980s, with the exception of a few countries and a few years, which are better explained by unreliable statistics.

III. Regional trends and developments

88. Regional appraisals have been made by the five regional commissions. They, like the statistical material presented previously, show that there are also common issues and problems that, although they vary by degree, characterize all regions.

A. *Africa**

89. Structural adjustment policies have been found to be gender biased since they ignore the unpaid labour of women. The fact is that unpaid labour in villages and families is the final lifeline for people all over the world when macro-economic measures do not work or even collapse.

1. *Employment*

90. In the services sector, there is a marked improvement in female employment in most African countries even though the proportion of women professionals has increased less rapidly than that of men. The sectoral

*Prepared by the Economic Commission for Africa.

distribution in agriculture, services and industry (1981-1987) shows that the participation of women in Africa as a whole is highest in agriculture and lowest in industry. However, the situation varies from subregion to subregion and from country to country within the subregions.

91. Employment in the informal sector continues to play a key role and to provide hope for survival for a greater majority of women and the urban poor. In many countries, particularly in West Africa, a great many women are involved in the informal sector, usually in small-scale projects.

92. In general, although many countries are involved in income-generating activities, e.g. handicrafts, gardening and textiles, many of these are centred on charitable activities. Projects in the informal sector should become more viable, economically sound and self-supporting. In some instances, it has been reported that women who own businesses are confronted with numerous economic constraints that reduce the viability of their business.

2. Education and training

93. During the last 10 years, there has been modest progress in the participation of female students at all levels of the school system, particularly at the primary school level. The increased enrolment of girls in primary school is largely the result of government development plans and the fact that education at the primary level is free in many countries. The number of female students decreases, however, at the higher secondary level and hence at university level because of the female dropout rate in most African countries. There are certain social and cultural factors that negatively affect female participation at higher levels of the school system, such as the increasing rate of teenage pregnancies and marriage in secondary schools that contribute significantly to the high female dropout rate.

94. With respect to non-formal education, national literacy programmes in several African countries have been the largest sustained adult education programmes with women being the majority of the participants. Efforts are being made to link these national literacy programmes with functional skills, income-generating activities and extension services.

95. Fewer girls than boys are enrolled in science subjects. Also, the majority of girls and women are cut off at an early age from a wide range of careers and interests in science-based training programmes. Many girls leaving school operate in an environment full of machinery and labour-saving devices. They should be exposed to science so that they can effectively participate in science- and technological-based activities.

3. Law and legislation

96. The Convention on the Elimination of All Forms of Discrimination against Women is an international bill of rights for women. What is required now is the implementation of the Convention by, for example, revising some laws such as the marriage, employment and education acts, to accommodate women's equality issues. Some Governments are already doing this by establishing law review commissions.

97. In general, the majority of women in Africa are not aware of their legal rights. In addition to establishing law review commissions, action-oriented strategies with a view to changing the socio-economic and legal position of women need to be developed.

4. Women at the decision-making level and legislation

98. The visible and public exercise of power by women is controversial in many societies. In most African countries, very few women are in politics. Political participation is a key issue for women because it is an indicator of their status as well as a tool to improve their condition in society. In many African countries, women have the right to vote and they do vote; the mere act of voting, however, cannot be regarded as a measure of political consciousness or participation. In many instances, poor rural and urban women are mobilized during political campaigns to vote. In such situations, women vote in high numbers but they do not participate in any other political activities, particularly at the decision-making level.

99. Although there has been an increase in the number of women entering the arena of decision-making and power, their path has not been easy. They had and still have to struggle against considerable odds in order to succeed in politics as well as getting into key positions in the government, parastatal organizations and institutions. There are still very few women in those areas of activity, to which access is, in most cases, restricted to those who hold higher academic qualifications. This situation continues to limit women's access to economic, social and political power. Thus, for instance, it is still very difficult for women to gain a foothold in those professions that bestow recognition and influence, especially when they are financially highly rewarding.

100. In general, although the number of women in high positions and at the decision-making level has increased, the situation is still very unsatisfactory.

5. Problems and constraints

(a) Structure

101. Structure is one of the major problems faced by Women in Development (WID) programmes, espe-

cially the location of women's affairs units in ministries. In most cases, national machinery is not located at a high central position within the government bureaucracy, is inadequately financed and is usually understaffed.

(b) Policy measures

102. Many countries have not yet adopted a national policy on women in development. This is a *sine qua non* for increased participation of women in national development.

6. Conclusions

103. Since 1985 and within the framework of the Strategies, some social and economic changes in favour of women in most countries in Africa have been apparent in different sectors. Governments have increasingly recognized the significant contribution of women to national development as evidenced by the efforts made by some to strengthen women's national machinery and women's affairs units in ministries.

104. The implementation of the Strategies, however, has been slow because of lack of financial and human resources, lack of national policy and lack of commitment by some Governments to WID.

105 Nevertheless, even though it is an exceedingly slow process, changes have occurred. In the employment sector, there is an undeniable tendency for women to move into the professional categories that were occupied almost exclusively by men until recently. In education and training, there has been an increase of girls' enrolment at all levels of the education system.

106. Much indeed still remains to be done, but the essential point is that Governments have to make crucial commitments if they are to implement the Forward-looking Strategies. This is why the Fourth Regional Conference on the Integration of Women in Development on the Implementation of the Forwardlooking Strategies on the Advancement of Women in Africa was a forum to define more clearly and set attainable, realistic targets for the region.

B. Asia and the Pacific*

107. In preparation for review and appraisal, the Economic and Social Commission for Asia and the Pacific (ESCAP) monitored the implementation of the Strategies in the Asian and Pacific region by means of a questionnaire sent to national focal points in April 1988. This report is based partly on the responses from nine countries.

1. Equality

108. The reports submitted by many of the signatory countries to the Convention express the view that the Convention has strengthened each country's political will to plan and monitor systematically its efforts to eliminate discrimination.

109. Many of those countries had instituted most of the legal measures prescribed in the Convention even before becoming a party to it. Some cite the Decade for Women as having stimulated the reform of laws that discriminated against women and the adoption of new ones that provide equal rights and opportunities.

110. In some countries, discriminatory legislative provisions in the social, economic and political spheres continue to exist, including provisions in the civil, penal and commercial codes and certain administrative rules and regulations. Civil codes in some instances have not been adequately studied to determine which laws still discriminate against women, and what is the legal capacity and status of women, married women in particular, regarding nationality, inheritance, ownership and control of property, freedom of movement, and the custody and nationality of children. In addition, there are cases where certain aspects of the law (e.g. customary provisions) are operating within multiple and conflicting legal systems.

111. Although much progress has been made in legislation, measures are necessary for its effective implementation and enforcement. De facto discrimination, particularly with reference to marital or family status, persists despite legislative action. Due to various degrees of legal literacy, the law as recourse has not automatically benefited all women equally. Socio-economic inequalities also affect women's ability to exercise their legal rights without fear of recrimination or intimidation.

112. Bridging the gap between the elimination of *de jure* and de facto discrimination against women is considered by those countries to be their most difficult task in attaining the goal of equal rights for women.

(a) Equality in social participation

113. Women's non-governmental organizations, which were strengthened during the Decade for Women, have continued to complement government efforts in promoting gender awareness among the public in order to change attitudes towards women. But there is evidence that not much progress has been achieved in increasing women's participation in mass communication media, which has been one of the major instruments propagating their traditional roles.

(b) Equality in political participation and decision-making

114. It is reported that women are becoming more visible in political life as they occupy a wider range of

*Prepared by the Economic and Social Commission for Asia and the Pacific.

public sector positions, such as ministers, directors, deputy directors, justices and local government heads. Although they still constitute a relatively small percentage of those holding public office at the national, provincial and local levels, such representation has been increasing in some countries. Women's participation at the local and village level public offices also continues to increase, though remaining low.

115. Effective participation of women in development has been impeded by the difficult international economic situation, the debt crisis, poverty, continued population growth, rising divorce rates, increasing migration and the growing incidence of female-headed households. Neither the expansion of employment for women nor the recognition that women constitute a significant proportion of producers has been accompanied by social adjustments to ease women's burden of child and household care. In fact, the economic recession had led to a reduction in investments, particularly in those services that allow greater societal sharing of the social and economic costs of child care and housework.

(c) *Institutional structures for women's advancement*

116. National focal points for the integration of women in the development process have been established, mostly during the Decade for Women. However, those focal points continue in most developing countries to be confronted by lack of resources and staff, high staff turnover, low commitment of staff to women's concerns, and lack of political and administrative mandates to influence policy formulation and coordinate the programmes on women of different government agencies. However, a few countries report the creation of a women's unit in each line agency to take responsibility for integrating women's concerns into the agency's policies and programmes.

2. *Development*

117. Since formal development plans usually serve as the source of government mandates, it has become imperative for women's concerns to be integrated into mainstream development planning. The continued low priority given to women in development planning is shown by the nature of planning for women's advancement in the region. Most countries report the inclusion of women's concerns in the social sector chapter of the national development plan. Some cite the inclusion of provisions on women in the different sections of the plan.

118. Barriers to women's equal opportunities in employment continue: high unemployment disadvantages women relative to men on account of women's lower skill levels, traditional attitudes concerning their role and protective legislation tending to raise labour costs incurred for hiring women workers. Complex protective legislation—such as maternity benefits, special health-care services, the right to protection of health and safety in work conditions and other labour standards, and social security coverage—had been adopted in many developing countries prior to the Decade for Women. Many of the protective laws are often violated with the consent of workers, including women, who fear for their jobs.

119. The rapid increase in married women's employment over the past decade is an important emerging trend. Possible explanations cited are the falling birth rate, lightened domestic chores and child-rearing owing to improved living standards, and a greater desire for self-realization among educated women. However, in the case of developing countries, the trend can be explained more by the economic necessity for additional family members to enter the labour force in order to augment family income. Even with the increasing participation by women, they continue to bear the primary responsibility for child care and domestic work in both developed and developing countries. That double burden partly explains women's relative disadvantage in employment, where interruptions in their working lives and preference for part-time work contribute to their narrower career opportunities.

(a) *Health*

120. Women's organizations in many developing countries have been involved in the local and national level planning and implementation and monitoring of health care. Some countries or areas have implemented measures to ensure women's participation in higher professional and managerial positions in health institutions.

121. Various health education and information programmes are reported by most countries. Programmes for training of nurses' aides, primary health care, family welfare and other public health and social services programmes are also used as vehicles to promote the proper use of essential drugs by women and their families. Most countries cite a variety of ongoing programmes that provide women with public health and related social welfare services. Programmes to promote the development and use of locally produced food for weaning infants have been established in most of them.

(b) *Education*

122. The main obstacle to women's emancipation is the pervasive influence of traditional social attitudes and customs, deeply rooted in what are referred to in

some cases as the feudal patriarchal system. This obstacle has been identified by almost all countries, regardless of their level of development and socio-economic system. Those social attitudes and values, exacerbated by pervasive poverty in many developing countries, are said to have resulted in different levels of human capital among men as compared with women, and explain, to a great extent, women's continued disadvantages in society. It is also observed that the disadvantages of women in rural areas are more severe.

123. To ensure that males and females have equal access to education at all levels, orientation for policy makers, planners and educational personnel and for parents has been undertaken. Although equal educational opportunities are guaranteed in the constitutions of many countries, women have often been confined to traditional fields of education. Efforts have been made in several countries or areas to encourage women to acquire education in science and technology, and other vocational training. To enable women to take up science, management and other technical subjects at all levels, incentives (scholarships) and counselling services have been provided to women in a number of countries.

124. Efforts have also been made to promote the functional literacy of women, with special emphasis on health, nutrition and economic skills for urban and rural women.

(c) Food, water and agriculture

125. Many countries report programmes that have been developed by the Government to increase productive capability in food production, off-farm employment opportunities, access to energy sources, safe and sufficient water, and irrigation facilities for rural women. However, the inheritance laws in a number of countries continue to include discriminatory provisions against women in rural areas.

(d) Industry, trade and commercial services

126. Government agencies in a number of countries have coordinated activities to integrate women's concerns in industrial policy-making. These agencies have initiated and implemented programmes and projects addressing the needs of small- and medium-scale enterprises in priority sectors and have assisted in developing women's associations in industries in the private sector. Skills training, credit and marketing assistance, technological assistance and other productivity guidelines have also been provided to women entrepreneurs and potential entrepreneurs. Support programmes are carried out in some countries to encourage women in the informal sector.

(e) Science and technology

127. Only a few countries have conducted evaluation studies on the role of women in scientific and technological development.

(f) Communications

128. Some countries cite the active role of non-governmental organizations in communication and mass media activities concerning women. Most Governments have no policies or guidelines to influence the media to promote equality between men and women.

(g) Housing, settlement, community development and transport

129. Only a few countries have given active consideration to women's needs of housing, settlement, community development and transport.

130. Government-supported programmes aimed at increasing women's land ownership and tenancy rights are reported by several countries.

131. In the transport sector, women participated in decision-making regarding issues of transport subsidies, choice of technology and transport routes. Women's role as operators and owners of the means of transport have been promoted.

(h) Energy

132. In a few countries, women participate in energy policy and strategy formulation. On energy use and energy conservation at household level, women are usually direct targets of campaign measures. Some countries cite major obstacles that authorities encounter in promoting equal participation of women in energy planning and management. Those most frequently cited are lack of gender awareness by the public, lack of appropriate education, skills and information among women, and men's dominant role as decision makers in that field.

(i) Environment

133. Little has been achieved in creating alternative means of livelihood for women and their families who have been deprived of their traditional livelihood owing to environmental degradation. Programmes, either informational or educational, have been organized by some countries in order to create awareness of environmental issues and to increase women's potential contribution in conserving and improving the environment.

(j) Social services

134. Some countries and areas have undertaken activities in order to raise public awareness of the need for shared responsibilities between men and women in

producing and rearing children. Measures have been introduced to provide shelter and support to abused women and children.

3. *Peace*

135. Special peace programmes with women's participation have been organized by several countries as part of the World Disarmament Campaign.

4. *Areas of special concern*

136. Assistance to women affected by drought and other natural disasters in some countries has been provided in the form of food security programmes and income-generating activities.

137. Destitution as an extreme form of poverty has had far-reaching effects on women, and the number of women affected has been increasing steadily. Governments have undertaken various measures to satisfy the special needs and concerns of destitute women.

138. The problem of victims of trafficking and involuntary prostitution constitute one of the most urgent concerns. Most responding Governments have taken legislative action to suppress the exploitation of women and to punish with imprisonment those trafficking in women or forcing women into prostitution. Some Governments have been providing social rehabilitation programmes. Programmes to increase public awareness on violence against women or prostitution have also been undertaken.

139. Women as the sole supporters of their families face particular social, economic and legal difficulties. Some Governments have given special attention to this group of women by ensuring their equal access to resources.

140. Almost all Governments provide some support for refugees and displaced women by means of food aid, education and training, health care, employment and economic opportunities.

C. *Europe**

141. Attention in the market economies of Europe and North America has been centred on the participation of women in the economy and on their situation in the labour market. It is noted in the latest *Economic Survey of Europe in 1987-1988* 12/ that one of the major dynamic factors during the last decade in employment growth was the rapid rise in the participation of women in the labour force. In 1987, in 15 countries of Western Europe combined, 60 per cent of women were members of the labour force, compared with just over 50 in 1975. On average, this implies nearly a percentage point increase in women's activity rates every year. While these have been increasing continuously during the 12-year

period considered, the participation rate of men has steadily fallen (from about 87 to 84 per cent between 1970 and 1987). As a result women accounted for more than two thirds of the growth of the labour force since 1975, and their share in the total increased from about 37 per cent in 1975 to nearly 42 per cent in 1987.

142. Experience over a longer period, however, suggests that the response of female participation rates to economic fluctuations is counter-cyclical and in the past few years the growth rate of the female labour force, compared to that of males, has not been as rapid as previously, especially during the recession of the early 1980s. With the exception of only three countries, the average annual growth rates of the female labour force between 1983 and 1986, which can be considered the period of recovery, were lower than in the four preceding years. The estimates for 1987, however, suggest a weakening of this downward trend: female labour-force growth still declined in comparison with the average for 1983-1986 in six countries, but stabilized or increased in the others.

143. Although women have entered the labour market in increasing numbers, their position in it seems to be weaker than that of men, as reflected in unemployment rates. For the 15 countries combined, the average unemployment rate of women in 1987 was close to 1 percentage point higher than that of men. With few exceptions, the data for individual countries confirm the higher rate of unemployment among women.

144. The estimates suggest that the difference between male and female unemployment rates has tended to narrow during the recession. Whereas in 1979 the unemployment rate of women in the 15 countries combined was nearly 2 percentage points higher than that of men, in 1983 it was less than half a point more. The data for 1987 suggest, moreover, that the difference between the two rates has increased again, but is still not as large as in 1979. Although account must be taken of the fact that unemployment in many countries is still very high and, consequently, that present conditions cannot be considered as "normal", the female-male difference in unemployment rates was less than 1 percentage point in 1987.

D. *Latin America and the Caribbean***

145. The region of Latin America and the Caribbean is currently experiencing the most severe economic and social crisis of the past 50 years. One of the effects of the crisis and of the debt has been an accelerating decline in

*Prepared by the Economic Commission for Europe
**Prepared by the Economic Commission for Latin America and the Caribbean.
12/ United Nations publication, Sales No. E.88.II.E.1.

the quality of life of the population, which has had a particularly dramatic effect on the living conditions of women. There has been a sharp drop in the funds earmarked for the implementation of social policies, particularly those relating to education, health and housing, and the social well-being of the population has been strongly affected.

1. Employment

146. Although participation in the labour force varies in accordance with the circumstances in each country, the incorporation of women has occurred on a scale that was unimaginable 30 years ago. The number of women in the labour force of Latin America and the Caribbean increased threefold between 1950 and 1980, rising from 10 million to 32 million.

147. None the less, the deterioration of the employment situation brought on by the crisis severely affects women, who form a majority of the unemployed and of those in the informal sector.

148. The services sector remains predominant in the economic participation of women and the process of development of services continues. Towards 1980, the percentages corresponding to this sector fluctuated between 38 per cent and 55 per cent of the total number of active women. Although their make up varies, personal services remain important, while the role played by social services is increasing. In most countries, office employees constitute the second most numerous group, and are steadily increasing.

149. The work performed by housewives cannot be ignored. Between 30 and 50 per cent of women over 25 are performing unpaid domestic tasks.

2. Education

150. A tremendous expansion has taken place in formal education and a growing number of women are enrolled in it. However, there are major differences between countries, between rural and urban areas, and between native, indigenous and black populations. In some countries, the illiteracy rates are as high as 90 per cent for elderly women, while in the 15-19 year age group, they do not exceed 15 per cent, and are the same for both sexes. In addition, in some countries, particularly those with high illiteracy rates, women still represent a minority of school enrolments and a majority of school drop-outs, which increases the difficulties they encounter in obtaining employment.

151. On the one hand, opportunities are now nearly equal at high-income levels; on the other, the most notable instances of discrimination have persisted among the rural poor and different ethnic and racial groups. Higher education for women still relates to skills considered as being most appropriate for women culturally, although there is no doubt that women are increasingly beginning to educate themselves for work and not merely to perform a traditional social role.

3. Health

152. In health, the majority of countries still fail to provide adequate free public services for a large percentage of the population, and curative medicine predominates. Health services tend to be concentrated in the urban areas. Since many of them are offered on a private basis, access is difficult for the majority of the population. Women's child-bearing role creates specific health requirements. Very frequent pregnancies combined with poor nutrition and lack of rest lead to debilitation, malnutrition and fatigue, resulting in high indices of mortality in childbirth. Adolescent pregnancies, which are on the rise, and induced abortions, which are very numerous and for the most part carried out clandestinely, constitute a threat to the lives of girls and women. All this is often compounded by cultural factors that invite discrimination against girls with regard to medical attention and nutrition. Despite the gravity of the situation, no progress has been made in the area of health and sex education for the population in general and for young people in particular.

4. Legislation

153. Legislation shows substantial progress. More than three quarters of the countries of the region have ratified or acceded to the Convention on the Elimination of All Forms of Discrimination against Women. The majority of them have also adopted domestic measures in the legal field in order to apply the Convention. In addition, in recent years most of the Governments in the region have set up specialized agencies to help to raise the status of women and have adopted plans and policies designed to ensure equality of opportunity. These national mechanisms are attached to ministries as government departments, divisions or offices in the family, social welfare, education, cultural, labour-planning and economic development sectors. However, most do not have enough resources to implement their programmes. Several countries have drawn up projects to amend provisions that discriminate against women, particularly provisions in their labour code (e.g. maternity privileges) and their penal code (e.g. rape). De facto discrimination still exists however, because of failure to comply with the law or the provisions in the covenants.

5. The family

154. The sharp deterioration of the current economic situation in Latin America and the Caribbean has resulted in serious family problems, which affect women

more than men. The crisis has caused traditions to deteriorate, the result often being instability and violence detrimental to women and children. In some countries, migration from the countryside to the city has increased, as has the number of households headed by women. In addition, the traditional allocation of roles, in which housework and the raising of children are regarded as the responsibility for women and not of men, persists.

6. General participation

155. Women, who represent half the population and in many countries more than half the electorate, still participate only minimally in the executive and legislative organs of their countries. The structure of their political participation is eminently pyramidal: the majority of them are among the lower party echelons and the higher the level of leadership, the fewer the women in it. While the political awareness of women has increased, significant obstacles to their participation in political life remain.

156. In recent decades in low-income districts of major cities, new social movements have emerged that are comprised of and led by women. Women form mothers' clubs, take part in social welfare programmes run by churches, take the lead in movements to obtain day-care centres or health facilities, participate in voluntary and vocational associations, establish organizations to design survival strategies to deal with the grave situation that they face or form pressure groups to obtain housing or infrastructure services. They also take part in associations of professionals and producers, federations of women employed in different branches of production and federations of peasant women.

157. Participation by women in social movements and their composing a social movement are phenomena that seem to suggest a broad cultural transformation linked to new approaches to policy-making. Women have played a basic role in the articulation of grievances and demands that they be settled. In this process, non-governmental organizations have made a decisive contribution to the design of projects for mobilizing and assisting women, from the low-income sector in particular.

E. Western Asia*

158. Arab women confront numerous development challenges. They are required to produce and participate in the process of development in all its aspects: economic, social and political. Women face obstacles to development deriving from the historical economic and other structural factors that have shaped the societies in which they live. Included in these are cultural values that, on the one hand, may emphasize materialism and, on the other, may call for women to return to their reproductive

and nurturing roles while relinquishing their other societal participatory roles.

159. Statistics on female participation in the region are often inadequate, but an examination of these, together with other information of a legal, economic or social type, suggests that in many countries, the Forward-looking Strategies have not yet been implemented.

1. Equality

160. Although the content of the Convention appears to be included in most of the constitutions of Arab States, only a few of them have ratified it, some with reservations on key provisions. Few States have implemented the Convention in the form of binding enabling legislation. The Convention has been met with resistance from fundamentalist political movements that allege that it equates men and women in inheritance, which is said to be against the teaching of Islam.

161. Inequality is still manifest in the Arab region in labour legislation as well as personal status legislation and laws pertaining to the right of children to obtain their mother's nationality. Moreover, in some Arab countries women are forbidden by law to be in certain leadership positions and to follow such occupations as that of judge or president, or even to participate in the country's legislative bodies.

162. Two factors are involved: (a) current ideological trends encourage women to stay at home in order to alleviate problems of unemployment; and .(b) laws do not offer sufficient protection to the majority of working women. Most women engaged in the labour market are not protected by law, by virtue of the fact that they are mainly agricultural labourers or working in the informal sector, although Arab labour legislation has abided by most regional and international recommendations concerning the protection of women against certain tedious jobs.

163 In terms of political participation, Palestinian women are highly active both in the occupied West Bank and Gaza Strip in activities related to the *Intifadah*, during which many have been imprisoned. Palestinian women are also active in organizations ranging from medical ones, such as the Red Crescent, to more directly political ones.

2. Development

164. More women are benefiting from education in the Arab world, but illiteracy continues to be a major impediment to woman's development and one that places them at a disadvantage with men. Moreover female participation in primary and preparatory education is

*Prepared by the Economic and Social Commission for Western Asia.

fairly low both in absolute terms and relative to the male population. The same holds true with regard to secondary education.

165. However, this situation may change rapidly if the trends recently identified by the United Nations Educational, Scientific and Cultural Organization (UNESCO) continue, since progress in women's participation on behalf of women is improving more rapidly than in some other developing regions.

166. The participation of women in the Arab labour force is fairly low. In 1975, an estimated 3.5 million females were in the Arab labour force, the equivalent of 9 per cent of the total. This number increased by 1980 to 4.2 million, but still constituted 9 per cent of the total labour force. Estimated projections for the year 2000 do not promise a marked improvement in the numbers of working women. However, the very few working women might be due to the concept of work employed in those statistics, that is, the highest percentage of female participation appears in those economies that are basically agricultural. Female agricultural labour is mostly accepted, however, a large proportion of female agricultural labour is unpaid.

167. Statistics on health conditions for women are scarce. However, the conditions of armed conflict under which women live in the area affect health conditions as does the fact that budgets allocated to defence in most Arab States are increasing, to the detriment of budgets allocated for other areas such as education and health.

168. A last important indicator of women's poor health conditions is the high fertility rates that greatly tax women's biological role. Moreover, most women in the Arab world suffer from malnutrition and the spread of anaemia.

3. *Peace*

169. Little improvement was noted during the Decade for Women in peace conditions in the region. The resolution of the conflict between Iran, Islamic Republic of and Iraq has been a positive factor. However, many Arab women, particularly Palestinian women, are still affected by the situations of armed conflict and occupation in which they find themselves.

PART TWO

REVIEW AND APPRAISAL AT THE NATIONAL LEVEL

170. Review and appraisal at the national level is largely based on what Governments perceive to have been their achievements. Absence of information may well reflect areas in which progress has not been sufficient to report. Considered together with global and regional analyses that have shown a marked slowing of progress,

the national reports suggest areas in which, on the one hand, greater action could lead to renewed progress and, on the other hand, new tactics must be adopted to ensure implementation of the Strategies.

IV. **Equality**

A. *Implementation of international standards at the national level*

1. *Convention on the Elimination of All Forms of Discrimination against Women*

171. Under the theme of equality, the main international instrument is the Convention. Signing the Convention means a declaration of intent by the State concerned, but not a commitment to implement the Convention. Only when the Convention is ratified or acceded to is a State bound to implement it.

172. By 31 October 1989, the Convention had been ratified or acceded to by 99 States (60%) out of a total of 169 States Members of the United Nations or observers; another 18 (11%) States have signed but not ratified the Convention; and 52 (30%) States have neither signed nor ratified, and are thus completely outside the Convention's coverage (see table 5). There are notable regional differences in acceptance of the Convention. Since the populations of countries vary, it is of interest to determine how much of the population in different regions is covered by the Convention. Over 60 per cent of the population of each region lives in a country that is a State party to the Convention. In Latin America, it is nearly 95 per cent. See figures V and VI.

173. CEDAW has met annually since 1982 and, in addition to reviewing reports of States parties, has made general recommendations to them. CEDAW recommended, in 1987, that States parties should adopt education and public information programmes that would help to eliminate prejudices and existing practices that hinder full social equality of women (Convention, article 5, and Forward-looking Strategies, paragraph 39). CEDAW appealed to States parties to consider withdrawing reservations made by 39 States, that appeared to be incompatible with the object and purpose of the Convention.

174. CEDAW also recommended that States parties should "make more use of temporary special measures such as positive action, preferential treatment or quota systems to advance women's integration into education, the economy, politics and employment. 13/ Such measures were considered particularly important with regard to article 8 of the Convention to ensure women the opportunity of representing their Government at the

13/ *Official Records of the General Assembly, Forty-third Session, Supplement No. 38* (A/43/38), para. 770.

Table 5. *Number and percentage of countries within each region having ratified or signed the Convention on the Elimination of All Forms of Discrimination against Women*

	Ratified before 1985		Ratified after 1985		Signed but not ratified		Not signed		Total	
	Number	(%)	Number	(%)	Number	(%)	Number	(%)	Number	(%)
Developed	23	66	7	20	3	9	2	6	35	100
Asia and the Pacific	12	25	3	6	5	10	28	58	48	100
Africa	17	33	11	22	6	12	17	33	51	100
Latin America and the Caribbean	23	66	3	9	4	12	5	14	35	100
Total	75		24		18		52		169	
Percentage	45		14		11		30		100	

international level and of participating in the work of international organizations without any discrimination. CEDAW further recommended that States parties should establish and/or strengthen national machinery at a high level of Government, monitor the situation of women comprehensively and carry out strategies and measures to eliminate discrimination. 13/ CEDAW also recommended that States parties should include in their periodic reports information on critical areas in the implementation of articles of the Convention that protect women against all kinds of violence in everyday life (A/44/38, p. 81), that ensure the application in practice of the principle of equal remuneration for work of equal value to overcome the gender-segregation in the labour market. It made a strong appeal for national statistics to ensure that data could be disaggregated according to gender (A/44/38, p. 82).

2. *Application of International Labour Organization conventions with reference to the Forward-looking Strategies*

175. The Forward-looking Strategies recommend that special measures should be taken to ratify the ILO conventions on equality of opportunities and treatment and equal pay. 14/ Since 1985, the Equal Remuneration Convention (No. 100), 1951, has been ratified by two countries: Cyprus (19 November 1987) and Malta (9 June 1988), bringing the total number of ratifications to 109. The Discrimination (Employment and Occupation) Convention (No. 111), 1958, has been ratified by three further countries: Cameroon (13 May 1988); San Marino (19 December 1986) and Democratic Yemen (3 January 1989), bringing the total number of ratifications to 110. These two instruments are among the ILO instruments that have received the largest number of ratifications.

176. In 1986, 1987, 1988 and 1989, the Committee of Experts on the Application of Conventions and Recommendations made observations on the application of the Equal Remuneration Convention (No. 100). The reports on the application of the Convention were due, under the Constitution of ILO, article 22, in 1986 and 1988.

177. Satisfaction on the progress in application of the Convention related to the following countries: 1986: Guyana, the Netherlands; 1987: Canada, Denmark, Norway; and 1988: Canada, Finland, France (New Caledonia), Guinea-Bissau, Mozambique. The information obtained on applications of this Convention was also considered by the Committee of Experts on the Application of Conventions and Recommendations at the relevant sessions of the International Labour Conference. The Committee of the Conference more particularly examined the cases of the following countries: 1986: Switzerland; 1987: the United Kingdom of Great Britain and Northern Ireland, Austria, Jamaica; 1988: India, Switzerland; and the United Kingdom.

178. In accordance with the Constitution, article 19, the Governing Body of ILO invited Governments to report on their law and practice respecting equal pay for men and women workers, as laid down in the Equal Pay Convention (No. 100) and Recommendation (No. 90), 1951. Reports were submitted by 130 States and six non-metropolitan territories. The report of the Committee of Experts 15/ on equal remuneration was considered by the Committee on the Application of Conventions

14/ *Report of the World Conference to Review and Appraise the Achievements ...*, para. 72.

15/ *Report of the Committee of Experts on the Application of Conventions and Recommendations*, Report III (Part 4B), International Labour Conference, 72nd, 73rd, 75th and 76th sessions, Geneva.

Figure V. Distribution of countries within each region having signed or ratified the Convention on the Elimination of All Forms of Discrimination against Women

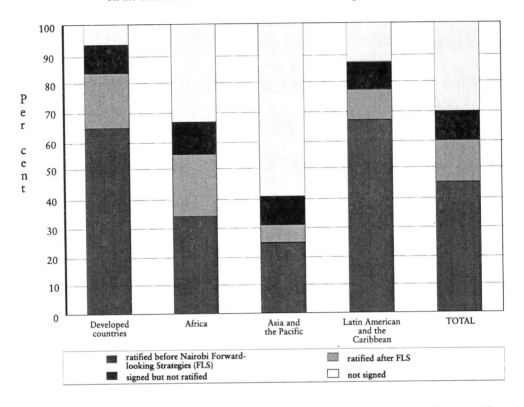

Figure VI. Distribution of the population by region and the countries by region, covered by the ratification of the Convention on the Elimination of All Forms of Discrimination against Women

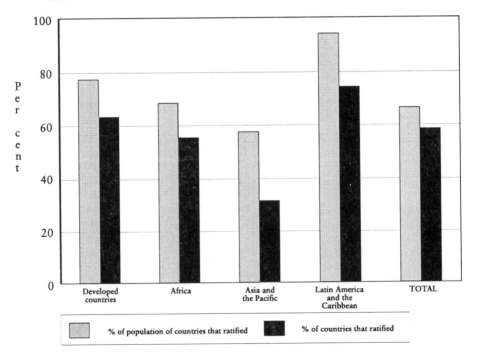

and Recommendations of the Conference, 16/ which expressed its gratification at the excellent quality of the survey, which embodied a thorough analysis of approaches and problems encountered in applying the principle of equal pay for equal work. The Committee concluded that ILO should continue to assign particular importance to the matter of equal pay, as basic to the acknowledgement of the value and dignity of all persons.

179. In 1986, 1987, 1988 and 1989, implementation of the Discrimination (Employment and Occupation) Convention (No. 111), 1958, was the subject of observations by the Committee on the Application of Conventions and Recommendations. 17/ The reports on application of the Convention were due, under article 22 of the ILO Constitution, in 1987 and 1989.

180. The Committee was able to express satisfaction relating to certain measures taken by the Governments to promote equality of opportunities and treatment free from sex discrimination: 1986: the Netherlands; 1987: Australia, the Central African Republic, Finland, Portugal; 1988: Belgium, Canada, Italy, Peru; 1989: Barbados and Spain. The information obtained on application of this Convention was also examined by the Committee on the Application of Conventions and Recommendations at the relevant sessions of the International Labour Conference.

181. In accordance with article 19 of the Constitution, the Governing Body invited 18/ Governments to report on their law and practice respecting the promotion of equality of opportunity and treatment in employment and occupation, as laid down in the Discrimination (Employment and Occupation) Convention (No. 111) and Recommendation (No. 111), 1958. Reports were submitted by 141 States and 18 non-metropolitan territories on this occasion. The report of the Committee of Experts 19/ on equality in employment and occupation was examined by the Committee on the Application of Conventions and Recommendations of the Conference, which drew attention to its excellent quality. The worker-representative members of the Committee proposed that the survey should be widely disseminated among all interested parties and should be used in promotional activities. This dissemination is to take place in the second half of 1989, thanks to contributions by two member States of ILO.

182. During its examination of the observations communicated by employers' and workers' organizations, the Committee of Experts noted that some of these related to equality of opportunities and treatment free from sex discrimination (see tables 6 and 7). The Committee continued to stress its continuing interest in receiving from employers' and workers' organizations

observations on the application of the international labour conventions. The Committee added that, in general, the submission of comments by employers' and workers' organizations under the usual ILO control system made it possible to examine particularly useful information and to avoid having frequent recourse to more formal and inflexible procedures of representations submitted under article 24 of the Constitution. During the period 1986-1989, no representations were submitted on matters of sex discrimination.

3. *United Nations Educational, Scientific and Cultural Organization conventions*

183. By 20 June 1989, 77 member States had become parties to the Convention against Discrimination in Education (1960), a number unchanged since 1987. However, when consultations were organized to measure the progress achieved in eliminating obstacles to the education of girls and to their access to all types of education, and which also serve to remind member States of their obligations in this field, the replies received were always more numerous than the States bound by the Convention against Discrimination in Education. For example, 84 States took part in the fourth consultation (23 C/72 and 23 C/ Resolution 2.5 of the General Conference). The questionnaire for the fifth consultation is currently being prepared. As previously, it will contain specific questions on the existence of any discrimination and on the provisions made to promote equality of opportunity and equal treatment for girls and women in education.

184. With regard to the Recommendation concerning the Status of Teachers, adopted by the Special Intergovernmental Conference on the Status of Teachers in 1966, a survey conducted among member States and international teachers' organizations concluded that there was no need to revise the text, but that it was preferable to continue to disseminate it, particularly in collaboration with ILO (24 C/16, para. 14). The four non-governmental organizations that represent the teaching profession will provide assistance for the regional or subregional workshops and seminars scheduled in the draft Programme

16/ *Report of the Committee on the Application of Conventions and Recommendations*, International Labour Conference, 72nd session, Geneva, 1986, provisional summary record 31/15.

17/ *Report of the Committee of Experts on the Application of Conventions and Recommendations*, Report III (Part 4A), International Labour Conference, 72nd, 73rd, 75th and 76th sessions, Geneva.

18/ International Labour Organization, *Official Bulletin*, vol. LXVII, 1984, Series A, No. 1, p. 10 (French version).

19/ *General Survey by the Committee of Experts on the Application of Conventions and Recommendations*, Report III (Part 4B), International Labour Conference, 72nd session, Geneva, 1986.

Table 6. *Comments on sex discrimination received from employers' and workers' organizations*

	1986	1987	1988	1989
Convention No. 100	13 (13)	1	12	-
Convention No. 111	1	6	3 (18)	9
Total	134	155	182	154

Source: APPL working paper (Geneva, ILO, 1989).
Note: The figures within brackets reflect comments on the occasion of the general survey.

Table 7. *Convention (No. 156) concerning workers with family responsibilities, 1981**

State	Ratification registered	State	Ratification registered
Argentina	17 March 1988	Portugal	2 May 1985
Finland	9 February 1983	San Marino	19 April 1988
France	16 March 1989	Spain	11 September 1985
Greece	10 June 1988	Sweden	11 August 1982
Netherlands	24 March 1988	Venezuela	27 November 1984
Niger	5 June 1985	Yemen	13 March 1989
Norway	22 June 1982	Yugoslavia	15 December 1987
Peru	16 June 1986		

and Budget for 1990-1991 to put the Recommendation into effect (UNESCO 25 C/15, p. 9, 1989).

185. "The Recommendation on the Development of Adult Education (1976) applies to adults of both sexes but emphasizes the need to eliminate 'the isolation of women from adult education ... and ... activities, including those which provide training for qualifications leading to activities or responsibilities which have hitherto been reserved for men'. The fourth International Conference on Adult Education, held in Paris in 1985, drew the attention of UNESCO in particular to the special requirements of life-long education for women: in the draft Programme and Budget for 1990-1991, provision is made for the first consultation of member States concerning the application of this Recommendation in order to make strategies for the development of education for adults, both men and women, more effective". (UNESCO 25C/15, p. 9, 1984).

B. *Constitutional and legal equality*

186. Of the 28 developing countries reporting on measures taken on constitutional and legal equality, about half say that they have achieved *de jure* equality. A few others indicate that inequality still exists in certain legal provisions, particularly those relating to property, family laws, employment legislation and application of laws. Several developing countries mention that they have ratified the Convention on the Elimination of All Forms of Discrimination against Women, including some that have not yet achieved *de jure* equality, but recognize the obligation to reformulate and modify existing laws that discriminate against women.

187. Almost all of the developed countries (15 of 17 countries) state that a main issue is the achievement of de facto equality. Although many of them consider that they achieved *de jure* equality some time ago and continued during the Decade for Women to make efforts towards de facto equality, the achievement of de facto equality remains a major issue. Only one of the developed countries states that *de jure* equality has not been achieved.

188. Measures taken to strengthen national machinery are mentioned by a few developing countries as a means of reinforcing equality.

189. Several countries, both developing and developed, have adopted national plans of action for the advancement of women in recent years. Some of these call for the integration of gender equality into all government policies.

190. Several international non-governmental organizations report that the achievement of constitutional and legal equality is one of their declared priorities, both within their own organizations and in their efforts to mobilize Governments to undertake the necessary steps to institutionalize measures ensuring equality. Some non-governmental organizations have given wide publicity to the Convention.

1. Methods used to eliminate legal discrimination

191. Some countries report special institutional measures to eliminate *de jure* discrimination; for example, by establishing special committees on sex discrimination to review existing legislation and advise on measures to remove elements of discrimination based on gender. Several countries, developing as well as developed, have made amendments to or revisions of existing laws to ensure the rights of women, to improve the status of women or to eliminate discrimination particularly in the field of civil law, for example, marriage, inheritance and child care.

192. Measures to eliminate de facto discrimination through legal literacy programmes, legal assistance and counselling for women are mentioned by several countries. One developing country mentions that legal counselling before regional and supreme courts is provided free of charge for women.

193. Several of the developed countries have taken special measures. A few countries report on governmental assistance to facilitate the test cases in court that could advance equality. One developed country states that individuals who assert a right under human rights legislation benefit from the services of a human rights commission staff, investigators, lawyers and legal aid without charge and can also be assisted to pursue court cases of a constitutional nature. One country mentions compliance of legal acts with the Constitution being supervised by a tribunal. Another country reports that assistance grants by the Government to companies are now tied to the compliance by the company with the Equal Treatment Act; furthermore if the Act is violated, women have the opportunity of applying to the Equality Commission.

194. A few countries maintain the importance of increasing support to research and relevant statistics on the life situation and standard of living of women and men, since these facts are very important tools in the development of official policies for equal status.

2. Special areas of discrimination in which legal measures have been taken

195. Several countries, mainly in Europe, Latin America and Asia emphasize the need for measures to prevent violence against women and children. Many countries, both developing and developed, report on reviews of legislation relating to sexual assaults and rape, and have strengthened provisions to prevent violence against women. A few developing countries mention the introduction of new national laws for the prevention of domestic violence. Some developing countries mention such measures as the elimination of articles lowering punishment for rape or other forms of violence in cases of "dishonest women"; revision of laws regarding adultery; permitting abortion for therapeutic or eugenic reasons, or in case of rape; and stricter penalization of violent behaviour in the family.

196. Some of the developed countries report on increased attention to the problems of domestic violence, including maltreatment of women and children, sexual abuse of children and sexual assaults on women. One country reports on amendments to the rules concerning prosecution for assault and rape, so that prosecution is no longer dependent on an accusation being made by the person subjected to the offence. This means that anyone who knows of a case of domestic violence can report it to the police, after which preliminary hearings can commence. By this measure, it has been established that such offences cannot be considered a private matter concerning only the parties involved.

197. Equal employment opportunity acts to eliminate discriminatory practices and to impose penalties in case of discriminatory retirement practices or dismissal have been adopted in a few of the developing countries. Labour laws are often said to take into consideration the ILO conventions regarding women's employment, including leave for sick children and the right to nurse infants.

198. Several developing countries report that there is equal pay for equal work. Many of the developed countries state that even though the principle of equal pay has long since been sanctioned by law, women still do not receive de facto equal pay for work of equal value. A few of these countries report on such measures as the allocation of additional resources to bolster efforts to implement equal pay, and a pay equity act requiring federally regulated larger companies to develop an employment equity plan and to report annually on the results. Also, all companies tendering on federal contracts worth $US 2,000 or more are required to commit themselves to the implementation of employment equity as a condition of their bid. One country mentions that the principle of equal pay was introduced in the 1940s, but despite this, de facto equal pay for work of equal value still does not exist. Another country considers the wage differences between sexes merely the result of the fact that women are often employed in lower qualified categories.

199. A few countries mention that studies have

been undertaken to develop methods for the evaluation of work in order to eliminate de facto discrimination.

C. *Equality in social participation*

200. Many countries recognize that equal social participation requires an environment that supports and encourages a successful integration of work and family responsibilities. One strategy mentioned by some countries is based on the premise that social responsibilities should be shared equally by women and men.

201. Several developing countries report that, as a result of equal opportunity laws, both the equal treatment of the sexes and job opportunities for women have increased. Furthermore, fringe benefits, retirement age and training are provided. A few countries mention re-engagement schemes for women workers forcing employers to re-hire women who have resigned because of pregnancy or child care. One country reports on incentive benefits given to employers for re-engaging women. A few countries state that they have ratified all ILO conventions that affect the social status of women. Some countries mention bilateral agreements with other countries on the employment of accompanying spouses to employees in the foreign service.

202. Measures taken to eliminate de facto discrimination are varied. Legislative measures in some countries include new equal status acts to eliminate de facto discrimination, pay equity acts, equal opportunity acts, acts on equality of men and women in appointing members of public committees, equality committees to ensure equality in personnel policies, and equal treatment acts to ensure equal admission to public service through anonymous tests.

203. Some countries mention the active promotion of career advancement and managerial responsibilities for women. One country reports on a programme adopted by the Government with the objective of changing social and cultural patterns in the behaviour of men and changing the stereotyping of women's traditional roles.

204. A few non-governmental organizations state that they have emphasized leadership training, management and entrepreneurial skills training in order to enable women and girls to participate in social and political life at all levels.

1. *Maternity leave and child care*

205. Child-care-leave acts are mentioned by many countries as one of the most important measures taken or that can be taken towards achieving de facto equality. A legal right to maternity leave exists in almost all developed countries. In one developed country, law asserts the principle of both parents sharing the responsibility for the care of children.

206. A few developing countries report on provisions for maternity leave. Most of the developed countries provide maternity leave, with or without pay, varying from about 3 to 18 months. In several of the developed countries compensation is paid at the rate of the insurable earnings. In one country, this is 90 per cent of the gross income during the first 12 months. In some other countries, one parent has the right to take full or partial leave of absence without pay for up to four years for child care. In several countries the parental benefits also apply for the father of the child.

207. In many developing countries, however, qualifying conditions, such as belonging to social security schemes, often exclude a high proportion of working women.

2. *Research and information dissemination*

208. Most of the developed countries mention measures to disseminate information free of charge on women's rights and opportunities, as well as to support research on women's topics to enhance equality between men and women and to abolish sex stereotyping in the society. Public legal information on women's rights is provided by various government departments, legal aid centres and women's organizations. A few Governments have published comprehensive reports on the situation of women in order to provide information on trends, facts and problems relevant to women and to serve as a basis for further policy and programme development.

209. Many countries recognize the influential role played by the mass media in combating discrimination and stressing equality. Some countries report on active work to raise public awareness of sex-discriminatory advertising and negotiations held between representatives of authorities concerned with equal opportunity, consumer authorities, advertisers and other organizations to start a self-control process for the prevention of discriminatory advertising. Special information is disseminated to schools. Several countries have introduced women's studies at universities, and educational material and curricula are being reviewed with the aim of eliminating sex-role stereotyping. One country mentions the introduction of parent-education classes to encourage parents to foster mutual respect, understanding and cooperation in the family.

210. A few of the developed countries have elaborated a time-use survey proposal to measure unpaid work in the household and in the community. The data is expected to be useful in policy areas including divorce, labour market practice, child-care provision, social and health service provision, and income maintenance. Another country has supported development and promotion

of a system of statistical indicators of the socio-economic status of women.

D. *Equality in political participation*

211. Globally, there is strong evidence that women are substantially underrepresented in politics and decision-making, as has been documented in reports presented to the Commission at its thirty-third (E/CN.6/ 1989/7) and thirty-fourth sessions. (E/CN.6/1990/2)

212. A few developed countries mention that the greatest success of the Forward-looking Strategies has been the establishment of constitutional and legal guarantees of equality and the appointment of women to key decision-making positions in government boards, commissions, high judicial offices, deputy ministry levels and diplomatic postings.

213. Most countries state that efforts have been made to increase the representation of women in politics, but only a few of the developed countries report on a substantial increase of women in decision-making positions during the past 10 years. In three of these countries, there are now more than 30 per cent women members of parliament, while a few other countries report on having reached a representation varying from about 5 to 15 per cent women.

214. Three of the developed countries that have the highest proportion of women in parliament stress that the increased representation of women is only valid in positions in directly elected political bodies. These Governments are now paying more attention to the underrepresentation of women in indirectly elected bodies, and setting up special committees to review the question. These countries have already passed new laws requiring presentation of both a male and a female candidate for each seat to public committees. In one of these countries, the Equal Status Act requires a minimum of 40 per cent female representatives on all official committees, boards and delegations. Another country has set up in the plan of action for equality the goal of increasing women's participation to 40 per cent by 1995. If the intermediate goal of 30 per cent representation of women has not been achieved by 1992, legislation will be considered to enforce the achievement of the final goal of equal representation.

215. Some developing countries mention appointments of women ambassadors, and other countries report on training programmes for women for improving their management and leadership skills.

216. Many of the developing countries mention primarily participation of women in non-governmental organizations and international conferences, exchange visits and other international cooperative and development activities. A few countries express also the active support of Governments in promoting women's participation in international meetings, of both official and non-governmental organizations.

217. Several of the developed countries assert that efforts are being taken to increase women's participation in international affairs. Information from the few countries that reported more specifically on this subject reveals that the rates of women in diplomatic and consular service range between 3 and 13 per cent.

218. One of the developed countries states that all representatives at meetings of international organizations are assigned the responsibility of including the women's perspective in each area of concern. To achieve the goal of at least 40-per-cent representation of each sex on all official committees and boards, the Ministry of Foreign Affairs, for example, has to submit the lists of proposed members for all delegations to the national machinery before delegates are appointed. An explanation is required if the list of proposed delegates contains less than 50 per cent women. In order to find female candidates for positions in international organizations, the Ministry has contacted the national machinery and non-governmental organizations. This has led, in practice, to a more equal representation at international meetings. The last delegation of that country to the General Assembly consisted of 11 women and 14 men.

219. A few developed countries mention that the proportion of women among the trainees for the Foreign Service has risen to between 40 and 50 per cent, partly due to the special encouragement given to women to apply to this sector.

220. Some of the developed countries recognize the value of the active work of non-governmental organizations on issues related to peace and disarmament, nationally and internationally. Some of them receive government grants annually to support activities, information and education concerning efforts towards peace and disarmament.

221. A few of the developed countries affirm that efforts have been made to improve the official development aid policies and programmes to developing countries. Special attention has been given to integrating women's perspectives and to ensuring that benefits from development projects reach women. Some countries mention increased voluntary contributions to the United Nations. In the national reports, both the developing and the developed countries recognize that promotion of women to decision-making positions in important areas of social life is identified as a problem. Even if various measures have been taken to get more women into decision-making positions, the progress is reported to be slow. This problem is often said to be associated with the slow improvement of women's overall social status, the

educational system, poor facilities for child care and too few women employed in important sectors of the economy.

222. A few developing countries recognize that there are too few women in political and decision-making positions when compared to the high rate of women in the labour force. Some developing countries mention new goals to expand women's participation in society. Measures taken in this direction are, for example, governmental support for training women for political participation, training in decision-making, encouragement of women's participation both in national and international politics, and measures to ensure that women's political interests are represented.

223. One developing country reports on the promotion of an equitable representation of women in decision-making positions, and the application of a quota system on the recruitment of women to public administration. Another country mentions the establishment of women's development units in all the main ministries.

224. A few developing countries report on increased women's participation in trade unions, rural movements and other non-governmental organizations. One developing country mentions the establishment of an all-woman political party.

225. One developing country states that even if women's participation in decision-making is, at present, trivial, it can see the signs of progressive changes due to improved education for women and increased awareness of women's rights and women's role in the development of the country.

226. Some of the developed countries mention that as there has not been any significant increase of women in politics, the political parties are now discussing the introduction of quotas for more equal sex representation.

227. A few of the developed countries mention governmental support for research to study and identify the barriers for women to reach higher positions in employment.

228. One developed country says that even though it has tried to increase the ratio of female members in all national advisory councils, the proportion of women has increased only to 6.6 per cent in 1988 from 2.4 per cent in 1975. This country has set up a goal of 15 per cent women to be represented in national advisory councils by the year 2000.

229. One of the developed countries mentions that women are now holding 30 per cent of the senior posts throughout the federal Government, and several countries report an increasing number of women being appointed to high judicial offices, deputy minister levels and to diplomatic and United Nations postings.

230. Some non-governmental organizations report on research activities being undertaken on women and political participation, on equal access to training and education, and on the role of women in development, including the implications of laws on the status of women. Sexist attitudes in educational systems and methods of training are also being identified as some of the obstacles to the increased participation of women.

E. *Obstacles in the area of equality*

1. *Legal obstacles*

231. Inequality in political participation is said by a few of the developed countries to be one of the greatest national concerns. The main obstacles mentioned for women are:

(a) Time constraints resulting from household duties, child-bearing and child rearing;

(b) Insufficient education in general and political education in particular;

(c) Women's reluctance to participate in politics, in particular high level politics; prevailing negative attitudes towards women's participation in public life; lack of confidence in and support for female candidates and politicians on the part of the electorate, including women; difficulty in combining a political career with a traditional role of women in the family and often in society; economic dependency or lack of financial means;

(d) Short historical tradition of political participation and lack of experience in campaigning, public debate, exposure to media.

232. Another obstacle, mentioned by several developed countries, is the uneven sharing of responsibilities for unpaid work at home, including the care of children. Some countries recognize a growing awareness of the fact that political work is often not compatible with the day-to-day responsibility for family and children. This has led to some political parties having started to provide child-minding facilities in connection with long meetings.

233. Still pending are the problems related to labour laws and their application. Similarly, there continues to be a need to review penal laws, especially those referring to the incrimination of adultery and to rape and sexual violence to minors. A few countries mention that even if they have *de jure* equality there are still other laws that contradict equality for women and that need to be identified and revised. Several countries mention the problem of women not being aware of the existing laws for equality. One country mentions also the time-lag between legislation and its implementation.

2. Obstacles to political and social participation

234. In the report submitted to the Commission at its thirty-third session on the priority theme for peace (E/CN.6/1989/7) it was noted that there are many reasons why women might not be elected to parliaments, but the most sure is that women are not, in most countries, put up as candidates for office. One reason that women are not put up as candidates is because they are not well-represented in the leadership of political parties. Indeed, in those countries where women do become candidates, they are more likely to be elected than men.

235. A few developing countries mention that the limited participation of women in labour unions, political parties and decision-making positions makes it difficult for women to control the means for improved living conditions. This is said to depend upon traditional attitudes, customs, lifestyle, poor political training and the social structure.

236. Some non-governmental organizations mention that there still is inequality in sharing economic and political power, and although some political parties and organizations have introduced a quota system or other affirmative action measures, the resistance within the parties to implement positive action programmes is still great. Some of these organizations also mention that they have observed remaining obstacles to reaching equality in political participation and decision-making in non-governmental organizations that almost automatically lead to the underrepresentation of women in the areas of overall development, employment, trade, industry, and science and technology.

237. Unemployment, lack of adequate housing, health care and other areas are considered by one country to be a much more serious problem than de facto equality. The task of taking care of the family falls heavily on women, narrowing women's opportunities for social participation.

238. In the original *World Survey on the Role of Women in Development*, 20/ it is stated that the basic questions of equity and equality need to be settled sooner rather than later. If they are not, the benefits of peace and economic development will be unequally shared and, consciously or unconsciously, distributed according to outmoded hierarchies or unfair structures.

3. Cultural obstacles

239. Several countries stress the obstacle provided by a system of traditional cultural values, beliefs and patterns that contributes to the reassertion of existing inequality, assigning women to demeaning roles and a status that prohibits them from enjoying full and equal participation in society. The efforts to change the socio-cultural structure have been inadequate, but it is also

recognized by some countries that this will take time. A few countries recognize that participation of women in management is much lower than women's participation in skilled employment. Some countries say that women are still regarded only as part of social welfare issues and family-planning programmes. There is concern, in many countries, that an upsurge in conservatism may lead to the maintenance or resuscitation of cultural practices that have been deemed inimical to women.

240. One trade union states that one reason for the lack of active participation of women in the work of non-governmental organizations, especially at the leadership level, is often due to the unequal sharing of family responsibilities and the inherent traditional management practices of organizations. A representative of another non-governmental organization said that young women are neglected in the third world because of the widespread gender bias against females. Girls are likely to be illiterate, malnourished, lack marketable skills for employment, and marry early and bear children, leading to a cycle of poverty.

V. Development

241. About half of the developing countries returning the questionnaire mention an increased awareness of the importance of integrating women into socio-economic development. A new concept seems to be emerging of seeing women's participation as a key economic factor in the whole development process, and rather than pursuing special women's projects, many countries try to mainstream women into general development projects.

242. Several countries have adopted special national plans or strategies to achieve this goal. Some developing countries report on national plans of action, including a wide range of comprehensive measures, for example, special committees to ensure that women's concerns are taken care of in legislation; appointing and training equality advocates to act on discrimination in hiring; the promotion of women workers; and the provision of child care.

243. Only a very few countries say they have no specific agenda for women in development. Several developing countries mention that the Decade for Women has provided a great impetus to the socio-economic development of women.

244. Some of the developing countries report on rapid socio-economic changes experienced in recent years that have had far-reaching effects on the status of women in general: smaller families, higher age at marriage, liberalized laws to protect women's rights, increased eco-

20/ United Nations publication, Sales No. E.86.IV.3.

nomic opportunities, greater access to education and improved health.

245. Several developing countries report on measures taken to promote the integration of women into economic development. The most common measures emphasize income-generating activities by the provision of vocational training and education to facilitate the integration of women into the labour market. Several countries mention provision of courses on skills for entrepreneurship to promote self-employment. Some developing countries also mention training for women to improve leadership skills for management and decision-making training or training on a more professional level for women.

246. A few non-governmental organizations stress the view of equality and peace as prerequisites for development regarding women and society. Some non-governmental organizations report on work for the promotion of integrated and participative development for both sexes in rural and urban areas.

A. Employment

247. It is noted in the *1989 World Survey* 3/ that while there is evidence that some women have improved their position through improved access to employment and more remunerated economic sectors, far more have become poor. Poverty among women is said to have increased, even within the richest countries, resulting in what has become known as the "feminization of poverty". 21/ It is also mentioned in the *1989 World Survey* that there has been a shift in the female labour force away from the categories of own-account workers and employees, towards the category of unpaid family workers. 22/

248. In rural areas of developing countries, women's training usually focuses on activities related to the traditional sector, such as handicrafts, thereby further marginalizing women from mainstream economic development. In the modern sector, women are trained for a limited number of occupations that are often at the bottom level of the skill hierarchy and usually not inducive to occupational mobility.

249. According to the *1989 World Survey*, interviews in Latin America have shown that women's wages, in most cases, account for 50 per cent of total family income. Even in families in which women are not in paid employment, the income that they generate by informal activities is often vital for the subsistence of their families, as is the case also in the African countries. Without the many, albeit unrecognized, contributions of these women, the economy would cease to function. 23/

250. In general, according to the national reports for the review and appraisal, employment among women

is reported to have increased substantially during the last decade in all regions. In this respect, a few developing countries underline the importance of revising the legislation to ensure equal opportunities for work for women.

251. A few developing countries stress the value of non-governmental organizations and cooperatives to promote self-employment among women. One country mentions, for example, a women's cooperative that has formed capital financing bodies to procure loans and credits. In another country, the Government actively supports women's cooperatives with credit.

252. Special measures in the field of occupational health are mentioned only by a very few developing countries. Examples of measures in this area include the right to maternity leave, safer working conditions for women, and especially pregnant women, minimum wage, and establishment of occupational health and safety officers in larger industries.

253. Several of the developed countries report on having taken measures to improve the professional position of women and to overcome the segregated labour market. The projects have included, for example, encouragement of girls to choose non-traditional professions, provision of preparatory courses for girls who want technical jobs, special programmes for the advancement of women in public employment focusing on making technical sectors accessible to women and encouraging the promotion of women to leading posts. One country mentions that women who combine studies with a working career receive social privileges.

254. Some of the developed countries mention special labour market policies and programmes for women. These programmes include motivation of women in respect to careers, financial assistance for training courses, ensuring women's access to specialized and advanced training, promotion of women's initiatives, creating jobs and improvement of the availability of child-care facilities.

255. In some developed countries, efforts have been concentrated on equal remuneration for equal work. One country reports that parliament must make a biannual report on the measures taken in the State public administration to ensure the application of the principle of sex equality, but very few enterprises in the private sector have voluntarily applied the professional equality plan. A few countries stress training and counselling service for women who want to return to work.

256. Some of the non-governmental organizations mention that conventions and labour standards have

21/ United Nations publication, Sales No. E.89.IV.2, p. 361.
22/ Ibid., p. 54.
23/ Ibid., p. 304.

been adopted in many countries through the active involvement of trade unions. They are also engaged in research and evaluation exercises to monitor that equal pay for work of equal value is embodied in agreements and legislation.

257. A few non-governmental organizations mention also having been engaged in training, research and information activities for their members in predominantly "male" occupations. Workshops have been organized to promote opportunities to develop self-help programmes for young women, and guidance and financial support have been given to unemployed youth.

B. Health

258. According to the *1989 World Survey*, statistics from Latin American countries, which information is fairly reliable, indicate that the declining maternal mortality rates continued throughout the period 1977-1984. Economic slow-down might later have had an effect on maternal mortality, but no definitive and clear-cut conclusion may be drawn from available statistics. 24/ The *1989 World Survey* also points out that the mortality rate of infants and children under the age of five has declined steadily in the period 1950-1980. However, the rate of decline has slowed noticeably since 1980, but excess female mortality seems more widespread among children aged from one to four years. 25/

259. Other studies, including those by the World Health Organization (WHO), indicate that the health problems caused by traditional practices, such as female circumcision, persist. In the report of the Secretary-General on the effects of the acquired immunodeficiency syndrome (AIDS) on the advancement of women (E/CN.6/1989/6/Add.1), the link between female circumcision and being infected by the AIDS virus by women is noted.

260. In the national reports, several developing countries assert the importance of improving the health status of women and children. Of primary concern is the high maternal and infant mortality rates.

261. Many developing countries report on improved measures, especially in the field of preventive health, including sanitation, nutrition, water and health education programmes. A few countries mention the provision of training of traditional birth attendants. One developing country points out that provision is made of legal, medical and social counselling to women in need.

262. Some more substantial health achievements are reported from a few developing countries, especially decreased infant and maternal mortality rates. One developing country mentions a decrease in the infant mortality rate from 64/1000 to 24/1000 during the period 1972-1987. Statistics on maternal mortality in develop-

ing countries are not often available, which to some extent reflects a lack of medical attention at childbirth.

263. Family-planning programmes seem to be receiving much attention in most of the developing countries according to the responses to the questionnaire. Many of them also report on successful programmes or on the extension and modernization of population programmes. A few countries mention that they have introduced family-life education in schools.

264. A few of the developed countries mention measures taken to improve the provision of health care to better meet the needs of women, particularly among more vulnerable groups such as the elderly. One country reports having new health and welfare plans that contain about 100 initiatives. Another country mentions a study showing that men and women have different patterns of illnesses and believe that such differences are significant when assigning priorities in health policies.

265. A few non-governmental organizations mention promotion of health education, participation in immunization and information campaigns on primary health care. They also report having undertaken workshops and symposia on family planning and genetic engineering.

266. One representative of a non-governmental organization mentions management training programmes conducted for professionals in developing countries in health, and family planning to help both men and women managers to use limited resources efficiently, to extend services to neglected groups of the population and to strengthen the institutional capacities of local groups. A strong network of trained managers in the developing world has been created in the field of population activities.

C. Education

267. It is noted in the *1989 World Survey* that improvements in the educational situation in general have slowed or stopped on a global basis, as was noted in chapter I. 26/

268. In the national reports, many developing countries report on high achievements in education both in general as well as specifically for girls. A few developing countries stress their achievements in having established compulsory education for both girls and boys. Illiteracy is still high in a few countries, but it is said to be improving. One country mentions projects trying to sensitize parents to girls' right to education. In general, the education of girls is said to have increased substantially, and a greater pro-

24/ Ibid., pp. 42 and 43.
25/ Ibid., pp. 43-45.
26/ Ibid., pp. 27-37.

portion of women are working in the formal sector as well as receiving training for employment.

269.　Many developing countries report having established or expanded functional literacy programmes for adults, and especially for rural women. These programmes focus at the same time on education in the fields of health, nutrition and home economics. Some of these programmes are carried out in collaboration with the United Nations Children's Fund (UNICEF) and other international organizations. A few developing countries underline the significant role of radio, television and videos in raising the level of education of rural women.

270.　A number of countries mention the introduction of educational programmes with the objective of both parents sharing parental and family responsibilities. A few developing countries mention the establishment of special courses on women's issues in colleges and universities.

271.　A number of countries report on measures taken to promote education and training for women in non-traditional areas such as high technology. Other measures mentioned were various training projects in new technologies and marketing techniques to enable women to gain economic independence.

272.　A few of the developed countries mention that much effort has been concentrated in the area of education to ensure that young girls pursue programmes of higher education and to incorporate perspectives relevant to women into the educational programmes at all levels. One country reports on efforts made to recruit more women to top positions in school administration.

273.　A few non-governmental organizations report on the implementation of participatory integrated development projects with women and assistance to national centres organizing training programmes for women workers, and production of a Development Kit to support development education programmes.

274.　Several non-governmental organizations mention provision of training in leadership and income-generating skills to prepare women and girls for social and political participation in both rural and urban areas. Educational programmes to reduce the high rate of illiteracy and rehabilitation programmes for school dropouts are sponsored by a number of non-governmental organizations. Seminars and workshops for project planning, management, communications and income-generating activities have been organized for middle- and top-level women to improve the situation of women generally and to influence policy-making.

D.　Food, water and agriculture

275.　It is reported in the 1989 World Survey that there is a growing concern to support women in their role of agricultural producers by substantial activities in contrast to developing small-scale, non-sustainable and insignificant projects often separate from primary development projects or programmes for women. There is increasing recognition of the need to integrate women into mainstream agricultural development, 27/ although the extent to which this is being put into effect is still modest. This recognition is essential if the full potential of the whole agricultural labour force, both male and female, is to be fully used to maximize output.

276.　Attempts by most national machinery to implement food and agricultural development programmes and projects for rural women have generally met with very modest success. The main reasons are insufficient human and financial resources, the lack of a country-wide network of regional or local branches and a lack of technical expertise. This results in low status among other governmental agencies and reinforces the isolation of separate women's units from the programmes and field activities of the sectoral ministries. The result has been for such national machinery to design and implement a series of small income-generating projects, mainly in crafts, vegetable gardens and small livestock production, that are seen as the main activities for rural women. They fail to address women's need for assistance with their primary agricultural responsibilities in food and cash-crop production. However, programming and implementation of agricultural projects are mostly effectively carried out by ministries of agriculture assisted and monitored by special women's units or focal points. The importance of adopting empowerment rather than welfare strategies for rural women is also emphasized.

277.　It is also pointed out in the 1989 World Survey that women's groups tend to suffer, on all levels, from a lack of training in management skills, financial resources and skilled human resources. 28/

278.　In the national reports, several developing countries report on different development projects undertaken in the rural areas with the objectives of improving women's situation socially and economically. A few countries say that Governments are now recognizing that women's work in rural areas is not valued enough. Women are recognized to be the key factor not only as food producers, but also in food processing, in food trading and in handicraft production.

279.　Development projects focusing on social conditions include most often measures to improve nutritional and health status, including water and sanitation projects. Functional literacy programmes carried out in rural areas often include some training of the more specific skills needed to accelerate the development process.

27/　Ibid., pp. 76-77.
28/　Ibid., p. 379.

280. Development projects with emphasis on improving the economic situation for rural women have included specific measures to establish an infrastructure for income-generating activities or to increase effectiveness in agriculture and food processing, training in home economics, trade, marketing and management.

281. A few developing countries have made efforts to develop small-scale industries in rural areas in order for women to be gainfully employed.

282. Several developed countries report on several projects undertaken in rural areas to create alternative jobs for women or jobs that can be combined with agricultural work. The projects include support for women's cooperatives and training to enable them to create their own enterprises. Special courses in agriculture, milk production, maintenance of machinery, tractor driving and economics are provided specifically for women. Some countries assert that, as a general principle, all education, health, family planning and social security policies, legislation and all other provisions apply equally to women in rural and urban areas.

283. One developed country mentions that the major problems rural women are facing are isolation, inadequate access to service and credit, unequal participation in decision-making and economic inequality. The fact that women play a significant role in the agricultural economy is increasingly recognized and documented. Efforts have accordingly been made to increase the number of women in senior positions in government departments concerned with issues pertaining to rural women.

284. A few non-governmental organizations mention cooperation with United Nations bodies in projects to train women in rural areas to form women's organizations and to create safe and accessible water supplies. They also report on efforts to educate and support women to become independent farmers; projects undertaken including legal counselling for women in rural areas, education of trainers for rural self-help groups and distribution of educational material on funding, food and health, water, sanitation and on basic skills in management, financial and commercial experience. Also, workshops for management training in the fields of agriculture, food science, food processing and technical education have been organized, especially in developing countries.

E. Industry

285. It is stated in the 1989 World Survey that women's entry into the industrial labour force has had both positive and negative effects on women. On the positive side, industrial employment offers women an entry into paid employment and, at times, greater bargaining power and entitlement to familial and societal resources. On the negative side, the majority of female industrial workers are employed in occupations that are ill-paid and repetitive and that have poor career prospects. 29/ Moreover, a vast number of women have found employment in industrial sectors that are being automated. Only a few industries, such as electronics, food-processing and textiles, have actively sought and recruited women workers for unskilled and semi-skilled jobs. These jobs require little training, and hence those industries can rely on a workforce that has the image of being prone to a high turnover. The share of women in management and highly skilled occupations has remained insignificant.

286. There are indications that manufacturing outwork is increasing in both developed and developing countries. According to the 1989 World Survey, women make up the bulk of these home-based workers, mainly because domestic piecework is a way of combining unpaid household work and child care with remunerated labour. Women receive little protection and few benefits as wage-earners, either as outworkers or as employees of small units. 30/

287. In the national reports, a few developing countries report that they have established national training programmes for women entrepreneurs to encourage private enterprises and self-employment. A few countries mention provision of small credit schemes without interest or collateral, or loans repayable in easy instalments for low-income groups, in collaboration with national machinery, commercial banks and cooperatives. One developing country mentions the establishment of a special women's bank to facilitate access to credit.

288. Several developing countries mention that they have taken measures to develop agro-based small-scale industries. One country encourages broadening the base of ownership by supporting private enterprises, including corporations, cooperatives and other collective organizations. Another country encourages women into the manufacturing, electronics and food industries.

289. Several of the developed countries state that they have taken special measures to expand the occupational range for women, including the reservation of places for women in training programmes in non-traditional fields and for higher paid occupations. One country reports on the planning of positive action for women in industry. Another country says that it did not have any particular policy for women in this field.

F. Trade and commerce

290. The high proportion of women working in the services sector has been universally recognized. In the

29/ Ibid., p. 129.
30/ Ibid., pp. 152, 201, 252.

1989 World Survey, it is reported that according to statistics compiled by ILO in developed countries, and in Latin America and the Caribbean, the services sector accounts for 60-80 per cent of the total female labour force. 31/ Although many female workers are still employed in agriculture, the service sector is already the largest employer of female workers in Asia; in Africa, women engaged in it outnumber those in industry by three to one. Studies on female employment attribute this situation to the following: women have easy access to some service occupations, especially those requiring no special skills; certain service occupations are traditionally conceived of as women's work; men's domination of some areas of the manufacturing sector; and the heavy dependence of the service sector on part-time employment.

291. In the *1989 World Survey* it is pointed out that despite the low levels of income, vulnerability of jobs and unsupportable conditions of work, women seem to be entering the informal sector in increasing numbers. Demographic pressure and diminishing opportunities in agriculture have no doubt played an important role. Perhaps a more important factor motivating many women to seek opportunities in the informal sector has been the constraints imposed on them by domestic cares and the bearing and rearing of children, and that increasing numbers of women in developing countries are responsible for supporting their children, partly because men are contributing little or nothing to the household income.

292. In the national reports, many developing countries report the provision of economic and technical assistance to women to generate enterprises and promote agricultural development. This often includes measures for easier access to bank loans, funds and grants. One country mentions policies of a more liberalized economy, for example, decreasing the control of fixed prices and lessening the tax burden.

293. One developed country mentions that the number of women entering the category of self-employed has risen three times as quickly as the number of self-employed men. Women are said to constitute over 27 per cent of business owners, primarily in the service and retail sectors. That country also mentions that the governmental bank and provincial governments offer financial and credit services, training and planning services and innovative programmes and conferences to encourage entrepreneurship and informal networks among women.

G. *Science and technology*

294. It is stated in the *1989 World Survey* that in the emerging industrial global restructuring, the comparative advantages of national economies will no longer be determined by natural endowments of raw materials and labour, but will be primarily based on technology. As manual skills and physical strength decline in importance, a country can improve its competitiveness by enhancing and more fully utilizing the cognitive skills of its female workforce. Creating opportunities for women will be a prudent policy, not only on the grounds of equity, but also for economic growth. 32/

295. The steady supply of personnel trained in the use and management of information technology is a vital condition for strengthening the manufacturing and trading base of developing countries, and is currently particularly important for industrializing countries.

296. It is mentioned in the *1989 World Survey* that experiences of the negative impact of technological change for women is not necessarily inherent in the technologies being introduced. The main cause is often insufficient support systems to enable women to benefit and make use of those technologies. Women are also disadvantaged since they are often excluded from new opportunities created because of lack of training to obtain the required knowledge and skills or lack of access to capital. 33/

297. A few developing countries mention measures to increase women's participation through the implementation of consciousness-raising education on equality between the sexes by the revision of school curricula and by the promotion of equal opportunities in vocational training. Some countries state that there are few women in this field because of traditional attitudes against women studying science and technology. One developing country states that they have strengthened the governmental machinery for development of science and technology for women.

298. Some of the developed countries mention support to research studies and demonstration projects that will broaden the understanding of technological change. Women's non-governmental organizations are given priority for funding under this programme. Another country provides scholarships to encourage women to undertake postgraduate studies in science and technology.

299. Several non-governmental organizations report on support through scholarships to women pursuing graduate studies in aerospace-related science and engineering. They also promote women's full integration and involvement in technological research programmes and energy aspects of food and agricultural development.

31/ Ibid., p. 145.
32/ Ibid., pp. 167-168.
33/ Ibid., p. 278.

H. *Communications*

300. A few developing countries mention that the national machinery is often the key factor in disseminating information, organizing workshops and seminars, publicizing newsletters, research summaries etc. on women's issues to raise consciousness and eliminate stereotypes of women. Workshops for psycho-social assistance to women, family education, motivation, self-respect and leadership have been organized in a few developing countries.

301. Some developing countries mention the use of the media to promote equal opportunities for women at work and to achieve women's participation in decision-making. One country mentions the distribution of films on equality, produced by ILO, and films on sexual education of children and family life, produced by ministries.

302. A few developing countries emphasize the positive use of mass media, radio and especially television, to discuss women in development. Special television campaigns for equity, equal pay, minority women, abused women, and against war toys for children have been produced in some countries.

303. Several developing countries state that they have established training courses for people working in the media to change visual images of attitudes towards women. One of the developing countries mentions training women in the production of audio-visual cassettes; another mentions production of audio-visual educational materials and the organization of the first film forum on women and the establishment of awards to women who do distinguish work in communications. A few developing countries say they have plans to increase women's participation in committees on communications.

304. Two of the developed countries report that the representation of women in management has increased to 26 per cent in the field of national broadcasting. A few of the developed countries say that their Governments are aiming to enhance the participation of women in creative and managerial capacities in the cultural sector. One developed country states that employment equity has been implemented in the National Broadcasting Corporation and the National Film Board.

305. A few countries mention the establishment of regulations on programmes abusive to women with guidelines to eliminate sex stereotyping in communications material. A National Film Board is said to have provided a forum for female film makers to bring women's perspectives into the media, provide practical training for women and respond to current community needs in the choice of films produced. Another country says it is addressing key policies in the restructuring of broadcasting.

I. *Housing, settlement, community development and transport*

306. Several of the developing countries mention planning projects providing low-cost housing to poor families and multiple purpose centres, or provision of loans for low-income persons, often women and young families. One country mentions plans to encourage the provision of fiscal and tax incentives to encourage the private sector to produce low-income housing.

307. One developing country reports on the adoption of development plans that aim at enhancing the role of women in housing in relation to policy, housing production, finance and estate management. The training of women in construction, housing and maintenance are part of this strategy.

308. A few of the developed countries mention specific governmental programmes to assist poorer people who are not able to afford suitable and adequate housing on the private market. Women have been increasingly able to benefit from these social housing programmes. One of the developed countries has encouraged the enrolment of women in architectural and engineering fields, and has appointed women as coordinators in technical schools and institutes.

309. One non-governmental organization reports on contributions to the redevelopment of inner city areas through projects and studies on housing and women. It has also advocated that more women should be appointed to town and city planning, and construction authorities and committees.

J. *Energy*

310. According to the *1989 World Survey* many of women's income-earning activities depend on adequate supplies of fuel and biomass energy. Some of the energy-intensive small industries are food processing, beer brewing, fish smoking, pottery and brick-making. New approaches have been tried that place improved stoves in the wider context of household fuel planning and cooking efficiency. Moreover, it is increasingly recognized that energy concepts and projects must be integrated into rural development programmes and that women's roles and needs in relation to energy resources must be viewed in a broader context. 34/

311. Some developing countries mention the establishment of demonstration centres for educating women on the use of energy conservation and simple technology, such as biogas and solar energy. One country states that the situation of women and girls as providers and consumers of energy has improved with the shift to alternative energy sources. Another country says that there were

34/ Ibid., pp. 94-97.

no major policies or measures specifically for women in the field of energy; however, its action plan is believed to have encouraged women's participation in community power associations.

312. One of the developed countries says that energy programmes are not differentiated by gender; however, special efforts have been made to encourage women to enter non-traditional occupations in the energy sector. Another country mentions that it has begun a new review of resource management law, in which the national machinery is involved to ensure that future processes and frameworks for decision-making are responsive and accessible to women.

K. *Environment*

313. According to the *1989 World Survey*, it is now recognized that the collection of firewood in rural areas is not a major cause of deforestation. The main causes are large-scale lumbering, agricultural expansion, over-use of existing agricultural land, burning forests to encourage fodder growth and over-grazing. Rapid urban growth also puts pressure on land. Agro-forestry has proved to be a promising approach by its integration of agriculture with forestry in order to produce outputs for sale, food and fuelwood. Forestry programmes have begun to emphasize gender issues as important for their success.

314. In the *1989 World Survey* it is mentioned that women have been especially hard hit by drought and desertification. They have been left to cultivate crops on the less fertile land and frequently have to compensate for declining yields by cultivating much larger areas of marginal land. The increased workload has shortened the time available for collecting fuel and water to meet their families' basic needs. 35/

315. Several developing countries mention the measures taken to increase the supply of water and improve sanitation. One country has set up a goal of providing water and sanitation to 90 per cent of the urban population. Another country has adopted programmes involving women against deforestation. Two countries say that there is growing interest in environmental issues, and mention also the important role of the work of non-governmental organizations in this area.

316. One country states that although there is no specific major policy for women on environmental issues, they recognize that non-governmental organizations are involved in environmental protection activities such as sanitation and water supply programmes. Rural women are said to have been integrated into the implementation of energy conservation such as utilization of agri-waste or biomass as sources of energy for household consumption and as income-generating activities.

317. One of the developed countries says that the environmental policies are not differentiated by gender. However, in ecological studies special attention is paid to the most susceptible groups.

L. *Social services*

318. Policies to develop social services that aim at easing the double burden of women, at home and at work, are reported to have been implemented in several developing countries. A number of countries state that the welfare of the family is an object of prime interest. Measures mentioned include provision of material and monetary aid for the protection of children, mothers, disabled and old people. One developing country reports on the adoption of more advanced social security measures that cover sickness, maternity leave, unemployment, occupational illness, disability and old age.

319. Several countries assert that the provision of child care is of high priority and some report on substantial contributions to provide affordable and quality childcare facilities to meet the growing demand. One developing country mentions that considerable progress has been made to assure the constitutional right to establish day nurseries for the age group 0-6 years (and also the universal right to education). Some countries mention cash subsidies to employers who provide child care, and others mention support for a wider use of flexible working hours.

M. *Remaining obstacles*

320. According to the *1989 World Survey*, in spite of the growth of agriculture, forestry and fisheries in recent years, there are several obstacles on the path to the progress of rural women: the lack of access to land and other factors of production, particularly credit, marketing and cooperatives, and to political institutions at the local and national levels; and the absence, or lack of implementation, of legal provisions protecting their civil and economic rights. 36/

321. Policies designed to achieve balanced rural development fail, often because of the absence of reliable statistics on the role of women in the economy. Land reform and settlement programmes often vest the property of land on the heads of household who, in most societies, are reported to be male spouses. The Green Revolution has often changed women's employment patterns for the worse, increasing their seasonality, and excluding women from skilled employment. Drought and desertification have borne especially hard on women, particularly in Africa where they have been assigned land of lower productivity and have had to collect fuelwood from farther away from their homes. The development of industries and urban areas and the crisis of small

35/ Ibid., p. 97.
36/ Ibid., pp. 101-111.

agriculture has increased the migration of males away from their homes, and has left women in charge of the farm work.

322. Women-only projects have generally been under-funded and have enjoyed limited institutional support. Mainstream projects have seldom taken the interests of women into account and, as has been the case with many land reform and resettlement projects, they have sometimes worked to women's detriment.

1. *Economic and infrastructural obstacles*

323. Several developing countries state that the predominant obstacles are the basic socio-economic problems including high level of poverty and lack of employment opportunities, institutional weakness, poor health conditions, low educational level, high levels of illiteracy, women's ignorance of their rights, traditional attitudes and social customs, lack of understanding of the concept of women in development, limited facilities of technical and vocational training, and the economic crisis.

324. One country stresses the importance of women's control of productive resources, as for example, accessibility to credits, loans, proximity of banking services, management capabilities, entrepreneurial skills, decision-making and capabilities of influencing policies.

325. Several developing countries assert that international factors are causing a decline in the standard of living. The debt burden is mentioned by many countries to have had a detrimental affect on the socio-economic development process in general, but especially women are said to suffer the most from the extra burden of falling employment opportunities. Conditions on funds of the International Monetary Fund (IMF) stipulating restrictions on public spending are said to cause bad results especially on education.

326. Several countries state that one of the main obstacles is the low educational level, the high levels of illiteracy or semi-literacy.

327. One country considers women's participation in the socio-economic development as marginal because of discriminatory legislation, lack of good marketing networks, lack of appropriate skills, lack of aggressiveness, lack of direction in the establishment of grass-root industries, and lack of qualified staff and training centres.

328. Also women's ignorance of legal rights and development facilities, because of a low level of education and poor communication, among other factors, are mentioned as obstacles.

329. Lack of statistics on women's input in agriculture as well as women's work in general do not reflect the value of women's work.

330. One international confederation of trade unions says that the majority of working women still face discrimination in the labour market and women are concentrated in a small number of sectors and occupations, in low-paying jobs or in the informal and agricultural sector doing unremunerated work. The nature of female labour is said to be a result of the combination of women's three social functions: motherhood, professional work and the practice of their equal rights as citizens. The lack of active participation of women in all aspects of the society is often said to be due to the unequal sharing of family responsibilities and the structure of organizations. The unwillingness of employers to discuss equal pay, positive action, child care, parental leave etc. are mentioned as a major barrier to the elimination of discriminatory practices.

2. *Tradition*

331. Traditional customs, sex roles and cultural prejudices are cited by many countries as being among the greatest obstacles to women's full participation in the development process. Reluctance of people to send their daughters to school due to the custom of early marriage is mentioned by one country. Another country says that cooperative participation is considered to be a male activity and that traditional attitudes are against women entrepreneurs. Laws and regulations prejudicial to women's interest hinder women from getting administrative jobs.

332. Several developing countries say that the obstacles to the realization of the principle of equal opportunity for women and men are due to deep-rooted subtle traditional attitudes, social awareness and stereotypes that pervade the whole society. Indicators of this are lower pay for typical "women's work", gender bias in career choices, limited mobility to managerial positions and a low level of consciousness of women's concerns, not the least among those who are supposed to implement policies in favour of equality. Increased participation of women in management is much slower than their participation in highly skilled professions and employment. One country mentions that there is also a tendency for occupations that are well paid to decrease in pay level on the entrance of women.

333. A number of countries recognize that women because of heavy domestic burdens, do not have the time to participate in training and literacy programmes or participate in politics. Another problem asserted by several countries is the insufficient organization of women.

334. Women's reproduction functions, childbirth and child care, are stated by a few countries to be an obstacle for women, making it more difficult for women to obtain a job.

335. Sex-segregated labour markets are mentioned

by a few developing and developed countries as an obstacle to development.

336. Some non-governmental organizations mention that sexual harassment in the workplace is still a problem for working women.

337. Access of rural women to power-structures and decision-making, and to male-dominated organizations is practically non-existent. They are also excluded from agrarian reform measures. One non-governmental organization mentions the problems of some development workers for rural women, who are often concentrated in cities, intervening without having any knowledge of the real conditions of life of rural women, their traditional activities or the technologies they use.

3. Health and other obstacles

338. A few countries declare that the poor health and social conditions, and particularly the high rates of maternal mortality are another obstacle to women's development.

339. One country mentions the lack of or poor transport facilities and lack of telephones as a major constraint to women's advancement.

340. One country points out that even if a country has a national socio-economic plan, half of the rural women do not benefit from it. Therefore, specific projects have to be established to increase the integration of rural women in the development process.

341. Some non-governmental organizations mention that they have intensified their assistance to national centres organizing training programmes for women workers, including training of women educators and leaders.

342. Many developing countries state that one of the main obstacles is posed by the debt burden, which reduces resources available for social development. In one country fewer women have been able to enter the labour market because the public sector, which employs most of the women, has stopped recruitment. The increased competition on the labour market is thought to have increased hostility against female employment. One country asserts that the severe socio-economic and political crisis tends to spread conservative views threatening the implementation of the Strategies. The priorities in the implementation of the programme for overcoming the economic crisis coincide with the priorities of the Forward-looking Strategies. A contributing factor to the crisis is the country's indebtedness, which directly affects the social status of women, thus making it more difficult for young women to find jobs.

VI. Peace

A. Participation in peace activities

343. Few data have been collected on the participation of women in decision-making processes at the international level. However, some data have been presented to the Commission at its thirty-fourth session on equality in political participation and decision-making (E/CN.6/1990/2) and on women in situations of armed conflict (E/CN.6/1990/4). In addition, information collected by the Division for the Advancement of Women as part of a longer term project in the context of the preparation of future priority themes also indicates levels of participation.

344. One example of the lack of participation is the thirty-ninth and fortieth rounds of the Talks on Mutual Reduction of Armed Forces and Armaments and Associated Measures in Central Europe, which were held at Vienna, Austria. Between 1975 and 1986, there were only 10 women in the 19 delegations to the Talks, nearly all of whom participated only at the end of the period (5 women out of a total of 92 delegates or 5%). However, the women who did participate often held important rank and their impact may have been greater than their number.

345. Women were not equally represented in the permanent missions to the United Nations in 1989. Out of a total of 1,689 representatives for 159 delegations, only 337 were women (20%); 57 delegations (36%) listed no women members. There were significant regional differences with the Latin America and Caribbean region having the highest percentage of women delegates: an average of 39 per cent, with several of these countries with over 50 per cent women representatives. Countries of the Western European and Others group had 26 per cent women representatives; Africa, 15 per cent; Asia and the Pacific, 12 per cent; and Eastern Europe, 4 per cent.

346. The gender composition of delegations in the First Committee of the General Assembly in 1985, 1987 and 1988 is of interest since the First Committee deals with disarmament and international security. It is a forum for interaction and decision-making on peace, all countries, including 45 in Africa; 26 in Latin America; 43 in Asia and the Pacific; 23 in Western Europe and Other (which includes Australia, New Zealand and North America); and 8 countries in Eastern Europe.

347. The numerical representation of women on the First Committee (see figure VII) does not reflect the importance that women accord to the subject of peace and the increasing interest and expertise that women have in this area. The total female participation at all levels for the period 1985-1988 is a mere 7.9 per cent. Even the

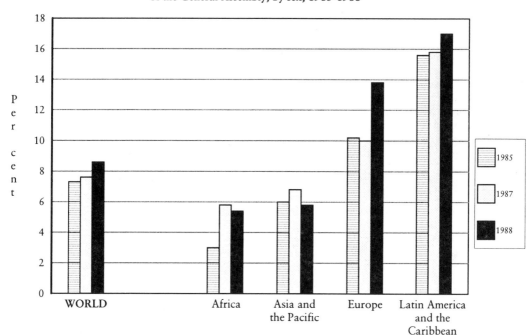

Figure VII. Composition of delegations to the First (Political and Security) Committee of the General Assembly, by sex, 1985-1988

region with the best record of female participation (Latin America and the Caribbean) has only 16.3 per cent females.

348. At the international level, patterns are similar to those of the participation of women in national decision-making: the areas of defence have the lowest participation of women, the economic areas a slightly higher participation and the more general areas, the highest participation, but still very unequal.

349. Less than one third of the developing countries providing national reports indicate specific measures taken for increasing women's active participation in the area of peace. Some of these countries mention support for the distribution of information on peace matters and the encouragement of activities that promote women's participation in the area of peace. A few other developing countries recognize the active participation of women's groups in international peace promotion by participation in international conferences and gatherings on peace and security, disarmament, international solidarity, against nuclear weapons and more specific peace cooperation with neighbouring countries.

350. A few developing countries mention the efforts of the national machinery for coordinating efforts together with women's international organizations directed towards peace and international solidarity. One country reports that the national women's organizations in two countries at war signed a peace agreement with

each other. Another country reports on the increasing importance women have gained in the area of peace since they actively participated in a movement for a peace zone proposal (now signed by over 100 countries). This has led to a growing awareness and the increased participation of women in efforts for peace.

351. Several of the developed countries report on women's participation in the area of peace. A few of these countries report an increase in women representatives to international gatherings in the area of arms control. Further, they mention efforts made by Governments to increase the number of nominations of women to senior positions in international organizations.

352. Several of the developed countries report on the recognition of the valuable work of non-governmental organizations on issues related to peace and disarmament, nationally and internationally. Some report on activities such as peace marches, national and international congresses, often organized by non-governmental organizations in which women are very strong. Many of these groups also support policies in favour of developing countries, and cooperate with women's organizations in South Africa, Central America and Palestine. Several Governments mention their active support to non-governmental organizations by annual financial assistance to support activities concerning peace. One country mentions that women comprise one third of the non-

governmental consultative group that interacts with the Government on arms control and disarmament.

353. Some non-governmental organizations state that working for peace is of high priority, and a number of them mention work with and for refugees. One non-governmental organization mentions the establishment of a fund for legal aid to children in crisis, for example due to apartheid. Other non-governmental organizations mention having worked together towards peace in the Middle East. Some non-governmental organizations report on the promotion of peace among their members through international and regional cooperation, exchange programmes and solidarity networks focusing on the role of women working for peace, especially in third world countries.

B. *Education for peace*

354. Education for peace is the aspect of peace most reflected in the national reports. More than half of the developing countries report on some measures taken to increase the awareness of the value of peace promotion. Measures mentioned, among others, are the dissemination of information on peace-related issues, promotion of disarmament and human rights, support for opportunities for full participation, support to conferences and seminars, and publicity campaigns on peace education.

355. A few developing countries mention that peace issues are integrated in the social studies curriculum in schools, including such subjects as tolerance, racial and sexual equality, and respect and understanding for others. One country mentions peace education for children on proletarian values and on international cooperation. One developing country mentions the Government's recognition of the importance of introducing the concept of peace to be part and parcel of children's upbringing, and says that measures have been taken to include practical law as a subject in school curricula.

356. Some of the developing countries mention the growing consciousness among women of the significant role they can play in peace promotion. One country mentions the role of the national machinery for coordination of action against racial discrimination and apartheid, especially in South Africa and Palestine. Women's organizations have started many projects and movements to foster peace in the family, neighbourhood and community. One country mentions publicity campaigns and a national movement created for the development of education for peace, with special concern for children.

357. Several developed countries mention that education for peace is reflected in the field of culture through the education programmes and school hand-

books. One country says that both the compulsory school curriculum and the upper secondary school underline the importance of international affairs in teaching. A few countries report that the subject of conflicts and their resolution is applied not only to matters of defence and peace, law and justice or religion and ideology, but also to all subjects and class committee proceedings and in other contexts where the relations between human beings are discussed. The objective is to help pupils to understand how conflicts can arise and how they can be resolved, and that teaching must be aimed at strengthening respect for fundamental human rights and liberties, as well as creating a disposition to strive for peace and an understanding of the necessity of international solidarity. Some countries report having produced special educational material on peace issues.

358. A few of the developed countries mention special working groups established by their Governments composed of representatives from various ministries and non-governmental organizations to stimulate and disseminate information on peace and disarmament. Peace education is also mentioned as one of the basic aims of the activities of women's non-governmental organizations. One country maintains that the most important role in peace education is played by the family.

359. Several developed countries report on governmental establishments of peace research institutes. Other countries mention the provision of funds directed towards research and information on peace efforts within the United Nations framework, or to research pertaining to women in international, regional and national institutions.

360. Some countries mention the regular dissemination of information on United Nations activities and on the work of the Conference on Security and Cooperation in Europe (CSCE) by the Ministry of Foreign Affairs.

C. *Violence against women*

361. It is suggested in the *1989 World Survey* that poverty and insecurity caused by agricultural or industrial displacement, by unemployment, underemployment or bad working conditions, and by rising costs that may follow economic adjustment policies, are possible factors in increasing domestic violence. 37/

362. Further, women's low status and economic dependence are factors in their subjection to sexual harassment, rape, incest and domestic violence. Like political repression and reaction, such physical violence is based on stereotypes of power and dominance, of worth and worthlessness, in other words, of inequality.

363. In their national reports, half of the develop-

37/ Ibid., p. 382.

ing countries mention the problem of violence against women. Most of these countries report that the topic of abused women is of national priority. Several developing countries state that both the Government and non-governmental organizations have taken increased interest in gender-based violence. A few countries have adopted national programmes for prevention of violence and assistance to victims of domestic violence.

364. Measures taken are mainly for the immediate protection and assistance to abused women, such as provision of shelters, legal aid, financial assistance and improved police action. A few countries report on some long-term preventive measures such as legislative reforms and efforts to change attitudes by community education.

365. Two developing countries mention the introduction of heavier penalties for domestic violence. Legislation on rape is reported as varying from rape not considered to be a crime to it being a penal offence carrying a penalty of up to 20 years. Two other developing countries mention the successful establishment of police stations, staffed and run by women, to deal with violence against women. A few other countries mention access to shelters, legal aid centres and counselling centres for abused women. These resources are often established by non-governmental organizations, some of which receive official support.

366. Other measures mentioned by developing countries are primarily information campaigns, development of audio-visual educational materials, television programmes, workshops etc. to increase public awareness of violence against women. A few countries have also started training programmes for community health workers, police and others who come into contact with abused women. One country reports on official encouragement to report cases of abuse; another country states that it is going to encourage the organization of women's interest groups.

367. Eleven developed countries report on measures taken to reduce the incidence and to mitigate the consequences of family violence. Several of these countries report on increased governmental attention and support to abused women. A few countries stress that emphasis is being placed more on the difficult and vulnerable position of the victims of violence. Some countries mention governmental support to ensure that the criminal trial and sentencing process is responsive to the needs of the victims. Criminal procedures have been changed to ease the burden on the victim when a sexual assault case goes to court. The most common support measures mentioned are the provision of shelters, professional and financial assistance, crisis centres, help to fund re-employment, seminars and the use of mass media to increase the awareness of the problem, and training of police on the dynamics of domestic violence.

368. A few countries mention the development of counselling centres for men with problems of violent behaviour.

369. Also, a number of non-governmental organizations are concerned about the increase of violent behaviour in society and in the family, especially violence against women and elderly women.

D. *Women under specific conflict situations*

370. The Strategies note the importance of the issues of women and children under apartheid (E/CN.6/1990/9), of Palestinian women and children (E/CN.6/1990/10), and of women in areas affected by armed conflicts, foreign intervention and threats to peace (E/CN.6/1990/4). Separate reports on each of these issues are before the Commission.

E. *Obstacles to the participation of women in peace*

371. The 1989 *World Survey* states that military expenditure continues to be one of the few growth areas in the world economy, and this expansion is not confined to the richer States. Figures assembled by the Stockholm International Peace Research Institute (SIPRI) show that the world continues to devote a large share of its resources to the development and preservation of military force. The 1989 *World Survey* also presents figures showing the imbalance of allocation of resources: every two days, hunger and related causes kill as many people as the atomic bomb dropped on Hiroshima in 1945, and every year, 7 million children are killed by diseases that are preventable or curable. The United Nations Educational, Scientific and Cultural Organization (UNESCO) has estimated that it would cost $US 300 million a year to immunize all unprotected children by 1990. This is less than the world spent on military purposes every three hours of 1988.

372. One developing country believes that the greatest obstacle to the progress of women and their participation in development is the armed conflicts or other action seeking to destroy national cultures. Another country mentions the problems of the low level of education and insufficient tools in communications.

373. Two developing countries regret that there has been so little participation in international efforts for peace due to the economic crisis.

VII. Areas of special concern

374. The Nairobi Conference identified 14 areas of special concern. Some of these correspond to particular groups, such as disabled or indigenous women; others correspond to women caught up in events, such as refugee

Figure VIII. Areas of special concern: Distribution of countries reporting on the implementation of the Forward-looking Strategies

P e r c e n t

70
60
50
40
30
20
10
0

drought · urban poor · elderly · young · abused · destitute · prostitution · deprived of trad. means of livelihood · sole supporters of families · disabled · detention · refugee · migrant · minority & indigenous

Field of Studies

Developed countries · Developing countries

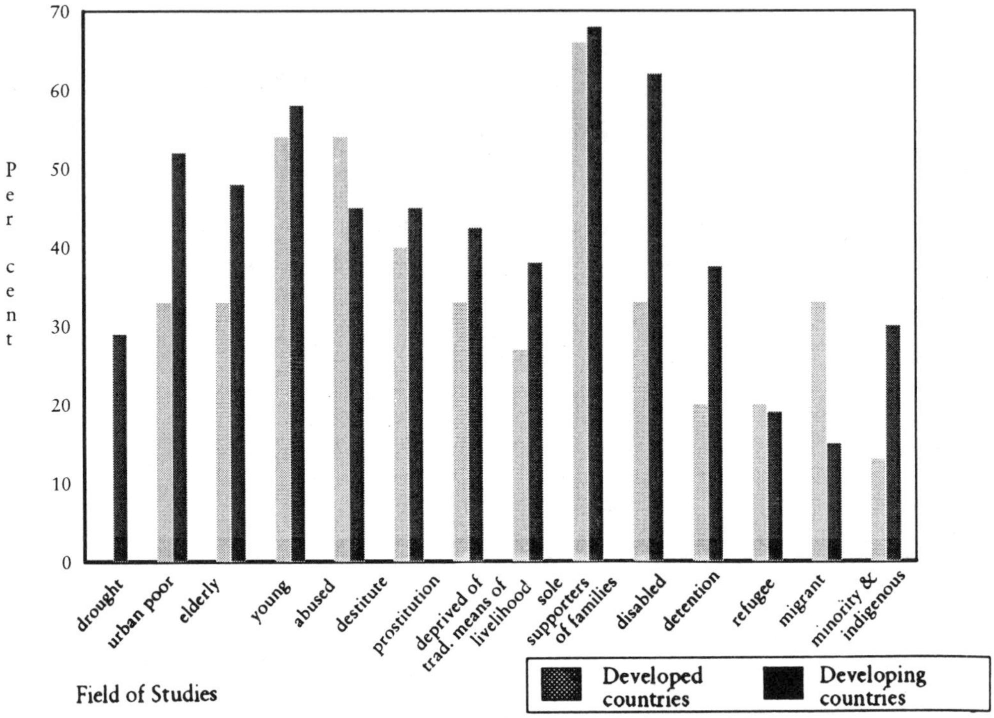

or migrant women. Most of these groups have in common a condition of vulnerability. Part I of the review and appraisal questionnaire, which 32 developing countries and 13 developed countries returned, reveals that in the areas of special concern about two thirds or more of the developing countries report that the Forward-looking Strategies have been implemented and priority has been given to sole-supporters of families, disabled women and young women; followed by urban poor women, elderly women, abused women and destitute women (see figure VIII).

375. Of the developed countries, more than half report that the Forward-looking Strategies have been implemented and that priority has been given to sole supporters of households, young women and abused women.

A. *Women as supporters of households*

376. Almost half of the developing countries that returned Part II of the questionnaire report on measures taken to improve the conditions for families with children. Several of the developing countries mention especially their concern for the often adverse social situation of the single-parent families, which mostly are female-headed. A few indicate that the number of sole-supported households are increasing steadily. Two countries report

up to 40 per cent of households are headed by women. These countries, however, do not report having taken any specific measures for helping these women.

377. Some non-governmental organizations addressed the problems of the increased number of single-parent families and the lack of child-care facilities that have left many women unable to seek regular or full-time employment. This has often led single-parent families living below the poverty line.

378. Several developing countries mention measures taken to improve the health of pregnant women, mothers and children. Other measures mentioned are the provision of allowances to children suffering from family disintegration, or aid such as day-care to ease the double burden of working women. A few countries mention measures such as agricultural programmes, skill training programmes and other employment generating activities for divorced women and widows.

379. A few countries have established special programmes targeting adolescent mothers in order to improve their social situation.

B. *Elderly women*

380. In addition to material provided for the review and appraisal of the Strategies, information is also avail-

able from the second review and appraisal of the implementation of the international plan of aging (E/1989/13).

381. Slightly over half of the countries answering the questionnaire deal with the problems of aging women. The answers are similar for all regions; there is no difference between developed and developing countries. A third of the countries expressing concern about elderly women state that it is a priority, but do not indicate any action; two thirds are implementing the Strategies, even if in some cases aging is not a priority.

382. Very little information is provided on obstacles found or measures taken. Several developing countries reaffirm their concern, and several others state the intention of setting up old people's homes, that pensions exist and, in one case, efforts have been made to enable elderly women to earn an income and to lead a productive old age by making handicrafts. Many developed countries emphasize income and social security. Measures taken range from the appointment of a minister to work for the elderly in special homes and rent subsidies to the extension of provision of pension rights to poor women over 65 and lower retirement age. Most of these measures are not gender specific. Besides economic obstacles, others were identified such as the problem of abuse in all forms, and loneliness.

383. The questionnaire for the review of the international plan on aging contained two specific questions on women, and the answers were generally provided by the national focal points on aging.

384. The first question was on the effect on elderly women of the change in the status of women. Slightly over half of the answers in both developing and developed countries indicate that there was no effect. Of the countries indicating positive effect, most cited the need for women to work as the cause for the inability or incapacity to assist the elderly. The economic crisis was thus evoked, but it was acknowledged that even with less time women were still the main group of care takers. One developed country mentions as an obstacle the unwillingness of the elderly to live with their children.

385. The second question regarded any special measures taken by Governments to assist elderly women, widows in particular. Over two thirds of the answers indicate no special measures. Of those who state that measures have been taken, most do not give specific information. The measures in developing countries centre on pensions and social assistance for widows, particularly civil servants or war widows. In the developed countries, besides widows' benefits, retirement age is sometimes earlier for women; this is being repealed by one country. Elderly mothers of large families receive support in some cases, as do war widows.

386. The information from the review of the international plan on aging (E/1989/13) reveals that very few countries have taken significant specific measures to help elderly women. This is consistent with the answers of the Nairobi review and appraisal.

387. Several countries express their concern for the health and social status of older women, widows and divorced women. A few countries have introduced pension schemes, and some countries are establishing special homes for the elderly. One developing country has established special agricultural programmes with focus on widows, divorced, disabled and landless women. Another developing country has undertaken projects for helping elderly women to improve their economic situation by marketing handicraft products.

388. Two non-governmental organizations mention conferences and seminars held to create awareness of the problems of older women. Violence against older women in families and in institutions in both developed and developing countries is said to be growing.

C. Women victims of trafficking and involuntary prostitution

389. Several developing countries report on measures taken to improve the social situation of women victims of prostitution or of trafficking in women. The measures mentioned are amendments of legislation to provide for stricter penalties and programmes to alleviate poverty; the latter measures include the provision of health care, education, employment training and legal protection.

390. A few of the developed countries mention action that has been taken to help women to escape from prostitution. One country mentions that it has taken steps to ratify the Convention for the Suppression of the Traffic in Persons and of the Exploitation of the Prostitution of Others (General Assembly resolution 317 (IV) of 2 December 1949).

D. Young women

391. Several developing countries express concern about young women. One country mentions the provision of skill-training programmes; another country mentions the provision of low-cost housing programmes; and a third country mentions encouraging women to engage in sports and art.

392. Several developed countries mention measures taken to improve the situation of young women. One country mentions the establishment of an Office of Youth Affairs to give the youth a voice in government policy-making. A few countries stress the need to achieve equality between boys and girls by trying to break sex segregation in schools and sports participation. Other measures mentioned are special programmes to assist

teenage parents by the provision of financial aid and encouragement for further education.

393. Non-governmental organizations report on cooperation with the specialized agencies of the United Nations in setting up a hostel for teenage mothers to provide information on child and family social welfare policies, and training in income-generating activities. Young women have been involved in service projects, fund-raising and leadership-training programmes.

E. Urban poor women

394. Several developing countries mention concern for poor women. A few countries mention measures taken to create employment for these women. Some others mention improved social welfare provisions, including low-cost housing to low-income people, and food assistance. One country mentions the improvement of urban planning.

395. A few developed countries mention that some general measures have been taken to improve social welfare policies in order to better meet the needs of poor people. One country mentions special support measures to long-term unemployed women.

F. Women with physical and mental disabilities

396. Several developing countries report on having established, or being in the stage of planning, rehabilitation and training centres to improve the situation of disabled women: physically or socially handicapped, mentally distressed and destitute. Two developing countries mention also the provision of financial assistance.

397. A few of the developed countries mention improvement of the situation of physically or mentally disabled women. Some countries seem to have a broader definition of criteria for classifying disability, which may be why the disabled gain more attention in these countries than in other countries. One country mentions the appointment of a minister responsible for the status of disabled persons. Other more common measures focus on rehabilitation and training for employment. One country mentions support also to non-governmental organizations working for disabled people.

G. Women in detention

398. A few developing countries mention concern for improving the situation of women in prisons. One country stresses the need for preventive measures.

399. Also, several developed countries mention the need to improve the conditions of women in prisons. Some special measures have been taken in the fields of health, maternity, training and counselling.

H. Refugee and migrant women

400. A few developing countries mention their concern for refugee women and children. Two countries report on measures such as the provision of social services, shelters and rehabilitation.

401. Several developed countries mention measures taken to improve the vulnerable situation of many migrant women. One country stresses the implementation of the policy to provide equal opportunities in all fields of economic and social life for migrants with native citizens. Migrants have the same access to social security, education, legal and social rights; children of immigrants have the right to receive supportive instruction in their mother tongue. Other special measures to strengthen the position of immigrant women are the promotion of migrant organizations through funding and research projects.

I. Minority and indigenous women

402. One developing country mentions measures taken to develop the potential of minority cultural communities by strengthening their organizations, training programmes, financial assistance for self-employment and training in social communication skills, and by the provision of maternal and child care.

403. Several developed countries report special concern for native women. One country mentions the publications on indigenous women in the economy for development of future policies. Two other countries stress measures to ensure full legal and political rights for aboriginal women. One country has a law requiring participation of native representatives in any changes to constitutional provisions relating to aboriginal people. A working group on native women and economic development has also been established, and special fundings are provided for the education and training of natives.

J. Women deprived of their traditional livelihood, destitute women and women affected by drought

404. One developing country mentions agricultural programmes for landless and destitute women. A few other developing countries mention provision for the training of rural women to achieve self-sufficiency and for emergency relief measures. Measures taken in these areas of concern are reported only from a few countries.

405. A few developed countries mention some general measures taken to improve the living conditions of women belonging to these groups. Some mention their activities in development programmes in the developing countries.

VIII. National machinery for the advancement of women

406. Although national machinery was not discussed in the Forward-looking Strategies under a specific section or chapter, a number of paragraphs in the Strategies were devoted to it. It should however be noted that the question of national machinery received less attention at the Nairobi Conference than at the previous women's world conferences. The Commission on the Status of Women identified the issue as one of the first priority themes for consideration at its thirty-third session under the rubric of equality, and the issue will be discussed again in 1991 under the rubric of development. Furthermore the Economic and Social Council requested in its resolution 1988/22 establishing the review and appraisal system that the issue of national machinery was of sufficient importance to be treated specifically in the questionnaire. The information in this chapter is based on the answers to the questionnaire and the reports of CEDAW, supplemented by information derived from a seminar organized by the Secretariat on the issue in September 1987 and on the subsequent debate at the Commission.

A. Trends

407. In the *Directory* presented to the Commission in 1989, detailed information on 91 units of national machinery was presented and the existence of another 37 noted. This means that between 55 and 75 per cent of all countries have designated a national machinery. To a large extent, the difference between the two figures can be attributed to national machinery that is nongovernmental rather than governmental and that does not play an active role internationally (see table 8); the signatories of the Convention and countries answering the review and appraisal questionnaire correspond largely to the core group of 91 units of machinery listed in the *Directory*.

Table 8. *Correlation between the ratification of the Convention on the Elimination of All Forms of Discrimination against Women and the existence of national machinery*

	Convention		
	Ratified by 8 August 1989	Not yet ratified	Total
National machinery exists	70	22	92
No national machinery	29	49	78
Total	99	71	170

B. Measures to implement the Forward-looking Strategies

408. Despite the present count, a significant number of countries do not have a national machinery. While most countries consider that the implementation of the Strategies requires an effective national machinery, some countries might face difficulties in implementing the Forward-looking Strategies due to the lack of one. Many of the small island countries, for example, do not have a national machinery. It is possible that specific designs are necessary, and many could benefit from some assistance in this area.

409. More important than numbers is the trend for Governments to upgrade or supplement the initial forms given the national machinery. Several units have become centrally organized and strategically located in order to have authority and to coordinate the various implementing bodies, and to process the essential information enabling it to be effective. Although the Mexico Plan of Action recommended that national machinery should be created as a transitional measure, 38/ it appears to be maturing and taking on more permanent features, irrespective of the type of country, and is related to the accumulation of experience and political commitment.

410. Measures can be distinguished concerning the creation or strengthening of national machinery and its activities and role.

1. The recent strengthening of national machinery

411. Several countries have created a national machinery since the Nairobi World Conference. Countries in which national machinery existed before 1985 have frequently taken measures to make it more effective by giving it higher status within the governmental system, often by up-grading its rank or that of its head (e.g. to ministerial rank). Giving power and authority to the national machinery to deal with women's issues at an inter-ministerial level by creating inter-ministerial working groups and establishing plans of action for all levels of implementation is another method of giving the authority to national machinery to integrate women's issues into sectoral plans and programmes to study the impact of budgets on women and to integrate women's concerns into budgets. In some cases, Governments directly increase the financial resources of their national machinery or provide it with budgetary autonomy.

412. In many countries, national machinery has evolved from relatively simple to more complex organi-

---

38/ *Report of the World Conference of the International Women's Year, Mexico City, 19 June-2 July 1975* (United Nations publication, Sales No. E.76.IV.1), paras. 34-36.

zations. This has occurred in countries with different political systems and at different levels of development. National machinery often started in a specific ministry, such as social welfare, or as a nongovernmental organization. There has often been both a horizontal and a vertical expansion; some countries set up special units in all relevant ministries, provide them with senior advisers or ensure that the sub-national levels in federal systems also have their equivalent to the national level machinery. In addition to spreading the goals of the work of national machinery for women to the sectors of government, national machinery establishes working relationships with non-governmental organizations and various public or private institutions that can be important, either in implementation or in advisory or information functions. Such changes are often accompanied by a period of training or study of organizational issues and of change in function, in particular a shift from direct implementation to policy-making, coordination and monitoring.

2. Functions and activities of national machinery

413. National machinery often began implementing the Forward-looking Strategies by disseminating them. In many countries, the national machinery adapted the Strategies to the national situation, often through a consultative process involving many types of organization at different levels, including grass-root levels. Some countries specifically attempted to set targets for implementation, others emphasized a comprehensive approach. An outgrowth of these efforts by many countries has been to establish specific long-term national plans for the advancement of women. It should be noted that developing countries, rather than dispersing their resources, prefer to concentrate their efforts on specific areas such as social participation, education and information, technical training and education for rural women, maternity education schemes, lobbying for minorities and health issues. There is also a focus on conditions for women's participation, with assistance for household tasks or, at a more general level, identifying women's needs and mobilizing women.

414. An area in which national machinery has generally taken action is that of introducing legal changes to eliminate discrimination in existing laws and in systematically checking laws for built-in discrimination. In many cases, this has a big impact on key issues such as marriage or inheritance. In other cases, the focus is placed more on employment questions such as recruitment (job advertising) and equal pay. In some developing countries, national machinery organizes legal literacy courses to encourage women to exercise their rights.

415. A clearly emerging area for concern for na-

tional machinery, once *de jure* discrimination is eliminated, is to introduce de facto equality. This is related to the importance given to the monitoring role of the machinery and can take many forms, ranging from continuing verification of implementation of policies and laws, to sanctioning illegal practices by fines, introducing accountability of responsible persons, setting up specialized recourses (e.g. Ombudsman) and coordinating with the media to spread information.

416. Finally, national machinery generally plays a vital role in coordination of efforts to improve women's status and in advising the Government and authorities. This is done directly, for example, by coordinating a long-term plan of action, or indirectly with the assistance of advisory councils or commissions, which can promote awareness, support the machinery or propose research.

C. Obstacles to the effectiveness of national machinery

417. Obstacles to the effectiveness of national machinery can be of internal origin or derive from problems encountered in the environment in which the machinery acts. As in the case of measures, there does not seem to be a significant difference between developed and developing countries in the types of obstacle identified.

1. Internal obstacles

418. Lack of resources is identified by very few countries as a problem for national machinery. This can possibly be explained by the fact that national machinery still has modest expectations or perceives an ability to achieve results with modest resources.

419. The most important obstacles identified concern problems of structure and management. The staff of some machinery has difficulties in the methodology of integrating the concept of the advancement of women into the mainstream of development. As reported by one country, it is a more crucial question than the lack of authority, since lack of understanding of the role of women can play in overall development leads to ineffectiveness: sectoral ministries misunderstand what is expected of them or they tend to neglect the provisions they are supposed to implement. Related to these problems is the weakness of focal points established in sectoral ministries or at lower levels, due not only to lack of status, as in some cases, but also to their insufficient training in how to integrate programmes. Moreover, sectoral ministries can have different priorities than those of the national machinery, and the governmental bureaucracy often lacks consciousness of women's issues. Most of the obstacles identified are mentioned by national machinery with complex structures, and are thus related to basic management functions.

2. External obstacles

420. In a few cases, external obstacles are interpreted in a broad sense, such as the economic crisis that is perceived as making it very difficult for national machinery to be effective, especially in favour of vulnerable groups.

421. Many countries highlight the negative environment in which machinery has to function, which involves a lack of political commitment but more often the traditional attitudes and roles of both men and women, which can translate itself, for example, into preference being given to the education of boys rather than girls. The gap between de jure and de facto equality is frequently identified as a major obstacle. Related obstacles are also identified, such as the insufficiency of existing laws, the time lag between the adoption of legislation and its implementation, and the ignorance of women of their own rights. Some countries underline the fact that some of these problems are more difficult to solve because of the scarcity of women in high decision-making posts.

D. Present priorities

422. In May 1989, a one-page questionnaire was sent to all the national machinery listed in the Directory presented to the Commission in order to identify those priority issues on which they were presently concentrating. The questionnaire to the national machinery focuses only on the main area of concern of national machinery in mid-1989, in contrast to the questionnaire on the review and appraisal, which attempted to cover all the Forward-looking Strategies. By 15 September 1989, 49 responses had been received and a clear picture had emerged of current concerns.

423. No major differences could be noted between the developed and developing countries. Developing countries are more interested in development issues and developed countries in equality, but most of the interest concentrates on these two themes, followed closely by the areas of special concern.

424. Under the theme "equality" there is consensus between developed and developing countries on two issues: achieving equality in political participation and eliminating stereotypes. There is therefore much interest in the cultural dimensions of inequality that appear to be the main component of de facto inequality.

425. Under the theme of "development", machinery in developed and developing countries alike express concern with employment. Developed countries focus mostly on job segregation and inequalities in pay, and developing countries on rural women and food as well as on income generation. The role of education is considered very important, particularly the acquisition of skills that

is often perceived as job oriented. Health and motherhood are also areas of concern, particularly in the developing countries. Other issues that emerge as being of priority concern are the double burden of women (in particular the problems of household work), violence against women (especially in Latin America) and prostitution. Finally, a number of units of national machinery are concerned with planning and programming as well as providing information on women.

PART THREE

REVIEW AND APPRAISAL AT THE INTERNATIONAL LEVEL

IX. The international level

426. Part three focuses on the efforts of the United Nations system since the Nairobi Conference to integrate the Strategies into its thinking, work programme and activities. The Commission and the General Assembly have received detailed reports on this area; work during the past biennium is presented in the report on monitoring (E/CN.6/1990/7). For purposes of the review and appraisal, major trends and problems encountered are emphasized.

427. The Decade for Women and its three Conferences (Mexico, Copenhagen and Nairobi) resulted in the creation of an unprecedented awareness of women's issues and momentum in this field, both at the national and international levels. Although the emphasis was placed on action, there was also concern for harmonization. For example, the entities of the United Nations system cooperated closely in producing the 1989 World Survey and in the review and appraisal of the Decade, sharing expertise and experience. This was helped by the annual ad hoc interagency meeting held immediately after each session of the Commission on the Status of Women acting as preparatory body for the Nairobi Conference. A number of components of the United Nations system had established focal points, and their regular meetings assisted in building an effective network transcending institutional and bureaucratic barriers.

428. The implementation of the Strategies was started immediately after their adoption, in 1985, by the General Assembly in its resolution 40/108. Many intergovernmental bodies issued mandates, requesting reports on action and monitoring: the Commission, the Economic and Social Council, the General Assembly, the regional commissions and the governing bodies of the various agencies. In addition, a number of units in the various components of the system were active in conducting research, training, publications, reporting and technical cooperation.

429. Following the adoption of the Strategies, there was wide concern that the issue of women could be forgotten or reduced in priority in favour of new ones. The Commission played a crucial role in ensuring that not only the progress made was not lost, but also that it would become irreversible. The Commission took a vigorous and determined lead in maintaining the momentum and in overseeing the incorporation of the Strategies throughout the United Nations system. The strengthening of the Commission, due largely to its own dynamism, deserves to be recalled. In a time of financial crisis, the Commission succeeded in having its sessions held on an annual rather than a biennial basis (Economic and Social Council resolution 1987/21), and began focusing its discussions on more substantive and technical issues through a balanced selection of priority themes in the areas of equality, development and peace, selected several years in advance in order to allow adequate planning and preparation of its work. Finally, the Council decided by resolution 1989/45 on the enlargement of the membership of the Commission from 32 to 45.

A. An overall view of the activities of the United Nations system

430. The activities of the system during the period 1988-1989 have already been described in the cross-organizational programme analysis of activities for the advancement of women presented to the Committee for Programme and Co-ordination in 1989 (E/1989/19). One indicator of the output of these activities can be found in information in the Women's Information System (WIS) as, except for technical cooperation, most of the activities appear in the form of either meetings or documents. An examination of the number of meetings organized and documents produced since 1986 provides an indication of the volume, the issues and countries that have been of concern to the United Nations system.

1. Meetings

431. Output under the heading of meetings include intergovernmental meetings such as the sessions of the Commission, seminars, expert groups and interagency meetings. Between January 1986 and December 1989, the United Nations system is estimated to have held roughly 380 meetings on the subject of women, an average of nearly a hundred a year. There are some annual fluctuations that can be linked to work programme cycles.

432. In terms of region covered, opposed to the venue of the meeting, 39 per cent of the meetings on women were not at a regional or country level, but a global or interregional one. Two regions emerge as receiving the most attention: Economic and Social Commission for Asia and the Pacific and the Economic Commission for Africa with 20 and 19 per cent, respectively. Together the Economic Commission for Europe, the Economic Commission for Latin America and the Caribbean and the Economic and Social Commission for Western Asia represent only 18 per cent of the geographical focus of meetings.

433. In terms of subject matter, roughly two thirds of the meetings were held on the three themes of the Decade for Women, but development dominates, followed by equality with less than 20 per cent. The theme of peace represents less than 1 per cent of the meetings held. Meetings of a general nature represent 22 per cent of the total, and meetings on technical cooperation about 13 per cent.

2. Documents produced by the United Nations system

434. Documents on women have been catalogued for the period from the Nairobi Conferences 1985 to 31 May 1989. During that period, WIS has collected 1,450 documents produced throughout the United Nations system on the subject of women. At the most, 5-10 per cent of documents produced by the United Nations system are estimated to have not been catalogued.

435. Not all documents have a geographical coverage or emphasis. However, whenever a document provides sufficient information on one or several countries, it is registered and the distribution by country or region shows the emphasis placed by the United Nations system on certain regions or countries. If there is a geographical im- balance, it could affect the conclusions of a global nature.

436. The distribution by region shows that three regions (Africa, Asia and the Pacific and Europe) each represent approximately 25 per cent of the references to specific countries; Latin America and the Caribbean and the Western Asia region have a much lower share: 16 per cent and 6 per cent respectively. These figures reflect the emphasis placed by the United Nations system on the different regions and influences the image projected of the regions. If a category of industrialized market economies is used, together they represent 30 per cent of the references.

437. Differences in the frequencies of country references within regions are more pronounced than those between the regions. A few countries in each region constitute the bulk of the references: between 1 and 4 countries account for 25 per cent of the references in each region, so that 14 countries, less than 10 per cent of the total, represent a quarter of all references. In Asia and the Pacific, two thirds of the countries represent only a fifth

of the references. In each region, the countries with a low reference frequency tend to be the smaller and less developed ones. Island countries, with a few exceptions, appear very infrequently in United Nations documents on women.

438. Since a document can cover different subjects, multiple descriptors of the contents are used. Taking a broad subject area, development clearly dominates the documentation produced by the system on women. Equality also receives considerable attention. Peace is represented significantly less than the first two themes, largely because most of the United Nations system is composed of development-oriented specialized agencies.

439. Under the theme of development, education is the subject most covered (over 250 references). The two other subthemes of the Decade for Women: employment and health, are much less frequent, as is food, including agriculture, rural development and water, which are in the 140-160 range of references. Topics having between 20 and 240 references include social services, housing (settlements and transport), industry and energy. Science and technology, environment and communications are all below 20 references.

440. The areas of special concern do not receive much attention since they are each below the level of 40 references: the areas of violence, destitution, prostitution and migration are between 20 and 40 references. All the other areas are below that level, for example, the special groups (youth, elderly, disabled, refugee, indigenous women).

B. Technical cooperation and research

441. Since the Nairobi World Conference, a concerted effort has been made to improve the capacity of the United Nations system to deliver technical cooperation for the benefit of women, both by incorporating it in mainstream activities and developing approaches to deal directly with women's concerns. This has included the development of guidelines for the incorporation of women's concerns by most of the operational agencies and institutions of staff training, as called for by the Strategies. Details are given in the biennial monitoring report, also before the Commission (E/CN.6/1990/7).

442. While the International Research and Training Institute for the Advancement of Women (INSTRAW) is mandated to promote research for women, the United Nations Development Fund for Women (UNIFEM) was established by the General Assembly as the only multilateral technical cooperation fund directed specifically to women. The main areas of activities of these two United Nations entities since the Nairobi World Conference are important to examine because of their impact

and catalytic role with respect to the United Nations system.

1. United Nations Development Fund for Women

443. UNIFEM is mandated to finance innovative and experimental activities directly benefiting women, in line with national and regional priorities; and to serve as a catalyst in attracting additional and specialized resources for women. It intervenes in priority sectors where it can make critical contributions to women and development by providing access to improved technologies, training and credit, and by encouraging an economic and social environment within which its efforts would be more effective.

444. The models and approaches developed by UNIFEM through its project-support experiences have contributed to mainstream development thinking and technical cooperation efforts in designing effective and sustainable strategies and programmes involving women as full partners in development. This illustrates the critical value of a special, autonomous fund, working in partnership with the United Nations Development Programme (UNDP) and other United Nations agencies, funds and programmes.

445. During the period 1985-1988, UNIFEM, in its catalytic role, was able to leverage nearly twice its own investments, for example, roughly $US 17 million. In addition to contributions made to the Fund by non-governmental organizations and individuals, the Fund receives its major resources through government pledges made at the United Nations Pledging Conference for Development Activities. In 1988, UNIFEM received $US 5.7 million in pledged contributions, which represents a 16 per cent increase over the previous year. This figure is expected to rise for 1989.

2. International Research and Training Institute for the Advancement of Women

446. INSTRAW is mandated to set up an integrated multi-disciplinary, methodological approach to women in development to be carried out through a network of cooperative arrangements. Following the Nairobi World Conference, efforts first focused on training to develop innovative methodologies in the preparation of multi-media training packages for women and development. Emphasis was also placed on training in planning and programming techniques for women in development.

447. More recently, in the framework of women and development, priority has been given to the programme on information, documentation and communication, including the publications programme. In this context, networking has become a main pillar of the mode of operation of INSTRAW through cooperative

arrangements and cost-sharing within and outside the United Nations system. An example of this approach can be found in the development of a major statistical thrust in the United Nations system to take into account the activities of women in national accounts. Renewed efforts are now being carried out to relate the international and national levels to the grass-roots level, and to set up feedback mechanisms to improve policies and programmes.

448. Financially, the pledges and contributions to the INSTRAW programme have continued to increase and, in 1989, reached a level of $US 1.2 million.

3. *Statistics and indicators*

449. One of the far-reaching recommendations in the Strategies concerns the measurement of women's contributions to development in national accounts. An expert group on the issue made several proposals with special reference to the informal sector. These included the following: (a) the promotion of the wider understanding and improved application of principles and recommendations on the coverage of subsistence, small-scale and non-monetary household production, contained in the United Nations System of National Accounts (SNA); (b) a review and analysis of the classification of industry, occupation and status in employment, with a view to suggesting ways in which women's concerns might be better taken into account of in the revisions currently being prepared; (c) an analysis, to the extent possible, of income and production flows in SNA by sex, on an experimental basis; and (d) an experimental compilation of supplementary statistics and estimates that would permit the development of augmented estimates of gross domestic product (GDP) in supplementary or satellite accounts, that is, estimates of GDP that take into account household domestic work and reproduction not currently included in the SNA production boundary.

450. In its discussion of the methodological development of economic accounts on women's contribution to development to supplement SNA, undertaken by the Statistical Office and INSTRAW, the Statistical Commission agreed that a technical report on methods of compilation, valuation and analysis in that field would be of great value to countries. The technical report should be aimed at assisting countries interested in developing their own statistics in that field and, ultimately, at providing national planners with a complete picture of production in the informal and household sectors, and of important activities in households outside the production boundary. The Commission has stressed the need to improve understanding of women's roles in the economy, to rectify inequities in women's economic situation and to provide a more accurate and comprehensive basis for social and economic planning.

451. The Statistical Office and INSTRAW are preparing the first draft of the report for mid-1990. It will draw extensively on existing work and on case studies of statistics on women in the informal sector and in development undertaken by INSTRAW and the Statistical Office in approximately 12 developing countries of Africa, Asia and Latin America, with support from UNDP and the Government of the Netherlands, and will take into account the conclusions of the expert group meetings on the revision of SNA and its harmonization with the System of Material Product Balances, held in 1989.

C. *Institutional coordination*

452. The organizations of the United Nations system have taken a number of steps to implement that part of the Forward-looking Strategies concerned with institutional coordination. In programmatic terms, the organizations of the system formulated and the Administrate Committee on Co-ordination proposed a system-wide medium-term plan for women and development for the period 1990-1991. The Economic and Social Council agreed to the plan in its resolution 1987/86. The plan will constitute the framework for the system-wide implementation of the Strategies. It has been considered so useful as a coordination device that the Council has already decided that a new plan should be formulated to cover the period 1996-2001 for all aspects of the advancement of women.

453. The first progress report on the implementation of the system-wide plan was presented to the Economic and Social Council, through the Commission on the Status of Women, in 1989. This showed that most of the organizations of the system had incorporated the provisions of the plan into their individual medium-term plans and programming documents. Furthermore, the basis for monitoring implementation was set through the preparation of a cross-organizational programme analysis on the advancement of women that was presented to the Committee for Programme and Co-ordination in 1989. That programme analysed the level of activity concerned with the advancement of women during the period 1988-1989, the biennium previous to the period in which the system-wide plan will come into effect and will constitute a baseline against which implementation can be measured.

454. At the intersecretariat level, a number of mechanisms have been set up to ensure coordinated action and to encourage joint work. The Division for the Advancement of Women continues to be the focal point of the United Nations system for the implementation of

the Forward-looking Strategies. At the centre of the process is the interagency meetings on women that take place immediately following the annual sessions of the Commission. These meetings, for which the Division for the Advancement of Women is the secretariat, plan to cooperate in the preparation of reports for the Commission, the Economic and Social Council and the General Assembly. In practice, all of the substantive reports presented to the central legislative bodies include substantive contributions from the relevant organizations of the United Nations system. Some, like the *1989 World Survey* are joint products. The meetings also provide an opportunity for substantive discussion of issues, for the monitoring of the system-wide medium-term plan and the work of other subsidiary bodies of the Administrative Committee on Co-ordination in terms of the advancement of women, each of which has been requested to deal with the issue in their specialized contexts. It has also taken the lead in developing joint approaches to operational activities for women and development.

455. In addition, the operational agencies of the system, through the Joint Consultative Group on Policy, which comprises UNDP, UNICEF, WFP and UNFPA, have undertaken activities, including the training of staff, to harmonize approaches towards women and development. At its second regular session in 1989, the Administrative Committee on Co-ordination, in its decision 1989/28 of 30 October 1989, concluded that:

"The organizations of the United Nations system, in this review and appraisal year, recommit themselves to full implementation of their responsibilities under the Strategies: in programmes, in policies, in institutional arrangements and in personnel practices. They will take the steps necessary to ensure that, when the next review and appraisal takes place in 1995, the hopes invested in the United Nations system will have increasingly been realized." (ACC/1989/DEC/24-32, p. 6)

456. The network of focal points set up during the Decade has been continued. A directory of the focal points is updated and published on a biennial basis. The organizations of the United Nations system use this network. In many of the organizations, the focal point is a unit especially set up to deal with women's questions; in others, it is a specially appointed coordinator.

457. In addition, a number of organizations have set up regional and sectoral information systems on women that collect and exchange publications and reports. Among the more elaborated systems is the Women's Information System (WINAP) maintained by ESCAP. At the global level, the Division for the Advancement of Women maintains the Women's Information System that has catalogued all United Nations system publications and reports since the Nairobi Conference. It has also collaborated with the Statistical Office and INSTRAW to establish a data bank on women (WISTAT). A common feature of both these systems is that they are conceived for personal computers, which enables networking both inside the United Nations system and the national machinery in different countries.

D. *Women in the United Nations system*

458. The Strategies called on the United Nations system to take all necessary measures to achieve an equitable balance between women and men staff members at managerial levels in all substantive areas, as well as in field posts. 39/ Progress in this area has been regularly reported to the General Assembly.

459. Long-term progress can be assessed by comparing the situation in 1984, prior to the Nairobi Conference, with that in 1988, the latest year for which data are available. A distinction is made by type of United Nations entity: the Secretariat of the United Nations, voluntary funds such as UNFPA and UNICEF, the specialized agencies such as ILO, FAO, WHO and others such as the International Court of Justice and the United Nations University. Four levels are compared: entry levels (P1-P2), middle Professionals (P3-P4), middle management (P5-D1) and senior management (D2 and above). The results are shown in tables 9 and 10.

460. In the four years under review, the total increase in the representation of women has been 3.6 percentage points, which corresponds to an overall increase to 21 per cent of Professional staff. The leading group has been the voluntary funds with an increase of 5.7 percentage points, which represents a 25 per cent increase, followed by the Secretariat with an increase of 4.2 points, representing a 20 per cent increase. At the entry level, the targets set by the General Assembly have been reached or are not far from being reached. However, equality is far from being reached at the middle and senior management levels.

461. It should be noted that this period was characterized by financial crisis and post reduction for many of the organizations, and that most have adopted affirmative action policies and targets.

39/ *Report of the World Conference to Review and Appraise the Achievements* ..., p. 85.

Table 9. *The distribution of women by United Nations entity and level in 1984 and 1988*
(Percentage)

Entity	Senior manage-ment	Middle manage-ment	Middle profes-sional	Entry level	Total
			1984		
United Nations Secretariat	3.3	7.4	25.7	32.9	20.3
United Nations voluntary funds	4.0	7.3	23.1	37.2	22.9
Specialized agencies	1.2	3.7	16.9	35.2	3.9
Other	0.0	1.3	17.7	44.4	13.1
Total	2.5	5.0	20.5	35.1	17.2
			1988		
United Nations Secretariat	4.5	10.3	30.2	37.5	24.5
United Nations voluntary funds	6.5	12.9	28.6	40.1	28.7
Specialized agencies	2.7	4.8	20.1	36.3	16.3
Other	0.0	2.9	18.9	56.5	15.1
Total	4.0	7.2	24.6	38.1	20.8

Table 10. *Changes between 1984 and 1988 by level and type of United Nations entity*
(Percentage points)

Entity	Senior manage-ment	Middle manage-ment	Middle profes-sional	Entry level	Total
United Nations Secretariat	1.2	3.0	4.5	4.5	4.2
United Nations voluntary funds	2.5	5.7	5.5	2.9	5.7
Specialized agencies	1.5	1.1	3.2	1.1	2.4
Other	0.0	1.7	1.2	12.1	2.0
Total	1.5	2.1	4.1	3.0	3.6

Document 94

General Assembly resolution on the occasion of the tenth anniversary of the adoption of the Convention on the Elimination of All Forms of Discrimination against Women, urging States that have not yet done so to ratify the Convention

A/RES/44/73, 8 December 1989

The General Assembly,

Bearing in mind that one of the purposes of the United Nations, as stated in Articles 1 and 55 of the Charter, is to promote universal respect for human rights and fundamental freedoms for all without distinction of any kind, including distinction as to sex,

Affirming that women and men should participate equally in social, economic and political development, should contribute equally to such development and should share equally in improved conditions of life,

Recalling its resolution 34/180 of 18 December 1979, by which it adopted the Convention on the Elimination of All Forms of Discrimination against Women,

Recalling also its previous resolutions on the Convention, in particular resolution 43/100 of 8 December 1988, and taking note of Economic and Social Council resolution 1989/44 of 24 May 1989,

Recalling further the decisions taken on 7 and 8 March 1988 at the Fourth Meeting of States Parties to the Convention, 1/

Aware of the important contribution that the implementation of the Nairobi Forward-looking Strategies for the Advancement of Women 2/ can make to eliminating all forms of discrimination against women and to achieving legal and de facto equality between women and men,

Noting the emphasis placed by the World Conference to Review and Appraise the Achievements of the United Nations Decade for Women: Equality, Development and Peace on the ratification of and accession to the Convention,

Bearing in mind that 18 December 1989 marks the tenth anniversary of the adoption of the Convention,

Having considered the report of the Committee on the Elimination of Discrimination against Women on its eighth session, 3/

Noting that the Committee agreed, in examining reports, to take due account of the different cultural and socio-economic systems of States parties to the Convention,

1. *Welcomes* the ratification of or accession to the Convention on the Elimination of All Forms of Discrimination against Women by an increasing number of Member States;

2. *Urges* all States that have not yet ratified or acceded to the Convention to do so as soon as possible;

3. *Emphasizes* the importance of the strictest compliance by States parties with their obligations under the Convention;

4. *Takes note* of the report of the Secretary-General 4/ and requests him to submit annually to the General Assembly a report on the status of the Convention;

5. *Takes note also* of the report of the Committee on the Elimination of Discrimination against Women on its eighth session;

6. *Endorses* general recommendation No. 10 of the Committee, made at its eighth session, on activities to commemorate the tenth anniversary of the adoption of the Convention, 5/ including the request that its report on the achievements of States parties and obstacles encountered by them in implementing the Convention be regularly updated, and requests that sufficient resources be provided for that purpose;

7. *Urges* States parties to the Convention to make all possible efforts to submit their initial as well as second and subsequent reports on the implementation of the Convention, in accordance with article 18 thereof and with the guidelines of the Committee, and to cooperate fully with the Committee in the presentation of the reports;

8. *Recognizes* the special relevance of the periodic reports of States parties to the Convention to the efforts of the Commission on the Status of Women to review and appraise the implementation of the Nairobi Forward-looking Strategies for the Advancement of Women in those countries;

9. *Strongly supports* the view of the Committee that the Secretary-General should accord higher priority to strengthening support for the Committee;

10. *Endorses* the proposal made by the Committee that a working group be convened to meet for three to five days prior to the ninth session of the Committee to prepare issues and questions relating to the second and subsequent periodic reports of the States parties to be considered at the ninth session of the Committee, 6/ and invites the Secretary-General to take the necessary action towards that end;

11. *Strongly encourages* the Committee to enhance its efforts to rationalize its procedures and expedite the consideration of periodic reports and to develop procedures and guidelines for the consideration of second reports;

12. *Takes note* of the proposals of the Secretary-General for full funding of the Committee and requests that the programme budget for 1990-1991 provide for attendance at all the Committee's meetings by relevant professional staff from the Division for the Advancement of Women of the Centre for Social Development and Humanitarian Affairs of the Secretariat, legal staff expert in human rights treaty implementation and adequate secretarial staff, and for the necessary facilities for the effective functioning of the Committee in order to enable it to carry out its mandate as efficiently as other human rights treaty bodies;

13. *Welcomes* the steps already taken by the Secretary-General and requests him, in view of the observance of the tenth anniversary of the adoption of the Convention on 18 December 1989, to facilitate and encourage, within existing resources, the dissemination of information relating to the Convention and the Committee, taking into account all the relevant general rec-

1/ See CEDAW/SP/14.
2/ *Report of the World Conference to Review and Appraise the Achievements of the United Nations Decade for Women: Equality, Development and Peace, Nairobi, 15-26 July 1985* (United Nations publication, Sales No. E.85.IV.10), chap. I, sect. A.
3/ *Official Records of the General Assembly, Forty-fourth Session, Supplement No. 38* (A/44/38).
4/ A/44/457.
5/ See *Official Records of the General Assembly, Forty-fourth Session, Supplement No. 38* (A/44/38), sect. V.
6/ Ibid., sect. II.B.

ommendations made by the Committee at its eighth session, in particular general recommendation No. 10;

14. *Requests* the Secretary-General to transmit the report of the Committee to the Commission on the Status of Women for information;

15. *Also requests* the Secretary-General to submit to the General Assembly at its forty-fifth session a report on the implementation of the present resolution, and to transmit the report to the Commission on the Status of Women at its thirty-fifth session.

Document 95

General Assembly resolution emphasizing the priority of implementation, monitoring, review and appraisal of the Nairobi Forward-looking Strategies for the Advancement of Women and calling on Member States to give priority to policies and programmes relating to employment, health and education

A/RES/44/77, 8 December 1989

The General Assembly,

Recalling all its relevant resolutions, in particular resolutions 40/108 of 13 December 1985, 42/62 of 30 November 1987 and 43/101 of 8 December 1988, in which, *inter alia*, it endorsed and reaffirmed the importance of the Nairobi Forward-looking Strategies for the Advancement of Women 1/ for the period up to the year 2000 and set out measures for their immediate implementation and for the overall achievement of the interrelated goals and objectives of the United Nations Decade for Women: Equality, Development and Peace,

Taking into consideration the resolutions adopted by the Economic and Social Council on issues relating to women since its resolution 1987/18 of 26 May 1987,

Reaffirming its resolution 40/30 of 29 November 1985, in which it emphasized that the elderly must be considered an important and necessary element in the development process at all levels within a given society, and that, consequently, elderly women should be considered contributors to as well as beneficiaries of development,

Reaffirming also its determination to encourage the full participation of women in economic, social, cultural, civil and political affairs and to promote development, cooperation and international peace,

Conscious of the important and constructive contribution to the improvement of the status of women made by the Commission on the Status of Women, the specialized agencies, the regional commissions and other organizations and bodies of the United Nations system and non-governmental organizations concerned,

Emphasizing once again the priority of the implementation, monitoring, review and appraisal of the Forward-looking Strategies,

Recognizing the advancement of women as one of

the priorities of the Organization for the biennium 1990-1991,

Recalling that the Commission will hold in 1990 a session of extended duration to review and appraise progress in the implementation of the Forward-looking Strategies,

1. *Takes note* of the report of the Secretary-General; 2/

2. *Reaffirms* the importance of resolutions 1, 2 and 4 adopted by the Commission on the Status of Women at its special session in 1987, 3/ in particular its recommendation that the implementation of the Forward-looking Strategies and the status of women in general should be incorporated as one of the priorities in the introduction to the medium-term plan of the Organization for the period 1992-1997;

3. *Reaffirms* the urgent need for the Forward-looking Strategies to be translated immediately into concrete action by Governments, within the framework of overall national priorities, as well as by the organizations and bodies of the United Nations system, the specialized agencies and intergovernmental and non-governmental organizations;

4. *Calls upon* Member States to give priority to policies and programmes relating to the subtheme "Employment, Health and Education", in particular to literacy, for the empowerment of women, especially those in the rural areas, to meet their own needs through self-

1/ *Report of the World Conference to Review and Appraise the Achievements of the United Nations Decade for Women: Equality, Development and Peace, Nairobi, 15-26 July 1985* (United Nations publication, Sales No. E.85.IV.10), chap.I, sect.A.
2/ A/44/511.
3/ See *Official Records of the Economic and Social Council, 1987, Supplement No. 2 (E/1987/15)*, chap. I, sect. C.

reliance and the mobilization of indigenous resources, as well as to issues relating to the role of women in economic and political decision-making, population, the environment and information;

5. *Reaffirms* the central role of the Commission in matters related to the advancement of women, and calls upon it to promote the implementation of the Forward-looking Strategies to the year 2000 based on the goals of the United Nations Decade for Women: Equality, Development and Peace and the subtheme "Employment, Health and Education", and urges all organizations of the United Nations system to cooperate effectively with the Commission in this task;

6. *Notes* the preparations for the session of the Commission in 1990 to review and appraise progress in the implementation of the Forward-looking Strategies;

7. *Requests* the Commission during its session in 1990 to consider the role of women in and their contribution to development so as to ensure adequate attention to issues concerning women in the process of preparing for the special session of the General Assembly devoted to international economic cooperation, in particular to the revitalization of economic growth and development of the developing countries and the international development strategy for the fourth United Nations development decade;

8. *Also requests* the Commission to consider at its session in 1990 the question of holding in 1995 a world conference on women, at the lowest possible cost, and to report thereon to the General Assembly at its forty-fifth session;

9. *Requests* the relevant United Nations bodies to continue to provide action-oriented input when reporting to the Commission on the priority themes;

10. *Emphasizes*, in the framework of the Forward-looking Strategies, the importance of the total integration of women in the development process, bearing in mind the specific and urgent needs of the developing countries, and calls upon Member States to establish specific targets at each level in order to increase the participation of women in professional, management and decision-making positions in their countries;

11. *Also emphasizes* the need to give urgent attention to redressing socio-economic inequities at the national and international levels as a necessary step towards the full realization of the goals and objectives of the Forward-looking Strategies;

12. *Urges* that particular attention be given by the United Nations and Governments to the situation of disabled women, and that Governments take steps to ensure the equalization of opportunities for these women in the economic, social and political fields;

13. *Endorses* the convening in 1991 of a high-level interregional consultation on women in public life, to be financed within existing resources and from voluntary and other contributions;

14. *Takes note with interest* of the conclusions and recommendations of the International Seminar on Women and Rural Development: Programmes and Projects, held at Vienna from 22 to 26 May 1989; 4/

15. *Requests* the Secretary-General, in formulating the system-wide medium-term plan for the advancement of women for the period 1996-2001, and in integrating the Forward-looking Strategies into activities mandated by the General Assembly, to pay particular attention to the strengthening of national machineries for the advancement of women and to specific sectoral themes that cut across the three objectives, equality, development and peace, and include, in particular, literacy, education, health, population, the environment and the full participation of women in decision-making;

16. *Also requests* the Secretary-General to continue updating the *World Survey on the Role of Women in Development*, 5/ bearing in mind its importance, placing particular emphasis on the adverse impact of the difficult economic situation affecting the majority of developing countries, in particular on the condition of women, and giving special attention to worsening conditions for the incorporation of women into the labour force as well as to the impact of reduced expenditures for social services on women's opportunities for education, health and child care, and to submit a preliminary version of the updated *World Survey on the Role of Women in Development* to the Economic and Social Council, through the Commission, in 1993 and a final version in 1994;

17. *Requests* Governments, when presenting candidatures for vacancies in the Secretariat, in particular at the decision-making level, to give priority to women's candidatures when the required qualifications exist, and requests the Secretary-General in reviewing these candidatures to give special consideration to candidates from underrepresented and unrepresented countries;

18. *Once again calls upon* the Secretary-General and the executive heads of the specialized agencies and other United Nations bodies to establish five-year targets at each level for the percentage of women in Professional and decision-making positions, taking into account the principle of equitable geographical distribution, in order that a definite upward trend in the implementation of General Assembly resolution 41/206 D of 11 December 1986 may be registered with regard to the number of

4/ See A/44/516, annex.
5/ E/CN.6/1988/7.

Professional and decision-making positions held by women by 1990, and to set additional targets every five years;

19. *Requests* the Secretary-General to invite Governments, organizations of the United Nations system, including the regional commissions and the specialized agencies, and intergovernmental and non-governmental organizations to report periodically to the Economic and Social Council, through the Commission, on activities undertaken at all levels to implement the Forward-looking Strategies;

20. *Also requests* the Secretary-General to continue to provide for the existing weekly radio programmes on women in the regular budget of the United Nations, making adequate provisions for broadcasts in different languages, and to develop the focal point for issues relating to women in the Department of Public Information of the Secretariat, which, in concert with the Centre for Social Development and Humanitarian Affairs of the Secretariat, should provide a more effective public information programme relating to the advancement of women;

21. *Further requests* the Secretary-General to include in his report on the implementation of the Forward-looking Strategies, to be submitted to the General Assembly at its forty-fifth session, an assessment of recent developments that are relevant to the priority themes to be considered at the subsequent session of the Commission and to transmit to the Commission a summary of relevant views expressed by delegations during the debate in the Assembly;

22. *Requests* the Secretary-General to report to the General Assembly at its forty-fifth session on measures taken to implement the present resolution;

23. *Decides* to consider these questions further at its forty-fifth session under the item entitled "Forward-looking Strategies for the advancement of women to the year 2000".

Document 96

General Assembly resolution calling for improvement of the situation of women in rural areas

A/RES/44/78, 8 December 1989

The General Assembly,

Recalling its resolution 34/14 of 9 November 1979, in which it endorsed the Declaration of Principles and the Programme of Action as adopted by the World Conference on Agrarian Reform and Rural Development, 1/ and other relevant resolutions,

Recalling also the importance given to the problems of rural women in the Nairobi Forward-looking Strategies for the Advancement of Women, 2/

Bearing in mind Economic and Social Council resolution 1988/29 of 26 May 1988, in which the Council urged Governments and development agencies of the United Nations system to pay particular attention to the role of women in rural development,

Taking note with satisfaction of the results of the International Seminar on Women and Rural Development: Programmes and Projects, held at Vienna from 22 to 26 May 1989, 3/

Recognizing that the economic and financial crises in many developing countries have severely affected the socio-economic status of women, especially in rural areas,

Recognizing also the urgent need to take appropriate measures aimed at improving further the situation of women in rural areas,

1. *Commends* the report of the Secretary-General on national experience relating to the improvement of the situation of women in rural areas; 4/

2. *Calls upon* Member States to make use of the report and the main conclusions and recommendations of the International Seminar on Women and Rural Development: Programmes and Projects, contained in the annex to the report, and to endeavour to reflect them, as appropriate, in national development strategies, paying special attention, *inter alia*, to:

(a) Setting up or strengthening national machineries for the advancement of women in order to ensure effective execution, monitoring and evaluation of national strategies in the field of rural development and, in particular, to strengthen liaison with agricultural and rural development institutions;

1/ See *Report of the World Conference on Agrarian Reform and Rural Development, Rome, 12-20 July 1979* (WCARRD/REP); transmitted to the members of the General Assembly by a note by the Secretary-General (A/34/485).
2/ *Report of the World Conference to Review and Appraise the Achievements of the United Nations Decade for Women: Equality, Development and Peace, Nairobi, 15-26 July 1985* (United Nations publication, Sales No. E.85.IV.10), chap. I, sect. A.
3/ See A/44/516, annex.
4/ A/44/516.

(b) Identifying and formulating more comprehensive priority development projects aimed at improving the situation of rural women and integrating them into national development plans at all levels;

(c) Taking measures designed to give rural women broader access to material and financial resources, that is, the provision of land, credit and loans, to promote the establishment and strengthening of rural women's associations and to encourage the development of women's cooperatives and other small enterprises;

3. *Requests* the organizations and funds of the United Nations system, donor organizations and countries to promote the realization of programmes and projects aimed at the improvement of the situation of rural women, and to provide, on request, training opportunities for national machineries in order to increase their effectiveness;

4. *Requests* the Secretary-General to prepare, in consultation with Member States, a report on the implementation of the present resolution and to submit it to the General Assembly at its forty-eighth session, through the Economic and Social Council.

Document 97

ECOSOC resolution recommending that a world conference on women be held in 1995 and requesting the CSW to act as preparatory body

E/RES/1990/12, 24 May 1990

The Economic and Social Council,

Bearing in mind General Assembly resolution 35/10 C of 3 November 1980, on special conferences of the United Nations,

Recalling its resolution 1987/20 of 26 May 1987, in which it recommended that world conferences to review and appraise the progress achieved in the implementation of the Nairobi Forward-looking Strategies for the Advancement of Women be held during the decade of the 1990s, on a date to be determined by the General Assembly not later than 1990, and in 2000,

Recalling that the General Assembly, in its resolution 44/77 of 8 December 1989, requested the Commission on the Status of Women to consider at its session in 1990 the question of holding in 1995 a world conference on women, at the lowest possible cost, and to report thereon to the Assembly at its forty-fifth session,

Bearing in mind that in its resolution 1987/20 the Council decided that the Commission on the Status of Women would be designated the preparatory body for those world conferences,

Convinced that without a major international event by which to focus national attention on the implementation of the Nairobi Forward-looking Strategies, the review and appraisal to take place in 1995 will not be given sufficient priority,

Reaffirming the continuing validity of the Nairobi Forward-looking Strategies, including the interrelationship between equality, development and peace, and stressing the need to ensure their full implementation by the year 2000,

1. *Recommends* that a world conference on women be held in 1995;

2. *Requests* the Commission on the Status of Women, as the preparatory body for the world conference, to include preparations for the conference in its regular work programme during the period 1991-1995 under the item concerning the monitoring of the implementation of the Nairobi Forward-looking Strategies for the Advancement of Women;

3. *Requests* the Secretary-General to include the relevant costs of preparing for and convening the world conference in the programme budget for the bienniums 1992-1993 and 1994-1995, within the respective budgetary limits;

4. *Also requests* the Secretary-General to make proposals on the preparation and convening of the world conference for submission to the Commission at its thirty-fifth session.

Document 98

ECOSOC resolution adopting the recommendations and conclusions arising from the first review and appraisal of the implementation of the Nairobi Forward-looking Strategies for the Advancement of Women to the year 2000 and urging Governments to implement the recommendations

E/RES/1990/15, 24 May 1990

The Economic and Social Council,

Recalling its resolution 1987/18 of 26 May 1987, in which it affirmed the appropriateness of a five-year circle of review and appraisal of the implementation of the Nairobi Forward-looking Strategies for the Advancement of Women,

Having reviewed the discussion held by the Commission on the Status of Women at its thirty-fourth session on the report of the Secretary-General 1/ on progress at the national, regional and international levels in the implementation of the Nairobi Forward-looking Strategies,

1. *Adopts* the recommendations and conclusions arising from the first review and appraisal of the implementation of the Nairobi Forward-looking Strategies for the Advancement of Women, annexed to the present resolution;

2. *Urges* Governments and international and non-governmental organizations to implement the recommendations;

3. *Requests* the Secretary-General to give wide distribution to the recommendations and conclusions;

4. *Also requests* the Secretary-General to include information on the implementation of the recommendations in his biennial monitoring report and in the report on the second regular review and appraisal of the Nairobi Forward-looking Strategies.

Annex

Recommendations and conclusions arising from the first review and appraisal of the implementation of the Nairobi Forward-looking Strategies for the Advancement of Women

I. INCREASING THE PACE OF IMPLEMENTATION OF THE NAIROBI FORWARD-LOOKING STRATEGIES FOR THE ADVANCEMENT OF WOMEN

1. After five years of implementation of the Nairobi Forward-looking Strategies for the Advancement of Women, and one third of the time set for achieving the objectives has elapsed, obstacles remain. Although the continued efforts of women throughout the world to achieve equality, development and peace have begun to have an effect at the grass-root level, their efforts have yet to be translated into improvements in the daily lives of most women. This success is largely invisible: it is not yet reflected in official statistics and not always found in government policy. The entrenched resistance to women's advancement and the reduction of resources available for change that has accompanied the world economic situation in the late 1980s have meant that there has been a loss of impetus and even stagnation in some areas where more progress would have been expected.

2. The pace of implementation of the Nairobi Forward-looking Strategies must be improved in the crucial last decade of the twentieth century. The cost to societies of failing to implement the Strategies will be high in terms of slowed economic and social development, misuse of human resources and reduced progress for society as a whole. For this reason, immediate steps should be taken to remove the more serious obstacles to the implementation of the Strategies.

A. *Equality*

3. The interdependence of the different political and social sectors on the one hand, and the legal and social situation on the other, needs to be recognized. However, *de jure* equality constitutes only the first step towards de facto equality. Most countries have enacted legal measures to ensure that women have equal opportunities before the law, that is, *de jure* equality. But de facto as well as *de jure* discrimination continues and visible political and economic commitment by Governments and non-governmental organizations will be required to eliminate it. One obstacle to eliminating de facto discrimination is that most women and men are not aware of women's legal rights or do not fully understand the legal and administrative systems through which they must be implemented. Some affirmative action measures require legal bases which still need to be created.

Recommendation I. Governments, in association with women's organizations and other non-governmental organizations, should take steps on a priority

1/ E/CN.6/1990/5.

basis to inform women and men of women's rights under international conventions and national law and to prepare or continue campaigns for women's "legal literacy" using formal and non-formal education at all levels, the mass media and other means; efforts to this end should have been undertaken by 1994.

The work of the Committee on the Elimination of Discrimination against Women should be widely publicized through forms of communication that are accessible to women in order to make them aware of their rights. National reports to the Committee should be widely disseminated within the respective countries and discussed by governmental and non-governmental organizations. Organizations of the United Nations system, particularly the International Labour Organization and the United Nations Educational, Scientific and Cultural Organization, should be requested to examine national experience in promoting legal literacy with a view to assisting Governments, non-governmental organizations and women's movements in mounting successful campaigns.

Recommendation II. Governments should take steps to put legal equality into practice, including measures to provide a link between individual women and official machinery such as the establishment of offices of ombudsmen or similar systems. Where possible, access to legal redress by collective and individual legal action by national machinery and non-governmental organizations should be facilitated in order to assist women in ensuring the implementation of their rights.

4. There is abundant evidence that practices denigrating the role and potential of women continue to constitute obstacles in many countries. Whether reflected in stereotyped images of male and female roles in textbooks or in the glorification of traditional roles in the mass media, the perpetuation of such images retards women's advancement by providing justification for an unequal *status quo.*

Recommendation III. In the area of education, both formal and non-formal, Governments should promote the training of teachers on gender issues, co-education and professional counselling. Governments should complete the revision of textbooks expeditiously, if possible by 1995, in accordance with national law and practice, in order to eliminate sex-biased presentations and should, in conjunction with women's groups, take steps to reduce the stereotyping of women in the mass media, whether by self-policing on the part of the media or by other measures.

Governments, non-governmental organizations, women's groups and all other entities concerned should take steps to amend formal and informal educational systems at all levels to promote change in the psychological, social and traditional practices that are the foundation of the de facto obstacles to women's progress.

The United Nations Secretariat, the United Nations Educational, Scientific and Cultural Organization and other appropriate organizations of the United Nations system should continue to analyse the extent and effects of stereotyping of women and implement innovative programmes to combat it.

5. Women have always been an important part of workforce and their role will continue to grow with development, industrialization, economic necessity and the expansion of women's access to the economy. In most countries, however, the participation of women and men in the economy continues to be unequal, characterized by job segregation, insufficient training opportunities, unequal pay for work of equal value, inadequate career prospects and lack of full participation in economic decision-making.

Recommendation IV. Governments, non-governmental organizations and private-sector enterprises should take special measures to increase the proportion of women involved in economic decision-making, including studies on the incidence of women in such positions in the public and private sectors, the promotion of training programmes, analysis of alternative policies to provide women with careers leading to economic decision-making, and the adjustment of national legislation.

The United Nations should study the incidence of women in economic decision-making world-wide, analyse innovative national programmes to increase the proportion of women in economic decision-making positions and publicize the results, within existing resources.

Recommendation V. Governments and other appropriate parties should make efforts to increase the number of women in paid employment, including the adoption of measures to eliminate sex segregation in the labour market and to improve women's working conditions. Governments and other appropriate parties should collect, maintain and improve statistics showing the relative remuneration of women and men. They should renew their efforts to close the gap between women's and men's pay, possibly by 1995, and take special measures to address the principle of equal pay for work of equal value. They should also take concrete steps to measure the economic value of women's unpaid work with a view to taking it into account in national policies by 1995.

The United Nations system should complete work on methodological aspects of measuring pay inequities between women and men, unpaid work and work in the informal sector and should publish studies of countries where such measurements have been made.

6. That women are grossly underrepresented in political decision-making has been amply documented. This means that decisions on public policies that affect women's equality are still in the hands of men, who may not have the same incentive to pursue them as women. Despite indications that in some countries women, by voting for candidates or parties that promise to promote their interests, are beginning to decide the outcome of elections, the incidence of women in parliaments, political parties and in formal government is still low. The situation will persist unless more women stand and are selected for office and are allowed to begin careers leading to senior management positions in the public sector and until women exercise their voting power in their own interests as well as in the interests of society.

7. The number of women in decision-making positions in intergovernmental and non-governmental organizations should be increased. Efforts should also be made to ensure women's participation in the process of selection and enrolment.

Recommendation VI. All civil service regulations should have clear statements on practices of recruitment, appointment, promotion, leave entitlement, training and development, and other conditions of service.

Governments, political parties, trade unions and professional and other representative groups should each aim at targets to increase the proportion of women in leadership positions to at least 30 per cent by 1995, with a view to achieving equal representation between women and men by the year 2000, and should institute recruitment and training programmes to prepare women for those positions.

Governments, political parties, trade unions and women's organizations should be encouraged to establish a list of qualified women which could be used to fill vacant positions. The importance of training women in the skills necessary for political and administrative careers should also be recognized.

The Interregional Consultation on Women in Public Life, to be held in September 1991, should have maximum participation by Governments and non-governmental organizations and should elaborate for the first half of the decade an agenda for political

action that will mobilize all women to participate actively in the political process.

The United Nations Secretariat, in cooperation with other institutions and in collaboration with Governments, should further develop and disseminate an accessible database on the composition of the highest decision-making bodies at the national, regional and international levels, disaggregated by sex. The United Nations system could assist national Governments to set up such databases.

B. *Development*

8. The experience of the past five years has confirmed the view expressed at the World Conference to Review and Appraise the Achievements of the United Nations Decade for Women: Equality, Development and Peace, held at Nairobi from 15 to 26 July 1985, that the advancement of women is not possible without development, and that without the advancement of women, development itself will be difficult to achieve.

9. Unfortunately, women in most developing countries were adversely affected by an overall economic crisis produced by the debt problem, deteriorating terms of trade, protectionism, internal imbalances and unequal patterns of income distribution. For the majority of women, economic and social developments during the 1980s have not resulted in the benefits anticipated at the beginning of the decade. On the contrary, there has been a dramatic reduction of economic development and the adjustment-oriented policies adopted have led to a serious reduction of public expenditure on education, health and housing. Those circumstances have affected the condition of women in a variety of negative ways.

10. An economic environment of growth with equitable distribution, both at the national level and in the international economic system, is essential, as is the recognition of women's full participation. The feminization of poverty reflects the underlying structural problems faced by women in the midst of economic change. Prevailing economic policies at the national and international levels have frequently failed to take into account potential negative effects on women or women's potential contribution and have accordingly not succeeded.

Recommendation VII. In order to help revitalize economic growth, international economic and social cooperation, together with sound economic policies, should be pursued. Structural adjustment and other economic reform measures should be designed and implemented so as to promote the full participation of women in the development process, while avoiding the negative economic and social effects. They should be accompanied by policies giving women equal access to credit, productive inputs, markets and decision-making and this should be incorporated fully into national economic policy and planning.

The international development strategy for the fourth United Nations development decade should take full account of women's contribution and potential and this should be an important part of monitoring its implementation. Relevant organizations of the United Nations system should continue to examine the effects of national and international economic policies on social progress, in particular the condition of women in developing countries.

11. The incorporation of women into the labour force has occurred on a scale unimaginable 30 years ago. Nevertheless, given unfavourable economic conditions in developing countries, the majority of women remain or are increasing in number in the informal sector of the economy.

Recommendation VIII. Governmental policies, non-governmental action and international cooperation should be directed towards supporting programmes to improve the living conditions of women in the informal sector.

These programmes should contribute, among other things, to the incorporation into the informal sector of appropriate technologies which could increase production in that sector and make domestic and international markets more accessible. Women in the informal sector should be encouraged to organize themselves so that they know their rights and are able to obtain the necessary support to exercise them.

Appropriate organizations at the international level should gather more detailed and accurate information related to women in the informal sector in order to identify the most efficient measures to ameliorate their condition.

12. Women are overrepresented among the poor because of the factors deriving from existing inequality between men and women in most societies. The number of women living in extreme poverty in many countries has increased during the period under review.

Recommendation IX. Governments, non-governmental organizations and international organizations should take concrete measures to eradicate poverty. These measures should have a multi-purpose approach and include educational skills and training designed to generate productive activities.

13. Since 1970, there has been a significant expansion in women's access to education, which has proved to be an important means of equipping women to play a full and equal role in society. Although some regions have achieved equality in access to education, considerable progress remains to be achieved in most developing countries at all levels of education, including universal primary education. Moreover, although improved access of girls to education is gradually eliminating illiteracy among the young, gender-related differences in illiteracy among adults continue to constitute an obstacle to women's legal, economic, social and political empowerment by denying women an essential tool for acquiring knowledge and skills. In addition, women who have access to education are often channelled into traditionally female specialities. Of particular concern for the future is the achievement of women's access to science and technology through education and training, which is now limited by budgetary constraints, especially in developing countries.

Recommendation X. Governments that have not already done so should reorient resources to ensure women's equal access to education and training at all levels and in all fields and, in collaboration with women's groups and non-governmental organizations, should make special efforts to remove all gender-related differences in adult literacy by the year 2000. Programmes should be established to ensure that parents and teachers provide equal educational opportunities for girls and boys. In particular, encouragement should be given to promoting the study by girls of scientific and technological subjects, particularly those corresponding to national development priorities, and to preparing girls for full participation in the economy and in public life. In order to fulfil these commitments, appropriate measures should be taken at the national and international levels to ensure revitalization of growth on a long-term basis.

The United Nations Educational, Scientific and Cultural Organization and other organizations of the United Nations system should give special priority to eliminating female illiteracy and to monitoring efforts to ensure that women have equal access to all levels of education and training.

14. The importance of food security and the critical role of women as producers of food—both domestic and cash crops—are indisputably recognized; none the less, the conditions of rural women are improving at a slow pace and in some cases have even deteriorated. Projects on their behalf have generally met with limited success. The main reasons are insufficient human and financial expertise, the lack of a country-wide network of regional or local branches of government agencies and the lack of technical expertise. All of these factors have been aggravated in developing countries by the current economic crisis, which has shifted resources to export-oriented farmers and deprived rural women of vital inputs and infrastructure.

Recommendation XI. Governments should take particular steps to ensure that new technologies are accessible to women and that women participate in the design and application of those technologies.

Recommendation XII. Governments and non-governmental organizations should adopt empowerment rather than welfare strategies to support women in their role as agricultural producers, with a view to improving their economic and social situation and to integrating them into mainstream agricultural development. Priority should be accorded to projects aimed at guaranteeing access of rural women to technology, credit, training, trade marketing, management and improved agricultural infrastructure and control of the use of land.

The United Nations system, mainly the Food and Agriculture Organizations of the United Nations, should collaborate with Governments in identifying and providing inputs that are needed to support the agricultural productive capacity of women.

The United Nations system should develop new methods of promoting the transfer of science and technology to women.

15. Since the beginning of the 1980s, there has been a decline in the standard of health and nutrition of women in parts of every developing region due, *inter alia*, to a decline in per capita expenditure on health. This is a particularly alarming situation since maternal and neonatal health are crucial to infant survival. Infant and child mortality rates have been rising in a number of countries after having declined for decades.

Recommendation XIII. Governments, international organizations, non-governmental organizations and the public in general should be aware of the decline in women's health in developing countries. Improvement of women's health by the provision of appropriate and accessible health services should be a priority within the goal of health for all by the year 2000. 2/

Women constitute the majority of health care workers in most countries. They should be enabled to play a much larger role in decision-making for health. Governments, international non-governmental organizations and women's organizations should undertake programmes aimed at improving women's health by ensuring access to adequate maternal and child health care, family planning, safe motherhood programmes, nutrition, programmes for female-specific diseases and other primary health care services in relation to the goal of health for all by the year 2000.

The World Health Organization and other organizations of the United Nations system should further develop emergency programmes to cope with the deteriorating conditions of women's health mainly in developing countries, with particular attention to nutrition, maternal health care and sanitation.

16. Women's access to information and services relating to population and family planning are improving only slowly in most countries. A woman's ability to control her own fertility continues to be a major factor enabling her to protect her health, achieve her personal objectives and ensure the strength of her family. All women should be in a position to plan and organize their lives.

Recommendation XIV. Governments, non-governmental organizations and women's movements should develop programmes to enable women to implement their decisions on the timing and spacing of their children. These programmes should include population education programmes linked to women's rights and the role of women in development, as well as the sharing of family responsibilities by men and boys. Social services should be provided to help women reconcile family and employment requirements.

Family planning programmes should be developed or extended to enable women to implement their decisions on the timing and spacing of their children and for safe motherhood.

The United Nations Secretariat, the United Nations Population Fund, the World Health Organization and other organizations of the United Nations system should develop collaborative programmes to link the role of women in development to questions related to population.

17. During the past five years, women's health, both physical and psychological, has been increasingly affected in many countries by the consumption and abuse of alcohol, narcotic drugs and psychotropic substances.

Recommendation XV. Governments and other competent national authorities should establish national policies and programmes on women's health with respect to the consumption and abuse of alcohol, narcotic drugs and psychotropic substances. Strong preventive as well as rehabilitative measures should be taken.

In addition, efforts should be intensified to reduce occupational health hazards faced by women and to discourage illicit drug use.

18. The emergence, since the Nairobi Conference, of new threats to the health and status of women, such as the alarming increase in sexually transmitted diseases and the acquired immunodeficiency syndrome (AIDS)

2/ See General Assembly resolution 36/43.

pandemic, requires urgent action from both medical and social institutions.

Recommendation XVI. Greater attention is also needed with respect to the issue of women and AIDS. Efforts in this regard should be an integral part of the World Health Organization Global Programme on AIDS. Urgent action and action-oriented research are also required by social institutions at all levels, in particular the United Nations system, national AIDS committees and non-governmental organizations, to inform women of the threat of AIDS to their health and status.

19. Urbanization, migration and economic changes have increased the proportion of families headed by women and the number of women entering the labour force. These women have experienced increasing difficulties in harmonizing their economic role with the demands on them to provide care for children and dependants. The double burden, rather than being reduced by greater sharing between spouses, has increased. Unless it is reduced, women will not be able to play their full and fair role in development.

Recommendation XVII. Governments and other appropriate bodies should, by 1995, establish social support measures with the aim of facilitating the combination of parental and other caring responsibilities and paid employment, including policies for the provision of services and measures to increase the sharing of such responsibilities by men and women and to deal with specific problems of female-headed households that include dependants.

The United Nations Secretariat, the United Nations Children's Fund and other appropriate organizations of the United Nations system should, as part of the International Year of the Family in 1994, make a special effort to analyse the issues of caring for children and dependants and sharing domestic, parental and other caring responsibilities, including the appraisal of national experience.

20. The issue of the environment affects the lives of everyone, women and men alike. Women's participation in making decisions on the environment is limited despite the high level of concern women express for the issue and their involvement in it. Women's concern for the environment in all its aspects can be an important force for a general mobilization of women that may have an impact on other areas, including equality and peace.

Recommendation XVIII. Governments should make efforts to involve individual women and women's groups in making decisions on the environment. Educational programmes should be developed on environmental issues and their relation to daily life.

The United Nations Conference on Environment and Development, to be held in 1992, should consider dealing with the issue of women and the environment with a view, *inter alia*, to mobilizing women at both the national and international levels and to ensuring that the experience and knowledge of women are fully taken into account.

21. The progress made in disarmament negotiations is welcomed. It is noted that this has not been matched by progress in social and economic development.

Recommendation XIX. Governments are urged to consider redirecting possible savings from disarmament to the improvement of social and economic development, including women's development.

C. Peace

22. Despite the progress made in some areas, international, regional and national conflicts persist, and women continue to number among their main victims. At the same time, women are no more prominent among those making decisions on conflicts than in the past.

Recommendation XX. Governments should be encouraged to increase the participation of women in the peace process at the decision-making level, including them as part of delegations to negotiate international agreements relating to peace and disarmament and establishing a target for the number of women participating in such delegations.

The United Nations and the international non-governmental organizations concerned should continue to monitor and support greater involvement of women in the peace process.

Recommendation XXI. In the context of an increased effort to resolve the long-standing conflicts affecting Palestinian and South African women, special efforts should be made to ensure that all women concerned fully participate in the peace process and in the construction of their societies. The reconstruction process should include as a priority special programmes of assistance to women. Such programmes should also be developed for the benefit of Namibian women.

23. The recognition that violence against women in the family and society is pervasive and cuts across lines of income, class and culture must be matched by urgent and effective steps to eliminate its incidence. Violence against women derives from their unequal status in society.

Recommendation XXII. Governments should take immediate measures to establish appropriate penalties for violence against women in the family, the work place and society. Governments and other relevant agencies should also undertake policies to prevent, control and reduce the impact of violence on women in the family, the work place and society. Governments and relevant agencies, women's organizations, non-governmental organizations and the private sector should develop appropriate correctional, educational and social services, including shelters, training programmes for law enforcement officers, the judiciary and health and social service personnel, as well as adequate deterrent and corrective measures. The number of women at all levels of law enforcement, legal assistance and the judicial system should be increased.

The United Nations system, Governments and non-governmental organizations should study the relationship between the portrayal of violence against women in the media and violence against women in the family and society, including possible effects of new transnational transmission technologies.

II. NATIONAL MACHINERY

24. The first few years of the implementation of the Nairobi Forward-looking Strategies have emphasized the importance of national machinery for the advancement of women in promoting the integration of women's needs and concerns into government policies and programmes, in mobilizing grass-roots support and in providing information at the national and international levels. National machinery, despite resource limitations, has been a significant factor in keeping the Strategies alive in individual countries. The effectiveness of national machinery has been found to depend on the political commitment of Governments, as reflected in appropriate resource levels, institutional location, competence in technical fields and ability to use information. Improving all of these factors is an important means of eliminating other obstacles.

Recommendation XXIII. National machinery should be established in every State by 1995, should be given an institutional location allowing it to have a direct effect on government policy and should be provided with sufficient resources of its own to collect and disseminate information on the situation of women and on the potential consequences of government policies on women and to contribute to their advancement. National machinery should continue to develop coherent policies for the advancement of women as part of national priorities and plans.

The United Nations system should support national machinery by providing advisory, training and information services relating to planning and management, training methods, evaluation and the acquisition and use of information; it should encourage mutual assistance and exchange of experience between units of national machinery.

Recommendation XXIV. The United Nations system should, within the existing regular budget, allocate sufficient resources to enable it to meet national requests and maintain coordinated international activities at a level that will make possible the implementation of the Nairobi Forward-looking Strategies for the Advancement of Women. Additionally, voluntary contributions to this end are to be encouraged.

III. PRIORITY THEMES FOR THE PERIOD 1993-1996

25. Based on this analysis, the Commission on the Status of Women should examine key priority themes in each of the areas of equality, development and peace.

A. *Equality*

1. Increased awareness by women of their rights, including legal literacy.

2. Equal pay for work of equal value, including methodologies for measurement of pay inequities and work in the informal sector.

3. Equality in economic decision-making.

4. Elimination of stereotyping of women in the mass media.

B. *Development*

1. Women in extreme poverty: integration of women's concerns in national development planning.

2. Women in urban areas: population, nutrition and health factors for women in development, including migration, drug consumption and AIDS.

3. Promotion of literacy, education and training, including technological skills.

4. Child and dependant care, including sharing of work and family responsibilities.

C. *Peace*

1. Women and the peace process.

2. Measures to eradicate violence against women in the family and society.

3. Women in international decision-making.

4. Education for peace.

Document 99

General Assembly resolution calling for efforts to increase the literacy of women

A/RES/45/126, 14 December 1990

The General Assembly,

Recalling that in the Universal Declaration of Human Rights 1/ and the International Covenant on Economic, Social and Cultural Rights 2/ the inalienable right of every individual to education is recognized,

Recalling also the special references to and recommendations on women's needs in relation to literacy, education and training contained in paragraphs 163 to 173 of the Nairobi Forward-looking Strategies for the Advancement of Women, 3/

Taking note of Commission on the Status of Women resolution 34/8 of 8 March 1990 on women and literacy, 4/

Taking note also of Economic and Social Council resolution 1990/15 of 24 May 1990, the annex to which contains the recommendations and conclusions arising from the first review and appraisal of the implementation of the Nairobi Forward-looking Strategies for the Advancement of Women, in which, *inter alia*, it is recommended that Governments should make special efforts to remove all gender-related differences in adult literacy by the year 2000 and that programmes should be established to ensure that parents and teachers provide equal educational opportunities for girls and boys,

Noting that in the Convention on the Elimination of All Forms of Discrimination against Women, 5/ States parties, *inter alia*, committed themselves to taking measures to ensure equal access to education for women and men,

Recalling its resolutions 42/104 of 7 December 1987, by which it proclaimed 1990 as International Literacy Year, and 44/127 of 15 December 1989, in which it called for continuing international efforts to promote literacy,

Recalling also the World Declaration on Education for All adopted by the World Conference on Education for All, 6/ in which it is recognized that literacy programmes are indispensable to the basic learning needs of all and that the most urgent priority is to ensure access to, and improve the quality of, education for girls and women, as well as to remove every obstacle that hampers their active participation,

Mindful of Economic and Social Council resolution 1990/12 of 24 May 1990, in which it recommended that a world conference on women be held in 1995,

Taking note of the Plan of Action for Implementing the World Declaration on the Survival, Protection and Development of Children in the 1990s, 7/ adopted by the World Summit for Children, held in New York on 29 and 30 September 1990, in which, *inter alia*, the adoption of measures was called for that emphasized the need to improve the current disparities between girls and boys in access to basic education and the need to reduce adult illiteracy by half, with an emphasis on female illiteracy, before the year 2000,

Mindful of the fact that the eradication of illiteracy, including illiteracy among women, is one of the paramount objectives of the International Development Strategy for the Fourth United Nations Development Decade, 8/

Recognizing that in many countries there is a significant gap between enrolment and retention levels of girls and boys in basic education programmes, just as there is a gap in literacy between adult men and women, which denies women of all ages the opportunity to participate fully in national development activities,

Bearing in mind that increased literacy levels have already been directly associated with reduced population growth in many parts of the world and that the promotion of women's literacy is an important element in ensuring the success of national objectives relating to population,

1. *Notes with appreciation* the commendable work done in connection with International Literacy Year by the specialized agencies and other organizations of the United Nations system, including the United Nations Educational, Scientific and Cultural Organization, with its Plan of Action for the Eradication of Illiteracy by the Year 2000, the United Nations Children's Fund and the United Nations Development Programme;

1/ Resolution 217 A (III).

2/ See resolution 2200 A (XXI), annex.

3/ *Report of the World Conference to Review and Appraise the Achievements of the United Nations Decade for Women: Equality, Development and Peace, Nairobi, 15-26 July 1985* (United Nations publication, Sales No. E.85.IV.10), chap. I, sect. A.

4/ See *Official Records of the Economic and Social Council, 1990, Supplement No. 5* (E/1990/25), chap. I, sect. C.

5/ Resolution 34/180, annex.

6/ *Final Report of the World Conference on Education for All: Meeting Basic Learning Needs, Jomtien, Thailand, 5-9 March 1990,* Inter-Agency Commission (UNDP, UNESCO, UNICEF, World Bank) for the World Conference on Education for All, New York, 1990, appendix 1.

7/ A/45/625, annex.

8/ See resolution 45/199, annex.

2. *Commends* those Governments that have launched national programmes aimed at meeting the objectives of the Year;

3. *Notes with satisfaction* the active involvement of many non-governmental organizations in the Year and, in particular, the establishment of the International Task Force on Literacy;

4. *Encourages* the Secretary-General and Member States, as well as intergovernmental and non-governmental organizations, to continue to support efforts to increase literacy by:

(a) Improving the educational opportunities for females of all ages, particularly children;

(b) Providing basic education to all without discrimination based on gender and in settings that are accessible and culturally acceptable;

(c) Encouraging the development of gender-specific indicators and measurements for assessing the impact of educational and training efforts in both domestic and international projects and programmes and for assessing the inclusion and participation of women of all ages in those efforts;

5. *Encourages* Member States to attempt to disaggregate by gender data in such areas as school enrolment, completion, participation and repetition rates;

6. *Urges* Member States to eliminate *de jure* and de facto barriers to schooling for women of all ages;

7. *Calls upon* Member States to give special attention and emphasis to the guidelines and recommendations developed for the Year when implementing measures to eliminate illiteracy;

8. *Encourages* the Secretary-General, in collaboration with relevant United Nations organizations, including the United Nations Educational, Scientific and Cultural Organization, the United Nations Children's Fund and the United Nations Development Programme,

to assist Member States in strengthening strategies to target resources to women of all ages, especially those most disadvantaged, and thereby work towards the elimination of illiteracy of women of all ages;

9. *Calls upon* Member States to accelerate the participation of women in literacy programmes, particularly in areas pertaining to the improvement of their socio-economic condition, including legal literacy and income-generating and skill-building activities;

10. *Encourages* Member States to increase the number of tutors and trainers with the necessary qualifications, to maximize their efforts to reach women and to increase the participation of non-governmental and private volunteer organizations, particularly women's organizations, in the implementation and management of literacy programmes and in policy and programme development;

11. *Requests* the Secretary-General to prepare for the world conference on women to be held in 1995 a report on the progress to increase female literacy made by Governments, intergovernmental and non-governmental organizations and the specialized agencies, regional commissions and other organizations of the United Nations system;

12. *Requests* the Committee on the Elimination of Discrimination against Women to pay particular attention to measures taken by Governments to increase female literacy, particularly by ensuring equal access to basic education for girls and boys;

13. *Requests* the Secretary-General in his next update to the *World Survey on the Role of Women in Development* 9/ to examine specifically the relationship between the literacy of women and their economic and social advancement.

9/ See United Nations publication, Sales No.E.89.IV.2.

Document 100

General Assembly resolution endorsing the ECOSOC recommendation that a world conference on women be held in 1995

A/RES/45/129, 14 December 1990

The General Assembly,

Recalling all its relevant resolutions, in particular resolution 44/77 of 8 December 1989, in which, *inter alia*, it endorsed and reaffirmed the importance of the Nairobi Forward-looking Strategies for the Advancement of Women 1/ for the period up to the year 2000 and

set out measures for their immediate implementation and for the overall achievement of the interrelated goals and

1/ *Report of the World Conference to Review and Appraise the Achievement of the United Nations Decade for Women: Equality, Development and Peace, Nairobi, 15-26 July 1985* (United Nations publication, Sales No. E.85.IV.10), chap. I, sect. A.

objectives of the United Nations Decade for Women: Equality, Development and Peace,

Taking into consideration the resolutions adopted by the Economic and Social Council on issues relating to women since its resolution 1987/18 of 26 May 1987,

Reaffirming its resolution 40/30 of 29 November 1985, in which it emphasized that the elderly must be considered an important and necessary element in the development process at all levels within a given society and that, consequently, elderly women should be considered contributors to as well as beneficiaries of development,

Reaffirming also its determination to encourage the full participation of women in economic, social, cultural, civil and political affairs and to promote development, cooperation and international peace,

Conscious of the important and constructive contribution to the improvement of the status of women made by the Commission on the Status of Women, the specialized agencies, the regional commissions and other organizations and bodies of the United Nations system and non-governmental organizations concerned,

Emphasizing once again the priority of the implementation, monitoring, review and appraisal of the Forward-looking Strategies,

Recognizing the advancement of women as one of the priorities of the Organization for the biennium 1990-1991,

Recognizing that the Commission held in 1990 a session of extended duration to review and appraise progress in the implementation of the Forward-looking Strategies,

1. *Takes note* of the report of the Secretary-General; 2/

2. *Also takes note* of the recommendations and conclusions arising from the first review and appraisal of the implementation of the Forward-looking Strategies, contained in the annex to Economic and Social Council resolution 1990/15 of 24 May 1990;

3. *Urges* Governments, international organizations and non-governmental organizations to implement the recommendations;

4. *Reaffirms* paragraph 2 of section I of the recommendations and conclusions, in which it is stated that the pace of implementation of the Forward-looking Strategies must be improved in the crucial last decade of the twentieth century since the cost to societies of failing to implement the Strategies would be high in terms of slowed economic and social development, misuse of human resources and reduced progress for society as a whole and, for that reason, immediate steps should be taken to remove the most serious obstacles to the implementation of the Strategies;

5. *Calls again upon* Member States to give priority to policies and programmes relating to the subtheme "Employment, health and education", in particular to literacy, for the empowerment of women, especially those in the rural areas, to meet their own needs through self-reliance and the mobilization of indigenous resources, as well as to issues relating to the role of women in economic and political decision-making, population, the environment and information;

6. *Reaffirms* the central role of the Commission on the Status of Women in matters related to the advancement of women, and calls upon it to continue promoting the implementation of the Forward-looking Strategies to the year 2000, based on the goals of the United Nations Decade for Women: Equality, Development and Peace and the subtheme "Employment, Health and Education", and urges all organizations of the United Nations system to cooperate effectively with the Commission in this task;

7. *Requests* the Commission, when considering the priority theme relating to development during its thirty-fifth and subsequent sessions, to ensure its early contribution to the work of the international meeting on population to be held in 1994 and to address the role of technologies in the development of developing countries;

8. *Endorses* Economic and Social Council resolution 1990/12 of 24 May 1990, in which the Council recommended that a world conference on women should be held in 1995 and requested that the Commission act as the preparatory body for the world conference;

9. *Takes note* of the invitation extended by the Government of Austria to host the world conference on women in 1995 at Vienna;

10. *Requests* the Commission, as the preparatory body for the world conference, to decide on the venue of the conference, not later than 1992, bearing in mind that preference should be given to those regions that have not yet hosted a world conference on women;

11. *Also requests* the Commission, in deciding on the preparation of documentation for the conference, to pay attention to Economic and Social Council resolution 1990/9 of 24 May 1990 concerning the second report on the implementation of the Forward-looking Strategies;

12. *Further requests* the Commission to focus the agenda of the world conference in 1995 on the Forward-looking Strategies as well as on the recommendations and conclusions arising from the first review and appraisal of the implementation of the Strategies; 3/

2/ A/45/489.
3/ E/CN.6/1990/5.

13. *Requests* the Commission to ask the Secretary-General to appoint not later than 1992 the Secretary-General of the conference;

14. *Requests* the relevant United Nations bodies to continue to provide action-oriented input when reporting to the Commission on the priority theme;

15. *Emphasizes*, in the framework of the Forward-looking Strategies, the importance of the total integration of women in the development process, bearing in mind the specific and urgent needs of the developing countries, and calls upon Member States to establish specific targets at each level in order to increase the participation of women in professional, management and decision-making positions in their countries;

16. *Also emphasizes* the need to give urgent attention to redressing socio-economic inequities at the national and international levels as a necessary step towards the full realization of the goals and objectives of the Forward-looking Strategies;

17. *Urges* that particular attention be given by the United Nations and Governments to the situation of disabled women and that Governments take steps to ensure the equalization of opportunities for these women in the economic, social and political fields;

18. *Also urges* the Commission, the relevant organizations of the United Nations and Governments to give particular attention to refugee women and children and migrant women, taking into account their contribution in the social, economic and political fields and the urgent need to avoid all kinds of discrimination against them;

19. *Endorses* the convening in 1991 of a high-level interregional consultation on women in public life, to be financed within existing resources and from voluntary and other contributions;

20. *Requests* the Secretary-General, in formulating the system-wide medium-term plan for the advancement of women for the period 1996-2001 and in integrating the Forward-looking Strategies into activities mandated by the General Assembly, to pay particular attention to the strengthening of national machineries for the advancement of women and to specific sectoral themes that cut across the three objectives, equality, development and peace, and include, in particular, literacy, education, health, population, the environment and the full participation of women in decision-making;

21. *Also requests* the Secretary-General to continue updating the *World Survey on the Role of Women in Development*, 4/ bearing in mind its importance, placing particular emphasis on the adverse impact of the difficult economic situation affecting the majority of developing countries, in particular on the condition of women, and giving special attention to worsening conditions for the incorporation of women into the labour force as well as to the impact of reduced expenditures for social services on women's opportunities for education, health and child care, and to submit a preliminary version of the updated *World Survey on the Role of Women in Development* to the Economic and Social Council, through the Commission, in 1993 and a final version in 1994;

22. *Requests* Governments, when presenting candidatures for vacancies in the Secretariat, in particular at the decision-making level, to give priority to women's candidatures, and requests the Secretary-General in reviewing these candidatures to give special consideration to female candidates from underrepresented and unrepresented developing countries;

23. *Requests* the Secretary-General to invite Governments, organizations of the United Nations system, including the regional commissions and the specialized agencies, and intergovernmental and non-governmental organizations to report periodically to the Economic and Social Council, through the Commission, on activities undertaken at all levels to implement the Forward-looking Strategies;

24. *Also requests* the Secretary-General to continue to provide for the existing weekly radio programmes on women in the regular budget of the United Nations, making adequate provisions for broadcasts in different languages, and to develop the focal point for issues relating to women in the Department of Public Information of the Secretariat, which, in concert with the Centre for Social Development and Humanitarian Affairs of the Secretariat, should provide a more effective public information programme relating to the advancement of women;

25. *Further requests* the Secretary-General to include in his report on the implementation of the Forward-looking Strategies, to be submitted to the General Assembly at its forty-sixth session, an assessment of recent developments that are relevant to the priority themes to be considered at the subsequent session of the Commission and to transmit to the Commission a summary of relevant views expressed by delegations during the debate in the Assembly;

26. *Requests* the Secretary-General to report to the General Assembly at its forty-sixth session on measures taken to implement the present resolution;

27. *Decides* to consider these questions further at its forty-sixth session under the item entitled "Forward-looking strategies for the advancement of women to the year 2000".

4/ See United Nations publications, Sales No. E.89.IV.2.

Document 101

General Assembly resolution calling for improvement in the status of women in the United Nations Secretariat

A/RES/45/239 C, 21 December 1990

[Editor's note: Similar resolutions have been adopted by the General Assembly since 1975 and every year since 1990.]

Improvement of the status of women in the Secretariat

The General Assembly,

Reaffirming that the United Nations shall place no restrictions on the eligibility of men and women to participate in any capacity and under conditions of equality in its principal and subsidiary organs,

Recalling Articles 97, 100 and 101 of the Charter of the United Nations,

Recalling its resolution 2715 (XXV) of 15 December 1970, in which it first addressed the question of the employment of women in the Professional category, and all relevant resolutions that have continued to focus on this area since then, particularly its resolution 40/258 B of 18 December 1985, in which it welcomed the action programme to improve the status of women in the Secretariat for 1985-1990,

Noting with satisfaction that the question of the improvement of the status of women in the secretariats of the United Nations system continues to be a standing item on the agenda of the Administrative Committee on Coordination,

Taking account of the relevant part of the report of the International Civil Service Commission, 1/

Taking note of the report of the Secretary-General on the improvement of the status of women in the Secretariat 2/ and section II.G of the report of the Secretary-General on the composition of the Secretariat, 3/

Noting with concern that, although there has been a slight increase in the percentage of women in the Secretariat, women fill only 7.1 per cent of posts at the D-1 level and above,

Reaffirming that the Fifth Committee is the appropriate Main Committee of the General Assembly entrusted with responsibility for administrative, budgetary and personnel matters, including, *inter alia*, the issue of representation of women in the Secretariat,

1. *Reiterates* its full support for the Secretary-General as the chief administrative officer of the Organization and his prerogatives and responsibilities under the Charter of the United Nations;

2. *Urges* the Secretary-General to continue his efforts to increase the number of women in posts subject to geographical distribution, particularly in senior policy-level and decision-making posts, in order to achieve an overall participation rate of 30 per cent by the end of 1990 and, to the extent possible to 35 per cent by 1995, taking into account the principle that the paramount consideration shall be the necessity of securing the highest standards of efficiency, competence and integrity with full respect for the principle of equitable geographical distribution;

3. *Also urges* the Secretary-General, all things being equal and to the extent possible, to accord priority to the participation of women at the D-1 level and above with a view to increasing the participation rate of women in posts at the D-1 level and above to 25 per cent of the total within the overall participation rate of women in 35 per cent of posts subject to geographical distribution by 1995.

4. *Reiterates its request* that the Secretary-General make every effort to increase the representation of women from developing countries, in particular at the D-1 level and above;

5. *Requests* the Secretary-General to make every effort to increase the representation of women from those countries with a low representation of women;

6. *Also requests* the Secretary-General, in accordance with General Assembly resolution 44/185 C of 19 December 1989, to develop an action programme for the advancement of women in the Secretariat for the period 1991-1995, incorporating as necessary the unfulfilled points of the 1985-1990 action programme and to report thereon to the Assembly at its forty-sixth session;

7. *Further requests* the Secretary-General to include in the action programme for the advancement of women in the Secretariat for the period 1991-1995: (a) a comprehensive evaluation and analysis by the Secretariat of the main obstacles to the improvement of the status of women in the Organization; (b) proposed measures to overcome the underrepresentation of women from certain Member States; and (c) a detailed programme of activities, including monitoring procedures and a timetable for their completion;

8. *Requests* the Secretary-General to maintain the existing Secretariat machinery and to consider the ade-

1/ *Official Records of the General Assembly, Forty-fifth Session, Supplement No. 30* and addendum (A/45/30 and Add.1), chap. VIII.
2/ A/45/548.
3/ A/45/541.

quacy of the existing machinery to implement the action programme, taking account of the workloads in the relevant offices, and to report thereon when submitting the action programme for the period 1991-1995;

9. *Requests* Member States to continue to support the efforts of the United Nations, the specialized agencies and related organizations to increase the participation of women in the Professional category and above by, *inter alia*, nominating more women candidates, especially for senior policy-level and decision-making posts, by encouraging women to apply for vacant posts and by creating national rosters of women candidates to be shared with the Secretariat, specialized agencies and related organizations.

Document 102

"Overview of the world's women", from The World's Women: Trends and Statistics, 1970-1990 *(extract)*

ST/ESA/STAT/SER.K/8, 1991

Words advocating the interests of women, however plausible and persuasive they may be, need numbers to influence policy and change the world. Numbers are also needed to better inform women of how their lives are changing or not changing—globally, regionally and nationally. That was one of the main conclusions of the World Conference of the International Women's Year, held in Mexico City in 1975, where women's leaders proclaimed 1976-1985 as the United Nations Decade for Women: Equality, Development and Peace, and called on the United Nations statistical services to compile and monitor indicators in several key categories for women: 1/

Family life. How are women's responsibilities in the family changing relative to men's? How are changes in households providing greater opportunities and affecting what women do?

Leadership and decision-making. How many women are represented in government, business and the community? Is their influence on the rise?

Health and child-bearing. Are women living longer, healthier lives? How does the health of women—and girls—compare with men's? What choices do women have in child-bearing? And what are the risks connected with child-bearing worldwide?

Education. Are women better educated today than 20 years ago? How does their education compare with men's?

Economic life. What do women contribute to production—and to development? How is that contribution valued—and measured?

Remarkably there were few indicators available in the early 1970s to answer even the most basic questions. Now there are. This book pieces together what's available to give a more coherent set of indicators and a clearer picture of where women stand.

Consider this: the number of illiterate women rose from 543 million in 1970 to 597 million in 1985, while the number of illiterate men rose from 348 million to 352 million.

And this: women work as much as or more than men everywhere, as much as 13 hours, on average, more each week according to studies in Asia and Africa.

And this: of 8,000 abortions in Bombay after parents learned the sex of the foetus through amniocentesis, only one would have been a boy. 2/

Numbers can thus give words considerable power — the power to change.

Regional trends—1970-1990

Over the past 20 years there have been important changes in what women do—out of choice or necessity, depending on the hardships and opportunities they face.

In *Latin America and the Caribbean*, women in urban areas made some significant gains according to indicators of health, child-bearing, education and economic, social and political participation. But there was little change in rural areas and the serious macroeconomic deterioration of many Latin American countries in the 1980s undercut even the urban gains as the decade progressed.

In *sub-Saharan Africa*, there was some improvement for women in health and education, but indicators in these fields are still far from even minimally acceptable levels in most countries. Fertility remains very high, and there are signs that serious economic decline—coupled with rapid population growth—is undermining even the modest gains in health and education. Women's economic and social participation and contribution is high in sub-Saharan

1/ See *Report of the World Conference of the International Women's Year, Mexico City, 19 June-2 July 1975* (United Nations publication, Sales No. E.76.IV.1), chap. II, sect. A, paras. 161-173.
2/ Government of India, Department of Women and Child Development, Ministry of Human Resource Development, *The Lesser Child: the Girl in India* (New Delhi, n.d.).

Africa. But given the large differences between men and women in other economic, social and political indicators at the start of the 1970s, the limited progress in narrowing those differences since then and the general economic decline, the situation for women in Africa remains grave.

In *northern Africa and western Asia*, women made substantial gains in health and education. Fertility declined slightly but remains very high—5.5 children in northern Africa and 5.3 in western Asia. Women in these regions continue to lag far behind in their economic participation and in social participation and decision-making.

In *southern Asia*, women's health and education improved somewhat. But as in Africa, indicators are still far from minimally acceptable levels — and are still very far from men's. Nor has economic growth, when it has occurred, helped women — apparently because of their low social, political and economic participation in both urban and rural areas.

In much of *eastern and south-eastern Asia*, women's levels of living improved steadily in the 1970s and 1980s. Many of the inequalities between men and women—in health, education and employment—were reduced in both urban and rural areas and fertility also declined considerably. Even so, considerable political and economic inequalities persist in much of the region—because women are confined to the lowest paid and lowest status jobs and sectors and because they are excluded from decision-making.

Throughout the *developed regions*, women generally are in good health and their fertility is low. But in other fields, indicators of the status of women show mixed results. Women's economic participation is high in eastern Europe and the USSR, northern Europe and northern America—lower in Australia, Japan, New Zealand and southern and western Europe. Everywhere occupational segregation and discrimination in wages and training work very much in favour of men. In political participation and decision-making, women are relatively well represented only in northern and western Europe and (at least until recently) the USSR.

Gaps in policy, investment and pay

Resounding throughout the statistics in this book is one consistent message. Major gaps in policy, investment and earnings prevent women from performing to their full potential in social, economic and political life.

Policy gaps

Integration of women in mainstream development policies. The main policy gap is that governments seldom integrate the concerns and interests of women into mainstream policies. Development policies typically emphasize export-oriented growth centred on cash crops, primary commodities and manufactures—largely controlled by men. Those policies typically neglect the informal sector and subsistence agriculture—the usual preserve of women. Even when women are included in mainstream development strategies, it is often in marginal women-in-development activities.

Much of this gap is embodied in laws that deny women equality with men in their rights to own land, borrow money and enter contracts. Even where women now have *de jure* equality, the failures to carry out the law deny equality de facto. Consider Uganda, which has a new constitution guaranteeing full equality for women. One women's leader there had this assessment: "We continue to be second-rate citizens—no, third-rate, since our sons come before us. Even donkeys and tractors sometimes get better treatment." 3/

Counting women's work. A second policy gap is that governments do not consider much of women's work to be economically productive and thus do not count it. If women's unpaid work in subsistence agriculture and housework and family care were fully counted in labour force statistics, their share of the labour force would be equal to or greater than men's. And if their unpaid housework and family care were counted as productive outputs in national accounts, measures of global output would increase 25 to 30 per cent.

Even when governments do consider women's work to be economically productive, they overlook or undervalue it. Until recently, labour force statistics counted production narrowly, excluding such activities as grinding grain and selling home-grown food at the market. The International Labour Organization widened the definition in 1982, but the application of the new standard is far from universal, and in most countries and regions only a small part of women's production is measured. Without good information about what women really do—and how much they produce—governments have little incentive to respond with economic policies that include women. 4/

Investment gaps

Education. There also are big gaps between what women could produce and the investments they command. Households—and governments—almost always invest less in women and girls than in men and boys. One

3/ Miria Matembe, "Speaking out for women in Abuja", *Africa Recovery*, vol. 3, No. 3 (United Nations publication, 1989).

4/ See *Improving Concepts and Methods for Statistics and Indicators on the Situation of Women*, Series F, No. 33 (United Nations publication, Sales No. E.84.XVII.3); *Methods of Measuring Women's Participation and Production in the Informal Sector*, Series F, No. 46 (United Nations publication, Sales No. E.90.XVII.16); and "Development of guidelines on national accounts for women's contribution to development", report of the Secretary-General to the Statistical Commission at its twenty-fifth session (E/CN.3/1989/12).

measure of this is enrolment in school: roughly 60 per cent of rural Indian boys and girls enter primary school, but after five years, only 16 per cent of the girls are still enrolled, compared with 35 per cent of the boys. 5/

The losses from investing less in girls' education are considerable. Studies in Malaysia show that the net return to education at all levels of wages and productivity is consistently 20 per cent higher for girls and young women than for boys and young men. 6/ And that does not include the second-round benefits of reduced fertility, improved nutrition and better family care.

One consequence of women's low educational achievement is that it puts them at a disadvantage to their husbands when making major life decisions about the work they do, the number of children they have and the way they invest family income.

Health services. Another investment gap is in health services. Women need, and too seldom receive, maternal health care and family planning services. And families often give lower priority to the health care of girls than boys. Where health services are being cut back, as they so often are under economic austerity programmes, the health needs of women are typically neglected.

Productivity. These gaps in investing in women's development persist in the investments that governments might make to increase their economic productivity. Governments give little or no support to activities in which women predominate—notably, the informal sector and subsistence agriculture. Indeed, government policies typically steer women into less productive endeavours. The infrastructure that might underpin their work is extremely inadequate. And the credit available to them from formal lending institutions is negligible. Often illiterate, usually lacking collateral and almost always discriminated against, women must rely on their husbands or on high-priced moneylenders if they want to invest in more productive ventures.

Pay gaps

Lower pay. There also are big gaps between what women produce and what they are paid. Occupational segregation and discrimination relegate women to low-paying, low-status jobs. And even when women do the same work as men, they typically receive less pay—30 to 40 per cent less on average world-wide. Nor are their prospects for advancement the same as men's, with deeply rooted prejudices blocking them from the top.

No pay. Another pay gap is that much of women's work is not paid and not recognized as economically productive. The work is considered to be of no economic importance and is not counted, which brings the discussion back to policy gaps.

Trends in child-bearing and family life

Giving women the means to regulate their child-bearing strengthens their control over their lives. Modern family planning methods make it far easier for women today to limit their fertility—and as important, to pick the timing and spacing of their births. Almost everywhere, the access to and the use of family planning are increasing, but not as rapidly as they might.

Fertility rates are declining in many developing countries but remain at quite high levels in most countries in Africa, in the southern Asia region and in countries of western Asia. Influencing the falling rates are broader use of effective family planning methods, changing attitudes about desired family size and reductions in infant mortality. With the spread of modern contraception, women are better able to limit their fertility. But safe contraception must be available and accepted by both women and men, and in some societies men often do not allow women to practise family planning.

The child-bearing gap between developed and developing regions remains wide. In Asia and Africa, a woman typically has her first child at about age 19 or even earlier, her last at 37, for a child-bearing span of 18 years. In some countries—such as Bangladesh, Mauritania, Nigeria, the Sudan and Yemen—girls often start having children at age 15. Compare this with developed regions, where a woman typically has her first child at 23 and her last at 30, for a span of only seven years. Women in developed regions have fewer children over a shorter span of years and thus need to devote a smaller part of their lives to child-bearing and parenting.

Family planning and health services have helped women in many ways—improving their overall health status and that of their children and increasing their opportunities to take an expanded role in society.

Child-bearing exposes women to a particular array of health risks. But the broader availability of family planning and maternal health services has reduced some of the risks of pregnancy and child-birth—delaying the first birth, allowing longer spacing between births, and reducing pregnancies among women who have had four or more births and thus face the greatest risk of haemorrhaging after giving birth. 7/ Complications from child-

5/ Jee Peng Tan and Michael Haines, "Schooling and demand for children: historical perspectives", World Bank Staff Working Paper, No. 697, Population and Development Series, No. 22 (Washington, D.C., World Bank, 1984).
6/ George Psacharopoulos, "Returns to education: a further international update and implication", *Journal of Human Resources,* vol. 20 (Fall 1985).
7/ Erica Royston and Sue Armstrong, eds., *Preventing Maternal Deaths* (Geneva, World Health Organization, 1989); and Judith S. McGuire and Barry M. Popkin, "Helping women improve nutrition in the developing world: beating the zero sum game", World Bank Technical Paper, No. 114 (Washington, D.C., World Bank, 1990).

bearing nevertheless remain a major (avoidable) cause of death for women in many developing countries — especially where family planning services are poor or hard to reach, where malnutrition is endemic among pregnant women and where births are not attended by trained personnel.

Healthier mothers are more likely to have full-term pregnancies and strong children. With more resources, they are better able to nurture their children. Better educated mothers are more likely to educate their children. The positive outcome: healthier, better educated families.

Poor women generally miss out on this positive cycle. Because they have little or no education, they have little knowledge of health practices and limited economic opportunities. They have no collateral for borrowing to invest in more productive activities. Simply trying to ensure that the family survives takes all their time. The unhappy outcome: sick, poorly educated families — and continuing poverty.

Poor teenage girls, the most vulnerable of mothers, face even greater obstacles. Cultural pressures, scant schooling and inadequate information about and access to family planning make them most likely to have unhealthy or unwanted pregnancies. In developed and developing countries alike, mothers aged 15-19 are twice as likely to die in childbirth as mothers in their early twenties, and those under 15 are five times as likely. 8/ They are less likely to obtain enough education or training to ensure a good future for themselves and their children.

Trends in marriages and households

In developed and developing regions alike, women now spend less time married and fewer years bearing and rearing children. Couples are marrying later and separating or divorcing more, in part because of their increased mobility and migration.

Throughout much of the world—the exceptions are in Asia and the Pacific—households are getting smaller and have fewer children. There are fewer multigenerational households, more single-parent families and more people living alone. Smaller households suggest the gradual decline of the extended family household, most evident in western developed countries, but also beginning to be apparent in developing countries. Also evident is a decline in the strength of kinship and in the importance of family responsibility combined with greater reliance on alternative support systems and greater variations in living arrangements.

Because more women are living (or forced to live) alone or as heads of households with dependants, their responsibility for their family's survival and their own has been increasing since 1970. Motherhood is more often unsupported by marriage and the elderly are more often unsupported by their children—trends that increase the burden on women. And even for women living with men, the man's income is often so inadequate that the woman must take on the double burden of household management and outside work to make ends meet.

Women face another burden that is invisible to the outside world: domestic violence. It is unmeasured but almost certainly very extensive. Domestic violence is masked by secretiveness and poor evidence, and there are social and legal barriers to its active prevention. Men's attacks on women in their homes are thought to be the least reported of crimes—in part because such violence is seen as a social ill, not a crime. Women's economic independence—and the corresponding ability to leave an abusive man—are essential for preventing violence and for fostering self-esteem. And as the awareness of women's rights becomes more universal and enforceable, more women will be opposing domestic violence.

Economic life

Economic growth in many of the developed regions has provided new opportunities for women in economic participation, production and income—despite persistent occupational and wage discrimination and the continuing exclusion of women's unpaid housework from economic measurement.

Some countries in Asia and a few in other developing regions were also able to sustain strong economic growth rates, again providing new opportunities for women despite even more pervasive social and economic obstacles to their economic advancement. But in most countries in the developing regions, as well as in eastern Europe and the USSR, the economic outlook was far worse in 1990 than in 1970. And world-wide the population living in the poorest countries increased dramatically. This mixed economic growth has created new obstacles to women's economic participation and their progress towards equality with men—seriously undercutting previous advances. And whether in circumstances of economic growth or decline, women have been called on to bear the greater burdens, and receive the fewest benefits. 9/

Women are the first to be dismissed from the salaried labour force by economic downturns and the

8/ Nafis Sadik, *Investing in Women: The Focus of the '90s* (New York, United Nations Population Fund).

9/ *Engendering Adjustment for the 1980s: Report of the Commonwealth Expert Group on Women and Structural Adjustment* (London, Commonwealth Secretariat Publications, 1989); Susan Joekes, "Gender and macro-economic policy", Association for Women in Development, Paper No. 4 (Blacksburg, Virginia, 1989); and *The Invisible Adjustment: Poor Women and the Economic Crisis* (Santiago, United Nations Children's Fund, Regional Office for the Americas and the Caribbean, 1989).

contractions under stabilization and adjustment programmes. With essentials less affordable because of rising inflation and falling subsidies, women have little choice but to work harder and longer. And when the demand for workers rises, as in Brazil in the late 1980s, the men find jobs at their old wages while the women must take jobs at even lower pay than before. 10/

Women's working world

Women's working world continues to differ from men's in the type of work, the pay, the status and the pattern of entering and leaving the work force. The biggest difference is that women continue to bear the burden of managing the household and caring for the family—and that men continue to control the resources for production and the income from it. In agriculture, for example, women continue to be left labour-intensive tasks that consume the most time. 11/

Women everywhere contribute to economic production. As officially measured, 46 per cent of the world's women aged 15 and over—828 million—are economically active. At least another 10-20 per cent of the world's women are economically productive but not counted as part of the labour force because of inadequate measurement.

Women are left to provide child care, to provide food and health care, to prepare and process crops, to market goods, to tend gardens and livestock and to weave cloth, carpets and baskets. Much of this work does not benefit from investment, making it very inefficient and forcing women to work very hard for meagre results. In the worst cases, technological investments end up exploiting women—improving their productivity but barring them from any access or control over the profits.

The pattern, then, is that women work as much or more than men. Although women spend less time in activities officially counted as economically productive and make much less money, they spend far more in home production. If a woman spends more time in the labour force, she still bears the main responsibility for home and family care, and sleep and leisure are sacrificed.

Economic participation

Men's participation in the labour force has fallen everywhere. Women's, by contrast, has fallen significantly only in sub-Saharan Africa, where economic crises have been most widespread. Women's share in the total labour force is increasing in most regions.

In many parts of the developed regions there have been increases in women's economic activity rates over the past two decades. Women's highest shares in wage and salaried employment are in eastern Europe and the Soviet Union, something that could change as new economic policies create widepread unemployment there.

In Africa, most public and wage employees are men, leaving women either in subsistence agriculture or to create whatever other opportunities they can in the informal sector.

In Asia and the Pacific, the picture is mixed. Women's economic activity rates (in official statistics) are very low (under 20 per cent) in southern and western Asia, but fairly high (35-40 per cent) in eastern and south-eastern Asia. Women's wage and salary employment rose considerably (from 44 to 57 per cent of the total, excluding southern Asia), reflecting significant expansion of economic opportunities for women.

In Latin America, women's economic participation grew fastest but remained at low levels (31 per cent in urban areas, 14 per cent in rural). The increase reflects greater opportunities in towns and cities as well as greater economic necessities arising from the ongoing economic crisis of the 1980s.

Occupational segregation and wage discrimination

Everywhere in the world the workplace is segregated by sex. Women tend to be in clerical, sales and domestic services and men in manufacturing and transport. Women work in teaching, care-giving and subsistence agriculture and men in management, administration and politics. Looking at job categories in more detail reveals even sharper segregation. For example, in teaching, women predominate in elementary or first level education while men predominate in higher education.

Women hold a mere 10-20 per cent of managerial and administrative jobs world-wide and less than 20 per cent of the manufacturing jobs. In Singapore barely 1 per cent of working women are in managerial work, compared with nearly 10 per cent for a much larger number of working men. Even when women work in male-dominated occupations, they are relegated to the lower echelons. Among all the organizations of the United Nations system, for example, women hold only 3 per cent of the top management jobs and 8 per cent of senior management positions, but 42 per cent of the entry-level civil service slots, suggesting that women are not usually promoted or hired directly into higher levels. Of the top 1,000 corporations in the United States, only two are headed by a woman, a mere 2/10 of 1 per cent. 12/

In every country having data, women's nonagricultural wage rates are substantially lower than men's. In some countries, the gap is around 50 per cent and only in very few is it less than 30 per cent. The average gap is between 30 per cent and 40 per cent and there is no sign that it is substantially narrowing.

10/ *The Invisible Adjustment...*
11/ McGuire and Popkin, op. cit.
12/ "Chief Executives of the *Business Week* 1000: A Directory", *Business Week*, 19 October 1989.

Even where women have moved into occupations dominated by men, their income remains lower. Take Canada, where women made solid inroads into administration, management, engineering, physical sciences, university teaching and law and medicine. Between 1971 and 1981 they accounted for nearly a third of the growth in these professions. Women in these professions earned about 15 per cent more than women in other professional categories, but they still lagged 15-20 per cent behind their male counterparts. 13/

The informal sector

One wedge of opportunity for women is the informal sector, including self-employment. Crucial to the survival strategies of many women, the informal sector also opens important long-term opportunities where salaried employment is closed to women, declining or inadequate. Women work in the informal sector because of necessity and convenience. It requires less skill and education. It has fewer biases in favour of men. And it is easier to reconcile with cultural norms that keep women near the home, for there is less conflict between working hours and household tasks. But informal employment is far less secure an employer than the formal workplace and productivity is often low.

Incomes may be lower in the informal sector for several reasons. One is the absence or high cost of credit. Another is lack of government support. A third is exploitation by larger firms controlling raw materials or markets. And although women's participation in the informal sector is increasing, the returns are declining. Studies show that there is greater difference in the earnings of men and women in the informal sector than in the formal. 14/

Women in the informal sector are vulnerable to even slight deteriorations in an economy. Especially in highly indebted countries, informal sector returns have fallen even more than formal sector returns, as more people are pushed into the informal sector. Despite the meagre earnings, the informal sector has been women's only recourse for surviving the economic crises in Africa and Latin America during the 1980s.

Public life and leadership

Women are poorly represented in the ranks of power, policy and decision-making. Women make up less than 5 per cent of the world's heads of State, heads of major corporations and top positions in international organizations. Women are not just behind in political and managerial equity, they are a long way behind. This is in spite of the fact that women are found in large numbers in low-level positions of public administrations, political parties, trade unions and businesses.

The picture barely improves at other decision-making levels. Fifty United Nations Member States have no woman in any of their top echelons of government. Although women have made some incursions in the past 20 years in parliaments and at middle management levels, their representation in these areas still averages less than 10 per cent and less than 20 per cent respectively. Their parliamentary representation would have to increase by 35 to 50 percentage points to reach parity with men. The eastern European and USSR parliaments are exceptions. Women have made up about a fourth of the parliamentary bodies there and played an important role. But recent elections show a significant drop in women's representation in these countries, just as parliaments—as a result of political changes—have become more important.

Women continue to be denied equal access to high-status and high-paying positions, but there has been some progress since the United Nations Decade for Women begun in 1976. Many countries have set up special offices to review complaints of discriminatory practice in political parties, parliaments, unions and professional organizations. Israel, Venezuela and several European countries have quotas to guarantee women more equal participation in the leadership of political parties. Trade unions in Canada, Norway and the United Kingdom have reserved a designated percentage of political seats for women. Women are also defining their own paths in politics. Increasing numbers are entering political life through non-governmental organizations, women's movements and associations of professional women. And women are increasingly active in the politics of their communities and locales.

Community and grass-roots participation have long been an extension of women's traditional place in the community and responsibility for the health and well-being of their families. The past 20 years have seen a burgeoning of groups headed by or heavily made up of women. Discriminatory practices, increasing poverty, violence against women, environmental threats, military build-ups, family and economic imperatives and the negative consequences of economic adjustment and stabilization programmes have all increased women's needs to band together to change conditions or policies. Women in both the developed and the developing regions have discovered that they can translate their efforts to protect themselves into effective political action.

Demands for equal status

International efforts to establish the rights of women culminated in 1979 with the General Assembly's adoption of the Convention on the Elimination of All Forms

13/ Katherine Marshall, "Women in male-dominated professions", *Canadian Social Trends* (Ottawa, Statistics Canada), Winter 1987.
14/ *Engendering Adjustment...*, p. 39.

Milestones of advocacy for women's equality

Women, more than ever, are on the global agenda, as a result of 30 years of constant advocacy and pressure.

1946 The United Nations Commission on the Status of Women is formed to monitor the situation of women and promote women's rights around the world.

1952 The Commission initiates the Convention on the Political Rights of Women, the first global mandate to grant women equal political rights under the law—the right to vote, hold office and exercise public functions.

1957 and 1962 Conventions initiated on the equality of married women, guaranteeing them equal rights in marriage and in dissolving marriage.

1967 Declaration on the Elimination of Discrimination against Women.

1975 International Women's Year. The World Conference on Women in Mexico City proclaims 1976-1985 as the United Nations Decade for Women: Equality, Development, Peace. Agencies are asked to collect thorough statistical information on women for the first time.

1979 The United Nations General Assembly adopts the Convention on the Elimination of all Forms of Discrimination against Women.

1980 The World Conference on Women in Copenhagen adopts the Programme of Action for the Second Half of the United Nations Decade for Women: Equality, Development and Peace. Agencies are asked to prepare the most recent data and time-trend analyses on the situation of women.

1985 The Nairobi World Conference reviews progress during the decade for women and adopts the Forward-looking Strategies for the Advancement of Women.

---

of Discrimination against Women (see annex II*). The Convention confronts stereotypes, customs and norms that give rise to the many legal, political and economic constraints on women. The legal status of women receives the broadest attention—for basic rights of political participation, civil rights and reproductive rights. One hundred two countries have ratified the Convention, legally binding themselves to incorporate the Convention's demands in their policies.

In 1985 the Nairobi Forward-Looking Strategies for the Advancement of Women were approved by 157 countries gathered to assess the achievements and failures of the United Nations Decade for Women (see annex I). The Strategies demand that governments:

- Play key roles in ensuring that both men and women enjoy equal rights in such areas as education, training and employment.

- Act to remove negative stereotypes and perceptions of women.

- Disseminate information to women about their rights and entitlements.

- Collect timely and accurate statistics on women and monitor their situation.

- Encourage the sharing and support of domestic responsibilities.

Even with progress in legislation, women—especially poor women—are still a long way from receiving social recognition for what they do. De facto discrimination on the grounds of sex is insidious but widespread. For example, the Bangladesh Constitution guarantees the equal rights of men and women and sanctions affirmative action programmes in favour of women, but as the data in the following chapters reveal, the status of women in Bangladesh is among the lowest in the world. It is encouraging, then, that policy makers there have stepped up efforts to implement programmes for women, particularly in health and education. 15/

Many societies deny women independence from family obligations and male control, particularly where girls are married at a very young age to much older men. According to estimates from the World Fertility Survey, almost half the women in Africa, 40 per cent in Asia and 30 per cent in Latin America are married by the age of 18. Men are on average four to eight years older. And a woman's social status is often linked entirely to her reproductive role. Failure to bear children—or even to bear sons—is cause for ostracism, divorce and even brutality in areas of Africa and southern Asia. 16/

The Nairobi Strategies restate demands in the 1957 and 1962 international conventions for equal status of women and men in marriage and in the dissolution of marriage. In addition to such reforms in marriage laws and practices, efforts to improve women's economic

*[Editor's note: Not reproduced here.]

15/ Rounaq Jahad, "Women and development in Bangladesh: challenges and opportunities" (Dhaka, Ford Foundation, 1989).

16/ Odile Frank, "Infertility in sub-Saharan Africa", Center for Policy Studies Working Paper, No. 97 (New York, The Population Council, 1983); and "The epidemiology of infertility—report of a WHO scientific group", Technical Report Series 582 (Geneva, World Health Organization, 1975).

status and autonomy—to reflect their economic responsibilities and contributions— can bring them closer to an equal footing with men in and out of the household.

Narrowing the gaps in the 1990s

The numbers throughout this book show the continuing gaps between men and women in policy, investment and pay. What's needed, of course, is equality of opportunity for women—in health, in education, in work and in decision-making at all levels. To get there is going to require extensive changes in policy, in government, in business and in the household, with women and men reworking the conventional assumptions about political, economic and family life. It is also going to require explicit initiatives to advance women's interests, initiatives informed by the analysis of numbers and grounded in the argument that advancing the interests of women benefits everyone.

The cost of these changes, especially when weighed against the benefit, would be small. Many of the policy changes cost nothing. Many of the required investments are small in relation to a country's gross domestic product — and in relation to military spending. True, closing the pay gap will cost something, and men will be the apparent losers. But better pay and incentives for women will increase productivity overall, so that everyone should benefit in the long run.

Many recent publications about women set out the agenda for action: the United Nations Population Fund's *Investing in Women*, the Commonwealth Secretariat's *Engendering Adjustment*, the World Bank's *Women in Development: A Progress Report on the World Bank Initiative*, UNDP's *Human Development Report 1990*, and UNICEF's *The Invisible Adjustment: Poor Women and the Economic Crisis*, among many others. 17/ Each gives its special emphasis to the broad agenda, with the recurring themes described below.

Counting what women do

National statistical services collect little data on women's economic contribution and income. One immediate need is to begin to quantify, and assign an economic value to, unpaid housework. Another is to measure women's paid work better. Also needed are disaggregations of all the main indicators by gender and improved compilation, analysis and dissemination of data already collected.

Putting women beside men at the centre of policy

The numbers in this book show how different women's situations are from men's—mainly because of the opportunities they lack. New laws can pave the way to better opportunities for women—in owning and managing productive resources, in entering contracts, in do-

ing many of the things men do in their daily work life. New policies—explicitly accommodating the special requirements of women for basic infrastructure, for access to credit and to markets, for technology and training and for child care—can do the same. This would cost little but require nothing short of a revolution in the way decisions are made in government, in business and in the household.

Investing in women's economic productivity

With the right policies, it will be possible to invest better in women's human capital and in their productive capital.

High maternal death rates are preventable. 18/ The nutrition of mothers is also easily improved — with modest resources yielding incalculable benefits in the long term. Ensuring that pregnant women have simple, regular prenatal care and a healthy diet with iron supplements would save hundreds of thousands of lives by reducing high-risk pregnancies and increasing the birthweight of newborns. Providing family planning, in addition to conferring considerable benefits on the health of mothers and their children, also has incalculable benefits in the long term, by reducing population growth.

All countries should increase the enrolment—and attendance—of girls at all levels of schooling and give them opportunities in all fields of study. Education does much for a woman's status — in society, in the workplace, in the family. It also enables women to take more control of their lives and to respond better to opportunities. Not least, it puts wives on more equal footing with their husbands in making important decisions about their families' future. Educational systems can also do much to eliminate the cultural and societal barriers that block women's opportunities. Of special concern, however, is dealing with the nearly 600 million illiterate women already missed by educational systems.

Agricultural extension has to be redirected to reach women farmers and respond better to the problems they face. Part of this involves using more women as extension and field workers, and part, developing and delivering technical packages that women can use. The counterpart to extension is rural infrastructure, to make women's efforts more productive and to give them better access to markets.

Credit programmes also need to be redirected to reach women generally. Programmes of small loans, such as those of the Grameen Bank in Bangladesh and of Women's World Banking in every region, are essential for women to respond to the opportunities they see in

17/ *Investing in Women...*; *Engendering Adjustment...*; *Women in Development...*, World Bank (Washington, D.C., 1990); *Human Development...*, United Nations Development Programme (New York and Oxford; Oxford University Press, 1990); *The Invisible Adjustment....*
18/ Royston and Armstrong, eds., op. cit.

farming, in small business, in training and in moving up the ladder everywhere. 19/ Governments also need to provide other support for women's entrepreneurial endeavors in the informal sector—and in the formal sector. Also of importance is developing and delivering time-saving technology for women's unpaid work.

Reducing the gaps in pay

The requirements here are obvious: put an end to occupational segregation and wage discrimination, and recognize women's unpaid work as economically productive. These are matters for legislators, business leaders, and statistical services. But these are also matters for men and, above all, women. Men are not going to open the doors to their domains. Women are. And equipped with better skills and different views of their role in life, they will.

In sum: the agenda for the 1990s is to invest more in women — and to broaden their opportunities. Investing in wider opportunities for women — in health, in education, in formal and informal work and in decision-making at all levels — is far more than an investment in women, for it is an investment in their families and societies. It is a way to lift people out of poverty. It is a way to slow population growth. It is a way to protect the environment. And it is a way to get onto a path of equitable, sustainable development.

19/ See Andreas Fuglesand and Dale Chandler, "Participation as process: what we can learn about Grameen Bank, Bangladesh" (Oslo, Norwegian Ministry of Development Cooperation, 1986); and "Women's World Banking: Background Paper 1980" (New York, Women's World Banking, Inc., 1980).

Document 103

General Assembly resolution on implementation of the Nairobi Forward-looking Strategies and requesting the CSW to give special attention to women in developing countries

A/RES/46/98, 16 December 1991

The General Assembly,

Recalling all its relevant resolutions, in particular resolution 44/77 of 8 December 1989, in which, *inter alia*, it endorsed and reaffirmed the importance of the Nairobi Forward-looking Strategies for the Advancement of Women 1/ for the period up to the year 2000 and set out measures for their immediate implementation and for the overall achievement of the interrelated goals and objectives of the United Nations Decade for Women: Equality, Development and Peace,

Recalling also its resolution 45/129 of 14 December 1990,

Taking into consideration the resolutions adopted by the Economic and Social Council on issues relating to women since its resolution 1987/18 of 26 May 1987,

Reaffirming its resolution 40/30 of 29 November 1985, in which it emphasized that the elderly must be considered an important and necessary element in the development process at all levels within a given society and that, consequently, elderly women should be considered contributors to as well as beneficiaries of development,

Reaffirming also its determination to encourage the full participation of women in economic, social, cultural, civil and political affairs and to promote development, cooperation and international peace,

Conscious of the important and constructive contribution to the improvement of the status of women made by the Commission on the Status of Women, the specialized agencies, the regional commissions and other organizations and bodies of the United Nations system and non-governmental organizations concerned,

Concerned that the resources available to the programme on the advancement of women of the Secretariat are insufficient to ensure adequate support to the Committee on the Elimination of Discrimination against Women and effective implementation of other aspects of the programme, especially the preparations for the Fourth World Conference on Women, to be held in 1995,

Regretting that the high-level inter-regional consultation on women in public life did not take place in 1991 as scheduled,

Recognizing the advancement of women as one of the priorities of the Organization for the biennium 1990-1991,

1. *Takes note* of the report of the Secretary-General; 2/

1/ *Report of the World Conference to Review and Appraise the Achievements of the United Nations Decade for Women: Equality, Development and Peace, Nairobi, 15-26 July 1985* (United Nations publication, Sales No. E.85.IV.10), chap. I, sect. A.
2/ A/46/439.

2. *Reaffirms* paragraph 2 of section I of the recommendations and conclusions arising from the first review and appraisal of the implementation of the Nairobi Forward-looking Strategies for the Advancement of Women, contained in the annex to Economic and Social Council resolution 1990/15 of 24 May 1990, which called for an improved pace in the implementation of the Strategies in the crucial last decade of the twentieth century, since the cost to societies of failing to implement the Strategies would be high in terms of slowed economic and social development, misuse of human resources and reduced progress for society as a whole;

3. *Urges* Governments, international organizations and non-governmental organizations to implement the recommendations;

4. *Calls again upon* Member States to give priority to policies and programmes relating to the subtheme "Employment, health and education", in particular to literacy, for the empowerment of women, especially those in the rural areas, to meet their own needs through self-reliance and the mobilization of indigenous resources, as well as to issues relating to the role of women in economic and political decision-making, population, the environment and information;

5. *Reaffirms* the central role of the Commission on the Status of Women in matters related to the advancement of women, and calls upon it to continue promoting the implementation of the Forward-looking Strategies to the year 2000, based on the goals of the United Nations Decade for Women: Equality, Development and Peace and the subtheme "Employment, health and education", and urges all organizations of the United Nations system to cooperate effectively with the Commission in this task;

6. *Requests* the Commission, when considering the priority theme relating to development during its thirty-sixth and subsequent sessions, to ensure its early contribution to the work of forthcoming major international conferences such as the United Nations Conference on Environment and Development, to be held in 1992, the World Conference on Human Rights, to be held in 1993, and the International Conference on Population and Development, to be held in 1994, and to address the impact of technologies on women;

7. *Also requests* the Commission to give special attention to women in developing countries, particularly in Africa and the least developed countries, who suffer disproportionately from the effects of the global economic crisis and the heavy external debt burden, and to recommend further measures for the equalization of opportunity and for integration of these women into the development process when considering the priority theme relating to development;

8. *Requests* the Secretary-General to ensure that appropriate staff from the secretariats of the Committee on the Elimination of Discrimination Against Women and the Commission on the Status of Women participate in the preparatory process for the World Conference on Human Rights, as well as in the Conference itself, in accordance with General Assembly resolution 40/108 of 13 December 1985;

9. *Endorses anew* Economic and Social Council resolution 1990/12 of 24 May 1990, in which the Council recommended that a world conference on women should be held in 1995 and requested that the Commission act as the preparatory body for the world conference;

10. *Requests* the Commission to decide on the venue of the Fourth World Conference on Women not later than at its thirty-sixth session, in accordance with Commission decision 35/102 of 8 March 1991, 3/ bearing in mind that preference should be given to the region that has not yet hosted a world conference on women;

11. *Requests* the Secretary-General to appoint not later than 1992 the Secretary-General of the Conference;

12. *Requests* the relevant United Nations bodies to continue to provide action-oriented input when reporting to the Commission on the priority theme relating to development;

13. *Notes with satisfaction* the publication of *The World's Women 1970-1990* 4/ through the cooperative efforts of various United Nations organizations;

14. *Recommends* the further development of methods of compilation and data collection in areas of concern identified by the Commission, with a view to preparing in all official languages, as a background document for the Fourth World Conference on Women, an updated edition of the publication mentioned in paragraph 13 above;

15. *Emphasizes*, in the framework of the Forward-looking Strategies, the importance of the total integration of women in the development process, bearing in mind the specific and urgent needs of the developing countries, and calls upon Member States to establish specific targets at each level in order to increase the participation of women in professional, management and decision-making positions in their countries;

16. *Emphasizes once again* the need to give urgent attention to redressing socio-economic inequities at the national and international levels as a necessary step towards the full realization of the goals and objectives of the Forward-looking Strategies;

17. *Welcomes* the creation of the ad hoc open-ended working group to elaborate standard rules on the

3/ See *Official Records of the Economic and Social Council, 1991, Supplement No. 8* (E/1991/28), chap. I, sect. D.
4/ United Nations publication, Sales No. E.90.XVII.3.

equalization of opportunities for persons with disabilities;

18. *Urges* that particular attention be given by the United Nations and Governments to the situation of women with disabilities and that Governments take steps to ensure the equalization of opportunities for these women in the economic, social and political fields;

19. *Takes note* of the Guidelines on the Protection of Refugee Women prepared by the Office of the United Nations High Commissioner for Refugees, 5/ which provide practical means of ensuring the protection of refugee women, and which are in keeping with decisions of the Economic and Social Council and the Commission on the Status of Women on this issue;

20. *Recommends* that all organizations of the United Nations system include in the policy analyses of development issues, as well as in proposals for major international conferences and in development projects, the potential contribution of ageing and elderly women, as relevant;

21. *Notes* the relevance of the interregional consultation on women in public life to the preparation for the Fourth World Conference on Women, and requests that the Commission at its thirty-sixth session make recommendations to the General Assembly through the Economic and Social Council for the convening of the consultation not later than 1993;

22. *Urges* the Commission, the relevant organizations of the United Nations system and Governments to give particular attention to refugee women and children and migrant women, taking into account their contribution in the social, economic and political fields and the urgent need to avoid any kind of discrimination against them;

23. *Requests* the Secretary-General, in formulating the system-wide medium-term plan for the advancement of women for the period 1996-2001 and in integrating the Forward-looking Strategies into activities mandated by the General Assembly, to pay particular attention to the strengthening of national machineries for the advancement of women and to specific sectoral themes that cut across the three objectives, equality, development and peace, and include, in particular, literacy, education, health, population, the impact of technology on the environment and its effect on women and the full participation of women in decision-making;

24. *Also requests* the Secretary-General to continue updating the *World Survey on the Role of Women in Development*, 6/ bearing in mind its importance, placing particular emphasis on the adverse impact of the difficult economic situation affecting the majority of developing countries, in particular on the condition of women, and giving special attention to worsening conditions for the incorporation of women into the labour force, as well as the impact of reduced expenditures for social services on women's opportunities for education, health and child care, and to submit a preliminary version of the updated *World Survey on the Role of Women in Development* to the Economic and Social Council, through the Commission, in 1993 and a final version in 1994;

25. *Requests* Governments, when presenting candidatures for vacancies in the Secretariat, in particular at the decision-making level, to give priority to women's candidatures, and requests the Secretary-General in reviewing these candidatures to give special consideration to female candidates from underrepresented and unrepresented developing countries and to assist those countries in identifying suitable women candidates to fill vacancies at the decision-making level;

26. *Requests* the Secretary-General to invite Governments, organizations of the United Nations system, including the regional commissions and the specialized agencies, and intergovernmental and non-governmental organizations to report periodically to the Economic and Social Council, through the Commission, on activities undertaken at all levels to implement the Forward-looking Strategies;

27. *Also requests* the Secretary-General to continue to provide for the existing weekly radio programmes on women in the regular budget of the United Nations, making adequate provisions for broadcasts in different languages, and to develop the focal point for issues relating to women in the Department of Public Information of the Secretariat, which, in concert with the Centre for Social Development and Humanitarian Affairs of the Secretariat, should provide a more effective public information programme relating to the advancement of women;

28. *Further requests* the Secretary-General to include in his report on the implementation of the Forward-looking Strategies, to be submitted to the General Assembly at its forty-seventh session, an assessment of recent developments that are relevant to the priority themes to be considered at the subsequent session of the Commission and to transmit to the Commission a summary of relevant views expressed by delegations during the debate in the Assembly;

29. *Requests* the Fifth Committee, in reviewing the programme on the advancement of women contained in the proposed programme budget for the biennium 1992-1993, to ensure that established staffing levels, temporary assistance and other objects of expenditure are sufficient

5/ See document EC/SCP/67, annex, of the Executive Committee of the Programme of the United Nations High Commissioner for Refugees.
6/ United Nations publication, Sales No. E.89.IV.2.

to ensure adequate support to the Committee on the Elimination of Discrimination against Women and effective implementation of other aspects of the programme, especially the preparations for the Fourth World Conference on Women, and, if proposed resources are found to be insufficient, to determine the appropriate resource levels;

30. *Requests* the Secretary-General to report to the General Assembly at its forty-seventh session on measures taken to implement the present resolution;

31. *Decides* to consider the question of the forward-looking strategies for the advancement of women to the year 2000 at its forty-seventh session under the item entitled "Advancement of women".

Document 104

Agenda 21, adopted by the United Nations Conference on Environment and Development, held in Rio de Janeiro from 3 to 14 June 1992— Chapter 24: Global action for women towards sustainable and equitable development (extract)

A/CONF.151/26/Rev.1 (Vol. 1), 1992

...

Programme area

Basis for action

24.1 The international community has endorsed several plans of action and conventions for the full, equal and beneficial integration of women in all development activities, in particular the Nairobi Forward-looking Strategies for the Advancement of Women, 1/ which emphasize women's participation in national and international ecosystem management and control of environment degradation. Several conventions, including the Convention on the Elimination of All Forms of Discrimination against Women (General Assembly resolution 34/180, annex) and conventions of ILO and UNESCO have also been adopted to end gender-based discrimination and ensure women access to land and other resources, education and safe and equal employment. Also relevant are the 1990 World Declaration on the Survival, Protection and Development of Children and the Plan of Action for implementing the Declaration (A/45/625, annex). Effective implementation of these programmes will depend on the active involvement of women in economic and political decision-making and will be critical to the successful implementation of Agenda 21.

Objectives

24.2 The following objectives are proposed for national Governments:

(*a*) To implement the Nairobi Forward-looking Strategies for the Advancement of Women, particularly with regard to women's participation in national ecosystem management and control of environment degradation;

(*b*) To increase the proportion of women decision makers, planners, technical advisers, managers and extension workers in environment and development fields;

(*c*) To consider developing and issuing by the year 2000 a strategy of changes necessary to eliminate constitutional, legal, administrative, cultural, behavioural, social and economic obstacles to women's full participation in sustainable development and in public life;

(*d*) To establish by the year 1995 mechanisms at the national, regional and international levels to assess the implementation and impact of development and environment policies and programmes on women and to ensure their contributions and benefits;

(*e*) To assess, review, revise and implement, where appropriate, curricula and other educational material, with a view to promoting the dissemination to both men and women of gender-relevant knowledge and appreciation of women's roles through formal and non-formal education, as well as through training institutions, in collaboration with non-governmental organizations;

(*f*) To formulate and implement clear governmental policies and national guidelines, strategies and plans for the achievement of equality in all aspects of society, including the promotion of women's literacy, education, training, nutrition and health and their participation in key decision-making positions and in management of the environment, particularly as it pertains to their access to resources, by facilitating better access to all forms of credit, particularly in the informal sector, taking measures towards ensuring women's access to property rights as well as agricultural inputs and implements;

(*g*) To implement, as a matter of urgency, in accordance with country-specific conditions, measures to ensure

1/ *Report of the World Conference to Review and Appraise the Achievements of the United Nations Decade for Women: Equality, Development and Peace, Nairobi, 15-26 July 1985* (United Nations publication, Sales No. E.85.IV.10), chapter I, sect. A.

that women and men have the same right to decide freely and responsibly the number and spacing of their children and have access to information, education and means, as appropriate, to enable them to exercise this right in keeping with their freedom, dignity and personally held values;

(h) To consider adopting, strengthening and enforcing legislation prohibiting violence against women and to take all necessary administrative, social and educational measures to eliminate violence against women in all its forms.

Activities

24.3 Governments should take active steps to implement the following:

(a) Measures to review policies and establish plans to increase the proportion of women involved as decision makers, planners, managers, scientists and technical advisers in the design, development and implementation of policies and programmes for sustainable development;

(b) Measures to strengthen and empower women's bureaux, women's non-governmental organizations and women's groups in enhancing capacity-building for sustainable development;

(c) Measures to eliminate illiteracy among females and to expand the enrolment of women and girls in educational institutions, to promote the goal of universal access to primary and secondary education for girl children and for women, and to increase educational and training opportunities for women and girls in sciences and technology, particularly at the post-secondary level;

(d) Programmes to promote the reduction of the heavy workload of women and girl children at home and outside through the establishment of more and affordable nurseries and kindergartens by Governments, local authorities, employers and other relevant organizations and the sharing of household tasks by men and women on an equal basis, and to promote the provision of environmentally sound technologies which have been designed, developed and improved in consultation with women, accessible and clean water, an efficient fuel supply and adequate sanitation facilities;

(e) Programmes to establish and strengthen preventive and curative health facilities, which include women-centred, women-managed, safe and effective reproductive health care and affordable, accessible, responsible planning of family size and services, as appropriate, in keeping with freedom, dignity and personally held values. Programmes should focus on providing comprehensive health care, including pre-natal care, education and information on health and responsible parenthood, and should provide the opportunity for all women to fully breastfeed at least during the first four months post-partum. Programmes should fully support women's productive and reproductive roles and well-being and should

pay special attention to the need to provide equal and improved health care for all children and to reduce the risk of maternal and child mortality and sickness;

(f) Programmes to support and strengthen equal employment opportunities and equitable remuneration for women in the formal and informal sectors with adequate economic, political and social support systems and services, including child care, particularly day-care facilities and parental leave, and equal access to credit, land and other natural resources;

(g) Programmes to establish rural banking systems with a view to facilitating and increasing rural women's access to credit and to agricultural inputs and implements;

(h) Programmes to develop consumer awareness and the active participation of women, emphasizing their crucial role in achieving changes necessary to reduce or eliminate unsustainable patterns of consumption and production, particularly in industrialized countries, in order to encourage investment in environmentally sound productive activities and induce environmentally and socially friendly industrial development;

(i) Programmes to eliminate persistent negative images, stereotypes, attitudes and prejudices against women through changes in socialization patterns, the media, advertising, and formal and non-formal education;

(j) Measures to review progress made in these areas, including the preparation of a review and appraisal report which includes recommendations to be submitted to the 1995 world conference on women.

24.4 Governments are urged to ratify all relevant conventions pertaining to women if they have not already done so. Those that have ratified conventions should enforce and establish legal, constitutional and administrative procedures to transform agreed rights into domestic legislation and should adopt measures to implement them in order to strengthen the legal capacity of women for full and equal participation in issues and decisions on sustainable development.

24.5 States parties to the Convention on the Elimination of All Forms of Discrimination against Women should review and suggest amendments to it by the year 2000, with a view to strengthening those elements of the Convention related to environment and development, giving special attention to the issue of access and entitlements to natural resources, technology, creative banking facilities and low-cost housing, and the control of pollution and toxicity in the home and workplace. States parties should also clarify the extent of the Convention's scope with respect to the issues of environment and development and request the Committee on the Elimination of Discrimination against Women to develop guidelines regarding the nature of reporting such issues, required under particular articles of the Convention.

A) Areas requiring urgent action

24.6 Countries should take urgent measures to avert the ongoing rapid environmental and economic degradation in developing countries that generally affects the lives of women and children in rural areas suffering drought, desertification and deforestation, armed hostilities, natural disasters, toxic waste and the aftermath of the use of unsuitable agro-chemical products.

24.7 In order to reach these goals, women should be fully involved in decision-making and in the implementation of sustainable development activities.

B) Research, data collection and dissemination of information

24.8 Countries should develop gender-sensitive databases, information systems and participatory action-oriented research and policy analyses with the collaboration of academic institutions and local women researchers on the following:

(a) Knowledge and experience on the part of women of the management and conservation of natural resources for incorporation in the databases and information systems for sustainable development;

(b) The impact of structural adjustment programmes on women. In research done on structural adjustment programmes, special attention should be given to the differential impact of those programmes on women, especially in terms of cut-backs in social services, education and health and in the removal of subsidies on food and fuel;

(c) The impact on women of environmental degradation, particularly drought, desertification, toxic chemicals and armed hostilities;

(d) Analysis of the structural linkages between gender relations, environment and development;

(e) The integration of the value of unpaid work, including work that is currently designated "domestic", in resource accounting mechanisms in order better to represent the true value of the contribution of women to the economy, using revised guidelines for the United Nations System of National Accounts, to be issued in 1993;

(f) Measures to develop and include environmental, social and gender impact analyses as an essential step in the development and monitoring of programmes and policies;

(g) Programmes to create rural and urban training, research and resource centres in developing and developed countries that will serve to disseminate environmentally sound technologies to women.

C) International and regional cooperation and coordination

24.9 The Secretary-General of the United Nations should review the adequacy of all United Nations institutions, including those with a special focus on the role of women, in meeting development and environment objectives, and make recommendations for strengthening their capacities. Institutions that require special attention in this area include the Division for the Advancement of Women (Centre for Social Development and Humanitarian Affairs, United Nations Office at Vienna), the United Nations Development Fund for Women (UNIFEM), the International Research and Training Institute for the Advancement of Women (INSTRAW) and the women's programmes of regional commissions. The review should consider how the environment and development programmes of each body of the United Nations system could be strengthened to implement Agenda 21 and how to incorporate the role of women in programmes and decisions related to sustainable development.

24.10 Each body of the United Nations system should review the number of women in senior policy-level and decision-making posts and, where appropriate, adopt programmes to increase that number, in accordance with Economic and Social Council resolution 1991/17 on the improvement of the status of women in the Secretariat.

24.11 UNIFEM should establish regular consultations with donors in collaboration with UNICEF, with a view to promoting operational programmes and projects on sustainable development that will strengthen the participation of women, especially low-income women, in sustainable development and in decision-making. UNDP should establish a women's focal point on development and environment in each of its resident representative offices to provide information and promote exchange of experience and information in these fields. Bodies of the United Nations system, governments and non-governmental organizations involved in the follow-up to the Conference and the implementation of Agenda 21 should ensure that gender considerations are fully integrated into all the policies, programmes and activities.

Means of implementation

Financing and cost evaluation

24.12 The Conference secretariat has estimated the average total annual cost (1993-2000) of implementing the activities of this chapter to be about $40 million from the international community on grant or concessional terms. These are indicative and order-of-magnitude estimates only and have not been reviewed by Governments. Actual costs and financial terms, including any that are non-concessional, will depend upon, *inter alia*, the specific strategies and programmes Governments decide upon for implementation.

...

Document 105

General Assembly resolution on implementation of the Nairobi Forward-looking Strategies and requesting the CSW to complete work on a declaration on the elimination of violence against women

A/RES/47/95, 16 December 1992

The General Assembly,

Recalling all its relevant resolutions, in particular resolution 44/77 of 8 December 1989, in which, *inter alia*, it endorsed and reaffirmed the importance of the Nairobi Forward-looking Strategies for the Advancement of Women 1/ for the period up to the year 2000 and set out measures for their immediate implementation and for the overall achievement of the interrelated goals and objectives of the United Nations Decade for Women: Equality, Development and Peace,

Recalling also its resolution 46/98 of 16 December 1991,

Taking into consideration the resolutions adopted by the Economic and Social Council on issues relating to women since the adoption of its resolution 1987/18 of 26 May 1987,

Reaffirming its determination to encourage the full participation of women in economic, social, cultural, civil and political affairs and to promote development, cooperation and international peace,

Conscious of the important and constructive contribution to the improvement of the status of women made by the Commission on the Status of Women, the specialized agencies, the regional commissions and other organizations and bodies of the United Nations system and non-governmental organizations concerned,

Concerned that the resources available to the programme on the advancement of women of the Secretariat are insufficient to ensure adequate support to the Committee on the Elimination of Discrimination against Women and effective implementation of other aspects of the programme, especially the preparations for the Fourth World Conference on Women: Action for Equality, Development and Peace, to be held in 1995,

Welcoming the completion of work on the draft declaration on the elimination of violence against women by the inter-sessional working group of the Commission on the Status of Women,

Recognizing the advancement of women as one of the priorities of the Organization for the biennium 1992-1993,

1. *Takes note* of the report of the Secretary-General, 2/

2. *Reaffirms* paragraph 2 of section I of the recommendations and conclusions arising from the first review and appraisal of the implementation of the Nairobi Forward-looking Strategies for the Advancement of Women, contained in the annex to Economic and Social Council resolution 1990/15 of 24 May 1990, which called for an improved pace in the implementation of the Strategies in the crucial last decade of the twentieth century, since the cost to societies of failing to implement the Strategies would be high in terms of slowed economic and social development, inadequate use of human resources and reduced progress for society as a whole;

3. *Urges* Governments, international organizations and non-governmental organizations to implement the recommendations;

4. *Calls again upon* Member States to give priority to policies and programmes relating to the subtheme "Employment, health and education", in particular to literacy, for self-reliance of women and the mobilization of indigenous resources, as well as to issues relating to the role of women in economic and political decision-making, population, the environment and information;

5. *Reaffirms* the central role of the Commission on the Status of Women in matters related to the advancement of women, and calls upon it to continue promoting the implementation of the Forward-looking Strategies to the year 2000, based on the goals of the United Nations Decade for Women: Equality, Development and Peace and the subtheme "Employment, health and education", and urges all relevant bodies of the United Nations system to cooperate effectively with the Commission in this task;

6. *Requests* the Commission, when considering the priority theme relating to development during its thirty-seventh and subsequent sessions, to ensure its early contribution to the preparatory work of forthcoming major international conferences such as the World Conference on Human Rights, to be held in 1993, the International Conference on Population and Development, to be held in 1994, the Fourth World Conference on Women: Action for Equality, Development and Peace, to be held in 1995, and the World Summit on Social Development to be held in 1995, and to address the impact of technologies on women;

1/ *Report of the World Conference to Review and Appraise the Achievements of the United Nations Decade for Women: Equality, Development and Peace, Nairobi, 15-26 July 1985* (United Nations publication, Sales No. E.85.IV.10), chap. I, sect. A.
2/ A/47/377.

7. *Also requests* the Commission to give special attention to women in developing countries, particularly in Africa and the least developed countries, who suffer disproportionately from the effects of the global economic crisis and the heavy external debt burden, and to recommend further measures for the equalization of opportunity and for integration of these women into the development process when considering the priority theme relating to development;

8. *Endorses* Economic and Social Council decision 1992/272 of 30 July 1992 concerning the preparations for the Fourth World Conference on Women, in which the Council took note of Commission on the Status of Women resolution 36/8 of 20 March 1992, 3/ and expresses its appreciation to the Government of China for its offer to act as host for the Conference, to be held in Beijing from 4 to 15 September 1995;

9. *Requests* the Secretary-General to take into account section A, paragraph 6, of Commission resolution 36/8 when appointing the Secretary-General of the Conference;

10. *Also requests* the Secretary-General to ensure that appropriate staff from the secretariats of the Committee on the Elimination of Discrimination against Women and the Commission on the Status of Women participate in the preparatory process for the World Conference on Human Rights, as well as in the Conference itself, in accordance with General Assembly resolution 40/108 of 13 December 1985;

11. *Recommends* the further development of methods of compilation and data collection in areas of concern identified by the Commission and urges Member States to improve and broaden collection of gender-disaggregated statistical information and make it available to the relevant bodies of the United Nations system with a view to having prepared, in all official languages, as a background document for the Fourth World Conference on Women, an updated edition of *The World's Women 1970-1990: Trends and Statistics*; 4/

12. *Emphasizes*, in the framework of the Forward-looking Strategies, the importance of the total integration of women in the development process, bearing in mind the specific and urgent needs of the developing countries, and calls upon Member States to establish specific targets at each level in order to increase the participation of women in professional, management and decision-making positions in their countries;

13. *Emphasizes once again* the need to give urgent attention to redressing socio-economic inequities at the national and international levels as a necessary step towards the full realization of the goals and objectives of the Forward-looking Strategies;

14. *Urges* the Commission to complete its work on the draft declaration on the elimination of violence against women and to submit it for information to the World Conference on Human Rights;

15. *Strongly urges* that particular attention be given by the relevant United Nations organizations and Governments to the special needs of women with disabilities, to elderly women and also to women in vulnerable situations such as migrant and refugee women and children;

16. *Endorses* the recommendation contained in section B of Commission resolution 36/8 that regional preparatory conferences should include in their agendas the issue of women in public life, as well as the request that the Secretary-General include information on women in public life in the preparation of the priority theme, "Peace: women in international decision-making", for the Commission at its thirty-ninth session in 1995;

17. *Welcomes* the recommendations on women, environment and development in all programme areas, adopted at the United Nations Conference on Environment and Development, in particular chapter 24 of Agenda 21, entitled "Global action for women towards sustainable and equitable development", 5/

18. *Urges* organs, organizations and bodies of the United Nations to ensure active participation of women in the planning and implementation of programmes for sustainable development, and requests Governments to consider nominating women as representatives to the Commission on Sustainable Development; 6/

19. *Requests* the Secretary-General, in formulating the system-wide medium-term plan for the advancement of women for the period 1996-2001 and in integrating the Forward-looking Strategies into activities mandated by the General Assembly, to pay particular attention to specific sectoral themes that cut across the three objectives, equality, development and peace, and include, in particular, literacy, education, health, population, the impact of technology on the environment and its effect on women and the full participation of women in decision-making, and to continue to assist Governments in strengthening their national machineries for the advancement of women;

20. *Also requests* the Secretary-General to con-

3/ See *Official Records of the Economic and Social Council, 1992, Supplement No. 4* (E/1992/24), chap. I. sect. C.
4/ United Nations publication, Sales No. E.90.XVII.3.
5/ *Report of the United Nations Conference on Environment and Development, Rio de Janeiro, 3-14 June 1992* (A/CONF.151/26/Rev.1 (Vol. I and Vol. I/Corr.1, Vol. II, Vol. III/Corr.1)) (United Nations publication, Sales No. E.93.I.8 and corrigendum), vol. I: Resolutions adopted by the Conference, resolution 1, annex II.
6/ See resolution 47/191.

tinue updating the *World Survey on the Role of Women in Development*, 7/ bearing in mind its importance, placing particular emphasis on the adverse impact of the difficult economic situation affecting the majority of developing countries, particularly on the condition of women, giving special attention to worsening conditions for the incorporation of women into the labour force, as well as the impact of reduced expenditures for social services on women's opportunities for education, health and child care, and to submit a preliminary version of the updated *World Survey on the Role of Women in Development* to the Economic and Social Council, through the Commission, in 1993 and a final version in 1994;

21. *Requests* Governments, when presenting candidatures for vacancies in the Secretariat, in particular at the decision-making level, to give priority to women's candidatures, and requests the Secretary-General in reviewing these candidatures to give special consideration to female candidates from underrepresented and unrepresented developing countries;

22. *Requests* the Secretary-General to invite Governments, organizations of the United Nations system, including the regional commissions and the specialized agencies, and intergovernmental and non-governmental organizations to report periodically to the Economic and Social Council, through the Commission, on activities undertaken at all levels to implement the Forward-looking Strategies;

23. *Also requests* the Secretary-General to continue to provide for the existing weekly radio programmes on women in the regular budget of the United Nations, making adequate provisions for broadcasts in different languages, and to develop the focal point for issues relating to women in the Department of Public Information of the Secretariat, which, in concert with the Centre for Social Development and Humanitarian Affairs of the Secretariat, should provide a more effective public information programme relating to the advancement of women;

24. *Further requests* the Secretary-General to include in his report on the implementation of the Forward-looking Strategies, to submitted to the General Assembly at its forty-eighth session, an assessment of recent developments that are relevant to the priority themes to be considered at the subsequent session of the Commission and to transmit to the Commission a summary of relevant views expressed by delegations during the debate in the Assembly;

25. *Recommends* that the Commission on the Status of Women, as the preparatory body for the Fourth World Conference on Women, should consider at its next session the relevance of the resolutions drafted at the World Conference to Review and Appraise the Achievements of the United Nations Decade for Women: Equality, Development and Peace, held in 1985, in order to avoid duplication of work, keeping in mind that those resolutions were neither adopted by the Conference nor considered by the General Assembly;

26. *Requests* the Secretary-General to report to the General Assembly at its forty-eighth session on measures taken to implement the present resolution;

27. *Also requests* the Secretary-General to report to the General Assembly at its forty-eighth session on the state of preparation for the Fourth World Conference on Women under the item entitled "Advancement of women".

28. *Decides* to consider the implementation of the Forward-looking Strategies for the period up to the year 2000 at its forty-eighth session under the item entitled "Advancement of women".

7/ United Nations publication, Sales No. E.89.IV.2.

Document 106

Vienna Declaration and Programme of Action, adopted by the World Conference on Human Rights, held in Vienna from 14 to 25 June 1993—Section II.A.3: The equal status and human rights of women (extract)

A/CONF.157/24 (Part I), 13 October 1993

...

3. *The equal status and human rights of women*

36. The World Conference on Human Rights urges the full and equal enjoyment by women of all human rights and that this be a priority for Governments and for the United Nations. The World Conference on Human Rights also underlines the importance of the integration and full participation of women as both agents and beneficiaries in the development process, and reiterates the objectives established on global action for women towards sustainable and equitable development set forth

in the Rio Declaration on Environment and Development and chapter 24 of Agenda 21, adopted by the United Nations Conference on Environment and Development (Rio de Janeiro, Brazil, 3-14 June 1992).

37. The equal status of women and the human rights of women should be integrated into the mainstream of United Nations system-wide activity. These issues should be regularly and systematically addressed throughout relevant United Nations bodies and mechanisms. In particular, steps should be taken to increase cooperation and promote further integration of objectives and goals between the Commission on the Status of Women, the Commission on Human Rights, the Committee for the Elimination of Discrimination against Women, the United Nations Development Fund for Women, the United Nations Development Programme and other United Nations agencies. In this context, cooperation and coordination should be strengthened between the Centre for Human Rights and the Division for the Advancement of Women.

38. In particular, the World Conference on Human Rights stresses the importance of working towards the elimination of violence against women in public and private life, the elimination of all forms of sexual harassment, exploitation and trafficking in women, the elimination of gender bias in the administration of justice and the eradication of any conflicts which may arise between the rights of women and the harmful effects of certain traditional or customary practices, cultural prejudices and religious extremism. The World Conference on Human Rights calls upon the General Assembly to adopt the draft declaration on violence against women and urges States to combat violence against women in accordance with its provisions. Violations of the human rights of women in situations of armed conflict are violations of the fundamental principles of international human rights and humanitarian law. All violations of this kind, including in particular murder, systematic rape, sexual slavery, and forced pregnancy, require a particularly effective response.

39. The World Conference on Human Rights urges the eradication of all forms of discrimination against women, both hidden and overt. The United Nations should encourage the goal of universal ratification by all States of the Convention on the Elimination of All Forms of Discrimination against Women by the year 2000. Ways and means of addressing the particularly large number of reservations to the Convention should be encouraged. *Inter alia*, the Committee on the Elimination of Discrimination against Women should continue its review of reservations to the Convention. States are urged to withdraw reservations that are contrary to the object and purpose of the Convention or which are otherwise incompatible with international treaty law.

40. Treaty monitoring bodies should disseminate necessary information to enable women to make more effective use of existing implementation procedures in their pursuits of full and equal enjoyment of human rights and non-discrimination. New procedures should also be adopted to strengthen implementation of the commitment to women's equality and the human rights of women. The Commission on the Status of Women and the Committee on the Elimination of Discrimination against Women should quickly examine the possibility of introducing the right of petition through the preparation of an optional protocol to the Convention on the Elimination of All Forms of Discrimination against Women. The World Conference on Human Rights welcomes the decision of the Commission on Human Rights to consider the appointment of a special rapporteur on violence against women at its fiftieth session.

41. The World Conference on Human Rights recognizes the importance of the enjoyment by women of the highest standard of physical and mental health throughout their life span. In the context of the World Conference on Women and the Convention on the Elimination of All Forms of Discrimination against Women, as well as the Proclamation of Teheran of 1968, the World Conference on Human Rights reaffirms, on the basis of equality between women and men, a woman's right to accessible and adequate health care and the widest range of family planning services, as well as equal access to education at all levels.

42. Treaty monitoring bodies should include the status of women and the human rights of women in their deliberations and findings, making use of gender-specific data. States should be encouraged to supply information on the situation of women *de jure* and de facto in their reports to treaty monitoring bodies. The World Conference on Human Rights notes with satisfaction that the Commission on Human Rights adopted at its forty-ninth session resolution 1993/46 of 8 March 1993 stating that rapporteurs and working groups in the field of human rights should also be encouraged to do so. Steps should also be taken by the Division for the Advancement of Women in cooperation with other United Nations bodies, specifically the Centre for Human Rights, to ensure that the human rights activities of the United Nations regularly address violations of women's human rights, including gender-specific abuses. Training for United Nations human rights and humanitarian relief personnel to assist them to recognize and deal with human rights abuses particular to women and to carry out their work without gender bias should be encouraged.

43. The World Conference on Human Rights urges Governments and regional and international organiza-

tions to facilitate the access of women to decision-making posts and their greater participation in the decision-making process. It encourages further steps within the United Nations Secretariat to appoint and promote women staff members in accordance with the Charter of the United Nations, and encourages other principal and subsidiary organs of the United Nations to guarantee the participation of women under conditions of equality.

44. The World Conference on Human Rights welcomes the World Conference on Women to be held in Beijing in 1995 and urges that human rights of women should play an important role in its deliberations, in accordance with the priority themes of the World Conference on Women of equality, development and peace.

Document 107

General Assembly resolution adopting the Declaration on the Elimination of Violence against Women

A/RES/48/104, 20 December 1993

The General Assembly,

Recognizing the urgent need for the universal application to women of the rights and principles with regard to equality, security, liberty, integrity and dignity of all human beings,

Noting that those rights and principles are enshrined in international instruments, including the Universal Declaration of Human Rights, 1/ the International Covenant on Civil and Political Rights, 2/ the International Covenant on Economic, Social and Cultural Rights, 2/ the Convention on the Elimination of All Forms of Discrimination against Women 3/ and the Convention against Torture and Other Cruel, Inhuman or Degrading Treatment or Punishment, 4/

Recognizing that effective implementation of the Convention on the Elimination of All Forms of Discrimination against Women would contribute to the elimination of violence against women and that the Declaration on the Elimination of Violence against Women, set forth in the present resolution, will strengthen and complement that process,

Concerned that violence against women is an obstacle to the achievement of equality, development and peace, as recognized in the Nairobi Forward-looking Strategies for the Advancement of Women, 5/ in which a set of measures to combat violence against women was recommended, and to the full implementation of the Convention on the Elimination of All Forms of Discrimination against Women,

Affirming that violence against women constitutes a violation of the rights and fundamental freedoms of women and impairs or nullifies their enjoyment of those rights and freedoms, and concerned about the long-standing failure to protect and promote those rights and freedoms in the case of violence against women,

Recognizing that violence against women is a manifestation of historically unequal power relations between men and women, which have led to domination over and discrimination against women by men and to the prevention of the full advancement of women, and that violence against women is one of the crucial social mechanisms by which women are forced into a subordinate position compared with men,

Concerned that some groups of women, such as women belonging to minority groups, indigenous women, refugee women, migrant women, women living in rural or remote communities, destitute women, women in institutions or in detention, female children, women with disabilities, elderly women and women in situations of armed conflict, are especially vulnerable to violence,

Recalling the conclusion in paragraph 23 of the annex to Economic and Social Council resolution 1990/15 of 24 May 1990 that the recognition that violence against women in the family and society was pervasive and cut across lines of income, class and culture had to be matched by urgent and effective steps to eliminate its incidence,

Recalling also Economic and Social Council resolution 1991/18 of 30 May 1991, in which the Council recommended the development of a framework for an international instrument that would address explicitly the issue of violence against women,

Welcoming the role that women's movements are playing in drawing increasing attention to the nature, severity and magnitude of the problem of violence against women,

1/ Resolution 217 A (III).
2/ See resolution 2200 A (XXI), annex.
3/ Resolution 34/180, annex.
4/ Resolution 39/46, annex.
5/ *Report of the World Conference to Review and Appraise the Achievements of the United Nations Decade for Women: Equality, Development and Peace, Nairobi, 15-26 July 1985* (United Nations publication, Sales No. E.85.IV.10), chap. I, sect. A.

Alarmed that opportunities for women to achieve legal, social, political and economic equality in society are limited, *inter alia*, by continuing and endemic violence,

Convinced that in the light of the above there is a need for a clear and comprehensive definition of violence against women, a clear statement of the rights to be applied to ensure the elimination of violence against women in all its forms, a commitment by States in respect of their responsibilities, and a commitment by the international community at large to the elimination of violence against women,

Solemnly proclaims the following Declaration on the Elimination of Violence against Women and urges that every effort be made so that it becomes generally known and respected:

Article 1

For the purposes of this Declaration, the term "violence against women" means any act of gender-based violence that results in, or is likely to result in, physical, sexual or psychological harm or suffering to women, including threats of such acts, coercion or arbitrary deprivation of liberty, whether occurring in public or in private life.

Article 2

Violence against women shall be understood to encompass, but not be limited to, the following:

(*a*) Physical, sexual and psychological violence occurring in the family, including battering, sexual abuse of female children in the household, dowry-related violence, marital rape, female genital mutilation and other traditional practices harmful to women, non-spousal violence and violence related to exploitation;

(*b*) Physical, sexual and psychological violence occurring within the general community, including rape, sexual abuse, sexual harassment and intimidation at work, in educational institutions and elsewhere, trafficking in women and forced prostitution;

(*c*) Physical, sexual and psychological violence perpetrated or condoned by the State, wherever it occurs.

Article 3

Women are entitled to the equal enjoyment and protection of all human rights and fundamental freedoms in the political, economic, social, cultural, civil or any other field. These rights include, *inter alia*:

(*a*) The right to life; 6/

(*b*) The right to equality; 7/

(*c*) The right to liberty and security of person; 8/

(*d*) The right to equal protection under the law; 7/

(*e*) The right to be free from all forms of discrimination; 7/

(*f*) The right to the highest standard attainable of physical and mental health; 9/

(*g*) The right to just and favourable conditions of work; 10/

(*h*) The right not to be subjected to torture, or other cruel, inhuman or degrading treatment or punishment. 11/

Article 4

States should condemn violence against women and should not invoke any custom, tradition or religious consideration to avoid their obligations with respect to its elimination. States should pursue by all appropriate means and without delay a policy of eliminating violence against women and, to this end, should:

(*a*) Consider, where they have not yet done so, ratifying or acceding to the Convention on the Elimination of All Forms of Discrimination against Women or withdrawing reservations to that Convention;

(*b*) Refrain from engaging in violence against women;

(*c*) Exercise due diligence to prevent, investigate and, in accordance with national legislation, punish acts of violence against women, whether those acts are perpetrated by the State or by private persons;

(*d*) Develop penal, civil, labour and administrative sanctions in domestic legislation to punish and redress the wrongs caused to women who are subjected to violence; women who are subjected to violence should be provided with access to the mechanisms of justice and, as provided for by national legislation, to just and effective remedies for the harm that they have suffered; States should also inform women of their rights in seeking redress through such mechanisms;

(*e*) Consider the possibility of developing national plans of action to promote the protection of women against any form of violence, or to include provisions for that purpose in plans already existing, taking into account, as appropriate, such cooperation as can be provided by non-governmental organizations, particularly those concerned with the issue of violence against women;

6/ Universal Declaration of Human Rights, article 3; and International Covenant on Civil and Political Rights, article 6.

7/ International Covenant on Civil and Political Rights, article 26.

8/ Universal Declaration of Human Rights, article 3; and International Covenant on Civil and Political Rights, article 9.

9/ International Covenant on Economic, Social and Cultural Rights, article 12.

10/ Universal Declaration of Human Rights, article 23; and International Covenant on Economic, Social and Cultural Rights, articles 6 and 7.

11/ Universal Declaration of Human Rights, article 5; International Covenant on Civil and Political Rights, article 7; and Convention against Torture and Other Cruel, Inhuman or Degrading Treatment or Punishment.

(f) Develop, in a comprehensive way, preventive approaches and all those measures of a legal, political, administrative and cultural nature that promote the protection of women against any form of violence, and ensure that the re-victimization of women does not occur because of laws insensitive to gender considerations, enforcement practices or other interventions;

(g) Work to ensure, to the maximum extent feasible in the light of their available resources and, where needed, within the framework of international cooperation, that women subjected to violence and, where appropriate, their children have specialized assistance, such as rehabilitation, assistance in child care and maintenance, treatment, counselling, and health and social services, facilities and programmes, as well as support structures, and should take all other appropriate measures to promote their safety and physical and psychological rehabilitation;

(h) Include in government budgets adequate resources for their activities related to the elimination of violence against women;

(i) Take measures to ensure that law enforcement officers and public officials responsible for implementing policies to prevent, investigate and punish violence against women receive training to sensitize them to the needs of women;

(j) Adopt all appropriate measures, especially in the field of education, to modify the social and cultural patterns of conduct of men and women and to eliminate prejudices, customary practices and all other practices based on the idea of the inferiority or superiority of either of the sexes and on stereotyped roles for men and women;

(k) Promote research, collect data and compile statistics, especially concerning domestic violence, relating to the prevalence of different forms of violence against women and encourage research on the causes, nature, seriousness and consequences of violence against women and on the effectiveness of measures implemented to prevent and redress violence against women; those statistics and findings of the research will be made public;

(l) Adopt measures directed towards the elimination of violence against women who are especially vulnerable to violence;

(m) Include, in submitting reports as required under relevant human rights instruments of the United Nations, information pertaining to violence against women and measures taken to implement the present Declaration;

(n) Encourage the development of appropriate guidelines to assist in the implementation of the principles set forth in the present Declaration;

(o) Recognize the important role of the women's movement and non-governmental organizations worldwide in raising awareness and alleviating the problem of violence against women;

(p) Facilitate and enhance the work of the women's movement and non-governmental organizations and cooperate with them at local, national and regional levels;

(q) Encourage intergovernmental regional organizations of which they are members to include the elimination of violence against women in their programmes, as appropriate.

Article 5

The organs and specialized agencies of the United Nations system should, within their respective fields of competence, contribute to the recognition and realization of the rights and the principles set forth in the present Declaration and, to this end, should, *inter alia*:

(a) Foster international and regional cooperation with a view to defining regional strategies for combating violence, exchanging experiences and financing programmes relating to the elimination of violence against women;

(b) Promote meetings and seminars with the aim of creating and raising awareness among all persons of the issue of the elimination of violence against women;

(c) Foster coordination and exchange within the United Nations system between human rights treaty bodies to address the issue of violence against women effectively;

(d) Include in analyses prepared by organizations and bodies of the United Nations system of social trends and problems, such as the periodic reports on the world social situation, examination of trends in violence against women;

(e) Encourage coordination between organizations and bodies of the United Nations system to incorporate the issue of violence against women into ongoing programmes, especially with reference to groups of women particularly vulnerable to violence;

(f) Promote the formulation of guidelines or manuals relating to violence against women, taking into account the measures referred to in the present Declaration;

(g) Consider the issue of the elimination of violence against women, as appropriate, in fulfilling their mandates with respect to the implementation of human rights instruments;

(h) Cooperate with non-governmental organizations in addressing the issue of violence against women.

Article 6

Nothing in the present Declaration shall affect any provision that is more conducive to the elimination of violence against women that may be contained in the legislation of a State or in any international convention, treaty or other instrument in force in a State.

Document 108

General Assembly resolution on implementation of the Nairobi Forward-looking Strategies and on the participation of non-governmental organizations in the Fourth World Conference on Women

A/RES/48/108, 20 December 1993

The General Assembly,

Recalling all its relevant resolutions, in particular resolution 44/77 of 8 December 1989, in which, *inter alia*, it endorsed and reaffirmed the importance of the Nairobi Forward-looking Strategies for the Advancement of Women 1/ for the period up to the year 2000 and set out measures for their immediate implementation and for the overall achievement of the interrelated goals and objectives of the United Nations Decade for Women: Equality, Development and Peace,

Recalling also its resolutions 46/98 of 16 December 1991 and 47/95 of 16 December 1992,

Taking into consideration the resolutions adopted by the Economic and Social Council on issues relating to women since the adoption of its resolution 1987/18 of 26 May 1987,

Reaffirming its determination to encourage the full participation of women in economic, social, cultural, civil and political affairs and to promote development, cooperation and international peace,

Conscious of the important and constructive contribution to the improvement of the status of women made by the Commission on the Status of Women, the specialized agencies, the regional commissions and other organizations and bodies of the United Nations system and non-governmental organizations concerned,

Concerned that the resources available in the Secretariat to the programme on the advancement of women are insufficient to ensure adequate support to the Committee on the Elimination of Discrimination against Women and effective implementation of other aspects of the programme, especially the preparations for the Fourth World Conference on Women: Action for Equality, Development and Peace, to be held in 1995,

Taking into account Commission on the Status of Women resolutions 36/8 of 20 March 1992 2/ and 37/7 of 25 March 1993 3/ on the preparations for the Fourth World Conference on Women,

Bearing in mind the important role non-governmental organizations play in all activities for the advancement of women and the fact that some of them, especially those from developing countries, do not enjoy consultative status with the Economic and Social Council,

Noting with satisfaction that the preparations for the Fourth World Conference on Women have entered a substantive stage, that the relevant United Nations bodies, China, as the host country, and other countries all attach great importance to the preparation of the Conference and that the various preparatory activities are being conducted in an in-depth and comprehensive manner,

Considering that 1994 will be a year of crucial importance to the preparations for the Fourth World Conference on Women, that the Commission on the Status of Women will convene an inter-sessional working group to deliberate the content of the Platform for Action and that the five regional commissions will convene their respective regional preparatory meetings for the Conference,

1. *Takes note* of the report of the Secretary-General; 4/

2. *Reaffirms* section I, paragraph 2, of the recommendations and conclusions arising from the first review and appraisal of the implementation of the Nairobi Forward-looking Strategies for the Advancement of Women, contained in the annex to Economic and Social Council resolution 1990/15 of 24 May 1990, which called for an improved pace in the implementation of the Forward-looking Strategies in the crucial last decade of the twentieth century, since the cost to societies of failing to implement them would be high in terms of slowed economic and social development, misuse of human resources and reduced progress for society as a whole;

3. *Urges* Governments, international organizations and non-governmental organizations to implement the recommendations;

4. *Calls again upon* Member States to give priority to policies and programmes relating to the subtheme "Employment, health and education", in particular to literacy, for self-reliance of women and the mobilization of indigenous resources, as well as to issues relating to

1/ *Report of the World Conference to Review and Appraise the Achievements of the United Nations Decade for Women: Equality, Development and Peace, Nairobi, 15-26 July 1985* (United Nations publication, Sales No. E.85.IV.10), chap. I, sect. A.
2/ See *Official Records of the Economic and Social Council, 1992, Supplement No. 4* (E/1992/24), chap. I, sect. C.
3/ Ibid., *1993, Supplement No. 7* (E/1993/27), chap. I, sect. C.
4/ A/48/413.

the role of women in economic and political decision-making, population, the environment, information and science and technology;

5. *Reaffirms* the central role of the Commission on the Status of Women in matters related to the advancement of women and calls upon it to continue promoting the implementation of the Forward-looking Strategies to the year 2000, based on the goals of the United Nations Decade for Women: Equality, Development and Peace and the subtheme "Employment, health and education", and urges all relevant bodies of the United Nations system to cooperate effectively with the Commission in this task;

6. *Requests* the Commission, when considering the priority theme relating to development during its thirty-eighth and subsequent sessions, to ensure its early contribution to the preparatory work for forthcoming major international conferences such as the International Conference on Population and Development, to be held in 1994, the Fourth World Conference on Women: Action for Equality, Development and Peace, to be held in 1995, and the World Summit for Social Development, to be held in 1995, and to address the impact of technologies on women;

7. *Also requests* the Commission to give special attention to women in developing countries, particularly in Africa and the least developed countries, who suffer disproportionately from the effects of the global economic crisis and the heavy external debt burden, and to recommend further measures for the equalization of opportunity and for the integration of the roles and perspective of women, as well as their needs, concerns and aspirations, into the entire development process when considering the priority theme of development;

8. *Emphasizes*, in the framework of the Forward-looking Strategies, the importance of the total integration of women of all ages in the development process, bearing in mind the specific and urgent needs of the developing countries, and calls upon Member States to establish specific targets at each level in order to increase the participation of women in professional, management and decision-making positions in their countries;

9. *Emphasizes once again* the need to give urgent attention to redressing socio-economic inequities at the national and international levels as a necessary step towards the full realization of the goals and objectives of the Forward-looking Strategies through meeting the practical and strategic needs of women;

10. *Strongly urges* that particular attention be given by the competent United Nations organizations and Governments to the special needs of women with disabilities, elderly women and also women in vulnerable situations such as migrant and refugee women and children;

11. *Takes note* of the report of the Secretary-General on the improvement of the situation of women in rural areas, 5/ and urges the international community and the competent United Nations bodies and organs to place more emphasis on the sharp increase in the incidence of poverty among rural women;

12. *Welcomes* the recommendations adopted at the United Nations Conference on Environment and Development on women, environment and development in all programme areas, in particular those set out in chapter 24 of Agenda 21, 6/ entitled "Global action for women towards sustainable and equitable development";

13. *Urges* organs, organizations and bodies of the United Nations to ensure active participation of women in the planning and implementation of programmes for sustainable development, and requests Governments, in the context of General Assembly resolution 47/191 of 22 December 1992, to consider nominating women as representatives to the Commission on Sustainable Development;

14. *Requests* the Secretary-General, in formulating the system-wide medium-term plan for the advancement of women for the period 1996-2001 and in integrating the Forward-looking Strategies into activities mandated by the General Assembly, to pay particular attention to specific sectoral themes that cut across the three objectives, equality, development and peace, and include, in particular, literacy, education, health, population, the impact of technology on the environment and its effect on women and the full participation of women in decision-making, and to continue to assist Governments in strengthening their national machineries for the advancement of women;

15. *Also requests* the Secretary-General to continue updating the *World Survey on the Role of Women in Development*, 7/ bearing in mind its importance, placing particular emphasis on the adverse impact of the difficult economic situation affecting the majority of developing countries, particularly on the condition of women, giving special attention to worsening conditions for the incorporation of women into the labour force, as well as the impact of reduced expenditures for social services on opportunities available to women for education, health and child care, and to submit a final version of the preliminary version 8/ of the updated *World Survey*

5/ A/48/187-E/1993/76.
6/ *Report of the United Nations Conference on Environment and Development, Rio de Janeiro, 3-14 June 1992* (A/CONF.151/26/Rev.1 (Vol. I, Vol. I/Corr.1, Vol. II, Vol. III and Vol. III/Corr.1)) (United Nations publication, Sales No. E.93.I.8 and corrigenda), vol. I: *Resolutions adopted by the Conference*, resolution 1, annex II.
7/ United Nations publication, Sales No. E.89.IV.2.
8/ A/48/70-E/1993/16.

on the Role of Women in Development to the Economic and Social Council, through the Commission on the Status of Women, in 1994;

16. *Requests* Governments, when presenting candidatures for vacancies in the Secretariat, in particular at the decision-making level, to give priority to candidatures of women, and requests the Secretary-General in reviewing those candidatures to give special consideration to female candidates from underrepresented and unrepresented developing countries;

17. *Requests* the Secretary-General to invite Governments, organizations of the United Nations system, including the regional commissions and the specialized agencies, and intergovernmental and non-governmental organizations to report periodically to the Economic and Social Council, through the Commission, on activities undertaken at all levels to implement the Forward-looking Strategies;

18. *Also requests* the Secretary-General to continue to provide for the existing weekly radio programmes on women in the regular budget of the United Nations, making adequate provisions for broadcasts in different languages, and to develop the focal point for issues relating to women in the Department of Public Information of the Secretariat, which, in concert with the Department for Policy Coordination and Sustainable Development, should provide a more effective public information programme relating to the advancement of women;

19. *Further requests* the Secretary-General to include in his report on the implementation of the Forward-looking Strategies, to be submitted to the General Assembly at its forty-ninth session, an assessment of recent developments that are relevant to the priority themes to be considered at the subsequent session of the Commission and to transmit to the Commission a summary of relevant views expressed by delegations during the debate in the Assembly;

20. *Requests* the Commission to examine the implications of the World Conference on Human Rights and the Vienna Declaration and Programme of Action 9/ adopted by the Conference for its central role in matters related to the rights of women within the United Nations system and to report to the Economic and Social Council at its substantive session of 1994;

21. *Requests* the Secretary-General to prepare a report for the Commission, for consideration at its thirty-eighth session, on steps to be taken by the Division for the Advancement of Women, in cooperation with other United Nations bodies, specifically the Centre for Human Rights of the Secretariat, to ensure that relevant human rights mechanisms of the United Nations, such as treaty-monitoring bodies, rapporteurs and working groups, regularly address violations of the rights of women, including gender-specific abuses;

22. *Recognizes* that the Declaration on the Elimination of Violence against Women, proclaimed in General Assembly resolution 48/104 of 20 December 1993, is essential to the attainment of full respect for the rights of women and is an important contribution to efforts aimed at achieving the objectives of the Nairobi Forward-looking Strategies by the year 2000;

23. *Requests* the Secretary-General to lend support to the convening of the regional preparatory meetings so as to lay a good foundation for the Fourth World Conference on Women;

24. *Also requests* the Secretary-General to give more support, from within existing resources, to the Division for the Advancement of Women, acting as secretariat of the Fourth World Conference on Women, by providing sufficient financial and human resources and giving wide publicity to the Conference and its preparatory activities;

25. *Appeals* to countries to compile their national reports in earnest and to forward them in time, both to their respective regional commissions and to the secretariat of the Conference;

26. *Invites* the Secretary-General to play a more active role in appealing to countries to contribute to the Trust Fund for the Fourth World Conference on Women, in order to finance additional activities of the preparatory process and the Conference itself, in particular the participation of least developed countries in the Conference and its preparatory meetings;

27. *Recommends* the further development of methods of compilation and data collection in areas of concern identified by the Commission on the Status of Women, and urges Member States to improve and broaden collection of gender-desegregated statistical information and make it available to the relevant bodies of the United Nations system with a view to preparing, in all official languages, as a background document for the Fourth World Conference on Women, an updated edition of *The World's Women 1970-1990: Trends and Statistics*; 10/

28. *Endorses* the recommendation contained in Commission on the Status of Women resolution 36/8 that regional preparatory conferences should include in their agendas the issue of women in public life, as well as the request for the Secretary-General to include information on the decision-making position of women in public life and in the fields of science and technology in the preparation of the priority theme on peace: "Women in inter-

9/ *Report of the World Conference on Human Rights, Vienna, 14-25 June 1993* (A/CONF.157/24 (Part I)), chap. III.
10/ United Nations publication, Sales No. E.90.XVII.3.

national decision-making", for the Commission at its thirty-ninth session, in 1995;

29. *Requests* the Secretary-General to make available for the Fourth World Conference on Women reports and decisions of the World Conference on Human Rights, the International Conference on Population and Development and the World Summit for Social Development;

30. *Decides*, taking into account Commission on the Status of Women resolution 37/7, to adopt the modalities for the participation in and contribution to the Fourth World Conference on Women and its preparatory process by the non-governmental organizations, particularly those from the developing countries, set out in the annex to the present resolution;

31. *Also requests* the Secretary-General to prepare a report for the Fourth World Conference on Women, to be held in Beijing in 1995, on the extent to which gender concerns have been included in the activities of the relevant human rights mechanisms of the United Nations, such as treaty-monitoring bodies, rapporteurs and working groups;

32. *Further requests* the Secretary-General to report to the General Assembly at its forty-ninth session on measures taken to implement the present resolution.

Annex

Participation of non-governmental organizations in the Fourth World Conference on Women and its preparatory body

Non-governmental organizations in consultative status with the Economic and Social Council that express the wish to attend the Conference and the meetings of the Commission on the Status of Women, acting as its preparatory body, will be accredited for participation. Others wishing to be accredited may apply to the Conference secretariat for that purpose in accordance with the following requirements:

(a) The secretariat of the Fourth World Conference on Women will be responsible for the receipt and preliminary evaluation, in accordance with the provisions set out below, of requests from non-governmental organizations for accreditation to the Conference and the Commission on the Status of Women acting as preparatory body;

(b) All such applications must be accompanied by information on the competence of the organization and on its relevance to the work of the preparatory body, indicating the particular areas of the preparations for the Conference to which such competence and relevance pertain, and should include the following:

(i) The purposes of the organization;

(ii) Information on its programmes and activities in areas relevant to the Conference and on the country or countries in which those programmes and activities are carried out;

(iii) Confirmation of its activities at the national and/or the international level;

(iv) Copies of its annual reports, with financial statements and a list of members of the governing body and their country of nationality;

(v) A description of its membership, indicating the total number of members of the governing body and their country of nationality;

(c) Non-governmental organizations seeking accreditation will be asked to confirm their interest in the goals and objectives of the Conference;

(d) In cases where the Conference secretariat believes, on the basis of the information provided in accordance with the present document, that an organization has established its competence and relevance to the work of the Commission on the Status of Women acting as preparatory body, it will recommend to the Commission that the organization be accredited. In cases where the Conference secretariat does not recommend the granting of accreditation, it will make such information available to members of the Commission at least one week prior to the start of each session;

(e) The Commission on the Status of Women will decide on all proposals for accreditation within twenty-four hours of the recommendations of the Conference secretariat having been taken up by the Commission in plenary session. Should a decision not be taken within that period, interim accreditation will be accorded until such time as a decision is taken;

(f) A non-governmental organization that has been granted accreditation to attend one session of the Commission on the Status of Women acting as preparatory body may attend all future sessions and the Conference;

(g) In recognition of the intergovernmental nature of the Fourth World Conference on Women, non-governmental organizations will have no negotiating role in the work of the Conference and its preparatory process;

(h) Relevant non-governmental organizations in consultative status with the Economic and Social Council may be given the opportunity briefly to address the Commission on the Status of Women acting as preparatory body in plenary meeting and its subsidiary bodies. Other relevant non-governmental organizations may also ask to speak briefly at such meetings. If the number of requests is too large, the Commission will request that non-governmental organizations form themselves into constituencies, with each constituency speaking through one spokesperson. Any oral intervention by a non-governmental organization should, in accordance with usual United Nations practice, be made at the discretion of the Chairman and with the consent of the Commission;

(i) Relevant non-governmental organizations may, at their own expense, make written presentations in the official languages of the United Nations during the preparatory process, as they deem appropriate. Those written presentations will not be issued as official documents unless they are in accordance with the rules of procedure of the Conference.

Document 109

Executive summary of the 1994 World Survey on the Role of Women in Development *(extract)*

ST/ESA/241, 1995

1. In its resolutions 44/77 of 8 December 1989 and 44/171 of 19 December 1989, the General Assembly requested the Secretary-General to submit the final version of the *1994 World Survey on the Role of Women in Development* to the Assembly in 1994. In accordance with Commission on the Status of Women resolution 36/8 of 20 March 1992, the *World Survey* will be one of the principal documents for the Fourth World Conference on Women: Action for Equality, Development and Peace. In accordance with Assembly resolution 48/108 of 20 December 1993, a preliminary executive summary of the *World Survey* was provided to the Economic and Social Council at its substantive session of 1994 (E/1994/86), through the Commission on the Status of Women.

2. This is the third of the quinquennial *World Surveys* to have been prepared. The first, a draft of which was available to the World Conference to Review and Appraise the Achievements of the Decade for Women at Nairobi in 1985, was issued in 1986. 1/ The second was issued in 1989. 2/ The *Surveys* are now timed to be issued in the year previous to the five-yearly review and appraisal of the Nairobi Forward-looking Strategies for the Advancement of Women. Each *Survey* has had a particular point of departure. The first explored the contribution of women to the economy so as to demonstrate that women were key participants in economic development. The second started to explore the relationship between the participation of women and the global adjustment process that was under way. The third *Survey* examines what has happened as a result of the restructuring process and the emergence of women as decisive elements in the global economy. It is intended, by examining the most recent information available, to project trends of how men and women, in playing their ascribed roles in society, affect and are affected by the global economy.

3. The first *World Survey* was one of the few studies examining the role of women in the economy. Since then, the question of women and development has started to be incorporated into many mainstream surveys of the global economy, and the situation of women in the recent past has been accurately described in these studies. The third *Survey*, therefore, concentrates on identifying trends and considering how a gender perspective might change the way development concepts are expressed.

4. Many specialized agencies have contributed sections to the text, including the International Labour Organization (ILO), the United Nations Educational, Scientific and Cultural Organization (UNESCO), the United Nations Industrial Development Organization (UNIDO), the International Trade Centre (ITC), the International Fund for Agricultural Development (IFAD) and the Food and Agriculture Organization of the United Nations (FAO); other organizations provided inputs to these. A first draft was circulated to the organizations of the United Nations system.

5. The full text of the *Survey*, including tables, reaches some 250 pages and will be available to the Fourth World Conference on Women. It will be submitted through the Commission on the Status of Women at its thirty-ninth session, acting as the preparatory committee for the Conference, and will constitute one of the factual bases for the Platform of Action to be adopted at the Conference.

6. In view of these considerations, and given the documentation constraints confronting the General Assembly, the Secretary-General is presenting only the executive summary of the document to the Assembly at its forty-ninth session. The Secretary-General recommends that the Assembly consider the summary at its current session and return to the full version at its fiftieth session under an agenda item entitled "Effective mobilization of women in development", taking into account also at that

1/ *World Survey on the Role of Women in Development* (United Nations publication, Sales No. E.86.IV.3).
2/ *1980 World Survey on the Role of Women in Development* (United Nations publication, Sales No. E.89.IV.2).

time the results of the Fourth World Conference on Women.

Executive summary

7. Since the last *Survey* in 1989, the world has experienced a fundamental change in its economic relations, in which women were a major factor. The 1980s ended with a slow-down in economic growth in developed and developing countries, and the 1990s have started with a recession followed by a slow and cautious recovery. Progress in developed and developing countries has been uneven. Many developing countries have encountered significant difficulties in implementing structural adjustment programmes. The relative positions of countries in the developing and the developed worlds have changed, and new growth poles have emerged. Markets have become further integrated through trade and global investment, and interdependence among economies has increased. This trend has been further reinforced by the conclusion of the Uruguay Round of multilateral trade negotiations, which sought to keep the world trade system open and promised its further liberalization.

8. These changes took place in a context where there has been a renewed emphasis on democratization and good governance, as well as on the use of the market to direct economic development. Perceptions of the meaning, causes and conditions of development have been greatly modified. Development discourse now emphasizes sustainability and the human dimension.

9. The world economy has changed and, in certain measure, it is women who have made many of the positive changes possible. Economic development and growth appears to be intricately related to the advancement of women. Where women have advanced, economic growth has usually been steady; where women have not been allowed to be full participants, there has been stagnation. The *Survey* is about this process, what it means and how it can be built upon for a more secure future for humankind. It looks at development through a gender lens: at poverty as a failure of development and how investing in the capacities of women represents a way out; at employment, where the participation of women is decisive in the transformation of the labour force; and at economic decision-making, where the absence of women at the top of large corporate bureaucracies and their growing presence in a dynamic middle sector affects development policies.

10. Despite its considerable significance for economic advancement and the sustainability of development, the change in the role of women in development has continued as a largely unnoticed evolutionary process. It is now possible to see many trends in this process

clearly for the first time in the statistical series contained in the Women's Indicators and Statistics Data Base (WISTAT), in a growing corpus of micro-studies, and in the work of the United Nations and the specialized agencies. To mark these trends, the *1994 World Survey* employs what is now called gender analysis.

11. Gender analysis views women and men in terms of the roles they play in society, roles which can change as societies change. By comparing women and men, rather than looking at women as a group seen in isolation, gender analysis illuminates a key aspect of the structure of society and makes it easier to identify obstacles to its improvement. Central to the analysis is the distinction between productive and reproductive roles, referring to production of goods and services and to the social reproduction of society over generations, and their interrelationship. Both roles are valuable and both can be performed by women and men alike. In the past, social reproductive roles were largely assigned to women and productive roles largely to men. This is changing, but the tension between the two remains and is a recurrent theme of the *1994 World Survey*.

12. Two types of changes have occurred over the past 10 years in what could be called the enabling environment for women in the economy. One is changes in the legal status of women in the direction of equality. The other is the longer-term effects of achieving equal access by women to education and training. Taken together, these changes have served to provide equal opportunities for an increasing proportion of women and have allowed them to participate fully in development, contributing with the particular skills and priorities that derive from their gender roles.

13. The gradual achievement of *de jure* equality for women is reflected in the increase in the number of States party to the Convention on the Elimination of All Forms of Discrimination against Women. In most of these States, ratification or accession has required the elimination of legal restrictions that had impeded women from obtaining access to the factors of production: land, capital and technology. While progress in exercising these rights has been less rapid, especially where there is a gap between constitutional principle, enabling legislation and customary behaviour, in States that are party to the Convention, especially those that have not registered reservations, progress towards equality in economic participation is evident.

14. In most regions of the world, there has been notable progress towards equality between men and women in access to education at all levels. By 1990, most regions had achieved or were close to achieving equality in primary school enrolment, a marked change from 1970. Even more rapid progress can be observed in

secondary and tertiary levels of education. There are regional differences however. In Africa and south Asia in particular, progress in eliminating the gap between girls and boys has been less rapid.

15. The rapid elimination of differences in access to education does not mean that the access problem has been solved. Although women are doing much better than before in terms of access to education and years of education attained, the situation remains problematic with regard to the content of curriculum materials, which are often gender biased, the social and organizational arrangements in schools, and the presence of women in decision-making positions in the school system at all levels. Girls are still channelled into typical female fields of study and career paths, especially with regard to the technological skills needed to meet the challenges of information and technological progress in order to enable women to continue to take on gainful employment. Adult illiteracy, a consequence of past inequality in access and which is far more prevalent among women than men, needs to be addressed as does the broader issue of training.

16. However, it can no longer be said for the women now entering the labour force for the first time that their educational backgrounds are inferior to those of men. The longer term consequences of this equality still needs to be seen, but its present-day effects are certain.

17. The impact of the economic reforms of the 1980s, while similar in terms of its direction, have had different consequences for men and women in terms of the distribution of the adjustment burden. Rapid technological innovation, accompanying changes in work organization, growing economic interdependence, and the globalization of markets and production affected the socio-economic position of women in a complex and multidimensional way, bringing them into the formal labour market in unprecedented numbers. This had both positive and negative aspects.

18. In developed countries, as a result of industrial restructuring in the context of persisting gender-related wage differentials, layoffs undertaken to achieve cost reduction were often geared towards higher paid workers. The workers and managers let go under these circumstances were more often men than women, since women were, on the whole, lower paid. General increases in living costs associated with recession meant that in many countries women chose to enter the labour market in circumstances that were often precarious and without social support. This had the consequence of narrowing the remuneration gap between women and men.

19. The increase in labour force participation was not, however, a matter of women replacing men in their jobs. It was rather a consequence of structural change and greater willingness on the part of women to accept initially lower pay in the growth sectors. It is also true that women, whose traditional labour history had involved frequent moves in and out of the labour force in connection with maternity or the need to provide care to dependants and a willingness to work on a part-time basis or do outwork, were more acceptable to the new model of the flexible firm. Moreover, a shift in the crucial service sector to businesses requiring highly skilled staff, coupled with the increase of qualified women and the relatively lower barriers to employment, have helped bring women into better paid jobs.

20. There is increasing evidence of a relationship between the advancement of women and economic performance. The very nature of restructuring policies has led to an increase in women in the labour force, initially as part of a lower paid labour force in labour-intensive industry. Subsequently, progress in the liberalization of markets has reinforced this participation and is beginning to reflect itself in a move of female labour into higher paid, more skilled sectors.

21. In the economies in transition, the short-run situation has been almost the opposite. Women had already achieved equality in labour force participation, but the economic restructuring of State-owned enterprises, in which a large share of the economically active female population was employed, has led to high unemployment among women. Women appear to be at a greater disadvantage than men in the context of transition. Evidence suggests that in the sectors most affected by reform, women are laid off first. When unemployed, women face greater difficulties than men in obtaining alternative employment. Privatization favoured those in the previous system who had access to capital, information and markets. In the former system these had been predominantly men, and this has carried over to the new economies. The initial evidence suggests that men are predominantly being employed in the new industries. However, it is not clear that these trends will persist, given the qualifications possessed by women, particularly in new growth areas after economic stabilization has been achieved.

22. The situation is further complicated by the fact that the new private sector firms are unable or unwilling to maintain the social support services that were part of employment under the former system, making it difficult for women to participate in economic activity on the same basis as before.

23. In developing countries, the effects of global restructuring varied by region. Structural adjustment inevitably began with stabilization policies that were intended to set the stage for the resumption of growth by

reducing inflation rates and achieving a sustainable balance-of-payments position. This inevitably meant an increase in living costs as subsidies were removed and prices for staple goods rose to market levels, and as government expenditure cuts were often accompanied by service charges for health care and education. It was women who bore the first brunt of coping with these changes within the household. Subsequently, women who previously had not been in the formal economically active population became economically active. At the same time, farmers who bought more food than they produced, small producers and public and urban informal sector workers, categories in which a relatively high proportion are women, have been among the hardest hit.

24. The changes in employment patterns that occurred in the context of economic restructuring affected women in particular ways. In the process of intra- and intersectoral employment shifts, women in large numbers accepted lower paid jobs with little security. However, it was often the case that women were employed while their spouses were not. If there had to be a choice between "low pay" or "no pay", women accepted low pay, while their spouses often chose no pay rather than accepting lower remuneration. However, jobs for men were often simply not available. As a consequence, women were often more able than men to obtain jobs in growth sectors.

25. This has been particularly the case in the economies promoting export-oriented trade regimes based on labour-intensive manufacturing and international cost reduction. In the export-oriented sectors, women have often been the preferred employees.

26. In Asia, where growth has been based on outward-oriented development strategies, women constituted the larger share of those employed in the export-oriented industries. Similar trends are being observed in Latin America and the Caribbean as economies in that region take steps towards greater economic liberalization. In contrast, production of tradeable goods largely based on primary commodities in Africa has tended to work against women, who predominate in the production of non-tradeable food crops.

27. The short-run effects of structural adjustment have been more difficult for women than for men. While it is difficult to evaluate the longer-term effects, it would seem that the major gender factor has been the inability of women to benefit from changes in the incentive structures that were due to the pre-existing, sex-related barriers to reallocation of labour. To the extent that this is addressed in current policies, some of the negative consequences may be mitigated. Similarly, where privatization benefits micro- and small-scale enterprises, into which women are moving rapidly, the adjustment process can have longer-term benefits for women. Market de-

regulation, which in effect allows firms to have high wage flexibility, has particularly benefited women in the short-run, because female employment has increased. This will be a long-term benefit, however, if women are able to obtain equal pay with men and upgrade their skills so as to move into high-productivity sectors.

28. Changes in world trade patterns have, as noted, led to increased female industrial employment in those countries where growth of exports has been particularly strong. In this sense, increases in trade from developed to developing countries has been, to some extent, determined by women workers. Whether this will translate into long-term benefits will also depend on whether women will be given the opportunities to refine their skills, since labour force quality is a major component in international competition. The growth in the importance of transnational corporations is also significant, since they have a clear preference for employment of women in export processing zones. It may also be positive to the extent that they implement in their subsidiaries the equal opportunity policies mandated in their headquarters countries. There is little evidence about whether any shift in international financial flows will improve the economic status of women, although should new investment reach firms owned by or employing women, this would be positive.

29. The *Survey* has explored, using the new data available from WISTAT, the relationship between economic growth and the participation of women in the labour force. The analysis shows that women benefit from economic growth, sometimes to a greater extent than men, but not everywhere and not always. Regional differences in this context are very important. The most relative benefit has been in the countries of eastern and south-eastern Asia, where growth has been export-based. However, the comparative data suggest that, as the economy grows and the labour market becomes tighter, competitiveness in skills assumes a greater role than labour cost in terms of the allocation of employment opportunities between women and men. Unless women are able to upgrade their skills and catch up with the technological upgrading of the economy in developing countries, the opportunities for them to benefit from economic growth to a greater extent than men will disappear.

30. The relationship between the global economic environment, the enabling environment and the role of women in the economy can be seen in the analysis of three central themes of the *Survey*: poverty; productive employment; and women and economic decision-making.

Poverty

31. Poverty is universally considered to be unacceptable; it represents a major failure of development.

Analysing its causes and solutions from a gender perspective can help illuminate the nature of development and help identify successful policies and programmes for both men and women.

32. The extent to which an evident increase in poverty is a longer-term global trend is still a matter of debate, but there is no question that there are more poor than ever in the world, that poverty is increasing in some regions, or that women and men experience poverty differently. Despite a renewal in economic growth worldwide, the number of people living in absolute poverty has increased in developing and developed regions alike.

33. A gender perspective looks at how and why women and men experience poverty differently and how they become poor through different processes. While poverty can be measured at different levels, ranging from the individual to the nation, a particularly appropriate level for gender analysis is the household, consisting of people living together in the same place for a common purpose. Households, with shared income and consumption, experience poverty and have to cope with it. In the household always, but especially where sharing is unequal, gender usually has significant consequences for well-being.

34. At the intra-household level, poverty is defined in terms of consumption. Poverty is the condition of deprivation; not having enough food, shelter and other essentials to meet basic needs. Consumption within the household is less determined by the income brought in by a member than by cultural and social factors determining who can bring in income and how the goods available for consumption are shared, factors which often favour men.

35. One approach to understanding poverty from a gender perspective is based on the concepts of entitlements and endowments. An entitlement is a right to command resources. An endowment consists of the skills, access and other resources that make it possible to exercise an entitlement. In that sense, poverty is a failure to ensure entitlements because of inadequate endowments. In gender terms, this can be seen in terms of asymmetries between women and men in their entitlements and endowments. Taken together, these asymmetries reproduce the vicious cycle of poverty and explain why men and women experience it differently.

36. In the household, it can mean that women have fewer entitlements to household goods, coupled with additional responsibilities. They have less command over labour, whether their own or of others to help them undertake activities. The division of labour between women and men is unfavourable to women, who must work longer hours at largely unremunerated tasks. Similarly, women receive less return for their labour in income terms than men, although they are more likely to use their income for household purposes. Moreover, most women have fewer entitlements to officially distributed resources, whether in the form of land, extension services or credit, especially in rural areas. This, in turn, prevents women from building up their skills and resources.

37. The strongest direct link between gender and poverty is found in the situation of female-headed households, the existence of which is considered to be a significant indicator of female poverty. While female headship formally should mean that a woman is the person most financially responsible for the household, that definition is not always used in census counts, when an adult male is usually assumed to be the head. Thus, when the head of a household is counted to be a woman, this usually means that there is no adult male present and the woman is the only support. In developing regions, there are major differences, with the highest percentage found in sub-Saharan Africa, although globally the percentage of female-headed households is highest in Europe and North America, where they constitute the poorest segment of otherwise relatively wealthy societies. Female headship can be the result of migration, family dissolution, male mortality or unpartnered fertility.

38. What is characteristic of these female-headed households is a high dependency ratio, coupled with fewer adult income earners. Unlike households with two or more adult income earners, female-headed households place women in a situation of having to undertake both productive and reproductive activities, with an inevitable trade-off between the two. Female-headed households in general are poorer because of this, and the welfare of children in them has been found to be generally less good in terms of nutrition, health and education, although this varied by region.

39. Education can be clearly identified as a mitigating factor for poverty. There has been progress in reducing the gap between boys and girls, but the progress has been less rapid in some regions, such as Africa, and in rural areas generally. For poor households generally, sending children to school can involve difficult choices, however positive the long-run results may be. However, a number of innovative programmes have demonstrated that illiteracy and low school attendance for girls can be addressed successfully. Similarly, training of women in economic sectors where their role is particularly important, such as agriculture, forestry and fishing, can lead to important economic returns. Education and training for members of refugee households, which are predominately female-headed, has also grown in importance.

40. Poverty is particularly acute in rural areas, and has particular consequences for women. A combination of factors, including cutbacks in services as part of restructuring, environmental degradation, consequences of

past discrimination reflected in female illiteracy, male out-migration leading to female-headed households, all coupled with women's traditional limited access to factors of production combine to feminize rural poverty. Least developed countries are themselves predominantly rural. Moreover, export-oriented growth in agriculture has directed resources towards export crops, which are usually controlled by men, rather than to food production, which is largely undertaken by women.

41. Much of what is known about gender aspects of rural poverty is derived from micro-studies; there is a general absence of data disaggregated by sex, a prerequisite for recognition of the role of women in agriculture. On the whole, the evidence suggests that economic activity of women in rural areas is increasing, but not their participation in decision-making.

42. Strengthened grass-roots organizations of women, especially at the community level, are becoming ever more important. These organizations have been found to be effective in increasing participation, but suffer from a lack of support and resources. National machinery for the advancement of women can help remedy this by encouraging increased participation by women. A variety of programmes to establish and strengthen these organizations can be envisaged in the context of democratization, including various types of information and promotional campaigns.

43. Rural poverty has to be addressed in terms of access to and control of productive resources. Access to land is of particular concern since, traditionally, land is passed from father to son and reform measures have tended to reinforce this pattern. Improvement of de jure access to land by women is an important factor in the success of rural development policies. Similarly, removing obstacles to the access of women to paid labour can help address this gender asymmetry. Provision of access to modern technology can also help.

44. Improved access to credit can be a major means of addressing poverty by releasing the productive abilities of women. While many credit programmes do not take women into account, especially poor women, women have proven to be better credit risks on the whole than men, particularly when credit has been accompanied by extension, training and assistance in marketing. It requires identifying the particular needs of women, including the need to balance the multiple roles played by both women and men.

45. Provision of extension services to women has been problematic. Not only are most extension agents men, but the programmes themselves have been designed primarily for male-dominated activities. As a result, many of these programmes are no longer adapted to reality. Programmes designed with a gender approach are more likely to be effective; they require a combination of research, recruitment of women extension agents, and training of male extension workers to be gender-sensitive.

46. Addressing rural poverty also implies recognizing the importance of non-agricultural work in rural areas. Many non-farm occupations and enterprises are particularly suited to women, including small-scale enterprises in food and beverage processing, handicrafts and petty trading. Support for these also requires efforts to provide access to the factors of production, including especially, credit technological information and marketing.

47. Assured health services, including family planning, for rural women, who may be particularly at risk as a result of maternity, need to be part of any poverty eradication programme in rural areas. Many of these services have been reduced as a result of restructuring and, in other cases, there have been gender effects such as, for example, when the introduction of fees has led to a relatively lower level of immunization for girls than for boys.

48. Migration to urban areas has been one consequence of continued rural poverty. While in some countries this migration has been predominately male, in others women have migrated in greater proportion, particularly where economic growth is higher. There have been some reciprocal benefits from this migration; remittances of urban migrants can help alleviate rural poverty, and care for the children of migrants by relatives in the rural areas relieves some of the burden on urban dwellers.

49. Urban poverty itself is an increasingly important issue, not only because urban populations are growing dramatically in the developing world, but also because the nature of and solutions to urban poverty are different. Urban life is based on a cash economy, which sharpens the effects of poverty by making households more vulnerable to price changes. Public services are more critical to well-being in urban areas and when access to them is lacking, poverty can be particularly acute. For recent migrants, there is a need to learn to deal with a new environment. Highest rates of urban growth are expected in Africa and Asia. Urban populations are typically young, with high proportions under 15 years of age and consequent implications for providing health and education facilities.

50. There are gender dimensions to the organization of urban space and housing, particularly since women are more likely to work outside the home. The relative location of workplace and home is important in terms of the ability of women to balance productive and reproductive tasks that are not fully shared. Also important is the provision of infrastructure, especially potable water, since water provision, even in urban areas, tends to be a female responsibility.

51. Health in urban areas has gender dimensions in terms of the effects of environmental degradation and often violent living conditions, the spread of the human immunodeficiency virus/acquired immunodeficiency syndrome (HIV/AIDS) and other infectious diseases, and occupational health issues that are gender specific. The stresses of urban life can be more acute for women given their multiple tasks. Of particular concern is an increasing trend towards early pregnancies among urban adolescent girls, since their long-term consequences can include significant reduction in opportunities. Because of the complexity of the services that need to be provided, the delivery of urban health programmes to women should be seen in a holistic manner.

52. In dealing with poverty, whether urban or rural, there are different roles for different actors in the process. Although there has been a tendency to de-emphasize the role of the State in the economy through privatization and other measures, the State still plays a critical role. Its function is to raise, allocate and reorganize public resources for the good of society as a whole and to create the legal and normative enabling environment for development. How the role is played depends on the priorities set by the State, which, in many countries, has not included the type of public investment and incentives that might address poverty. The State, however, can provide the normative basis for change, as reflected in laws and programmes, can increase the access of women to productive resources and can act to help provide equal opportunities. This can be reinforced by community and other non-governmental organizations.

53. Women have considerably less influence than men on the priorities set for public action. The market, in contrast, responds to a multiplicity of individual choices, where influence is a function of resources. Women have less influence in the market because they do not have the same control over their labour as men and they face structural limitations on access to other means of production.

54. The conclusion is to use public action, by the State and by organizations, to extend the entitlements of the poor and increase their endowments so that they can be empowered to improve their own situations. As the less empowered of the poor, when entitlements are extended to women the effect in terms of poverty eradication is particularly great. This requires of women to take advantage of their rights and responsibilities as citizens to make use of the State.

Productive employment

55. One of the greatest economic changes over the past decade has been the rapid influx of women into the paid labour force and the emerging general patterns of employment, which are more like those typical for women than for men. Productive employment by women is also a critical factor in the eradication of poverty, both at the household level and for national economies. The employment of women relative to men is increasing, as are their qualifications, but it is underpaid, poorly regulated and has a short-term perspective.

56. Globally, over one third of all women aged 15 years and older are in the formal labour force, although there are conspicuous regional differences. Female economic activity has increased over the past two decades in almost all regions, and if under-reported activity in the informal sector were to be counted the proportion would be even higher. The greatest growth in employment is in manufacturing and services. There has also been growth in the proportion of women in the category of technical and professional workers. However, although there has been an upward trend in the proportion of women in managerial and administrative categories, few women have reached the top ranks of corporate management.

57. Information on the exact extent of the economic participation of women is still uneven, partly because of the way participation is defined and partly because of under-counting of unpaid work and work in the informal sector. It is therefore likely that the economic participation of women is much higher than official statistics show.

58. The entry of women into the labour force is a function of both economic necessity and a desire to exercise their right to work. It has been abetted by a trend towards more flexible working patterns and practices in response to competitive pressures. This has resulted in "atypical" or "non-standard" modes of work, such as part-time and temporary work, outwork and homework, which have been more accepted by women in the light of their family responsibilities. To some extent, this reflected a proliferation of low-income jobs and a decline of higher paid employment which had been the domain of men. Consequently, a notable rise in female employment was accompanied by a decline in male employment and a shift for men towards part-time and other atypical forms of employment. However, women continue, on average, to earn less than men, a situation that is only partially attributable to job differences.

59. Evidence, particularly from the economies in transition, suggests that the entry of women into the labour force is now a permanent feature and that, rather than considering themselves as a reserve labour force, they want to remain at work because of preference. This has made the transition to market economies in those countries particularly difficult for women, who have experienced relatively higher rates of unemployment than men. In the Asia and Pacific region, women have pro-

vided the bulk of growth in the labour force in countries with export-oriented industrialization.

60. Technological change is a major factor in the employment of women. In the past, women workers tended to be displaced when cheap labour was replaced by technology. Whether this will continue in the future is an unanswered question. In manufacturing when the purpose of technology is to replace labour-intensive work, female industrial workers can be the group most affected. However, when productivity improvements are the motive, women are frequently beneficiaries. Given skill upgrading, introduction of technology can have positive effects on women by making a qualitative change in the nature of the work. Some information technologies have the effect, as a result of globalization, of creating employment in developing countries through such clerical tasks as remote data-entry. It can also lead to atypical patterns of employment, including homework, and divide the labour force between a highly skilled, stable, core staff and peripheral workers who can be taken on or let go quickly. The group into which women will fall will depend on whether they are able to acquire the requisite skills.

61. The introduction of new technologies to agriculture, likewise, can have either positive or negative effects. The immediate effect of the introduction of high-yielding varieties of grain, for example, especially in Asia, was to generate employment for women, because tasks like sowing seeds, weeding and harvesting had been traditionally performed by women. Over the longer term, the introduction of other technologies has tended to replace women's labour. Some evidence suggests that the development of appropriate technology for tasks now performed by women is a means to their empowerment.

62. A new global study of women in the manufacturing sector by UNIDO, summarized in the *Survey*, demonstrates that the participation rate of women in that sector has increased faster than that of men. It suggests, however, that there are many patterns and identifiable groups of countries fitting them. Moreover, women are concentrated in the lower end of the spectrum; few are involved in administrative and management functions. In countries having export-oriented industries there appears to be a preference for hiring women workers, at least partly because of their lower cost or willingness to work on a subcontracting or outwork basis. When there is stagnation in the large enterprises in the modern sector, new job opportunities are often found in labour-intensive micro- or small-scale industries.

63. Female employment in manufacturing, as is the case with employment generally, is also conditioned by the socio-cultural norms about their public participation and whether their employment is given the same value as that of men.

64. In each of 12 country groups identified, ranging from industrialized countries with a high concentration of women in the tertiary sector through least developed countries with a traditional socio-economic role for women, there are specific challenges and policies to meet them.

65. One consequence of massive unemployment and underemployment in many developing countries has been an increasing internal and international migration of women to obtain employment. For sending countries, the remittances of women workers can be significant. For receiving countries, the migrant workers provide labour in areas where national supply is inadequate. The conditions under which migration occurs are not always favourable to women, and strategies, such as training and orientation to national conditions, have been identified to improve the situation of female migrants.

66. The increase in the rates of economic activity of women has often been accompanied by a decrease in the quality of working conditions. Some of the factors involved in the qualitative issues are outlined below. One is whether work takes place in the public, the formal private or the informal sector. Work in the public sector, with generally non-discriminatory rules, provides better protection for employees. This sector has been shrinking as a result of restructuring. Work in developing countries is typically in agriculture or the informal sector, where conditions are unregulated and often precarious.

67. In industrialized countries, much of the growth in the participation of women in the labour force has been accounted for by part-time work. As noted, this atypical type of employment is becoming common in developing countries as well. The issue is how to provide social protection, career development and employment security to these part-time workers.

68. There is also continued evidence of occupational segregation, leading to lower pay and limited occupational mobility. This, however, is partly offset by the growing economic importance of some of the fields in which women have traditionally been represented. There is, even here, evidence of wage differentials that cannot be explained solely by occupation, regardless of sector.

69. While there has been an increase in the understanding that social protection needs to be accorded to workers, particularly in terms of services such as child care that enable women and men to reconcile their productive and reproductive roles, this has been affected by problems of global restructuring, which reduced the likelihood that these facilities would be provided either by the State or by the enterprises and reduced the incentives for men to share in this role.

70. There has been an increase in women members in trade unions, but this lags behind women's numbers

in the labour force and women are not well represented in trade union leadership or in associations of employers. Organizing in associations and unions has been found to strengthen the bargaining power of women and protect their interests where it occurs.

Women and economic decision-making

71. The increase in the importance of women in the formal economy, the recognition of their role in eradicating poverty, and the changes that have already occurred in women's access to education and other human resources development assets, have not yet been reflected in their participation in economic decision-making. It is clear that these changes in the underlying structure of the economy will not automatically lead to changes in decision-making processes or structures.

72. Economic decision makers include persons occupying a wide variety of positions whose decisions can determine the direction of economic policy in both long-term and immediate ways. They include top executives of national public bodies dealing with economic matters; senior managers of public and private enterprises at the national and international levels; entrepreneurs at various levels; senior managers of international and regional financial institutions; and members of the boards of trade unions and professional and business organizations.

73. While data exist on women in management occupations, there are no regular global statistics on the proportion of women among economic decision makers. There are many reasons why there should be more women in top decision-making positions, ranging from women's equal rights to such positions, the growing proportion of women in the labour force, the increasing proportion of women among persons in technical, professional, administrative and management occupations, and the advantage to the economy from drawing on the skills and abilities of women, derived from their experience.

74. In terms of the general category of managers, women hold between 10 and 30 per cent of what ILO classifies as management positions, but there are less than 5 per cent in top management. In the 1,000 largest non-United States of America corporations, only 1 per cent of top management positions are filled by women, and in the 1,000 largest United States corporations the figure is only 8 per cent, mostly in second-level top management. These corporations comprise the bulk of transnational business. A similar situation is found in the boards of trade unions and the boards of professional and employers' organizations.

75. In government, where only 6 per cent of ministerial positions in 1993 were held by women, women held an even lower proportion of top posts dealing with the economy. While there was a larger percentage of women in sub-ministerial level decision-making posts, again the proportion was lower in those dealing with the economy. The situation is no different for international economic decision-making. Neither the United Nations, the specialized agencies, the Bretton Woods institutions nor the regional development banks have many women in decision-making positions, either in government delegations or in the secretariats themselves.

76. Changes in the composition of third-level students of law, business, science and technology, where women are achieving parity in most regions, should mean that the pool from which the next generation of economic decision makers is drawn will contain as many women as men.

77. Overall, there is a very slow rate of increase in the proportion of women in top decision-making, regardless of the level of development of the country. This contrasts with the growth in the number of women employed and the significant increase of women among entrepreneurs. This, coupled with the increase in young women with appropriate training, could lead to an increase in women in economic decision-making at a far faster rate than heretofore, if structural obstacles that are gender-based can be surmounted.

78. One basic obstacle is the lack of assured, upward career paths for women in corporate structures, whether public or private, starting with recruitment and extending through career development. Recruitment of women to corporate careers has been slow, in part because women were considered less desirable in them owing to their presumed reproductive role and the fact that many women chose education in fields that did not lead to recruitment for economic management.

79. Once recruited, women have had to deal with corporate cultures that, consciously or not, are male-oriented. Ranging from work-hour norms, through networks, through achievement criteria based on perceptions and stereotyped expectations, reinforced by administrative procedures, these corporate cultures have tended to create obstacles to the promotion of women. Taken together, the factors form a "glass ceiling", an invisible but impassable barrier that prevents women from rising professionally upward, regardless of their education and experience. Even if women manage to reach higher levels of management, their minority status can produce unnecessary stresses that make mobility both difficult and, occasionally, undesired.

80. Many women, rather than seeking careers in larger corporations, are choosing to become entrepreneurs, owning or running small and medium-sized modern enterprises. While the statistics on the number of entrepreneurs are not always comparable, over time statistics have shown that the gap between women and men

in the category has been diminishing over the past 20 years. The enterprises created are different from those owned by men, and centre on delivery of modern services and other growth sectors.

81. This development has been facilitated by the increase in educational access and the growth in sectors where women's gender-derived skills in communication, multi-tasking and non-hierarchical decision-making are particularly important. At the same time, these enterprises face special obstacles in terms of obtaining financial resources, access to management training and technical assistance, building networks and not having social support facilities.

82. Many of these factors come together in terms of trade development, as women seek to take advantage of trade-driven growth. Women entrepreneurship finds expression at all levels of trade, but must work against the variety of constraints already noted. A number of steps are being taken to create an enabling environment that will permit women to compete fully in trade development. The Women in Trade Development programme of ITC involves a series of interventions defined to help create that environment.

Promoting the effective participation of women in development

83. The current role of women in development is the result of trends unleashed by changes in the enabling environment coupled with the nature of global economic change. Market forces and the policy choices underlying them have propelled women into a decisive position in much of the global and national economy. However, the changes have not been fast enough, are not sufficiently secure and are not occurring everywhere. To equalize and accelerate the process, policies should be adopted by Governments, by enterprises and by women themselves to address the main obstacles.

84. It is increasingly clear that gender should be taken into account in global and national policy-making. Developments over the past decade, especially global economic restructuring, have proven that economic change is not gender neutral. Yet there is little evidence that economic policy makers have considered gender as a key variable in their policy-making. Gender could be taken into account by such means as:

(*a*) Examining the gender-related employment effects of policies such as export promotion or technological change;

(*b*) Ensuring that the transition to a flexible market does not merely lead to low wages as a proxy for productivity, but rather develops the skills of workers to provide a transition to industries built on skilled workforces with productivity based on output;

(*c*) Taking into account when defining economic policies the types of employment that both men and women will be able to undertake, giving appropriate value to sharing of reproductive roles between women and men.

85. In that poverty reflects a failure of development, it leads to a cycle that undermines future development and has significant gender dimensions. It is obvious that these gender dimensions should be addressed. A major dimension of poverty is that men and women experience poverty differently at the level of the household and, therefore, by aggregation in the economy as a whole. It follows that women constitute the most significant entry-point for poverty-alleviation strategies; women are less the problem of poverty than the basis for its solution. Not having benefited in the past from opportunities that would have built up their endowments because programmes were directed primarily towards men, yet charged in reality with the responsibility for coping with lack of consumption, women have been denied the necessary entitlements to lift themselves and their families from poverty. This could be addressed by a range of actions which will increase women's endowments and entitlements. Actions might include:

(*a*) Ensuring equal access to education by girls, especially from poor families and in rural areas, through programmes that support their enrolment and retention in schools;

(*b*) Providing adult women with training and non-formal education related to their work to help compensate for past lack of educational opportunity;

(*c*) Changing laws and regulations to give women equal access to productive resources and gainful employment, including, especially for poor rural women, land and credit;

(*d*) Ensuring that new employment opportunities are designed to meet both need for income and performance of family responsibilities;

(*e*) Increasing access for women, especially in rural areas, to land and credit in their own right;

(*f*) Promoting community and public services that would allow women and men, especially heads of single-parent households, to accommodate their need to earn income with the need to maintain the family, including, especially, child and dependent care;

(*g*) Encouraging the development of organizations of women, at the community level, that can help empower poor women.

86. Eradicating poverty means ensuring that women can be productively employed on equal terms. The growing incidence of the globalization of markets,

production and finance, technological transformation, economic restructuring, transition to market economies, and changes in work organizations and production processes, as well as demographic trends, will continue to create opportunities and risks for women workers. They pose new challenges for their social protection, working conditions, appropriate legislative framework and enforcement and active labour-market policies. They provide challenges to the roles of Governments, employers, the trade unions and the other relevant institutions and actors at the national, regional and international levels in the promotion of gender equality in the world of work.

87. An integrated approach to employment could involve a number of actions, such as:

(a) Creating a legislative framework that enables equal participation, including reforms of labour codes, so that men and women are treated equally and all appropriate economic activity is covered;

(b) Taking steps to enforce equality norms by establishing institutions to supervise conditions in both the public and the private sectors, to provide accessible recourse to individuals and to ensure certain sanctions for violation of norms;

(c) Providing training and retraining to women workers to facilitate their skill acquisition and upgrade their skills, especially for workers in sectors undergoing structural change;

(d) Addressing occupational stereotyping through the educational and training systems in schools, enterprises, unions and the media;

(e) Taking steps to ensure that jobs are classified and remunerated according to the principle of equal pay for work of equal value, including appropriate legislation;

(f) Establishing the norm that family responsibility should be shared by men and women alike and should be supported by public and private institutions, creating "family friendly" societies;

(g) Creating public services and encouraging private provision of child and dependent care as part of the work environment;

(h) Studying new methods of permitting men and women to mesh careers with family commitment through flexible work schedules, location and the possibility of part-time work with associated social security benefits;

(i) Taking steps to address the occupational health and safety of women reflected in unsafe work environments and sexual harassment;

(j) Providing training and access to resources for self-employment and entrepreneurship;

(k) Encouraging the development of the participation of women at all levels in existing organizations such as trade unions and other workers' and employers' organizations, and formation of new organizations, especially of those in atypical jobs;

(l) Implementing affirmative action programmes in those areas where there are present-day consequences of past discrimination, especially in terms of access to decision-making;

(m) Increasing the amount of research and data collection on gender factors in employment.

88. To achieve these ends, a variety of actors must be involved. The Government has a responsibility to be a model employer, but, more important, it has the role of promoting the kinds of public laws and policies that will help provide a more gender-responsive world of work but will not inhibit the efficiency of the market. Employers and trade unions have the responsibility, through collective bargaining, to ensure that employment practices provide an environment in which women and men can reconcile productive and reproductive roles. Non-governmental organizations and national women's machineries can provide support to the promotion of equality between men and women through supporting innovative programmes and monitoring developments.

89. Policies may have to take into account several major trends that pose new challenges for women in the world of work. The changing nature of the formal sector in the light of global economic restructuring will make growing demands on women to adjust to new opportunities as national economies shift in emphasis to greater competitiveness and efficiency. In central and eastern Europe, the shift from a public, full-employment economy to a privatized economy makes particular demands on women to break into new market-oriented occupations. The retrenchment of the public sector, with the unemployment of many who used to work in that sector, requires adjustment.

90. A second trend is the emergence of an intermediate sector between the formal sector of large enterprises and the increasingly crowded informal sector. This sector, made up of small and medium-sized enterprises, provides opportunities for women if they can obtain the skills, experience, financing and networking necessary to make them profitable.

91. A third trend is the growth of the informal sector itself, blurring the lines between the household and the enterprise with the growth of subcontracting, home-based work and self-employment. This will require a form of regulation and social protection if the growth is not to be accompanied by exploitation.

92. A final trend is the growth in flexibility and deregulation in the economy, which, on the positive side, can provide better opportunities to balance productive and reproductive roles but which, on the negative side,

could lead to a lack of social protection as well as a lessened quality and security of employment. Which side prevails will depend on the policies and practices adopted.

93. Finally, unless policies and programmes are implemented to increase the participation of women in economic decision-making, the opportunities to address poverty and improve the world of work are unlikely to be translated into reality. Particular responsibility for creation of opportunities rests with the public sector, which could consider a range of actions, such as:

(*a*) Ensuring that appropriate third-level education opportunities are open to both women and men to equip them for managerial and entrepreneurial careers;

(*b*) Implementing and enforcing legislation on equal employment opportunities, including preventing sexual harassment;

(*c*) Encouraging private sector bodies to accelerate the move of women to executive positions through moni-toring, information dissemination and establishment of voluntary norms;

(*d*) Furthering networking among women executives, including sharing of information on developments and opportunities;

(*e*) Promoting the establishment of gender-neutral recruitment and promotion policies by corporations, as well as the public sector, through sensitization and models;

(*f*) Setting up in the public sector and encouraging in the private sector the norm of dual-career managerial couples, including appropriate policies for parental leave, job-sharing and flexible career patterns;

(*g*) Encouraging more women to undertake entrepreneurship, by developing an integrated approach to expedite financing, technical assistance services, information, training and counselling.

...

Document 110

Commission on Human Rights resolution appointing a Special Rapporteur on violence against women

Commission on Human Rights resolution 1994/45(ESCOR, 1994, Suppl. No. 4, p. 140), 11 March 1994

The Commission on Human Rights,

Recalling its resolution 1993/46 of 8 March 1993 on integrating the rights of women into the human rights mechanisms of the United Nations, in which it also decided to consider at its fiftieth session the appointment of a special rapporteur on violence against women.

Also recalling that the World Conference on Human Rights welcomed the decision of the Commission on Human Rights to consider at its fiftieth session the appointment of a special rapporteur on violence against women.

Welcoming the adoption by the General Assembly, in its resolution 48/104 of 20 December 1993, of the Declaration on the Elimination of Violence against Women, which recognizes that violence against women both violates and impairs or nullifies the enjoyment by women of human rights and fundamental freedoms, and expresses concern about the long-standing failure to protect and promote these rights and freedoms in relation to violence against women.

Deeply concerned at continuing and endemic violence against women, and noting that the Declaration on the Elimination of Violence against Women sets out various forms of physical, sexual and psychological violence against women,

Mindful that the Vienna Declaration and Programme of Action (A/CONF.157/23), adopted by the World Conference on Human Rights, affirmed that gender-based violence and all forms of sexual harassment and exploitation, including those resulting from cultural prejudice and international trafficking, are incompatible with the dignity and worth of the human person and must be eliminated.

Alarmed by the marked increase in acts of sexual violence directed notably against women and children, as expressed in the Final Declaration of the International Conference for the Protection of War Victims (Geneva, 30 August–1 September 1993), and reiterating that such acts constitute grave breaches of international humanitarian law,

Bearing in mind that the Vienna Declaration and Programme of Action calls for action to integrate the equal status and human rights of women into the mainstream of United Nations system-wide activity, stresses the importance of working towards the elimination of violence against women in public and private life and urges the eradication of all forms of discrimination against women,

Recalling the outcome of the World Conference on Human Rights as reflected in the Vienna Declaration and

Programme of Action, which affirmed that the human rights of women and of the girl child are an inalienable, integral and indivisible part of universal human rights and that the full and equal participation of women in political, civil, economic, social and cultural life, at the national, regional and international levels, and the eradication of all forms of discrimination on the grounds of sex are priority objectives of the international community,

Also recalling that the Vienna Declaration and Programme of Action affirmed that the human rights of women should form an integral part of United Nations human rights activities, including the promotion of all human rights instruments as they relate to women, and urged Governments, institutions, intergovernmental and non-governmental organizations to intensify their efforts for the protection and promotion of the human rights of women and the girl child,

Bearing in mind that the programme of action for the equal status and human rights of women adopted in the Vienna Declaration and Programme of Action (part II.B.3) sets out a series of measures to be taken to further the full and equal enjoyment by women of all human rights as a priority for Governments and the United Nations, and recognizing the importance of the integration and the full participation of women as both agents and beneficiaries in the development process,

Welcoming the report of the Secretary-General (E/CN.4/1994/34) submitted in response to the request contained in Commission resolution 1993/46 of 8 March 1993 to consult with all United Nations human rights bodies, including the treaty bodies, on the implementation of the resolution and in particular the action taken to create a focal point in the Centre for Human Rights for the human rights of women,

Considering that the Vienna Declaration and Programme of Action called on the United Nations to encourage the goal of universal ratification by all States of the Convention on the Elimination of All Forms of Discrimination against Women by the year 2000 and to avoid, as far as possible, the resort to reservations,

Reaffirming that discrimination on the basis of sex is contrary to the Charter of the United Nations, the Universal Declaration of Human Rights, the Convention on the Elimination of All Forms of Discrimination against Women and other international human rights instruments, and that its elimination is an integral part of efforts towards the elimination of violence against women,

Stressing that the effective implementation of the Convention on the Elimination of All Forms of Discrimination against Women will contribute to the elimination of violence against women and that the Declaration on

the Elimination of Violence against Women strengthens and complements this process,

Recognizing the need to promote and strengthen national and international efforts to improve the status of women in all areas in order to foster the elimination of discrimination and gender-based violence against women,

Looking forward to the Fourth World Conference on Women: Action for Equality, Development and Peace to be held in Beijing in 1995, and urging that human rights of women should play an important role in its deliberations,

Recognizing the important role of the women's movement and of non-governmental organizations in promoting the human rights of women,

1. *Condemns* all violations of the human rights of women, including acts of gender-based violence against women;

2. *Calls for*, in accordance with the Declaration on the Elimination of Violence against Women, the elimination of gender-based violence in the family, within the general community and where perpetrated or condoned by the State and emphasizes the duty of Governments to refrain from engaging in violence against women and to exercise due diligence to prevent, investigate and, in accordance with national legislation, to punish acts of violence against women and to take appropriate and effective action concerning acts of violence against women, whether those acts are perpetrated by the State or by private persons, and to provide access to just and effective remedies and specialized assistance to victims;

3. *Condemns* all violations of the human rights of women in situations of armed conflict, recognizes them to be violations of international human rights and humanitarian law, and calls for a particularly effective response to violations of this kind, including in particular murder, systematic rape, sexual slavery and forced pregnancy;

4. *Calls* for the elimination of violence against women in public and private life, of all forms of sexual harassment, exploitation and trafficking in women, the elimination of gender bias in the administration of justice and the eradication of the harmful effects of certain traditional or customary practices, cultural prejudices and religious extremism;

5. *Urges* Governments to intensify their efforts to promote and protect the human rights of women and eliminate violence against women, in accordance with the Vienna Declaration and Programme of Action (A/CONF.157/23) adopted by the World Conference on Human Rights and the Declaration on the Elimination of Violence against Women, through the adoption of all appropriate means and measures, at the national, regional and international levels;

6. *Decides* to appoint, for a three-year period, a special rapporteur on violence against women, including its causes and its consequences, who will report to the Commission on an annual basis beginning at its fifty-first session;

7. *Invites* the Special Rapporteur, in carrying out this mandate, and within the framework of the Universal Declaration of Human Rights and all other international human rights instruments, including the Convention on the Elimination of All Forms of Discrimination against Women and the Declaration on the Elimination of Violence against Women, to:

(a) Seek and receive information on violence against women, its causes and its consequences from Governments, treaty bodies, specialized agencies, other special rapporteurs responsible for various human rights questions and intergovernmental and non-governmental organizations, including women's organizations, and to respond effectively to such information;

(b) Recommend measures, ways and means, at the national, regional and international levels, to eliminate violence against women and its causes, and to remedy its consequences;

(c) Work closely with other special rapporteurs, special representatives, working groups and independent experts of the Commission on Human Rights and the Sub-Commission on Prevention of Discrimination and Protection of Minorities and with the treaty bodies, taking into account the Commission's request that they regularly and systematically include in their reports available information on human rights violations affecting women, and cooperate closely with the Commission on the Status of Women in the discharge of its functions;

8. *Requests* the Chairman of the Commission, after consultation with the other members of the Bureau, to appoint as Special Rapporteur an individual of recognized international standing and experience in addressing the human rights of women;

9. *Requests* all Governments to cooperate with and assist the Special Rapporteur in the performance of the tasks and duties mandated and to furnish all information requested;

10. *Requests* the Secretary-General to provide the Special Rapporteur with all necessary assistance, in particular the staff and resources required to perform all mandated function, especially in carrying out and following up on missions undertaken either separately or jointly with other special rapporteurs and working groups, and adequate assistance for periodic consultations with the Committee on the Elimination of Discrimination against Women and all other treaty bodies;

11. *Also requests* the Secretary-General to ensure that the reports of the Special Rapporteur are brought to the attention of the Commission on the Status of Women to assist in the Commission's work in the area of violence against women;

12. *Calls* for intensified effort at the international level to integrate the equal status of women and the human rights of women into the mainstream of United Nations system-wide activity and to address these issues regularly and systematically throughout relevant United Nations bodies and mechanisms;

13. *Recognizes* the particular role of the Commission on the Status of Women in promoting equality between women and men;

14. *Encourages* the strengthening of cooperation and coordination between the Commission on Human Rights, the Commission on the Status of Women, the Committee on the Elimination of Discrimination against Women and other treaty bodies, the United Nations Development Fund for Women, the United Nations Development Programme and other United Nations agencies;

15. *Calls* for closer cooperation and coordination between the Centre for Human Rights and the Division for the Advancement of Women;

16. *Renews* its call to Governments to include gender-disaggregated data, including information on the *de jure* and de facto situation of women, in the information they provide to special rapporteurs, treaty bodies and to all other United Nations bodies and mechanisms concerned with human rights, and notes that the Vienna Declaration and Programme of Action calls on all special rapporteurs, working groups, the treaty bodies and other mechanisms of the Commission and the Sub-Commission to make use of such data in their deliberations and findings;

17. *Renews* its request to the secretariat to ensure that special rapporteurs, experts, working groups, treaty bodies and other mechanisms of the Commission and the Sub-Commission are fully apprised of the particular human rights violations suffered by women, and, in view of the fact that the Vienna Declaration and Programme of Action encourages training for United Nations human rights and humanitarian relief personnel to assist them to recognize and deal with the human rights violations particular to women and to carry out their work without gender bias, requests the Centre for Human Rights to take action in this regard;

18. *Requests* all special rapporteurs, experts, working groups, treaty bodies, and other mechanisms of the Commission and the Sub-Commission, in the discharge of their mandates, regularly and systematically to include in their reports available information on human rights violations against women;

19. *Requests* Governments and the United Nations to include in their human rights education activities information on the human rights of women;

20. *Notes* that the Fourth World Conference on Women: Action for Equality, Development and Peace, to be held in Beijing in 1995, may consider the question of means of integrating the human rights of women into the mainstream of United Nations system-wide activity;

21. *Decides* to continue its consideration of the question as a matter of high priority at its fifty-first session;

22. *Recommends* the following draft decision to the Economic and Social Council for adoption:

Question of integrating the rights of women into the human rights mechanisms of the United Nations and the elimination of violence against women

The Economic and Social Council, taking note of Commission on Human Rights resolution 1994/45 of 4

March 1994, approves:

(a) The Commission's decision to appoint a special rapporteur on violence against women, including its causes and its consequences;

(b) The Commission's request to the Secretary-General to provide the Special Rapporteur with all necessary assistance, in particular the staff and resources required to perform all mandated functions, especially in carrying out and following up on missions undertaken either separately or jointly with other rapporteurs and working groups, and adequate assistance for periodic consultations with the Committee on the Elimination of Discrimination against Women and all other treaty bodies;

(c) The Commission's request to the Special Rapporteur to report to the Commission on an annual basis, beginning at its fifty-first session.

[Adopted as Economic and Social Council decision 1994/254 of 22 July 1994.]

Document 111

Report of the Secretary-General to the General Assembly on the status of the Convention on the Elimination of All Forms of Discrimination against Women

A/49/308, 12 August 1994

I. Introduction

1. By its resolution 34/180 of 18 December 1979, the General Assembly adopted the Convention on the Elimination of All Forms of Discrimination against Women. In its subsequent resolutions 35/140, 36/131, 37/64, 38/109, 39/130, 40/39, 41/108, 42/60, 42/62, 43/100, 44/73, 45/124 and 47/94, the Assembly urged States that had not yet ratified or acceded to the Convention to do so as soon as possible and requested the Secretary-General to report on the status of the Convention. In its resolution 45/124 of 14 December 1990, the Assembly requested the Secretary-General to submit this report annually. In accordance with those resolutions, the Secretary-General has submitted at each session of the Assembly a report on the status of the Convention (A/35/428, A/36/295 and Add.1, A/37/349 and Add.1, A/38/378, A/39/486, A/40/623, A/41/608 and Add.1, A/42/627, A/43/605, A/44/457, A/45/426, A/46/462, A/47/368 and A/48/354).

2. In its resolution 47/94 of 16 December 1992, the General Assembly repeated its request for the annual submission of the report on the status of the Convention. The Assembly further requested the Secretary-General to

submit to the Assembly at its forty-ninth session a report on the implementation of that resolution and to make the report available to the Commission on the Status of Women at its thirty-ninth session.

3. By its resolution 1994/7 of 21 July 1994, the Economic and Social Council requested the Secretary-General to submit to the General Assembly at its forty-ninth session a report on the working methods of the Committee on the Elimination of Discrimination against Women and its capacity to fulfil its mandate effectively, including a comparison with the working situation of other treaty bodies. It also requested the General Assembly, in the light of the present report, to review the Committee's working situation and, in this context, also to consider the possibility of amending article 20 of the Convention to allow for sufficient meeting time for the Committee.

II. Status of the Convention on the Elimination of All Forms of Discrimination against Women

4. The Convention was opened for signature in New York on 1 March 1980 and, in accordance with its article 27, entered into force on 3 September 1981.

5. As at 1 August 1994, 134 States had become parties to the Convention, 88 States had ratified it, 40

States had acceded and 6 States had succeeded to it. In addition, seven States had signed it without yet ratifying it. Since the last progress report, Albania, Armenia, the Bahamas, Bosnia and Herzegovina, Lithuania, the Republic of Moldova, Tajikistan and the former Yugoslav Republic of Macedonia have become parties to the Convention. The Bahamas acceded with reservations. No reservations to the Convention were withdrawn during the reporting period. The Government of Finland objected to the reservations made by the Government of Maldives upon accession. The Government of the Netherlands objected to the reservations and declarations made by the Governments of India, Morocco and Maldives upon ratification or accession. The complete list of States that have signed and ratified, acceded or succeeded to the Convention, as well as the dates of their signatures and the dates of receipt of the instruments of ratification, accession or succession, is contained in annex I to the present report. Reservations made upon ratification or accession are contained in annex II, and objections to the application of the Convention are contained in annex III to the present report.

III. The Committee on the Elimination of Discrimination against Women: working methods and capacity to fulfil its mandate

6. The Committee on the Elimination of Discrimination against Women shares many similarities in its working methods with other human rights treaty monitoring bodies. There are, however, a number of key differences. Table 1 summarizes the similarities and differences between the Committee and the other five human rights treaty bodies.

7. It should be noted that many of the provisions in the Convention, which cover the full range of issues relating to discrimination against women and the impairment of women's civil, political, economic, social and cultural rights, also fall within the mandates of the Human Rights Committee and the Committee on Economic, Social and Cultural Rights.

8. The monitoring of compliance with the Convention through the consideration of reports submitted by States parties remains the central activity and object of concern of the Committee. In that sense the mandate of the Committee is the same as that of other human rights treaty bodies.

9. The mandate of the Committee on the Elimination of Discrimination against Women under article 21 of the Convention includes the drafting of suggestions and general recommendations based on the examination of reports and information received from States parties. These have assumed increasing importance in its work.

10. In addition, the Committee now contributes to international conferences that bear on the status and advancement of women. On request it has forwarded its views on specific issues to other human rights bodies such as the Commission on Human Rights. In the light of the objectives expressed in the Vienna Declaration and Programme of Action, adopted by the World Conference on Human Rights on 25 June 1993, 1/ such contributions and involvement can be expected to increase in the future.

11. One of the other human rights treaty bodies meets alternately at Geneva and in New York. Under the provisions of article 20, the Committee normally meets at United Nations Headquarters or at any other convenient place as determined by the Committee. Historically, the meetings alternated between New York and Vienna, where the secretariat of the Committee was located. However, since the Committee's secretariat has been transferred to New York, all meetings are expected normally to be held there.

12. As of 1 August 1994, there were 134 States parties to the Convention. The number of ratifications to the other human rights treaties as of 30 June 1994 stood as follows: the Convention on the Elimination of Racial Discrimination, 139; the Covenant on Civil and Political Rights, 127; the Covenant on Economic, Social and Cultural Rights, 129; the Convention against Torture, 82; and the Convention on the Rights of the Child, 161.

A. Consideration of reports of States parties

Meeting time

13. Unlike other human rights instruments, article 20 of the Convention on the Elimination of All Forms of Discrimination against Women contains a limitation on the allowed meeting time. It states that the Committee "shall normally meet for a period of not more than two weeks annually in order to consider the reports submitted" by States parties. This time-limit has proved to be increasingly inadequate, as evidenced by the backlog of reports, to be detailed below, which have been submitted as required under article 18 and which await consideration. As a result, the Economic and Social Council in resolution 1992/17 recommended that three weeks be allocated until the backlog in reports had been eliminated. The General Assembly in its resolution 47/94 supported the Committee's request for additional meeting time and requested an extension of the sessions in 1993 and 1994. In spite of this, a considerable backlog remains.

14. Although the Committee has increased the scope of its activities, the Convention foresees no assign-

1/ *Report of the World Conference on Human Rights, Vienna, 14-25 June 1993* (A/CONF.157/24 (Part I)), chap. III.

Table 1. *Consideration of reports by the human rights treaty bodies*

As at 1 June 1994	Human Rights Committee	Committee on Economic, Social and Cultural Rights	Committee on the Elimination of Racial Discrimination	Committee against Torture	Committee on the Rights of the Child	Committee on the Elimination of Discrimination against Women
Treaty ratifications	127	129	139	82	161	133
Number of members	18	18	18	10	10	23
Current mandated regular meeting time	3 three-week sessions per year	1 three-week session per year a/	2 two-week sessions per year	2 two-week sessions per year	2 three-week sessions per year b/	1 two-week session per year c/
Number of reports considered per session	5-7	5-6	12-13	6	6	15-16
Number of reports considered per year	15-20	12	25	12	12	15-16
Average number of meetings per country report	3 (2 for initial reports)	3	2	2	3	1 1/2 meetings for initial reports; 1 meeting for subsequent reports
Number of overdue reports	95	129	392 d/	46	80	117
Reporting periods	First report within one year after entry into force; subsequent reports every five years	First report within one year after entry into force; subsequent reports every five years	First report within two years after entry into force; subsequent reports every two years (Economic and Social Council resolution 1988/4)	First report within one year after entry into force; subsequent reports every four years	First report within two years after entry into force; subsequent reports every five years	First report within one year after entry into force; subsequent reports every four years
Secretariat servicing	Centre for Human Rights	Centre for Human Rights	Centre for Human Rights	Centre for Human Rights	Centre for Human Rights	Division for the Advancement of Women

a/ In 1993 and 1994, the Committee on Economic, Social and Cultural Rights met for 2 three-week sessions as a result of the authorization of an extraordinary session in 1993 and 1994.
b/ In 1994, the Committee on the Rights of the Child met for 3 three-week sessions as a result of the authorization of a special session.
c/ The Committee on the Elimination of Discrimination against Women currently meets for 1 three-week session per year as a result of the authorization of the General Assembly.
d/ This number reflects the more frequent reporting requirements of the Convention on the Elimination of Racial Discrimination and the fact that the Committee on the Elimination of Racial Discrimination has been considering reports for eight years longer than any other treaty body.

ments beyond the consideration of reports of States parties and the drafting of suggestions and general recommendations based on this review. The Committee normally allocates some meeting time during the sessions for the drafting and consideration of suggestions and general recommendations, discussion of procedural matters and working methods, and contributions to international conferences and events relevant to its work. These discussions take place in two standing working groups whose findings are in the end presented to the plenary meetings.

15. The other human rights treaty bodies have longer and more flexible meeting schedules:

(a) The Committee on the Elimination of Racial Discrimination meets twice a year for sessions of two weeks in duration;

(b) The Human Rights Committee is authorized to meet for three sessions of three weeks duration each year. An additional three weeks is allotted for working groups;

(c) The Committee on Economic, Social and Cultural Rights ordinarily should meet once each year for three weeks, in addition to a pre-sessional working group of one week's duration. However, it currently meets for 2 three-week sessions per year, as a result of the decisions by the Economic and Social Council to authorize extraordinary sessions for 1993 2/ and 1994. 3/ This increase was authorized to permit the Committee to deal with the backlog of reports. In its decision regarding the 1994 session, the Council also authorized a special three-day meeting of the Committee's pre-sessional working group in order to prepare for the consideration of States parties reports;

(d) The Committee against Torture meets twice a year for two week sessions;

(e) The Committee on the Rights of the Child currently meets for two regular sessions of three weeks' duration per year, with each session being preceded by a one-week working group. A special three-week session plus an additional week-long pre-session working group were authorized for 1994 by the General Assembly following a request by the Committee in its fourth session for additional meeting time to deal with the anticipated avalanche of reports. 4/ The Committee has requested the authorization of the General Assembly to hold three regular sessions from 1995 onwards. 5/ Prior to considering any reports of States parties, the Committee spent 2 three-week sessions discussing general matters such as working methods. It also devotes considerable time each session to thematic reports, matters of technical assistance and the methods of work of the Committee.

Number of reports of States parties received and considered

16. Following the initial report which is due one year after ratification, States parties are required under the Convention to submit periodic reports every four years. Following their initial reports, the reporting periodicity under the other treaties is as follows: every two years under the Convention on the Elimination of Racial Discrimination; every four years under the Convention against Torture; and every five years under the Covenant on Civil and Political Rights, the Covenant on Economic, Social and Cultural Rights and the Convention on the Rights of the Child.

17. From 1982 up to 30 June 1994, 145 reports were received by the Committee on the Elimination of Discrimination against Women since 1982. Table 2 shows the number of reports received, considered and pending consideration. The number submitted to the other treaty bodies is as follows: the Committee on Economic, Social and Cultural Rights, 241 since 1977; the Human Rights Committee, 316 since 1977; the Committee on the Elimination of Racial Discrimination, 739 since 1969; the Committee against Torture, 67 since 1988; and the Committee on the Rights of the Child, 41 since 1992.

18. Since its establishment in 1981, the Committee on the Elimination of Discrimination against Women has held 13 sessions in which it reviewed 69 initial reports of States parties, 35 second periodic reports, 9 third periodic reports, 4 combined first and second periodic reports and 3 combined second and third periodic reports for a total of 120 reports. In addition, it considered two reports on an exceptional basis. At its thirteenth session, in 1994, the Committee on the Elimination of Discrimination against Women considered 16 reports in three weeks; 12 reports are presently scheduled for the upcoming fourteenth session. In 1993, the Committee considered 15 reports in three weeks. In 1992, 11 reports were reviewed in two weeks, compared with 11 in 1991 and 12 in 1990.

(a) The Committee on the Rights of the Child by comparison has dealt with an average of six country reports at each three-week session since it began considering reports in 1993;

(b) The Human Rights Committee typically considers 4 to 5 reports per session or between 13 and 14 reports over a period of nine weeks each year;

(c) The Committee on Economic, Social and Cultural Rights hears five to six global reports in a three-week session;

2/ Economic and Social Council decision 1992/259.
3/ Economic and Social Council decision 1993/296.
4/ CRC/C/20, p. 4, recommendation No. 1.
5/ See CRC/C/24, p. 4, recommendation No. 1.

Table 2. *Statistics on reporting to the Committee on the Elimination of Discrimination against Women*

A. Reports received by the Committee (as at 1 June 1994)

Year	Initial	1+2 combined	1+2+3 combined	Second	2+3 combined	Third	Exceptional reports
1982	7						
1983	12						
1984	5						
1985	4						
1986	14			2			
1987	11			8			
1988	5			7			
1989	2			9			
1990	5			5		3	
1991	3	3	1	2	1	7	
1992	1	3		5	2	4	
1993	1	2	1	2	2	5	
1994	2	1		2	1		2

B. Number of reports considered (as at 1 June 1994)

Year	Session	Initial	1+2 combined	1+2+3 combined	Second	2+3 combined	Third	Exceptional reports
1982	First	0						
1983	Second	7						
1984	Third	6						
1985	Fourth	5						
1986	Fifth	8						
1987	Sixth	8						
1988	Seventh	11			2			
1989	Eighth	6			3			
1990	Ninth	7					5	
1991	Tenth	2					8	
1992	Eleventh	1	1	1	6			
1993	Twelfth	1	1	2	4	1	2	
1994	Thirteenth	4	2		3	4		2
1995	Fourteenth	3	2	1	3		3	

C. Number of reports awaiting discussion (as at 1 June 1994)

Initial	1+2 combined	1+2+3 combined	Second	2+3 combined	Third
6	6	2	6	3	10

D. Total number of reports received and awaiting consideration: 33

(*d*) The Committee against Torture has considered an average of 12 reports in 4 weeks, or 6 per two-week session, each year since it began hearing reports;

(*e*) Over the past 10 years, the Committee on the Elimination of Racial Discrimination has heard an average of 29 reports per year in the space of six weeks.

19. The relatively high number of ratifications leads inevitably to an increase in the number of reports to be considered. However, the total number of reports received has remained relatively constant, indicating that the degree of compliance with reporting obligations is declining. It was suggested by the Secretariat to the Committee that the delay in considering reports, once submitted, was a factor in non-compliance. 6/ In 1987, 19 reports of States parties were submitted to the Committee on the Elimination of Discrimination against Women under article 18; in 1993, the number was 12 and as of 30 June 1994, 6 reports had been received.

20. In addition, like other treaty bodies, the Committee has begun to ask for reports on an exceptional basis. For example, like the Committee on the Elimination of Racial Discrimination and the Human Rights Committee, the Committee, being concerned about the alleged violations of human rights inflicted upon women in the territory of the former Yugoslavia, requested during its twelfth session that the States of the territory of the former Yugoslavia submit a report on an exceptional basis. 7/ Those reports were presented and considered during the Committee's thirteenth session. It may be expected, in the light of the Committee's commitment to look into similar grave violations of rights being experienced by women in any part of the world, that it will request special reports in the future whenever events in States parties to the Convention give rise to concern regarding the well-being, status or advancement of women and the Committee wishes to act on an ad hoc basis.

Time allocated per report

21. One of the most striking disparities in the working conditions of the treaty bodies lies in the amount of time available for the consideration of reports of States parties. The Committee on the Elimination of Discrimination against Women allots one and a half three-hour meetings for the initial report of a State party and only 1 three-hour meeting for subsequent periodic reports. The time allocation does not increase even when the Committee is considering combined reports, which has become an increasingly frequent practice; initial and second periodic reports are considered in one and a half meetings and second and subsequent periodic reports are considered in one meeting. During the thirteenth session, the Committee observed that the number of reports considered at each session was much too high for the allotted time and was much greater than that considered by other treaty bodies.

(*a*) By comparison, the Committee on the Elimination of Racial Discrimination devotes two three-hour meetings to each report;

(*b*) The Human Rights Committee allots at least three full meetings per country report and two meetings for initial reports;

(*c*) This time-frame is in line with the practice of the Committee on Economic, Social and Cultural Rights, which devotes 1 three-hour meeting to reports dealing with specified articles of the Covenant, and 3 three-hour meetings when considering "global" or comprehensive reports from State parties;

(*d*) The Committee against Torture normally spends 2 three-hour meetings on each report;

(*e*) The Committee on the Rights of the Child allots 3 three-hour meetings for each report.

22. It should be noted that both the Committee against Torture and the Committee on the Elimination of Racial Discrimination are limited in their mandates relative to the other treaty bodies, as the Conventions which they monitor focus on one particular human rights issue rather than an entire range of concerns. This lessens the time required for each inquiry they conduct. Therefore, when considering the amount of time each treaty body has at its disposal to spend per report, the more appropriate comparisons are between the Committee on the Elimination of Discrimination against Women and the bodies monitoring treaties that are global in scope, that is, the Human Rights Committee, the Committee on Economic, Social and Cultural Rights and the Committee on the Rights of the Child. Notwithstanding, even for initial reports the Committee on the Elimination of Discrimination against Women spends less time per report than the Committee against Torture or the Committee on the Elimination of Racial Discrimination.

23. The Convention includes a large number of issues that also fall within the mandates of the Covenant on Civil and Political Rights and the Covenant on Economic, Social and Cultural Rights. In addition, the Committee's reporting guidelines have become more detailed and precise in recent years in an effort to improve the quality of reports and facilitate the effective enjoyment of the rights under the Convention among States parties. The allotted time in many cases borders on being simply inadequate to permit the Committee to probe policies,

6/ CEDAW/C/1994/6.

7/ *Official Records of the General Assembly, Forty-eighth Session, Supplement No. 38* (A/48/38), para. 1.

issues and areas that would permit it to gain access to the real advancement of women in many of these countries.

24. The consequence of this report presentation schedule is that the Committee on the Elimination of Discrimination against Women is seriously constrained in its ability to inquire into the situation of women. In its report on the thirteenth session, the Committee observed that its work programme had already reached the level at which the expected quality of results could no longer be ensured. 8/ At the second meeting of the chairpersons of treaty bodies, held in 1988, it was noted that a thorough examination of a report and a genuinely constructive dialogue with a State party required at least two meetings (A/44/98, para. 40). With less time, the principle of constructive dialogue threatens to become dangerously superficial. Under these circumstances, reporting risks becoming a strictly pro forma exercise in which States parties escape both the searching scrutiny of the Committee and the opportunity to benefit from more extensive dialogue. The result can only be the ultimate weakening of the Convention as an instrument and catalyst for the protection of women's human rights and a potential undermining or discrediting of the existing treaty regime.

Backlog of reports

25. As of 30 June 1994, the Committee had received but not yet considered 33 reports, one third of which were combined reports, comprising either initial and second, second and third or initial, second and third reports. While the actual number of outstanding reports has been even higher at certain points in the past, the backlog total actually comprises 46 distinct reporting obligations. The current number results from the practice of allowing combined reports, the first of which were considered at the eleventh session.

26. As at 1 June 1994, reports had been awaiting consideration by the Committee from between 1 and 52 months, or on average more than 20 months. By the time the fourteenth session is convened in January 1995, the earliest point at which any report can now be considered, the upper limit will be 59 months, or nearly five years. Eight reports date from 1991 or earlier, 7 reports from 1992, 12 from 1993 and 6 from 1994. In contrast, the Committee on the Elimination of Racial Discrimination expects to have only three reports awaiting consideration at the end of its next session, in August 1994.

27. In 1985, at the fourth session of the Committee on the Elimination of Discrimination against Women, the time lapse between receipt and consideration of reports averaged 18 months. In 1990, at the ninth session, the time lapse was 27 months. At the twelfth session, the time lapse 34 months, or nearly three years. At the thirteenth

session, with the exception of special reports from the States of the territory of the former Yugoslavia, States parties waited on average 29 months to have their reports heard. 9/ By the fourteenth session, the average delay will be 38 months.

28. As is evident from these figures, the general trend is towards longer and longer delays. Were there to be substantially greater compliance by States parties with the actual reporting obligations under the Convention, the burden on the Committee would be greater and, under the present time constraints, the delay would be dramatically worse.

29. A lengthy time lapse between submission and consideration obviously jeopardizes the entire reporting procedure, as it lessens the validity of the information received and at times renders both empirical and policy information completely outdated and inapplicable. It increases the possibility that those compiling the report will neither be available to respond to or benefit from the observations of the Committee nor remain responsible for implementing the Convention. Supplementary reports have frequently been required to reflect changes in the situation since the original report. This both increases the burden of reporting on States parties and places an increased strain on secretariat resources, as additional time is required to process and analyse the reports and additional translation services are needed.

30. A central purpose of periodic reports is to assess any progress or deterioration in the status of women and the effect of the Convention in furthering the advancement of women. Where periodic or initial and periodic reports are combined, or where additional reports become needed because the original reports have become obsolete in important respects, such an assessment becomes impossible and an important goal of the reporting process is frustrated.

31. Finally, as noted earlier, the long delay constitutes a disincentive to reporting to the very States parties that are complying with their obligations under the Convention, as well as to States that are overdue.

Overdue reports

32. As at 1 June 1994 there were 38 initial reports, 39 second periodic reports and 40 third periodic reports due but not yet received from States parties for a total of 117 reports overdue. The delay in reporting in other treaty bodies stands as follows.

(*a*) For the Committee on the Elimination of Racial

8/ Ibid., *Forty-ninth Session, Supplement No. 38* (A/49/38), para. 796.
9/ Excluded from these calculations are updated reports and subsequent periodic reports which were received in the interim and considered at the same session.

Discrimination, 392 reports 10/ formally outstanding. However, combined reports are accepted by the Committee and it is now actually waiting for reports from about 80 States parties;

(*b*) For the Human Rights Committee, 20 initial, 23 second periodic, 37 third periodic and 13 fourth periodic reports for a total of 93 reports are overdue;

(*c*) The Committee on Economic, Social and Cultural Rights currently has 105 reports outstanding;

(*d*) For the Committee against Torture, 23 initial and 23 periodic reports are overdue;

(*e*) For the Committee on the Rights of the Child, 80 initial reports are outstanding.

33. Because of the problem of seriously overdue reports, the Committee on Economic, Social and Cultural Rights has begun to schedule for consideration the situation in States parties that have consistently failed to report or whose reports are long overdue. The chairpersons of the treaty bodies recommended at the last session that, as a last resort and to the extent appropriate, each treaty body follow this practice (A/47/628, para. 71).

34. The Committee on the Elimination of Discrimination against Women faces a similar problem, as there are States parties who have long ratified the Convention, yet whose initial reports have not been submitted. Annex IV shows the situation of overdue reports for the Committee. As at 30 June 1994, there were 16 States parties whose reports were 5 years or more overdue; 12 of these were more than 8 years overdue and 8 of these were more than 10 years overdue. However, should the Committee in the future take measures such as those of the Committee on Economic, Social and Cultural Rights to assess the progress in the advancement of women in all States parties to the Convention, whether or not they have complied with their reporting obligations, the constraints of the existing limitation in article 20 would become even more burdensome.

Preparation of concluding comments

35. Since its eleventh session, the Committee on the Elimination of Discrimination against Women has presented concluding comments at the end of the consideration of States parties' reports. Originally they were delivered by the Chair and included in the session report of the Committee to the General Assembly. However, during the thirteenth session, the Committee decided to adopt the practice now becoming common to all human rights treaty bodies and prepare a more detailed concluding comment to be included in the final report of the Committee. The comment is designed to highlight the most important points raised during the constructive dialogue, identify particular areas of progress as well as

issues and areas of concern that the Committee wishes the State party to report on in its next periodic report. Meeting time is required in order for the Committee to finalize its comments. At its thirteenth session, the time was not sufficient and concluding comments on the reports of three States were deferred to the next session of the Committee.

Role of non-governmental organizations

36. Non-governmental organizations have taken on increasing importance in recent years in the promotion of human rights, particularly as providers of alternative sources of information. In recognition of their evolving significance, their role at the national, regional and international levels was formally recognized in the Vienna Declaration and Programme of Action. 11/ Their participation in the reporting process under international instruments is particularly valuable, as it allows treaty bodies to obtain a balanced and comprehensive view of the human rights situation on the ground that might otherwise remain undisclosed or unavailable to the experts. Furthermore, the regional or international focus of many such groups often places them in a unique position to impart information about supranational and regional trends.

37. Both the Committee on the Rights of the Child and the Committee on Economic, Social and Cultural Rights have taken steps to increase the participation of non-governmental organizations in the reporting process and other work of their respective committees. To this end, they have set aside time for the organizations to make oral statements to their committees during the regular sessions. The pre-session working groups of the two committees also receive oral and written submissions from non-governmental organizations.

38. National and international non-governmental organizations have observer status at Committee sessions. The Committee on the Elimination of Discrimination against Women receives reports from non-governmental organizations on an ad hoc and informal basis and has often commented on the value of the additional information received and had occasion to question the representatives of States parties about matters relevant to the Convention which were disclosed in their reports. The

10/ This very high number is a result of a number of factors: the Convention on the Elimination of Racial Discrimination was the first convention to enter into force and its committee began receiving reports eight years before any other; that Convention has a much shorter reporting periodicity than others, two years as opposed to four or five. In practice, States parties report only every four or five years or more, and the Committee expects a comprehensive report only every four years with an update every two years.

11/ *Report of the World Conference on Human Rights, Vienna, 14-25 June 1993* (A/CONF.157/24 (Part I)), chap. III, para. 38.

Committee also encourages States parties to consult with national non-governmental organizations in the preparation of their reports wherever possible and commends their presence during the consideration of reports. In addition, the Committee invited non-governmental organizations to contribute information 12/ which was used in preparing the background report for the discussion on violence against women which gave rise to general recommendation No. 19.

39. At present, however, non-governmental organizations do not make formal representations to the Committee, nor do they participate in the dialogue between States parties and the Committee during the presentation of the reports. While the Secretariat provides the addresses of the Committee members to interested non-governmental organizations, no substantial servicing, such as translation and dissemination of reports, is currently available.

B. Preparation of suggestions and general recommendations

40. Under article 21, the Committee may make suggestions and general recommendations based on the examination of reports and information received from States parties. Since its inception, the Committee has formulated 21 general recommendations. As of this time, the Committee on the Elimination of Racial Discrimination has adopted 17 general recommendations and a number of additional decisions; the Human Rights Committee has adopted 23 general comments; 13/ the Committee on Economic, Social and Cultural Rights has adopted 4 general comments, some of which are quite lengthy and detailed; the Committee against Torture, while empowered to do so, has not yet adopted any general comments; and the Committee on the Rights of the Child has adopted 18 conclusions and recommendations. 14/

41. In the early years, the recommendations of the Committee on the Elimination of Discrimination against Women were relatively brief and were either directed at either technical and reporting procedures or designed to merely highlight particular issues and areas of concern. However, recent recommendations have become more lengthy and detailed as the Committee endeavours to make the experience it has gained through the consideration of a large number of country reports available for the benefit of all States parties. As a consequence, the recommendations have become an increasingly important source of jurisprudence on the Convention and information to all States parties. In this sense, the Committee's general recommendations are now similar to those adopted by the Human Rights Committee and the Committee on Economic, Social and Cultural Rights.

42. The Committee on the Elimination of Discrimination against Women is now directing its attention to an elaboration of the specific provisions of the Convention. Recommendations now generally concern substantive issues. For example, general recommendation No. 19 contains a detailed analysis of the phenomenon and persistence of violence against women and suggestions for States parties as to methods of its eradication and remedies which should be available to women who are victims of violence. The most recent general recommendation, No. 21, concerning the equality of women in marriage and family relations, contains an elaboration of articles 9, 15 and 16. Future recommendations are planned which will deal with the nature of the guarantees and the obligations of States parties under articles 2, 7 and 8.

43. In addition, the Committee has forwarded six suggestions to other bodies within the United Nations system on matters relating to the Convention.

44. Detailed recommendations are important to the dissemination of the Committee's work, the development of the Convention jurisprudence and the integration of gender issues into the work of the United Nations system. At the same time, they place increasing demands on the secretariat and require considerably more in the way of both preparation and meeting time for the Committee.

C. Activities undertaken by other treaty bodies but not undertaken by the Committee

45. A number of activities are undertaken by other treaty bodies, but not by the Committee, which have implications for the work of those bodies. For example, in addition to their other activities, both the Human Rights Committee and the Committee against Torture are required to consider communications and individual petitions submitted under the optional protocols to their respective instruments.

46. Taking note of the recommendation of the World Conference on Human Rights that new procedures be adopted to strengthen the implementation of the commitment to women's equality and that the possibility

12/ Official Records of the General Assembly, Forty-sixth Session, Supplement No. 38 (A/46/38), para. 389.

13/ The general comments formulated by the Human Rights Committee and the Committee on Economic, Social and Cultural Rights are approximately equivalent in purpose and scope to the general recommendations of the Committee on the Elimination of Discrimination against Women and the Committee on the Elimination of Racial Discrimination.

14/ This number reflects the practice of that Committee to formulate all administrative and procedural matters as formal recommendations. To date, there has been no substantive consideration of the articles of that Convention.

of an optional protocol in particular be examined, 15/ the Committee on the Elimination of Discrimination against Women, through its suggestion No. 5, 16/ expressed its desire to have an expert group meeting convened to discuss the issue. The Economic and Social Council, in its resolution 1994/7 of 21 July 1994, decided that the Commission examine at its thirty-ninth session, in cooperation with the Committee and taking into consideration the results of any expert meeting on the question that might be convened prior to that session, the feasibility of an optional protocol. It is not, however, anticipated that an expert meeting on the subject will be convened, since resources for it are not available in the regular budget and none have been forthcoming from extra-budgetary sources.

47. In the event that a protocol were to be adopted, it would increase the amount of time required for Committee sessions and place additional demands on secretariat time and resources.

48. Several of the treaty bodies engage in general discussions on themes or issues of relevance to their concerns or the implementation of their respective conventions, some of which are also of concern to the Committee. For example, during its last session, on 16 May 1994, the Committee on Economic, Social and Cultural Rights held a meeting on the effect of structural adjustment programmes and safety nets on human rights. This same issue was also identified during the thirteenth session of the Committee on the Elimination of Discrimination against Women as an issue of great impact and importance in the enjoyment of women's human rights. Moreover, the Committee on Economic, Social and Cultural Rights in its last session identified the situation of women as one of the most pressing issues on its own agenda.

D. Additional activities of the treaty bodies

49. Under article 17 of the Convention, the Committee on the Elimination of Discrimination against Women has a broad mandate to consider the progress made in the implementation of the Convention and, through it, advances in the interests and status of women in the States parties generally. The other treaty bodies are similarly charged with the responsibility to oversee a particular area or issue of concern within the field of human rights. Thus, in comparing the resources of the Committee with the other treaty bodies and their respective abilities to carry out their mandates, it is useful to review the activities undertaken by the other treaty bodies in the pursuit of their particular objectives.

Discussion of special issues and topics

50. Both the Committee on the Rights of the Child and the Committee on Economic, Social and Cultural

Rights devote one day during each session to a general discussion of a special issue relating to the mandate of their respective committees. Among the purposes of such general discussions identified by the Committee on Economic, Social and Cultural Rights are the development of a deeper appreciation of the standards contained in the treaty, consultation with experts, involvement of the general public and establishing the foundations for the drafting of general comments. That Committee has recognized the importance of contributions from outside in successfully realizing these objectives.

51. In preparation for its general discussions, the Committee on the Rights of the Child submits its agenda and identified areas of concern to specialized agencies and solicits their input. It also convenes working groups on such topics and meets with other agencies and bodies within the United Nations. For example, it has a standing working group on economic and social indicators whose members participated in a seminar on social and economic indicators held in January 1993 and organized by the Centre for Human Rights.

52. The Committee on the Elimination of Discrimination against Women in recent sessions has also recognized the importance of general discussions on emerging trends in the situation of women. For example, during the eleventh session the increase of female-headed households was identified as one such matter. During the twelfth session, there were repeated calls to have general discussions on new trends. However, in the light of the time constraints that the Committee currently faces, regular and systematic consideration of issues of importance to the implementation of the Convention has not yet been possible.

Regional meetings

53. In addition to its regular meetings, the Committee on the Rights of the Child conducts informal regional meetings which are funded by UNICEF. The purpose of these meetings is to allow on-site visits and inspections of conditions in States parties to the Convention on the Rights of the Child and to permit briefings to develop an understanding of the application of the Convention in particular regional situations. Activities such as these strengthen the capacity of the Committee to monitor the implementation of the Convention and to advance the interests of children generally.

54. Where the situation in a State party warrants and needed information is unavailable by other means, the Committee on Economic, Social and Cultural Rights

---

15/ Report of the World Conference on Human Rights, Vienna, 14-25 June 1993 (A/CONF.157/24 (Part II)), chap. III, sect. II, para. 40.
16/ Official Records of the General Assembly, Forty-ninth Session, Supplement No. 38 (A/49/38), p. 10.

may request that the State party accept a mission consisting of one or two of the Committee's experts.

55. The Committee on the Elimination of Discrimination against Women currently has no provision or resources for such activities. The Committee of Chairpersons has emphasized the value of holding meetings outside Geneva, New York and Vienna (see A/47/628, para. 86), but notes that financial and other requirements tend to make their cost prohibitive.

Input into world conferences

56. On its own initiative, the Committee on the Elimination of Discrimination against Women made a substantive contribution to the Third World Conference on Women held at Nairobi in 1985. In the light of the decision taken at the Vienna World Conference on Human Rights to increase coordination among human rights bodies and to mainstream women's human rights, it will be important for the Committee to contribute to any and all world conferences that have a bearing on the status and rights of women.

57. At its twelfth session, the Committee formulated a detailed suggestion to the World Conference on Human Rights. 17/ During its thirteenth session, it formulated a suggestion to the International Conference on Population and Development which will be held at Cairo in September 1994. 18/ Extensive consideration was also given to the Committee's input into the upcoming Fourth World Conference on Women to be held at Beijing in September 1995, including the structure and content of the report on the history, implementation and future of the Convention. The Committee also made a recommendation to the World Summit for Social Development, to be held at Copenhagen in March 1995, including the need for gender to be reflected throughout the conference document and for attention to the impact of economic adjustment policies on women and children. The Committee expressed the view that it was highly desirable that experts from both developed and developing countries participated in the preparatory meetings to help Member States understand that the Convention was an important normative instrument that may offer guidelines to social development initiatives and that its implementation was indispensable to social development. 19/

IV. Implementation of General Assembly resolution 47/94

A. *Secretariat servicing*

58. In its resolution 47/94, the General Assembly requested the Secretary-General to continue his efforts to provide Secretariat staff and technical resources for the effective performance by the Committee of its functions and ensure adequate support to the Committee.

59. Since 1981, the Committee has been substantively and technically serviced by the Division for the Advancement of Women, now part of the Department for Policy Coordination and Sustainable Development. Servicing of the Committee by the Division currently includes the following tasks. The Secretariat receives and processes the reports of States parties. Processing and pre-analysis of a report involves: a consideration of the structure and adequacy of the report, including the degree of compliance with the reporting guidelines established by the Committee; consideration of reports of States parties submitted to other treaty bodies and the extraction of information relevant to the Convention; an analysis of the fulfilment or deficiencies of the Government with respect to specific articles of the Convention; and the provision of statistical background material to the report. In addition, the Secretariat corresponds with States parties regarding the reports and maintains contact with Committee members throughout the year. Furthermore, the Secretariat is required to engage in detailed analysis and consideration of particular provisions of the Convention. Such analyses may provide needed background material for the preparation of general recommendations or be used to assist the Committee in the development of the jurisprudence of the Convention and the elaboration of specific articles.

60. The view has been expressed by the Committee and supported by the General Assembly, that technical and substantive support for the Committee should be strengthened within existing resources. At the time the General Assembly adopted the Convention in 1979, no statement of programme budget implications was issued, nor has one been issued subsequently with regard to Secretariat servicing. The servicing of the Committee has been absorbed within the regular work programme of the Division. The regular staff resources of the Division have decreased since 1985.

B. *Publicity*

61. In response to the request of the General Assembly for continued dissemination of information relating to the Committee, the Convention and the concept of legal literacy, the Division dedicated an issue of its publication Women 2000 (No. 3, 1992) to women's equal rights, wherein it deals with the Convention, the Committee, the role of non-governmental organizations, the concept of temporary special measures, legal literacy

17/ Ibid., *Forty-eighth Session, Supplement No. 38* (A/48/38), p. 6, suggestion No. 4.
18/ Ibid., *Forty-ninth Session, Supplement No. 38* (A/49/38), p. 10, suggestion No. 6.
19/ Ibid., para. 832.

and the communications procedure. The Centre for Human Rights is in the process of publishing a fact sheet on the Convention.

62. Resources have been set aside in the 1994 budget to issue volume 3 of the sales publication on the work of the Committee. It is foreseen that future programme budgets will allow continuation of this publication.

C. Technical and advisory services

63. The General Assembly welcomed also the initiatives taken to provide regional training courses for government officials of States parties as well as for States considering acceding to the Convention and urged the Secretariat to support such initiatives. Consequently, until this year, the Division provided technical assistance to States parties in the preparation of reports where they were either overdue or inadequate. It also organized training seminars for States parties and non-ratifying States that were designed to familiarize government officials and non-governmental organizations with the Convention and the reporting process. The resources for these activities were provided from the regular programme of technical cooperation of the Organization. However,

with the reorganization of the resources of the regular programme, and the transfer of the Division to the Department for Policy Coordination and Sustainable Development, these resources are no longer available. Efforts are being undertaken to work with the Centre for Human Rights in its programme of advisory services.

D. Interaction between the Committee and the Commission

64. Consistent with the recommendation of the General Assembly that meetings of the Committee be scheduled to allow for the timely transmission of the results of its work to the Commission on the Status of Women in the same year, the results of the Committee's work on its twelfth and thirteenth sessions were presented to the Commission by way of conference room papers. 20/ The Committee's fourteenth session is also scheduled in such a way that a similar procedure can be followed.

20/ E/CN.6/1993/CRP.2 on the Committee's twelfth session and E/CN.6/1994/CRP.1 on the Committee's thirteenth session.

Document 112

Report of the Secretary-General to the General Assembly on violence against women migrant workers

A/49/354, 1 September 1994

I. Introduction

1. In its resolution 48/110 of 20 December 1993 on violence against women migrant workers, the General Assembly reiterated its concern about the plight of women migrant workers who become victims of physical, mental and sexual harassment and abuse, and requested the Secretary-General to report to the General Assembly at its forty-ninth session on the implementation of the resolution, taking note of the relevant views of the Commission on the Status of Women in its discussion on the subject of violence against women at its thirty-eighth session.

2. The resolution followed on General Assembly resolution 47/96 on the same subject, which had requested the Secretary-General to seek the views of Member States and organizations of the United Nations system on the problem and to report orally on findings, through the Commission on the Status of Women and the Economic and Social Council. For this purpose, the views of Member States and organizations of the United Nations system were requested, a request that was reiterated in 1994.

3. Thirteen Member States and seven organizations of the United Nations system provided information. 1/ Oral reports were presented by the Secretariat to the Commission on the Status of Women, the Economic and Social Council and the General Assembly in 1993. The discussion of the priority theme "Peace: measures to eradicate violence against women in the family and society" included reference to the issue of violence against women migrant workers. The information provided by these sources, as well as reports by several non-governmental organizations, has been used to compile this report.

4. At its thirty-eighth session, the Commission on the Status of Women adopted resolution 38/7 on violence against women migrant workers which, *inter alia*, re-

1/ Austria, Belarus, Burkina Faso, Czech Republic, Liechtenstein, Mauritius, Morocco, Philippines (initial reply and update), Portugal, Russia, Syrian Arab Republic, Thailand, Turkey and the United Kingdom; UNOG, ECA, ECLAC, INSTRAW, FAO, IFAD and UNIDO.

quested the Secretary-General to see to the development of concrete indicators to determine the situation of women migrant workers in sending and receiving countries as a basis for future action and further requested the Secretary-General to submit a copy of the present report to the Commission at its thirty-ninth session, including in it reports to be submitted by the Special Rapporteur on violence against women, the Centre for Human Rights, relevant United Nations functional bodies and specialized agencies, intergovernmental organizations and non-governmental organizations. It should be noted that the present report reflects information received by the Secretariat as at 30 August 1994, but that the recently appointed Special Rapporteur has not yet submitted reports, although she was consulted on this report.

5. It should be noted that migration can be either internal or international. The present report, derived from its mandate, is restricted to international migration. It should also be noted that what is considered internationally to be meant by violence against women is enumerated in the Declaration on the Elimination of Violence against Women adopted by the General Assembly in its resolution 48/104. This includes physical, sexual and psychological abuse occurring within the general community, including rape, sexual abuse, sexual harassment and intimidation at work, in educational institutions and elsewhere, trafficking in women and forced prostitution.

II. International migration by women

6. International migration has been a fact throughout human history. Statistics reported by the United Nations for 1985 based on 1970 and 1980 census rounds, plus the number of refugees reported by the Office of the United Nations High Commissioner for Refugees (UNHCR) for that year, estimate a world level of migrants at over 105 million persons. 2/ Similarly, data from the 1980 census round for 125 countries showed that 48 million persons had been migrants, half of them women. 3/ Somewhat over half of the migrants (and 60 per cent of the women migrants) were living in developed countries. Some countries, in all regions, have sufficiently large foreign-born populations to be considered receiving countries. These include countries such as Cameroon, Côte d'Ivoire, Ghana, South Africa, the United Republic of Tanzania and Zimbabwe in Africa; Argentina, Brazil, Canada, the United States and Venezuela in the Americas; Bangladesh, Hong Kong, India, Iran, Israel, Japan, Kuwait, Malaysia, the Republic of Korea, Saudi Arabia, Singapore and Turkey in Asia; Belgium, France, Germany, Italy, Netherlands, Poland, Sweden, Switzerland and the United Kingdom in Europe; and Australia and New Zealand in Oceania.

7. Most of the migrants are permanent, having left their home countries for other countries with no intention of returning. A large proportion of female migrants, especially to Europe and North America, migrated to join spouses or parents who had previously migrated. Many of these migrants join the labour force of the receiving country, but on the same basis as citizens.

8. A growing phenomenon has been temporary migration, people who have migrated for work with an intention to return. This had been a factor in Europe for some time, and more men than women were involved. It has been estimated that by 1990, Western European countries had about 16 million foreigners, most of whom were admitted as workers or their immediate families. 4/ In Asia, significant numbers of women from Indonesia, Malaysia, the Philippines, Sri Lanka or Thailand have been found to be temporary migrant workers. 5/ Many of these workers went to Europe, while others went to areas of Western Asia or East Asia. For example, in Kuwait, 103,501 women were employed as domestic workers in 1989, constituting 5.1 per cent of the population of the country. Almost all were non-Kuwaiti Asian. 6/ In Saudi Arabia, there were 219,000 non-Saudi Asian female workers in 1986. 7/ There were, additionally, many migrants who were refugees, of which the number and the proportion of women among them has been rising. In many cases, their migration would also be permanent and they would be dealt with in receiving countries on the same basis as citizens. In other countries, they are considered to be temporary migrants.

9. Most of the statistical information on migrant women comes from the receiving countries, rather than from sending countries. However, for example, a 1991

2/ Persons identified as migrants because they lived outside their countries of birth. United Nations, Population Division of the Department for Economic and Social Information and Policy Analysis, "Population Distribution and Migration: the emerging issues" in Population Distribution and Migration (ST/ESA/SER.R/133). The data are from Christian Skoog, "The quality and use of census data on international migration", paper presented to the XIII World Congress of Sociology, Bielefeld, Germany, 18-23 July 1994.
3/ The figure refers to the foreign-born population in those countries. United Nations, Department for Economic and Social Information and Policy Analysis, International Migration Policies and the Status of Female Migrants: Proceedings of the United Nations Expert Group Meeting on International Migration Policies and the Status of Female Migration (ST/ESA/SER.R/), New York, 1994, table IV.1.
4/ Ibid., pp. 5-6.
5/ Ibid., pp. 5-11.
6/ Nasra M. Shah, "Migration between Asian countries", chap. XII of Population Distribution and Migration, citing Kuwait, Directory of Civil Information: Population and Labor Force. Kuwait, Public Authority for Civil Information, July 1989.
7/ Ibid., citing Manolo Abella, "International migration in the Middle East: patterns and implications for sending countries". Paper pre,, sented at the Informal Expert Group Meeting on International Migration, Geneva, Switzerland, 16-19 July 1991.

Survey of Overseas Workers conducted by the National Statistics Office of the Philippines estimated the number of Filipino contract workers at 721,100, of whom 40.6 per cent were women. Women overseas workers were concentrated in Asia (72 per cent), with the rest in Europe (11 per cent), North America (8 per cent) and elsewhere (9 per cent). In Europe, Filipino women workers exceeded men. 8/

10.   There are limited statistics on migrant workers from other countries, and even where figures are available, they are often not disaggregated by sex. Much of migration is undocumented and therefore difficult to quantify. In Africa, for example, movement to neighbouring countries for economic purposes, both temporary and long-term, is often not reported since the migrants merge easily into the population of the host countries which have similar ethnic compositions. A similar situation exists in some countries in Latin America. As a study of the Population Division of the United Nations notes, "... the pervasive view is that most undocumented migrants are men". 9/ There are indications, however, that the numbers of women migrant workers are relatively large. Existing reports, estimates, and anecdotal information provide a broad picture of the situations of women migrant workers, and the conditions that make them particularly vulnerable to violence.

11.   A major motivation for migration is usually a belief that this will lead to an improved economic status. This is true for men and women alike. In the past, women would become migrant workers by accompanying their husbands or fathers and then enter the labour force of the receiving country. More recently, based on relative opportunities in the international labour market, women are beginning to migrate on their own, often, as men had done in the past, leaving their families behind. In some countries, women are actively recruited for temporary jobs overseas. Migration is inevitably from less developed to more developed countries.

12.   For temporary migrants, a major economic aspect is remittances to families who remain in the home country. These remittances are used in the household to maintain consumption and to provide a basis for later investment. For Governments of sending countries, the remittances can constitute a significant source of foreign exchange. The survey in the Philippines showed that the average contract worker remitted 76,741 pesos monthly to his or her family. 10/ It has been estimated globally that in 1989, migrant remittances amounted to US$ 65 billion, compared with the US$ 47 billion provided as official development assistance by member States of the Organisation for Economic Cooperation and Development (OECD) to developing countries in that year. 11/ While temporary male migration is often related to agri-

cultural labour, construction or industries, temporary female migration has tended to concentrate in the services sector, especially domestic service. In some countries there have been national policies that actively encourage female emigration. In one case, this income remitted to the home country by women workers was said to be the second largest source of foreign exchange. 12/

A.   *Recruitment of women migrant workers*

13.   Although a small percentage of migrant workers are hired through official governmental recruitment agencies in the receiving country or, in some cases, through agencies in the sending countries, the vast majority, especially women migrant domestic workers, are hired through personal contacts with friends or family members already working in destination countries. "Employment exchanges", consisting of notice boards where offers of domestic work are posted, often exist in agencies such as welfare centres that do not directly arrange contacts. In addition, there are many illegal recruitment agencies, which are responsible for the migration of large numbers of women. In western Asia, women migrants are nearly all hired through private, unmonitored placement agencies.

14.   One study, based on interviews with a large sample of returned migrants and their families, found that the processing fees demanded by recruitment agencies vary from country to country, though in most cases, they are very high relative to what the prospective migrant will earn. 13/ It was noted that because of the size of these fees, many women have to borrow money from private money lenders, who charge exorbitant fees, or from relatives and friends. There are, however, few studies in other countries about the means by which women migrant workers are recruited.

15.   Little information is available also on the various types of contracts negotiated through formal recruitment agencies (although some countries do have standard contracts), the type of agreements reached between migrant women and their employers, or the extent to which the employer abides by the contract clauses. There is some indication that formal contracts are not always

8/ Second reply of the Government of the Philippines to the Secretary-General, July 1994.
9/ United Nations, Department for Economic and Social Information and Policy Analysis, op. cit., pp. 5-12.
10/ Second reply of the Government of the Philippines.
11/ International Organization for Migration, "Migration and Development", chap. XXVI in United Nations, *Population Distribution and Migration*, 1994.
12/ Frank Eelens and J. D. Speckman, "Recruitment of Labor Migrants for the Middle East: the Sri Lankan Case", *International Migration Review*, XXIV, No. 2 (Summer 1990), p. 299.
13/ Eelens and Speckman, loc. cit., p. 318.

honoured by employers since there is little or no governmental or legal enforcement.

16. Women wishing to migrate legally must negotiate a difficult labyrinth of immigration laws and regulations, which vary from country to country. Quotas, waiting lists, arbitrary and changing rules, and legal, financial, and language barriers prevent all but the most persistent and knowledgeable from becoming legal residents. Immigration regulations for employers often discourage them from hiring foreign workers legally and make the small risk of employing cheap illegal labour worthwhile.

17. Cases have been reported of women being recruited for jobs that they believed legitimate and discovering, upon arrival, that they were being trafficked for the purpose of prostitution.

18. Further, when legal visas expire, especially short-term entertainment visas, women often prefer or are forced to stay on illegally rather than return to their home countries.

B. *Types of work performed by migrant women*

19. Historically, migrant women have found employment primarily in a limited number of "female" occupations, such as domestic service, sewing, waitressing, teaching, nursing, secretarial and clerical work and low-level factory work. Migrant women, like women generally, were less likely to find employment in higher-paid occupations such as construction or heavy industry. Some have also found employment in prostitution.

20. For many migrant women, domestic service has been a particularly important means of entry into the labour market. Domestic work was viewed, for the most part, as secure employment, providing women with at least a minimum level of food and shelter and/or a regular source of income. Poor rural women often migrated to urban areas to take advantage of opportunities for domestic and other forms of employment that wealthier or more highly educated women workers did not want. When changes in the national labour force and wage structures reduced the supply of national domestic workers, their place has often been taken by migrants.

21. The prevalence of migrant women in domestic service bears further elaboration. While traditional divisions of labour valued female work within the home as a substantial, if unpaid, contribution to the welfare of the family, industrialization allowed women to move out of the home while still maintaining primary or exclusive responsibility for domestic work. This role was devalued as a necessary but invisible and lower status function. Domestic work continues to be unrecognized as an essential activity with substantial economic importance. Instead, the role of household domestic worker was inherited by other, less economically privileged, women. Progressively, the domestic services sector became reserved almost entirely for immigrant women workers, regarded as low-skilled labour doing low-prestige work.

22. In a number of countries in western Asia, after 1975, due to an increasing demand for domestic servants coupled with religious and social restrictions that limit native women from participating actively in the labour force, the proportion of migrant workers had reached a high level. For example, among 1,316,014 migrant workers in one Gulf State, 517,436 were women. 14/ An estimated 230,000 Indonesian women between 1983 and 1990 migrated to countries of that region, mostly as domestic help. Sri Lankan women were found to predominate as domestic servants in those countries, amounting to 47 per cent in 1979, and 57 per cent in 1985. 15/

23. Similarly, foreign maids in Hong Kong, Taiwan, Malaysia and Singapore are common. In Hong Kong, for example, official employment contracts for foreign maids increased from 44 in 1975 to more than 100,000 by early 1993. About 90 per cent of these women were Filipino, with others from Thailand, Indonesia, India and Sri Lanka. 16/

24. The United Kingdom reported that in the period from January-August 1993, clearance was granted under immigration rules for 8,613 domestic workers, the majority of whom were female. 17/ It can be anticipated that similar patterns exist in other European countries.

25. Wages for foreign women domestic workers, legal or illegal, are lower in many countries on average than that of their national counterparts in the same job, than national legal minimums, and than in other employment. sectors. 18/ The majority of migrant domestic women servants must accept live-in conditions as a prerequisite to employment. Room and board are usually counted as part of salary.

14/ Middle East Watch: Women's Rights Project, *Punishing the Victim: Rape and Mistreatment of Asian Maids in Kuwait*, vol. 4, issue 8, p. 4. Estimates from the Ministry of Planning.
15/ Eelens and Speckman, loc. cit.
16/ Immigration Department Statistics cited by May-an Villalba, "Understanding Asian Women in Migration: Towards a theoretical framework", in Isis International, *Women in Action*, 2 and 3/1993, Quezon City, Philippines, Isis International, 1993.
17/ Reply of the United Kingdom.
18/ Gabriella Arena, "Lavoro femminile ed immigraziones: dai Paesi Afro-Asiatici a Roma", *Studi Emigrazione*, No. 70, Anno XX, June 1983; Colectivo Ioé, "El servicio doméstico en España entre el trabajo invisible y la economía sumergida, Informe de Investigación, Madrid, 1990; Nony Ardill and Nigel Cross, *Undocumented Lives: Britain's Unauthorised Migrant Workers*, London, Runnymede Trust, 1988, all cited in Patricia Weinert, *Foreign Female Domestic Workers: Help Wanted*, World Employment Programme Research, International Migration for Employment Working Paper (MIG WP.50), Geneva, ILO, 1991.

26. While live-in servants may live in nicer neigh-bourhoods than non-resident domestics, their working conditions may be worse and they have far less mobility and social life. In one study, 72 per cent of domestic servants were found to get no days off at all, and only 13 per cent received a regular day off each week. 19/ In many cases, employers restrict domestic servants from leaving the house, do not allow use of the telephone, or do not permit visitors. Personal documents, such as passports, are usually retained by the employer. Regula-tions often require permission from the authorities to change employers, and a change of employer would not necessarily improve working conditions.

27. Migrant women domestic workers accept low wages and poor work conditions because their salaries are nevertheless higher, in the case of Asian women from poor countries four or five times higher, than those earned by white-collar professionals in their home coun-try and perhaps ten times what most women from their region would earn.

28. Some countries, in fact, explicitly exclude do-mestic work from their labour laws. 20/ Under those circumstances, foreign domestic workers will lack legal protection either as immigrants or domestic workers. In most countries, social welfare programmes are not open to illegal residents, and in many they are not open to legal foreigners on temporary work permits.

C. Trafficking

29. Trafficking for the purpose of prostitution con-tinues to be one type of migration. While it is condemned in international law, it continues to exist. In some regions this is related to what is termed sex tourism. Often this involves women recruited as entertainers or to work in restaurants and factories who are then diverted to pros-titution either from the outset or when temporary visas expired.

30. One study estimated that 20,000 to 30,000 women and girls from one country who had expected to work in restaurants and factories were prisoners of debt bondage in brothels in a neighbouring country. Police complicity through the extortion of protection money, direct arrangements for border crossings and transpor-tation, and patronage of the brothels was docu-mented. Publicity forced Government attention to the problem. 21/

31. Press reports suggest that women from Eastern Europe are increasingly being trafficked and the phenome-non probably exists in most regions, usually unreported. 22/

III. International norms governing migrant workers

32. The rights of migrant workers and other mi-grants have been a matter of international concern for many years. Starting with the various conventions dealing with slavery, through various International Labour Or-ganization (ILO) conventions, to the omnibus Interna-tional Convention on the Protection of the Rights of All Migrant Workers and Members of Their Families, the international community has set out norms for dealing with this population group.

A. Early conventions related to trafficking

33. Among the first international norms related to women migrant workers were those intended to deal with international trafficking in women. Some of these ante-dated the League of Nations, others were a result of work by the League.

1. Agreement for the Suppression of the White Slave Traffic

34. The international agreement concluded on 18 May 1904 covers traffic in women for prostitution in another country. Under the terms of this agreement, the States Parties are required to carry out monitoring activi-ties to detect traffickers in women at stations, ports of embarkation, and during journeys. The arrival of persons who are obviously perpetrators, co-perpetrators, or victims of trafficking in women must be reported to the authori-ties at their destination, to the appropriate diplomatic or consular officials, or to any other competent body.

35. The States Parties are also required, within the limits laid down by law, to take statements from foreign-ers coming into the country to establish their identity and civil status and to determine, and if necessary investigate, the person(s) responsible for their decision to leave their native country. In the case of trafficking victims, this information must be communicated to the authorities in the women's country of origin with a view to the possible return of the women to their own country.

36. The convention also requires States Parties to send women back to their country of origin if they or the persons who have authority over them request their return. Other provisions cover the cost of this return trip. There are also provisions for States Parties to monitor the activities of bureaux and agencies which arrange employ-ment abroad for women or girls, where possible and within

19/ Grete Brochman, *The Middle East Avenue. Female Migration from Sri Lanka. Causes and Consequences*, Oslo, Institute for Social Research, 1990, cited in Weinert, op. cit., p. 24.
20/ See Middle East Watch, op. cit.
21/ Asia Watch and the Women's Rights Project, *A Modern Form of Slavery: Trafficking of Burmese Women and Girls into Brothels in Thailand*, New York, Human Rights Watch, 1991.
22/ Periodic reports to the Economic and Social Council on suppres-sion of the traffic in persons and of the exploitation of the prostitution of others have been prepared by the Secretary-General at different points. See, for example, E/1994/76 and addenda.

the limits laid down by law. Thus, the implementation of these provisions would allow the authorities to identify women migrant workers lured into forced prostitution and return them to their countries, in contrast to the many reported cases in which they are sent to jail as illegal immigrants and for other infractions of immigration laws.

2. International Convention for the Suppression of the White Slave Traffic

37. A second convention for the suppression of the white slave traffic took place on 4 May 1910. It contains provisions for the punishment of persons who traffic in women. The provisions of this convention oblige States Parties to take measures or put forward proposals to their legislatures to make it an offence for anyone to recruit, transport, or kidnap a woman below the age of majority, in order to satisfy the desires of any other person, or to commit an immoral act, even if the woman agrees and if the various actions which constitute the offence take place in different countries. The same provisions apply when women of full age are recruited by means of deception, as frequently happens to illegal women migrant workers. The convention also contains provisions governing extradition, and these could also be applicable to women migrant workers. Sufficient evidence exists to confirm that perpetrators are not punished accordingly and that what is missing is the will to implement these provisions.

3. Convention to Combat the Traffic in Women and Children

38. The international convention adopted on 30 September 1921 by the League of Nations adds to the two previous instruments provisions that the States Parties are required, among other things, to take legal and administrative measures for issuing permits and monitoring employment bureaux and placement agencies in order to protect women and children who are looking for work in another country. They are also required to take legal and administrative measures specifically to combat the traffic in women and children. The convention explicitly refers to the obligation to ensure that notices are posted at railway stations and ports, warning women and children of the dangers of the traffic in persons and indicating where they can obtain accommodation and assistance.

39. Again these provisions pertain directly to the current situation of women migrant workers, as the victims of unscrupulous agencies which continue trafficking regardless of prohibitions.

40. The Convention for the Suppression of the Traffic in Women of Full Age of 11 October 1933, was intended to supplement the three previous conventions.

4. The Slavery Convention

41. The Slavery Convention, adopted on 25 September 1926 by the League of Nations, could also be used to advocate the cause of women migrant workers. It defines slavery as "The status or condition of a person over whom any or all of the powers attaching to the right of ownership are exercised". The slave trade means and includes "all acts involved in the capture, acquisition, or disposal of a person with intent to reduce him to slavery".

42. The Convention also contains provisions requiring States to take measures to ensure that forced labour does not produce situations comparable to slavery and to reinforce national and international efforts to abolish slavery, the slave trade, and similar practices. States Parties further agree to adopt legal and other measures to bring about the complete elimination of certain practices, irrespective of whether they fall under the Convention's definition of slavery. This includes debt bondage, whereby a person pledges his own services or those of another person over whom he has authority as security for a debt.

B. ILO Convention

43. Several ILO conventions have provisions designed to protect the rights of migrant workers, and therefore cover women migrant workers.

1. Migration for Employment Convention (Revised)

44. The Migration for Employment Convention (Revised) of 1949 defines a migrant worker as a person who migrates from one country to another with a view to working for an employer and not in a self-employed capacity. Among other things, the Convention requires the States Parties to maintain a reasonable and free service or ensure that such a service is maintained in order to assist migrant workers and to supply them with correct information. The States Parties are also required, in so far as national legislation allows, to take all the appropriate steps against misleading propaganda concerning emigration and immigration. Each of the States Parties agrees that its employment services and other services which are concerned with migration will cooperate with the equivalent services of other States. The activities carried out by public employment services must be free for migrant workers.

45. These provisions are aimed at combating one of the problems which make women migrant workers vulnerable in gaining access to service concerned with migration.

46. A total of 40 countries are party to the Convention, of whom many are major receiving countries for migrant labour.

2. Migrant Workers (Supplementary Provisions) Convention, 1975 (No. 143)

47. The Migrant Workers (Supplementary Provisions) Convention, 1975 (No. 143) requires States to respect the basic human rights of all migrant workers. Each of the States Parties must systematically establish whether migrant workers are working illegally in its territory, whether migration for employment is taking place from its territory as the starting-point, end-point, or as a country of transit, and whether migrating persons find themselves in circumstances which conflict with international, multilateral, bilateral or national regulations and agreements, either on arrival or during their stay and employment. Furthermore, the States Parties to the Convention are required to take necessary and appropriate measures within their jurisdictions or in cooperation with other States to combat the clandestine migration and illegal employment of migrants.

48. Each of the States Parties must also take appropriate measures against persons who organize illegal or clandestine migration for the purposes of employment and against persons who have employees who have entered the country illegally. At the national and international level the States Parties are required to take measures on this matter to create systematic contacts and exchanges of information with other States.

49. All of the measures must be designed to ensure that persons responsible for the illegal migration of workers can be prosecuted, irrespective of the country in which they undertake their activities. National regulations must be adopted for the effective detection of cases of illegal employment of migrant workers and for administrative, civil and criminal sanctions, including terms of imprisonment for illegally employing migrant workers, organizing migration with a view to abusive employment, or deliberately assisting such forms of migration for profit or otherwise.

50. Seventeen States have ratified the Convention.

C. United Nations conventions

51. Several conventions prepared under the auspices of the United Nations set international norms relative to women migrant workers.

1. Convention for the Suppression of the Traffic in Persons and of the Exploitation of the Prostitution of Others

52. This Convention was adopted by the General Assembly on 2 December 1949 and takes precedence over the other conventions in relation to States which are parties to the 1949 convention and one or more of the other conventions. Each of the other conventions is deemed to have been terminated when all the States which are parties to the conventions become parties to the 1949 Convention.

53. In reference to emigration and immigration, the 1949 Convention requests that States Parties take measures to combat the traffic in persons for the purposes of prostitution and to monitor employment agencies. The Convention also specifically requires measures to protect immigrants and emigrants at places of arrival and departure and during journeys; other measures pertain to traffickers and victims.

54. A total of 67 States are party to this Convention, including many of those identified as sending or receiving countries of women migrant workers.

2. Convention on the Elimination of All Forms of Discrimination against Women

55. The Convention on the Elimination of All Forms of Discrimination against Women of 18 December 1979 requires the States Parties to take measures to eliminate all forms of discrimination against women. Article 6 deals with the traffic in women and requires States to take any appropriate measures, including legislation, to combat all forms of traffic in women and the exploitation of prostitution by women.

56. The Committee on the Elimination of Discrimination against Women, the monitoring body for the Convention, has indicated in its recommendation No. 19 on violence against women that the Convention, under its various articles, covers violence against women, including as workers.

3. International Convention on the Protection of the Rights of All Migrant Workers and Members of Their Families

57. On 18 December 1990, the General Assembly adopted the International Convention on the Protection of the Rights of All Migrant Workers and Members of Their Families. This Convention stipulates among other things that migrant workers or the members of their families must not be held in slavery or servitude and that forced labour may not be demanded of them.

58. The Convention also makes provision for sanctions against persons or groups who use violence against migrant workers, employ them in irregular circumstances, or who threaten or intimidate them.

59. To date, only Egypt and Morocco have ratified or acceded to the Convention and Mexico, Chile and the Philippines have signed without ratifying. The Convention has not, accordingly, entered into force.

4. United Nations human rights conventions

60. Women migrant workers, like everyone else, are entitled to protections accorded by the various United Nations human rights conventions and other instruments.

IV. Reported incidence of violence against women migrant workers

61. There are only limited indicators of violence against women migrant workers. Statistics on violence against women generally are collected infrequently and are not yet accurate. There is considerable evidence that violence against women in the family and in society is widespread, universal and possibly growing. It can be expected that women migrant workers are likely to be victims of violence, especially when, as in a number of circumstances, their employment situation, coupled with their status as foreigners, leaves them vulnerable. However, it should be noted that a number of the replies from Governments indicated that they had no record of any incidents of violence against women migrant workers, or that there had been very few reported.

62. For some types of violence reporting is unlikely, given the nature of the conditions under which violence would occur. It should be noted that under the terms of the Declaration on the Elimination of Violence against Women, as well as the Convention on the Elimination of All Forms of Discrimination against Women, trafficking for the purpose of prostitution is, by definition, violence. It is also illegal in almost all States. Still, some of the studies noted above, as well as others, suggest that the phenomenon exists. When the person who is a victim of trafficking is a migrant, the fact of illegality and the likelihood of repatriation can be disincentives to report incidences of violence.

63. Domestic service, by its nature, leaves women migrant workers vulnerable, since the place of work is usually the household and public regulation is not always effective there. There is considerable documentation about the incidence of physical violence and other forms of coercion against migrant women in domestic service in several countries. 23/ Some 80 per cent of all complaints reported by the Sri Lankan Bureau of Foreign Employment concerned female domestic workers in the Middle East. Sexual harassment by the male head of household was one of the three most common problems. 24/

V. Steps being taken to reduce violence against women migrant workers

64. Migrant workers, because they cross national boundaries, are in some measure an international responsibility. Eliminating violence against women migrant workers can be seen as an essential part of implementing the Declaration on the Elimination of Violence against Women as well as other relevant norms.

65. In many countries, as indicated by replies to the Secretary-General's request for information, measures exist or are being taken to deal with the question. Some of these are general economic and social policies designed to reduce the need for migration, others are to provide adequate legal remedies for women migrant workers and still others are social measures designed to deal with the effects of violence.

A. Measures being taken in sending countries

66. With regard to addressing the causes of migrations, the President of the Philippines announced, in an address on 1 May 1994, the adoption of a national jobs programme to create 1.1 million jobs annually and steps to increase the availability of housing and to encourage the development of cooperatives and other livelihood projects. 25/ Similarly, Thailand reports that a number of preventive measures are being administered by the Department of Labour Protection to discourage Thai women from working abroad by improving employment prospects in their own country. 26/

1. Legal measures

67. The Philippines noted that it had enacted legislation to curb trafficking in women as mail-order brides or in other ways. Policy directives had been issued to suppress the trafficking in and prostitution of women, and a selective ban had been imposed on the employment of Filipino entertainers and domestic servants in receiving countries that did not provide legal protection for them, or where they were otherwise endangered. 27/

68. Regulation of recruiting firms is another measure that has been taken in some countries. 28/

2. Social measures

69. Measures have been taken to reduce the vulnerability of women migrant workers by providing orientation prior to departure. The Philippines reports that rules of the Philippine Overseas Employment Administration require entertainers, nurses and domestics applying for overseas work to undergo pre-deployment orientation to increase their awareness and to prepare them for the social, cultural and job realities in their destinations.

70. Measures have also been taken to provide assistance to migrant workers in the receiving countries. This can include routine assistance by embassy and consular officials, as well as the negotiation of bilateral agreements with receiving States. The Philippines reports

23/ See, for example, Middle East Watch, op. cit.

24/ Malsiri Dias, "Female Overseas Contract Workers: Sri Lanka", in Asian and Pacific Development Centre (eds.), *Trade in Domestic Helpers, Causes, Mechanisms and Consequences*, Kuala Lumpur, APDAC, 1989, p. 212, cited in Weinert, op. cit.

25/ Second reply of the Government of the Philippines.

26/ Reply of the Government of Thailand.

27/ First reply of the Government of the Philippines.

28/ See Eelans and Speckman, loc. cit.

that its Overseas Workers Welfare Administration is employing more women officers in its front-line units and its overseas operations, especially at job sites with predominately women workers. It also maintains several social centres to serve the social, cultural and recreational needs of Filipino workers abroad. 29/

71. For migrant workers who have encountered abuse, measures are being considered to provide support services upon return. A plan to provide a programme of intervention, containing support, rights and resources components has been reported. 30/

B. Measures being taken in receiving countries

72. Most countries reporting indicate that women migrant workers have the same rights as nationals of their countries and that, therefore, there are no special measures necessary. In that sense, they would have similar difficulties or ease in exercising rights as women who were nationals of the country, compounded by the problems caused by language and different customs. A number of countries have taken steps to deal with the specific difficulties faced by women migrant workers. It should be noted that protection under the laws does not necessarily apply to migrants who have arrived illegally in the receiving country. These workers are, by reason of their illegality, particularly vulnerable to violence.

1. Legal measures

73. A number of countries have adopted measures to ensure that migrant workers receive equal treatment under the laws of the country. Mauritius reports that with a view to reinforce measures of control over companies employing foreign labour, the Ministry of Labour and Industrial Relations established on 21 February 1994 a Foreign Labour Inspection Squad, whose main objective is to ensure the full protection of the rights of migrant workers as provided by national labour legislation and their contracts of employment. 31/

2. Social measures

74. A number of countries have reported existing or proposed programmes to provide training and orientation to women migrant workers about their rights. This includes special vocational and language training. 32/ In the United Kingdom, the Employment Service applies the principle of equal opportunity in its programmes and services as relevant to women migrant workers, helping them to have the necessary access to employment facilities and to solve language difficulties. 33/

75. Non-governmental sources indicate that, in addition, there have been networks and organizations of and for migrant women workers in a number of places. Examples include Solidarity with Women in Distress

(SOLWODI) in Germany, the Filipino Women's Council in Rome, the National Organization of Immigrant and Visible Minority Women of Canada and BABAYLAN, a Philippine Women's Network in Europe. 34/

VI. Conclusions

76. The information available suggests that migration of women workers is growing and likely to continue. They will be subject to many of the same situations of violence as women in the receiving countries, made more acute by the type of work undertaken by women migrant workers and the difficulties caused by their status as migrants.

77. An international framework of protection is found in a number of international conventions that are directly relevant to the issues of violence against women migrant workers, including the Convention on the Elimination of All Forms of Discrimination against Women.

78. It is worth recalling that the issues of migrant women has been a concern for some time: migrant women are found among the areas of special concern in the Nairobi Forward-looking Strategies for the Advancement of Women. The issue of migrant women was considered by the Commission on the Status of Women under the priority theme Equality in 1991. The report of the Secretary-General to that session of the Commission concluded that:

"Governments of receiving countries should ensure that all migrants, especially women, are given information, in a language that they know, on their legal rights and obligations. Such information should include legal advice to female migrants, especially on how to acquire and maintain legal status, on marriage and divorce, domestic violence, labour laws, legislation on sex discrimination, and welfare and other social entitlements, including family planning. Counselling services should also be provided. Associations of and for migrant women should be used to disseminate information among migrants, provide counselling and other social and legal services, identify problems and communicate with decision-makers. Migrant women should be entitled to the same rights as migrant men. Governments should periodically review and, where necessary, revise migration policies and legislation, as well as their implementation, to prevent discriminatory practices against women."

29/ First reply of the Government of the Philippines.
30/ Second reply of the Government of the Philippines.
31/ Reply of the Government of Mauritius.
32/ Replies of the Governments of Burkina Faso and the Russian Federation.
33/ Reply of the Government of the United Kingdom.
34/ Reported in Isis International, op. cit., pp. 71-77.

79. Partly on the basis of that report the Commission on the Status of Women adopted resolution 35/6 on women migrant workers which, *inter alia*, calls upon States to sign and ratify the International Convention on the Protection of the Rights of All Migrant Workers and Members of Their Families, encourages the establishment of services to assist migrant workers and requests organizations of the United Nations system to assist in disseminating information among migrant workers.

80. On the basis of oral reports to the Commission on the Status of Women, as well as material on migrant women contained in the report of the Secretary-General on urban women, the Commission adopted resolution 38/7 on violence against women migrant workers. In this resolution, the Commission called upon Member States to adopt measures to implement the Declaration on the Elimination of Violence against Women, including applying it to women migrant workers, called for consultations between the sending and receiving States for women migrant workers to identify problem areas and measures to address them; and called upon these States to ensure the protections foreseen under the relevant international conventions.

81. From these measures already proposed, as well as those being enacted, a number of conclusions should be drawn.

—It is important to address the causes of migration in the sending countries and, for those who wish to migrate and return, to provide protection against unscrupulous recruiters and orientation to migrants about their rights and responsibilities and the likely conditions in the receiving countries.

—The desirability of negotiations between sending and receiving countries about the conditions of migrants is clear.

—Receiving countries should accord legal migrants equal treatment before their laws and provide the necessary information about these rights, accessible institutions and appropriate support programmes.

—An effort should be made to study the situation of undocumented migrant workers with a view to determining measures that can help resolve their status and thereby reduce their vulnerability to violence.

—Networks of women migrant workers should be encouraged and supported.

82. The size of the phenomenon of violence against women migrant workers is not known. To properly monitor the issue, statistics and indicators should be collected. As a first step, statistics that are disaggregated by sex, should be maintained by both sending and receiving countries on migrants. This will permit determination of the growth of international migration and its flow. The statistics should indicate the occupations to which the migrants are going. Periodic studies should be undertaken to indicate changes in the conditions of work.

83. In order to monitor violence against women migrant workers it is necessary, first, to monitor violence against women generally as called for in the Declaration on the Elimination of Violence against Women. The adoption of the Declaration provides categories of acts that should be counted. In view of their special vulnerability, the incidence of violence against women migrant workers should be counted as a category within national indicators.

Document 113

Programme of Action, adopted by the International Conference on Population and Development, held in Cairo from 5 to 13 September 1994—Chapter IV and Principle 4: Gender equality, equity and empowerment of women (extract)

A/CONF.171/13, 18 October 1994

...

Annex

*Programme of Action of the International Conference on Population and Development**

Principle 4

Advancing gender equality and equity and the empowerment of women, and the elimination of all kinds of violence against women, and ensuring women's ability to control their own fertility, are cornerstones of population and development-related programmes. The human rights of women and the girl child are an inalienable, integral and indivisible part of universal human rights. The full and equal participation of women in civil, cultural, eco-

* The official language of the Programme of Action is English, with the exception of paragraph 8.25, which was negotiated in all six official languages of the United Nations.

nomic, political and social life, at the national, regional and international levels, and the eradication of all forms of discrimination on grounds of sex, are priority objectives of the international community.

...

Chapter IV
Gender equality, equity and empowerment of women

A. *Empowerment and status of women*

Basis for action

4.1. The empowerment and autonomy of women and the improvement of their political, social, economic and health status is a highly important end in itself. In addition, it is essential for the achievement of sustainable development. The full participation and partnership of both women and men is required in productive and reproductive life, including shared responsibilities for the care and nurturing of children and maintenance of the household. In all parts of the world, women are facing threats to their lives, health and well-being as a result of being overburdened with work and of their lack of power and influence. In most regions of the world, women receive less formal education than men, and at the same time, women's own knowledge, abilities and coping mechanisms often go unrecognized. The power relations that impede women's attainment of healthy and fulfilling lives operate at many levels of society, from the most personal to the highly public. Achieving change requires policy and programme actions that will improve women's access to secure livelihoods and economic resources, alleviate their extreme responsibilities with regard to housework, remove legal impediments to their participation in public life, and raise social awareness through effective programmes of education and mass communication. In addition, improving the status of women also enhances their decision-making capacity at all levels in all spheres of life, especially in the area of sexuality and reproduction. This, in turn, is essential for the long-term success of population programmes. Experience shows that population and development programmes are most effective when steps have simultaneously been taken to improve the status of women.

4.2. Education is one of the most important means of empowering women with the knowledge, skills and self-confidence necessary to participate fully in the development process. More than 40 years ago, the Universal Declaration of Human Rights asserted that "everyone has the right to education". In 1990, Governments meeting at the World Conference on Education for All in Jomtien, Thailand, committed themselves to the goal of universal access to basic education. But despite notable efforts by countries around the globe that have appreciably expanded access to basic education, there are approximately 960 million illiterate adults in the world, of whom two thirds are women. More than one third of the world's adults, most of them women, have no access to printed knowledge, to new skills or to technologies that would improve the quality of their lives and help them shape and adapt to social and economic change. There are 130 million children who are not enrolled in primary school and 70 per cent of them are girls.

Objectives

4.3. The objectives are:

(*a*) To achieve equality and equity based on harmonious partnership between men and women and enable women to realize their full potential;

(*b*) To ensure the enhancement of women's contributions to sustainable development through their full involvement in policy- and decision-making processes at all stages and participation in all aspects of production, employment, income-generating activities, education, health, science and technology, sports, culture and population-related activities and other areas, as active decision makers, participants and beneficiaries;

(*c*) To ensure that all women, as well as men, are provided with the education necessary for them to meet their basic human needs and to exercise their human rights.

Actions

4.4. Countries should act to empower women and should take steps to eliminate inequalities between men and women as soon as possible by:

(a) Establishing mechanisms for women's equal participation and equitable representation at all levels of the political process and public life in each community and society and enabling women to articulate their concerns and needs;

(b) Promoting the fulfilment of women's potential through education, skill development and employment, giving paramount importance to the elimination of poverty, illiteracy and ill health among women;

(c) Eliminating all practices that discriminate against women; assisting women to establish and realize their rights, including those that relate to reproductive and sexual health;

(d) Adopting appropriate measures to improve women's ability to earn income beyond traditional occupations, achieve economic self-reliance, and ensure women's equal access to the labour market and social security systems;

(e) Eliminating violence against women;

(f) Eliminating discriminatory practices by employers against women, such as those based on proof of contraceptive use or pregnancy status;

(g) Making it possible, through laws, regulations and other appropriate measures, for women to combine the roles of child-bearing, breast-feeding and child-rearing with participation in the workforce.

4.5. All countries should make greater efforts to promulgate, implement and enforce national laws and international conventions to which they are party, such as the Convention on the Elimination of All Forms of Discrimination against Women, that protect women from all types of economic discrimination and from sexual harassment, and to implement fully the Declaration on the Elimination of Violence against Women and the Vienna Declaration and Programme of Action adopted at the World Conference on Human Rights in 1993. Countries are urged to sign, ratify and implement all existing agreements that promote women's rights.

4.6. Governments at all levels should ensure that women can buy, hold and sell property and land equally with men, obtain credit and negotiate contracts in their own name and on their own behalf and exercise their legal rights to inheritance.

4.7. Governments and employers are urged to eliminate gender discrimination in hiring, wages, benefits, training and job security with a view to eliminating gender-based disparities in income.

4.8. Governments, international organizations and non-governmental organizations should ensure that their personnel policies and practices comply with the principle of equitable representation of both sexes, especially at the managerial and policy-making levels, in all programmes, including population and development programmes. Specific procedures and indicators should be devised for gender-based analysis of development programmes and for assessing the impact of those programmes on women's social, economic and health status and access to resources.

4.9. Countries should take full measures to eliminate all forms of exploitation, abuse, harassment and violence against women, adolescents and children. This implies both preventive actions and rehabilitation of victims. Countries should prohibit degrading practices, such as trafficking in women, adolescents and children and exploitation through prostitution, and pay special attention to protecting the rights and safety of those who suffer from these crimes and those in potentially exploitable situations, such as migrant women, women in domestic service and schoolgirls. In this regard, international safeguards and mechanisms for cooperation should be put in place to ensure that these measures are implemented.

4.10. Countries are urged to identify and condemn the systematic practice of rape and other forms of inhuman and degrading treatment of women as a deliberate instrument of war and ethnic cleansing and take steps to assure that full assistance is provided to the victims of such abuse for their physical and mental rehabilitation.

4.11. The design of family health and other development interventions should take better account of the demands on women's time from the responsibilities of child-rearing, household work and income-generating activities. Male responsibilities should be emphasized with respect to child-rearing and housework. Greater investments should be made in appropriate measures to lessen the daily burden of domestic responsibilities, the greatest share of which falls on women. Greater attention should be paid to the ways in which environmental degradation and changes in land use adversely affect the allocation of women's time. Women's domestic working environments should not adversely affect their health.

4.12. Every effort should be made to encourage the expansion and strengthening of grass-roots, community-based and activist groups for women. Such groups should be the focus of national campaigns to foster women's awareness of the full range of their legal rights, including their rights within the family, and to help women organize to achieve those rights.

4.13. Countries are strongly urged to enact laws and to implement programmes and policies which will enable employees of both sexes to organize their family and work responsibilities through flexible work-hours, parental leave, day-care facilities, maternity leave, policies that enable working mothers to breast-feed their children, health insurance and other such measures. Similar rights should be ensured to those working in the informal sector.

4.14. Programmes to meet the needs of growing numbers of elderly people should fully take into account that women represent the larger proportion of the elderly and that elderly women generally have a lower socioeconomic status than elderly men.

B. *The girl child*

Basis for action

4.15. Since in all societies discrimination on the basis of sex often starts at the earliest stages of life, greater equality for the girl child is a necessary first step in ensuring that women realize their full potential and become equal partners in development. In a number of countries, the practice of prenatal sex selection, higher rates of mortality among very young girls, and lower rates of school enrolment for girls as compared with boys suggest that "son preference" is curtailing the access of girl children to food, education and health care. This is often compounded by the increasing use of technologies to determine foetal sex, resulting in abortion of female foetuses. Investments made in the girl child's health, nutrition and education, from infancy through adolescence, are critical.

Objectives

4.16. The objectives are:

(a) To eliminate all forms of discrimination against the girl child and the root causes of son preference, which results in harmful and unethical practices regarding female infanticide and prenatal sex selection;

(b) To increase public awareness of the value of the girl child, and concurrently, to strengthen the girl child's self-image, self-esteem and status;

(c) To improve the welfare of the girl child, especially in regard to health, nutrition and education.

Actions

4.17. Overall, the value of girl children to both their family and society must be expanded beyond their definition as potential child-bearers and caretakers and reinforced through the adoption and implementation of educational and social policies that encourage their full participation in the development of the societies in which they live. Leaders at all levels of the society must speak out and act forcefully against patterns of gender discrimination within the family, based on preference for sons. One of the aims should be to eliminate excess mortality of girls, wherever such a pattern exists. Special education and public information efforts are needed to promote equal treatment of girls and boys with respect to nutrition, health care, education and social, economic and political activity, as well as equitable inheritance rights.

4.18. Beyond the achievement of the goal of universal primary education in all countries before the year 2015, all countries are urged to ensure the widest and earliest possible access by girls and women to secondary and higher levels of education, as well as to vocational education and technical training, bearing in mind the need to improve the quality and relevance of that education.

4.19. Schools, the media and other social institutions should seek to eliminate stereotypes in all types of communication and educational materials that reinforce existing inequities between males and females and undermine girls' self-esteem. Countries must recognize that, in addition to expanding education for girls, teachers' atti-

tudes and practices, school curricula and facilities must also change to reflect a commitment to eliminate all gender bias, while recognizing the specific needs of the girl child.

4.20. Countries should develop an integrated approach to the special nutritional, general and reproductive health, education and social needs of girls and young women, as such additional investments in adolescent girls can often compensate for earlier inadequacies in their nutrition and health care.

4.21. Governments should strictly enforce laws to ensure that marriage is entered into only with the free and full consent of the intending spouses. In addition, Governments should strictly enforce laws concerning the minimum legal age of consent and the minimum age at marriage and should raise the minimum age at marriage where necessary. Governments and non-governmental organizations should generate social support for the enforcement of laws on the minimum legal age at marriage, in particular by providing educational and employment opportunities.

4.22. Governments are urged to prohibit female genital mutilation wherever it exists and to give vigorous support to efforts among non-governmental and community organizations and religious institutions to eliminate such practices.

4.23. Governments are urged to take the necessary measures to prevent infanticide, prenatal sex selection, trafficking in girl children and use of girls in prostitution and pornography.

C. *Male responsibilities and participation*

Basis for action

4.24. Changes in both men's and women's knowledge, attitudes and behaviour are necessary conditions for achieving the harmonious partnership of men and women. Men play a key role in bringing about gender equality since, in most societies, men exercise preponderant power in nearly every sphere of life, ranging from personal decisions regarding the size of families to the policy and programme decisions taken at all levels of Government. It is essential to improve communication between men and women on issues of sexuality and reproductive health, and the understanding of their joint responsibilities, so that men and women are equal partners in public and private life.

Objective

4.25. The objective is to promote gender equality in all spheres of life, including family and community life, and to encourage and enable men to take responsibility for their sexual and reproductive behaviour and their social and family roles.

Actions

4.26.   The equal participation of women and men in all areas of family and household responsibilities, including family planning, child-rearing and housework, should be promoted and encouraged by Governments. This should be pursued by means of information, education, communication, employment legislation and by fostering an economically enabling environment, such as family leave for men and women so that they may have more choice regarding the balance of their domestic and public responsibilities.

4.27.   Special efforts should be made to emphasize men's shared responsibility and promote their active involvement in responsible parenthood, sexual and reproductive behaviour, including family planning; prenatal, maternal and child health; prevention of sexually transmitted diseases, including HIV; prevention of unwanted and high-risk pregnancies; shared control and contribution to family income, children's education, health and nutrition; and recognition and promotion of the equal value of children of both sexes. Male responsibilities in family life must be included in the education of children from

the earliest ages. Special emphasis should be placed on the prevention of violence against women and children.

4.28.   Governments should take steps to ensure that children receive appropriate financial support from their parents by, among other measures, enforcing child-support laws. Governments should consider changes in law and policy to ensure men's responsibility to and financial support for their children and families. Such laws and policies should also encourage maintenance or reconstitution of the family unit. The safety of women in abusive relationships should be protected.

4.29.   National and community leaders should promote the full involvement of men in family life and the full integration of women in community life. Parents and schools should ensure that attitudes that are respectful of women and girls as equals are instilled in boys from the earliest possible age, along with an understanding of their shared responsibilities in all aspects of a safe, secure and harmonious family life. Relevant programmes to reach boys before they become sexually active are urgently needed.

...

Document 114

Report of the Secretary-General to the General Assembly on the improvement of the status of women in the Secretariat

A/49/587, 1 November 1994

Advancement of women

*Human resources management:
other human resources questions*

*Improvement of the status of women
in the Secretariat*

REPORT OF THE SECRETARY-GENERAL

I. Introduction

1.   At its forty-eighth session, the General Assembly adopted resolution 48/106 of 20 December 1993 on the improvement of the status of women in the Secretariat. Recalling previous resolutions and decisions and in accordance with the Charter of the United Nations, the Assembly urged the Secretary-General to accord greater priority to the recruitment and promotion of women in posts subject to geographical distribution. In achieving the targets of 35 per cent in posts subject to geographical distribution and 25 per cent representation of women for posts at the D-1 level and above by 1995, set in resolutions 45/125 of 14 December 1990, 45/239 C of 21 December 1990, 46/100 of 16 December 1991 and 47/93

of 16 December 1992, particular attention was to be focused on senior policy-level and decision-making posts and on those areas of the Secretariat where the levels of representation were below average. In the resolution the Assembly also called for an increase in the representation levels of women from developing countries, particularly those which are unrepresented or underrepresented, including countries in transition.

2.   To further the Secretary-General's efforts in this regard, the General Assembly, in resolution 48/106, called for a strengthening, from within existing resources, of the Focal Point for Women in the Secretariat "... to ensure authority of enforcement and responsibility of accountability and to enable it more effectively to monitor and facilitate progress in the 1995 action programme".

3.   By resolution 48/106 and also resolution 48/108 of 20 December 1993 on the implementation of the Nairobi Forward-looking Strategies for the Advancement of Women, the General Assembly encouraged the support and active participation of Member States in improving the status of women in the Secretariat through such measures as: identifying and submitting more

women candidates, encouraging women to apply for vacant posts, creating national rosters, and sharing information with the Secretariat.

4. The past year has been marked by vigorous efforts by the Office of Human Resources Management (OHRM) to integrate the goals and targets for the improvement of the status of women into the overall strategy for the management of the Organization's human resources set out in document A/C.5/49/5. It is the view of the Secretary-General that the adoption of a pro-active, more people-centred human resources strategy built on the principles of the Charter will enhance the ability of the Secretariat to recruit and retain personnel of the highest calibre and integrity, and, within this context, serve as the most conducive means of enhancing the status of women. It is anticipated that strengthened planning capacity and career development, along with better conditions of service, will make it possible to attract and retain more women and enable the Secretariat to achieve the goals set by the General Assembly.

5. The present report is divided into three sections. Section II offers an account of the current status of women in the Secretariat in posts subject to geographical distribution, as at 30 June 1994. In keeping with the Secretary-General's view that the efforts to improve the status of women must include women in all categories, this section also reports on the representation of women in posts with special language requirements and in the General Service and related categories. Section III provides an analysis of the constraints confronted by women and sheds light on actions that have been taken to improve the status of women. Section IV sets out the strategic plan of action for the improvement of the status of women in the Secretariat based on the 1991-1995

Action Programme. It translates the Secretary-General's pro-active policy for attainment of gender balance into tangible and measurable objectives, targets and measures; and an implementation plan which takes into account the existing attitudinal, administrative and managerial constraints. It also addresses the issues and concerns of women in other categories and reaffirms the Secretary-General's conviction that full gender parity must be achieved by the year 2000.

II. Current situation

A. Women in posts subject to geographical distribution

6. As shown in table 1, steady progress has been achieved since 30 June 1993, when the overall percentage of women in posts subject to geographical distribution was 31.3 per cent. By 30 June 1994, the percentage had risen to 32.6 per cent, representing a 1.3 percentage point increase. The percentage of women at levels D-1 and above, which was 12.3 per cent at 30 June 1993, rose to 15.1 per cent by 30 June 1994. Representation at the D-1 and D-2 levels increased from 12.8 and 13.6 in 1993 to 14.7 and 18.7, respectively, in 1994. It is significant that these increases were achieved at a time when the Organization was undergoing restructuring, a freeze on recruitment was in place until April of 1994, and a new system for placement and promotion was introduced.

7. In spite of the steady progress, the overall picture of representation at senior levels is below target. However, women at D-2 and D-1 levels increased by eight posts compared to 1993 figures. In addition, the welcome trend towards increased numbers of women at the P-5 levels has continued by the addition of 19 women, helping to form the critical mass at mid-level needed for

Table 1. *Number and percentage of staff in posts subject to geographical distribution*

Level	30 June 1993				30 June 1994			
	Women	Men	Total	%	Women	Men	Total	%
USG	3	18	21	14.3	2	17	19	10.5
ASG	1	14	15	6.7	2	16	18	12.5
D-2	9	57	66	13.6	14	61	75	18.7
D-1	31	211	242	12.8	34	198	232	14.7
P-5	103	372	475	21.7	122	375	497	24.5
P-4	203	463	666	30.5	246	481	727	33.8
P-3	239	396	635	37.7	240	371	611	39.2
P-2	209	237	446	46.9	168	201	369	45.5
P-1	6	1	7	60.0	2	0	2	100.0
Total	804	1 769	2 573	31.3	830	1 720	2 550	32.6

Source: Reports of the Secretary-General on the composition of the Secretariat (A/48/559 and A/49/527).

the promotion of women staff members to the D-1 level and above. The slower progress in increasing the representation of women at the D-1 level and above is in some part due to the lack of seniority in grade of women promoted to the P-5 level in years before. Among other strategies, it will thus be important to identify qualified women with accumulated seniority, or, as appropriate, to invoke the mechanism of accelerated promotion for particularly deserving candidates. A strategy being utilized to prepare women for assumption of higher level managerial and supervisory posts is temporary assignment of women to higher level vacant posts and/or assigning them to duties of officer-in-charge.

8. A study undertaken by the Steering Committee for Improvement of the Status of Women in 1994 in Departments and Offices indicates that out of 26 surveyed, 10 have attained the overall 35 per cent target and five have reached the 25 per cent target and five have reached the 25 per cent target at the D-1 level and above, but the rest have fallen below expectations. Statistics thus bear out the Secretary-General's conclusion that the pace of progress must be accelerated and such measures as those set out in the strategic plan of action should be adopted if decisive action is to be taken to meet the targets.

9. One device that could play a role in increasing the percentage of women at decision-making levels is the Senior Review Group, established by the Secretary-General in late 1993 for the filling of posts at the Director (D-2) level. The Senior Review Group can certainly play an important role in bringing more women into decision-making levels by systematically reviewing all eligible internal candidates, as well as ensuring that all existing special

measures to promote women have been applied in the consideration of internal and external women candidates.

10. As indicated in table D1 in the report of the Secretary-General on the composition of the Secretariat (A/49/527), representation of women in posts subject to geographical distribution as a percentage of all staff in 1994 continued to show imbalances among regions and countries of origin. Eastern Europe (0.75), the Middle East (1.25) and Africa (2.94) registered the lowest representation among the regions. The highest percentages were registered by North America and the Caribbean (9.53), Western Europe (8.00) and Asia and the Pacific (6.78). It should be noted that the percentage for the Asia-Pacific region is based on representation mainly by Asia; the Pacific area is underrepresented. The regional imbalance is also reflected in the percentage of women staff grouped by region of origin as of 30 June 1994 (A/49/527, table D2). Eastern Europe (2.29), the Middle East (3.86), Africa (9.04) and Latin America (9.52) have the lowest representation of women in a range from 2.29 per cent for Eastern Europe to 29.28 per cent for North America and the Caribbean.

11. Of the Member States within range or over-represented, women account for approximately one third of the representation. Figures vary widely among countries, and more women are represented at the lower levels, P-1 to P-4 posts.

B. *Women in posts subject to special language requirements*

12. As shown in table 2, a comparative analysis of the status of women in posts with special language re-

Table 2. *Percentage of women in posts with special language requirements 1975, 1980, 1985 and 1994 a/ (as at June of each year)*

Levels	1975		1980		1985		1994	
	M	F	M	F	M	F	M	F
P-5	33	11	41	15	108	39	95	36
P-4	145	49	169	83	226	122	211	130
P-3	227	126	279	150	218	113	230	120
P-2	111	39	89	43	130	53	20	19
P-1	4	3	0	2	0	0	0	0
Total	520	228	578	293	683	327	556	305
Grand total	748		871		1 010		861	
Female %	30.5		33.6		32.4		35.4	

Source: Reports of the Secretary-General on the composition of the Secretariat: A/10184, A/35/528, A/40/652, A/48/559 and A/49/527.

a/ It should be noted that posts with special language requirements are from levels P-1 to P-5 inclusive.

quirements covering the period 1975 through 1994 reveals a 4.9 per cent increase in the representation level of women, from 30.5 per cent in 1975 to 35.4 per cent in 1994. Further statistical analysis reveals that, however welcome this increase, the patterns of regional representation noted in respect of posts subject to geographical distribution prevail in this traditionally gender-blind category of Professional staff. There is every reason to believe that the active support of Member States in these regions in proposing women candidates to sit for a competitive language examination will yield significant results in improving the status of women in posts with special language requirements.

C. Women in the General Service and related categories

13. The majority of women working in the United Nations system are in the General Service and related categories. In fact, there are more than four times as many women in the General Service than in the Professional category. Promotion to the G-7 level is understandably limited by the pyramidal structure of grading, and a recent study undertaken by the Focal Point for Women on stagnation of staff at levels G-5/G-6 and G-7 indicates that only some 6 per cent of the total General Service staff population will reach the G-7 level to perform paraprofessional functions during an average career span of 25 years.

14. The G to P Competitive Examination has come to be regarded as the most objective avenue for promotion from the General Service to the Professional category. It is moreover significant that, as in the case of competitive examinations to fill posts with special language requirements, the removal of extraneous factors leads to a more gender-balanced representation.

15. Recent in-house studies have revealed issues of concern to women in the General Service and related categories which merit greater attention. These include such areas as training opportunities and career development. These concerns will receive particular attention in the context of the overall human resources management strategies proposed by the Office of Human Resources Management as well as in the strategic plan of action proposed in this report.

III. Constraints and some improvements

A. Women in the Professional category: the glass ceiling

16. Constraints to the advancement of women are many, varied and well entrenched. Often subtle and difficult to pinpoint because they relate to the "social" environment, they create invisible walls that hamper the efforts to introduce change and make progress slow and difficult.

17. It is gratifying to note that such strategic measures as the issuance of the landmark administrative instruction ST/AI/382 in March 1993, on special measures to improve the status of women in the Secretariat, and concerted efforts to increase the pool of qualified women candidates at the middle levels have contributed to the sizeable gains in the P-4 and P-5 levels during 1992-1994. The impact of a growing pool of P-5 women staff members qualified to assume higher level duties has not yet translated into promotions of women to the D-1 level and above, in part because these women have not accumulated the required seniority. Such mechanisms as cumulative seniority and judicious use of accelerated promotions in particularly deserving cases as appropriate will be applied, to increase the representation of women at the senior and policy-making levels. OHRM will devote careful attention to maintaining the pool of P-5 women candidates and to providing training as needed for their further career development. The strategic plan of action presented in this report includes strategies to facilitate the promotion of women to levels D-1 and above. These have been formulated bearing in mind the constraints listed below, which have been identified within the Secretariat.

1. Years in grade

18. A study of women in a single grade for 10 years or longer carried out by the Focal Point for Women indicates that many well-qualified women staff members remain in one grade for 10 years or longer. Enhanced planning capacity and career development will serve the interests of both the Organization and staff—men and women—in clarifying where and when opportunities for mobility and career advancement will arise. A management culture and management tools are being developed to recognize staff contributions to the Organization's work programmes as well as staff mobility and flexibility in adapting to a wider range of functions. Measures will be implemented to facilitate the advancement of this pool of qualified, senior women staff members, including to the extent possible considering their candidatures before looking externally for other women candidates.

2. Placement and promotion system

19. It is too early to assess the impact of the introduction of a new placement and promotion system in November 1993. The new system replaced the grade-by-grade annual promotion review with a system for announcing vacancies to which all interested persons could apply. While a comparative analysis of both systems would not be appropriate because of the different nature and cycles of the systems, a detailed analysis of the number of men and women recruited or promoted during the full year 1994 would indicate whether the new

Table 3. *Percentage of women promoted through the appointment and promotion bodies (from January to June 1994)*

Levels	Men	Women	Total	Percentage of women
D-1	5	2	7	28
P-5	9	5	14	36
P-4	10	12	22	54
P-3	11	16	27	59
P-2/P-1	0	6	6	100
Total	35	41	76	54

Source: Data provided by the secretariat of the appointment and promotion bodies.

Table 4. *Percentage of women recruited through the appointment and promotion bodies (from January to June 1994)*

Levels	Men	Women	Total	Percentage of women
D-1	1	1	2	50
P-5	4	1	5	20
P-4	15	2	17	12
P-3	6	15	21	71
P-2/P-1	1	2	3	6
Total	27	21	48	44

Source: Data provided by the secretariat of the appointment and promotion bodies.

system offers greater opportunities to improve the status of women in the Secretariat.

20. As shown in table 3, preliminary figures indicate that more women than men have been promoted at levels P-2 through P-4, while more men than women have been promoted at the P-5 and D-1 levels. A total of 76 staff members, 54 per cent of whom are women, were promoted during the same period. As foreseen in the Secretary-General's bulletin ST/SGB/267, entitled "Placement and promotion", of 15 November 1993, the new system will be reviewed, updated and refined by 1995 in the light of experience and the long-term needs of the Organization. Special attention will be given in the context of this review to determining how the system could better facilitate the promotion and recruitment of women.

3. *Recruitment*

21. Table 4 indicates the percentage of women recruited through the appointment and promotion bodies during the first half of 1994. The data reveal that a much higher percentage of women than men was recruited at levels P-1/P-2 and P-3, 67 and 71 per cent, with a significant drop to 12 and 20 per cent for women at the P-4 and P-5 levels, respectively. Recruitment at the D-1 level was equally divided between men and women candidates. Thus, while some gains have been achieved, efforts must be made to accelerate the recruitment of women at middle and senior management levels and to ensure the steady and deliberate application of recruitment policies geared towards achieving the representation targets set by the General Assembly. The multiple roles played by women and their varied experiences, including volunteer work, should be given greater weight in evaluating candidatures and the contributions they can make to the work of the Organization, particularly those women rejoining the workforce.

4. *Career progression*

22. In line with the spirit of the overall strategy for the management of the Organization's human resources set out in document A/C.5/49/5, and the strategic plan of action for women, career development plans and career development will play a prominent role in facilitating the advancement of women in the Secretariat.

5. *Access to qualified/experienced women*

23. Women comprise on average a lower percentage of the applicants for senior management vacancies. The paucity of women applicants, combined with the relatively small pool of women in service, contributes greatly to frustrating the effort to increase the representation of women. The response of women candidates to vacancies in certain fields traditionally viewed as male-dominated and technical—such as engineering— yields an even lower percentage of applicants or none at all. It is a generally recognized fact that women qualified in diverse technical fields can be identified in the newly independent States and countries in transition, as well as in Asian, African and Latin American developing countries. Efforts are under way to reach them.

24. External and internal competitive examinations have opened an avenue to recruit and promote women. External examinations, in particular, yielded a significant increase in the number of women recruits from 31 per cent in 1985 to 51 per cent in 1992. From 1985 through 1993, in nine rounds of the internal G to P Competitive Examinations, 63 per cent of the 177 staff promoted were women. The expansion and publicity of these examinations, especially in unrepresented or underrepresented Member States in the case of external examinations, are considered useful devices in targeting recruitment and promotion mechanisms to balance geographical and gender distribution. Accordingly, the

Examinations and Tests Section of OHRM is publicizing the national competitive examinations through the mass media and encourages all qualified women to apply.

6. Mobility

25. The Secretary-General considers that greater mobility will not only better serve the Organization but will serve the interests of individual staff in terms of their careers, experience and job satisfaction. However, it should be borne in mind that mobility can be a double-edged sword for dual-career families and single-parent families, where primary care is generally entrusted to women. OHRM will revisit such issues as strengthening systems to facilitate spousal employment and flexible working hours.

B. Women in the General Service and related categories: the glass ceiling

26. It should be recalled that, while there is a general acceptance among women in the General Service and related categories that the G to P Competitive Examination is a means of advancement to the Professional category, the number of available posts is considerably smaller than the number of General Service staff seeking access to Professional status. The small number of posts at the entry level has served to frustrate those, including women, in the General Service category who cannot be placed because of a shortage of posts. The allocation of posts for internal examinations is 30 per cent; consideration is being given to the possibility of proposing an increase to 40 per cent.

27. The Focal Point for Women intends to conduct further research into the avenues which can be pursued to identify means of enhancing the job satisfaction of senior General Service staff. Consideration must be given to identifying other avenues in addition to the competitive examination process for qualified women at the G-6 and G-7 levels to obtain job satisfaction and recognition of their contributions to the Organization.

C. Sexual harassment

˙ 28. It is considered that the issuance on 29 October 1992 of two administrative instructions, ST/AI/379 entitled "Procedures for dealing with sexual harassment" and ST/IC/1992/67 entitled "Guidelines for promoting equal treatment of men and women in the Secretariat", has sensitized both men and women to such issues and may well have served as a deterrent to such behaviour. Efforts have to be made to dispel the perception that those reporting incidents of sexual harassment will be placed in a situation detrimental to their career development and relations within the work environment.

29. With this in mind, an integral aspect of training programmes for managers, staff going on mission assignment and others will be an emphasis on the equal treatment of men and women and on issues related to sexual harassment. Moreover, the implementation of the system of accountability and responsibility and the new performance appraisal system should help to change the management culture of the Organization and render it more responsive also in this particular area.

IV. Strategic plan of action for the improvement of the status of women in the Secretariat (1995-2000)

A. Introduction

30. Reflective of the Secretary-General's commitment to the improvement of the status of women in the Secretariat is his intention to issue strict instructions to all departments, offices and organs of the Secretariat to adhere to the "succession plan for women", being devised as the centre-piece of the strategic plan of action for the improvement of the status of women in the Secretariat. The plan would give the Secretariat, for the first time, a planning capability and management tools to ensure that the 35 per cent overall target will be achieved by 1995, and the 25 per cent at levels D-1 and above as soon as possible and not later than June 1997.

31. The strategic plan of action, 1995-2000 (hereinafter called "the plan") is based on the Action Programme for the Improvement of the Status of Women in the Secretariat (1991-1995) but updates it to reflect the human resources management strategies and policies proposed by the Secretary-General in documents A/49/527 and A/C.5/49/5. Taking into account the mandates and requests of the General Assembly, the plan will set viable objectives and goals attainable within the current and anticipated capacity of the Organization. The Secretary-General will ensure the implementation of the plan through the issuance of clear and specific instructions as to the authority and responsibility of all managers to implement it, and the criteria by which performance will be appraised.

B. Goals and objectives

32. The long-term goals of the plan are to create conditions of equality and opportunity for women to participate fully in the work of the Secretariat and to achieve complete parity by the year 2000.

33. The objectives of the plan are:

(a) To achieve the target of 35 per cent overall representation of women in posts subject to geographical distribution by 1995 through the identification and setting of appropriate rates of recruitment and promotion;

(b) To achieve the 25 per cent representation of women at the D-1 level and above as soon as possible and not later than June 1997 through setting appropriate rates of recruitment/promotion at these levels;

(c) To identify and adopt recruitment and promotion policies and procedures which support the Secretariat's efforts to reach the targets and objectives;

(d) To establish clear opportunities for career development and improved conditions of work for the female staff in posts with special language requirements and in the General Service and related categories;

(e) To formulate specific actions and identify viable means to facilitate the implementation of the plan.

34. A recent assessment undertaken by the Focal Point for Women in the Office of Human Resources Management shows that the target of 35 per cent overall will be achieved if the "succession plan for women" that is being drawn up for the strategic plan is strictly followed. The 25 per cent target at levels D-1 and above is expected to be achieved around 1997, if the rates of recruitment and promotion proposed by the succession plan are implemented at these levels.

35. The assessment was based on the rate of attrition and replacement of vacancies in the Secretariat in the past five years and projected the number of men and women on available geographical posts from 1995 to the year 2000. The assumption was that the trends in recruitment and attrition from the past five years will continue during the next five years and that no significant changes would take place in the number of posts subject to geographical distribution.

36. The results also indicated that the Secretariat must accelerate promotion and recruitment of women gradually to a rate of at least 50 per cent to achieve better gender balance by the year 2000. Accordingly, the plan incorporates the results of this study into a model which would be used to test a few scenarios for reaching gender balance and set new annual targets and succession planning.

37. The succession plan for women will develop recruitment and promotion models and attempt to predict their impact, over a five-year period, on the grading structure and gender balance of the Secretariat.

38. These models will:

(a) Estimate available vacancies by grade for levels P-1/P-2 to Under-Secretary-General for the years 1995-2000;

(b) Estimate the targeted number of recruitments and/or promotions of women to be attained in each grade for each of the years in the period 1995-2000, if the overall target is set at 50/50 per cent representation by the year 2000;

(c) Test the likely impact of several "what if" scenarios in the combination of promotion/recruitment

actions balanced against anticipated attrition rates at each grade level and over the years of the plan;

(d) Select the scenario which will balance the aspirations of women on board with the role of recruitment in closing the wide gaps in the representation levels of men and women at the higher levels (D-1 and above). The selected scenario will be built on principles that foster equality in conditions of work and job opportunities, offer training opportunities and encourage mobility of staff so as to maintain a steady influx of junior Professional women at the P-1 to P-3 levels, build the pool of women in middle grades at P-4 and P-5 levels, and close the gender gap at the senior, policy-making D-1 and D-2 levels;

(e) Synchronize vacancies with the requirements of departmental staffing needs;

(f) Tie the success of the plan to the initiatives and monitoring role of OHRM and the accountability of the departments.

C. Implementation

39. To effect change, planning and targeting must be coupled with commitment and strategic action in such areas as planning and information/database development, recruitment, placement and promotion monitoring, appraisal and follow-up. The endorsement of this approach by the General Assembly is essential to achieving success. The strategic actions to be undertaken are as follows:

(a) Planning and information/database development

Planning and the development of timely and accurate information and database resources are essential to establish a human resources management planning and career management capacity. The strategic plan of action for women could provide a model for a human resources plan for the Secretariat and will be integrated into the planning capability of OHRM when this is established.

(b) Networking with other databases on women

Every opportunity will be taken to network with regional and international databases, including those of the regional commissions, universities, research institutions, professional women's associations and Governments. Special attention will be devoted to rosters available in developing countries and regions.

(c) Upgrading the internal roster of women

OHRM will continue upgrading its roster capability, cross-referencing to reflect the diverse experiences of staff members, and facilitate the identification of candidates eligible for placement in posts in various occupational groups.

(d) Broad advertising and communication

OHRM will endeavour to advertise widely in professional journals as well as newspapers and direct mailings tailored to the requirements of the post being advertised and/or to the targeted countries which are unrepresented or underrepresented by women and/or in terms of geographical distribution.

(e) Recruitment missions

To increase the Organization's access to qualified women, particularly in unrepresented or underrepresented countries, the work programme of the Focal Point for Women and the Recruitment and Placement Division will include strategically targeted recruitment missions. During 1994 and 1995, recruitment missions will be scheduled to coincide with regional preparatory meetings for the Fourth World Conference on Women, deemed to represent an ideal opportunity to widen the net for recruiting qualified women from all regions.

(f) Management culture

It is essential to develop a management culture which is supportive in both word and deed of measures to achieve equality between men and women in the workplace, empowering both and giving both the scope to contribute to the work of the Organization to their maximum potential. Such a culture will require the active concern and involvement of managers at all levels in the optimum development and management of their human resources capacity.

(g) Mobility

Greater interagency cooperation will be sought in facilitating spouse employment and efforts will also be undertaken to encourage Governments to permit spouse employment in their respective duty stations.

(h) In-service training

Field mission assignments serve as excellent opportunities for women to expand their fields of expertise and gain valuable experience and skills, often offering the possibility to serve at a higher level. Similar opportunities between offices away from Headquarters and Headquarters would serve experience-building. A planned rotation system would also ensure that a return to the respective duty station would avoid the creation of job insecurity or placement difficulties.

(i) Career development

Women especially need to be encouraged to look after and actively engage their supervisors in their career development. Managers need to be encouraged to demonstrate flexibility and interest in facilitating such efforts.

(j) Training

OHRM is preparing training packages designed to foster the desired changes in management culture, enhance awareness and ability to deal with gender discrimination and sexual harassment issues, and provide skills training. More women at the P-5 and D-1 levels will be included in management training programmes to encourage their participation in the change in management culture, by promoting better understanding among both women and men of different leadership styles, exploring better means of working together, and creating a more responsive working environment for all.

(k) General Service and related categories

Within the context of the local recruitment of staff and through their assignment to peace-keeping, peace-making and other field operations, mobility should continue to be afforded also to staff in the General Service and related categories. These assignments should be effected through a roster capability. Such measures would give all qualified and deserving staff the opportunity to gain experience, knowledge and expertise and, as shown in previous field missions, often offer the opportunity to perform functions at a higher level.

A roster capability with senior G-6 and G-7 women could also be established in certain fields, such as Personnel Management, Personnel Administration, Recruitment, Finance and Administration to allow for quick replacement of Professional staff going away on mission. This would permit on-the-job training at a higher level for those staff selected.

D. Monitoring, appraisal and follow-up

40. Monitoring, appraisal and follow-up are essential components of the plan and will be continuous. Monitoring will measure day-to-day activities against the short-term goals as well as such general and long-term objectives of the plan as the numerical targets and timetables, set under the succession plan for achieving equitable gender balance in posts subject to geographical distribution. Compliance with criteria established for the development of the management system will be monitored.

41. The various components of the plan will be developed as pilot projects fully compatible and integrated with such Secretariat-wide systems as the Integrated Management Information System, the accountability and responsibility system and the performance appraisal system. Progress will be evaluated against the stated objectives and goals and will be reported to the General Assembly on a regular basis. Revisions and follow-up action will be undertaken on the basis of experience gained and further guidance offered by the General Assembly.

42. The assignment of responsibilities and roles within the Secretariat to specific, identifiable organizational units and officials and the establishment of the performance appraisal system, which will also evaluate performance in this regard, are viewed as important means of strengthening the spirit of commitment to implementing the plan. Authority commensurate with the responsibility delegated will empower officials to take the actions required in achieving stated goals. Clear policies and the communication of these as well as decisions to all staff will enhance transparency in human resources management.

E. *Focal Point for Women in the Secretariat*

43. The Focal Point for Women will continue to work closely with the divisions of OHRM and advise the Assistant Secretary-General for Human Resources Management on ways of improving the placement, promotion and recruitment processes as well as strategies to improve the environment and working conditions of women.

44. The activities of the Focal Point for Women are currently financed from extrabudgetary resources. While specific proposals to fund these activities with regular budget resources will be included in the proposed programme budget for the biennium 1996-1997, the uncertainty as to the availability of future extrabudgetary funding casts a doubt as to the immediate future of the unit. As an interim solution, Member States are encouraged to provide voluntary contributions to strengthen the capacity of the Focal Point to carry out the strategic plan.

F. *Member States*

45. The Secretary-General will continue to urge Member States to include women among those lists of nationals proposed for vacancies and to assist in contacting and encouraging qualified women to apply for positions with the United Nations and to publicize vacancies.

Material support is also being invited in the form of the non-reimbursable secondment or financing of experts to assist the Office of Human Resources Management, in particular the Focal Point for Women, in the conduct of goal-specific studies or activities.

46. The commitment and active support of Member States is also critical. The Secretary-General will continue to identify and draw to the attention of Member States the ways in which they can play a decisive role in achieving the goals and objectives set for the improvement of the status of women in the Secretariat.

V. Conclusion

47. As preparations progress for the Organization's fiftieth anniversary and the Fourth World Conference on Women in 1995, it is appropriate to recall that the Charter of the United Nations sets the foundation of the commitment to create conditions of equality and opportunity for women and men of the highest calibre. General Assembly resolutions 48/106 and 48/108 refer to the shared responsibility of the Member States and the Secretary-General in this regard, identifying the diverse and complementary roles of each. These as well as previous relevant resolutions entrust the Secretary-General with fulfilling specific mandates and achieving specific goals in improving the status of women in the Secretariat, in particular at decision-making levels. Guided by the resolutions, the Secretary-General has taken action to fulfil these mandated responsibilities to the extent possible. It is increasingly clear, however, that the full involvement of Member States as active partners is required, if the objectives and goals set by the General Assembly are to be met. Thus, the strategic plan of action for the improvement of the status of women in the Secretariat outlined in the present report envisages courses of action to be pursued by the Secretary-General as well as ways in which Member States can actively support the Secretary-General in his efforts.

Document 115

Preliminary report of the Special Rapporteur on violence against women to the Commission on Human Rights

E/CN.4/1995/42, 22 November 1994

Further promotion and encouragement of human rights and fundamental freedoms, including the question of the programme and methods of work of the Commission

Alternative approaches and ways and means within the United Nations system for improving the effective enjoyment of human rights and fundamental freedoms

Preliminary report submitted by the Special Rapporteur on violence against women, its causes and consequences, Ms. Radhika Coomaraswamy, in accordance with Commission on Human Rights resolution 1994/45

Introduction

1. At its fiftieth session on 4 March 1994, the Commission on Human Rights adopted resolution 1994/45, entitled "The question of integrating the rights of women into the human rights mechanism of the United Nations and the elimination of violence against women", in which it decided to appoint, for a three-year-period, a special rapporteur on violence against women, including its causes and consequences.

2. In the same resolution, the Commission on Human Rights invited the Special Rapporteur, in carrying out that mandate, and within the framework of the Universal Declaration of Human Rights and all other international human rights instruments, including the Convention on the Elimination of All Forms of Discrimination against Women and the Declaration on the Elimination of Violence against Women, to:

(a) Seek and receive information on violence against women, its causes and consequences from Governments, treaty bodies, specialized agencies, other special rapporteurs responsible for various human rights questions and intergovernmental and non-governmental organizations, including women's organizations, and to respond effectively to such information;

(b) Recommend measures, ways and means, at the national, regional and international levels, to eliminate violence against women and its causes, and to remedy its consequences;

(c) Work closely with other special rapporteurs, special representatives, working groups and independent experts of the Commission on Human Rights and the Sub-Commission on Prevention of Discrimination and Protection of Minorities and with the treaty bodies, taking into account the Commission's request that they regularly and systematically include in their reports available information on human rights violations affecting women, and cooperate closely with the Commission on the Status of Women in the discharge of its functions.

3. Pursuant to paragraph 8 of the above-mentioned resolution, the Chairman of the fiftieth session of the Commission on Human Rights, after consultation with the members of the Bureau, appointed Ms. Radhika Coomaraswamy (Sri Lanka) as Special Rapporteur on violence against women, its causes and consequences.

4. By its decision 1994/254 of 22 July 1994, the Economic and Social Council endorsed Commission on Human Rights resolution 1994/45.

5. In that resolution the Commission also called for the elimination of gender-based violence in the family, within the general community and where perpetrated or condoned by the State. It also emphasized the duty of Governments to take appropriate and effective action concerning acts of violence against women, whether those acts are perpetrated by the State or by private persons.

6. Furthermore, in accordance with paragraph 10 of the same resolution, the Special Rapporteur was mandated to carry out field missions, either separately or jointly, with other special rapporteurs and working groups, as well as to consult periodically with the Committee on the Elimination of Discrimination against Women. In addition, the Commission requested the Secretary-General to ensure that the reports of the Special Rapporteur were brought to the attention of the Commission on the Status of Women to assist in the Commission's work in the area of violence against women.

I. Mandate and working methods of the Special Rapporteur

A. General

7. The different forms of violence against women include, as spelled out in the above resolution, all violations of the human rights of women in situations of armed conflict, and in particular, murder, systematic rape, sexual slavery and forced pregnancy, as well as all forms of sexual harassment, exploitation and trafficking in women, the elimination of gender bias in the administra-

tion of justice and the eradication of the harmful effects of certain traditional or customary practices, cultural prejudice and religious extremism.

8. The Special Rapporteur has understood her mandate to contain two components. The first consists of setting out the elements of the problem before her, the international legal standards and a general survey of incidents and issues as they relate to the many problem areas. The second component consists of identifying and investigating factual situations, as well as allegations which may be forwarded to the Special Rapporteur by concerned parties.

9. With regard to the second component, the Special Rapporteur deems it useful to take a more specific approach by endeavouring to identify more precisely situations of violence against women. For this purpose the Special Rapporteur, in a spirit of dialogue, will approach concerned Governments and request clarifications on allegations regarding violence against women that she may have received. This method of direct dialogue with Governments is consistent with the approach of the Commission on Human Rights, which invited the Special Rapporteur "to seek and receive information on violence against women, its causes and consequences, from Governments" and further requested "all Governments to cooperate with and assist the Special Rapporteur in the performance of the tasks and duties mandated and to furnish all information requested".

10. Taking into consideration the alarming situation of violence against women throughout the world, the Special Rapporteur intends to establish dialogue with Governments concerning allegations and prospective field missions with a view to assisting the Governments concerned to find durable solutions for the elimination of violence against women in their societies.

11. In addition to inquiring into specific allegations and in accordance with paragraph 10 of resolution 1994/45, the Special Rapporteur is planning to undertake a number of field missions in connection with her first and second reports, to be submitted in 1996 and 1997, respectively. These field visits will cover all geopolitical regions. In particular, the Special Rapporteur envisages visiting the Asian, African and Eastern European regions in 1995, and the Latin American, Western European and other and Asian regions in 1996.

12. On 29 July 1994, the Secretary-General sent a note verbale to Governments transmitting the Special Rapporteur's request, with reference to paragraph 7 (a) of resolution 1994/45, for relevant information and contributions in order to assist her in her work.

13. Information and materials were requested in the areas of:

(a) Violence in the family (including domestic violence, traditional practices, infanticide, incest, etc.);

(b) Violence in the community (including rape, sexual assault, sexual harassment, commercialized violence such as trafficking in women, prostitution, labour exploitation, pornography, women migrant workers, etc.);

(c) Violence by the State (including violence against women in detention and custodial violence, as well as violence against women in situations of armed conflict and against refugee women).

14. In particular, the Special Rapporteur expressed her interest in receiving, with respect to any of the above issues, information on national legislation, relevant court cases, training programmes for judges and lawyers, police practice and training procedures, special policies and institutions concerned with women victims of violence, as well as statistical data. Governments were also asked to submit information on national plans of action with regard to violence against women, referred to in article 4 (e) of the Declaration on the Elimination of Violence against Women (General Assembly resolution 48/104).

15. At the time of submission of the present report, replies had been received from Angola, Argentina, Burkina Faso, Brunei Darussalam, China, Cyprus, Denmark, Ecuador, Finland, Germany, Iraq, Kuwait, Luxembourg, Malta, Mauritania, Mexico, New Zealand, Peru, the Philippines, San Marino, Slovenia, St. Vincent and the Grenadines, Switzerland, the Syrian Arab Republic, Turkey, the United Kingdom of Great Britain and Northern Ireland, the United States of America and Yugoslavia.

16. Requests for information on violence against women, its causes and consequences, were also addressed to treaty bodies, other special rapporteurs responsible for various human rights questions, specialized agencies, United Nations bodies and organs, and intergovernmental and non-governmental organizations, including women's organizations.

17. The Special Rapporteur received responses from the Division for the Advancement of Women, the Crime Prevention and Criminal Justice Branch of the United Nations Office at Vienna, the Economic and Social Commission for Asia and the Pacific, the Economic Commission for Latin America and the Caribbean, the Office of the United Nations High Commissioner for Refugees, the International Court of Justice, the United Nations Research Institute for Social Development, the United Nations African Institute for the Prevention of Crime and the Treatment of Offenders, the Food and Agriculture Organization of the United Nations, the United Nations Educational, Scientific and Cultural Organization and the World Health Organization, as well as from the United Nations Development Programme offices in Burundi, El Salvador, the Gambia,

Guatemala, Guyana, India, the Libyan Arab Jamahiriya, Madagascar, Pakistan, Panama, Peru, Senegal, the Sudan, Turkey, the United Republic of Tanzania and Venezuela.

18. Replies were also received from the Conference on Security and Cooperation in Europe, the Commonwealth Secretariat, the Council of Europe, the Inter-American Court of Human Rights, the Inter-Parliamentary Union, the International Organization for Migration and Interpol, as well as the following non-governmental organizations: Amnesty International, Baha'i International Community, Coalition Against Trafficking in Women, Education International, Human Rights Watch/Women's Rights Project, Inter-African Committee on Traditional Practices, International Federation of Business and Professional Women, International Fellowship of Reconciliation, International Institute of Humanitarian Law, Medical Women's International Association, Socialist Women International, World Education Fellowship.

19. The Special Rapporteur will use the information received mainly in her second and third reports when she will be reporting on specific issues in greater detail.

B. The United Nations system and initiatives against violence against women

20. The issue of violence against women has only recently found its place on the international human rights agenda. In the 1970s, women's issues were generally related to problems of political and economic discrimination and to equitable participation in the development process by women of the third world. The major international legal instrument concerned with women's rights *per se*, the 1979 Convention on the Elimination of All Forms of Discrimination against Women, concentrated on "discrimination". The issue of gender-based violence is not specifically addressed in the Convention although it is clearly fundamental to its provisions.

21. At the World Conference to Review and Appraise the Achievements of the United Nations Decade for Women: Equality, Development and Peace, held at Nairobi in July 1985, the issue of violence against women was once again only raised as an afterthought to issues of discrimination, health and economic and social issues.

22. Paragraph 258 of the Nairobi Forward-looking Strategies for the Advancement of Women, adopted by the World Conference, states:

"Violence against women exists in various forms in everyday life in all societies. Women are beaten, mutilated, burned, sexually abused and raped. Such violence is a major obstacle to the achievement of peace and the other objectives of the Decade and should be given special attention. Women victims of violence should be given particular attention and

comprehensive assistance. To this end, legal measures should be formulated to prevent violence and to assist women victims. National machinery should be established in order to deal with the question of violence against women within the family and society. Preventive policies should be elaborated, and institutionalized forms of assistance to women victims provided."

23. In 1986, an expert group meeting on violence in the family with special emphasis on its effects on women was organized under the auspices of the Division for the Advancement of Women.

24. The issue of violence against women was taken up by the Economic and Social Council in recommendations and conclusions arising from the first review and appraisal of the implementation of the Nairobi Forward-looking Strategies, annexed to its resolution 1990/15 of 24 May 1990, in which it recognized that:

"Violence against women in the family and society is pervasive and cuts across lines of income, class and culture must be matched by urgent and effective steps to eliminate its incidence. Violence against women derives from their unequal status in society."

Consequently, Governments were called upon to take immediate measures to establish appropriate penalties for, as well as reduce the impact of, violence against women in the family, the workplace and society (recommendation XXII).

25. In the same year, at the Eighth United Nations Congress on the Prevention of Crime and Treatment of Offenders, it was stated that violence against women was seen as a result of the power imbalance between women and men, and that violence sustained that imbalance.

26. In March 1991, the Commission on the Status of Women, at its thirty-fifth session, in draft resolution II, recommended to the Economic and Social Council for adoption that a framework for an international instrument be developed in consultation with the Committee for the Elimination of Discrimination against Women that would address explicitly the issue of violence against women.

27. Subsequently, the Economic and Social Council, upon the recommendation of the Commission on the Status of Women, adopted resolution 1991/18 of 30 May 1991, entitled "Violence against women in all its forms", in which *inter alia* it urged Member States to adopt, strengthen and enforce legislation prohibiting violence against women and to take all appropriate administrative, social and educational measures to protect women from all forms of physical and mental violence; and, more importantly, recommended the development of a framework for an international instrument that would explicitly address the issue.

28. As a result, in November 1991, another expert meeting on violence against women was convened at Vienna, under the auspices of the Division for the Advancement of Women. The Expert Group recommended, *inter alia*, the improvement of reporting by States on violence against women to the Committee on the Elimination of Discrimination against Women (CEDAW), and the appointment of a special thematic rapporteur on violence against women, as well as preparing a draft United Nations declaration on violence against women, to be submitted to the Commission on the Status of Women and to CEDAW.

29. In 1992, CEDAW, at its eleventh session, took the important step of formally including under gender-based discrimination gender-based violence

"that is violence which is directed against a woman because she is a woman or which affects women disproportionately. It includes acts which inflict physical, mental or sexual harm or suffering, threats such as acts, coercion, and other deprivation of liberty. Gender-based violence may breach specific provisions of the Convention, regardless whether those provisions expressly mention violence."

States parties were, therefore, requested to take appropriate and effective measures to overcome all forms of gender-based violence, whether by public or private act" (General recommendation 19, entitled "Violence against women", 1992).

30. In 1993, the Commission on the Status of Women had before it at its thirty-seventh session a draft declaration on violence against women, as contained in a report of the Secretary-General (E/CN.6/1993/12), and subsequently decided to convene an inter-sessional working group, which met in September 1992, to develop further the draft declaration on violence against women.

31. Also in 1993, upon the recommendation of the Commission on the Status of Women, the Economic and Social Council, in its resolution 1993/10 of 27 July 1993, urged the General Assembly to adopt the draft declaration on the elimination of violence against women, and in resolution 1993/26 also of 27 July 1993, entitled "Violence against women in all its forms", urged Governments to give their full support to its adoption.

32. The process of anchoring the issue of violence against women firmly on the international agenda culminated in the adoption, without a vote, by the General Assembly at its forty-eighth session, of resolution 48/104 on 20 December 1993, in which it proclaimed the Declaration on the Elimination of Violence Against Women.

33. This Declaration is the first international human rights instrument to deal exclusively with violence against women. It affirms that violence against women both violates and impairs or nullifies the enjoyment by women of human rights and fundamental freedoms and is concerned about the long-standing failure to protect and promote those rights and freedoms in relation to violence against women. For the first time also, a clear and comprehensive definition of violence against women has been attempted in article 1 of the Declaration (see chap. II).

34. Also in 1993, a parallel process advocating the elimination of violence against women emerged in other human rights mechanisms of the United Nations. The Commission on Human Rights, at its forty-ninth session, in its resolution 1993/46 of 8 March 1993, condemned all acts of violence and violations of human rights directed specifically against women and decided to consider the appointment of a special rapporteur on violence against women at its fiftieth session.

35. Similarly, the Vienna Declaration and Programme of Action adopted by the World Conference on Human Rights, held at Vienna in June 1993, contains important provisions in the field of the human rights of women. Part I, paragraph 18, reads as follows:

"The human rights of women and of the girl-child are an inalienable, integral and indivisible part of universal human rights. The full and equal participation of women in political, civil, economic, social and cultural life, at the national, regional and international levels, and the eradication of all forms of discrimination on grounds of sex are priority objectives of the international community.

"Gender-based violence and all forms of sexual harassment and exploitation, including those resulting from cultural prejudice and international trafficking, are incompatible with the dignity and worth of the human person, and must be eliminated. This can be achieved by legal measures and through national action and international cooperation in such fields as economic and social development, education, safe maternity and health care, and social support.

"The human rights of women should form an integral part of the United Nations human rights activities, including the promotion of all human rights instruments relating to women.

"The World Conference on Human Rights urges Governments, institutions, intergovernmental and non-governmental organizations to intensify their efforts for the protection and promotion of human rights of women and the girl-child."

36. It is further stated, in Part II, paragraph 37 of the Vienna Declaration and Programme of Action, that:

"The equal status of women and the human rights of women should be integrated into the mainstream of United Nations system-wide activity. These issues should be regularly and systematically addressed throughout relevant United Nations bodies and mechanisms. In particular, steps should be taken to increase cooperation and promote further integration of objectives and goals between the Commission on the Status of Women, the Commission on Human Rights, the Committee on the Elimination of Discrimination against Women, the United Nations Development Fund for Women, the United Nations Development Programme and other United Nations agencies. In this context, cooperation and coordination should be strengthened between the Centre for Human Rights and the Division for the Advancement of Women."

37. In particular, in Part II, paragraph 38 of the Vienna Declaration and Programme of Action:

"The World Conference on Human Rights stresses the importance of working towards the elimination of violence against women in public and private life, the elimination of all forms of sexual harassment, exploitation and trafficking in women, the elimination of gender bias in the administration of justice and the eradication of any conflicts which may arise between the rights of women and the harmful effects of certain traditional or customary practices, cultural prejudices and religious extremism. The World Conference calls upon the General Assembly to adopt the draft declaration on violence against women and urges States to combat violence against women in accordance with its provisions. Violations of the human rights of women in situations of armed conflict are violations of the fundamental principles of international human rights and humanitarian law. All violations of this kind, including in particular murder, systematic rape, sexual slavery, and forced pregnancy, require a particularly effective response."

38. With regard to the effective integration of the human rights of women into United Nations activities, Part II, paragraph 40, states:

"Treaty monitoring bodies should disseminate necessary information to enable women to make more effective use of existing implementation procedures in their pursuit of full and equal enjoyment of human rights and non-discrimination. New procedures should also be adopted to strengthen implementation of the commitment to women's equality and the human rights of women. The Commission on the Status of Women and the Committee on the Elimination of Discrimination against Women should

quickly examine the possibility of introducing the right of petition through the preparation of an optional protocol to the Convention on the Elimination of All Forms of Discrimination against Women. The World Conference on Human Rights welcomes the decision of the Commission on Human Rights to consider the appointment of a special rapporteur on violence against women at its fiftieth session."

39. At its fiftieth session, the Commission on Human Rights, in its resolution 1994/45 of 4 March 1994, decided to appoint a special rapporteur on violence against women, including its causes and consequences.

40. As part of the preparatory process for the Fourth World Conference on Women, to be held in Beijing in 1995, a draft platform of action is being elaborated. In Section II.C of this draft platform, as approved by the Commission on the Status of Women, at its thirty-eighth session, in its resolution 38/10, violence against women is recognized as a global problem, taking various forms in both public and private life, which constitutes a violation of basic human rights, instilling fear and insecurity in women's lives.

41. Lastly, on 9 June 1994 the General Assembly of the Organization of American States adopted the Inter-American Convention on the Prevention, Punishment and Eradication of Violence against Women (the "Convention of Belém do Pará").

42. It is evident that the human rights of women, and more specifically their integration into the mainstream of United Nations activities in the field of human rights, is gaining increasing political attention on the international human rights agenda. The appointment of a special rapporteur on violence against women by the Commission on Human Rights should be seen as one important step in this direction, as well as the culmination of joint efforts of active and interested Governments, non-governmental organizations and women's groups worldwide.

43. With regard to the integration of the human rights of women into the mainstream of United Nations human rights activities, and in accordance with paragraphs 10, 11 and 12 of Commission resolution 1994/45 and paragraph (b) of Economic and Social Council decision 1994/254, the Special Rapporteur has been closely following the preparatory process for the Fourth World Conference on Women, to be held in Beijing in September 1995. In this connection, the Special Rapporteur has met with representatives of the secretariat for the World Conference at the Division for the Advancement of Women and participated at the Arab Regional Preparatory Meeting for the World Conference on Women, held at Amman from 6 to 10 November 1994.

44. In addition, the Special Rapporteur will meet with the members of the Committee on the Elimination of Discrimination against Women at its fourteenth session, in January 1995, and is planning to attend the thirty-ninth session of the Commission on the Status of Women, in March 1995.

45. On the basis of the above, as well as in an attempt to give full justice to the complexity of the issue, the Special Rapporteur has prepared this preliminary report in which she recalls the terms of her mandate, her interpretation of these terms and the working methods in the introduction. Chapter I focuses on the nature of the problem and the specific causes and consequences of violence against women. Chapter II outlines the relevant international legal standards and human rights instruments applicable to violence against women. Chapter III addresses the general issues concerning the problems arising from such violence in the family, the community and where perpetrated or condoned by the State. Finally, in chapter V the Special Rapporteur submits conclusions and preliminary recommendations based on her analysis of the information available at the time of the finalization of the present report. 1/

II. The nature of the problem—causes and consequences of violence against women

A. *General*

46. The human rights tradition privileges a certain type of human personality—an individual endowed with rights, guided by reason and empowered with dignity. Since the Universal Declaration of Human Rights, this has been the vision which has sustained many of the political, economic and social experiments of the modern world. In recent times it has provided the firm foundation for the development of democracy, justice and equality in many societies.

47. Violence against human beings has been one of the major factors which has prevented the realization of human rights goals in the twentieth century. War, repression, and the brutalization of public and private life have destroyed the possibility of human rights being enjoyed as a universal phenomenon. Violence against women, in particular, has inhibited women as a group from enjoying the full benefits of human rights. Women have been vulnerable to acts of violence in the family, in the community and by States. The recorded incidents of such violence have reached such unprecedented proportions that they have shocked the conscience of the world. As a result, the international community has decided to take concerted action against incidents of violence against women as part of the general campaign for human rights. 2/

48. Women are vulnerable to violence because of their female sexuality (resulting in, *inter alia*, rape and female genital mutilation); because they are related to a man (domestic violence, dowry deaths, sati) or because they belong to a social group, where violence against women becomes a means of humiliation directed at the group (rape in times of armed conflict or ethnic strife). Women are subject to violence in the family (battering, sexual abuse of female children, dowry related violence, incest, deprivation of food, marital rape, female genital mutilation), to violence in the community (rape, sexual abuse, sexual harassment, trafficking in women, forced prostitution) and violence by the State (women in detention and rape during times of armed conflict).

B. *Historically unequal power relations*

49. As is stated in the Preamble to the United Nations Declaration on the Elimination of Violence against Women, violence against women is a manifestation of historically unequal power relations between men and women. Violence is part of a historical process and is not natural or born of biological determinism. The system of male dominance has historical roots and its functions and manifestations change over time. 3/ The oppression of women is therefore a question of politics, requiring an analysis of the institutions of the State and society, the conditioning and socialization of individuals, and the nature of economic and social exploitation. The use of force against women is only one aspect of this phenomenon, which relies on intimidation and fear to subordinate women.

50. Women are subject to certain universal forms of abuse such as rape and domestic violence. In addition, certain cultural forms are specific to regions and countries. These include female genital mutilation, virginity tests, bride burning or the binding of the feet of female children. It is argued that any attempt to universalize women's experience is to conceal other forms of oppression such as those based on race, class or nationality. This reservation must be noted and acknowledged. And yet it must be accepted that there are patterns of patriarchal domination which are universal, though this domination

1/ The Special Rapporteur would like to thank Ms. Tej Thapa, Ms. Natasha Balendra and Ms. Mala Dharmananda for their research assistance in the preparation of this report.

2/ For a discussion of this campaign see Women's Leadership Institute Report, *Women, Violence and Human Rights*, Center for Women's Global Leadership, Rutgers University, 1992. Also see Charlotte Bunch, "Women's rights as human rights: Toward a revision of human rights", in 12 *Human Rights Quarterly*, 486 (1990).

3/ For a discussion of the historical aspects of power relations, see Gerda Lerner, *The Creation of Patriarchy*, Oxford University Press, New York, 1986.

takes a number of different forms as a result of particular and different historical experiences. 4/

51. If the roots of female subordination lie in historical power relations within society, then the institutions of State and civil society must accept responsibility for female subordination, including violence against women. The State bears a primary responsibility not only to refrain from encouraging acts of violence against women but actively to intervene in preventing such acts from taking place. State institutions such as prisons and detention centres are often the sites of violence against women. Rape is often used as an instrument of torture. State inaction in situations of violence against women is one of the major factors that allows such violence to continue.

52. In fact, in modern times, the State has become an arena of conflict: on the one hand, it may act according to legislation and practices which are against women's interests; but on the other hand, the State may emerge as the major instrument in transforming certain legislative, administrative and judicial practices which empower women to vindicate their rights. The negligence of the State may be the cause of increased violence against women, while the active intervention of the State may actually be the catalyst for reforming power relations within society. 5/

53. Among the historical power relations responsible for violence against women are the economic and social forces which exploit female labour and the female body. Economically disadvantaged women are more vulnerable to sexual harassment, trafficking and sexual slavery. They are also employed as bonded labour and low-paid labour in many economic enterprises throughout the world. As migrant workers, they often face innumerable hardships in foreign countries. 6/ Economic exploitation is an important aspect of modern female labour. In addition, a study of 90 societies in relation to wife beating found that economic equality was a key factor which prevented violence against women. 7/ Denying women economic power and economic independence is a major cause of violence against women because it prolongs their vulnerability and dependence. Unless economic relations in a society are more equitable towards women, the problem of violence against women will continue. 8/

54. The institution of the family is also an arena where historical power relations are often played out. On the one hand, the family can be the source of positive nurturing and caring values where individuals bond through mutual respect and love. On the other hand, it can be a social institution where labour is exploited, where male sexual power is violently expressed and where a certain type of socialization disempowers women. Female sexual identity is often created by the family environment. The negative images of the self which often inhibit women from realizing their full potential may be linked to familial expectation. The family is, therefore, the source of positive humane values, yet in some instances it is the site for violence against women and a socialization process which may result in justifying violence against women. 9/

55. Modern technology may also be a factor impinging on the question of violence against women. "Ecofeminists" have continuously pointed out that modern technology has resulted in the destruction of the lifestyle of rural women in many parts of the globe. 10/ Others have pointed to the growth of sweat shops and similar sites for the economic exploitation of female labour spawned by modern technology and its needs. Economic systems which value profits often do so at the expense of female labour. This is particularly true of production processes involved in free trade zones and home-based production. Since female labour is devalued in these sectors, they often become sites for violence against women. Rape and sexual harassment of these workers remain an important social problem in many developing societies. 11/

56. The area which is particularly relevant to the

4/ Annie Bunting, "Theorizing women's cultural diversity in feminist international human rights strategies", in 20 *Journal of Law and Society* 6 (1993). Also, Radhika Coomaraswamy, "To bellow like a cow: women, ethnicity and the discourse of rights", in Rebecca Cook, ed., *Human Rights of Women: National and International Perspectives* (forthcoming 1994).

5/ See generally, A. Borchost, and B. Siim, "Women and the advanced welfare State—A new kind of patriarchal power" in A.S. Sassoon ed. *Women and the State. The Shifting Boundaries between Public and Private*, London, Hutchinson, 1987. Also see B. Friedan, *The Feminine Mystique*, Hammondsworth, Penguin, 1986; and D. Dahlerup, "Confusing concepts—confusing realities: A theoretical discussion of the patriarchal State" in Sasson, ibid.

6/ Middle East Watch, Women's Rights Project, *Punishing the Victim: Rape and Mistreatment of Asian Maids in Kuwait*, New York, August 1992.

7/ David Levinson, *Family Violence in Cross Cultural Perspective*, Newbury Park, Sage, 1989.

8/ See Isabella Bakker ed. *The Strategic Silence, Gender and Economic Policy*, London, Zed, 1994. Also see Susan Bullock, *Women and Work*, London, Zed, 1994; S.P. Joekas, *Women and the World Economy*, New York, Oxford, 1987 and United Nations Centre for Transnational Corporations, *Women Workers in Multinational Corporations in Developing Countries*, UNCTC, Geneva, ILO, 1985.

9/ N. Chodorow, *The Reproduction of Mothering. Psychoanalysis and the Sociology of Gender*, Berkeley, University of California Press, 1978.

10/ See Maria Mies and Vandana Shiva, *Ecofeminism*, London, Zed, 1994.

11/ See, for example, Carol Aloysius, "Working women need protection from sexual harassment", Sri Lanka, *Sunday Observer*, 23 May 1993.

problem of violence against women in the context of technology is the issue of reproductive technology. Though reproductive technology has allowed women greater freedom and greater choice with regard to the important function of childbirth, it has also created innumerable health problems for women, problems which are often ignored by the medical establishment. These health problems have resulted in female deaths which in other circumstances might have been avoided. Women's access to adequate health care becomes a crucial factor in this regard. In addition, reproductive technology which allows for preselection of the sex of the child has resulted in the killing of female foetuses and selective abortion. The practice of surrogate motherhood which has developed recently has also resulted in the exploitation of the bodies of women from the third world. Modern technology has been the means of liberation and choice for many women, but for others it has resulted in death and exploitation. 12/

57. In the context of the historical power relations between men and women, women must also confront the problem that men control the knowledge systems of the world. Whether it be in the field of science, culture, religion or language, men control the accompanying discourse. Women have been excluded from the enterprise of creating symbolic systems or interpreting historical experience. 13/ It is this lack of control over knowledge systems which allows them not only to be victims of violence, but to be part of a discourse which often legitimizes or trivializes violence against women. The ability to minimize women's experience of violence ensures that no remedial action is taken by either States or individuals. Part of the campaign to eliminate violence against women must be to challenge the systems of knowledge and the discourse of individuals which trivialize women's experience of violence. 14/ Women are also denied access to knowledge because they are refused education in many parts of the world. The right to female education must therefore be the first step towards articulating a more sensitive history of violence against women.

C. Sexuality

58. In addition to historical power relations, the causes of violence against women are also closely linked to the question of female sexuality. Violence is often used as an instrument to control female sexual behaviour. It is for this reason that violence against women often finds sexual expression. Rape, sexual harassment, trafficking, female genital mutilation, all involve forms of violence which are an assault on female sexuality. 15/

59. The control of female sexual behaviour is an important aspect of many law codes. 16/ The purpose of this control is to ensure chastity so as to make certain that

the children of a woman are born to the correct father. This control also ensures that property will not be inherited by those who are not of the same lineage. This desire to ensure chastity may take different forms. Female genital mutilation is perhaps its most extreme manifestation. This form of violence against women curtails female sexual expression so that women will remain chaste and faithful to their husbands.

60. In many traditions, concepts of honour are linked to a woman's sexuality. Violence against women is often justified by the argument that that honour has been violated by a woman's sexual behaviour. 17/ Such concepts of honour also find collective expression in many societies. In this context, violence against women who are seen as being the property of the males in a rival social group becomes a means of defiling the honour of that social group. Female sexuality has been a battleground in feudal and in modern vendettas where male prestige and honour are challenged.

61. If attitudes towards female sexuality are often the cause of violence against women, it becomes important for society to "protect" its women from the violence of "the other". This protection often entails restrictions being placed on women, whether in the form of dress codes or the freedom of movement. It also implies that women who respect these rules are protected, but that those who assert equality and independence are more vulnerable to violence. Women who challenge the codes of dress and the restrictions on movement are often targets of male violence.

62. Many authors who have analysed the subordination of women argue that fear of rape and male sexual assault remains the most important aspect of life for women in all societies. 18/ Attitudes toward female sexuality are seen as primary factors responsible for violence against women. These attitudes not only condition the

12/ G. Corea et al, *Man-Made Woman. How New Reproductive Technologies Affect Women*, London, Hutchinson, 1985. See also, M. Stanworth ed. *Reproductive Technologies*, Oxford, Polity Press, 1987.

13/ See G. Lerner, op. cit,; also L. Irigary, "This sex which is not one" in S. Gunew ed., *A Reader in Feminist Knowledge*, London, Rutledge, 1991.

14/ See Gayatri Spivak, "Feminism and deconstruction, again" in Teresa Brennan ed., *Between Feminism and Psychoanalysis*, London, Methuen, 1989.

15/ See S. Brownmiller, *Against Our Will*, Hammondsworth, Penguin, 1977. See also S. Firestone, *The Dialectic of Sex*, London Women's Press, 1979.

16/ See Lerner, op. cit., chap. 5.

17/ See Laura Moghaizel, "The Arab and the Mediterranean world: Legislation towards crimes of honour" in M. Schuler ed., *Empowerment and the Law: Strategies of Third World Women*, Washington D.C., OEF, 1986.

18/ See S. Brownmiller, op. cit.

behaviour of men and women in society, but often end up justifying violence against women. Themes such as the vindication of honour, concepts of family shame and the need for protecting "proper" women while punishing others are some of the factors which have conditioned male attitudes towards female sexuality and the use of violence against women.

D. *Cultural ideology*

63. Besides history and sexuality, the prevalence of ideologies which justify the subordinate position of women is another cause of violence directed against women. In many ideologies a traditional legitimacy is given to using violence against women in certain instances. In both the developed and the developing world, there have been cultural sanctions in the past for husbands chastising or beating their wives in certain circumstances. These sanctions have been included in law codes in different cultural heritages. 19/

64. The ideologies which justify the use of violence against women base their discussion on a particular construction of sexual identity. The construction of masculinity often requires that manhood be equated with the ability to exert power over others, especially through the use of force. Masculinity gives man power to control the lives of those around him, especially women. The construction of femininity in these ideologies often requires women to be passive and submissive, to accept violence as part of a woman's estate. Such ideologies also link a woman's identity and self-esteem to her relationship to her father, husband or son. An independent woman is often denied expression in feminine terms. In addition, standards of beauty, defined by women, often require women to mutilate themselves or damage their health, whether with regard to foot binding, anorexia nervosa and bulimia. 20/ It is important to reinvent creatively these categories of masculinity and femininity, devoid of the use of force and ensuring the full development of human potential. 21/

·65. Article 4 of the Declaration on the Elimination of Violence against Women states clearly that "States should condemn violence against women and should not invoke custom, tradition or religious consideration to avoid their obligations with respect to its elimination". 22/ Unfortunately international experience points to a different reality. Custom, tradition and religion are frequently invoked to justify the use of violence against women. They form an ideological framework which is resistant to change and transformation.

66. It is universally accepted that the spirit of all the world's religions is dedicated to equality, including equality between the sexes. Though interpretations may vary, there is no question that all the world's religions are committed to the pursuit of equality and human rights. However, certain man-made practices performed in the name of religion not only denigrate individual religions but violate internationally accepted norms of human rights, including women's rights. Recent religious movements, often termed "fundamentalist", have sought to clothe these discriminatory practices with religious sanctity. In most societies there is an ongoing dialogue between women interested in women's rights and those who are close to religious traditions. It is the concern of the international community that this dialogue results in the elimination of man-made practices which violate human rights and the spirit of equality contained in the world's religions. This question should be high on the list of priorities. Religious considerations should never be used to justify the use of violence against women. 23/

67. Certain customary practices and some aspects of tradition are often the cause of violence against women. Besides female genital mutilation, a whole host of practices violate female dignity. Foot binding, male preference, early marriage, virginity tests, dowry deaths, sati, female infanticide and malnutrition are among the many practices which violate a woman's human rights. Blind adherence to these practices and State inaction with regard to these customs and traditions have made possible large-scale violence against women. States are enacting new laws and regulations with regard to the development of a modern economy and modern technology and to developing practices which suit a modern democracy, yet it seems that in the area of women's rights change is slow to be accepted.

68. Not all customs and traditions are unprotective of women's rights. There are certain traditions and customary practices in all parts of the world which actually promote and defend women's rights and women's dignity. However, those customs and traditions which involve violence against women must be challenged and eliminated as violating the basic tenants of international human rights law. 24/

19/ See S. Brownmiller op. cit.; also G. Lerner, op. cit.
20/ Naomi Wolf, *The Beauty Myth*, New York, William Morrow, 1991.
21/ See Linda Bell, *Rethinking Ethics in the Midst of Violence*, Lanham, Rowman and Littlefield, 1993. See also C. Gilligan, *In a Different Voice: Psychological Theory and Women's Development*, Cambridge, Harvard University Press, 1982.
22/ General Assembly resolution 48/104.
23/ D.L. Eck and D. Jain, *Speaking of Faith: Cross Cultural Perspectives on Women, Religion and Social Change*, New Delhi, Kali, 1986.
24/ See, for example, A. Sen, "More than 100 million women are missing" in *New York Review of Books*, 20 December 1990, or A. El-Dareer, *Women, Why Do You Weep? Circumcision and its Consequences*, London, Zed, 1982 or M. Kishwar, "Dowry deaths, the real murders", *Indian Times*, 9 April 1989.

69. Elements of the national and international media may also be blamed for causing attitudes which give rise to violence against women. The media sometimes reproduce negative stereotypes of women. More importantly, by often glamourizing the culture of violence they allow for the widespread acceptance of violence as a means of resolving conflict in society or in the home. Pornography is perhaps the extreme manifestation of media violence against women. Although this question involves important issues concerning the right to freedom of expression, the portrayal of violence against women in pornographic literature and film, where women are shown bound, battered, tortured, humiliated and degraded, is a major problem for those confronting violence against women in their societies. Pornography is both a symptom and a cause of violence against women. Pornography in itself violates female dignity but, in addition, it often promotes attitudes and practices which result in violence being directed against women. 25/

E. *Doctrines of privacy*

70. Doctrines of privacy and the concept of the sanctity of the family are other causes for violence against women to persist in society. In the past, the State and the law intervened with regard to violence in the home only when violence became a public nuisance. Otherwise, the doctrine of privacy allowed for violence to continue unabated. The public/private distinction, which has been at the root of most legal systems, including human rights law, has created major problems for the vindication of women's rights. However, in recent times the approach to law has changed. States are increasingly reaching into the privacy of the home. In developing countries the regulation of reproductive rights has become an important concern. States are now increasingly being held responsible for human rights offences committed within the home. States are required, by standards of due diligence, to prevent as well as punish crimes of violence which take place in the private domain. 26/

F. *Patterns of conflict resolution*

71. Patterns of conflict resolution within a given society are often responsible for violence being directed against women. The study of wife battery, as mentioned above, points to this aspect as being the second most important factor when it comes to wife abuse in different societies. 27/ Studies in the mid-twentieth century have also concluded that militarization leads to greater abuse with regard to women. 28/ Levels of repression and militarization may, therefore, be directly related to the increase of incidents of violence against women. Rape as an instrument of war is perhaps the greatest manifestation of this phenomenon. Societies which socialize indi-

viduals to resolve conflicts non-violently are less likely to entertain problems of violence against women than societies where violence is an important part of the conflict resolution process.

G. *Government inaction*

72. Perhaps the greatest cause of violence against women is government inaction with regard to crimes of violence against women. There appears to be a permissive attitude, a tolerance of perpetrators of violence against women, especially when this violence is expressed in the home. The seriousness of the crime is rarely acknowledged. There exists also a non-recognition of such crimes in the laws of many countries, especially in relation to domestic violence, marital rape, sexual harassment and violence associated with traditional practices. As a result, in most societies crimes of violence against women are invisible. In addition, even where crimes of violence against women are recognized in the law, they are rarely prosecuted with vigour. In the context of norms recently established by the international community, a State that does not act against crimes of violence against women is as guilty as the perpetrators. States are under a positive duty to prevent, investigate and punish crimes associated with violence against women. 29/

H. *Consequences*

73. The consequences of violence directed against women are difficult to ascertain because the crimes are often invisible and there is very little data on the subject. However, it is very clear that fear is perhaps the greatest consequence. Fear of violence prevents many women from living independent lives. Fear curtails their movement, so that women in many parts of the world do not venture out alone. Fear requires that they dress in a manner that is "unprovocative" so that no-one can say that "they asked for it" if they are violently assaulted. Fear of violence requires that they seek out male protection to prevent violence being directed at them. This protection can result in a situation of vulnerability and

25/ See A. Dworkin, *Pornography: Men Possessing Women*, London, Women's Press, 1981. Also C. MacKinnon, "Sexuality, pornography and method: Pleasure under patriarchy", in *Ethics*, vol. 99, No 2.

26/ See C. Pateman, "Feminist critiques of the public/private dichotomy" in A. Phillips ed. *Feminism and Equality*, Oxford, Basil Blackwell, 1986.

27/ See David Levinson, op. cit.

28/ W. Reich, *The Mass Psychology of Fascism*, Hammondsworth, Pelican, reprint 1972.

29/ See Dorothy Q. Thomas and Michele E. Beasley Esq, op. cit. Also see Kenneth Roth, "Domestic violence as an international human rights issue", in Rebecca Cook, ed. *Human Rights of Women: National and International Perspectives* (forthcoming 1994).

dependence which is not conducive to women's empowerment. Women's potential remains unrealized and energies which could be directed towards the amelioration of society are often stifled.

74. In certain cultural contexts, especially those in which female genital mutilation is practised, a woman is denied her existence as a sexual being with needs and expectations. This denial of female sexuality through the mutilation of the body has to be seen as a violation of a fundamental human right.

75. Women who are at the receiving end of violence have serious health problems. In recent times, studies have been conducted on the harmful physical and emotional impact of violence against women, such as on the harmful effects of female genital mutilation on the health of women. Other forms of abuse also result in physical injury to the body of the victim. In addition there are psychological effects. Abused women are subject to depression and personality disorders. They manifest high levels of anxiety and somatic disorders. These psychological effects have a negative effect on the women as they paralyse them and inhibit their self-determination. What is termed the "traumatic syndrome of abused women" includes lack of volitional autonomy, fear, anguish, depression and in some cases suicide. 30/

76. Violence in the family, in particular, has serious consequences for both women and children. Children often show signs of post-trauma stress and have behavioural and emotional disorders. In addition, a Canadian study shows that males coming from homes where there is spousal abuse are 1,000 per cent more likely to beat their own wives than those who come from families where there is no such abuse. 31/ The consequence of tolerating violence in the first instance is to perpetuate a cycle of violence in the family and in society.

77. In terms of development, violence prevents women from participating fully in the life of the family and the community and in society. Energies which might be directed towards social good and development are curtailed. Women's potential and their contribution towards development and growth is an important aspect of the development process. Violence against women prevents women as well as society from realizing their full potential. 32/

78. The cost to society in terms of violence against women is phenomenal. Much of the cost is hidden since statistics on this issue are rare. But the United States, for example, spent US$ 27.6 million on refugee accommodation for victims of violence in 1987 alone. 33/ This does not take into account the medical, legal and other expenses associated with these projects. There are similar statistics for other countries which have set up accommodation for victims of violence. 34/ The material cost of

the consequences of violence is superseded by the more intangible costs relating to the quality of life, the suppression of human rights and the denial of women's potential to participate fully in their society.

III. International legal standards

A. *Protection from violence*

79. Women have been invisible in the development and growth of modern international law. Though law is assumed to be gender-neutral, the norms and standards of international law are generally unconcerned with the "women's" question. 35/ In recent times this approach has changed, especially in the field of international human rights law. The problems associated with gender inequality and violence against women have gained increasing recognition by the international community. There is a concerted effort to eradicate violence against women as part of a worldwide campaign on women's human rights.

80. Many international legal instruments dealing with human rights include the protection of women from violence in their provisions. The Universal Declaration of Human Rights, in article 1, states that "all human beings are born free and equal in dignity and rights". Article 2 provides that "everyone is entitled to all the rights and freedoms set forth in this Declaration, without distinction of any kind, such as race, colour, sex, language, religion, political or other opinion, national or social origin, property, birth or other status". Article 3 of the Universal Declaration provides that "everyone has the right to life, liberty and security of person". Article 5 provides that "no one shall be subjected to torture or to cruel, inhuman or degrading treatment or punishment". The non-discrimination clause, taken together with articles 3 and

30/ See Pan American Health Organization. Also, see United Nations, Division for the Advancement of Women, Department of Policy Coordination and Sustainable Development, *Report of the Expert Group Meeting on Measures to Eradicate Violence against Women* (MAV/1993/1), New York, 1993. Also see Jane Francis Connors, *Violence against Women in the Family* (ST/CSDHA/2), New York, United Nations, 1989.

31/ *Women—Challenges to the Year 2000*, (United Nations publication, Sales No. E.91.I.21). Also see Jane Francis Connors, op. cit.

32/ See Roxanne Carillo, *Battered Dreams: Violence Against Women as an Obstacle for Development*, New York, UNIFEM, Sales publication No. WE 011, 1992.

33/ Ibid., p. 5.

34/ *Women - Challenges to the Year 2000*, op. cit.

35/ See Hilary Charlesworth, Christine Chinkin and Shelley Wright, "Feminist approaches to international law", *Am J. Int L* 85 (1991) 613 and Andrew Byrnes, "Women, Feminism and International Human Rights Law-Methodological Myopia, Fundamental Flaw or Meaningful Marginalisation", 12 *Aust YB Int'l* 205 (1992). Also see Rebecca J. Cook, "Women's international human rights—A bibliography", in 24 *N.Y.U.J Int'l and Pol.* 857 (1992).

5, means that any form of violence against women which can be construed as a threat to her life, liberty or security of person or which constitutes torture or cruel, inhuman or degrading treatment is not in keeping with the Universal Declaration and is therefore a violation of the international obligations of Member States.

81. Other instruments, such as the International Covenant on Civil and Political Rights and the International Covenant on Economic, Social and Cultural Rights, likewise prohibit violence against women. Article 2 of the International Covenant on Civil and Political Rights contains a non-discrimination clause similar to that contained in article 2 of the Universal Declaration. In addition, article 26 of the Covenant argues:

> "All persons are equal before the law and are entitled without any discrimination to the equal protection of the law. In this respect, the law shall prohibit any discrimination and guarantee to all persons equal and effective protection against discrimination on any ground such as ... sex."

This, taken in conjunction with article 6.1 of the Covenant, which protects the right to life, article 7, which protects everyone from torture or cruel, inhuman or degrading treatment or punishment, and article 9.1, which protects the right to liberty and security of person, means that the Covenant may be construed as covering the issue of gender-based violence.

82. Article 3 of the International Covenant on Economic, Social, and Cultural Rights guarantees the equal right of men and women to the enjoyment of all rights set forth in that Covenant and many of the substantive rights set out in the Covenant cannot be enjoyed by women if gender-based violence is widespread. For example, article 7 of the International Covenant on Economic and Social Rights ensures the right of everyone to the enjoyment of just and favourable conditions of work. This, by implication, entails that women must be free of violence and harassment at the workplace.

83. In times of war, the Convention relative to the Protection of Civilian Persons in Time of War, of 12 August 1949 (the Fourth Geneva Convention), states clearly in its article 27 that "Women shall be especially protected against any attack on their honour in particular against rape, enforced prostitution or any form of indecent assault." This section is echoed in common article 3 of the Geneva Conventions and in Protocol II to the Geneva Conventions.

84. The most extensive instrument dealing exclusively with the rights of women, however, is the Convention on the Elimination of All Forms of Discrimination against Women, which came into force in September 1981. Although this instrument does not explicitly deal with violence against women, except in the areas of trafficking and prostitution (art. 6), many of the anti-discrimination clauses contained in it provide for the protection of women from violence. Additionally, many of the recent recommendations of the monitoring body of the Convention, the Committee for the Elimination of Discrimination Against Women (CEDAW), especially General recommendation No. 19, have addressed the issue of gender-based violence and provide the sole source of legally binding material at the international level dealing expressly with violence against women.

85. The Convention on the Elimination of All Forms of Discrimination against Women is perhaps best described as an international bill of rights for women as it sets out in detail both what is to be regarded as discrimination against women and the measures that have to be taken in order to eliminate this discrimination. Women's rights are conceptualized as human rights and a "non-discrimination" model is adopted, so that women's rights are seen to be violated if women are denied the same rights as men. Article 1 of the Convention defines discrimination against women as

> "any distinction, exclusion or restriction made on the basis of sex which has the effect or purpose of impairing or nullifying the recognition, enjoyment or exercise by women, irrespective of their marital status, on a basis of equality of men and women, of human rights and fundamental freedoms in the political, economic, social, cultural, civil or any other field".

Violence is not expressly mentioned but a proper interpretation of the definition allows it to be included by implication.

86. Furthermore, CEDAW has on various occasions recommended that the issue of violence against women be included in the reports submitted to it by the State Parties. In General recommendation 12, adopted in 1989, the Committee requested that States include in their reports information about violence against women and the measures taken to eliminate such violence.

87. General recommendation No. 19, 36/ formulated in 1992, deals entirely with violence against women and explicitly states that gender-based violence is a form of discrimination which seriously inhibits a woman's ability to enjoy rights and freedoms on a basis of equality with men and asks that State parties have regard to this when reviewing their laws and policies. The recommendation further states that when reporting under the Convention States parties should take this into consideration. It also argues that the definition of "discrimination" in

---

36/ Committee on the Elimination of Violence against Women, Eleventh session, General recommendation 19 (CEDAW/C/1992/L.1/Add.15).

article 1 of the Convention includes gender-based violence, which is in turn defined in recommendation 19 as "violence directed against a woman because she is a woman or which affects women disproportionately. It includes physical, mental, or sexual harm or suffering, threats of such acts, coercion and other deprivations of liberty".

88. General recommendation 19 also deals with specific articles of the Convention and how they relate to violence against women. The specific areas discussed are (i) traditional attitudes, customs and practices (arts. 2 (f), 5 and 10 (c)), (ii) all forms of traffic and exploitation of prostitution of women (art. 6), (iii) violence and equality in employment (art. 11), (iv) violence and health (art. 12), (v) rural women (art. 14) and (vi) family violence (art. 16).

89. General recommendation 19 argues that certain traditions and customs and practices whereby women are regarded as subordinate or as having stereotyped roles perpetuate various practices, including violence and coercion, and that such prejudices and beliefs may be used to justify gender-based violence as a form of protection or control of women, as a result of which women are deprived of the equal enjoyment of their human rights and fundamental freedoms.

90. With regard to prostitution, and traditional as well as new forms of trafficking, the recommendation states that these activities put women at special risk of violence and abuse. States parties are directed to take special preventative and punitive steps against such violence.

91. On the question of employment, General recommendation 19 states that gender-specific violence such as sexual harassment in the workplace can seriously impair equality in employment. With regard to health issues, States are directed to provide a support service for all victims of gender-based violence, including refuge, specially trained health workers, rehabilitation and counselling services.

92. The General recommendation also recognizes that rural women are at special risk of violence because of the persistence of traditional attitudes in many rural communities and it imposes an obligation on States to ensure that services for victims of violence are accessible to rural women. Where necessary, special services should be provided for isolated communities.

93. Violence in the family is seen to be widespread and present in every part of the world and measures necessary to eradicate family violence are listed.

94. General recommendation 19 also directs State parties, in their reports, to describe the extent of each problem in their countries, the measures taken to prevent and punish the occurrence of such problems, and the effectiveness of such measures.

95. The Declaration on the Elimination of Violence against Women deals exclusively with violence against women. The document is a comprehensive statement of international standards with regard to the protection of women from violence. Although the Declaration is not legally binding, it sets out international norms which States have recognized as being fundamental in the struggle to eliminate all forms of violence against women.

96. This Declaration is the first real set of international standards to deal specifically with the problem of violence against women. For the purposes of the Declaration, violence against women is defined in article 1 as

"any act of gender-based violence that results in, or is likely to result in, physical, sexual, or psychological harm or suffering to women, including threats of such acts, coercion or arbitrary deprivation of liberty, whether occurring in public or private life".

97. The Preamble to the Declaration clearly locates the roots of gender-based violence in "historically unequal power relations between men and women, which have led to domination over and discrimination against women by men and to the prevention of the full advancement of women", recognizing that "violence against women is one of the crucial social mechanisms by which women are forced into a subordinate position compared with men". The Preamble also identifies groups of women who are especially vulnerable to violence. These include women belonging to minority groups, refugee women, migrant women, women living in rural or remote communities, destitute women, women in detention, female children, women with disabilities, elderly women and women in situations of armed conflict. Vulnerability and historicity are thus seen as the dual principles which are responsible for violence against women.

98. Violence against women is defined in the Declaration as including, but not being limited to, physical, sexual and psychological violence that occurs in the family. Such violence includes battering, sexual abuse of female children in the household, dowry related violence, marital rape, female genital mutilation and other traditional practices harmful to women, non-spousal violence and violence related to exploitation. The Declaration also points to the prevalence of violence in the general community, including rape, sexual abuse, sexual harassment and intimidation at work, in educational institutes and elsewhere, trafficking in women and forced prostitution. Finally it recognizes violence which is either perpetrated or condoned by the State. The definition of violence contained in the Declaration appears, therefore, to be a broad one whereby violence is not strictly construed as meaning only the actual use of physical force, but implies the right to inquire against all forms of action which disempower women because of the fear of violence,

whether the fear is instilled by the State, actors in the community or members of the family.

B. *State responsibility*

99. The problem of violence against women brings into sharp focus an issue that has been troubling the international community—State responsibility for the actions of private citizens. In the past, a strict judicial interpretation had made the State responsible only for actions for which it or its agents are directly accountable. In this case it would relate to issues such as women in custody and women in detention and perhaps the problem of women during armed conflict. The question of domestic violence, rape and sexual harassment, etc., were seen as the actions of individuals and thus beyond the "human rights" responsibility of the State.

100. It is a recognized part of general international human rights law that States are responsible for (i) the protection of the rights of individuals to exercise their human rights, (ii) investigation of alleged violations of human rights, (iii) punishment of the violators of human rights, (iv) provision of effective remedies for the victims of human rights violations. Yet States are rarely held responsible for ignoring their obligations with regard to women's rights. 37/ The reason for this is twofold. States do not consider women's rights as human rights, especially those rights which are exercised in the home or the community, and they do not see such violations as an "internationally recognized justiciable wrong". Secondly, States do not consider themselves responsible for violations of women's rights by private actors.

101. The earlier sections of this chapter clearly show that women's rights have become an integral part of international human rights law and that violence against women is a violation of human rights for which States are accountable. States therefore have an international obligation with regard to the protection of these rights as part of the general regime of international human rights law.

102. Except for categories such as "pirates" and "international war criminals", private individuals and agencies are not generally bound by international human rights law. But States may be responsible for their failure to meet international obligations even when violations originate in the conduct of private individuals. State responsibility for the violation of women's human rights by private actors is anticipated by customary international law. States are held legally responsible for acts or omissions of private persons in the following instances:

(a) The person is an agent of the State;

(b) Private acts are covered by provisions of a treaty obligation;

(c) There is State complicity in the wrongs perpetrated by private actors;

(d) State failure to exercise due diligence in the control of private actors.

103. The "due diligence" standard has been generally accepted as a measure of evaluating a State's responsibility for violation of human rights by private actors. 38/

104. The standards developed by customary international law have been expanded by international and regional human rights conventions and recent judicial decisions. For example, in the 1988 *Valesquez* case, the Inter-American Court of Human Rights imposed liability on Honduras for its lack of due diligence in preventing unexplained "disappearances", whether by the State or private actors. 39/ States were also held responsible for the organization of the government apparatus and structures of public power in order to make them capable of juridically ensuring free and full enjoyment of human rights.

105. Besides complying with the "due diligence" standard for the protection of human rights, States are required by international human rights instruments to ensure equal protection of the law for their citizens. If data collected provides evidence of systematic, discriminatory, non-prosecution by the State of crimes of violence against women, then, it is argued, States have violated their responsibility under international human rights law. 40/ Research does suggest that the investigation, prosecution and sentencing of, for example, crimes of domestic violence occur with much less frequency than of other similar crimes. Wife murderers receive greatly reduced sentences, domestic battery is rarely investigated and rape frequently goes unpunished. These examples stand in direct contrast to the treatment of violent crimes against male victims. The pervasiveness of domestic violence and its frequent non-prosecution by Governments, as well as the new emphasis on equal protection of the law as a central human rights concern, have made it possible to conceptualize crimes such as domestic violence as a human rights issue and to hold Governments accountable for this discrimination. 41/

37/ Rebecca J. Cook, "State responsibility for violation of women's human rights", in 7 *Harvard Human Rights Journal*, 1994, 125, p. 166.
38/ See Moore, *Int. Arb.* 495 (1872). For discussion of this issue with regard to women's rights, see Rebecca J. Cook, op. cit, and Dorothy Q. Thomas and Michelle E. Beasley Esq, "Domestic violence as a human rights issue", in *Human Rights Quarterly*, 1993, 15, pp. 36-62.
39/ *Valesquez Rodriguez Case Honduras*, 4 *Inter.Am.Ct. HR* (Ser.C.), 1988.
40/ See Dorothy Q. Thomas and Michele E. Beasley Esq., op. cit. Also see Kenneth Roth, "Domestic violence as an international human rights issue, in Rebecca Cook, ed. *Human Rights of Women: National and International Perspectives* (forthcoming 1994).
41/ See Dorothy Q. Thomas and Michele E. Beasley, op. cit.

106. This emerging trend towards holding States responsible for actions of certain private actors is reflected both in the Convention on the Elimination of All Forms of Discrimination against Women and the Declaration on the Elimination of Violence Against Women. Discrimination under the Convention is not restricted to actions by or on behalf of the State; this is expressly acknowledged, in regard to violence, in General Recommendation 19. Article 2 (e) of the Convention states that States parties are required "to take all appropriate measures to eliminate discrimination against women by any person, organization or enterprise". This provision expressly covers State responsibility for violations by private actors. Article 16 explicitly refers to discrimination in the family and Recommendation 19 clearly includes family violence within its purview. 42/

107. The Declaration sums up the current standards in operation as they relate specifically to the question of violence against women. Article 4 (c) proclaims that States should "exercise due diligence to prevent, investigate and, in accordance with national legislation, punish acts of violence against women, *whether those acts are perpetrated by the State or by private persons*". All States are not only responsible for their own conduct or the conduct of their agents, but are now also responsible for their failure to take necessary steps to prosecute private citizens for their behaviour, in compliance with international standards. This emergence of State responsibility for violence in society plays an absolutely crucial role in efforts to eradicate gender-based violence and is perhaps one of the most important contributions of the women's movement to the issue of human rights.

C. *Obligations of the State*

108. The obligations of the State with regard to the elimination of violence against women are comprehensively spelt out in article 4 of the Declaration on the Elimination of Violence against Women. The State is obliged to condemn violence against women and is expected not to invoke custom, tradition, or religion to avoid the obligation; the State is expected to pursue all "appropriate means", "without delay" in adopting a policy of eliminating violence against women. Among other obligations of the State outlined in article 4 are:

(a) Ratification of the Convention on the Elimination of All Forms of Violence against Women (art. 4 (a));

(b) Specific directives with regard to the development of legal and administrative mechanisms to ensure effective justice for victims of violence (art. 4 (d));

(c) To ensure that there is specialized assistance in terms of support and rehabilitation for women victims of violence (art. 4 (g));

(d) Training of judicial and police officials (art. 4 (i));

(e) Reform of educational curricula (art. 4 (j));

(f) Promotion of research (art. 4 (k));

(g) Full reporting of the problem of violence against women to international human rights mechanisms (art. 4 (m)).

109. A basic premise of both the Convention and the Declaration appears to be that the law and legal institutions have an important role to play in realizing the gender equality and elimination of violence envisaged in these instruments. It is possible to perceive the emphasis given, in these international instruments, to law as a tool that can be used in combination with other mechanisms to deliver justice and equity to women. However, both documents refrain from placing an undue reliance on strictly legal mechanisms at the expense of other methods. They make provision for the use of non-legal mechanisms, such as rehabilitation and education of the judiciary and other officials to make them sensitive to issues of gender, as necessary complements to the law in efforts to eliminating gender-based violence.

110. The Convention was the first international instrument to target tradition and culture as influential forces in shaping gender roles and family values. The Declaration followed in its footsteps in this regard. Among the obligations of the State set out in the Declaration is the obligation to "adopt all appropriate measures, especially in the field of education, to modify the social and cultural patterns of conduct of men and women and to eliminate prejudices, customary practices and all other practices based on the idea of the inferiority or superiority of either of the sexes and on stereotyped roles for men and women" (art. 4). This is a landmark in the battle against gender-based violence, as such prejudices are most prominent in the areas of culture, community and family, which are precisely the spheres of most importance to many women. If, therefore, the State were able to bring about fundamental changes in the patterns of socialization which tend to disempower women and create an atmosphere in which violence against them appears more legitimate, it would be a significant step towards the elimination of gender-based violence.

111. In this regard, it should be mentioned that some of the States that have ratified the Convention have entered reservations indicating that they will accept it only in so far as it does not conflict with certain national customs, practices, or laws. This has caused much disagreement as it is widely felt that many of these reservations are incompatible with the basic obligations of the Convention. States should, therefore, be requested to be more circumspect about entering reservations, and con-

42/ Rebecca J. Cook, op. cit., p. 166.

sider whether the contemplated reservation is compatible with the spirit of the Convention.

112. Another of the obligations imposed on States by these international instruments should help to alleviate a major problem with regard to the elimination of violence against women, which is the lack of statistics available on the issue. Both the Convention and the Declaration impose an obligation on States to encourage research and the compilation of statistics on the subject of gender-based violence. Article 4 (k) of the Declaration directs States to

"Promote research, collect data and compile statistics, especially concerning domestic violence, relating to the prevalence of different forms of violence against women and encourage research on the causes, nature, seriousness and consequences of violence against women and on the effectiveness of measures implemented to prevent and redress violence against women; those statistics and findings of the research will be made public".

Such statistics and research should help both by providing the basic material with which those working in the field of gender-based violence can make their programmes more effective, and by making the problem of violence more visible to the general public and the international community at large.

D Obligations of the international community

113. The Declaration sees the international community as an essential actor in the process of eliminating violence against women (art. 5). The directives to United Nations specialized agencies, bodies and organs are intended to ensure that they promote awareness of the issue of violence against women in their programmes, collect data on the problem and periodically analyse the trends, formulate guidelines and manuals on the issue and cooperate with non-governmental organizations in addressing it. The United Nations system should, therefore, be seen as a data bank and as an awareness-raising instrument in attempting to make the international community more sensitive to the needs of women, particularly in the area of violence against women.

E. Regional conventions

114. On 9 June 1994, at Belém do Pará, countries of the Latin American region adopted the Inter-American Convention on the Prevention, Punishment and Eradication of Violence against Women (Convention of Belém do Pará). Violence against women is defined in its article 1 as "any act or conduct, based on gender, which causes death or physical, sexual or psychological harm or suffering to women, whether in the public or private sphere". Like the United Nations Declaration, the Con-

vention of Belém do Pará divides violence against women into three broad categories: violence which occurs in the family, in the community and where it is perpetrated or condoned by the State (art. 2). However, in relation to the family, unlike the Declaration, the Convention explicitly includes people who do not and have never shared the same residence within the definition of a family or domestic unit, thus recognizing that people involved in an interpersonal relationship do not necessarily live together. This is of fundamental importance as many of the protections and remedies against violence in the family available to both the married woman and the woman living with her partner are at present unavailable to the woman who is not cohabiting with her partner.

115. Article 7 sets out State obligations in regard to the eradication of gender-based violence which are very similar to the obligations set out in the United Nations Declaration. Article 8, however, sets out additional obligations which generally deal with a broader agenda, namely that of education and the development of a mass consciousness in relation to violence against women. Among the obligations set out here, but not in the United Nations Declaration are the obligation to "promote awareness and observance of the right of women to be free from violence, and the right of women to have their human rights respected and protected" (art. 8 (a)) and the obligation to "encourage the communications media to develop appropriate media guidelines in order to contribute to the eradication of violence against women in all its forms, and to enhance respect for the dignity of women" (art. 8 (g)).

116. Chapter IV of the Convention of Belém do Pará sets out the mechanisms of protection available under the Convention. Under article 10 the States parties are obliged to include in their national reports to the Inter-American Commission of Women information on measures adopted to prevent and prohibit violence against women and to assist women affected by violence, as well as any difficulties they observe in applying those measures, and the factors that contribute to violence against women. This is similar to the obligation imposed by the Convention on the Elimination of All Forms of Discrimination against Women to report to CEDAW. However, unlike that Convention, the Convention of Belém do Pará also provides an individual right of petition and a right for non-governmental organizations to lodge complaints with the Inter-American Commission of Human Rights. Article 12, in this regard, provides that "any person or group of persons, or any non-governmental entity legally recognized in one or more member States of the Organization, may lodge petitions with the Inter-American Commission of Human Rights containing denunciations or complaints of violations of article 7 of

this Convention by a State party, and the Commission shall consider such claims in accordance with the norms and procedure established by the American Convention on Human Rights and the Statutes and Regulations of the Inter-American Commission of Human Rights for lodging and considering petitions".

IV. General issues concerning the problems arising from violence in the family, in the community and perpetrated or condoned by the State

A. *Violence in the family*

1. *Domestic violence*

(a) *Introduction*

117. The family has been traditionally considered as a retreat, a place where individuals are able to find security and shelter. The family has been romanticized as the "private haven" where peace and harmony prevail. Recent research, however, points to the fact that the family may be a "cradle of violence" and that females within the home are often subjected to violence in the family. 43/

118. There are many types of domestic violence. Young girls and children are often victims of sexual assault within the family. Elderly family members and the infirm may also be subject to ill-treatment. Female domestic servants are another category which is often at the receiving end of violence. In extended families, mothers-in-law are often violent towards their daughters-in-law. Though there are many incidents of assault directed against the husband, studies show that they are not so frequent and rarely result in serious injury. Despite all those different types of domestic violence, the most prevalent is the violence of the husband against the wife.

(b) *Causes*

119. The causes of violence against women in the home have been analysed in detail by a United Nations report on violence against women in the family. Among the causes discussed are:

(i) Alcohol and drug abuse by the perpetrator: in one study of 60 battered women, drinking accompanied 93 per cent of the incidents. In other studies alcoholism was linked to violence in 40 per cent of the cases; 44/

(ii) A cycle of violence: the childhood of the abusive man may have been disrupted by violence in the family. Studies conclude that violence by parents begets violence in the next generation. 45/ Violence in this context is seen as learned behaviour;

(iii) "Provocation": it has been argued that in some cases the victim provokes the abuser. But research indicates that while such incidents may take place they are not the norm. The only real pattern with regard to "provocative" behaviour is the seeming failure on the part of the woman to comply with the husband's authority; 46/

(iv) Economic and social factors: early studies on domestic violence point to, *inter alia*, economic and social factors such as unemployment, low wages and inadequate housing, as being causes of domestic violence. Research in developing countries seems to augment these findings. Poverty seems to aggravate violence, because of stress and frustration factors. However, violence against women also exists in wealthier circles; 47/

(v) Culture: certain cultural factors may precipitate violence against women;

(vi) Structural inequality: the general structures of society and the family which accept male dominance and female submissiveness as the norm may help legitimate violence against women.

120. Violence against women within the family is a significant pattern in all countries of the globe. Of the 487 murders committed by men in England and Wales during the period from 1885 to 1905, 124 or more than a quarter, were murders of women by their husbands, while a further 115 were of mistresses or girlfriends by their men. 48/ Twentieth century figures for the United Kingdom reveal that this pattern has not changed. 49/ Similar statistics have also been found when using samples from the United States of America. 50/ Official statistics on male violence against women, other than criminal homicide, similarly reveal that the victim is most likely to be the wife of the offender. The First Report of the British-Crime Survey found that 10 per cent of all assault victims were women who had been assaulted by their present or previous husbands or lovers. 51/

43/ Jane Francis Connors, op. cit., (note 30), p. 14.
44/ Ibid, p. 26.
45/ Ibid.
46/ Ibid., p. 27.
47/ Ibid., p. 28.
48/ Dobash and Dobash, *Violence against Wives*, Scottish Home and Health Department, p. 15.
49/ *Criminal Statistics, 1982, England and Wales*, Cmnd. 9048, London, HM Stationery Office, Table 4.4; E. Gibson and S. Klein, *Murder (1957-1968)*, Home Office Research Study No. 3, London, HM Stationery Office, 1969.
50/ H. von Hentig, *The Criminal and His Victim*, New Haven, Connecticut, Shoe String, 1948. M. E. Wolfgang, *Patterns in Criminal Homicide*, Philadelphia, University of Pennsylvania, 1958.
51/ *Criminal Statistics, England and Wales, 1980*, Cmnd. 8376, London, HM Stationery Office, Table 2.5.

121. While statistics on domestic violence are more scarce in developing countries, it would appear that a similar situation exists there. For example, a retrospective study of 170 cases of murder of women in Bangladesh between 1983 and 1985 revealed that 50 per cent occurred within the family. 52/ In Papua New Guinea, of villagers interviewed, 55 per cent of females and 65 per cent of males felt that a man could use force to control his wife. 53/ In Thailand, statistics indicate that more than 50 per cent of married women studied in Bangkok's biggest slum are regularly beaten by their husbands. 54/ In Santiago, Chile, it has been found that 80 per cent of women acknowledged being victims of violence in their own homes. 55/ In Sri Lanka, 60 per cent of women interviewed in a sample survey responded that they had been subjected to domestic violence during their period of cohabitation. 56/ The recent case in the United States of the alleged murder by the athlete O.J. Simpson of his wife and her friend has served to highlight the issue of domestic violence in the international media.

122. The traditional legal systems sanctioned violence in the family by recognizing the husband's "right to chastisement". 57/ This right was recognized by courts 58/ in many jurisdictions. In addition many legal systems allowed men to use force to extract "conjugal duties" and the crime of marital rape was unrecognized. The legal systems were therefore relatively unconcerned with abused women unless there was serious injury or a public nuisance. In some countries the defence of "honour" allowed for the easy acquittal of husbands who killed their wives. 59/

(c) *Criminalization*

123. In many jurisdictions this approach has changed. Today many States recognize the importance of protecting the victim of wife abuse and of punishing the perpetrator of the crime. One of the major questions facing law reformers is whether to "criminalize" wife battery. There is a sense that domestic violence is a crime between those who are linked by the bonds of intimacy. The question of intimacy, i.e. whether wife-battery should be treated as an ordinary crime or whether there should be an emphasis on counselling and mediation, poses a major dilemma for policy makers.

124. The question of whether the criminal justice system or a system of mediation and conciliation is most appropriate in dealing with domestic violence is one which arises constantly. Advocates of the criminal justice approach point to the symbolic power of the law and argue that arrest, prosecution and conviction, with punishment, is a process that carries the clear condemnation of society for the conduct of the abuser and acknowledges his personal responsibility for the activity. In addition,

some research studies reveal that intervention by the criminal justice system is the most effective mechanism for stopping acts of violence both in the short term and in the long term. The Minneapolis Domestic Violence Experiment was designed to assess which of the three police responses—conducting informal mediations between the parties involved, ordering the suspect to leave the residence for eight hours or arresting the suspect—was the most effective in preventing subsequent assault. During a six-month period, research revealed that 19 per cent of those involved in mediation and 24 per cent of those ordered to leave, repeated the assault, but only 10 per cent of those who were arrested indulged in further violence towards their spouses. 60/

125. Despite these advantages of the criminal justice model, it is critical that those involved in policy making in this area should take account of the cultural, economic and political realities of their countries. Whilst it is important to attach a criminal label to this type of activity it is impossible to ignore that it takes place within the family, between persons who are emotionally and financially involved with each other. Any policy which fails to acknowledge the singular nature of these crimes and which is unaccompanied by attempts to provide support for the victim and help for the abuser will be doomed to failure. Thus, for example, policy makers considering the domestic violence programme of London, Ontario, 61/ which is often cited as a model for domestic violence treatment where a charging policy exists, must take account of the fact that the police force, which receives intensive training in how to deal with wife battering, funds a family consultant service that provides a 24-hour crisis intervention service, whilst a community service exists which includes a battered women's advo-

---

52/ I. Shamin, *Case study from Bangladesh*, Dhaka, University of Dhaka, Department of Sociology, 1987.

53/ APDC, Asia and Pacific Women's Resource and Action Series, *Law*, Kuala Lumpur, Asia Pacific Development Corporation, 1993, p. 17.

54/ Ibid., p. 15.

55/ Ibid.

56/ S. Deraniyagala, "An investigation into the incidence and causes of domestic violence in Colombo, Sri Lanka", *Women in Need*, Colombo, 1992.

57/ W. Blackstone, *Commentaries on the Laws of England*, 1775.

58/ *Bradley v State*, 2 Miss. 156 1824, p. 158.

59/ Cases on conjugal duty. Also see Human Rights Watch women's rights project, *Criminal Injustice, Violence against Women in Brazil*, Human Rights Watch, New York, 1991.

60/ Minneapolis Domestic Violence Experiment. Also see "Developments in the Law—Legal responses to domestic violence", 106 *Harvard Law Review*, 1993, p. 1523.

61/ See *Confronting Violence. A Manual for Commonwealth Action*, Women and Development Programme, Human Resource Development Group, Commonwealth Secretariat, London, June 1992.

'cacy clinic to provide emotional and legal counselling for women, as well as a treatment group for men who batter.

(d) *Police action*

126. A criminal justice approach is fundamentally dependent on the role of the police. Since the police will be the body called upon for an initial response in a complex situation, it is important that there be clear standards with regard to police action in the context of domestic violence.

127. In most jurisdictions the power of the police to enter the private premises of the individual is limited, and this acts as an important guarantee which protects the lives of ordinary women and men from arbitrary State interference. In the context of domestic violence, however, too great an adherence to this guarantee can protect the violent man at the expense of the woman. In order to guard against this eventuality, a number of Australian states have introduced legislation to clarify and extend police powers of entry to investigate offences of domestic violence. Some legislations allow the police to enter if requested to do so by a person who apparently resides on the premises or where the officer has reason to believe that a person on those premises is under threat of attack or has recently been under threat of attack or an attack on such a person is imminent. 62/ This type of provision allows the police quicker and easier access to premises and thus an opportunity either to prevent or put a stop to the violence therein.

128. Although the power to arrest for domestic crime is usually the same as for any other crime, officers are often uncertain as to their legal powers and this is so even in cases of very serious violence. Many commentators argue that the police should be given special powers of arrest in situations of domestic violence and that they should be mandated to implement these powers. They believe that arrest not only provides the woman with immediate safety, but gives her a feeling of power, leaving the man with an immediate message that his behaviour is unacceptable, a message which is said to have long-term effects on his future behaviour. Australia, Canada and England have instituted policies for the management of domestic violence which generally advocate a presumption of arrest unless there are good, clear reasons for not arresting. 63/ Such policies make it clear to the officer on the ground what type of behaviour is expected of her/him.

129. In many cases of domestic violence, immediate release of the offender on bail may be dangerous for the victim and, certainly, release without prior warning to the victim may have serious consequences for her. A number of Australian jurisdictions attempt to strike a balance between the interests of the offender and the victim by specifying conditions designed to protect the victim to be attached to the release of the offender. Thus, the offender can be released on condition that he does not drink or approach his spouse, while bail may not be granted where the offender has previously broken protective bail conditions. 64/

130. It is essential that police officers are made aware that domestic violence is a serious issue which is neither a normal part of family life nor a private problem that will not profit from police intervention. The Musasa project in Zimbabwe introduced intensive education directed at police officers on the ground. As the programme progressed, the feedback indicated that women were receiving more sympathetic and prompt assistance at the police stations than was the case previously. 65/

131. Some countries have introduced police units that have been specially and intensively trained for the purpose of dealing with spousal assault. Specific police stations for dealing with women's issues, including domestic violence, have been set up in Brazil. From the outset, the stations had two full-time police officers, eight investigators, three clerks and two prison warders, all of them women. These police stations have proved to be very successful and 41 such stations now exist in São Paulo. 66/ Special police desks, units and stations are increasingly becoming a means of refining police methods when it comes to the question of domestic violence.

(e) *Legislation*

132. Legislation with regard to domestic violence is a modern phenomenon. In the past, domestic violence was dealt with under the laws for general criminal assault. This has proved to be unsatisfactory. There is an increasing belief that special laws should be drafted, having special remedies and procedures which are most effective with regard to crime between "intimates". Though contained within the framework of criminal laws, these procedures would try to meet the special needs posed by domestic violence.

133. The first problem which arises with regard to legislation is to allow for prosecution of husbands who

62/ *Justices Act* section 1959 (Tas) 106F; *Crimes Act* 1900 (NSW: Act) section 349A; *Crimes Act* (NSW) section 375F.

63/ See *Confronting Violence* ... op. cit.

64/ *Bail Act* 1978 (NSW) section 37; *Bail Act* 1980 (Qld); *Bail Act* 1985 (SA) section 11; *Bail Act* 1982 (WA); *Domestic Violence Ordinance* 1986 (ACT) section 24.

65/ Sheelagh Stewart, "Working the system: Sensitizing the police to the plight of women", in M. Schuler, *Freedom from Violence, Women, Law and Development*, OEF (Overseas Educational Fund) International, 1992.

66/ L. Eluf, "A new approach to law enforcement: The special women's police station", in M. Schuler, *Freedom From Violence*, op. cit.

beat their wives even if the wives, under pressure, want to withdraw their claims. In response to this, some countries have instructed police and prosecutors to proceed with the cases even in situations where the woman indicated that she would rather not proceed. 67/ This mandatory prosecution has been one strategy employed. In addition since the wife will be the main witness, some jurisdictions have introduced legislation making the wife a "compellable witness" except in certain situations. Other jurisdictions move away from compulsory prosecution to advocacy support. In the United States of America many cities have been able dramatically to increase victim participation by providing advocates for battered women. In San Francisco, it was found that 70 per cent of women who initially wanted charges dropped agreed to cooperate once advocates addressed their concerns. 68/

134. In addition to the criminal punishment attached to assault, even in a domestic violence context, most jurisdictions recognize quasi-criminal remedies. The most important of these are the "protection" or "bound over" orders. In most jurisdictions there is a procedure whereby someone can complain to a magistrate or a justice that violence has taken place and the violent party is then "bound over" to keep the peace or be of good behaviour. The standard of proof is lower than with strictly criminal proceedings and this may provide some women with appropriate relief. Law reformers in Australia, for example, recognized the potential of the "bind over" process in cases of domestic violence. 69/ In general terms, the legislation provides for a court order, obtained on the balance of probabilities, protecting the victim against further attacks or harassment. Breach of the order is a criminal offence and the police may arrest, without a warrant, a person who has contravened a protection order. Orders that can be made include forbidding the offender to approach the woman and limiting his access to certain premises, even the matrimonial home that he legally owns.

135. In addition to quasi-criminal remedies, civil law remedies are also available to women victims of violence. The most useful civil law remedy in relation to cases of domestic violence is probably the remedy known as an injunction or an interdict, which is used to support a primary cause of action. Where domestic violence is concerned, an injunction can be granted as incidental or ancillary proceedings for divorce, nullity or judicial separation or other civil proceedings, such as assault or battery. Such incidental relief could, for example, take the form of an order directing that the husband refrain from making contact with his wife or that he vacate the shared matrimonial home. Some jurisdictions have enacted legislation removing the requirement of applying

for principle relief and allow the woman to apply for injunctive relief independently of any other legal action. 70/ This is very useful as a battered woman is then able to apply for an order directing her husband not to molest or harass her without having to apply for primary or principle relief, such as divorce, at the same time. Another civil remedy which is available in the United States of America in certain states is an action in tort 71/ claiming damages from the marital partner.

(f) Training professionals

136. Generally, all levels of the legal system are ignorant of the dynamics of domestic violence. Most police, prosecutors, magistrates and judges adhere to traditional values that support the family as an institution and the dominance of the male party within it. It is therefore necessary to train law enforcers and medical and legal professionals who come in contact with victims to understand gender violence, to appreciate the trauma of the victim and to take proper evidence for criminal proceedings. However, it is often very difficult to gain the cooperation of professionals for training of this type. Professionals in law and medicine are particularly resistant to learning from anyone outside their specialty. The Musasa project in Zimbabwe found that cooperation of the police and magistrates was facilitated by involving a legal professional in the education process and by ensuring that the content was dependable and informed. Another effective technique was to facilitate a workshop with one part of the legal system acting as host to another.

(g) Community support services

137. The nature of the crime of domestic violence requires the intervention of the community to assist and support the victims. In this regard, hospitals are an important starting point since they are often the first place that victims of violence go to. Student doctors must be made aware of the dynamics and incidence of family violence and must be taught to ask appropriate questions of patients who may be abused. Refresher programmes

67/ See *Confronting Violence* ..., op. cit., p. 26.

68/ L. Heise and J. R. Chapman "Reflections on a movement: The U.S. battle against woman abuse", in M. Schuler, *Freedom from Violence*, op. cit.

69/ *Crimes Act* 1990 (NSW) Part XVA; *De Facto Relationships Act* 1959 (Tas) section 106; *Domestic Violence Ordinance* 1986 (ACT); *Justices Amendment Act* (No. 2) 1988 (NT) sections 99-100.

70/ Australia, *Family Law Act*, 1975 sections. 114, 70C; Hong Kong, *Domestic Violence Order*, 1986; Jamaica, *Matrimonial Causes Act* 1989, section 10; United Kingdom, *Matrimonial Homes Act*, 1983, *Domestic Proceedings and Magistrates Court Act*, 1978, etc.

71/ See "Developments in the law—Legal responses to domestic violence", 106 *Harvard Law Review*, 1993, p. 1531.

should be initiated on the subject, the issue should be addressed in professional and academic journals and guidelines which assist in the identification of abuse and suggest appropriate treatment for battered women should be developed and used in hospitals and surgeries.

138. Community workers should be trained to provide information to the victim on the law and law enforcement, the available financial and other support offered by the State, the procedures for obtaining such assistance, and other organizations such as refuges, that might offer assistance. Community workers can play an important role in identifying violence, raising awareness about such issues and in directing victims to the correct procedures for seeking redress.

139. "Shelters" provide battered women with a safe haven and somewhere to go. They provide survival, safety, support, self esteem and information. The Musasa project in Zimbabwe strove to give women power over their own lives. 72/ Care must be taken that the shelters are of a decent standard, well funded and well staffed. They must be well planned and take into account religious and cultural differences that may exist between residents. Finally, any shelter or refugee system must be viewed only as a component of a coordinated and multifaceted approach to domestic violence. States should be required to encourage the setting up of shelters for women victims of violence and to provide resources for their activities.

140. Many commentators feel that any relief given to the women victims must be accompanied by "counselling" of the battered. Treatment programmes for batterers have been established in a number of countries, including Canada, the United States and Australia. The primary aim of such programmes is to prevent recidivism and studies show that six months to a year after completing treatment, 60 to 84 per cent of men have not physically abused their partners, whereas perhaps two thirds of non-treated men would have recidivated. 73/ It would therefore appear that such programmes can act as viable sentencing options for the courts, especially in cases where the women prefer that their partners get "help" rather than punishment. The establishment of counselling as an alternative sentence recognizes the intimate nature of the crime and may be more acceptable to the women victims of violence.

141. In conclusion, it would appear that an integrated approach is necessary in dealing with battered women. Most commentators propose a multidisciplinary strategy, with lawyers, psychologists, social workers and others working together to gain a holistic understanding of each particular case and the needs of the individual victim. Giving attention to the real life context of the battered woman, her hopelessness, dependency, restricted options, and her consequent need for empowerment underpins the Chilean approach, for example, to wife abuse. 74/ The aim is to work with the battered woman to develop her capacity to decide her own future.

142. Most of the strategies discussed in this paper have been short-term ones. However, in order effectively to confront violence against the woman at home, these short-term measures must merge with longer-term ones. Education and training can provide this link. Formal education in schools can be used to eliminate stereotypical attitudes; the subject of family violence should be part of the curriculum and peaceful methods of conflict resolution explored. Informal methods of education can also be used, first to advise women of available options and support systems and also to convey the message to both women and men that family violence is to be deplored. Here attention should be paid to the particular national and cultural context so that suitable strategies can be used. In some countries it may be appropriate to produce simple booklets. 75/ Other countries have used poster campaigns. 76/ Some countries may find video and television advertising effective. Where literacy is high, newspaper campaigns can be effective, as can public speaking and easy writing competitions. Papua New Guinea, for example, has mounted a multi-pronged education campaign, consisting of the dissemination of posters and leaflets to all aid posts, health centres, clinics, hospitals, schools, post offices, banks and churches, and radio advertising and radio plays. 77/ To cater for the non-literate population, street theatre and video have been used, an approach which has been taken in Jamaica. 78/ A concerted effort at raising awareness is perhaps the most effective measure against domestic violence in the long term.

2. Traditional practices

(a) Introduction

143. In many societies, women are subject to violence because of traditional practices. Among such practices which violate women's human rights are female genital mutilation, son preference, gender difference in

72/ Sheelagh Srewert, "Working the system: Sensitizing the police to the plight of women", in M. Schuler, *Freedom from Violence*, op. cit.

73/ Z. Eisikovts and J. Edleson, Intervening with Men who Batter: A Critical Review of the Literature. *Social Sciences Review*, 1989.

74/ N. Gonzalez, "A new concept of mediation: An interdisciplinary approach to domestic violence", in M. Schuler, op. cit.

75/ See *Confronting Violence. A Manual for Commonwealth Action, Women and Development Programme, Human Resource Development Group, Commonwealth Secretariat, London, June 1992, p. 43.*

76/ Ibid.

77/ Ibid.

78/ Ibid.

nutrition, early childhood marriage, violence related to dowry, widow burning and virginity tests. All these practices have received international attention as aspects of the problem of women's human rights.

144. Valuable ground-breaking and informative research on the issue of traditional practices affecting the health of women and children has already been carried out by the Special Rapporteur on traditional practices affecting the health of women and children of the Sub-Commission on Prevention of Discrimination and Protection of Minorities, as well as its Working Group on traditional practices, the Inter-African Committee for Traditional Practices, the World Health Organization and numerous other institutions. The intention of the Special Rapporteur, therefore, is to argue that, on the basis of these materials and documentation, traditional practices should be construed as a definite form of violence against women which cannot be overlooked nor be justified on the grounds of tradition, culture or social conformity.

145. The delicate nature of questioning the very existence of these age-old practices, which are deeply rooted in the tradition, culture and power inequities of societies and often serve as initiation rituals by which young women are integrated and accepted into a community, as well as the lack of information and education in many regions where these practices are prevalent, are all factors which contribute to the continuing existence of these practices despite the United Nations repeated condemnation of all practices that affect the health of women and children and its repeated calls for their complete eradication. In this connection, the Special Rapporteur would like to draw the attention of the Commission on Human Rights to the Plan of Action for the Elimination of Harmful Traditional Practices affecting the Health of Women and Children, prepared in connection with two regional seminars organized by the Centre for Human Rights in Burkina Faso for the African region and in Sri Lanka for the Asian region. This Plan of Action will be available to the Commission on Human Rights at its present session for consideration (E/CN.4/Sub.2/1994/10).

(b) *Female genital mutilation*

146. The number of sexually mutilated women and girls in Africa and in some parts of Asia has increased to 100 million in 1994. According to the World Health Organization, a further 2 million girls are estimated to be at risk of the practices each year—most of them live in 26 African countries, a few in Asian countries, and their numbers are increasing among immigrant populations in Europe, Australia, Canada and the United States of America. 79/ Infibulation is practised in Somalia,

Djibouti, the northern part of the Sudan, some parts of Ethiopia, Egypt and Mali. Excision and circumcision occur in the Gambia, the northern part of Ghana, Nigeria, Liberia, Senegal, Sierra Leone, Guinea, Guinea-Bissau, Burkina Faso, parts of Benin, Côte d'Ivoire, parts of Tanzania, Togo, Uganda, Kenya, Chad, Central African Republic, Cameroon and Mauritania. 80/ Outside Africa a certain form of female circumcision is practised in Indonesia, Malaysia and Yemen. Minority communities and immigrant communities drawn from the above countries, living in other parts of the world, also practise some form of female genital mutilation.

147. Female genital mutilation takes various forms, ranging from clitoridectomy (partial or total removal of the clitoris) and excision (the removal of the clitoris and the labia minora), which account for approximately 85 per cent of female genital mutilations, to its most extreme form, namely infibulation (the complete removal of the clitoris and the labia minora, as well as the inner surface of the labia majora; the vulva is then stitched together so that only a small opening is preserved in the vagina to allow for the passage of urine and menstrual blood. 81/

148. The procedures are generally carried out by traditional birth attendants or elderly women of the village designated for this task using special knives, scissors, scalpels, pieces of glass or razor blades. Unintended damage occurs because of crude tools, poor light and septic conditions. Anaesthetics and antiseptics are generally not used. The age at which circumcision is carried out varies from a few days to seven years. 82/

149. These deliberately inflicted acts of violence may cause grave physical and psychological damage to women and girls, in the short and long term. The pain and traumatic experience itself may scar the minds of young women. Sexual intercourse and childbirth may be extremely painful and result in complications. Other health consequences have been recorded, such as haemorrhage, shock, infection, tetanus, gangrene, urine retention, injury to adjacent tissue, as well as more long-term problems such as bleeding, infertility, incontinence, fistulae and increasingly HIV/AIDS.

150. According to the World Health Organization, along with an increasing awareness of the dangerous repercussions of female genital mutilation, attitudes are

79/ F. Hosken, "General and sexual mutilation of females", in *WIN News*, Lexington, January 1994.

80/ Final report of the Special Rapporteur on traditional practices affecting the health of women and children, Mrs. Halima Embarek Warzazi, (E/CN.4/Sub.2/1991/6), para. 11.

81/ World Health Organization, Division of Family Health, *Female Genital Mutilation—the Practice*, Geneva, WHO, July 1994.

82/ E/CN.4/Sub.2/1991/6, para. 13.

gradually changing towards the gradual elimination of harmful traditional practices, especially among the more educated, urban communities. However, at the same time, a trend to "medicalize" the practice of female genital mutilation, that is to carry out the operation in clinical conditions to reduce the health risks, has been detected.

"The World Health Organization continues to advise unequivocally that female genital mutilation must not be institutionalized, nor should any form of female genital mutilation be performed by any health professionals in any setting, including hospitals or other health establishments." 83/

151. Except for industrialized societies where female genital mutilation is practised by immigrant populations, few countries have legislation prohibiting female genital mutilation. The criminalization of the practice of female circumcision has occurred only in countries such as France and the United Kingdom.

152. Since female genital mutilation is a sensitive issue in many societies, women's groups have preferred to rely on education, information and awareness-raising to combat the practice. They argue that legal strategies are not effective against customary practices. Since there is cultural acceptance and even celebration of the practice, in some societies, they argue that it is important to approach the question as a health issue, relying on doctors and educationalists as the major catalysts for change.

153. But, some argue that this is not enough. Since female genital mutilation is violence against women and since such violation has become of increasing concern to the international community, it is believed that legal strategies which give expression to international norms should be pursued. Legal prohibition of such a practice, accompanied by criminal sanctions, would be in keeping with international human rights standards. Such a strategy of prohibiting the practice, and criminalizing associated conduct must be accompanied by education programmes aimed at raising awareness among the people. A concerted international and national campaign should be conducted to raise consciousness about the pervasiveness of this practice and the need for its eradication.

(c) *Son preference and gender difference in nutrition*

154. Given the present number of men in India and in China, there should today be 30 million more women in India and 38 million more women in China than there are. 84/

155. The prevalence of son preference, more marked in Asian societies and historically rooted in the patriarchal system, cannot be ignored. Son preference has

been defined in a report of the Working Group on Traditional Practices affecting the Health of Women and Children of the Sub-Commission as "the preference of parents for male children which often manifests itself in neglect, deprivation or discriminatory treatment of girls to the detriment of their mental and physical health" (E/CN.4/1986/42, para. 143). Son preference has also been found to be directly associated with a high mortality risk for women.

156. The entire life cycle of a woman can be affected by this practice, from its most extreme forms of foetal or female infanticide to neglect of the girl child and woman over her brother and husband as far as adequate nutrition, basic health care, access to education and information, recreation and economic options are concerned. Such sayings as "To have a son is good economics and good politics, whereas bringing up a girl is like watering the neighbour's garden" illustrate the attitude in societies where son preference is prevalent. The male child, and later the man, are considered to ensure the continuity and protection of family property, to provide "an extra pair of hands" by bringing in a bride and to provide for parents in their old age.

157. By contrast, the young woman has a subordinate and vulnerable status. Already at the foetal stage, amniocentesis tests, sonography and increasingly developed technological methods for sex determination often lead to the abortion of the female foetus. The girl continues to be subjected to violence and discrimination through differentiating food practices, resulting in malnutrition and retarded growth. Her sexuality is often controlled through physically and mentally violent practices. During sickness, the woman is not provided with medical care, generally to the benefit of the sick male. Son preference and gender discrimination continue to affect women's access to education and their low literacy rate, and seem to be instrumental in promoting the practice of early marriage, which may prove equally detrimental to the physical and mental health of young women.

158. In families where food is scarce, the more nutritious food is kept for the male child. A WHO report of 1985 shows these preferential feeding practices and gender bias in nutrition. 85/ The same report points to differential treatment in health care and access to education.

159. This gender bias from birth which discriminates against women when it comes to nutrition, education and health amounts to violence against women. However, legal strategies are unlikely to be effective in

83/ Ibid.
84/ Roxanne Carillo, op. cit. (note 32).
85/ WHO, 1985, Offset Publication No. 90, *Women, Health and Development*.

this context. Initially, there must be an attempt to collect gender disaggregated data so that the problem of gender bias becomes more apparent. Special education and health programmes must be devised to prevent these discriminatory practices.

(d) Early marriage and dowry related violence

160. In India, 11,259 dowry related deaths were recorded in the last three years, 86/ in Nepal, 40 per cent of girls under the age of 15 are already married. 87/

161. Traditional marriage and related practices obviously still prevail in a number of societies, especially in the Asian and African regions and may range from death as a result of dowry debts to early marriage, childhood pregnancy, nutritional taboos and delivery practices to bride/widow burning.

162. In many societies the payment of a dowry is required for the groom to marry. In addition, the expenses for the marriage are also borne by the bride's family. Failure to provide the agreed amount of dowry could mark the beginning of violence within the family for the woman. She may be verbally abused, mentally and physically tortured, starved and, in certain communities, even burnt alive by the husband and/or his family members. 88/

163. Early marriage is intended to guarantee a woman's virginity, relieve her family of the burden of a mouth to feed and ensure a long cycle of fertility to produce a number of sons. Yet early marriage generally leads to early childhood/teenage pregnancy, which in its turn, as stated at the Second United Nations Regional Seminar on Traditional Practices affecting the Health of Women and Children, lessens the life expectancy of girls, adversely affects their health, nutrition, education and employment opportunities and lowers their economic participation rate. Furthermore, maternal and child mortality rates are found to be extremely high in areas such as South Asia, where the use of traditional birth practices has been recorded.

164. Violence related to the institution of marriage is of grave concern to those interested in women's rights as human rights. The Governments of India and of Bangladesh have sought to criminalize violence related to the dowry. The Indian penal code contains provisions with regard to dowry deaths, which allow for such crime to be deduced from circumstantial evidence and for the strengthening of police powers. The crime also carries the maximum penalty. 89/ The proper implementation of these provisions is absolutely necessary if dowry deaths are to be prevented.

165. The age of marriage is also a factor which contributes to the violation of women's human rights. According to a WHO report, over 50 per cent of first births in many developing countries are to women aged less than 19. 90/ Early marriage of the female child should be prohibited. Marriage of female children under the age of 18 should not be encouraged and States should adjust their laws accordingly.

(e) Other practices

166. In many traditional societies, pregnancy and childbirth are events surrounded by numerous myths and practices. As a result of dietary restrictions, many women are undernourished during maternity and have a low intake of essential proteins and vitamins, which in turn has implications for the health of the new-born. Labour and childbirth are often characterized by unhygienic conditions, unskilled assistance, as well as by religious rituals practised by traditional birth attendants. It must, however, be mentioned that some religious rituals may have a supporting effect on the women themselves and are felt to be reassuring. 91/

167. In India, the practice of widow-burning or sati, which has had a resurgence in recent years, has been outlawed both by national and State Governments. Though this is welcome, there is still concern that the practice may occur in small communities and that effective implementation of the laws is absolutely necessary. 92/

168. In many societies, women are subject to virginity tests on their marriage night or as part of a prosecution for rape or sexual abuse. A recent report by Human Rights Watch highlights this practice in Turkey. 93/ State agencies should not collaborate in the practice of virginity tests as it is a violation of a woman's human rights. In addition, action should be taken to prevent customary practices which degrade women by forcing them to submit to virginity tests whether in State-run dormitories, State orphanages, or by private families.

169. From the above facts, it seems painfully obvious that violence against women manifests itself in its possibly most blatant form through traditional practices affecting the health of women and children. These cul-

86/ APDC, op. cit. (note 53).
87/ UNICEF South Asia Regional Office, Kathmandu, Working Papers presented to the Second United Nations Regional Seminar on Harmful Traditional Practices affecting the Health of Women and Children, Colombo, 1994 (E/CN.4/Sub.2/1994/10).
88/ Ibid.
89/ Criminal law (Amendment) Act 1983—amending section 30YB Penal Code 1860.
90/ WHO, 1985, op. cit.
91/ Final report of the Special Rapporteur on traditional practices ..., op. cit. (note 80).
92/ The Commission of Sati (Prevention) Act of 1987, New Delhi.
93/ Human Rights Watch Women's Project, "Matter of power - State control of women's virginity in Turkey", June 1994.

turally conditioned practices are not only dangerous to women's health, at times even resulting in their death, but also violate the basic human rights of women and seriously impair their dignity. Though the infliction on them of different forms of physical and mental violence throughout their life span, girls and women are denied their human right to be free and independent, and to live in a secure environment within their families, homes and communities.

(f) Traditional laws

170. Certain traditional practices and sanctions which are violent towards women are justified by special legislation. The public stoning and lashing of women serve to institutionalize violence against women. The Special Rapporteur has received many allegations of such violent punishments being inflicted on women in the Islamic Republic of Iran, for example. It is important that research be conducted with regard to these laws to ascertain their impact on the full enjoyment of human rights by women and that these laws be reconsidered in the light of universally accepted human rights standards.

(g) Death threats

171. Women who defy traditional practices and related legislation often are sometimes at the receiving end of death threats and violence, for example the writer Taslima Nasreen of Bangladesh and Asma Jehangir of Pakistan. In Algeria, according to information received by the Special Rapporteur, women have been killed or have received death threats, especially in March 1994. Among the victims was Mme Meziane, the director of a school in Bet Khadem. This tradition of violence against women who do not conform to cultural norms is frequent in many societies. Government inaction in the face of such threats results in women being denied their fundamental human rights—especially the right to life. It is important that Governments investigate and prosecute those who issue such death threats with seeming impunity (see report of the Special Rapporteur on the right to freedom of opinion and expression, Mr. A. Hussain (E/CN.4/ 1995/32)). Non-State actors should be held internationally accountable for their activities with regard to violence against women.

B. Violence in the community

1. Rape and sexual assault

(a) Introduction

172. Rape has often been described as the primary instrument of control in a patriarchal society. 94/ Clinical tests show that rapists present very normal attributes. Most rapists are in fact known to their victims. 95/

173. Effective prosecution for rape is one of the fundamental demands of the women's movement. Rape occurs in the family in the form of marital rape or incest; rape occurs in the community, it is used as an instrument of torture by States against women in detention; and rape occurs in situations of armed conflict and in refugee camps. Women's vulnerability to rape is one of the main factors which prevent their empowerment and their enjoying equality with men.

174. For a long time, women have argued that rape is a form of torture inflicted by both private and public actors in violation of the international human rights instruments. 96/ Rape prevents women from living in security and dignity and therefore violates international standards set out in the International Covenants and the Universal Declaration (see chap. III).

175. States have an international legal obligation to investigate, prosecute and punish rapists. State discrimination in not pursuing cases involving violence against women has been documented by some groups. 97/ This non-prosecution is a serious issue and can only be overcome by raising awareness among the police, the judiciary and the general community.

(b) Police action

176. The police are often insensitive to issues concerning rape. They are often suspicious of complainants, particularly if there is no sign of injury, if the woman knows the offender, if she delays reporting the rape or if she appears unnaturally calm or unemotional. If the woman is seen as being morally dubious, as she will be if she is living with her boyfriend, is sexually experienced or is a prostitute, the allegation will be completely in doubt. Police stations are the traditional rape reception agencies and the police response to complainants requires priority attention. Education and training are essential for prejudice and negative attitudes to be eliminated and practical approaches to a complaint imparted. In Malaysia, women-only rape squads have been formed by the police and a policy directive established that only women police officers handle rape victims. 98/

94/ See Kate Millet, *Politics*, New York, Virago Press; and Susan Brownmiller, *Against Our Will*, London, Penguin.
95/ Catherine Mackinnon, "Sexuality, pornography, and method, Pleasure under patriarchy", in *Ethnic* 1989, vol. 99, No. 2.
96/ *Token Gestures: Women's Human Rights and UN Reporting: The UN Special Rapporteur on Torture*, International Human Rights Law Group, Washington, D.C., June 1993.
97/ Human Rights Watch Women's Rights Project, *Criminal Justice, Violence against Women in Brazil*, New York, 1991.
98/ See I. Fernandez, "Mobilizing on all fronts: A comprehensive strategy to end violence against women", in M. Schuler, *Freedom from Violence*, Women, Law and Development, OEF International, 1992.

In the United Kingdom, police have developed "rape suites". These are specifically designed interview rooms, equipped with a bathroom and examination couch. The victim is interviewed and examined in the "suite", which is separate from the main station interviewing area and provides pleasant and comfortable surroundings. 99/ In Brazil there are women-only police stations which deal with the problem of violence against women.

(c) Services

177. Many countries have established what are sometimes called "rape crisis centres". Some of these operate a telephone advice service or a short-term residential facility for victims. Most provide sympathetic and knowledgeable support to victims. These rape crisis centres provide integrated services to women victims of violence. Centre staff accompany the victim to the police station and the hospital to give her support. They provide her with legal and counselling services and work closely with hospitals, the police station and the prosecutor's office. They are basically intended to give the woman victim courage to face the difficult and often embarrassing procedures that the legal process requires. 100/ These centres are augmented by non-governmental organizations and government services, which include information networks, hotlines and counselling services.

178. Hospitals are another important institution which needs to be sensitized with regard to women and rape. In Malaysia, the rape crisis centres have been set up in the hospitals and a special room in the hospital is designated for the examination of rape victims; the police are called there to take the report from the victim; only one doctor examines the victim; and a volunteer from a women's organization is called to counsel her during this period and provide her with information and support so that she can make decisions regarding treatment and police action. 101/

(d) Legislation

179. The criminal laws which exist with regard to rape also pose certain problems. In most cases rape is defined as sexual intercourse with a woman, against her will and without her consent. Questions emerge as to what is "sexual intercourse", what is "consent" and what are the relevant rules of evidence which should govern a case concerning rape.

(e) Sexual intercourse

180. Most jurisdictions consider sexual intercourse for the purposes of rape to exist only where there is penile penetration of the vagina. However, frequently, the offender is unable or chooses not to penetrate his victim in this manner, but may force her to perform acts of oral sex, penetrate her with other parts of the body or other objects or demean her in other ways. A number of jurisdictions, especially in the Commonwealth, have thus taken the view that this concentration on penile penetration is misplaced. Some define sexual intercourse to include anal and oral acts of sex. 102/ Others go further and include the insertion of objects into specified orifices while some others also cover cunnilingus. 103/ These jurisdictions which have redefined rape to include acts beyond penile penetration seek to stress the demeaning and violent aspects of rape, rather than its sexual nature.

(f) Sexual assault within marriage

181. In many countries sexual assault by a husband on his own wife is not regarded as unlawful sexual intercourse and thus is not a crime. This is based on the assumption that the wife gives herself up to the husband by entering into the contract of marriage. Some jurisdictions have, however, done away with this marital immunity. 104/

(g) The complainant's consent

182. In most countries, rape is defined by statute or by common law as sexual intercourse without the consent of or against the will of the victim. Research from all jurisdictions indicates that any woman who has to prove that she did not consent will face enormous difficulty unless she shows signs of fairly serious injury. She will face particular difficulty if she knows or has had a sexual relationship with the man in the past. Thus a number of jurisdictions have attempted to shift the emphasis of the crime away from her consent. Most take as

99/ See *Confronting Violence: A Manual for Commonwealth Action*, Women and Development Programme, Human Resource Development Group, Commonwealth Secretariat, London, June 1992.

100/ See, for example, Elizabeth Shrader Cox, "Developing strategies: Efforts to eradicate violence against women", in M. Schuler, *Freedom From Violence*, Women, Law and Development, OEF International, 1992.

101/ See I. Fernandez, op. cit.

102/ *South Australia Criminal Law Consolidation Act*, 1976, section 3.

103/ Victoria, *Crimes Act* 1958, section 2A(1); NSW, *Crimes Act* 1900, section 61A; New Zealand, *Crimes Act* 1961, section 128.

104/ *Crimes Act* 1900 (New South Wales) section 61A(4); *Crimes Act* 1958 (Victoria) section 62(2); *Criminal Code* (Queensland) section 347; *Criminal Code* (Tasmania) section 185; *Criminal Code* (Canada) section 246.8; *Crimes Act* 1961 (New Zealand) section 124(4). Scotland: *HM Advocate v Duffy* (1982) SCCR 182; *Stallard v HM Advocate* (1989) SCCR 248. Wales; *R v R* (1991) 141 NLJ 383.

their inspiration the Michigan *Criminal Sexual Conduct Act* 105/ which eliminated consent as an element of the crime, focusing on the conduct of the offender, rather than the consent of the victim. Thus, "criminal sexual conduct" is committed when sexual intercourse occurs where the accused uses force or coercion or in circumstances where the victim is deemed to be incapable of giving consent, with force or coercion receiving a wide statutory definition.

183.   Related to this concept of consent is the question of whether consent which is grudging or elicited following substantial pressure being applied should be inoperative. It would appear appropriate that consent be vitiated where it is gained by the imposition of the other person's position of authority over, or professional or other trusting relation to the victim. Thus, following certain incidents and revelations in Bihar and Maharashtra, legislation in India has shifted the burden of proof in cases of women raped in State institutions, i.e. custodial rape, so that those in power have to prove that a rape did not take place. 106/ Some jurisdictions have introduced the crime of "inducing sexual connection by coercion", which occurs where sexual activity takes place when the offender knows that the complainant consents because of the offender's position of power. 107/ Similarly, others provide that where consent to sexual intercourse is obtained by virtue of a "non-violent threat", defined as intimidatory or coercive conduct or other threat, not involving a threat of physical force, in circumstances where the victim could not reasonably be expected to resist the threat and where the offender is aware that submission is gained because of the threat, the offender is liable to six years' imprisonment. 108/

(h) *Evidence*

(i) *Corroboration*

184.   Where most crimes are concerned, the accused can be convicted on the testimony of one individual, but where the crime is sexual, the evidence of the victim alone is insufficient and it is essential that it be corroborated in some way. Additionally, in a number of countries, although corroborating evidence is not specifically required, there is a rule of law that the judge must tell the jury that it is unwise to convict on the uncorroborated testimony of the victim. In some countries, the testimony of the victim has to be corroborated by four male witnesses. 109/Many countries have recently recognized that there is little justification for the requirement of corroboration and that it seriously impedes the conviction of sexual offenders, and have thus done away with the requirement. Canada, for example, provides that no corroboration is required for conviction and that the

judge shall not instruct the jury that it is unsafe to convict in the absence of corroboration. 110/

185.   Evidence of the victim's past sexual history with men other than the accused is often introduced in rape trials either to prove that the woman is of "notoriously bad character", for example a prostitute or highly promiscuous and thus likely to have consented to intercourse, or to prove that she is unreliable and thus her evidence is suspect. The complainant faces a barrage of questions in cross examination about her past sexual, social and medical experiences which seek to protect the defendant and denigrate the character of the victim. Although it is rare for the complainant's past sexual history to have any bearing on the particular complaint, evidence on the topic will affect a jury and inevitably lead to the acquittal of the accused. Many countries have, therefore introduced reforms which seek to limit the introduction of evidence concerning the complainant's sexual history. The Canadian provision states that evidence of the complainant's past sexual activity with the accused may be freely admitted, but no evidence may be adduced as to the complainant's past sexual history with any other person, unless it is evidence which falls within three limited categories. Even if the evidence falls within one of these categories, it is admissible only after reasonable notice in writing of the evidence and its particulars have been given to the prosecution and the judge has conducted a closed hearing, after which she decides that the evidence falls within one of the categories. 111/ In Australia, the legislation of New South Wales absolutely prohibits evidence of sexual reputation, while evidence of sexual experience is inadmissible except in specific circumstances. 112/

(ii) *Court proceedings*

186.   Current court practice and procedures can exacerbate the complainant's ordeal during trial. These include long time lag between incident and trial, lack of information about the progress of the case and the whereabouts of the offender, and the demeanour of the prosecutors, judicial officers and other persons with whom she may have to deal. A number of jurisdictions have legislated with these points in mind. In New Zealand, for

105/ *Confronting Violence: A Manual for* Commonwealth Action, *Commonwealth Secretariat, 1987.*

106/ Criminal Law (Amendment) Act 1983.

107/ *Crimes Act* 1961 section 129A (NA).

108/ *Crimes Act* 1900 section 65A (NSW).

109/ A. Jahagirt and H. Jilani, *The Hudood Ordinance: A Divine Sanction,* Lahore, Rhodas Book, 1990.

110/ *Criminal Code* section 246.4.

111/ *Criminal Code* section 246.

112/ *Crimes Act* 1900 section 409B.

example, the Victims of Offences Act 1987 directs prosecutors, judicial officers, counsel, officials and other persons who deal with victims to treat them with courtesy, compassion and respect for their personal dignity and privacy. Victims are to be informed of the services and remedies available to them and the conduct of the proceedings. They should be protected from intimidation, their views on bail and any fears they should have about the offender are to be imparted to the court deciding any bail application and they are to be notified of the release or escape of the offender. In some countries, provisions have been introduced to limit the number of persons who can be present at the trial. Some provide for *in camera* proceedings, some provide that the court is to be closed to all except specified persons when the complainant gives her evidence and others allow her to give evidence in written form.

(iii) Sentencing

187. Light sentences in sexual assault cases not only trivialize the experience of the individual victim, but also carry the wider implication that female sexual victimization is unimportant. Criticism of sentencing practice in cases of rape has led some jurisdictions to set minimum penalties. In the United Kingdom, for example, courts have laid down specific guidelines concerning rape offenders. 113/ These proceed on the basis that the offender should receive a custodial sentence, unless the circumstances are most exceptional and that the minimum penalty, in the absence of mitigating factors, should be five years' imprisonment. Particularly dangerous offenders, such as serial rapists, should be sentenced to at least 15 years' imprisonment, while in some cases, for example where the offender is a psychopath, he should be imprisoned for life. Some jurisdictions provide that the sentencing judge should receive an oral or written statement from the prosecutor about the physical or emotional harm that the victim has suffered. 114/

(iv) Treatment programme for offenders

188. The value of treatment programmes is more readily accepted in the United States than in Britain. One well established programme is a treatment unit set up in South Florida State Hospital which aims to rehabilitate incarcerated rapists and other serious sex offenders, largely by means of group discussion and self-help enterprises. Wives and girl-friends are drawn into the system and special attention is given to after-care following a gradual transition to the community. For instance, ex-offenders are given pocket telephones which they can use to dial another ex-offender volunteer for support whenever they feel the urge to re-offend creeping up on them. 115/ The possible value of such treatment programmes should be evaluated before they are set up and care must be taken to ensure that such programmes are not used as a substitute for prosecution.

Public education

189. In addition to the education of police officers, judges and other court officials, it is essential that the general public is also educated and a mass consciousness raised. In Malaysia, exhibitions and theatrical presentations, including talks and discussion sessions, were made to women's groups, schools, communities and professional groups such as nurses, police and counsellors. Many women's groups were mobilized to continue the consciousness raising programmes. To enable these groups to develop educational programmes, training sessions were held and a campaign kit, pamphlets and rape counselling booklets were produced as resources. Finally, in order to equip the leaders with the necessary skills for public speaking, representative action and writing, training sessions for them were organized. The media's role was also emphasized. Articles and reports began to appear in the press. The electronic media made an effort to have special reports on rape at prime news times. One newspaper even carried a survey for four continuous weeks with cases of rape victims. 116/ In the end, effective public opinion will be the most formidable weapon against rape in society.

2. Sexual harassment

(a) Introduction

190. Sexual harassment in the workplace and elsewhere has become an increasingly important issue on the agenda for women's rights, with recent reports pointing to the widespread occurrence of the phenomenon and its serious and disturbing effects. In designing strategies to combat the phenomenon, it is of vital importance that an adequate definition of sexual harassment be first agreed upon. Behaviour which falls within this definition is bound to be very diverse and would include behaviour which is considered "normal" in today's social context, as well as behaviour which falls within the definition of many legally recognized sexual offences. The search for an adequate definition of sexual harassment is likely to be difficult and will vary with cultural values and norms. However, there are two vital ingredients to such conduct. First, it is conduct which is unwanted by the recipient, in

113/ *Billam Case* (1986) 1 All ER 985.
114/ *New Zealand, Victims of Offences Act 1987* section 8.
115/ Howard League Working Party, *Unlawful Sex*, Waterlow, 1985, pp. 104-106.
116/ See I. Fernandez, "Mobilizing on all fronts: A comprehensive strategy to end violence against women", M. Schuler, *Freedom from Violence*, Women, Law and Development, OEF International, 1992.

other words, unwelcome sexual attention. Second, it is conduct which from the recipient's point of view is offensive or threatening. 117/

(b) Legal strategies

191. Some examples of sexual harassment fall within the definition of the crimes of rape, sexual assault, indecent assault or common assault. Where this is the case and since many countries have criminal laws against such activities, the woman can complain to the police, who may choose to institute a criminal prosecution against the offender. In some cases, if the police choose not to prosecute, the woman herself may prosecute privately. The woman also has the option, whether or not a criminal prosecution is being instituted, to pursue a civil action in either contract or tort, depending on the circumstance in which the offence was committed.

192. When sexual harassment takes the form of acts of violence or indecency, it is regarded as a criminal offence. The German penal code imposes penalties on individuals who abuse their authority to obtain sexual favours; while in Denmark, sexual harassment is condemned under section 220 of the Penal Code, which prohibits any abuse of the subordination or financial dependence of an individual with a view to obtaining sexual favours outside of marriage. 118/

193. In most countries, women walking in public places or travelling on public transport are subject to a great deal of harassment. In India, certain sections of the Penal Code establish the offence of insulting the modesty of a woman, whether by word, gesture or act. 119/ Further, the Delhi Metropolitan Council has criminalized "Eve teasing", which is defined as words, spoken or written, or signs or visible representations or gestures, or acts or reciting or singing indecent words in a public place by a man to the annoyance of a woman. 120/

194. Where sexual harassment occurs in the workplace, other non-criminal legal remedies may also be available. For example, the United Kingdom *Sex Discrimination Act 1975*, while not specifically prohibiting sexual harassment, proscribes sex discrimination, defined as treating a woman less favourably than a man, and makes it unlawful for an employer to discriminate against her by dismissing her or subjecting her to any other detriment for the sole reason that she is a woman. Courts have concluded that sexual harassment is sex discrimination and that proven harassment may render an employer liable in damages. 121/

195. In the United States of America, any discrimination is prohibited at work on the grounds of sex. 122/ In 1977, a United States court acknowledged for the first time that sexual harassment constituted a form of sex discrimination. 123/ Subsequently, United States case law expanded the concept of sexual harassment in two directions. First, by providing for what is called a "quid pro quo" case of sexual harassment. This form of sexual harassment consists in extorting sexual favours against the threat of punishment or the promise of professional advantage. 124/ Secondly, the courts accepted that sexual harassment took place, even if the victim was not subjected to blackmail, if the actions of the individual engaged in harassment caused a degradation of the victim's working environment. 125/

196. Remedies for sexual harassment in the workplace are also available under employment protection legislation which exists in some countries to protect workers from unfair dismissal. 126/ For example, Greek legislation allows for the termination of a contract of employment in the event of changes to the conditions of the contract which are unfavourable to the employee. 127/ It has been successfully applied in a case in which the court found that an employee was entitled to resign or to claim compensation in the event of dismissal on the grounds of an unfavourable change to the contract of employment after having been harassed by the employer. 128/

197. Recently, specific provisions aimed at discouraging sexual harassment in the workplace and elsewhere, such as educational institutions, have been enacted in a number of countries. For example, the Canadian Federal Human Rights Act prohibits sexual harassment in employment and in the provision of goods and services where these come within the jurisdiction of the federal Government. This legislation is complemented at federal level by the sexual harassment provisions of the Canada Labour Code which requires employers to issue

117/ See *Confronting Violence: A Manual for Commonwealth Action*, Commonwealth Secretariat, June 1992, p.110.
118/ *Measures to Combat Sexual Harassment at the Workplace: Action Taken in the Member States of the European Community*, European Parliament, Directorate General for Research, Division for Budgetary and Cultural Affairs and Comparative Law, Luxembourg, January 1994, p. 23.
119/ *Indian Penal Code*, section 509; see also Southern Nigeria, *Penal Code*, section 360; Botswana, *Penal Code*, section 143; Singapore, *Penal Code*, sections 354 and 354A.
120/ Delhi, *Prohibition of Eve Teasing Bill*, reported in *Women's International Network News*, Summer, vol. 0, No. 3, 1984.
121/ For example, *Strathclyde Regional Council v Porcelli* (1986) IRLR 134; *Wileman v Milenic Engineering Ltd* (1988) IRLR 144.
122/ Title VII of the 1964 Civil Rights Act, article 703.
123/ *Barnes v Costle*.
124/ *Henison v City of Dundee*, 1982.
125/ *Bundy v Jackson*, 1982.
126/ For example, *Employment Protection (Consolidation) Act (UK)*, 1978.
127/ Law No. 2112 on termination of employment dated 11 March 1920, as amended on 17 October 1953.
128/ Cass, Plen, Ass. 13/87 Jur. Trib. 36; 78 (Decision 13/87).

a sexual harassment policy which condemns sexual harassment, indicates that disciplinary measures will be taken against transgressors, provides for procedures to deal with instances of harassment and informs employees of their rights under the Human Rights Act. In Portugal, legislation establishes that an employer must impose disciplinary measures on anyone who by his/her conduct, provokes or creates conditions that lead to the demoralization of workers and more particularly women. 129/

198. In a number of jurisdictions, liability for sexual harassment in the workplace extends beyond the individual offending employee and renders the employer vicariously liable. In Denmark, under the Equal Opportunities Act the employer could be held liable for sex discrimination which includes sexual harassment and the situation is similar in the United Kingdom under the Sex Discrimination Act. Likewise, in Denmark, Germany and Ireland the employer may be held liable for unfair dismissal on the grounds of sexual harassment, whilst in France the employer is considered liable in the event that he has not taken the necessary preventive measures. 130/ This has two advantages for the complainant. First, she is assured of adequate compensation if she is successful, because the employer is usually financially viable. Second, the threat of imposition of vicarious liability results in employers taking positive steps to ensure that offences of this nature do not happen.

(c) *Other strategies*

199. The nature of sexual misconduct is such that women have tended to concentrate on legal remedies and more or less formal methods of complaint. Organizations concerned with sexual harassment have been established in a number of countries. In the United Kingdom, Women Against Sexual Harassment (WASH) publicizes the issue, provides training for employers and support and advice for complainants of harassment. In Canada, the Women's Legal Education and Action Fund (LEAF) conducts test cases and provides assistance in claims of sexual harassment, as does its British sister organization, the Women's Legal Defence Fund. 131/

200. Throughout the world, trade unions have issued guidelines and protocols to raise awareness and address the issue. In 1981, for example, in the United Kingdom the National Association of Local Government Officers (NALGO), the largest white collar union, issued guidelines for members on combating sexual harassment at work. NALGO's lead has been followed by other trade unions in the United Kingdom and elsewhere. 132/ For example, in Italy, in November 1989, the Italian Confederation of Workers' Unions, the Italian Workers' Union and the Italian General Confederation of Labour adopted a joint position from which to combat sexual harassment in the workplace. 133/

201. Codes of conduct and protocols dealing with sexual harassment have also been issued by human rights commissions. The New Zealand Human Rights Commission, for example, issued "Eliminating Sexual Harassment—A Guide for Employers", which suggests strategies for approaching workplace harassment and provides a guide for those in charge of the management of the problem in 1986. Similar guides have been produced by the Canadian and Australian Commissions, while the Report of the Commission of Inquiry (Integrity Commission) in Guyana, issued in 1987, suggested the formulation of a code of conduct for persons holding positions in public life. 134/

202. Sexual harassment of women in the workplace, educational institutions and elsewhere defines the role of women in sexual terms and serves to perpetuate their subordinate role in society. Sexual harassment constitutes a form of sex discrimination, for it not only degrades the woman but reinforces and reflects the idea of non-professionalism on the part of women workers, who are consequently regarded as less able to perform their duties than their male colleagues. Accordingly, it should be treated as a serious and important issue.

203. Government bodies can do much to increase awareness of the seriousness of sexual harassment and the procedures that can be invoked to confront it. Arresting pamphlets have been issued in Australia, Canada, New Zealand and the United Kingdom which could be used by other countries in developing strategies to deal with sexual harassment. The Australian Human Rights and Equal Opportunities Commission, moreover, conducted a major campaign about sexual harassment in 1990, which was effective in sensitizing the community about the issue. This campaign, entitled SHOUT (Sexual

129/ Article 40(2) of Order in Council No. 49,408; Regime Juridico do Contrato Individual de Trabalho, Order in Council No. 49,408 of 24 November 1969.

130/ *Measures to Combat Sexual Harassment at the Workplace: Action Taken in the Member States of the European Community*, European Parliament, Directorate General for Research, Division for Budgetary and Cultural Affairs and Comparative Law, Luxembourg, January 1994, pp. 24-25.

131/ See *Confronting Violence. A Manual for Commonwealth Action*, Commonwealth Secretariat, June 1992, p. 113.

132/ Ibid.

133/ *Measures to Combat Sexual Harassment at the Workplace: Action Taken in the Member States of the European Community*, European Parliament, Directorate General for Research, Division for Budgetary and Cultural Affairs and Comparative Law, Luxembourg, January 1994, p.56.

134/ See *Confronting Violence*, op. cit., p. 114.

Harassment is Out), consisted of a poster, magazine and radio advertizing campaign, with the facility of a toll free telephone line for women who wished to provide information about sexual harassment. 135/

(d) The United Nations system

204. The Special Rapporteur has received certain allegations with regard to sexual harassment within the United Nations system. She will, in due course, write to the United Nations officials concerned with a request for clarification. However, it is important to state in this preliminary report that the United Nations system must be above reproach with regard to such issues. Effective rules and procedures must exist for vindicating the rights of women who are subject to sexual harassment.

3. Prostitution and trafficking

(a) General description

205. Prostitutes are a heterogenous group, with different interests, different understandings of their rights and positions, and different vulnerabilities. The "call-girl" or "escort" is relatively better off and more independent than the girl-child who is trafficked into foreign countries where she has no economic basis or cultural or familial ties. The prostitute or commercial sex worker (hereinafter, "CSW") in industrialized countries may belong to fairly sophisticated unions (albeit largely unrecognized) or movements whose agendas often conflict with those of feminist organizations working ostensibly on their behalf; the CSW in developing countries does not have access to effective networks of support or organization.136/ Some women become prostitutes through the exercise of "rational choice"; others become prostitutes as a result of coercion, deception or economic enslavement. A discussion of prostitution must accept the premise that prostitution as a phenomenon is the aggregate of social and sexual relations which are historically, culturally and personally specific. The only common denominator shared by the international community of prostitutes is an economic one: prostitution is an income generating activity, marked by a degree of commercial indifference between client and worker.

206. The size of the CSW population worldwide is not known, and estimates are unhelpful. In Thailand, for instance, the estimated number of female prostitutes ranges from 70,000 to 2 million. 137/ CSWs are relatively well-remunerated compared to the average unskilled female labourer. 138/ In the Republic of Korea, for instance, a CSW earns between US$ 4,500 and 9,000 per year, while the female worker in the garment industry earns US$ 135 to 480 per year; in the Netherlands, a CSW earns US$ 30,000 per annum, while a woman in the garment industry earns US$ 15,000. 139/ The income

earned by the CSW is trivial however compared to the massive profits realized by those who are organizationally involved in the commercial sex industry (travel agencies, hotels/bars, airline companies, "pimps" and "madams"). 140/ The economic advantages which accrue all around account for the continued growth, and indifference to the attendant problems, of the commercial sex industry.

(b) Nature of the abuse

207. As a result of these enormous economic incentives, CSWs are particularly vulnerable to economic exploitation. While the extent of domination and bondage varies according to the socio-economic conditions faced by each CSW, they are all subject to a certain degree of exploitation. They usually only realize a small percentage of their earnings: in Germany, for example, the CSW gets only DM 80 of the DM 350 that is charged for her services. 141/ The condition of the German prostitute in this example, however, is markedly better than the condition of prostitutes who are held in debt-bondage and who see no percentage of their labour earnings at all.

135/ Ibid.

136/ At the First and Second World Whores Conference (Amsterdam 1986 and Brussels 1987, respectively), the concerns of prostitutes in developed countries were distinctly different from those of feminist organizations representing third world prostitutes. The Third World groups were concerned with issues of exploitation and systemic power imbalances; the Western groups were concerned with issues of personal autonomy and morality.

137/ Newsweek, 29 June 1992.

138/ This does not apply to women held in debt bondage or other kinds of forced prostitution.

139/ United Nations, Economic and Social Council for Asia and the Pacific, 1986. See also Heishoo Shin, "Women's sexual services and economic development", October 1991, Ph.D. thesis, unpublished.

140/ One writer has estimated that sex is the most valuable subsector of the annual US$ 3 billion tourist industry in Thailand. See, Steven Schlosstein, Asia's New Little Dragons, Chicago, Contemporary Books, 1991. While writers such as Schlosstein, Enloe and Truong have emphasized the growth of tourism as a chief instigator of the increase in the CSW population worldwide, it should be noted that the local demand for prostitutes in most countries is greater than the foreign demand. The sex tourist generates more income than the local commercial sex client per CSW contact, but the volume in client numbers is greater in the local population. See, A Modern Form of Slavery, Asia Watch.

Cynthia Enloe in Does Khaki Become You? (London, Pandora Books, 1988) points to a direct correlation between an increase in military presence in a population and a dramatic rise in prostitution in the same population. Military bases notoriously incorporate prostitution into the "rest and recreation" culture for soldiers. The role of Governments in helping military bases procure prostitutes is not an innocent one.

141/ See, "In pursuit of an illusion: Thai women in Europe", Women's Information Centre/Foundation for Women, Bangkok, 1988, No. 96.

Because prostitution is illegal in most countries, or highly regulated in countries where it is legal, CSWs face enormous legal and moral isolation. Their legal status is vulnerable, and their social status is highly stigmatized. In countries where prostitution is illegal, they are subject to detention and possible abuse if they lodge a complaint, or they have to bribe local police officers to help them. 142/ The rape of a prostitute in some countries does not amount to justiciable rape. The situation is not that different even where prostitution has been legalized: a prostitute may be subject to abuse, including rape, from the police as well as from her pimp or manager, in spite of having a justiciable claim. The social stigma which attaches to the vocation of prostitution isolates many women from their families and friends, a particularly tragic irony since many prostitutes are working in order to support their parents and children. 143/

208.   CSWs are also subject to extensive health hazards. Sexually transmitted diseases (STDs) are prevalent among CSWs. Few CSWs have enough autonomy to be able to refuse intercourse with a client or to insist on condom usage. HIV/AIDS is a very real risk factor for all CSWs. In a study conducted by Asia Watch, 14 out of 19 girl prostitutes in Thailand tested seropositive. Male to female transmission of HIV/AIDS is three times more efficient than female to male transmission, 144/ which means that the virus spreads rapidly through prostitution communities, primarily via male clients. Shared use of depo provera needles among women in brothels or shared use of heroin needles among drug prostitutes also accounts for a rise in the rate of HIV/AIDS transmission in the prostitute community. 145/ Because of their illegal status, prostitutes by and large do not or cannot seek adequate medical attention. Their economic vulnerability requires that they hide their medical status as much as possible from clients and managers, although CSWs working in brothels are known to be forcibly tested for HIV/AIDS infection in direct contravention of World Health Organization guidelines. 146/

209.   Prostitutes are very dependent on the various organizational and structural edifices which profit from their labour, such as those who can manipulate the law (police officers, brothel owners, immigration officials), those who control the advertising and entertainment industries, including the pornographic and mail-order bride industries, or those who control travel agencies, airlines, restaurants and sex-shops. The violence they face from these groups ranges from beatings for refusing clients to withholding clients, and therefore income, from CSWs who have erred in some way. Women prostitutes report that clients ask them to perform bizarre, humiliating and painful acts derived in part from pornographic

literature and in part from the licence afforded them by the private, anonymous nature of commercial sex. The international market for prostitution, in part owing to the fear of HIV/AIDS, has been marked in recent years by the demand for "fresh" or virgin girls. The premium placed on virginity has created a climate in which older commercial sex workers must portray themselves as something other than what they are. 147/ The urban experienced CSW increasingly finds her vocational position threatened by young rural naive girls who are fast becoming the CSW of choice for many clients, and she is consequently forced into situations of greater dependence on these abusive structural supports.

210.   Trafficking of women and children for the purposes of prostitution is a critical barometer of the nature of abuse that takes place within the sex industry. The rise in trafficking of women in many parts of the world is linked, among other things, to the increasing fear of HIV/AIDS (and the perceived need therefore to recruit untainted blood), the increase of sex tourism deriving from the pressure on developing countries to generate more foreign currency income, and continuing societal condonation of the imperatives of male sexuality. 148/

211.   Women who are trafficked are by and large not aware of what awaits them; some women contact pimps or managers directly, but the larger percentage of trafficked women are sold into bondage by their parents,

142/   The abuse of prostitutes while in detention is in direct contravention of the Minimum Standards on the Treatment of Prisoners.
143/   Stigma does not necessarily attach to prostitution everywhere. Certain African countries are known to have very liberal postures towards prostitution: women move in and out of prostitution in an autonomous manner, with the full knowledge of their families and communities. There are communities in Nepal and India which condone prostitution as an income-generating activity to such an extent that they have developed well-established rituals to reconstitute the virginity of a prostitute when she retires and gets married. The prostitute, at the end of the ceremonial rites, regains not just her virginity but communal respect.
144/   Newsweek, 29 June 1992.
145/   Thanh-Dam Truong, Sex, Money and Prostitution in South East Asia, London, Zed Books, 1990.
146/   The WHO Guidelines expressly require consent from a person before any medical intrusion is made upon the person's body.
147/   Brothel owners are known to sell a woman's virginity several times over. The prices clients pay for a virgin is usually very high and the misrepresentation is motivated by lucrative concerns. A Modern Form of Slavery: Trafficking of Burmese Women and Girls into Brothels in Thailand, New York, Human Rights Watch, 1993.
148/   From Thailand to the Netherlands, police and other officials have claimed that incidents of rape would increase if men could not satisfy their needs through prostitutes. Under this reckoning (for which there appears to be absolutely no proof), the chaste woman should be grateful that her husband visits prostitutes and thus does not rape her or other chaste women.

husbands, boyfriends, or they are deceived or coerced, sometimes by friends or elders in the village. The "mail-order bride-business" accounts for some percentage of trafficking in women: women who believe they will find a wealthy husband and a safe family environment in another country may in fact be forced into prostitution upon arrival. 149/

212. Women who are trafficked into other countries for the purpose of prostitution generally work out of the most abusive of brothels, bars and salons. The conditions faced by these women are appalling. Asia Watch and the Women's Rights Group conducted a comprehensive study of girls and women trafficked from Burma into Thailand. 150/ The study found that women trafficked into brothels in Thailand work between 10 and 14 hours a day, with an average of 10 clients per day. The average size of the rooms these women live and work out of measure two by two and a half metres. If they are lucky, they get a few days off during menstruation. The workers generally receive a little over a dollar a day from the brothel owner, although the clients pay much more directly to the brothel owner. They are expected to pay for their food and lodgings out of this money. Many of these women are held in debt-bondage as they are expected to repay the amount forwarded to their parents by the recruiting agents. They may also be illegally confined to the brothels, through the practice of withholding passports or through more physically abusive means. In one known incident, five girl prostitutes in Thailand were burned to death in a brothel because they had been chained to their beds and could not get away.

213. Of the 30 women interviewed by Asia Watch, only two were above 20 years of age. The report cites accounts of 10-year-old girls who pass out from pain when raped by clients. In Thailand, the sexual intercourse experienced by girls 15 years or younger always constitutes statutory rape. Instead of punishing the rapist, i.e. the client or the brothel owner as an accomplice to the rape, in Thailand the girls who do complain are often arrested and sent back to the brothel upon payment of a fine. Women who are trafficked are usually smuggled across borders with the bribed complicity of the border guards. Victims of trafficking report extensive police usage of brothels for free. Their status as illegal immigrants is further disabling, rendering them highly vulnerable to sexual, economic and physical abuse. Health care is virtually non-existent for them, except for the provision of birth control pills or depo provera. 151/ Rehabilitation and deportation centres often serve as scouting grounds for corrupt police and brothel owners to recruit sex workers at inexpensive rates. 152/

(c) *Legislation*

214. Most States have either outlawed prostitution or have imposed heavy regulations on the practice of prostitution. 153/ However, virtually no model legislation adopted by any one State has adequately or effectively been able to deal with the problems related to the practice of prostitution, and the commercial sex industry has continued to thrive, undeterred by legal hurdles. The stigma attached to prostitutes makes them very reluctant to come forward and register with the authorities. Their clients likewise feel freer in clandestine conditions. The commercial sex industry, therefore, has many incentives for evading the law, and because prostitution functions mainly in the darker spaces of a community, relying on word of mouth, coded language and community and State complicity, evading the law has not been difficult.

215. Several international instruments address the issue of prostitution directly. States should be actively encouraged to accede to the International Covenant on Civil and Political Rights and the Convention on the Elimination of All Forms of Discrimination Against Women. Article 6 of this Convention, in particular, obligates States parties to take all appropriate measures to "suppress all forms of traffic in women and exploitation of prostitution of women". Such measures could involve enacting legislation to prosecute all those involved in the exploitative organizations surround-

---

149/ Khin Titisa, *Providence and Prostitution*, International Reports: Women and Society Series, London, 1990.

150/ *A Modern Form of Slavery*, op. cit. (note 147). Women and girls are also trafficked from China and other parts of the world into Thailand. While recent focus with regard to trafficking has been on Thailand, the Philippines and the Republic of Korea, trafficking in women is not confined to these countries. It is estimated that 200,000 women have been trafficked from Nepal to India. Women are trafficked from Bangladesh into Pakistan, from South Asia and South-East Asia into Europe and from South America into Europe and North America.

151/ If a prostitute becomes pregnant while in the brothel, she must either have a forced (and in Thailand, illegal) abortion or, if she carries the child to term, the child is usually sold by the brothel owner without the woman's consent or knowledge.

152/ Some of the abuses cited in this report are specific to the particularly oppressive regime in Myanmar. Asia Watch notes that even when sex workers from Myanmar are deported back to that country, the Government of Myanmar has been known to refuse re-entry for those who are not ethnically Burmese, and that the Government of Thailand has been complicitous in this explicitly racist practice. The Government of Myanmar also actively prosecutes women who were trafficked against their will upon re-entry into Myanmar.

153/ In Peru, for example, where prostitution is legal but heavily regulated, most prostitutes do not register as required, preferring to work illegally in spite of the fact that they are then subject to greater police harassment.

ing prostitution and trafficking, including brothel owners, pimps, airlines; increasing the statutory age for rape to 18, and actively prosecuting clients who violate this law; and establishing commissions of inquiry to investigate allegations of abuse and complicity by government agents.

216. The Special Rapporteur also notes with interest the work of the Working Group on Contemporary Forms of Slavery of the Sub-Commission on Prevention of Discrimination and Protection of Minorities in connection with a draft programme of action for prevention of traffic in persons and the exploitation of the prostitution of others (E/CN.4/1994/71, annex) and calls upon the Commission on Human Rights to consider the draft programme at its present session.

217. States that have not acceded to the Convention for the Suppression of the Traffic in Persons and of the Exploitation of the Prostitution of Others should urgently be encouraged to do so. The Convention calls on States parties to protect all persons from the abuses of trafficking and exploitation of prostitution. It mandates that States parties make suitable provisions for the care and maintenance of victims, repatriate victims of trafficking only with the agreement of the State of destination, and bear the cost of repatriation to a certain extent when the victim is unable to do so (art. 19).

218. States should pay particular attention to stopping the recruitment of young girls into prostitution, by monitoring carefully employment and recruitment agencies, as well as advertising and pornography agencies. The Convention on the Rights of the Child requires States to take all appropriate "legislative, administrative, social and educational measures to protect the child from all forms of physical or mental violence, injury or abuse, neglect or negligent treatment, maltreatment or exploitation, including sexual abuse". The growing trend of forcing younger and younger girls into prostitution is a problem that needs urgent and serious affirmative action. The reports of the Special Rapporteur on the sale of children, child prostitution and child pornography have raised awareness of the pervasive nature of these practices. 154/

219. Trafficking and the abuse and exploitation of prostitutes does constitute violence against women. Many groups argue that the only way to control and regulate such violence is to legalize prostitution. Legislation allows for the enactment of health and labour regimes which would protect the CSW. However, most societies and cultures do not accept this position. They believe that moral condemnation and criminalizing activity associated with prostitution and trafficking are the only means available for eradicating violence against women in this sphere.

4. Violence against women migrant workers

(a) General description

220. Migrant women workers, whether internal or international, represent an upward trend in women's economic activity. Although such women are typically lower paid than their male counterparts, they are increasingly becoming the most important, if not the only, breadwinners in their families. 155/ It has been estimated that the female migrant population has outnumbered the male migrant population by wide margins since the 1980s. Of international female migrant workers 72 per cent are found in Asia, 11 per cent in Europe, 8 per cent in North America and 9 per cent elsewhere. 156/

221. Poverty alleviation is the principal motivating factor for migrant workers, who often earn several times more in the host country than they could earn at home. There are compelling advantages which accrue to both the sending and receiving Governments of migrant workers as well. The foreign exchange remittances by international female migrant workers are of great importance to the Governments of the sending countries, which tend to be poorer than the receiving countries. In Sri Lanka, for instance, the foreign exchange remittances repatriated by female migrant workers have been estimated to be the second most important source of foreign exchange income to the Government. 157/ The receiving country is usually in need of a specific form of labour for which there is either no willing or available labour power. These interests constitute the basis for the phenomenon of international migrant workers.

222. The profile of the female migrant labour force is quite varied, ranging from skilled labour (nurses, secretaries, teachers) to unskilled labour (domestic workers, waitresses, low-level factory workers). The skilled labour force is better educated and more highly remunerated, paralleling the same phenomenon in the non-migrant labour force, although the national worker tends to be better paid than the non-national worker. While certain forms of abuse are universally experienced by women, the unskilled worker, and in particular the domestic worker, experiences violence directed against her to a greater degree and of a different kind.

223. Internal unskilled migrants tend to travel either with their husband and children or in groups of

154/ Report of the Special Rapporteur on the sale of children, child prostitution and pornography to the General Assembly at its forty-ninth session.
155/ Patricia Weinert, Foreign Female Domestic Workers: Help Wanted, Geneva, ILO, March 1991.
156/ Advancement of women: violence against migrant women workers, Report of the Secretary-General, (A/49/354).
157/ Eelens and Speckman, International Migration Review, XXIV, No. 2, Summer 1990, p. 229.

men and women. Language is usually not a problem and they are better protected against violence from persons outside their migrant group. 158/ International unskilled migrants do not have all of these advantages. They are very often working illegally, the language is foreign, and they are isolated from their social group. Although studies show that the literacy rate among foreign domestic workers is higher than the literacy rate of their national counterparts, the majority of migrant women are not well educated enough to be effectively apprised of their rights. 159/ Their position in the receiving country is thus very vulnerable, often in clandestine conditions, at the mercy of the employer and the recruitment agencies.

(b) Nature of the abuse

224. The nature of the abuse faced by international female migrants varies. Its chronic under-reporting (and under-investigation of reported cases) makes it very difficult to document with any certainty the extent of the problem. The abuses that are reported fall into two categories: non-physical abuse and physical violence. The nature of these abuses is outlined below.

(i) Non-physical abuse

225. A widely reported form of non-physical abuse is the common practice of withholding the migrant woman's passport or documentation papers. Employers claim to be protecting the woman (she might lose the passport), but whatever the motivation for this practice may be, it has the effect of entrapping the woman inside her employer's compound, especially in countries which require aliens to carry evidence of their legal status on them at all times. For the woman who seeks refuge in her embassy when fleeing the employer's house, she has no proof of citizenship with which to claim her right to protection.

226. Labour laws do not apply to the illegal worker and some countries explicitly exclude legal domestic workers from the labour laws altogether. Migrant women report that employers withhold their wages or pay them substantially less than originally agreed, holding them effectively in debt bondage. Domestic workers and "sweat-shop" workers, in particular, report long working hours; in one study, 72 per cent of domestic workers reported having no days off at all. 160/ Domestic workers also report under-feeding by employers; often they are allowed only left-overs. These common abuses create conditions under which women suffer assault in isolation and allow employers to behave with near total impunity.

(ii) Physical violence

227. One of the most comprehensive reports documenting physical abuse against migrant women is the 1992 report of Middle East Watch on the mistreatment of Asian maids in Kuwait. 161/ The nature of the problems documented in this report are similar to those documented in other reports on other regions, such as in Hong Kong, Singapore and parts of North Africa, although it is important to note that incidents of such abuse have increased dramatically in post-war Kuwait, perhaps as a result of a rise in hostility towards foreigners.

228. Of the 60 cases investigated by Middle East Watch, two thirds of the cases concerned physical abuse by the employer, including kicking, beating, slapping, punching and hair-pulling. One third of these 60 cases directly involved the rape or sexual assault of maids. 162/ Often the beatings accompany the rape or attempted rape. In the most egregious cases, the physical and mental trauma accompanying the assault or rape was severe enough to require hospitalization. 163/ The Middle East Watch report noted that while not all Asian maids suffered at the hands of their Kuwaiti employers, such abuses were disturbingly prevalent.

229. Female migrant workers also suffer often at the hands of the police. There are documented cases of women who report rape by employers being sent back by the police to the employer or being physically or sexually assaulted at the police station. Women who lodge such complaints are often detained at the police station for arbitrary lengths of time. Migrant women in Kuwait who try to flee their employers' houses and injure themselves in the process have been charged with violating the Kuwaiti law against suicide. 164/ The police also notoriously do not follow up on most of the cases that are reported to them.

(c) Legislation

230. Both sending and receiving Governments have encountered difficulties in regulating the flow of migrant workers. The bulk of migrant workers are recruited through private, unregistered agencies, which evade immigration and labour laws with ease. 165/

158/ See Jan Bremen, Of Peasants, Migrants and Paupers, Oxford, Clarendon Press, 1985.
159/ See Weinert, op. cit.
160/ See A/49/354 (note 156).
161/ Punishing the Victim, Middle East Watch, August 1992.
162/ Ibid.
163/ Ibid. It should be noted that lack of adequate medical care is an acute problem among migrant women, especially those facing abuse.
164/ Ibid.
165/ The pernicious role that these unregulated recruitment agencies play deserves mention. Women recruited through these agencies are charged an exorbitant recruitment fee, with a debt interest of 15 to 30 per cent. Women who were under the impression that they were hired for domestic or factory help have realized too late that they were being trafficked for prostitution instead. The base contracts which govern a migrant woman's working conditions are negotiated by the recruitment agencies; the woman herself is left out of the negotiating process and remains in the dark as to the terms she has signed onto.

Countries such as Bangladesh and India, that have tried to restrict exit for nationals seeking to migrate, have experienced instead a mass illegal exodus of workers, despite all efforts. Receiving countries, whose own national labour force is unwilling to work in the low-prestige, low-pay jobs typically occupied by migrant workers, have little incentive to regulate the conditions of the migrant workers. The attempts at regularization in various European countries have failed to legalize more than a handful of migrant workers; most migrants do not surface for fear of deportation. Italy has tried to crack down on the illegal labour force by instituting fines and prison terms; this approach has been criticized because it is difficult to enforce and because it punishes the vulnerable labourer rather than the employer.

231. In recent years, a few countries have made efforts to reach out to the female migrant population. In 1981, Canada instituted the Foreign Domestic Worker's Programme (FDW) as part of its broader Employment Authorization Programme. The purpose of the FDW was to regulate better the employment of foreign domestic workers, specifically through contracts detailing issues such as wage rates, hours and benefits. The FDW also simplified the process by which migrants could acquire permanent legal resident status, by requiring only two years of consecutive work with a specific employer doing a specific job. While the FDW represents a significant step forward in the process of legitimizing and protecting migrant domestic workers, it has also been charged with artificially forcing wages down and restricting mobility in an attempt to keep the national labour force from being attracted to domestic work.

232. The Government of the Philippines under President Corazon Aquino established the Overseas Workers Welfare Administration (OWWA), which is charged, *inter alia*, with regulating recruitment agencies and providing orientation to migrants prior to their departure. The Government also pledged to create 1.1 million jobs annually, to increase the availability of affordable housing, and to encourage the development of income-generating cooperatives. The Government of Mauritius has recently established the Foreign Labour Inspection Squad (as of 21 February 1994) which, like OWWA, is charged with regulating recruitment agencies and reaching out to migrant workers before they leave. These are important efforts which actively try to support the migrant woman, rather than threatening her into clandestine conditions.

(d) *International instruments*

233. There are many international instruments which can be mobilized to prevent abuse against migrant women. These instruments basically recognize the duty of the sending State to apprise its citizens of their rights and obligations, and the duty of the receiving State to assure human rights protection to the citizens of other countries. There follows below a list of recommendations deriving in part from these international instruments and in part from reports prepared by human rights organizations.

(i) States must act affirmatively to regulate private recruitment agencies, which constitute the original site from which migrant women are drawn. Administrative agencies, such as OWWA in the Philippines, should be established for this purpose. 166/

(ii) Both sending and receiving countries should establish outreach programmes for migrant women, providing legal, social and educational assistance.

(iii) Police stations should have trained female officers charged with helping migrant women who come in to report cases of abuse. Migrant women held in detention should come into contact with male officers only when a female officer is also present.

(iv) Embassies should be equipped to help their migrant citizens effectively, both when they seek refuge and when they are held in custody. 167/

(v) Migrant women should not be excluded from the protection of the national minimum labour standards. Employers should be actively prosecuted for violating national labour standards.

(vi) Further, States should ensure that their national labour standards conform with the various guidelines and recommendations put forth by the International Labour Organization. 168/

166/ Such administrative organizations could be charged with developing a standardized contract which must be used by all recruitment agencies.

167/ A tax of 1 per cent on all remittances repatriated by migrant women has been recommended by the Sri Lankan Women's Chamber of Industry and Commerce to create a fund for the purpose of helping migrant women who seek help while abroad.

168/ The following ILO conventions and standards are particularly relevant in this context: Forty Hour Week Convention and Reduction of Hours of Work Recommendation (limiting the hours of work to 40 per week, and requiring that overtime be compensated); Protection of Wages Convention and Recommendation (requiring contracts with specified wages and other terms); Weekly Rest (Industry) Convention (requiring at least one rest day per week, with the express provision that such rest day should coincide with the rest day observed by other workers). The other international instruments which should be mobilized to provide protection for migrant women are the International Covenant on Economic, Social and Cultural Rights, the Convention on the Elimination of All Forms of Discrimination against Women, and the International Convention on the Protection of the Rights of All Migrant Workers and Members of Their Families.

(vii) A basic problem underlying the presence of abuse is Government indifference or inaction. Many States have protective laws which are not enforced. States should, therefore, be held accountable for such inaction.

(viii) Trade unions should be encouraged to help realize the rights of migrant women.

(ix) The General Assembly at its forty-eighth session in December 1993 adopted resolution 48/110, entitled "Violence against women migrant workers", in which, called upon all countries, particularly the sending and receiving States, to cooperate in taking appropriate steps to ensure that the rights of women migrant workers were protected. The General Assembly also called upon competent bodies and specialized agencies of the United Nations system, other intergovernmental organizations and non-governmental organizations to inform the Secretary-General of the extent of the problem of violence against women migrant workers and to recommend further measures to implement the purposes of the resolution. This last provision is noteworthy and concerned groups and agencies who have relevant information should actively be encouraged to report to the Secretary-General on a regular basis.

234. The economic interests that lead to migration are compelling; migration cannot be stopped, nor should it be prohibited. Rather than trying to control migration, efforts should be directed at providing maximum protection for migrant women. Providing effective legal mechanisms by which such migrant women can be officially recognized and counted as a population equally deserving of State protection must be the starting point for effective redress of abuse against this vulnerable group.

5. *Pornography*

(a) *Introduction*

235. Pornography has become a major issue for women's movements all over the world. Many feminists view pornography as the very essence of patriarchy; indeed, the theory is advanced that it is the mainstay of male power and female subjugation. Pornography eroticizes domination 169/ and power differentiation. In other words pornography makes power sexual, it also turns women's subordination into a natural phenomenon. Pornography sexualizes rape, battery, sexual harassment, prostitution and child sexual abuse; it thereby celebrates, promotes, authorizes and legitimates them.

236. There is a school of thought that certain types of pornography are about sexual expression and identity. Some argue that such pornography or erotica liberate female sexuality. However, certain prominent writers argue that what pornography does goes beyond its content: it eroticizes hierarchy, it sexualizes inequality. From this perspective pornography is neither harmless fantasy nor a corrupt and confused misrepresentation of an otherwise natural and healthy sexual situation. It institutionalizes the sexuality of male supremacy, fusing the eroticization of dominance and submission with the social construction of males and females. Thus, pornography in itself represents a form of violence against women by constructing a situation which glamorizes the degradation and maltreatment of women, and asserts their subordinate function as mere receptacles for male lust. 170/

237. Furthermore, it would also appear that exposure to certain types of pornography actually causes more violence against women. The first instances of such violence occur with the making of the pornography. Many of the models are raped, killed and threatened in the making of the material. In addition, experimental research on pornography shows that certain materials cause measurable harm to women through increasing men's propensity to be violent. They significantly increase attitudinal measures known to correlate with rape and self-reports of aggressive acts—measures such as hostility towards women, propensity to rape, condoning rape, and predicting that one would rape or force sex on a woman if one knew one would not get caught. In addition to the experimental evidence, there is a great deal of anecdotal evidence which seems to point to a causative relationship between the consumption of pornography and sexual violence. 171/

(b) *Free speech*

238. The most contentious issue faced by those who wish to eliminate pornography is how to define pornography in a manner that does not deny free speech and artistic creativity. In jurisdictions within the United States of America, the free speech argument has been more persuasive than arguments which see pornography as violence against women. The Williams Committee on Obscenity and Film Censorship (1979) considered that

169/ C. Mackinnon, "Pornography, civil rights and speech", in 20 *Harvard Civil Rights—Civil Liberties Law Review* 1985, pp. 1-70.
170/ Ibid.
171/ See, for instance, D. Zillman, *Connections Between Sex and Aggression*, Donnerstein and Berkowitz, 1984; "Reactions in aggressive erotic films as a factor of violence against women", *Social Psychology*, 1981, pp. 710-724. Malmuth and Check, "The effects of mass media exposure on acceptance of violence against women: A field experiment", *J. Research Personality*, 1981, 15, pp. 436-446

for material to be pornographic it must have a certain function or intention, to arouse its audience sexually, and also a certain content, explicit representations of sexual material (organs, postures, activity etc.). "A work has to have both this function and this content to be a piece of pornography." 172/

239. In this definition, "intention" and "explicitness" remain the key to pornography. "Explicitness" is the only thing that can be measured relatively objectively. The intention of the author or photographer is, on the other hand, hard to prove and the sexual arousal of the consuming public cannot seriously be "measured".

240. Such definitions fail to address the issue that most pornography represents a form of violence against women and that the evidence shows that it is directly causative of further violence against women. In this context the definition put forward by Andrea Dworkin and Catherine MacKinnon provided a major breakthrough in defining pornography by conceptualizing it as "a practice of sex discrimination which sexualizes the subordination of women and which eroticizes violence against women". They then define pornography specifically, descriptively and objectively for what it depicts and communicates about the sexualized subordination of women:

> "We define pornography as the sexually explicit subordination of women through pictures or words that also includes women dehumanized as sexual objects, things, or commodities, enjoying pain or humiliation or rape, being tied up, cut up, mutilated, bruised, or physically hurt, in postures of sexual submission or servility or display, reduced to body parts, penetrated by objects or animals, or presented in scenarios of degradation, torture, injury, shown as filthy or inferior, bleeding, bruised or hurt in a context that makes these conditions sexual." 173/

241. Such a definition squarely locates the issue of pornography in the area of violence against women.

(c) *Legislation*

242. In most countries, there is in fact no legislation against pornography. What there is instead is legislation against "obscenity" and "indecency". Material is usually taken to be obscene if, taken as a whole, it has the effect of corrupting and depraving persons who are likely, having regard to all relevant circumstances, to read, see or hear the matter contained or embodied in it. Attention is focused on the possible harm to the male consumer, whilst the wider notion of harm, that of violence against women, goes unaddressed. It is, therefore, necessary to find new ways of legislating which address the issue of pornography in terms of the concerns relating to the violent subordination of women.

(d) *Criminal law—incitement to sexual hatred*

243. In the United Kingdom, the Campaign against Pornography and Censorship (CPC), launched in 1989, took up the campaign for legislating against pornography on the grounds of incitement to sexual hatred and violence, using the United Kingdom Race Relations Act 1976 as a model. The incitement section of the Act is criminal legislation which provides a precedent for restraints on freedom of expression that can be oppressive and harmful to a particular group on the grounds of race. It could also be used as a model for restraints on freedom of expression that, as in the case of pornography, can be harmful and oppressive to a particular group on the grounds of gender. Legislation against pornography is then possible on the grounds that it can act as an "incitement to sexual hatred" and "contribute to acts of violence against women in the form of sexual abuse, sexual assault, sexual harassment, rape and murder", as well as to sexism and sex discrimination. The incitement legislation, being criminal legislation, puts the power of enforcement in the hands of the police and the "State". The potential for abuse in this form of legislation, however, would be virtually eliminated, if there were a concrete, specific and unambiguous definition of pornography.

(e) *Civil law—the sex discrimination model*

244. CPC also proposed legislation against pornography as a form of discrimination against women on the grounds of sex. Civil sex discrimination legislation against pornography would enable women to take action on grounds of harm done to them by pornography. It would enable women to take a stand on their own behalf against the pornography industry and enable them to obtain compensation for harm or injury.

245. Catherine Mackinnon and Andrea Dworkin attempted a similar strategy by drawing up the Minneapolis Ordinance in the United States of America in 1983. They argued that pornography, as defined by them (see para. 240 above), violated women's civil rights and the right not to be discriminated against. The legal process would necessitate an individual woman making a complaint that pornography had infringed her rights or her ability to exercise, or benefit from, equal opportunities.

246. The above strategy has been followed in Australia where in a recent case, two women who had been

. 172/ *The Williams Committee on Obscenity and Film Censorship*, London, 1979, p. 103.
173/ C. Mackinnon, op. cit.

employed in a construction site complained of sex discrimination when their male colleagues hung pornographic posters on their "crib" walls. They sued their employers and the trade union and accused them of aiding and abetting these acts of sex discrimination. The Tribunal found for the women and allowed them a measure of compensation for the violation of their rights. 174/ This trend towards seeing pornography as an act of sex discrimination is an important landmark in the struggle for women's equality and for the elimination of violence against women.

(f) Child pornography

247. The problem of child pornography, often involving the girl child, has been an important concern of the Commission on Human Rights, reflected in the reports of the Special Rapporteur on the sale of children, child prostitution and child pornography, Mr. Vitit Muntarbhorn, as well as in the reports of the Working Group on Contemporary Forms of Slavery of the Sub-Commission. The Special Rapporteur on the sale of children urges that not only the production and distribution of child pornography but also its possession should be criminalized. 175/

C. Violence perpetrated or condoned by the State

1. Custodial violence against women

(a) Nature of the abuse

248. Custodial violence against women is a widespread and troubling phenomenon. Abuse of power by government agents, usually police or military personnel, under non-transparent and highly unequal conditions, together with the impunity accorded to such agents, constitute the bases on which custodial violence ferments and grows. Governmental anxiety to apprehend alleged perpetrators, especially those who are perceived as threats to national security, national identity and national morality creates a general climate of non-accountability. Governments using military force to suppress their people are particularly unresponsive to charges of military custodial violence. 176/

249. Custodial violence is indifferent to the nature of the alleged criminal activity under which women are apprehended. Women are vulnerable to abuse whether accused of petty theft, sexually deviant behaviour or affiliation with a "wanted" criminal. The nature of the abuse ranges from physical or verbal harassment and humiliation to sexual and physical torture. Amnesty International reports that thousands of women held in custody are routinely raped in police detention centres worldwide. Torture to extract confessions or information is taking increasingly sophisticated and abhorrent forms,

from rape with electrically charged metal rods to the refined use of psychotropic drugs. 177/ The psychological and gynaecological sequelae of these extreme forms of custodial violence are further compounded by inadequate or unavailable medical treatment.

250. Prolonged illegal detentions and deprivation of food, sleep and water are also routine abuses faced by women in police custody. Even in States which have obligated themselves to provide legal counsel to accused persons, attorneys are not made available to them. Many detained women, especially in countries with lower literacy rates, do not know which law they have been detained under or what the alleged offence is. According to a study carried out by Human Rights Watch, "out of 90 women interviewed in a jail in Pakistan, 91 per cent did not know under what law they had been accused. Sixty-two per cent had no legal assistance whatsoever, and of those who had lawyers almost half had never met them". 178/

251. Governments fighting armed opposition movements are known to use torture routinely as a means of extracting information. Women detained in police or military custody in many countries are commonly subjected to beatings, burns, shocks, rape and molestation. "Disappearances" and extra-judicial killings at the hands of custodial authorities have been reported in Afghanistan, Brazil, Burundi, Cambodia, Chad, Chile, India, Lebanon, Myanmar, Sri Lanka and Uganda. 179/ A "disappearance" is defined as a situation in which there exists reasonable grounds to believe that a person has been taken into custody by government agents despite government statements to the contrary. The whereabouts and fate of the abductee are kept concealed. Defining the boundaries of custody or police detention is difficult in this regard because it is nearly impossible to prove that government agents are responsible for the abduction. Persons released after temporary disappearances report that while the abduction appeared to be carried out

174/ *Horne & McIntosh v. Press Clough Joint Venture and Metals and Engineering Workers Union*, Equal Opportunity Tribunal, Western Australia, 1994.

175/ See report of the Working Group on Contemporary Forms of Slavery on its nineteenth session (E/CN.4/Sub.2/1994/33) and interim report of the Special Rapporteur on the sale of children, child prostitution and child pornography to the General Assembly at its forty-ninth session (A/49/478).

176/ Military abuse of power is unchecked in large part because the mandate the military is given in national security crises is itself very broad. The rise in recent years of "disappearances" as a military strategy against allegedly subversive persons is a compelling example of the untethered powers allowed military forces.

177/ *Torture*, 1:92, vol. 2, 1992, IRTC, Copenhagen.

178/ *Double Jeopardy: Police Abuse of Women in Pakistan*, Asia Watch, Women's Rights Project, New York, 1992, p. 44.

179/ *Disappearances and Political Killings*, London, Amnesty International, 1994.

by government agents, the further interrogation and torture were not clearly attributable to the military or police.

252. The emergence of "special laws" in certain countries has led to an increase in custodial abuse of women. In 1980, there were 70 women in jail in all of Pakistan; by 1987, there were 125 women in detention in the state of Punjab alone, and 91 in the state of Sindh. Most of these women faced trial under Pakistan's Hudood Ordinances. 180/ A 1988 survey showed that 78 per cent of female detainees alleged maltreatment at the hands of the police; 72 per cent claimed sexual abuse. 181/ The Hudood Ordinances in Pakistan make extra-marital sex, which is defined to include rape, illegal, non-compoundable, non-bailable and punishable by death. 182/ Under them, women can be arrested without a warrant and detained without charge for prolonged periods in the absence of female officers. Women detainees have reported sexual torture, including having chilies forced into their vaginas with sticks by police officers in attempts to get them to confess to adultery. 183/ Gang rape, beatings, molestation and sexual harassment are common treatment for women accused of sexually deviant behaviour. Such custodial violence passes undetected because medical examinations are not provided.

253. The extent of police mistreatment both in detention settings and in non-custodial settings in India has received much attention lately. It provides a good example of the widespread nature of the abuse. In September 1989, the Rajasthani Government admitted that police officers were under trial in 50 rape cases. In New Delhi, 14 cases of rape involving 20 police officers at 12 different police stations were reported between 1 January and 11 February 1990. 184/

254. Preventive detention laws are increasingly becoming the legal instruments through which police derive their impunity. The Terrorist and Disruptive Activities (Prevention) Act in India, the Anti-Subversion Law in Indonesia, the Public Security Law in the Republic of Korea, the Prevention of Terrorism Act in Sri Lanka, to name just a few, are all instruments which allow police to detain persons who "might" commit crimes for prolonged periods without trial. Such legislation, by virtue of the wide and unchecked latitude given to police, creates a dangerous space within which the treatment of detainees cannot be questioned. The length of time and the highly obscure nature of these detentions pose a special threat for women who may get pregnant following police rape and be forced to go through pregnancy without medical care.

255. Police complicity in prostitution and trafficking rings throughout the world also accounts for some custodial violence. 185/ Police frequent brothels and threaten prostitutes with detention or deportation in order to secure free sexual services. The police involvement in the trafficking of female prostitutes into Thailand and the abuse these women suffer at the hands of the police has been well documented by Asia Watch. 186/ Women who are trafficked into the Middle East from Asia also face abuse at the hands of the police, ranging from rape to physical assault, when simply appearing at the police station to lodge a complaint. 187/

(b) Legislation

256. Many countries have penal and jail codes which generally conform, with exceptions, to the Standard Minimum Rules on the Treatment of Prisoners, adopted in 1955 by the First United Nations Congress on the Prevention of Crime and the Treatment of Offenders. These codes are, however, rarely followed. In the context of violence against women in custody, the Jail Code of Bangladesh stands out as a commendable piece of legislation. Under the Jail Code, male and female prisoners are segregated and male officers are barred access to the women's quarters. Women have to be chaperoned by a female officer when being questioned or examined by a male officer. Such protective measures can go a long way towards redressing the violence women face in custody. In India, many states have created special police cells to deal specifically with women in custody, in large part as the result of pressure from women's advocacy groups, although the conditions of the cells themselves have not been improved.

257. Bringing state legislation into conformity with the guidelines set forth in the Standard Minimum Rules on the Treatment of Prisoners is a necessary step in the amelioration of violence against women in custody. These Rules require the segregation of men and

180/ A. Jahangir and H. Jilani, The Hudood Ordinances: A Divine Sanction, Lahore, Rhotas Books, 1990.

181/ Double Jeopardy, op. cit. Amnesty International and the U.S. State Department country reports both confirm regular torture and rape of women detainees in Pakistan.

182/ See Jahangir and Jilani, op. cit. Men are subject to trial for violation of the Hudood Ordinances also, but the larger percentage of those charged are women.

183/ Double Jeopardy ..., op. cit. Police in Pakistan notoriously refuse to register complaints of rape.

184/ Cited in India: Torture, Rape and Deaths in Custody, London, Amnesty International, 1992.

185/ A discussion of custodial violence against women must address the fact that abuse of women by police occurs in non-custodial settings also. The psychological and physical conditions are such, however, that they are tantamount to official custody.

186/ A Modern Form of Slavery, op. cit. (see note 147).

187/ See Middle East Watch Women's Rights Project, Punishing the Victim: Rape and Mistreatment of Asian Maids in Kuwait, New York, August 1992.

women, and the segregation of pre-trial and convicted persons. They further require that women in custody be guarded by female officers and interrogated only in the presence of at least one other female officer. Medical care and examinations as outlined in the Standard Minimum Rules must be followed in order to ensure that abuse of women is detected early on. Pre-natal and post-natal care is also expressly provided for in the Standard Minimum Rules.

258. The Body of Principles for the Protection of All Persons under Any Form of Detention or Imprisonment, adopted by the General Assembly in its resolution 43/173 of 9 December 1988, also sets forth rules for the prevention and detection of ill-treatment of those in custody. Other relevant international instruments are the Convention against Torture and Other Cruel, Inhuman or Degrading Treatment or Punishment, the International Covenant on Civil and Political Rights, and the Convention on the Elimination of All Forms of Discrimination against Women.

259. States should be encouraged to become parties to the Convention against Torture and Other Cruel, Inhuman or Degrading Treatment or Punishment. There should also be constitutional protection against torture. In addition, States must play an active role in prosecuting authorities accused of abuse of women detainees. State protection of its agents is the single most important factor in the continuance of incidences of abuse of women detainees. Especially in countries witnessing internal strife, where police and military authorities are given a broad mandate, governmental vigilance must be increased to redress abuse of power. Legal instruments which make it easier to press claims against government agents and which allow for meaningful remedies should be passed by all States, in which police misconduct occurs. An active judiciary which protects the rights of the citizens is also necessary if the right to be free from torture is to be vindicated.

(c) Custodial rape

260. Recent legislation in India with regard to custodial rape, that is rape in any state owned institution, shifts the burden of criminal proof so that the State now has the responsibility to show that the alleged rape did not take place. This dramatic piece of legislation was a response to the agitation of India's many women's groups. This approach is based on the belief that state institutions which serve the public interest must be beyond reproach, so much so, that even the rules of evidence have been changed in order to ensure safety to women when they are placed in the custody of the State.

2. Violence against women in situations of armed conflict

(a) General

261. Rape of women and girls in situations of armed conflict, whether civil or international, constitutes by definition a grave breach of international human rights and humanitarian law. The Fourth Geneva Convention of 1949 states that "Women shall be especially protected against any attack on their honour, in particular against rape, enforced prostitution, or any form of indecent assault" (art. 27). Article 147 includes in the list of acts constituting grave breaches of the Convention "wilfully causing great suffering or serious injury to body or health". The International Committee of the Red Cross has interpreted this to include rape. [188] In addition, acts of sexual assault against women are outlawed by international humanitarian law through normative provisions prohibiting violence against the physical integrity, dignity and security of the person. They include common article 3 of the Geneva Conventions, in so far as it prohibits "violence to life and person", "cruel treatment", "torture" or "outrages upon personal dignity", and Protocol II Additional to the Geneva Conventions, relating to the protection of non-international armed conflicts, which expressly forbids "outrages upon personal dignity, in particular humiliating and degrading treatment, rape, enforced prostitution and any form of indecent assault" (art. 4.2 (e)).

262. The Vienna Declaration and Programme of Action, adopted by the World Conference on Human Rights in June 1993, states:

"Violations of the human rights of women in situations of armed conflict are violations of the fundamental principles of international human rights and humanitarian law. All violations of this kind, including in particular murder, systematic rape, sexual slavery, and forced pregnancy, require a particularly effective response" (Part II, para. 38).

263. Yet, although rape is one of the most widely used types of violence against women and girls, it remains the least condemned war crime; throughout history, the rape of hundreds of thousands of women and children in all regions of the world has been a bitter reality.

264. At the international level, with regard to the prosecution of war crimes, there seems to be a newly emerging trend, namely the setting up of international expert commissions and tribunals. The international community has adopted a more institutionalized response to the atrocities committed in the territories of the former Yugoslavia and in Rwanda in particular. The

188/ Dorothy Q. Thomas and Regan E. Ralph, "Rape in war, challenging the tradition of impunity", in *SAIS Review*, 1994, p. 81.

precursors to such tribunals were the International Military Tribunal at Nuremberg and the International Military Tribunal for the Far East (Tokyo Tribunal). Although rape as a war crime was not an issue before these early tribunals, they set the precedent for international prosecution of alleged war crimes.

265. In the case of the former Yugoslavia, the United Nations Security Council established first a commission of experts pursuant to its resolution 780 (1992) and then the International Tribunal for the Prosecution of Persons Responsible for Serious Violations of International Humanitarian Law Committed in the Territory of the Former Yugoslavia since 1991. In the context of the armed conflict in Rwanda, a commission of experts was established pursuant to Security Council resolution 935 (1994) to examine and analyse grave violations of international humanitarian law in Rwanda. It is imperative that such tribunals make a special effort to investigate allegations of and to prosecute gender-specific war crimes of violence against women.

266. The Special Rapporteur notes with interest that the Commission of Experts mandated to obtain and analyse information on violations of international humanitarian law in the former Yugoslavia conducted investigations which encompassed violations of international humanitarian law against persons, including extra-judicial executions, torture and other violations of international humanitarian law, particularly in detention camps. Special emphasis was given in these investigations to allegations of rape and sexual assault.

267. Furthermore, the report of the Secretary-General pursuant to paragraph 2 of Security Council resolution 808 (1993), discussing the competence of the International Tribunal for the former Yugoslavia, refers to crimes against humanity as being inhumane acts of a very serious nature, such as wilful killing, torture or rape, committed as part of a widespread or systematic attack against any civilian population on national, political, ethnic, racial or religious grounds, and states that "in the conflict in the territory of the former Yugoslavia, such inhuman acts have taken the form of so-called 'ethnic cleansing' and widespread and systematic rape and other forms of sexual assault, including forced prostitution". 189/ These developments are most welcome in the context of prosecution for international war crimes.

(b) *Nature of abuse*

268. In recent times, there has been extensive documentation of violence against women in times of armed conflict. United Nations documentation on the former Yugoslavia is a case in point. In the spring of 1993, an investigation committee of the European Community

stated that the mass rape and/or sexual torture of women in Bosnia and Herzegovina must be considered systematic, ordered acts and an important element of Serb warfare strategy. Additionally, the establishment for the first time of camps explicitly intended for sexual torture marks a definite escalation of violence against women in armed conflicts. The final report of the Commission of Experts identified five patterns of rape and sexual assault and concluded that, in Bosnia and Herzegovina, "these patterns strongly suggest that a systematic rape policy existed in certain areas ... practices of 'ethnic cleansing', sexual assault and rape were carried out by some parties so systematically that they strongly appear to be the product of a policy". 190/ Rape is, therefore, evidently widely used as another repugnant instrument for ethnic cleansing and for increasing inter-ethnic hatred.

269. In March 1994, the United Nations/Organization of American States International Civilian Mission in Haiti issued a press release condemning the use of rape against women as an unacceptable violation of the rights of Haitian women, which appear to form an integral part of the political violence and terror, in which armed civilian auxiliaries, "attachés", members of the Front for the Advancement and Progress of Haiti and the armed forces of Haiti had all been implicated. 191/

270. Most recently, the massacres, the hunting of survivors, the attacks on schools and churches, the rape and abduction of women and girls and violence against children characterizing the armed conflict in Rwanda have all been described in first-hand testimonies. According to a detailed report on the situation, "soldiers and militiamen raided homes, hospitals and camps for the displaced, looking for Tutsi women to rape. Girls as young as five have been raped. Some women and girls were macheted and then raped immediately afterwards,

189/ Report of the Secretary-General pursuant to paragraph 2 of Security Council resolution 808 (1993) (S/25704), paragraph 48.
190/ Letter dated 24 May 1994 from the Secretary-General to the President of the Security Council and annex (Final report of the Commission of Experts established pursuant to Security Council resolution 780 (1992)) (S/1994/674).
191/ United Nations/OAS International Civilian Mission in Haiti, Press release, Port-au-Prince, 21 March 1994. The High Commissioner for Human Rights and the Special Rapporteur have received a petition from the Catholic Women's Community of Germany (Katholische Frauengemeinschaft Deutschlands) containing approximately 2,000 signatures against the practice of systematic rape of women and children in Haiti. The signatories also demand the documentation of rapes in Haiti, the prosecution of perpetrators and an end to impunity, and protection and assistance for women victims of rape, reiteration of rape as a war crime in international agreements, the recognition of gender-specific reasons such as rape, as a basis for the right to seek asylum, the establishment of an international criminal court and the recognition of rape as an international crime in an international criminal code.

while others were allegedly gang raped, sometimes in public places. Some were acquired as a concubine or a second 'wife'. Fearful of death, many young women saw surrender as the only way to survive". 192/

271. In addition, human rights groups and non-governmental organizations have extensively documented other cases of violence against women in situations of armed conflict.

(a) During the armed conflict in Bangladesh in 1971, it is estimated that 200,000 civilian women and girls were victims of rape committed by Pakistani soldiers. 193/

(b) During 1992 alone, 882 women were reportedly gang raped by Indian security forces in Jammu and Kashmir. 194/ Militant groups in Kashmir have also been accused of using rape as an instrument of armed struggle.

(c) In Peru, rape of women by security forces is a common practice in the ongoing armed conflict between the Communist Party of Peru—Shining Path—and government counter-insurgency forces. 195/

(d) In Myanmar, in 1992, government troops raped women in a Rohingya Muslim village after the men had been inducted into forced labour. 196/

272. However, until recently the silence over the issue of rape in wartime has denied the historical meaning of rape and its structural importance in gender relations. Public discussion on the issue of rape in wartime took place for the first time in 1992, when reports were received of the rape and deliberate impregnation of thousands of women whose rights had been violated by all parties to the conflict in the territories of the former Yugoslavia.

273. For the first time also, after nearly 50 years, Korean women survivors of the Second World War used as "comfort women" by the Japanese imperial forces have broken their silence and come forward to tell their stories. It is estimated that more than 200,000 Asian women, mainly Koreans, were forcibly recruited by the Japanese army command to serve as sexual slaves of soldiers in brothels, so-called "military comfort houses".

(c) *Motives*

274. The underlying motives for rape in wartime should be looked at closely in order to recognize the scope of this extreme act of violence against women perpetrated by sexual means, as well as to understand the gravity of the situation at present, when the systematic and deliberate use of rape as a weapon of war marks an escalation in violence against women worldwide.

275. Rape is used as an instrument to exert violence, 197/ possibly as a manifestation of anger, in order to punish, intimidate, coerce, humiliate and degrade. In

one human rights report concerning rape in internal armed conflict, it is stated that:

"reported cases often involve the insertion of foreign objects into the vagina and anus combined with other forms of torture including electric shock to the genitals and breasts; rape of pregnant women and of minors; and gang rape by police and security force personnel. Often women are raped while blindfolded, so they cannot identify their attackers. Usually, they are told they or their family members will be killed if they report the rape". 198/

276. In addition, culturally and socially conditioned links between male sexuality, virility, potency and violence have been observed: especially in the case of gang rape, the perpetrators are generally seeking to prove their masculine identity *vis-à-vis* the woman, as well as themselves. This coincides with the fact that the occurrence of rape is particularly high in situations where male power has become unstable. In these cases, rape may be committed because a violation of the gender stereotype is perceived by the aggressor, i.e. the woman poses a threat to the man by being politically active, engaging in resistance movements or propaganda, so that rape essentially constitutes a sexual punishment for the trespass of a perceived gender boundary. 199/

277. Rape in situations of armed conflict, however, may essentially differ in character, in the sense that it is not perceived as a sexual but rather an aggressive act, which gives satisfaction from the humiliation and helplessness of the victim. 200/ Naturally, individual incidents of rape are committed for personal motives of sexual fulfilment in times of conflict as in peace, but it is the increasing evidence of rape used on a massive scale and in a deliberate manner to further the causes of one warring faction over another that it is intended to analyse in this section.

192/ African Rights, *Rwanda: Death, Despair and Defiance*, London, 1994.
193/ Ruth Seifert, *War and Rape: Analytical Approaches*, Women's International League for Peace and Freedom, Switzerland, April 1993, p. 12. See also Dorothy Q. Thomas and Regan E. Ralph, "Rape ..." loc. cit., p. 81.
194/ Asia Watch, *The Human Rights Crisis in Kashmir: A Pattern of Impunity*, Human Rights Watch, New York, 1993, p. 103.
195/ Human Rights Watch/Americas, *Untold Terror: Violence against Women in Peru's Armed Conflict*, New York, December 1992, p. 2.
196/ Asia Watch, *Myanmar: Rape, Forced Labour and Religious Persecution in Northern Araken*, New York, Human Rights Watch, 1992.
197/ Ruth Seifert, 1993, op. cit., p. 2.
198/ Human Rights Watch/Americas, op. cit.
199/ Ibid., p. 18.
200/ Ruth Seifert, "Mass rapes: Their logic in Bosnia-Herzegovina and elsewhere", in *Women's Studies International Forum*, Spring 1995 (forthcoming), p. 2.

278. Distinctive patterns of rape have been discernible in situations of armed conflict, whether in Korea during the Second World War or in the territories of the former Yugoslavia. Women are abused and raped by looters and civilians, sometimes people known to them, prior to military action in their own homes, or in public in their villages to serve as a deterrent for any resistance to the forthcoming military action, to suffocate dissent and to force collaboration. Upon the arrival of the military, the women are raped, sometimes killed and otherwise deported to detention camps. During deportation, women also may have to endure physical abuse. In the detention camps, they are once again raped and are sometimes required to serve as sexual slaves to the enemy soldiers, often having to endure other forms of sexual torture, beating and threats. Furthermore, the detention of women in hotels or similar facilities for the sole purpose of sexually entertaining soldiers, members of the camps and surrounding enemy communities has also been documented. 201/

279. A further characteristic of this atrocious practice is the use of rape as a method to terrorize civilian populations in villages and to force ethnic groups to leave. An escalation in the atrocities committed against women during armed conflicts is the practice of forced pregnancy and maternity. After being subjected to deliberate attempts to impregnate them, women are detained until it is too late for them to obtain an abortion, in an attempt to humiliate the ethnic group of the victim and to "dilute" it.

280. The raping of the women of a community, culture or nation is also conducted because of a belief that such rape is the symbolic rape of the body of that community, the destruction of the fundamental elements of a society and culture 202/ —"the ultimate humiliation of the male enemy". 203/ Women are victims in the fight for male honour. The inability to protect women's sexual purity is seen as an act of humiliation. 204/

281. Rape by enemy troops is also increasingly used as war propaganda. This sometimes leads to inflation of figures. The incidence of rape by one's own troops is diminished whereas the enemy troops' sins are exaggerated in order to incite hatred and aggression against them. Yet the number of reported cases of rape is never accurate because of the widespread fear of reporting incidents of rape and the social stigma associated with being raped. Severe traumatization, feelings of guilt and shame are accompanied by the fear of rejection by husband or family and by the fear of reprisals against themselves and their families. Some victims of rape are driven to commit suicide as a result of all these consequences; others end up as prostitutes as their only way of survival after rejection by the family.

282. It has been found that a lack of trust in the judicial system and the national legislation and their effectiveness, as well as the fear of (publicly) awakening bad memories, are major reasons for silence. 205/ This distrust has largely been created by the condoning of this practice by commanding officers through inactivity, in most reported cases.

283. In his reports, the Special Rapporteur on the situation of human rights in the territory of the former Yugoslavia, Mr. Mazowiecki, has repeatedly emphasized that, in the case of Bosnia and Herzegovina, he "is not aware of any attempts by any of those in positions of power, either military or political, to stop the rapes". 206/ Similarly, the civil strife in Peru, as documented by Human Rights Watch, has always been characterized by the Government's failure to prosecute the agents of abuse and to guarantee women equal protection under the law. 207/

(d) *Impunity*

284. It is exactly this official failure to condemn or punish rape that gives it overt political sanction, which allows rape and other forms of sexual torture and ill-treatment to become tools of military strategy. 208/ In certain contexts, in situations of armed conflict, institutions and mechanisms of justice have completely broken down. This ensures a certain anarchy, and rape is one of the consequences.

285. The impunity described above is further proof of women's powerlessness against a State that turns a blind eye to rape. The sad reality is that where no one is held accountable for gross human rights abuses and impunity for perpetrators prevails, women have no protection against rape and no way of seeking redress after they have been assaulted.

(e) *"Comfort women"*

286. It is precisely this question of impunity that the former "comfort women" victims of the Second World War are addressing in their recent testimonies. 209/

287. Between 1932 and 1945, the Japanese impe-

201/ S/1994/674, paragraph 249.
202/ Ruth Seifert (1995), op. cit., p. 7.
203/ Various sources, including Asia Watch, *The Crisis in Kashmir, A Pattern of Impunity*, New York, Human Rights Watch, 1993.
204/ Dorothy Q. Thomas, op. cit., p. 89.
205/ Rape and abuse of women in the territory of the former Yugoslavia, Report of the Secretary-General (E/CN.4/1994/5), 30 June 1993.
206/ E/CN.4/1993/50, para. 260.
207/ Human Rights Watch/Americas, op. cit. (note 195).
208/ J. Vickers, *Women and War*, London, Zed Books, 1993, p. 21.
209/ For a detailed study see Karen Parker and Jennifer F. Chew "Compensation for Japan's WW II war rape victims", in *Hastings International and Comparative Review*, vol. 17, No.3, Spring 1994.

rial forces are reported to have practised a policy of systematic mobilization of women of colonized or occupied areas by force, pretext or kidnapping, in order to use them as sexual slaves for the armed forces. Most of the women were young girls between the ages of 11 and 20.

288. The "comfort women" or "jugun ianfu" had to endure multiple rape on an everyday basis in the "military comfort houses", which were strictly regulated by the military and set up in such places as north-east China or Manchuria, other parts of China, the Philippines, Korea, and the Dutch East Indies, Malaysia, Indonesia. Allegedly, soldiers were encouraged by their commanding officers to use the "comfort women" facilities rather than civilian brothels "for the purpose of stabilizing soldiers' psychology, encouraging their spirit and protecting them from venereal infections", as well as a measure to prevent looting and widespread raping during military attacks on villages. 210/

289. It is only after having overcome their own sense of guilt and shame, as well as the social stigma associated with being a victim of rape, and only after the discovery of official documentary evidence in the Japanese national archives of the "comfort women" operation, that the few survivors have finally spoken out. They are demanding (a) disclosure by the Government of Japan of all records and information in its possession concerning the issue, (b) an official public apology recognizing Japanese guilt, (c) the provision of due reparation to the surviving victims and their families and (d) the punishment of the perpetrators. The Filipino and Korean "comfort women" have also filed law suits against the Government of Japan. These demands may be seen as setting the framework for future action with regard to State accountability for violence against women in times of armed conflict.

290. In July 1992, an apology was delivered by the Japanese Prime Minister, admitting that the Japanese military had forced tens of thousands of women to work as sex slaves in a vast network of Government-run brothels. However, the question of compensation has still to be determined and the act has still to be recognized as a crime under international humanitarian law.

291. Nearly 50 years have passed since the end of the Second World War. And yet this issue should not be considered a matter of the past but of today. It is a crucial question that would set a legal precedent at the international level for the prosecution of perpetrators of systematic rape and sexual slavery in times of armed conflict. A symbolic gesture of compensation would introduce a remedy of "compensation" for women victims of violence perpetrated during times of armed conflict.

292. The right to appropriate compensation under international law is well recognized. In the *Chorzow Factory* case, it was clearly established that any breach of an engagement invokes an obligation even though the precise amount of loss cannot be clearly established. 211/ The Special Rapporteur on the right to restitution, compensation and rehabilitation for victims of gross violations of human rights and fundamental freedoms, Mr. T. van Boven, has said "there is no doubt that the obligation to provide for compensation as a means to repair a wrongful act or a wrongful situation is a well established principle in international law". 212/

3. *Refugees and displaced women*

(a) *General*

293. An estimated 20 million people worldwide are refugees, and another estimated 24 million are internally displaced persons. 213/ Refugees and internally displaced persons are victims of persecution, human rights abuses and ethnic or militant conflict. They live outside the communal culture familiar to them, often in countries very different from their own. They also often face linguistic, racial and legal discrimination, and in many cases their physical and psychological security is not assured. Access to food, medicine, shelter and water is likewise usually very difficult to obtain, in part owing to the exigencies of armed or hostile conflicts. 214/ Refugees pose very particular protection problems: in particular, they require protection from forced returns, from violent attacks, from unjustified and prolonged periods of detention and from exploitation by State and Government officials.

294. Women and children constitute approximately 80 per cent of most refugee populations. In addition to the fears and problems which they share in common with all refugees, women and girls are vulnerable to gender-based discrimination and gender-specific violence and exploitation. They are at risk in the communities from which they are fleeing, at risk during flight

210/ Paper prepared by the non-governmental organization Korean Women Drafted for Military Sexual Slavery by Japan, Seoul, August 1994.

211/ 1928 PCIJ, p. 29.

212/ E/CN.4/Sub.2/1990/10, para. 33.

213/ See *Seeking Refuge, Finding Terror: Widespread Rape of Somali Women in North Eastern Kenya*, Africa Watch, 1993; also Susan Forbes Martin, *Refugee Women*, Women and World Development Series, London, Zed Books, 1991. Although the Special Rapporteur refers to refugee women, it should be pointed out that the nature and extent of the abuse faced by refugee women is not always distinct from the abuse faced by refugee girls. Accounts of the rape of 4-year-old girls are as common as accounts of the rape of 40-year-old women.

214/ Malnutrition is the principal cause of mortality in refugee camps.

and at risk in the refugee camps where they seek protection. The male perpetrators of the exploitation and violence against refugee women include military personnel, immigration personnel, bandit or pirate groups, other male refugees and rival ethnic groups. Data on Vietnamese boat people of the Office of the United Nations High Commissioner for Refugees indicate that 39 per cent of the women among them are abducted and/or raped by pirates while at sea. 215/

295. Family structures, which could otherwise be a basis of stability and protection, are often radically altered in refugee situations. Separation from or loss of members of the family may lead to women becoming heads of household. With children to support and often no prior income generating experience, most of these women are dependent on external support structures, and are consequently more vulnerable to exploitation. Even when families remain intact during and after flight, the extraordinary circumstances of being refugees change the traditional dynamics of male-female relationships. Frustrations arising from such changes can result in increased incidence of domestic violence and depression. 216/ It has been noted, however, that despite these changes women continue to remain responsible for most domestic activities and, interestingly, become the principal conductors of preserving and passing on the culture they have taken with them. 217/

(b) *Nature of the abuse*

296. The persecution which leads women to seek asylum elsewhere often takes the form of sexual assault or torture; 218/ a common reason given by refugees as the cause for flight is to ensure the safety of the women. In one report it is alleged that for almost half of the Somali refugee women who reported being raped in the Kenyan refugee camps, rape was a factor in causing them to become refugees in the first instance. 219/ The use of rape as an instrument of persecution in the former Yugoslavia is well documented. 220/ Victims of such violations are reluctant to speak about their experiences, especially since rape victims continue to be stigmatized and faulted in most cultures. 221/ As with rape or sexual assaults in non-refugee populations, there generally are few hard facts to document in detail the problem of sexual violence against refugee women.

297. Women and girl refugees in flight from the terror of their communities are susceptible to exploitation, rape, abduction and murder. Women separated from male members of their families or travelling with small children are particularly vulnerable to sexual exploitation and manipulation. Piracy attacks involving killings, abductions, rape and sexual assault in South-East Asia have received much attention because the at-

tacks often focus directly on women. Young girls on board the vessel are raped or assaulted by the pirates while the other passengers are forced to stand by. Witnesses have reported boat people being forced to offer young girls and women as ransom in exchange for the lives of the other passengers. An anti-piracy programme set up by the Royal Thai Government and UNHCR from 1982 to 1991 did lead to a decrease in the number of such attacks, but also led the pirates to intensify attacks, killing everyone on board after raping the women to avoid eyewitness evidence against them. 222/ Women refugees in flight also report being held and raped repeatedly for weeks in border jails, 223/ and being abducted and prostituted against their will. 224/

298. Fears of sexual assault and rape do not subside once women reach the refugee camps. The security situation in the camps is generally unsatisfactory and in some cases very poor. On occasion women are raped on their way to communal toilets at night, or in their beds

215/ Richard Mollica and Linda Son, "Cultural dimensions in treatment and evaluation of sexual trauma: An overview", in *Psychiatric Clinics of North America*, 1989, 12(2):363-379.

216/ Susan Forbes Martin, *Refugee Women*, op. cit. Child and spouse abandonment by men in refugee camps is not an infrequent phenomenon.

217/ Ibid. The author cites, for example, the Afghan refugee camps in Afghanistan where the use of purdah has been intensified, affecting even those groups of Afghan women who did not practise purdah while in Afghanistan.

218/ One study notes that sexual torture can consist of, *inter alia*, "rape of women by specially trained dogs, use of electric currents upon the sexual organs ... the insertion of penis-shaped objects into the body-openings (these can be made of metal or other materials to which an electrical current is later connected, are often grotesquely large and cause subsequent physical damage)". From Inger Agger, *Journal of Traumatic Stress*, vol. 2, No. 3, 1989.

The verdict is still out on the issue of whether rape trauma syndrome (RTS) should be accepted as evidence in rape trials. Whether or not this debate is ever resolved, groups concerned with refugee women should watch for symptoms that are associated with RTS in assessing the needs of refugee women.

219/ See *Seeking Refuge* ..., op. cit. (note 213).

220/ "Note on certain aspects of sexual violence against refugee women" (A/AC.96/822), Executive Committee of the High Commissioner's Programme, 12 October 1993.

221/ One Somali woman described the war in her country: "The war in Somalia is an anarchist war. It is a war on the women. Any woman between the ages of 18 and 40 is not safe from being forcibly removed to the army camps to be raped and violated. And that's only the beginning. If her husband finds out, he kills her for the shame of it all; if they know that he has found out, they kill him, too; if he goes into hiding instead, and she won't tell where he is, they kill her." Quoted in Martin, *Refugee Women*, op. cit., p. 24.

222/ Martin, *Refugee Women*, op. cit.

223/ Roberta Aichison, in *Cultural Survival Quarterly*, vol. 8, No. 2, Summer 1984.

224/ "Note on certain aspects of sexual violence ...", op. cit. (note 220)

with their husbands and children nearby. Most camps are not lit, and night patrols to ensure greater protection are infrequent or absent. 225/ Some of the attacks in the Somali camps in Kenya are by Kenyan police; these attacks tend to be more brutal in the aftermath of an attack by bandit gangs. The bandit community, which is believed to be responsible for most of the incidents, is nomadic and as indigent as the refugee community. Some of the attackers are other, male, refugees, but the identities of the rapists are generally unknown since they are seldom caught. 226/

299. Women may also be exploited and manipulated through offers of protection in exchange for sexual favours. Women with children are very vulnerable to this kind of manipulation. There have been reported cases of children being held as ransom in exchange for the mother's sexual services. Absence of sufficient legal documentation compounds the problem for refugee women in this regard. When the procedures for securing the proper documentation are not effective or the papers remain in the custody of the male head of the household, an abandoned woman, or a woman without documentation may face great difficulty in proving that she is legally resident in the country of asylum. The absence of effective mechanisms of documentation leaves the woman refugee vulnerable to sexual and other exploitation.

300. Forced prostitution of refugee women, especially if they are not accompanied by an adult male, is a prevalent problem. Cases of minors being sold into prostitution have been reported in many countries with refugee populations. The abuse of young refugee girls for sexual purposes has been documented in recent years as a growing phenomenon.

301. Lack of access to health care and food is one of the main problems faced by refugee women and internally displaced women. Several countries have used food as a weapon, impeding the assistance efforts of international humanitarian groups. In Angola, both Government and rebel troops have deliberately starved displaced persons and planted mines in otherwise arable land. Similar strategies in Ethiopia, Mozambique, and the Sudan have lead to the death of hundreds of thousands of refugees and displaced persons often predominantly women and children. Discriminatory practices in the distribution of food and other supplies, and especially, in the provision of health services, are a widespread problem requiring systemic revision.

302. Internally displaced women may be more vulnerable to abuse than refugee women because the Government that caused the displacement is the same Government that is primarily responsible for their safety and access to services. There is no international agency with an explicit mandate to help internally displaced

persons, although the International Committee of the Red Cross, as well as some non-governmental organizations, do actively intervene on their behalf.

303. Increasingly, the United Nations High Commissioner for Refugees has also been involved with the situation of internally displaced persons. While UNHCR has no general competence for internally displaced persons, the organization has frequently been specifically requested by the Secretary-General or the competent principal organs of the United Nations to intervene on behalf of internally displaced persons. UNHCR involvement with the internally displaced has often been in the context of the voluntary repatriation of refugees, where return movements and rehabilitation and reintegration programmes have included both returning refugees and displaced persons in circumstances where it is neither reasonable nor feasible to treat the two categories differently.

304. Women are also subject to persecution arising out of discriminatory gender-specific norms and customs. Amnesty International has reported the case of a woman being flogged in public because she was found wearing lipstick under her veil. Women are also flogged or persecuted in other ways for adultery, and there are documented cases of girls killed for losing their virginity. 227/ Persecution as a result of transgressing social mores is not specifically referred to in the definition of persecution contained in the Convention relating to the Status of Refugees. The difficulty of talking about traumatic experiences, combined with the non-inclusion of gender-specific persecution in the Convention, creates special problems for such women trying to make a case for refugee status protection to the authorities. 228/

(c) *Legal standards*

305. Both international law and the national law of asylum countries govern the protection of refugee women. The basic international instrument for the protection of refugees is the 1951 Convention relating to the Status of Refugees and its 1967 Protocol. The United Nations High Commissioner for Refugees is charged with providing international protection to refugees and with seeking durable solutions to their problems. The Convention defines a refugee as a person who has a well-founded

225/ UNHCR, *Guidelines for the Protection of Refugee Women*, 1991.
226/ *Seeking Refuge*, op. cit.
227/ The practice of *sati* in India can be seen as a form of gender-specific persecution, arising from a combination of communal conventions and ineffective State intervention.
228/ The existing bank of jurisprudence on the meaning of persecution includes rape but does not include, for example, infanticide, bride-burning, *sati*, forced marriage, forced sterilization, forced abortions or domestic violence.

fear of persecution arising from nationality, race, religion, membership of a particular social group, or political opinion. The European Parliament in 1984 determined that women facing cruel or inhuman treatment as a result of seeming to have transgressed social mores should be considered a particular social group for purposes of determining refugee status.

306. The Executive Committee of UNHCR has acknowledged that gender can be a factor in persecution on the basis of one of the five listed categories, and moreover, that women can in certain circumstances be considered to constitute a "particular social group". The Executive Committee of the High Commissioner's Programme, in Conclusion No. 39 on Refugee Women and International Protection (1985), recognized that States, in the exercise of their sovereignty, are free to adopt the interpretation that women asylum seekers who face harsh or inhumane treatment due to having transgressed the social mores of the society in which they live may be considered a "particular social group".

307. In addition to the 1951 Convention, women refugees are also protected by all international human rights instruments and mechanisms, and in particular the Convention on the Elimination of All Forms of Discrimination against Women, the Declaration on the Protection of Women and Children in Emergency and Armed Conflict, the International Covenants on Civil and Political Rights and on Economic, Social and Cultural Rights and, more generally, by the Universal Declaration of Human Rights. The Convention on the Rights of the Child also provides international protection for the human rights of girls.

308. National laws and policies in part determine what legal status an individual receives once she arrives in the country of asylum, where she will live and what assistance will be provided to her. It has been pointed out that assistance and protection is afforded to refugees presumptively in many developing countries, whereas extensive evidentiary hurdles need to be overcome in most industrialized countries.

309. Criminal acts of violence against refugee women are punishable under national laws. In part because of extensive international organization and non-governmental organization involvement in refugee situations, however, Governments have tended either to abdicate responsibility or to act in nominal and ineffective ways.

310. UNHCR notes that protection is at the heart of the problem faced by female refugees. The Special Rapporteur, therefore, puts forward the following steps which need to be taken in order to enhance protection from violence for these women and girls, both during flight and in the refugee camps.

(a) The security and design of refugee camps generally must be improved. Poorly lit camps, latrines at unsafe distances and lack of privacy all create tense and hostile living conditions for women.

(b) Trained female officers are vitally important at all points of the refugees' journey. Female officers should be deployed at border checkpoints and detention centres, as well as in the refugee camps. Women refugees, particularly those travelling alone, should not be left in custody without a female officer present.

(c) Women and girls need greater access to medical services and female doctors and nurses. Not only are women the main health care providers for other members of their families, but creating better access to health care will also help identify protection problems.

(d) Participation by refugee women in the organizational structures of the refugee camps has been an effective means of enhancing coping processes, promoting self-sufficiency and promoting protection. Women should be involved in food and supply distribution efforts, in the provision of health care services and in decisions on repatriation. In some situations UNHCR trains refugee women to act as counsellors in the handling of other rape victims. Additionally, programmes to teach income-generating skills should be implemented. Refugee women who have turned to prostitution note that other income-generating vocations are not open to them.

(e) All States should actively investigate and prosecute all Government and military personnel who are reported to have abused, either through physical or psychological duress, women and children refugees. States' indifference to the actions of their agents only perpetuates the imbalance already inherent in the refugee situation.

. (f) An agency similar in purpose to the UNHCR should be established for the protection of internally displaced people.

(g) The inclusion of gender-defined social groups should be recognized as falling within the definition of a "particular social group" as a legitimate group for purposes of establishing persecution.

(h) Refugee women and girls should be allowed to exercise choice as to where they will remain. There should be efficient procedures by which a woman feeling threatened in a given camp can be moved to a safer camp. Women and girl refugees should also be given a choice in the decision to repatriate or move to a second asylum country.

311. There is no international instrument specifically designed to address the needs of internally displaced persons. However, it should be emphasized that internally displaced women can avail themselves of the protections guaranteed in the international human rights instruments mentioned above. International humanitar-

ian law, namely the four Geneva Conventions of 1949 and the two Additional Protocols thereto of 1966, often also apply to the case of internally displaced persons since they provide legal protection in times of conflict or war.

312. Refugees may live for years, even lifetimes, away from their homes. The upheaval and constant uncertainty that invades their existence is made worse in the case of women and girls by the fact that, by virtue of their gender, they are often uniquely subject to highly traumatic sexual and violent abuse. States facing armed conflict within their borders must pay special attention to the particular needs of internally displaced women and girls. States who host refugee women and girls must extend to them non-discriminatory and vigilant protection.

313. The issue of violence against indigenous women and women who belong to a minority has emerged in many discussions at the national and international levels. These women are often subject to double discrimination as indigenous people or as belonging to minorities, as well as being women. Special programmes should be devised to assist these women in challenging this dual-edged violence which affects their lives.

V. Conclusions and preliminary recommendations

314. The Special Rapporteur has intended in this first report to provide a general overview of the issues relating to violence against women, including its causes and consequences. Subsequent reports will deal more specifically with the areas of violence in the family, violence in the community and violence by the State. These reports will contain detailed recommendations with regard to eliminating violence against women in these spheres.

315. As a preliminary measure at the national level, however, States could be called upon to meet their responsibilities contained in the Declaration on the Elimination of Violence against Women. More specifically, States should be called upon:

(a) To condemn violence against women and not invoke custom, tradition or religion to avoid their obligations to eliminate such violence;

(b) To ratify the Convention on the Elimination of All Forms of Discrimination against Women without reservation;

(c) To formulate national plans of action to combat violence against women;

(d) To initiate strategies to develop legal and administrative mechanisms to ensure effective justice for women victims of violence;

(e) To ensure the provision of specialized assistance for the support and rehabilitation of women victims of violence;

(f) To train and sensitize judicial and police officials with regard to issues concerning violence against women;

(g) To reform educational curricula so as to instil values which will prevent violence against women;

(h) To promote research with regard to the issues concerning violence against women;

(i) To ensure proper reporting of the problem of violence against women to international human rights mechanisms.

316. At the international level, the Special Rapporteur reiterates the call contained in the Vienna Declaration and Programme of Action to incorporate human rights and the equal status of women into the mainstream of United Nations action in the field of human rights and requests the Commission on Human Rights to make available the present report to the Fourth World Conference on Women, to be held in Beijing in 1995.

317. Finally, the Special Rapporteur encourages the formulation of an optional protocol to the Convention on the Elimination of All Forms of Discrimination against Women allowing for an individual right of petition once local remedies are exhausted. This will ensure that women victims of violence will have a final recourse under an international human rights instrument to have their rights established and vindicated.

Document 116

General Assembly resolution on implementation of the Nairobi Forward-looking Strategies

A/RES/49/161, 23 December 1994

[Editor's note: Since 1985, resolutions calling for the implementation of the Nairobi Forward-looking Strategies have been adopted each year by the General Assembly.]

The General Assembly,

Recalling all its relevant resolutions, in particular resolution 44/77 of 8 December 1989, in which, *inter alia*, it endorsed and reaffirmed the importance of the Nairobi Forward-looking Strategies for the Advancement of Women 1/ for the period up to the year 2000 and set out measures for their immediate implementation and for the overall achievement of the interrelated goals and objectives of the United Nations Decade for Women: Equality, Development and Peace,

Recalling also its resolutions 46/98 of 16 December 1991, 47/95 of 16 December 1992 and 48/108 of 20 December 1993,

Taking into consideration the resolutions adopted by the Economic and Social Council on issues relating to women since the adoption of its resolution 1987/18 of 26 May 1987,

Reaffirming its determination to encourage the full participation of women in economic, social, cultural, civil and political affairs and to promote development, cooperation and international peace,

Conscious of the important and constructive contribution to the improvement of the status of women made by the Commission on the Status of Women, the specialized agencies, the regional commissions and other organizations and bodies of the United Nations system and non-governmental organizations concerned,

Concerned that the resources available in the Secretariat to the programme on the advancement of women are insufficient to ensure adequate support to the Committee on the Elimination of Discrimination against Women and effective implementation of other aspects of the programme, especially the preparations for the Fourth World Conference on Women: Action for Equality, Development and Peace, to be held in 1995,

Taking into account Commission on the Status of Women resolutions 36/8 of 20 March 1992, 2/ 37/7 of 25 March 1993 3/ and 38/10 of 18 March 1994 4/ on the preparations for the Fourth World Conference on Women,

Bearing in mind the important role non-governmental organizations play in all activities for the advancement of women and the fact that some of them, especially those from developing countries, do not enjoy consultative status with the Economic and Social Council,

Noting with satisfaction that the preparations for the Fourth World Conference on Women have entered a substantive stage, that the relevant United Nations bodies, China, as the host country, and other countries all attach great importance to the preparations for the Conference and that the various preparatory activities are being conducted in an in-depth and comprehensive manner,

Considering that 1995 will be a year of crucial importance to the preparations for the Fourth World Conference on Women and that the Commission on the Status of Women will deliberate the content of the Platform for Action at its thirty-ninth session,

Welcoming the report of the Secretary-General 5/ containing the executive summary of the 1994 *World Survey on the Role of Women in Development,*

Expressing its satisfaction that the Programme of Action of the International Conference on Population and Development 6/ establishes that the empowerment of women is a key issue for the Fourth World Conference on Women,

Also expressing its satisfaction that the regional preparatory conferences for the Fourth World Conference on Women have produced plans or platforms for their regions, which provide useful inputs for the Platform for Action of the Conference,

1. *Takes note* of the report of the Secretary-General; 7/

2. *Reaffirms* section I, paragraph 2, of the recommendations and conclusions arising from the first review and appraisal of the implementation of the Nairobi Forward-looking Strategies for the Advancement of Women,

1/ *Report of the World Conference to Review and Appraise the Achievements of the United Nations Decade for Women: Equality, Development and Peace, Nairobi, 15-26 July 1985* (United Nations publication, Sales No. E.85.IV.10), chap. I, sect. A.

2/ See *Official Records of the Economic and Social Council, 1992, Supplement No. 4* (E/1992/24), chap. I, sect. C.

3/ Ibid., *1993, Supplement No. 7* (E/1993/27), chap. I, sect. C.

4/ Ibid., *1994, Supplement No. 7* (E/1994/27), chap. I, sect. C.

5/ A/49/378.

6/ *Report of the International Conference on Population and Development, Cairo, 5-13 September 1994* (A/CONF.171/13), chap. I, resolution 1, annex.

7/ A/49/349.

contained in the annex to Economic and Social Council resolution 1990/15 of 24 May 1990, which called for an improved pace in the implementation of the Forward-looking Strategies in the crucial last decade of the twentieth century, since the cost to societies of failing to implement them would be high in terms of slowed economic and social development, misuse of human resources and reduced progress for society as a whole;

3. *Urges* Governments, international organizations and non-governmental organizations to implement the recommendations;

4. *Calls again upon* Member States to give priority to policies and programmes relating to the sub-theme "Employment, health and education", in particular to literacy for self-reliance of women and the mobilization of indigenous resources, as well as to issues relating to the role of women in economic and political decision-making, population, the environment, information and science and technology;

5. *Reaffirms* the central role of the Commission on the Status of Women in matters related to the advancement of women, and calls upon it to continue promoting the implementation of the Forward-looking Strategies to the year 2000, based on the goals of the United Nations Decade for Women: Equality, Development and Peace and the sub-theme "Employment, health and education", and urges all relevant bodies of the United Nations system to cooperate effectively with the Commission in this task;

6. *Requests* the Commission, when considering the priority theme relating to development during its thirty-ninth session, to ensure its early contribution to the preparatory work for forthcoming major international conferences to be held in 1995, namely, the Fourth World Conference on Women: Action for Equality, Development and Peace and the World Summit for Social Development, and to address the impact of technologies on women;

7. *Also requests* the Commission to give special attention to women in developing countries, particularly in Africa and the least developed countries, who suffer disproportionately from the effects of the global economic crisis and the heavy external debt burden, and to recommend further measures for the equalization of opportunity and for the integration of the roles and perspective of women, as well as their needs, concerns and aspirations, into the entire development process when considering the priority theme of development;

8. *Emphasizes*, in the framework of the Forward-looking Strategies, the importance of the total integration of women of all ages in the development process, bearing in mind the specific and urgent needs of the developing countries, and calls upon Member States to establish specific targets at each level in order to increase the participation of women in professional, management and decision-making positions in the countries;

9. *Emphasizes once again* the need to give urgent attention to redressing socio-economic inequities at the national and international levels as a necessary step towards the full realization of the goals and objectives of the Forward-looking Strategies through meeting the practical and strategic needs of women;

10. *Strongly urges* that particular attention be given by the competent United Nations organizations and Governments to the special needs of women with disabilities, elderly women and also women in vulnerable situations such as migrant and refugee women and children;

11. *Urges* the international community and the competent United Nations bodies and organs to place more emphasis on the sharp increase in the incidence of poverty among rural women;

12. *Welcomes* the recommendations adopted at the United Nations Conference on Environment and Development on women, environment and development in all programme areas, in particular those set out in chapter 24 of Agenda 21, 8/ entitled "Global action for women towards sustainable and equitable development";

13. *Welcomes also* the recommendations of the International Conference on Population and Development regarding the advancement of women, contained in the Programme of Action of the Conference; 9/

14. *Urges* organs, organizations and bodies of the United Nations system to ensure the active participation of women in the planning and implementation of programmes for sustainable development, and requests Governments, in the context of General Assembly resolution 47/191 of 22 December 1992, to consider nominating women as representatives to the Commission on Sustainable Development;

15. *Requests* the Secretary-General, in formulating the system-wide medium-term plan for the advancement of women for the period 1996-2001 and in integrating the Forward-looking Strategies into activities mandated by the General Assembly, to pay particular attention to specific sectoral themes that cut across the three objectives, equality, development and peace, and to include, in particular, literacy, education, health, population, the impact of technology on the environment and its effect on women and the full participation of women in decision-making, and to continue to assist Governments in strengthening their national machineries for the advancement of women;

8/ *Report of the United Nations Conference on Environment and Development, Rio de Janeiro, 3-14 June 1992* (United Nations publication, Sales No. E.93.I.8 and corrigenda), vol. I: *Resolutions adopted by the Conference*, resolution 1, annex II.
9/ *Report of the International Conference on Population and Development, Cairo, 5-13 September 1994* (A/CONF.171/13), resolution 1, annex.

16. *Also requests* the Secretary-General to continue updating the *World Survey on the Role of Women in Development*, 10/ bearing in mind its importance, placing particular emphasis on the adverse impact of the difficult economic situation affecting the majority of developing countries, particularly on the condition of women, giving special attention to worsening conditions for the incorporation of women into the labour force, as well as the impact of reduced expenditures for social services on opportunities available to women for education, health and child care;

17. *Requests* Governments, when presenting candidatures for vacancies in the Secretariat, in particular at the decision-making level, to give priority to candidatures of women, and requests the Secretary-General in reviewing those candidatures to give special consideration to female candidates from underrepresented and unrepresented developing countries;

18. *Requests* the Secretary-General to invite Governments, organizations of the United Nations system, including the regional commissions and the specialized agencies, and intergovernmental and non-governmental organizations to report periodically to the Economic and Social Council, through the Commission on the Status of Women, on activities undertaken at all levels to implement the Forward-looking Strategies;

19. *Also requests* the Secretary-General to continue to provide for the existing weekly radio programmes on women in the regular budget of the United Nations, making adequate provisions for broadcasts in different languages, and to develop the focal point for issues relating to women in the Department of Public Information of the Secretariat, which, in concert with the Department for Policy Coordination and Sustainable Development, should provide a more effective public information programme relating to the advancement of women;

20. *Further requests* the Secretary-General to include in his report on the implementation of the Forward-looking Strategies, to be submitted to the General Assembly at its fiftieth session, an assessment of recent developments that are relevant to the priority themes to be considered at the subsequent session of the Commission and to transmit to the Commission a summary of relevant views expressed by delegations during the debate in the Assembly;

21. *Requests* the Commission to continue to examine the implications of the World Conference on Human Rights and the Vienna Declaration and Programme of Action 11/ adopted by the Conference for its central role in matters related to the rights of women within the United Nations system and to report to the Economic and Social Council at its substantive session of 1995;

22. *Requests* the Secretary-General to prepare a report for the Commission, for consideration at its thirty-ninth session, on steps to be taken by the Division for the Advancement of Women, in cooperation with other United Nations bodies, specifically the Centre for Human Rights of the Secretariat, to ensure that relevant human rights mechanisms of the United Nations, such as treaty-monitoring bodies, rapporteurs and working groups, regularly address violations of the rights of women, including gender-specific abuses;

23. *Recognizes* that the Declaration on the Elimination of Violence against Women, proclaimed by the General Assembly in its resolution 48/104 of 20 December 1993, is essential to the attainment of full respect for the rights of women and is an important contribution to efforts aimed at achieving the objectives of the Forward-looking Strategies by the year 2000;

24. *Expresses its satisfaction* for the smooth conclusion of the regional preparatory meetings, the results of which constitute important inputs to the Platform for Action, the final document of the Fourth World Conference on Women;

25. *Requests* the Secretary-General to give more support, from within existing resources, to the Division for the Advancement of Women, acting as secretariat of the Fourth World Conference on Women, by providing sufficient financial and human resources and giving wide publicity to the Conference and its preparatory activities;

26. *Appeals* to countries that have not done so to compile their national reports in earnest and to forward them in time to the secretariat of the Conference;

27. *Decides* that, in order to support developing countries, in particular the least developed among them, in participating fully and effectively in the Conference and its preparatory process, each least developed country, to the extent that extrabudgetary funds are available, may be provided from the trust fund established by the Secretary-General for the preparations for the Conference with travel expenses and, on an exceptional basis, daily subsistence allowance for representatives attending the thirty-ninth session of the Commission, which is the preparatory body for the Conference, and the Conference itself;

28. *Expresses its gratitude and appreciation* to the Governments, organizations and individuals that have already contributed to the Trust Fund for the Fourth World Conference on Women;

29. *Recommends* the further development of methods of compilation and data collection in areas of

10/ United Nations publication, Sales No. E.89.IV.2.
11/ *Report of the World Conference on Human Rights, Vienna, 14-25 June 1993* (A/CONF.157/24 (Part I)), chap. III.

concern identified by the Commission, and urges Member States to improve and broaden collection of gender-disaggregated statistical information and make it available to the relevant bodies of the United Nations system with a view to preparing, in all official languages, as a background document for the Fourth World Conference on Women, an updated edition of *The World's Women 1970-1990: Trends and Statistics*; 12/

30. *Endorses* the request by the Commission that the Secretary-General should include information on the decision-making position of women in public life and in the fields of science and technology in the preparation of the priority theme on peace, "Women in international decision-making", for the Commission at its thirty-ninth session, in 1995;

31. *Requests* the Secretary-General to make available for the Fourth World Conference on Women reports and decisions of the World Conference on Human Rights, the International Conference on Population and Development and the World Summit for Social Development;

32. *Emphasizes* that the success of the Fourth World Conference on Women will depend largely on the follow-up to the Conference;

33. *Invites* United Nations bodies and specialized agencies and other relevant intergovernmental organizations to consider making concrete commitments and specifying actions to meet the global priorities for the advancement of women by the year 2000 which will be reflected in the Platform for Action;

34. *Invites* Member States similarly to consider specific action which they could take in their own countries to bring about change by the year 2000;

35. *Decides*, taking into account Commission on the Status of Women resolution 38/10, to adopt the modalities for the participation in and contribution to the Fourth World Conference on Women and its preparatory process by non-governmental organizations, particularly those from the developing countries, set out in the annex to General Assembly resolution 48/108;

36. *Requests* the Secretary-General to prepare a report for the Fourth World Conference on Women, to be held at Beijing in 1995, on the extent to which gender concerns have been included in the activities of the relevant human rights mechanisms of the United Nations, such as treaty-monitoring bodies, rapporteurs and working groups;

37. *Requests* that the report of the Fourth World Conference on Women be submitted to the General Assembly at its fiftieth session for consideration and action;

38. *Requests* the Secretary-General to prepare for the consideration of the General Assembly at its fiftieth session a report on follow-up to the Fourth World Conference on Women, taking into consideration the recommendations made at the Conference;

39. *Also requests* the Secretary-General to report to the General Assembly at its fiftieth session on measures taken to implement the present resolution.

12/ United Nations publication, Sales No. E.90.XVII.3.

Document 117

General Assembly resolution calling attention to the concerns of older women in development policies and requesting that special attention be paid to discrimination against older women in the implementation of the Convention on the Elimination of All Forms of Discrimination against Women

A/RES/49/162, 23 December 1994

The General Assembly,

Recalling its resolution 44/76 of 8 December 1989, in which it pointed out that age segregation, in addition to sex stereotyping, makes the social and economic problems of elderly women even more acute, and that they are often viewed only as beneficiaries and not as contributors to development,

Also recalling its resolution 40/30 of 29 November 1985, in which it emphasized that the elderly must be

considered an important and necessary element in the development process at all levels within a given society,

Further recalling Commission on the Status of Women resolution 36/4 of 20 March 1992, 1/ in which the Commission emphasized the need to adopt an approach for the advancement of women that takes into

1/ See *Official Records of the Economic and Social Council, 1992, Supplement No. 4* (E/1992/24), chap. I, sect. C.

account all stages of life, so as to identify measures that respond to women's needs,

Calling attention to the urgent need to develop and improve the publication of statistics by sex and by age, and to identify and evaluate the different forms of activities of older women which are not normally recognized as having an economic value, in particular in the informal sectors,

Taking into consideration the proceedings of the International Symposium on Population Structure and Development, held at Tokyo in September 1987, which called attention to the fact that the United Nations had estimated that there were 208 million women aged 60 and above in 1985, of which about half lived in the developed and half in the developing world, and that by the year 2025 this number had been projected to increase to 604 million elderly women for the world as a whole, of which nearly 70 per cent would be living in the developing countries,

1. *Takes note with appreciation* of the joint publication of the International Research and Training Institute for the Advancement of Women and the Statistics Division of the United Nations Secretariat entitled *The Situation of Elderly Women: Available Statistics and Indicators* 2/ and encourages both organizations to continue their pioneering work in this field;

2. *Requests* the Committee on the Elimination of Discrimination against Women to pay particular attention to discrimination on grounds of age when evaluating national reports on the implementation of the Convention on the Elimination of All Forms of Discrimination against Women; 3/

3. *Invites* the competent organs of the United Nations to adopt an approach that, in all their strategies and programmes for the advancement of women, takes into account all stages of life;

4. *Invites* the international development agencies and organizations, including the United Nations Development Fund for Women and the United Nations Development Programme, to take account of the potential of elderly women as a human resource for development and to include older women in their development strategies and programmes, and encourages Governments to ensure the inclusion of women, regardless of age, in development projects covered by national and multilateral financial institutions;

5. *Invites* the Preparatory Committee for the World Summit for Social Development to ensure that older women's concerns and contributions to development are considered under the three main agenda items of the Summit: "Elimination of poverty", "Social integration" and "Employment";

6. *Urges* the Commission on the Status of Women, as the preparatory body for the Fourth World Conference on Women: Action for Equality, Development and Peace, to ensure that older women's concerns and contributions to development are recognized and incorporated into the strategies, programmes and policies of the Platform for Action which deal with equality, development and peace;

7. *Requests* the Secretary-General to report to the General Assembly at its fiftieth session on the implementation of the present resolution under the item entitled "Advancement of women".

2/ INSTRAW/SER.B/44.
3/ Resolution 34/180, annex.

Document 118

General Assembly resolution calling on States to ratify the Convention on the Elimination of All Forms of Discrimination against Women and urging compliance with the Convention

A/RES/49/164, 23 December 1994

The General Assembly,

Bearing in mind that one of the purposes of the United Nations, as stated in Articles 1 and 55 of the Charter, is to promote universal respect for human rights and fundamental freedoms for all without distinction of any kind, including distinction as to sex,

Affirming that women and men should participate equally in social, economic and political development, should contribute equally to such development and should share equally in improved conditions of life,

Recalling its resolution 34/180 of 18 December 1979, by which it adopted the Convention on the Elimination of All Forms of Discrimination against Women,

Recalling also its previous resolutions on the Convention, and taking note of Economic and Social Council resolution 1994/7 of 21 July 1994,

Welcoming the growing number of States parties to the Convention, which now stands at one hundred and thirty-four,

Noting with deep concern that the Convention is still one of the human rights instruments with a large number of reservations, many of which run contrary to the object and purpose of the Convention, despite the fact that some States parties have withdrawn their reservations to it,

Recalling the Vienna Declaration and Programme of Action 1/ adopted by the World Conference on Human Rights on 25 June 1993, in which the Conference stipulated that the human rights of women and the girl child were an inalienable, integral and indivisible part of universal human rights,

Recalling also that, in the Vienna Declaration and Programme of Action, the Conference recommended the adoption of new procedures to strengthen implementation of the commitment to women's equality and human rights, including a call upon the Commission on the Status of Women and the Committee on the Elimination of Discrimination against Women to examine quickly the possibility of introducing the right of petition through the preparation of an optional protocol to the Convention,

Taking note of the decision adopted at the Sixth Meeting of States Parties to the Convention, on 4 February 1992, 2/

Aware of the important contribution that the implementation of the Nairobi Forward-looking Strategies for the Advancement of Women 3/ can make to eliminating all forms of discrimination against women and to achieving legal and de facto equality between women and men,

Having considered the reports of the Committee on the Elimination of Discrimination against Women on its twelfth 4/ and thirteenth 5/ sessions,

Taking note of the suggestions and general recommendations made by the Committee in accordance with its mandate, as demonstrated most recently by the Committee at its thirteenth session, at which the Committee adopted suggestion No. 6 on the International Conference on Population and Development and general recommendation No. 21 related to articles 9, 15 and 16 of the Convention as its contribution to the International Year of the Family, as well as other general recommendations made by the Committee,

Noting that the workload of the Committee has increased because of the growing number of States parties to the Convention, that the annual session of the Committee is still the shortest of all the annual sessions of the human rights treaty bodies and that, in spite of the recommendation by the Economic and Social Council in its resolution 1992/17 of 30 July 1992, which was supported by the General Assembly in its resolution 47/94

of 16 December 1992, that three weeks be allowed for each session of the Committee to enable the Committee to consider the reports submitted by the States parties until the backlog in reports has been eliminated, a considerable backlog still remains,

Convinced of the need to adopt measures to enable the Committee to consider in a thorough and timely manner the reports submitted by States parties and to discharge all its responsibilities under the Convention,

Taking note of the report of the Secretary-General on the working methods of the Committee and its capacity to fulfil its mandate effectively, which included a comparison of other treaty bodies, 6/

Welcoming the efforts of the Committee to improve further its working methods by adopting concluding observations containing specific suggestions and recommendations,

Recalling that, under article 17, paragraph 9, of the Convention, the Secretary-General is required to provide the necessary staff and facilities for the effective performance of the functions of the Committee,

Recalling also its resolutions 44/73 of 8 December 1989, 45/124 of 14 December 1990 and 47/94 of 16 December 1992, in which, *inter alia*, it strongly supported the view of the Committee that the Secretary-General should accord higher priority to strengthening support for the Committee,

Strongly supporting general recommendation No. 19 of the Committee on violence against women, and calling upon States parties to prepare their periodic reports in accordance with this and other general recommendations of the Committee,

Noting with satisfaction the appointment of a Special Rapporteur of the Commission on Human Rights on violence against women, including its causes and consequences,

1. *Expresses its satisfaction* with the increasing number of States that have ratified or acceded to the Convention on the Elimination of All Forms of Discrimination against Women, and supports the general recommendation of the Committee on the Elimination of Discrimination against Women to draw attention to

---

1/ *Report of the World Conference on Human Rights, Vienna, 14-25 June 1993* (A/CONF.157/24 (Part I)), chap. III.

2/ *See* CEDAW/SP/1992/4.

3/ *Report of the World Conference to Review and Appraise the Achievements of the United Nations Decade for Women: Equality, Development and Peace, Nairobi, 15-26 July 1985* (United Nations publication, Sales No. E.85.IV.10), chap. I, sect. A.

4/ *Official Records of the General Assembly, Forty-eighth Session, Supplement No. 38* (A/48/38).

5/ Ibid., *Forty-ninth Session, Supplement No. 38* (A/49/38).

6/ A/49/308, sect. III.

those reservations which are incompatible with the objective and purpose of the Convention;

2. *Urges* all States that have not yet ratified or acceded to the Convention to do so as soon as possible;

3. *Emphasizes* the importance of the strictest compliance by States parties with their obligations under the Convention;

4. *Encourages* States to consider limiting the extent of any reservation they lodge to the Convention, to formulate any reservations as precisely and as narrowly as possible and to ensure that no reservation is incompatible with the object and purpose of the Convention or otherwise contrary to international law;

5. *Requests* States parties to the Convention to review their reservations regularly, with a view to withdrawing them expeditiously so that the Convention may be fully implemented;

6. *Takes note* of the report of the Secretary-General on the status of the Convention on the Elimination of All Forms of Discrimination against Women, 7/ and requests him to continue to report annually to the General Assembly;

7. *Takes note also* of the reports of the Committee on the Elimination of Discrimination against Women on its twelfth 8/ and thirteenth 9/ sessions;

8. *Recommends* that the States parties to the Convention, in the light of the reports mentioned in paragraphs 6 and 7 above, review the working situation of the Committee and its capacity to fulfil its mandate more effectively, and in this context also that the States parties consider the possibility of amending article 20 of the Convention so as to allow for sufficient meeting time for the Committee;

9. *Requests* the States parties to the Convention to meet in 1995 in order to consider the review of article 20 of the Convention mentioned in paragraph 8 above;

10. *Invites* States parties to the Convention to make all possible efforts to submit their initial as well as their second and subsequent periodic reports on the implementation of the Convention, in accordance with article 18 thereof and with the guidelines provided by the Committee, and to cooperate fully with the Committee in the presentation of their reports;

11. *Welcomes* the efforts made by the Committee to rationalize its procedures and expedite the consideration of periodic reports, and strongly encourages the Committee to continue those efforts;

12. *Welcomes also*, in accordance with general recommendation No. 11 of the Committee, 10/ the initiatives taken to provide regional training courses on the preparation and drafting of reports of States parties for government officials and training and information

seminars for States considering acceding to the Convention, and urges the relevant organs and organizations of the United Nations to support such initiatives;

13. *Requests* the Secretary-General to continue his efforts to provide secretariat staff, including legal staff members expert in human rights treaty implementation, and technical resources for the effective performance by the Committee of its functions;

14. *Strongly supports* the view of the Committee that the Secretary-General should accord higher priority, within existing resources, to strengthening technical and substantive support for the Committee, in particular to assist in preparatory research;

15. *Requests* the Secretary-General to continue to provide for, facilitate and encourage, within existing resources, the dissemination of information relating to the Committee, its decisions and recommendations, the Convention and the concept of legal literacy, taking into account the Committee's own recommendations to that end;

16. *Supports* the request of the Committee at its twelfth and thirteenth sessions for additional meeting time, with adequate support from the Secretariat, so as to allow for the Committee to meet once a year for three weeks for its fourteenth and fifteenth sessions, and recommends that the request made by the Committee for additional meeting time be considered within the existing level of budgetary resources;

17. *Requests* the Secretary-General to ensure adequate support to the Committee, and also requests that sufficient resources be provided for that purpose from within the existing regular budget to enable the Committee to deal in a thorough and timely manner with reports submitted by States parties;

18. *Decides* that, at its fifty-first session, it will review once again whether the backlog of the Committee in considering reports has been reduced;

19. *Recommends* that meetings of the Committee be scheduled, whenever possible, to allow for the timely transmission of the results of its work to the Commission on the Status of Women, for information, in the same year;

20. *Requests* the Secretary-General to submit to the General Assembly at its fifty-first session a report on the implementation of the present resolution and to make the report available to the Commission on the Status of Women at its forty-first session.

7/ 49/308, chap. II.
8/ *Official Records of the General Assembly, Forty-eighth Session, Supplement No. 38* (A/48/38).
9/ *Ibid., Forty-ninth Session, Supplement No. 38* (A/49/38).
10/ *Official Records of the General Assembly, Forty-fourth Session, Supplement No. 38* (A/44/38), sect. V.

Document 119

"Overview of the world's women in 1995", from The World's Women
1995: Trends and Statistics *(extract)*

ST/ESA/STAT/SER.K/12, 1995

Issues of gender equality are moving to the top of the global agenda but better understanding of women's and men's contributions to society is essential to speed the shift from agenda to policy to practice. Too often, women and men live in different worlds—worlds that differ in access to education and work opportunities, and in health, personal security and leisure time. *The World's Women 1995* provided information and analyses to highlight the economic, political and social differences that still separate women's and men's lives and how these differences are changing.

How different are these worlds? Anecdote and misperception abound, in large part because good information has been lacking. As a result, policy has been ill-informed, strategy unfounded and practice unquestioned. Fortunately, this is beginning to change. It is changing because advocates of women's interests have done much in the past 20 years to sharpen people's awareness of the importance of gender concerns. It is changing because this growing awareness has, by raising new questions and rephrasing old, greatly increased the demand for better statistics to inform and focus the debate. And it is changing because women's contributions—and women's rights—have moved to the centre of social and economic change.

The International Conference on Population and Development, held in Cairo in 1994, was a breakthrough. It established a new consensus on two fundamental points:

—Empowering women and improving their status are essential to realizing the full potential of economic, political and social development.

—Empowering women is an important end in itself. And as women acquire the same status, opportunities and social, economic and legal rights as men, as they acquire the right to reproductive health and the right to protection against gender-based violence, human well-being will be enhanced.

The International Conference on Population and Development drew together the many strands of thought and action initiated by two decades of women's conferences. It was also the culmination of an active effort by women's issues. At the United Nations Conference on Environment and Development in Rio de Janeiro in 1992, non-governmental organizations pushed for understanding the link between women's issues and sustainable development. At the World Conference on Human Rights in Vienna in 1993, women's rights were finally accepted as issues of international human rights.

At the Population Conference and later at the World Summit for Social Development, held in Copenhagen in 1995, the terms of discourse shifted. Not only were women on the agenda—women helped set the agenda. The empowerment of women was not merely the subject of special sessions about women's issues. It was accepted as a crucial element in any strategy seeking to solve social, economic and environmental problems. And building on the advances made in the recognition of women's human rights at the World Conference in Vienna, women's human rights became a focus of the debate in Cairo. The rights approach, advanced by women's groups, was added to the core objectives of development policy and the movement for women's equality.

To promote action on the new consensus, this second edition of *The World's Women* builds on the first, presenting statistical summaries of health, schooling, family life, work and public life. Each has to be seen in proper context, however. Yes, there have been important changes in the past 25 years and women have generally made steady progress, but is impossible to make sweeping global statements. Women's labour force participation rates are up in much of the world, but down in countries wracked by war and economic decline. Girl's education is improving, but there are hundreds of millions of illiterate women and girls who do not complete primary schooling, especially in Africa and southern Asia.

It is also important to look at a range of indicators. Women's political participation may be high in the Nordic countries, but in employment Nordic women still face considerable job segregation and wage discrimination. Women's higher education may be widespread in western Asia, but in many of those countries there are few or no women in important political positions and work opportunities are largely limited to unpaid family labour.

The World's Women presents few global figures, focusing instead on country data and regional averages (see the box on regional trends). There are myriad differences among countries in every field and *The World's Women* tries to find a meaningful balance between detailed country statements and broad generalization. Generalizations are primarily drawn at the regional and subregional levels where there is a high degree of uniformity among countries. For all the topics covered, *The World's Women* has tapped as many statistical sources as possible, with detailed references as a basis for further study. Specialized studies are used when they encompass several countries, preferably in more than one region, so as to avoid presenting conclusions relevant in only one country.

Indicators relevant to specific age groups are crucial to understanding women's situation. The Programme of Action of the International Conference on Population and Development identified equality for the girl-child as a necessary first step in ensuring that women realize their full potential and become equal partners with men. This edition of *The World's Women* responds to this concern by highlighting the experience of the girl-child. Evidence of prenatal sex selection and differences in mortality, health, school enrolment and even work indicates that girls and boys are not treated equally.

The experience of the elderly is more difficult to describe from the few available data. Although elderly people constitute a valuable component of societies' human resources, data on the elderly are insufficient for regional generalizations. Considering that the numbers of elderly are growing rapidly in all regions, this gap needs to be addressed.

Education for empowerment
In the Programme of Action of the International Conference on Population and Development, education is considered one of the most important means to empower women with the knowledge, skills and self-confidence necessary to participate fully in development processes. Educated women marry later, want fewer children, are more likely to use effective methods of contraception and have greater means to improve their economic livelihood.

Through widespread promotion of universal primary education, literacy rates for women have increased over the past few decades—to at least 75 per cent in most countries of Latin America and the Caribbean and eastern and south-eastern Asia. But high rates of illiteracy among women still prevail in much of Africa and in parts of Asia. And when illiteracy is high it almost always is accompanied by large differences in rates between women and men.

At intermediate levels of education, girls have made progress in their enrolment in school through the second level. The primary-secondary enrolment ratio is now about equal for girls and boys in the developed regions and Latin America and the Caribbean and is approaching near equality in eastern, south-eastern and western Asia. But progress in many countries was reversed in the 1980s, particularly among those experiencing problems of war, economic adjustment and declining international assistance—as in Africa, Latin America and the Caribbean, and eastern Europe.

In higher education enrolments, women equal or exceed men in many regions. They outnumber men in the developed regions outside western Europe, in Latin America and the Caribbean and western Asia. Women are not as well represented in other regions, and in sub-Saharan Africa and southern Asia they are far behind—30 and 38 women per 100 men.

The Framework for Action to implement the World Declaration on Education for All states that it is urgent to improve access to education for girls and women—and to remove every obstacle that hampers their active participation. Priority actions include eliminating the social and cultural barriers that discourage—or even exclude—girls and women from the benefits of regular education programmes.

Seeking influence
Despite progress in women's higher education, major obstacles still arise when women strive to translate their high-level education into social and economic advancement. In the world of business, for example, women rarely account for more than 1 or 2 per cent of top executive positions. In the more general category of administration and management including middle levels, women's share rose in every region but one between 1980 and 1990. Women's participation jumped from 16 to 33 per cent in developed regions outside Europe. In Latin America, it rose from 18 to 25 per cent.

In the health and teaching professions—two of the largest occupational fields requiring advanced training—women are well represented in many countries but usually at the bottom levels of the status and wage hierarchy. Similarly, among the staff of an international group of agriculture research institutes, women's participation at the non-scientific and trainee levels is moderate, but there are few women at management and senior scientific levels.

The information people receive through newspapers, radio and television shapes their opinions about the world. And the more decision-making positions women hold in the media, the more they can influence output—breaking stereotypes that hurt women, attracting greater attention to issues of equality in the home and in public life, and providing young women with new images, ideas and ideals. Women now make up more than half of the communications students in a large number of countries and are increasingly visible as presenters, announcers and reporters, but they remain poorly represented in the more influential media occupations such as programme managers and senior editors.

In the top levels of government, women's participation remains the exception. At the end of 1994 only 10 women were heads of state or government; of these 10 countries only Norway had as many as one third women

Regional trends

Latin America and the Caribbean

- Fertility has declined significantly—dropping 40 per cent or more over the past two decades in 13 of the region's 33 countries. The total fertility rate has fallen from 4.8 to 3.2. But adolescent fertility remains high—13 per cent of all births are to mothers below age 20. In Central America, 18 per cent are.

- Maternal mortality has declined in most countries of Latin America but the incidence of unsafe abortion in South America is the highest in the world.

- Literacy has reached 85 per cent or more across most of the region, and girls outnumber boys at both secondary and tertiary levels of education.

- Latin America's recorded labour force participation rate for women (34 per cent) is low, but in the Caribbean it is much higher (49 per cent).

- Latin America and the Caribbean are as urbanized as the developed regions, with 74 per cent of the population in urban areas. But the rate of growth is h 0.9 per cent—which strains housing, water and sanitation and other infrastructure.

Sub-Saharan Africa

- Minimal progress is seen in the basic social and economic indicators. Health and education gains have faltered in the face of economic crises and civil strife. Literacy remains the lowest in the world, 43 per cent of adult women and 67 per cent of adult men, and the difference between women's and men's literacy rates is the highest.

- Fertility is the highest in the world at about six children per woman.

- Women's labour force participation has dropped throughout the past two decades—the only region where this occurred.

- Urban areas are growing at a rate of 5 per cent a year, but with new housing and economic growth at a standstill, many live in poverty and squalor. Africa's urban migrants are predominantly male, shifting the sex ratio in rural areas to 106 women per 100 men.

- Estimated HIV infection rates continue to soar, and unlike any other region, the percentage of women infected with HIV is estimated to be as high if not higher than the percentage of men. In Uganda and in Zambia, the life expectancy of both women and men has already declined because of the disease, and eight other countries are beginning to see similar effects.

Northern Africa and western Asia

- In the past two decades, many countries in the region have invested in girls' education—bringing the primary-secondary enrolment ratio for girls to 67 in northern Africa (from 50 in 1970) and 84 in western Asia, and raising women's literacy to 44 per cent in the region. But women's illiteracy in northern Africa remains high, and girls' enrolment still lags behind boys'.

- Women are entering the labour force in increasing numbers—up from 8 per cent in 1970 to 21 in 1990 in northern Africa and from 22 to 30 per cent in western Asia. Still, these numbers are the lowest in the world. Also low is women's share of decision-making positions in government and business.

- Marriage among girls aged 15-19 has declined significantly in northern Africa and to a lesser degree in western Asia—from 38 per cent to 10 per cent in northern Africa and from 24 per cent to 17 per cent in western Asia. Teenage fertility, however, remains fairly high.

- Fertility—which was traditionally high—has declined significantly in the past 20 years, especially in northern Africa. It remains high (with total fertility rates over 5) in several countries in western Asia. These countries also have low female literacy.

Southern Asia

- Many health and education indicators remain low. Although it has risen by 10 years in the past two decades, life expectancy remains lower in southern Asia than in any other region but sub-Saharan Africa—58 for both women and men. Equal life expectancies are also exceptional—in all other regions, women have an advantage of several years.

ministers or subministers. Some progress has been made in the appointment of women to ministerial or subministerial positions but these positions are usually tenuous for them. Most countries with women in top ministerial positions do not have comparable representation at the subministerial level. And in other countries, where significant numbers of women have reached the subminis-terial levels, very few have reached the top. Progress for women in parliaments has also been mixed and varies widely among regions. It is strongest in northern Europe, where it appears to be rising steadily.

Missing from this summary is women's remarkable advance in less traditional paths to power and influence. The importance of the United Nations Decade for

- One in 35 women dies of pregnancy-related complications. Maternal mortality has declined but still remains high.
- Nearly two thirds of adult women are illiterate—and the percentage of girls enrolled in primary and secondary levels of schooling is far below all other regions except sub-Saharan Africa.
- Women continue to marry early—41 per cent of girls aged 15-19 are already married—and adolescent fertility remains high.
- More women are counted in the labour force but most are still relegated to unpaid family labour or low-paying jobs. Although women's representation at the highest levels of government is generally weakest in Asia, four of the world's 10 current women heads of state or government hold office in this region.

Eastern and south-eastern Asia

- Development indicators continue to improve. Infant mortality has declined significantly in south-eastern Asia in the past two decades.
- Literacy is nearly universal in most countries for men but not for women. However, girls and boys now have nearly equal access to primary and secondary education.
- Adolescent marriage rates in eastern Asia are the lowest in the world— only 2 per cent of women and less than 1 per cent of men aged 15-19 are married—and household size is shrinking.
- Eastern Asia reports the largest average decline in fertility, from 4.7 to 2.3, and its contraceptive use now exceeds that of developed regions. Fertility has also declined in south-eastern Asia, but is still generally higher than in eastern Asia.
- Women's participation in the labour force is as high as in developed regions—approximately 55 per cent.

Developed regions

- Basic health and education indicators generally indicate high levels of well-being but in eastern Europe some show signs of deterioration.

- Currently, women in 13 countries have a life expectancy of 80 years or more and 11 more countries are expected to reach that level after the year 2000. Men's life expectancy has increased little during the past two decades in eastern Europe, however, partly due to a rise in death rates for middle-aged men. Women's life expectancy in eastern Europe has increased much less than in other regions.
- Fertility continues to fall—from 2.3 in 1975 to 1.9 in 1995. But teenage pregnancy is relatively high in some countries—Bulgaria, the Republic of Moldova, Ukraine and the United States.
- Traditional family structure and size are changing. People are marrying later or not at all, and marriages are less stable. Remarriage rates have dropped—especially for women—and single parent families now make up 10-25 per cent of all families. The population is ageing and becoming increasingly female as it does.
- Women's labour force participation increased significantly for regions outside of eastern Europe from 38 per cent in 1970 to 52 per cent in 1990. In eastern Europe, where women's labour force participation was already 56 per cent in 1970, the increase was small (to 58 per cent).
- Women continue to earn less than men—in manufacturing, women's average wage is three quarters that of men's. And women and men tend to work in different jobs—women in clerical, sales and service, and men in production and transport. And men commonly do work which is accorded higher pay and status. For example, the majority of school administrators are men while most teachers are women, and the majority of hospital consultants are men while most nurses are women.
- Women work longer hours than men in the majority of these countries—at least 2 hours longer than men do in 13 out of 21 countries studied. Much of the unpaid work is done by women—for example, women contribute roughly three quarters of total child care at home.

Women and international women's conferences should not be underestimated, for these forums enabled women to develop the skills required for exercising power and influence, to mobilize resources and articulate issues and to practise organizing, lobbying and legislating. Excluded from most political offices, many women have found a voice in non-governmental organizations (NGOs) at the grass roots, national and international levels. NGOs have taken issues previously ignored—such as violence against women and rights to reproductive health—and brought them into the mainstream policy debate.

Since the women's conference in Nairobi in 1985, many grass-roots groups have been working to create new awareness of women's rights, including their rights within the family, and to help women achieve those rights. They have set agendas and carved out a space for women's issues. And as seen in recent United Nations conferences, NGOs as a group can wield influence broad enough to be active partners with governments in deciding national policies and programmes.

Reproductive health—reproductive freedom

With greater access to education, employment and contraception, many women are choosing to marry later and have fewer children. Those who wait to marry and begin child-bearing have better access to education and greater opportunities to improve their lives. Women's increased access to education, to employment and to contraception, coupled with declining rates of infant mortality, have contributed to the worldwide decline in fertility.

The number of children women bear in developed regions is now below replacement levels at 1.9 per woman. In Latin America and in most parts of Asia it has also dropped significantly. But in Africa women still have an average of six children and in many sub-Saharan African countries women have as many or more children now than they did 20 years ago.

Adolescent fertility has declined in many developing and developed countries over the past 20 years. In Central America and sub-Saharan Africa, however, rates are five to seven times higher than in developed regions. Inadequate nutrition, anaemia and early pregnancies threaten the health and life of young girls and adolescents.

Too many women lack access to reproductive health services. In developing countries maternal mortality is a leading cause of death for women of reproductive age. WHO estimates that more than half a million women die each year in childbirth and millions more develop pregnancy-related health complications. The deteriorating economic and health conditions in sub-Saharan Africa led to an increase in maternal mortality during the 1980s, where it remains the highest in the world. An African woman's lifetime risk of dying from pregnancy-related causes is 1 in 23, while a North American woman's is 1 in 4,000. Maternal mortality also increased in some countries of eastern Europe.

Pregnancy and childbirth have become safer for women in most of Asia and in parts of Latin America. In developed countries attended delivery is almost universal, but in developing countries only 55 per cent of births take place with a trained attendant and only 37 per cent in hospitals or clinics. Today new importance is being placed on women's reproductive health and safe motherhood as advocates work to redefine reproductive health as an issue of human rights.

The Programme of Action of the International Conference on Population and Development set forth a new framework to guide government actions in population, development and reproductive health—and to measure and evaluate programmes designed to realize these objectives. Instead of the traditional approach centred on family planning and population policy objectives, governments are encouraged to develop client-centred management information systems in population and development and particularly reproductive health, including family planning and sexual health programmes.

Fewer marriages—smaller households

Rapid population changes, combined with many other social and economic changes, are being accompanied by considerable changes in women's household and family status. Most people still marry but they marry later in life, especially women. In developing regions, consensual unions and other non-formal unions remain prevalent, especially in rural areas.

As a result of these changes, many women—many more women than men—spend a significant part of their life without a partner, with important consequences for their economic welfare and their children's.

In developed regions, marriage has become both less frequent and less stable, and cohabitation is on the rise. Marriages preceded by a period of cohabitation have clearly increased in many countries of northern Europe. And where divorce once led quickly to remarriage, many postpone marriage or never remarry.

Since men have higher rates of remarriage, marry at an older age, and have shorter life expectancy, most older men are married, while many older women are widows. Among women 60 and older, widowhood is significant everywhere—from 40 per cent in the developed regions and Latin America to 50 per cent in Africa and Asia. Moreover, in Asia and Africa, widowhood also affects many women at younger ages.

Between 1970 and 1990 household size decreased significantly in the developed regions, in Latin America and the Caribbean and in eastern and south-eastern Asia. Households are the smallest in developed regions, having declined to an average of 2.8 persons per household in 1990. In eastern Asia the average household size has declined to 3.7, in south-eastern Asia to 4.9. In Latin American countries the average fell to 4.7 persons per household, and in the Caribbean to 4.1. In northern African countries household size increased on average from 5.4 to 5.7.

In developed countries the decline in the average household size reflects an increase in the number of one-person households, especially among unmarried adults and the elderly. In developing regions the size of the household is more affected by the number of children, although a shift from extended households to nuclear households also has come effect. Household size remains high in countries where fertility has not yet fallen significantly—for instance, in some of the African and western Asian countries.

Work—paid and unpaid

Women's access to paid work is crucial to their self-reliance and the economic well-being of dependent family members. But access to such work is unequal between women and men. Women work in different occupations than men, almost always with lower status and pay.

In developing countries many women work as unpaid family labourers in subsistence agriculture and household enterprises. Many women also work in the informal sector, where their remuneration is unstable, and their access to funds to improve their productivity is limited at best. And whatever other work women do, they also have the major responsibility for most household work, including the care of children and other family members.

The work women do contributes substantially to the well-being of families, communities and nations. But work in the household—even when it is economic—is inadequately measured, and this subverts policies for the credit, income and security of women and their families.

Over the past two decades, women's reported economic activity rates increased in all regions except sub-Saharan Africa and eastern Asia, and all of these increases are large except in eastern Europe, central Asia and Oceania. In fact, women's labour force participation increased more in the 1980s than in the 1970s in many regions. In contrast, men's economic activity rates have declined everywhere except central Asia.

The decline in women's reported labour force participation in sub-Saharan Africa stands out as an exception—dropping from a high of 57 per cent in 1970 to 54 per cent in 1980 to 53 per cent in 1990.

In 1990 the average labour force participation rate among women aged 15 and over ranged from a high of 56-58 per cent in eastern and central Asia and eastern Europe to a low in northern Africa of 21 per cent. The participation rates of men vary within a more limited range of 72-83 per cent. Because so many women in developing countries work in agriculture and informal household enterprises where their contributions are underreported, their recorded rates of economic activity should be higher in many cases. The estimated increase in southern Asia—from 25 per cent of women economically active in 1970 to 44 per cent in 1990—may be due largely to changes in the statistical methods used rather than to significant changes in work patterns.

Although work in subsistence production is crucial to survival, it goes largely underreported in population and agricultural surveys and censures. Most of the food eaten in agricultural households in developing countries is produced within the family holding, much of it by women. Some data show the extent of women's unreported work in agriculture. In Bangladesh, India and Pakistan, government surveys using methods to improve the measurement of subsistence work report that more than half of rural women engage in such activities as tending poultry or cattle, planting rice, drying seeds, collecting water and preparing dung cakes for fuel. Direct observation of women's activities suggests that almost all women in rural areas contribute economically in one way or another.

The informal sector—working on own-account and is small family enterprises—also provides women with important opportunities in areas where salaried employment is closed or inadequate. In five of the six African countries studied by the Statistical Division of the United Nations Secretariat, more than one third of women economically active outside agriculture work in the informal sector, and in seven countries of Latin America 15-20 per cent. In nine countries in Asia the numbers vary—from less than 10 per cent of economically active women in western Asia to 41 per cent in the Republic of Korea and 65 per cent in Indonesia.

Although fewer women than men participate in the labour force, in some countries—including Honduras, Jamaica and Zambia—more women than men make up the informal sector labour force. In several other countries, women make up 40 per cent or more of the informal sector.

In addition to the invisibility of many of women's economic activities, women remain responsible for most housework, which also goes unmeasured by the System of National Accounts. But time-use data for many developed countries show almost everywhere that women work at least as many hours each week as men, and in large number of countries they work at least two hours more than men. Further, the daily time a man spends on work tends to be the same throughout his working life. But a woman's working time fluctuates widely and at times is extremely heavy—the result of combining paid work, household and child-care responsibilities.

Two thirds to three quarters of household work in developed regions is performed by women. In most countries studied, women spend 30 hours or more on housework each week while men spend around 10 hours. Among household tasks, the division of labour remains clear and definite in most countries. Few men do the laundry, clean the house, make the beds, iron the clothes. And most women do little household repair and maintenance. Even when employed outside the home, women do most of the housework.

Efforts to generate better statistics

The first world conference on women in Mexico in 1975 recognized the importance of improving statistics on women. Until the early 1980s women's advocates and women's offices were the main forces behind this work. Big efforts had not yet been launched in statistical offices—either nationally or internationally.

The collaboration of the Statistical Division of the United Nations Secretariat with the International Research and Training Institute for the Advancement of Women (INSTRAW)—beginning in 1982—on a training programme to promote dialogue and understanding between policy makers and statisticians laid the groundwork for a comprehensive programme of work.

By the time of the world conference in Nairobi in 1985 some progress was evident. The Statistical Division compiled 39 key statistical indicators on the situation of women for 172 countries, and important efforts at the national level included the preparation of *Women and Men in Sweden*, first published in 1984 and with sales of 100,000.

Since Nairobi numerous developments have strengthened and given new momentum to this work. The general approach in development strategy has moved from women in development to gender and development. The focus has shifted from women in isolation to women in relation to men—to the roles each has, the relationships between them and the different impacts of policies and programmes.

In statistics the focus has likewise moved from attention to women's statistics to gender statistics. There now is a recognition, for example, that biases in statistics apply not only to women but also to men in their roles in the household. That recognition reaches beyond the disaggregation of data by sex to assessing statistical systems in terms of gender. It asks:

—Do the topics investigated on statistics and the concepts and definitions used in data collection reflect the diversities of women's and men's lives?

—Will the methods used in collecting data take into account stereotypes and cultural factors that might produce bias?

—Are the ways data are compiled and presented well suited to the needs of policy makers, planners and others who need such data?

The first *World's Women: Trends and Statistics*, issued in 1991, presented the most comprehensive and authoritative compilation of global indicators on the status of women ever available. The book's data have informed debates at international conferences and national policy meetings and provided a resource to the press and others. Its publication greatly contributed to the understanding of data users and created, for the first time, a substantial global audience for statistical gender-based information. This audience has demanded, in turn, more and better data. The book also stimulated more work on the compilation of statistics and led to *The World's Women 1995* being prepared as an official conference document for the Fourth World Conference on Women in Beijing in 1995.

As gender issues receive greater priority in the work programmes of international organizations, support to the Statistical Division of the United Nations Secretariat and to national efforts to improve this work have gathered strength at UNFPA, UNICEF, UNDP, WFP, UNIFEM and INSTRAW, among others. ILO, FAO, WHO, UNESCO and UNHCR are also rethinking statistical recommendations and guidelines in their work to better understand women's activities and situations, and products of this change are evident in *The World's Women 1995*.

The World's Women 1995 shows considerable development in the statistics available on women and men—and in ways of presenting them effectively. But it also points to important needs for new work—to be addressed in the Platform for Action of the Fourth World Conference on Women. Some problems identified by the first world conference—such as the measurement of women's economic contribution and the definition of the concepts of household and household head—are still unresolved. But significant improvements have been made in many areas. Data users know much more today than 20 years ago about how women's and men's situations differ in social, political and economic life. And consumers of data are also asking many more questions that are increasing the demand for more refined statistics. Still other areas not commonly addressed in the regular production of official statistics have only begun to be explored: the male role in the family, women in poverty and women's human rights, including violence against women.

Important in today's more in-depth approach are:

—Identification of the data needed to understand the disparities in the situation, contributions and problems of women and men.

—Evaluation of existing concepts and methods against today's changed realities.

—Development of new concepts and methods to yield unbiased data.

—The preparation of statistics in formats easily accessible to a wide array of users.

None of this is easy—or without cost. Every step requires considerable effort and expertise. All require integrated approaches that pull together today's often fragmented, specialized efforts and take a fresh look at methods and priorities—in, say, education, employment, criminal justice, business, credit and training. All require a broader, more integrated treatment of social and economic data. And all require special efforts to improve international comparability. But required above all—for true national, regional and global assessments of the social, political and economic lives of women and men—is agreement on what the key issues are and support for how to address them.

The objective is always to produce timely statistics on women and men that can inform policy, refine strategy and influence practice. After two decades of efforts, improved gender statistics are doing much to inform policy debate and implementation. But to provide truly effective monitoring at all levels requires continuity and reinforcing the dialogue between statisticians and the consumers of statistics—policy makers, researchers, advocates and the media.

...

Document 120

Overview of the report of the Secretary-General to the CSW on the second review and appraisal of the implementation of the Nairobi Forward-looking Strategies for the Advancement of Women (extract)

E/CN.6/1995/3, 10 January 1995, and E/CN.6/1995/3/Add.1, 24 February 1995

I. Overview of the global economic and social framework

1. Since the adoption in 1985 of the Nairobi Forward-looking Strategies for the Advancement of Women, 1/ the world has experienced far-reaching economic, political and social changes. In response to the economic crisis of the 1980s, greater emphasis was placed on policies of structural adjustment, economic liberalization and improved governance. These policies, together with the expansion of the world trade and international financial markets and with rapid technological innovation, strengthened long-term trends towards globalization, integration of markets and internationalization of production. As a consequence of these trends, the world economy became more interdependent and thus more vulnerable to economic and political upheavals as national economic policies acquired widespread international ramifications. Together, these changes led to economic restructuring that has shaped the development process in recent years and has had a significant impact—both positive and negative—on women's participation in development and on their economic, political and social status.

2. Perceptions of the meaning, causes and conditions of development have been significantly modified. The development debate now emphasizes sustainability and human-centred and gender-responsive development. In parallel with the evolution of the development debate there have been changes in the perception and content of what are known as Women in Development issues. The role of women in development is no longer perceived as almost exclusively linked with broad issues of public health and population policies such as nutrition, child-rearing and family planning; women are now recognized as agents of change, as an economic force in themselves and as a valuable resource without which progress in development would be limited. While there have been many global changes over the past decade, the most dramatic for the lives of most individual women have been the changes in the economy.

3. A number of shifts in economic activity have come to be understood as resulting from the interaction between the allocation by women of their time and incomes and economic variables that include prices, consumption patterns and production techniques. Women's actions in the economic sphere have come to be viewed as actively shaping economic development and not merely being influenced by it. Consequently, within the Women in Development agenda there has been a shift towards greater emphasis on economic growth, sound economic policies and productive employment as the areas of prime concern for the economic advancement of women.

4. More often than not, the economic reforms of the past decade were part of something larger than the simple restructuring of an economic domain. In many developing economies and economies in transition, economic reforms were part of a movement towards greater democracy, freedom and human rights. Precipitated to some extent by failures in economic development caused by extensive governmental intervention in resource allocation and production decision-making, the rapid process of democratization led to new opportunities as well as to new obstacles for women's advancement.

1/ *Report of the World Conference to Review and Appraise the Achievements of the United Nations Decade for Women: Equality, Development and Peace, Nairobi, 15-26 July 1985* (United Nations publication, Sales No. E.85.IV.10), chap. I, sect. A.

5. While providing genuine opportunities for women in transitional and developing economies to participate in the political, economic and social life of their societies on an equal footing with men, democratization unleashed a variety of competitive claims on economic resources and on the political agenda by different political, ethnic, cultural and religious groups. The absence of democratic institutions and the other elements of civil society that serve to separate conflicting interests and turn the power struggle into a truly democratic process for all led, at least initially, to the marginalization of vulnerable groups that lacked a sufficient economic and political power base.

6. These changes have been found in all regions but have been particularly marked in terms of the situation of women in Eastern Europe, the Commonwealth of Independent States the Baltic States and other transitional States whose economies have deteriorated, especially in terms of ability to influence the process of economic and political decision-making. There, the general absence of the necessary civil institutions, an effective women's movement and of formal women's organizations capable of articulating women's interests and fighting for them in the competitive free-market environment led, at least during the first years of reform, to the exclusion of women from full participation in economic and political decision-making and to a loss of equality in terms of economic opportunities and advancement.

7. Changes in the work and lives of women all over the world are intricately related to changes in the global economic, social and political environment and to policy responses made within that framework. The traditional division of labour, differential access to factors of production and differences in the consumption patterns of men and women cause apparently gender-neutral policies to have a gender-specific outcome. Numerous studies show that the short-term costs of adjustment and stabilization are often distributed disproportionately so that women come to bear a greater share of the burden. On the other hand, there is evidence of a strong relationship between economic growth and the economic advancement of women. 2/ International economic conditions therefore form a backdrop against which the progress made in the implementation of the Nairobi Forward-looking Strategies for the Advancement of Women should be assessed.

A. *Trends in the global economy and in economic restructuring as they relate to the advancement of women*

8. Three interrelated sets of phenomena have shaped the world economy in the recent past and will continue to do so in the foreseeable future. They include:

(a) The various responses to the economic and political crisis of the 1980s (structural adjustment in developing countries, industrial restructuring and the change of emphasis in macroeconomic policy-making in the developed market economies and economic and political transition in the economies in the former USSR and Eastern Europe);

(b) Rapid technological innovation and its implications for the organization of work and for income distribution;

(c) Growing economic interdependence and globalization of markets and production.

Together, these phenomena comprised what was termed a process of economic restructuring. This process affected women's socio-economic position in a complex and multidimensional way, causing changes in the level, patterns and conditions of female employment and modifying women's social roles.

1. *Developing countries: structural adjustment and its impact on women*

9. The world recession profoundly affected the majority of developing countries, particularly in Africa, Latin America and the Caribbean, and the Middle East. Those in Asia as a whole proved more resilient, though here, too, individual countries, such as the Philippines, were adversely affected by external shocks and global developments. Reduced demand for primary products, falling commodity prices, high and rising interest rates, the virtual disappearance after 1982 of private bank lending, and, in the case of the Middle East, the collapse of the regional oil economy in the mid-1980s all contributed to a steady worsening of the balance of payments and the virtual doubling of the external debt burden in the period 1983-1993. For the most part, the response of the developing countries has been to institute programmes of stabilization and structural adjustment designed to bring their economies into line with the new realities of the international marketplace and undertaken, more often than not, under the auspices of the international financial institutions.

10. In the past decade a large number of developing countries went through the experience of structural adjustment. In fact, the decade came to be known as the "decade of structural adjustment" as the World Bank made 59 adjustment loans between 1980 and 1988 3/ to assist countries with protracted balance-of-payments problems to stabilize their economies and correct distortions causing inefficiency. Policies were thus directed

2/ See the discussion in *Women in the World Economy: the 1994 World Survey on the Role of Women in Development.*

3/ F. Nixson, "The third world and the global economy: recent trends and future prospects", *Developments in Economics:*

towards allocative efficiency, international competitiveness, market deregulation, "getting prices right", reduction of budget deficits and control of inflation. In the developing countries these policies were employed within the context of structural adjustment, which came to be viewed not only as a response to economic disequilibria but also as a prerequisite for long-term sustainable development. The divergence in economic performance among regions at the end of the decade reflected the varied experience of structural adjustment programmes. In some countries, the reform programme resulted in the resumption of growth, while in others political tensions and the erosion of human capital have hampered growth and decreased the production base. In recent years, some critics have argued that structural adjustment policies have not incorporated country- and gender-specific issues sufficiently.

11. While structural adjustment policies have been gender-neutral in design and implementation, it is now widely recognized that the social and economic inequalities of women in many countries have rendered them specially vulnerable to the effects of structural adjustment. However, this recognition has yet to be translated into gender-sensitive development planning. Methodological and theoretical difficulties, together with a lack of proper gender-disaggregated time-series data on the impact on women of structural adjustment, preclude any in-depth empirical assessment of the gender-related aspects. A significant body of analysis nevertheless exists and is based on inferences from the effects of economic policies on main macroeconomic aggregates and a priori knowledge of differences in the ways women and men allocate their labour and income and of differences in their access to productive resources and public services. The uneven distribution of the short-term costs of structural adjustment between men and women is particularly evident with respect to decline in real income, loss of employment opportunities, deterioration of employment conditions and exacerbation of pressures related to reproduction and maintenance of human resources in the context of lagged supply response, rising prices and cut-offs in public expenditure.

12. The structural adjustment policies of the 1980s lacked gender awareness both at the conceptual level and in implementation. The underlying macroeconomic model did not take account of the fact that women are often unable to respond adequately to the opportunities presented in the context of expenditure-switching policies and to changes in relative prices and the incentives resulting from them for the reallocation of resources, because of persisting inequalities in gender relations and constraints posed by the sexual division of labour. Some analysts suggest that the social costs of adjustment have been shifted from the State to the household and to women in the household. As a result, structural adjustment policies in the 1980s were less efficient in the reallocation of female than of male labour, and less sustainable than they could have been if gender issues were taken into account. Economic development theory and planning have not yet addressed this problem fully.

13. However, should the emphasis on human investment that is being written into the third generation of structural adjustment packages continue, women could benefit from this new departure. 4/ This, however, requires a conscious effort on the part of national and international policy makers to write a gender dimension into all projects and programmes, as much at the formulation stage as at the implementation level.

(a) *Latin America and the Caribbean*

14. Structural adjustment has been particularly intense in the economies of Latin America, where external indebtedness aggravated by falling commodity prices and increased interest rates caused a deep recession throughout the 1980s. The average annual growth rate of GDP in Latin America and the Caribbean in the 1980s was only 1 per cent as against 5.5 per cent in the 1970s. 5/ The decade was indeed "lost" for development as the annual average change in per capita GDP reached -0.1 per cent after having been at 2.0 per cent during the preceding decade 6/ (table 1). These changes were accompanied by worsening of income distribution which is now more inequitable in Latin America and the Caribbean than anywhere else in the world. 7/

15. In the Latin American region, the adjustment process was both recessionary and regressive, and this was reflected above all in real wages and in employment. Thus, serious problems and difficulties remain, most obviously in the form of persistently high rates of poverty, the inequitable income distribution and, quite often, a deterioration in the provision of social services, which not only renders current democratic processes fragile, but

4/ Since early 1994, the International Monetary Fund has placed greater emphasis on social sector policies. Recognizing the important developmental gains from improving the status and quality of life of women, in the context of both programmes and the policy dialogue with member Governments the Fund has underscored the importance of improving women's access to education, health care, and family planning. The Fund is exploring, in close consultation with the Bank, the modalities of providing gender-sensitivity training for Fund staff, in order to enhance their effectiveness in both the design of adjustment programmes and the provision of technical assistance.

5/ *World Economic Survey, 1990* (United Nations publication, Sales No. E.90.II.C.1), p. 3.

6/ *World Economic Survey, 1993* (United Nations publication, Sales No. E.93.II.C.1), p. 209.

7/ ECLAC, *Panorama social de America Latina y el Caribe*, 1993 ed. (Santiago, 1993).

Table 1. *Growth of world output and per capita GDP, 1971-1994*
(annual average percentage changes)

	Growth of GDP (annual rates)						Growth of real GDP per capita (annual percentage change)	
	1971-1980	1981-1990	1991	1992	1993	1994	1974-1983	1984-1993
World	3.9	2.9	0.3	0.8	1.1	2.5		
Developed market economies	3.1	2.6	0.7	1.6	1.0	2.5	2.3	2.1
Economies in transition	5.2	2.5	-9.0	-16.8	-10.0	-6.0	..	-2.9
Developing economies	5.6	3.2	3.4	4.9	5.2	5.0	1.8	1.9
Latin America and Caribbean	5.5	1.0	2.8	2.1	3.3	2.7	0.9	0.5
Africa	4.9	0.5	1.6	0.9	1.7	2.2	0.7	-1.1
West Asia	6.5	-0.2	-0.2	5.7	3.5	3.5	-1.8	-2.9
South and East Asia	5.8	7.0	5.3	5.2	5.4	6.2	3.5	3.8
China	5.9	9.0	8.0	13.2	13.4	10.0	4.9	8.4
Mediterranean	5.3	3.2	-5.6	-1.9	-0.3	4.0	2.2	-0.9

Source: *World Economic Survey, 1990* and *1993* (United Nations publications, Sales Nos. E.90.II.C.1 and E.91.II.C.1); *World Economic and Social Survey, 1994* (United Nations publication, Sales No. E.94.II.C.1). Forecast is based on Project LINK. Estimates are rounded to the nearest half percentage point. Growth of world output, 1971-1994, and per capita GDP, by country groups.

also calls into question the sustainability and indeed the very nature of the economic recovery so far achieved. In addition, only a handful of countries have managed to fully consolidate the adjustment and stabilization policies undertaken, and the process is marked by many interruptions. 8/

16. The impact of the debt problem and the structural adjustment programmes has been especially severe in the Caribbean countries, with direct consequences for women's unpaid work, migration, human rights violations, domestic violence, sexual exploitation and availability of and access to health services. As for the particular case of Haiti, it was said that the difficulties were so extreme that they went beyond the parameters of the situation in the rest of Latin America and the Caribbean. 9/

17. The growth of the informal sector was the main variable in the readjustment of the Latin American labour market in the early 1980s. The rise in unemployment and informality was accompanied by massive declines in wage and a sharp rise in the precariousness of employment. Temporary and part-time work became increasingly widespread, while the overall quality of employment declined. Aside from the difficulty of measuring female participation in the informal and precarious sector, it can be said that the poorest women workers are to be found in the urban informal sector and that, if domestic employment is added, women's participation is above 70 per cent in most cases. Information on some countries of the region, based on household surveys, shows that women account for between 8 per cent (Panama) and 64 per cent (Cochabamba, Bolivia) of the informal sector workforce. 10/

8/ ECLAC, "Women in Latin America and the Caribbean in the 1990s: diagnostic elements and proposals" (LC/L.836; CRM.6/4).

9/ ECLAC, "Report of the Regional Conference on the Integration of Women into the Economic and Social Development of Latin America and the Caribbean, Mar del Plata, Argentina, 25-29 September 1994" (PLE/2/Rev.1).

10/ ECLAC, 1994. "Women and urban employment in Latin America: the significance of changes in the 1990s" (DDR/3). See also M. Pollack, "Feminization of the informal sector in Latin America and the Caribbean?" *Mujer y Desarrollo*, No. 11 (LC/L.731).

(b) *Sub-Saharan Africa*

18. In Africa, particularly sub-Saharan Africa, economic conditions remain bleak, despite some modest improvement in current growth. Economic decline hit bottom in the mid-1980s when even nominal GDP growth rates turned negative. 11/ Out of the region's 45 countries, 28 suffered a decline in real GDP per capita. The decade of 1990s started with a minor improvement as growth in 1993 picked up to 1.7 per cent, which is still, however, well below the average annual population growth rate of 2.9 per cent for the period of 1985-1990. There has also been some modest improvement in sub-Saharan Africa's terms of trade, which suffered a decline during the 1980s and the early 1990s.

Table 2. *Sub-Saharan Africa: selected economic and development indicators, 1980 and 1990*

	1980	1990	Percentage change
Per capita GNP	582	335	-42.4
Per capita consumption	465	279	-40.0
Investment (percentage of GDP)	20.2	14.2	-29.7
Exports of goods	54.9	38.5	-29.9
Total external debt	56.2	146.9	161.4
Per capita food production index	107	94	-12.1
Memo item: Women in labour force	39.3	37.6	-4.3

Source: *African Development Indicators* (Washington, D.C., World Bank, 1992).

19. Poverty and deprivation in sub-Saharan Africa continue to deepen. A regional classification by integrated poverty index 12/ reveals that 36 out of the 45 countries in sub-Saharan Africa were in the severe poverty group. 13/ The situation has been aggravated by civil conflicts, 14/ which have destroyed physical capital, institutions and infrastructure in at least eight countries. 15/ To make matters worse, the region has been hit hard by the AIDS epidemic, which is inflicting high costs on the economy and society through its adverse effects on productivity and savings. Africa is home to 50 per cent of all HIV-infected people and the proportion of women among AIDS victims in Africa is larger than in North America and Europe and continues to grow. 16/

20. Despite the resumption in the early 1990s of the inflow of capital to developing economies, Africa remains excluded from access to international financial resources. In conjunction with the terms-of-trade decline,

the persistently negative net financial resources transfer to Africa led to a significant worsening of external balances in African and particularly sub-Saharan economies. In addition, official development assistance may not be as forthcoming as it was in the 1980s because of greater demands on it around the world and the shrinking supply of resources. There is therefore a considerable risk that the inflow of resources to the African region will be inadequate in comparison to its development needs and the restoration of economic stability. This will, of course, have serious consequences for investment and growth in the region.

21. General economic decline, deindustrialization and political instability in Africa have inhibited the implementation of the Nairobi Forward-looking Strategies in that region. Government expenditure cuts have led to widespread layoffs in public-sector enterprises. Employment in the private sector is also in decline as a result of aggregate demand deflation caused by stabilization and adjustment policies. The urban unemployment rate is currently between 15 and 20 per cent, up from 10 per cent in the 1970s. Women, although a minority in the public sector, 17/ appear to have fared worse than men as a result of public sector retrenchment. In Benin, for example, women's share in parastatal employment was only 6 per cent, but their share among workers laid off was 21 per cent. 18/

22. Women in Africa have long been concentrated in the informal sector in such activities as petty trade, small-scale production and personal services. Despite the widespread perception of the informal sector as infinitely elastic with respect to the absorption of female labour, recent figures indicate the opposite. Table 3 shows that

11/ "Population distribution and migration. Proceedings of the United Nations Expert Meeting on Population Distribution and Migration, Santa Cruz, Bolivia, 18-22 January 1993" (ESA/P/WP.12).

12/ The Integrated Poverty Index is calculated by combining the head-count measure of poverty and the income-gap ratio, income distribution below the poverty line and the annual rate of growth per capital GNP.

13/ I. Jazairy, M. Alamgir and T. Panuccio, *The State of World Rural Poverty. An Introduction into its Causes and Consequences* (New York, New York University Press, 1992).

14/ Civil strife in Algeria, Burundi, Kenya, Liberia, Rwanda, Sierra Leone, Sudan and Zaire and the civil war in Angola reduced or brought to a halt economic activities, displaced population, destroyed infrastructure and precluded economic reforms.

15/ *Global Economic Prospects and the Developing Countries* (World Bank, Washington, D.C., 1994).

16/ *Report on the World Social Situation, 1993* (United Nations publication, Sales No. E.93.IV.2), p. 39.

17/ G. Standing, "Feminization through flexible labour", *World Development*, vol. 17, No. 7 (July 1989).

18/ V. Moghadam, "An overview of global employment and unemployment in a gender perspective" (UNU/WIDER, 1994).

the percentage share of women in the informal sector in selected sub-Saharan African countries declined between 1985 and 1990. In 1990 the share of women in the informal sector in these countries was lower than it had been in the 1970s in all but two countries. That the female share of informal-sector employment declined despite the increase in the supply of female labour brought about by the "added worker" 19/ effect of structural adjustment indicates that women may have encountered difficulties in entering the sector that had traditionally provided them with income-earning opportunities. One explanation might be competition from the men who lost their jobs in the public sector as a result of structural adjustment policies. In most African countries men predominate in public-sector employment and consequently constitute the majority of redundant workers when public expenditures are contracted under policies of structural adjustment. They are better equipped with capital and business contacts, and their entry into the sector may have driven women's businesses out. On the other hand, informal-sector employment is by definition very difficult to measure. Given the low unemployment figures for women in the region and the fact that poor women in Africa simply cannot afford to be unemployed, the declining rates of informal-sector participation may mean greater precariousness for sources of women's income as they resort to informal survival responses at times of economic hardship.

23. The most likely explanation of the declining share of women in the informal sector, however, is the overall economic decline of sub-Saharan Africa. Reduction in real income and contraction of aggregate demand has caused a decline in demand for informal-sector goods and services. The shortage of investable funds and the high cost of credit have not been conducive to the sector's expansion and are likely to drive a number of informal entrepreneurs out of business. Poor access to credit and labour crowding have made women entrepreneurs particularly vulnerable to the decline in informal-sector earnings and loss of business. Despite the limited counteracting influence of the substitution effect (i.e., the increase in demand for the cheaper goods and services of the informal sector owing to the downward pressure on income), the information available (table 3) seems to suggest that the net effect on women's business in the informal sector was that of contraction.

(c) *Asia and the Pacific*

24. During the recession of the 1980s and early 1990s, the economies of East Asia as a whole proved relatively more resilient to the worsening of the external economic environment largely because of greater outward orientation of economic policies and greater diver-

sification of the production base. The economies of the region grew on average by 7 per cent annually during the 1980s and have maintained over 5 per cent growth since the beginning of the current decade. Economic performance has, however, varied from 1.7 per cent growth in the Philippines to 8 per cent growth in Malaysia, Singapore, Thailand and Viet Nam. 20/ There has been a notable decline in the dependency of economic growth in the region on the performance of the developed market economies; as intraregional trade has been growing faster than the total trade of these economies, the structure of their exports has continued to veer towards manufactures and the inflow of external capital has increased. The economies of East Asia are likely to remain the fastest growing in the 1990s, but rates of growth are expected to slow down as they begin to run into infrastructure and environmental constraints.

25. The South Asian economies grew on average by 5 per cent annually during the 1980s. Unlike growth in the rest of the developing world, this was an improvement over the preceding decade. Faced with external financial crises, major economies in the region embarked on structural adjustment and stabilization policies. Future prospects for growth depend on the maintenance and consistency of these reforms. The inward looking import-substitution policies followed by the economies of the region for decades led to the inhibition of factor-market flexibility and, in some cases, to the loss of economic stability. The region continues to be home to the majority of the world's poor. In 1990 the proportion of the population of South Asia whose income and consumption fell below the nationally defined poverty line was 49 per cent. 21/ Most of the region's poor are concentrated in the rural areas, and poverty among women is on the rise. 22/

26. In the 1980s widespread poverty and unemployment 23/ in the countries of South and South-

19/ The effects of structural adjustment on women are often described in terms of "added worker effect" and the "discouraged worker effect". The "added worker effect" is increase in the supply of female labour in response to a decline in household income. The "discouraged worker effect" results from the decline in employment opportunities.

20/ *World Economic and Social Survey, 1994* (United Nations publication, Sales No. E.94.II.C.1).

21/ *World Development Report, 1992. Development and Environment* (New York, Oxford University Press, 1992).

22/ I. Jazairy, M. Alamgir and T. Panuccio, *op. cit.*, p. 84.

23/ In Sri Lanka and the Philippines, for example, the rates of unemployment among women have been higher than among men throughout the period since the Nairobi Conference. (See "Review and appraisal of the implementation of the Nairobi Forward-looking Strategies for the Advancement of Women" (E/ESCAP/RUD/SOCWD/1).)

Table 3. *Female share of employment in the informal sector, 1970-1990*

Country	1970	1980	1985	1990
Congo	26.7	26.9	26.8	24.6
Ghana	32.0	32.0	32.0	27.3
Guinea	31.9	32.0	32.0	26.8
Liberia	42.8	43.2	43.0	39.3
Madagascar	33.3	33.1	32.8	29.0
Kenya	31.3	31.0	31.1	36.7
Nigeria	29.8	30.0	30.0	25.9
Somalia	32.1	31.9	32.0	34.6
Togo	38.6	39.0	39.0	32.2
United Republic of Tanzania	30.3	30.0	30.0	28.4
Zaire	37.3	37.0	37.0	24.9

Source: *African Employment Report* (ILO, Geneva, 1990). Cited in S. Baden, "The impact of recession and structural adjustment on women in developing countries", ILO paper, December 1993.

Table 4. *Advancement of women in Asia and the Pacific: selected indicators, 1970-1990*

	1970	1980	1990
Education a/			
First level	66.00	78.00	84.00
Second level	58.00	70.00	77.00
Third level	46.00	63.00	84.00
Science and technology b/	33.00	45.00	70.00
Economic activity c/	28.00	42.00	48.00
Employment in professional, technical, administrative and management fields	27.00	47.00	55.00
Wage ratio d/			
Agriculture	74.00	78.00	79.00
Manufacturing	72.00	60.00	64.83

Source: WISTAT, version 3, 1994.

a/ Average ratio of girls to boys in enrolment in schools (number of girls per 100 boys).

b/ Average ratio of girls to boys in science and technology fields at third level of education.

c/ Average ratio of women to men in the economically active population (number of women per 100 men).

d/ Percentages.

East Asia prompted a flow of international migration from the region to the capital-exporting economies of Western Asia. A significant number of women from Indonesia, Malaysia, the Philippines, Sri Lanka, India, Bangladesh and Thailand became temporary migrant workers in the Western Asia region. In Kuwait, for example, 103,501 migrant women were employed as domestic workers in 1989, constituting 5.1 per cent of the population of the country. In Saudi Arabia, there were 219,000 non-Saudi Asian female workers in 1986. 24/ However, the collapse of the oil economy, the Gulf crisis of early 1991 and the eight years of the Iran-Iraq war led to a decline of capital surplus in the region. In some cases capital surplus disappeared completely and some countries had to turn to international capital markets to borrow money to finance wars and later reconstruction efforts. The adverse economic and political circumstances in West Asia have caused a decline in opportunities for migrant women and men, thereby worsening the external payments position of the economies from which migration had originated.

27. If only the quantitative aspect is considered, it is possible to say that Asian women have benefited from the economic success of the region. These benefits are captured in the increase in labour force participation, sustained over the last two decades, in the increased access to education for girls at all levels, and in an increase in the ratio of women's to men's earnings, as income accruing to women through productive employment has increased.

28. Examined from a gender perspective, the development experience of the East and South-East Asian economies suggests that female advancement is directly related to policies of external openness and export promotion and inversely related to policies of import substitution and protectionism. However, the fact that female employment expansion took place in these economies in the context of comparative advantage in labour-intensive production should not be overlooked. As countries climb the "ladder of comparative advantage", there is constant pressure to upgrade production and modify micro- and macroeconomic management so as to take account of changes in economic structure and relative prices. In terms of the future of female employment in export-oriented industries in the economies where development in the last two decades has been driven by export expansion, the need for technological upgrading translates into the need for skills acquisition and better education and qualifications for female workers. Otherwise the benefits accruing to women thus far from export-led development will simply vanish with growth. Recent evidence suggests

24/ "Violence against migrant women workers" (A/49/354).

that the share of female labour in export-oriented industries is declining as skill requirements in export industries shift with shifts in comparative advantage. This, together with evidence of poor access for women to retraining, indicates that the gains to women's employment from the expansion of export-oriented industries might have been a short-lived phenomenon. 25/

29. The emergence of China as a major growth pole and trading power in the region should serve as a catalyst of economic growth and intraregional trade. It should also pose significant competition for already established exporters of labour-intensive manufactures in and outside the region. China's index of comparative advantage correlates significantly with that of four other large developing countries—Egypt, India, Indonesia and Turkey. 15/ Arguably, China's growing exports present a threat to female employment in such industries as electronics, toys, textiles and apparel in the first generation of newly industrializing countries where the eventual tightening of the labour market and rising labour costs pushed real wages up. However, economic history shows that, as far as female aggregate employment is concerned, shifts in comparative advantage do not always result in winners and losers. Owing to a strong upward trend in female employment in the non-tradable service sector, women's aggregate employment in the industrialized market economies continues to grow despite increasing cost competitiveness of the developing economies.

30. The outlook for the developing countries as a whole in the 1990s is considerably brighter than in the previous decade. One indicator of improved growth is the net transfer of financial resources, and this reached $54 billion in 1993, an amount not seen since the early 1980s. 20/ After years of lost access to foreign credit and of capital flight, the Latin American economies emerged from the depths of the debt crisis as "emerging markets" attracting a considerable inflow of financial resources from the beginning of the 1990s. After almost a decade of being negative figures, net financial transfers to the region reached US$ 12 billion in 1992 and are estimated at almost US$ 19 billion for 1993. The inflow of foreign direct investment and greater access for the economies in question to international credit markets are largely attributed to the success of the Brady Plan in reducing the face value of their commercial debt and to comprehensive macro- and micro-economic reforms that improved their competitiveness and creditworthiness. 26/

31. The inflow of foreign capital to developing countries creates new jobs and increases the demand for labour, including that of women. Given progress in economic reforms and political stability, the inflow of foreign capital can expand employment opportunities for women in developing countries and thus foster their economic advancement. It should be noted, however, that the conditions underlying competitiveness are changing and are coming to rely less on natural assets like cheap labour and more on created assets in the form of knowledge and skills. Emerging patterns of flows and stocks of foreign direct investment reveal that such assets have become the main determinant of foreign direct investment location. In view of women's poorer educational level—or rather its less appropriate orientation, given modern needs—women in developing countries are less likely to benefit from the inflows of foreign direct investment and the expansion of the export industries associated with it.

2. *Economies in transition: 27/ economic and political restructuring and its impact on women*

32. While the former centrally planned economies of Central and Eastern Europe and the Soviet Union were sheltered to some extent from the global economic crisis of the early 1980s by an autarchic trade and production regime, towards the end of the decade they too experienced a decline in economic performance that was caused by a tightening of the resource constraint on extensive growth, the inability to sustain growth through technological progress, severe monetary disequilibria, and attempts at economic reform in the context of structural rigidities and distortions. Since the end of the 1980s these countries have embarked on the road of transition to a market economy and this has proved to be costly in terms of real income and output decline, loss of employment and security, a rapid deterioration in social conditions and deepening gender inequalities.

33. The fundamental changes in trading patterns that followed the disintegration of the Council on Mutual Economic Assistance (CMEA) and the internal payments system led to a rapid deterioration in the current account and to an accumulation of external debt. Lack of commitment to tight monetary policy and at times its political infeasibility fuelled inflation rates, which in some countries approached a dangerously high near-hyper-inflation level. In response to high inflation, some countries in the

25/ S. Baden, "The impact of recession and structural adjustment on women's work in developing countries", paper prepared for the ILO, 1993.

26/ Current debt-service to export ratio of major recipients of private capital among developing countries is 0.22 as compared with 0.29 in the period 1982-1987. Their debt to export ratio in 1990-1992 declined to 1.75 from 1.86 in 1982-1987 (*Global Economic Prospects and the Developing Countries* ..., p. 11).

27/ Economies in transition include the countries of Eastern Europe (Albania, Bulgaria, Croatia, the Czech Republic, Hungary, Poland, Romania, Slovakia, Slovenia and the Federal Republic of Yugoslavia), the republics of the former Soviet Union cooperating within the Commonwealth of Independent States, and the Baltic States of Estonia, Latvia and Lithuania.

Table 5. *Rates of growth of GDP and external debt indicators a/ of economies in transition, 1983-1994*

	1983-1988	1989	1990	1991	1992	1993	1994 b/
Economies in transition	3.4	2.1	-6.3	-9.0	-16.8	-8.6	-6.0
Eastern Europe	3.3	0.0	-11.8	-12.0	-6.2	0.8	2.2
Albania	-	-	-9.0	-29.4	-6.0	11.0	6.0
Bulgaria	3.7	-1.4	-9.1	-16.7	-13.0	-4.2	-0.5
Former Czechoslovakia	2.0	1.3	-4.7	-15.9	-7.2		
Czech Republic						-0.5	2.0
Slovakia						-4.7	0.0
German Democratic Republic	4.2	2.4	-25.1				
Hungary	1.9	3.8	-4.0	-11.9	-5.0	-2.0	0.0
Poland	4.2	0.2	-12.0	-7.6	0.0	4.0	4.2
Romania	2.4	-5.8	-7.4	-13.7	-15.0	1.0	1.2
Former Soviet Union and successor States	3.5	3.0	-4.0	-8.0	-20.0	-12.0	-9.2

External debt and debt indicators for economies in transition, 1983-1993 b/
(billions of dollars)

Former Soviet Union	27.1	53.9	59.8	67.5	78.7	86.1	
Eastern Europe	65.1	82.6	91.1	99.5	95.4	95.6	

Source: *World Economic Survey, 1993 and 1994* (United Nations publications, Sales Nos. E.93.II.C.1 and E.94.II.C.1).
a/ Average growth rates and annual percentage changes.
b/ Forecast.

region embarked on "shock-therapy" macroeconomic stabilization. 28/ Where policy makers were able to conduct a consistent monetary policy, this approach worked although inflation still remained relatively high and the decline in output and income continued. Real wage decline took place in all the economies in transition, but its magnitude varied from about 12 to 15 per cent in Hungary and the Czech Republic to around 30 per cent in Poland. 29/

34. The process of market building in economies in transition involves, *inter alia*, changes in property rights and ownership structures. 30/ Privatization in the transition economies varies in terms of its methods, speed and degree of success. Privatization methods include sales through local auctions, the distribution of privatization vouchers, the use of mutual funds and other financial intermediaries, and sometimes "spontaneous" privatization by the current management. If the privatization of small-scale enterprises, shops and restaurants has been relatively fast and painless, that of large-scale government-owned enterprises has involved many economic problems (such as the difficulty of making an adequate estimate of the market value of the enterprise to be

privatized) and social problems (such as the displacement of workers and the loss of social benefits and job security). The emerging private economy covers a wide range of activities, from catering to commercial law; and it takes a variety of forms, from limited liability and joint stock companies to micro-enterprises and sole proprietorship.

35. Privatization raises many complex issues with respect to its impact on the economic status of women. Generally speaking, it tends to increase their chances of being laid off and to worsen their conditions of employment. At the same time, it offers opportunities for higher incomes and for entrepreneurship. Although it is rather difficult to determine with certainty the direction of the impact of privatization on women in transitional econo-

28/ "Shock therapy" involves a sharp cut of budget deficits, liberalization of prices and imports, devaluation of exchange rates, interest rate increases and tight control of money supply growth.
29/ "The role of women in the transition processes: facing a major challenge" (E/ECE/RW/HLM/5).
30/ J. Musil, "New social contracts: responses of the State and the social partners to the challenges of restructuring and privatization", *Labour and Society*, vol. 16, No. 4, p. 1.

mies because the process is still at an early stage and because gender-disaggregated data are lacking, it is possible to identify some early trends. It seems that, so far, privatization undertaken in the context of stabilization policies and slow institutional change has adversely affected women's economic position. Where restructuring is directed at increasing the profitability of privatized and commercialized enterprises, female clerical and administrative jobs tend to be cut before male production-line jobs because of perceptions of female labour as "expensive" owing to the associated social benefits and protective legislation enjoyed by women in the past, and of women as less efficient workers because of the burden of family responsibilities. Consequently, the privatization of large State firms had strong and immediate impact on female employment because of the large numbers of women employed by them in administrative and clerical positions. Because of the special protective measures that underpinned women's participation in the labour force in the past and because of a resurgence of traditional stereotypes of gender relations, women have had difficulty in securing their jobs in privatized firms, or getting new jobs after being laid off. An industrial establishment survey carried by ILO in East-Central Europe in 1990-1993 shows a marked tendency for managers to give pronounced preference in recruitment to men, even in previously "women-dominated" sectors. 31/

36. In the course of privatization and cost/production restructuring, the sectoral distribution of female employment is changing. An ILO survey of Russian industry shows that, as privatized and commercialized State-owned enterprises undergo restructuring, there is a relatively small decline in the share of female employment in the declining sectors of heavy industry and an increase in the share of female employment in light, "feminized" industries like textiles, garments and food-processing. This trend points towards strengthening the already existing segregation of employment in industry, "which inevitably leads to a decline in their relative wages and benefits".

37. As transition progresses, female employment dynamics are beginning to resemble those of industrialized market economies. Despite the advantageous position of women in the services sector at the beginning of reform, they seem to be unable to consolidate their advantage in this sector. As trade, banking, insurance and financial services become more profitable men move into these sectors in increasing numbers changing the employment ratio to their advantage. In Poland, for example, in the period 1989-1992 the employment share of women declined in trade, banking, insurance and community and social services, while that of men increased dramatically. Male employment in trade increased by 62 per cent and

in banking and insurance by 80 per cent. Similar changes in the female and male shares of employment in trade, banking, insurance and financial services took place in the Czech Republic. There, thus, appears to be a clear tendency towards convergence of high employment shares of women (see table 6) in these branches with those much lower ones in industrialized market economies. The less profitable services like education, health and social care continue to be women-dominated and women's employment share in them is increasing.

38. Unemployment is becoming a key area of concern for women in the transitional economies. While the steep decline in real income has made women's wages a necessity for the survival of the household, jobs have become scare and competition for them has intensified. The vast majority of women were little prepared for the loss of job security and the need to compete for employment in a market environment. Although highly educated, women appear to be losing jobs to men even in previously "women-dominated" sectors of the economy. The rate of female unemployment is on the rise in all the economies in transition except for the Czech Republic. Women constitute by far the largest share of all those registered as unemployed and are believed to be the majority of those who are not registered. The duration of unemployment is longer for women than for men. In the Russian Federation, for example, the average time of registered unemployment is 4.6 months for women and less than 2 months for men. 32/

39. The position of women in the labour market is further complicated by resurgence of the stereotyping of gender roles and a decline in the availability of social services, particularly in the area of child care, provided in the past by the State and by enterprises. As a result of budgetary pressures and privatization, child-care facilities have become less available and more expansive. The social costs of transition have thus been shifted from the State to the household and ultimately to women.

40. Growing unemployment among men, lack of child-care facilities and increasing social tensions have precipitated the return of traditional attitudes towards the role of women. A public opinion survey conducted in 1991 in the Russian Federation reveals that a growing number of men feel that women's place is the home. In the media and the press, social problems have been openly blamed on "too much emancipation of women". Measures, such as extended maternity leave and early retirement, have been introduced to encourage women to stay at home. As a result there is little sensitivity to

31/ L. Paukert, "Women's employment in East-Central European countries during the period of transition to a market economy system", working paper prepared for the ILO, 1993.
32/ "Regional review and appraisal of the Nairobi Forward-looking Strategies for the Advancement of Women" (E/ECE/RW/HLM/1).

Table 6. *Share of women in the banking and insurance industries in selected economies in transition, 1993*

Country	Women's share (percentage)
Azerbaijan a/	48.80
Belarus a/	88.10
Czech Republic	68.58
Georgia a/	75.50
Hungary b/	74.38
Kazakhstan a/	85.30
Poland	75.00
Romania	79.38
Russian Federation a/	90.20
Slovakia	79.40
Ukraine a/	88.80
Uzbekistan a/	61.10

Source: Economic Commission for Europe, "Regional review and appraisal of Nairobi Forward-looking Strategies" (E/ECE/RW/HLM).
a/ 1990.
b/ Financial intermediaries.

Table 7. *Women's share in unemployment: selected countries, 1991*

Country	Women's share (percentage)
Bulgaria	62.0
Hungary a/	40.0
Kazakhstan b/	70.0
Poland	52.0
Yugoslavia	53.0
Romania	85.0-90.0
Russian Federation c/	90.0
Slovak Republic	58.0
Ukraine d/	65.0

Source: Compiled from several sources, and M. Fong, "Economic restructuring and women's status in Eastern Europe", UNU/WIDER research paper (Helsinki, 1991), pp. 6-9.
a/ Quoted as "over 40 per cent".
b/ National report of Kazakhstan.
c/ 1993 figure of ECE, 1994 (E/ECE/RW/HELM/1).
d/ National report of Ukraine. Quoted as "over 65 per cent".

women's issues and to the growing "feminization of unemployment".

41. So far, women in Eastern Europe, the Commonwealth of Independent States and the Baltic States have had to endure a greater share of the hardship of transition. Their participation in political decision-making has declined, putting them in a poor position to influence the process of reform. At the same time, unemployment among women has grown and they presently account for a greater share of the unemployed. Their incomes have also declined and poverty among women and the households headed by women has increased. The balance between their economic and reproductive roles has shifted towards a greater emphasis on the latter owing to the strengthening of the traditional gender contract. Their distress has been intensified by growing social problems, and rapid criminalization of society in many economies in transition. Sexual harassment against women, sexual abuse and prostitution, previously reported to the United Nations Committee on the Elimination of Discrimination against Women as non-existent, are a reality now. So there is a real danger that women in that area might be further marginalized and find themselves on the periphery of major economic and political structures. This would have serious implications for social equilibrium in the region and for the sustainability of the transition process. Failure to incorporate

women would also lead to a less than optimal economic performance in the transition period as 50 per cent of the labour force that is highly educated and skilled would remain underutilized.

3. *Developed market economies: growing flexibility in markets and women's work*

42. After the recession of the early 1980s, the developed market economies experienced an unusually long period of economic expansion that slowed towards the end of the decade and ended with the shallow recession of the early 1990s (see table 1). The current recovery has been slow: in 1993 growth picked up in the United States and Canada but remained unchanged in Japan and declined in the major economies of Western Europe, except for the United Kingdom, where the economy started to grow again.

43. Recession and the slow recovery pushed the rate of unemployment up from 6 per cent in 1990 to 7.3 per cent in 1992 and 7.7 per cent in 1993. 20/ While relatively low in the United States and Japan, unemployment has become a major problem in Western Europe, where rates reached 10-12 per cent in 1993. The unemployment rate is expected to increase in 1994 and possibly in 1995.

44. Among the pressing macroeconomic concerns of the developed market economies are structural fiscal

Table 8. *Unemployment rates by sex: selected OECD countries, 1973-1992 (Percentage share)*

	1973	1979	1990	1992
United States				
Men	2.3	3.1	4.1	6.0
Women	2.3	3.2	3.3	4.4
Japan				
Men	1.0	1.6	1.4	1.4
Women	0.5	1.1	1.3	1.3
United Kingdom				
Men	2.1	3.8	6.3	11.5
Women	0.3	1.3	2.0	3.2
France				
Men	2.3	3.1	5.6	6.5
Women	1.3	3.5	7.8	8.5
Sweden				
Men	1.6	1.3	1.3	5.4
Women	2.1	1.6	1.2	3.5

Source: *World Economic and Social Survey, 1994* (United Nations publication, Sales No. E.94.II.C.1).

deficits and a resurgence of inflation. Their macroeconomic policies have therefore been directed at fiscal consolidation and they have assumed an anti-inflationary stance that might conflict with the objective of a speedy economic recovery.

45. The micro- and macroeconomic reforms of the late 1980s and early 1990s encompassed a tightening of fiscal and monetary polices, flexibility and deregulation of financial, product and labour markets, and an industrial restructuring, that in part reflected a longer-term trend of structural shifts involving changes in the roles of industry and services in economic growth. Industrial restructuring was also manifested in the move towards a "flexible firm" to foster competitiveness and greater mobility in an environment of ever-changing markets. These policies have had a distinct impact on women's position in the labour market, and on their rates, quality and conditions of employment.

46. The long-term trend in the developed market economies has been towards increasing rates of female labour force participation for women and declining rates for men (see figure I). Against this long-term trend, there are cyclical changes in the rates of female labour force participation that are the result of recession, short-term macroeconomic policies and micro-economic reforms.

47. The general worsening of the employment situation in the OECD economies is currently a major concern for policy makers in these countries. There has been an increase in the rates of long-term unemployment and country reports from the European region indicate that about 50 per cent of the unemployed in some countries has been out of work for 12 months or more. 32/ While there are variations in rates and patterns of unemployment among the developed market economies, it appears that in the majority of OECD countries unemployment rates for women are either comparable to those for men or lower. However, in Denmark, France, Germany, Italy and the Netherlands, unemployment rates for women are significantly higher than those for men. 32/

48. A consistent increase in the rate of female labour force participation has taken place in the context of the expansion of the services sector. The share of total employment and women's employment in this sector have increased in all the OECD countries, 25/ while the shares of employment in agriculture and industry have declined, which explains the decline in male labour force participation (see figure II).

49. Policies directed at the enhancement of internal and external competitiveness were centred around the deregulation and flexibilization of financial, product and labour markets. They focused primarily on wage-bargaining institutions, tax and social spending policies and employment legislation perceived as hampering wage flexibility. At the micro-level, the flexibilization of markets was matched by industrial restructuring directed at lean production strategies and the evolution of flexible firms, capable of rapid expansion and contraction with a small number of permanent employees and the remainder employed as temporary and casual workers, outworkers and subcontractors. While benefiting female employment in terms of the supply of jobs, flexibilization has led to a trade-off between the quality and quantity of female employment. The positive aspects of the process must be weighted against the potential for undermining existing employment protection, social security provisions, and access to training and for the fragmentation of career prospects. Concern has been voiced that women may have been used as part of deregulation strategy by virtue of their association with flexible employment.

50. Present data indicate that part-time employment is increasingly a female phenomenon, and the majority of those employed part-time in almost all the developed market economies are women.

51. The increase in the part-time employment of women has been a factor contributing to increased occupational segregation and persisting inequality in economic rewards, salaries and benefits. While in some economies the proportion of women in "male-dominated" occupations has increased slightly as a result

**Figure I. Labour-force participation rates, by sex, total
Organisation for Economic Co-operation and Development**
(Percentage)

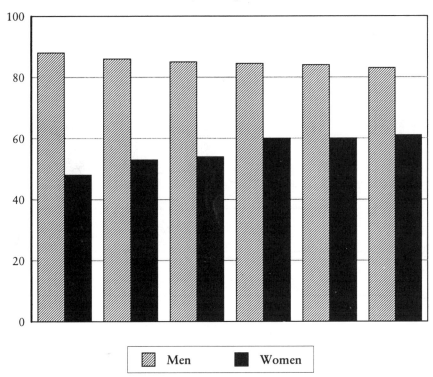

Men   Women

of affirmative action by the Government, employment segregation continues to persist. In France, for example, nurses, midwives, beauticians, secretaries, social assistants, cashiers, switchboard and telephone operators and receptionists are highly "feminized" occupational categories in which women constitute more than 90 per cent of employees. 32/

52. The increase in female labour force participation has not led to women achieving equal status or bargaining power in the labour market. As wage demands are increasingly being tied to increases in productivity, women's concentration in the services sector has contributed to an overall weakening of their wage bargaining power since increased productivity is not easily measured in this sector. National reports show that women's earnings are lower than men's in most of the reporting countries. Women earn between 50 and 90 per cent of men's earnings, but rates vary considerably across countries. In 1990, women's wages in non-agricultural industries in Japan were only 49.6 per cent of men's; and in Germany women earned 73.1 per cent of men's wages, while in France the figure was 80.8 per cent and in Australia, 90.8 per cent.

B. Gender aspects of internal and external migration

53. Migration, involving as it does millions of people around the world, is intricately linked with important economic, social, political, cultural and environmental factors. As such, it has gender-specific characteristics that however are often masked by data aggregates established without regard to gender. The data collected and published under the heading of "migrants and dependents" do not permit a full exploration of the extent, causes and consequences of migration from a gender perspective. Nevertheless, the available data, however limited, suggest that both internal and external migration may have distinct gender patterns that vary with level of development, development strategies, type of economic growth and political factors.

1. Internal migration

54. Internal migration, which exceeds external migration by at least an order of magnitude, continues to be viewed primarily in terms of rural-urban flows and the growth of urban areas despite the growing importance of urban-urban and rural-rural flows. The world's urban

Figure II. Changes in female share of total employment: by sectors, 1973-1992
(Percentage change)

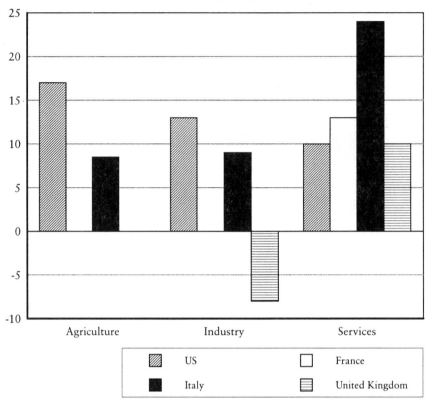

Source: OECD, Labour Force Statistics, cited 1971-1991 (Paris, 1993).

Table 9. *Women's share in part-time employment: selected OECD economies, 1973-1992*
(Percentage)

	1979	1983	1990	1991	1992
Austria	87.8	88.4	89.1	89.7	..
Belgium	88.9	84.0	88.6	89.3	..
Canada	72.1	71.3	71.0	70.5	70.0
Denmark	86.9	84.7	75.7	75.5	..
France	82.2	84.4	83.6	83.7	83.7
Germany	91.6	91.9	89.7	89.6	..
Italy	61.4	64.8	67.2	65.4	67.9
Japan	70.1	72.8	70.7	69.9	69.3
United Kingdom	92.8	89.8	86.2	86.1	85.4
United States	68.0	66.8	67.6	67.2	66.4

Source: OECD, *Labour Force Statistics, 1971-1991* (Paris, 1993).

Table 10. *Ratio of women to men in total, urban and rural population (1990 round)*

Region/ age group	Total population	Urban population	Rural population
Africa/15-19	0.997	0.989	1.100
Africa/20-24	1.002	0.885	1.097
Latin America/15-19	0.984	1.061	0.873
Latin America/20-24	1.006	1.089	0.882
Western Europe/15-19	0.956	0.972	0.913
Western Europe/20-24	0.956	0.988	0.865
Asia and Pacific/15-19	0.946	0.930	0.963
Asia and Pacific/20-24	0.944	0.909	0.969
East Asia/15-19	0.938	0.936	0.938
East Asia/20-24	0.935	0.956	0.864
South-east Asia/15-19	0.968	0.987	0.968
South-east Asia/20-24	0.986	1.003	0.982
Eastern Europe/15-19	0.948	0.939	0.934
Eastern Europe/20-24	0.952	0.958	0.929

Source: WISTAT, 1994.

population is estimated to have grown by about 500 million people over the period 1975-1985 and about half of this gain has been attributed to net rural-urban migration. Recent estimates suggest that 43 per cent of the world's population currently live in urban areas as compared to only 37 per cent in the 1970s. Some projections show that by the year 2005 urban population will reach a staggering 58 per cent. 33/ In recent years average annual population growth rates in urban areas, particularly in sub-Saharan Africa, Latin America and Asia, have been high and positive, while average annual growth in rural areas has, with few exceptions, been low or negative. This suggests that a significant part of population growth is due to migration from rural to urban areas.

55. The gender pattern of rural/urban migration can be derived from the population sex ratios given in table 10 below. Although largely insufficient to support any definite conclusions, these ratios suggest that in low-income developing economies with a large agricultural sector men predominate among migrants from rural to urban areas and that in the newly industrialized and highly urbanized economies of Latin America and East Asia women migrate more than men. For example, in Africa, sex ratios in rural areas indicate that more men migrate to cities than women; and in Latin America they indicate that more women than men leave their villages for the city. In Asia, in general, men tend to predominate in the rural-urban migration flow, while in East Asia women in the 20-24 age group slightly outnumber men

among rural-to-urban migrants. In Western Asia, rural and urban sex ratios reflect the predominance of males among city migrants.

56. It should be noted that the patterns of rural-to-urban migration observed in each of these regions are consistent with regional trends in economic development with respect to trade orientation, the inflow of FDI and the gender characteristics of employment in export-processing industries. The creation of EPZs in the context of export-promotion policies has undoubtedly contributed to fostering female migration from rural to urban areas in the first and second generation of the newly industrialized economies of East and South-East Asia and Latin America.

2. *External migration*

57. In the past two decades external (international) migration for economic or political reasons has involved millions of people. Census data largely for the 1970s and 1980s suggest that the number of migrants in the mid-1980s exceeded 105 million. 33/ Although more recent data on the extent of external migration are not available, increasing globalization and growing interdependence in the world economy, the greater mobility of capital, regional integration and the reconfiguration of nation States in Europe and the former Soviet Union suggest that

33/ *Population Distribution and Migration* (United Nations publication, forthcoming).

external migration may currently involve significantly more people than it did in the 1980s.

58. There is a general lack of adequate data on the gender composition of the external migration flows, and little attention as yet has been paid to such important issues as their gender-specific impact. It is therefore difficult to identify specific ways in which women migrants influence the process of external migration or are impacted by it. Clearly, women migrants may experience a significant change in lifestyle associated with a move to a society with greater gender equality or considerable hardship, when migrating as refugees in the context of war, famine or drought.

59. With their statistics on foreign-born population, national population censuses provide the most comprehensive data on the extent of female migration. Census data for the 1970s and 1980s show that women accounted on average for slightly more than 50 per cent of the total inflow of migrants into developed countries. In developing countries, they represented 45.4 per cent of the total foreign-born population; and their share in the total number of people living outside their countries of origin averaged 48.1 per cent. Of course, these averages mask significant variations within and between regions. In the Americas and Europe women accounted for more than half of the foreign-born population; in Africa and Asia they were less than half of that category; and they were strongly underrepresented in the countries of Western Asia.

60. In the absence of data for the 1990s it cannot be determined whether the share of women in international migration flows has changed. It is nevertheless clear that women account for about one half of all international migration. Gender-disaggregated reporting of data on international migration and greater attention to its gender-specific consequences are necessary if a better understanding of the process itself and of the role of women in it is to be achieved.

C. Trends in international trade and their influence on the advancement of women

61. The relationship between the growth of international trade and increasing female participation in productive employment hinges on the employment-creating potential of trade and its influence on the nature and orientation of national economic development by bringing domestic resources allocation into line with comparative advantage. Those developing countries that opened their economies to international trade experienced a dramatic rise in the participation of women in industrial employment.

62. There are at least three reasons why this happened. First, production for the external market led to an increase in the demand for labour. Secondly, there was a significant expansion in trade flows and a change in their composition. Thirdly, as labour-intensive manufactured exports came to dominate export flows from the developing countries, unit labour cost minimization became a matter of priority for export-oriented industries. In this context, female labour, which is universally cheaper than male labour, enjoyed a unit labour cost advantage. The evidence shows that, in countries with export-oriented production, female labour was systematically preferred over male labour by transnational corporations and domestic export-oriented industries.

63. As a result of the expansion of international and intra-industry trade, women's participation in industrial production, and particularly in light manufacturing, has increased dramatically. The global average for women's participation in the manufacturing labour force stands today at about 30 per cent, which is almost the same as the share of women in the global labour force. 34/ However, this increase reflects the industrialization process in developing countries, which typically begins with the production of labour-intensive items as economies begin to diversify away from primary production. In the industrialized and former centrally planned economies, (except for the Asian economies in transition) women's participation in industrial production has actually declined.

64. Trade expansion did not, however, prove to be a zero-sum game in terms of the aggregate female employment as had been predicted. Despite competition from developing countries, female employment continued to rise in the developed economies. The strong and sustained upward trend in women's employment in the non-tradable services sector is thought to have been largely responsible for this development. The decline in female industrial employment was primarily due to the long-term process of structural change in the composition of gross domestic product (GDP) rather than to the competitive pressure from the developing countries only. Some job losses to competition from developing countries, particularly in the manufacturing industries, were, however, inevitable, but the bulk of the burden fell most heavily on low-skilled, overwhelmingly male, labourers.

65. The trade-driven, export-oriented development strategies followed by first- and second-generation of newly industrializing countries 35/ came to be known as "female-led" as much as "export-led" owing to the high share of women in the export-oriented industries. The women-manufactured exports of these countries

34/ About 854 million women were estimated to be economically active in 1990, accounting for 32.1 per cent of the global labour force. See *Women in Manufacturing: Participation Patterns, Determinants and Trends* (Vienna, UNIDO, 1993).

accounted for most of manufactures exported from South to North. In this sense, South/North trade in manufactures was not only labour-intensive but also "female-labour intensive". In some countries, particularly in East and South-east Asia and Latin America, the share of female employment in export-oriented industries reached as much as 95 per cent in the 1980s. 25/ In Mexico, the share of women's employment in the export-processing zones was 77 per cent in the early 1980s. In the Republic of Korea and Singapore women accounted for between 68 and 83 per cent of the labour force in textiles and clothing and between 59 and 90 per cent in electronics.

66. Although trade liberalization in the developing countries has led to a steep increase in the employment of women in export-oriented industries, providing them with better income opportunities, most of the jobs that went to women were low-wage long-hours production-line jobs or sub-contracting jobs with no opportunity for the acquisition of new skills and without wage-bargaining power. That is to say that while trade expansion led to an increase in the supply of jobs for women, the quality of those jobs was often poor and they were insecure, paid only a fraction of male wage for the same job and lacked social protection. 36/ Thus, the increase in the industrial employment of women in the context of outward-oriented development was based on explicitly inferior treatment of female labour. Female employment in export-oriented economies is also highly segregated as the proportion of women employed in "feminized" industries greatly exceeds that in total industrial employment, suggesting that the female labour force is highly concentrated in these industries and underrepresented elsewhere. When the qualitative aspects of this process are weighted against the quantitative indicators of greater job availability, the overall assessment of the impact of export-oriented development is hardly consonant with female advancement.

67. Recent evidence suggests that the share of women's employment in the export-oriented industries is declining in the "mature" newly industrializing countries. In view of women's relatively poor educational levels—or rather their less appropriate orientation given modern needs—women in developing countries are less likely to benefit from export-oriented production than they were. It is doubtful that trade expansion lays the ground for any special long-term benefits for women in developing countries in terms of their placement in the labour market and of improved access to employment on better terms in the future. As countries move along the development spectrum, they move away from reliance on unskilled labour-intensive manufacturing (as in Singapore) and unless their skills acquisition keeps pace with the country's industrial and technology development,

women's employment opportunities will fall away with such growth. 37/

68. An open trading system is the key to economic growth and prosperity, which in turn is a *sine qua non* for political stability and democracy. Inasmuch as growth and stability are important factors influencing the economic advancement of women, free trade is instrumental in achieving this objective. There is no doubt that any shrinking of the volume of world trade would do immense harm to the world economy and to prospects for sustainable development in the developing countries. Development experiences (or rather the lack thereof) in the 1980s showed that the adverse consequences of economic decline often affect women to a greater extent than men. On the other hand, growth based on free trade and principles of comparative advantage has proved to be greatly beneficial to women. The resurgence in the mid-1970s of protectionist pressures and their proliferation in the 1980s under the strain of recession posed a serious threat to free trade and, by extension, to women's jobs and economic advancement.

69. The main achievement of the Uruguay Round of multilateral trade negotiations was that its successful conclusion served to uphold the principles of free trade. The Round, which took three years to devise and seven to complete, was the most ambitious in the history of GATT. The agreement under the Uruguay Round comes into effect on 1 January 1995, subject to ratification. Although implementation of the major agreements will be spread over the next 10 years and will not be as thorough and swift as exporting countries would have liked, significant new market-opening rules were introduced. The main provisions of the agreement, and those of utmost importance to the developing countries, aim at broadening market access, bringing trade in services and in textiles and clothing under the GATT regulation, providing a comprehensive framework for the future liberalization of trade in agriculture products, and curbing the proliferation of non-tariff trade barriers and unilateral protectionist measures.

70. The liberalization of trade resulting from the Uruguay Round should lead to a significant increase in world trade and income, which is expected to increase by US$ 213-274 billion annually. It is expected that everybody stands to gain, particularly in the long run. The gender-specific dimensions of these gains (and of the unavoidable short-term losses) are less obvious, however. Some of the largest projected increases in trade are in areas of great importance to developing countries. Trade in clothing is expected to increase by 60 per cent and

35/ Recent trends suggest that Malaysia, Thailand, Indonesia, the Philippines and China have replaced four original newly industrializing countries as the engine of growth in the region.

in textiles by 34 per cent. It should be noted that these are the sectors that usually lead the industrialization process at the early stages when a developing country is just beginning to diversify from primary production. These are also the sectors where production is "female-intensive"—i.e., where the share of women in total employment is high. The dismantlement of the Multifibre Arrangement (MFA), which controlled trade in textiles since 1973 should speed up the shift in comparative advantage and hence in the global division of labour, leading to the take-off of the industrialization process in the least developed countries. As industrialization at its early stages is often "female-led", women stand to benefit in terms of the increase in the availability of productive employment.

71. In a large number of primary-producing economies, diversification into the production of manufactured exports is nevertheless going to be a slow process. Most of the short- to medium-term gains are likely to accrue to Asian and Latin American exporters of manufactured goods. Given changes in consumer demand, shifts in comparative advantage of established exporters of manufactured goods and gender-related differences in education, it is unlikely that women in these economies will continue to hold onto their share of employment in export-oriented industries.

72. Primary producers and exporters of tropical products in Africa stand to benefit least from the liberalization of trade, at least in the short run, because of the low-income elasticities of their exports and the already low tariffs on most of them. Furthermore, women in many African countries are not involved in the production of export crops either because the gender-related division of labour does not permit them to switch to the production of tradable crops or because, as such production becomes profitable, deliberate efforts are made to turn cash-crop production over to men. 38/ Some of the developing countries—net importers of food—might see their terms of trade decline since the prices of their food imports are likely to rise as a short-term result of the Uruguay Round. The increase in trade in services is likely to benefit women, given their high propensity of employment in this sector.

73. Despite the obvious advantages for women in the liberalization of international trade, the extent to which they benefit will vary with their level of education and the nature of their economic environment. In the short-run, nationally and internationally, there will be winners and losers. Trade-adjustment assistance and skill-building programmes are therefore necessary to assist male and female workers who are displaced as a result of greater competition from abroad. Lately, however, there is some evidence of unequal access to retraining for women. 25/

D. *Other factors affecting the implementation of the Nairobi Forward-looking Strategies*

74. The Nairobi Forward-looking Strategies call for equal rights for women in social, legal and economic domains. They specifically emphasize the right to independent and full access to productive resources, and they call for the greater integration of women into every stage of the development process, for the reduction of poverty among women, particularly at the times of economic distress caused by recession or structural adjustment, and for the advancement of women to positions of economic and political power in business and government. They also call for greater recognition in national accounts and economic statistics of women's paid, unpaid and informal-sector work and for the facilitation of women's access to productive employment through the greater availability and the improvement of the conditions of such employment. In that respect, emphasis was also given to the need to reduce widespread employment segregation by encouraging women to work in male-dominated environments.

75. The World Conference on Human Rights, held at Vienna in 1993, reaffirmed the importance of human rights in relation to all other aspects of global life. It specifically reaffirmed the importance of the equal rights of women and men, as well as a rights-based focus on issues of peace and development. In terms of women's *de jure* human rights, the provisions of the Vienna Declaration and Programme of Action reflected the considerable progress in placing these in the legal structure. The fact that, by the end of 1994, over 138 States were party to the Convention on the Elimination of All Forms of Discrimination against Women placed the laws of those countries within the norms set out in the Convention. At the same time, the enjoyment of these rights in terms of women's de facto situation did not improve at the same rate, as is noted below.

76. The reliance on democratic means for electing and changing governments, through competitive elections, that has characterized recent years, has opened the prospect for women of using the exercise of their political rights to improve their own status. At the same time, enjoyment of these rights has been constrained by the negative effects of previous systems which constitute a base of inequality upon which reform processes have been built. After the shift towards democracy, in the absence of strong and independent national machinery to raise women's issues into public debate, independent women's movements have continued to be excluded from the process of economic and political decision-making.

36/ J. Henshall Momsen, "Attitudes to women factory workers in Malaysia" in *Women and Development in the Third World* (London, Routledge, 1991).

Women's participation in parliament and at all levels of economic decision-making have only increased dramatically in a few countries and in others it has declined.

77. Where a resurgence of democracy has coincided with the spread of political instability, women continue to be the majority of the countless victims of political and ethnic violence. Much therefore remains to be done before the world can claim that the objectives of the Nairobi Forward-looking Strategies have been achieved.

Document 121

Annex II (on an optional protocol to the Convention) to the report of the fourteenth session of CEDAW (extract)

E/CN.6/1995/CRP.1, 3 February 1995

Annex II

Background

1. The Vienna Declaration and Programme of Action, adopted by consensus by States Members of the United Nations at the 1993 World Conference on Human Rights, stresses the need for women to make effective use of existing procedures under international human rights instruments. It also emphasizes the need for the adoption of new procedures and, in particular, a petition procedure for the Convention on the Elimination of All Forms of Discrimination against Women. It states that the "Commission on the Status of Women and the Committee on the Elimination of Discrimination against Women should quickly examine the possibility of introducing the right of petition through the preparation of an optional protocol to the Convention".

2. The question of the preparation of a protocol to the Convention was discussed by the Committee at its thirteenth session in 1994. In its suggestion No. 5, the Committee asked the Commission on the Status of Women to request that an expert group meeting be convened during 1994, "composed of 5 to 10 independent experts with a knowledge of the different forms of civilization and of the principal legal systems". The expert group was asked to prepare a draft optional protocol to the Convention and the report of that meeting was to be presented to the Committee for its comments and to the Commission for action. The Committee also designated one of its members to prepare a paper on the subject for its 1995 session.

3. The Committee regrets that, at the thirty-eighth session in 1994, the Commission on the Status of Women did not convene an expert group meeting. The Commission decided however that, at its thirty-ninth session in 1995, in cooperation with the Committee, it would examine the feasibility of introducing the right of petition through the preparation of an optional protocol to the Convention, taking into account the results of any governmental expert group meeting on the question that might have been convened. The decision of the Commission on the Status of Women was echoed by the Economic and Social Council in its resolution 1994/7.

4. Bearing in mind the decision of the Commission on the Status of Women, and in order to expedite matters, the Maastricht Centre for Human Rights at the University of Limberg, in conjunction with the International Human Rights Law Group, with the financial assistance of the Netherlands and the Australian Governments, convened an expert group meeting during 1994. Participants were drawn from different regions and from different legal systems, had a knowledge of international law and experience of the other human rights treaty bodies and included three members of the Committee. The draft optional protocol prepared by the expert group drew on existing international and regional procedures. The draft, together with other relevant documents, served as the basis for discussion by the Committee at its fourteenth session. As a result of those discussions, the overwhelming majority of the members of the Committee suggested that the following ideas be submitted to the Commission on the Status of Women for consideration. One member of the Committee expressed her reservation with regard to paragraphs 8 and 12 to 26.

Elements of an optional protocol

5. States parties to the Convention should have the option to ratify or accede to the optional protocol. "State party" in this section means one that has ratified or acceded to the optional protocol.

6. Two procedures should be envisaged: a communications procedure and an inquiry procedure.

7. Communications may be submitted by an individual, group or organization suffering detriment from a violation of rights in the Convention or claiming to be directly affected by the failure of a State party to comply with its obligations under the Convention or by a person or group having a sufficient interest in the matter.

8. Communications would be in writing and confidential.

9. The admissibility of a communication would be subject to the following:

(a) The communication would be inadmissible if a State party to the Convention had not ratified or acceded to the optional protocol;

(b) It should not be anonymous;

(c) It should disclose an alleged violation of rights or an alleged failure of a State party to give effect to obligations under the Convention;

(d) It should relate to acts or omissions that occurred after the State party ratified or acceded to the Convention, unless the violation or failure to give effect to those obligations or the impact continued after the protocol took effect for that State party;

(e) It should not be an abuse of the right to submit a communication;

(f) A communication would be declared inadmissible by the Committee if all domestic remedies had not been exhausted, unless the Committee considered that requirement unreasonable. If the same matter was being examined under another international procedure, the Committee would declare the communication inadmissible unless it considered that procedure unreasonably prolonged;

(g) The communication would be inadmissible if the author, within a reasonable period, failed to provide adequate substantiating information.

10. Pending examination of a communication, the Committee should have the right to request that the status quo be preserved, and a State party should give an undertaking to that effect, in order to avoid irreparable harm. Such a request should be accompanied by information confirming that no inference could be drawn that the Committee had determined the merits of the communication.

11. While the State party would be informed confidentially of the nature of the communication, the author's identity would not be revealed without that person's consent. The State party would, within a specified period, provide replies or information about any remedy. While the process of examination continued, the Committee would work in cooperation with the parties to facilitate a settlement which, if reached, would be contained in a confidential report of the Committee.

12. The Committee would examine communications in the light of all information provided by the State party, or by the author or received from other relevant sources. All such information would be transmitted to the parties for comment. The Committee would set its procedures, hold closed meetings when examining communications and, as a whole Committee, adopt and transmit views and any recommendations to the parties. While examining a communication, the Committee might, with the agreement of the State party concerned, visit its territory.

13. When the whole Committee considered that the communication had been justified, it might recommend remedial measures or measures designed to give effect to obligations under the Convention. The State party would remedy violations and implement recommendations. It would also ensure that an appropriate remedy (which might include adequate reparation) was provided. It would also provide the Committee within a set period with details of the remedial measures taken.

14. The Committee should have the power to initiate and continue discussions concerning such measures and remedies and have the power to invite the State party to include such information in its reports under article 18 of the Convention.

15. The Committee would, in its confidential report, summarize the nature of communications received, its examination of them, the replies and statements of the States parties concerned and its views and recommendations.

16. The Committee would have the power to delegate to a working group its responsibilities under this section. The working group would report to the Committee and the Committee alone would have the power to adopt views and make recommendations.

Inquiry procedure

17. If the Committee received reliable information indicating a serious or systematic violation by a State party of rights under the Convention or of a failure to give effect to its Convention obligations, the Committee should have the right to invite that State party to cooperate in examining the information and in submitting observations on it. After considering those observations and any other relevant information, the Committee should have the power to designate one or more of its members to conduct an inquiry and report urgently to the Committee.

18. Such an inquiry would be conducted with the cooperation of the State party and might, with its agreement, include a visit to its territory.

19. Following the examination of the findings, which would be transmitted to the State party, the latter would have a set period in which to make observations in response.

20. The inquiry would be conducted confidentially and at all stages with the cooperation of the States parties.

21. The Committee would encourage the State party to discuss the steps taken by it as a consequence of the inquiry. Those discussions might be continued until

a satisfactory outcome was achieved. The Committee might ask the State party to report on its response to the inquiry in its report under article 18 of the Convention.

22. After completing all those steps, the Committee would be empowered to publish a report.

23. When ratifying or acceding to the optional protocol the State party would undertake to assist the Committee in its inquiries and to prevent any obstacles to, or victimization of, any person who provides the Committee with information or assists it in its inquiries.

General matters

24. States parties would publicize the protocol and its procedures, the Committee's views and any recommendations concerning a communication received or inquiry conducted.

25. The Committee would develop rules and procedures that would enable it to conduct its work fairly, efficiently and, as necessary, urgently.

26. Meeting time of not less than three weeks per annum and resources, including expert legal advice, would be made available to enable the Committee to conduct its work under the Convention.

27. Procedures for the signing, ratification, accession and entry into force of the protocol should be prescribed.

28. No State-to-State communication procedure should be included and no reservations permitted.

29. Procedures for amendment and denunciation and the authentic texts of the protocol should be prescribed.

Document 122

Copenhagen Declaration on Social Development, adopted by the World Summit for Social Development, held in Copenhagen from 6 to 12 March 1995—Commitment 5, on the achievement of equality and equity between women and men (extract)

A/CONF.166/9, 1995

...

Commitment 5

We commit ourselves to promoting full respect for human dignity and to achieving equality and equity between women and men, and to recognizing and enhancing the participation and leadership roles of women in political, civil, economic, social and cultural life and in development.

To this end, at the national level, we will:

(a) Promote changes in attitudes, structures, policies, laws and practices in order to eliminate all obstacles to human dignity, equality and equity in the family and in society, and promote full and equal participation of urban and rural women and women with disabilities in social, economic and political life, including in the formulation, implementation and follow-up of public policies and programmes;

(b) Establish structures, policies, objectives and measurable goals to ensure gender balance and equity in decision-making processes at all levels, broaden women's political, economic, social and cultural opportunities and independence, and support the empowerment of women, including through their various organizations, especially those of indigenous women, those at the grass-roots level,

and those of poverty-stricken communities, including through affirmative action, where necessary, and also through measures to integrate a gender perspective in the design and implementation of economic and social policies;

(c) Promote full and equal access of women to literacy, education and training, and remove all obstacles to their access to credit and other productive resources and to their ability to buy, hold and sell property and land equally with men;

(d) Take appropriate measures to ensure, on the basis of equality of men and women, universal access to the widest range of health-care services, including those relating to reproductive health care, consistent with the Programme of Action of the International Conference on Population and Development; 1/

(e) Remove the remaining restrictions on women's rights to own land, inherit property or borrow money, and ensure women's equal right to work;

(f) Establish policies, objectives and goals that enhance the equality of status, welfare and opportunity of

1/ See *Report of the International Conference on Population and Development, Cairo, 5-13 September 1994* (A/CONF.171/13 and Add.1).

the girl child, especially in regard to health, nutrition, literacy and education, recognizing that gender discrimination starts at the earliest stages of life;

(g) Promote equal partnership between women and men in family and community life and society, emphasize the shared responsibility of men and women in the care of children and support for older family members, and emphasize men's shared responsibility and promote their active involvement in responsible parenthood and responsible sexual and reproductive behaviour;

(h) Take effective measures, including through the enactment and enforcement of laws, and implement policies to combat and eliminate all forms of discrimination, exploitation, abuse and violence against women and girl children, in accordance with relevant international instruments and declarations;

(i) Promote and protect the full and equal enjoyment by women of all human rights and fundamental freedoms;

(j) Formulate or strengthen policies and practices to ensure that women are enabled to participate fully in paid work and in employment through such measures as positive action, education, training, appropriate protection under labour legislation and facilitating the provision of quality child care and other support services.

At the international level, we will:

(k) Promote and protect women's human rights

and encourage the ratification of, if possible by the year 2000, the avoidance, as far as possible, of the resort to reservations to, and the implementation of the provisions of the Convention on the Elimination of All Forms of Discrimination against Women 2/ and other relevant instruments, as well as the implementation of the Nairobi Forward-looking Strategies for the Advancement of Women, 3/ the Geneva Declaration for Rural Women 4/ and the Programme of Action of the International Conference on Population and Development;

(l) Give specific attention to the preparations for the Fourth World Conference on Women, to be held at Beijing in September 1995, and to the implementation and follow-up of the conclusions of that Conference;

(m) Promote international cooperation to assist developing countries, at their request, in their efforts to achieve equality and equity and the empowerment of women;

(n) Devise suitable means to recognize and make visible the full extent of the work of women and all their contributions to the national economy, including contributions in the unremunerated and domestic sectors.

...

1/ See *Report of the International Conference on Population and Development, Cairo, 5-13 September 1994* (A/CONF.171/13 and Add.1).

Document 123

Report of the Secretary-General to the General Assembly on the Convention on the Elimination of All Forms of Discrimination against Women, including the text of the proposed amendment to article 20 of the Convention (extract)

A/50/346, 11 August 1995

I. Introduction

1. By its resolution 34/180 of 18 December 1979, the General Assembly adopted the Convention on the Elimination of All Forms of Discrimination against Women. In its subsequent resolutions 35/140, 36/131, 37/64, 38/109, 39/130, 40/39, 41/108, 42/60, 42/62, 43/100, 44/73, 45/124, 47/94 and 49/164, the Assembly urged States that had not yet ratified or acceded to the Convention to do so as soon as possible and requested the Secretary-General to report on the status of the Convention. In its resolution 45/124 of 14 December 1990, the Assembly requested the Secretary-General to submit this report annually. In accordance with those resolutions, the Secretary-General has submitted at each session of the Assembly a report on the status of the

Convention (A/35/428, A/36/295 and Add.1, A/37/349 and Add.1, A/38/378, A/39/486, A/40/623, A/41/608 and Add.1, A/42/627, A/43/605, A/44/457, A/45/426, A/46/462, A/47/368, A/48/354 and A/49/308).

2. In its resolution 49/164 of 23 December 1994, on the Convention on the Elimination of All Forms of Discrimination against Women, the General Assembly recommended "that the States parties to the Convention, in the light of the reports mentioned in paragraphs 6 and 7 above, review the working situation of the Committee and its capacity to fulfil its mandate more effectively, and in this context also that the States parties consider the possibility of amending article 20 of the Convention so as to allow for sufficient meeting time for the Committee". It also "requested the States parties to the Conven-

tion to meet in 1995 in order to consider the review of article 20 of the Convention mentioned in paragraph 8 above". The reports mentioned in the resolution included the report of the Secretary-General on the working methods of the Committee and its capacity to fulfil its mandate 1/ as well as the reports of the Committee on its twelfth 2/ and thirteenth 3/ sessions.

3. In its decision 49/448 on "Consideration of the request for the revision of article 20, paragraph 1, of the Convention on the Elimination of All Forms of Discrimination against Women", the "General Assembly, on the recommendation of the Third Committee, 4/ aware that the Governments of Denmark, Finland, Iceland, Norway and Sweden have made a written request 5/ for the revision of article 20, paragraph 1, of the Convention on the Elimination of All Forms of Discrimination against Women 6/ by replacing the words 'normally meet for a period of not more than two weeks annually in order' by the words 'meet annually for a period necessary', and having noted that article 26 of the Convention stipulates that the General Assembly shall decide upon the steps, if any, to be taken in respect of such a request decided: (*a*) to request the States parties to the Convention to consider the request for a revision of article 20, paragraph 1, at a meeting to be convened in 1995; and (*b*) to request the States parties at the meeting to limit the scope of any revision of the Convention to article 20, paragraph 1, thereof".

4. In pursuance of General Assembly decision 49/448, the 8th meeting of State parties took place at United Nations Headquarters in New York on 22 May 1995. On the basis of its discussion the meeting of States parties adopted resolution 8/1 on "Proposed amendment to article 20, paragraph 1, of the Convention on the Elimination of All Forms of Discrimination against Women". The resolution is contained in annex I to the present report.

II. Status of the Convention on the Elimination of all Forms of Discrimination against Women

5. The Convention was opened for signature in New York on 1 March 1980 and, in accordance with its article 27, entered into force on 3 September 1981.

6. As at 1 August 1995, 143 States had ratified the Convention, of which 49 States had acceded and 5 had succeeded to it. In addition, six States had signed it without yet ratifying it. Since the last progress report (A/49/308), the following States parties have ratified, acceded or succeeded to the Convention: Cameroon, Chad, Comoros, Georgia, Kuwait, Malaysia, Papua New Guinea, Uzbekistan.

7. Reservations were made upon ratification to the Convention by Malaysia and Kuwait.

8. An objection was received during the period 1 August 1994 to 1 August 1995 from Norway.

9. One reformulation of a reservation made upon accession was made by the Libyan Arab Jamahiriya.

10. One withdrawal of a reservation and declaration was received from the United Kingdom of Great Britain and Northern Ireland.

Annex I

Draft resolution 8/1

Proposed amendment to article 20, paragraph 1, of the Convention on the Elimination of All Forms of Discrimination against Women

The States parties to the Convention on the Elimination of All Forms of Discrimination against Women,

Recalling General Assembly resolution 49/164 of 23 December 1994 on the Convention on the Elimination of All Forms of Discrimination against Women,

Noting the proposed revision of article 20, paragraph 1, of the Convention on the Elimination of All Forms of Discrimination against Women by replacing the words "normally meet for a period of not more than two weeks annually in order" by the words "meet annually for a period necessary" put forward by the Governments of Denmark, Finland, Iceland, Norway and Sweden, in accordance with article 26 of the Convention,

Further noting General Assembly decision 49/448 in accordance with article 26 requesting that the current meeting of States parties consider the proposed amendment and to limit the scope of any revision of the Convention to article 20, paragraph 1,

Reiterating the importance of the Convention on the Elimination of All Forms of Discrimination against Women as well as the contribution of the Committee on the Elimination of Discrimination against Women to the United Nations efforts to eliminate discrimination against women,

Noting that the workload of the Committee on the Elimination of Discrimination against Women has increased because of the growing number of States parties of the Convention and that the annual session of the Committee is the shortest of all the annual sessions of the human rights treaty bodies,

Recalling recommendation 22 of the Committee on the Elimination of Discrimination against Women at its fourteenth session on the meeting time of the Committee,

Convinced of the need to adopt measures to enable the Committee, in accordance with its mandate, to con-

1/ A/49/308, chap. III.
2/ *Official Records of the General Assembly, Forty-eighth Session, Supplement No. 38* (A/48/38).
3/ Ibid., *Forty-ninth Session, Supplement No. 38 (A/49/38).*
4/ A/49/607, para. 38.
5/ A/C.3/49/26.
6/ General Assembly resolution 34/180, annex.

sider in a thorough and timely manner the reports submitted by States parties and to discharge all its responsibilities under the Convention,

Also convinced that an adequate amount of time for the meetings of the Committee is a vital factor in ensuring in future years the continued effectiveness of the Committee on the Elimination of Discrimination against Women,

1. *Decide* to replace article 20, paragraph 1, of the Convention on the Elimination of All Forms of Discrimination against Women with the following text: "The Committee shall normally meet annually in order to consider the reports submitted in accordance with article 18 of the present Convention. The duration of the meetings of the Committee shall be determined by a meeting of the States parties to the present Convention, subject to the approval of the General Assembly.";

2. *Recommend* that the General Assembly take note with approval of this amendment at its fiftieth session;

3. *Decide* that the amendment shall enter into force following consideration by the General Assembly and when it has been accepted by a two-thirds majority of States parties which shall have so notified the Secretary-General as depositary of the Convention.

...

Document 124

Report of the Secretary-General to the General Assembly on traffic in women and girls

A/50/369, 24 August 1995

I. Introduction

1. In its resolution 49/166 of 23 December 1994 on traffic in women and girls, the General Assembly expressed its grave concern over the worsening problem of trafficking in women and girl children, particularly the internationalization of the traffic, and requested that Governments, relevant United Nations bodies and specialized agencies, as well as intergovernmental and nongovernmental organizations, take a number of specific steps to address the problem. Among other measures, the Assembly encouraged States to consider ratifying the Convention for the Suppression of the Traffic in Persons and of the Exploitation of the Prostitution of Others (resolution 317 (IV), annex) and other relevant international instruments, and invited further consideration of the problem by the Special Rapporteur of the Commission on Human Rights on violence against women, the Working Group on Contemporary Forms of Slavery of the Subcommission on Prevention of Discrimination and Protection of Minorities, the World Summit for Social Development, the Fourth World Conference on Women: Action for Equality, Development and Peace and the Ninth United Nations Congress on the Prevention of Crime and the Treatment of Offenders. The Assembly requested the Secretary-General to submit to the Assembly at its fiftieth session a preliminary report on the implementation of the resolution.

II. Trafficking: nature and scope of the problem and recent developments

2. Trafficking has been a long-standing concern of the United Nations. The importance of traffic in persons has increased and taken new forms in recent years because of changes in the global economy. Trafficking, which mainly affects women, has become a world-wide phenomenon and is often highly organized. The focus of attention has increasingly shifted to international dimensions of trafficking and away from the issue as a purely domestic concern.

3. The Convention on the Elimination of All Forms of Discrimination against Women (resolution 34/180, annex), in article 6 calls upon States parties to "take all appropriate measures, including legislation, to suppress all forms of traffic in women and exploitation of prostitution of women". This article is first and foremost addressed to those who profit from the sexual exploitation of girls and women. The Convention, which entered into force on 3 September 1981, is the most comprehensive document on women's rights in existence. As of 24 July 1995, 96 States had signed the Convention and 143 had ratified or acceded to it.

4. Trafficking also affects children, in particular girl children, with regard to sexual exploitation, child labour, intercountry adoption and other forms of illegal activities and/or exploitation. The Convention on the Rights of the Child (resolution 44/25, annex), adopted by the General Assembly in 1989 and since ratified by 177 States, is an international instrument that promotes and protects the human rights of children in different areas (civil, cultural, economic, political and social rights). This Convention specifically addresses the issue of trafficking in its article 35:

"States Parties shall take all appropriate national, bilateral and multilateral measures to prevent the abduction of, the sale of or traffic in children for any purpose or in any form."

The Convention protects children from being victims of any form of trafficking and also guarantees their protection from trafficking in several other articles, including: article 3, dealing with the best interest of the child; article 11, dealing with illicit transfer and non-return; article 21, on adoption; article 32, on child labour; article 34, on sexual exploitation; article 36, dealing with other forms of exploitation; and article 39, dealing with physical and psychological rehabilitation.

5. Prohibitions against trafficking in women have been set forth by international conventions beginning with the International Agreement of 18 May 1904 for the Suppression of the White Slave Traffic, and include the International Convention of 4 May 1910 for the Suppression of the White Slave Traffic, the International Convention of 30 September 1921 for the Suppression of the Traffic in Women and Children, the 1926 Slavery Convention and the 1949 Convention for the Suppression of the Traffic in Persons and of the Exploitation of the Prostitution of Others (resolution 317 (IV), annex). Under the 1949 Convention, the States parties agreed, in article 1: "to punish any person who, to gratify the passions of another: 1. Procures, entices or leads away, for purposes of prostitution, another person, even with the consent of that person; 2. Exploits the prostitution of another person, even with the consent of that person." In the preamble, it declares that prostitution and traffic in persons are "incompatible with the dignity and worth of the human persons and endanger the welfare of the individual, the family and the community". The 1949 Convention was elaborated before the contemporary extensive system of treaty-based human rights protection existed within the United Nations.

6. The linkage between trafficking and the violation of women's human rights has also been clearly established. The Vienna Declaration and Programme of Action, adopted by the World Conference on Human Rights on 25 June 1993, 1/ states that "Gender-based violence and all forms of sexual harassment and exploitation, including those resulting from cultural prejudice and international trafficking, are incompatible with the dignity and worth of the human person, and must be eliminated." The Declaration on the Elimination of Violence against Women (resolution 48/104) includes in article 2, the following definition: "Physical, sexual and psychological violence occurring within the general community, including rape, sexual abuse, sexual harassment and intimidation at work, in educational institutions and elsewhere, trafficking in women and forced prostitution". The Commission on Human Rights, in paragraph 4 of its resolution 1994/45 listed trafficking among the

forms of violence against women and as a violation of their human rights and called for its elimination.

7. The increasing international dimension of trafficking of women and girls was raised in the report of the Secretary-General to the General Assembly at its forty-ninth session on violence against women migrant workers (A/49/354).

8. As part of its response to that report, the General Assembly, in its resolution 49/166, condemned the "illicit and clandestine movement of persons across national and international borders, largely from developing countries and some countries with economies in transition, with the end goal of forcing women and girl children into sexually or economically oppressive and exploitative situations for the profit of recruiters, traffickers and crime syndicates, as well as other illegal activities related to trafficking, such as forced domestic labour, false marriages, clandestine employment and false adoption". While focusing on international dimensions of trafficking, the Assembly goes beyond a narrow view of trafficking only for the purpose of prostitution to incorporate other aspects of forced labour and deceptive practices.

9. In addition to the World Conference on Human Rights, other recent United Nations conferences have included the issue of trafficking in their final documents. In its Programme of Action, the International Conference on Population and Development, held at Cairo from 5 to 13 September 1994, stated: 2/

"All States and families should give the highest possible priority to children. The child has the right to standards of living adequate for its well-being and the right to the highest attainable standards of health, and the right to education. The child has the right to be cared for, guided and supported by parents, families and society and to be protected by appropriate legislative, administrative, social and educational measures from all forms of physical or mental violence, injury or abuse, neglect or negligent treatment, maltreatment or exploitation, including sale, trafficking, sexual abuse and trafficking in its organs." (Principle 11)

"...

"4.9. Countries should take full measures to eliminate all forms of exploitation, abuse, harassment and violence against women, adolescents and children. This implies both preventive actions and rehabilitation of victims. Countries should prohibit degrading practices, such as trafficking in women,

1/ Report of the World Conference on Human Rights, Vienna, 14-25 June 1993 (A/CONF.157/24 (Part I), chap. III, sect. I, para. 18).
2/ See A/CONF.171/13, chap. I, resolution 1, annex.

adolescents and children and exploitation through prostitution, and pay special attention to protecting the rights and safety of those who suffer from these crimes and those in potentially exploitable situations, such as migrant women, women in domestic service and schoolgirls. In this regard, international safeguards and mechanisms for cooperation should be put in place to ensure that these measures are implemented."

"...

"7.39. Active and open discussion of the need to protect women, youth and children from any abuse, including sexual abuse, exploitation, trafficking and violence, must be encouraged and supported by educational programmes at both national and community levels. Governments should set the necessary conditions and procedures to encourage victims to report violations of their rights. Laws addressing those concerns should be enacted where they do not exist, made explicit, strengthened and enforced, and appropriate rehabilitation services provided. Governments should also prohibit the production and the trade of child pornography."

"...

"10.16.   The objectives are:

"...

"(c) To prevent all international trafficking in migrants, especially for the purposes of prostitution;"

"...

"10.18. Governments of both receiving countries and countries of origin should adopt effective sanctions against those who organize undocumented migration, exploit undocumented migrants or engage in trafficking in undocumented migrants, especially those who engage in any form of international traffic in women, youth and children. Governments of countries of origin, where the activities of agents or other intermediaries in the migration process are legal, should regulate such activities in order to prevent abuses, especially exploitation, prostitution and coercive adoption."

10. In commitment 6 of the Copenhagen Declaration on Social Development 3/ the World Summit for Social Development stated:

"At the international level, we will:

"...

"(y) Intensify and coordinate international support for education and health programmes based on respect for human dignity and focused on the protection of all women and children, especially against exploitation, trafficking and harmful practices, such as child prostitution, female genital mutilation and child marriages."

11. In the Programme of Action, 4/ the World Summit stated:

"17. International support for national efforts to promote a favourable political and legal environment must be in conformity with the Charter of the United Nations and principles of international law and consistent with the Declaration on Principles of International Law concerning Friendly Relations and Cooperation among States in accordance with the Charter of the United Nations. Support calls for the following actions:

"...

"(b) Coordinating policies, actions and legal instruments and/or measures to combat terrorism, all forms of extremist violence, illicit arms trafficking, organized crime and illicit drug problems, money laundering and related crimes, trafficking in women, adolescents, children, migrants and human organs, and other activities contrary to human rights and human dignity;"

"...

"63. There is need for intensified international cooperation and national attention to the situation of migrant workers and their families. To that end:

"...

"(d) Governments of both receiving countries and countries of origin should adopt effective sanctions against those who organize undocumented migration, exploit undocumented migrants or engage in trafficking in undocumented migrants;"

"...

"78. In order to address the concerns and basic human needs related to undocumented migrants:

"(a) Governments are urged to cooperate in reducing the causes of undocumented migration, safeguarding the basic human rights of undocumented migrants, preventing their exploitation and offering them appropriate means of appeal according to national legislation and punishing criminals who organize trafficking in human beings;"

"...

"79. Addressing the problems created by violence, crime, substance abuse and the production, use and trafficking of illicit drugs, and the rehabilitation of addicts requires:

3/ See A/CONF.166/9, chap. I, resolution 1, annex I.
4/ Ibid., annex II.

"(k) Combating trafficking in women and children through national and internationally coordinated measures, at the same time establishing or strengthening institutions for the rehabilitation of the victims of the trafficking of women and children."

12. At its thirty-ninth session, the Commission on the Status of Women adopted resolution 39/6 on traffic in women and girls. 5/ In addition to including similar provisions to those adopted by the General Assembly, the Commission invited Governments to combat trafficking in women and children through nationally and internationally coordinated measures, at the same time establishing or strengthening institutions for the protection of the victims of trafficking and to ensure for victims the necessary assistance, including legal support services that are linguistically and culturally accessible, towards their full protection, treatment and rehabilitation; and to consider the development of standard minimum rules for the humanitarian treatment of trafficked persons, consistent with internationally-recognized human rights standards. It welcomed the adoption of resolution 1994/5 by the Subcommission on Prevention of Discrimination and Protection of Minorities recommending that Governments adopt legislation to prevent child prostitution and child pornography. It also drew attention to the report of the Special Rapporteur of the Commission on Human Rights on the sale of children, child prostitution and child pornography. It requested the Secretary-General to focus the International Day for the Abolition of Slavery, 2 December 1996, on the problem of trafficking in human persons, especially women and children, and to devote one meeting of the fifty-first session of the General Assembly to the discussion of the problem.

13. In regional preparatory conferences for the Fourth World Conference on Women, the issue of trafficking has been raised in those of Asia and the Pacific, Latin America and the Caribbean. In the Jakarta Plan of Action adopted by the regional conferences for Asia and the Pacific, Europe and Latin America and the Caribbean, Governments included, among actions to be taken:

"Child prostitution and forced prostitution must be made illegal and heavy punishment imposed on traffickers and agents. Laws should be reformulated to shift the bias against prostitutes that currently exists in many countries." (para. E.1.x.)

14. The Regional Programme of Action for the Women of Latin America and the Caribbean, 1995-2001 states:

"Promoting the adoption and implementation of an international convention against all forms of overt and covert sexual exploitation, including sex tourism and child prostitution, which provides for the establishment of social services to assist victims of all forms of sexual exploitation and for the prosecution of traffickers and managers of the sex industry." (strategic action V.1.g)

15. The Regional Platform of Action—Women in a Changing World—Call for Action from an ECE Perspective, adopted by the European region, states:

"Special measures should be adopted to eliminate trafficking in women and to assist women and children victims of sex trade, sexual violence, forced prostitution and forced labour, with special attention to migrant women. Countries of origin and recipient countries should enforce existing legislation in order to protect the rights of women and girl victims and to sanction the offenders. Specific actions should be developed at the intergovernmental level to prevent further abuse, including the dismantling of international networks of trafficking. Special measures for the social, medical and psychological care of these victims should be designed based on cooperation between Governments and non-governmental organizations." (para. 84)

16. The draft Platform for Action to be adopted by the Fourth World Conference on Women (A/CONF.177/L.1) includes strategic objective D.3, "Adopt special measures to eliminate trafficking in women and to assist female victims of violence due to prostitution and trafficking", which includes the following actions, most of which were adopted during the thirty-ninth session by the Commission on the Status of Women acting as preparatory committee for the Fourth World Conference on Women:

"*Actions to be taken*

"131. By Governments of countries of origin, transit and destination, regional and international organizations, as appropriate:

"(a) Consider the ratification and enforcement of international conventions on trafficking in persons and on slavery;

"(b) Take appropriate measures to address the root factors, including external factors, that encourage trafficking in women and girls for prostitution, [other commercial sex work], forced marriages and forced labour in order to eliminate trafficking in women, including by strengthening existing legislation with a view to providing better protection of the rights of women and girls and to punishing the perpetrators, through both criminal and civil measures;

"(c) Step up cooperation and concerted action by

5/ *Official Records of the Economic and Social Council, 1995, Supplement No. 6* (E/1995/26), chap. I, sect. C.

all relevant law enforcement authorities and institutions with a view to dismantling [national and international] networks in trafficking;

"(d) [Allocate resources to provide comprehensive programmes designed [to heal victims of trafficking] including through job training, legal assistance and confidential health care] and take measures to cooperate with non-governmental organizations to provide for the social, medical and psychological care of the victims of trafficking;

"(e) Develop educational and training programmes and policies and consider enacting legislation aimed at preventing sex tourism and trafficking, giving special emphasis to the protection of young women and children."

17. Trafficking across international borders is by definition illegal. The very nature of undocumented status makes illegal migrants vulnerable to various forms of exploitation. The question must be asked, however, whether trafficking is the same as illegal migration. It would seem that the two are related, but different. Migration across frontiers without documentation does not have to be coerced or exploitative. At the same time, persons can be trafficked with their consent. A distinction could be made in terms of the purpose for which borders are crossed and whether movement occurs through the instrumentality of another person. Under this distinction, trafficking of women and girls would be defined in terms of "the end goal of forcing women and girl children into sexually or economically oppressive and exploitative situations" and the fact that it is done "for the profit of recruiters, traffickers and crime syndicates" (General Assembly resolution 49/166).

18. The analysis of how trafficking is being approached in recent international declarations, programmes of action and resolutions suggests that there is still some ambiguity in how the issue should be addressed and whether, in terms of the increasingly international dimensions of the problem, the existing international instruments are effective or whether they need to be reviewed.

III. Activities of United Nations bodies and agencies to address the problem of trafficking

19. The issue of trafficking is now being addressed in a variety of different intergovernmental and other United Nations forums. An examination of how this takes place indicates both the potential of the United Nations to deal with the issue and the need for a greater degree of coordination.

20. The Commission on the Status of Women has had, periodically, a concern with trafficking and with prostitution. Most recently the issue has arisen in the context of drafting the Declaration on the Elimination of Violence against Women. At its thirty-ninth session, the Commission adopted resolution 39/6 as noted in paragraph 12 above.

21. The Convention on the Elimination of All Forms of Discrimination against Women and the Convention on the Rights of the Child are the two human rights treaties that specifically address trafficking, as noted above. The Committee on the Elimination of Discrimination against Women, in examining periodic reports of States parties to the Convention has addressed the issue of trafficking. An analysis of the Convention's article 6 notes that most States parties report the enactment of laws prohibiting and penalizing all forms of traffic in women and the exploitation of prostitution. The Committee focused on the legal situation, particularly prohibition, criminalization, prosecution and punishment as it relates to the prostitute, the client and any third person profiting from the prostitution of others. Most States parties do not favour prohibition of prostitution, but rather social measures to prevent it. Attention has been focused on the position of prostitutes, including the exercise of human rights, rather than on measures taken to prevent the trafficking of women.

22. The analysis, together with other information, led the Committee to adopt in 1992 general recommendation 19 dealing with violence against women. 6/ In paragraph 14 of the general recommendation, relating to article 6 of the Convention, it is stated that:

"Poverty and unemployment increase opportunities for trafficking in women. In addition to established forms of trafficking there are new forms of sexual exploitation, such as sex tourism, the recruitment of domestic labour from developing countries to work in developed countries and organized marriages between women from developing countries and foreign nationals. These practices are incompatible with the equal enjoyment of rights by women and with respect for their rights and dignity. They put women at special risk of violence and abuse."

23. Although the Committee has tried to define the scope of traffic in women and exploitation of the prostitution of women, it has not clarified what kind of reporting is expected from the States parties in the implementation of article 6.

24. The Committee on the Rights of the Child, a 10-member expert body that monitors the implementation of the Convention on the Rights of the Child, regularly addresses the question of trafficking in children, including girls, during the review of State party reports,

6/ *Official Records of the General Assembly, Forty-seventh Session, Supplement No. 38* (A/47/38), chap. I.

i.e., sexual exploitation, including prostitution; sex tourism and pornography; child labour, including slavery and forced labour; and intercountry adoption.

25. In some of its concluding observations on State parties reports, which it began to examine in 1992, the Committee explicitly stated the need to fight against trafficking in children. Thus, in countries where cases of abuse, sale or traffic in children exist in relation to intercountry adoption, the Committee has usually suggested to the Government to ratify the Hague Convention on Protection of Children and Cooperation in respect of Intercountry Adoption (1993) (see para. 41 below). The Committee has also expressed its concern on reports of the forced labour of children, the exploitation of child labour in the informal and agricultures sectors and the trafficking of children which have been brought to its attention.

26. The 1949 Convention for the Suppression of the Traffic in Persons and of the Exploitation of the Prostitution of Others, in addition to requiring protection for all persons against trafficking and exploitation of prostitution, in its article 21, requires States parties to:

"... communicate to the Secretary-General of the United Nations such laws and regulations as have already been promulgated in their States, and thereafter annually such laws and regulations as may be promulgated, relating to subjects of the present Convention, as well as all measures taken by them concerning the application of the Convention. The information received shall be published periodically by the Secretary-General and sent to all Members of the United Nations and to non-member States ..."

27. The Convention currently has 69 States parties. Ratification, accession or succession to the Convention has been slow, if steady. Between 1949 and 1960, 27 States became party; between 1961 and 1970, 11 States; between 1971 and 1980, 10; and between 1981 and 1990, 11. Since 1990, 10 more States have become party, although 6 of these were successors to States that had previously been party.

28. Reports relating to the implementation of the Convention are considered by the Working Group on Contemporary Forms of Slavery of the Subcommission on Prevention of Discrimination and Protection of Minorities of the Commission on Human Rights. The mandate of the Working Group comprises a review of developments in the field of slavery, examination of any information from credible sources on the subject and recommendations for remedial action (Economic and Social Council decision 16 (LVI) of 17 May 1974). The United Nations Voluntary Trust Fund on Contemporary Forms of Slavery was established by the General Assembly at its forty-sixth session in 1991 (General Assembly resolution 46/122 of 17 December 1991). The purpose of the Fund is to assist representatives of non-governmental organizations dealing with contemporary forms of slavery to participate in the Working Group. The Fund should also extend assistance, humanitarian, legal and financial aid to individuals whose human rights have been severely violated as a result of contemporary forms of slavery.

29. The Commission on Human Rights itself has recently dealt with the issue. In its resolution 1995/25 of 3 March 1995, entitled "Traffic in women and girls", the Commission urged Governments to combat the problem of trafficking in women and girls to insure that victims were provided with assistance, support, legal advice, protection, treatment and rehabilitation. It was recommended that the problem be considered in implementation of all relevant international instruments.

30. The Special Rapporteur of the Commission on Human Rights on violence against women considered the issue of prostitution and trafficking in her preliminary report, submitted to the Commission on Human Rights in accordance with resolution 1994/45 of 4 March 1994. She described the nature of the problem as being the economic exploitation, health hazards and lack of health care, appalling work conditions, vulnerability to violence and lack of legal protection for women who are trafficked for the purposes of prostitution. The Special Rapporteur noted that the increase in international trafficking of women and recruitment of younger and younger girls "in many parts of the world is linked, among other things, to the increasing fear of HIV/AIDS (and the perceived need therefore to recruit untainted blood), the increase of sex tourism ... and continuing societal condonation of the imperatives of male sexuality ... Women who are trafficked are by and large not aware of what awaits them ... the larger percentage of trafficked women are sold into bondage by their parents, husbands, boyfriends ... or they are deceived or coerced." These practices thrive despite legal prohibitions and regulations owing in some measure to the complicity of policies and other enforcement officials.

31. The Special Rapporteur recommended that States be actively encouraged to accede to the International Covenant on Civil and Political Rights, the Convention for the Suppression of the Traffic in Persons and of the Exploitation of the Prostitution of Others, and the Convention on the Elimination of All Forms of Discrimination against Women. On the basis of her findings and the extensive materials and documentation received from varied sources on this issue, the Special Rapporteur is intending to carry out a field mission in the course of 1996 on the issue of trafficking and forced prostitution in women and girls.

32. Regarding the implementation of article 6 of

the Convention on the Elimination of All Forms of Discrimination against Women, the Special Rapporteur suggested that measures taken to combat trafficking could include legislation to prosecute all persons involved in exploitation of women through prostitution and trafficking, including brothel owners, pimps and airlines; increasing the statutory age for rape to 18 and actively prosecuting clients who violate this law; and establishing commissions of inquiry to investigate allegations of abuse and complicity by government agents.

33. The Special Rapporteur further emphasized the need to monitor employment, recruitment, advertising and pornography agencies to stop the recruitment of young girls into prostitution. While some groups argue for legalized prostitution regulated by health and labour laws as a way to decrease trafficking, forced prostitution and related abuses, the Special Rapporteur noted that "most societies and cultures ... believe that moral condemnation and criminalizing activity associated with prostitution and trafficking are the only means available for eradicating violence against women in this sphere".

34. In his report to the General Assembly at its forty-ninth session (A/49/478, annex), the Special Rapporteur of the Commission on Human Rights on the sale of children, child prostitution and child pornography emphasized that child prostitution was an enormous national and international issue. He reported that INTERPOL had established a Standing Working Party on Offences against Minors to improve transnational cooperation in preventing and combating child exploitation. He reviewed the serious problem of child prostitution and reported a number of activities to increase awareness and counter trafficking of children for the purposes of prostitution. The Special Rapporteur noted that the problem of trafficking and prostitution of girls had been given greater attention in recent years in a number of countries.

35. Under the crime prevention and criminal justice programme, the Commission on Crime Prevention and Criminal Justice and the Ninth Congress on the Prevention of Crime and the Treatment of Offenders have considered trafficking but have not addressed particular gender aspects of the issue. One approach is the consideration of traffic in girls and boys, reflected in Commission resolution 3/2 on "International traffic in minors". 7/ This topic was also a priority at the Ninth Congress, where international cooperation for the prosecution of illicit traffic in children had been solicited (resolution 7).

36. During the fourth session of the Commission, attention was focused on the complicity of organized criminal activities in the illegal trafficking in minors. In document E/CN.15/1995/4, on the world situation with regard to international traffic in minors, the Secretary-

General concluded that the international traffic in minors was a serious criminal offence that was conducted basically by criminal organizations with international connections. The Commission prepared a draft resolution for the Economic and Social Council requesting that the Secretary-General initiate the views of Member States on an international convention on traffic in children.

37. At the same session of the Commission, a note by the Secretariat on additional measures to combat alien-smuggling also highlighted women as an especially vulnerable group of smuggled illegal migrants (E/CN.15/1995/3, paras. 9, 12 and 13). This issue has also been raised in the context of organized smuggling of illegal migrants. On the recommendation of the Commission, the Economic and Social Council adopted resolution 1994/14 of 25 July 1994. At its fourth session, the Commission also recommended draft resolution E/CN.15/1995/L.4 dated 24 July 1995 on criminal justice action to combat the organized smuggling of illegal migrants across national boundaries for adoption by the Council. In the resolution (1995/10), the Council determined that the problem required international scrutiny and requested that Member States review and reinforce laws to combat all aspects of trafficking and penalize traffickers.

38. The available data on forced prostitution and trafficking were reviewed for *The World's Women 1995: Trends and Statistics* and summarized in the section on violence against women. The data, while limited, suggested that these problems are widespread in many countries and that little attention was being given by Governments to improving measurement techniques and data sources.

39. At the regional level, the Economic and Social Commission for Asia and the Pacific (ESCAP) has included activities related to the issue in its programme. For example, in 1991, it organized a workshop on the promotion of community awareness for the prevention of prostitution (ST/ESCAP/1078).

IV. Developments regarding the issue of trafficking outside the United Nations

40. Trafficking has been given attention by other intergovernmental bodies, especially in Europe. The Council of Europe held a seminar at Strasbourg in 1991 on action against traffic in women and forced prostitution as violations of human rights and human dignity and a working conference at Amsterdam in July 1991 on trafficking in women. The conference was attended by non-governmental organizations from 14 European

7/ *Official Records of the Economic and Social Council, 1994, Supplement No. 11* (E/1994/31), chap. I.C.

countries. Conference participants concluded that the widening gap between rich and poor countries increased the vulnerability of women from third world countries to trafficking and abuse and that strategies should aim to empower women rather than control or suppress abuse and violence, since efforts at control and suppression often led to negative consequences for trafficked women. They called for a new international convention against traffic in persons to replace the 1949 Convention (see para. 5), measures coordinated among European countries to safeguard the rights of trafficked women while prosecuting traffickers and support for national groups and organizations to increase awareness of the problem and develop policies to combat trafficking. They recommended international collaboration for the support of grass-roots organizations to offer education and legal and social assistance to women considering migration and to migrant prostitutes. The participants noted that law enforcement, government, health and judicial systems that ignored the situation of trafficked women and girls, that punished complaints by deportation, that failed to prosecute traffickers and exempted illegal migrants from equal protection under the law made trafficking easier and more profitable and violated the human rights of women. Businesses, including hotels, entertainment and airlines, that promoted and benefit from sex tourism contributed to trafficking in women and girls.

41. The Hague Convention on Protection of Children and Cooperation in respect of Intercountry Adoption (1993) is an international instrument whose goal it is to regulate intercountry adoption through international cooperation so that cases of abuse, sale and trafficking linked to this activity can be eliminated. This treaty was adopted on 1 May 1993, and as at 1 September of the same year, 4 States had ratified this international instrument and 15 had signed it.

42. The International Workshop on International Migration and Traffic in Women, held in Thailand in October 1994, was organized by the Foundation for Women, Thailand, the Women's Studies Centre, Chiangmai, and the Women and Autonomy Centre of Leiden University in the Netherlands. It was a forum for nongovernmental organizations from a variety of countries that reviewed the experiences of trafficked women, studies conducted in three sending countries and four receiving countries and papers presented on the problem in a dozen countries and regions. As one outcome of the workshop, the Global Alliance Against Traffic in Women was formed. Subsequently, the Global Alliance submitted a statement on prostitution and trafficking to the Special Rapporteur on violence against women at Geneva in February 1995.

43. The Ministry of Foreign Affairs of the Nether-lands, the Department of the Law of International Organizations and the Netherlands Institute of Human Rights of Utrecht University and the Centre of Human Rights of the University of Limburg organized a conference at Utrecht from 15 to 19 November 1994 on combatting traffic in persons. The conference suggested in its final conclusions that the Commission on Human Rights should establish a thematic special rapporteur or a thematic working group on traffic in persons. It also suggested that the Commission consider the usefulness of the Working Group on Contemporary Forms of Slavery and, if appropriate, consider strengthening its mandate. 8/

44. The Coalition against Trafficking in Women with its long-standing concern about the issue of trafficking, has undertaken a number of activities. The Coalition, in collaboration with UNESCO, brought together a group of experts to elaborate a convention broadly prohibiting sexual exploitation and asking that States suppress all prostitution, sex tourism, mail order bride markets, and trafficking in women.

V. Conclusions

45. The concern with trafficking in women as an international problem is growing, and being considered in a variety of different forums. The problem has been addressed, variously, in terms of: (a) its human rights dimensions, including as discrimination against women and violence against women; (b) migration and its regulation; (c) crime prevention; and (d) social services. In most cases, the aspects have been considered separately and at least four subsidiary bodies of the Economic and Social Council (the Commission on Human Rights, the Commission on the Status of Women, the Commission on Population and Development and the Commission on Crime Prevention and Criminal Justice) have indicated a legislative interest in the problem. At least two international treaties, the 1949 Convention for the Suppression of the Traffic in Persons and of the Exploitation of the Prostitution of Others and the Convention on the Elimination of All Forms of Discrimination against Women address the issue. In addition, the Convention on the Rights of the Child stipulates that States must take all necessary measures to prevent the trafficking in girls, in particular through preventive measures such as education and training of special professional groups and rehabilitation policies.

46. Steps requested by General Assembly resolution 49/166, including the gathering and sharing of information about all aspects of traffic in women and girls,

8/ Netherlands Institute of Human Rights, *Combating Traffic in Persons*, Proceedings of the Conference on Traffic in Persons, Utrecht and Maastricht, 15-19 November 1994, Special No. 17, Utrecht, 1995.

efforts to increase public awareness, the adoption of measures to prevent traffic and establish sanctions against traffickers and the provision of support, legal advice, protection, treatment and rehabilitation for victims of trafficking, all imply the desirability of a comprehensive approach to the issue.

47. In the light of the various injunctions arising from recent international conferences including, most recently, the Fourth World Conference on Women, it might be desirable to undertake a full appraisal of the most appropriate means to ensure the desired comprehensive approach to the issue. This could include the preparation of a comprehensive report by the Secretary-General on measures to address international trafficking, including information needs and availability, adequacy of existing international instruments and means of harmonizing different approaches to aspects of the problem, both at the intergovernmental and the inter-secretariat levels.

Document 125

Report of the Secretary-General to the General Assembly on the effective mobilization and integration of women in development: gender issues in macroeconomic policy-making and development planning

A/50/399, 22 September 1995

I. Introduction

1. Reports on the effective mobilization of women in development have been submitted to the General Assembly, through the Economic and Social Council, regularly on a biennial basis for a number of years, starting at the forty-second session.

2. At that session, by its resolution 42/178 of 11 December 1987, the General Assembly recognized the significant contribution of women to the overall economy and recommended the intensification of efforts to promote the integration of women in development; it also urged Governments to include measures for the involvement of women, both as agents and as beneficiaries, in national development plans, and to review the impact on women of development policies and programmes. Subsequent reports have emphasized coordination of activities of organizations of the United Nations system relating to women in development (A/44/290), the effective mobilization of women in the implementation of the International Development Strategy for the Fourth United Nations Development Decade (A/46/464) and how gender was dealt with in Agenda 21 (A/48/393).

3. The 1994 World Survey on the Role of Women in Development 1/ analysed changes in the role of women in development in the context of global economic restructuring, focusing, among other issues, on the impact of development policies on women. The Second Review and Appraisal of the Implementation of the Nairobi Forward-looking Strategies for the Advancement of Women, in its analysis of factors affecting the implementation of the Strategies, considered a broad range of macroeconomic and international trade polices and their impact on the economic and social status of women.

4. Accordingly, building on the work already undertaken, the present report, the fourth of the biennial reports on the effective mobilization and integration of women in development, focuses on gender issues in entrepreneurship, macroeconomic policy-making and development planning. The choice of this theme reflects the growing recognition in academic circles and among development practitioners of the need to consider gender as a variable in the design of economic policies if their implementation is to produce an outcome that is both efficient and socially desirable.

5. The need for the explicit incorporation of gender issues in the design of economic policies, particularly policies of structural adjustment, has frequently been emphasized in the context of expert group meetings organized by the Division for the Advancement of Women of the Department for Policy Coordination and Sustainable Development 2/ and by various international development institutions. 3/ The growing evidence from analyses that have taken gender into account provides the

1/ United Nations publication, Sales No. E.95.IV.1.

2/ See, for example, the reports of the Secretary-General on the negative effects of the international economic situation on the improvement of the status of women (E/CN.6/1990/3); the integration of women in the process of development (E/CN.6/1992/8); and women in extreme poverty: integration of women's concerns in national development planning (E/CN.6/1993/3).

3/ See Commonwealth Secretariat, "Engendering adjustment for the 1990s"; report of a Commonwealth expert group on women and structural adjustment (1989); and "Women's economic potential to overcome poverty"; advance report of the findings and recommendations of the International Round Table on Women's Economic Potential to Overcome Poverty, Bonn/königswinter, 27-30 November 1994.

basis for questioning whether the current economic models that underpin national and international economic policy fully factor in this critical variable. The present report explores the wider question of economic policy from this perspective.

II. Engendering development: evolution of the concept

6. Consideration of the meaning and determinants of development and of development policies has produced a succession of approaches over the past three decades. The early preoccupation of development practitioners with economic growth gave way to strategies to secure basic needs and achieve national self-reliance as development came to be redefined in terms of poverty reduction. The lessons and experience of a decade of structural adjustment precipitated yet another reassessment of what development is all about. The notion of sustainable human development emphasizes the enlargement of the choices and opportunities available to people and views development as a participatory, people-centred and all-inclusive process. The experience of development policies over the past decade gave rise to a new growth theory combining efficiency with equity and providing a framework for analysing endogenous sources of growth. For most of the time, however, the presence of women in distinct parts of economic production was largely overlooked by the prevailing paradigm. That failure limited development efforts and their impact. Economic growth, project efficiency and social justice call for a new approach to development that systematically includes women.

7. Over the last decade, women-in-development issues, previously treated as an adjunct to the main goal of economic development, gradually gained a greater prominence within the development agenda and efforts, however tentative, were made to introduce gender variables into the analysis of variations in economic policy outcomes. The early attempt to "add women as an afterthought" 4/ to the pre-existing model of development gave way to a realization that the success of development itself was highly contingent on women's full participation in it. Numerous studies demonstrated that investment in women was not only a matter of social justice but an integral part of development strategy leading to a more efficient use of resources, economic growth and a sustainable development process. The impermeability of some countries to economic reforms and the disappointing results achieved in others have been linked to a failure to consider the gender dimension of economic adjustment, among other factors.

8. The Third United Nations Development Decade ended with a new awareness of the need to give explicit consideration to the economic and social role of women when planning for development. The earlier model of the

"integration" of women in development was subjected to much criticism, particularly as being limited from the perspective of women's strategic gender interest. 5/ As a result, building on what has been achieved so far, the women-in-development approach evolved into the "gender and development" approach, which focuses on gender relations as they constrain or advance efforts to promote economic development and reduce poverty and seeks not only to integrate women into development, but to "look for the potential in development initiative to transform unequal social/gender relations and to empower women". 6/

9. Gender analysis, now widely accepted in the field of development as an analytical framework, seeks to remedy the nearly complete disregard for gender in economic theory and policy-making by stressing the gender dimension of micro- and macroeconomic policies and the need to include gender as a variable in economic policy-making and development planning. A corollary of the gender approach is that there is not a self-contained set of "women's issues". It is rather the case that there are many issues concerning economic transformation, the allocation of resources, savings, investment, growth, human capital formation, poverty, the labour market, inequality and the role of the State that could be better understood if disaggregation by sex took place at the outset of conceptualization and formulation of policies instead of passing references to women in an otherwise unaltered analysis.

10. Although recognized by national and international development agencies as well as in academic circles, the gender aspect of economic policy-making has not been used as a planning and policy-making tool and there is no "sustainable dialogue between planners and those within the research community who might help them towards a gender analysis". 7/ To bridge this gap, it is necessary to bring the tools of economic analysis

4/ Diane Elson, "Gender issues in development strategies"; paper prepared for the United Nations seminar on the Integration of Women in Development, Vienna, 9-11 December 1991).

5/ The two-stage "gender planning" model developed by Moser distinguishes, from both a policy and an operational viewpoint, between the practical or present interests of women (current inadequacies in the living and working conditions of women, for example) and strategic needs which target more egalitarian gender relations, either by reducing the basis of women's economic disadvantage or by modifying the gender division of labour so that it does not constrict women's income earning potential (C. Moser, *Gender Planning and Development: Theory, Practice and Training* (New York, Routhledge, 1993)).

6/ Rosi Braidotti and others, *Women, the Environment and Sustainable Development: Towards a Theoretical Synthesis* (London, Zed Books, 1994), p. 82.

7/ Susan Bullock, *Women and Work* (London, Zed Books, 1994), p. 30.

together with gender realities so that the gender dimension can be included in policy formulation and analysis.

III. Women's access to productive employment and entrepreneurship

11. Sustainable development requires a dynamic equilibrium of human and natural resources. Given women's role in both production and social reproduction, sustainable development is, by definition, a process where women's role is central. During the United Nations Decade for Women and following the adoption of the Nairobi Forward-looking Strategies, the centrality of women's role to development found recognition in numerous policies and programmes adopted by Governments and international development and finance institutions to enhance women's integration in development. Those efforts, however, focused primarily on the effects of development on women, including reinforcement of discrimination, neglecting to some extent their role as an underutilized economic resource that affects allocative and production efficiency. Although considerable progress has been achieved in access to education and health services, less has been accomplished in other areas, and improvements in educational attainments and greater access to paid employment have not always been translated into greater economic autonomy and advancement.

12. Two issues should be considered of growing importance in the formulation of gender-sensitive economic policies: women's increasing access to productive employment, especially in growth sectors; and women's growing roles as entrepreneurs.

A. *Women in the labour market*

13. Women play an important economic role in societies throughout the world, providing a substantial contribution to national income and development. In the past 20 years, new patterns in the economic participation of women have emerged. Their participation rates and labour force attachment have been growing steadily, and some estimates suggest that they will approximate those of men by the year 2000 in most industrialized economies and in some developing countries. 8/

14. In the past 20 years women have been entering the labour market in increasing numbers and their average share in the labour force has increased significantly in all regions except sub-Saharan Africa and Central Asia. Economic activity rates for women are on the rise everywhere, while those for men are declining. Most labour economists agree that the rise in female labour-force participation rates is a secular and international phenomenon. While previously noted trends showed that women were concentrated in a limited number of sectors

or in lower-paid and less stable employment, those sectors have shown the greatest dynamism in the context of global restructuring, suggesting that many assumptions about the role of women in the labour market will have to be reconsidered.

15. Demographic developments, economic necessity and changes in employment patterns and labour demand have been the forces behind the great influx of women into the formal job market. Today, in developing countries, women account for 31 per cent of the labour force (see table 1). National reports from industrialized countries indicate that in those countries women constitute approximately half of the labour force. The increase has been particularly dramatic in the past 20 years: in Portugal, for example, the female labour force grew from 21.3 to 43.7 per cent in the period 1970-1990. 9/

16. The new opportunities embodied in rising rates of economic activity should provide women with the resources necessary for greater economic autonomy and self-reliance. However, women's share in unemployment often exceeds their share in the labour force in most developing countries, in economies in transition (where they account for the greater share of the unemployed), and in some industrialized countries where comparative statistics are available (table 2). To some extent, the increased share of women in economic activity, as for example in Eastern Europe, can be misleading as an indicator of growing economic autonomy, given the fact that unemployment is heavily skewed towards young female school-leavers entering the labour force. In Poland, almost 60 per cent of all unemployed school-leavers in 1990 were women.

17. It should also be noted that many economically active women are underemployed. In developing countries, underemployment of female labour is characterized by low and/or declining marginal productivity and seasonal employment. The structural underemployment of women inherited from centrally planned economic systems has been perpetuated in unemployment among women with higher and specialized education and lack of opportunity to re-enter the labour force at a level corresponding to their education and experience. This has been further exacerbated by such widespread practices as mandatory part-time work, extended child-care leave and administrative leave and early-retirement policies instituted by enterprises undergoing downsizing and restructuring.

8/ *World Labour Report, 1994* (Geneva, International Labour Office, 1994).

9/ United Nations Population Fund, *National Perspectives on Population and Development: synthesis of 168 national reports prepared for the International Conference on Population and Development, 1994*, p. 30.

Table 1. *Economic activity rates, by sex: 1970-1990*
(Percentage)

	1970		1980		1990	
	Women	*Men*	*Women*	*Men*	*Women*	*Men*
Developed regions						
Eastern Europe	56	79	56	77	58	74
Western Europe	37	78	42	75	51	72
Developing regions	40	81	46	78	54	75
Africa						
Northern	8	82	12	79	21	75
Africa						
Sub-Saharan	57	90	54	89	53	83
Latin America and the Caribbean						
Latin America	22	85	25	82	34	82
Caribbean	38	81	42	77	49	72
Asia and the Pacific						
Eastern Asia	57	86	58	83	56	80
Southern Asia	25	88	24	85	44	78
Central Asia	55	76	56	77	58	79
Western Asia	22	83	26	81	30	77
Oceania	47	88	46	86	48	76

Source: The World's Women, 1995: Trends and Statistics (United Nations publication, Sales No. E.95.XVII.2).

18. The International Labour Organization (ILO) defines the underemployed as those who would like additional work, who work for low wages or whose skills are underutilized. 10/ According to this definition, underemployment is currently a characteristic of the female labour force in the industrialized countries, where, in the context of the deregulation of factor and product markets and in response to growing unemployment, job creation has been geared towards part-time, temporary and casual work. Current data indicate that, as the percentage of households headed by women has steadily increased, more and more women have been seeking full-time paid work but have ended up in only part-time jobs 11/ (see table 3).

19. The steadily rising rates of economic participation, however, do not reveal the full extent of women's contribution to development because they do not fully recognize work done at home and outside the formal economy. Nor does the income women receive provide a full measure of their contribution to the economy. Some advances have been made in the area of wage equity over the past 40 years, but progress varies between regions and age groups. While in some industrialized economies the earnings of young women have almost reached parity with those of men of the same age, 12/ women's earnings in most of the developing world continue to fall short of

men's. 13/ The wage differential is particularly significant in the developing countries and in those industrializing countries where labour standards were allowed to deteriorate under the pressure to compete successfully in the world market for manufactured goods and to attract foreign investment (see table 4). Women's wages in manufacturing are lower in most countries. In Japan, for example, women in manufacturing typically earn only 40 per cent of the wage earned by men.

20. Empirical research has shown that 40 to 80 per cent of the differential in the average hourly pay for men and women in many developing and some developed economies can be ascribed to discrimination, so that productivity-related characteristics and differences in hu-

10/ See Shirley Nuss and others, "Women in the world of work: statistical analysis and projections to the year 2000", *Women, Work and Development*, No. 18 (Geneva, International Labour Office, 1989).

11/ Economic Commission for Europe, "Regional review and appraisal of the Nairobi Forward-looking Strategies: report by the secretariat" (E/ECE/RW/HLM/1), 15 August 1994.

12/ *The Economist*, 5 March 1994.

13/ International Institute of Labour Studies, "Women workers in a changing global environment: framework for discussion"; paper prepared for the International Forum on Equality for Women in the World of Work: Challenges for the Future, Geneva, 1-3 June 1994.

Table 2. *Female share in the unemployed and economically active populations:*
selected countries or territories, 1975-1991/92
(Percentage)

	1975		1985		1991/92	
	Unemployed	Economically active	Unemployed	Economically active	Unemployed	Economically active
Developing countries						
Barbados	57.1	43.3	59.4	47.2	64.5	48.3
Brazil	28.3	24.4	33.8	27.2	33.2	35.2
Chile	35.2	24.8	30.8	28.0	31.2	31.0
Costa Rica	38.3	19.7	30.1	21.6	36.0	29.8
Ghana	21.5	41.9	30.7	40.6	10.0	..
Jamaica	67.2	44.6	66.2	45.8	68.3	46.5
Panama	45.6	25.8	47.1	26.7	50.1	29.2
Puerto Rico	25.5	28.3	26.1	29.4	29.6	37.6
Republic of Korea	22.5	33.3	22.8	34.0	29.5	40.0
Syrian Arab Republic	9.2	13.2	25.5	16.0	37.5	18.0
Thailand	38.5	47.1	60.8	45.9	51.0	47.1
Trinidad and Tobago	37.5	27.8	36.3	29.7	45.5	33.8
Venezuela	22.1	23.3	25.0	26.7	34.7	30.9
Industrialized countries						
Austria	54.1	39.6	39.6	40.2	45.1	41.0
Belgium	54.1	32.2	55.9	33.8	61.7	41.3
Denmark	31.9	40.0	55.6	44.2	49.4	46.5
Finland	34.8	45.0	46.6	46.6	38.6	47.0
France	56.6	37.7	53.8	39.6	54.1	43.8
Germany	42.0	37.2	44.1	37.7	52.2	38.5
Greece	34.6	25.9	42.5	26.4	61.9	36.8
Italy	54.6	30.1	57.4	31.7	58.0	37.1
Netherlands	21.7	28.6	34.6	31.0	55.9	39.7
Norway	47.5	35.0	54.9	40.5	41.1	45.2
Portugal	44.8	30.9	56.9	24.1	61.1	42.3
Switzerland	23.3	35.3	45.9	36.7	42.9	44.2
Turkey	11.4	36.5	16.4	34.0	26.9	31.4
United Kingdom	18.7	37.1	31.2	38.7	26.2	43.3
United States	44.0	39.1	45.6	41.5	42.8	45.1

Source: International Labour Office, *Year Book of Labour Statistics*, 1985 and 1990.

man capital are responsible for the remaining differential. However, earnings discrimination is perhaps a less important aspect of labour-market gender discrimination. More important is access to and participation in markets. Studies in rural development in Africa have demonstrated that women sometimes face extreme discrimination in access to non-farm wage employment, which is largely determined by education, wage and sex. While men with a secondary education had a 0.75 per cent probability of employment, women with the same education and age characteristics had only half that probability. 14/ Employment prospects for women with primary education or less were only a fraction of those for men, suggesting that discrimination may apply differently at different levels of education. 15/

21. The distribution of the female labour force

14/ See P. Collier, "Women in development: defining the issues", Policy, Planning and Research Working Paper (World Bank, 1988).
15/ Ibid.

Table 3. *Women's share in part-time employment: selected OECD economies, 1979-1992*
(*Percentage*)

	1979	1983	1990	1991	1992
Austria	87.8	88.4	89.1	89.7	..
Belgium	88.9	84.0	88.6	89.3	..
Canada	72.1	71.3	71.0	70.5	70.0
Denmark	86.9	84.7	75.7	75.5	..
France	82.2	84.4	83.6	83.7	83.7
Germany	91.6	91.9	89.7	89.6	..
Italy	61.4	64.8	67.2	65.4	67.9
Japan	70.1	72.8	70.7	69.9	69.3
United Kingdom	92.8	89.8	86.2	86.1	85.4
United States	68.0	66.8	67.6	67.2	66.4

Source: Organisation for Economic Co-operation and Development, *Employment Outlook*, July 1993.

continues to show a high concentration in a single sector while the male labour force is more evenly distributed. 16/ Other than in sub-Saharan Africa and Southern Asia, where women are concentrated in agriculture, services tend to provide most of the jobs that go to women. The services sector has now become "feminized" in most countries. Women's employment is concentrated in public services, teaching, administrative and commercial enterprises and domestic services, in which women often account for 90 per cent of employees. Industry remains a modest source of employment for women, except in Eastern Europe and Southern and Eastern Asia, where, in some countries, women account for the greater proportion of the labour force in export industries.

22. There have been trends over the past decade towards a reduction in occupational segregation by sex as women in some countries have entered higher-level professional jobs. But at the same time the share of women's employment in "feminized" occupations has increased, thereby reinforcing gender differences by employment sector at the bottom of the labour market. 17/ To some extent, a marked shift towards services, which now account for some 65 per cent of GDP and for between 50 and 70 per cent of all jobs in the industrialized countries, has served to increase the importance of women's employment since women now account for 55 to 80 per cent of employment in the services sector. In the economies in transition, where gender segregation in the labour market is more marked than in other industrialized economies, structural changes in the economy and privatization have caused a redistribution of female employment in the services sector from the sectors that have become more prestigious in terms of pay and status, like insurance and banking, to the sectors with an already high concentration of women employees and a low return on their labour, like education, nursing and social care.

23. In the developing economies the direction of segregation of female labour is similar to that in the industrialized economies, and women are underrepresented in the higher-paid professions and occupations and overrepresented in low-pay and low-status occupations. The adjustment-related labour shedding in the public sector in the past decade has to some extent reinforced this segregation pattern as the female labour made redundant moved into the already overcrowded flexible-entry sectors, such as the informal sector and services, which did not happen in the case of men.

24. Other trends in female employment in developing countries include the growth of female industrial employment in the context of the growth of export-oriented manufacturing and a partial reversal of the job-related migration pattern of the 1970s, as demand restraint and trade liberalization policies drastically curtailed the availability of jobs in urban areas and reduced real incomes. Despite rising agricultural prices and agricultural wage rates, women in developing countries have not been able to benefit fully from these developments owing to constraints on the reallocation of their labour and the persistence of limited access to land, credit and extension services.

25. Women the world over are currently employed at a higher rate than men in sectors which ignite economic growth and promote innovation and social change. There appears to be a positive correlation between the importance of the sector in terms of its share of GDP and the concentration of female labour. The same is true in terms of the growth potential of a sector and women's representation in its labour force, that is to say that women

16/ *The World's Women, 1995: Trends and Statistics* (United Nations publication, Sales No. E.95.XVII.2), p. 113.
17/ See Economic Commission for Europe, "Women's access to employment and entrepreneurship" (E/ECE/RW/HLM/4), 1994.

Table 4. *Women's wages as a percentage of men's wages, by region, 1970-1990*

	Agriculture			Non-agriculture			Manufacturing		
	1970	*1980*	*1990*	*1970*	*1980*	*1990*	*1970*	*1980*	*1990*
Africa									
Mean	70.00	58.51	69.21	61.46	81.79	89.43	63.50	60.00	73.25
Maximum	75.00	67.52	83.63	61.46	114.00	113.50	63.50	62.00	97.00
Minimum	65.00	49.00	55.00	61.46	64.30	73.00	63.50	55.00	49.00
Latin America and the Caribbean									
Mean	77.00	67.55	87.58	..	74.52	68.86	82.00	70.25	74.75
Maximum	83.00	78.11	98.21	..	81.24	75.97	82.00	81.00	94.00
Minimum	70.00	52.16	74.81	..	69.97	64.62	82.00	51.00	65.00
Western Europe and other States									
Mean	81.70	80.31	85.17	68.84	77.16	78.35	66.04	75.00	74.64
Maximum	111.00	98.00	98.55	86.93	87.43	90.80	80.00	90.00	89.00
Minimum	56.00	63.12	64.45	57.53	64.69	65.15	55.00	61.00	59.00
Asia and the Pacific									
Mean	74.00	78.57	79.31	91.51	69.78	68.22	60.00	44.00	41.00
Maximum	90.00	91.55	92.20	91.51	101.53	89.80	84.00	86.00	97.00
Minimum	48.00	57.15	60.76	91.51	44.40	49.61	60.00	44.00	41.00
Eastern Europe									
Mean	73.00	..	74.00	69.18	70.40	75.39	68.80	69.67	72.75
Maximum	73.00	..	74.00	69.18	72.39	82.00	69.60	73.00	78.00
Minimum	73.00	..	74.00	69.18	68.41	71.00	68.00	68.00	68.00

Source: *Women's Indicators and Statistics Database (Wistat)*, version 3, CD-ROM (United Nations publication, Sales No. E.95.XVII.6).

are concentrated in the fastest-growing sectors of the economy and the fastest-growing occupations. Of the 20 occupations that will generate the greatest number of new jobs by the year 2005, the majority are in services and belong to the heavily feminized category. 18/ Trends in the labour force participation of women together with patterns of global economic restructuring and transformation suggest that in the future more women will emerge as workers and entrepreneurs. "What women want from their jobs has meshed much better with the needs of the market-place than what men want. Their prospective success should make everyone more optimistic about economic growth." 19/

26. Taking account of this new trend in the global economy would seem to be important in formulating employment policies to maximize growth.

B. *Entrepreneurship*

27. In recent years there has been a reversal of an earlier trend towards diminishing self-employment

among women, and it has been estimated that by the end of the 1980s the rate of growth of women's self-employment exceeded that of their overall employment. 20/ Data from the Women's Indicators and Statistics Database (Wistat) show that the ratio of women to men

18/ Occupations that are likely to generate most of the new jobs in the period 1990-2005 are: salespersons (retail); registered nurses; cashiers; general office clerks; truck drivers; general managers and top executives; janitors and cleaners, including maids and housekeepers; nursing aides, orderlies and attendants; food counter and related workers; waiters and waitresses; teachers (elementary and secondary school); receptionists and information clerks; system analysis and computer scientists; food preparation workers; child-care workers; gardeners/groundkeepers; accountants and auditors; computer programmers; and guards; of these, 13 occupations are on the list of occupations with a very high concentration of women (see *The World's Women, 1995*, and Economic Commission for Europe, E/ECE/RW/HLM/1 and 2, 1994).

19/ *The Economist*, 23 August 1986, p. 13.

20/ S. Washington, "Women at work", *OECD Observer*, No. 176 (1992).

among employers and own-account workers has increased in almost all regions in the past 20 years.

28.   As women have gained a major place for themselves in the labour market and greater access to productive resources, it has become increasingly irrelevant and unrealistic to continue to rely on the marginalization approach as a premise for the analysis of women in development. According to the *1994 World Survey on the Role of Women in Development*, women's enterprises account for a significant share — in some cases as large as 40 per cent — of the newly-created businesses. In the United States, the rate of growth of businesses owned by women was four times the overall growth rate of new businesses between 1982 and 1987 (see table 5). There are at least 6.5 million women business owners in the United States according to the latest estimates by the National Foundation for Women Business Owners. In 1992, businesses owned by women employed more people than all the Fortune 500 companies combined. 21/ Women entrepreneurs represent a rising force that holds great promise for development. Their impact is based on the role entrepreneurship plays in long-term economic growth, on the special role small- and medium-sized enterprises and the informal sector (where women's businesses are concentrated) play in economic development, and on the major social benefits associated with the greater economic autonomy and access to markets and decision-making that are inevitably linked to women's access to and ability to command resources.

29.   Comparative studies of economic development suggest that, as industrialization progresses, the importance for economic growth of entrepreneurship and innovation increases relative to that of capital and labour. Entrepreneurial activity improves allocative efficiency and reduces X-inefficiency. 22/ It promotes international technology transfer, thereby facilitating economic growth, restructuring and development. In fact, entrepreneurship is regarded as a fourth factor of production that is particularly crucial for long-term growth and development: studies of long-term growth have shown that the residual that is unexplained by change in the stock of capital and labour is responsible for some 50 per cent of variations in economic growth. 23/ This "residual" growth is fuelled by the introduction of "new combinations" of means of production and technological progress, both of which can be directly attributed to entrepreneurship.

30.   The development experience of the past decade has shown that development strategies emphasizing import substitution and central planning have prompted a greater interest by Governments and international development institutions in small-scale economic activities and a participatory economic development process. Owing to the importance of women's incomes to both national productivity and individual and family welfare, as well as the significance of the role of the informal sector in poverty reduction, Governments and donor agencies are funding an increasing number of programmes in developing countries targeted at female microentrepreneurs. 24/ Such programmes aim at reducing the vulnerability of women working in the informal sector by assuring them access to credit, better working conditions and appropriate technology, training and infrastructural support, as well as helping them with marketing. 25/

31.   In the economies undergoing structural adjustment and economic transition, entrepreneurship, with its

21/ National Association for Female Executives, *Women in the American Workforce and Power Structure: A Contemporary Snapshot* (June 1993).

22/ X-inefficiency is the notion that individual firms—and economies as a whole—are more likely to operate inside the frontiers of their production possibilities than on them, because producers do not exert sufficient effort at all times to maximize output and there is a gap between actual and minimum attainable supply costs. The concept suggests that the costs of increasing output are zero and that therefore output can be raised, when X-inefficiency exists, without corresponding increases in factor input.

23/ Angus Maddison, *Phases of Capitalist Development* (New York, Oxford University Press, 1982).

24/ There is no consensus in the literature on a definition of microenterprises, which is typically a function of the number of persons employed in the business. The Georgia Institute of Technology has found 50 different definitions used in 75 countries (World Bank, "Employment and development of small enterprises", Sector Policy Paper, (Washington, D.C., 1987)). Definitions may be based on capital invested, or the number of employees, or other criteria. According to ILO, small enterprises include "... modern industrial firms of up to 50 employees, family units of three or four people, village industries, associations, companies, cooperatives, owner-operators, mini-firms and the self-employed in the non-structured sector of the economy". While there is no lower limit to the size of a "small enterprise", fixing an upper limit usually depends on the interests of the person or body concerned and on the particular economic sector where the definition is to be used. From the managerial perspective, a small enterprise may be described as one where operational and administrative decisions are made by one or two people, but definitions vary when small enterprises are considered from the perspective of financiers, labour officers, traders, services personnel or manufactures. In the World Bank sector policy paper on small enterprises it is suggested that the upper limit of $250,000 for fixed assets should be used to classify an enterprise as "small", but no lower limit is set. Whatever the definitions used and despite the diversity in terminology (small enterprises, small and medium-scale enterprises, microenterprises, mini-firms, etc.), it seems to be a fact that women's enterprises are generally among the very smallest in the sector.

25/ UNCTAD secretariat, "Women as entrepreneurs and decision makers in the least developed countries"; paper prepared for the Expert Group Meeting on Women and Economic Decision-Making, New York, 7-11 November 1994.

Table 5. *Women-owned businesses as a percentage of all United States firms and receipts, 1987*

	Women-owned firms, 1987	Percentage change 1982-1987	Women-owned firm receipts
All industries	30.40	57.50	13.94
Agricultural services	13.44	146.20	9.39
Mining	21.82	33.30	12.82
Construction	5.71	63.00	8.74
Manufacturing	21.70	109.40	13.63
Transportation, communication and public utilities	13.46	105.10	14.32
Wholesale trade	18.79	157.00	14.32
Retail trade	35.63	26.50	15.68
Finance, insurance and real estate	35.64	77.50	14.42
Services	38.21	76.60	14.65
Unclassified industries	26.58	–21.60	12.43

Source: United States Department of Commerce, 1987 Economic Censuses: Women-Owned Business (Bureau of the Census, 1990).

growing female component, is playing a key role in the success of policy reforms that aim at creating a foundation for long-term sustainable growth. While stabilization policies of demand restraint are designed to put a floor under a downward spiral in key economic indicators and are critical for the resumption of growth, long-term sustained economic development requires an improvement in the economy's productive capacity that can only be accomplished by active policies on the supply side. Such policies aim at the realignment of relative prices, exchange rate competitiveness and the liberalization of trade and markets but are not necessarily sufficient to ensure the appropriate supply-side responses needed for structural change. Rather, they create conditions for the emergence of productive entrepreneurship, which is the ultimate force behind the introduction of new know-how and the attainment of the greater allocative and organizational efficiency of markets. In developed and developing economies, the loci of entrepreneurship tend to reside with the activities of small and medium enterprises in the formal sector; in the case of the latter, mostly in the informal sector.

32. In developing countries, formal-sector enterprises represent only a fraction of all small-scale enterprises. The bulk of small-scale production appears to take place in informal-sector enterprises with fewer than 10 workers. The average size of an enterprise in Sierra Leone, for example, is 1.9 persons; in Bangladesh it is fewer than three persons. The importance of the informal sector is overwhelming, especially in sub-Saharan Africa, where the great majority of least-developed countries are to be found. It has been estimated that over 90 per cent of new jobs in urban areas in this region in the 1990s will be created in that sector. An assessment of informal microenterprises in Ecuador has found that they play a key role in generating urban employment and that the microenterprise sector accounts for about two thirds of the labour employed in the private sector. 26/

33. Outside the agricultural sector, women's businesses in developing countries tend to be concentrated in the small and medium enterprises, often in the informal sector, that developed rapidly in those countries in the 1970s and 1980s as a result of rapid urbanization and, to some extent, the diversion of resources from the formal economy caused by acute economic distortions and excessive government regulation. By and large, informal-sector enterprises emerge to fill gaps in demand for goods and services that are not effectively captured by the modern formal sector. In Latin America and sub-Saharan Africa, women's share in the informal sector exceeds that in the total labour force, and economically active women are more likely than men to be in this sector. 27/ A number of sources indicate that women own and/or operate about one third of all informal businesses. 28/ As small-scale entrepreneurs, women operate businesses in craft production, carpet weaving, pottery making, food processing and the brewing of beer and in trade and street vending. Data suggest, however, that women are found in the informal sector more often than men because of lack of opportunity or other obstacles to wage employment.

34. The expansion of small and medium enterprises in the past decade can be traced to the restructuring of the global economy, globalization and the flexibilization of production and, consequently, to the growth of industrial outwork, subcontracting and home-based production. While their role as business owners in the formal sector in developing countries is often negligible, women account for 43 per cent of small-business owners in Egypt, 49 per cent in Jamaica, 37 per cent in Thailand,

26/ M. Baydas, "Discrimination against women in formal credit markets: reality or rhetoric?", *World Development*, vol. 22, No. 7 (1994), p. 1075.

27/ S. Joekes and A. Weston, *Women and the New Trade Agenda* (United Nations Development Fund for Women (UNIFEM), 1994), p. 67.

28/ M. Berger, "Giving women credit: the strengths and limitations of credit as a tool for alleviating poverty", *World Development*, vol. 17, No. 7 (July 1989), p. 1021.

and 61 per cent in Honduras. In Zambia, 60 per cent of rural non-farm enterprises are owned by women and, in Zimbabwe, 62 per cent of rural non-farm enterprises and 77 per cent of urban non-farm enterprises have female proprietorship. 29/ But the growth in self-employment among women in developing countries and the economies in transition is largely a "supply driven" phenomenon, rooted to a greater extent in the need for survival and in economic necessity than in attractive market opportunities. Women's remuneration also remains lower than that of men: "data gathered on Latin America and Africa show that women's informal businesses have lower revenues, lower asset bases, and smaller profit margins than men's; in Peru, for example, women's business assets are just one half those of men". 30/

35. From the perspective of the characteristics of the sector, women-owned small business is a vital component of successful economic restructuring and adjustment. It is an important source of efficiency, growth and economic and political decentralization, which contributes to economic welfare and development. It is also a powerful tool of low-cost job creation, and this is particularly important during periods of stabilization and structural adjustment and as a component of development strategy in economies with a relatively high labour endowment. In addition to employment generation, small and medium enterprises create a positive economy-wide externality by providing on-the-job training for semi-skilled workers, many of whom are women. Increasing concern for the environmental sustainability of development again points to small enterprises as a hopeful solution, since their scale of operation and labour-intensive technologies put less strain on the environment.

36. The literature on entrepreneurship distinguishes between productive, unproductive and destructive entrepreneurship and between entrepreneurial activities and rent-seeking activities, which are of questionable value to society as a whole. Research shows that the welfare of society is much more likely to be affected by the direction of entrepreneurial activities than by the number of persons who carry them out. In that sense, it can be argued that the marginal social product associated with women-owned and/or operated businesses exceeds the marginal private product, owing to the externalities resulting from the economic empowerment of women and to a tendency towards productive activities rather than rent-seeking or arbitrage because of greater fiscal constraints facing women entrepreneurs and because they are poorly placed in society to lobby for political patronage.

37. Women, particularly in developing economies and economies in transition, are often driven to self-employment as a result of worsening economic conditions. It is sometimes argued that their businesses are better characterized as income-generating rather than entrepreneurial in the classical, Schumpeterian sense of the concept. On this count, several observations are in order. Innovative entrepreneurship requires a complex infrastructure and developed markets that are unlikely to exist in developing countries or in most of the economies in transition. The concept of innovative entrepreneurship is therefore too narrow a criterion for dividing women's individual economic activity into an entrepreneurial category and a merely income-generating category. Women's entrepreneurial businesses in developing economies fulfil an important market-making function, often operating where markets do not exist or are segmented and do not operate perfectly. Their entrepreneurial skills therefore affect the effectiveness of markets and enhance allocative efficiency.

38. Between the very broad and very narrow definitions of entrepreneurship there remains a large area that includes not only innovativeness in the use and combination of existing resources but also management, leadership and marketing. From the managerial perspective, women-managed businesses are inherently entrepreneurial, because women's managerial style differs qualitatively from that of men and the practices followed in women-managed enterprises are beginning to change how business institutions are run. 31/ They also challenge the social attitudes and expectations about gender behaviour that determine the parameters of the participation of women and men in economic and political decision-making. The resulting change in the gender system—the way our culture determines what is "male" and what is "female"—contributes to both the greater economic efficiency and greater equity of the development process.

39. Studies have shown that entrepreneurial activities help women towards social and economic empowerment. As women's incomes rise, their control over productive resources, including their own labour, increases. They acquire a greater voice in decision-making at all levels, starting with the household and extending to the economic and political domains. Other benefits include a lower incidence of malnutrition and disease among their families and more education for their children, as well as a reduction in violence directed towards women.

40. In industrialized market economies a desire to secure economic autonomy and to escape from male

29/ S. Joekes and A. Weston, op. cit., p. 66.
30/ C. Grown and J. Sebstad, "Introduction: towards a wider perspective on women's employment", World Development, vol. 17, No. 7 (July 1989), p. 937.
31/ Women in a Changing Global Economy: 1994 World Survey on the Role of Women in Development (United Nations publication, Sales No. E.95.IV.1), p. 85.

Table 6. *Business credit to women, 1993*

Institutions by type	Women clients (Percentage of total)	Payment rate (Percentage)
Commercial bank programmes		
Indonesia Bank Rakyat (BRI)/KUPEDES Programme	23	98
Bank Pembanguran Daerah (BPD)/Baden Kredit Kecamatan Programme, Indonesia	60	80
Poverty-lending banks		
Grameen Bank, Bangladesh	94	87
Self Employment Women's Association (SEWA) Cooperative Bank, India	100	97
Banco Solidario (BancoSol), Bolivia (commercial bank)	7	98
National boards		
National Board for Small Scale Industries, Ghana: Credit Scheme for Small Enterprises	43	72
Enhancing Opportunities for Women in Development (ENOWID)	100	95
Non-governmental organizations		
Asociación Dominicana para el Desarrollo de la Mujer (ADOPEM), Dominican Republic	100	95
Kenya Rural Enterprise Programme (KREP)	63	95
Credit Union Association, Ghana	30	..
Affiliate network institutions		
FINCA International, Washington, D.C.	96	97
ACCION International, Washington, D.C.	54	95
Friends of Women's World Banking/India	100	95
Women's World Banking Ghana Limited	..	88
Women's World Banking New York	97	96

Source: The World's Women, 1995; national report of Ghana, 1994.

domination are most frequently cited by women as reasons for starting their own businesses. Women microentrepreneurs in developing economies chose own-account economic activity because of the lower barriers to entry into small-scale entrepreneurship and constraints on their access to the labour market. In both developed and developing countries, poor access to credit is the most frequently mentioned obstacle to the launching and expansion of women-owned businesses. Although formal capital markets are legally open to women, financial resources are largely unavailable to them owing to many factors inherent in tradition and society. Factors limiting women's access to formal credit markets are related to institutional requirements, to cultural and social norms and to the type of productive activities in which women's businesses predominate.

41. Credit is either unavailable or very limited for small entrepreneurs, and for women in particular, because they usually do not own marketable land rights and hence have no collateral. From the point of view of commercial credit institutions in developing countries, lending to small enterprises is not a very attractive option for diversifying their loan portfolios, and there are sound reasons for this. In developing countries, where inflation rates are high, credit rationing and fixed interest rates favour large loans because of lower administrative costs. As a result, formal credit institutions prefer to work with large and less risky customers. Women microentre-

preneurs often lack real assets and creditworthiness and are unfamiliar with the accounting practices that commercial banks require. In Kenya, for example, banks still require land certificates to be presented with applications for credit. 32/ Also, in some countries, financial institutions permit only one loan per household. As a result, women's participation in formal small-scale enterprise lending programmes rarely exceeds 20 per cent and can be as low as 16 per cent. 33/

42. Evidence from banks that have been lending to the poor and to low-income women entrepreneurs shows that the higher unit cost of small-scale lending may not inhibit commercial lending to microenterprises if financial infrastructure is sufficiently developed and diversified. Thus, there may be a case, based on the long-term social opportunity costs, for applying the infant-industry argument to subsidies to innovative credit schemes for women entrepreneurs, the infant industry in this case being financial services. Lately, however, it has been argued that highly subsidized interest rates on loans given to the poor are dysfunctional, and credit programmes are increasingly being designed to be self-sustaining in accordance with the revolving fund concept, whereby deposits are mobilized and funds are made available on a continuing basis to participants at market rates of interest. 34/ Despite the 95 to 97 per cent recovery rate on loans to women entrepreneurs (see table 6), their access to credit remains limited and appears to be in decline in some countries. 35/

43. The evidence frequently used in the literature on women microentrepreneurs to demonstrate the financial constraints faced by women-owned businesses is often interpreted too easily as a loan-supply problem, overlooking the possibility that the observed lack of participation by women in formal credit markets might be caused by a lack of demand for credit or possibly access to informal sources of credit, even though most women microentrepreneurs report a need for credit. 36/ Studies have revealed that for the majority of women in developing countries formal credit institutions may not be a satisfactory source of financial resources owing to the high opportunity cost of applying for credit and the high transaction costs they face in the credit market. Other factors that act as a constraint on the demand for credit by low-income women entrepreneurs include the remote location of financial institutions, complicated procedures for loan application and poor understanding of financial rules and regulations.

44. It has recently been emphasized that current models of the demand for credit by women entrepreneurs do not reflect the risk involved in indebtedness. 37/ It has also been noted that high interest rates put most women off, and that, in their view, their small business is not enough to push them into such debt to risk the security of their children and families. 38/ Low-income women farmers in sub-Saharan Africa, many of whom are just emerging from a subsistence life-style, have been reluctant to take advantage of the increased availability of credit to them because of their low cash incomes and a general aversion to risk. In this respect, it has been argued that greater availability of credit to rural women farmers should not be viewed as a perfect substitute for subsidizing production inputs when designing programmes directed at raising the productivity of rural women. 39/

45. The study of Ecuadorian microenterprises already referred to has shown, however, that women entrepreneurs are as likely to apply for loans as their male counterparts: in the statistical sample used by the study, women represented a higher proportion of those entrepreneurs who applied for loans. 40/ The study showed that women borrowers were subject to rationing of loan size; that is, they were granted loans in amounts smaller than requested. Discrimination against women entrepreneurs in terms of the size of the loan rather than the number of loans granted suggests that, to be successful in borrowing, female entrepreneurs need to establish their creditworthiness in order to provide the information, which, if lacking, allows lenders to resort to nonprice mechanisms of loan-rationing.

46. Given the problem of inadequate information that is inherent in credit-allocation decision-making, redirecting public credit to women as a target group is only a partial solution to their poor access to loanable funds. To make financial assets more accessible to women, it is important to encourage and facilitate their greater reliance on the savings market. Greater access by women to the savings market contributes to the development of female entrepreneurship on several fronts. Savings can finance long-term investment in sectors where women's enterprises predominate, thereby rectifying a current misallocation of capital and increasing the aggregate savings rate. Also, the accumulation of assets facilitates access to formal credit and improves creditworthiness. For reasons already mentioned, the credit market is intrinsically male-biased, whereas women's predominance in the informal

32/ National report of Kenya, 1994.
33/ M. Berger, loc. cit., pp. 1019-1020.
34/ UNCTAD Expert Group Meeting on Women in Development in the Least Developed Countries, held at Niamey on 24 January 1995.
35/ National report of Ghana, 1994.
36/ M. Baydas, loc. cit., p. 1074.
37/ D. Adams and J. von Pischke, "Microenterprise credit programs: déjà vu", World Development, vol. 20, No. 10 (1992).
38/ National report of Ghana, 1994.
39/ C. Gladwin, ed., Structural Adjustment and African Women Farmers (Gainesville, University of Florida Press, 1991).
40/ M. Baydas, loc. cit.

savings market suggests that the savings market is likely to be gender-neutral. 41/ Greater efficiency will, however, be required of financial systems in dealing with small transactions and assisting women entrepreneurs in building long-term working relations with financial institutions.

47. The overwhelming emphasis in the past on the credit side rather than on the savings side of the market in the context of programmes targeting women entrepreneurs has left savings institutions underdeveloped and inaccessible to women. National reports indicate that the rate and pattern of savings differ significantly between women and men. A survey in a rural district of Namibia 42/ found that only 45 per cent of households headed by women had savings as compared to 73 per cent of households headed by men. Women saved annually only 23 per cent of the amount saved by men and usually kept their savings at home. The design of savings schemes attractive to women should therefore be a priority in the formulation of programmes directed at facilitating women's access to financial resources.

48. Other obstacles to the development of businesses owned by women include an adverse economic and regulatory environment, inadequate physical infrastructure and marketing, poor access to new technology, and a lack of vocational and managerial training. Rigid social and cultural norms and lack of sharing of domestic responsibilities exacerbate the problems women face when operating businesses.

IV. Gender in models of development economics

49. A broad consensus has emerged in the field of development on the importance of greater attention to the situation of women if elimination of absolute poverty is to be achieved and economic growth is to become sustainable. Research has shown that investing in women promotes growth and efficiency, reduces poverty, helps future generations and promotes development. The analysis in the preceding section of two gender-related aspects of economic growth demonstrates the need to consider gender factors in policy-making. Yet discussions of gender have continued to be removed from mainstream economic and development policy-making in terms of both the focus and place of analysis. Reports on women in development continue to focus on the welfare impact of development policies on women, while little or no attention is paid to the effects of gender relations on the outcomes of economic policies. Women-in-development and, lately, gender-in-development issues remain sidelined in special reports or special policy initiatives, rather than being given systematic consideration when policies and programmes for structural change are being formulated. The contention of the present report is that, without explicit consideration of gender in policy for-

mulation, certain significant costs of economic inefficiency and resource misallocation are likely to persist, with a consequent reduction in growth and in social equity.

50. There is a reciprocal relationship between gender and development: development strategies and the economic policies pursued in the context of those strategies have a gender-specific impact; and gender differences in access to productive resources, factor markets, income and allocation of income have an impact on the efficiency and sustainability of economic policy outcomes. While the impact of development policies on women is a well-documented and widely addressed issue in the literature on women and development, the significance of gender for economic policy-making has received, as yet, far less attention. Economic analysis that is gender-aware has the potential to promote a better understanding of development and to facilitate the formulation of the policies required for its sustainability.

A. Gender in neoclassical development economics

51. In the early literature on women in development it was argued extensively that women become marginalized as, in the course of development, their household-based subsistence activities become increasingly subsumed into wider, market-based activities. Economic marginalization sets in motion what can be termed a "vicious circle of inequality", as a lack of participation in development leads to an unequal share of the benefits of development and that in turn reduces women's competitiveness in the job market. This approach suggests that economic development is "bad" for women because it sharpens gender inequalities and worsens the burden on women of unpaid and unrecognized work. The standard prescription has been to increase investment in women's human capital to reduce the discrimination women face in the labour market.

52. In the field of development economics, gender is not integrated into macroeconomic development modelling and its treatment is often limited to a few passing references to the impact of development on women. According to Nobel laureate W. Arthur Lewis, the author of a well-known structural change model, women benefit from growth even more than men: "woman gains freedom from drudgery, is emancipated from the seclusion of the household, and gains at last the chance to be a full human being, exercising her mind and her talents in the same way as men". 43/ Structural change models com-

41/ P. Collier, *op. cit.*
42/ National report of Namibia, 1994.
43/ W. A. Lewis, *The Theory of Economic Growth* (London, Allen and Unwin (1955)). Cited in D. Elson, "Gender issues in development strategies"; paper prepared for the seminar on integration of women in development, Vienna, 9-11 December 1991.

pletely omit gender from the analysis of the reallocation of labour from the subsistence sector with zero or declining marginal product of labour to the high-productivity modern industrial sector. These models treat labour supply as infinite and the reallocation of labour surplus as occurring smoothly, unhindered by the sexual division of labour and social practices. In real life, however, productivity, wage differentials and changes in relative prices do not always provide a sufficient inducement for the intersectoral transfer of at least 50 per cent of the labour force.

B. Gender and the structuralist perspective in development economics

53. Although structuralists disagree with neoclassical economists on the extent to which changes in relative prices can precipitate supply response in developing economies, they do not include gender among the "bottlenecks" that have a potential to inhibit such a response. The structuralist approach to stabilization policies points, *inter alia*, to the redistribution of income from labour to capital as the hidden equilibrating factor between supply and demand, but no attention is paid to the fact that labour is gendered and that income distribution occurs along gender lines, often leaving women worse off relative to men, as suggested by the ample research on the allocation of household income and household expenditure patterns. The equilibrating factor, in this case, lies in the implicit assumption of the infinite elasticity of female labour and income to absorb the shocks of stabilization and compensate for any shortfall in household income. 44/

54. Another point of structuralist criticism of neoclassical economics is the assumption of the infinite elasticity of the supply of agricultural and primary product exports in response to devaluation-induced changes in relative prices. Although sceptical of this assumption, the structuralist approach does not consider the sexual division of labour in the agricultural sector as a factor limiting supply response. However, the literature on structural adjustment and rural women provides abundant examples of how women's unwillingness and/or inability to sacrifice time and land to the production of cash crops at the expense of traditional food crops limits the response of supply to changes in price signals. Furthermore, it has also been suggested that the low substitutability of male labour for female labour reduces the ability of men to reallocate their labour in accordance with changes in market opportunities. 45/ This has important effects on the welfare of the household and the economic outcomes of adjustment. Hence, the failure to account for the gender aspects of resource reallocation in response to price signals may cause a sub-optimal policy outcome and worsen gender inequality, which in turn poses a threat to the sustainability of economic reforms.

C. Gender and outward-oriented development

55. It is generally agreed among mainstream economists that outward orientation in economic development has been the single most important factor responsible for rapid economic development and the reduction of inequality in the first and second generations of the newly industrialized economies and the other developing economies that have opened their economies to trade in the past decade. Policies of trade liberalization bring domestic resource allocation closer to international opportunity costs and shape their production structures in accordance with comparative advantage. Outward orientation in development policy renders interference by Governments with trade and the economy obsolete and replaces it with the policies of better governance that have been identified as those most conducive to growth, economic stability and poverty reduction. Looked at from a gender perspective, the long list of virtues of outward orientation can be expanded by the addition of the positive impact it has had on women's economic participation. Trade expansion has clearly benefited women's access to paid employment in many developing countries, albeit with some qualifications. But in the context of ongoing globalization and the introduction of new technologies and the ever-changing organization of production, the employment benefits accruing to women thus far from the liberalization of trade may be short-lived unless technological upgrading is matched by an upgrading of skills and better education for female workers.

56. Even a casual examination of employment trends, economic growth rates and the expansion of exports as a share of GDP suggests a relationship between these three factors. Empirical analyses confirm that there is a strong causal relationship between the expansion of female employment, particularly in labour-intensive light manufacturing, and patterns and the rates of export growth. Those developing countries that export an increasing proportion of their manufacturing output to the North tend to show a rise in the share of female labour in the manufacturing sectors: the results of regression analyses undertaken for the study of the impact of the trade regime adopted by 15 Asian countries show that a 1 per cent increase in exports as a share of GNP is associated with a 0.2 per cent increase in female non-

44/ D. Elson, "Gender-aware analysis and development economics", *Journal of International Development*, vol. 5, No. 2 (1993), pp. 237-247.
45/ C. Blackden and E. Morris-Hughes, *Paradigm Postponed: Gender and Economic Adjustment in Sub-Saharan Africa*. Human Resources and Poverty Division, Technical Note No. 13 (World Bank, August 1993), p. 8.

agricultural employment. 46/ The exports of those developing countries that rely on export-promotion development strategies are best described as female-labour intensive, and the economic growth of those countries has been as much female led as export led.

57. Outward orientation in development has enabled many developing countries to make better use of their resources as they have opened their economies to international competition and brought their production structures into line with comparative advantage. The female labour force has been an underutilized and undervalued resource that could be employed at a lower cost than male labour. Gender-based wage differentials have reinforced the viability of labour-intensive manufacturing exports to economies where labour costs are higher, thus enabling the economies that pursue export promotion to grow faster. The questions whether women have been able to benefit from the expansion of trade, other than in terms of greater access to paid employment and whether the benefits are of a long-term nature have been widely debated in the literature, and the conclusions reached have not been entirely optimistic.

58. One argument frequently made in the context of this debate is that opportunities to earn independent incomes tend to strengthen women's decision-making power in the household and that this positively affects the treatment of girl-children in the household and helps to break up the intragenerational perpetuation of the feminization of poverty. Thus, export production serves women's interests to the extent that it contributes to an increase in the supply of employment opportunities open to women. From the perspective of promoting egalitarian gender relations, trade-related gains in employment have not led to any improvement in the quality of female jobs. Most remain poorly paid, and gender-related wage differentials have persisted. 47/ In terms of the occupational and sectoral distribution of female employment, there has been a notable increase in the employment of women in trade-related services, where their prospects for higher remuneration are better.

59. With regard to the future of female employment in export-oriented industries in the economies where development in the past two decades has been driven by export expansion, the need for technological upgrading translates into the need for skills acquisition and better education and training for female workers. Failing this, the benefits thus far accruing to women from export-led development will simply vanish with growth. Recent evidence suggests that the share of female labour in export-oriented industries is declining as skill requirements shift with shifts in comparative advantage. This, together with evidence of poor access for women to retraining, indicates that the gains to women's employ-

ment from the expansion of export-oriented industries may have been short-lived.

60. Despite the prediction that expanding international trade, based on comparative advantage, must inevitably result in winners and losers, the anticipated negative effects of competition from developing countries on female employment in the industrialized countries have not materialized, as least as far as aggregate employment is concerned. The expansion of international trade seems, on the contrary, to have created better business opportunities for women entrepreneurs in developed economies. Business surveys in the United States, for example, show that women-owned businesses have a somewhat higher propensity to export and import than other businesses. A 1992 survey found that the proportion of exporters among women-owned small businesses was higher than among small businesses in general. The most recent Census Department figures show that 7.5 per cent of surveyed women-owned businesses report some share of revenues from exports, compared to 6.1 per cent of male-owned businesses. Some 22 per cent of members of the National Association of Women Business Owners said that they were considering becoming involved in international trade. 48/

61. Analysis of women-owned businesses involved in international trade shows that women may have an affinity for exporting owing to their different management style and greater attention to building long-term business relationships. A more pragmatic explanation would be that women's businesses are often founded during downturn periods of slow domestic growth, a situation that prompts business owners to look abroad for better business opportunities. 49/

V. Gender in economic policy: some examples

62. Micro-economic theory, dominated by the marginalist paradigm and the equilibrium perspective, makes only passing reference to the economic topics of special importance to women. Even less attention is devoted to such issues at the macro level; gender-specific differences when shown in macroeconomic data receive no macroeconomic explanation. The models used in discussing the economics of the household and gender-related issues are based on assumptions that often harbour male biases. An example of this is the basic premise of the neoclassical approach, the idea of the individual as characterized by the well-defined preference function, which is not compatible with gender differentiation of

46/ F. Perkins, "Are women benefiting from economic development?", IPA Review, vol. 46, No. 4 (1994), pp. 45-49.
47/ S. Joekes and A. Weston, op. cit., p. 59.
48/ B. Norton, "Why women's businesses are getting ahead in exporting", Working Woman, vol. 19, No. 7 (July 1994).
49/ Ibid.

economic agents because women often lack control over productive assets and autonomy in decision-making. 50/ Policy advice formulated on the basis of these models is couched in gender-neutral terms but often leads to gender-specific results that escape the attention of economic policy makers for lack of the methodological and statistical tools for addressing them. The result is that, at present, gender issues in economic theory and policy-making are "hidden by the invisible hand". 51/

63. Gender inequalities in access to and participation in markets cause markets to fail to allocate resources efficiently. Factor markets are particularly important, since their inefficiency can inhibit growth and/or worsen income distribution. Gender discrimination in these markets leads to a sub-optimal allocation of resources that entails long-term social opportunity costs, thus providing a rationale for subsidizing innovative credit schemes, designed to provide credit to low-income producers and entrepreneurs. The relative immobility of the female labour force in response to market signals obstructs allocative efficiency in the labour market, and there are social opportunity costs in the loss of efficiency and misallocation of resources resulting from female labour being "locked up" in non-market work. On the other hand, there are positive externalities to female non-market work that can be viewed in terms of the production of a public good and that therefore present a case for public-policy intervention.

64. Mainstream economists paid little attention to the household until the last 20 years or so. Thus far, household behaviour has usually been modelled in economic theory on the behaviour of individual economic agents: in macroeconomic analysis the household is considered in terms of providing factor inputs, savings and consumption, and micro-economic analysis considers primarily its consumption role. Such constructs of micro-economic theory as "comparative advantage", "utility maximization" and "preference functions" are applied to the household in the same way as they are applied to the individual economic agent. The household is treated as a unit that maximizes the joint utility function of its members. Despite the analytical shortcomings of the aggregation of individual family members into a joint utility function, the micro-economic model of the household claims that it behaves as if it were a single entity maximizing joint utility and welfare. Gender neutrality is in this case assumed to be inconsequential and benevolent.

65. The conceptual framework underlying economic analysis and much development policy-making relies on the representation of the household as an altruistic collectivity where all available resources are pooled and distributed efficiently among its members, taking equally into account the welfare of each member. Despite the fact that this model does not justify the treatment of the household as a unity (see box) and, as a remedy to that, simply assumes that altruism prevails in the family, it has been widely used to analyse and shape a range of development policies and projects.

66. If equality of outcome entails equality of access to resources, there are strong gender arguments for directing transfers to women as individuals in order to avoid leakages at the household level. It has been rightly argued that education, health care, credit and food are not "household public goods"; 52/ they are individual goods that are rival and exclusive in consumption. Research shows that failure to account for gender-based asymmetries in the intrahousehold allocation of resources weakens development projects. Policies directed at raising the productivity of the agricultural sector or developing entrepreneurship do not achieve the desired results unless they take into account the fact that within a single household separate economic accounting units exist and the pattern of the exchange of labour and distribution of resources among them reflects the differences in the bargaining power of its members, which in turn depends on their entitlement. Women, however, are usually considered to be entitled to less and, as a result, their bargaining power is weaker. In this respect, the cooperative conflict model is a better tool for development policy-making, because it provides a rationale for an intrahousehold approach to policy formulation. Currently, however, the cooperative conflict model, although widely discussed in the literature on human development and the structuralist perspective on macroeconomic policy-making, remains more of a dissent against the neoclassical unitary approach than an active tool of development planning.

67. Economic growth, inflation and monetary and fiscal policies may each have a differential impact on women. Yet in its discussion of aggregates, macroeconomics entirely omits gender issues. This inadequacy of macroeconomics stems from the neglect of one whole area of production; the unpaid production of human resources. The work carried out by women in reproduction and the maintenance of human resources is excluded from national accounts, and the link between the paid and the unpaid economy is therefore lost. This has im-

50/ D. Elson, loc. cit., p. 240.

51/ S. Feiner and B. Roberts, "Hidden by the invisible hand: neoclassical economic theory and textbook treatment of race and gender", Gender and Society, vol. 4, No. 2 (June 1990), pp. 159-181.

52/ I. Palmer, "Social and gender issues in macroeconomic policy advice"; paper presented at the International Round Table on Women's Economic Potential to Overcome Poverty, Bonn/Königswinter, 27-30 November 1994.

The household models in economic theory

1. New household economics: the joint welfare maximization model

The model extends the micro-economic framework of maximization behaviour to the analysis of the household. To deal with the problem of the aggregation of individual preferences into a joint welfare function, the model deploys an assumption that "since blood is thicker than water ... preferences of different members [of the household] are interrelated by a 'social welfare function' which takes into account the deservingness or ethical worth of the consumption levels of each of the members. The family acts as if it were maximizing their joint welfare function". a/ The model also assumes maximizing behaviour, stable preferences and equilibrium in implicit or explicit markets to provide a systematic analysis of the household. The problems which might cause maximization failure, such as utility comparisons and joint utility maximization, are addressed by assuming implicit markets and altruistic behaviour of the household head. b/

2. New institutional economics: implicit contracts and household bargaining model— cooperative conflict model c/

The new institutional economics focuses on the evolution of social institutions that create the context in which individual decisions are made. It views the household as an institutional mode of production and exchange. The household is seen as an institutional response to basic needs based on long-term constructs between individuals related by birth or marriage. Decision-making within the household reflects contractual rights and obligations, as well as economic incentives. Institutional economics rejects the assumption of altruism, postulating differences in terms of domestic trade that are the function of the relative bargaining power of participants. Deploying the bargaining format of the institutional economics, the cooperative conflict model addresses issues of gender and power within the household. This model assumes that members of the household cooperate as long as the outcomes of their cooperation are preferable to those without cooperation. In this assumption, it departs from utility maximization by positing that individuals in the household do not bargain solely on the grounds of their self-interest, i.e., "utility". Instead, their bargaining strategies depend on perceived notions of what they are entitled to. Entitlement depends on perceived contributions, and because women's contribution is largely "invisible", no matter how much time or energy they expect, they are considered to be entitled to less.

a/ P. Samuelson, "Social indifference curves", *Quarterly Journal of Economics*, vol. LXX, No. 1 (1956), p. 10.

b/ G. Becker, *A Treatise on the Family* (Cambridge, Mass., Harvard University Press, 1991).

c/ A. K. Sen, "Gender and cooperative conflicts", in I. Tinker, ed., *Persistent Inequalities* (Oxford, Oxford University Press, 1990), pp. 123-149.

portant practical consequences. When macroeconomic policies are formulated, the gender dimension of the consequences of changes in market signals and of the reallocation of resources is lost. Implicit in this approach is that women's ability to compensate at the household level for the decline in output and for changes in the composition and level of aggregate demand is treated as infinitely elastic, obscuring the impact of macroeconomic policy on the human resource base of economic activity. This in turn is likely to have a negative impact on international economic competitiveness, balance of payments and economic growth, as the shortfall in human skills resulting from the adverse impact of macroeconomic policy remains unaccounted for and unplanned for in terms of appropriate supportive measures and resources, thus rendering the policy unsustainable.

68. Repressed financial markets and credit rationing favour capital intensity and may perpetuate discrimination. Small enterprises, including the bulk of businesses owned by women, are forced to seek credit in the informal market where they are obliged to pay interest rates several times higher than in the formal financial sector. To the extent that financial repression discourages the development of small-scale production, it hurts the economic participation of women. Regulated credit hurts women indirectly by interfering with the efficient allocation of resources and inhibiting economic growth.

69. Policies of trade liberalization and external openness, together with supporting macroeconomic policies involving exchange-rate management and the maintenance of international competitiveness, have been shown to be beneficial for women in terms of improving their economic position and their bargaining power in the family. The loss of competitiveness and real exchange-rate appreciation, on the other hand, tend to affect women to a greater extent than men because employers still feel free to discriminate against them.

70. The link between taxation policies and em-

ployment, structural change and economic growth can be better understood if the gender aspects of taxation are addressed at the outset of policy-making. The main taxation issues that have a gender-specific impact are the unit of taxation, the progressiveness of taxation, the balance between direct and indirect taxation and the availability of tax rebates relating to dependency status and child care. The importance of these issues varies according to the level of economic development: while to women in the industrialized economies personal taxation issues are of greater importance, in developing countries, where women's income is often below the taxable threshold, it is the balance between direct and indirect taxation, sectoral taxation policies and the progressiveness of the tax schedule that are relevant to women's employment and access to productive resources.

71.   More progressive personal taxation schedules, the choice of joint or individual income as the unit of taxation and reduced reliance on regressive taxation will all tend to be to the advantage of women and will provide incentives for women to seek paid employment. Provision for tax rebates for such expenses as child care is also desirable in order to encourage high participation rates. Taxation that penalizes exports and the agricultural sector tends to worsen the economic position of women.

VI. Conclusions: strategies for increasing the participation of women in economic development

72.   Economic policies and development strategies affect women everywhere, often to a greater extent than men. Some have the potential to liberate women's skills and contributions while others intensify the conditions which prevent that from happening. Cross-country analyses of access by women to productive employment and entrepreneurship show that a growth strategy of protection and capital intensity has been inimical to promoting gender equality in access to markets. It also shows that macroeconomic policies deployed to address allocative distortions have often worsened women's position relative to men. It is important, however, to keep in perspective that the "negative impact" on women of structural adjustment policies has been due first of all to the rigidity of their socially ascribed roles and their limited access to productive resources, which were already in existence prior to the introduction of economic reform. Another reason why economic policies some-

times lead to gender-asymmetric outcomes is that gender remains outside the context of their formulation. Here, the issue is not limited to the gender-inequitable outcomes of macroeconomic policies: it is the efficiency and sustainability of those policies that is at stake if gender remains outside the subject-matter of macroeconomic development planning.

73.   Strategies for the integration of women in development in the 1990s have to be focused on introducing gender awareness into every step of macroeconomic policy-making and development planning. Forging the link between macroeconomic policy instruments and the ultimate goal of development—poverty alleviation— requires the explicit articulation of the gender dimension of all economic activity in both the theory and application of macroeconomic development. Gender analysis should be an integral part of the design of policies and programmes aimed at promoting economic growth, stability and the alleviation of poverty.

74.   Taking gender into account in development policies will require a modification of the underlying assumptions about development. Such a modification would entail combining efficiency and equity factors in the conceptualization and implementation of development policies. The elimination of gender-based distortion in the allocation of resources should be seen as complementary to efficiency, rather than in opposition to it. Furthermore, if equity in outcomes of the development process in terms of gender entails equality of opportunity, then it should be approached on the basis of the recognition of similarities rather than differences between women and men. For example, an extra cost of maternity leave and child care to employers of women should not function as a tax on female employment.

75.   A central conclusion of the present analysis is that all economic policy questions, at the national or international level, need to be subject to examination in terms of their gender dimensions. Careful attention to this procedure can help ensure that the effective mobilization of women for development is a central part of development policies, planning and programmes. A possible future step would be to begin to develop theoretical and econometric models that could begin to factor in gender issues and thereby help refine economic policy decisions.

Document 126

Report of the Secretary-General to the General Assembly on the improvement of the situation of women in rural areas

A/50/257/Rev.1, 28 September 1995

I. Introduction

1. In its resolution 48/109 of 20 December 1993, the General Assembly requested the Secretary-General to prepare a report on the improvement of the situation of women in rural areas and to submit it, through the Economic and Social Council, to the Assembly at its fiftieth session. Reports on the subject have been submitted to the Assembly in 1985 (A/40/239 and Add.1), 1989 (A/44/516) and 1993 (A/48/187-E/1993/76).

2. The issue of rural women has been on the international agenda for a long time. It has been addressed in various conferences and agreements, as reflected in the final documents of the three World Conferences on Women, in 1975, 1980 and 1985, the World Conference on Agrarian Reform and Rural Development, in 1979, the World Summit for Children, in 1990, the United Nations Conference on Environment and Development, in 1992, the World Conference on Human Rights and the International Conference on Population and Development, in 1994, and the World Summit for Social Development, in 1995. It was considered at the Summit on the Economic Advancement of Rural Women, organized in 1992 under the auspices of the International Fund for Agricultural Development (IFAD). Issues related to rural women can be found throughout the critical areas of concern in the Platform for Action adopted at the Fourth World Conference on Women. 1/ Considerable information has thus been collected, analysed and presented over the past two decades about the situation of women in rural areas.

3. The report requested by the General Assembly seeks to update that information, taking into account a number of new and emerging perspectives on the issue. Over the past decade, there has been no radical change in the issues relating to rural women and the types of actions necessary to address them. In policy terms, there is a general consensus about what should be done, as expressed in the reports of international conferences and the resolutions adopted by intergovernmental bodies and expert seminars and meetings. These include:

    (a) Access to land, capital/credit, technology;

    (b) Access to gainful employment;

    (c) Support for non-agricultural activities;

    (d) Access to markets;

    (e) At least a minimum level of social infrastructure;

    (f) Availability of basic health and family planning services;

    (g) Access to education, including adult education, aimed at eliminating illiteracy;

    (h) Access to water, electricity, energy resources;

    (i) Social support measures, e.g., child-care facilities and social security;

    (j) Access to decision-making at all levels;

    (k) Empowerment of women;

    (l) Community organization and training.

4. These affirmations have been made in various ways over the past 20 years. There is considerable evidence that, as is the case with the global economy as a whole and with developing countries in general, rural societies are beginning to undergo fundamental changes.

5. Demographic projections now suggest that around the year 2006, half of the world's population will be living in urban areas and the proportion of women living in rural areas will continue to decline globally as it has in some regions already.

6. The importance of rural women in the next century will rest more on their impact on the economy and society than on their numbers. It will be related to their contribution to food security and to economic growth, as well as to the maintenance of social cohesion.

7. Taking into account previous analyses, the report seeks to examine the trends that will affect the status of rural women in the twenty-first century. The analysis centres on the changes in the world in terms of the patterns of growth in the global economy, urbanization and environmental degradation. It then examines two issues that are of growing, but somewhat unrecognized importance, for rural women: food security and the impact of rural-urban migration.

II. Trends and issues affecting rural women

8. Rural women the world over are an integral and vital force in the development processes that are the key to socio-economic progress. Rural women include farmers, as well as domestic servants. They form the backbone of the agricultural labour force across much of the developing world and produce an estimated 35 to 45 per cent of the gross domestic product and well over half of the

---

1/ See *Report of the Fourth World Conference on Women, Beijing, 4-15 September 1995* (A/CONF.177/20), chap.I.

developing world's food. Yet, more than half a billion rural women are poor and lack access to resources and markets. In fact, their number is estimated to have increased by 50 per cent over the past 20 years and, at the present time, they outnumber poor men.

9. The situation of rural women is beginning to be affected by the growing interdependence of the global economy, by urbanization and by the increasing concern with food security.

A. Changes in the global economy

10. As has been shown in the *1994 World Survey on the Role of Women in Development* 2/ and in the second review and appraisal of the implementation of the Nairobi Forward-looking Strategies for the Advancement of Women, changes in the global economy have had a noticeable gender dimension. There has been recovery in some parts of the developing world, but stagnation in others. The interdependence of national economies has continued to grow. These changes have particular effects on rural women, depending on where they live.

11. In a separate study, on the effective mobilization and integration of women in development (A/50/399), it is noted that one consequence of economic change is the extensive incorporation of women into the economically active population, especially in the sectors showing the greatest growth. These growth sectors are non-agricultural.

12. Traditionally, the role of agriculture in economic development has been viewed as that of establishing a framework for industrialization by providing factor inputs and low-priced food. Disillusion in the 1980s with industrialization-at-any-cost development strategies that were extremely costly in terms of imports and other scarce resources brought about renewed interest in agriculture, but as a vehicle for economic growth and productive employment.

13. More than three quarters of the population of developing countries depend directly on agriculture for their livelihood. Agricultural development is therefore the *sine qua non* of national economic development if economic progress is to reach the majority of the population without a long wait for "trickle-down" effects. Agriculture is also important in the sense that its failure to keep pace with industrialization can act as a constraint on sustainable industrial growth and the development of other sectors, because it constitutes an important source of effective demand for industry.

14. The neglect of agriculture, a by-product of decades of inward-oriented industrialization in developing countries, has been a cause of severe internal imbalances and widespread poverty, inequality and unemployment. Policies of overvalued exchange rates, high effective protection and repressed financial markets have had a negative effect on agricultural growth. However, the process of redressing the bias against agriculture created by such policies has sometimes led to a worsening of the gender bias in agricultural economic activity, because of the absence of gender awareness in economic adjustment policies. Failure to take account of gender barriers to the intra- and inter-sectoral reallocation of resources in the design of adjustment policies so as to correct their adverse effects on gender balance in access to and command of productive resources has led to a shift in relative income-earning ability in agricultural production in favour of men, albeit with some regional variations. Persistent inadequacies in women's access to land, credit, extension services and technology suggest that men rather than women have been able to benefit from incentives under expanded commercial agriculture. Women own-account farmers, agricultural labourers and subsistence producers have largely remained in low-productivity and low-income activities.

B. Urbanization

15. A significant factor in the future of rural development is the accelerating trend towards urbanization. Whether through rural-urban migration or the growth of smaller towns to sizes that will define them as urban, according to United Nations projections, the urbanization process will result in 62 per cent of the population living in urban areas within 30 years (see table 1).

16. At the same time, even as its relative proportion declines, the total rural population in the world is projected to continue to grow larger, at least until 2025, when it begins to decline slowly (see table 2). As is the case today, most of the rural dwellers will be in developing countries. However, their number will be dwarfed by the 5 billion urban residents in 2025, 4 billion of whom will be in the less developed regions. This will amount to an increase of 2.6 billion people from 1995, all of whom will have to be fed through increased agricultural productivity.

17. Urban growth occurs both because of natural growth in urban populations and because of rural-urban migration. In the early stages, migration is the dominant factor. Migration is not gender neutral and it is the gender difference in migration that can strongly affect the situation of rural women in a given country.

18. There is growing evidence that in low-growth areas, it is men who migrate, while in high-growth areas, women migrate at a higher rate, particularly younger women. This can be seen in table 3, which shows the ratio of women to men in urban and rural areas among the

2/ *Women in a Changing Global Economy: 1994 World Survey on the Role of Women in Development* (United Nations publication, Sales No. E.95.IV.1).

Table 1. *Total world population and pecentage of population residing in urban areas*

Region	1970		1995		2025	
	Total population (in thousands)	Percent urban	Total population (in thousands)	Percent urban	Total population (in thousands)	Percent urban
World total	3 697 141	36.59	5 716 426	45.21	8 294 341	61.07
More developed regions	1 002 607	67.52	1 166 598	74.92	1 238 406	83.98
Less developed regions	2 694 535	25.08	4 549 828	37.59	7 055 935	57.05
Least developed countries	302 737	12.62	575 407	22.40	1 162 279	43.49

Source: World Urbanization Prospects: The 1994 Revision (United Nations publication, Sales No. E.95.XIII.12), tables A.3 and A.5.

young adult cohorts. 3/ In regions that have experienced greater and more rapid economic growth, it appears that post-school-age women migrate at a greater rate than men. In countries that have had less growth, it is young men who have been more likely to migrate.

19. The patterns of rural-to-urban migration observed in each of these regions are consistent with regional trends in economic development with respect to trade orientation, the inflow of foreign direct investment and the type of employment in export-processing industries. The creation of export-processing zones in the context of export-promotion policies has undoubtedly contributed to fostering female migration from rural to urban areas in the first and second generation of the newly industrialized economies of East and South-East Asia and Latin America and the Caribbean.

20. Migration has effects on the rural economy generally and on gender relations which need to be examined. On the one hand, male migration can undercut agriculture when food production is affected by traditional sex-based divisions of labour and when women lack access to credit, technology and markets. On the other hand, female migration can erode traditional systems as migrants take on new urban values, institutions such as the extended family become less effective because of physical distance and kin-based obligations become less important. At the same time, remittances from migrants can become a significant part of the rural economy.

C. Food security

21. The transformation of societies towards an urban base provides opportunities as well as problems. The strategic role of rural areas in the production of food becomes more important as urban populations increase in size, and food production can be a source of economic growth, since an increasing share of production will have to be marketed rather than self-consumed. Moreover, the increase in cash income of the rural population can provide a stimulus for the urban economy through increases in consumption of basic goods. Owing to the fact that, in a large number of the developing countries, women predominate in food production and marketing, this should provide enhanced opportunities for rural women.

22. All development strategies include concerns about food, agriculture and population. These three factors constitute the concept of sustainable food security. The Food and Agriculture Organization of the United Nations (FAO) defines food security to mean "that food is available at all times, that all persons have means of access to it, that it is nutritionally adequate in terms of quantity, quality and variety, and that it is acceptable within the given culture". 4/

23. Trends in per capita food production and food supplies in the present decade are similar to a large extent to the trends in per capita output, which is similar to the situation a decade ago. During the past three decades, the number of countries that were able to meet their daily per capita requirements has increased from fewer than 25 to more than 50. The rate of agricultural production growth at the global level has been about 2.3 per cent between 1970 and 1990 and thus has exceeded population growth so that per capita supplies of food have increased. However, wide regional disparities remained: the situation

3/ There are few global indicators of rural/urban migration. However, an estimate of the gender composition of migration can be seen from the ratio of women to men in urban and rural populations compared to the national average. If there are more men than the national average in urban areas, the migration has been primarily of males. If there are more women than the national average in urban areas, migration has been primarily of females.

4/ FAO Committee on World Food Security, Twentieth Session, Rome, 25-28 April 1995 (CFS: 95/4).

Table 2. *Rural population and average annual rate of change of rural population in the world, 1965-1970, 1985-1990 and 2020-2025*

Region	Rural population (in thousands)			Rate of change		
	1970	1990	2025	1965-1970	1985-1990	2020-2025
World total	2 344 356	3 007 383	3 229 007	1.71	1.06	-0.37
Less developed regions	2 018 685	2 705 976	3 030 649	2.18	1.22	-0.28
More developed regions	325 671	301 407	198 357	-0.96	-0.28	-1.63

Source: World Urbanization Prospects: The 1994 Revision (United Nations publication, Sales No. E.95.XIII.12), table 18.

Table 3. *Ratio of women to men in total, urban and rural population*
(1990 census round)
(Number of women for each 100 men)

Region	Age group	Total population	Urban population	Rural population
Africa	15-19	99.7	98.9	110.0
	20-24	100.2	88.5	109.7
Latin America	15-19	98.4	106.1	87.3
	20-24	100.6	108.9	88.2
Western Europe	15-19	95.6	97.2	91.3
	20-24	95.6	98.8	86.5
Asia and Pacific	15-19	94.6	93.0	96.3
	20-24	94.4	90.9	96.9
East Asia	15-19	93.8	93.6	93.8
	20-24	93.5	95.6	86.4
South-East Asia	15-19	96.8	98.7	96.8
	20-24	98.6	100.3	98.2
Eastern Europe	15-19	94.8	93.9	93.4
	20-24	95.2	95.8	92.9

Source: Women's Indicators and Statistics Database (WISTAT), version 3, 1994.

improved in East Asia but worsened in sub-Saharan Africa and there was no progress in Latin America. 5/

24. The International Conference on Nutrition, held in December 1992, drew attention to the fact that more than 780 million people, or 20 per cent of the population in developing countries, suffer from chronic malnutrition and each year about 13 million children below the age of five die from infectious diseases that can be attributed to hunger or malnutrition.

25. Any approach to food security needs to take into account the role of rural women, their status and opportunities regarding all these issues. Although rural women are at the end of the distribution chain for productive resources and social services, they are at the beginning of the food production chain. In developing countries rural women are responsible for more than 55 per cent of the food grown; in Africa they produce 70 per cent of the food. Moreover, women comprise 67 per cent of the agricultural labour force in developing countries. 6/

5/ *Agriculture: Towards 2010* (Rome, FAO, 1993).
6/ *Women in a Changing Global Economy* ..., p. 35.

III. Major factors in rural women's role as food producers

26. One of the major findings over the past 20 years has been that, in most developing countries, women are the predominant producers of food for domestic consumption. They perform this function while facing considerable constraints. An examination of these factors can provide a basis for determining how best to overcome the constraints and thereby help increase the effectiveness of women in addressing the issue of food security.

27. In contrast to more developed countries, where growth in agricultural production has been based on application of technology and increased size of productive units, food production in developing countries remains centred on smaller holdings managed by households that provide the bulk of the labour input required by the productive systems.

28. There are a number of gender dimensions to food production, relating to labour input, to land use, to access to capital and technology and to environmentally sound production practices. These four factors are linked and, if addressed, can help ensure that food production increases with accompanying benefits for rural households and for society as a whole.

A. Labour availability and use

29. Food production in developing countries is labour-intensive. For households, ensuring that there will be family members available to do necessary work is an essential economic element. Women and men alike provide labour input, although their tasks often differ. There is a close relationship between having children and agricultural production, and having large numbers of children is often perceived by women and men alike as an economic necessity. As one analyst noted, there is a certain paradox, with the increase of women's responsibilities and duties, higher demand on their time and energy, they are "less likely to see the utility for themselves of having fewer children, even though population densities in the little land left for subsistence families are rapidly increasing". 7/ There are now seen to be a number of incentives for rural women to have larger numbers of children, with the consequent impact on their abilities to increase production.

30. While there is a correlation between the decline of fertility and increases in income, at least to a certain level, there is an underlying assumption that higher income encourages people to invest in hired labour or mechanization and thereby release children and pay more attention to their education. However, a number of studies indicate that men and women invest increased incomes differently and men were not necessarily willing

to hire labour to replace that of their spouses and children. Others indicate that rural women may perceive the need to have many children, especially sons, as long-term risk insurance, as widows are able to keep their property largely through sons' productive activity and status.

31. The strong motivation of rural women in developing countries to have more children is also related to infant mortality. To reduce fertility, it is necessary to ensure the survival of children through improvement of maternal and child nutrition, availability of health care and clean water. This, in turn, is related to increases in income. Increases in income involve improved nutrition and application of labour-saving technologies, although that depends on whether the increases in income are passed on as greater food entitlements for the family, particularly to the more nutritionally vulnerable members, and as investment in higher labour productivity, again in particular to the most work-stressed members.

B. Intra-household relations

32. To a larger extent than in urban areas, the rural household is a production unit as well as one whose primary economic function is the management of consumption. Women, men and children in the household are expected to contribute to household income, by working the household's land, by working as salaried labour and by other means. The effectiveness of the household as an economic unit depends in large measure on the intra-household relations between women and men. As Waring noted in 1988: "Family resources and decisions impinge not only on rates of fertility, mortality, and migration, but also on transfer of activities from the unpaid, largely unmeasured household sector to the market sector, which is a fundamental determinant of the rate of growth of gross national product". 8/

33. Most households have a division of labour based on gender. The precise division of tasks varies by country and culture, although a common feature is that women are given primary responsibility for the tasks associated with preparing food, providing fuel and water, raising children and taking care of the elderly and the sick. They frequently have the responsibility for subsistence production of food, as well as for certain tasks in commercial production.

34. While the economics of subsistence agriculture has begun to be studied, the gender dimensions of household production are less known. There is evidence from micro-studies that an examination of intra-household

7/ Jodi L. Jacobson, *Gender Bias: Roadblock to Sustainable Development*, World Watch Paper No. 110 (September 1992).
8/ Marilyn Waring, *If Women Counted: A New Feminist Economics* (New York, Harper and Row, 1988).

gender differences in food production would show that women make a significant contribution to the household economy and, by aggregation, to national food security. However, the extent of this contribution has not yet been generally measured.

35. A variety of studies, including national reports prepared for the Fourth World Conference on Women, have shown the considerable contribution of women farmers to food production. For example, in the Lao People's Democratic Republic, as a result of women's rice farming, national rice production was said to have doubled between 1976 and 1985. In Viet Nam, female peasants contributed significantly to changes in the rural economic structure and increased rate of production growth. Food production there went up from 18.4 million tons in 1986 to 21.5 million in 1989, 1990 and 1991, converting Viet Nam from a food importer to a food exporter. In China, the output value produced by women was estimated to account for between 50 and 60 per cent of the gross agricultural output value.

36. The migration of men in order to find seasonal work, especially in Latin America and Asia, and the displacement of pastoral households, especially in Africa, in practice, both increase women's role in livestock production and their workload. This role is not recognized at the policy-making level or in legal terms. As a result, the provision of services and external inputs, both technical and financial, bypasses women in all three continents and has not kept up with women's increasing role in livestock production. Government policies continue to encourage male-oriented activities, namely, beef production, large commercial dairy centres and large-scale cattle trade. To reach women, focus should be on small-scale activities, e.g., milk-based products, small ruminants and other small stock.

37. An additional gender factor is that women's systematic lack of access to cash can create biases in the perception of who is producing what and earning what within the household. 9/ Women are often not able to exercise rights of ownership and use of resources, including their labour, to the same degree as men. Often, women are not recognized as holders of rights on their own account, but rather are considered, to a lesser or greater degree, dependants of men. In rural areas, women who work in the field, in family productive units and in a work-paid system, paid by job or by production, are generally seen as helpers of their husbands.

38. The growing number of female-headed households in developing countries represents a challenge for improving household food security. In general, female-headed households tend to be poorer, own less land, and often lack access to credit and technology. However, according to studies undertaken in Kenya and Malawi,

household food security and the nutritional status of individual members can be significantly better in female-headed households, as women tend to spend a greater proportion of their income on food. One of the study's conclusions was that, although there is a strong argument that income is a major determinant of household food security, it is also true that the level of income controlled by women has a positive impact on household caloric intake, an impact that is over and above the effect of income. This finding suggests that gender may influence the composition of diets within households, as was indicated in the Malawi case by the higher proportion of food budgets allocated to alcoholic beverages by male-headed households and the higher proportion of calories directed to young children by the poorer de facto female-headed households. In other terms, the female gender of the head compensates for the difference in income at low levels of income. Clearly, it is not the female-headedness *per se* that leads to this pattern of behaviour, but the intersection between income and gender of the head. 10/

39. In its study on the state of world rural poverty, IFAD concluded that since the food security of households is usually dependent on women's earnings, low-paying jobs and lack of regular employment for women often mean inadequate food security and poor family nutrition. Support for rural women should focus on generating off-farm and on-farm regular employment and on improving wage incomes. Improving technical skills of women through better education and training also improves their access to better jobs. 11/

40. When intra-household relations are asymmetric, in terms of ability to contribute to or benefit from economic activity, the household may not be able to manage its resources efficiently, particularly when women's skills are not used effectively. This is often attributable to cultural factors which, for example, can preclude women from decision-making on land use or from marketing activities.

41. Intra-household relations are crucial for policy design and implementation, and further examination of this factor, particularly in terms of women's role as the main producers of food, will be necessary.

C. Land distribution and income

42. Of all of the factors that determine food production, access to land is the most important. Women's

9/ A. K. Sen, "Gender and cooperative conflicts", in I. Tinker, ed., *Persistent Inequalities: Women and World in Development* (New York, Oxford University Press, 1992), pp. 123-149.
10/ E. Kennedy and P. Peters, "Household food security and child nutrition: The interaction of income and gender of household head", *World Development*, vol. 20, No. 8, p. 1084.
11/ *The State of World Rural Poverty* (Rome, IFAD, 1992), p. 293.

lesser access to land has been a common factor in most societies and still constitutes one of the main obstacles to their full participation in rural development. The existing practices, including of inheritance, favour male ownership of land. Even in those countries where women are legally entitled to own land, de facto implementation of this right is rare. Indeed, the issue of access to land was a major concern reflected in the Beijing Declaration and Platform for Action.

43. Of particular importance to rural women is the development of legal measures and administrative regulations to improve their secure access to land. This may involve designating women as individual or joint owners of plots distributed in agrarian reforms, giving them separate tenancy rights in settlement schemes, improving their rights to claim a fair share of family resources upon divorce, abandonment or widowhood, and so forth. A second area of concern is the review of civil codes that treat women as legal minors, requiring, for example, their husband's signature to open bank accounts or to obtain credit. Equally important for rural women, especially in Asia and Latin America, is new labour legislation supporting their equitable access to rural labour markets, mandating equal pay for equal work, and improving working conditions, while enforcing legal standards. A fourth priority is to improve rural women's access to informal sector markets by eliminating discriminatory licensing and price-control measures.

44. When they are automatically designated as heads of household men can control most household economic resources and are normally indirect recipients of project resources targeted at households. These principles hold even when men are not the primary source of household income and when women manage important household resources and conduct various household enterprises on a relatively autonomous basis. In most societies, there is still male control of land, major livestock resources, a large share of subsistence output and the bulk of household income. Women are, in general, dependent on men for final decisions with respect to virtually everything that affects their lives, and are therefore more vulnerable to poverty.

45. Rural women's customary land rights have also been threatened by agrarian reform programmes which have tended to redistribute land titles primarily to men. Although all the land reform legislation of Asia brought the land to the beneficiary "household" or "family", it allowed the allocation of land within the household to be governed by prevailing custom and law, which decreed the man to be the "head of the household". Land was allotted to the "tenant" or "tiller", who was always presumed to be a man. Thus, although the agrarian reform legislation during the period 1945-1985 did not

specifically or explicitly discriminate against women, the application of the law in the context of existing customs and inheritance laws often resulted in their losing their right to land.

46. A review of Latin American agrarian reform shows that in all countries, except Cuba and Nicaragua, only one member of the household can officially be designated as a beneficiary. Even though female heads of households may, in principle, apply for land, administrative practices and additional criteria defining potential beneficiaries have essentially excluded women. More recently, a review of 165 national reports submitted to the United Nations Secretariat in 1994 during the preparations for the Fourth World Conference on Women gave a clear picture of the situation in that area. The existing male preference in ownership of land is found in all regions of the world.

47. Often there are no legal provisions for women to keep the land in case of death of the husband, separation or divorce. The difficulties that rural women encounter in obtaining access to land are even greater for female-headed households, whose number is growing. When women do not own land they often cannot qualify for agricultural services, in particular for credit and extension services, where ownership is a requirement.

48. Market incentives can work in developing countries but only if due consideration is given to the social and legal framework. Where the distribution of land ownership and opportunities is highly skewed towards men, market mechanisms tend to bring more benefits to them, at least in the short run.

D. *Protection and regeneration of the resource base*

49. There is a pronounced and obvious connection between food security and environmental degradation. The drive towards food security sometimes overtaxes the environment, and environmental degradation often limits the capacity to produce enough food. Various studies have shown that there has been increasing reduction of arable land through soil degradation, erosion, deforestation and desertification. This factor, if unchecked, can affect future abilities to maintain food security.

50. An important link between women and the environment is in terms of the above factor. In most developing countries, food production is undertaken mainly by women, and therefore, issues related to food security, land rights and environmentally sustainable land-use practices are central to their lives. Gender imbalances in access to resources impact negatively on women's ability to play vital custodial roles in sustainable environment practices. There is some evidence that the labour-intensive food production practices of women can be environmentally sound and could, if used more exten-

sively, both increase food production and protect the resource base. Similarly, it seems likely that women would be particularly receptive to new technologies and techniques that would be beneficial for maintaining land quality.

51. The link between rural women and environmental protection can be seen in terms of forestry. The depletion of forestry resources, in particular, has had a significant negative impact on women. Apart from their value as a productive resource, trees protect the quality of the soil and water and most tropical farming systems are unsustainable without trees as part of the system. Forests provide food, fodder and fibre products which fall within women's responsibility. Small-scale enterprises dependent on forestry products are among the major employers of rural women, particularly the landless and resource poor.

52. Little attention has been given to the asset-creating activities in which women engage, such as through trade involving natural resources and their products, or to the ways in which the use of such resources involves them in the wider social and political life of their families or communities.

53. For example, one analysis has suggested that community forestry projects have frequently assumed women to be interested only in species for fuelwood, in contrast with men's interest in, for example, trees to produce building materials to sell for cash. While women often do have pressing fuel needs, their own responses to narrowly focused fuelwood projects have in many instances revealed the broader scope of their interests and needs. Policies designed from a narrow view of women's roles "risk not only ignoring large parts of their spectrum of interests and activities, but also entrenching women in narrowly defined domestic roles and thus reinforcing, rather than rectifying, gender inequalities". 12/

54. The relationship between women and the environment also includes such issues as their rights of access, control and participation in decision-making over natural resources. The lack of women's rights in that area might demotivate women to invest in sound environmental management and enforce the degradation of the natural resource base.

IV. The impact of rural-urban migration on rural women

55. Gender differences in rural-urban migration has not been well-studied. In part this is because female migration has been neglected as part of a general neglect of women in social sciences research. It also reflects inadequacies in existing data on women's migration, and on women's role and socio-economic status in general. 13/

56. Lack of economic opportunities in rural areas, whether caused by population pressure on finite land resources or lack of non-agricultural development, often leaves younger people little alternative to migration in order to obtain employment. A study prepared by the International Training and Research Institute for the Advancement of Women (INSTRAW) noted that the number of female migrants is increasing world wide. Though more women migrate for family reasons, including to accompany other family members, to get married or to join the spouse, than for economic reasons, a significant proportion of women migrate for economic reasons, including for education, which is usually intended to assist them in seeking better employment in the future. 14/

57. In Asia, for example, in India, Bangladesh and Thailand, men migrate mostly during the slack season, because of underemployment or loss of employment owing to the mechanization of agriculture, for educational purposes, or for psychosocial reasons such as prestige. During the dry season, available non-farm employment opportunities are mainly jobs related to infrastructure, such as construction and maintenance, and they also go to men.

58. There is growing evidence that women also migrate for economic reasons, and not only to join spouses. In Africa, factors such as level of education, age, marital status and ethnicity are associated with migration to the cities. According to studies in eight countries—Burundi, Ghana, Kenya, Mali, Nigeria, Senegal, Togo and Uganda—it was found that both married and unmarried women had strong motivation to migrate. In every country, except Mali, non-marital reasons for migration appear to be more common in rural-urban migration. In Kenya, small plot holdings in densely populated districts proved unproductive to sustain women on the farms in rural areas. Since 1969, the process of rural-urban migration has progressively shifted from a high dominance of unmarried male migrants to one in which women, both unmarried and married, as well as children, have become an important component of migration.

59. In Asia, women basically fall into two categories: some are forced out of independent rural production for the market into casual labour, while others, generally younger women, are no longer able to make a sufficient contribution to the rural household economy. In the Philippines, for example, 7 out of 10 females employed in the service sector in urban areas are migrants

12/ Melissa Leach, "Gender and the environment: traps and opportunities", Development in Practice, vol. 1, No. 2 (February 1992), p. 15.
13/ Internal Migration of Women in Developing Countries (United Nations publication, Sales No. E.94.XIII.3).
14/ The Migration of Women: Methodological Issues in the Measurement and Analysis of Internal and International Migration (Santo Domingo, INSTRAW, 1994), p. 48.

and more than half of these are young and single. 15/ The expansion of the service sector mainly in urban areas of Thailand was the main factor attracting female migrants from the rural areas. Those migrants were relatively less educated, and migrated to Bangkok on a short-term basis to earn supplementary income. The female migrants with higher levels of education had demonstrated considerable independence and moved for economic reasons. In the Republic of Korea, the rate of female migration has slightly exceeded the male rate in the past few decades, with the largest differences occurring between the ages of 15 and 29. Migration rates were associated positively with educational attainment, and the educational selectivity of migration was stronger for females than for males. 16/

60. Major reasons for the out-migration of rural women in Latin America are lack of access to land and mechanization of agricultural production, while, at the same time, there are vast job opportunities for them in the cities, especially in textiles, food processing and other labour-intensive industries, as well as in the informal sector of the economy, such as domestic services or street vending. 17/

61. Male migration to urban areas tends to conserve the traditional kinship relations and patriarchal and seniority values, thus reinforcing gender asymmetries in intra-household distribution and management of productive resources. In general, no significant difference has been found in the number of children of couples who live together and of those in which the males are temporary migrants. Though the husband's departures and returns, if he is a seasonal migrant, may change the timing of births, this does not seem to increase or decrease childbearing. Migration might help modify knowledge, attitudes and practice towards contraception, but it might also promote higher fertility to compensate for separation. Migration has also been one of the causes of the spread of the acquired immunodeficiency syndrome (AIDS) and venereal diseases.

62. While male migration may not change traditional roles in rural society, it may be that female migration will have a longer-term impact not only on the migrants themselves, but also on the women who remain in the rural areas. The relative economic independence that accompanies migration provides an alternative model to that traditionally ascribed to rural women.

63. The migration of women to urban areas may serve to emancipate them from the patriarchal control of the family, particularly when women manage to find a job and become relatively economically independent. However, there is also evidence that women tend to send their income back to their families and thus remain financially dependent and under their control. Over the

short run, this can provide a source of capital for rural development, although it also appears that rural-urban migration is typically one-way.

64. Education and the mass media intensify the process of urbanization in terms of cultural modernization, which undermines the traditional commitments to kin. The relocation of economic activity from the family to the market and increases in mobility and migration reduce parental leverage and, to a certain extent, destabilize the traditional division of labour.

65. The interrelations between rural-urban migration, seen in gender terms, as well as the rural economy and society, merit further study. The fact that these flows of people are tending to blur the distinction between rural and urban areas can be an important factor in designing both urban and rural development policies.

V. Conclusions

66. The evident importance of women as food producers in a rapidly urbanizing world suggests that strong priority should be given to implementing those actions found in the Beijing Declaration and Platform for Action designed to provide rural women with equal access to productive resources. In paragraph 58 (n), for example, the following action is called for:

"Formulate and implement policies and programmes that enhance the access of women agricultural and fisheries producers (including subsistence farmers and producers, especially in rural areas) to financial, technical, extension and marketing services; provide access to and control of land, appropriate infrastructure and technology in order to increase women's incomes and promote household food security, especially in rural areas and, where appropriate, encourage the development of producer-owned, market-based cooperatives." 18/

67. Linkages between urbanization/industrialization and agricultural/rural development are in many ways reflected in the changing status and roles of rural women. Rural women are an important link between rural and urban areas: they maintain food security and the general well-being of their households. A gender approach to

15/ "Special problems of female heads of households in agriculture and rural development in Asia and the Pacific" (Bangkok, Economic and Social Commission for Asia and the Pacific, 1985) (E/ESCAP/AD.6/8).

16/ *Migration and Urbanization: Interrelationship with Socio-economic Development and Evolving Policy Issues*, Population Studies Series, No. 114 (1992) (ST/ESCAP/1133).

17/ M. d. L. A. Crummett, "The women's movement", *Ceres-The FAO Review*, No. 137 (1992).

18/ See *Report of the Fourth World Conference on Women, Beijing*, 4-15 September 1995 (A/CONF.177/20), chap. I.

socio-economic issues deserves to be addressed by, and incorporated in, regional development policies, plans, programmes and projects. Investment in rural women can make development programmes more productive. Since women produce a large proportion of food, it makes sense to improve their status and access to productive resources, capital, markets and information. Efforts should be made at all levels towards fostering rural and urban development. In view of the preparations for the forthcoming World Food Summit, to be held in November 1996, the role of women in food production and food security should receive greater prominence in the elaboration of the documents for that meeting.

68. The evident importance of gender issues in rural-urban migration and the close links between women's status in urban areas and in rural areas, suggest that gender aspects of the rural-urban continuum should be an important factor to be considered in the prepara-

tions for the United Nations Conference on Human Settlements (Habitat II).

69. The limited amount of information available on the economic contribution of rural women within the household, including in subsistence agriculture, suggests the need for greater efforts to document this phenomenon, including by implementing the action called for in chapter IV, section H, of the Platform for Action, as follows:

"Improving data collection on the unremunerated work which is already included in the United Nations System of National Accounts, such as in agriculture, particularly subsistence agriculture, and other types of non-market production activities." 19/

19/ Ibid.

Document 127

Report of the Fourth World Conference on Women, held in Beijing from 4 to 15 September 1995; including the Agenda, the Beijing Declaration and the Platform for Action (extract)

A/CONF.177/20, 17 October 1995

Agenda

...

1. Opening of the Conference.
2. Election of the President.
3. Adoption of the rules of procedure.
4. Adoption of the agenda and other organizational matters.
5. Election of officers other than the President.
6. Organization of work, including the establishment of the Main Committee.
7. Credentials of representatives to the Conference:
    (a) Appointment of the members of the Credentials Committee;
    (b) Report of the Credentials Committee.
8. General exchange of views:
    (a) Second review and appraisal of the implementation of the Nairobi Forward-looking Strategies for the Advancement of Women to the year 2000;
    (b) Main conclusions and recommendations of regional preparatory conferences;
    (c) National priorities and commitments.

9. Platform for Action.
10. Adoption of the Declaration and the Platform for Action of the Fourth World Conference on Women.
11. Adoption of the report of the Conference.

...

Chapter I

Resolutions adopted by the Conference

Resolution 1
*Beijing Declaration and Platform for Action**

The Fourth World Conference on Women,

Having met in Beijing from 4 to 15 September 1995,

1. *Adopts* the Beijing Declaration and Platform for Action, which are annexed to the present resolution;

2. *Recommends* to the General Assembly of the United Nations at its fiftieth session that it endorse the Beijing Declaration and Platform for Action as adopted by the Conference.

* Adopted at the 16th plenary meeting, on 15 September 1995; for the discussion, see chapter V.

Beijing Declaration

1. We, the Governments participating in the Fourth World Conference on Women,

2. Gathered here in Beijing in September 1995, the year of the fiftieth anniversary of the founding of the United Nations,

3. Determined to advance the goals of equality, development and peace for all women everywhere in the interest of all humanity,

4. Acknowledging the voices of all women everywhere and taking note of the diversity of women and their roles and circumstances, honouring the women who paved the way and inspired by the hope present in the world's youth,

5. Recognize that the status of women has advanced in some important respects in the past decade but that progress has been uneven, inequalities between women and men have persisted and major obstacles remain, with serious consequences for the well-being of all people,

6. Also recognize that this situation is exacerbated by the increasing poverty that is affecting the lives of the majority of the world's people, in particular women and children, with origins in both the national and international domains,

7. Dedicate ourselves unreservedly to addressing these constraints and obstacles and thus enhancing further the advancement and empowerment of women all over the world, and agree that this requires urgent action in the spirit of determination, hope, cooperation and solidarity, now and to carry us forward into the next century.

We reaffirm our commitment to:

8. The equal rights and inherent human dignity of women and men and other purposes and principles enshrined in the Charter of the United Nations, to the Universal Declaration of Human Rights and other international human rights instruments, in particular the Convention on the Elimination of All Forms of Discrimination against Women and the Convention on the Rights of the Child, as well as the Declaration on the Elimination of Violence against Women and the Declaration on the Right to Development;

9. Ensure the full implementation of the human rights of women and of the girl child as an inalienable, integral and indivisible part of all human rights and fundamental freedoms;

10. Build on consensus and progress made at previous United Nations conferences and summits — on women in Nairobi in 1985, on children in New York in 1990, on environment and development in Rio de Janeiro in 1992, on human rights in Vienna in 1993, on population and development in Cairo in 1994 and on social development in Copenhagen in 1995 with the objective of achieving equality, development and peace;

11. Achieve the full and effective implementation of the Nairobi Forward-looking Strategies for the Advancement of Women;

12. The empowerment and advancement of women, including the right to freedom of thought, conscience, religion and belief, thus contributing to the moral, ethical, spiritual and intellectual needs of women and men, individually or in community with others and thereby guaranteeing them the possibility of realizing their full potential in society and shaping their lives in accordance with their own aspirations.

We are convinced that:

13. Women's empowerment and their full participation on the basis of equality in all spheres of society, including participation in the decision-making process and access to power, are fundamental for the achievement of equality, development and peace;

14. Women's rights are human rights;

15. Equal rights, opportunities and access to resources, equal sharing of responsibilities for the family by men and women, and a harmonious partnership between them are critical to their well-being and that of their families as well as to the consolidation of democracy;

16. Eradication of poverty based on sustained economic growth, social development, environmental protection and social justice requires the involvement of women in economic and social development, equal opportunities and the full and equal participation of women and men as agents and beneficiaries of people-centred sustainable development;

17. The explicit recognition and reaffirmation of the right of all women to control all aspects of their health, in particular their own fertility, is basic to their empowerment;

18. Local, national, regional and global peace is attainable and is inextricably linked with the advancement of women, who are a fundamental force for leadership, conflict resolution and the promotion of lasting peace at all levels;

19. It is essential to design, implement and monitor, with the full participation of women, effective, efficient and mutually reinforcing gender-sensitive policies and programmes, including development policies and programmes, at all levels that will foster the empowerment and advancement of women;

20. The participation and contribution of all actors of civil society, particularly women's groups and net-

works and other non-governmental organizations and community-based organizations, with full respect for their autonomy, in cooperation with Governments, are important to the effective implementation and follow-up of the Platform for Action;

21. The implementation of the Platform for Action requires commitment from Governments and the international community. By making national and international commitments for action, including those made at the Conference, Governments and the international community recognize the need to take priority action for the empowerment and advancement of women.

We are determined to:

22. Intensify efforts and actions to achieve the goals of the Nairobi Forward-looking Strategies for the Advancement of Women by the end of this century;

23. Ensure the full enjoyment by women and the girl child of all human rights and fundamental freedoms and take effective action against violations of these rights and freedoms;

24. Take all necessary measures to eliminate all forms of discrimination against women and the girl child and remove all obstacles to gender equality and the advancement and empowerment of women;

25. Encourage men to participate fully in all actions towards equality;

26. Promote women's economic independence, including employment, and eradicate the persistent and increasing burden of poverty on women by addressing the structural causes of poverty through changes in economic structures, ensuring equal access for all women, including those in rural areas, as vital development agents, to productive resources, opportunities and public services;

27. Promote people-centred sustainable development, including sustained economic growth, through the provision of basic education, life-long education, literacy and training, and primary health care for girls and women;

28. Take positive steps to ensure peace for the advancement of women and, recognizing the leading role that women have played in the peace movement, work actively towards general and complete disarmament under strict and effective international control, and support negotiations on the conclusion, without delay, of a universal and multilaterally and effectively verifiable comprehensive nuclear-test-ban treaty which contributes to nuclear disarmament and the prevention of the proliferation of nuclear weapons in all its aspects;

29. Prevent and eliminate all forms of violence against women and girls;

30. Ensure equal access to and equal treatment of women and men in education and health care and enhance women's sexual and reproductive health as well as education;

31. Promote and protect all human rights of women and girls;

32. Intensify efforts to ensure equal enjoyment of all human rights and fundamental freedoms for all women and girls who face multiple barriers to their empowerment and advancement because of such factors as their race, age, language, ethnicity, culture, religion, or disability, or because they are indigenous people;

33. Ensure respect for international law, including humanitarian law, in order to protect women and girls in particular;

34. Develop the fullest potential of girls and women of all ages, ensure their full and equal participation in building a better world for all and enhance their role in the development process.

We are determined to:

35. Ensure women's equal access to economic resources, including land, credit, science and technology, vocational training, information, communication and markets, as a means to further the advancement and empowerment of women and girls, including through the enhancement of their capacities to enjoy the benefits of equal access to these resources, *inter alia*, by means of international cooperation;

36. Ensure the success of the Platform for Action, which will require a strong commitment on the part of Governments, international organizations and institutions at all levels. We are deeply convinced that economic development, social development and environmental protection are interdependent and mutually reinforcing components of sustainable development, which is the framework for our efforts to achieve a higher quality of life for all people. Equitable social development that recognizes empowering the poor, particularly women living in poverty, to utilize environmental resources sustainably is a necessary foundation for sustainable development. We also recognize that broad-based and sustained economic growth in the context of sustainable development is necessary to sustain social development and social justice. The success of the Platform for Action will also require adequate mobilization of resources at the national and international levels as well as new and additional resources to the developing countries from all available funding mechanisms, including multilateral, bilateral and private sources for the advancement of women; financial resources to strengthen the capacity of national, subregional, regional and international institutions; a commitment to equal rights, equal responsibilities and equal opportunities and to the equal participation of women and men in all national, regional and interna-

tional bodies and policy-making processes; and the establishment or strengthening of mechanisms at all levels for accountability to the world's women;

37. Ensure also the success of the Platform for Action in countries with economies in transition, which will require continued international cooperation and assistance;

38. We hereby adopt and commit ourselves as Governments to implement the following Platform for Action, ensuring that a gender perspective is reflected in all our policies and programmes. We urge the United Nations system, regional and international financial institutions, other relevant regional and international institutions and all women and men, as well as non-governmental organizations, with full respect for their autonomy, and all sectors of civil society, in cooperation with Governments, to fully commit themselves and contribute to the implementation of this Platform for Action.

Chapter I

Mission statement

1. The Platform for Action is an agenda for women's empowerment. It aims at accelerating the implementation of the Nairobi Forward-looking Strategies for the Advancement of Women 1/ and at removing all the obstacles to women's active participation in all spheres of public and private life through a full and equal share in economic, social, cultural and political decision-making. This means that the principle of shared power and responsibility should be established between women and men at home, in the workplace and in the wider national and international communities. Equality between women and men is a matter of human rights and a condition for social justice and is also a necessary and fundamental prerequisite for equality, development and peace. A transformed partnership based on equality between women and men is a condition for people-centred sustainable development. A sustained and long-term commitment is essential, so that women and men can work together for themselves, for their children and for society to meet the challenges of the twenty-first century.

2. The Platform for Action reaffirms the fundamental principle set forth in the Vienna Declaration and Programme of Action, 2/ adopted by the World Conference on Human Rights, that the human rights of women and of the girl child are an inalienable, integral and indivisible part of universal human rights. As an agenda for action, the Platform seeks to promote and protect the full enjoyment of all human rights and the fundamental freedoms of all women throughout their life cycle.

3. The Platform for Action emphasizes that women share common concerns that can be addressed only by working together and in partnership with men towards the common goal of gender* equality around the world. It respects and values the full diversity of women's situations and conditions and recognizes that some women face particular barriers to their empowerment.

4. The Platform for Action requires immediate and concerted action by all to create a peaceful, just and humane world based on human rights and fundamental freedoms, including the principle of equality for all people of all ages and from all walks of life, and to this end, recognizes that broad-based and sustained economic growth in the context of sustainable development is necessary to sustain social development and social justice.

5. The success of the Platform for Action will require a strong commitment on the part of Governments, international organizations and institutions at all levels. It will also require adequate mobilization of resources at the national and international levels as well as new and additional resources to the developing countries from all available funding mechanisms, including multilateral, bilateral and private sources for the advancement of women; financial resources to strengthen the capacity of national, subregional, regional and international institutions; a commitment to equal rights, equal responsibilities and equal opportunities and to the equal participation of women and men in all national, regional and international bodies and policy-making processes; and the establishment or strengthening of mechanisms at all levels for accountability to the world's women.

Chapter II

Global framework

6. The Fourth World Conference on Women is taking place as the world stands poised on the threshold of a new millennium.

7. The Platform for Action upholds the Convention on the Elimination of All Forms of Discrimination against Women 3/ and builds upon the Nairobi Forward-looking Strategies for the Advancement of Women, as well as relevant resolutions adopted by the Economic and Social Council and the General Assembly. The formulation of the Platform for Action is aimed at establishing a basic group of priority actions that should be carried out during the next five years.

8. The Platform for Action recognizes the impor-

* For the commonly understood meaning of the term "gender", see annex IV to the present report.
1/ Report of the World Conference to Review and Appraise the Achievements of the United Nations Decade for Women: Equality, Development and Peace, Nairobi, 15-26 July 1985 (United Nations publication, Sales No. E.85.IV.10), chap. I, sect. A.
2/ Report of the World Conference on Human Rights, Vienna, 14-25 June 1993 (A/CONF.157/24 (Part I)), chap. III.
3/ General Assembly resolution 34/180, annex.

tance of the agreements reached at the World Summit for Children, the United Nations Conference on Environment and Development, the World Conference on Human Rights, the International Conference on Population and Development and the World Summit for Social Development, which set out specific approaches and commitments to fostering sustainable development and international cooperation and to strengthening the role of the United Nations to that end. Similarly, the Global Conference on the Sustainable Development of Small Island Developing States, the International Conference on Nutrition, the International Conference on Primary Health Care and the World Conference on Education for All have addressed the various facets of development and human rights, within their specific perspectives, paying significant attention to the role of women and girls. In addition, the International Year for the World's Indigenous People, 4/ the International Year of the Family, 5/ the United Nations Year for Tolerance, 6/ the Geneva Declaration for Rural Women, 7/ and the Declaration on the Elimination of Violence against Women 8/ have also emphasized the issues of women's empowerment and equality.

9.   The objective of the Platform for Action, which is in full conformity with the purposes and principles of the Charter of the United Nations and international law, is the empowerment of all women. The full realization of all human rights and fundamental freedoms of all women is essential for the empowerment of women. While the significance of national and regional particularities and various historical, cultural and religious backgrounds must be borne in mind, it is the duty of States, regardless of their political, economic and cultural systems, to promote and protect all human rights and fundamental freedoms. 9/ The implementation of this Platform, including through national laws and the formulation of strategies, policies, programmes and development priorities, is the sovereign responsibility of each State, in conformity with all human rights and fundamental freedoms, and the significance of and full respect for various religious and ethical values, cultural backgrounds and philosophical convictions of individuals and their communities should contribute to the full enjoyment by women of their human rights in order to achieve equality, development and peace.

10.   Since the World Conference to Review and Appraise the Achievements of the United Nations Decade for Women: Equality, Development and Peace, held at Nairobi in 1985, and the adoption of the Nairobi Forward-looking Strategies for the Advancement of Women, the world has experienced profound political, economic, social and cultural changes, which have had both positive and negative effects on women. The World Conference

on Human Rights recognized that the human rights of women and the girl child are an inalienable, integral and indivisible part of universal human rights. The full and equal participation of women in political, civil, economic, social and cultural life at the national, regional and international levels, and the eradication of all forms of discrimination on the grounds of sex are priority objectives of the international community. The World Conference on Human Rights reaffirmed the solemn commitment of all States to fulfil their obligations to promote universal respect for, and observance and protection of, all human rights and fundamental freedoms for all in accordance with the Charter of the United Nations, other instruments related to human rights and international law. The universal nature of these rights and freedoms is beyond question.

11.   The end of the cold war has resulted in international changes and diminished competition between the super-Powers. The threat of a global armed conflict has diminished, while international relations have improved and prospects for peace among nations have increased. Although the threat of global conflict has been reduced, wars of aggression, armed conflicts, colonial or other forms of alien domination and foreign occupation, civil wars, and terrorism continue to plague many parts of the world. Grave violations of the human rights of women occur, particularly in times of armed conflict, and include murder, torture, systematic rape, forced pregnancy and forced abortion, in particular under policies of ethnic cleansing.

12.   The maintenance of peace and security at the global, regional and local levels, together with the prevention of policies of aggression and ethnic cleansing and the resolution of armed conflict, is crucial for the protection of the human rights of women and girl children, as well as for the elimination of all forms of violence against them and of their use as a weapon of war.

13.   Excessive military expenditures, including global military expenditures and arms trade or trafficking, and investments for arms production and acquisition have reduced the resources available for social development. As a result of the debt burden and other economic difficulties, many developing countries have undertaken structural adjustment policies. Moreover, there are structural adjustment programmes that have been poorly designed and implemented, with resulting detrimental

4/ General Assembly resolution 45/164.
5/ General Assembly resolution 44/82.
6/ General Assembly resolution 48/126.
7/ A/47/308-E/1992/97, annex.
8/ General Assembly resolution 48/104.
9/ Vienna Declaration and Programme of Action, *Report of the World Conference on Human Rights* ..., chap. III, para. 5.

effects on social development. The number of people living in poverty has increased disproportionately in most developing countries, particularly the heavily indebted countries, during the past decade.

14. In this context, the social dimension of development should be emphasized. Accelerated economic growth, although necessary for social development, does not by itself improve the quality of life of the population. In some cases, conditions can arise which can aggravate social inequality and marginalization. Hence, it is indispensable to search for new alternatives that ensure that all members of society benefit from economic growth based on a holistic approach to all aspects of development: growth, equality between women and men, social justice, conservation and protection of the environment, sustainability, solidarity, participation, peace and respect for human rights.

15. A world-wide movement towards democratization has opened up the political process in many nations, but the popular participation of women in key decision-making as full and equal partners with men, particularly in politics, has not yet been achieved. South Africa's policy of institutionalized racism — apartheid — has been dismantled and a peaceful and democratic transfer of power has occurred. In Central and Eastern Europe the transition to parliamentary democracy has been rapid and has given rise to a variety of experiences, depending on the specific circumstances of each country. While the transition has been mostly peaceful, in some countries this process has been hindered by armed conflict that has resulted in grave violations of human rights.

16. Widespread economic recession, as well as political instability in some regions, has been responsible for setting back development goals in many countries. This has led to the expansion of unspeakable poverty. Of the more than 1 billion people living in abject poverty, women are an overwhelming majority. The rapid process of change and adjustment in all sectors has also led to increased unemployment and underemployment, with particular impact on women. In many cases, structural adjustment programmes have not been designed to minimize their negative effects on vulnerable and disadvantaged groups or on women, nor have they been designed to assure positive effects on those groups by preventing their marginalization in economic and social activities. The Final Act of the Uruguay Round of multilateral trade negotiations 10/ underscored the increasing interdependence of national economies, as well as the importance of trade liberalization and access to open, dynamic markets. There has also been heavy military spending in some regions. Despite increases in official development assistance (ODA) by some countries, ODA has recently declined overall.

17. Absolute poverty and the feminization of poverty, unemployment, the increasing fragility of the environment, continued violence against women and the widespread exclusion of half of humanity from institutions of power and governance underscore the need to continue the search for development, peace and security and for ways of assuring people-centred sustainable development. The participation and leadership of the half of humanity that is female is essential to the success of that search. Therefore, only a new era of international cooperation among Governments and peoples based on a spirit of partnership, an equitable, international social and economic environment, and a radical transformation of the relationship between women and men to one of full and equal partnership will enable the world to meet the challenges of the twenty-first century.

18. Recent international economic developments have had in many cases a disproportionate impact on women and children, the majority of whom live in developing countries. For those States that have carried a large burden of foreign debt, structural adjustment programmes and measures, though beneficial in the long term, have led to a reduction in social expenditures, thereby adversely affecting women, particularly in Africa and the least developed countries. This is exacerbated when responsibilities for basic social services have shifted from Governments to women.

19. Economic recession in many developed and developing countries, as well as ongoing restructuring in countries with economies in transition, have had a disproportionately negative impact on women's employment. Women often have no choice but to take employment that lacks long-term job security or involves dangerous working conditions, to work in unprotected home-based production or to be unemployed. Many women enter the labour market in under-remunerated and undervalued jobs, seeking to improve their household income; others decide to migrate for the same purpose. Without any reduction in their other responsibilities, this has increased the total burden of work for women.

20. Macro- and micro-economic policies and programmes, including structural adjustment, have not always been designed to take account of their impact on women and girl children, especially those living in poverty. Poverty has increased in both absolute and relative terms, and the number of women living in poverty has increased in most regions. There are many urban women living in poverty; however, the plight of women living in rural and remote areas deserves special attention given

10/ See *The Results of the Uruguay Round of Multilateral Trade Negotiations: The Legal Texts* (Geneva, GATT secretariat, 1994).

the stagnation of development in such areas. In developing countries, even those in which national indicators have shown improvement, the majority of rural women continue to live in conditions of economic underdevelopment and social marginalization.

21. Women are key contributors to the economy and to combating poverty through both remunerated and unremunerated work at home, in the community and in the workplace. Growing numbers of women have achieved economic independence through gainful employment.

22. One fourth of all households world wide are headed by women and many other households are dependent on female income even where men are present. Female-maintained households are very often among the poorest because of wage discrimination, occupational segregation patterns in the labour market and other gender-based barriers. Family disintegration, population movements between urban and rural areas within countries, international migration, war and internal displacements are factors contributing to the rise of female-headed households.

23. Recognizing that the achievement and maintenance of peace and security are a precondition for economic and social progress, women are increasingly establishing themselves as central actors in a variety of capacities in the movement of humanity for peace. Their full participation in decision-making, conflict prevention and resolution and all other peace initiatives is essential to the realization of lasting peace.

24. Religion, spirituality and belief play a central role in the lives of millions of women and men, in the way they live and in the aspirations they have for the future. The right to freedom of thought, conscience and religion is inalienable and must be universally enjoyed. This right includes the freedom to have or to adopt the religion or belief of their choice either individually or in community with others, in public or in private, and to manifest their religion or belief in worship, observance, practice and teaching. In order to realize equality, development and peace, there is a need to respect these rights and freedoms fully. Religion, thought, conscience and belief may, and can, contribute to fulfilling women's and men's moral, ethical and spiritual needs and to realizing their full potential in society. However, it is acknowledged that any form of extremism may have a negative impact on women and can lead to violence and discrimination.

25. The Fourth World Conference on Women should accelerate the process that formally began in 1975, which was proclaimed International Women's Year by the United Nations General Assembly. The Year was a turning-point in that it put women's issues on the agenda. The United Nations Decade for Women (1976-1985) was a world-wide effort to examine the status and

rights of women and to bring women into decision-making at all levels. In 1979, the General Assembly adopted the Convention on the Elimination of All Forms of Discrimination against Women, which entered into force in 1981 and set an international standard for what was meant by equality between women and men. In 1985, the World Conference to Review and Appraise the Achievements of the United Nations Decade for Women: Equality, Development and Peace adopted the Nairobi Forward-looking Strategies for the Advancement of Women, to be implemented by the year 2000. There has been important progress in achieving equality between women and men. Many Governments have enacted legislation to promote equality between women and men and have established national machineries to ensure the mainstreaming of gender perspectives in all spheres of society. International agencies have focused greater attention on women's status and roles.

26. The growing strength of the non-governmental sector, particularly women's organizations and feminist groups, has become a driving force for change. Non-governmental organizations have played an important advocacy role in advancing legislation or mechanisms to ensure the promotion of women. They have also become catalysts for new approaches to development. Many Governments have increasingly recognized the important role that non-governmental organizations play and the importance of working with them for progress. Yet, in some countries, Governments continue to restrict the ability of non-governmental organizations to operate freely. Women, through non-governmental organizations, have participated in and strongly influenced community, national, regional and global forums and international debates.

27. Since 1975, knowledge of the status of women and men, respectively, has increased and is contributing to further actions aimed at promoting equality between women and men. In several countries, there have been important changes in the relationships between women and men, especially where there have been major advances in education for women and significant increases in their participation in the paid labour force. The boundaries of the gender division of labour between productive and reproductive roles are gradually being crossed as women have started to enter formerly male-dominated areas of work and men have started to accept greater responsibility for domestic tasks, including child care. However, changes in women's roles have been greater and much more rapid than changes in men's roles. In many countries, the differences between women's and men's achievements and activities are still not recognized as the consequences of socially constructed gender roles rather than immutable biological differences.

28. Moreover, 10 years after the Nairobi Conference, equality between women and men has still not been achieved. On average, women represent a mere 10 per cent of all elected legislators world wide and in most national and international administrative structures, both public and private, they remain underrepresented. The United Nations is no exception. Fifty years after its creation, the United Nations is continuing to deny itself the benefits of women's leadership by their underrepresentation at decision-making levels within the Secretariat and the specialized agencies.

29. Women play a critical role in the family. The family is the basic unit of society and as such should be strengthened. It is entitled to receive comprehensive protection and support. In different cultural, political and social systems, various forms of the family exist. The rights, capabilities and responsibilities of family members must be respected. Women make a great contribution to the welfare of the family and to the development of society, which is still not recognized or considered in its full importance. The social significance of maternity, motherhood and the role of parents in the family and in the upbringing of children should be acknowledged. The upbringing of children requires shared responsibility of parents, women and men and society as a whole. Maternity, motherhood, parenting and the role of women in procreation must not be a basis for discrimination nor restrict the full participation of women in society. Recognition should also be given to the important role often played by women in many countries in caring for other members of their family.

30. While the rate of growth of world population is on the decline, world population is at an all-time high in absolute numbers, with current increments approaching 86 million persons annually. Two other major demographic trends have had profound repercussions on the dependency ratio within families. In many developing countries, 45 to 50 per cent of the population is less than 15 years old, while in industrialized nations both the number and proportion of elderly people are increasing. According to United Nations projections, 72 per cent of the population over 60 years of age will be living in developing countries by the year 2025, and more than half of that population will be women. Care of children, the sick and the elderly is a responsibility that falls disproportionately on women, owing to lack of equality and the unbalanced distribution of remunerated and unremunerated work between women and men.

31. Many women face particular barriers because of various diverse factors in addition to their gender. Often these diverse factors isolate or marginalize such women. They are, *inter alia*, denied their human rights, they lack access or are denied access to education and vocational training, employment, housing and economic self-sufficiency and they are excluded from decision-making processes. Such women are often denied the opportunity to contribute to their communities as part of the mainstream.

32. The past decade has also witnessed a growing recognition of the distinct interests and concerns of indigenous women, whose identity, cultural traditions and forms of social organization enhance and strengthen the communities in which they live. Indigenous women often face barriers both as women and as members of indigenous communities.

33. In the past 20 years, the world has seen an explosion in the field of communications. With advances in computer technology and satellite and cable television, global access to information continues to increase and expand, creating new opportunities for the participation of women in communications and the mass media and for the dissemination of information about women. However, global communication networks have been used to spread stereotyped and demeaning images of women for narrow commercial and consumerist purposes. Until women participate equally in both the technical and decision-making areas of communications and the mass media, including the arts, they will continue to be misrepresented and awareness of the reality of women's lives will continue to be lacking. The media have a great potential to promote the advancement of women and the equality of women and men by portraying women and men in a non-stereotypical, diverse and balanced manner, and by respecting the dignity and worth of the human person.

34. The continuing environmental degradation that affects all human lives has often a more direct impact on women. Women's health and their livelihood are threatened by pollution and toxic wastes, large-scale deforestation, desertification, drought and depletion of the soil and of coastal and marine resources, with a rising incidence of environmentally related health problems and even death reported among women and girls. Those most affected are rural and indigenous women, whose livelihood and daily subsistence depends directly on sustainable ecosystems.

35. Poverty and environmental degradation are closely interrelated. While poverty results in certain kinds of environmental stress, the major cause of the continued deterioration of the global environment is the unsustainable patterns of consumption and production, particularly in industrialized countries, which are a matter of grave concern and aggravate poverty and imbalances.

36. Global trends have brought profound changes in family survival strategies and structures. Rural to urban migration has increased substantially in all regions. The global urban population is projected to reach 47 per

cent of the total population by the year 2000. An estimated 125 million people are migrants, refugees and displaced persons, half of whom live in developing countries. These massive movements of people have profound consequences for family structures and well-being and have unequal consequences for women and men, including in many cases the sexual exploitation of women.

37. According to World Health Organization (WHO) estimates, by the beginning of 1995 the number of cumulative cases of acquired immunodeficiency syndrome (AIDS) was 4.5 million. An estimated 19.5 million men, women and children have been infected with the human immunodeficiency virus (HIV) since it was first diagnosed and it is projected that another 20 million will be infected by the end of the decade. Among new cases, women are twice as likely to be infected as men. In the early stage of the AIDS pandemic, women were not infected in large numbers; however, about 8 million women are now infected. Young women and adolescents are particularly vulnerable. It is estimated that by the year 2000 more than 13 million women will be infected and 4 million women will have died from AIDS-related conditions. In addition, about 250 million new cases of sexually transmitted diseases are estimated to occur every year. The rate of transmission of sexually transmitted diseases, including HIV/AIDS, is increasing at an alarming rate among women and girls, especially in developing countries.

38. Since 1975, significant knowledge and information have been generated about the status of women and the conditions in which they live. Throughout their entire life cycle, women's daily existence and long-term aspirations are restricted by discriminatory attitudes, unjust social and economic structures, and a lack of resources in most countries that prevent their full and equal participation. In a number of countries, the practice of prenatal sex selection, higher rates of mortality among very young girls and lower rates of school enrolment for girls as compared with boys suggest that son preference is curtailing the access of girl children to food, education and health care and even life itself. Discrimination against women begins at the earliest stages of life and must therefore be addressed from then onwards.

39. The girl child of today is the woman of tomorrow. The skills, ideas and energy of the girl child are vital for full attainment of the goals of equality, development and peace. For the girl child to develop her full potential she needs to be nurtured in an enabling environment, where her spiritual, intellectual and material needs for survival, protection and development are met and her equal rights safeguarded. If women are to be equal partners with men, in every aspect of life and development, now is the time to recognize the human dignity and worth of the girl child and to ensure the full enjoyment of her human rights and fundamental freedoms, including the rights assured by the Convention on the Rights of the Child, 11/ universal ratification of which is strongly urged. Yet there exists world-wide evidence that discrimination and violence against girls begin at the earliest stages of life and continue unabated throughout their lives. They often have less access to nutrition, physical and mental health care and education and enjoy fewer rights, opportunities and benefits of childhood and adolescence than do boys. They are often subjected to various forms of sexual and economic exploitation, paedophilia, forced prostitution and possibly the sale of their organs and tissues, violence and harmful practices such as female infanticide and prenatal sex selection, incest, female genital mutilation and early marriage, including child marriage.

40. Half the world's population is under the age of 25 and most of the world's youth — more than 85 per cent — live in developing countries. Policy makers must recognize the implications of these demographic factors. Special measures must be taken to ensure that young women have the life skills necessary for active and effective participation in all levels of social, cultural, political and economic leadership. It will be critical for the international community to demonstrate a new commitment to the future — a commitment to inspiring a new generation of women and men to work together for a more just society. This new generation of leaders must accept and promote a world in which every child is free from injustice, oppression and inequality and free to develop her/his own potential. The principle of equality of women and men must therefore be integral to the socialization process.

Chapter III

Critical areas of concern

41. The advancement of women and the achievement of equality between women and men are a matter of human rights and a condition for social justice and should not be seen in isolation as a women's issue. They are the only way to build a sustainable, just and developed society. Empowerment of women and equality between women and men are prerequisites for achieving political, social, economic, cultural and environmental security among all peoples.

42. Most of the goals set out in the Nairobi Forward-looking Strategies for the Advancement of Women have not been achieved. Barriers to women's empowerment remain, despite the efforts of Governments, as well as non-governmental organizations and women and men everywhere. Vast political, economic and ecological

11/ General Assembly resolution 44/25, annex.

crises persist in many parts of the world. Among them are wars of aggression, armed conflicts, colonial or other forms of alien domination or foreign occupation, civil wars and terrorism. These situations, combined with systematic or de facto discrimination, violations of and failure to protect all human rights and fundamental freedoms of all women, and their civil, cultural, economic, political and social rights, including the right to development and ingrained prejudicial attitudes towards women and girls, are but a few of the impediments encountered since the World Conference to Review and Appraise the Achievements of the United Nations Decade for Women: Equality, Development and Peace, in 1985.

43. A review of progress since the Nairobi Conference highlights special concerns — areas of particular urgency that stand out as priorities for action. All actors should focus action and resources on the strategic objectives relating to the critical areas of concern which are, necessarily, interrelated, interdependent and of high priority. There is a need for these actors to develop and implement mechanisms of accountability for all the areas of concern.

44. To this end, Governments, the international community and civil society, including non-governmental organizations and the private sector, are called upon to take strategic action in the following critical areas of concern:

- The persistent and increasing burden of poverty on women
- Inequalities and inadequacies in and unequal access to education and training
- Inequalities and inadequacies in and unequal access to health care and related services
- Violence against women
- The effects of armed or other kinds of conflict on women, including those living under foreign occupation
- Inequality in economic structures and policies, in all forms of productive activities and in access to resources
- Inequality between men and women in the sharing of power and decision-making at all levels
- Insufficient mechanisms at all levels to promote the advancement of women
- Lack of respect for and inadequate promotion and protection of the human rights of women
- Stereotyping of women and inequality in women's access to and participation in all communication systems, especially in the media
- Gender inequalities in the management of natural resources and in the safeguarding of the environment

- Persistent discrimination against and violation of the rights of the girl child

Chapter IV

Strategic objectives and actions

45. In each critical area of concern, the problem is diagnosed and strategic objectives are proposed with concrete actions to be taken by various actors in order to achieve those objectives. The strategic objectives are derived from the critical areas of concern and specific actions to be taken to achieve them cut across the boundaries of equality, development and peace — the goals of the Nairobi Forward-looking Strategies for the Advancement of Women — and reflect their interdependence. The objectives and actions are interlinked, of high priority and mutually reinforcing. The Platform for Action is intended to improve the situation of all women, without exception, who often face similar barriers, while special attention should be given to groups that are the most disadvantaged.

46. The Platform for Action recognizes that women face barriers to full equality and advancement because of such factors as their race, age, language, ethnicity, culture, religion or disability, because they are indigenous women or because of other status. Many women encounter specific obstacles related to their family status, particularly as single parents; and to their socio-economic status, including their living conditions in rural, isolated or impoverished areas. Additional barriers also exist for refugee women, other displaced women, including internally displaced women as well as for immigrant women and migrant women, including women migrant workers. Many women are also particularly affected by environmental disasters, serious and infectious diseases and various forms of violence against women.

A. Women and poverty

47. More than 1 billion people in the world today, the great majority of whom are women, live in unacceptable conditions of poverty, mostly in the developing countries. Poverty has various causes, including structural ones. Poverty is a complex, multidimensional problem, with origins in both the national and international domains. The globalization of the world's economy and the deepening interdependence among nations present challenges and opportunities for sustained economic growth and development, as well as risks and uncertainties for the future of the world economy. The uncertain global economic climate has been accompanied by economic restructuring as well as, in a certain number of countries, persistent, unmanageable levels of external debt and structural adjustment programmes. In addition,

all types of conflict, displacement of people and environmental degradation have undermined the capacity of Governments to meet the basic needs of their populations. Transformations in the world economy are profoundly changing the parameters of social development in all countries. One significant trend has been the increased poverty of women, the extent of which varies from region to region. The gender disparities in economic power-sharing are also an important contributing factor to the poverty of women. Migration and consequent changes in family structures have placed additional burdens on women, especially those who provide for several dependants. Macroeconomic policies need rethinking and reformulation to address such trends. These policies focus almost exclusively on the formal sector. They also tend to impede the initiatives of women and fail to consider the differential impact on women and men. The application of gender analysis to a wide range of policies and programmes is therefore critical to poverty reduction strategies. In order to eradicate poverty and achieve sustainable development, women and men must participate fully and equally in the formulation of macroeconomic and social policies and strategies for the eradication of poverty. The eradication of poverty cannot be accomplished through anti-poverty programmes alone but will require democratic participation and changes in economic structures in order to ensure access for all women to resources, opportunities and public services. Poverty has various manifestations, including lack of income and productive resources sufficient to ensure a sustainable livelihood; hunger and malnutrition; ill health; limited or lack of access to education and other basic services; increasing morbidity and mortality from illness; homelessness and inadequate housing; unsafe environments; and social discrimination and exclusion. It is also characterized by lack of participation in decision-making and in civil, social and cultural life. It occurs in all countries — as mass poverty in many developing countries and as pockets of poverty amidst wealth in developed countries. Poverty may be caused by an economic recession that results in loss of livelihood or by disaster or conflict. There is also the poverty of low-wage workers and the utter destitution of people who fall outside family support systems, social institutions and safety nets.

48. In the past decade the number of women living in poverty has increased disproportionately to the number of men, particularly in the developing countries. The feminization of poverty has also recently become a significant problem in the countries with economies in transition as a short-term consequence of the process of political, economic and social transformation. In addition to economic factors, the rigidity of socially ascribed gender roles and women's limited access to power, education, training and productive resources as well as other emerging factors that may lead to insecurity for families are also responsible. The failure to adequately mainstream a gender perspective in all economic analysis and planning and to address the structural causes of poverty is also a contributing factor.

49. Women contribute to the economy and to combating poverty through both remunerated and unremunerated work at home, in the community and in the workplace. The empowerment of women is a critical factor in the eradication of poverty.

50. While poverty affects households as a whole, because of the gender division of labour and responsibilities for household welfare, women bear a disproportionate burden, attempting to manage household consumption and production under conditions of increasing scarcity. Poverty is particularly acute for women living in rural households.

51. Women's poverty is directly related to the absence of economic opportunities and autonomy, lack of access to economic resources, including credit, land ownership and inheritance, lack of access to education and support services and their minimal participation in the decision-making process. Poverty can also force women into situations in which they are vulnerable to sexual exploitation.

52. In too many countries, social welfare systems do not take sufficient account of the specific conditions of women living in poverty, and there is a tendency to scale back the services provided by such systems. The risk of falling into poverty is greater for women than for men, particularly in old age, where social security systems are based on the principle of continuous remunerated employment. In some cases, women do not fulfil this requirement because of interruptions in their work, due to the unbalanced distribution of remunerated and unremunerated work. Moreover, older women also face greater obstacles to labour-market re-entry.

53. In many developed countries, where the level of general education and professional training of women and men are similar and where systems of protection against discrimination are available, in some sectors the economic transformations of the past decade have strongly increased either the unemployment of women or the precarious nature of their employment. The proportion of women among the poor has consequently increased. In countries with a high level of school enrolment of girls, those who leave the educational system the earliest, without any qualification, are among the most vulnerable in the labour market.

54. In countries with economies in transition and in other countries undergoing fundamental political, eco-

nomic and social transformations, these transformations have often led to a reduction in women's income or to women being deprived of income.

55. Particularly in developing countries, the productive capacity of women should be increased through access to capital, resources, credit, land, technology, information, technical assistance and training so as to raise their income and improve nutrition, education, health care and status within the household. The release of women's productive potential is pivotal to breaking the cycle of poverty so that women can share fully in the benefits of development and in the products of their own labour.

56. Sustainable development and economic growth that is both sustained and sustainable are possible only through improving the economic, social, political, legal and cultural status of women. Equitable social development that recognizes empowering the poor, particularly women, to utilize environmental resources sustainably is a necessary foundation for sustainable development.

57. The success of policies and measures aimed at supporting or strengthening the promotion of gender equality and the improvement of the status of women should be based on the integration of the gender perspective in general policies relating to all spheres of society as well as the implementation of positive measures with adequate institutional and financial support at all levels.

Strategic objective A.1. *Review, adopt and maintain macroeconomic policies and development strategies that address the needs and efforts of women in poverty*

Actions to be taken

58. By Governments:

(a) Review and modify, with the full and equal participation of women, macroeconomic and social policies with a view to achieving the objectives of the Platform for Action;

(b) Analyse, from a gender perspective, policies and programmes — including those related to macroeconomic stability, structural adjustment, external debt problems, taxation, investments, employment, markets and all relevant sectors of the economy — with respect to their impact on poverty, on inequality and particularly on women; assess their impact on family well-being and conditions and adjust them, as appropriate, to promote more equitable distribution of productive assets, wealth, opportunities, income and services;

(c) Pursue and implement sound and stable macroeconomic and sectoral policies that are designed and monitored with the full and equal participation of women, encourage broad-based sustained economic growth, address the structural causes of poverty and are geared towards eradicating poverty and reducing gender-based inequality within the overall framework of achieving people-centred sustainable development;

(d) Restructure and target the allocation of public expenditures to promote women's economic opportunities and equal access to productive resources and to address the basic social, educational and health needs of women, particularly those living in poverty;

(e) Develop agricultural and fishing sectors, where and as necessary, in order to ensure, as appropriate, household and national food security and food self-sufficiency, by allocating the necessary financial, technical and human resources;

(f) Develop policies and programmes to promote equitable distribution of food within the household;

(g) Provide adequate safety nets and strengthen State-based and community-based support systems, as an integral part of social policy, in order to enable women living in poverty to withstand adverse economic environments and preserve their livelihood, assets and revenues in times of crisis;

(h) Generate economic policies that have a positive impact on the employment and income of women workers in both the formal and informal sectors and adopt specific measures to address women's unemployment, in particular their long-term unemployment;

(i) Formulate and implement, when necessary, specific economic, social, agricultural and related policies in support of female-headed households;

(j) Develop and implement anti-poverty programmes, including employment schemes, that improve access to food for women living in poverty, including through the use of appropriate pricing and distribution mechanisms;

(k) Ensure the full realization of the human rights of all women migrants, including women migrant workers, and their protection against violence and exploitation; introduce measures for the empowerment of documented women migrants, including women migrant workers; facilitate the productive employment of documented migrant women through greater recognition of their skills, foreign education and credentials, and facilitate their full integration into the labour force;

(l) Introduce measures to integrate or reintegrate women living in poverty and socially marginalized women into productive employment and the economic mainstream; ensure that internally displaced women have full access to economic opportunities and that the qualifications and skills of immigrant and refugee women are recognized;

(m) Enable women to obtain affordable housing and access to land by, among other things, removing all obstacles to access, with special emphasis on meeting the needs of women, especially those living in poverty and female heads of household;

(n) Formulate and implement policies and programmes that enhance the access of women agricultural and fisheries producers (including subsistence farmers and producers, especially in rural areas) to financial, technical, extension and marketing services; provide access to and control of land, appropriate infrastructure and technology in order to increase women's incomes and promote household food security, especially in rural areas and, where appropriate, encourage the development of producer-owned, market-based cooperatives;

(o) Create social security systems wherever they do not exist, or review them with a view to placing individual women and men on an equal footing, at every stage of their lives;

(p) Ensure access to free or low-cost legal services, including legal literacy, especially designed to reach women living in poverty;

(q) Take particular measures to promote and strengthen policies and programmes for indigenous women with their full participation and respect for their cultural diversity, so that they have opportunities and the possibility of choice in the development process in order to eradicate the poverty that affects them.

59. By multilateral financial and development institutions, including the World Bank, the International Monetary Fund and regional development institutions, and through bilateral development cooperation:

(a) In accordance with the commitments made at the World Summit for Social Development, seek to mobilize new and additional financial resources that are both adequate and predictable and mobilized in a way that maximizes the availability of such resources and uses all available funding sources and mechanisms with a view to contributing towards the goal of poverty eradication and targeting women living in poverty;

(b) Strengthen analytical capacity in order to more systematically strengthen gender perspectives and integrate them into the design and implementation of lending programmes, including structural adjustment and economic recovery programmes;

(c) Find effective development-oriented and durable solutions to external debt problems in order to help them to finance programmes and projects targeted at development, including the advancement of women, *inter alia*, through the immediate implementation of the terms of debt forgiveness agreed upon in the Paris Club in December 1994, which encompassed debt reduction, including cancellation or other debt relief measures and develop techniques of debt conversion applied to social development programmes and projects in conformity with the priorities of the Platform for Action;

(d) Invite the international financial institutions to examine innovative approaches to assisting low-income countries with a high proportion of multilateral debt, with a view to alleviating their debt burden;

(e) Ensure that structural adjustment programmes are designed to minimize their negative effects on vulnerable and disadvantaged groups and communities and to assure their positive effects on such groups and communities by preventing their marginalization in economic and social activities and devising measures to ensure that they gain access to and control over economic resources and economic and social activities; take actions to reduce inequality and economic disparity;

(f) Review the impact of structural adjustment programmes on social development by means of gender-sensitive social impact assessments and other relevant methods, in order to develop policies to reduce their negative effects and improve their positive impact, ensuring that women do not bear a disproportionate burden of transition costs; complement adjustment lending with enhanced, targeted social development lending;

(g) Create an enabling environment that allows women to build and maintain sustainable livelihoods.

60. By national and international non-governmental organizations and women's groups:

(a) Mobilize all parties involved in the development process, including academic institutions, non-governmental organizations and grass-roots and women's groups, to improve the effectiveness of anti-poverty programmes directed towards the poorest and most disadvantaged groups of women, such as rural and indigenous women, female heads of household, young women and older women, refugees and migrant women and women with disabilities, recognizing that social development is primarily the responsibility of Governments;

(b) Engage in lobbying and establish monitoring mechanisms, as appropriate, and other relevant activities to ensure implementation of the recommendations on poverty eradication outlined in the Platform for Action and aimed at ensuring accountability and transparency from the State and private sectors;

(c) Include in their activities women with diverse needs and recognize that youth organizations are increasingly becoming effective partners in development programmes;

(d) In cooperation with the government and private sectors, participate in the development of a comprehensive national strategy for improving health, education and social services so that girls and women of all ages living in poverty have full access to such services; seek funding to secure access to services with a gender perspective and to extend those services in order to reach the rural and remote areas that are not covered by government institutions;

(e) In cooperation with Governments, employers, other social partners and relevant parties, contribute to the development of education and training and retraining policies to ensure that women can acquire a wide range of skills to meet new demands;

(f) Mobilize to protect women's right to full and equal access to economic resources, including the right to inheritance and to ownership of land and other property, credit, natural resources and appropriate technologies.

Strategic objective A.2. *Revise laws and administrative practices to ensure women's equal rights and access to economic resources*

Actions to be taken

61. By Governments:

(a) Ensure access to free or low-cost legal services, including legal literacy, especially designed to reach women living in poverty;

(b) Undertake legislative and administrative reforms to give women full and equal access to economic resources, including the right to inheritance and to ownership of land and other property, credit, natural resources and appropriate technologies;

(c) Consider ratification of Convention No. 169 of the International Labour Organization (ILO) as part of their efforts to promote and protect the rights of indigenous people.

Strategic objective A.3. *Provide women with access to savings and credit mechanisms and institutions*

Actions to be taken

62. By Governments:

(a) Enhance the access of disadvantaged women, including women entrepreneurs, in rural, remote and urban areas to financial services through strengthening links between the formal banks and intermediary lending organizations, including legislative support, training for women and institutional strengthening for intermediary institutions with a view to mobilizing capital for those institutions and increasing the availability of credit;

(b) Encourage links between financial institutions and non-governmental organizations and support innovative lending practices, including those that integrate credit with women's services and training and provide credit facilities to rural women.

63. By commercial banks, specialized financial institutions and the private sector in examining their policies:

(a) Use credit and savings methodologies that are effective in reaching women in poverty and innovative in reducing transaction costs and redefining risk;

(b) Open special windows for lending to women, including young women, who lack access to traditional sources of collateral;

(c) Simplify banking practices, for example by reducing the minimum deposit and other requirements for opening bank accounts;

(d) Ensure the participation and joint ownership, where possible, of women clients in the decision-making of institutions providing credit and financial services.

64. By multilateral and bilateral development cooperation organizations:

Support, through the provision of capital and/or resources, financial institutions that serve low-income, small-scale and micro-scale women entrepreneurs and producers, in both the formal and informal sectors.

65. By Governments and multilateral financial institutions, as appropriate:

Support institutions that meet performance standards in reaching large numbers of low-income women and men through capitalization, refinancing and institutional development support in forms that foster self-sufficiency.

66. By international organizations:

Increase funding for programmes and projects designed to promote sustainable and productive entrepreneurial activities for income-generation among disadvantaged women and women living in poverty.

Strategic objective A.4. *Develop gender-based methodologies and conduct research to address the feminization of poverty*

Actions to be taken

67. By Governments, intergovernmental organizations, academic and research institutions and the private sector:

(a) Develop conceptual and practical methodologies for incorporating gender perspectives into all aspects of economic policy-making, including structural adjustment planning and programmes;

(b) Apply these methodologies in conducting gender-impact analyses of all policies and programmes, including structural adjustment programmes, and disseminate the research findings.

68. By national and international statistical organizations:

(a) Collect gender and age-disaggregated data on

poverty and all aspects of economic activity and develop qualitative and quantitative statistical indicators to facilitate the assessment of economic performance from a gender perspective;

(b) Devise suitable statistical means to recognize and make visible the full extent of the work of women and all their contributions to the national economy, including their contribution in the unremunerated and domestic sectors, and examine the relationship of women's unremunerated work to the incidence of and their vulnerability to poverty.

B. Education and training of women

69. Education is a human right and an essential tool for achieving the goals of equality, development and peace. Non-discriminatory education benefits both girls and boys and thus ultimately contributes to more equal relationships between women and men. Equality of access to and attainment of educational qualifications is necessary if more women are to become agents of change. Literacy of women is an important key to improving health, nutrition and education in the family and to empowering women to participate in decision-making in society. Investing in formal and non-formal education and training for girls and women, with its exceptionally high social and economic return, has proved to be one of the best means of achieving sustainable development and economic growth that is both sustained and sustainable.

70. On a regional level, girls and boys have achieved equal access to primary education, except in some parts of Africa, in particular sub-Saharan Africa, and Central Asia, where access to education facilities is still inadequate. Progress has been made in secondary education, where equal access of girls and boys has been achieved in some countries. Enrolment of girls and women in tertiary education has increased considerably. In many countries, private schools have also played an important complementary role in improving access to education at all levels. Yet, more than five years after the World Conference on Education for All (Jomtien, Thailand, 1990) adopted the World Declaration on Education for All and the Framework for Action to Meet Basic Learning Needs, 12/ approximately 100 million children, including at least 60 million girls, are without access to primary schooling and more than two thirds of the world's 960 million illiterate adults are women. The high rate of illiteracy prevailing in most developing countries, in particular in sub-Saharan Africa and some Arab States, remains a severe impediment to the advancement of women and to development.

71. Discrimination in girls' access to education persists in many areas, owing to customary attitudes, early marriages and pregnancies, inadequate and gender-biased teaching and educational materials, sexual harassment and lack of adequate and physically and otherwise accessible schooling facilities. Girls undertake heavy domestic work at a very early age. Girls and young women are expected to manage both educational and domestic responsibilities, often resulting in poor scholastic performance and early drop-out from the educational system. This has long-lasting consequences for all aspects of women's lives.

72. Creation of an educational and social environment, in which women and men, girls and boys, are treated equally and encouraged to achieve their full potential, respecting their freedom of thought, conscience, religion and belief, and where educational resources promote non-stereotyped images of women and men, would be effective in the elimination of the causes of discrimination against women and inequalities between women and men.

73. Women should be enabled to benefit from an ongoing acquisition of knowledge and skills beyond those acquired during youth. This concept of lifelong learning includes knowledge and skills gained in formal education and training, as well as learning that occurs in informal ways, including volunteer activity, unremunerated work and traditional knowledge.

74. Curricula and teaching materials remain gender-biased to a large degree, and are rarely sensitive to the specific needs of girls and women. This reinforces traditional female and male roles that deny women opportunities for full and equal partnership in society. Lack of gender awareness by educators at all levels strengthens existing inequities between males and females by reinforcing discriminatory tendencies and undermining girls' self-esteem. The lack of sexual and reproductive health education has a profound impact on women and men.

75. Science curricula in particular are gender-biased. Science textbooks do not relate to women's and girls' daily experience and fail to give recognition to women scientists. Girls are often deprived of basic education in mathematics and science and technical training, which provide knowledge they could apply to improve their daily lives and enhance their employment opportunities. Advanced study in science and technology prepares women to take an active role in the technological and industrial development of their countries, thus necessitating a diverse approach to vocational and technical training. Technology is rapidly changing the world and has also affected the developing countries. It is essential

12/ *Final Report of the World Conference on Education for All: Meeting Basic Learning Needs, Jomtien, Thailand, 5-9 March 1990,* Inter-Agency Commission (UNDP, UNESCO, UNICEF, World Bank) for the World Conference on Education for All, New York, 1990, appendix 1.

that women not only benefit from technology, but also participate in the process from the design to the application, monitoring and evaluation stages.

76.   Access for and retention of girls and women at all levels of education, including the higher level, and all academic areas is one of the factors of their continued progress in professional activities. Nevertheless, it can be noted that girls are still concentrated in a limited number of fields of study.

77.   The mass media are a powerful means of education. As an educational tool the mass media can be an instrument for educators and governmental and non-governmental institutions for the advancement of women and for development. Computerized education and information systems are increasingly becoming an important element in learning and the dissemination of knowledge. Television especially has the greatest impact on young people and, as such, has the ability to shape values, attitudes and perceptions of women and girls in both positive and negative ways. It is therefore essential that educators teach critical judgement and analytical skills.

78.   Resources allocated to education, particularly for girls and women, are in many countries insufficient and in some cases have been further diminished, including in the context of adjustment policies and programmes. Such insufficient resource allocations have a long-term adverse effect on human development, particularly on the development of women.

79.   In addressing unequal access to and inadequate educational opportunities, Governments and other actors should promote an active and visible policy of mainstreaming a gender perspective into all policies and programmes, so that, before decisions are taken, an analysis is made of the effects on women and men, respectively.

Strategic objective B.1.   *Ensure equal access to education*

Actions to be taken

80.   By Governments:

(a)   Advance the goal of equal access to education by taking measures to eliminate discrimination in education at all levels on the basis of gender, race, language, religion, national origin, age or disability, or any other form of discrimination and, as appropriate, consider establishing procedures to address grievances;

(b)   By the year 2000, provide universal access to basic education and ensure completion of primary education by at least 80 per cent of primary school-age children; close the gender gap in primary and secondary school education by the year 2005; provide universal primary education in all countries before the year 2015;

(c)   Eliminate gender disparities in access to all areas of tertiary education by ensuring that women have equal access to career development, training, scholarships and fellowships, and by adopting positive action when appropriate;

(d)   Create a gender-sensitive educational system in order to ensure equal educational and training opportunities and full and equal participation of women in educational administration and policy- and decision-making;

(e)   Provide — in collaboration with parents, non-governmental organizations, including youth organizations, communities and the private sector — young women with academic and technical training, career planning, leadership and social skills and work experience to prepare them to participate fully in society;

(f)   Increase enrolment and retention rates of girls by allocating appropriate budgetary resources; by enlisting the support of parents and the community, as well as through campaigns, flexible school schedules, incentives, scholarships and other means to minimize the costs of girls' education to their families and to facilitate parents' ability to choose education for the girl child; and by ensuring that the rights of women and girls to freedom of conscience and religion are respected in educational institutions through repealing any discriminatory laws or legislation based on religion, race or culture;

(g)   Promote an educational setting that eliminates all barriers that impeded the schooling of pregnant adolescents and young mothers, including, as appropriate, affordable and physically accessible child-care facilities and parental education to encourage those who are responsible for the care of their children and siblings during their school years, to return to or continue with and complete schooling;

(h)   Improve the quality of education and equal opportunities for women and men in terms of access in order to ensure that women of all ages can acquire the knowledge, capacities, aptitudes, skills and ethical values needed to develop and to participate fully under equal conditions in the process of social, economic and political development;

(i)   Make available non-discriminatory and gender-sensitive professional school counselling and career education programmes to encourage girls to pursue academic and technical curricula in order to widen their future career opportunities;

(j)   Encourage ratification of the International Covenant on Economic, Social and Cultural Rights 13/ where they have not already done so.

13/ General Assembly resolution 2200 A (XXI), annex.

Strategic objective B.2. *Eradicate illiteracy among women*

Actions to be taken

81. By Governments, national, regional and international bodies, bilateral and multilateral donors and non-governmental organizations:

(a) Reduce the female illiteracy rate to at least half its 1990 level, with emphasis on rural women, migrant, refugee and internally displaced women and women with disabilities;

(b) Provide universal access to, and seek to ensure gender equality in the completion of, primary education for girls by the year 2000;

(c) Eliminate the gender gap in basic and functional literacy, as recommended in the World Declaration on Education for All (Jomtien);

(d) Narrow the disparities between developed and developing countries;

(e) Encourage adult and family engagement in learning to promote total literacy for all people;

(f) Promote, together with literacy, life skills and scientific and technological knowledge and work towards an expansion of the definition of literacy, taking into account current targets and benchmarks.

Strategic objective B.3. *Improve women's access to vocational training, science and technology, and continuing education*

Actions to be taken

82. By Governments, in cooperation with employers, workers and trade unions, international and non-governmental organizations, including women's and youth organizations, and educational institutions:

(a) Develop and implement education, training and retraining policies for women, especially young women and women re-entering the labour market, to provide skills to meet the needs of a changing socio-economic context for improving their employment opportunities;

(b) Provide recognition to non-formal educational opportunities for girls and women in the educational system;

(c) Provide information to women and girls on the availability and benefits of vocational training, training programmes in science and technology and programmes of continuing education;

(d) Design educational and training programmes for women who are unemployed in order to provide them with new knowledge and skills that will enhance and broaden their employment opportunities, including self-employment, and development of their entrepreneurial skills;

(e) Diversify vocational and technical training and improve access for and retention of girls and women in education and vocational training in such fields as science, mathematics, engineering, environmental sciences and technology, information technology and high technology, as well as management training;

(f) Promote women's central role in food and agricultural research, extension and education programmes;

(g) Encourage the adaptation of curricula and teaching materials, encourage a supportive training environment and take positive measures to promote training for the full range of occupational choices of non-traditional careers for women and men, including the development of multidisciplinary courses for science and mathematics teachers to sensitize them to the relevance of science and technology to women's lives;

(h) Develop curricula and teaching materials and formulate and take positive measures to ensure women better access to and participation in technical and scientific areas, especially areas where they are not represented or are underrepresented;

(i) Develop policies and programmes to encourage women to participate in all apprenticeship programmes;

(j) Increase training in technical, managerial, agricultural extension and marketing areas for women in agriculture, fisheries, industry and business, arts and crafts, to increase income-generating opportunities, women's participation in economic decision-making, in particular through women's organizations at the grassroots level, and their contribution to production, marketing, business, and science and technology;

(k) Ensure access to quality education and training at all appropriate levels for adult women with little or no education, for women with disabilities and for documented migrant, refugee and displaced women to improve their work opportunities.

Strategic objective B.4. *Develop non-discriminatory education and training*

Actions to be taken

83. By Governments, educational authorities and other educational and academic institutions:

(a) Elaborate recommendations and develop curricula, textbooks and teaching aids free of gender-based stereotypes for all levels of education, including teacher training, in association with all concerned — publishers, teachers, public authorities and parents' associations;

(b) Develop training programmes and materials for teachers and educators that raise awareness about the status, role and contribution of women and men in the family, as defined in paragraph 29 above, and society; in this context, promote equality, cooperation, mutual respect and shared responsibilities between girls and boys from pre-school level onward and develop, in particular, educational modules to ensure that boys have the skills necessary to take care of their own domestic needs and to share responsibility for their household and for the care of dependants;

(c) Develop training programmes and materials for teachers and educators that raise awareness of their own role in the educational process, with a view to providing them with effective strategies for gender-sensitive teaching;

(d) Take actions to ensure that female teachers and professors have the same opportunities as and equal status with male teachers and professors, in view of the importance of having female teachers at all levels and in order to attract girls to school and retain them in school;

(e) Introduce and promote training in peaceful conflict resolution;

(f) Take positive measures to increase the proportion of women gaining access to educational policy- and decision-making, particularly women teachers at all levels of education and in academic disciplines that are traditionally male-dominated, such as the scientific and technological fields;

(g) Support and develop gender studies and research at all levels of education, especially at the postgraduate level of academic institutions, and apply them in the development of curricula, including university curricula, textbooks and teaching aids, and in teacher training;

(h) Develop leadership training and opportunities for all women to encourage them to take leadership roles both as students and as adults in civil society;

(i) Develop appropriate education and information programmes with due respect for multilingualism, particularly in conjunction with the mass media, that make the public, particularly parents, aware of the importance of non-discriminatory education for children and the equal sharing of family responsibilities by girls and boys;

(j) Develop human rights education programmes that incorporate the gender dimension at all levels of education, in particular by encouraging higher education institutions, especially in their graduate and postgraduate juridical, social and political science curricula, to include the study of the human rights of women as they appear in United Nations conventions;

(k) Remove legal, regulatory and social barriers, where appropriate, to sexual and reproductive health education within formal education programmes regarding women's health issues;

(l) Encourage, with the guidance and support of their parents and in cooperation with educational staff and institutions, the elaboration of educational programmes for girls and boys and the creation of integrated services in order to raise awareness of their responsibilities and to help them to assume those responsibilities, taking into account the importance of such education and services to personal development and self-esteem, as well as the urgent need to avoid unwanted pregnancy, the spread of sexually transmitted diseases, especially HIV/AIDS, and such phenomena as sexual violence and abuse;

(m) Provide accessible recreational and sports facilities and establish and strengthen gender-sensitive programmes for girls and women of all ages in education and community institutions and support the advancement of women in all areas of athletics and physical activity, including coaching, training and administration, and as participants at the national, regional and international levels;

(n) Recognize and support the right of indigenous women and girls to education and promote a multicultural approach to education that is responsive to the needs, aspirations and cultures of indigenous women, including by developing appropriate education programmes, curricula and teaching aids, to the extent possible in the languages of indigenous people, and by providing for the participation of indigenous women in these processes;

(o) Acknowledge and respect the artistic, spiritual and cultural activities of indigenous women;

(p) Ensure that gender equality and cultural, religious and other diversity are respected in educational institutions;

(q) Promote education, training and relevant information programmes for rural and farming women through the use of affordable and appropriate technologies and the mass media — for example, radio programmes, cassettes and mobile units;

(r) Provide non-formal education, especially for rural women, in order to realize their potential with regard to health, micro-enterprise, agriculture and legal rights;

(s) Remove all barriers to access to formal education for pregnant adolescents and young mothers, and support the provision of child care and other support services where necessary.

Strategic objective B.5. *Allocate sufficient resources for and monitor the implementation of educational reforms*

Actions to be taken

84. By Governments:

(a) Provide the required budgetary resources to the educational sector, with reallocation within the educational sector to ensure increased funds for basic education, as appropriate;

(b) Establish a mechanism at appropriate levels to monitor the implementation of educational reforms and measures in relevant ministries, and establish technical assistance programmes, as appropriate, to address issues raised by the monitoring efforts.

85. By Governments and, as appropriate, private and public institutions, foundations, research institutes and non-governmental organizations:

(a) When necessary, mobilize additional funds from private and public institutions, foundations, research institutes and non-governmental organizations to enable girls and women, as well as boys and men on an equal basis, to complete their education, with particular emphasis on under-served populations;

(b) Provide funding for special programmes, such as programmes in mathematics, science and computer technology, to advance opportunities for all girls and women.

86. By multilateral development institutions, including the World Bank, regional development banks, bilateral donors and foundations:

(a) Consider increasing funding for the education and training needs of girls and women as a priority in development assistance programmes;

(b) Consider working with recipient Governments to ensure that funding for women's education is maintained or increased in structural adjustment and economic recovery programmes, including lending and stabilization programmes.

87. By international and intergovernmental organizations, especially the United Nations Educational, Scientific and Cultural Organization, at the global level:

(a) Contribute to the evaluation of progress achieved, using educational indicators generated by national, regional and international bodies, and urge Governments, in implementing measures, to eliminate differences between women and men and boys and girls with regard to opportunities in education and training and the levels achieved in all fields, particularly in primary and literacy programmes;

(b) Provide technical assistance upon request to developing countries to strengthen the capacity to monitor progress in closing the gap between women and men in education, training and research, and in levels of achievement in all fields, particularly basic education and the elimination of illiteracy;

(c) Conduct an international campaign promoting the right of women and girls to education;

(d) Allocate a substantial percentage of their resources to basic education for women and girls.

Strategic objective B.6. *Promote life-long education and training for girls and women*

Actions to be taken

88. By Governments, educational institutions and communities:

(a) Ensure the availability of a broad range of educational and training programmes that lead to ongoing acquisition by women and girls of the knowledge and skills required for living in, contributing to and benefiting from their communities and nations;

(b) Provide support for child care and other services to enable mothers to continue their schooling;

(c) Create flexible education, training and retraining programmes for life-long learning that facilitate transitions between women's activities at all stages of their lives.

C. *Women and health**

89. Women have the right to the enjoyment of the highest attainable standard of physical and mental health. The enjoyment of this right is vital to their life and well-being and their ability to participate in all areas of public and private life. Health is a state of complete physical, mental and social well-being and not merely the absence of disease or infirmity. Women's health involves their emotional, social and physical well-being and is determined by the social, political and economic context of their lives, as well as by biology. However, health and well-being elude the majority of women. A major barrier for women to the achievement of the highest attainable standard of health is inequality, both between men and women and among women in different geographical regions, social classes and indigenous and ethnic groups. In national and international forums, women have emphasized that to attain optimal health throughout the life cycle, equality, including the sharing of family responsibilities, development and peace are necessary conditions.

90. Women have different and unequal access to and use of basic health resources, including primary health services for the prevention and treatment of childhood diseases, malnutrition, anaemia, diarrhoeal diseases, communicable diseases, malaria and other tropical diseases and tuberculosis, among others. Women also have different and unequal opportunities for the protection, promotion and maintenance of their health. In many developing countries, the lack of emergency obstetric services is also of particular concern. Health policies and

---

* The Holy See expressed a general reservation on this section. The reservation is to be interpreted in terms of the statement made by the representative of the Holy See at the 4th meeting of the Main Committee, on 14 September 1995 (see chap. V of the present report, para. 11).

programmes often perpetuate gender stereotypes and fail to consider socio-economic disparities and other differences among women and may not fully take account of the lack of autonomy of women regarding their health. Women's health is also affected by gender bias in the health system and by the provision of inadequate and inappropriate medical services to women.

91. In many countries, especially developing countries, in particular the least developed countries, a decrease in public health spending and, in some cases, structural adjustment, contribute to the deterioration of public health systems. In addition, privatization of health-care systems without appropriate guarantees of universal access to affordable health care further reduces health-care availability. This situation not only directly affects the health of girls and women, but also places disproportionate responsibilities on women, whose multiple roles, including their roles within the family and the community, are often not acknowledged; hence they do not receive the necessary social, psychological and economic support.

92. Women's right to the enjoyment of the highest standard of health must be secured throughout the whole life cycle in equality with men. Women are affected by many of the same health conditions as men, but women experience them differently. The prevalence among women of poverty and economic dependence, their experience of violence, negative attitudes towards women and girls, racial and other forms of discrimination, the limited power many women have over their sexual and reproductive lives and lack of influence in decision-making are social realities which have an adverse impact on their health. Lack of food and inequitable distribution of food for girls and women in the household, inadequate access to safe water, sanitation facilities and fuel supplies, particularly in rural and poor urban areas, and deficient housing conditions, all overburden women and their families and have a negative effect on their health. Good health is essential to leading a productive and fulfilling life, and the right of all women to control all aspects of their health, in particular their own fertility, is basic to their empowerment.

93. Discrimination against girls, often resulting from son preference, in access to nutrition and health-care services endangers their current and future health and well-being. Conditions that force girls into early marriage, pregnancy and child-bearing and subject them to harmful practices, such as female genital mutilation, pose grave health risks. Adolescent girls need, but too often do not have, access to necessary health and nutrition services as they mature. Counselling and access to sexual and reproductive health information and services for adolescents are still inadequate or lacking completely, and a young woman's right to privacy, confidentiality, respect and informed consent is often not considered. Adolescent girls are both biologically and psychosocially more vulnerable than boys to sexual abuse, violence and prostitution, and to the consequences of unprotected and premature sexual relations. The trend towards early sexual experience, combined with a lack of information and services, increases the risk of unwanted and too early pregnancy, HIV infection and other sexually transmitted diseases, as well as unsafe abortions. Early child-bearing continues to be an impediment to improvements in the educational, economic and social status of women in all parts of the world. Overall, for young women early marriage and early motherhood can severely curtail educational and employment opportunities and are likely to have a long-term, adverse impact on the quality of their lives and the lives of their children. Young men are often not educated to respect women's self-determination and to share responsibility with women in matters of sexuality and reproduction.

94. Reproductive health is a state of complete physical, mental and social well-being and not merely the absence of disease or infirmity, in all matters relating to the reproductive system and to its functions and processes. Reproductive health therefore implies that people are able to have a satisfying and safe sex life and that they have the capability to reproduce and the freedom to decide if, when and how often to do so. Implicit in this last condition are the right of men and women to be informed and to have access to safe, effective, affordable and acceptable methods of family planning of their choice, as well as other methods of their choice for regulation of fertility which are not against the law, and the right of access to appropriate health-care services that will enable women to go safely through pregnancy and childbirth and provide couples with the best chance of having a healthy infant. In line with the above definition of reproductive health, reproductive health care is defined as the constellation of methods, techniques and services that contribute to reproductive health and well-being by preventing and solving reproductive health problems. It also includes sexual health, the purpose of which is the enhancement of life and personal relations, and not merely counselling and care related to reproduction and sexually transmitted diseases.

95. Bearing in mind the above definition, reproductive rights embrace certain human rights that are already recognized in national laws, international human rights documents and other consensus documents. These rights rest on the recognition of the basic right of all couples and individuals to decide freely and responsibly the number, spacing and timing of their children and to have the information and means to do so, and the right

to attain the highest standard of sexual and reproductive health. It also includes their right to make decisions concerning reproduction free of discrimination, coercion and violence, as expressed in human rights documents. In the exercise of this right, they should take into account the needs of their living and future children and their responsibilities towards the community. The promotion of the responsible exercise of these rights for all people should be the fundamental basis for government- and community-supported policies and programmes in the area of reproductive health, including family planning. As part of their commitment, full attention should be given to the promotion of mutually respectful and equitable gender relations and particularly to meeting the educational and service needs of adolescents to enable them to deal in a positive and responsible way with their sexuality. Reproductive health eludes many of the world's people because of such factors as: inadequate levels of knowledge about human sexuality and inappropriate or poor-quality reproductive health information and services; the prevalence of high-risk sexual behaviour; discriminatory social practices; negative attitudes towards women and girls; and the limited power many women and girls have over their sexual and reproductive lives. Adolescents are particularly vulnerable because of their lack of information and access to relevant services in most countries. Older women and men have distinct reproductive and sexual health issues which are often inadequately addressed.

96. The human rights of women include their right to have control over and decide freely and responsibly on matters related to their sexuality, including sexual and reproductive health, free of coercion, discrimination and violence. Equal relationships between women and men in matters of sexual relations and reproduction, including full respect for the integrity of the person, require mutual respect, consent and shared responsibility for sexual behaviour and its consequences.

97. Further, women are subject to particular health risks due to inadequate responsiveness and lack of services to meet health needs related to sexuality and reproduction. Complications related to pregnancy and childbirth are among the leading causes of mortality and morbidity of women of reproductive age in many parts of the developing world. Similar problems exist to a certain degree in some countries with economies in transition. Unsafe abortions threaten the lives of a large number of women, representing a grave public health problem as it is primarily the poorest and youngest who take the highest risk. Most of these deaths, health problems and injuries are preventable through improved access to adequate health-care services, including safe and effective family planning methods and emergency obstet-ric care, recognizing the right of women and men to be informed and to have access to safe, effective, affordable and acceptable methods of family planning of their choice, as well as other methods of their choice for regulation of fertility which are not against the law, and the right of access to appropriate health-care services that will enable women to go safely through pregnancy and childbirth and provide couples with the best chance of having a healthy infant. These problems and means should be addressed on the basis of the report of the International Conference on Population and Development, with particular reference to relevant paragraphs of the Programme of Action of the Conference. 14/ In most countries, the neglect of women's reproductive rights severely limits their opportunities in public and private life, including opportunities for education and economic and political empowerment. The ability of women to control their own fertility forms an important basis for the enjoyment of other rights. Shared responsibility between women and men in matters related to sexual and reproductive behaviour is also essential to improving women's health.

98. HIV/AIDS and other sexually transmitted diseases, the transmission of which is sometimes a consequence of sexual violence, are having a devastating effect on women's health, particularly the health of adolescent girls and young women. They often do not have the power to insist on safe and responsible sex practices and have little access to information and services for prevention and treatment. Women, who represent half of all adults newly infected with HIV/AIDS and other sexually transmitted diseases, have emphasized that social vulnerability and the unequal power relationships between women and men are obstacles to safe sex, in their efforts to control the spread of sexually transmitted diseases. The consequences of HIV/AIDS reach beyond women's health to their role as mothers and caregivers and their contribution to the economic support of their families. The social, developmental and health consequences of HIV/AIDS and other sexually transmitted diseases need to be seen from a gender perspective.

99. Sexual and gender-based violence, including physical and psychological abuse, trafficking in women and girls, and other forms of abuse and sexual exploitation place girls and women at high risk of physical and mental trauma, disease and unwanted pregnancy. Such situations often deter women from using health and other services.

100. Mental disorders related to marginalization, powerlessness and poverty, along with overwork and

14/ *Report of the International Conference on Population and Development, Cairo, 5-13 September 1994* (United Nations publication, Sales No. E.95.XIII.18), chap. I, resolution 1, annex.

stress and the growing incidence of domestic violence as well as substance abuse, are among other health issues of growing concern to women. Women throughout the world, especially young women, are increasing their use of tobacco with serious effects on their health and that of their children. Occupational health issues are also growing in importance, as a large number of women work in low-paid jobs in either the formal or the informal labour market under tedious and unhealthy conditions, and the number is rising. Cancers of the breast and cervix and other cancers of the reproductive system, as well as infertility, affect growing numbers of women and may be preventable, or curable, if detected early.

101. With the increase in life expectancy and the growing number of older women, their health concerns require particular attention. The long-term health prospects of women are influenced by changes at menopause, which, in combination with life-long conditions and other factors, such as poor nutrition and lack of physical activity, may increase the risk of cardiovascular disease and osteoporosis. Other diseases of ageing and the inter-relationships of ageing and disability among women also need particular attention.

102. Women, like men, particularly in rural areas and poor urban areas, are increasingly exposed to environmental health hazards owing to environmental catastrophes and degradation. Women have a different susceptibility to various environmental hazards, contaminants and substances and they suffer different consequences from exposure to them.

103. The quality of women's health care is often deficient in various ways, depending on local circumstances. Women are frequently not treated with respect, nor are they guaranteed privacy and confidentiality, nor do they always receive full information about the options and services available. Furthermore, in some countries, over-medicating of women's life events is common, leading to unnecessary surgical intervention and inappropriate medication.

104. Statistical data on health are often not systematically collected, disaggregated and analysed by age, sex and socio-economic status and by established demographic criteria used to serve the interests and solve the problems of subgroups, with particular emphasis on the vulnerable and marginalized and other relevant variables. Recent and reliable data on the mortality and morbidity of women and conditions and diseases particularly affecting women are not available in many countries. Relatively little is known about how social and economic factors affect the health of girls and women of all ages, about the provision of health services to girls and women and the patterns of their use of such services, and about the value of disease prevention and health promotion programmes

for women. Subjects of importance to women's health have not been adequately researched and women's health research often lacks funding. Medical research, on heart disease, for example, and epidemiological studies in many countries are often based solely on men; they are not gender specific. Clinical trials involving women to establish basic information about dosage, side-effects and effectiveness of drugs, including contraceptives, are noticeably absent and do not always conform to ethical standards for research and testing. Many drug therapy protocols and other medical treatments and interventions administered to women are based on research on men without any investigation and adjustment for gender differences.

105. In addressing inequalities in health status and unequal access to and inadequate health-care services between women and men, Governments and other actors should promote an active and visible policy of mainstreaming a gender perspective in all policies and programmes, so that, before decisions are taken, an analysis is made of the effects for women and men, respectively.

Strategic objective C.1. Increase women's access throughout the life cycle to *appropriate, affordable, and quality health care, information and related services*

Actions to be taken

106. By Governments, in collaboration with non-governmental organizations and employers' and workers' organizations and with the support of international institutions:

(a) Support and implement the commitments made in the Programme of Action of the International Conference on Population and Development, as established in the report of that Conference and the Copenhagen Declaration on Social Development and Programme of Action of the World Summit for Social Development 15/ and the obligations of States parties under the Convention on the Elimination of All Forms of Discrimination against Women and other relevant international agreements, to meet the health needs of girls and women of all ages;

(b) Reaffirm the right to the enjoyment of the highest attainable standards of physical and mental health, protect and promote the attainment of this right for women and girls and incorporate it in national legislation, for example; review existing legislation, including health legislation, as well as policies, where necessary, to reflect a commitment to women's health and to ensure

15/ *Report of the World Summit for Social Development, Copenhagen, 6-12 March 1995* (A/CONF.166/9), chap. I, resolution 1, annexes I and II.

that they meet the changing roles and responsibilities of women wherever they reside;

(c) Design and implement, in cooperation with women and community-based organizations, gender-sensitive health programmes, including decentralized health services, that address the needs of women throughout their lives and take into account their multiple roles and responsibilities, the demands on their time, the special needs of rural women and women with disabilities and the diversity of women's needs arising from age and socio-economic and cultural differences, among others; include women, especially local and indigenous women, in the identification and planning of health-care priorities and programmes; remove all barriers to women's health services and provide a broad range of health-care services;

(d) Allow women access to social security systems in equality with men throughout the whole life cycle;

(e) Provide more accessible, available and affordable primary health-care services of high quality, including sexual and reproductive health care, which includes family planning information and services, and giving particular attention to maternal and emergency obstetric care, as agreed to in the Programme of Action of the International Conference on Population and Development;

(f) Redesign health information, services and training for health workers so that they are gender-sensitive and reflect the user's perspectives with regard to interpersonal and communications skills and the user's right to privacy and confidentiality; these services, information and training should be based on a holistic approach;

(g) Ensure that all health services and workers conform to human rights and to ethical, professional and gender-sensitive standards in the delivery of women's health services aimed at ensuring responsible, voluntary and informed consent; encourage the development, implementation and dissemination of codes of ethics guided by existing international codes of medical ethics as well as ethical principles that govern other health professionals;

(h) Take all appropriate measures to eliminate harmful, medically unnecessary or coercive medical interventions, as well as inappropriate medication and over-medication of women, and ensure that all women are fully informed of their options, including likely benefits and potential side-effects, by properly trained personnel;

(i) Strengthen and reorient health services, particularly primary health care, in order to ensure universal access to quality health services for women and girls; reduce ill health and maternal morbidity and achieve world wide the agreed-upon goal of reducing maternal mortality by at least 50 per cent of the 1990 levels by the year 2000 and a further one half by the year 2015; ensure that the necessary services are available at each level of the health system and make reproductive health care accessible, through the primary health-care system, to all individuals of appropriate ages as soon as possible and no later than the year 2015;

(j) Recognize and deal with the health impact of unsafe abortion as a major public health concern, as agreed in paragraph 8.25 of the Programme of Action of the International Conference on Population and Development; 14/

(k) In the light of paragraph 8.25 of the Programme of Action of the International Conference on Population and Development, which states: "In no case should abortion be promoted as a method of family planning. All Governments and relevant intergovernmental and non-governmental organizations are urged to strengthen their commitment to women's health, to deal with the health impact of unsafe abortion 16/ as a major public health concern and to reduce the recourse to abortion through expanded and improved family-planning services. Prevention of unwanted pregnancies must always be given the highest priority and every attempt should be made to eliminate the need for abortion. Women who have unwanted pregnancies should have ready access to reliable information and compassionate counselling. Any measures or changes related to abortion within the health system can only be determined at the national or local level according to the national legislative process. In circumstances where abortion is not against the law, such abortion should be safe. In all cases, women should have access to quality services for the management of complications arising from abortion. Post-abortion counselling, education and family-planning services should be offered promptly, which will also help to avoid repeat abortions", consider reviewing laws containing punitive measures against women who have undergone illegal abortions;

(l) Give particular attention to the needs of girls, especially the promotion of healthy behaviour, including physical activities; take specific measures for closing the gender gaps in morbidity and mortality where girls are disadvantaged, while achieving internationally approved goals for the reduction of infant and child mortality — specifically, by the year 2000, the reduction of mortality rates of infants and children under five years of age by one third of the 1990 level, or 50 to 70 per 1,000 live births, whichever is less; by the year 2015 an infant mortality rate below 35 per 1,000 live births and an under-five mortality rate below 45 per 1,000;

16/ Unsafe abortion is defined as a procedure for terminating an unwanted pregnancy either by persons lacking the necessary skills or in an environment lacking the minimal medical standards or both (based on World Health Organization, *The Prevention and Management of Unsafe Abortion*, Report of a Technical Working Group, Geneva, April 1992 (WHO/MSM/92.5)).

(m) Ensure that girls have continuing access to necessary health and nutrition information and services as they mature, to facilitate a healthful transition from childhood to adulthood;

(n) Develop information, programmes and services to assist women to understand and adapt to changes associated with ageing and to address and treat the health needs of older women, paying particular attention to those who are physically or psychologically dependent;

(o) Ensure that girls and women of all ages with any form of disability receive supportive services;

(p) Formulate special policies, design programmes and enact the legislation necessary to alleviate and eliminate environmental and occupational health hazards associated with work in the home, in the workplace and elsewhere with attention to pregnant and lactating women;

(q) Integrate mental health services into primary health-care systems or other appropriate levels, develop supportive programmes and train primary health workers to recognize and care for girls and women of all ages who have experienced any form of violence especially domestic violence, sexual abuse or other abuse resulting from armed and non-armed conflict;

(r) Promote public information on the benefits of breast-feeding; examine ways and means of implementing fully the WHO/UNICEF International Code of Marketing of Breast-milk Substitutes, and enable mothers to breast-feed their infants by providing legal, economic, practical and emotional support;

(s) Establish mechanisms to support and involve non-governmental organizations, particularly women's organizations, professional groups and other bodies working to improve the health of girls and women, in government policy-making, programme design, as appropriate, and implementation within the health sector and related sectors at all levels;

(t) Support non-governmental organizations working on women's health and help develop networks aimed at improving coordination and collaboration between all sectors that affect health;

(u) Rationalize drug procurement and ensure a reliable, continuous supply of high-quality pharmaceutical, contraceptive and other supplies and equipment, using the WHO Model List of Essential Drugs as a guide, and ensure the safety of drugs and devices through national regulatory drug approval processes;

(v) Provide improved access to appropriate treatment and rehabilitation services for women substance abusers and their families;

(w) Promote and ensure household and national food security, as appropriate, and implement pro-

grammes aimed at improving the nutritional status of all girls and women by implementing the commitments made in the Plan of Action on Nutrition of the International Conference on Nutrition, 17/ including a reduction world wide of severe and moderate malnutrition among children under the age of five by one half of 1990 levels by the year 2000, giving special attention to the gender gap in nutrition, and a reduction in iron deficiency anaemia in girls and women by one third of the 1990 levels by the year 2000;

(x) Ensure the availability of and universal access to safe drinking water and sanitation and put in place effective public distribution systems as soon as possible;

(y) Ensure full and equal access to health-care infrastructure and services for indigenous women.

Strategic objective C.2. *Strengthen preventive programmes that promote women's health*

Actions to be taken

107. By Governments, in cooperation with non-governmental organizations, the mass media, the private sector and relevant international organizations, including United Nations bodies, as appropriate:

(a) Give priority to both formal and informal educational programmes that support and enable women to develop self-esteem, acquire knowledge, make decisions on and take responsibility for their own health, achieve mutual respect in matters concerning sexuality and fertility and educate men regarding the importance of women's health and well-being, placing special focus on programmes for both men and women that emphasize the elimination of harmful attitudes and practices, including female genital mutilation, son preference (which results in female infanticide and prenatal sex selection), early marriage, including child marriage, violence against women, sexual exploitation, sexual abuse, which at times is conducive to infection with HIV/AIDS and other sexually transmitted diseases, drug abuse, discrimination against girls and women in food allocation and other harmful attitudes and practices related to the life, health and well-being of women, and recognizing that some of these practices can be violations of human rights and ethical medical principles;

(b) Pursue social, human development, education and employment policies to eliminate poverty among women in order to reduce their susceptibility to ill health and to improve their health;

(c) Encourage men to share equally in child care and household work and to provide their share of finan-

17/ *Final Report of the International Conference on Nutrition, Rome, 5-11 December 1992* (Rome, Food and Agriculture Organization of the United Nations, 1993), Part II.

cial support for their families, even if they do not live with them;

(d) Reinforce laws, reform institutions and promote norms and practices that eliminate discrimination against women and encourage both women and men to take responsibility for their sexual and reproductive behaviour; ensure full respect for the integrity of the person, take action to ensure the conditions necessary for women to exercise their reproductive rights and eliminate coercive laws and practices;

(e) Prepare and disseminate accessible information, through public health campaigns, the media, reliable counselling and the education system, designed to ensure that women and men, particularly young people, can acquire knowledge about their health, especially information on sexuality and reproduction, taking into account the rights of the child to access to information, privacy, confidentiality, respect and informed consent, as well as the responsibilities, rights and duties of parents and legal guardians to provide, in a manner consistent with the evolving capacities of the child, appropriate direction and guidance in the exercise by the child of the rights recognized in the Convention on the Rights of the Child, and in conformity with the Convention on the Elimination of All Forms of Discrimination against Women; ensure that in all actions concerning children, the best interests of the child are a primary consideration;

(f) Create and support programmes in the educational system, in the workplace and in the community to make opportunities to participate in sport, physical activity and recreation available to girls and women of all ages on the same basis as they are made available to men and boys;

(g) Recognize the specific needs of adolescents and implement specific appropriate programmes, such as education and information on sexual and reproductive health issues and on sexually transmitted diseases, including HIV/AIDS, taking into account the rights of the child and the responsibilities, rights and duties of parents as stated in paragraph 107 (e) above;

(h) Develop policies that reduce the disproportionate and increasing burden on women who have multiple roles within the family and the community by providing them with adequate support and programmes from health and social services;

(i) Adopt regulations to ensure that the working conditions, including remuneration and promotion of women at all levels of the health system, are non-discriminatory and meet fair and professional standards to enable them to work effectively;

(j) Ensure that health and nutritional information and training form an integral part of all adult literacy programmes and school curricula from the primary level;

(k) Develop and undertake media campaigns and information and educational programmes that inform women and girls of the health and related risks of substance abuse and addiction and pursue strategies and programmes that discourage substance abuse and addiction and promote rehabilitation and recovery;

(l) Devise and implement comprehensive and coherent programmes for the prevention, diagnosis and treatment of osteoporosis, a condition that predominantly affects women;

(m) Establish and/or strengthen programmes and services, including media campaigns, that address the prevention, early detection and treatment of breast, cervical and other cancers of the reproductive system;

(n) Reduce environmental hazards that pose a growing threat to health, especially in poor regions and communities; apply a precautionary approach, as agreed to in the Rio Declaration on Environment and Development, adopted by the United Nations Conference on Environment and Development, 18/ and include reporting on women's health risks related to the environment in monitoring the implementation of Agenda 21; 19/

(o) Create awareness among women, health professionals, policy makers and the general public about the serious but preventable health hazards stemming from tobacco consumption and the need for regulatory and education measures to reduce smoking as important health promotion and disease prevention activities;

(p) Ensure that medical school curricula and other health-care training include gender-sensitive, comprehensive and mandatory courses on women's health;

(q) Adopt specific preventive measures to protect women, youth and children from any abuse — sexual abuse, exploitation, trafficking and violence, for example — including the formulation and enforcement of laws, and provide legal protection and medical and other assistance.

Strategic objective C.3. *Undertake gender-sensitive initiatives that address sexually transmitted diseases, HIV/AIDS, and sexual and reproductive health issues*

Actions to be taken

108. By Governments, international bodies including relevant United Nations organizations, bilateral and multilateral donors and non-governmental organizations:

18/ *Report of the United Nations Conference on Environment and Development, Rio de Janeiro, 3-14 June 1992*, vol. I, *Resolutions Adopted by the Conference* (United Nations publication, Sales No. E.93.I.8 and corrigenda), resolution 1, annex I.
19/ Ibid., resolution 1, annex II.

(a) Ensure the involvement of women, especially those infected with HIV/AIDS or other sexually transmitted diseases or affected by the HIV/AIDS pandemic, in all decision-making relating to the development, implementation, monitoring and evaluation of policies and programmes on HIV/AIDS and other sexually transmitted diseases;

(b) Review and amend laws and combat practices, as appropriate, that may contribute to women's susceptibility to HIV infection and other sexually transmitted diseases, including enacting legislation against those socio-cultural practices that contribute to it, and implement legislation, policies and practices to protect women, adolescents and young girls from discrimination related to HIV/AIDS;

(c) Encourage all sectors of society, including the public sector, as well as international organizations, to develop compassionate and supportive, non-discriminatory HIV/AIDS-related policies and practices that protect the rights of infected individuals;

(d) Recognize the extent of the HIV/AIDS pandemic in their countries, taking particularly into account its impact on women, with a view to ensuring that infected women do not suffer stigmatization and discrimination, including during travel;

(e) Develop gender-sensitive multisectoral programmes and strategies to end social subordination of women and girls and to ensure their social and economic empowerment and equality; facilitate promotion of programmes to educate and enable men to assume their responsibilities to prevent HIV/AIDS and other sexually transmitted diseases;

(f) Facilitate the development of community strategies that will protect women of all ages from HIV and other sexually transmitted diseases; provide care and support to infected girls, women and their families and mobilize all parts of the community in response to the HIV/AIDS pandemic to exert pressure on all responsible authorities to respond in a timely, effective, sustainable and gender-sensitive manner;

(g) Support and strengthen national capacity to create and improve gender-sensitive policies and programmes on HIV/AIDS and other sexually transmitted diseases, including the provision of resources and facilities to women who find themselves the principal caregivers or economic support for those infected with HIV/AIDS or affected by the pandemic, and the survivors, particularly children and older persons;

(h) Provide workshops and specialized education and training to parents, decision makers and opinion leaders at all levels of the community, including religious and traditional authorities, on prevention of HIV/AIDS and other sexually transmitted diseases and on their repercussions on both women and men of all ages;

(i) Give all women and health workers all relevant information and education about sexually transmitted diseases including HIV/AIDS and pregnancy and the implications for the baby, including breast-feeding;

(j) Assist women and their formal and informal organizations to establish and expand effective peer education and outreach programmes and to participate in the design, implementation and monitoring of these programmes;

(k) Give full attention to the promotion of mutually respectful and equitable gender relations and, in particular, to meeting the educational and service needs of adolescents to enable them to deal in a positive and responsible way with their sexuality;

(l) Design specific programmes for men of all ages and male adolescents, recognizing the parental roles referred to in paragraph 107 (e) above, aimed at providing complete and accurate information on safe and responsible sexual and reproductive behaviour, including voluntary, appropriate and effective male methods for the prevention of HIV/AIDS and other sexually transmitted diseases through, *inter alia*, abstinence and condom use;

(m) Ensure the provision, through the primary health-care system, of universal access of couples and individuals to appropriate and affordable preventive services with respect to sexually transmitted diseases, including HIV/AIDS, and expand the provision of counselling and voluntary and confidential diagnostic and treatment services for women; ensure that high-quality condoms as well as drugs for the treatment of sexually transmitted diseases are, where possible, supplied and distributed to health services;

(n) Support programmes which acknowledge that the higher risk among women of contracting HIV is linked to high-risk behaviour, including intravenous substance use and substance-influenced unprotected and irresponsible sexual behaviour, and take appropriate preventive measures;

(o) Support and expedite action-oriented research on affordable methods, controlled by women, to prevent HIV and other sexually transmitted diseases, on strategies empowering women to protect themselves from sexually transmitted diseases, including HIV/AIDS, and on methods of care, support and treatment of women, ensuring their involvement in all aspects of such research;

(p) Support and initiate research which addresses women's needs and situations, including research on HIV infection and other sexually transmitted diseases in women, on women-controlled methods of protection, such as non-spermicidal microbicides, and on male and female risk-taking attitudes and practices.

Strategic objective C.4. *Promote research and disseminate information on women's health*

Actions to be taken

109. By Governments, the United Nations system, health professions, research institutions, non-governmental organizations, donors, pharmaceutical industries and the mass media, as appropriate:

(a) Train researchers and introduce systems that allow for the use of data collected, analysed and disaggregated by, among other factors, sex and age, other established demographic criteria and socio-economic variables, in policy-making, as appropriate, planning, monitoring and evaluation;

(b) Promote gender-sensitive and women-centred health research, treatment and technology and link traditional and indigenous knowledge with modern medicine, making information available to women to enable them to make informed and responsible decisions;

(c) Increase the number of women in leadership positions in the health professions, including researchers and scientists, to achieve equality at the earliest possible date;

(d) Increase financial and other support from all sources for preventive, appropriate biomedical, behavioural, epidemiological and health service research on women's health issues and for research on the social, economic and political causes of women's health problems, and their consequences, including the impact of gender and age inequalities, especially with respect to chronic and non-communicable diseases, particularly cardiovascular diseases and conditions, cancers, reproductive tract infections and injuries, HIV/AIDS and other sexually transmitted diseases, domestic violence, occupational health, disabilities, environmentally related health problems, tropical diseases and health aspects of ageing;

(e) Inform women about the factors which increase the risks of developing cancers and infections of the reproductive tract, so that they can make informed decisions about their health;

(f) Support and fund social, economic, political and cultural research on how gender-based inequalities affect women's health, including etiology, epidemiology, provision and utilization of services and eventual outcome of treatment;

(g) Support health service systems and operations research to strengthen access and improve the quality of service delivery, to ensure appropriate support for women as health-care providers and to examine patterns with respect to the provision of health services to women and use of such services by women;

(h) Provide financial and institutional support for research on safe, effective, affordable and acceptable methods and technologies for the reproductive and sexual health of women and men, including more safe, effective, affordable and acceptable methods for the regulation of fertility, including natural family planning for both sexes, methods to protect against HIV/AIDS and other sexually transmitted diseases and simple and inexpensive methods of diagnosing such diseases, among others; this research needs to be guided at all stages by users and from the perspective of gender, particularly the perspective of women, and should be carried out in strict conformity with internationally accepted legal, ethical, medical and scientific standards for biomedical research;

(i) Since unsafe abortion 16/ is a major threat to the health and life of women, research to understand and better address the determinants and consequences of induced abortion, including its effects on subsequent fertility, reproductive and mental health and contraceptive practice, should be promoted, as well as research on treatment of complications of abortions and post-abortion care;

(j) Acknowledge and encourage beneficial traditional health care, especially that practised by indigenous women, with a view to preserving and incorporating the value of traditional health care in the provision of health services, and support research directed towards achieving this aim;

(k) Develop mechanisms to evaluate and disseminate available data and research findings to researchers, policy makers, health professionals and women's groups, among others;

(l) Monitor human genome and related genetic research from the perspective of women's health and disseminate information and results of studies conducted in accordance with accepted ethical standards.

Strategic objective C.5. *Increase resources and monitor follow-up for women's health*

Actions to be taken

110. By Governments at all levels and, where appropriate, in cooperation with non-governmental organizations, especially women's and youth organizations:

(a) Increase budgetary allocations for primary health care and social services, with adequate support for secondary and tertiary levels, and give special attention to the reproductive and sexual health of girls and women and give priority to health programmes in rural and poor urban areas;

(b) Develop innovative approaches to funding health services through promoting community participation and local financing; increase, where necessary, budgetary allocations for community health centres and community-based programmes and services that address women's specific health needs;

(c) Develop local health services, promoting the incorporation of gender-sensitive community-based participation and self-care and specially designed preventive health programmes;

(d) Develop goals and time-frames, where appropriate, for improving women's health and for planning, implementing, monitoring and evaluating programmes, based on gender-impact assessments using qualitative and quantitative data disaggregated by sex, age, other established demographic criteria and socio-economic variables;

(e) Establish, as appropriate, ministerial and inter-ministerial mechanisms for monitoring the implementation of women's health policy and programme reforms and establish, as appropriate, high-level focal points in national planning authorities responsible for monitoring to ensure that women's health concerns are mainstreamed in all relevant government agencies and programmes.

111. By Governments, the United Nations and its specialized agencies, international financial institutions, bilateral donors and the private sector, as appropriate:

(a) Formulate policies favourable to investment in women's health and, where appropriate, increase allocations for such investment;

(b) Provide appropriate material, financial and logistical assistance to youth non-governmental organizations in order to strengthen them to address youth concerns in the area of health, including sexual and reproductive health;

(c) Give higher priority to women's health and develop mechanisms for coordinating and implementing the health objectives of the Platform for Action and relevant international agreements to ensure progress.

D. *Violence against women*

112. Violence against women is an obstacle to the achievement of the objectives of equality, development and peace. Violence against women both violates and impairs or nullifies the enjoyment by women of their human rights and fundamental freedoms. The long-standing failure to protect and promote those rights and freedoms in the case of violence against women is a matter of concern to all States and should be addressed. Knowledge about its causes and consequences, as well as its incidence and measures to combat it, have been greatly expanded since the Nairobi Conference. In all societies, to a greater or lesser degree, women and girls are subjected to physical, sexual and psychological abuse that cuts across lines of income, class and culture. The low social and economic status of women can be both a cause and a consequence of violence against women.

113. The term "violence against women" means any act of gender-based violence that results in, or is likely to result in, physical, sexual or psychological harm or suffering to women, including threats of such acts, coercion or arbitrary deprivation of liberty, whether occurring in public or private life. Accordingly, violence against women encompasses but is not limited to the following:

(a) Physical, sexual and psychological violence occurring in the family, including battering, sexual abuse of female children in the household, dowry-related violence, marital rape, female genital mutilation and other traditional practices harmful to women, non-spousal violence and violence related to exploitation;

(b) Physical, sexual and psychological violence occurring within the general community, including rape, sexual abuse, sexual harassment and intimidation at work, in educational institutions and elsewhere, trafficking in women and forced prostitution;

(c) Physical, sexual and psychological violence perpetrated or condoned by the State, wherever it occurs.

114. Other acts of violence against women include violation of the human rights of women in situations of armed conflict, in particular murder, systematic rape, sexual slavery and forced pregnancy.

115. Acts of violence against women also include forced sterilization and forced abortion, coercive/forced use of contraceptives, female infanticide and prenatal sex selection.

116. Some groups of women, such as women belonging to minority groups, indigenous women, refugee women, women migrants, including women migrant workers, women in poverty living in rural or remote communities, destitute women, women in institutions or in detention, female children, women with disabilities, elderly women, displaced women, repatriated women, women living in poverty and women in situations of armed conflict, foreign occupation, wars of aggression, civil wars, terrorism, including hostage-taking, are also particularly vulnerable to violence.

117. Acts or threats of violence, whether occurring within the home or in the community, or perpetrated or condoned by the State, instil fear and insecurity in women's lives and are obstacles to the achievement of equality and for development and peace. The fear of violence, including harassment, is a permanent constraint on the mobility of women and limits their access to resources and basic activities. High social, health and economic costs to the individual and society are associated with violence against women. Violence against women is one of the crucial social mechanisms by which women are forced into a subordinate position compared with men. In many cases, violence against women and girls occurs in the family or within the home, where

violence is often tolerated. The neglect, physical and sexual abuse, and rape of girl children and women by family members and other members of the household, as well as incidences of spousal and non-spousal abuse, often go unreported and are thus difficult to detect. Even when such violence is reported, there is often a failure to protect victims or punish perpetrators.

118. Violence against women is a manifestation of the historically unequal power relations between men and women, which have led to domination over and discrimination against women by men and to the prevention of women's full advancement. Violence against women throughout the life cycle derives essentially from cultural patterns, in particular the harmful effects of certain traditional or customary practices and all acts of extremism linked to race, sex, language or religion that perpetuate the lower status accorded to women in the family, the workplace, the community and society. Violence against women is exacerbated by social pressures, notably the shame of denouncing certain acts that have been perpetrated against women; women's lack of access to legal information, aid or protection; the lack of laws that effectively prohibit violence against women; failure to reform existing laws; inadequate efforts on the part of public authorities to promote awareness of and enforce existing laws; and the absence of educational and other means to address the causes and consequences of violence. Images in the media of violence against women, in particular those that depict rape or sexual slavery as well as the use of women and girls as sex objects, including pornography, are factors contributing to the continued prevalence of such violence, adversely influencing the community at large, in particular children and young people.

119. Developing a holistic and multidisciplinary approach to the challenging task of promoting families, communities and States that are free of violence against women is necessary and achievable. Equality, partnership between women and men and respect for human dignity must permeate all stages of the socialization process. Educational systems should promote self-respect, mutual respect, and cooperation between women and men.

120. The absence of adequate gender-disaggregated data and statistics on the incidence of violence makes the elaboration of programmes and monitoring of changes difficult. Lack of or inadequate documentation and research on domestic violence, sexual harassment and violence against women and girls in private and in public, including the workplace, impede efforts to design specific intervention strategies. Experience in a number of countries shows that women and men can be mobilized to overcome violence in all its forms and that effective public measures can be taken to address both the causes and the consequences of violence. Men's groups mobilizing against gender violence are necessary allies for change.

121. Women may be vulnerable to violence perpetrated by persons in positions of authority in both conflict and non-conflict situations. Training of all officials in humanitarian and human rights law and the punishment of perpetrators of violent acts against women would help to ensure that such violence does not take place at the hands of public officials in whom women should be able to place trust, including police and prison officials and security forces.

122. The effective suppression of trafficking in women and girls for the sex trade is a matter of pressing international concern. Implementation of the 1949 Convention for the Suppression of the Traffic in Persons and of the Exploitation of the Prostitution of Others, 20/ as well as other relevant instruments, needs to be reviewed and strengthened. The use of women in international prostitution and trafficking networks has become a major focus of international organized crime. The Special Rapporteur of the Commission on Human Rights on violence against women, who has explored these acts as an additional cause of the violation of the human rights and fundamental freedoms of women and girls, is invited to address, within her mandate and as a matter of urgency, the issue of international trafficking for the purposes of the sex trade, as well as the issues of forced prostitution, rape, sexual abuse and sex tourism. Women and girls who are victims of this international trade are at an increased risk of further violence, as well as unwanted pregnancy and sexually transmitted infection, including infection with HIV/AIDS.

123. In addressing violence against women, Governments and other actors should promote an active and visible policy of mainstreaming a gender perspective in all policies and programmes so that before decisions are taken an analysis may be made of their effects on women and men, respectively.

Strategic objective D.1. *Take integrated measures to prevent and eliminate violence against women*

Actions to be taken

124. By Governments:

(a) Condemn violence against women and refrain from invoking any custom, tradition or religious consideration to avoid their obligations with respect to its elimination as set out in the Declaration on the Elimination of Violence against Women;

(b) Refrain from engaging in violence against women and exercise due diligence to prevent, investigate and, in accordance with national legislation, punish acts

20/ General Assembly resolution 317 (IV), annex.

of violence against women, whether those acts are perpetrated by the State or by private persons;

(c) Enact and/or reinforce penal, civil, labour and administrative sanctions in domestic legislation to punish and redress the wrongs done to women and girls who are subjected to any form of violence, whether in the home, the workplace, the community or society;

(d) Adopt and/or implement and periodically review and analyse legislation to ensure its effectiveness in eliminating violence against women, emphasizing the prevention of violence and the prosecution of offenders; take measures to ensure the protection of women subjected to violence, access to just and effective remedies, including compensation and indemnification and healing of victims, and rehabilitation of perpetrators;

(e) Work actively to ratify and/or implement international human rights norms and instruments as they relate to violence against women, including those contained in the Universal Declaration of Human Rights, 21/ the International Covenant on Civil and Political Rights, 13/ the International Covenant on Economic, Social and Cultural Rights, 13/ and the Convention against Torture and Other Cruel, Inhuman or Degrading Treatment or Punishment; 22/

(f) Implement the Convention on the Elimination of All Forms of Discrimination against Women, taking into account general recommendation 19, adopted by the Committee on the Elimination of Discrimination against Women at its eleventh session; 23/

(g) Promote an active and visible policy of mainstreaming a gender perspective in all policies and programmes related to violence against women; actively encourage, support and implement measures and programmes aimed at increasing the knowledge and understanding of the causes, consequences and mechanisms of violence against women among those responsible for implementing these policies, such as law enforcement officers, police personnel and judicial, medical and social workers, as well as those who deal with minority, migration and refugee issues, and develop strategies to ensure that the revictimization of women victims of violence does not occur because of gender-insensitive laws or judicial or enforcement practices;

(h) Provide women who are subjected to violence with access to the mechanisms of justice and, as provided for by national legislation, to just and effective remedies for the harm they have suffered and inform women of their rights in seeking redress through such mechanisms;

(i) Enact and enforce legislation against the perpetrators of practices and acts of violence against women, such as female genital mutilation, female infanticide, prenatal sex selection and dowry-related violence, and give vigorous support to the efforts of non-governmental and community organizations to eliminate such practices;

(j) Formulate and implement, at all appropriate levels, plans of action to eliminate violence against women;

(k) Adopt all appropriate measures, especially in the field of education, to modify the social and cultural patterns of conduct of men and women, and to eliminate prejudices, customary practices and all other practices based on the idea of the inferiority or superiority of either of the sexes and on stereotyped roles for men and women;

(l) Create or strengthen institutional mechanisms so that women and girls can report acts of violence against them in a safe and confidential environment, free from the fear of penalties or retaliation, and file charges;

(m) Ensure that women with disabilities have access to information and services in the field of violence against women;

(n) Create, improve or develop as appropriate, and fund the training programmes for judicial, legal, medical, social, educational and police and immigrant personnel, in order to avoid the abuse of power leading to violence against women and sensitize such personnel to the nature of gender-based acts and threats of violence so that fair treatment of female victims can be assured;

(o) Adopt laws, where necessary, and reinforce existing laws that punish police, security forces or any other agents of the State who engage in acts of violence against women in the course of the performance of their duties; review existing legislation and take effective measures against the perpetrators of such violence;

(p) Allocate adequate resources within the government budget and mobilize community resources for activities related to the elimination of violence against women, including resources for the implementation of plans of action at all appropriate levels;

(q) Include in reports submitted in accordance with the provisions of relevant United Nations human rights instruments, information pertaining to violence against women and measures taken to implement the Declaration on the Elimination of Violence against Women;

(r) Cooperate with and assist the Special Rapporteur of the Commission on Human Rights on violence against women in the performance of her mandate and furnish all information requested; cooperate also with other competent mechanisms, such as the Special Rapporteur of the Commission on Human Rights on torture and the Special Rapporteur of the Commission on Hu-

21/ General Assembly resolution 217 A (III).
22/ General Assembly resolution 39/46, annex.
23/ Official Records of the General Assembly, Forty-seventh Session, Supplement No. 38 (A/47/38), chap. I.

man Rights on summary, extrajudiciary and arbitrary executions, in relation to violence against women;

(s) Recommend that the Commission on Human Rights renew the mandate of the Special Rapporteur on violence against women when her term ends in 1997 and, if warranted, to update and strengthen it.

125. By Governments, including local governments, community organizations, non-governmental organizations, educational institutions, the public and private sectors, particularly enterprises, and the mass media, as appropriate:

(a) Provide well-funded shelters and relief support for girls and women subjected to violence, as well as medical, psychological and other counselling services and free or low-cost legal aid, where it is needed, as well as appropriate assistance to enable them to find a means of subsistence;

(b) Establish linguistically and culturally accessible services for migrant women and girls, including women migrant workers, who are victims of gender-based violence;

(c) Recognize the vulnerability to violence and other forms of abuse of women migrants, including women migrant workers, whose legal status in the host country depends on employers who may exploit their situation;

(d) Support initiatives of women's organizations and non-governmental organizations all over the world to raise awareness on the issue of violence against women and to contribute to its elimination;

(e) Organize, support and fund community-based education and training campaigns to raise awareness about violence against women as a violation of women's enjoyment of their human rights and mobilize local communities to use appropriate gender-sensitive traditional and innovative methods of conflict resolution;

(f) Recognize, support and promote the fundamental role of intermediate institutions, such as primary health-care centres, family-planning centres, existing school health services, mother and baby protection services, centres for migrant families and so forth in the field of information and education related to abuse;

(g) Organize and fund information campaigns and educational and training programmes in order to sensitize girls and boys and women and men to the personal and social detrimental effects of violence in the family, community and society; teach them how to communicate without violence and promote training for victims and potential victims so that they can protect themselves and others against such violence;

(h) Disseminate information on the assistance available to women and families who are victims of violence;

(i) Provide, fund and encourage counselling and rehabilitation programmes for the perpetrators of violence and promote research to further efforts concerning such counselling and rehabilitation so as to prevent the recurrence of such violence;

(j) Raise awareness of the responsibility of the media in promoting non-stereotyped images of women and men, as well as in eliminating patterns of media presentation that generate violence, and encourage those responsible for media content to establish professional guidelines and codes of conduct; also raise awareness of the important role of the media in informing and educating people about the causes and effects of violence against women and in stimulating public debate on the topic.

126. By Governments, employers, trade unions, community and youth organizations and non-governmental organizations, as appropriate:

(a) Develop programmes and procedures to eliminate sexual harassment and other forms of violence against women in all educational institutions, workplaces and elsewhere;

(b) Develop programmes and procedures to educate and raise awareness of acts of violence against women that constitute a crime and a violation of the human rights of women;

(c) Develop counselling, healing and support programmes for girls, adolescents and young women who have been or are involved in abusive relationships, particularly those who live in homes or institutions where abuse occurs;

(d) Take special measures to eliminate violence against women, particularly those in vulnerable situations, such as young women, refugee, displaced and internally displaced women, women with disabilities and women migrant workers, including enforcing any existing legislation and developing, as appropriate, new legislation for women migrant workers in both sending and receiving countries.

127. By the Secretary-General of the United Nations:

Provide the Special Rapporteur of the Commission on Human Rights on violence against women with all necessary assistance, in particular the staff and resources required to perform all mandated functions, especially in carrying out and following up on missions undertaken either separately or jointly with other special rapporteurs and working groups, and adequate assistance for periodic consultations with the Committee on the Elimination of Discrimination against Women and all treaty bodies.

128. By Governments, international organizations and non-governmental organizations:

Encourage the dissemination and implementation of the UNHCR Guidelines on the Protection of Refugee

Women and the UNHCR Guidelines on the Prevention of and Response to Sexual Violence against Refugees.

Strategic objective D.2. Study the causes and consequences of *violence against women and the effectiveness of preventive measures*

Actions to be taken

129. By Governments, regional organizations, the United Nations, other international organizations, research institutions, women's and youth organizations and non-governmental organizations, as appropriate:

(a) Promote research, collect data and compile statistics, especially concerning domestic violence relating to the prevalence of different forms of violence against women, and encourage research into the causes, nature, seriousness and consequences of violence against women and the effectiveness of measures implemented to prevent and redress violence against women;

(b) Disseminate findings of research and studies widely;

(c) Support and initiate research on the impact of violence, such as rape, on women and girl children, and make the resulting information and statistics available to the public;

(d) Encourage the media to examine the impact of gender role stereotypes, including those perpetuated by commercial advertisements which foster gender-based violence and inequalities, and how they are transmitted during the life cycle, and take measures to eliminate these negative images with a view to promoting a violence-free society.

Strategic objective D.3. *Eliminate trafficking in women and assist victims of violence due to prostitution and trafficking*

Actions to be taken

130. By Governments of countries of origin, transit and destination, regional and international organizations, as appropriate:

(a) Consider the ratification and enforcement of international conventions on trafficking in persons and on slavery;

(b) Take appropriate measures to address the root factors, including external factors, that encourage trafficking in women and girls for prostitution and other forms of commercialized sex, forced marriages and forced labour in order to eliminate trafficking in women, including by strengthening existing legislation with a view to providing better protection of the rights of women and girls and to punishing the perpetrators, through both criminal and civil measures;

(c) Step up cooperation and concerted action by all relevant law enforcement authorities and institutions with a view to dismantling national, regional and international networks in trafficking;

(d) Allocate resources to provide comprehensive programmes designed to heal and rehabilitate into society victims of trafficking, including through job training, legal assistance and confidential health care, and take measures to cooperate with non-governmental organizations to provide for the social, medical and psychological care of the victims of trafficking;

(e) Develop educational and training programmes and policies and consider enacting legislation aimed at preventing sex tourism and trafficking, giving special emphasis to the protection of young women and children.

E. *Women and armed conflict*

131. An environment that maintains world peace and promotes and protects human rights, democracy and the peaceful settlement of disputes, in accordance with the principles of non-threat or use of force against territorial integrity or political independence and of respect for sovereignty as set forth in the Charter of the United Nations, is an important factor for the advancement of women. Peace is inextricably linked with equality between women and men and development. Armed and other types of conflicts and terrorism and hostage-taking still persist in many parts of the world. Aggression, foreign occupation, ethnic and other types of conflicts are an ongoing reality affecting women and men in nearly every region. Gross and systematic violations and situations that constitute serious obstacles to the full enjoyment of human rights continue to occur in different parts of the world. Such violations and obstacles include, as well as torture and cruel, inhuman and degrading treatment or punishment, summary and arbitrary executions, disappearances, arbitrary detentions, all forms of racism and racial discrimination, foreign occupation and alien domination, xenophobia, poverty, hunger and other denials of economic, social and cultural rights, religious intolerance, terrorism, discrimination against women and lack of the rule of law. International humanitarian law, prohibiting attacks on civilian populations, as such, is at times systematically ignored and human rights are often violated in connection with situations of armed conflict, affecting the civilian population, especially women, children, the elderly and the disabled. Violations of the human rights of women in situations of armed conflict are violations of the fundamental principles of international human rights and humanitarian law. Massive violations of human rights, especially in the form of genocide, ethnic cleansing as a strategy of war and its consequences, and rape, including systematic rape of women in war situations, creating a mass exodus of

refugees and displaced persons, are abhorrent practices that are strongly condemned and must be stopped immediately, while perpetrators of such crimes must be punished. Some of these situations of armed conflict have their origin in the conquest or colonialization of a country by another State and the perpetuation of that colonization through state and military repression.

132. The Geneva Convention relative to the Protection of Civilian Persons in Time of War, of 1949, and the Additional Protocols of 1977 24/ provide that women shall especially be protected against any attack on their honour, in particular against humiliating and degrading treatment, rape, enforced prostitution or any form of indecent assault. The Vienna Declaration and Programme of Action, adopted by the World Conference on Human Rights, states that "violations of the human rights of women in situations of armed conflict are violations of the fundamental principles of international human rights and humanitarian law". 25/ All violations of this kind, including in particular murder, rape, including systematic rape, sexual slavery and forced pregnancy require a particularly effective response. Gross and systematic violations and situations that constitute serious obstacles to the full enjoyment of human rights continue to occur in different parts of the world. Such violations and obstacles include, as well as torture and cruel, inhuman and degrading treatment or summary and arbitrary detention, all forms of racism, racial discrimination, xenophobia, denial of economic, social and cultural rights and religious intolerance.

133. Violations of human rights in situations of armed conflict and military occupation are violations of the fundamental principles of international human rights and humanitarian law as embodied in international human rights instruments and in the Geneva Conventions of 1949 and the Additional Protocols thereto. Gross human rights violations and policies of ethnic cleansing in war-torn and occupied areas continue to be carried out. These practices have created, *inter alia*, a mass flow of refugees and other displaced persons in need of international protection and internally displaced persons, the majority of whom are women, adolescent girls and children. Civilian victims, mostly women and children, often outnumber casualties among combatants. In addition, women often become caregivers for injured combatants and find themselves, as a result of conflict, unexpectedly cast as sole manager of household, sole parent, and caretaker of elderly relatives.

134. In a world of continuing instability and violence, the implementation of cooperative approaches to peace and security is urgently needed. The equal access and full participation of women in power structures and their full involvement in all efforts for the prevention and resolution of conflicts are essential for the maintenance and promotion of peace and security. Although women have begun to play an important role in conflict resolution, peace-keeping and defence and foreign affairs mechanisms, they are still underrepresented in decision-making positions. If women are to play an equal part in securing and maintaining peace, they must be empowered politically and economically and represented adequately at all levels of decision-making.

135. While entire communities suffer the consequences of armed conflict and terrorism, women and girls are particularly affected because of their status in society and their sex. Parties to conflict often rape women with impunity, sometimes using systematic rape as a tactic of war and terrorism. The impact of violence against women and violation of the human rights of women in such situations is experienced by women of all ages, who suffer displacement, loss of home and property, loss or involuntary disappearance of close relatives, poverty and family separation and disintegration, and who are victims of acts of murder, terrorism, torture, involuntary disappearance, sexual slavery, rape, sexual abuse and forced pregnancy in situations of armed conflict, especially as a result of policies of ethnic cleansing and other new and emerging forms of violence. This is compounded by the life-long social, economic and psychological traumatic consequences of armed conflict and foreign occupation and alien domination.

136. Women and children constitute some 80 per cent of the world's millions of refugees and other displaced persons, including internally displaced persons. They are threatened by deprivation of property, goods and services and deprivation of their right to return to their homes of origin as well as by violence and insecurity. Particular attention should be paid to sexual violence against uprooted women and girls employed as a method of persecution in systematic campaigns of terror and intimidation and forcing members of a particular ethnic, cultural or religious group to flee their homes. Women may also be forced to flee as a result of a well-founded fear of persecution for reasons enumerated in the 1951 Convention relating to the Status of Refugees and the 1967 Protocol, including persecution through sexual violence or other gender-related persecution, and they continue to be vulnerable to violence and exploitation while in flight, in countries of asylum and resettlement and during and after repatriation. Women often experience difficulty in some countries of asylum in being recognized as refugees when the claim is based on such persecution.

137. Refugee, displaced and migrant women in

24/ United Nations, *Treaty Series*, vol. 75, No. 973, p. 287.
25/ *Report of the World Conference on Human Rights* ..., chap. III, sect. II, para. 38.

most cases display strength, endurance and resourcefulness and can contribute positively to countries of resettlement or to their country of origin on their return. They need to be appropriately involved in decisions that affect them.

138. Many women's non-governmental organizations have called for reductions in military expenditures world wide, as well as in international trade and trafficking in and the proliferation of weapons. Those affected most negatively by conflict and excessive military spending are people living in poverty, who are deprived because of the lack of investment in basic services. Women living in poverty, particularly rural women, also suffer because of the use of arms that are particularly injurious or have indiscriminate effects. There are more than 100 million anti-personnel land-mines scattered in 64 countries globally. The negative impact on development of excessive military expenditures, the arms trade, and investment for arms production and acquisition must be addressed. At the same time, maintenance of national security and peace is an important factor for economic growth and development and the empowerment of women.

139. During times of armed conflict and the collapse of communities, the role of women is crucial. They often work to preserve social order in the midst of armed and other conflicts. Women make an important but often unrecognized contribution as peace educators both in their families and in their societies.

140. Education to foster a culture of peace that upholds justice and tolerance for all nations and peoples is essential to attaining lasting peace and should be begun at an early age. It should include elements of conflict resolution, mediation, reduction of prejudice and respect for diversity.

141. In addressing armed or other conflicts, an active and visible policy of mainstreaming a gender perspective into all policies and programmes should be promoted so that before decisions are taken an analysis is made of the effects on women and men, respectively.

Strategic objective E.1. *Increase the participation of women in conflict resolution at decision-making levels and protect women living in situations of armed and other conflicts or under foreign occupation*

Actions to be taken

142. By Governments and international and regional intergovernmental institutions:

(a) Take action to promote equal participation of women and equal opportunities for women to participate in all forums and peace activities at all levels, particularly at the decision-making level, including in the United Nations Secretariat with due regard to equitable geographical distribution in accordance with Article 101 of the Charter of the United Nations;

(b) Integrate a gender perspective in the resolution of armed or other conflicts and foreign occupation and aim for gender balance when nominating or promoting candidates for judicial and other positions in all relevant international bodies, such as the United Nations International Tribunals for the former Yugoslavia and for Rwanda and the International Court of Justice, as well as in other bodies related to the peaceful settlement of disputes;

(c) Ensure that these bodies are able to address gender issues properly by providing appropriate training to prosecutors, judges and other officials in handling cases involving rape, forced pregnancy in situations of armed conflict, indecent assault and other forms of violence against women in armed conflicts, including terrorism, and integrate a gender perspective into their work.

Strategic objective E.2. *Reduce excessive military expenditures and control the availability of armaments*

Actions to be taken

143. By Governments:

(a) Increase and hasten, as appropriate, subject to national security considerations, the conversion of military resources and related industries to development and peaceful purposes;

(b) Undertake to explore new ways of generating new public and private financial resources, *inter alia*, through the appropriate reduction of excessive military expenditures, including global military expenditures, trade in arms and investment for arms production and acquisition, taking into consideration national security requirements, so as to permit the possible allocation of additional funds for social and economic development, in particular for the advancement of women;

(c) Take action to investigate and punish members of the police, security and armed forces and others who perpetrate acts of violence against women, violations of international humanitarian law and violations of the human rights of women in situations of armed conflict;

(d) While acknowledging legitimate national defence needs, recognize and address the dangers to society of armed conflict and the negative effect of excessive military expenditures, trade in arms, especially those arms that are particularly injurious or have indiscriminate effects, and excessive investment for arms production and acquisition; similarly, recognize the need to combat illicit arms trafficking, violence, crime, the production and use of and trafficking in illicit drugs, and trafficking in women and children;

(e) Recognizing that women and children are particularly affected by the indiscriminate use of anti-personnel land-mines:

(i) Undertake to work actively towards ratification, if they have not already done so, of the 1981 Convention on Prohibitions or Restrictions on the Use of Certain Conventional Weapons Which May Be Deemed to Be Excessively Injurious or to Have Indiscriminate Effects, particularly the Protocol on Prohibitions or Restrictions on the Use of Mines, Booby Traps and Other Devices (Protocol II), 26/ with a view to universal ratification by the year 2000;

(ii) Undertake to strongly consider strengthening the Convention to promote a reduction in the casualties and intense suffering caused to the civilian population by the indiscriminate use of land-mines;

(iii) Undertake to promote assistance in mine clearance, notably by facilitating, in respect of the means of mine-clearing, the exchange of information, the transfer of technology and the promotion of scientific research;

(iv) Within the United Nations context, undertake to support efforts to coordinate a common response programme of assistance in de-mining without unnecessary discrimination;

(v) Adopt at the earliest possible date, if they have not already done so, a moratorium on the export of anti-personnel land-mines, including to non-governmental entities, noting with satisfaction that many States have already declared moratoriums on the export, transfer or sale of such mines;

(vi) Undertake to encourage further international efforts to seek solutions to the problems caused by antipersonnel land-mines, with a view to their eventual elimination, recognizing that States can move most effectively towards this goal as viable and humane alternatives are developed;

(f) Recognizing the leading role that women have played in the peace movement:

(i) Work actively towards general and complete disarmament under strict and effective international control;

(ii) Support negotiations on the conclusion, without delay, of a universal and multilaterally and effectively verifiable comprehensive nuclear-test-ban treaty that contributes to nuclear disarmament and the prevention of the proliferation of nuclear weapons in all its aspects;

(iii) Pending the entry into force of a comprehensive nuclear-test-ban treaty, exercise the utmost restraint in respect of nuclear testing.

Strategic objective E.3. *Promote non-violent forms of conflict resolution and reduce the incidence of human rights abuse in conflict situations*

Actions to be taken

144. By Governments:

(a) Consider the ratification of or accession to international instruments containing provisions relative to the protection of women and children in armed conflicts, including the Geneva Convention relative to the Protection of Civilian Persons in Time of War, of 1949, the Protocols Additional to the Geneva Conventions of 1949 relating to the Protection of Victims of International Armed Conflicts (Protocol I) and to the Protection of Victims of Non-International Armed Conflicts (Protocol II); 24/

(b) Respect fully the norms of international humanitarian law in armed conflicts and take all measures required for the protection of women and children, in particular against rape, forced prostitution and any other form of indecent assault;

(c) Strengthen the role of women and ensure equal representation of women at all decision-making levels in national and international institutions which may make or influence policy with regard to matters related to peace-keeping, preventive diplomacy and related activities and in all stages of peace mediation and negotiations, taking note of the specific recommendations of the Secretary-General in his strategic plan of action for the improvement of the status of women in the Secretariat (1995-2000) (A/49/587, sect. IV).

145. By Governments and international and regional organizations:

(a) Reaffirm the right of self-determination of all peoples, in particular of peoples under colonial or other forms of alien domination or foreign occupation, and the importance of the effective realization of this right, as enunciated, *inter alia*, in the Vienna Declaration and Programme of Action, 2/ adopted by the World Conference on Human Rights;

(b) Encourage diplomacy, negotiation and peaceful settlement of disputes in accordance with the Charter of the United Nations, in particular Article 2, paragraphs 3 and 4 thereof;

(c) Urge the identification and condemnation of the systematic practice of rape and other forms of inhuman and degrading treatment of women as a deliberate instrument of war and ethnic cleansing and take steps to

26/ See *The United Nations Disarmament Yearbook*, vol. 5: 1980 (United Nations publication, Sales No. E.81.IX.4), appendix VII.

ensure that full assistance is provided to the victims of such abuse for their physical and mental rehabilitation;

(d) Reaffirm that rape in the conduct of armed conflict constitutes a war crime and under certain circumstances it constitutes a crime against humanity and an act of genocide as defined in the Convention on the Prevention and Punishment of the Crime of Genocide; 27/ take all measures required for the protection of women and children from such acts and strengthen mechanisms to investigate and punish all those responsible and bring the perpetrators to justice;

(e) Uphold and reinforce standards set out in international humanitarian law and international human rights instruments to prevent all acts of violence against women in situations of armed and other conflicts; undertake a full investigation of all acts of violence against women committed during war, including rape, in particular systematic rape, forced prostitution and other forms of indecent assault and sexual slavery; prosecute all criminals responsible for war crimes against women and provide full redress to women victims;

(f) Call upon the international community to condemn and act against all forms and manifestations of terrorism;

(g) Take into account gender-sensitive concerns in developing training programmes for all relevant personnel on international humanitarian law and human rights awareness and recommend such training for those involved in United Nations peace-keeping and humanitarian aid, with a view to preventing violence against women, in particular;

(h) Discourage the adoption of and refrain from any unilateral measure not in accordance with international law and the Charter of the United Nations, that impedes the full achievement of economic and social development by the population of the affected countries, in particular women and children, that hinders their well-being and that creates obstacles to the full enjoyment of their human rights, including the right of everyone to a standard of living adequate for their health and well-being and their right to food, medical care and the necessary social services. This Conference reaffirms that food and medicine must not be used as a tool for political pressure;

(i) Take measures in accordance with international law with a view to alleviating the negative impact of economic sanctions on women and children.

Strategic objective E.4. *Promote women's contribution to fostering a culture of peace*

Actions to be taken

146. By Governments, international and regional intergovernmental institutions and non-governmental organizations:

(a) Promote peaceful conflict resolution and peace, reconciliation and tolerance through education, training, community actions and youth exchange programmes, in particular for young women;

(b) Encourage the further development of peace research, involving the participation of women, to examine the impact of armed conflict on women and children and the nature and contribution of women's participation in national, regional and international peace movements; engage in research and identify innovative mechanisms for containing violence and for conflict resolution for public dissemination and for use by women and men;

(c) Develop and disseminate research on the physical, psychological, economic and social effects of armed conflicts on women, particularly young women and girls, with a view to developing policies and programmes to address the consequences of conflicts;

(d) Consider establishing educational programmes for girls and boys to foster a culture of peace, focusing on conflict resolution by non-violent means and the promotion of tolerance.

Strategic objective E.5. *Provide protection, assistance and training to refugee women, other displaced women in need of international protection and internally displaced women*

Actions to be taken

147. By Governments, intergovernmental and non-governmental organizations and other institutions involved in providing protection, assistance and training to refugee women, other displaced women in need of international protection and internally displaced women, including the Office of the United Nations High Commissioner for Refugees and the World Food Programme, as appropriate:

(a) Take steps to ensure that women are fully involved in the planning, design, implementation, monitoring and evaluation of all short-term and long-term projects and programmes providing assistance to refugee women, other displaced women in need of international protection and internally displaced women, including the management of refugee camps and resources; ensure that refugee and displaced women and girls have direct access to the services provided;

(b) Offer adequate protection and assistance to women and children displaced within their country and find solutions to the root causes of their displacement with a view to preventing it and, when appropriate, facilitate their return or resettlement;

27/ General Assembly resolution 260 A (III), annex.

(c) Take steps to protect the safety and physical integrity of refugee women, other displaced women in need of international protection and internally displaced women during their displacement and upon their return to their communities of origin, including programmes of rehabilitation; take effective measures to protect from violence women who are refugees or displaced; hold an impartial and thorough investigation of any such violations and bring those responsible to justice;

(d) While fully respecting and strictly observing the principle of non-refoulement of refugees, take all the necessary steps to ensure the right of refugee and displaced women to return voluntarily to their place of origin in safety and with dignity, and their right to protection after their return;

(e) Take measures, at the national level with international cooperation, as appropriate, in accordance with the Charter of the United Nations, to find lasting solutions to questions related to internally displaced women, including their right to voluntary and safe return to their home of origin;

(f) Ensure that the international community and its international organizations provide financial and other resources for emergency relief and other longer-term assistance that takes into account the specific needs, resources and potentials of refugee women, other displaced women in need of international protection and internally displaced women; in the provision of protection and assistance, take all appropriate measures to eliminate discrimination against women and girls in order to ensure equal access to appropriate and adequate food, water and shelter, education, and social and health services, including reproductive health care and maternity care and services to combat tropical diseases;

(g) Facilitate the availability of educational materials in the appropriate language — in emergency situations also — in order to minimize disruption of schooling among refugee and displaced children;

(h) Apply international norms to ensure equal access and equal treatment of women and men in refugee determination procedures and the granting of asylum, including full respect and strict observation of the principle of non-refoulement through, *inter alia*, bringing national immigration regulations into conformity with relevant international instruments, and consider recognizing as refugees those women whose claim to refugee status is based upon the well-founded fear of persecution for reasons enumerated in the 1951 Convention 28/ and the 1967 Protocol 29/ relating to the Status of Refugees, including persecution through sexual violence or other gender-related persecution, and provide access to specially trained officers, including female officers, to interview women regarding sensitive or painful experiences, such as sexual assault;

(i) Support and promote efforts by States towards the development of criteria and guidelines on responses to persecution specifically aimed at women, by sharing information on States' initiatives to develop such criteria and guidelines and by monitoring to ensure their fair and consistent application;

(j) Promote the self-reliant capacities of refugee women, other displaced women in need of international protection and internally displaced women and provide programmes for women, particularly young women, in leadership and decision-making within refugee and returnee communities;

(k) Ensure that the human rights of refugee and displaced women are protected and that refugee and displaced women are made aware of these rights; ensure that the vital importance of family reunification is recognized;

(l) Provide, as appropriate, women who have been determined refugees with access to vocational/professional training programmes, including language training, small-scale enterprise development training and planning and counselling on all forms of violence against women, which should include rehabilitation programmes for victims of torture and trauma; Governments and other donors should contribute adequately to assistance programmes for refugee women, other displaced women in need of international protection and internally displaced women, taking into account in particular the effects on the host countries of the increasing requirements of large refugee populations and the need to widen the donor base and to achieve greater burden-sharing;

(m) Raise public awareness of the contribution made by refugee women to their countries of resettlement, promote understanding of their human rights and of their needs and abilities and encourage mutual understanding and acceptance through educational programmes promoting cross-cultural and interracial harmony;

(n) Provide basic and support services to women who are displaced from their place of origin as a result of terrorism, violence, drug trafficking or other reasons linked to violence situations;

(o) Develop awareness of the human rights of women and provide, as appropriate, human rights education and training to military and police personnel operating in areas of armed conflict and areas where there are refugees.

148. By Governments:

(a) Disseminate and implement the UNHCR

28/ United Nations, *Treaty Series*, vol. 189, No. 2545.
29/ Ibid., vol. 606, No. 8791.

Guidelines on the Protection of Refugee Women and the UNHCR Guidelines on Evaluation and Care of Victims of Trauma and Violence, or provide similar guidance, in close cooperation with refugee women and in all sectors of refugee programmes;

(b) Protect women and children who migrate as family members from abuse or denial of their human rights by sponsors and consider extending their stay, should the family relationship dissolve, within the limits of national legislation.

Strategic objective E.6. *Provide assistance to the women of the colonies and non-self-governing territories*

Actions to be taken

149. By Governments and intergovernmental and non-governmental organizations:

(a) Support and promote the implementation of the right of self-determination of all peoples as enunciated, *inter alia*, in the Vienna Declaration and Programme of Action by providing special programmes in leadership and in training for decision-making;

(b) Raise public awareness, as appropriate, through the mass media, education at all levels and special programmes to create a better understanding of the situation of women of the colonies and non-self-governing territories.

F. *Women and the economy*

150. There are considerable differences in women's and men's access to and opportunities to exert power over economic structures in their societies. In most parts of the world, women are virtually absent from or are poorly represented in economic decision-making, including the formulation of financial, monetary, commercial and other economic policies, as well as tax systems and rules governing pay. Since it is often within the framework of such policies that individual men and women make their decisions, *inter alia*, on how to divide their time between remunerated and unremunerated work, the actual development of these economic structures and policies has a direct impact on women's and men's access to economic resources, their economic power and consequently the extent of equality between them at the individual and family levels as well as in society as a whole.

151. In many regions, women's participation in remunerated work in the formal and non-formal labour market has increased significantly and has changed during the past decade. While women continue to work in agriculture and fisheries, they have also become increasingly involved in micro, small and medium-sized enterprises and, in some cases, have become more dominant in the expanding informal sector. Due to, *inter alia*, difficult economic situations and a lack of bargaining power resulting from gender inequality, many women have been forced to accept low pay and poor working conditions and thus have often become preferred workers. On the other hand, women have entered the workforce increasingly by choice when they have become aware of and demanded their rights. Some have succeeded in entering and advancing in the workplace and improving their pay and working conditions. However, women have been particularly affected by the economic situation and restructuring processes, which have changed the nature of employment and, in some cases, have led to a loss of jobs, even for professional and skilled women. In addition, many women have entered the informal sector owing to the lack of other opportunities. Women's participation and gender concerns are still largely absent from and should be integrated in the policy formulation process of the multilateral institutions that define the terms and, in cooperation with Governments, set the goals of structural adjustment programmes, loans and grants.

152. Discrimination in education and training, hiring and remuneration, promotion and horizontal mobility practices, as well as inflexible working conditions, lack of access to productive resources and inadequate sharing of family responsibilities, combined with a lack of or insufficient services such as child care, continue to restrict employment, economic, professional and other opportunities and mobility for women and make their involvement stressful. Moreover, attitudinal obstacles inhibit women's participation in developing economic policy and in some regions restrict the access of women and girls to education and training for economic management.

153. Women's share in the labour force continues to rise and almost everywhere women are working more outside the household, although there has not been a parallel lightening of responsibility for unremunerated work in the household and community. Women's income is becoming increasingly necessary to households of all types. In some regions, there has been a growth in women's entrepreneurship and other self-reliant activities, particularly in the informal sector. In many countries, women are the majority of workers in non-standard work, such as temporary, casual, multiple part-time, contract and home-based employment.

154. Women migrant workers, including domestic workers, contribute to the economy of the sending country through their remittances and also to the economy of the receiving country through their participation in the labour force. However, in many receiving countries, migrant women experience higher levels of unemployment compared with both non-migrant workers and male migrant workers.

155. Insufficient attention to gender analysis has meant that women's contributions and concerns remain too often ignored in economic structures, such as financial markets and institutions, labour markets, economics as an academic discipline, economic and social infrastructure, taxation and social security systems, as well as in families and households. As a result, many policies and programmes may continue to contribute to inequalities between women and men. Where progress has been made in integrating gender perspectives, programme and policy effectiveness has also been enhanced.

156. Although many women have advanced in economic structures, for the majority of women, particularly those who face additional barriers, continuing obstacles have hindered their ability to achieve economic autonomy and to ensure sustainable livelihoods for themselves and their dependants. Women are active in a variety of economic areas, which they often combine, ranging from wage labour and subsistence farming and fishing to the informal sector. However, legal and customary barriers to ownership of or access to land, natural resources, capital, credit, technology and other means of production, as well as wage differentials, contribute to impeding the economic progress of women. Women contribute to development not only through remunerated work but also through a great deal of unremunerated work. On the one hand, women participate in the production of goods and services for the market and household consumption, in agriculture, food production or family enterprises. Though included in the United Nations System of National Accounts and therefore in international standards for labour statistics, this unremunerated work — particularly that related to agriculture — is often undervalued and under-recorded. On the other hand, women still also perform the great majority of unremunerated domestic work and community work, such as caring for children and older persons, preparing food for the family, protecting the environment and providing voluntary assistance to vulnerable and disadvantaged individuals and groups. This work is often not measured in quantitative terms and is not valued in national accounts. Women's contribution to development is seriously underestimated, and thus its social recognition is limited. The full visibility of the type, extent and distribution of this unremunerated work will also contribute to a better sharing of responsibilities.

157. Although some new employment opportunities have been created for women as a result of the globalization of the economy, there are also trends that have exacerbated inequalities between women and men. At the same time, globalization, including economic integration, can create pressures on the employment situation of women to adjust to new circumstances and to find new sources of employment as patterns of trade change. More analysis needs to be done of the impact of globalization on women's economic status.

158. These trends have been characterized by low wages, little or no labour standards protection, poor working conditions, particularly with regard to women's occupational health and safety, low skill levels, and a lack of job security and social security, in both the formal and informal sectors. Women's unemployment is a serious and increasing problem in many countries and sectors. Young workers in the informal and rural sectors and migrant female workers remain the least protected by labour and immigration laws. Women, particularly those who are heads of households with young children, are limited in their employment opportunities for reasons that include inflexible working conditions and inadequate sharing, by men and by society, of family responsibilities.

159. In countries that are undergoing fundamental political, economic and social transformation, the skills of women, if better utilized, could constitute a major contribution to the economic life of their respective countries. Their input should continue to be developed and supported and their potential further realized.

160. Lack of employment in the private sector and reductions in public services and public service jobs have affected women disproportionately. In some countries, women take on more unpaid work, such as the care of children and those who are ill or elderly, compensating for lost household income, particularly when public services are not available. In many cases, employment creation strategies have not paid sufficient attention to occupations and sectors where women predominate; nor have they adequately promoted the access of women to those occupations and sectors that are traditionally male.

161. For those women in paid work, many experience obstacles that prevent them from achieving their potential. While some are increasingly found in lower levels of management, attitudinal discrimination often prevents them from being promoted further. The experience of sexual harassment is an affront to a worker's dignity and prevents women from making a contribution commensurate with their abilities. The lack of a family-friendly work environment, including a lack of appropriate and affordable child care, and inflexible working hours further prevent women from achieving their full potential.

162. In the private sector, including transnational and national enterprises, women are largely absent from management and policy levels, denoting discriminatory hiring and promotion policies and practices. The unfavourable work environment as well as the limited number of employment opportunities available have led many

women to seek alternatives. Women have increasingly become self-employed and owners and managers of micro, small and medium-scale enterprises. The expansion of the informal sector, in many countries, and of self-organized and independent enterprises is in large part due to women, whose collaborative, self-help and traditional practices and initiatives in production and trade represent a vital economic resource. When they gain access to and control over capital, credit and other resources, technology and training, women can increase production, marketing and income for sustainable development.

163. Taking into account the fact that continuing inequalities and noticeable progress coexist, rethinking employment policies is necessary in order to integrate the gender perspective and to draw attention to a wider range of opportunities as well as to address any negative gender implications of current patterns of work and employment. To realize fully equality between women and men in their contribution to the economy, active efforts are required for equal recognition and appreciation of the influence that the work, experience, knowledge and values of both women and men have in society.

164. In addressing the economic potential and independence of women, Governments and other actors should promote an active and visible policy of mainstreaming a gender perspective in all policies and programmes so that before decisions are taken, an analysis is made of the effects on women and men, respectively.

Strategic objective F.1. *Promote women's economic rights and independence, including access to employment, appropriate working conditions and control over economic resources*

Actions to be taken

165. By Governments:

(a) Enact and enforce legislation to guarantee the rights of women and men to equal pay for equal work or work of equal value;

(b) Adopt and implement laws against discrimination based on sex in the labour market, especially considering older women workers, hiring and promotion, the extension of employment benefits and social security, and working conditions;

(c) Eliminate discriminatory practices by employers and take appropriate measures in consideration of women's reproductive role and functions, such as the denial of employment and dismissal due to pregnancy or breast-feeding, or requiring proof of contraceptive use, and take effective measures to ensure that pregnant women, women on maternity leave or women re-entering the labour market after childbearing are not discriminated against;

(d) Devise mechanisms and take positive action to enable women to gain access to full and equal participation in the formulation of policies and definition of structures through such bodies as ministries of finance and trade, national economic commissions, economic research institutes and other key agencies, as well as through their participation in appropriate international bodies;

(e) Undertake legislation and administrative reforms to give women equal rights with men to economic resources, including access to ownership and control over land and other forms of property, credit, inheritance, natural resources and appropriate new technology;

(f) Conduct reviews of national income and inheritance tax and social security systems to eliminate any existing bias against women;

(g) Seek to develop a more comprehensive knowledge of work and employment through, *inter alia*, efforts to measure and better understand the type, extent and distribution of unremunerated work, particularly work in caring for dependants and unremunerated work done for family farms or businesses, and encourage the sharing and dissemination of information on studies and experience in this field, including the development of methods for assessing its value in quantitative terms, for possible reflection in accounts that may be produced separately from, but consistent with, core national accounts;

(h) Review and amend laws governing the operation of financial institutions to ensure that they provide services to women and men on an equal basis;

(i) Facilitate, at appropriate levels, more open and transparent budget processes;

(j) Revise and implement national policies that support the traditional savings, credit and lending mechanisms for women;

(k) Seek to ensure that national policies related to international and regional trade agreements do not have an adverse impact on women's new and traditional economic activities;

(l) Ensure that all corporations, including transnational corporations, comply with national laws and codes, social security regulations, applicable international agreements, instruments and conventions, including those related to the environment, and other relevant laws;

(m) Adjust employment policies to facilitate the restructuring of work patterns in order to promote the sharing of family responsibilities;

(n) Establish mechanisms and other forums to enable women entrepreneurs and women workers to contribute to the formulation of policies and programmes being developed by economic ministries and financial institutions;

(o) Enact and enforce equal opportunity laws, take positive action and ensure compliance by the public and private sectors through various means;

(p) Use gender-impact analyses in the development of macro and micro-economic and social policies in order to monitor such impact and restructure policies in cases where harmful impact occurs;

(q) Promote gender-sensitive policies and measures to empower women as equal partners with men in technical, managerial and entrepreneurial fields;

(r) Reform laws or enact national policies that support the establishment of labour laws to ensure the protection of all women workers, including safe work practices, the right to organize and access to justice.

Strategic objective F.2. *Facilitate women's equal access to resources, employment, markets and trade*

Actions to be taken

166. By Governments:

(a) Promote and support women's self-employment and the development of small enterprises, and strengthen women's access to credit and capital on appropriate terms equal to those of men through the scaling-up of institutions dedicated to promoting women's entrepreneurship, including, as appropriate, non-traditional and mutual credit schemes, as well as innovative linkages with financial institutions;

(b) Strengthen the incentive role of the State as employer to develop a policy of equal opportunities for women and men;

(c) Enhance, at the national and local levels, rural women's income-generating potential by facilitating their equal access to and control over productive resources, land, credit, capital, property rights, development programmes and cooperative structures;

(d) Promote and strengthen micro-enterprises, new small businesses, cooperative enterprises, expanded markets and other employment opportunities and, where appropriate, facilitate the transition from the informal to the formal sector, especially in rural areas;

(e) Create and modify programmes and policies that recognize and strengthen women's vital role in food security and provide paid and unpaid women producers, especially those involved in food production, such as farming, fishing and aquaculture, as well as urban enterprises, with equal access to appropriate technologies, transportation, extension services, marketing and credit facilities at the local and community levels;

(f) Establish appropriate mechanisms and encourage intersectoral institutions that enable women's cooperatives to optimize access to necessary services;

(g) Increase the proportion of women extension workers and other government personnel who provide technical assistance or administer economic programmes;

(h) Review, reformulate, if necessary, and implement policies, including business, commercial and contract law and government regulations, to ensure that they do not discriminate against micro, small and medium-scale enterprises owned by women in rural and urban areas;

(i) Analyse, advise on, coordinate and implement policies that integrate the needs and interests of employed, self-employed and entrepreneurial women into sectoral and inter-ministerial policies, programmes and budgets;

(j) Ensure equal access for women to effective job training, retraining, counselling and placement services that are not limited to traditional employment areas;

(k) Remove policy and regulatory obstacles faced by women in social and development programmes that discourage private and individual initiative;

(l) Safeguard and promote respect for basic workers' rights, including the prohibition of forced labour and child labour, freedom of association and the right to organize and bargain collectively, equal remuneration for men and women for work of equal value and non-discrimination in employment, fully implementing the conventions of the International Labour Organization in the case of States Parties to those conventions and, taking into account the principles embodied in the case of those countries that are not parties to those conventions in order to achieve truly sustained economic growth and sustainable development.

167. By Governments, central banks and national development banks, and private banking institutions, as appropriate:

(a) Increase the participation of women, including women entrepreneurs, in advisory boards and other forums to enable women entrepreneurs from all sectors and their organizations to contribute to the formulation and review of policies and programmes being developed by economic ministries and banking institutions;

(b) Mobilize the banking sector to increase lending and refinancing through incentives and the development of intermediaries that serve the needs of women entrepreneurs and producers in both rural and urban areas, and include women in their leadership, planning and decision-making;

(c) Structure services to reach rural and urban women involved in micro, small and medium-scale enterprises, with special attention to young women, low-income women, those belonging to ethnic and racial minorities, and indigenous women who lack access to capital and assets; and expand women's access to financial markets by identifying and encouraging financial supervisory and regulatory reforms that support financial institutions' direct and indirect efforts to better meet the credit and other financial needs of the micro, small and medium-scale enterprises of women;

(d) Ensure that women's priorities are included in public investment programmes for economic infrastructure, such as water and sanitation, electrification and energy conservation, transport and road construction; promote greater involvement of women beneficiaries at the project planning and implementation stages to ensure access to jobs and contracts.

168. By Governments and non-governmental organizations:

(a) Pay special attention to women's needs when disseminating market, trade and resource information and provide appropriate training in these fields;

(b) Encourage community economic development strategies that build on partnerships among Governments, and encourage members of civil society to create jobs and address the social circumstances of individuals, families and communities.

169. By multilateral funders and regional development banks, as well as bilateral and private funding agencies, at the international, regional and subregional levels:

(a) Review, where necessary reformulate, and implement policies, programmes and projects, to ensure that a higher proportion of resources reach women in rural and remote areas;

(b) Develop flexible funding arrangements to finance intermediary institutions that target women's economic activities, and promote self-sufficiency and increased capacity in and profitability of women's economic enterprises;

(c) Develop strategies to consolidate and strengthen their assistance to the micro, small and medium-scale enterprise sector, in order to enhance the opportunities for women to participate fully and equally and work together to coordinate and enhance the effectiveness of this sector, drawing upon expertise and financial resources from within their own organizations as well as from bilateral agencies, Governments and non-governmental organizations.

170. By international, multilateral and bilateral development cooperation organizations:

Support, through the provision of capital and/or resources, financial institutions that serve low-income, small and micro-scale women entrepreneurs and producers in both the formal and informal sectors.

171. By Governments and/or multilateral financial institutions:

Review rules and procedures of formal national and international financial institutions that obstruct replication of the Grameen Bank prototype, which provides credit facilities to rural women.

172. By international organizations:

Provide adequate support for programmes and projects designed to promote sustainable and productive entrepreneurial activities among women, in particular the disadvantaged.

Strategic objective F.3. *Provide business services, training and access to markets, information and technology, particularly to low-income women*

Actions to be taken

173. By Governments in cooperation with non-governmental organizations and the private sector:

(a) Provide public infrastructure to ensure equal market access for women and men entrepreneurs;

(b) Develop programmes that provide training and retraining, particularly in new technologies, and affordable services to women in business management, product development, financing, production and quality control, marketing and the legal aspects of business;

(c) Provide outreach programmes to inform low-income and poor women, particularly in rural and remote areas, of opportunities for market and technology access, and provide assistance in taking advantage of such opportunities;

(d) Create non-discriminatory support services, including investment funds for women's businesses, and target women, particularly low-income women, in trade promotion programmes;

(e) Disseminate information about successful women entrepreneurs in both traditional and non-traditional economic activities and the skills necessary to achieve success, and facilitate networking and the exchange of information;

(f) Take measures to ensure equal access of women to ongoing training in the workplace, including unemployed women, single parents, women re-entering the labour market after an extended temporary exit from employment owing to family responsibilities and other causes, and women displaced by new forms of production or by retrenchment, and increase incentives to enterprises to expand the number of vocational and training centres that provide training for women in non-traditional areas;

(g) Provide affordable support services, such as high-quality, flexible and affordable child-care services, that take into account the needs of working men and women.

174. By local, national, regional and international business organizations and non-governmental organizations concerned with women's issues:

Advocate, at all levels, for the promotion and support of women's businesses and enterprises, including those in the informal sector, and the equal access of women to productive resources.

Strategic objective F.4. *Strengthen women's economic capacity and commercial networks*

Actions to be taken

175. By Governments:

(a) Adopt policies that support business organizations, non-governmental organizations, cooperatives, revolving loan funds, credit unions, grass-roots organizations, women's self-help groups and other groups in order to provide services to women entrepreneurs in rural and urban areas;

(b) Integrate a gender perspective into all economic restructuring and structural adjustment policies and design programmes for women who are affected by economic restructuring, including structural adjustment programmes, and for women who work in the informal sector;

(c) Adopt policies that create an enabling environment for women's self-help groups, workers' organizations and cooperatives through non-conventional forms of support and by recognizing the right to freedom of association and the right to organize;

(d) Support programmes that enhance the self-reliance of special groups of women, such as young women, women with disabilities, elderly women and women belonging to racial and ethnic minorities;

(e) Promote gender equality through the promotion of women's studies and through the use of the results of studies and gender research in all fields, including the economic, scientific and technological fields;

(f) Support the economic activities of indigenous women, taking into account their traditional knowledge, so as to improve their situation and development;

(g) Adopt policies to extend or maintain the protection of labour laws and social security provisions for those who do paid work in the home;

(h) Recognize and encourage the contribution of research by women scientists and technologists;

(i) Ensure that policies and regulations do not discriminate against micro, small and medium-scale enterprises run by women.

176. By financial intermediaries, national training institutes, credit unions, non-governmental organizations, women's associations, professional organizations and the private sector, as appropriate:

(a) Provide, at the national, regional and international levels, training in a variety of business-related and financial management and technical skills to enable women, especially young women, to participate in economic policy-making at those levels;

(b) Provide business services, including marketing and trade information, product design and innovation, technology transfer and quality, to women's business enterprises, including those in export sectors of the economy;

(c) Promote technical and commercial links and establish joint ventures among women entrepreneurs at the national, regional and international levels to support community-based initiatives;

(d) Strengthen the participation of women, including marginalized women, in production and marketing cooperatives by providing marketing and financial support, especially in rural and remote areas;

(e) Promote and strengthen women's micro-enterprises, new small businesses, cooperative enterprises, expanded markets and other employment opportunities and, where appropriate, facilitate the transition from the informal to the formal sector, in rural and urban areas;

(f) Invest capital and develop investment portfolios to finance women's business enterprises;

(g) Give adequate attention to providing technical assistance, advisory services, training and retraining for women connected with the entry to the market economy;

(h) Support credit networks and innovative ventures, including traditional savings schemes;

(i) Provide networking arrangements for entrepreneurial women, including opportunities for the mentoring of inexperienced women by the more experienced;

(j) Encourage community organizations and public authorities to establish loan pools for women entrepreneurs, drawing on successful small-scale cooperative models.

177. By the private sector, including transnational and national corporations:

(a) Adopt policies and establish mechanisms to grant contracts on a non-discriminatory basis;

(b) Recruit women for leadership, decision-making and management and provide training programmes, all on an equal basis with men;

(c) Observe national labour, environment, consumer, health and safety laws, particularly those that affect women.

Strategic objective F.5. *Eliminate occupational segregation and all forms of employment discrimination*

Actions to be taken

178. By Governments, employers, employees, trade unions and women's organizations:

(a) Implement and enforce laws and regulations and encourage voluntary codes of conduct that ensure that international labour standards, such as International Labour Organization Convention No. 100 on equal pay and workers' rights, apply equally to female and male workers;

(b) Enact and enforce laws and introduce implementing measures, including means of redress and access to justice in cases of non-compliance, to prohibit direct and indirect discrimination on grounds of sex, including by reference to marital or family status, in relation to access to employment, conditions of employment, including training, promotion, health and safety, as well as termination of employment and social security of workers, including legal protection against sexual and racial harassment;

(c) Enact and enforce laws and develop workplace policies against gender discrimination in the labour market, especially considering older women workers, in hiring and promotion, and in the extension of employment benefits and social security, as well as regarding discriminatory working conditions and sexual harassment; mechanisms should be developed for the regular review and monitoring of such laws;

(d) Eliminate discriminatory practices by employers on the basis of women's reproductive roles and functions, including refusal of employment and dismissal of women due to pregnancy and breast-feeding responsibilities;

(e) Develop and promote employment programmes and services for women entering and/or re-entering the labour market, especially poor urban, rural and young women, the self-employed and those negatively affected by structural adjustment;

(f) Implement and monitor positive public- and private-sector employment, equity and positive action programmes to address systemic discrimination against women in the labour force, in particular women with disabilities and women belonging to other disadvantaged groups, with respect to hiring, retention and promotion, and vocational training of women in all sectors;

(g) Eliminate occupational segregation, especially by promoting the equal participation of women in highly skilled jobs and senior management positions, and through other measures, such as counselling and placement, that stimulate their on-the-job career development and upward mobility in the labour market, and by stimulating the diversification of occupational choices by both women and men; encourage women to take up non-traditional jobs, especially in science and technology, and encourage men to seek employment in the social sector;

(h) Recognize collective bargaining as a right and as an important mechanism for eliminating wage inequality for women and to improve working conditions;

(i) Promote the election of women trade union officials and ensure that trade union officials elected to represent women are given job protection and physical security in connection with the discharge of their functions;

(j) Ensure access to and develop special programmes to enable women with disabilities to obtain and retain employment, and ensure access to education and training at all proper levels, in accordance with the Standard Rules on the Equalization of Opportunities for Persons with Disabilities; 30/ adjust working conditions, to the extent possible, in order to suit the needs of women with disabilities, who should be assured legal protection against unfounded job loss on account of their disabilities;

(k) Increase efforts to close the gap between women's and men's pay, take steps to implement the principle of equal remuneration for equal work of equal value by strengthening legislation, including compliance with international labour laws and standards, and encourage job evaluation schemes with gender-neutral criteria;

(l) Establish and/or strengthen mechanisms to adjudicate matters relating to wage discrimination;

(m) Set specific target dates for eliminating all forms of child labour that are contrary to accepted international standards and ensure the full enforcement of relevant existing laws and, where appropriate, enact the legislation necessary to implement the Convention on the Rights of the Child and International Labour Organization standards, ensuring the protection of working children, in particular, street children, through the provision of appropriate health, education and other social services;

(n) Ensure that strategies to eliminate child labour also address the excessive demands made on some girls for unpaid work in their household and other households, where applicable;

(o) Review, analyse and, where appropriate, reformulate the wage structures in female-dominated professions, such as teaching, nursing and child care, with a view to raising their low status and earnings;

(p) Facilitate the productive employment of documented migrant women (including women who have been determined refugees according to the 1951 Convention relating to the Status of Refugees) through greater recognition of foreign education and credentials and by adopting an integrated approach to labour market training that incorporates language training.

30/ General Assembly resolution 48/96, annex.

Strategic objective F.6. *Promote harmonization of work and family responsibilities for women and men*

Actions to be taken

179. By Governments:

(a) Adopt policies to ensure the appropriate protection of labour laws and social security benefits for part-time, temporary, seasonal and home-based workers; promote career development based on work conditions that harmonize work and family responsibilities;

(b) Ensure that full and part-time work can be freely chosen by women and men on an equal basis, and consider appropriate protection for atypical workers in terms of access to employment, working conditions and social security;

(c) Ensure, through legislation, incentives and/or encouragement, opportunities for women and men to take job-protected parental leave and to have parental benefits; promote the equal sharing of responsibilities for the family by men and women, including through appropriate legislation, incentives and/or encouragement, and also promote the facilitation of breast-feeding for working mothers;

(d) Develop policies, *inter alia*, in education to change attitudes that reinforce the division of labour based on gender in order to promote the concept of shared family responsibility for work in the home, particularly in relation to children and elder care;

(e) Improve the development of, and access to, technologies that facilitate occupational as well as domestic work, encourage self-support, generate income, transform gender-prescribed roles within the productive process and enable women to move out of low-paying jobs;

(f) Examine a range of policies and programmes, including social security legislation and taxation systems, in accordance with national priorities and policies, to determine how to promote gender equality and flexibility in the way people divide their time between and derive benefits from education and training, paid employment, family responsibilities, volunteer activity and other socially useful forms of work, rest and leisure.

180. By Governments, the private sector and non-governmental organizations, trade unions and the United Nations, as appropriate:

(a) Adopt appropriate measures involving relevant governmental bodies and employers' and employees' associations so that women and men are able to take temporary leave from employment, have transferable employment and retirement benefits and make arrangements to modify work hours without sacrificing their prospects for development and advancement at work and in their careers;

(b) Design and provide educational programmes through innovative media campaigns and school and community education programmes to raise awareness on gender equality and non-stereotyped gender roles of women and men within the family; provide support services and facilities, such as on-site child care at workplaces and flexible working arrangements;

(c) Enact and enforce laws against sexual and other forms of harassment in all workplaces.

G. *Women in power and decision-making*

181. The Universal Declaration of Human Rights states that everyone has the right to take part in the Government of his/her country. The empowerment and autonomy of women and the improvement of women's social, economic and political status is essential for the achievement of both transparent and accountable government and administration and sustainable development in all areas of life. The power relations that prevent women from leading fulfilling lives operate at many levels of society, from the most personal to the highly public. Achieving the goal of equal participation of women and men in decision-making will provide a balance that more accurately reflects the composition of society and is needed in order to strengthen democracy and promote its proper functioning. Equality in political decision-making performs a leverage function without which it is highly unlikely that a real integration of the equality dimension in government policy-making is feasible. In this respect, women's equal participation in political life plays a pivotal role in the general process of the advancement of women. Women's equal participation in decision-making is not only a demand for simple justice or democracy but can also be seen as a necessary condition for women's interests to be taken into account. Without the active participation of women and the incorporation of women's perspective at all levels of decision-making, the goals of equality, development and peace cannot be achieved.

182. Despite the widespread movement towards democratization in most countries, women are largely underrepresented at most levels of government, especially in ministerial and other executive bodies, and have made little progress in attaining political power in legislative bodies or in achieving the target endorsed by the Economic and Social Council of having 30 per cent women in positions at decision-making levels by 1995. Globally, only 10 per cent of the members of legislative bodies and a lower percentage of ministerial positions are now held by women. Indeed, some countries, including those that are undergoing fundamental political, economic and social changes, have seen a significant decrease in the number of women represented in legislative bodies. Al-

though women make up at least half of the electorate in almost all countries and have attained the right to vote and hold office in almost all States Members of the United Nations, women continue to be seriously underrepresented as candidates for public office. The traditional working patterns of many political parties and government structures continue to be barriers to women's participation in public life. Women may be discouraged from seeking political office by discriminatory attitudes and practices, family and child-care responsibilities, and the high cost of seeking and holding public office. Women in politics and decision-making positions in Governments and legislative bodies contribute to redefining political priorities, placing new items on the political agenda that reflect and address women's gender-specific concerns, values and experiences, and providing new perspectives on mainstream political issues.

183. Women have demonstrated considerable leadership in community and informal organizations, as well as in public office. However, socialization and negative stereotyping of women and men, including stereotyping through the media, reinforces the tendency for political decision-making to remain the domain of men. Likewise, the underrepresentation of women in decision-making positions in the areas of art, culture, sports, the media, education, religion and the law have prevented women from having a significant impact on many key institutions.

184. Owing to their limited access to the traditional avenues to power, such as the decision-making bodies of political parties, employer organizations and trade unions, women have gained access to power through alternative structures, particularly in the non-governmental organization sector. Through non-governmental organizations and grass-roots organizations, women have been able to articulate their interests and concerns and have placed women's issues on the national, regional and international agendas.

185. Inequality in the public arena can often start with discriminatory attitudes and practices and unequal power relations between women and men within the family, as defined in paragraph 29 above. The unequal division of labour and responsibilities within households based on unequal power relations also limits women's potential to find the time and develop the skills required for participation in decision-making in wider public forums. A more equal sharing of those responsibilities between women and men not only provides a better quality of life for women and their daughters but also enhances their opportunities to shape and design public policy, practice and expenditure so that their interests may be recognized and addressed. Non-formal networks and patterns of decision-making at the local community level that reflect a dominant male ethos restrict women's ability to participate equally in political, economic and social life.

186. The low proportion of women among economic and political decision makers at the local, national, regional and international levels reflects structural and attitudinal barriers that need to be addressed through positive measures. Governments, transnational and national corporations, the mass media, banks, academic and scientific institutions, and regional and international organizations, including those in the United Nations system, do not make full use of women's talents as top-level managers, policy makers, diplomats and negotiators.

187. The equitable distribution of power and decision-making at all levels is dependent on Governments and other actors undertaking statistical gender analysis and mainstreaming a gender perspective in policy development and the implementation of programmes. Equality in decision-making is essential to the empowerment of women. In some countries, affirmative action has led to 33.3 per cent or larger representation in local and national Governments.

188. National, regional and international statistical institutions still have insufficient knowledge of how to present the issues related to the equal treatment of women and men in the economic and social spheres. In particular, there is insufficient use of existing databases and methodologies in the important sphere of decision-making.

189. In addressing the inequality between men and women in the sharing of power and decision-making at all levels, Governments and other actors should promote an active and visible policy of mainstreaming a gender perspective in all policies and programmes so that before decisions are taken, an analysis is made of the effects on women and men, respectively.

Strategic objective G.1. *Take measures to ensure women's equal access to and full participation in power structures and decision-making*

Actions to be taken

190. By Governments:

(a) Commit themselves to establishing the goal of gender balance in governmental bodies and committees, as well as in public administrative entities, and in the judiciary, including, *inter alia*, setting specific targets and implementing measures to substantially increase the number of women with a view to achieving equal representation of women and men, if necessary through positive action, in all governmental and public administration positions;

(b) Take measures, including, where appropriate, in electoral systems that encourage political parties to integrate women in elective and non-elective public positions in the same proportion and at the same levels as men;

(c) Protect and promote the equal rights of women and men to engage in political activities and to freedom of association, including membership in political parties and trade unions;

(d) Review the differential impact of electoral systems on the political representation of women in elected bodies and consider, where appropriate, the adjustment or reform of those systems;

(e) Monitor and evaluate progress in the representation of women through the regular collection, analysis and dissemination of quantitative and qualitative data on women and men at all levels in various decision-making positions in the public and private sectors, and disseminate data on the number of women and men employed at various levels in Governments on a yearly basis; ensure that women and men have equal access to the full range of public appointments and set up mechanisms within governmental structures for monitoring progress in this field;

(f) Support non-governmental organizations and research institutes that conduct studies on women's participation in and impact on decision-making and the decision-making environment;

(g) Encourage greater involvement of indigenous women in decision-making at all levels;

(h) Encourage and, where appropriate, ensure that government-funded organizations adopt non-discriminatory policies and practices in order to increase the number and raise the position of women in their organizations;

(i) Recognize that shared work and parental responsibilities between women and men promote women's increased participation in public life, and take appropriate measures to achieve this, including measures to reconcile family and professional life;

(j) Aim at gender balance in the lists of national candidates nominated for election or appointment to United Nations bodies, specialized agencies and other autonomous organizations of the United Nations system, particularly for posts at the senior level.

191. By political parties:

(a) Consider examining party structures and procedures to remove all barriers that directly or indirectly discriminate against the participation of women;

(b) Consider developing initiatives that allow women to participate fully in all internal policy-making structures and appointive and electoral nominating processes;

(c) Consider incorporating gender issues in their political agenda, taking measures to ensure that women can participate in the leadership of political parties on an equal basis with men.

192. By Governments, national bodies, the private sector, political parties, trade unions, employers' organizations, research and academic institutions, subregional and regional bodies and non-governmental and international organizations:

(a) Take positive action to build a critical mass of women leaders, executives and managers in strategic decision-making positions;

(b) Create or strengthen, as appropriate, mechanisms to monitor women's access to senior levels of decision-making;

(c) Review the criteria for recruitment and appointment to advisory and decision-making bodies and promotion to senior positions to ensure that such criteria are relevant and do not discriminate against women;

(d) Encourage efforts by non-governmental organizations, trade unions and the private sector to achieve equality between women and men in their ranks, including equal participation in their decision-making bodies and in negotiations in all areas and at all levels;

(e) Develop communications strategies to promote public debate on the new roles of men and women in society, and in the family as defined in paragraph 29 above;

(f) Restructure recruitment and career-development programmes to ensure that all women, especially young women, have equal access to managerial, entrepreneurial, technical and leadership training, including on-the-job training;

(g) Develop career advancement programmes for women of all ages that include career planning, tracking, mentoring, coaching, training and retraining;

(h) Encourage and support the participation of women's non-governmental organizations in United Nations conferences and their preparatory processes;

(i) Aim at and support gender balance in the composition of delegations to the United Nations and other international forums.

193. By the United Nations:

(a) Implement existing and adopt new employment policies and measures in order to achieve overall gender equality, particularly at the Professional level and above, by the year 2000, with due regard to the importance of recruiting staff on as wide a geographical basis as possible, in conformity with Article 101, paragraph 3, of the Charter of the United Nations;

(b) Develop mechanisms to nominate women candidates for appointment to senior posts in the United

Nations, the specialized agencies and other organizations and bodies of the United Nations system;

(c) Continue to collect and disseminate quantitative and qualitative data on women and men in decision-making and analyse their differential impact on decision-making and monitor progress towards achieving the Secretary-General's target of having women hold 50 per cent of managerial and decision-making positions by the year 2000.

194. By women's organizations, non-governmental organizations, trade unions, social partners, producers, and industrial and professional organizations:

(a) Build and strengthen solidarity among women through information, education and sensitization activities;

(b) Advocate at all levels to enable women to influence political, economic and social decisions, processes and systems, and work towards seeking accountability from elected representatives on their commitment to gender concerns;

(c) Establish, consistent with data protection legislation, databases on women and their qualification for use in appointing women to senior decision-making and advisory positions, for dissemination to Governments, regional and international organizations and private enterprise, political parties and other relevant bodies.

Strategic objective G.2. *Increase women's capacity to participate in decision-making and leadership*

Actions to be taken

195. By Governments, national bodies, the private sector, political parties, trade unions, employers' organizations, subregional and regional bodies, non-governmental and international organizations and educational institutions:

(a) Provide leadership and self-esteem training to assist women and girls, particularly those with special needs, women with disabilities and women belonging to racial and ethnic minorities to strengthen their self-esteem and to encourage them to take decision-making positions;

(b) Have transparent criteria for decision-making positions and ensure that the selecting bodies have a gender-balanced composition;

(c) Create a system of mentoring for inexperienced women and, in particular, offer training, including training in leadership and decision-making, public speaking and self-assertion, as well as in political campaigning;

(d) Provide gender-sensitive training for women and men to promote non-discriminatory working relationships and respect for diversity in work and management styles;

(e) Develop mechanisms and training to encourage women to participate in the electoral process, political activities and other leadership areas.

H. *Institutional mechanisms for the advancement of women*

196. National machineries for the advancement of women have been established in almost every Member State to, *inter alia*, design, promote the implementation of, execute, monitor, evaluate, advocate and mobilize support for policies that promote the advancement of women. National machineries are diverse in form and uneven in their effectiveness, and in some cases have declined. Often marginalized in national government structures, these mechanisms are frequently hampered by unclear mandates, lack of adequate staff, training, data and sufficient resources, and insufficient support from national political leadership.

197. At the regional and international levels, mechanisms and institutions to promote the advancement of women as an integral part of mainstream political, economic, social and cultural development, and of initiatives on development and human rights, encounter similar problems emanating from a lack of commitment at the highest levels.

198. Successive international conferences have underscored the need to take gender factors into account in policy and programme planning. However, in many instances this has not been done.

199. Regional bodies concerned with the advancement of women have been strengthened, together with international machinery, such as the Commission on the Status of Women and the Committee on the Elimination of Discrimination against Women. However, the limited resources available continue to impede full implementation of their mandates.

200. Methodologies for conducting gender-based analysis in policies and programmes and for dealing with the differential effects of policies on women and men have been developed in many organizations and are available for application but are often not being applied or are not being applied consistently.

201. A national machinery for the advancement of women is the central policy-coordinating unit inside government. Its main task is to support government-wide mainstreaming of a gender-equality perspective in all policy areas. The necessary conditions for an effective functioning of such national machineries include:

(a) Location at the highest possible level in the Government, falling under the responsibility of a Cabinet minister;

(b) Institutional mechanisms or processes that facilitate, as appropriate, decentralized planning, implementation and monitoring with a view to involving non-governmental organizations and community organizations from the grass-roots upwards;

(c) Sufficient resources in terms of budget and professional capacity;

(d) Opportunity to influence development of all government policies.

202. In addressing the issue of mechanisms for promoting the advancement of women, Governments and other actors should promote an active and visible policy of mainstreaming a gender perspective in all policies and programmes so that, before decisions are taken, an analysis is made of the effects on women and men, respectively.

Strategic objective H.1. *Create or strengthen national machineries and other governmental bodies*

Actions to be taken

203. By Governments:

(a) Ensure that responsibility for the advancement of women is vested in the highest possible level of government; in many cases, this could be at the level of a Cabinet minister;

(b) Based on a strong political commitment, create a national machinery, where it does not exist, and strengthen, as appropriate, existing national machineries, for the advancement of women at the highest possible level of government; it should have clearly defined mandates and authority; critical elements would be adequate resources and the ability and competence to influence policy and formulate and review legislation; among other things, it should perform policy analysis, undertake advocacy, communication, coordination and monitoring of implementation;

(c) Provide staff training in designing and analysing data from a gender perspective;

(d) Establish procedures to allow the machinery to gather information on government-wide policy issues at an early stage and continuously use it in the policy development and review process within the Government;

(e) Report, on a regular basis, to legislative bodies on the progress of efforts, as appropriate, to mainstream gender concerns, taking into account the implementation of the Platform for Action;

(f) Encourage and promote the active involvement of the broad and diverse range of institutional actors in the public, private and voluntary sectors to work for equality between women and men.

Strategic objective H.2. *Integrate gender perspectives in legislation, public policies, programmes and projects*

Actions to be taken

204. By Governments:

(a) Seek to ensure that before policy decisions are taken, an analysis of their impact on women and men, respectively, is carried out;

(b) Regularly review national policies, programmes and projects, as well as their implementation, evaluating the impact of employment and income policies in order to guarantee that women are direct beneficiaries of development and that their full contribution to development, both remunerated and unremunerated, is considered in economic policy and planning;

(c) Promote national strategies and aims on equality between women and men in order to eliminate obstacles to the exercise of women's rights and eradicate all forms of discrimination against women;

(d) Work with members of legislative bodies, as appropriate, to promote a gender perspective in all legislation and policies;

(e) Give all ministries the mandate to review policies and programmes from a gender perspective and in the light of the Platform for Action; locate the responsibility for the implementation of that mandate at the highest possible level; establish and/or strengthen an inter-ministerial coordination structure to carry out this mandate, to monitor progress and to network with relevant machineries.

205. By national machinery:

(a) Facilitate the formulation and implementation of government policies on equality between women and men, develop appropriate strategies and methodologies, and promote coordination and cooperation within the central Government in order to ensure mainstreaming of a gender perspective in all policy-making processes;

(b) Promote and establish cooperative relationships with relevant branches of government, centres for women's studies and research, academic and educational institutions, the private sector, the media, non-governmental organizations, especially women's organizations, and all other actors of civil society;

(c) Undertake activities focusing on legal reform with regard, *inter alia*, to the family, conditions of employment, social security, income tax, equal opportunity in education, positive measures to promote the advancement of women, and the perception of attitudes and a culture favourable to equality, as well as promote a gender perspective in legal policy and programming reforms;

(d) Promote the increased participation of women as both active agents and beneficiaries of the development process, which would result in an improvement in the quality of life for all;

(e) Establish direct links with national, regional and international bodies dealing with the advancement of women;

(f) Provide training and advisory assistance to government agencies in order to integrate a gender perspective in their policies and programmes.

Strategic objective H.3. *Generate and disseminate gender-disaggregated data and information for planning and evaluation*

Actions to be taken

206. By national, regional and international statistical services and relevant governmental and United Nations agencies, in cooperation with research and documentation organizations, in their respective areas of responsibility:

(a) Ensure that statistics related to individuals are collected, compiled, analysed and presented by sex and age and reflect problems, issues and questions related to women and men in society;

(b) Collect, compile, analyse and present on a regular basis data disaggregated by age, sex, socio-economic and other relevant indicators, including number of dependants, for utilization in policy and programme planning and implementation;

(c) Involve centres for women's studies and research organizations in developing and testing appropriate indicators and research methodologies to strengthen gender analysis, as well as in monitoring and evaluating the implementation of the goals of the Platform for Action;

(d) Designate or appoint staff to strengthen gender-statistics programmes and ensure coordination, monitoring and linkage to all fields of statistical work, and prepare output that integrates statistics from the various subject areas;

(e) Improve data collection on the full contribution of women and men to the economy, including their participation in the informal sector(s);

(f) Develop a more comprehensive knowledge of all forms of work and employment by:

(i) Improving data collection on the unremunerated work which is already included in the United Nations System of National Accounts, such as in agriculture, particularly subsistence agriculture, and other types of non-market production activities;

(ii) Improving measurements that at present underestimate women's unemployment and underemployment in the labour market;

(iii) Developing methods, in the appropriate forums, for assessing the value, in quantitative terms, of unremunerated work that is outside national accounts, such as caring for dependants and preparing food, for possible reflection in satellite or other official accounts that may be produced separately from but are consistent with core national accounts, with a view to recognizing the economic contribution of women and making visible the unequal distribution of remunerated and unremunerated work between women and men;

(g) Develop an international classification of activities for time-use statistics that is sensitive to the differences between women and men in remunerated and unremunerated work, and collect data disaggregated by sex. At the national level, subject to national constraints:

(i) Conduct regular time-use studies to measure, in quantitative terms, unremunerated work, including recording those activities that are performed simultaneously with remunerated or other unremunerated activities;

(ii) Measure, in quantitative terms, unremunerated work that is outside national accounts, work to improve methods to assess its value, and accurately reflect its value in satellite or other official accounts that are separate from, but consistent with core national accounts;

(h) Improve concepts and methods of data collection on the measurement of poverty among women and men, including their access to resources;

(i) Strengthen vital statistical systems and incorporate gender analysis into publications and research; give priority to gender differences in research design and in data collection and analysis in order to improve data on morbidity; and improve data collection on access to health services, including access to comprehensive sexual and reproductive health services, maternal care and family planning, with special priority for adolescent mothers and for elder care;

(j) Develop improved gender-disaggregated and age-specific data on the victims and perpetrators of all forms of violence against women, such as domestic violence, sexual harassment, rape, incest and sexual abuse, and trafficking in women and girls, as well as on violence by agents of the State;

(k) Improve concepts and methods of data collection on the participation of women and men with disabilities, including their access to resources.

207. By Governments:

(a) Ensure the regular production of a statistical publication on gender that presents and interprets topical data on women and men in a form suitable for a wide range of non-technical users;

(b) Ensure that producers and users of statistics in each country regularly review the adequacy of the official statistical system and its coverage of gender issues, and prepare a plan for needed improvements, where necessary;

(c) Develop and encourage the development of quantitative and qualitative studies by research organizations, trade unions, employers, the private sector and non-governmental organizations on the sharing of power and influence in society, including the number of women and men in senior decision-making positions in both the public and private sectors;

(d) Use more gender-sensitive data in the formulation of policy and implementation of programmes and projects.

208. By the United Nations:

(a) Promote the development of methods to find better ways to collect, collate and analyse data that may relate to the human rights of women, including violence against women, for use by all relevant United Nations bodies;

(b) Promote the further development of statistical methods to improve data that relate to women in economic, social, cultural and political development;

(c) Prepare a new issue of *The World's Women* at regular five-year intervals and distribute it widely;

(d) Assist countries, upon request, in the development of gender policies and programmes;

(e) Ensure that the relevant reports, data and publications of the Statistical Division of the United Nations Secretariat and the International Research and Training Institute for the Advancement of Women on progress at the national and international levels are transmitted to the Commission on the Status of Women in a regular and coordinated fashion.

209. By multilateral development institutions and bilateral donors:

Encourage and support the development of national capacity in developing countries and in countries with economies in transition by providing resources and technical assistance so that countries can fully measure the work done by women and men, including both remunerated and unremunerated work, and, where appropriate, use satellite or other official accounts for unremunerated work.

I. *Human rights of women*

210. Human rights and fundamental freedoms are the birthright of all human beings; their protection and promotion is the first responsibility of Governments.

211. The World Conference on Human Rights reaffirmed the solemn commitment of all States to fulfil their obligation to promote universal respect for, and observance and protection of, all human rights and fundamental freedoms for all, in accordance with the Charter of the United Nations, other instruments relating to human rights, and international law. The universal nature of these rights and freedoms is beyond question.

212. The promotion and protection of all human rights and fundamental freedoms must be considered as a priority objective of the United Nations, in accordance with its purposes and principles, in particular with the purpose of international cooperation. In the framework of these purposes and principles, the promotion and protection of all human rights is a legitimate concern of the international community. The international community must treat human rights globally, in a fair and equal manner, on the same footing, and with the same emphasis. The Platform for Action reaffirms the importance of ensuring the universality, objectivity and non-selectivity of the consideration of human rights issues.

213. The Platform for Action reaffirms that all human rights — civil, cultural, economic, political and social, including the right to development — are universal, indivisible, interdependent and interrelated, as expressed in the Vienna Declaration and Programme of Action adopted by the World Conference on Human Rights. The Conference reaffirmed that the human rights of women and the girl child are an inalienable, integral and indivisible part of universal human rights. The full and equal enjoyment of all human rights and fundamental freedoms by women and girls is a priority for Governments and the United Nations and is essential for the advancement of women.

214. Equal rights of men and women are explicitly mentioned in the Preamble to the Charter of the United Nations. All the major international human rights instruments include sex as one of the grounds upon which States may not discriminate.

215. Governments must not only refrain from violating the human rights of all women, but must work actively to promote and protect these rights. Recognition of the importance of the human rights of women is reflected in the fact that three quarters of the States Members of the United Nations have become parties to the Convention on the Elimination of All Forms of Discrimination against Women.

216. The World Conference on Human Rights reaffirmed clearly that the human rights of women throughout the life cycle are an inalienable, integral and indivisible part of universal human rights. The International Conference on Population and Development reaffirmed women's reproductive rights and the right to

development. Both the Declaration of the Rights of the Child 31/ and the Convention on the Rights of the Child 11/ guarantee children's rights and uphold the principle of non-discrimination on the grounds of gender.

217. The gap between the existence of rights and their effective enjoyment derives from a lack of commitment by Governments to promoting and protecting those rights and the failure of Governments to inform women and men alike about them. The lack of appropriate recourse mechanisms at the national and international levels, and inadequate resources at both levels, compound the problem. In most countries, steps have been taken to reflect the rights guaranteed by the Convention on the Elimination of All Forms of Discrimination against Women in national law. A number of countries have established mechanisms to strengthen women's ability to exercise their rights.

218. In order to protect the human rights of women, it is necessary to avoid, as far as possible, resorting to reservations and to ensure that no reservation is incompatible with the object and purpose of the Convention or is otherwise incompatible with international treaty law. Unless the human rights of women, as defined by international human rights instruments, are fully recognized and effectively protected, applied, implemented and enforced in national law as well as in national practice in family, civil, penal, labour and commercial codes and administrative rules and regulations, they will exist in name only.

219. In those countries that have not yet become parties to the Convention on the Elimination of All Forms of Discrimination against Women and other international human rights instruments, or where reservations that are incompatible with the object or purpose of the Convention have been entered, or where national laws have not yet been revised to implement international norms and standards, women's *de jure* equality is not yet secured. Women's full enjoyment of equal rights is undermined by the discrepancies between some national legislation and international law and international instruments on human rights. Overly complex administrative procedures, lack of awareness within the judicial process and inadequate monitoring of the violation of the human rights of all women, coupled with the underrepresentation of women in justice systems, insufficient information on existing rights and persistent attitudes and practices perpetuate women's de facto inequality. De facto inequality is also perpetuated by the lack of enforcement of, *inter alia*, family, civil, penal, labour and commercial laws or codes, or administrative rules and regulations intended to ensure women's full enjoyment of human rights and fundamental freedoms.

220. Every person should be entitled to participate in, contribute to and enjoy cultural, economic, political and social development. In many cases women and girls suffer discrimination in the allocation of economic and social resources. This directly violates their economic, social and cultural rights.

221. The human rights of all women and the girl child must form an integral part of United Nations human rights activities. Intensified efforts are needed to integrate the equal status and the human rights of all women and girls into the mainstream of United Nations system-wide activities and to address these issues regularly and systematically throughout relevant bodies and mechanisms. This requires, *inter alia*, improved cooperation and coordination between the Commission on the Status of Women, the United Nations High Commissioner for Human Rights, the Commission on Human Rights, including its special and thematic rapporteurs, independent experts, working groups and its Subcommission on Prevention of Discrimination and Protection of Minorities, the Commission on Sustainable Development, the Commission for Social Development, the Commission on Crime Prevention and Criminal Justice, and the Committee on the Elimination of Discrimination against Women and other human rights treaty bodies, and all relevant entities of the United Nations system, including the specialized agencies. Cooperation is also needed to strengthen, rationalize and streamline the United Nations human rights system and to promote its effectiveness and efficiency, taking into account the need to avoid unnecessary duplication and overlapping of mandates and tasks.

222. If the goal of full realization of human rights for all is to be achieved, international human rights instruments must be applied in such a way as to take more clearly into consideration the systematic and systemic nature of discrimination against women that gender analysis has clearly indicated.

223. Bearing in mind the Programme of Action of the International Conference on Population and Development 14/ and the Vienna Declaration and Programme of Action 2/ adopted by the World Conference on Human Rights, the Fourth World Conference on Women reaffirms that reproductive rights rest on the recognition of the basic right of all couples and individuals to decide freely and responsibly the number, spacing and timing of their children and to have the information and means to do so, and the right to attain the highest standard of sexual and reproductive health. It also includes their right to make decisions concerning reproduction free of discrimination, coercion and violence, as expressed in human rights documents.

31/ General Assembly resolution 1386 (XIV).

224. Violence against women both violates and impairs or nullifies the enjoyment by women of human rights and fundamental freedoms. Taking into account the Declaration on the Elimination of Violence against Women and the work of Special Rapporteurs, gender-based violence, such as battering and other domestic violence, sexual abuse, sexual slavery and exploitation, and international trafficking in women and children, forced prostitution and sexual harassment, as well as violence against women, resulting from cultural prejudice, racism and racial discrimination, xenophobia, pornography, ethnic cleansing, armed conflict, foreign occupation, religious and anti-religious extremism and terrorism are incompatible with the dignity and the worth of the human person and must be combated and eliminated. Any harmful aspect of certain traditional, customary or modern practices that violates the rights of women should be prohibited and eliminated. Governments should take urgent action to combat and eliminate all forms of violence against women in private and public life, whether perpetrated or tolerated by the State or private persons.

225. Many women face additional barriers to the enjoyment of their human rights because of such factors as their race, language, ethnicity, culture, religion, disability or socio-economic class or because they are indigenous people, migrants, including women migrant workers, displaced women or refugees. They may also be disadvantaged and marginalized by a general lack of knowledge and recognition of their human rights as well as by the obstacles they meet in gaining access to information and recourse mechanisms in cases of violation of their rights.

226. The factors that cause the flight of refugee women, other displaced women in need of international protection and internally displaced women may be different from those affecting men. These women continue to be vulnerable to abuses of their human rights during and after their flight.

227. While women are increasingly using the legal system to exercise their rights, in many countries lack of awareness of the existence of these rights is an obstacle that prevents women from fully enjoying their human rights and attaining equality. Experience in many countries has shown that women can be empowered and motivated to assert their rights, regardless of their level of education or socio-economic status. Legal literacy programmes and media strategies have been effective in helping women to understand the link between their rights and other aspects of their lives and in demonstrating that cost-effective initiatives can be undertaken to help women obtain those rights. Provision of human rights education is essential for promoting an understanding of the human rights of women, including knowledge of recourse mechanisms to redress violations of their rights. It is necessary for all individuals, especially women in vulnerable circumstances, to have full knowledge of their rights and access to legal recourse against violations of their rights.

228. Women engaged in the defence of human rights must be protected. Governments have a duty to guarantee the full enjoyment of all rights set out in the Universal Declaration of Human Rights, the International Covenant on Civil and Political Rights and the International Covenant on Economic, Social and Cultural Rights by women working peacefully in a personal or organizational capacity for the promotion and protection of human rights. Non-governmental organizations, women's organizations and feminist groups have played a catalytic role in the promotion of the human rights of women through grass-roots activities, networking and advocacy and need encouragement, support and access to information from Governments in order to carry out these activities.

229. In addressing the enjoyment of human rights, Governments and other actors should promote an active and visible policy of mainstreaming a gender perspective in all policies and programmes so that, before decisions are taken, an analysis is made of the effects on women and men, respectively.

Strategic objective I.1 *Promote and protect the human rights of women, through the full implementation of all human rights instruments, especially the Convention on the Elimination of All Forms of Discrimination against Women*

Actions to be taken

230. By Governments:

(a) Work actively towards ratification of or accession to and implement international and regional human rights treaties;

(b) Ratify and accede to and ensure implementation of the Convention on the Elimination of All Forms of Discrimination against Women so that universal ratification of the Convention can be achieved by the year 2000;

(c) Limit the extent of any reservations to the Convention on the Elimination of All Forms of Discrimination against Women; formulate any such reservations as precisely and as narrowly as possible; ensure that no reservations are incompatible with the object and purpose of the Convention or otherwise incompatible with international treaty law and regularly review them with a view to withdrawing them; and withdraw reservations that are contrary to the object and purpose of the Convention on the Elimination of All Forms of Discrimination against Women or which are otherwise incompatible with international treaty law;

(d) Consider drawing up national action plans identifying steps to improve the promotion and protection of human rights, including the human rights of women, as recommended by the World Conference on Human Rights;

(e) Create or strengthen independent national institutions for the protection and promotion of these rights, including the human rights of women, as recommended by the World Conference on Human Rights;

(f) Develop a comprehensive human rights education programme to raise awareness among women of their human rights and raise awareness among others of the human rights of women;

(g) If they are States parties, implement the Convention by reviewing all national laws, policies, practices and procedures to ensure that they meet the obligations set out in the Convention; all States should undertake a review of all national laws, policies, practices and procedures to ensure that they meet international human rights obligations in this matter;

(h) Include gender aspects in reporting under all other human rights conventions and instruments, including ILO conventions, to ensure analysis and review of the human rights of women;

(i) Report on schedule to the Committee on the Elimination of Discrimination against Women regarding the implementation of the Convention, following fully the guidelines established by the Committee and involving non-governmental organizations, where appropriate, or taking into account their contributions in the preparation of the report;

(j) Enable the Committee on the Elimination of Discrimination against Women fully to discharge its mandate by allowing for adequate meeting time through broad ratification of the revision adopted by the States parties to the Convention on the Elimination of All Forms of Discrimination against Women on 22 May 1995 relative to article 20, paragraph 1, 32/ and by promoting efficient working methods;

(k) Support the process initiated by the Commission on the Status of Women with a view to elaborating a draft optional protocol to the Convention on the Elimination of All Forms of Discrimination against Women that could enter into force as soon as possible on a right of petition procedure, taking into consideration the Secretary-General's report on the optional protocol, including those views related to its feasibility;

(l) Take urgent measures to achieve universal ratification of or accession to the Convention on the Rights

of the Child before the end of 1995 and full implementation of the Convention in order to ensure equal rights for girls and boys; those that have not already done so are urged to become parties in order to realize universal implementation of the Convention on the Rights of the Child by the year 2000;

(m) Address the acute problems of children, *inter alia*, by supporting efforts in the context of the United Nations system aimed at adopting efficient international measures for the prevention and eradication of female infanticide, harmful child labour, the sale of children and their organs, child prostitution, child pornography and other forms of sexual abuse and consider contributing to the drafting of an optional protocol to the Convention on the Rights of the Child;

(n) Strengthen the implementation of all relevant human rights instruments in order to combat and eliminate, including through international cooperation, organized and other forms of trafficking in women and children, including trafficking for the purposes of sexual exploitation, pornography, prostitution and sex tourism, and provide legal and social services to the victims; this should include provisions for international cooperation to prosecute and punish those responsible for organized exploitation of women and children;

(o) Taking into account the need to ensure full respect for the human rights of indigenous women, consider a declaration on the rights of indigenous people for adoption by the General Assembly within the International Decade of the World's Indigenous People and encourage the participation of indigenous women in the working group elaborating the draft declaration, in accordance with the provisions for the participation of organizations of indigenous people.

231. By relevant organs, bodies and agencies of the United Nations system, all human rights bodies of the United Nations system, as well as the United Nations High Commissioner for Human Rights and the United Nations High Commissioner for Refugees, while promoting greater efficiency and effectiveness through better coordination of the various bodies, mechanisms and procedures, taking into account the need to avoid unnecessary duplication and overlapping of their mandates and tasks:

(a) Give full, equal and sustained attention to the human rights of women in the exercise of their respective mandates to promote universal respect for and protection of all human rights — civil, cultural, economic, political and social rights, including the right to development;

(b) Ensure the implementation of the recommendations of the World Conference on Human Rights for

32/ See CEDAW/SP/1995/2.

the full integration and mainstreaming of the human rights of women;

(c) Develop a comprehensive policy programme for mainstreaming the human rights of women throughout the United Nations system, including activities with regard to advisory services, technical assistance, reporting methodology, gender-impact assessments, coordination, public information and human rights education, and play an active role in the implementation of the programme;

(d) Ensure the integration and full participation of women as both agents and beneficiaries in the development process and reiterate the objectives established for global action for women towards sustainable and equitable development set forth in the Rio Declaration on Environment and Development; 18/

(e) Include information on gender-based human rights violations in their activities and integrate the findings into all of their programmes and activities;

(f) Ensure that there is collaboration and coordination of the work of all human rights bodies and mechanisms to ensure that the human rights of women are respected;

(g) Strengthen cooperation and coordination between the Commission on the Status of Women, the Commission on Human Rights, the Commission for Social Development, the Commission on Sustainable Development, the Commission on Crime Prevention and Criminal Justice, the United Nations human rights treaty monitoring bodies, including the Committee on the Elimination of Discrimination against Women, and the United Nations Development Fund for Women, the International Research and Training Institute for the Advancement of Women, the United Nations Development Programme, the United Nations Children's Fund and other organizations of the United Nations system, acting within their mandates, in the promotion of the human rights of women, and improve cooperation between the Division for the Advancement of Women and the Centre for Human Rights;

(h) Establish effective cooperation between the United Nations High Commissioner for Human Rights and the United Nations High Commissioner for Refugees and other relevant bodies, within their respective mandates, taking into account the close link between massive violations of human rights, especially in the form of genocide, ethnic cleansing, systematic rape of women in war situations and refugee flows and other displacements, and the fact that refugee, displaced and returnee women may be subject to particular human rights abuse;

(i) Encourage incorporation of a gender perspective in national programmes of action and in human rights and national institutions, within the context of human rights advisory services programmes;

(j) Provide training in the human rights of women for all United Nations personnel and officials, especially those in human rights and humanitarian relief activities, and promote their understanding of the human rights of women so that they recognize and deal with violations of the human rights of women and can fully take into account the gender aspect of their work;

(k) In reviewing the implementation of the plan of action for the United Nations Decade for Human Rights Education (1995-2004), take into account the results of the Fourth World Conference on Women.

Strategic objective I.2. *Ensure equality and non-discrimination under the law and in practice*

Actions to be taken

232. By Governments:

(a) Give priority to promoting and protecting the full and equal enjoyment by women and men of all human rights and fundamental freedoms without distinction of any kind as to race, colour, sex, language, religion, political or other opinions, national or social origins, property, birth or other status;

(b) Provide constitutional guarantees and/or enact appropriate legislation to prohibit discrimination on the basis of sex for all women and girls of all ages and assure women of all ages equal rights and their full enjoyment;

(c) Embody the principle of the equality of men and women in their legislation and ensure, through law and other appropriate means, the practical realization of this principle;

(d) Review national laws, including customary laws and legal practices in the areas of family, civil, penal, labour and commercial law in order to ensure the implementation of the principles and procedures of all relevant international human rights instruments by means of national legislation, revoke any remaining laws that discriminate on the basis of sex and remove gender bias in the administration of justice;

(e) Strengthen and encourage the development of programmes to protect the human rights of women in the national institutions on human rights that carry out programmes, such as human rights commissions or ombudspersons, according them appropriate status, resources and access to the Government to assist individuals, in particular women, and ensure that these institutions pay adequate attention to problems involving the violation of the human rights of women;

(f) Take action to ensure that the human rights of women, including the rights referred to in paragraphs 94 to 96 above, are fully respected and protected;

(g) Take urgent action to combat and eliminate violence against women, which is a human rights violation, resulting from harmful traditional or customary practices, cultural prejudices and extremism;

(h) Prohibit female genital mutilation wherever it exists and give vigorous support to efforts among non-governmental and community organizations and religious institutions to eliminate such practices;

(i) Provide gender-sensitive human rights education and training to public officials, including, *inter alia*, police and military personnel, corrections officers, health and medical personnel, and social workers, including people who deal with migration and refugee issues, and teachers at all levels of the educational system, and make available such education and training also to the judiciary and members of parliament in order to enable them to better exercise their public responsibilities;

(j) Promote the equal right of women to be members of trade unions and other professional and social organizations;

(k) Establish effective mechanisms for investigating violations of the human rights of women perpetrated by any public official and take the necessary punitive legal measures in accordance with national laws;

(l) Review and amend criminal laws and procedures, as necessary, to eliminate any discrimination against women in order to ensure that criminal law and procedures guarantee women effective protection against, and prosecution of, crimes directed at or disproportionately affecting women, regardless of the relationship between the perpetrator and the victim, and ensure that women defendants, victims and/or witnesses are not revictimized or discriminated against in the investigation and prosecution of crimes;

(m) Ensure that women have the same right as men to be judges, advocates or other officers of the court, as well as police officers and prison and detention officers, among other things;

(n) Strengthen existing or establish readily available and free or affordable alternative administrative mechanisms and legal aid programmes to assist disadvantaged women seeking redress for violations of their rights;

(o) Ensure that all women and non-governmental organizations and their members in the field of protection and promotion of all human rights — civil, cultural, economic, political and social rights, including the right to development — enjoy fully all human rights and freedoms in accordance with the Universal Declaration of Human Rights and all other human rights instruments and the protection of national laws;

(p) Strengthen and encourage the implementation of the recommendations contained in the Standard Rules on the Equalization of Opportunities for Persons with Disabilities, 30/ paying special attention to ensure non-

discrimination and equal enjoyment of all human rights and fundamental freedoms by women and girls with disabilities, including their access to information and services in the field of violence against women, as well as their active participation in and economic contribution to all aspects of society;

(q) Encourage the development of gender-sensitive human rights programmes.

Strategic objective I.3. *Achieve legal literacy*

Actions to be taken

233. By Governments and non-governmental organizations, the United Nations and other international organizations, as appropriate:

(a) Translate, whenever possible, into local and indigenous languages and into alternative formats appropriate for persons with disabilities and persons at lower levels of literacy, publicize and disseminate laws and information relating to the equal status and human rights of all women, including the Universal Declaration of Human Rights, the International Covenant on Civil and Political Rights, the International Covenant on Economic, Social and Cultural Rights, the Convention on the Elimination of All Forms of Discrimination against Women, the International Convention on the Elimination of All Forms of Racial Discrimination, 33/ the Convention on the Rights of the Child, the Convention against Torture and Other Cruel, Inhuman or Degrading Treatment or Punishment, the Declaration on the Right to Development 34/ and the Declaration on the Elimination of Violence against Women, as well as the outcomes of relevant United Nations conferences and summits and national reports to the Committee on the Elimination of Discrimination against Women;

(b) Publicize and disseminate such information in easily understandable formats and alternative formats appropriate for persons with disabilities, and persons at low levels of literacy;

(c) Disseminate information on national legislation and its impact on women, including easily accessible guidelines on how to use a justice system to exercise one's rights;

(d) Include information about international and regional instruments and standards in their public information and human rights education activities and in adult education and training programmes, particularly for groups such as the military, the police and other law enforcement personnel, the judiciary, and legal and health professionals to ensure that human rights are effectively protected;

33/ General Assembly resolution 2106 A (XX), annex.
34/ General Assembly resolution 41/128, annex.

(e) Make widely available and fully publicize information on the existence of national, regional and international mechanisms for seeking redress when the human rights of women are violated;

(f) Encourage, coordinate and cooperate with local and regional women's groups, relevant non-governmental organizations, educators and the media, to implement programmes in human rights education to make women aware of their human rights;

(g) Promote education on the human and legal rights of women in school curricula at all levels of education and undertake public campaigns, including in the most widely used languages of the country, on the equality of women and men in public and private life, including their rights within the family and relevant human rights instruments under national and international law;

(h) Promote education in all countries in human rights and international humanitarian law for members of the national security and armed forces, including those assigned to United Nations peace-keeping operations, on a routine and continuing basis, reminding them and sensitizing them to the fact that they should respect the rights of women at all times, both on and off duty, giving special attention to the rules on the protection of women and children and to the protection of human rights in situations of armed conflict;

(i) Take appropriate measures to ensure that refugee and displaced women, migrant women and women migrant workers are made aware of their human rights and of the recourse mechanisms available to them.

J. Women and the media

234. During the past decade, advances in information technology have facilitated a global communications network that transcends national boundaries and has an impact on public policy, private attitudes and behaviour, especially of children and young adults. Everywhere the potential exists for the media to make a far greater contribution to the advancement of women.

235. More women are involved in careers in the communications sector, but few have attained positions at the decision-making level or serve on governing boards and bodies that influence media policy. The lack of gender sensitivity in the media is evidenced by the failure to eliminate the gender-based stereotyping that can be found in public and private local, national and international media organizations.

236. The continued projection of negative and degrading images of women in media communications — electronic, print, visual and audio — must be changed. Print and electronic media in most countries do not provide a balanced picture of women's diverse lives and contributions to society in a changing world. In addition,

violent and degrading or pornographic media products are also negatively affecting women and their participation in society. Programming that reinforces women's traditional roles can be equally limiting. The world-wide trend towards consumerism has created a climate in which advertisements and commercial messages often portray women primarily as consumers and target girls and women of all ages inappropriately.

237. Women should be empowered by enhancing their skills, knowledge and access to information technology. This will strengthen their ability to combat negative portrayals of women internationally and to challenge instances of abuse of the power of an increasingly important industry. Self-regulatory mechanisms for the media need to be created and strengthened and approaches developed to eliminate gender-biased programming. Most women, especially in developing countries, are not able to access effectively the expanding electronic information highways and therefore cannot establish networks that will provide them with alternative sources of information. Women therefore need to be involved in decision-making regarding the development of the new technologies in order to participate fully in their growth and impact.

238. In addressing the issue of the mobilization of the media, Governments and other actors should promote an active and visible policy of mainstreaming a gender perspective in policies and programmes.

Strategic objective J. 1. *Increase the participation and access of women to expression and decision-making in and through the media and new technologies of communication*

Actions to be taken

239. By Governments:

(a) Support women's education, training and employment to promote and ensure women's equal access to all areas and levels of the media;

(b) Support research into all aspects of women and the media so as to define areas needing attention and action and review existing media policies with a view to integrating a gender perspective;

(c) Promote women's full and equal participation in the media, including management, programming, education, training and research;

(d) Aim at gender balance in the appointment of women and men to all advisory, management, regulatory or monitoring bodies, including those connected to the private and State or public media;

(e) Encourage, to the extent consistent with freedom of expression, these bodies to increase the number of programmes for and by women to see to it that women's needs and concerns are properly addressed;

(f) Encourage and recognize women's media networks, including electronic networks and other new technologies of communication, as a means for the dissemination of information and the exchange of views, including at the international level, and support women's groups active in all media work and systems of communications to that end;

(g) Encourage and provide the means or incentives for the creative use of programmes in the national media for the dissemination of information on various cultural forms of indigenous people and the development of social and educational issues in this regard within the framework of national law;

(h) Guarantee the freedom of the media and its subsequent protection within the framework of national law and encourage, consistent with freedom of expression, the positive involvement of the media in development and social issues.

240. By national and international media systems:

Develop, consistent with freedom of expression, regulatory mechanisms, including voluntary ones, that promote balanced and diverse portrayals of women by the media and international communication systems and that promote increased participation by women and men in production and decision-making.

241. By Governments, as appropriate, or national machinery for the advancement of women:

(a) Encourage the development of educational and training programmes for women in order to produce information for the mass media, including funding of experimental efforts, and the use of the new technologies of communication, cybernetics space and satellite, whether public or private;

(b) Encourage the use of communication systems, including new technologies, as a means of strengthening women's participation in democratic processes;

(c) Facilitate the compilation of a directory of women media experts;

(d) Encourage the participation of women in the development of professional guidelines and codes of conduct or other appropriate self-regulatory mechanisms to promote balanced and non-stereotyped portrayals of women by the media.

242. By non-governmental organizations and media professional associations:

(a) Encourage the establishment of media watch groups that can monitor the media and consult with the media to ensure that women's needs and concerns are properly reflected;

(b) Train women to make greater use of information technology for communication and the media, including at the international level;

(c) Create networks among and develop information programmes for non-governmental organizations, women's organizations and professional media organizations in order to recognize the specific needs of women in the media, and facilitate the increased participation of women in communication, in particular at the international level, in support of South-South and North-South dialogue among and between these organizations, *inter alia*, to promote the human rights of women and equality between women and men;

(d) Encourage the media industry and education and media training institutions to develop, in appropriate languages, traditional, indigenous and other ethnic forms of media, such as story-telling, drama, poetry and song, reflecting their cultures, and utilize these forms of communication to disseminate information on development and social issues.

Strategic objective J.2. *Promote a balanced and non-stereotyped portrayal of women in the media*

Actions to be taken

243. By Governments and international organizations, to the extent consistent with freedom of expression:

(a) Promote research and implementation of a strategy of information, education and communication aimed at promoting a balanced portrayal of women and girls and their multiple roles;

(b) Encourage the media and advertising agencies to develop specific programmes to raise awareness of the Platform for Action;

(c) Encourage gender-sensitive training for media professionals, including media owners and managers, to encourage the creation and use of non-stereotyped, balanced and diverse images of women in the media;

(d) Encourage the media to refrain from presenting women as inferior beings and exploiting them as sexual objects and commodities, rather than presenting them as creative human beings, key actors and contributors to and beneficiaries of the process of development;

(e) Promote the concept that the sexist stereotypes displayed in the media are gender discriminatory, degrading in nature and offensive;

(f) Take effective measures or institute such measures, including appropriate legislation against pornography and the projection of violence against women and children in the media.

244. By the mass media and advertising organizations:

(a) Develop, consistent with freedom of expression, professional guidelines and codes of conduct and other forms of self-regulation to promote the presentation of non-stereotyped images of women;

(b) Establish, consistent with freedom of expression, professional guidelines and codes of conduct that address violent, degrading or pornographic materials concerning women in the media, including advertising;

(c) Develop a gender perspective on all issues of concern to communities, consumers and civil society;

(d) Increase women's participation in decision-making at all levels of the media.

245. By the media, non-governmental organizations and the private sector, in collaboration, as appropriate, with national machinery for the advancement of women:

(a) Promote the equal sharing of family responsibilities through media campaigns that emphasize gender equality and non-stereotyped gender roles of women and men within the family and that disseminate information aimed at eliminating spousal and child abuse and all forms of violence against women, including domestic violence;

(b) Produce and/or disseminate media materials on women leaders, *inter alia*, as leaders who bring to their positions of leadership many different life experiences, including but not limited to their experiences in balancing work and family responsibilities, as mothers, as professionals, as managers and as entrepreneurs, to provide role models, particularly to young women;

(c) Promote extensive campaigns, making use of public and private educational programmes, to disseminate information about and increase awareness of the human rights of women;

(d) Support the development of and finance, as appropriate, alternative media and the use of all means of communication to disseminate information to and about women and their concerns;

(e) Develop approaches and train experts to apply gender analysis with regard to media programmes.

K. *Women and the environment*

246. Human beings are at the centre of concern for sustainable development. They are entitled to a healthy and productive life in harmony with nature. Women have an essential role to play in the development of sustainable and ecologically sound consumption and production patterns and approaches to natural resource management, as was recognized at the United Nations Conference on Environment and Development and the International Conference on Population and Development and reflected throughout Agenda 21. Awareness of resource depletion, the degradation of natural systems and the dangers of polluting substances has increased markedly in the past decade. These worsening conditions are destroying fragile ecosystems and displacing communities, especially women, from productive activities and are an increasing threat to a safe and healthy environment. Poverty and environmental degradation are closely interrelated. While poverty results in certain kinds of environmental stress, the major cause of the continued deterioration of the global environment is the unsustainable pattern of consumption and production, particularly in industrialized countries, which is a matter of grave concern, aggravating poverty and imbalances. Rising sealevels as a result of global warming cause a grave and immediate threat to people living in island countries and coastal areas. The use of ozone-depleting substances, such as products with chlorofluorocarbons, halons and methyl bromides (from which plastics and foams are made), are severely affecting the atmosphere, thus allowing excessive levels of harmful ultraviolet rays to reach the Earth's surface. This has severe effects on people's health such as higher rates of skin cancer, eye damage and weakened immune systems. It also has severe effects on the environment, including harm to crops and ocean life.

247. All States and all people shall cooperate in the essential task of eradicating poverty as an indispensable requirement for sustainable development, in order to decrease the disparities in standards of living and better meet the needs of the majority of the people of the world. Hurricanes, typhoons and other natural disasters and, in addition, the destruction of resources, violence, displacements and other effects associated with war, armed and other conflicts, the use and testing of nuclear weaponry, and foreign occupation can also contribute to environmental degradation. The deterioration of natural resources displaces communities, especially women, from income-generating activities while greatly adding to unremunerated work. In both urban and rural areas, environmental degradation results in negative effects on the health, well-being and quality of life of the population at large, especially girls and women of all ages. Particular attention and recognition should be given to the role and special situation of women living in rural areas and those working in the agricultural sector, where access to training, land, natural and productive resources, credit, development programmes and cooperative structures can help them increase their participation in sustainable development. Environmental risks in the home and workplace may have a disproportionate impact on women's health because of women's different susceptibilities to the toxic effects of various chemicals. These risks to women's health are particularly high in urban areas, as well as in low-income areas where there is a high concentration of polluting industrial facilities.

248. Through their management and use of natural resources, women provide sustenance to their families

and communities. As consumers and producers, caretakers of their families and educators, women play an important role in promoting sustainable development through their concern for the quality and sustainability of life for present and future generations. Governments have expressed their commitment to creating a new development paradigm that integrates environmental sustainability with gender equality and justice within and between generations as contained in chapter 24 of Agenda 21. 19/

249. Women remain largely absent at all levels of policy formulation and decision-making in natural resource and environmental management, conservation, protection and rehabilitation, and their experience and skills in advocacy for and monitoring of proper natural resource management too often remain marginalized in policy-making and decision-making bodies, as well as in educational institutions and environment-related agencies at the managerial level. Women are rarely trained as professional natural resource managers with policy-making capacities, such as land-use planners, agriculturalists, foresters, marine scientists and environmental lawyers. Even in cases where women are trained as professional natural resource managers, they are often underrepresented in formal institutions with policy-making capacities at the national, regional and international levels. Often women are not equal participants in the management of financial and corporate institutions whose decision-making most significantly affects environmental quality. Furthermore, there are institutional weaknesses in coordination between women's non-governmental organizations and national institutions dealing with environmental issues, despite the recent rapid growth and visibility of women's non-governmental organizations working on these issues at all levels.

250. Women have often played leadership roles or taken the lead in promoting an environmental ethic, reducing resource use, and reusing and recycling resources to minimize waste and excessive consumption. Women can have a particularly powerful role in influencing sustainable consumption decisions. In addition, women's contributions to environmental management, including through grass-roots and youth campaigns to protect the environment, have often taken place at the local level, where decentralized action on environmental issues is most needed and decisive. Women, especially indigenous women, have particular knowledge of ecological linkages and fragile ecosystem management. Women in many communities provide the main labour force for subsistence production, including production of seafood; hence, their role is crucial to the provision of food and nutrition, the enhancement of the subsistence and informal sectors and the preservation of the environ-

ment. In certain regions, women are generally the most stable members of the community, as men often pursue work in distant locations, leaving women to safeguard the natural environment and ensure adequate and sustainable resource allocation within the household and the community.

251. The strategic actions needed for sound environmental management require a holistic, multidisciplinary and intersectoral approach. Women's participation and leadership are essential to every aspect of that approach. The recent United Nations global conferences on development, as well as regional preparatory conferences for the Fourth World Conference on Women, have all acknowledged that sustainable development policies that do not involve women and men alike will not succeed in the long run. They have called for the effective participation of women in the generation of knowledge and environmental education in decision-making and management at all levels. Women's experiences and contributions to an ecologically sound environment must therefore be central to the agenda for the twenty-first century. Sustainable development will be an elusive goal unless women's contribution to environmental management is recognized and supported.

252. In addressing the lack of adequate recognition and support for women's contribution to conservation and management of natural resources and safeguarding the environment, Governments and other actors should promote an active and visible policy of mainstreaming a gender perspective in all policies and programmes, including, as appropriate, an analysis of the effects on women and men, respectively, before decisions are taken.

Strategic objective K.1. *Involve women actively in environmental decision-making at all levels*

Actions to be taken

253. By Governments, at all levels, including municipal authorities, as appropriate:

(a) Ensure opportunities for women, including indigenous women, to participate in environmental decision-making at all levels, including as managers, designers and planners, and as implementers and evaluators of environmental projects;

(b) Facilitate and increase women's access to information and education, including in the areas of science, technology and economics, thus enhancing their knowledge, skills and opportunities for participation in environmental decisions;

(c) Encourage, subject to national legislation and consistent with the Convention on Biological Diversity, 35/

35/ United Nations Environment Programme, *Convention on Biological Diversity* (Environmental Law and Institutions Programme Activity Centre), June 1992.

the effective protection and use of the knowledge, innovations and practices of women of indigenous and local communities, including practices relating to traditional medicines, biodiversity and indigenous technologies, and endeavour to ensure that these are respected, maintained, promoted and preserved in an ecologically sustainable manner, and promote their wider application with the approval and involvement of the holders of such knowledge; in addition, safeguard the existing intellectual property rights of these women as protected under national and international law; work actively, where necessary, to find additional ways and means for the effective protection and use of such knowledge, innovations and practices, subject to national legislation and consistent with the Convention on Biological Diversity and relevant international law, and encourage fair and equitable sharing of benefits arising from the utilization of such knowledge, innovation and practices;

(d) Take appropriate measures to reduce risks to women from identified environmental hazards at home, at work and in other environments, including appropriate application of clean technologies, taking into account the precautionary approach agreed to in the Rio Declaration on Environment and Development; 18/

(e) Take measures to integrate a gender perspective in the design and implementation of, among other things, environmentally sound and sustainable resource management mechanisms, production techniques and infrastructure development in rural and urban areas;

(f) Take measures to empower women as producers and consumers so that they can take effective environmental actions, along with men, in their homes, communities and workplaces;

(g) Promote the participation of local communities, particularly women, in identification of public service needs, spatial planning and the provision and design of urban infrastructure.

254. By Governments and international organizations and private sector institutions, as appropriate:

(a) Take gender impact into consideration in the work of the Commission on Sustainable Development and other appropriate United Nations bodies and in the activities of international financial institutions;

(b) Promote the involvement of women and the incorporation of a gender perspective in the design, approval and execution of projects funded under the Global Environment Facility and other appropriate United Nations organizations;

(c) Encourage the design of projects in the areas of concern to the Global Environment Facility that would benefit women and projects managed by women;

(d) Establish strategies and mechanisms to increase the proportion of women, particularly at grass-roots levels, involved as decision makers, planners, managers, scientists and technical advisers and as beneficiaries in the design, development and implementation of policies and programmes for natural resource management and environmental protection and conservation;

(e) Encourage social, economic, political and scientific institutions to address environmental degradation and the resulting impact on women.

255. By non-governmental organizations and the private sector:

(a) Assume advocacy of environmental and natural resource management issues of concern to women and provide information to contribute to resource mobilization for environmental protection and conservation;

(b) Facilitate the access of women agriculturists, fishers and pastoralists to knowledge, skills, marketing services and environmentally sound technologies to support and strengthen their crucial roles and their expertise in resource management and the conservation of biological diversity.

Strategic objective K.2. *Integrate gender concerns and perspectives in policies and programmes for sustainable development*

Actions to be taken

256. By Governments:

(a) Integrate women, including indigenous women, their perspectives and knowledge, on an equal basis with men, in decision-making regarding sustainable resource management and the development of policies and programmes for sustainable development, including in particular those designed to address and prevent environmental degradation of the land;

(b) Evaluate policies and programmes in terms of environmental impact and women's equal access to and use of natural resources;

(c) Ensure adequate research to assess how and to what extent women are particularly susceptible or exposed to environmental degradation and hazards, including, as necessary, research and data collection on specific groups of women, particularly women with low income, indigenous women and women belonging to minorities;

(d) Integrate rural women's traditional knowledge and practices of sustainable resource use and management in the development of environmental management and extension programmes;

(e) Integrate the results of gender-sensitive research into mainstream policies with a view to developing sustainable human settlements;

(f) Promote knowledge of and sponsor research on the role of women, particularly rural and indigenous women, in food gathering and production, soil conservation, irrigation, watershed management, sanitation, coastal zone and marine resource management, integrated pest management, land-use planning, forest conservation and community forestry, fisheries, natural disaster prevention, and new and renewable sources of energy, focusing particularly on indigenous women's knowledge and experience;

(g) Develop a strategy for change to eliminate all obstacles to women's full and equal participation in sustainable development and equal access to and control over resources;

(h) Promote the education of girls and women of all ages in science, technology, economics and other disciplines relating to the natural environment so that they can make informed choices and offer informed input in determining local economic, scientific and environmental priorities for the management and appropriate use of natural and local resources and ecosystems;

(i) Develop programmes to involve female professionals and scientists, as well as technical, administrative and clerical workers, in environmental management, develop training programmes for girls and women in these fields, expand opportunities for the hiring and promotion of women in these fields and implement special measures to advance women's expertise and participation in these activities;

(j) Identify and promote environmentally sound technologies that have been designed, developed and improved in consultation with women and that are appropriate to both women and men;

(k) Support the development of women's equal access to housing infrastructure, safe water, and sustainable and affordable energy technologies, such as wind, solar, biomass and other renewable sources, through participatory needs assessments, energy planning and policy formulation at the local and national levels;

(l) Ensure that clean water is available and accessible to all by the year 2000 and that environmental protection and conservation plans are designed and implemented to restore polluted water systems and rebuild damaged watersheds.

257. By international organizations, non-governmental organizations and private sector institutions:

(a) Involve women in the communication industries in raising awareness regarding environmental issues, especially on the environmental and health impacts of products, technologies and industry processes;

(b) Encourage consumers to use their purchasing power to promote the production of environmentally safe products and encourage investment in environmentally sound and productive agricultural, fisheries, commercial and industrial activities and technologies;

(c) Support women's consumer initiatives by promoting the marketing of organic food and recycling facilities, product information and product labelling, including labelling of toxic chemical and pesticide containers with language and symbols that are understood by consumers, regardless of age and level of literacy.

Strategic objective K.3. *Strengthen or establish mechanisms at the national, regional and international levels to assess the impact of development and environmental policies on women*

Actions to be taken

258. By Governments, regional and international organizations and non-governmental organizations, as appropriate:

(a) Provide technical assistance to women, particularly in developing countries, in the sectors of agriculture, fisheries, small enterprises, trade and industry to ensure the continuing promotion of human resource development and the development of environmentally sound technologies and of women's entrepreneurship;

(b) Develop gender-sensitive databases, information and monitoring systems and participatory action-oriented research, methodologies and policy analyses, with the collaboration of academic institutions and local women researchers, on the following:

(i) Knowledge and experience on the part of women concerning the management and conservation of natural resources for incorporation in the databases and information systems for sustainable development;

(ii) The impact on women of environmental and natural resource degradation, deriving from, *inter alia*, unsustainable production and consumption patterns, drought, poor quality water, global warming, desertification, sealevel rise, hazardous waste, natural disasters, toxic chemicals and pesticide residues, radioactive waste, armed conflicts and its consequences;

(iii) Analysis of the structural links between gender relations, environment and development, with special emphasis on particular sectors, such as agriculture, industry, fisheries, forestry, environmental health, biological diversity, climate, water resources and sanitation;

(iv) Measures to develop and include environmental, economic, cultural, social and gender-sensitive analyses as an essential step in the development and monitoring of programmes and policies;

(v) Programmes to create rural and urban training, research and resource centres that will disseminate environmentally sound technologies to women;

(c) Ensure the full compliance with relevant international obligations, including where relevant, the Basel Convention and other conventions relating to the transboundary movements of hazardous wastes (which include toxic wastes) and the Code of Practice of the International Atomic Energy Agency relating to the movement of radioactive waste; enact and enforce regulations for environmentally sound management related to safe storage and movements; consider taking action towards the prohibition of those movements that are unsafe and insecure; ensure the strict control and management of hazardous wastes and radioactive waste, in accordance with relevant international and regional obligations and eliminate the exportation of such wastes to countries that, individually or through international agreements, prohibit their importation;

(d) Promote coordination within and among institutions to implement the Platform for Action and chapter 24 of Agenda 21 by, *inter alia*, requesting the Commission on Sustainable Development, through the Economic and Social Council, to seek input from the Commission on the Status of Women when reviewing the implementation of Agenda 21 with regard to women and the environment.

L   *The girl child*

259.   The Convention on the Rights of the Child recognizes that "States Parties shall respect and ensure the rights set forth in the present Convention to each child within their jurisdiction without discrimination of any kind, irrespective of the child's or his or her parent's or legal guardian's race, colour, sex, language, religion, political or other opinion, national, ethnic or social origin, property, disability, birth or status" (art. 2, para. 1). 11/ However, in many countries available indicators show that the girl child is discriminated against from the earliest stages of life, through her childhood and into adulthood. In some areas of the world, men outnumber women by 5 in every 100. The reasons for the discrepancy include, among other things, harmful attitudes and practices, such as female genital mutilation, son preference — which results in female infanticide and prenatal sex selection — early marriage, including child marriage, violence against women, sexual exploitation, sexual abuse, discrimination against girls in food allocation and other practices related to health and well-being. As a result, fewer girls than boys survive into adulthood.

260.   Girls are often treated as inferior and are socialized to put themselves last, thus undermining their self-esteem. Discrimination and neglect in childhood can initiate a lifelong downward spiral of deprivation and exclusion from the social mainstream. Initiatives should be taken to prepare girls to participate actively, effectively and equally with boys at all levels of social, economic, political and cultural leadership.

261.   Gender-biased educational processes, including curricula, educational materials and practices, teachers' attitudes and classroom interaction, reinforce existing gender inequalities.

262.   Girls and adolescents may receive a variety of conflicting and confusing messages on their gender roles from their parents, teachers, peers and the media. Women and men need to work together with children and youth to break down persistent gender stereotypes, taking into account the rights of the child and the responsibilities, rights and duties of parents as stated in paragraph 267 below.

263.   Although the number of educated children has grown in the past 20 years in some countries, boys have proportionately fared much better than girls. In 1990, 130 million children had no access to primary school; of these, 81 million were girls. This can be attributed to such factors as customary attitudes, child labour, early marriages, lack of funds and lack of adequate schooling facilities, teenage pregnancies and gender inequalities in society at large as well as in the family as defined in paragraph 29 above. In some countries the shortage of women teachers can inhibit the enrolment of girls. In many cases, girls start to undertake heavy domestic chores at a very early age and are expected to manage both educational and domestic responsibilities, often resulting in poor scholastic performance and an early drop-out from schooling.

264.   The percentage of girls enrolled in secondary school remains significantly low in many countries. Girls are often not encouraged or given the opportunity to pursue scientific and technological training and education, which limits the knowledge they require for their daily lives and their employment opportunities.

265.   Girls are less encouraged than boys to participate in and learn about the social, economic and political functioning of society, with the result that they are not offered the same opportunities as boys to take part in decision-making processes.

266.   Existing discrimination against the girl child in her access to nutrition and physical and mental health services endangers her current and future health. An estimated 450 million adult women in developing countries are stunted as a result of childhood protein-energy malnutrition.

267.   The International Conference on Population and Development recognized, in paragraph 7.3 of the

Programme of Action, 14/ that "full attention should be given to the promotion of mutually respectful and equitable gender relations and particularly to meeting the educational and service needs of adolescents to enable them to deal in a positive and responsible way with their sexuality", taking into account the rights of the child to access to information, privacy, confidentiality, respect and informed consent, as well as the responsibilities, rights and duties of parents and legal guardians to provide, in a manner consistent with the evolving capacities of the child, appropriate direction and guidance in the exercise by the child of the rights recognized in the Convention on the Rights of the Child, and in conformity with the Convention on the Elimination of All Forms of Discrimination against Women. In all actions concerning children, the best interests of the child shall be a primary consideration. Support should be given to integral sexual education for young people with parental support and guidance that stresses the responsibility of males for their own sexuality and fertility and that help them exercise their responsibilities.

268. More than 15 million girls aged 15 to 19 give birth each year. Motherhood at a very young age entails complications during pregnancy and delivery and a risk of maternal death that is much greater than average. The children of young mothers have higher levels of morbidity and mortality. Early child-bearing continues to be an impediment to improvements in the educational, economic and social status of women in all parts of the world. Overall, early marriage and early motherhood can severely curtail educational and employment opportunities and are likely to have a long-term adverse impact on their and their children's quality of life.

269. Sexual violence and sexually transmitted diseases, including HIV/AIDS, have a devastating effect on children's health, and girls are more vulnerable than boys to the consequences of unprotected and premature sexual relations. Girls often face pressures to engage in sexual activity. Due to such factors as their youth, social pressures, lack of protective laws, or failure to enforce laws, girls are more vulnerable to all kinds of violence, particularly sexual violence, including rape, sexual abuse, sexual exploitation, trafficking, possibly the sale of their organs and tissues, and forced labour.

270. The girl child with disabilities faces additional barriers and needs to be ensured non-discrimination and equal enjoyment of all human rights and fundamental freedoms in accordance with the Standard Rules on the Equalization of Opportunities for Persons with Disabilities. 30/

271. Some children are particularly vulnerable, especially the abandoned, homeless and displaced, street children, children in areas in conflict, and children who are discriminated against because they belong to an ethnic or racial minority group.

272. All barriers must therefore be eliminated to enable girls without exception to develop their full potential and skills through equal access to education and training, nutrition, physical and mental health care and related information.

273. In addressing issues concerning children and youth, Governments should promote an active and visible policy of mainstreaming a gender perspective into all policies and programmes so that before decisions are taken, an analysis is made of the effects on girls and boys, respectively.

Strategic objective L.1. *Eliminate all forms of discrimination against the girl child*

Actions to be taken

274. By Governments:

(a) By States that have not signed or ratified the Convention on the Rights of the Child, take urgent measures towards signing and ratifying the Convention, bearing in mind the strong exhortation made at the World Conference on Human Rights to sign it before the end of 1995, and by States that have signed and ratified the Convention, ensure its full implementation through the adoption of all necessary legislative, administrative and other measures and by fostering an enabling environment that encourages full respect for the rights of children;

(b) Consistent with article 7 of the Convention on the Rights of the Child, 11/ take measures to ensure that a child is registered immediately after birth and has the right from birth to a name, the right to acquire a nationality and, as far as possible, the right to know and be cared for by his or her parents;

(c) Take steps to ensure that children receive appropriate financial support from their parents, by, among other measures, enforcing child-support laws;

(d) Eliminate the injustice and obstacles in relation to inheritance faced by the girl child so that all children may enjoy their rights without discrimination, by, *inter alia*, enacting, as appropriate, and enforcing legislation that guarantees equal right to succession and ensures equal right to inherit, regardless of the sex of the child;

(e) Enact and strictly enforce laws to ensure that marriage is only entered into with the free and full consent of the intending spouses; in addition, enact and strictly enforce laws concerning the minimum legal age of consent and the minimum age for marriage and raise the minimum age for marriage where necessary;

(f) Develop and implement comprehensive policies, plans of action and programmes for the survival, protection, development and advancement of the girl child to promote and protect the full enjoyment of her human rights and to ensure equal opportunities for girls; these plans should form an integral part of the total development process;

(g) Ensure the disaggregation by sex and age of all data related to children in the health, education and other sectors in order to include a gender perspective in planning, implementation and monitoring of such programmes.

275. By Governments and international and non-governmental organizations:

(a) Disaggregate information and data on children by sex and age, undertake research on the situation of girls and integrate, as appropriate, the results in the formulation of policies, programmes and decision-making for the advancement of the girl child;

(b) Generate social support for the enforcement of laws on the minimum legal age for marriage, in particular by providing educational opportunities for girls.

Strategic objective L.2. *Eliminate negative cultural attitudes and practices against girls*

Actions to be taken

276. By Governments:

(a) Encourage and support, as appropriate, non-governmental organizations and community-based organizations in their efforts to promote changes in negative attitudes and practices towards girls;

(b) Set up educational programmes and develop teaching materials and textbooks that will sensitize and inform adults about the harmful effects of certain traditional or customary practices on girl children;

(c) Develop and adopt curricula, teaching materials and textbooks to improve the self-image, lives and work opportunities of girls, particularly in areas where women have traditionally been underrepresented, such as mathematics, science and technology;

(d) Take steps so that tradition and religion and their expressions are not a basis for discrimination against girls.

277. By Governments and, as appropriate, international and non-governmental organizations:

(a) Promote an educational setting that eliminates all barriers that impede the schooling of married and/or pregnant girls and young mothers, including, as appropriate, affordable and physically accessible child-care facilities and parental education to encourage those who have responsibilities for the care of their children and siblings during their school years to return to, or continue with, and complete schooling;

(b) Encourage educational institutions and the media to adopt and project balanced and non-stereotyped images of girls and boys, and work to eliminate child pornography and degrading and violent portrayals of the girl child;

(c) Eliminate all forms of discrimination against the girl child and the root causes of son preference, which result in harmful and unethical practices such as prenatal sex selection and female infanticide; this is often compounded by the increasing use of technologies to determine foetal sex, resulting in abortion of female foetuses;

(d) Develop policies and programmes, giving priority to formal and informal education programmes that support girls and enable them to acquire knowledge, develop self-esteem and take responsibility for their own lives; and place special focus on programmes to educate women and men, especially parents, on the importance of girls' physical and mental health and well-being, including the elimination of discrimination against girls in food allocation, early marriage, violence against girls, female genital mutilation, child prostitution, sexual abuse, rape and incest.

Strategic objective L.3. *Promote and protect the rights of the girl child and increase awareness of her needs and potential*

Actions to be taken

278. By Governments and international and non-governmental organizations:

(a) Generate awareness of the disadvantaged situation of girls among policy makers, planners, administrators and implementors at all levels, as well as within households and communities;

(b) Make the girl child, particularly the girl child in difficult circumstances, aware of her own potential, educate her about the rights guaranteed to her under all international human rights instruments, including the Convention on the Rights of the Child, legislation enacted for her and the various measures undertaken by both governmental and non-governmental organizations working to improve her status;

(c) Educate women, men, girls and boys to promote girls' status and encourage them to work towards mutual respect and equal partnership between girls and boys;

(d) Facilitate the equal provision of appropriate services and devices to girls with disabilities and provide their families with related support services, as appropriate.

Strategic objective L.4. *Eliminate discrimination against girls in education, skills development and training*

Actions to be taken

279. By Governments:

(a) Ensure universal and equal access to and completion of primary education by all children and eliminate the existing gap between girls and boys, as stipulated in article 28 of the Convention on the Rights of the Child; 11/ similarly, ensure equal access to secondary education by the year 2005 and equal access to higher education, including vocational and technical education, for all girls and boys, including the disadvantaged and gifted;

(b) Take steps to integrate functional literacy and numeracy programmes, particularly for out-of-school girls in development programmes;

(c) Promote human rights education in educational programmes and include in human rights education the fact that the human rights of women and the girl child are an inalienable, integral and indivisible part of universal human rights;

(d) Increase enrolment and improve retention rates of girls by allocating appropriate budgetary resources and by enlisting the support of the community and parents through campaigns and flexible school schedules, incentives, scholarships, access programmes for out-of-school girls and other measures;

(e) Develop training programmes and materials for teachers and educators, raising awareness about their own role in the educational process, with a view to providing them with effective strategies for gender-sensitive teaching;

(f) Take actions to ensure that female teachers and professors have the same possibilities and status as male teachers and professors.

280. By Governments and international and non-governmental organizations:

(a) Provide education and skills training to increase girls' opportunities for employment and access to decision-making processes;

(b) Provide education to increase girls' knowledge and skills related to the functioning of economic, financial and political systems;

(c) Ensure access to appropriate education and skills-training for girl children with disabilities for their full participation in life;

(d) Promote the full and equal participation of girls in extracurricular activities, such as sports, drama and cultural activities.

Strategic objective L.5. *Eliminate discrimination against girls in health and nutrition*

Actions to be taken

281. By Governments and international and non-governmental organizations:

(a) Provide public information on the removal of discriminatory practices against girls in food allocation, nutrition and access to health services;

(b) Sensitize the girl child, parents, teachers and society concerning good general health and nutrition and raise awareness of the health dangers and other problems connected with early pregnancies;

(c) Strengthen and reorient health education and health services, particularly primary health care programmes, including sexual and reproductive health, and design quality health programmes that meet the physical and mental needs of girls and that attend to the needs of young, expectant and nursing mothers;

(d) Establish peer education and outreach programmes with a view to strengthening individual and collective action to reduce the vulnerability of girls to HIV/AIDS and other sexually transmitted diseases, as agreed to in the Programme of Action of the International Conference on Population and Development and as established in the report of that Conference, recognizing the parental roles referred to in paragraph 267 of the present Platform for Action;

(e) Ensure education and dissemination of information to girls, especially adolescent girls, regarding the physiology of reproduction, reproductive and sexual health, as agreed to in the Programme of Action of the International Conference on Population and Development and as established in the report of that Conference, responsible family planning practice, family life, reproductive health, sexually transmitted diseases, HIV infection and AIDS prevention, recognizing the parental roles referred to in paragraph 267;

(f) Include health and nutritional training as an integral part of literacy programmes and school curricula starting at the primary level for the benefit of the girl child;

(g) Emphasize the role and responsibility of adolescents in sexual and reproductive health and behaviour through the provision of appropriate services and counselling, as discussed in paragraph 267;

(h) Develop information and training programmes for health planners and implementors on the special health needs of the girl child;

(i) Take all the appropriate measures with a view to abolishing traditional practices prejudicial to the health of children, as stipulated in article 24 of the Convention on the Rights of the Child. 11/

Strategic objective L.6. *Eliminate the economic exploitation of child labour and protect young girls at work*

Actions to be taken

282. By Governments:

(a) In conformity with article 32 of the Convention on the Rights of the Child, 11/ protect children from economic exploitation and from performing any work that is likely to be hazardous or to interfere with the child's education, or to be harmful to the child's health or physical, mental, spiritual, moral or social development;

(b) Define a minimum age for a child's admission to employment in national legislation, in conformity with existing international labour standards and the Convention on the Rights of the Child, including girls in all sectors of activity;

(c) Protect young girls at work, *inter alia*, through:

(i) A minimum age or ages for admission to employment;

(ii) Strict monitoring of work conditions (respect for work time, prohibition of work by children not provided for by national legislation, and monitoring of hygiene and health conditions at work);

(iii) Application of social security coverage;

(iv) Establishment of continuous training and education;

(d) Strengthen, where necessary, legislation governing the work of children and provide for appropriate penalties or other sanctions to ensure effective enforcement of the legislation;

(e) Use existing international labour standards, including, as appropriate, ILO standards for the protection of working children, to guide the formulation of national labour legislation and policies.

Strategic objective L.7. *Eradicate violence against the girl child*

Actions to be taken

283. By Governments and, as appropriate, international and non-governmental organizations:

(a) Take effective actions and measures to enact and enforce legislation to protect the safety and security of girls from all forms of violence at work, including training programmes and support programmes, and take measures to eliminate incidents of sexual harassment of girls in educational and other institutions;

(b) Take appropriate legislative, administrative, social and educational measures to protect the girl child, in the household and in society, from all forms of physical or mental violence, injury or abuse, neglect or negligent treatment, maltreatment or exploitation, including sexual abuse;

(c) Undertake gender sensitization training for those involved in healing and rehabilitation and other assistance programmes for girls who are victims of violence and promote programmes of information, support and training for such girls;

(d) Enact and enforce legislation protecting girls from all forms of violence, including female infanticide and prenatal sex selection, genital mutilation, incest, sexual abuse, sexual exploitation, child prostitution and child pornography, and develop age-appropriate safe and confidential programmes and medical, social and psychological support services to assist girls who are subjected to violence.

Strategic objective L.8. *Promote the girl child's awareness of and participation in social, economic and political life*

Actions to be taken

284. By Governments and international and non-governmental organizations:

(a) Provide access for girls to training, information and the media on social, cultural, economic and political issues and enable them to articulate their views;

(b) Support non-governmental organizations, in particular youth non-governmental organizations, in their efforts to promote the equality and participation of girls in society.

Strategic objective L.9. *Strengthen the role of the family* * *in improving the status of the girl child*

Actions to be taken

285. By Governments, in cooperation with non-governmental organizations:

(a) Formulate policies and programmes to help the family, as defined in paragraph 29 above, in its supporting, educating and nurturing roles, with particular emphasis on the elimination of intra-family discrimination against the girl child;

(b) Provide an environment conducive to the strengthening of the family, as defined in paragraph 29 above, with a view to providing supportive and preventive measures which protect, respect and promote the potential of the girl child;

(c) Educate and encourage parents and caregivers to treat girls and boys equally and to ensure shared responsibilities between girls and boys in the family, as defined in paragraph 29 above.

Chapter V

Institutional arrangements

286. The Platform for Action establishes a set of actions that should lead to fundamental change. Immediate action and accountability are essential if the targets are to be met by the year 2000. Implementation is primarily the responsibility of Governments, but is also dependent on a wide range of institutions in the public,

---

*As defined in para. 29 above.

private and non-governmental sectors at the community, national, subregional/regional and international levels.

287. During the United Nations Decade for Women (1976-1985), many institutions specifically devoted to the advancement of women were established at the national, regional and international levels. At the international level, the International Research and Training Institute for the Advancement of Women (INSTRAW), the United Nations Development Fund for Women (UNIFEM), and the Committee to monitor the Convention on the Elimination of All Forms of Discrimination against Women were established. These entities, along with the Commission on the Status of Women and its secretariat, the Division for the Advancement of Women, became the main institutions in the United Nations specifically devoted to women's advancement globally. At the national level, a number of countries established or strengthened national mechanisms to plan, advocate for and monitor progress in the advancement of women.

288. Implementation of the Platform for Action by national, subregional/regional and international institutions, both public and private, would be facilitated by transparency, by increased linkages between networks and organizations and by a consistent flow of information among all concerned. Clear objectives and accountability mechanisms are also required. Links with other institutions at the national, subregional/regional and international levels and with networks and organizations devoted to the advancement of women are needed.

289. Non-governmental and grass-roots organizations have a specific role to play in creating a social, economic, political and intellectual climate based on equality between women and men. Women should be actively involved in the implementation and monitoring of the Platform for Action.

290. Effective implementation of the Platform will also require changes in the internal dynamics of institutions and organizations, including values, behaviour, rules and procedures that are inimical to the advancement of women. Sexual harassment should be eliminated.

291. National, subregional/regional and international institutions should have strong and clear mandates and the authority, resources and accountability mechanisms needed for the tasks set out in the Platform for Action. Their methods of operation should ensure efficient and effective implementation of the Platform. There should be a clear commitment to international norms and standards of equality between women and men as a basis for all actions.

292. To ensure effective implementation of the Platform for Action and to enhance the work for the advancement of women at the national, subregional/re-

gional and international levels, Governments, the United Nations system and all other relevant organizations should promote an active and visible policy of mainstreaming a gender perspective, *inter alia*, in the monitoring and evaluation of all policies and programmes.

A. *National level*

293. Governments have the primary responsibility for implementing the Platform for Action. Commitment at the highest political level is essential to its implementation, and Governments should take a leading role in coordinating, monitoring and assessing progress in the advancement of women. The Fourth World Conference on Women is a conference of national and international commitment and action. This requires commitment from Governments and the international community. The Platform for Action is part of a continuing process and has a catalytic effect as it will contribute to programmes and practical outcomes for girls and women of all ages. States and the international community are encouraged to respond to this challenge by making commitments for action. As part of this process, many States have made commitments for action as reflected, *inter alia*, in their national statements.

294. National mechanisms and institutions for the advancement of women should participate in public policy formulation and encourage the implementation of the Platform for Action through various bodies and institutions, including the private sector, and, where necessary, should act as a catalyst in developing new programmes by the year 2000 in areas that are not covered by existing institutions.

295. The active support and participation of a broad and diverse range of other institutional actors should be encouraged, including legislative bodies, academic and research institutions, professional associations, trade unions, cooperatives, local community groups, non-governmental organizations, including women's organizations and feminist groups, the media, religious groups, youth organizations and cultural groups, as well as financial and non-profit organizations.

296. In order for the Platform for Action to be implemented, it will be necessary for Governments to establish or improve the effectiveness of national machineries for the advancement of women at the highest political level, appropriate intra- and inter-ministerial procedures and staffing, and other institutions with the mandate and capacity to broaden women's participation and integrate gender analysis into policies and programmes. The first step in this process for all institutions should be to review their objectives, programmes and operational procedures in terms of the actions called for in the Platform. A key activity should be to promote

public awareness and support for the goals of the Platform for Action, *inter alia*, through the mass media and public education.

297. As soon as possible, preferably by the end of 1995, Governments, in consultation with relevant institutions and non-governmental organizations, should begin to develop implementation strategies for the Platform and, preferably by the end of 1996, should have developed their strategies or plans of action. This planning process should draw upon persons at the highest level of authority in government and relevant actors in civil society. These implementation strategies should be comprehensive, have time-bound targets and benchmarks for monitoring, and include proposals for allocating or reallocating resources for implementation. Where necessary, the support of the international community could be enlisted, including resources.

298. Non-governmental organizations should be encouraged to contribute to the design and implementation of these strategies or national plans of action. They should also be encouraged to develop their own programmes to complement government efforts. Women's organizations and feminist groups, in collaboration with other non-governmental organizations, should be encouraged to organize networks, as necessary, and to advocate for and support the implementation of the Platform for Action by Governments and regional and international bodies.

299. Governments should commit themselves to gender balance, *inter alia*, through the creation of special mechanisms, in all government-appointed committees, boards and other relevant official bodies, as appropriate, as well as in all international bodies, institutions and organizations, notably by presenting and promoting more women candidates.

300. Regional and international organizations, in particular development institutions, especially INSTRAW, UNIFEM and bilateral donors, should provide financial and advisory assistance to national machinery in order to increase its ability to gather information, develop networks and carry out its mandate, in addition to strengthening international mechanisms to promote the advancement of women through their respective mandates, in cooperation with Governments.

B. *Subregional/regional level*

301. The regional commissions of the United Nations and other subregional/regional structures should promote and assist the pertinent national institutions in monitoring and implementing the global Platform for Action within their mandates. This should be done in coordination with the implementation of the respective regional platforms or plans of action and in close collaboration with the Commission on the Status of Women, taking into account the need for a coordinated follow-up to United Nations conferences in the economic, social, human rights and related fields.

302. In order to facilitate the regional implementation, monitoring and evaluation process, the Economic and Social Council should consider reviewing the institutional capacity of the United Nations regional commissions within their mandates, including their women's units/focal points, to deal with gender issues in the light of the Platform for Action, as well as the regional platforms and plans of action. Consideration should be given, *inter alia*, and, where appropriate, to strengthening capacity in this respect.

303. Within their existing mandates and activities, the regional commissions should mainstream women's issues and gender perspectives and should also consider the establishment of mechanisms and processes to ensure the implementation and monitoring of both the Platform for Action and the regional platforms and plans of action. The regional commissions should, within their mandates, collaborate on gender issues with other regional intergovernmental organizations, non-governmental organizations, financial and research institutions and the private sector.

304. Regional offices of the specialized agencies of the United Nations system should, as appropriate, develop and publicize a plan of action for implementing the Platform for Action, including the identification of timeframes and resources. Technical assistance and operational activities at the regional level should establish well-identified targets for the advancement of women. To this end, regular coordination should be undertaken among United Nations bodies and agencies.

305. Non-governmental organizations within the region should be supported in their efforts to develop networks to coordinate advocacy and dissemination of information about the global Platform for Action and the respective regional platforms or plans of action.

C. *International level*

1. *United Nations*

306. The Platform for Action needs to be implemented through the work of all of the bodies and organizations of the United Nations system during the period 1995-2000, specifically and as an integral part of wider programming. An enhanced framework for international cooperation for gender issues must be developed during the period 1995-2000 in order to ensure the integrated and comprehensive implementation, follow-up and assessment of the Platform for Action, taking into account the results of global United Nations summits and confer-

ences. The fact that at all of these summits and conferences, Governments have committed themselves to the empowerment of women in different areas, makes coordination crucial to the follow-up strategies for this Platform for Action. The Agenda for Development and the Agenda for Peace should take into account the Platform for Action of the Fourth World Conference on Women.

307. The institutional capacity of the United Nations system to carry out and coordinate its responsibility for implementing the Platform for Action, as well as its expertise and working methods to promote the advancement of women, should be improved.

308. Responsibility for ensuring the implementation of the Platform for Action and the integration of a gender perspective into all policies and programmes of the United Nations system must rest at the highest levels.

309. To improve the system's efficiency and effectiveness in providing support for equality and women's empowerment at the national level and to enhance its capacity to achieve the objectives of the Platform for Action, there is a need to renew, reform and revitalize various parts of the United Nations system. This would include reviewing and strengthening the strategies and working methods of different United Nations mechanisms for the advancement of women with a view to rationalizing and, as appropriate, strengthening their advisory, catalytic and monitoring functions in relation to mainstream bodies and agencies. Women/gender units are important for effective mainstreaming, but strategies must be further developed to prevent inadvertent marginalization as opposed to mainstreaming of the gender dimension throughout all operations.

310. In following up the Fourth World Conference on Women, all entities of the United Nations system focusing on the advancement of women should have the necessary resources and support to carry out follow-up activities. The efforts of gender focal points within organizations should be well integrated into overall policy, planning, programming and budgeting.

311. Action must be taken by the United Nations and other international organizations to eliminate barriers to the advancement of women within their organizations in accordance with the Platform for Action.

General Assembly

312. The General Assembly, as the highest intergovernmental body in the United Nations, is the principal policy-making and appraisal organ on matters relating to the follow-up to the Conference, and as such, should integrate gender issues throughout its work. It should appraise progress in the effective implementation of the Platform for Action, recognizing that these issues cut across social, political and economic policy. At its fiftieth

session, in 1995, the General Assembly will have before it the report of the Fourth World Conference on Women. In accordance with its resolution 49/161, it will also examine a report of the Secretary-General on the follow-up to the Conference, taking into account the recommendations of the Conference. The General Assembly should include the follow-up to the Conference as part of its continuing work on the advancement of women. In 1996, 1998 and 2000, it should review the implementation of the Platform for Action.

Economic and Social Council

313. The Economic and Social Council, in the context of its role under the Charter of the United Nations and in accordance with General Assembly resolutions 45/264, 46/235 and 48/162, would oversee system-wide coordination in the implementation of the Platform for Action and make recommendations in this regard. The Council should be invited to review the implementation of the Platform for Action, giving due consideration to the reports of the Commission on the Status of Women. As coordinating body, the Council should be invited to review the mandate of the Commission on the Status of Women, taking into account the need for effective coordination with other related commissions and Conference follow-up. The Council should incorporate gender issues into its discussion of all policy questions, giving due consideration to recommendations prepared by the Commission. It should consider dedicating at least one high-level segment before the year 2000 to the advancement of women and implementation of the Platform for Action with the active involvement and participation, *inter alia*, of the specialized agencies, including the World Bank and IMF.

314. The Council should consider dedicating at least one coordination segment before the year 2000 to coordination of the advancement of women, based on the revised system-wide medium-term plan for the advancement of women.

315. The Council should consider dedicating at least one operational activities segment before the year 2000 to the coordination of development activities related to gender, based on the revised system-wide medium-term plan for the advancement of women, with a view to instituting guidelines and procedures for implementation of the Platform for Action by the funds and programmes of the United Nations system.

316. The Administrative Committee on Coordination (ACC) should consider how its participating entities might best coordinate their activities, *inter alia*, through existing procedures at the inter-agency level for ensuring system-wide coordination to implement and help follow up the objectives of the Platform for Action.

Commission on the Status of Women

317. The General Assembly and the Economic and Social Council, in accordance with their respective mandates, are invited to review and strengthen the mandate of the Commission on the Status of Women, taking into account the Platform for Action as well as the need for synergy with other related commissions and Conference follow-up, and for a system-wide approach to its implementation.

318. As a functional commission assisting the Economic and Social Council, the Commission on the Status of Women should have a central role in monitoring, within the United Nations system, the implementation of the Platform for Action and advising the Council thereon. It should have a clear mandate with sufficient human and financial resources, through the reallocation of resources within the regular budget of the United Nations to carry the mandate out.

319. The Commission on the Status of Women should assist the Economic and Social Council in its coordination of the reporting on the implementation of the Platform for Action with the relevant organizations of the United Nations system. The Commission should draw upon inputs from other organizations of the United Nations system and other sources, as appropriate.

320. The Commission on the Status of Women, in developing its work programme for the period 1996-2000, should review the critical areas of concern in the Platform for Action and consider how to integrate in its agenda the follow-up to the World Conference on Women. In this context, the Commission on the Status of Women could consider how it could further develop its catalytic role in mainstreaming a gender perspective in United Nations activities.

Other functional commissions

321. Within their mandates, other functional commissions of the Economic and Social Council should also take due account of the Platform for Action and ensure the integration of gender aspects in their respective work.

Committee on the Elimination of Discrimination against Women and other treaty bodies

322. The Committee on the Elimination of Discrimination against Women, in implementing its responsibilities under the Convention on the Elimination of All Forms of Discrimination against Women, should, within its mandate, take into account the Platform for Action when considering the reports submitted by States parties.

323. States parties to the Convention on the Elimination of All Forms of Discrimination against Women are invited, when reporting under article 18 of the Convention, to include information on measures taken to implement the Platform for Action in order to facilitate the Committee on the Elimination of Discrimination against Women in monitoring effectively women's ability to enjoy the rights guaranteed by the Convention.

324. The ability of the Committee on the Elimination of Discrimination against Women to monitor implementation of the Convention should be strengthened through the provision of human and financial resources within the regular budget of the United Nations, including expert legal assistance and, in accordance with General Assembly resolution 49/164 and the decision made by the meeting of States parties to the Convention held in May 1995, sufficient meeting time for the Committee. The Committee should increase its coordination with other human rights treaty bodies, taking into account the recommendations in the Vienna Declaration and Programme of Action.

325. Within their mandate, other treaty bodies should also take due account of the implementation of the Platform for Action and ensure the integration of the equal status and human rights of women in their work.

United Nations Secretariat

Office of the Secretary-General

326. The Secretary-General is requested to assume responsibility for coordination of policy within the United Nations for the implementation of the Platform for Action and for the mainstreaming of a system-wide gender perspective in all activities of the United Nations, taking into account the mandates of the bodies concerned. The Secretary-General should consider specific measures for ensuring effective coordination in the implementation of these objectives. To this end, the Secretary-General is invited to establish a high-level post in the office of the Secretary-General, using existing human and financial resources, to act as the Secretary-General's adviser on gender issues and to help ensure system-wide implementation of the Platform for Action in close cooperation with the Division for the Advancement of Women.

Division for the Advancement of Women

327. The primary function of the Division for the Advancement of Women of the Department for Policy Coordination and Sustainable Development is to provide substantive servicing to the Commission on the Status of Women and other intergovernmental bodies when they are concerned with the advancement of women, as well as to the Committee on the Elimination of Discrimination against Women. It has been designated a focal point for the implementation of the Nairobi Forward-looking Strategies for the Advancement of Women. In the light of the review of the mandate of the Commission on the

Status of Women, as set out in paragraph 313 above, the functions of the Division for the Advancement of Women will also need to be assessed. The Secretary-General is requested to ensure more effective functioning of the Division by, *inter alia*, providing sufficient human and financial resources within the regular budget of the United Nations.

328. The Division should examine the obstacles to the advancement of women through the application of gender-impact analysis in policy studies for the Commission on the Status of Women and through support to other subsidiary bodies. After the Fourth World Conference on Women it should play a coordinating role in preparing the revision of the system-wide medium-term plan for the advancement of women for the period 1996-2001 and should continue serving as the secretariat for inter-agency coordination for the advancement of women. It should continue to maintain a flow of information with national commissions, national institutions for the advancement of women and non-governmental organizations with regard to implementation of the Platform for Action.

Other units of the United Nations Secretariat

329. The various units of the United Nations Secretariat should examine their programmes to determine how they can best contribute to the coordinated implementation of the Platform for Action. Proposals for implementation of the Platform need to be reflected in the revision of the system-wide medium-term plan for the advancement of women for the period 1996-2001, as well as in the proposed United Nations medium-term plan for the period 1998-2002. The content of the actions will depend on the mandates of the bodies concerned.

330. Existing and new linkages should be developed throughout the Secretariat in order to ensure that the gender perspective is introduced as a central dimension in all activities of the Secretariat.

331. The Office of Human Resources Management should, in collaboration with programme managers world wide, and in accordance with the strategic plan of action for the improvement of the status of women in the Secretariat (1995-2000), continue to accord priority to the recruitment and promotion of women in posts subject to geographical distribution, particularly in senior policy-level and decision-making posts, in order to achieve the goals set out in General Assembly resolutions 45/125 and 45/239 C and reaffirmed in General Assembly resolutions 46/100, 47/93, 48/106 and 49/167. The training service should design and conduct regular gender-sensitivity training or include gender-sensitivity training in all of its activities.

332. The Department of Public Information should seek to integrate a gender perspective in its general information activities and, within existing resources, strengthen and improve its programmes on women and the girl child. To this end, the Department should formulate a multimedia communications strategy to support the implementation of the Platform for Action, taking new technology fully into account. Regular outputs of the Department should promote the goals of the Platform, particularly in developing countries.

333. The Statistical Division of the Department for Economic and Social Information and Policy Analysis should have an important coordinating role in international work in statistics, as described above in chapter IV, strategic objective H.3.

International Research and Training Institute for the Advancement of Women

334. INSTRAW has a mandate to promote research and training on women's situation and development. In the light of the Platform for Action, INSTRAW should review its work programme and develop a programme for implementing those aspects of the Platform for Action that fall within its mandate. It should identify those types of research and research methodologies to be given priority, strengthen national capacities to carry out women's studies and gender research, including that on the status of the girl child, and develop networks of research institutions that can be mobilized for that purpose. It should also identify those types of education and training that can be effectively supported and promoted by the Institute.

United Nations Development Fund for Women

335. UNIFEM has the mandate to increase options and opportunities for women's economic and social development in developing countries by providing technical and financial assistance to incorporate the women's dimension into development at all levels. Therefore, UNIFEM should review and strengthen, as appropriate, its work programme in the light of the Platform for Action, focusing on women's political and economic empowerment. Its advocacy role should concentrate on fostering a multilateral policy dialogue on women's empowerment. Adequate resources for carrying out its functions should be made available.

Specialized agencies and other organizations of the United Nations system

336. To strengthen their support for actions at the national level and to enhance their contributions to coordinated follow-up by the United Nations, each organization should set out the specific actions they will undertake, including goals and targets to realign priori-

ties and redirect resources to meet the global priorities identified in the Platform for Action. There should be a clear delineation of responsibility and accountability. These proposals should in turn be reflected in the system-wide medium-term plan for the advancement of women for the period 1996-2001.

337. Each organization should commit itself at the highest level and, in pursuing its targets, should take steps to enhance and support the roles and responsibilities of its focal points on women's issues.

338. In addition, specialized agencies with mandates to provide technical assistance in developing countries, particularly in Africa and the least developed countries, should cooperate more to ensure the continuing promotion of the advancement of women.

339. The United Nations system should consider and provide appropriate technical assistance and other forms of assistance to the countries with economies in transition in order to facilitate solution of their specific problems regarding the advancement of women.

340. Each organization should accord greater priority to the recruitment and promotion of women at the Professional level to achieve gender balance, particularly at decision-making levels. The paramount consideration in the employment of the staff and in the determination of the conditions of service should be the necessity of securing the highest standards of efficiency, competence and integrity. Due regard should be paid to the importance of recruiting the staff on as wide a geographical basis as possible. Organizations should report regularly to their governing bodies on progress towards this goal.

341. Coordination of United Nations operational activities for development at the country level should be improved through the resident coordinator system in accordance with relevant resolutions of the General Assembly, in particular General Assembly resolution 47/199, to take full account of the Platform for Action.

2. Other international institutions and organizations

342. In implementing the Platform for Action, international financial institutions are encouraged to review and revise policies, procedures and staffing to ensure that investments and programmes benefit women and thus contribute to sustainable development. They are also encouraged to increase the number of women in high-level positions, increase staff training in gender analysis and institute policies and guidelines to ensure full consideration of the differential impact of lending programmes and other activities on women and men. In this regard, the Bretton Woods institutions, the United Nations, as well as its funds and programmes and the specialized agencies, should establish regular and substantive dialogue, including dialogue at the field level, for more efficient and effective coordination of their assistance in order to strengthen the effectiveness of their programmes for the benefit of women and their families.

343. The General Assembly should give consideration to inviting the World Trade Organization to consider how it might contribute to the implementation of the Platform for Action, including activities in cooperation with the United Nations system.

344. International non-governmental organizations have an important role to play in implementing the Platform for Action. Consideration should be given to establishing a mechanism for collaborating with non-governmental organizations to promote the implementation of the Platform at various levels.

Chapter VI

Financial arrangements

345. Financial and human resources have generally been insufficient for the advancement of women. This has contributed to the slow progress to date in implementing the Nairobi Forward-looking Strategies for the Advancement of Women. Full and effective implementation of the Platform for Action, including the relevant commitments made at previous United Nations summits and conferences, will require a political commitment to make available human and financial resources for the empowerment of women. This will require the integration of a gender perspective in budgetary decisions on policies and programmes, as well as the adequate financing of specific programmes for securing equality between women and men. To implement the Platform for Action, funding will need to be identified and mobilized from all sources and across all sectors. The reformulation of policies and reallocation of resources may be needed within and among programmes, but some policy changes may not necessarily have financial implications. Mobilization of additional resources, both public and private, including resources from innovative sources of funding, may also be necessary.

A. National level

346. The primary responsibility for implementing the strategic objectives of the Platform for Action rests with Governments. To achieve these objectives, Governments should make efforts to systematically review how women benefit from public sector expenditures; adjust budgets to ensure equality of access to public sector expenditures, both for enhancing productive capacity and for meeting social needs; and achieve the gender-related commitments made in other United Nations summits and conferences. To develop successful national implementation strategies for the Platform for Action, Governments should allocate sufficient resources, includ-

ing resources for undertaking gender-impact analysis. Governments should also encourage non-governmental organizations and private-sector and other institutions to mobilize additional resources.

347. Sufficient resources should be allocated to national machineries for the advancement of women as well as to all institutions, as appropriate, that can contribute to the implementation and monitoring of the Platform for Action.

348. Where national machineries for the advancement of women do not yet exist or where they have not yet been established on a permanent basis, Governments should strive to make available sufficient and continuing resources for such machineries.

349. To facilitate the implementation of the Platform for Action, Governments should reduce, as appropriate, excessive military expenditures and investments for arms production and acquisition, consistent with national security requirements.

350. Non-governmental organizations, the private sector and other actors of civil society should be encouraged to consider allocating the resources necessary for the implementation of the Platform for Action. Governments should create a supportive environment for the mobilization of resources by non-governmental organizations, particularly women's organizations and networks, feminist groups, the private sector and other actors of civil society, to enable them to contribute towards this end. The capacity of non-governmental organizations in this regard should be strengthened and enhanced.

B. *Regional level*

351. Regional development banks, regional business associations and other regional institutions should be invited to contribute to and help mobilize resources in their lending and other activities for the implementation of the Platform for Action. They should also be encouraged to take account of the Platform for Action in their policies and funding modalities.

352. The subregional and regional organizations and the United Nations regional commissions should, where appropriate and within their existing mandates, assist in the mobilization of funds for the implementation of the Platform for Action.

C. *International level*

353. Adequate financial resources should be committed at the international level for the implementation of the Platform for Action in the developing countries, particularly in Africa and the least developed countries. Strengthening national capacities in developing countries to implement the Platform for Action will require striving for the fulfilment of the agreed target of 0.7 per cent of the gross national product of developed countries for overall official development assistance as soon as possible, as well as increasing the share of funding for activities designed to implement the Platform for Action. Furthermore, countries involved in development cooperation should conduct a critical analysis of their assistance programmes so as to improve the quality and effectiveness of aid through the integration of a gender approach.

354. International financial institutions, including the World Bank, the International Monetary Fund, the International Fund for Agricultural Development and the regional development banks, should be invited to examine their grants and lending and to allocate loans and grants to programmes for implementing the Platform for Action in developing countries, especially in Africa and the least developed countries.

355. The United Nations system should provide technical cooperation and other forms of assistance to the developing countries, in particular in Africa and the least developed countries, in implementing the Platform for Action.

356. Implementation of the Platform for Action in the countries with economies in transition will require continued international cooperation and assistance. The organizations and bodies of the United Nations system, including the technical and sectoral agencies, should facilitate the efforts of those countries in designing and implementing policies and programmes for the advancement of women. To this end, the International Monetary Fund and the World Bank should be invited to assist those efforts.

357. The outcome of the World Summit for Social Development regarding debt management and reduction as well as other United Nations world summits and conferences should be implemented in order to facilitate the realization of the objectives of the Platform for Action.

358. To facilitate implementation of the Platform for Action, interested developed and developing country partners, agreeing on a mutual commitment to allocate, on average, 20 per cent of official development assistance and 20 per cent of the national budget to basic social programmes should take into account a gender perspective.

359. Development funds and programmes of the United Nations system should undertake an immediate analysis of the extent to which their programmes and projects are directed to implementing the Platform for Action and, for the next programming cycle, should ensure the adequacy of resources targeted towards eliminating disparities between women and men in their technical assistance and funding activities.

360. Recognizing the roles of United Nations funds, programmes and specialized agencies, in particular the special roles of UNIFEM and INSTRAW, in the promotion of the empowerment of women, and therefore in the implementation of the Platform for Action within their respective mandates, *inter alia*, in research, training and information activities for the advancement of women as well as technical and financial assistance to incorporate a gender perspective in development efforts, the resources provided by the international community need to be sufficient and should be maintained at an adequate level.

361. To improve the efficiency and effectiveness of the United Nations system in its efforts to promote the advancement of women and to enhance its capacity to further the objectives of the Platform for Action, there is a need to renew, reform and revitalize various parts of the United Nations system, especially the Division for the Advancement of Women of the United Nations Secretariat, as well as other units and subsidiary bodies that have a specific mandate to promote the advancement of women. In this regard, relevant governing bodies within the United Nations system are encouraged to give special consideration to the effective implementation of the Platform for Action and to review their policies, programmes, budgets and activities in order to achieve the most effective and efficient use of funds to this end. Allocation of additional resources from within the United Nations regular budget in order to implement the Platform for Action will also be necessary.

...

Chapter V

Adoption of the Beijing Declaration and Platform for Action

1. At the 16th plenary meeting, on 15 September 1995, the Conference considered agenda item 10 (Beijing Declaration and Platform for Action of the Fourth World Conference on Women). The Chairperson of the Main Committee of the Conference, Patricia B. Licuanan (Philippines), made a statement.

2. At the same meeting, the representative of the Philippines, on behalf of the States Members of the United Nations that are members of the Group of 77, introduced a draft resolution (A/CONF.177/L.9) whereby the Conference would adopt the Beijing Declaration and Platform for Action and recommend them to the General Assembly for endorsement at its fiftieth session. The Conference then adopted the draft resolution (for the text, see chap. I, resolution 1).

3. After the draft resolution was adopted, representatives of the following States made general and interpretative statements or expressed reservations on the Beijing Declaration and Platform for Action: Peru, Kuwait, Egypt, Philippines, Holy See, Malaysia, Iran (Islamic Republic of), Libyan Arab Jamahiriya, Ecuador, Indonesia, Mauritania, Oman, Malta, Argentina, Brunei Darussalam, France, Yemen, Sudan, Dominican Republic, Costa Rica, United Arab Emirates, Venezuela, Bahrain, Lebanon, Tunisia, Mali, Benin, Guatemala, India, Algeria, Iraq, Vanuatu, Ethiopia, Morocco, Djibouti, Qatar, Nicaragua, Togo, Liberia, Syrian Arab Republic, Pakistan, Nigeria, Comoros, Bolivia, Colombia, Bangladesh, Honduras, Jordan, Ghana, Central African Republic, Cambodia, Maldives, South Africa, United Republic of Tanzania, Brazil, Panama, El Salvador, Madagascar, Chad, Cameroon, Niger, Gabon, United States of America and Canada. The observer for Palestine also made a statement.

Reservations and interpretative statements on the Beijing Declaration and Platform for Action

4. The representatives of a number of countries made statements which they requested the secretariat of the Conference to place on record. Those statements are set out below.

5. The representative of Argentina submitted the following written statement:

> The concept of family as used in the Conference documents is understood to mean the union of a man and a woman, who produce, nourish and educate their children. No definition or recommendation contained in these documents weakens the parents' primary responsibility for bringing up their children, including providing education on sexual matters, a responsibility which should be respected by States pursuant to the Convention on the Rights of the Child.

> No reference in these documents to the right to control matters related to sexuality, including sexual and reproductive health, may be interpreted as restricting the right to life or abrogating the condemnation of abortion as a method of birth control or an instrument of population policy (in accordance with article 75, paragraph 23, of the Constitution of Argentina, article 16 of the Convention on the Elimination of All Forms of Discrimination against Women and paragraph 42 of the Vienna Programme of Action, adopted by the World Conference on Human Rights). No proposal contained in the documents may be interpreted to justify programmes of female or male sterilization as an adjustment variable in eradicating poverty.

> The Argentine delegation participated in the consensus on paragraph 106 (k) of the Platform for Action, which recommends that Governments should con-

sider reviewing laws containing punitive measures against women who have undergone abortions. This position was taken in view of the legal tradition of Argentina, the practice of our courts and the attenuating circumstances that have generally been considered; this does not constitute, however, a proposal to decriminalize abortion or exempt from criminal responsibility those who may be accomplices or participants in this offence.

The references to the Programme of Action of the International Conference on Population and Development contained in the documents of the Fourth World Conference on Women should be understood in the context of the reservations formulated by the Government of the Argentine Republic and included in the report of that Conference (A/CONF.171/13 and Add.1).

With regard to all that is relevant to the documents of the Fourth World Conference on Women, the Argentine delegation maintains the same reservations which it submitted concerning the Regional Programme of Action for the Women of Latin America and the Caribbean, adopted in Santiago, Chile, in June 1995.

6.   The representative of Costa Rica submitted the following written statement:

Costa Rica is a State in which the strict rule of law prevails; it is respectful of the law, being fully devoted to respect for human rights and the promotion of tolerance; and it participates in the world-wide consensus that inequalities exist which place women at a disadvantage, and that this situation should be rectified.

Accordingly, Costa Rica has adopted, signed and ratified all the instruments which promote equality of rights and opportunities between women and men, and it has been adapting its national legislation to these instruments, especially in relation to the Convention on the Elimination of All Forms of Discrimination against Women.

Nevertheless, we are aware that new challenges exist in our country, that much remains to be resolved with regard to improving the situation of women and that the advancement of women is crucial to the achievement of sustainable human development.

Aware that the series of measures contained in the Platform for Action of the Fourth World Conference on Women is consistent with the policies promoted in our country for the advancement of women, we wish to confirm to the international community that we support the Platform, that this support is respectful of the socio-cultural diversity of nations and that

the Platform will be incorporated at the national level into the current legal system, in strict concordance with our best traditions, beliefs and values.

From this point of view, Costa Rica wishes to state that, in matters relating to sexuality, it understands any references in the Platform to women's rights to mean, as in the case of men, the capacity of women or men to achieve and maintain their sexual and reproductive health in a framework of relations of equality and mutual respect.

In relation to the strategic objective of the Platform which proposes the reduction in military expenditure and limiting the available arms, which is based on chapter IV, paragraph 70, subparagraph 12, of the Programme of Action of the World Summit for Social Development on the topic of social integration, Costa Rica reiterates its devotion to peace and the statement it made at that Conference concerning the need for conflicts and differences among nations and peoples and among social groups to be resolved through negotiation, dialogue and the quest for consensus, and that the resources being spent for weapons could be much better spent on the social development of peoples.

Lastly, we wish to confirm and reiterate to the international community that it is a priority task of both women and men to seek to eliminate all forms of discrimination in accordance with the principle of respect for human rights and fundamental freedoms.

7.   The representative of the Dominican Republic submitted the following written statement:

Pursuant to the rules of procedure of the Fourth World Conference on Women, the Dominican Republic supports the general agreement reached on the Platform for Action and reaffirms its commitment to comply with that agreement.

The Dominican Republic, as a signatory to the American Convention on Human Rights, and in accordance with the Constitution and laws of the Republic, confirms that every person has the right to life, and that life begins at the moment of conception.

Consequently, it accepts the content of the terms "reproductive health", "sexual health", "maternity without risk", "reproductive rights", "sexual rights" and "regulation of fertility" in the Platform for Action, but it makes an express reservation to the content of these terms, or any others, if they include abortion or interruption of pregnancy as a component.

We confirm the position taken by our country at the International Conference on Population and Development, and these reservations apply to all regional and international agreements referring to these concepts.

In accordance with the above-mentioned rules of procedure, we request that this statement of reservations be included in full in the final report of this Conference.

8. The representative of Egypt submitted the following written statement:

The participation of Egypt in the Fourth World Conference on Women reflects its conviction of the importance of women's issues and their promotion. It is an extension of Egypt's participation in the three preceding conferences on women, in addition to its having been host to one of the most important international conferences, the International Conference on Population and Development.

The Egyptian delegation would like to register the fact that its understanding of the texts included in the Platform for Action of the Fourth World Conference on Women that refer to sexual and reproductive relations rests on the basis that these relations are within the framework of a marital bond and that the family is understood to be the basic unit of society. Egypt's compliance with the recommendations contained in the Platform for Action will be conditional on complete respect for the rights of national sovereignty and various moral and religious values and conformity to our Constitution and the precepts of law and with the divine guidance of our true and tolerant religious law.

The Egyptian delegation would also like to register the fact that its reading and understanding of the paragraphs relating to inheritance rights in the Platform for Action, particularly paragraph 274 (d), will be against the background of complete respect for the laws of inheritance in the Islamic Shariah and in accordance with the provisions of the law and the Constitution.

The Egyptian delegation requests that this statement in its entirety should be included in the official report of the Fourth World Conference on Women.

9. The representatives of Estonia, Latvia and Lithuania submitted the following written statement:

Estonia, Latvia and Lithuania wish to express a reservation regarding paragraph 5 of the Platform for Action. We feel it is essential that the mission statement reflect a strong commitment by the international community to all the world's women and that the message should be all-encompassing. Paragraph 5 in its present form is exclusionary and contradicts the principle of universality, which

should apply to all States Members of the United Nations.

The changes in the present paragraph are also a violation of the rules of procedure in light of the fact that new language was introduced to unbracketed text already agreed to in document A/CONF.177/L.1 at the preparatory meeting for the Conference in March 1995.

The concerns and needs of countries with economies in transition have been marginalized by paragraph 5, thus weakening the Platform for Action. For this reason, our delegations regrettably feel obligated to place this reservation on record.

10. The representative of Guatemala submitted the following written statement:

My delegation wishes to state that, consistent with the national interest of Guatemala, it is submitting the following reservation, with the request that it be included in the final report of the Fourth World Conference on Women:

(a) Guatemala has the sovereign right to implement the recommendations contained in the Platform for Action in accordance with the provisions of its Political Constitution, national legislation and international treaties and conventions to which it is a party, and therefore none of the provisions and recommendations of this Conference and of the Platform for Action may or should be interpreted as contradicting the aforesaid legal instruments. In addition, these recommendations will be implemented in accordance with the development priorities of our country, in full respect for the diverse religious, ethical and cultural values and philosophical beliefs of our multi-ethnic, multilingual and multicultural people, and in accordance with universally recognized international human rights;

(b) Guatemala confirms all its reservations to the Programme of Action of the International Conference on Population and Development and its reservations to the Declaration and Programme of Action of the World Summit for Social Development, especially in relation to the topics, terms, conditions and provisions contained in the aforesaid documents which are repeated and re-utilized in this Platform for Action.

In addition, the Government of Guatemala reserves the right to interpret the Platform for Action expressly in accordance with its unconditional respect for the right to life from the moment of conception and its unconditional respect for the right of parents to choose the upbringing of their children. It endorses and guarantees the social, economic and juridical protection of the family on the legal basis of marriage, equal rights of spouses, responsible parenthood, the right of persons to decide freely the number and spacing of their children, and the dignity of motherhood.

In conformity with the ethical, moral, legal, cultural and natural criteria of the Guatemalan people, Guatemala interprets the concept of gender solely as female and male gender in reference to women and men and reserves its position on the interpretation of the term "lifestyle", because its meaning is not clear in these documents.

11. The representative of the Holy See submitted the following written statement:

"When one looks at the great process of women's liberation," one sees that the journey has been a difficult one, with its "share of mistakes," but headed toward a better future for women. Those are the words of Pope John Paul II. And he goes on to say: "This journey must go on!" The Holy See delegation joins its voice to his: This great journey must go on!

Women's voyage has been marked by false starts and disappointments, as well as by luminous achievements. There have been times, as in the industrial revolution, when old forms of oppression were exchanged for new, as well as times when intelligence and good will have triumphed.

The documents before us reflect that complex and uneven history of women's search. They are full of promise, but often short on concrete commitment, and in certain respects one could ask if the long-term consequences will really serve the good of women.

The delegation of the Holy See has worked hard, in a constructive way and in a spirit of good will to make the documents more responsive to women. Certainly, the living heart of these documents lies in their sections on the needs of women in poverty, on strategies for development, on literacy and education, on ending violence against women, on a culture of peace, and on access to employment, land, capital and technology. My delegation is pleased to note a close correspondence between these points and Catholic social teaching.

My delegation would be remiss in its duty to women, however, if it did not also indicate several critical areas where it strongly disagrees with the text.

My delegation regrets to note in the text an exaggerated individualism, in which key, relevant, provisions of the Universal Declaration of Human Rights are slighted—for example, the obligation to provide "special care and assistance" to motherhood. This

selectivity thus marks another step in the colonization of the broad and rich discourse of universal rights by an impoverished, libertarian rights dialect. Surely this international gathering could have done more for women and girls than to leave them alone with their rights!

Surely we must do more for the girl child in poor nations than give lip service to providing access to education, health and social services while carefully avoiding any concrete commitment of new and additional resources to that end.

Surely we can do better than to address the health needs of girls and women by paying disproportionate attention to sexual and reproductive health. Moreover, ambiguous language concerning unqualified control over sexuality and fertility could be interpreted as including societal endorsement of abortion and homosexuality.

A document that respects women's dignity should address the health of the whole woman. A document that respects women's intelligence should devote at least as much attention to literacy as to fertility.

Because my delegation is hopeful that out of these documents, which are in some ways at odds with themselves, the good for women will ultimately prevail, it wishes to associate itself with the consensus only on those above-mentioned aspects of the documents that the Holy See considers to be positive and at the service of the real well-being of women.

Unfortunately, the Holy See's participation in the consensus can be only a partial one because of numerous points in the documents which are incompatible with what the Holy See and other countries deem favourable to the true advancement of women. These points are indicated in the reservations which my delegation has set out below.

My delegation is confident that women themselves will overcome the limitations of and bring out what is best in these documents. As John Paul II has so well put it, "The path that lies ahead will be long and difficult, nevertheless we must have courage to set out on that path and the courage to go on to the end."

I would ask that the text of this statement, the reservations formally indicated below, as well as the statement of interpretation of the term "gender" be included in the report of the Conference.

Reservations and statements of interpretation

The Holy See, in conformity with its nature and particular mission, in partially joining the consensus on the documents of the Fourth World Conference on Women, wishes to express its position regarding those documents and make reservations on some of the concepts used in them.

The Holy See wishes to reaffirm the dignity and worth of women and the equal rights of men and women and regrets the failure of the Platform for Action to explicitly reassert this concept.

The Holy See, in line with the Universal Declaration of Human Rights, stresses that the family is the basic unit of society and is based on marriage as an equal partnership between husband and wife, to which the transmission of life is entrusted. It regrets that in the Platform for Action references were not made to such a fundamental societal unit without banal qualifying language (see, for example, strategic objective L.9).

The Holy See can only interpret such terms as "women's right to control their sexuality", "women's right to control ... their fertility" or "couples and individuals" as referring to the responsible use of sexuality within marriage. At the same time, the Holy See firmly condemns all forms of violence against and exploitation of women and girls.

The Holy See reaffirms the reservations it expressed at the conclusion of the International Conference on Population and Development, held in Cairo from 5 to 13 September 1994, which are included in the report of that Conference, concerning the interpretation given to the terms "reproductive health", "sexual health" and "reproductive rights". In particular, the Holy See reiterates that it does not consider abortion or abortion services to be a dimension of reproductive health or reproductive health services. The Holy See does not endorse any form of legislation which gives legal recognition to abortion.

With regard to the terms "family planning" or "widest range of family planning services" and other terms concerning family-planning services or regulation of fertility, the Holy See's actions during this Conference should in no way be interpreted as changing its well-known position concerning those family planning methods that the Catholic Church considers morally unacceptable or concerning family planning services that do not respect the liberty of spouses, the human dignity or the human rights of those concerned. The Holy See in no way endorses contraception or the use of condoms, either as a family planning measure or in HIV/AIDS prevention programmes.

The Holy See maintains that nothing in the Platform for Action or in other documents referenced therein is to be interpreted as requiring any health professional or health facility to perform, cooperate with, refer or arrange for services to which they have objections on the basis of religious belief or moral or ethical conviction.

The Holy See interprets all references to the term "forced pregnancy" as a specific instrument of armed conflict, in the context in which that term appears in the Vienna Declaration and Programme of Action, part II, paragraph 38.

The Holy See interprets the term "gender" as described in the statement set out below.

The Holy See does not associate itself with the consensus on the entire chapter IV, section C, concerning health; it wishes to place a general reservation on the entire section and it would ask that this general reservation be noted in the chapter. This section devotes a totally unbalanced attention to sexual and reproductive health in comparison to women's other health needs, including means to address maternal mortality and morbidity. Furthermore, the Holy See cannot accept ambiguous terminology concerning unqualified control over sexuality and fertility, particularly as it could be interpreted as a societal endorsement of abortion or homosexuality. The reservation on this chapter does not, however, indicate any reduction in the Holy See's commitment towards the promotion of the health of women and the girl child.

The Holy See does not join the consensus and expresses a reservation on paragraph 232 (f), with its reference to a text (para. 96) on a right of women to "control over ... their sexuality". This ambiguous term could be understood as endorsing sexual relationships outside heterosexual marriage. It asks that this reservation be noted on the paragraph. On the other hand, however, the Holy See wishes to associate itself with the condemnation of violence against women asserted in paragraph 96, as well as with the importance of mutuality and shared responsibility, respect and free consent in conjugal relations as stated in that paragraph.

The Holy See, with regard to the entire section on human rights, with the exception of quotations from or restatements of already existing human rights instruments, expresses its concern about an excessive individualism in its treatment of human rights. The Holy See further recalls that the mandate of the Fourth World Conference on Women did not include the affirmation of new human rights.

With regard to the phrase "Women's rights are human rights", the Holy See interprets this phrase to mean that women should have the full enjoyment of all human rights and fundamental freedoms.

With regard to all references to international agreements, the Holy See reserves its position in this regard, in particular on any existing international agreements mentioned in the documents, consistent with its manner of acceptance or non-acceptance of them.

The Holy See requests that these reservations, together with the following statement of interpretation on the term "gender", be included in the report of the Conference.

Statement of interpretation of the term "gender"

In accepting that the word "gender" in this document is to be understood according to ordinary usage in the United Nations context, the Holy See associates itself with the common meaning of that word, in languages where it exists.

The term "gender" is understood by the Holy See as grounded in biological sexual identity, male or female. Furthermore, the Platform for Action itself clearly uses the term "Both genders".

The Holy See thus excludes dubious interpretations based on world views which assert that sexual identity can be adapted indefinitely to suit new and different purposes.

It also dissociates itself from the biological determinist notion that all the roles and relations of the two sexes are fixed in a single, static pattern.

Pope John Paul insists on the distinctiveness and complementarity of women and men. At the same time, he has applauded the assumption of new roles by women, stressed the degree to which cultural conditioning has been an obstacle to women's progress, and exhorted men to assist in "the great process of women's liberation" ("Letter to Women", 6).

In his recent "Letter to Women", the Pope explained the Church's nuanced view in the following way: "One can also appreciate that the presence of a certain diversity of roles is in no way prejudicial to women, provided that this diversity is not the result of an arbitrary imposition, but is rather an expression of what is specific to being male and female."

12. The representative of Honduras submitted the following written statement:

The Government of the Republic of Honduras, in accordance with its belief in democracy, joins the consensus of all the peoples of the world in adopting the Platform for Action, regarding it as an effective instrument for the promotion and advancement of women to the year 2001 and in the new millennium.

Accordingly, it reaffirms its desire and commitment to take the necessary actions to bring about the implementation of the Platform.

The Constitution of Honduras provides that all men and women are born free and equal before the law, that there are no privileged classes and that all Hondurans are equal before the law (article 60).

Articles 65, 111 and 112 provide that the right to life is inviolable and that the family, marriage and de facto union are under the protection of the State.

The American Convention on Human Rights, of which our country is a signatory, reaffirms that every individual has the right to life from the moment of conception, on the basis of the moral, ethical, religious and cultural principles that should govern human behaviour.

Accordingly, Honduras shares the concepts relating to reproductive health, sexual health and family planning in the Platform for Action, provided that abortion or interruption of pregnancy is not included as a family planning method.

The Government of the Republic reaffirms that the family is the basic unit of society and therefore commits itself to strengthening all actions aimed at achieving greater levels of well-being, bringing into harmony the various segments of society.

Lastly, we invite the international community to support Governments and peoples in their efforts to ensure that the implementation of the Platform for Action is as successful as anticipated and that our women will finally achieve equity, development and peace, which are so necessary to the advancement of our peoples.

13. The representative of Indonesia submitted the following written statement:

While expressing our delegation's satisfaction on the adoption of the Beijing Declaration and Platform for Action by consensus, my delegation at the same time feels unhappy about the fact that there have been numerous reservations made by the delegations attending the Conference. This may give the public the false impression that our joint commitment to implement the Platform for Action, which is crucial to the goals of equality, development and peace for all women, will be difficult to realize.

The concerns reflected in the reservations—and my delegation also has reservations on certain paragraphs which are not consistent with the national interest of Indonesia—should not in any way constitute an obstacle to our genuine endeavour to implement the Platform for Action, since we all know that the spirit and objective of international cooperation in this regard is indeed a matter of mutual respect and support for our common cause.

Finally, my delegation wishes to request that its reservation be duly recorded in the report of the Conference.

14. The representative of the Islamic Republic of Iran submitted the following written statement:

I would like to register the reservation of the Islamic Republic of Iran on the following issues:

Although the family is the basic unit of society and as such plays a significant role in the advancement of women and promotion of human development, the Platform for Action falls short in recognizing its contribution and the importance of its stability and integrity.

Concerning paragraphs 96 and 232 (f), our understanding is that the provisions of those paragraphs can only be interpreted in the context of health and the framework of marital relations between men and women. The Islamic Republic of Iran holds that the rights referred to in those paragraphs fall in the category of existing human rights and do not establish any new rights.

The Islamic Republic of Iran upholds the principle that safe and responsible sexual relationships between men and women can only be legitimized within the framework of marriage. Moreover, the phrase "couples and individuals" should also be interpreted in that context.

Concerning programmes aimed at sexual and reproductive health, education and services, the Islamic Republic of Iran believes that such education and services should be guided by ethical and moral values and respect the responsibilities, rights and duties of parents, taking into account the evolving capacities of adolescents.

With respect to the issue of inheritance, the Islamic Republic of Iran interprets the references in the Platform for Action to this matter in accordance with the principles of the economic system of Islam.

The concept of equality in our interpretation takes into account the fact that although women are equal in their human rights and dignity with men, their different roles and responsibilities underline the need for an equitable system of rights, where the particular priorities and requirements of the woman in her multiple roles are accounted for.

The Islamic Republic of Iran affirms its commitment to the implementation of the Platform for Action with full respect for Islam and the ethical values of our society.

15. The representative of Iraq submitted the following written statement:

The delegation of Iraq has reservations with regard to paragraph 96 of the Platform for Action because it is incompatible with our social and religious values. Our reservation also applies to paragraph 232 (f) because of its allusion to paragraph 96.

The delegation of Iraq accepts the text of paragraph 274 (d) on the basis of its understanding that this does not conflict with the Islamic Shariah.

16. The representative of Israel submitted the following written statement:

The delegation of Israel to the Fourth World Conference on Women wishes to submit the following interpretative statement on paragraph 46 of the Platform for Action.

Israel would have preferred that explicit reference be made to the particular barriers faced by women because of their sexual orientation. However, in light of the interpretation given to the words "other status" by, *inter alia*, the United Nations Human Rights Committee, we interpret the words "other status" to include sexual orientation.

17. The representative of Japan submitted the following written statement:

My delegation would like to confirm its interpretation concerning paragraph 106 (k). The delegation of Japan joined the consensus on paragraph 106 (k) on the following understanding.

There has been a continuing debate on this issue in many countries. Some countries, including Japan, have undertaken a review of the relevant laws, while others have not. Bearing this in mind, my delegation confirms its understanding that relevant national laws can only be reviewed at the national or local level with due regard to national and legislative circumstances.

18. The representative of Kuwait submitted the following written statement:

My country's delegation attaches great importance to the Platform for Action adopted by this Conference and believes in its significant contribution to the advancement of women. However, at the same time, it would like to register a reservation to anything which constitutes a contravention of the Islamic Shariah and the customs and practices of our Islamic society, particularly paragraphs 232 (f), 106 (k) and 94 to 96.

The delegation of Kuwait would like to have its reservation recorded in the report of the Conference.

19.   The representative of the Libyan Arab Jamahiriya submitted the following written statement:

My delegation greatly appreciates the efforts
made by the Main Committee and working groups
of the Conference towards producing formulas
which represent the common positions of the participating delegations and respect the beliefs of different societies and their private affairs. In this
context, the Libyan delegation has made every possible effort in its discussions with all the working
groups and in meetings to join in the global
consensus towards which this Platform for Action
is directed.

In view of our belief in the importance of the dialogue between the different cultures and civiliza-
tions of the peoples of the world for the achievement
of universal social peace, we do not accept the right
of any nation or civilization to impose its culture or
political, economic or social orientations on any
other nation or people. In view also of our belief in
the sovereign right of every State to draw up domestic policies in keeping with its religious beliefs, local
laws and priorities for social and economic development, it is our understanding that the terms and
expressions which appear in this document and their
application will be within the limits of what is
permitted by our beliefs and the laws and traditions
which shape our behaviour as a society. On this
basis, our country's delegation would like to express
reservations with regard to the following:

(a)   The expression "sexual relations and sexual
behaviour" between men and women, adult or otherwise, outside of a lawful marital relationship,
which has appeared in a number of articles;

(b)   The expression "sexual education and reproductive health" used with reference to the unmarried and outside the ambit of parental responsibility,
supervision and care;

(c)   The term "individuals" linked with the basic
right of all couples to decide freely and responsibly
the number, spacing and timing of their children.
This right is not accorded in our society outside the
framework of a lawful marital relationship. This
expression appears in paragraphs 95 and 223;

(d)   The entire text of paragraph 96 because it is
inconsistent with our social and cultural values. The
same applies to paragraph 232 (f);

(e)   Everything included in and intended by the text
appearing in paragraph 106 (k), since it is contrary
to local laws based on the Islamic Shariah. The same
applies to the text appearing in paragraph 106 (j)
regarding abortion, since local laws do not permit

the performance of abortion except to save the
mother's life;

(f)   The text of paragraph 274 (d), which will be
interpreted and implemented in accordance with the
Islamic Shariah, which guarantees females the right
of inheritance.

We hope that this statement and these reservations
will be included in the official report of the Conference.

20.   The representative of Malaysia submitted the
following written statement:

The Beijing Declaration and Platform for Action are
an achievement for all women world wide. My
delegation is gratified to join the international community in expressing our commitment to the Platform, especially on those provisions dealing with
poverty, education, health, the elimination of violence against women in civil and armed conflicts,
and the active participation of women in decision-
making and economic development for their advancement and empowerment. However, we cannot
help noting a number of differences among delegations arising from the stand on certain issues by one
group of countries. While this group may adopt their
own cultural standards and priorities, their insistence on others has inevitably resulted in the Platform for Action being accompanied by a number of
reservations.

I wish to state that certain provisions within the
Platform for Action remain unacceptable to us, but
in the interest of achieving a consensus, we do not
wish to stand in the way of its adoption. Nevertheless, in view of the differing cultural norms and the
lack of clarity of certain words and phrases in the
Platform, I wish to make the following reservations
and clarifications on behalf of the Malaysian delegation.

First, the interpretation of the term "family", and
the terms "individual and couples" throughout the
document refer to the traditional family formed out
of a marriage or a registered union between a man
and a woman and comprising children and extended
family members.

Second, we are of the conviction that reproductive
rights should be applicable only to married couples
formed of the union between a man and a woman.

Third, we wish to state that the adoption of paragraph 96 does not signify endorsement by the Government of Malaysia of sexual promiscuity, any
form of sexual perversion or sexual behaviour that
is synonymous with homosexuality or lesbianism.

Fourth, in the context of paragraph 106 (k) we wish

to support the view that attention should be given to the prevention of unsafe abortions and the provision of humane management of complications from abortions as part of reproductive health care. However, abortion is not legal or permissible in Malaysia and can only be performed on medical grounds.

Fifth, in the context of paragraph 108 (k), while agreeing that adolescent health is an area requiring attention due to the increasing problems of unwanted teenage pregnancies, unsafe abortions, sexually transmitted diseases and HIV/AIDS, we believe that parental guidance should not be abdicated and that sexual permissiveness and unhealthy sexual and reproductive practices by adolescents should not be condoned.

May I request that these reservations be entered into the records of this Conference.

21. The representative of Malta submitted the following written statement:

In joining the consensus on the Platform for Action, the delegation of Malta would like to state that it reserves its position on the use of such terms as "reproductive health", "reproductive rights" and "control of fertility" as used in different parts of the document. The interpretation given by Malta is consistent with its national legislation, which considers the termination of pregnancy through induced abortion as illegal.

The delegation of Malta further reserves its position on those parts of the Platform for Action wherein reference is made to the Programme of Action of the International Conference on Population and Development. In this respect the delegation of Malta reaffirms its reservations as contained in the report of that Conference (A/CONF.171/13 and Add.1).

In particular the delegation of Malta cannot accept without reservation the expression "circumstances in which abortion is not against the law", the termination of pregnancy through procedures of induced abortion being illegal in Malta.

The delegation of Malta reserves its position on the wording "such abortion should be safe" since it feels that this phrase could lend itself to multiple interpretations, implying among other things that abortion can be completely free of medical and other psychological risks while ignoring altogether the rights of the unborn.

Furthermore, the delegation of Malta reserves its position on the use of the wording "international human rights instruments" and "United Nations consensus documents" wherever used in the Platform for Action consistent with its previous acceptance or non-acceptance of them.

We request that these reservations be recorded in the report of the Conference.

22. The representative of Mauritania submitted the following written statement:

My country's delegation would like to enter reservations with regard to any matter that conflicts with the Islamic Shariah and Islamic values, especially paragraph 96 concerning sexual rights, paragraph 232 (f), paragraph 106 (j) concerning illegal abortions, and paragraph 274 (d) concerning inheritance.

23. The representative of Morocco submitted the following written statement:

The delegation of Morocco reserves its position on paragraphs 96 and 106 (k) of the Platform for Action, whose content is in contradiction with the precepts of Islam and is not in conformity with its spiritual values and cultural traditions. Morocco also expresses its reservations on paragraph 232 (f), which refers to paragraph 96, and on paragraph 274 (d).

The delegation of the Kingdom of Morocco requests that its reservations be included in the report of the Conference.

24. The representative of Nepal submitted the following written statement:

The interpretation of paragraph 26 for Nepal shall preclude the freedom of conversion of one's own or someone else's religion.

25. The representative of Paraguay submitted the following written statement:

The Government of Paraguay expresses its satisfaction that chapter IV, section C, of the Platform for Action is in conformity with the content of its National Constitution, especially article 61 thereof, which provides that "the State recognizes the right of everyone to freely and responsibly decide the number of children they plan to have, as well as the time span between one child and another. Through a coordinated effort with the appropriate organizations, they are also entitled to receive education, scientific guidance, and adequate services. Special plans will be implemented to ensure reproductive health and maternal-child health care for low-income people."

The delegation of Paraguay points out that the concept of "methods ... for regulation of fertility which are not against the law", as referred to in paragraph 94 of the Platform for Action, will be interpreted in conformity with its national legislation.

The Government of Paraguay interprets the term "gender", which is used in the documents adopted at this Conference, as referring to both sexes, man and woman, and has incorporated this term, as defined, into its national documents.

26. The representative of Peru submitted the following written statement:

Pursuant to article 34 of the rules of procedure of the Conference, the delegation of Peru joins in the general agreement on the adoption of the Beijing Declaration and Platform for Action, in so far as the principles and commitments established by this Conference are compatible with those embodied in the Political Constitution of Peru. However, in accordance with the position it took at the International Conference on Population and Development and reaffirmed at the World Summit for Social Development, and at the sixth session of the Regional Conference on the Integration of Women into the Economic and Social Development of Latin America and the Caribbean, the delegation of Peru wishes to express its reservation with regard to the interpretation of the following points:

The community and the State protect the family and promote marriage, recognizing them as natural and basic institutions of society. The family and marriage essentially derive from the personal relation that is established between a man and a woman.

The right to life and the consideration of a person from the moment of conception as a subject of law in every respect are fundamental human rights. Therefore, the terms "reproductive health", "reproductive rights" and "sexual or reproductive health" as used in the Platform for Action must not include abortion as a method of birth control or family planning.

The concepts referring to population policy must always be understood within the context of the protection and promotion of the family and marriage, responsible fatherhood and motherhood and the freedom of choice of the family and the individual.

It is understood that sexual rights refer solely to heterosexual relationships.

The criteria established for allocating resources can in no way be understood as restricting the right of Governments to have access to such resources.

The reference to "existing" intellectual property rights with regard to the knowledge, innovations and practices of women of indigenous and local communities, including practices relating to traditional medicines, biological diversity and indigenous technologies, may in no way be construed as restricting the rights of countries and their inhabitants under national and international law.

27. The representative of the Russian Federation submitted the following written statement:

Paragraph 83 (p)

The Russian Federation takes the word "respected" in paragraph 83 (p) to mean that gender equality and cultural, religious and other diversity should be respected in educational institutions.

Paragraph 191 (c)

The Russian Federation understands paragraph 191 (c) to mean that political parties shall themselves determine the procedure for appointing women to their leadership bodies and that the State shall not put pressure on them to do so, while at the same time creating equal opportunities for the activities of political parties. Under Russian law, this provision applies not only to political parties but also to political movements.

Paragraph 204 (e)

The Russian Federation understands paragraph 204 (e) regarding mandates to review policies and programmes in the context of ensuring equal rights and equal opportunities. The basic principles for implementing this policy are enshrined in the Constitution of the Russian Federation.

Paragraph 258 (c)

The delegation of the Russian Federation takes it that paragraph 258 (c) relates to no other question than the transboundary movement of hazardous and radioactive waste. The Russian Federation believes that it is necessary to aim for full compliance of Governments, international governmental organizations and non-governmental organizations with existing international principles and rules governing the transboundary movement of hazardous and radioactive waste through the adoption of special measures, including the establishment of a national legal framework and the definition of the various categories of waste. The movement of such materials should not pose a threat to public health.

28. The representative of South Africa submitted the following written statement:

The South African delegation interprets paragraph 96, which reads, "The human rights of women include their right to have control over and decide freely and responsibly on matters related to their sexuality, including sexual and reproductive health, free of coercion, discrimination and violence", to include the right to be free from coercion, discrimination and violence based on sexual orientation.

The South African delegation wants to make it very clear that it does not want to be associated with any form of discrimination.

29. The representative of Tunisia submitted the following written statement:

The Tunisian delegation, by virtue of the powers vested in it, has the honour to confirm that Tunisia will interpret paragraphs 96, 232 (f) and 274 (d) of the Platform for Action within its fundamental laws and texts.

The foregoing was stated at the meetings of the Main Committee held on 13 and 14 September 1995. Tunisia will reject any provision that is contrary to its fundamental laws and texts. The delegation of Tunisia requests that this reservation be included in the documents of the Conference.

30. The representative of the United States of America submitted the following written statement:

Interpretative statement on the Beijing Declaration

The United States understands that the phrase "hereby adopt and commit ourselves as Governments to implement the ... Platform for Action" contained in the Beijing Declaration, and other similar references throughout the texts, are consistent with the fact that the Platform, Declaration and commitments made by States (unless such States indicate to the contrary) are not legally binding, and that they consist of recommendations concerning how States can and should promote the objectives of the Conference. The commitment referred to in the Declaration, therefore, constitutes a general commitment to undertake meaningful implementation of the Platform's recommendations overall, rather than a specific commitment to implement each element of the Platform. Accordingly, the United States accepts this phrase on this basis, on the understanding that it does not alter the status of the documents or the recommendations contained therein.

The United States understands that the references in the Declaration and Platform for Action to "sustainable development" are to be interpreted consistently with established principles and policies on this matter. As was recognized in Agenda 21, our long-term objective of enabling all people to achieve sustainable livelihoods involves integration simultaneously of policies related to issues of development, sustainable resource management and poverty eradication.

At the World Summit for Social Development, States further acknowledged that economic development, social development and environmental protection are interdependent and mutually reinforcing components of sustainable development.

Reservation on paragraph 5 of the Platform for Action

As the United States has stated on a number of occasions during the Conference and in the preparations for it, as a result of domestic funding constraints it cannot agree to an increase in funding for matters dealt with in the Platform for Action other than in the context of reallocation of existing resources, or unless sources of funding other than governmental assessments are involved. Accordingly, the United States reserves on paragraph 5 of the Platform for Action. The United States fully supports the objectives of the Conference and is willing to work with others to ensure that there is a proper allocation of resources within the United Nations system and other international organizations, to address commitments made in the Platform. In this context, the United States notes as well that many of the most critical actions to be taken in accordance with the Platform do not require additional funds from the international community and can be accomplished through actions at the national and local level.

Interpretative statements on individual paragraphs in the Platform for Action

Paragraph 17

The United States understands that the phrase "radical transformation of the relationship between women and men in paragraph 17 is a reference to the realization of full equality between women and men. It is in that context that the United States accepts this paragraph.

Paragraph 26

Paragraph 26 of the Platform recognizes the important role that non-governmental organizations play and the importance of working with them for progress. The United States recognizes the need for Governments to create an enabling environment for non-governmental organizations and that such an environment is critical to the successful implementation of the Platform. The United States understands that Governments, in requesting that non-governmental organizations take action to implement the Platform, are thereby committing themselves to facilitating the efforts of such organizations in this regard.

Paragraph 46

The United States Government has a firm policy of non-discrimination on the basis of sexual orientation and considers that the omission of this reference in paragraph 46 and elsewhere in the Platform for Action in no way justifies such discrimination in any country.

Paragraph 96

The United States understands and accepts that paragraph 96, which concerns, *inter alia*, equal relationships between women and men, applies existing norms of human rights law to these important areas of the lives of women and men, and thus emphasizes the importance of freedom from coercion, discrimination and violence in relations between men and women.

Paragraph 131

While the United States recognizes that human rights violations can and do occur in situations of foreign occupation around the world, the United States continues to have reservations, as it did at the World Conference on Human Rights in Vienna, about any implication that foreign occupation is a human rights violation *per se*.

Paragraph 166 (l)

The United States understands the intention of the inclusion of "equal remuneration for men and women for work of equal value" to be to promote pay equity between men and women and accepts the recommendation on that basis. The United States implements it by observing the principle of "equal pay for equal work".

Paragraph 206 (b), (e) and (f)

With respect to paragraph 206 (b), (e) and (f), the United States will seek to develop more comprehensive knowledge as well as to improve data collection on the issue of unwaged work, to the extent that funds are available. We plan to consult, in a cooperative manner, with appropriate research and documentation organizations.

Paragraphs 234-245

A number of institutions, organizations and others have been requested to take actions to implement the Platform. Although many institutions have participated here as observers, and non-governmental organizations have provided helpful inputs into the deliberations, Governments alone will adopt the Platform. As a result, it is necessary to underscore the fact that when the Platform mentions the actions these other actors may take, it thereby invites and encourages the suggested actions; it does not, and cannot, require such actions.

In this context, we understand that references to actions the media may take (such as those in chapter IV, section J, and in paragraph 33) are in the nature of suggestions and recommendations, and may not be construed to impinge on the freedom of the press, speech and expression, which are fundamental democratic freedoms.

Paragraph 247

The United States would like to underscore that it interprets the second sentence in paragraph 247 to mean that these listed occurrences can cause environmental degradation in certain circumstances but not in others. The United States also remains concerned about the reference to "the use and testing of nuclear weaponry" in this paragraph, which appears not to have been reviewed fully in the working group.

Paragraph 293

The United States understands and accepts that references to commitments in paragraph 293, references to what the Platform "requires" in paragraphs 4 and 5, and other similar references throughout the texts, including the Declaration, are consistent with the fact that the Platform, Declaration and commitments made by States (unless such States indicate to the contrary) are not legally binding, and that they consist of recommendations concerning how States can and should promote the human rights of women. Accordingly, the United States understands and accepts that such terms as used in these documents suggest practical measures to help promote the human rights of women, and do not alter the status of the documents or the recommendations contained therein.

Paragraph 353

The United States reiterates that, with respect to paragraph 353, it is not one of the countries that have accepted an "agreed target" for official development assistance or have made a commitments to fulfil such a target. We believe that national Governments, not international donors, must have primary responsibility for their country's development. Targets detract from the more important issues of the effectiveness and quality of aid and the policies of the recipient country. The United States has traditionally been one of the largest aid donors in volume terms and will continue to work with developing countries to provide aid in support of their efforts.

In addition, the United States understands and accepts the reference in paragraph 353 to increasing the share of official development assistance for social development programmes to apply to only those countries that have accepted the target.

31.   The representative of Vanuatu submitted the following written statement:

The Republic of Vanuatu has come to the Fourth World Conference on Women in Beijing for two purposes: first, to show solidarity with the world community concerning the advancement and rights of women, and second, to learn from other countries about what can be done to improve the situation of women.

In this respect, the delegation of Vanuatu has fully participated in the plenary meetings of the Conference as well as in the Main Committee and the working groups.

The delegation of Vanuatu recognizes the spirit of conciliation and compromise that has gone into the finalization of the Platform for Action. At the same time, the delegation notes that Vanuatu is a small country which has grown out of a strong fundamental traditional past and which now is changing in the midst of modern social, economic and political evolution.

While therefore endorsing the Platform for Action of this important Conference, the Vanuatu delegation wishes to state that its endorsement of the Platform is made with full respect for the constitu-tional, religious and traditional principles which the sovereign State has inherited and kept for the good government of our nation.

32.   The representative of Venezuela submitted the following written statement:

With a view to speeding up the general debate in order to arrive at a consensus on the Platform for Action, the official delegation of Venezuela makes the following statement of reservations and requests that it be included in full in the final report of the Conference.

The concepts of family planning, sexual health, reproductive health, maternity without risk, regulation of fertility, reproductive rights and sexual rights are acceptable provided that they do not include abortion or voluntary interruption of pregnancy.

Similarly, Venezuela expresses a reservation with regard to the concept of unwanted pregnancy, since the reference to "unwanted pregnancy" could be argued in the opposite sense, as implying acceptance of the right of a woman who has become pregnant against her will to terminate the pregnancy (by abortion), an act which is illegal in Venezuela.

Venezuela also expresses a reservation with regard to references to "unsafe abortion", because abortion under any circumstances is illegal in Venezuela, except when it is essential in order to save a woman's life.

Document 128

Report of the Secretary-General to the General Assembly on improvement of the status of women in the Secretariat

A/50/691, 27 October 1995

I.   Introduction

1.   At its forty-ninth session, the General Assembly adopted resolutions 49/167 of 23 December 1994 on the improvement of the status of women in the Secretariat and 49/222 A and B of 23 December 1994 and 14 July 1995, respectively, concerning the question of women in the context of the Secretary-General's new strategy for human resources management. In those resolutions, the Assembly recalled the goal set in its earlier resolutions, 45/125 of 14 December 1990, 45/239 C of 21 December 1990, 46/100 of 16 December 1991 and 47/93 of 16 December 1992, to accord greater priority to the recruitment and promotion of women in posts subject to geographical distribution in order to achieve by 1995 the targets of 35 per cent representation of women in posts subject to geographical distribution and 25 per cent representation for posts at the D-1 level and above. In resolution 49/167, the General Assembly urged the Secretary-General to implement fully his strategic plan of action for the improvement of the status of women in the Secretariat (1995-2000) (see A/49/587 and Corr.1). The long-term goals of the plan of action include the creation of conditions of equality and opportunity for men and women to participate fully in the work of the Secretariat and to achieve gender parity, 50 per cent women in posts subject to geographical distribution, by the year 2000. In section III of its resolution 49/222 A, the Assembly, *inter alia*,

Table 1. *Number and percentage of staff in posts subject to geographical distribution, 1993-1995*

	30 June 1993				30 June 1994				30 June 1995			
Level	Women	Men	Total	% women	Women	Men	Total	% women	Women	Men	Total	% women
USG	3	18	21	14.29	2	17	19	10.53	2	18	20	10.0
ASG	1	14	15	6.67	2	16	18	11.11	2	12	14	14.3
D-2	9	57	66	13.64	14	61	75	18.67	14	58	72	19.4
D-1	31	211	242	12.81	34	198	232	14.66	39	188	227	17.2
P-5	103	372	475	21.68	122	375	497	24.55	136	345	481	28.3
P-4	203	463	666	30.48	246	481	727	33.84	234	460	694	33.7
P-3	239	396	635	37.64	240	371	611	39.28	250	379	629	39.7
P-2	209	237	446	46.86	168	201	369	45.53	180	198	378	47.6
P-1	6	1	7	85.71	2	0	2	100.00	0	0	0	0.0
Total	804	1 769	2 573	31.25	830	1 720	2 550	32.55	857	1 658	2 515	34.1

Source: Reports of the Secretary-General on the composition of the Secretariat (A/48/559, A/49/527 and A/50/540).

requested the Secretary-General to include full implementation of the plan of action as a specific performance indicator in the performance appraisal of all managers. The Assembly also requested the Secretary-General to enable, from within existing resources, the Focal Point for Women effectively to monitor and to facilitate progress in the implementation of the plan of action.

2. Over the past year, the Secretary-General has pursued the goals of General Assembly resolutions 49/167 and 49/222 A and B. In particular, the individual responsibility of managers for the effective implementation of the strategies to improve the status of women, both qualitatively and quantitatively, in the Secretariat has been incorporated through the performance appraisal system within the overall system of accountability and responsibility. Training programmes have included components designed to sensitize managers to gender-related issues and to ways in which they can fulfil their individual responsibility to help integrate the gender perspective into all aspects of the work of the Organization.

3. During the past year, strategies have focused on meeting the targets of an overall participation rate of 35 per cent women in posts subject to geographical distribution and 25 per cent women in posts at the D-1 level and above by 1995, in accordance with resolutions 45/125, 45/239 C, 46/100 and 47/93. More forward-looking strategies have also sought to meet the target of 50 per cent women in posts subject to geographical distribution and 50 per cent women in high-level posts by the year 2000.

4. The Office of Human Resources Management (OHRM), through the Office of the Focal Point for Women, participated in the preparatory work for the Fourth World Conference on Women, held at Beijing from 4 to 15 September 1995. The elements of the Platform for Action relating to women's participation in decision-making and in power structures 1/ are particularly relevant to the subject-matter of the present report.

5. The current report is divided into six sections. Sections II to VI contain a discussion of the current situation, recent developments, the new management culture and its impact on women, implementation of the plan of action and conclusions.

II. Current situation

A. *Women in posts subject to geographical distribution*

6. The percentage of women in posts subject to geographical distribution has increased 1.5 percentage points during the period under review, from 32.6 per cent on 30 June 1994 to 34.1 per cent on 30 June 1995 (see table 1). The percentage of women at the D-1 level and above has increased 2 percentage points during the same period, from 15.1 per cent on 30 June 1994 to 17.1 per cent on 30 June 1995. The major reason for the increase was the concerted effort of programme managers,

1/ See *Report of the Fourth World Conference on Women, Beijing, 4-15 September 1995* (A/CONF.177/20), chap. I, resolution 1, annex II, chap. IV, sect. G.

Table 2. *Number and percentage of staff in posts with special language requirements, 1994 and 1995* a/

	30 June 1994				30 June 1995			
				%				%
Level	Wmen	Men	Total	women	Women	Men	Total	women
P-5	36	95	131	27.5	39	91	130	30.0
P-3	120	230	350	34.3	121	237	358	33.8
P-2	19	20	39	48.7	31	23	54	57.4
P-1	0	0	0	0.0	0	0	0	0.0
Total	305	556	861	35.4	317	582	899	35.3

Source: Reports of the Secretary-General on the composition of the Secretariat (A/49/527 and A/50/540).

a/ It should be noted that posts with special language requirements are from levels P-1 to P-5 inclusive.

OHRM and the appointment and promotion bodies to carefully review recommendations of staff put forward for promotion and to ensure that, where candidates were equally qualified, women were recommended and selected. This approach led for the first time to a higher proportion of women being approved for promotion than men, 51.42 per cent during the period 1 July 1994 to 30 June 1995. It may be noted that, while the percentage of women promoted to the D-1 level was only 29.2 per cent, or 7 out of 24 posts, the percentage of women promoted to the P-5 level was 58.9 per cent, or 33 out of 56 posts.

7. The percentage of women at the Assistant Secretary-General and Under-Secretary-General levels remained the same, two at each level, or 11.8 per cent. Intensified efforts will have to be made to appoint or promote women to the higher levels if the target of 50 per cent women in higher-level posts established by the Assembly in resolution 49/167 and endorsed by the Beijing Conference is to be met in the next five years.

8. In resolution 45/239 C, the Assembly, *inter alia*, urged the Secretary-General to increase the number of women from developing countries. As indicated in table D.1 of the report of the Secretary-General on the composition of the Secretariat (A/50/540), the representation of women in posts subject to geographical distribution as a percentage of all staff in 1995 continued to show imbalances in the same regions and countries of origin reported in 1994. Three regions: Eastern Europe (1.11), the Middle East (1.35) and Africa (3.02) continued to register the lowest representation among the regions. The highest percentages were registered by North America and the Caribbean (9.74), Western Europe (7.87) and Asia and the Pacific (7.63). However, the percentage for Asia and the Pacific reflects mainly the situation in Asia, as the Pacific area is largely underrepresented. The pattern of regional imbalance is also reflected in the percentage of women staff grouped by region of origin as a percentage of women staff only, as of 30 June 1995 (A/50/540, table D.2). Eastern Europe (3.26), the Middle East (3.96), Africa (8.86) and Latin America (9.45) have the lowest representation of women. Higher ranges are found in North America and the Caribbean (28.58), Western Europe (23.10) and Asia and the Pacific (22.40).

9. During the period under review, four men were appointed to D-2 posts subject to geographical distribution; no women were appointed at that level. Eight men and three women were promoted from the D-1 to the D-2 level. No women were placed in posts relating to peace-keeping, peacemaking or to the international tribunals, at the D-2 level or above. As indicated in the previous report of the Secretary-General (A/49/587 and Corr.1), a Senior Review Group was established in 1993 to review the filling of D-2 posts, with a view to providing the Secretary-General with structured advice that ensures both that personnel policies and recruitment guidelines are consistently implemented and to ensuring that staff members aspiring to these posts are satisfied that their candidacies are given adequate consideration. This Group plays an important role in assisting the Secretary-General to meet the mandated senior-level targets.

10. As part of the Organization's efforts to improve the status of women, the Under-Secretary-General

for Administration and Management, by a memorandum dated 5 October 1995, requested all heads of departments and offices to apply recently announced procedures for filling their vacancies in a more timely manner and, as part of this effort, to submit quarterly plans for filling a proportion of those vacancies over the next biennium with women candidates. Heads of departments and offices were informed of their department's or office's levels of representation of women in posts subject to geographical distribution and in posts at the decision-making levels, with a view to helping them evaluate the existing situation and to assisting them to set their own recruitment and promotion targets to advance the Organization in reaching Secretariat-wide targets. A recent study prepared in the Office of the Focal Point for Women has shown that, to reach the target of 50 per cent by the year 2000, approximately two of every three vacancies should be filled by women.

B. Women in posts subject to special language requirements

11. As shown in table 2, the number of women in posts subject to special language requirements was 35.4 per cent on 30 June 1994. The level of representation at 30 June 1995 was 35.3 per cent. This represents a decrease of 0.1 per cent, and reflects a slightly lower representation of women at the P-5 and P-4 levels. Within this group, moreover, the staffing complement of certain language services still consists predominantly of male staff. It might be noted, however, that, had the target been applied to posts subject to special language requirements, the Secretariat would have met a 35 per cent representation level for 1995.

C. Women in the General Service and related categories

12. The percentage of women in the General Service category has risen from 56.1 per cent in June 1994 to 57.8 per cent in June 1995. The percentage of women in the combined Field Service, Security Service, Trades and Crafts and Public Information Assistants categories is only 14.5 per cent, having risen 0.4 percentage points from 14.1 in 1994.

13. In order to alleviate the career bottleneck of General Service staff, to respond to proposals made by the Steering Committee on the Improvement of the Status of Women in the Secretariat in its first report, and to harmonize the G to P and national competitive examinations, it has been decided that qualified staff in this category should be invited to apply to sit for P-3 national competitive examinations, provided that they meet the same educational, experience and nationality requirements applicable to external candidates. The Secretary-

General proposes to do this on an experimental basis during the biennium 1996-1997. Currently, General Service staff may also apply to take the P-2 national competitive examinations, provided that they meet the same criteria.

14. Training opportunities have increased in both number and scope over the past year. Examples of available training provided to staff in the General Service and related categories have included: general orientation programmes; computer training, for more than 3,800 staff, of whom 2,800 were women; training of staff in the Executive Office of OHRM in providing more reliable and timely responses to the needs of programme managers and individual staff, for 130 staff, of whom 101 were women; and external studies programmes to upgrade substantive skills, for more than 142 staff, of whom 53 were women.

D. Promotion and placement

15. The strict application and monitoring of the special measures announced in administrative instruction ST/AI/382 has yielded a promotion rate of 51.42 per cent for women over the past year (see table 3). This is the first occasion that a rate of more than 50 per cent has been achieved. The special measures require that due regard be paid to achieving gender equality in the Secretariat, even when financial crises or measures lead to periods of down-sizing and/or a freeze on recruitment.

Table 3. *Percentage of women promoted through the appointment and promotion bodies to the P-3 to D-1 levels (30 June 1994–30 June 1995)*

Level	Men	Women	Total	Percentage of women
D-1	17	7	24	29.2
P-5	23	33	56	58.9
P-4	29	26	55	47.3
P-3	16	24	40	60.0

Source: OHRM, Secretariat of the Appointments and Promotions Board.

16. Despite the application of these measures, it has been noted that women of all categories tend to stay longer in grade than their male counterparts. This situation will be addressed by OHRM in 1996, in the context of preparing for the triennial review of those staff who have not benefited from the promotion system, as described in the report of the Secretary-General on a strat-

Table 4. *Percentage of women appointed through the appointment and promotion bodies at the P-2 to D-1 levels (30 June 1994–30 June 1995)*

Level	Men	Women	Percentage of women
D-1	3	2	40.0
P-5	4	3	42.9
P-4	14	7	33.3
P-3	21	18	46.2
P-2	26	30	53.6

Source: Report of the Secretary-General on the composition of the Secretariat (A/50/540).

egy for the management of the human resources of the Organization (see A/C.5/49/5, para. 8).

E. *Appointments*

17. Table 4 indicates the percentage of women recruited after consideration by the appointment and promotion bodies. The data reveal that a higher percentage of women were recruited at the P-1/P-2 and P-3 levels, largely through national competitive and G to P examinations. As shown in table 4, some increases over 1994 levels were also achieved at the P-4, P-5 and D-1 levels.

F. *Distribution of women across departments and offices and in occupational groups*

18. Table 5 indicates the gender distribution, by department or office, of Secretariat staff in posts subject to geographical distribution. Of the 32 entities reviewed, three have achieved a representation of more than 55 per cent women (United Nations Special Commission, Department of Administration and Management and Office of Human Resources Management); three have more than 45 per cent women (United Nations Joint Staff Pension Fund, Department of Public Information and Office of Programme Planning, Budget and Accounts); nine have more than 35 per cent women (Department for Policy Coordination and Sustainable Development, Office of the United Nations High Commissioner for Refugees, United Nations Office at Geneva, United Nations International Drug Control Programme, Department for Development Support and Management Services, United Nations Environment Programme, Department of Political Affairs, Office of Legal Affairs and Office of Internal Oversight Services); 11 have over 25 per cent women (Department for Economic and Social Information and Policy Analysis, Interorganizational bodies (Joint Inspec-

tion Unit (JIU)), Consultative Committee on Administrative Questions (CCAQ), International Computing Centre (ICC), Information Systems Coordination Committee (ISCC), Office of Conference and Support Services, Executive Office of the Secretary-General, Economic and Social Commission for Asia and the Pacific, Department of Peace-keeping Operations, United Nations Office at Vienna, Economic Commission for Latin America and the Caribbean, Economic and Social Commission for Western Asia, Department of Humanitarian Affairs, and Department of Peace-keeping Operations/Field Administration and Logistics Division); and six have not yet reached a representation of 25 per cent women in posts subject to geographical distribution (United Nations Conference on Trade and Development, Economic Commission for Europe, United Nations Centre for Human Settlements (Habitat), Economic Commission for Africa, Regional Commissions Liaison Office and United Nations Compensation Commission).

19. A recent report of the Joint Inspection Unit, entitled "Advancement of the status of women in the United Nations in an era of 'human resources management' and 'accountability': a new beginning?" (A/49/176), highlighted the uneven distribution of women in various occupational groups. If the level of women's representation of between 30 and 35 per cent and above is considered to form a critical mass, the Secretariat can be considered to have achieved that status in such occupational groups as political affairs, legal affairs, public information, administration, social affairs, economic affairs, human resources and human rights. Numbers alone, however, will neither guarantee that the "glass ceiling" barring access to the upper echelons will be shattered nor lead to a more even distribution of women across occupational groups. As departments begin to look more closely at the desirable mix of occupations within their staffing complement, gender issues must be integrated into strategic human resources planning and greater attention must be given to creating opportunities for women to serve the Organization at the higher levels.

III. Recent developments

20. During the course of the year, attention was focused on the status of women in the Secretariat in a variety of forms, as indicated in the present section.

A. *Administrative Committee on Coordination*

21. Following a request by the Steering Committee for the Improvement of the Status of Women in the Secretariat, the Secretary-General took the initiative of placing an item on the status of women in the secretariats of the United Nations system on the agenda of the spring

Table 5. Gender distribution of staff in the United Nations Secretariat by department or office and by grade: Professional and higher-level staff in posts subject to geographical distribution(as at 30 June 1995)

Department/office	USG F	USG M	ASG F	ASG M	D-2 F	D-2 M	D-1 F	D-1 M	P-5 F	P-5 M	P-4 F	P-4 M	P-3 F	P-3 M	P-2 F	P-2 M	P-1 F	P-1 M	Total F	Total M	Grand total	% women
55% and over																						
UNSCOM	0	0	0	0	0	0	0	0	1	0	0	0	0	0	0	0	0	0	1	0	1	100.0
DAM	0	1	0	0	1	0	1	1	4	4	6	4	4	2	3	1	0	0	19	13	32	59.4
DAM/OHRM	0	0	0	1	2	1	2	2	7	6	11	11	11	9	9	4	0	0	42	34	76	55.3
45% and over																						
UNJSP	0	0	0	0	0	0	0	3	2	4	7	3	7	8	1	0	0	0	17	18	35	48.6
DPI a/	1	0	0	1	1	4	5	12	14	24	28	35	48	35	22	22	0	0	119	133	252	47.2
DAM/OPPBA	0	0	0	1	0	4	0	4	7	9	13	11	15	14	5	5	0	0	40	48	88	45.5
35% and over																						
DPCSD	0	1	1	0	1	5	2	12	7	14	16	13	8	5	5	3	0	0	40	53	93	43.0
UNHCR	0	1	0	1	0	0	0	2	2	5	7	11	6	8	7	3	0	0	22	31	53	41.5
UNOG	0	1	0	0	0	1	2	8	7	7	5	11	13	21	11	13	0	0	38	62	100	38.0
UNDCP	0	1	0	0	0	2	0	0	1	8	7	6	3	8	6	3	0	0	17	28	45	37.8
DDSMS	0	1	0	0	1	3	0	7	6	13	16	21	9	9	2	2	0	0	34	56	90	37.8
UNEP	1	0	0	0	0	0	1	3	2	3	2	5	1	1	2	3	0	0	9	15	24	37.5
DPA	0	1	0	2	1	7	4	9	12	20	14	22	13	12	4	8	0	0	48	81	129	37.2
OLA	0	1	0	0	1	3	0	10	8	11	5	7	5	9	8	8	0	0	27	49	76	35.5
OIOS	0	1	0	0	0	1	1	2	2	5	8	11	2	7	4	4	0	0	17	31	48	35.4
25% and over																						
DESIPA	0	1	0	0	0	3	1	12	12	10	13	24	9	22	10	15	0	0	45	87	132	34.1
INTORG b/	0	0	0	0	0	1	0	0	0	2	1	1	1	0	0	0	0	0	2	4	6	33.3
DAM/OCSS	0	0	0	1	1	4	4	10	9	14	11	21	9	26	6	12	0	0	40	88	128	31.3
EOSG	0	2	1	1	1	1	3	2	1	3	1	3	1	4	0	2	0	0	8	18	26	30.8
ESCAP	0	1	0	0	1	0	3	9	2	21	10	32	11	20	14	11	0	0	41	94	135	30.4
DPKO	0	0	0	1	0	4	2	7	2	7	6	16	6	6	3	3	0	0	19	44	63	30.2
UNOV	0	0	0	0	1	1	2	5	2	7	4	11	1	11	5	2	0	0	15	37	52	28.8
ECLAC	0	1	0	0	1	1	0	10	7	18	8	32	12	23	9	18	0	0	37	103	140	26.4
ESCWA	0	1	0	0	1	0	0	3	2	11	4	20	4	6	5	4	0	0	16	45	61	26.2
DHA	0	1	0	0	0	3	0	5	3	11	1	7	3	1	3	2	0	0	10	30	40	25.0
DPKO/FALD	0	0	0	2	0	3	0	8	3	19	5	16	7	9	5	3	0	0	20	60	80	25.0
24% and under																						
UNCTAD	0	0	0	0	1	3	2	23	5	39	9	41	20	37	15	18	0	0	52	161	213	24.4
ECE	0	1	0	0	1	0	2	5	2	14	7	19	6	18	4	13	0	0	22	70	92	23.9
UNCHS	0	0	0	1	0	1	0	3	1	4	2	8	3	9	2	3	0	0	8	29	37	21.6
ECA	0	1	0	0	1	1	1	10	3	32	7	36	12	39	9	13	0	0	32	131	163	19.6
REGCOM	0	0	0	0	0	1	0	0	0	0	0	1	0	0	0	0	0	0	0	1	1	0.0
UNCC	0	0	0	0	0	1	0	1	0	1	0	1	0	0	0	0	0	0	0	4	4	0.0
Total	2	18	2	12	14	58	39	188	136	345	234	460	250	379	180	198	0	0	857	1 658	2 515	34.1

Source: Reports of the Secretary-General on the composition of the Secretariat (A/48/559, A/49/527 and A/50/540). It should be noted that percentages for offices with less than 20 staff on board are not significant.

a/ Including information centres.

b/ Including the secretariats of CCAQ, ICC, ISCC and JIU.

session of the Administrative Committee on Coordination (ACC). After an extensive discussion of the item, ACC adopted a comprehensive statement reaffirming the strong commitment of executive heads to ensuring that the advancement of women is a policy priority within the organizations of the common system and to taking the necessary action to improve the status of women in their respective secretariats. The statement addressed measures to facilitate the recruitment of women, encourage their mobility, promote a supportive work environment and foster the necessary attitudinal changes. The statement stressed that management commitment at the highest level is key to the achievement of gender equality goals and that particular attention must be paid to increasing the number of women in senior managerial positions. The statement, which was endorsed by the General Assembly in its resolution 49/222 B, is contained in the annex to the present report.

B. Steering Committee for the Improvement of the Status of Women in the Secretariat

22. The Steering Committee for the Improvement of the Status of Women in the Secretariat, in its capacity as an advisory body to the Secretary-General, continued to provide support and guidance during the course of the year. This included monitoring the efforts to appoint and promote more women staff and to improve their conditions of work. One of the most important contributions of the Committee during the year was the survey it conducted on the constraints preventing the achievement of the goal of equality for women. Twenty-eight heads of departments and offices, regional commissions, programmes and funds, including the United Nations Children's Fund (UNICEF), the United Nations Development Programme (UNDP) and the United Nations Population Fund (UNFPA), responded to the questionnaire. The Steering Committee concluded that the survey was also a useful instrument to raise awareness and to sensitize managers. The survey indicated that, in addition to long-standing constraints, restructuring and decentralization, the lack of competitive salaries and limited opportunities for spouse employment were affecting the Organization's ability to meet its targets for the advancement of women.

23. Many of the Steering Committee's recommendations have been incorporated into the Secretary-General's human resources management strategy. These include: recommendations towards meeting the 50 per cent representation target; means to permit qualified General Service staff to sit for P-2/P-3 national competitive examinations; and the need to appraise the performance of managers and supervisors in achieving the goal of gender balance. The Steering Committee has also noted the usefulness of studying successful practices in other organizations inside and outside the United Nations system.

C. International Women's Day celebrations in Copenhagen and New York

24. On 8 March 1995, International Women's Day, a special celebration was held at Copenhagen on the occasion of the World Summit for Social Development. The event, which was addressed by the Secretary-General, was attended by many heads of State. On 14 March 1995, the Group on Equal Rights for Women, the Franklin and Eleanor Roosevelt Institute and the United Nations Association-USA jointly sponsored a similar full-day commemoration in New York to honour Mrs. Eleanor Roosevelt, one of the small number of women delegates at the first session of the General Assembly of the United Nations in London in 1946. Mrs. Roosevelt was also honoured for her contributions to the drafting of the Universal Declaration of Human Rights, adopted in 1948. The focus of the day encompassed, as well, the status of women in the United Nations and what has been achieved over the 50-year period. The Roosevelt Institute published Women in the United Nations, 2/ a volume containing the statements made at the 14 March commemoration.

D. Fourth World Conference on Women

25. The culminating event of the year was the Fourth World Conference on Women, held at Beijing from 4 to 15 September 1995. In addition to its comprehensive proposals along sectoral areas, the Conference, in its Platform for Action, reviewed the situation of women in decision-making and in power structures. In paragraph 193 of the Platform for Action the United Nations was called on to implement existing and adopt new employment policies and measures in order to achieve overall gender equality, particularly at the Professional level and above, by the year 2000. It was stated that this should be achieved with due regard to the importance of recruiting staff on as wide a geographical basis as possible, in conformity with Article 101, paragraph 3, of the Charter of the United Nations. The United Nations was also requested to continue to monitor progress towards achieving the Secretary-General's target of having women hold 50 per cent of managerial and decision-making positions by the year 2000. 3/

26. With respect to institutional arrangements, the Conference invited the Secretary-General to establish a high-level post in the Office of the Secretary-General, using existing human and financial resources, to act as

2/ Published at Hyde Park, New York, in 1995.
3/ Report of the Fourth World Conference on Women ...

the Secretary-General's adviser on gender issues and to help ensure system-wide implementation of the Platform for Action in close cooperation with the Division for the Advancement of Women. 4/ This proposal will be addressed by the Secretary-General in the context of his report on the implementation of the outcome of the Conference, to be considered by the General Assembly at its current session.

IV. New management culture: impact on the status of women

A. *Accountability, training and gender sensitivity*

27. In developing his human resources management strategy, the Secretary-General made a deliberate effort to integrate the objectives set for the advancement of women into the new management culture envisaged for the Secretariat. To date, 4,500 staff at the Professional level and above and supervisors at the senior General Service levels have been trained in the new performance appraisal system (PAS). PAS includes a mandatory performance indicator to evaluate the extent to which managers and supervisors achieve gender balance and demonstrate sensitivity to the multi-cultural environment in their immediate office, as called for in Assembly resolution 49/222 A, section III. Responsiveness, client-service orientation and gender sensitivity are, moreover, emphasized in the people management training programme for senior managers at the D-1 and D-2 levels Secretariat-wide. So that the programme can offer a gender-balanced perspective and training environment, it has been expanded to include women staff at the P-5 level with managerial responsibilities.

B. *Measures to combat harassment, including sexual harassment*

28. In January 1995, a joint staff-management task force began examining the effectiveness of the Organization's policies and procedures established in October 1992 to deal with sexual harassment in the workplace. The task force recognized that the creation of a safe work environment, as called for in the Secretary-General's human resources management strategy, required that the concept be expanded to address all forms of harassment in the workplace. Despite the added dimension of a multi-cultural environment, instances of harassment in the United Nations workplace, as in the public and private sectors, are often characterized by abuse of power, with victims fearful of retaliation. Preliminary indications received through pilot Secretariat training sessions suggest that staff are extremely reluctant to come forward to report harassment. This would appear to be borne out by the low number of cases of reported harassment submitted since the 1992 policies were effected.

29. The Staff Management Coordination Committee, at its nineteenth session, held at Amman, in June 1995, agreed to a task force proposal to survey United Nations staff to gauge the degree to which harassment exists in the United Nations workplace. The survey will be the first of its breadth and scope, making it a benchmark-setting exercise for the United Nations and its family of organizations and agencies. Staff at all Secretariat, UNICEF, UNDP and UNFPA duty stations will be guaranteed anonymity in completing the questionnaire. The survey, which is currently being developed and will be reviewed by a series of departmental focus groups over the next few months, is scheduled for release in early 1996. Existing policies and mechanisms to deal with harassment will be re-examined, and strengthened as needed, in the light of the data yielded by the survey. This activity, when implemented, will assist in meeting the request of the Beijing Conference in its Platform for Action.

C. *Consolidation of special measures to improve the status of women*

30. While administrative instruction ST/AI/382 on special measures to improve the status of women in the Secretariat is regarded as a landmark document, it was considered that a streamlining and consolidation of all existing bulletins, administrative instructions and other policy issuances on achieving gender balance would increase the efficiency of the special measures and enhance the ability of OHRM to effect and monitor their implementation. The work of an interdepartmental task force has now been completed and the new instruction, to be announced by a Secretary-General's bulletin, is being finalized for issuance in the near future.

V. Implementation of the Strategic Plan of Action for the Improvement of the Status of Women in the Secretariat (1995-2000)

31. It will be recalled that the plan of action updated the Action Programme for the Improvement of the Status of Women in the Secretariat (1991-1995) and incorporated salient aspects of more current human resources development strategies. The Platform for Action adopted at Beijing included, in paragraph 331, a request to OHRM, in collaboration with programme managers world wide, to give priority to key issues relating to the advancement of women in the Secretariat in accordance with the plan of action. The present section assesses the steps taken to implement the measures proposed by the Secretary-General in his previous report to the General Assembly (see A/49/587 and Corr.1).

4/ Ibid., para. 326.

A. Goals and objectives

32. The long-term goals of the plan of action are to create conditions of equality and opportunity for women to participate fully in the work of the Secretariat and to achieve gender parity by the year 2000. When considering the Secretariat's efforts to achieve these objectives, the following should be borne in mind:

(a) Although the representation of women in the Secretariat has reached only 34.1 per cent in posts subject to geographical distribution at 30 June 1995, thus falling 0.9 per cent short of the target, it is hoped that representation levels will come closer to the 35 per cent target by year's end. Preliminary statistics on the early separation programme indicate that approximately twice as many men as women at the senior Professional levels will separate under the programme. The higher proportion of senior-level posts encumbered by men thus vacated will provide additional opportunities to improve the gender balance at those levels;

(b) The representation of women at the D-1 level and above is 17.1 per cent, falling significantly short of the goals of reaching 25 per cent by June 1997 and 50 per cent by the year 2000;

(c) The goal of establishing recruitment and promotion policies and strategies supportive of the targets and objectives to improve the status of women in the Secretariat has been furthered by the Secretary-General's new strategy for human resources management, outlined in document A/C.5/49/5 and endorsed by the General Assembly in its resolution 49/222 A. The human resources management strategy, together with the ACC statement endorsed by the Assembly in its resolution 49/222 B, represent important and intentional steps forward in integrating measures to improve the status of women within the overall human resources management policies of the United Nations system as a whole.

B. Implementation of policies and strategies

33. The plan of action, as detailed in paragraph 39 of the report of the Secretary-General (A/49/587 and Corr.1), identified 11 areas in which action is needed. Progress made in each area is discussed in the following paragraphs.

(a) *Planning and information/human resources database development*

34. Provision has been made for these activities in the restructured OHRM. A new Planning and Development Service has just begun its work. The Service will develop overall human resources planning strategies, by projecting vacancies, determining the staff function requirements of organizational units, inventorying the skills of staff on board and developing strategies to match

the two. Performance appraisal and management systems and career development and management systems, including succession planning and targeted training for staff of all categories, are integral elements of such strategies. The Service will also be responsible for the human resources management information system, which will serve as the underlying support in developing systems and strategies.

(b) *Networking with other databases on women*

(c) *Upgrading internal and external rosters of women*

(d) *Advertising these activities*

35. The above areas are among the main activities of the new Specialist Services Division of OHRM, created on 1 September 1995. Searches at a representative number of universities and in various regions have been initiated to identify potential candidates among students from many of the 51 unrepresented and underrepresented countries. The internal roster will, in fact, be a skills inventory. Both the skills inventory and the external roster will categorize staff by occupational groups, thus enabling a more efficient matching of skills and vacancies. This activity, which is to include staff at all duty stations, will be greatly facilitated by the extension of the Integrated Management Information System (IMIS) to cover all duty stations.

(e) *Recruitment missions*

36. Although no recruitment missions were undertaken during the period under review, candidates from 31 unrepresented, underrepresented and below mid-point represented countries participated in the P-2 and P-3 national competitive examinations. In addition, at the Fourth World Conference on Women, the representative of OHRM and the Office of the Focal Point for Women took the opportunity to address a letter dated 8 September 1995 to the 114 heads of delegations representing unrepresented, underrepresented and below mid-point represented countries, encouraging their delegations to submit the names of women candidates qualified for United Nations employment opportunities. All 189 States participating in the Conference received recruitment kits and an OHRM brochure on *Employment Opportunities at the United Nations*, as well as copies of the report of the Secretary-General setting out the strategic plan of action (A/49/587 and Corr.1), the ACC statement on women (A/C.5/49/62) and a sample recruitment application form. The representative of OHRM, on behalf of the Focal Point for Women, discussed recruitment and gender issues with many of the delegations. Follow-up action includes screening possible candidates for recruitment or rostering.

(f) Management culture

37. With the introduction of the performance appraisal system, the Secretary-General has put into place an important element of the system of accountability and responsibility as set out in document A/C.5/49/1, which was discussed by the General Assembly at its forty-ninth session. As detailed in section IV above, measures have been built into the performance appraisal system to hold managers accountable for how they deal with gender-related issues.

(g) Mobility and conditions of work

38. Developing and implementing systems of planned rotation by occupational group will be among the tasks of the newly created Planning and Development Service of OHRM. Pursuant to paragraph 6 of General Assembly resolution 49/167, work continues at the level of the ACC Consultative Committee on Administrative Questions (CCAQ) on such matters as the exchange of women staff between the organizations of the common system. The CCAQ task force on work/life issues has discussed such matters as flexi-time and flexi-place, spouse employment, parental leave and child and elderly care as part of the need to recognize that women usually have dual roles in the home and at the workplace. An evaluation of problems relating to spouse employment is being undertaken to identify ways to facilitate the movement of staff, their spouses and families between duty stations. Member States that host United Nations organizations and agencies could assist in this regard by permitting, on an exceptional basis, the spouses of staff members, male or female, the right to work. The ACC statement mentioned in paragraph 21 above envisaged the introduction of provisions to this effect in host country agreements and other efforts in each United Nations location to promote the employment of spouses.

(h) In-service training

39. A number of women staff members have been placed in higher-level posts, thereby gaining greater hands-on managerial experience. After serving in field missions, several women staff members without prior experience in the political area have been able to assume positions as political affairs or humanitarian affairs officers on return from mission. Others, having benefited from the opportunity of exercising wider responsibilities in the field, have moved to positions of higher responsibility in their own departments in recognition of their acquired experience and demonstrated ability. Determined efforts will be made to record in a more systematic way relevant work experiences in the performance records of all staff and to track the variables (academic background, mission assignment, higher-level responsi-

bilities, the grant of special post allowances and training) in order to facilitate movement across occupational groups.

(i) Career development

40. The work of the recently created Planning and Development Service will also include the systematic development of career development and management systems. As policies and guidelines are set for the career development of all categories of staff in the global Secretariat, the Operational Services Division created on 1 September 1995 will add career development counselling to the package of other services it provides through its seven clusters to all Headquarters departments and offices, offices away from Headquarters and field missions. While career development counselling services will begin to be offered by March/April 1996, the clusters are already providing a broad range of support services, including recruitment, placement and promotion support, staff entitlement and benefit administration and job classification. These services will eventually be replicated in the human resources management units of all offices away from Headquarters.

(j) Training

41. As mentioned in section IV above, training for new staff and for senior- and middle-level managers to develop the managerial skills required to change the Organization's management culture has, over the past year, incorporated gender balance and gender sensitivity and diversity issues. In the short term, OHRM is including in these programmes all staff with supervisory or managerial responsibility. In the long term, such training will be mandatory for all staff.

(k) General Service and related categories

42. The formulation and implementation of career development and counselling systems discussed in paragraph 40 above will broaden the scope and awareness of opportunities for staff in the General Service and related categories. Over the past two years, career development opportunities presented through field mission assignments have been somewhat diminished as a result of the closing of missions in Cambodia (UNTAC), Mozambique (ONUMOZ), Somalia (UNOSOM) and South Africa (UNOMSA) and the down-sizing of other missions. None the less, the remaining field missions continue to offer opportunities to staff in the General Service and related categories. A recent administrative instruction (ST/AI/404) limiting the duration of mission assignments of both General Service and Professional staff to two years aims to keep open the opportunity for the rotation of a greater number of staff so as to maximize the opportunities for individual staff to gain mission

experience. The instruction also ensures that posts will be blocked for staff who return on completion of an assignment of up to two years.

43. OHRM also plans to develop a roster of staff skills in the General Service and related categories in order to enhance the Organization's capacity to expeditiously identify and select staff with the required mix of skills for mission and other assignments. A system of regular rotation of staff with finance, personnel administration and recruitment skills has already been implemented for the deployment of staff of OHRM and the Office of Programme Planning, Budget and Accounts, through the Department of Peace-keeping Operations' Field Administration and Logistics Division, to and from a number of field missions.

(l) *Other activities*

44. With the issuance of administrative instruction ST/AI/399 concerning indebtedness to third parties, progress has been made in ensuring that legitimate obligations arising from court-mandated spousal and/or child support cases are fully respected.

C. *Monitoring, appraisal and follow-up*

45. Every effort will be made to ensure effective follow-up, and to monitor implementation, of the recommendations for the advancement of women in the Secretariat contained in the Platform for Action adopted by the Beijing Conference, through the sustained implementation of the strategic plan of action. Within the Secretariat, this will entail measures to ensure the equal opportunity of women to participate in the work of the Organization in its broadest aspects; to ensure the equal participation of women in decision-making positions; to give women access to the full range of occupational groups in the Secretariat; and to provide a work environment free of harassment, including sexual harassment.

46. As indicated in paragraph 30 above, the forthcoming issuance of a consolidated and updated instruction setting forth all of the special measures to improve the status of women in the Secretariat will serve as an important mechanism to facilitate the monitoring and appraisal of the implementation of measures to achieve equality between women and men staff members.

47. Departments and offices will be expected to report on their efforts to implement the special measures in the context of the system reaffirmed in October 1995 by the Under-Secretary-General for Administration and Management for the quarterly reporting on departmental plans for filling vacancies (see para. 10 above). This, in turn, will form the basis for a comprehensive monitoring system that will for the first time render feasible managerial accountability to the Secretary-General.

48. The measures required to strengthen policies and systems to identify, deal with and eliminate harassment, including sexual harassment, in the United Nations workplace should emerge more clearly when the results of the Secretariat-wide questionnaire are known, towards the middle of 1996. The questionnaire will be designed to assess the scope of the problem and to analyse the main factors that inhibit staff from coming forward to expose harassment that exists and managers from taking action to redress such situations. Action will be taken to upgrade, where necessary, existing counselling and support services, as well as the disciplinary machinery, and to establish new policies not only for dealing with harassment but also for creating a supportive culture of civility and respect among all staff.

D. *Office of the Focal Point for Women in the Secretariat*

49. The Focal Point for Women continues to report directly to the Assistant Secretary-General for Human Resources Management and to function as an integral part of his Office. Within OHRM, the Focal Point will continue to work closely with the newly reorganized divisions of OHRM, as follows: with the Specialist Services Division, on executive search, networking and roster upgrading and in identifying qualified women candidates and eliminating possibilities of discrimination; with the Operational Services Division, on placement, promotion, recruitment, career counselling and mediation issues; and with the Planning and Development Service, on succession planning, rotation and career management policies and systems.

50. The activities of the Office of the Focal Point are currently financed from extrabudgetary sources. It has not yet proved possible to place this activity on a more secure footing through funding under the regular budget, and extrabudgetary financing is again forecast for the 1996-1997 budget period. Deep concern exists about the continued flow of such resources, particularly when the Organization is facing serious financial difficulties. Concern has also been expressed that the current staff resources of one D-1 and one General Service level staff are extremely limited in view of the workload related to the implementation of the plan of action, as well as the monitoring, appraisal and follow-up arising from the Beijing Conference. In a letter dated 10 October 1994, the Under-Secretary-General for Administration and Management called upon those 26 Member States that had expressed support for the programme to provide voluntary contributions to strengthen the capacity of the Office of the Focal Point to better implement and monitor the plan of action and to undertake much-needed studies. So far, no Member State has responded to this call.

51. The Focal Point works in close collaboration with a network of departmental focal points, both at Headquarters and in the field, who in turn assist department heads and chiefs of administration or executive offices in monitoring policy implementation and in alerting the Focal Point in OHRM to problems encountered. The occasion of the Fourth World Conference on Women provided an opportunity for the focal points or their representatives from 11 departments and offices Secretariat-wide (Department of Development Support and Management Services, Department for Economic and Social Information and Policy Analysis, Department for Policy Coordination and Sustainable Development, United Nations Office at Vienna, Economic Commission for Africa, Economic Commission for Europe, Economic Commission for Latin America and the Caribbean, Economic and Social Commission for Asia and the Pacific, Economic and Social Commission for Western Asia, United Nations Conference on Trade and Development and United Nations Environment Programme) to meet and exchange views with one another, with the representative of OHRM and with other women staff members and women representing several agencies and organizations of the United Nations system (United Nations Children's Fund, United Nations Development Fund for Women, United Nations Population Fund, World Food Programme, Office of the United Nations High Commissioner for Refugees, United Nations University, International Research and Training Institute for the Advancement of Women, International Trade Centre UNCTAD/GATT, International Labour Organization, Food and Agriculture Organization of the United Nations, World Health Organization, International Fund for Agricultural Development, United Nations Industrial Development Organization and International Atomic Energy Agency).

52. The purpose of the meeting was to exchange views on progress made to implement the strategic plan of action; to seek ways and means to strengthen the effectiveness of the plan; and to review how the ad hoc inter-agency mechanism for examining such issues as system-wide strategies for meeting numerical and qualitative targets for women might be placed on a more regular basis. The recent report of the Joint Inspection Unit, entitled "The advancement of women through and in the programmes of the United Nations system: What happens after the Fourth World Conference on Women?" (A/50/509) also emphasized this need. Meeting participants also exchanged views on methods to (a) mainstream gender issues throughout the programmes of the United Nations in the context of the system-wide medium-term plan for women; (b) improve the status of women throughout the secretariats of the organizations and agencies; (c) prepare analytical studies using common data; (d) maintain regular communications and exchange information and data among focal points and interested staff; and (e) create and maintain advisory support and mentoring systems to apprise women staff, particularly new staff and those coming through the G to P examination, of ways to secure access to the necessary information and advice.

E. Member States

53. Member States, particularly those that are unrepresented or underrepresented and those whose desirable range is below the mid-point or that have few women staff in posts subject to geographical distribution, are encouraged to submit the names of qualified, suitable women candidates for vacancies, which are circulated regularly through the permanent missions or in international journals and media. The Secretariat is determined to reduce the time of recruitment for both successful candidates from the P-2 and P-3 national competitive examinations and those for higher-level posts. To assist in this regard, Member States are encouraged to prepare their own rosters of women candidates by occupational groups. These rosters should be screened in accordance with the guidelines and requirements set out in the 1995 brochure, *Employment Opportunities at the United Nations*. This will help to reduce the time lag between the issuance of vacancy announcements and the submission of candidates. In view of the low percentage of women at senior levels, Member States are particularly encouraged to include on their rosters and to transmit to the Secretariat suitable candidates for positions at the D-1 level and above as they are announced. Although offers of new appointments will resume only once the cash flow crisis has ended, efforts will continue to identify qualified, suitable women candidates for posts within the United Nations.

54. The Specialist Services Division of OHRM will undertake recruitment missions at universities and conduct executive searches, through professional organizations and agencies. Member States are urged to transmit to the Secretariat the names of appropriate agencies or institutions they would suggest be contacted for this purpose.

55. In view of the very limited resources available to the Office of the Focal Point for Women, the Secretary-General reiterates the request made in his previous report to the General Assembly (A/49/587 and Corr.1) for material support in the form of the secondment of experts from Governments or in the form of resources to assist the Office of the Focal Point in undertaking essential studies for the implementation of the plan of action.

56. The achievement of the goals of the plan of

action will require the full support and commitment of all Member States.

F. Non-governmental organizations and professional bodies

57. The United Nations intends to work more closely with non-governmental organizations and other professional organizations in areas such as networking, executive search and exchange of information on gender-sensitivity training, research and other issues. These organizations, world wide, are also viewed as a potential source of candidates for recruitment in the United Nations system.

VI. Conclusions

58. As the General Assembly considers the follow-up to the Fourth World Conference on Women, it is important that the recommendations of the Platform for Action regarding women in decision-making, in power structures and in managerial positions, to be applied at the national, regional and international levels, be similarly applied to women within the United Nations and its system of organizations.

59. The Secretary-General intends to vigorously pursue the achievement of the objectives set by the General Assembly with respect to the improvement of the status of women through the implementation of the strategic plan of action and the Platform for Action. To this end, the General Assembly may wish to consider extending the target of 50 per cent women and men in posts subject to geographical distribution by the year 2000, as set by the General Assembly in resolution 49/167, to all other categories of posts; namely, to posts with special language requirements as well as field mission and mission replacement posts, irrespective of the type or duration of the appointment, or of the series of Staff Rules under which an appointment is made. The percentage should apply both overall and within each category.

60. Moreover, to address an identified impediment to the advancement of women, Member States that are host countries to United Nations organizations may also wish to consider the proposal in paragraph 38 above, to permit on an exceptional basis the spouses of staff members to work.

61. With Member States as active partners, the Secretary-General hopes to achieve the goal of parity and equal opportunity within the United Nations Secretariat for women and men by the year 2000.

Annex

Statement on the status of women in the secretariats of the United Nations system, adopted by the Administrative Committee on Coordination at its first regular session of 1995

1. The members of the Administrative Committee on Coordination (ACC) reaffirm their strong commitment to ensuring that the advancement of women is a policy priority within the organizations of the common system and to taking necessary measures to improve the status of women in their respective secretariats. Key to the achievement of gender equality goals is management commitment at the highest levels.

2. ACC is conscious that progress to date has, with some exceptions, been limited. While the overall proportion of women has increased in most organizations, the number of women in senior and policy-making positions remains low. A concerted effort needs to be made to implement existing policies fully, as well as to develop new initiatives to increase the participation of women at senior levels.

3. In the development of action plans, in the context of the overall human resources management strategies of the organizations of the system, emphasis will be placed on clear, specific, short-term targets, preferably at the level of organizational units. Efforts will be made to increase the flexibility with which the system deals with women candidates, to remove obstacles to their recruitment, retention, promotion and mobility and to create a supportive environment. In addition to developing specific policies and monitoring mechanisms, Executive Heads intend to hold senior managers accountable for the implementation of these policies at the level at which the targets are set.

4. In the light of the above, consideration will be given by members of ACC to the following to facilitate recruitment of women:

(a) The feasibility of treating all women staff members of common-system organizations as internal candidates in applying for vacant posts in any organization of the system;

(b) Requesting organizations to utilize their field presences to prospect for women candidates in all disciplines;

(c) In cases where member States are to submit candidatures, urging Governments to submit at least one or more qualified female candidate for each position.

5. In order to encourage the mobility of women, consideration will be given to:

(a) Developing a system for inter-agency mobility of women staff to increase their experience;

(b) Facilitating spouse employment through amending the organizations' staff rules, where necessary;

(c) Encouraging the further development of spouse employment opportunities which encompass not only the common system and other governmental and intergovernmental organizations, but also, to the extent possible, the non-governmental and multinational sectors, as well as introducing relevant provisions in host country agreements; and organizing efforts at each United Nations location to promote spouse employment, led in the field by Resident Coordinators and in each headquarters city by a lead agency.

6. With respect to the promotion of a supportive work environment and to the fostering of the necessary attitudinal changes, organizations will consider the intro-

duction of measures which would lead to a climate conducive to the equal participation of men and women in the work of the organizations. Such measures would be related, *inter alia*, to the work/family issues currently under review, such as flexible working hours, part-time work, job-sharing schemes, child care and special leave arrangements.

7. In addition, those organizations which have not already done so are encouraged to introduce appropriate policies and procedures to combat sexual harassment.

8. While the focus of these measures remains the advancement of women at all levels, ACC is conscious that particular attention must be paid to increasing the number of women in senior managerial positions.

Document 129

Report of the Secretary-General to the General Assembly on implementation of the outcome of the Fourth World Conference on Women: Action for Equality, Development and Peace

A/50/744, 10 November 1995

Summary

The present report has been prepared in response to General Assembly resolution 49/161 of 23 December 1994. It provides an overview of the provisions and recommendations for action contained in the Declaration and Platform for Action adopted by consensus by the Fourth World Conference on Women, held in Beijing from 4 to 15 September 1995. The report focuses, in particular, on those recommendations which have immediate implications for action at the international level, including those requiring consideration by the General Assembly at its fiftieth session.

I. Introduction

1. The General Assembly, in its resolution 49/161 of 23 December 1994, requested the Secretary-General to prepare for consideration by the Assembly at its fiftieth session a report on the follow-up to the Fourth World Conference on Women, held in Beijing from 4 to 15 September 1995. The present report is being submitted to the General Assembly in accordance with that request. The report of the Fourth World Conference on Women is currently before the Assembly. 1/

2. The General Assembly's decision, in its resolution 45/129 of 14 December 1990, to convene a Fourth World Conference on Women in 1995 was adopted against the background of a strong concern, reflected in

Economic and Social Council resolutions 1990/12, 1990/14 and 1990/15, at the pace of implementation of the Nairobi Forward-looking Strategies for the Advancement of Women, 2/ in particular with regard to the objectives of ensuring equality for women, promoting their integration in development and advancing their participation in efforts to promote peace. The themes of the United Nations Decade for Women—equality, development and peace—were also chosen as the themes of the Fourth World Conference on Women.

3. In its resolution 47/95 of 16 December 1992, the General Assembly accepted with appreciation the offer of the Government of China to host the Conference.

4. The Conference was attended by 17,000 representatives of Governments, non-governmental organizations, international organizations and the media. Over 30,000 participants attended a parallel forum organized by non-governmental organizations at Huairou.

5. The Commission on the Status of Women served as the preparatory committee for the Conference and the Division for the Advancement of Women of the Depart-

1/ Report of the Fourth World Conference on Women, Beijing, 4-15 September 1995 (A/CONF.177/20).
2/ Report of the World Conference to Review and Appraise the Achievements of the United Nations Decade for Women: Equality, Development and Peace, Nairobi, 15-26 July 1985 (United Nations publication, Sales No. E.85.IV.10), chap. I, sect. A.

ment for Policy Coordination and Sustainable Development of the Secretariat served as the secretariat of the Conference; Mrs. Gertrude Mongella was appointed as its Secretary-General.

6. The preparatory activities for the Conference were characterized by intense collaboration among Governments, the Secretariat and the organizations of the United Nations system, and by the unprecedented involvement and strong support of other intergovernmental organizations and an extremely broad spectrum of non-governmental actors at the international, regional, subregional and national levels.

7. Activities at the national level were wide-ranging and included the preparation of national reports on the review and appraisal of the implementation of the Nairobi Forward-looking Strategies. Such reports were submitted by 165 Member and Observer States. Several countries also convened national meetings and/or set up national preparatory committees.

8. Each of the five regional commissions of the United Nations convened a regional preparatory meeting. These meetings, which were held at Jakarta, Vienna, Mar del Plata, Argentina, Dakar and Amman, resulted in regional plans or programmes of action that provided regional perspectives for the Platform for Action. Consultations organized with representatives of youth organizations at each regional meeting resulted in youth statements on the Platform for Action and further mobilization of youth activities at national and regional level.

9. Support for the Conference at the international level was furthered by the establishment by the Secretary-General of an Advisory Group composed of 19 eminent persons. The Group met three times prior to the Conference. It provided valuable advice to the Secretary-General and assisted in mobilizing political interest and public attention for the Conference.

10. A Trust Fund, to which a number of Member States and other donors contributed generously, augmented the resources available from the regular budget for the preparatory work.

II. Follow-up to the Fourth World Conference on Women

A. *Response of the international community and the United Nations system*

11. The Beijing Declaration and Platform for Action 3/ were adopted by consensus on 15 September 1995 by 189 Governments. The Declaration embodies the commitment of the international community to advance the goals of equality, development and peace and to implement the Platform for Action, ensuring that a gender perspective is reflected in all policies and programmes. The Platform for Action sets out measures for national and international action for the advancement of women.

12. The Fourth World Conference on Women was a conference of commitment. During the Conference, Governments, non-governmental organizations and intergovernmental bodies made specific commitments to implement the goals and objectives of the Conference. Those commitments must be sustained and translated into concrete policies and actions.

13. The Conference brought together the cross-cutting issues of development, equality and peace, and analysed them from a gender perspective. It defined an agenda for action to empower women in the social, political and economic spheres, in both private and public life, and to eliminate all forms of discrimination against women. It emphasized the connection between advancement of women and progress for society as a whole. It reaffirmed clearly that societal issues must be addressed from a gender perspective in order to ensure sustainable development. This agenda, and the approaches it embodies, must guide follow-up action at all levels.

14. As agreed in Beijing, the set of actions set out in the Platform for Action "should lead to fundamental change". To that end "immediate action and accountability are essential if the targets are to be met by the year 2000. Implementation is primarily the responsibility of Governments, but is also dependent on a wide range of institutions in the public, private and non-governmental sectors at the community, national, subregional/regional and international levels" (para. 286).

15. The overriding message of the Fourth World Conference on Women was that the issues addressed in the Platform for Action are global and universal. Deeply entrenched attitudes and practices perpetuate inequality and discrimination against women, in public and private life, in all parts of the world. Accordingly, implementation will require changes in values, attitudes, practices and priorities at the national, regional and international levels. A clear commitment to international norms and standards of equality between men and women, and measures to protect and promote the human rights of women and girl children as an integral part of universal human rights must underlie all action. Institutions at all levels must be reoriented to expedite implementation. An active and visible policy of mainstreaming a gender perspective should be promoted by Governments, the United Nations system and all other relevant organizations.

3/ *Report of the Fourth World Conference on Women ...*, chap. I, resolution 1, annexes I and II respectively.

16. National-level action and supporting action at the international and regional levels should be focused on the 12 critical areas of concern addressed by the Platform for Action (see chap. IV):

(a) The persistent and increasing burden of poverty on women;

(b) Inequalities and inadequacies in, and unequal access to, education and training;

(c) Inequalities and inadequacies in and unequal access to health care and related services;

(d) Violence against women;

(e) The effects of armed or other kinds of conflict on women, including those living under foreign occupation;

(f) Inequality in economic structures and policies, in all forms of productive activities and in access to resources;

(g) Inequality between men and women in the sharing of power and decision-making at all levels;

(h) Insufficient mechanisms at all levels to promote the advancement of women;

(i) Lack of respect for, and inadequate promotion and protection of, the human rights of women;

(j) Stereotyping of women and inequality in women's access to and participation in all communication systems, especially in the media;

(k) Gender inequalities in the management of natural resources and in the safeguarding of the environment;

(l) Persistent discrimination against and violation of the rights of the girl child.

17. Effective action will require the broadest possible cooperation. As indicated in paragraph 306:

"The Platform for Action needs to be implemented through the work of all bodies and organizations of the United Nations system during the period 1995-2000, specifically and as an integral part of wider programming. An enhanced framework for international cooperation for gender issues must be developed ... in order to ensure the integrated and comprehensive implementation, follow-up and assessment of the Platform for Action, taking into account the results of global United Nations summits and conferences. The fact that at all of these summits and conferences, Governments have committed themselves to the empowerment of women in different areas, makes coordination crucial to the follow-up strategies for this Platform for Action. The Agenda for Development and the Agenda for Peace should take into account the Platform for Action of the Fourth World Conference on Women."

18. The Platform for Action further states (para. 307) that "the institutional capacity of the United Nations system to carry out and coordinate its responsibility for implementing the Platform for Action, as well as its expertise and working methods to promote the advancement of women, should be improved" and that "responsibility for ensuring the implementation of the Platform for Action and the integration of a gender perspective into all policies and programmes of the United Nations system must rest at the highest levels" (para. 308).

19. The Secretary-General is in agreement with the Conference's conclusion that "to improve the system's efficiency and effectiveness in providing support for equality and women's empowerment at the national level and to enhance its capacity to achieve the objectives of the Platform for Action, there is a need to renew, reform and revitalize various parts of the United Nations system" (para 309). At the level of the United Nations and its agencies, the strengthening of the capacity of the system to support an integrated, effective follow-up to the Fourth World Conference as part of the overall effort to ensure the coordinated implementation of the results of the series of recent global conferences should be a key objective in pursuing further the ongoing reform process.

20. There must be a new unity of purpose and action in the Organization and the system as a whole contributing to the provision of effective, coordinated support for national action; coherent support for policy-making by the concerned intergovernmental bodies to further the key role of the Organization in respect of standard-setting, policy coordination and advocacy; mutual feedback and reinforcement between national and international action; and effective mainstreaming that ensures that the gender dimension is fully integrated in all aspects of the work of the United Nations.

21. In accordance with chapters V and VI of the Platform for Action, effective implementation of the Conference recommendations will require that existing machinery and institutions sharpen their focus, set clear priorities for action, evaluation and coordination, establish accountability mechanisms and use available resources efficiently.

22. Against this background, the Secretary-General intends to pursue vigorously his efforts to create a stronger, better coordinated programme for the advancement of women. In this regard a key new role will be played by his Senior Adviser (see paras. 54-57 below) and, at the system-wide level, by the proposed Administrative Committee on Coordination task force (see paras. 53 and 89 below).

23. Within the United Nations itself, the requirements from the Platform for Action have given added force to the provisions of General Assembly resolution 48/111 of 20 December 1993, in which it urged that interaction between the International Research and Training Institute for the Advancement of Women (INSTRAW) and the United Nations Development Fund for Women (UNIFEM), the Division for the Advancement of Women, the Commission on the Status of Women, and the Committee on the Elimination of Discrimination against Women be reviewed and rationalized within the context of ongoing efforts to revitalize the Economic and Social Council in pursuance of a stronger, more unified programme for the advancement of women.

24. Accordingly, the Secretary-General will review the different United Nations mechanisms for the advancement of women with a view to making them more mutually supportive and effective, eliminating any duplication and ensuring that the essential linkages are strengthened between the standard-setting and normative work of the Organization and operational activities. A key element of this review and, more generally, a central objective of the overall reform process, should be the enhancement of the capacity of the Organization in support of global policy-making and mainstreaming, mobilizing in a coordinated way the contributions of all parts of the Organization and the system. The Secretary-General will be guided, inter alia, by the Platform of Action, which envisages "reviewing and strengthening the strategies and working methods of different United Nations mechanisms for the advancement of women with a view to rationalizing and, as appropriate, strengthening their advisory, catalytic and monitoring functions in relation to mainstream bodies and agencies. Women/gender units are important for effective mainstreaming, but strategies must be further developed to prevent inadvertent marginalization as opposed to mainstreaming of the gender dimension throughout all operations" (para. 309).

25. The capacity of UNIFEM to provide effective operational support for follow-up action at the national level and to exercise a catalytic role in promoting an effective inter-agency coordination at the country level, through the resident coordinator system, and in bringing country-level experience to bear on relevant aspects of the work of the system at the global level will need to be fully utilized.

26. Proposals for strengthening the research and training capacity of the Organization in pursuance of a stronger, more unified programme for the advancement of women, as outlined in successive reports of the Secretary-General (E/1993/82, A/48/591 and A/49/365-E/1994/119), are already before the General Assembly. They require further consideration pursuant to the relevant Economic and Social Council and General Assembly resolutions on the merger of INSTRAW and UNIFEM. The objectives embodied in those resolutions should be actively pursued as an integral part of the effort to enhance the capacity of the Organization to promote a coherent and sustained follow-up to the Conference.

27. Enhancing coordination and improving the substantive services provided to the Commission on the Status of Women, the Committee on the Elimination of Discrimination against Women and other relevant bodies is another critical objective. The Division for the Advancement of Women has a key responsibility in this regard in support of global policy-making and mainstreaming.

28. The decisions to be taken by the General Assembly at its current session, including on the role and support requirements of the Commission on the Status of Women and other relevant bodies, and subsequent deliberations in those bodies should further the process of renewal, reform and revitalization referred to in paragraph 309 of the Platform for Action. In that light, the Secretary-General, in consultation with the chairpersons of these bodies and drawing on the advice of the proposed high-level board referred to in paragraph 61 below, will submit a further report to the General Assembly at its fifty-first session on ways to enhance the capacity of the Organization to support the ongoing follow-up to the Conference in the most integrated and effective way.

29. The mobilization of adequate resources is another key requirement for the effective implementation of the Platform for Action. The Conference made a strong call for such global mobilization. As stated in paragraph 345:

"To implement the Platform for Action, funding will need to be identified and mobilized from all sources and across all sectors. The reformulation of policies and reallocation of resources may be needed within and among programmes, but some policy changes may not necessarily have financial implications. Mobilization of additional resources both public and private, including resources from innovative sources of funding, may also be necessary."

In paragraph 361 there is a call for effective and efficient use of funds by the United Nations system in its efforts to promote the advancement of women and to enhance its capacity to further the objectives of the Platform for Action. The Platform underlines the need "to renew, reform and revitalize various parts of the United Nations system" and to allocate "additional resources from within the United Nations regular budget in order to implement the Platform for Action". It further states (para. 310):

"In following up the Fourth World Conference on Women, all entities of the United Nations system focusing on the advancement of women should have the necessary resources and support to carry out follow-up activities. The efforts of gender focal points within organizations should be well integrated into overall policy, planning, programming and budgeting."

30. The following paragraphs recall specific provisions of the Platform for Action concerning follow-up, focusing on the recommendations in its chapters V and VI, and immediate actions required to initiate their implementation. Follow-up by the United Nations system as a whole will be covered in greater detail in future reports to the General Assembly and other concerned intergovernmental bodies, including through the revised system-wide medium-term plan for the advancement of women for the period 1996-2001. 4/

B. Specific provisions of the Platform for Action relating to follow-up

1. National level

31. Governments, according to paragraph 293 of the Platform for Action, "have the primary responsibility for implementing the Platform for Action". Governments are called upon "to take a leading role in coordinating, monitoring and assessing progress in the advancement of women". Governments, with financial and advisory assistance from regional and international organizations (para. 300), are called upon (para. 296) "to establish or improve the effectiveness of national machineries for the advancement of women at the highest political level, appropriate intra- and inter-ministerial procedures and staffing, and other institutions with the mandate and capacity to broaden women's participation and integrate gender analysis into policies and programmes".

32. In paragraph 297 Governments are called upon to begin as soon as possible to develop implementation strategies for the Platform for Action, preferably by the end of 1995, with a view to completion by the end of 1996. National planning should be broad-based and participatory, comprehensive and time-bound, and should include proposals for allocating or reallocating resources for implementation.

33. The United Nations resident coordinators at the country level will have a key role in assisting Governments in these efforts (para. 341).

2. Regional/subregional level

34. In its paragraphs 301-305, 351 and 352, the Platform for Action recommends actions to be taken at the regional and subregional levels. The regional commissions of the United Nations and other subregional/regional structures are called upon to promote and assist national institutions in monitoring and implementing the global Platform for Action within their mandates. This should be done, according to paragraph 301, "in coordination with the implementation of the respective regional platforms or plans of action and in close collaboration with the Commission on the Status of Women, taking into account the need for a coordinated follow-up to United Nations conferences in the economic, social, human rights and related fields".

35. In order to facilitate regional implementation, monitoring and evaluation, as called for in paragraph 302, the Economic and Social Council should "consider reviewing the institutional capacity of the United Nations regional commissions within their mandates, including their women's focal points/units, to deal with gender issues in the light of the Platform for Action, as well as the regional platforms or plans of action. Consideration should be given, inter alia, and, where appropriate, to strengthening capacity in this respect". The Platform also calls for regular coordination by United Nations agencies and bodies at the regional level in relation to technical assistance and operational activities (para. 304).

36. The Secretary-General will make every effort to strengthen the gender dimension in all the activities of the regional commissions and to ensure that their capacities are fully utilized to follow up the Platform for Action, and to assist in the coordination of relevant activities by United Nations organizations, including the development of concerted action programmes in support of the objectives of the Conference at the regional level.

3. International level

37. In section C of chapter V the Platform for Action contains detailed recommendations on the responsibilities to be exercised by the United Nations intergovernmental machinery in respect of the follow-up to the Conference. It places special emphasis on its role in promoting the development of an enhanced framework for international cooperation for gender issues and the comprehensive implementation of the Platform, integrating the results of other global United Nations conferences.

38. With respect to the United Nations system, the Platform for Action calls for the integration of a gender

4/ Official Records of the Economic and Social Council, 1993, Supplement No. 9 (E/1993/29).

perspective into all policies and programmes through mainstreaming actions and stresses that responsibility for ensuring implementation of the Platform must rest at the highest level. Accordingly, the Secretary-General will propose to the Administrative Committee on Coordination the establishment of an inter-agency task force on the empowerment and the advancement of women. This task force will be an integral part of the arrangements being established under the aegis of the Administrative Committee for the integrated and coordinated follow-up to United Nations conferences (see also paras. 53 and 89 below). In paragraph 336, the Platform recommends that each organization set out the specific actions it will undertake, including goals and targets to realign priorities and redirect resources to meet the global priorities identified in the Platform for Action, with clear delineation of responsibility and accountability. These new orientations should be reflected in the revised system-wide medium-term plan for the advancement of women for the period 1996-2001. 4/ The Secretary-General will ensure that this task is given priority attention.

(a) *General Assembly*

39. In paragraph 312 the Platform for Action points out that the General Assembly "is the principal policy-making and appraisal organ on matters relating to the follow-up to the Conference, and as such should integrate gender issues throughout its work", recognizing that these issues cut across social, political and economic policy. The General Assembly is invited "to include the follow-up to the Conference as part of its continuing work on advancement of women" and to review its implementation in 1996, 1998 and 2000.

40. As part of the ongoing rationalization of the work of the General Assembly, care must be taken to ensure that the advancement of women remains a major focus, and that the gender dimension is fully integrated in the consideration of all issues before it, including those relating to peace and security.

(b) *Economic and Social Council*

41. According to paragraphs 313 to 316 of the Platform for Action, the Economic and Social Council should oversee system-wide coordination of implementation of the Platform and make recommendations in this regard. It should review the implementation of the Platform giving due consideration to reports of the Commission on the Status of Women.

42. The Platform recommends that the General Assembly and the Economic and Social Council review and strengthen the mandate of the Commission on the Status of Women taking into account the need for effec-

tive coordination with other related commissions and Conference follow-up.

"The Council should incorporate gender issues into its discussion of all policy questions, giving due consideration to recommendations prepared by the Commission. It should consider dedicating at least one high-level segment before the year 2000 to the advancement of women ... with active ... participation ... of the specialized agencies, including the World Bank and the International Monetary Fund." (para. 313)

The Council is also requested to consider dedicating at least one coordination segment before the year 2000 to coordination of the advancement of women, based on the system-wide medium-term plan, 4/ and one operational activities segment to the coordination of development activities related to gender (paras. 314 and 315).

43. In paragraph 321 the Platform for Action calls upon other functional commissions of the Economic and Social Council to "take due account of the Platform for Action and ensure the integration of gender aspects in their respective work".

44. The recommendations on the Economic and Social Council in the Platform for Action should be seen in the light of efforts to coordinate the follow-up to recent global conferences, taking into consideration the importance of mainstreaming gender issues, on the one hand, and ensuring continuing attention to the specific measures required to ensure the advancement of women, on the other. At its substantive session of 1995 the Council decided that, each year, within the framework of its coordination segment, it would carry out a review of cross-cutting themes common to major international conferences and/or contribute to an overall review of the implementation of the programme of action of a given conference.

(c) *Commission on the Status of Women*

45. The Commission on the Status of Women has been assisting the Economic and Social Council on issues relating to the advancement of women since 1946. The Platform for Action makes recommendations on the role of the Commission in paragraphs 317 to 320. It calls for a review and strengthening of the Commission's mandate, taking into account, *inter alia*, the need for synergy with other functional commissions. It states that the Commission should have a central role, within the United Nations system, in monitoring the implementation of the Platform and in assisting the Council in coordination of reporting on implementation. It notes the need for the allocation of sufficient resources in support of the Commission.

46. The Platform for Action calls upon the Commission, in developing its work programme for the period 1996-2000, to "review the critical areas of concern in the Platform for Action and consider how to integrate in its agenda the follow-up to the World Conference on Women. In this context, the Commission ... should consider how it could further develop its catalytic role in mainstreaming a gender perspective in United Nations activities" (para. 320). The follow-up to the Conference is already included in the provisional agenda of the Commission for its fortieth session, in 1996.

47. The Secretary-General intends to put forward proposals to the Commission at its next session to assist the Commission in developing its work programme to follow up the Platform for Action, including with respect to monitoring implementation of the recommendations in the Platform at all levels, and in enhancing its role in the coordinated follow-up to the continuum of conferences, taking into consideration related intergovernmental and inter-agency follow-up processes.

(d) Committee on the Elimination of Discrimination against Women

48. The Committee on the Elimination of Discrimination against Women was established in 1981 to monitor the implementation of the Convention on the Elimination of All Forms of Discrimination against Women. It is a treaty body devoted specifically to the rights of women. The Platform for Action underscores its important role in securing enjoyment by women of their human rights. In paragraph 324 the Platform states that the ability of the Committee to monitor implementation of the Convention should be strengthened "through the provision of human and financial resources within the regular budget of the United Nations, including expert legal assistance and ... sufficient meeting time for the Committee" in keeping with the decision made by the meeting of the States parties in May 1995. It also calls for the Committee to "increase its coordination with other human rights treaty bodies, taking into account the recommendations of the Vienna Declaration and Programme of Action". 5/

49. The Secretary-General will make every effort to provide coordinated secretariat support to the Committee, bearing in mind that the promotion of the enjoyment by women of their human rights is central to the overall effort for the advancement of the status of women. The Committee is expected to consider the implications for its work of the outcome of the Fourth World Conference on Women at its fifteenth session, in January 1996.

(e) Role of the Secretary-General

50. The Secretary-General is strongly committed to assuming "responsibility for coordination of policy within the United Nations for the implementation of the Platform for Action and for the mainstreaming of a system-wide gender perspective in all activities of the United Nations", as requested in paragraph 326 of the Platform for Action.

51. In his statement to the closing session of the Conference, the Secretary-General indicated that he would ensure that the recommendations addressed to him were implemented swiftly and effectively, and that he was committed to integrating the gender perspective into all aspects of the work of the Organization. He added that he would work with his colleagues, the executive heads of the United Nations specialized agencies and the United Nations programmes and funds to ensure a coordinated system-wide response, integrating the follow-up of this Conference with that of other global conferences.

52. The Secretary-General welcomes the emphasis on policy coordination and mainstreaming in paragraph 326. These requirements were a major consideration in the restructuring of the economic and social sectors and, in particular, in the location of the Division for the Advancement of Women in the Department for Policy Coordination and Sustainable Development. In the same context, the Secretary-General requested the Administrator of the United Nations Development Programme (UNDP) to assist him in ensuring policy coherence and coordination of operational activities. These requirements will continue to guide the Secretary-General in integrating the gender dimension in the programme management and human resource development strategies of the Organization and in ensuring a coordinated follow-up within the United Nations to recent global conferences, all of which have addressed the advancement of women as a central issue.

53. In relation to the system as a whole, at the initiative of the Secretary-General, the Administrative Committee on Coordination, at its first session for 1995, adopted a comprehensive statement reaffirming the strong commitment of executive heads to ensuring that the advancement of women is a policy priority within the organizations of the common system and to taking the necessary action to improve the status of women in their respective secretariats. At its most recent session, on 12 and 13 October 1995, the Administrative Committee on Coordination agreed that the gender perspective must be fully integrated into the work of the inter-agency task forces, under lead agency arrangements, which will fol-

5/ Report of the World Conference on Human Rights, Vienna, 14-25 June 1993 (A/CONF.157/24 (Part I)), chap. III.

low up recent global conferences on the basis of cross-sectoral themes (see para. 89 below). As the Platform for Action encompasses but goes well beyond these themes, the Administrative Committee also decided to consider, following the current session of the General Assembly, the best means of promoting sustained and coordinated follow-up to the Platform, and of ensuring that the improvement of the status of women in all its aspects is placed in the mainstream of the work of the system.

54. The Secretary-General has given careful consideration in this context to the invitation "to establish a high-level post in the Office of the Secretary-General, using existing human and financial resources, to act as [his] adviser on gender issues and to help ensure system-wide implementation of the Platform for Action in close cooperation with the Division for the Advancement of Women" (para. 326).

55. The Secretary-General is strongly of the view that, for effective mainstreaming, all organizational entities must exercise their line responsibilities for implementing relevant recommendations in the Platform for Action, without duplication. In this light, and in view of ongoing efforts to streamline high-level posts and to avoid additional managerial layers, the Secretary-General does not consider it appropriate to request an appropriation for an additional high-level post and related requirements at the present time.

56. Using existing human and financial resources, the Secretary-General would propose to integrate the functions referred to in paragraph 54 above into the portfolio of one of his Senior Advisers in the Executive Office of the Secretary-General. The Senior Adviser to the Secretary-General would not have line responsibilities or duplicate the work of units working on issues relating to the advancement of women. Rather, the Senior Adviser would have a role of overview and coordination, assisting the Secretary-General to ensure that the gender perspective is integrated into overall policy-making and programming, including in the political area, and is taken into account in all aspects of the work of the system and in furthering the Organization's linkages with civil society. The Secretary-General will propose that his Senior Adviser chair, in this capacity, the Administrative Committee on Coordination task force referred to in paragraph 89 below. Within the Executive Office of the Secretary-General, this senior official would also ensure that all statements and reports emanating from the Secretary-General are gender-sensitive. The Senior Adviser would also serve as a spokesperson for the Secretary-General on the above matters.

57. The Senior Adviser would draw upon the expertise and assistance of all existing entities working in this area, including the Division for the Advancement of Women of the Department for Policy Coordination and Sustainable Development, as well as UNIFEM, INSTRAW, the Focal Point on Women in the Department of Administration and Management and other concerned units within United Nations departments, funds and programmes.

58. As part of the effort to broaden participation and strengthen accountability, as well as to integrate effectively the gender dimension in the work of the Organization, the Secretary-General is requesting all United Nations departments and offices to review their programmes to determine how they can contribute to the implementation of the recommendations of the Conference. The Secretary-General will also ensure that the gender dimension is fully integrated in the perspective of the next medium-term plan, for the period 1998-2001.

59. Likewise, with respect to the status of women within the United Nations itself, the Secretary-General will pursue his efforts to integrate the measures in his strategic plan of action for the improvement of the status of women in the Secretariat (1995-2000) (see A/49/587 and Corr.1) within his overall human resources management strategy for the Organization as a whole. He intends to hold all programme managers accountable for implementation.

60. The participatory and inclusive character of the preparatory process and of the Conference itself was a key element in its success. The Secretary-General believes it essential that the follow-up to the Conference should also be as broadly based as possible. In particular, he considers it important that the expectations and concerns of major constituencies and groups on gender-related issues should be fully taken into account in implementing the Platform for Action, within the United Nations as well as the system as a whole.

61. To that end, the Secretary-General proposes to establish a high-level board on the advancement of women to advise him on the follow-up to the Conference. The board, which would consist of 15 to 20 eminent persons representing a broad range of experience and disciplines, would contribute to the building and strengthening of partnerships between the United Nations and major constituencies on gender-related issues; assist the Secretary-General and his Senior Adviser in promoting knowledge and understanding of, and mobilizing support for, United Nations activities for the advancement of women in general and the follow-up to the Conference in particular; and bring to the attention of the Secretary-General and, through him, to concerned intergovernmental and inter-agency bodies, emerging issues related to the implementation of the Platform for Action, and ways and means

of addressing them. The Secretary-General trusts that the Board will be a source of innovative ideas and approaches in the follow-up to the Conference, and a source of strong support to the Organization in its efforts to improve the status of women.

(f) United Nations Secretariat

(i) Division for the Advancement of Women

62. The Division for the Advancement of Women of the Department for Policy Coordination and Sustainable Development is the principal unit within the United Nations Secretariat dealing with issues relating to the improvement of the status of women. The placement of the Division within the Department by the Secretary-General during the restructuring of the economic and social sectors was aimed at ensuring the integration of gender issues in policy formulation and coordination, including the servicing of the intergovernmental machinery. Effective substantive support of the intergovernmental machinery, especially the Commission on the Status of Women, will require the involvement and cooperation of all organizations of the United Nations system, including in particular UNIFEM and INSTRAW.

63. In paragraphs 327 and 328 the Platform for Action notes that:

"The primary function of the Division for the Advancement of Women of the Department for Policy Coordination and Sustainable Development is to provide substantive servicing to the Commission on the Status of Women and other intergovernmental bodies when they are concerned with the advancement of women, as well as to the Committee on the Elimination of Discrimination Against Women. It has been designated focal point for the implementation of the Nairobi Forward-looking Strategies."

The Platform states (para. 328):

"The Division should examine the obstacles to the advancement of women through the application of gender-impact analysis in policy studies for the Commission on the Status of Women and through support to other subsidiary bodies. After the Fourth World Conference on Women it should play a co-ordinating role in preparing the revision of the system-wide medium-term plan ... 1996-2001 and should continue serving as the secretariat for inter-agency coordination for the advancement of women. It should continue to maintain a flow of information with national commissions, national institutions for the advancement of women and non-governmental organizations with regard to the implementation of the Platform for Action."

The Platform requests the Secretary-General "to ensure more effective functioning of the Division by, *inter alia*, providing sufficient human and financial resources within the regular budget of the United Nations" (para. 327).

64. As indicated above, the Division for the Advancement of Women will have a key role to play with respect to the implementation of the recommendations of the Conference, in support of the work of the intergovernmental machinery, of the organizations of the United Nations system and of other actors in the implementation of the Platform for Action and in promoting the integration of a gender perspective in all policies and programmes. There are, in particular, three areas in which the reinforcement of the Division is called for in order to enable it to carry out its new and expanded functions, in collaboration with other parts of the Secretariat and system, namely, capacity for gender analysis; the advancement of human rights of women; and the promotion of a system-wide approach to the implementation of the Platform, including outreach activities.

65. Gender-impact analysis of United Nations policies and programmes — a major prerequisite for mainstreaming — requires review of, interaction with and input into a wide range of activities in all areas covered by the Organization. Pursuant to paragraph 328 of the Platform for Action and to respond to follow-up action by the Commission on the Status of Women and the Economic and Social Council, the Division will, in particular, need to enhance its capacity to conduct and coordinate studies, applying gender impact analysis, to examine relationships between the advancement of women and other global issues dealt with by the United Nations and ways and means of promoting consistency and coherence in mainstreaming the gender dimension throughout the Organization. In addition to policy studies for the Commission on the Status of Women, outputs will include recommendations to the Secretary-General, the Committee on the Elimination of Discrimination against Women and, as appropriate, the Economic and Social Council and the General Assembly.

66. The role of the Division for the Advancement of Women in ensuring that the overall regime of protection of the human rights of women is strengthened is stressed in both the Platform for Action and the Vienna Declaration and Programme of Action. 5/ This implies a broader role in providing gender-based information to various human rights treaty bodies, as well as in taking steps "to ensure that the human rights activities of the United Nations regularly address violations of women's human rights, including gender-specific abuses". 6/ In view of the importance accorded to the elimination of

6/ Ibid., para. 42.

violence against women by the Platform for Action and previous intergovernmental decisions—including, *inter alia*, resolution 39/5 of the Commission on the Status of Women—the Division, together with other relevant United Nations bodies, will be called upon to provide enhanced support to the Special Rapporteur on Violence against Women and to assist in monitoring implementation of the Declaration on the Elimination of Violence against Women (see General Assembly resolution 48/104). In this regard, the Division will need to develop its database on the subject. In addition, the Division will be required to support the Commission on the Status of Women in relation to the communications procedure (Economic and Social Council resolution 1993/11) and in pursuing the proposal in the Platform for Action to elaborate a draft optional protocol to the Convention on the Elimination of All Forms of Discrimination against Women on the right to petition.

67. A third area relates to inter-agency coordination and the monitoring of intergovernmental decisions concerning the implementation of the Platform for Action, in support of the coordinating and monitoring roles of the Commission on the Status of Women and the Economic and Social Council, and to accompanying outreach activities with entities outside the system. A decentralized model of implementation places a high premium on monitoring as a means of maintaining consistency and avoiding duplication of effort at all levels. Given the scope and diversity of the Platform for Action, the Division will need, in the exercise of its functions, to interact with a wider range and larger number of institutions and actors than in the past. It will play a central role in developing further the system-wide medium-term plan for the advancement of women, 4/ which will need to reflect new methodologies and concepts.

68. The number of non-governmental organizations involved in the Conference and in the parallel NGO Forum was unprecedented. The process of mobilizing this vast and diverse support for the advancement of women will require considerable expansion of the Division's outreach capacity, including through publications, increased use of new information technologies, support for dissemination of information through mass media and women's networks, advisory services and database and network linkages.

69. The programme activities and the related resource requirements resulting from the new orientations and additional responsibilities outlined above were not included in the proposed programme budget for the biennium 1996-1997, 7/ before the General Assembly at the present session, which specifically provides for revision on the basis of the outcome of the Conference. A separate statement will be submitted in this regard.

(ii) *Other units of the United Nations Secretariat referred to in the Platform for Action*

70. The Platform for Action recommends (para. 331) that the Office of Human Resources Management:

"… continue to accord priority to the recruitment and promotion of women in posts subject to geographical distribution, particularly in senior policy-level and decision-making posts, in order to achieve the goals set out in General Assembly resolutions 45/125 and 45/239 C and reaffirmed in General Assembly resolutions 46/100, 47/93, 48/106 and 49/167. The training service should design and conduct regular gender-sensitivity training or include gender-sensitivity training in all of its activities."

71. The General Assembly has before it at its present session a separate report of the Secretary-General on the improvement of the status of women in the Secretariat (A/50/691), which addresses the requirements referred to above, including plans to reach the target of 50 per cent women by the year 2000 and developments in the area of training. Gender-equality issues will also be addressed in the medium-term plan for the period 1998-2001 in the context of the Secretary-General's overall strategy for human resource management, approved by the General Assembly in its resolution 49/222 B of 20 July 1995. Implementation of the strategic plan of action for the improvement of the status of women in the Secretariat (1995-2000) (see A/49/587 and Corr.1) will be monitored closely.

72. The Platform for Action further states

"The Department of Public Information should seek to integrate a gender perspective in its general information activities and, within existing resources, strengthen and improve its programmes on women and the girl child. To this end, the Department should formulate a multimedia communications strategy to support the implementation of the Platform for Action, taking new technology fully into account. Regular outputs of the Department should promote the goals of the Platform, particularly in developing countries." (para. 332)

73. In formulating such a communications strategy, the Department of Public Information will build on the momentum generated in the media by its information activities in support of the Fourth World Conference on Women, and integrate this strategy within the overall information programme to follow up the current cycle of major United Nations development conferences. Utilizing the full array of promotional activities and multimedia products undertaken by the Department, the

7/ *Official Records of the General Assembly, Fiftieth Session, Supplement No. 6 (A/50/6/Rev.1).*

communications strategy will draw on the Department's network of information centres and services located in 67 countries and the inter-agency coordination mechanism, the Joint United Nations Information Committee.

74. With respect to the Statistical Division of the Department for Economic and Social Information and Policy Analysis, in paragraph 333 the Platform for Action recommends that the Statistical Division should have an important coordinating role in international work in statistics, as described in chapter IV, strategic objective H.3.

75. In the period 1996-2001, implementation of the interrelated mandates of the International Conference on Population and Development, held at Cairo from 5 to 13 September 1994, the World Summit for Social Development, held at Copenhagen from 6 to 12 March 1995, and the Fourth World Conference on Women will require the development and dissemination of indicators on women and men with respect to the informal sector, unremunerated work, poverty, youth, elderly and disabled persons (para. 206 (e)-(h) and (k) and para. 208 (b)). It will also require the compilation and dissemination of the database and methodologies underlying these indicators, as well as the provision of technical support for work at the national level in these fields (para. 206 (b)). Statistical concepts and methods will need to be developed to measure and value unremunerated work. This would involve developing an international classification of activities for time-use statistics that is sensitive to the differences between women and men in remunerated and unremunerated work (para. 206 (g)), and working on the analytical framework and policy uses of supplementary accounts to the 1993 System of National Accounts that recognize the economic contribution of women. In this regard, the Statistical Division will interact with the inter-agency task force referred to above (para. 38), as well as with the Administrative Committee on Coordination task force on basic social services for all (see para. 89 below), which will address, *inter alia*, database issues emerging from the International Conference on Population and Development, the World Summit for Social Development, as well as the Fourth World Conference on Women.

(g) *United Nations Development Fund for Women*

76. As indicated in the Platform for Action:

"UNIFEM has the mandate to increase options and opportunities for women's economic and social development in developing countries by providing technical and financial assistance to incorporate the women's dimension into development at all levels. Therefore, UNIFEM should review and strengthen,

as appropriate, its work programme in the light of the Platform for Action, focusing on women's political and economic empowerment. Its advocacy role should concentrate on fostering a multilateral policy dialogue on women's empowerment. Adequate resources for carrying out its functions should be made available." (para. 335)

77. The operational role of UNIFEM in the follow-up to the Fourth World Conference on Women will be consolidated. It will continue to focus its work at the country level within the context of the resident coordinator system. UNIFEM will also work to bring its experience in programme countries to the attention of other organizations in the United Nations system with a view to strengthening the gender perspective of development programmes and increasing synergy with other United Nations organizations. UNIFEM will concentrate, as specified in the Platform for Action, on women's economic and political empowerment. With respect to women's economic empowerment, UNIFEM will concentrate on globalization and economic restructuring with a focus on trade and structural adjustment policies, gender-sensitive development policy and the promotion of sustainable livelihoods, including thorough new approaches to both micro-enterprise development and natural resource management. Its work with respect to political empowerment will focus on strengthening the role of women in governance, women's human rights, conflict prevention and peace-building, and empowering women to participate effectively in the global conference processes and the implementation of conference outcomes.

78. UNIFEM will support women's organizations to increase leadership opportunities for decision-making and advocacy for women. UNIFEM will play a key role in supporting the implementation of the Platform for Action at the country level, including through the proposed inter-agency task force, and the resident coordinator system.

(h) *International Research and Training Institute for the Advancement of Women*

79. The Platform for Action states:

"INSTRAW has a mandate to promote research and training on women's situation and development. In the light of the Platform for Action, INSTRAW should review its work programme and develop a programme for implementing those aspects of the Platform for Action that fall within its mandate. It should identify those types of research and research methodologies to be given priority, strengthen national capacities to carry out women's studies and gender research, including that on the status of the girl child, and develop networks of research institutions that can be mobilized for that purpose. It should also identify those types of education and training that can be effectively supported and promoted by the Institute." (para. 334)

80. Research and training activities to further the advancement of women requiring priority attention in the light of the Fourth World Conference on Women and other global United Nations conferences will include the study and understanding of the obstacles to the full recognition of women's participation in sustainable development, including methodological/conceptual development; concrete research and training programmes focusing on ways and means to solve the extreme poverty affecting women world wide, in particular in developing countries; and the dissemination of research findings and analytical tools to assist the efforts of intergovernmental agencies, governmental officials and policy makers, as well as academic and research centres and non-governmental organizations. Sections A and E to L in chapter IV of the Platform for Action are of particular relevance to the work of the Institute.

(i) *Other organizations of the United Nations system*

81. In paragraphs 336 to 344 of the Platform for Action, the specialized agencies and organizations of the United Nations are called upon to strengthen their support for actions at the national level and to enhance their contributions to coordinated follow-up by the United Nations.

"... each organization should set out the specific actions they will undertake, including goals and targets to realign priorities and redirect resources to meet the global priorities identified in the Platform for Action. There should be a clear delineation of responsibility and accountability. These proposals should in turn be reflected in the system-wide medium-term plan for the advancement of women for the period 1996-2001." (para. 336)

The Platform for Action additionally calls for gender mainstreaming and gender focal points in each agency.

82. The Platform for Action also recommends that "the Administrative Committee on Coordination consider how its participating entities might best coordinate their activities, *inter alia*, through existing procedures at the inter-agency level for ensuring system-wide coordination to implement and help follow up objectives of the Platform for Action" (para. 316).

83. Each organization should "take steps to enhance and support the roles and responsibilities of its focal points on women issues" (para. 337); "cooperate more [when providing technical assistance] to ensure the

continuing promotion of the advancement of women" (para. 338); "provide appropriate technical assistance and other forms of assistance to the countries with economies in transition in order to facilitate solution of their specific problems regarding the advancement of women" (para. 339); and "accord greater priority to the recruitment and promotion of women at the Professional level to achieve gender balance, particularly at decision-making levels ... Due regard should be paid to the importance of recruiting the staff on as wide a geographical basis as possible. Organizations should report regularly to their governing bodies on progress towards this goal" (para. 340). The Platform for Action proposes that "coordination of United Nations operational activities for development at the country level should be improved through the resident coordinator system in accordance with relevant resolutions of the General Assembly, in particular General Assembly resolution 47/199, to take full account of the Platform" (para. 341).

84. Paragraphs 342 to 344 of the Platform for Action encourage international financial institutions, in implementing the Platform:

"To review and revise policies, procedures and staffing to ensure that investments and programmes benefit women and thus contribute to sustainable development. They are also encouraged to increase the number of women in high-level positions, increase staff training in gender analysis and institute policies and guidelines to ensure full consideration of the differential impact of lending programmes and other activities on women and men. In this regard, the Bretton Woods institutions, the United Nations, as well as its funds and programmes and the specialized agencies, should establish regular and substantive dialogue, including dialogue at the field level, for more efficient and effective coordination of their assistance in order to strengthen the effectiveness of their programmes for the benefit of women and their families." (para. 342)

85. Moreover, in paragraph 354, the Platform for Action proposes that the international financial institutions and regional development banks "should be invited to examine their grants and lending and to allocate loans and grants to programmes for implementing the Platform for Action in developing countries, especially in Africa and the least developed countries". The International Monetary Fund (IMF) and the World Bank along with the organizations and bodies of the United Nations system are invited to assist countries with economies in transition to design and implement policies and programmes for the advancement of women (para. 356).

86. The Platform for Action recommends that consideration should be given "to inviting the World Trade

Organization to consider how it might contribute to the implementation of the Platform for Action, including activities in cooperation with the United Nations system" (para. 343).

87. These recommendations will be brought to the attention of all concerned organizations, and their responses will be covered in subsequent reports. The concerned organizations, including the Bretton Woods institutions and the World Trade Organization, will be invited to participate in the proposed inter-agency task force (see para. 38 above).

88. The revised system-wide medium-term plan for the advancement of women for the period 1996-2001, which will reflect the proposals for action agreed to in Beijing and at other recent global conferences, will provide a basis for monitoring the implementation by the United Nations system of the Platform for Action and related recommendations on gender issues formulated by other conferences. It will provide a mechanism for mobilizing and monitoring joint activities and for identifying gaps in the implementation of the Platform. The plan is scheduled for review by the Commission on the Status of Women, the Administrative Committee on Coordination, the Committee for Programme and Coordination and the Economic and Social Council in 1996.

89. At the second regular session for 1995 of the Administrative Committee on Coordination, held on 12 and 13 October, executive heads agreed that monitoring the follow-up by the United Nations system to the International Conference on Population and Development, the World Social Summit for Development and the Fourth World Conference on Women will be a main concern of the Committee in the period ahead. The Administrative Committee on Coordination decided that it will, to the extent possible, undertake this work on the basis of cross-sectoral themes, bringing together related results of recent global conferences. The Committee also decided to strengthen coordinated support for follow-up action at the country level, through inter-agency task forces organized around three interrelated themes: (a) the enabling environment for social and economic development; (b) employment and sustainable livelihoods; and (c) basic social services for all. It directed that the gender dimension should be taken fully into account in the work of each of these task forces. Noting that the Platform for Action adopted by the Fourth World Conference on Women encompasses but goes well beyond these themes, the Secretary-General, following action by the General Assembly, will propose to the Administrative Committee on Coordination the establishment of a goal-oriented, inter-agency task force on the empowerment and advancement of women in order to promote sustained and coordinated follow-up to the Platform for Action and to ensure that the improvement of the status of women in all its aspects is placed in the mainstream of the work of the system. The experience of the Ad Hoc Inter-Agency Group on Women, a network of focal points on women's issues that has been meeting within the framework of the Administrative Committee on Coordination since International Women's Year, in 1975, will be drawn upon in this regard.

(j) *Non-governmental organizations*

90. As noted above, the Conference was characterized by the unprecedented involvement of civil society, including the participation of an unprecedented number of non-governmental organizations. In recognition of this contribution, the Platform for Action states that the active support and participation of a broad and diverse range of institutional actors should be encouraged, including "legislative bodies, academic and research institutions, professional associations, trade unions, cooperatives, local community groups, non-governmental organizations, including women's organizations and feminist groups, the media, religious groups, youth organizations and cultural groups, as well as financial and non-profit organizations" (para. 295).

91. The Platform for Action provides for a role for non-governmental organizations in the design and implementation of national strategies or plans of action (para. 297). It further states that non-governmental organizations should be encouraged "to develop their own programmes to complement government efforts. Women's organizations and feminist groups, in collaboration with other non-governmental organizations, should be encouraged to organize networks, as necessary, and to advocate for and support the implementation of the Platform for Action by Governments and regional and international bodies" (para. 298). The Platform calls for strengthening the capacity of non-governmental organizations to mobilize and contribute resources towards implementation of the Platform (para. 350). Underscoring the role that non-governmental organizations have in implementing the Platform for Action, the Platform calls for consideration to be given to "establishing a mechanism for collaborating with non-governmental organizations to promote the implementation of the Platform at various levels" (para. 344).

92. The Secretary-General attaches great importance to the continued mobilization of all elements of civil society in promoting an effective follow-up to the Conference and expects that the Commission on the Status of Women will give consideration to means of promoting the effective implementation of the provisions of the Platform for Action relating to non-governmental organizations, including the establishment of appropriate

mechanisms to enhance collaboration with these organizations.

III. Recommendations for action by the General Assembly at its fiftieth session

93. Consideration by the General Assembly of the report on the Fourth World Conference on Women should serve to consolidate the commitments entered into by Member States and the international community in Beijing. To that end, the Assembly at its current session may wish to consider taking the following action:

(a) Calling upon Member States and the international community to commit themselves to full and effective implementation of the Platform for Action through the early development of specific implementation strategies, including the establishment or improvement of national machineries for the advancement of women and measures to integrate the gender dimension into all policies and programmes;

(b) Calling upon the organizations of the United Nations system to extend their full support to Governments and the international community in the implementation of the Platform for Action in the context of an integrated follow-up to all recent global conferences;

(c) Inviting all elements of civil society to contribute actively to the fulfilment of the objectives of the Platform for Action;

(d) Deciding to review the implementation of the Platform for Action on a biennial basis;

(e) Inviting the Economic and Social Council to utilize its high-level, coordination and operational activities segments to further policy coordination and inter-agency cooperation towards the achievement of the objectives of the Platform for Action, in accordance with the recommendations of the Conference;

(f) Inviting the Economic and Social Council to review and strengthen the mandate of the Commission on the Status of Women, taking into account the need for effective coordination with other related commissions and Conference follow-up, so as to enable the Commission to play a central role, within the United Nations system, in monitoring the implementation of the Platform for Action, and in assisting the Council in coordination of reporting on implementation;

(g) Inviting the Commission on the Status of Women, in developing its work programme for the period 1996-2000, to consider modalities for maximizing its contribution to the follow-up to the Conference, including monitoring of implementation, policy development with respect to the critical areas of concern in the Platform for Action and the strengthening of its catalytic role in mainstreaming a gender perspective in United Nations activities;

(h) Also inviting, within their mandates, all other United Nations organs and their subsidiary bodies to take due account of the Platform for Action and to ensure the integration of the gender dimension in their respective policy-making activities;

(i) Calling for mobilization of resources from all sources to further the implementation of the Platform for Action, including sustained contributions to voluntarily funded programmes of the United Nations system for activities on gender and development;

(j) Noting the commitment of the Secretary-General to exercise responsibility for coordination of policy within the United Nations for the implementation of the Platform for Action and for the mainstreaming of a system-wide gender perspective in all activities of the United Nations at all levels, and the arrangements being made by the Secretary-General in this regard;

(k) Noting the intention of the Secretary-General to establish a high-level advisory board on the advancement of women to ensure that the expectations and concerns of major constituencies on gender-related issues are fully taken into account in implementing the Platform for Action;

(l) Noting the key roles to be played by the Administrative Committee on Coordination, through, *inter alia*, the proposed inter-agency task force, the regional commissions and the resident coordinator system, in contributing to the coordinated implementation of the Platform for Action at the inter-agency, regional and national levels;

(m) Providing for the strengthening of the capacity of relevant entities within the United Nations to contribute, in a coordinated manner, to the effective follow-up to the Conference.

Document 130

General Assembly resolution on the girl child

A/RES/50/154, 21 December 1995

The General Assembly,

Recalling the Beijing Declaration and the Platform for Action of the Fourth World Conference on Women, 1/ the Copenhagen Declaration on Social Development and the Programme of Action of the World Summit for Social Development, 2/ the Programme of Action of the International Conference on Population and Development, 3/ the Vienna Declaration and Programme of Action of the World Conference on Human Rights, 4/ Agenda 21 adopted by the United Nations Conference on Environment and Development, 5/ the Plan of Action for Implementing the World Declaration on the Survival, Protection and Development of Children in the 1990s of the World Summit for Children, 6/ the World Declaration on Education for All and the Framework for Action to Meet Basic Learning Needs 7/ adopted at the World Conference on Education for All: Meeting Basic Learning Needs,

Recalling also that discrimination against the girl child and the violation of the rights of the girl child was identified as a critical area of concern in the Platform for Action of the Fourth World Conference on Women in the achievement of equality, development and peace for women, and that the advancement and empowerment of women throughout their life-cycle must begin with the girl child,

Noting with appreciation that the World Summit for Children sensitized the entire world to the plight of children,

Reaffirming the equal rights of women and men as enshrined in the Preamble to the Charter of the United Nations, and recalling the Convention on the Elimination of All Forms of Discrimination against Women 8/ and the Convention on the Rights of the Child, 9/

1. *Urges* all States to eliminate all forms of discrimination against the girl child and to eliminate the violation of the human rights of all children, paying particular attention to the obstacles faced by the girl child;

2. *Also urges* all States, international organizations as well as non-governmental organizations, individually and collectively to set goals and to develop and implement gender-sensitive strategies to address the needs of children, in particular those of girls, in accordance with the Convention on the Rights of the Child and the goals, strategic objectives and actions contained in the Platform for Action of the Fourth World Conference on Women;

3. *Requests* all States, international organizations as well as non-governmental organizations to increase awareness of the potential of the girl child and to promote the participation of girls and young women, on an equal basis and as partners with boys and young men, in social, economic and political life and in the development of strategies and in the implementation of actions aimed at achieving gender equality, development and peace;

4. *Calls upon* Member States and organizations and bodies of the United Nations system, in particular, the United Nations Children's Fund, the United Nations Educational, Scientific and Cultural Organization, the Food and Agriculture Organization of the United Nations and the World Health Organization, to take into account the rights and the particular needs of the girl child, especially in education, health and nutrition, and to eliminate negative cultural attitudes and practices against the girl child;

5. *Urges* all States to eliminate all forms of violence against children, in particular the girl child;

6. *Calls upon* States, international organizations as well as non-governmental organizations to help mobilize the necessary financial resources and political support to achieve goals, strategies and actions relating to the survival, development and protection of the girl child in all programmes for children;

7. *Requests* the Secretary-General to ensure that the goals and actions relating to the girl child receive full attention in the implementation of the Platform for Action of the Fourth World Conference on Women through the work of all organizations and bodies of the United Nations system;

1/ A/CONF.177/20 and Add.1, chap. I, resolution 1, annexes I and II.
2/ A/CONF.166/9, chap. I, resolution 1, annexes I and II.
3/ *Report of the International Conference on Population and Development, Cairo, 5-13 September 1994* (United Nations publication, Sales No. E.95.XIII.18), chap. I, resolution 1, annex.
4/ A/CONF.157/24 (Part I), chap. III.
5/ *Report of the United Nations Conference on Environment and Development, Rio de Janeiro, 3-14 June 1992* (A/CONF.151/26/Rev.1 (Vol. I and Vol. I/Corr.1, Vol. II, Vol. III and Vol. III/Corr.1)) (United Nations publication, Sales No. E.93.I.8 and corrigenda), vol. I: *Resolutions Adopted by the Conference,* resolution 1, annex II.
6/ See A/45/625, annex.
7/ *Final Report of the World Conference on Education for All: Meeting Basic Learning Needs, Jomtien, Thailand, 5-9 March 1990,* Inter-Agency Commission (UNDP, UNESCO, UNICEF, World Bank) for the World Conference on Education for All, New York, 1990, appendix 1.
8/ Resolution 34/180, annex.
9/ Resolution 44/25, annex.

8. *Also requests* the Secretary-General, as Chairman of the Administrative Committee on Coordination, to urge all the organizations and bodies of the United Nations system focusing on the advancement of women to make commitments to goals and actions relating to the girl child in the revision and implementation of the system-wide medium-term plan for the advancement of women for the period 1996-2001, 10/ as well as in the medium-term plan for the period 1998-2002.

10/ E/1993/43, annex.

Document 131

General Assembly resolution calling for the improvement of the situation of women in rural areas

A/RES/50/165, 22 Dceember 1995

[Editor's note: The first resolution on the situation of women in rural areas was adopted in 1975.]

The General Assembly,

Recalling its resolution 34/14 of 9 November 1979, in which it endorsed the Declaration of Principles and the Programme of Action as adopted by the World Conference on Agrarian Reform and Rural Development, 1/ and its resolutions 44/78 of 8 December 1989 and 48/109 of 20 December 1993,

Recalling also the importance attached to the problems of rural women by the Nairobi Forward-looking Strategies for the Advancement of Women 2/ and by the Beijing Declaration and the Platform for Action adopted by the Fourth World Conference on Women on 15 September 1995, 3/

Recalling further its resolution 47/174 of 22 December 1992, in which it welcomed the adoption of the Geneva Declaration for Rural Women by the Summit on the Economic Advancement of Rural Women, held at Geneva in February 1992, 4/ and urged all States to work for the achievement of the goals endorsed in the Declaration,

Welcoming the growing awareness of Governments of the need for strategies and programmes to improve the situation of women in rural areas,

Noting with deep concern that the economic and financial crises in many developing countries have severely affected the socio-economic status of women, especially in rural areas, and the continuing rise in the number of rural women living in poverty,

Recognizing the urgent need to take appropriate measures aimed at further improving the situation of women in rural areas,

1. *Takes note* of the report of the Secretary-General; 5/

2. Invites Member States, in their efforts to implement the outcome of the United Nations Conference on Environment and Development, the World Conference on Human Rights, the International Conference on Population and Development, the World Summit for Social Development and the Fourth World Conference on Women, bearing in mind also the Geneva Declaration for Rural Women, to attach greater importance to the improvement of the situation of rural women in their national development strategies, paying special attention to both their practical and their strategic needs, by, *inter alia*:

(a) Integrating the concerns of rural women into national development policies and programmes, in particular by placing a higher priority on budgetary allocation related to the interests of rural women;

(b) Strengthening national machineries and establishing institutional linkages among governmental bodies in various sectors and non-governmental organizations that are concerned with rural development;

(c) Increasing the participation of rural women in the decision-making process;

(d) Undertaking necessary measures to give rural women full and equal access to productive resources, including the right to inheritance and to ownership of land and other property, credit/capital, natural resources, appropriate technologies, markets and information, and meeting their basic requirements in water and sanitation;

1/ See *Report of the World Conference on Agrarian Reform and Rural Development, Rome, 12-20 July 1979* (WCARRD/REP), transmitted to the General Assembly by a note by the Secretary-General (A/34/485).
2/ *Report of the World Conference to Review and Appraise the Achievements of the United Nations Decade for Women: Equality, Development and Peace, Nairobi, 15-26 July 1985* (United Nations publication, Sales No. E.85.IV.10), chap. I, sect. A.
3/ A/CONF.177/20, chap. I, resolution 1, annexes I and II.
4/ A/47/308-E/1992/97, annex.
5/ A/50/257/Rev.1-E/1995/61/Rev.1.

(e) Investing in the human resources of rural women, particularly through health and literacy programmes and social support measures;

3. *Requests* the international community and relevant United Nations organizations and bodies to promote the realization of the programmes and projects aimed at the improvement of the situation of rural women within the overall framework of integrated follow-up to recent global conferences;

4. *Invites* the World Food Summit to be convened by the Food and Agriculture Organization of the United Nations in 1996 to give due consideration to the issue of improving the situation of rural women, taking into account their role in food production and food security, and the United Nations Conference on Human Settlements (Habitat II) to give due consideration to the gender aspects of rural-urban migration and its impact on the situation of rural women, in formulating relevant strategies and actions;

5. *Requests* the Secretary-General to prepare, in consultation with Member States and relevant United Nations organizations, a report on the implementation of the present resolution and to submit it, through the Economic and Social Council, to the General Assembly at its fifty-second session, taking into account possible measures to improve the reporting procedure.

Document 132

General Assembly resolution on traffic in women and girls

A/RES/50/167, 22 December 1995

[Editor's note: A similar resolution was also adopted in 1994.]

The General Assembly,

Reaffirming the principles set forth in the Universal Declaration of Human Rights, 1/ the Convention on the Elimination of All Forms of Discrimination against Women, 2/ the International Covenants on Human Rights, 3/ the Convention against Torture and Other Cruel, Inhuman or Degrading Treatment or Punishment, 4/ the Convention on the Rights of the Child 5/ and the Declaration on the Elimination of Violence against Women, 6/

Recalling that the Vienna Declaration and Programme of Action, adopted by the World Conference on Human Rights on 25 June 1993, 7/ affirmed the human rights of women and the girl child as an inalienable, integral and indivisible part of universal human rights,

Welcoming the Programme of Action of the International Conference on Population and Development 8/ which, *inter alia*, called upon all Governments to prevent all international trafficking in migrants, especially for the purpose of prostitution, and for the adoption by Governments of both receiving countries and countries of origin of effective sanctions against those who organize undocumented migration, exploit undocumented migrants or engage in trafficking in undocumented migrants, especially those who engage in any form of international traffic of women and children,

Recalling the recognition by the World Summit for Social Development, held at Copenhagen from 6 to 12 March 1995, 9/ of the danger to society of the trafficking in women and children,

Welcoming the initiatives taken by the Commission on Crime Prevention and Criminal Justice 10/ and the Ninth United Nations Congress on the Prevention of Crime and the Treatment of Offenders, held at Cairo from 29 April to 8 May 1995, 11/ towards criminalizing clandestine traffic in illegal migrants,

Concurring with the conclusion in the Platform for Action adopted by the Fourth World Conference on Women at Beijing on 15 September 1995, 12/ that the effective suppression of trafficking in women and girls for the sex trade is a matter of pressing international concern,

Recalling its resolution 49/166 of 23 December 1994, and taking note of Commission on the Status of Women resolution 39/6 of 29 March 1995, 13/

Acknowledging the work done by intergovernmental and non-governmental organizations in compiling information on the scale and complexity of the problem

---

1/ Resolution 217 A (III).
2/ Resolution 34/180, annex.
3/ Resolution 2200 A (XXI), annex.
4/ Resolution 39/46, annex.
5/ Resolution 44/25, annex.
6/ Resolution 48/104.
7/ A/CONF.157/24 (Part I), chap. III.
8/ *Report of the International Conference on Population and Development, Cairo, 5-13 September 1994* (United Nations publication, Sales No. E.95.XIII.18), chap. I, resolution 1, annex, chap. X.
9/ See A/CONF.166/9.
10/ See *Official Records of the Economic and Social Council, 1995*, Supplement No. 10 (E/1995/30), chap. I, sect. B.III.
11/ See A/CONF.169/16.
12/ A/CONF.177/20, chap. I, resolution 1, annex II.
13/ See *Official Records of the Economic and Social Council, 1995*, Supplement No. 6 (E/1995/26), chap. I, sect. C.

of trafficking, in providing shelters for trafficked women and children and in effecting their voluntary repatriation to their countries of origin,

Noting with concern the increasing number of women and girl children from developing countries and from some countries with economies in transition who are being victimized by traffickers, and acknowledging that the problem of trafficking also victimizes young boys,

Convinced of the need to eliminate all forms of sexual violence and sexual trafficking, including for prostitution and other forms of commercial sex, which are violations of the human rights of women and girl children and are incompatible with the dignity and worth of the human person,

Realizing the urgent need for the adoption of effective measures nationally, regionally and internationally to protect women and girl children from this nefarious traffic,

1. *Takes note with appreciation* of the report of the Secretary-General on the traffic in women and girls; 14/

2. *Appeals* to Governments to take appropriate measures to address the root factors, including external factors, that encourage trafficking in women and girls for prostitution and other forms of commercialized sex, forced marriages and forced labour, so as to eliminate trafficking in women, including by strengthening existing legislation with a view to providing better protection of the rights of women and girls and to punishing perpetrators, through both criminal and civil measures;

3. *Invites* Governments to combat trafficking in women and children through nationally and internationally coordinated measures, at the same time establishing or strengthening institutions for the protection of the victims of trafficking of women and children, and to ensure for victims the necessary assistance, including legal support services that are linguistically and culturally accessible, for their full protection, treatment and rehabilitation;

4. *Also invites* Governments to consider the development of standard minimum rules for the humanitarian treatment of trafficked persons, consistent with human rights standards;

5. *Urges* concerned Governments to support comprehensive, practical approaches by the international community to assist women and children victims of transnational trafficking to return home and be reintegrated into their home societies;

6. *Encourages* Member States to consider signing and ratifying or acceding to the Convention for the Suppression of the Traffic in Persons and the Exploitation of the Prostitution of Others, 15/ international agreements on the suppression of slavery and other relevant international instruments;

7. *Invites* the United Nations High Commissioner for Human Rights, in addressing the obstacles to the realization of the human rights of women, in particular, through his contacts with the Special Rapporteur of the Commission on Human Rights on violence against women and the Special Rapporteur of the Commission on Human Rights on the sale of children, child prostitution and child pornography, to include the traffic in women and girls among his priority concerns;

8. *Also encourages* the Centre for Human Rights of the Secretariat to include the traffic in women and girls in its programme of work under its advisory, training and information services, with a view to providing assistance to member Governments, upon their request, in instituting preventive measures against trafficking through education and appropriate information campaigns;

9. *Requests* the Commission on Human Rights to encourage the Working Group on Contemporary Forms of Slavery of the Subcommission on Prevention of Discrimination and Protection of Minorities to continue to address the issue of the traffic in women and girls under its draft programme of action on the traffic in persons and the exploitation of the prostitution of others; 16/

10. *Requests* the Commission on Crime Prevention and Criminal Justice to consider appropriate follow-up to the Ninth United Nations Congress on the Prevention of Crime and the Treatment of Offenders on measures to address the problem of trafficking in women and children and to submit a report thereon to the Secretary-General, through the usual channels, for inclusion in his report to the General Assembly;

11. *Invites* relevant intergovernmental and nongovernmental organizations to provide advisory services to Governments, upon their request, in planning and setting up rehabilitation programmes for victims of trafficking and in training personnel who will be directly involved in the implementation of these programmes;

12. *Decides* to focus the International Day for the Abolition of Slavery, 2 December 1996, on the problem of trafficking in human persons, especially women and children, and to devote one meeting of the fifty-first session of the General Assembly to the discussion of this problem;

13. *Requests* the Secretary-General to submit to the General Assembly at its fifty-first session, under the item entitled "Advancement of women", a comprehensive report on the implementation of the present resolution, with due regard for possible measures to improve the reporting procedure.

14/ A/50/369.
15/ Resolution 317 (IV), annex.
16/ See E/CN.4/Sub.2/1995/28/Add.1.

Document 133

General Assembly resolution on violence against women migrant workers

A/RES/50/168, 22 December 1995

[Editor's note: A resolution on violence against women migrant workers was first adoted in 1992. Similar resolutions were also adopted in 1993, 1994 and 1995.]

The General Assembly,

Recalling its resolutions 47/96 of 16 December 1992, 48/110 of 20 December 1993 and 49/165 of 23 December 1994, as well as Commission on the Status of Women resolution 38/7 of 18 March 1994, 1/ and taking note of Commission on the Status of Women resolution 39/7 of 31 March 1995 2/ and Commission on Human Rights resolution 1995/20 of 24 February 1995, 3/

Taking note of the report of the Secretary-General, 4/

Taking note with concern of the report of the Working Group on Contemporary Forms of Slavery of the Subcommission on Prevention of Discrimination and Protection of Minorities on its twentieth session, 5/ in particular its observations with respect to the treatment of migrant workers,

Acknowledging the preliminary report of the Special Rapporteur of the Commission on Human Rights on violence against women, its causes and its consequences, 6/

Stressing that the promotion of the human rights of women constitutes an integral part of human rights activities of the United Nations, as reaffirmed in the Vienna Declaration and Programme of Action, adopted by the World Conference on Human Rights on 25 June 1993, 7/

Affirming the Programme of Action of the International Conference on Population and Development, 8/ which called upon all countries to take full measures to eliminate all forms of exploitation, abuse, harassment and violence against women,

Welcoming the Copenhagen Declaration on Social Development and the Programme of Action of the World Summit for Social Development, adopted by the World Summit on 12 March 1995, 9/ which declared that countries should take concrete measures against the exploitation of migrants,

Welcoming also the Beijing Declaration and the Platform for Action, adopted by the Fourth World Conference on Women on 15 September 1995, 10/ which recognized the vulnerability to violence and other forms of abuse of women migrants, including women migrant workers, whose legal status in the host country depends on employers who may exploit their situations,

Noting the large numbers of women from developing countries and from some countries with economies in transition who continue to venture forth to more affluent countries in search of a living for themselves and their families, as a consequence of poverty, unemployment and other socio-economic conditions, while acknowledging the primary duty of States to work for conditions that provide employment and security to their citizens,

Concerned by the continuing reports of grave abuses and acts of violence committed against the persons of women migrant workers by some employers in some host countries,

Encouraged by some measures adopted by some receiving countries to alleviate the plight of women migrant workers residing within their areas of jurisdiction,

Reiterating that acts of violence directed against women impair or nullify their enjoyment of their human rights and fundamental freedoms,

1. *Determines* to prevent and eliminate all forms of violence against women and girls;

2. *Calls upon* States Members of the United Nations to adopt measures for the effective implementation of the Declaration on the Elimination of Violence against Women, 11/ including applying them to women migrant workers, as well as all relevant measures emanating from recent world conferences;

3. *Encourages* Member States to enact and/or reinforce penal, civil, labour and administrative sanctions in domestic legislation to punish and redress the wrongs done to women and girls who are subjected to any form of violence, whether in the home, the workplace, the community or society;

4. *Also encourages* Member States to adopt and/or implement and periodically to review and analyse legislation to ensure its effectiveness in eliminating violence against women, emphasizing the prevention of violence and the prosecution of offenders, and to take measures

1/ *Official Records of the Economic and Social Council, 1994,* Supplement No.7 (E/1994/27), chap. I, sect. C.
2/ Ibid., *1995, Supplement No.6* (E/1995/26), chap. I. sect. C.
3/ Ibid., Supplement No. 3 (E/1995/23 and Corr.1 and 2), chap. II.
4/ A/50/378.
5/ E/CN.4/Sub.2/1995/28 and Add.1.
6/ E/CN.4/1995/42.
7/ A/CONF.157/24 (Part I), chap. III.
8/ *Report of the International Conference on Population and Development, Cairo, 5-13 September 1994* (United Nations publication, Sales No. E.95.XIII.18), chap. I, resolution 1, annex.
9/ A/CONF.166/9, chap. I, resolution 1, annexes I and II.
10/ A/CONF.177/20, chap. I, resolution a, annexes I and II.
11/ Resolution 48/104.

to ensure the protection of women subjected to violence and that they have access to just and effective remedies, including compensation and indemnification and healing of victims, and for the rehabilitation of perpetrators;

5. *Reiterates* the need for States concerned, specifically the sending and receiving States of women migrant workers, to conduct regular consultations for the purpose of identifying problem areas in promoting and protecting the rights of women migrant workers and ensuring health, legal and social services for them, adopting specific measures to address these problems, setting up, as necessary, linguistically and culturally accessible services and mechanisms to implement these measures and, in general, creating conditions that foster greater harmony and tolerance between women migrant workers and the rest of the society in which they reside;

6. *Encourages* Member States to consider signing and ratifying or acceding to the International Convention on the Protection of the Rights of All Migrant Workers and Members of Their Families, 12/ as well as the Slavery Convention of 1926; 13/

7. *Recommends* that the issue of violence against women migrant workers be included in the agenda of the inter-agency meeting that precedes the regular session of the Commission on the Status of Women;

8. Requests the Secretary-General to convene a meeting of an expert group, with the participation of the Special Rapporteur of the Commission on Human Rights on violence against women and under the regular programme of the Division for the Advancement of Women

of the Secretariat, to submit recommendations for improving coordination of the various efforts of United Nations agencies on the issue of violence against women migrant workers and to develop concrete indicators as a basis for determining the situation of women migrant workers for submission, through normal channels, to the General Assembly at its fifty-first session;

9. *Requests* the United Nations High Commissioner for Human Rights, the Centre for Human Rights of the Secretariat and the Special Rapporteur, as well as all relevant bodies and programmes in the United Nations system, when addressing the issue of violence against women, to give particular attention to the issue of violence perpetrated against women migrant workers and to submit reports thereon to the General Assembly;

10. *Invites* trade unions to support the realization of the rights of women migrant workers by assisting them in organizing themselves so as to enable them better to assert their rights;

11. *Requests* the Secretary-General to report to the General Assembly at its fifty-first session on the implementation of the present resolution, including on reports received from all authorities and bodies in the United Nations system, Member States, intergovernmental organizations and other concerned bodies, with due regard for possible measures to improve the reporting procedure.

12/ Resolution 45/158, annex.
13/ United Nations, *Treaty Series*, vol. 212, No. 2861.

Document 134

General Assembly resolution on rape and abuse of women in the areas of armed conflict in the former Yugoslavia

A/RES/50/192, 22 December 1995

The General Assembly,

Guided by the purposes and principles of the Charter of the United Nations, the Universal Declaration of Human Rights, 1/ the International Covenants on Human Rights, 2/ the Convention on the Prevention and Punishment of the Crime of Genocide, 3/ the Convention against Torture and Other Cruel, Inhuman or Degrading Treatment or Punishment, 4/ the Convention on the Elimination of All Forms of Discrimination against Women, 5/ the Convention on the Rights of the Child 6/ and other instruments of human rights and international humanitarian law, including the Geneva Conventions of

12 August 1949 7/ and the Additional Protocols thereto, of 1977, 8/

Recalling its resolution 3074 (XXVIII) of 3 December 1973, entitled "Principles of international coopera-

1/ Resolution 217 A (III).
2/ Resolution 2200 A (XXI), annex.
3/ Resolution 260 A (III).
4/ Resolution 39/46, annex.
5/ Resolution 34/180, annex.
6/ Resolution 44/25, annex.
7/ United Nations, *Treaty Series,* vol. 75, No. 970-973.
8/ Ibid., vol. 1125, No. 17512 and 17513.

tion in the detection, arrest, extradition and punishment of persons guilty of war crimes and crimes against humanity", as well as Commission on Human Rights resolution 1994/77 of 9 March 1994, 9/ entitled "Rape and abuse of women in the territory of the former Yugoslavia", General Assembly resolutions 48/143 of 20 December 1993 and 49/205 of 23 December 1994, both entitled "Rape and abuse of women in the areas of armed conflict in the former Yugoslavia", and relevant resolutions of the Commission on the Status of Women,

Reaffirming the relevant Security Council resolutions, in particular resolution 798 (1992) of 18 December 1992, in which, *inter alia*, the Council strongly condemned those acts of unspeakable brutality,

Welcoming the initialling of the General Framework Agreement for Peace in Bosnia and Herzegovina and the annexes thereto 10/ by the Republic of Bosnia and Herzegovina, the Republic of Croatia and the Federal Republic of Yugoslavia (Serbia and Montenegro) and other parties thereto at Dayton, Ohio, on 21 November 1995,

Noting with deep concern all reports of the Special Rapporteur of the Commission on Human Rights on the situation of human rights in the territory of the former Yugoslavia, regarding rape and abuse of women in the territory of the former Yugoslavia, particularly in the Republic of Bosnia and Herzegovina,

Convinced that this heinous practice constitutes a deliberate weapon of war in fulfilling the policy of ethnic cleansing carried out by Serbian forces in the Republic of Bosnia and Herzegovina, and recalling General Assembly resolution 47/121 of 18 December 1992, in which the Assembly stated, *inter alia*, that the abhorrent policy of ethnic cleansing was a form of genocide,

Desirous of ensuring that persons accused of authorizing, aiding and perpetrating rape and sexual violence as a weapon of war in the areas of armed conflict in the former Yugoslavia will be brought to justice without further delay by the International Tribunal for the Prosecution of Persons Responsible for Serious Violations of International Humanitarian Law Committed in the Territory of the Former Yugoslavia since 1991, where appropriate,

Underlining, in this context, the need for the protection of the rape victims and the provision of effective guarantees of privacy and confidentiality of the rape victims, and desirous of facilitating their participation in the proceedings of the International Tribunal and ensuring that further traumatization will be prevented,

Deeply alarmed at the situation facing victims of rape in armed conflicts in different parts of the world and any use of rape as a weapon of war, in particular in the Republic of Bosnia and Herzegovina,

Noting with appreciation the efforts of Governments and the work of the United Nations High Commissioner for Refugees, the United Nations Educational, Scientific and Cultural Organization, humanitarian organizations, and non-governmental organizations aimed at supporting the victims of rape and abuse and alleviating their suffering,

Welcoming the report of the Secretary-General of 4 August 1995, 11/ submitted pursuant to resolution 49/205,

1. *Strongly condemns* the abhorrent practice of rape and abuse of women and children in the areas of armed conflict in the former Yugoslavia, which constitutes a war crime;

2. *Expresses its outrage* that the systematic practice of rape has been used as a weapon of war and an instrument of ethnic cleansing against women and children in the Republic of Bosnia and Herzegovina;

3. *Reaffirms* that rape in the conduct of armed conflict constitutes a war crime and that under certain circumstances it constitutes a crime against humanity and an act of genocide as defined in the Convention on the Prevention and Punishment of the Crime of Genocide, and calls upon States to take all measures required for the protection of women and children from such acts and to strengthen mechanisms to investigate and punish all those responsible and bring the perpetrators to justice;

4. *Also reaffirms* that all persons who perpetrate or authorize crimes against humanity or other violations of international humanitarian law are individually responsible for those violations and that those in positions of authority who have failed to ensure that persons under their control comply with the relevant international instruments are accountable, together with the perpetrators;

5. *Reminds* all States of their obligation to cooperate with the International Tribunal for the Prosecution of Persons Responsible for Serious Violations of International Humanitarian Law Committed in the Territory of the Former Yugoslavia since 1991 and also with the Office of the Prosecutor in the investigation and prosecution of persons accused of using rape as a weapon of war;

6. *Calls upon* States to put experts, including experts in the prosecution of crimes of sexual violence, as well as adequate resources and services, at the disposal of the Chief Prosecutor and the International Tribunal;

7. *Urges* all States and relevant organizations to continue to give serious consideration to the recommendations in the reports of the Special Rapporteur of the

9/ *Official Records of the Economic and Social Council, 1994, Supplement No.4* and corrigendum, (E/1994/24 and Corr.1), chap.II, sect.A.
10/ See A/50/790-S/1995/999.
11/ A/50/329.

Commission on Human Rights on the situation of human rights in the former Yugoslavia, in particular the recommendation concerning provision for the continuation of necessary medical and psychological care to victims of rape within the framework of programmes to rehabilitate women and children traumatized by war, as well as the provision of protection, counselling and support to victims and witnesses;

8. *Recognizes* the extraordinary suffering of the victims of rape and sexual violence and the necessity for an appropriate response to provide assistance to those victims, and expresses its concern, in particular, for the welfare of those victims who are currently among the internally displaced or otherwise affected by the war and who have experienced severe trauma and require psychosocial and other assistance;

9. *Also urges* all States and all relevant intergovernmental and non-governmental organizations, as well as the United Nations Children's Fund, the Office of the United Nations High Commissioner for Refugees, the United Nations High Commissioner for Human Rights, the United Nations Educational, Scientific and Cultural Organization and the World Health Organization, to continue to provide to the victims of such rape and abuse appropriate assistance for their physical and mental rehabilitation and to extend their support to the community-based assistance programmes;

10. *Demands* that the parties cooperate fully with the International Committee of the Red Cross, the United Nations High Commissioner for Human Rights, the Special Rapporteur of the Commission on Human Rights and her staff, as well as other mechanisms of the Commission on Human Rights, the United Nations High Commissioner for Refugees, the monitoring and other missions of the European Union and the Organization for Security and Cooperation in Europe, including by providing full access;

11. *Encourages* the new Special Rapporteur to continue to pay particular attention to the use of rape as a weapon of war, particularly in the Republic of Bosnia and Herzegovina;

12. *Requests* the Secretary-General to submit a report, as appropriate, to the General Assembly at its fifty-first session on the implementation of the present resolution;

13. *Decides* to continue its consideration of this question at its fifty-first session.

Document 135

General Assembly resolution on follow-up to the Fourth World Conference on Women and full implementation of the Beijing Declaration and Platform for Action

A/RES/50/203, 22 December 1995

The General Assembly,

Recalling its resolutions 45/129 of 14 December 1990, 46/98 of 16 December 1991 and 47/95 of 16 December 1992, as well as Economic and Social Council resolution 1990/12 of 24 May 1990 and Council decision 1992/272 of 30 July 1992, recommending that a world conference on women be held in 1995,

Reaffirming the importance of the outcome of the previous World Conferences on Women, held at Mexico City in 1975, 1/ at Copenhagen in 1980 2/ and at Nairobi in 1985, 3/

Building on the consensus reached and the progress made at previous United Nations conferences and summits, for children in New York in 1990, 4/ on environment and development at Rio de Janeiro in 1992, 5/ on human rights at Vienna in 1993, 6/ on population and development at Cairo in 1994 7/ and on social development at Copenhagen in 1995, 8/ towards achieving equality, development and peace,

Expressing its satisfaction that the Fourth World Conference on Women: Action for Equality, Develop-

1/ See *Report of the World Conference of the International Women's Year, Mexico City, 19 June-2 July 1975* (United Nations publication, Sales No. E/76.IV.1).

2/ See *Report of the World Conference of the United Nations Decade for Women: Equality, Development and Peace, Copenhagen, 14-30 July 1980* (United Nations publication, Sales No. E/80.IV.3 and corrigendum).

3/ See *Report of the World Conference to Review and Appraise the Achievements of the United Nations Decade for Women: Equality, Development and Peace, Nairobi, 15-26 July 1985* (United Nations publication, Sales No. E.85.IV.10).

4/ A/45/625, annex.

5/ See *Report of the United Nations Conference on Environment and Development, Rio de Janeiro, 3-14 June 1992* (A/CONF.151/26/Rev.1 (Vol. I and publication, Sales No. E.93.I.8 and corrigenda).

6/ See A/CONF.157/24 (Part I).

7/ See *Report of the International Conference on Population and Development, Cairo, 5-13 September 1994* (United Nations publication, Sales No. E.95.XIII.18).

8/ See A/CONF.166/9.

ment and Peace reached a successful conclusion and adopted the Beijing Declaration 9/ and the Platform for Action, 10/

Expressing its profound gratitude to the Government of the People's Republic of China for having made it possible for the Conference to be held at Beijing and for the excellent facilities, staff and services so graciously placed at the disposal of the Conference,

Recognizing the significance of the outcome of the Conference to make a real change for the empowerment of women and thus to the fulfilment of the goals adopted in the Nairobi Forward-looking Strategies for the Advancement of Women, 11/

Deeply convinced that the Beijing Declaration and the Platform for Action are important contributions to the advancement of women worldwide and must be translated into effective action by all States, the United Nations system and other organizations concerned, as well as non-governmental organizations,

Recognizing that the implementation of the Platform for Action rests primarily at the national level, that Governments, non-governmental organizations and public and private institutions should be involved in the implementation process and that national mechanisms also have an important role to play,

Bearing in mind that promotion of international cooperation is essential for the effective implementation of the Beijing Declaration and the Platform for Action,

Recognizing that the implementation of the Platform for Action requires commitment from Governments and the international community,

Recognizing also the important role played by States, the United Nations, the regional commissions and other international organizations, as well as non-governmental organizations and women's organizations, in the preparatory process of the Conference and the importance of their involvement in the implementation of the Platform for Action,

Taking into account the fact that the follow-up to the Conference should be undertaken on the basis of an integrated approach to the advancement of women within the framework of a coordinated follow-up to and implementation of the results of the major international conferences in the economic, social and related fields, as well as the overall responsibilities of the General Assembly and the Economic and Social Council,

Bearing in mind its resolution 50/42 of 8 December 1995,

Expressing its appreciation to the Secretary-General, the Secretary-General of the Conference and the staff of the Secretariat for the effective preparations and services provided for the Conference,

1. *Takes note* of the report of the Fourth World Conference on Women, 12/ as adopted on 15 September 1995;

2. *Endorses* the Beijing Declaration and the Platform for Action as adopted by the Conference;

3. *Calls upon* States, the United Nations system and all other actors to implement the Platform for Action, in particular by promoting an active and visible policy of mainstreaming a gender perspective at all levels, including in the design, monitoring and evaluation of all policies, as appropriate, in order to ensure effective implementation of the Platform;

4. *Stresses* that Governments have the primary responsibility for implementing the Platform for Action, that commitment at the highest level is essential for its implementation and that Governments should take a leading role in coordinating, monitoring and assessing progress in the advancement of women;

5. *Calls upon* States, with the assistance of non-governmental organizations, to disseminate the Beijing Declaration and the Platform for Action widely;

6. *Emphasizes* that Governments should, as soon as possible and no later than 1996, develop comprehensive implementation strategies or plans of action, including time-bound targets and benchmarks for monitoring, in order to implement the Platform for Action fully;

7. *Calls upon* Governments to create a national machinery where it does not exist and to strengthen, as appropriate, existing national machineries for the advancement of women;

8. *Encourages* non-governmental organizations to contribute to the design and implementation of these strategies or national plans of action in addition to their own programmes that complement government efforts;

9. *Recognizes* the importance attached to the regional monitoring of the global and regional platforms for action by regional commissions and other subregional or regional structures, within their mandates, in consultation with Governments, and the necessity of promoting cooperation among national Governments of the same region in this respect;

10. *Invites* the Economic and Social Council, in order to facilitate the regional implementation, monitoring and evaluation process, to consider reviewing the institutional capacity of the United Nations regional commissions, within their mandates, including their

9/ A/CONF.177/20 and Add.1, chap. I, resolution 1, annex I.
10/ Ibid., annex II.
11/ *Report of the World Conference to Review and Appraise the Achievements of the United Nations Decade for Women: Equality, Development and Peace, Nairobi, 15-26 July 1985* (United Nations publication, Sales No. E.85.IV.10), chap. I, sect. A.
12/ A/CONF.177/20 and Add.1.

women's units or focal points, to deal with gender-related issues in the light of the Platform for Action, as well as the regional platforms and plans of action, and to give consideration, *inter alia*, and where appropriate, to strengthening the capacity in this respect;

11. *Calls upon* States to take action to fulfil the commitments made at the Conference for the advancement of women and for the strengthening of international cooperation, and reaffirms that adequate financial resources should be committed at the international level for the implementation of the Platform for Action in the developing countries, in particular in Africa, and in the least developed countries;

12. *Recognizes* that implementation of the Platform for Action in the countries with economies in transition requires continued international cooperation and assistance, as indicated in the Platform for Action;

13. *Stresses* that full and effective implementation of the Platform for Action will require a political commitment to make available human and financial resources for the empowerment of women, the integration of a gender perspective in budgetary decisions on policies and programmes, as well as adequate financing of specific programmes for securing equality between women and men;

14. *Reaffirms* that, in order to implement the Platform for Action, a reformulation of policies and reallocation of resources may be needed, but that some policy changes may not necessarily have financial implications;

15. *Reaffirms also* that, in order to implement the Platform for Action, adequate mobilization of resources at the national and international levels, as well as new and additional resources to the developing countries, in particular in Africa, and the least developed countries, from all available funding mechanisms, including multilateral, bilateral and private sources for the advancement of women, will also be required;

16. *Calls upon* those States committed to the 20:20 initiative to integrate a gender perspective fully into its implementation, as referred to in paragraph 358 of the Platform for Action;

17. Recognizes that the creation of an enabling environment is necessary to ensure the full participation of women in economic activities;

18. *Reaffirms* that the implementation of the Platform for Action will require immediate and concerted action by all to create a peaceful, just and humane world based on all human rights and fundamental freedoms, including the principle of equality for all people of all ages and from all walks of life, and to this end, recognizes that broad-based and sustained economic growth in the context of sustainable development is necessary to sustain social development and social justice;

19. *Considers*, in relation to the United Nations, that the Platform for Action should be implemented through the work of all the bodies and organizations of the system during the period 1995-2000, specifically and as an integral part of wider programming;

20. *Considers also* that an enhanced framework for international cooperation for gender-related issues must be developed during the period 1995-2000 in order to ensure the integrated and comprehensive implementation, follow-up and assessment of the Platform for Action, taking into account the results of global United Nations summits and conferences;

21. *Decides* that the General Assembly, the Economic and Social Council and the Commission on the Status of Women, in accordance with their respective mandates and in accordance with Assembly resolution 48/162 of 20 December 1993 and other relevant resolutions, shall constitute a three-tiered intergovernmental mechanism that will play the primary role in the overall policy-making and follow-up, and in coordinating the implementation and monitoring of the Platform for Action, reaffirming the need for a coordinated follow-up to and implementation of the results of major international conferences in the economic, social and related fields;

22. *Also decides* to appraise the progress on a regular basis and to include in the agenda of its forthcoming sessions, starting from 1996, an item entitled "Implementation of the outcome of the Fourth World Conference on Women", with a view to assessing, in the year 2000, the progress achieved in the implementation of the Nairobi Forward-looking Strategies for the Advancement of Women and the Platform for Action in an appropriate forum;

23. *Invites* the Economic and Social Council to consider devoting to this matter one high-level segment, one coordination segment and one operational segment, before the year 2000, taking into account the multi-year programme of work of the Commission on the Status of Women and all other functional commissions of the Council;

24. *Also invites* the Economic and Social Council to review and strengthen the mandate of the Commission on the Status of Women, taking into account the Platform for Action as well as the need for synergy with all other related commissions and conference follow-up, and for a system-wide approach to its implementation;

25. *Decides* that the Commission on the Status of Women, as a functional commission assisting the Economic and Social Council, shall have a central role in the monitoring of the implementation of the Platform for Action within the United Nations system and in advising the Council thereon;

26. *Decides* that the Economic and Social Council should oversee system-wide coordination in the implementation of the Platform for Action, ensure overall coordination of the follow-up to and implementation of the results of all United Nations international conferences in the economic, social and related fields and report thereon to the General Assembly;

27. *Requests* the Commission on the Status of Women to develop its multi-year programme of work for the period 1996-2000 at its fortieth session so that it can review the critical areas of concern in the Platform for Action and to consider how it could integrate into its programme of work the follow-up to the Conference and how it could develop its catalytic role in mainstreaming a gender perspective in United Nations activities, taking into account the need for a focused and thematic approach to the review of the Platform for Action and the contribution that can be made by all other functional commissions of the Council;

28. *Also requests* the Commission on the Status of Women to forward its recommendations on the multi-year programme of work to the Economic and Social Council so that the Council can take a decision on the programme of work at its meeting in 1996, reviewing, coordinating and harmonizing the different programmes of work, including the reporting systems of all the commissions in the area of the advancement of women;

29. *Invites* all other functional commissions of the Economic and Social Council, within their mandates, to take due account of the Platform for Action and to ensure the integration of gender aspects in their respective work;

30. *Requests* the Secretary-General to assume responsibility for the coordination of policy within the United Nations for the implementation of the Platform for Action and the mainstreaming of a system-wide gender perspective in all activities of the United Nations system, including training, in accordance with paragraph 326 of the Platform for Action;

31. *Also requests* the Secretary-General to disseminate the Beijing Declaration and the Platform for Action as widely as possible, including to the competent organs of the United Nations and the specialized agencies;

32. *Further requests* the Secretary-General to report, through the Commission on the Status of Women and the Economic and Social Council, to the General Assembly at its fifty-first session on ways to enhance the capacity of the Organization and of the United Nations system to support the ongoing follow-up to the Conference in the most integrated and effective way, including human and financial requirements;

33. *Requests* the Secretary-General to ensure the more effective functioning of the Division for the Advancement of Women of the Secretariat in order to carry out all the tasks foreseen for it in the Platform for Action by, *inter alia*, providing sufficient human and financial resources within the regular budget of the United Nations;

34. *Also requests* the Secretary-General, in cooperation with the Administrator of the United Nations Development Programme, to ask the resident coordinators fully to apply a gender perspective in integrating the follow-up to the Conference into the coordinated follow-up to recent global United Nations conferences;

35. *Further requests* the Secretary-General to report annually to the Commission on the Status of Women and to the General Assembly, through the Economic and Social Council, on the measures taken and the progress achieved in the implementation of the Beijing Declaration and the Platform for Action;

36. *Requests* the Committee on the Elimination of Discrimination against Women, within its mandate, to take into account the Platform for Action when considering reports submitted by States parties, and invites States parties to include information on measures taken to implement the Platform for Action in their reports;

37. *Notes* the importance of the activities undertaken by the United Nations Development Fund for Women and the International Research and Training Institute for the Advancement of Women in the implementation of the Platform for Action;

38. *Encourages* international financial institutions to review and revise policies, procedures and staffing to ensure that investments and programmes benefit women and thus contribute to sustainable development;

39. *Invites* the World Trade Organization to consider how it might contribute to the implementation of the Platform for Action, including through activities in cooperation with the United Nations system.

Document 136

Memorandum to United Nations staff consolidating special measures introduced over the years for the achievement of gender equality (extract) *

ST/AI/412, 5 January 1996

1. The Organization's policy for the achievement of gender equality is restated in Secretary-General's bulletin ST/SGB/282, which is being issued concurrently with the present instruction and supersedes all prior bulletins that introduced special measures for women.

2. The present instruction consolidates into one administrative issuance all the special measures introduced over the years to implement the principle of equal treatment of men and women stated in Article 8 of the Charter of the United Nations, and to increase the number of women at the Professional level and above. Administrative instruction ST/AI/382 of 3 March 1993 is hereby superseded. Departmental memoranda implementing all prior special measures are also cancelled.

Special measures applicable to the recruitment, appointment and promotion of women to posts at the Professional level and above

3. The purpose of the following special measures is to give effect to the Secretary-General's goals, which the General Assembly urged the Secretary-General to implement, 1/ of bringing the gender balance in the Secretariat to 35 per cent women overall in Professional posts by 1995, to 25 per cent women at the D-1 level and above by June 1997, and to 50-50 parity between men and women both overall and for positions at the D-1 level and above by the year 2000. Those goals apply Secretariat-wide to all categories of posts, including posts subject to geographical distribution, language posts, mission and mission-replacement posts, irrespective of the type or duration of the appointment (permanent, fixed-term, limited duration, one year or less) or of the series of the Staff Rules under which an appointment is to be given (100, 200 and 300 series). Progress towards gender parity is to be monitored overall, by category of posts at each level and for positions at the D-1 level and above.

4. The following special measures shall apply throughout the Secretariat to the filling of all vacant posts at the Professional level and above in every department or office that has not reached parity between men and women both overall and at the D-1 level and above. They shall remain in effect until the Secretary-General is satisfied that substantial progress towards parity has been made.

5. Whenever the Secretary-General has found it necessary to impose a recruitment freeze, requests for exceptions to the freeze shall be considered in a more favourable light if the recommended candidate is a woman.

6. In order to avoid the apparent circumvention of recruitment policies through the use of short-term appointments, the appointment of staff for periods of up to 11 months shall be exercised strictly on a one-time basis and the practice of perpetuating short-term contracts by means of short breaks in service shall be discontinued. A staff member serving under a short-term contract or a contract of less than one year at the P-2 or P-3 level may not receive an appointment of one year or more unless he or she successfully passes a competitive examination in the appropriate occupational group. Eligibility for such examinations shall be limited to candidates encumbering established posts who are nationals of Member States that are unrepresented, underrepresented or below the mid-point of their desirable range.

7. Since the present gender distribution within the Secretariat does not provide a sufficient pool of women candidates who could be promoted to higher-level posts within the time-frame set by the Secretary-General and the General Assembly, the following special provisions shall apply to increase the pool of women eligible for consideration in all decisions on appointment, particularly to higher-level posts. Women who have been in the service of the Organization, including United Nations programmes, for at least one year, under any type of appointment or as consultants, shall be eligible to apply as internal candidates for vacancies at the Professional levels and above, i.e. they may apply for United Nations internal vacancy announcements. In accordance with staff regulation 4.4, the same considerations shall apply to women serving with specialized agencies and subsidiary organs within the common system. If found eligible to apply for an internal vacancy announcement under this provision, a woman candidate shall be expected to document that she meets the qualifications and experience requirements for the post, due regard being paid also to the principle of equitable geographic distribution. Appointments of one year or more at the P-2 and P-3 levels shall be subject to the provisions of paragraph 6 above.

8. The Office of Human Resources Management shall assist all departments and offices, in particular those

---

* *Personnel Manual* index No. 1176.
1/ Resolution 49/167 of 23 December 1994.

falling short of the targets set out in paragraph 3 above, in identifying women candidates who meet the minimum qualifications for any vacant post. For that purpose, the Office of Human Resources Management shall review potential women candidates within the department or office concerned and outside, including those serving in other departments or offices, in regional commissions, or on mission appointment. The Office of Human Resources Management shall also seek women candidates outside the Organization by advertising the post in appropriate publications and by seeking assistance from Governments and other external sources such as universities or professional women's associations.

9. Vacancies for posts at the P-5 level and above in departments and offices that do not have gender parity at those levels must be advertised internally and externally, except when the Office of Human Resources Management has agreed to waive the requirement of an external vacancy announcement, as may be done when fully qualified and suitable women candidates have already been identified from within the Organization or from the roster or another direct source of recruitment.

10. If any candidate is to be recruited over the normal maximum desirable range for a given country, such exceptions should be made only for women, in limited cases, in relation to posts for which they are the best qualified candidates.

11. Similarly, and in order to expand the pool of women available for recruitment at the lower Professional levels, exceptionally well qualified women serving under short-term appointments or appointments of less than one year at the P-2 or P-3 levels and encumbering an established post may, on a limited basis, be allowed to take the competitive examination referred to in paragraph 6 above, even though they are nationals of Member States above the mid-point of their desirable range or of overrepresented Member States.

12. On a trial basis, General Service staff members, the majority of whom are women, shall be allowed to take the P-3 national competitive examination when they meet the requirements as to education, experience and nationality applicable to other candidates. The results shall be reported to the General Assembly at its fifty-first session, with the request that the measure be approved for the future, should the results be positive.

13. In order to increase the number of women considered for promotion, the rules on seniority may be flexibly applied so that the cumulative seniority of a woman staff member is considered for purposes of regular and accelerated promotions. The cumulative seniority of a woman staff member shall be calculated as an average of the years in her present grade and the years accrued in her immediately preceding grade. For instance,

if seniority in her present P-5 grade is three years and seniority in her previous P-4 grade is seven years, cumulative seniority should be five years in her present grade. This policy shall be applied as needed to afford women the requisite seniority for promotion and shall not apply in those cases where averaging would have an adverse impact on a woman's eligibility for promotion.

14. The Office of Human Resources Management or the local personnel office shall make every effort to identify qualified women staff members who, under normal seniority criteria or according to the averaging technique outlined above, have the minimum requisite seniority for accelerated promotion. Those staff members shall be encouraged to apply for the post to be filled and, if appropriate under the applicable placement and promotion procedures, shall be reviewed by departments or offices and by the appointment and promotion bodies.

15. Vacancies in the category and level of posts falling short of the target figures set out in paragraph 3 above shall be filled, when there are one or more female candidates, by one of those candidates provided that (a) her qualifications meet all the requirements for the vacant post and (b) her qualifications are substantially equal or superior to those of competing male candidates. Particular emphasis should be given to demonstrated performance and potential, as well as to increasing the number of women from developing countries, particularly those countries that are unrepresented or underrepresented. When the qualifications of one or more female candidates match all the requirements for the vacant post and the department recommends a male candidate, the department must submit to the Office of Human Resources Management for transmission to the appointment and promotion bodies a written analysis, with appropriate supporting documentation, indicating how the qualifications of the recommended candidate are superior to those of the female candidates who were not recommended.

16. Except for posts filled through competitive examination, foreseeable vacancies that occur may not be filled by a male candidate until the Office of Human Resources Management has certified that, despite the best efforts of all concerned for a period of at least six months, it has not been possible to identify and secure a qualified woman candidate. In filling vacancies at the P-5 level and above, departments and offices recommending a male candidate shall also be required to demonstrate that they have considered both internal and external candidates.

17. Similar principles shall apply for all appointments that are not subject to review by the appointment and promotion bodies, whether the appointment is made under the 100, 200 or 300 series of the Staff Rules. In

every case, no male candidate shall be appointed until serious efforts to find suitable women candidates have been made and documented and the Office of Human Resources Management or the relevant personnel office is satisfied that, despite the best efforts of all concerned, it has not been possible to identify and secure a qualified woman candidate.

Special measures applicable to career development

18. Heads of departments and offices are requested to emphasize upward mobility and career development opportunities for all their staff, General Service and related categories as well as Professionals, women as well as men. The purpose of the following measures is to ensure that women are properly considered in respect of several particularly important aspects of the process.

19. Whenever temporary assignment against a higher-level post becomes available owing to temporary staff movements (mission assignment or replacement, sabbatical or other leave) or to the time required to fill a vacancy, all departments and offices are requested to undertake a review of their qualified women staff at the appropriate level for temporary assignment against higher-level posts, leading, when the necessary conditions are met, to the grant of a special post allowance or to the assumption of responsibilities as officer-in-charge. The performance of higher functions for a significant period shall be recorded in the staff member's file even if it does not lead to the grant of a special post allowance or the assumption of responsibilities as officer-in-charge. If temporary assistance is obtained, it should be at the lower level of the post whose incumbent has been assigned to higher-level functions. In the event that there are no qualified women in the department or office, the Office of Human Resources Management should be consulted to provide names of women from other departments or offices who would be suitable for such temporary assignments.

20. Women in both the Professional category and above and those in the General Service and related categories are encouraged to inform the Department of Peace-keeping Operations and/or the Office of Human Resources Management of their interest in serving in special missions or in established missions. The Department of Peace-keeping Operations and the Office of Human Resources Management shall ensure that those women are seriously considered as and when mission assignments become available. All programme managers are requested to release such staff for available mission assignments.

Training and increased awareness of gender issues

21. To foster better understanding between men and women and to erode subjective obstacles to the advancement of women within the Organization, the Office of Human Resources Management shall institute compulsory training programmes designed to foster the desired changes in management culture, enhance awareness and ability to deal with issues of gender discrimination, harassment, including sexual harassment, and provide skills training.

22. The Office of Human Resources Management shall ensure that women at the P-5 and D-1 levels are included in people management skills and other management training programmes to encourage their participation in the change in management culture, by promoting better understanding among both women and men of different leadership styles, exploring better means of working together and creating a more responsive working environment for all.

23. Induction and orientation courses shall explain the principle of gender equality mandated by Article 8 of the Charter and provide guidelines for promoting equal treatment of men and women in the Secretariat. Induction and orientation courses shall also provide information on the functioning, power structure and value system of the Organization and on where information can be obtained in relation to career development and opportunities.

24. All departments and offices shall encourage mentoring of all newly recruited women by experienced staff members. Mentoring may entail introducing the new staff members to office personnel, providing informal guidance on the workings of the office, offering career advice and familiarizing the new staff member with avenues of recourse for addressing problems that may arise.

25. All supervisors are requested to ensure that copies of Secretary-General's bulletin ST/SGB/282 and of the present instruction are distributed desk to desk and to discuss these documents with their staff.

Work/family issues

26. The Secretary-General is committed to promote a supportive work environment and to foster the necessary attitudinal changes. To that effect, the feasibility of a number of measures that would facilitate equal participation of men and women in the work of the Organization is under active consideration in the Secretariat. Such measures include flexible working hours, part-time work, job-sharing schemes, child and elder care, special leave arrangements and the preparation of guidelines to help to resolve conflicts between mobility and family commitments. The existing rules will be amended in due course to reflect the decisions taken by the Secretary-General, after consultation with the staff, in the light of the ongoing review.

Impact of reorganization/retrenchment

27. Whenever the Secretary-General has found it necessary to reorganize one or more departments or offices or to retrench a number of posts, a formal monitoring process shall be established within the Office of Human Resources Management, in close cooperation with each department or office concerned, in order to ensure that women are not disproportionately affected by the exercise. Goals shall be set by each department or office, in close consultation with the Office of Human Resources Management, to provide a basis for monitoring and analysis.

Record-keeping

28. Each department or office shall be responsible for maintaining statistics showing the current distribution of women and men at each level and category, including General Service and related categories, in terms of both posts subject to geographical distribution and the total number of staff, and their projected proportions for the following two years. The heads of departments or offices shall submit quarterly reports to the Assistant Secretary-General for Human Resources Management, using a format designed for that purpose in consultation with the Integrated Management Information System, as shown in the annex to the present instruction. All recommendations for filling posts, whether by recruitment, extension or promotion shall be accompanied by an explanation of how the recommended action will affect the representation of women at the level concerned and overall.

29. For the purpose of assisting departments and offices in identifying women candidates for available vacancies, the Office of Human Resources Management shall maintain a roster of external candidates that reflects gender. For the same purpose, the Office of Human Resources Management shall also develop and maintain a skills database of all staff members, including General Service and related categories, by occupational groupings and reflecting relevant data, including but not limited to gender, educational qualifications and any area of special knowledge or experience, technical and language skills, years of work experience and positions held.

30. The Office of Human Resources Management shall maintain an inventory of posts and staff by gender, occupation, level and duty station, based on the quarterly departmental summaries described in paragraph 28 above, and shall include gender distribution statistics in its regular statistical summaries. The Office of Human Resources Management shall include in its summaries statistical analyses on the number and percentage of women by nationality on all promotion registers and appointment lists, and specifying what percentage of those promoted or appointed from outside, within each grade, are women. The Office of Human Resources Management shall report regularly to the Secretary-General on the results achieved. The data shall be included in the annual reports of the Secretary-General on the composition of the Secretariat and the improvement of the status of women. Progress in meeting the objectives of the special measures shall be described by narratives for those of a qualitative nature and by numerical means, including the use of tables, bar charts and other visual representations, for those that are quantifiable.

...

Document 137

Memorandum from the Secretary-General to United Nations staff on policies to achieve gender equality in the United Nations*

ST/SGB/282, 5 January 1996

1. Article 8 of the Charter of the United Nations provides that the United Nations shall place no restrictions on the eligibility of men and women to participate in any capacity and under conditions of equality in its principal and subsidiary organs. Full compliance with this Article within the Secretariat, and the full participation of women in all aspects of the work of the Organization, are imperative, not only for reasons of equity, but also to enhance Secretariat effectiveness and the credibility and the leadership role of the United Nations in advancing the status of women worldwide.

2. The purpose of the present Bulletin is to reiterate the policy of the Organization and my strong commitment with respect to achieving gender equality in the United Nations, through the full implementation of the strategic plan of action for the improvement of the status of women in the Secretariat (1995-2000). 1/ The strategic plan, which was endorsed by the General Assembly in its resolution 49/167 of 23 December 1994, establishes the goal of gender parity by the year 2000 overall and in policy-level positions (D-1 and above).

3. Requirements to effect the change necessary to achieve the goals of the strategic plan include determined

*Personnel Manual index No. 1175.

1/ Report of the Secretary-General on the improvement of the status of women in the Secretariat (A/49/587), sect. IV.

managerial commitment and action, particularly at the highest levels; a clear implementation strategy, including specific, short-term targets; effective monitoring; accountability of managers; appropriate training; measures to encourage the mobility of women staff; and the creation of a supportive working environment, free from harassment and conducive to the equal participation of men and women in the work of the Organization.

4. I intend to hold senior managers accountable for the full implementation of the strategic plan. Managers will be required to report regularly on the results of the actions they have taken in this regard.

5. In promoting and guiding this effort, I will continue to rely on the valuable support and assistance of the Steering Committee for the Improvement of the Status of Women in the Secretariat.

6. In order to facilitate coherent action within the Secretariat, in line with the policy outlined in the present Bulletin, the special measures introduced over the years to improve the status of women have been consolidated into a single administrative instruction, which is being issued concurrently with the present Bulletin (ST/AI/412). Bulletins ST/SGB/220 of 15 October 1986, ST/SGB/226 of 11 May 1987, ST/SGB/227 of 2 November 1987, ST/SGB/229 of 16 November 1988, ST/SGB/232 of 28 November 1989, ST/SGB/237 of 18 March 1991 and ST/SGB/252 of 20 October 1992 are hereby superseded.

(Signed) Boutros BOUTROS-GHALI
Secretary-General

Document 138

Report of the Secretary-General to the CSW on the elaboration of a draft optional protocol to the Convention on the Elimination of All Forms of Discrimination against Women

E/CN.6/1996/10, 10 January 1996, E/CN.6/1996/10/Add.1, 9 February 1996, and E/CN.6/1996/Add.2, 29 February 1996

Introduction

1. The Economic and Social Council, in its resolution 1995/29 of 24 July 1995, requested the Secretary-General to invite Governments and intergovernmental and non-governmental organizations to submit their views on an optional protocol to the Convention on the Elimination of All Forms of Discrimination against Women, including their views on feasibility, taking into account the elements suggested by the Committee on the Elimination of Discrimination against Women in suggestion 7, adopted at its fourteenth session. 1/ The resolution further requested the Secretary-General to submit to the Commission on the Status of Women at its fortieth session—if possible, six weeks prior to the commencement of the session—a comprehensive report, including a synthesis, on the views expressed. The Council decided that the Commission should establish an in-session open-ended working group for a two-week period at its fortieth session to consider the report requested of the Secretary-General with a view to elaborating a draft optional protocol to the Convention. The present report is submitted in accordance with those requests.

I. Background

2. The adoption in 1979 of the Convention on the Elimination of All Forms of Discrimination against Women by the General Assembly (resolution 34/180) concluded a period of six years of negotiations and drafting in the Commission on the Status of Women and the Third Committee of the General Assembly. During that period, little attention was given to the possibility of introducing a right of petition, or individual complaints procedure, under the Convention, to supplement the reporting requirements established for States parties. 2/

3. An expert group meeting on violence against women was convened by the Division for the Advancement of Women, Department for Policy Coordination and Sustainable Development of the United Nations Secretariat, from 11 to 15 November 1991 in response to Economic and Social Council resolution 1991/18, on violence against women in all its forms. The experts recommended, *inter alia*, the consideration of an optional protocol, or protocols, to the Convention, which would be open to ratification or accession by States parties to the Convention (E/CN.6/1992/4).

1/ See *Official Records of the General Assembly, Fiftieth Session, Supplement No. 38* (A/50/38), chap. I.B.
2/ See A/32/218 (1977), para. 151, and E/CN.6/SR.673, paras. 93-94. See also Lars Adam Rehof, *Guide to the travaux préparatoires of the United Nations Convention on the Elimination of All Forms of Discrimination against Women* (Dordrechet, Martinus Nijhoff Publishers, 1993).

4. The question of the elaboration of an optional protocol under the Convention was subsequently raised in 1992 in the Committee on the Elimination of Discrimination against Women, in conjunction with the Committee's discussion on the question of violence against women. At that time, the Committee was of the view that a procedural optional protocol could be considered at a future time as an instrument to strengthen the Convention. 3/ In its suggestion 4, addressed to the World Conference on Human Rights, the Committee, *inter alia*, recommended, with a view to placing the Convention on the same footing as other human rights conventions, that "a study should be prepared on the feasibility of drafting optional protocols". 4/

5. The World Conference on Human Rights recommended that "new procedures should also be adopted to strengthen implementation of the commitment to women's equality and the human rights of women. The Commission on the Status of Women and the Committee on the Elimination of Discrimination against Women should quickly examine the possibility of introducing the right of petition through the preparation of an optional protocol to the Convention on the Elimination of All Forms of Discrimination against Women." 5/

6. In response to that recommendation, the Committee, at its thirteenth session, in 1994, adopted suggestion 5, in which it proposed that the Commission request the Secretary-General to convene an expert group meeting to prepare a draft optional protocol to the Convention, providing for a complaints procedure. The report of such a meeting should be presented first to the Committee for its comments and then to the Commission for action. 6/

7. In response to the proposal of the Commission, the Economic and Social Council adopted resolution 1994/7, in which it decided "that the Commission on the Status of Women shall examine at its thirty-ninth session, in cooperation with the Committee and taking into account the results of any governmental expert meeting on this question that may be convened prior to that session, the feasibility of introducing the right of petition through the preparation of an optional protocol to the Convention".

8. Although a governmental expert group meeting was not convened prior to the fourteenth session of the Committee, one of the Committee's experts prepared a note on the issue which was presented to the Committee. The note included a draft of an optional protocol which had been prepared by a meeting convened in Maastricht, Netherlands, 29 September-1 October 1994, in which three members of the Committee had participated. After an extensive discussion at its fourteenth session of the question of an optional protocol, the Committee adopted suggestion 7, containing elements for an optional proto-

col. The Council took note of suggestion 7 in its resolution 1995/29.

9. The Platform for Action, adopted at the Fourth World Conference on Women, requested Governments to "support the process initiated by the Commission on the Status of Women with a view to elaborating a draft optional protocol to the Convention on the Elimination of All Forms of Discrimination against Women that could enter into force as soon as possible on a right of petition procedure, taking into consideration the Secretary-General's report on the optional protocol, including those views related to its feasibility". 7/

10. At present, three of the major international human rights treaties currently in force have complaints procedures, giving their supervisory bodies authority to receive and consider communications. Article 1 of the First Optional Protocol of the International Covenant on Civil and Political Rights establishes the competence of the Human Rights Committee "to receive and consider communications from individuals subject to its jurisdiction who claim to be victims of a violation by [that] State party of any of the rights set forth in the Covenant". 8/ Article 14 of the International Convention on the Elimination of All Forms of Racial Discrimination establishes the competence of the Committee "to receive and consider communications from individuals or groups of individuals within its jurisdiction claiming to be victims of a violation by [a] State party of any of the rights set forth in this Convention". 9/ Article 22 of the Convention against Torture and Other Cruel, Inhuman or Degrading Treatment or Punishment establishes the competence of the Committee against Torture "to receive and consider communications from or on behalf of individuals subject to its jurisdiction who claim to be victims of a violation by a State party of the provisions of the Convention". 10/ The International Convention on the Protection of the Rights of All Migrant Workers and Members of Their Families, which has not yet entered into force, also provides for a communications procedure in its article 77, which establishes the competence of the Committee "to receive and consider communications from or on

3/ *Official Records of the General Assembly, Forty-seventh Session, Supplement No. 38* (A/47/38), para. 455 (b).
4/ Ibid., *Forty-eighth Session, Supplement No. 38* (A/48/38), chap. I.A, para. 6 (b).
5/ See "Report of the World Conference on Human Rights" (A/CONF.157/24, part I), chap. III, sect. II, para. 40.
6/ *Official Records of the General Assembly, Forty-ninth Session, Supplement No. 38* (A/49/38), chap. I.B.
7/ A/CONF.177/20, chap. I, annex II, sect. I, para. 230 (k).
8/ See *Human Rights: Compilation of International Instruments* (United Nations publication, Sales No. E.94.XIV.1), vol. I, part one.
9/ General Assembly resolution 2106 A (XX).
10/ General Assembly resolution 39/46.

behalf of individuals subject to [a State party's] jurisdiction who claim that their individual rights as established by the present Convention have been violated by that State party". 11/

11. The Committee on Economic, Social and Cultural Rights, established under the International Covenant on Economic, Social and Cultural Rights, has since its fifth session been considering the preparation of an optional protocol and its principal characteristics under that Covenant which would aim at introducing a complaints procedure. To that end, the Committee submitted a consolidated analytical paper to the World Conference on Human Rights (A/CONF.157/PC/62/Add.5). A further report on the matter was submitted by one of the Committee's experts to the Committee at its eleventh session, analysing the possible provisions of an optional protocol under the Covenant and offering a draft for such a protocol (E/C.12/1994/12). The report takes into account the discussions held in the Committee, as reflected in the Committee's report to the Conference, and work done with regard to an optional protocol under the Convention on the Elimination of All Forms of Discrimination against Women. It also draws from existing communications procedures under United Nations human rights treaties, particularly the first optional protocol to the International Covenant on Civil and Political Rights.

12. The Commission on the Status of Women has a mandate for considering confidential and non-confidential communications on the status of women. In accordance with that mandate, set forth in Economic and Social Council resolution 1993/11, the Commission is empowered to make recommendations to the Council on what action should be taken on emerging trends and patterns of discrimination against women revealed by such communications.

13. The Economic and Social Council, in its resolution 1503 (XLVIII) of 27 May 1970, adopted a procedure for dealing with communications relating to violations of human rights and fundamental freedoms. The "1503 procedure" addresses cases in which there seems to be reliable evidence of a consistent pattern of gross violations of human rights and fundamental freedoms.

14. In accordance with Council resolution 1995/29, the Secretary-General addressed a note verbale, dated 14 August 1995, to Member States, drawing their attention to the resolution and inviting them to submit the requested information to the Secretariat no later than 15 November. Subsequently, a second note verbale, dated 20 November 1995, was sent out in which the Secretary-General informed delegations that, in view of time constraints, the deadline for submission of comments was extended to 1 December 1995. The note informed delegations that comments received after that date could not be processed in the report of the Secretary-General.

15. A total of 15 responses was received in response to the two notes verbales, from the following Member States: Australia, Austria, Liechtenstein, Netherlands, Germany, Finland, New Zealand, Turkey, Mexico, Peru, Colombia, Ecuador, Norway, Ukraine, and Japan.

16. The following 19 non-governmental organizations also submitted comments: International Human Rights Law Group, Dutch section of the International Commission of Jurists (NCJM), Women for Women's Human Rights, Japan Christian Women's Temperance Union, Change, Human Rights Watch, Japanese Association of International Women's Rights, Japan Federation of Bar Associations, Norsk Folkehjelp, Forum for Women and Development, CLADEM, Asian Women's Human Rights Council, Caribbean Association for Feminist Research and Action, International Women's Human Rights Law Clinic, Center for Women's Global Leadership, New Zealand Human Rights Commission, Foundation for Women, Ain O Salish Kendra, Danish Women's Society.

17. In accordance with the request contained in Council resolution 1995/29, the present report first gives a synopsis of the replies; it then reflects comprehensively the views and comments received from Governments and summarizes the comments received from non-governmental organizations, in accordance with suggestion 7. General comments regarding the introduction of a right of petition under the Convention are reflected first and are organized in accordance with the major points addressed.

II. Synopsis of replies received

18. All replies addressed the question of the introduction of a right of petition through an optional protocol to the Convention. The overwhelming majority of comments expressed support for the process initiated by the Commission and the Economic and Social Council. Support was also expressed specifically for an optional protocol, particularly in the framework of related action taken at the World Conference on Human Rights and the Fourth World Conference on Women. The Committee's suggestion 7 on the issue was commended and seen as an important basis for initiating the preparatory work on a protocol. Reasons for support were expressed.

19. A number of Member States submitted their preliminary views as input for further discussion during the fortieth session of the Commission on the Status of Women. Several Member States identified issues and

11/ General Assembly resolution 45/158.

questions which, in their view, needed further clarification and elaboration or which might constitute problems in, or hinder, the elaboration of an optional protocol. It was noted that the possible development of an optional protocol warranted careful consideration. Member States expressed their expectation for constructive discussions and negotiations on it during the upcoming session of the Commission.

20. Several submissions addressed the question of the relationship between an optional protocol to the Convention and other existing procedures, including those under other international human rights instruments. While some noted that a complaints procedure would put the Convention on an equal footing with other instruments and welcomed the innovative character of the proposed inquiry procedure, others saw a need for further discussion of the complementarity and normative consistency between the proposed optional protocol and other existing procedures, including the communications procedure of the Commission on the Status of Women. The questions of overall streamlining and avoidance of duplication and of mainstreaming women's human rights in other human rights mechanisms were raised, as was the question of whether existing instruments and procedures were able effectively to address violations of the human rights of women.

21. A number of comments addressed the question of the nature of the rights contained in the Convention and their justiciability. In that regard, several categories of obligations of States parties arising from the provisions of the Convention were identified, and the programmatic nature of obligations was noted. It was noted that the nature of the provisions of the Convention might have a bearing on the type of mechanisms and remedies that are proposed. The question of the impact of the rights contained in the Convention on third parties—i.e., the legal relationship among individuals—was addressed. It was suggested that further analysis and discussion of the justiciability of rights and the nature of States parties' obligations and of related mechanisms might usefully take place, including the two main procedures proposed by the Committee: a communications procedure and an inquiry procedure.

22. Several comments referred to the question of standing under an optional protocol. Note was taken with interest of the proposals put forward in that regard by the Committee in suggestion 7 which seemed to indicate a very broad approach. The examples of relevant provisions in other existing instruments on the question of standing were made. It was also suggested that further clarification and discussions of that point were necessary, including the requirement that a claimant be subject to the jurisdiction of the State party.

23. Concerning the admissibility of communications, a lack of clarity was perceived in the Committee's formulation as it pertained to the question of non-retroactivity of norms. Likewise, the formulation of the Committee's proposal regarding the exhaustion of national and international remedies and of interim measures pending examination were identified for further discussion. While the innovative proposal concerning remedies was noted, it was also mentioned that that question warranted further consideration so as to take account of the diverse nature of the obligations contained in the Convention.

24. Several comments indicated that further consideration would need to be given to the publication of the Committee's report on the results of the proceedings under an optional protocol. The question of the binding nature of the Committee's views and recommendations was raised.

25. While the proposal for an inquiry procedure was seen as an important contribution to the enforcement of the Convention, procedural questions regarding the Committee's powers to initiate an inquiry were raised.

26. A number of comments referred to the need to address the resource implications of an optional protocol and to strengthen the capacity of the Committee and of the Division for the Advancement of Women in order to implement tasks arising from an optional protocol.

III. Views and comments expressed by Governments and other entities

A. *General comments*

1. *Views on an optional protocol*

27. Australia expressed its support for the development of an optional protocol to the Convention which it thought would improve the complaints procedures available to deal with issues involving the violation of the human rights of women. Liechtenstein stated that it was to become a State party to the Convention before the end of 1995 and welcomed the process initiated by the Commission concerning the elaboration of an optional protocol. Colombia found the suggestion put forward at the World Conference on Human Rights in 1993—that the Commission and the Committee should quickly examine the possibility of introducing the right of petition through the preparation of an optional protocol to the Convention—to be very positive. Ecuador expressed its support for the Council resolution on suggestion 7 of the Committee. Turkey considered in a positive way the preparation of an additional optional protocol to the Convention. Austria, bearing in mind paragraph 40 of the Vienna Declaration and Programme for Action, welcomed the procedure set out in Council resolution

1995/29 with the aim of elaborating a draft optional protocol. It supported the introduction of a right of petition in form of an optional protocol to the Convention and welcomed the ideas put forward in suggestion 7.

28. The Netherlands was convinced that the Committee on the Elimination of Discrimination against Women should be empowered to receive and investigate complaints. The addition of an optional protocol would make that possible. It noted that an attempt to draft such a protocol was made in Maastricht in September 1994 during a meeting of independent experts. It stated that it would in the near future make every effort to ensure that the international community consider the approval of an optional protocol along the lines set out in the Maastricht proposal. The Netherlands emphasized that the existence of an optional protocol did not mean that the importance of the reporting procedure should not be recognized in full and that the introduction of such a protocol should not adversely affect the other activities of the Committee. The Division for the Advancement of Women, Department for Policy Coordination and Sustainable Development of the United Nations Secretariat, should be well prepared for any such expansion of the duties of the Committee.

29. Finland stated that it had supported and continued to support the drafting of an optional protocol to the Convention. Peru welcomed the preparation of an optional protocol because it believed that such a protocol would contribute to achieving the goals of the Convention. Norway strongly supported the process initiated by the Commission on the Status of Women with a view to elaborating a draft optional protocol. It was convinced that the mechanisms foreseen in the draft optional protocol were feasible. New Zealand stated that the possible development of an optional protocol to the Convention was an important issue which warranted careful consideration.

30. Germany had not completed its opinion-forming process on whether it was feasible and actually possible to draft an optional protocol to the Convention. Nevertheless, Germany wished to put up for consideration a number of points which it perceived as posing serious problems and/or hindering the elaboration of an optional protocol. Its stance complied with that of the Beijing Platform for Action which, in its paragraph 230 (k) also referred to the feasibility of such an undertaking.

31. Japan noted that the possibility of establishing an optional protocol to the Convention should be examined carefully, taking into account existing mechanisms and the ongoing consideration of such mechanisms. If an optional protocol were drafted to promote the status of women, it should be formulated in such a way that it

would be accepted and therefore ratified, approved or acceded to by as many States parties as possible.

2. *Reasons provided in explanation of support and of issues*

32. Australia considered that the development of an optional protocol to the Convention would promote the effectiveness of the Convention by addressing weakness in the monitoring and enforcement mechanisms of the Convention. Australia noted that it was important, however, for an optional protocol not to work against efforts to have issues concerning the human rights of women dealt with more effectively by mainstream human rights bodies. It stated that the Human Rights Committee should continue to investigate complaints submitted by women claiming that their human rights had been violated.

33. In expressing its full support for the relevant recommendations of the World Conference on Human Rights and the Fourth World Conference on Women, the Netherlands stated that a right of petition could make an important contribution to the interpretation and practical application of the Convention. Furthermore, with the introduction of an optional protocol, the Convention would then be placed on an equal footing with other human rights conventions that embodied a right of petition, such as the International Covenant on Civil and Political Rights, the Convention on the Elimination of Racial Discrimination, and the Convention against Torture. The addition of a communications procedure was seen as crucial if women all over the world were to be afforded the opportunity of seeking redress for violations of their human rights.

34. Mexico was convinced that the establishment of an individual complaints procedure under the Women's Convention would strengthen the promotion and protection of women's rights recognized under the Convention. It considered the elements contained in suggestion 7 an important basis for initiating the preparatory work for a possible optional protocol and for the elaboration of the procedure for communications which such an instrument would need to put forward for cases of violations of rights contained in the Convention or where a State party did not comply with its obligations under the Convention.

35. Peru noted that a major study on an optional protocol would seem to be useful, similar to the analysis that must be presented to the national Congress in all cases of an international nature in the field of human rights, and which, according to the Constitution, required the approval of the legislature.

36. Germany pointed out that a problem would seem to arise from the fact that the members of the

Committee were not lawyers. Shifting the responsibility for examination to a "legal service" seemed to be of doubtful value when it came to ensuring effective legal protection, apart from the statutory expenses thus incurred, which would have to be made up for by cutbacks in other areas.

3. Relationship with existing international procedures

37. Australia noted that there was possible overlap between the operation of an optional protocol under the Convention and the First Optional Protocol to the International Covenant on Civil and Political Rights, concerning discrimination on the basis of sex. Consideration would need to be given to minimizing potential normative conflict and inconsistency between the Committees.

38. Mexico stated the need to discuss further how to avoid unnecessary duplication with other existing communications mechanisms. In particular, the ability of the Commission on the Status of Women to receive communications needed to be taken into account.

39. Austria suggested that existing elements in established human rights instruments be taken into consideration—in particular, the Optional Protocol to the International Covenant on Civil and Political Rights, and relevant practice.

40. Germany noted that where individual regulations coincided with, *inter alia*, the International Covenant on Civil and Political Rights and the European Convention on the Protection of Human Rights and Fundamental Freedoms, the mutual relation between the provisions must be clarified and examined.

41. Japan noted that the Convention prescribed recognition, enjoyment or exercise by women of human rights and fundamental freedoms in the political, economic, social, cultural, civil or any other field. The existing petition mechanisms were available only for the protection of civil and political rights. In addition, note should be taken of the fact that the Committee on Economic, Social and Cultural Rights had been considering the possibility of drafting an optional protocol to its Covenant, in order to establish a petition system.

42. New Zealand recognized the positive part which such an instrument could have in promoting States' compliance with the provisions of international human rights instruments. It had supported efforts to strengthen international human rights machinery, and although it was conscious of the limitations of an already overburdened system, it was anxious to find effective ways of addressing violations of the human rights of women. In its generic comments on the feasibility of an optional protocol which applied equally to other proposed human rights instruments, New Zealand was aware that there were existing avenues intended to pro-

tect the rights of women, although the efficacy of those procedures had been questioned. The existence, for example, of such instruments and procedures was not widely known nor were they fully utilized by women. Among them was the communications procedure of the Commission on the Status of Women, the International Covenant on Civil and Political Rights, and the 1503 Procedure. New Zealand noted that consideration was also being given to the question of developing an optional protocol under the International Covenant on Economic, Social and Cultural Rights. New Zealand would welcome an analysis of the degree to which those and other existing instruments and procedures were able effectively to address violations of the human rights of women, before adopting any new human rights instrument. Care should be taken to avoid duplication, with a view to streamlining the mechanisms available for redress under existing and proposed instruments while at the same time ensuring that any new instrument enhanced existing procedures.

43. Finland noted that the complaints about the defective application of the Convention or about the violation of women's human rights were submitted to the Commission on the Status of Women for examination. Then the representatives of Governments on the Commission had handled the cases. Finland stated that it was clear that the members of the Commission on the Status of Women could not be regarded as independent experts. Nevertheless, such a condition was a requirement for members in many quasi-judicial United Nations organs, such as the Committee established on the basis of the Covenant on Civil and Political Rights. When creating specific monitoring procedures, a central guarantee of protection of law was that an independent expert committee was responsible for surveillance. The observance of that requirement was particularly important in the context of international surveillance of human rights, which was based on the procedure of individual petition.

44. Colombia, while noting in general the major provisions contained in the 1503 Procedure, by which the Council established procedures for the submission of communications, and of human rights instruments, such as the Optional Protocol under the International Covenant on Civil and Political Rights, pointed out that certain important aspects were omitted from those procedures.

4. The nature of rights contained in the Convention and the question of justiciability

45. Australia noted that the obligations imposed upon or accepted by States Parties to the Convention were complex and variable. It asked whether those obligations were of a type that might form the basis of an enforceable system of individual rights. It believed there

was a need to consider in more detail the nature and types of obligations imposed by the Convention, particularly from the perspective of determining whether they were capable of investigation and adjudication via a complaints and inquiry procedure. It recommended that consideration should also be given to the means to address any perceived problems in that regard.

46. Finland stated that the starting-point of the elements suggested by the Committee was that the appeal and examination procedure would concern all material provisions of the Convention. It went on to state that those provisions, however, had been drawn up in a way which made it problematic to refer to them directly in order to secure the rights. Most of the articles had been formulated into political targets so that the States parties had wide freedom of action on the form of securing the rights. Finland indicated that the nature of the provisions of the Convention would determine what kind of surveillance mechanism could be created for them. Therefore it must be determined which provisions were suitable as the object of a juridical examination in a procedure of individual petition and were, consequently, justiciable. The inquiry procedure might be possible also with regard to such rights which by their nature were not suitable for the procedure of individual petition. The optional protocol to be elaborated might, as was evident from the principles adopted by the Committee, include elements from both approaches. The principles adopted by the Committee on the forms to be followed in the procedure of individual petition and the inquiry procedure could also be the basis for discussion and development in that work when strengthening various aspects of the feasibility of the optional protocol in question.

47. Finland went on to state that, on the other hand, the relevant principles contained certain points whose acceptability or suitability in the optional protocol was not self-evident. It was not necessary to include a certain portion of those points in the protocol or even in the rules of procedure, whereas some of them were provisions which were normally provided for in the above-mentioned document.

48. New Zealand noted that the obligations in the Convention were of both a civil and political and of an economic, social and cultural nature. It also noted that there were different categories of obligations outlined in the Convention. Care should be taken to ensure that, whatever mechanisms and remedies were proposed, they should take into account the varying nature and category of obligations in the Convention. New Zealand went on to state that full consideration of the provisions of the Convention indicated that there were at least five different categories of obligation in the provisions of the Convention, as follows:

(a) Outright obligations on States parties: "to refrain from engaging in any act or practice of discrimination against women", as stated in article 2 (d) and similarly phrased in articles 2 (g), 6, 9.1, 9.2, 11.3, 14.1, 15.1, 15.2, 15.4, 16.2 and 24;

(b) A mix of outright obligations and obligations to undertake appropriate measures: "to eliminate discrimination against women in the political and public life of the country and in particular ... ensure to women, on equal terms with men, the right (a) to vote in all elections and public referenda and to be eligible for election to all publicly elected bodies", as stated in article 7 (a)-7 (c) and similarly phrased in articles 11 (a)-11 (f) and 13 (a)-13 (c);

(c) Obligations to undertake certain activities: "to pursue by all appropriate means and without delay a policy of eliminating discrimination against women", as stated in article 2 and similarly phrased in articles 2 (a)-2 (c), 7, 10, 10 (a)-10 (b), 10 (d)-10 (e), 10 (g)-10 (h) and 11.2 (a)-11.2 (d);

(d) Undertakings to take appropriate measures: "to eliminate discrimination against women by any person, organization or enterprise", as stated in article 2 (e) and similarly phrased in articles 2 (c), 2 (f), 5 (b), 8 10 (f), 12.1, 12.2 and 14.2;

(e) Undertakings to change perceptions: "to modify the social and cultural patterns of conduct of men and women", as stated in article 5 (a) and similarly phrased in article 10 (c).

49. New Zealand, while appreciating that jurisprudence on any issue develops over time, would see value, prior to the adoption of an optional protocol, in further analysis of how the justiciability of the provisions of the Convention might affect the feasibility of a right of petition. In that regard, New Zealand commended the excellent work being undertaken by the Committee in providing interpretive observations on each of the substantive articles and encouraged it to complete its work in that area as soon as possible.

50. Japan noted that the Convention imposed on States Parties the obligation "to undertake all appropriate measures" to eliminate discrimination against women in various fields, but it did not specify in each provision the extent to which States Parties were obliged to do so. Regarding the admissibility of communications, suggestion 7 mentioned that a communication "should disclose an alleged violation of rights or an alleged failure of a State party to give effect to obligations under the Convention". In that connection, it should be pointed out that it was almost impossible for the Committee to determine whether States parties were complying with certain obligations, such as the obligation to take all appropriate measures to modify the social and cultural patterns of conduct of men and women (art. 5 (a)).

51. Germany noted that the Convention did not specify concrete rights but incorporated a wide array of programmatic obligations assumed by States parties in myriad areas, with States parties enjoying the resulting freedom to devise their individual ways of attaining the objectives stipulated. To exemplify that problem, Germany referred to article 2 of the Convention.

52. Germany went on to state that an individual complaints procedure would, on the other hand, provide for judicial and/or quasi-judicial procedures, facilitating, *inter alia*, the enforcement of rights to participation. That would entail incalculable consequences in terms of international law and economic, financial and social policy. In so far as part III of the Convention might be regarded as a series of guarantees which could imply rights to participation, attention must be drawn to the fact that the rights to participation were covered by numerous specific conventions with supervisory mechanisms of their own, so that there was no need to regulate that matter. Germany did not see how an individual complaints procedure which, by its nature, referred to individual rights, might be elaborated in addition to the monitoring mechanisms under article 17 and subsequent articles that were already provided for in the Convention.

53. Germany noted moreover, that reservations arose from the problem of the impact of those guarantees on third parties—i.e., on the legal relationship between individuals. The Convention was geared to have such an effect, as can be seen, for example, in articles 2 (e), 10 (e), 11, and 14 (e). Binding decisions of a quasi-judicial body might extensively encroach upon the autonomy in contracts and entail financial burdens on private persons.

5. *General comments received from non-governmental organizations*

54. All submissions received from non-governmental organizations expressed support for the elaboration of an optional protocol. Several pointed out that such a protocol would provide women with a new mechanism for protecting their rights and would open up opportunities for women to seek remedies for violations of their rights, and guarantees of their rights, at the international level. It was pointed out that, although domestic compliance was the most effective way to see international human rights observed, internationally enforceable law was a powerful incentive for Governments to live up to those obligations. While stressing that an optional protocol should contain the elements contained in suggestion 7, a number of non-governmental organizations called on the Commission on the Status of Women to take as a starting-point for its discussion the draft optional protocol adopted by the independent expert group in Maastricht.

55. Several non-governmental organizations stressed the necessity of ensuring implementation of the provisions of the Convention by introducing the right to petition. They stated that an optional protocol would strengthen Governments' commitment to the implementation of the Convention. It would also compensate for the inadequacy or non-existence of national or regional mechanisms of redress and remedy, and would allow women to secure the enjoyment of their human rights. An optional protocol would be a deterrent to State-sanctioned human rights violations. It would encourage Governments to resolve matters domestically and create incentives for them to reform their laws and practices in accordance with international standards and to comply with obligations under the Convention.

56. A number of non-governmental organizations stressed that an optional protocol would strengthen implementation of the Convention by making the rights contained in it, where ratified, justiciable, and reflect their status as autonomous and fundamental to the advancement of women. It would be an invaluable method for developing international jurisprudence on equality and provide more detailed guidance as to the content of the norms stated in the Convention. An optional protocol would lead to the interpretation of the Convention's provisions through practical application to specific cases and the development of precedents. An optional protocol, covering all the substantive provisions of the Convention, would be an essential tool to increase the Convention's practical effectiveness. It was considered a means by which substantive standards could be applied and where binding decisions could be reached.

57. Certain non-governmental organizations pointed out that an optional protocol would put the Convention on an equal footing with other international human rights instruments endowed with rights of petition, such as the International Covenant on Civil and Political Rights, the International Convention on the Elimination of All Forms of Racial Discrimination and the International Convention against Torture and Other Cruel, Inhuman or Degrading Treatment, and would allow redress of individual grievances. Potentially, it could correct women's under-usage of international human rights mechanisms. It was pointed out that there were currently no United Nations procedures focused specifically on women's human rights which addressed individual cases or widespread violations with a view to providing redress. Furthermore, it would help to integrate women's human rights into mainstream human rights mechanisms by allowing other human rights bodies to refer to the Committee's views and jurisprudence under an optional protocol for detailed analysis of the nature and scope of specific aspects of gender discrimination.

58. A number of non-governmental organizations stated that an optional protocol would serve to create broader public awareness about women's human rights, the Convention, and human rights education, and thus have a positive educative effect.

59. Several non-governmental organizations stressed that the validation of the reporting procedure through an optional protocol was the next essential stage. Further interpretation and practical application of the Convention would sustain the vitality of international cooperation. It would be a signal for the importance attached to the elimination of gender-based discrimination through practical means and a critical element for increasing the enforcement of international human rights treaties. Lack of national accountability under the Convention could also be addressed, and the role of the Committee on the Elimination of Discrimination against Women as a mediating body between Governments and complainants would be reinforced.

60. A few non-governmental organizations also pointed out that an optional protocol should apply to all the substantive articles (1-16) of the Convention. In that regard it was noted that the justiciability of many provisions of the Convention was clearly established, including those stated as guarantees of equality or non-discrimination. Guarantees of equality and non-discrimination had been accepted as justiciable in relation to both civil and political rights and economic, social and cultural rights as shown in the cases of the International Covenant on Civil and Political Rights and the International Convention on the Elimination of All Forms of Racial Discrimination. Even those which were formulated only as duties to take appropriate measures to achieve a general goal could be subject to interpretation by the Committee, since it should be possible to identify minimum core obligations under such provisions. Any determination of non-justiciability should rest with the Committee, rather than excluding *a priori* any of the substantive provisions from the purview of the protocol.

B. *Comments received regarding the elements of an optional protocol, as contained in suggestion 7* 12/

"5. States parties to the Convention should have the option to ratify or accede to the optional protocol. 'State party' in this section means one that has ratified or acceded to the optional protocol."

61. Ukraine pointed out that it was necessary to reflect the procedure for signing and ratifying the optional protocol. Therefore, after the term "State", the text should specify "which has signed and ratified the optional protocol".

62. A few non-governmental organizations commented that no State could be required to ratify the protocol. It would indeed be optional. It would be applicable only to States that were already States parties to the Convention and chose to ratify or accede to the optional protocol. No additional obligations would be imposed upon States parties to the Convention which chose not to ratify the protocol.

"6. Two procedures should be envisaged: a communications procedure and an inquiry procedure."

63. While non-governmental organizations expressed their strong support for the adoption of an optional protocol per se, many specified their support for both an individual and an inquiry procedure. It was also recommended that States ratifying a protocol should not be permitted to opt out of one of the procedures.

"7. Communications may be submitted by an individual, group or organization suffering detriment from a violation of rights in the Convention or claiming to be directly affected by the failure of a State party to comply with its obligations under the Convention or by a person or group having a sufficient interest in the matter."

64. Australia called attention to the innovative proposal that the Committee be able to consider communications from groups and organizations. It noted that the standing proposed was broader than the standing available under the First Optional Protocol to the International Covenant on Civil and Political Rights. Australia considered that the issue of standing under an optional protocol needed further consideration and discussion.

65. Australia wished to see further elaboration on the express requirement for "detriment to be suffered" by an individual, group or organization lodging a communication. That might imply that violation of a right under the Convention was not itself a sufficient detriment to ground a cause of action. Inclusion of that express requirement might operate to exclude consideration of systemic discrimination.

66. The fact that the right of petition was not restricted to individuals was welcomed by the Netherlands. It went further than the First Optional Protocol to the International Covenant on Civil and Political Rights and article 22 of the Convention against Torture, but was in line with article 14.1 of the International Convention on the Elimination of All Forms of Racial Discrimination. The broad definition of those entitled to submit a communication, which avoided the word "victim", was also a positive development.

67. Finland noted that the personal scope of the right of appeal required further consideration.

12/ Some of the elements did not receive any comment.

68. Mexico noted that the right of petition—i.e., to submit communications—should be limited to individuals or to persons having suffered an injury because of a violation of the rights contained in the Convention or to a person or persons who considered themselves to be directly affected by lack of compliance by the State party with the provisions of the Convention. The person or persons thus affected must be subject to the jurisdiction of the said State party.

69. Colombia believed that the proposed protocol must include the requirement that the person or group of persons who directed a complaint alleging to be victims of a violation of rights in the Convention by a State party must be under the jurisdiction of that State party. Colombia further believed that only natural persons could have human rights, and not juridical persons. For that reason, one could not speak of violations of the rights of organizations, as was suggested.

70. Japan stated that eligibility to submit communications should be limited to individuals who claimed to be victims of a violation by a State party of the rights in the Convention, following the example set by the First Optional Protocol under the International Covenant on Civil and Political Rights, if an optional protocol was to be drafted. Therefore, the Committee should not receive any communication from an individual, group or organization who claimed to be directly affected by the failure of a State party to comply with its obligations under the Convention or from a person or group who had a sufficient interest in the matter.

71. Many non-governmental organizations provided comments regarding this element. They expressed their strong support for broad standing criteria in an optional protocol. In particular, they pointed out that standing should be granted both to individuals and to groups and organizations alleging detriment or having suffered directly. That would first of all allow non-governmental organizations and others to represent the interests of victimized groups or individuals who might face danger of persecution, personal reprisal or social stigmatization if pursuing claims themselves and would be in line with practice established in other procedures. That was especially important where the majority of women were poor, illiterate and/or not aware of their rights. A number of non-governmental organizations stated that women often had insufficient resources to proceed alone. Individual complaints might be difficult because of the intimidating nature of official procedures, and the support of a group might be the deciding factor in pursuing a complaint.

72. Furthermore, non-governmental organizations stated that the possibility for group complaints was necessary because, as far as certain violations were concerned, it was more common for a group of women to be affected by the same event or the same perpetrator. Group complaints were essential since they would permit petitions by organizations on behalf of other women, especially in cases where victims would be endangered. Among the examples mentioned were refugee women, women victims of trafficking, or violence in the family.

73. In addition, some non-governmental organizations suggested that they and groups with a sufficient interest in the protection of women's equality and in the Convention should have standing in the proceedings so that they could actively cooperate with the Committee in providing evidence and information regarding a Government's violations of the Convention. Also, certain matters might be better served by a class action approach which could potentially improve the lot of an indefinite number of victims.

74. It was also suggested that an optional protocol must be applicable to both actions by a Government and to a Government's failure to act against violations carried out by private persons, groups or organizations.

"8. Communications would be in writing and confidential."

75. Australia stated that it would be important to ensure that the communications procedure did not indirectly discriminate against or disenfranchise individuals or groups. It noted that the element specified that the Committee would accept written communications only. While recognizing that a written complaint was likely to be most easily dealt with by the Committee and by States parties, Australia considered that the procedure could be deemed discriminatory against women who had low levels of print literacy. Consideration should be given to providing for a range of alternative modes of communication.

76. Australia also stated that the issue of confidentiality needed to be considered in the context of the rules and procedures of the Committee. In accordance with current practices, although there were good reasons for preserving confidentiality at various stages of the communications procedure, further consideration should be given to the circumstances in which there should be a discretion to waive confidentiality.

"9. The admissibility of a communication would be subject to the following:

"(a) The communication would be inadmissible if a State party to the Convention had not ratified or acceded to the optional protocol;

"(b) It should not be anonymous;

"(c) It should disclose an alleged violation of rights or an alleged failure of a State party to give effect to obligations under the Convention;

"(d) It should relate to acts or omissions that occurred after the State party ratified or acceded to the Convention, unless the violation or failure to give effect to those obligations or the impact continued after the protocol took effect for that State party."

77. Ukraine stated the need to specify "as a State party that has signed and ratified the Convention".

78. The Netherlands stated that it was not clear whether the element meant that communications relating to violations that took place before the optional protocol came into effect in the State which was the subject of the complaint would be declared inadmissible. If that were the case, it would seem better to base the right of petition on the date on which the Convention, and not the protocol, came into force, since accession to the protocol changed nothing with regard to the obligations of States parties under the Convention.

79. Colombia saw a lack of clarity in the element. The principle of non-retroactivity of norms must be upheld and, as a consequence, it must be established that a communication must refer to an act or omission that took place after the optional protocol entered into force in the respective State party.

"9. The admissibility of a communication would be subject to the following:

"... (e) It should not be an abuse of the right to submit a communication."

80. Colombia stated that a further prerequisite for admissibility should be that a communication not contain offensive or insulting language directed at the State against which the communication is lodged.

"9. The admissibility of a communication would be subject to the following:

"... (f) A communication would be declared inadmissible by the Committee if all domestic remedies had not been exhausted, unless the Committee considered that requirement unreasonable. If the same matter was being examined under another international procedure, the Committee would declare the communication inadmissible unless it considered that procedure unreasonably prolonged".

81. Finland noted that the question of the exhaustion of national and international legal remedies required further consideration.

82. New Zealand would welcome further debate on the matter: it welcomed the provision of inadmissibility if the same matter was being considered under another international procedure. Such a provision would go some considerable way to meeting New Zealand's desire for streamlined processes and non-duplication of efforts.

83. Mexico noted that, contrary to what was suggested in terms of inadmissibility in the second sentence, one of the causes for inadmissibility for communications must always be that the matter was being examined by another international procedure, no matter how long that procedure took. Mexico also believed that further discussion and analysis were needed regarding the criteria that would be used to decide whether exhaustion of domestic remedies was "not reasonable" and how the determination of their exhaustion would be made.

84. Colombia stated that, with regard to the first sentence, it would be clearer to state that communications were inadmissible if available domestic remedies had not been exhausted, except in cases where it had been shown convincingly that such remedies were inefficient or that they were being unjustifiably prolonged. Regarding the second sentence of point (f), Colombia noted that the formulation would give the Committee the ability to judge the efficiency and efficacy of other organs established under treaties, which would be unprecedented and very undesirable. Instead, it would be advisable to avoid duplication of existing procedures, by simply stating that a communication was inadmissible when the same matter was under consideration by another international procedure.

85. A few non-governmental organizations stated that the Convention did not respond adequately when domestic remedies were limited or non-existent, and an optional protocol would allow redress when women were not able to achieve it domestically. Likewise, the optional protocol should make it clear that the requirement of exhaustion of domestic remedies could be waived in cases in which the remedy sought was unavailable or ineffective, unduly prolonged or did not include due process protections, or where access to domestic remedies had been denied. Those exceptions were well established in the jurisprudence of United Nations human rights bodies. In such cases, an optional protocol would become an important fall-back mechanism to address women's rights.

86. It was suggested that the reasonable requirement of the exhaustion of domestic remedies should not obstruct the filing of claims but rather enable States parties that provided effective domestic remedies to address a complaint before it reached the international level. In turn, the eventuality of an international review enhanced the possibility that those complaints would be taken seriously. Thus, an optional protocol would advance the principle and practice of accountability on a domestic as well as international level.

"9. The admissibility of a communication would be subject to the following:

"...(g) The communication would be inadmissible if the author, within a reasonable period, failed to provide adequate substantiating information.

"10. Pending examination of a communication, the Committee should have the right to request that the status quo be preserved, and a State party should give an undertaking to that effect, in order to avoid irreparable harm. Such a request should be accompanied by information confirming that no inference could be drawn that the Committee had determined the merits of the communication."

87. New Zealand noted that element 10 proposed an innovation unprecedented in international human rights instruments: the right of the Committee to request that "the status quo be preserved ... in order to avoid irreparable harm" during consideration of a communication. As the intention of such a provision was unclear, further discussion on the issue might be warranted.

88. Colombia noted lack of clarity in the drafting of element 10. The proposal that the Committee had the right to request that the status quo be maintained seemed to suggest that the alleged violation should be maintained. Therefore, the words que no hay indicios de que should be deleted.

"11. While the State party would be informed confidentially of the nature of the communication, the author's identity would not be revealed without that person's consent. The State party would, within a specified period, provide replies or information about any remedy. While the process of examination continued, the Committee would work in cooperation with the parties to facilitate a settlement which, if reached, would be contained in a confidential report of the Committee."

89. The Netherlands stated that there must be scope for publicizing the results of the settlement with the agreement of the interested parties.

90. Mexico stated that communications must, without exception, be brought to the attention of the State party that was alleged of a violation of, or lack of compliance with, a provision of the Convention, even if that was done confidentially and with the necessary safeguards for the security of the person or persons who had brought the complaint.

91. Colombia noted, with regard to element 11, the need to ask in which specific cases the Committee would, without having concluded the proceedings, work with the parties to facilitate a settlement, given that that in fact would mean acceptance that a violation existed. Colombia further noted the importance of ensuring the right of the State party to be represented at those sessions of the Committee in which it dealt with cases in which the said State party had an interest. That was the case in similar situations in, *inter alia*, the committees established under the Covenant on Civil and Political Rights

and the Convention on the Elimination of Racial Discrimination.

92. Certain non-governmental organizations noted that any provision authorizing the Committee to facilitate a settlement should stipulate that the settlement must be on the basis of respect for the rights and obligations set forth in the Convention, to guard against the possibility that a complainant might be intimidated or coerced to agree to a settlement.

"12. The Committee would examine communications in the light of all information provided by the State party, or by the author or received from other relevant sources. All such information would be transmitted to the parties for comment. The Committee would set its procedures, hold closed meetings when examining communications and, as a whole Committee, adopt and transmit views and any recommendations to the parties. While examining a communication, the Committee might, with the agreement of the State party concerned, visit its territory."

93. Colombia pointed out that it would be logical for the Economic and Social Council, with its vast experience in the field of human rights and with the goal of maintaining necessary consistency, to establish the procedure. That would not prevent the Committee from establishing its own rules of procedure.

94. Japan noted that the Committee would examine a communication in the light of all information provided by the State party concerned and the author of the communication, but not in the light of information received from other relevant sources. In examining information thus provided, due respect should be given to the facts established through due process of law.

95. A few non-governmental organizations stated that the procedures available to the Committee for examining responses must include the ability to take oral or written evidence, on-site visits, and urgent measures requesting interim action to prevent irreparable harm.

"13. When the whole Committee considered that the communication had been justified, it might recommend remedial measures or measures designed to give effect to obligations under the Convention. The State party would remedy violations and implement recommendations. It would also ensure that an appropriate remedy (which might include adequate reparation) was provided. It would also provide the Committee within a set period with details of the remedial measures taken."

96. New Zealand noted that the element proposed that appropriate remedies, which might include adequate reparation, could be provided and that that aspect of the

proposal warranted further consideration. If provision were to be made for reparations, there was need for further interpretative work on the obligations of States parties under the Convention. New Zealand supported the work that the Committee had already done in preparing interpretative observations. However, further work in regard to remedies might be required to take into account the diverse nature of obligations contained in the Convention—for example, by providing for a range of remedies consistent with the nature of those obligations.

97. New Zealand commended the Committee for the innovative measure it proposed for possible inclusion in an optional protocol—in particular, in element 13 which suggested that a State party would provide the Committee with details of remedial measures taken to implement the recommendations on a communication issued by the Committee. New Zealand saw that proposal as providing constructive practical measures for the implementation of the optional protocol.

98. Some non-governmental organizations noted that remedial measures might include the reform or repeal of national legislation, payment of damages or provision of other forms of reparation, or steps to prevent future violations, such as reform of administrative procedures, similar to the practice of the Human Rights Committee.

99. Japan noted that a petition procedure under an optional protocol might infringe upon the independence of the judicial systems of States parties. In preparing an optional protocol to the Convention it was necessary to recognize that the views and recommendations of the Committee, which should be of a general nature, should not be legally binding on the States parties and that it should be up to each State party whether to take measures.

"14. The Committee should have the power to initiate and continue discussions concerning such measures and remedies and have the power to invite the State party to include such information in its reports under article 18 of the Convention."

100. A few non-governmental organizations commented that the procedure must provide for the adoption of views by the Committee and its powers to make recommendations, including discussions with the State party of the remedial measures taken, as well as the requirement of including relevant information in the reports under article 18 of the Convention.

"15. The Committee would, in its confidential report, summarize the nature of communications received, its examination of them, the replies and statements of the States parties concerned and its views and recommendations."

101. The Netherlands stated that, according to the Maastricht draft optional protocol, the report would not be entirely confidential. Article 9.3 of the Maastricht draft optional protocol states: "The Committee shall include in its annual report an account of the substance of the communication and its examination of the matter, a summary of the explanations and statements of the State party concerned, of its own views and recommendations, and the response of the State party concerned to those views and recommendations." 13/ That could take place in consultation with the parties concerned.

102. Finland noted that the question of the publicity of the decisions required further consideration.

103. A few non-governmental organizations pointed out that an optional protocol should call on States parties to publicize the protocol and its procedures and the Committee's views and any recommendations concerning a communication received or an inquiry conducted.

"16. The Committee would have the power to delegate to a working group its responsibilities under this section. The working group would report to the Committee and the Committee alone would have the power to adopt views and make recommendations."

104. Ukraine noted that the procedure for establishing the working groups needed to be specified.

105. A few non-governmental organizations noted that the Committee would adopt a decision on the merits and issue a declaratory judgement to the effect that the country was or was not in violation of its obligations under the Convention. If a violation was found, it should establish appropriate remedies, and notify the relevant State of its findings. The Government would be obligated to take all necessary steps to implement any specific remedy and to report back on measures taken to comply with the Committee's decision. Requiring governmental response would substantially increase accountability for violations of women's rights.

"17. If the Committee received reliable information indicating a serious or systematic violation by a State party of rights under the Convention or of a failure to give effect to its Convention obligations, the Committee should have the right to invite that State party to cooperate in examining the information and in submitting observations on it. After considering those observations and any other relevant information, the Committee should have the power to designate one or more of its members to conduct an inquiry and report urgently to the Committee."

13/ E/C.12/1994/12.

106. The Netherlands was of the opinion that the fact that such a procedure was being drafted constituted an important contribution to the enforcement of the Convention. In terms of United Nations conventions it was a relatively new procedure. Its adoption in a protocol would provide a suitable incentive for other bodies to follow the example of the Committee.

107. New Zealand noted the proposal of an inquiry procedure undertaken with the cooperation of the State party. It stated that the inquiry procedure was very similar to that which already existed under the 1503 Procedure. New Zealand would welcome further discussion on the possible duplication between the two procedures, including duplication in regard to the distinction made between gross violations of human rights and fundamental freedoms as contained in the 1503 Procedure and systematic violations and breaches as referred to in element 17.

108. With regard to a possible inquiry procedure, Mexico considered that such a procedure could be initiated exclusively on the basis of a communication, and as such, must follow the same requirements and procedures envisaged for the complaints procedure. Mexico furthermore saw a need for further analysis concerning the modes of financing of the activities which the Committee would be undertaking and which would determine whether the inquiry procedure proposed in points 17 and 18 would be included.

109. Japan noted that the Convention against Torture had institutionalized a procedure under which the Committee concerned might proceed with an inquiry if it received reliable information which appeared to contain well-founded indications that torture was being systematically practised (art. 20). Suggestion 7 envisaged that the Committee might initiate an inquiry if it received reliable information indicating a serious or systematic violation by a State party of rights under the Convention or failure to give effect to its Convention obligations. In that connection, two questions should be raised if an optional protocol were to be drafted: whether it was appropriate for the Committee to initiate an inquiry procedure; and if so, whether it was appropriate to establish as criteria for taking such action that a violation be "systematic" and/or that it be "serious", in light of the fact that the latter had not been used in connection with the existing international human rights treaty petition procedures. Those questions should be examined thoroughly.

110. A large number of non-governmental organizations stressed the need to include an inquiry procedure in the proposed optional protocol. Such a procedure would not duplicate the reporting procedure established under article 18 of the Convention. They stressed that the Committee should have the authority, on its own initiative and unhampered by political and other considerations, to examine any allegations concerning serious or systematic violations of the articles of the Convention. While requiring a high threshold for initiating its use, as indicated by the phrase "serious or systematic", without it, the Committee would have to ignore evidence of serious or systematic violations that did not result in a formal complaint. The inquiry procedure would facilitate the examination of widespread violations, such as *Fatwa*-related violence, violations that crossed national borders and implicated several Governments, such as trafficking, or violence against women in conflict situations. It was suggested that the inquiry procedure should be based on the precedent of article 20 of the Convention against Torture. Broader inquiries could also have an educational effect in bringing to light violations and/or neglect by States of particular practices.

"18. Such an inquiry would be conducted with the cooperation of the State party and might, with its agreement, include a visit to its territory."

111. Some non-governmental organizations stated that, while seeking the cooperation of the Government(s) concerned, the Committee should continue to investigate even if a Government did not cooperate. The need for the Committee to have power to conduct on-site investigations and to publish a report at the conclusion of its investigation was stressed.

"19. Following the examination of the findings, which would be transmitted to the State party, the latter would have a set period in which to make observations in response."

112. New Zealand commended the Committee for the innovative proposal that allowed Governments a set period in which to submit observations.

"20. The inquiry would be conducted confidentially and at all stages with the cooperation of the States parties.

"21. The Committee would encourage the State party to discuss the steps taken by it as a consequence of the inquiry. Those discussions might be continued until a satisfactory outcome was achieved. The Committee might ask the State party to report on its response to the inquiry in its report under article 18 of the Convention."

113. Some non-governmental organizations stated that, after releasing its finding, the Committee should continue to monitor the situation and request updates from Governments.

"22. After completing all those steps, the Committee would be empowered to publish a report."

114. The Netherlands stated that it was unclear whether the element could be acted upon against the will of the State concerned. If that was so, the Committee must be able to impose sanctions on States that refused to attach any consequences to the outcome of the inquiry.

"23. When ratifying or acceding to the optional protocol the State party would undertake to assist the Committee in its inquiries and to prevent any obstacles to, or victimization of, any person who provides the Committee with information or assists it in its inquiries."

115. New Zealand commended the Committee for the innovative proposal regarding the proposed safeguards indicated in the element.

116. Certain non-governmental organizations noted that the element would broaden the duty of cooperation which appeared in other human rights instruments by encompassing the duty to protect against victimization not only by the State itself but also by private individuals. As illustrated by the example of violence against women in the family, only the State was in a position to prevent such victimization.

"24. States parties would publicize the protocol and its procedures, the Committee's views and any recommendations concerning a communication received or inquiry conducted.

"25. The Committee would develop rules and procedures that would enable it to conduct its work fairly, efficiently and, as necessary, urgently.

"26. Meeting time of not less than three weeks per annum and resources, including expert legal advice, would be made available to enable the Committee to conduct its work under the Convention."

117. New Zealand stated that the resource implications of an optional protocol need to be addressed. For some years New Zealand, along with many others, has been seriously concerned about the inadequate resources provided to the Committee to support its work. Referring to points 25 and 26, New Zealand is of the view that in order to discharge the additional responsibilities and workload which would arise from the adoption of an optional protocol, the United Nations would need to commit the necessary resources to support the Committee's work. Accordingly, New Zealand recommends the preparation of an analysis of the resource implications of an optional protocol, including recommendations for future funding, for presentation to the Commission on the Status of Women.

118. Australia notes that the effective operation of an optional protocol will depend on adequate resources being made available, including additional meeting times for the Committee for the handling of complaints.

119. Mexico sees a need to analyse further ways to strengthen the capacity of the Committee in order to enable it to assume efficiently the tasks which would arise from the implementation of the optional protocol.

120. Japan notes that once the optional protocol enters into force, additional work related to it would impose an extra burden on the Committee as well as its secretariat, the Division for the Advancement of Women. With the current budget and at the present level of human resources, they would be unable to shoulder such an extra burden. It is therefore necessary to examine carefully the financial implications and human resources requirements arising from such new mandates.

121. A few non-governmental organizations pointed out that a condition for a strong optional protocol was the provision of adequate human and financial resources for the Committee.

"27. Procedures for the signing, ratification, accession and entry into force of the protocol should be prescribed."

122. New Zealand would wish to ensure that application of relevant provisions to territories under a State's jurisdiction would take account of the unique constitutional and legal status of the self-governing territories of New Zealand. It would be pleased to assist in the drafting of appropriate language to take account of that situation in due course.

"28. No State-to-State communication procedure should be included and no reservations permitted."

123. The Netherlands supported the prohibition of reservations to the protocol.

124. A few non-governmental organizations proposed that the optional protocol could allow State-to-State complaints of non-compliance to be heard by the Committee, since States might in the future be more willing to resort to such a procedure, which therefore should not be foreclosed by omitting it from an optional protocol. The inclusion of such a procedure would reinforce the principle that human rights obligations were obligations *erga omnes*.

"29. Procedures for amendment and denunciation and the authentic texts of the protocol should be prescribed."

125. There were no responses to element 29.

Addendum

1. In accordance with Economic and Social Council resolution 1995/29 of 24 July 1995 on the elaboration of a draft optional protocol to the Convention on the Elimination of All Forms of Discrimination against Women, the Secretary-General prepared a comprehensive report, including a synthesis, on the views expressed

in accordance with paragraph 5 of that resolution (E/CN.6/1996/10). After the report was completed, the views of the Governments of Cuba and China were received. They are reported below.

2. Cuba observed that, in keeping with the attention and priority given to women's issues in the country, the question of introducing the right of petition through an optional protocol to the Convention was being considered by the relevant authorities of the country with a view to determining the position which Cuba would take in the working group that was to meet during the fortieth session of the Commission on the Status of Women, to be held in March 1996.

3. The Cuban Government was also giving constant attention to examining its existing mechanisms and procedures in the light of international human rights instruments, particularly those dealing with women's human rights. To that end, a comprehensive evaluation of the feasibility of an optional protocol was being made at the national level, involving a joint effort in which all institutions concerned with women's issues in Cuba were participating.

4. Cuba also noted that, in the course of national consideration of the issue, particular attention would be paid to existing mechanisms, in order to ensure that the decisions ultimately taken made a real and substantive contribution to the handling of human rights issues without unnecessary duplication.

5. China stated that, since the Commission on the Status of Women and the Commission on Human Rights had already established special mechanisms to review communications and since the United Nations was practising thrift, another mechanism, such as an optional protocol, might cause a duplication of work and duties and a waste of human and financial resources. Those would certainly add an extra load to the United Nations heavy financial burden. The Secretary-General was requested to give serious consideration to the above-mentioned facts.

6. In accordance with resolution 1995/29 of the Economic and Social Council, the Commission on the Status of Women should establish an in-session open-ended working group at its fortieth session to consider the report of the Secretary-General with a view to elaborating a draft optional protocol to the Convention. Considering that an optional protocol would be legally binding on the States parties and should reflect their views, it was recommended that a drafting group of experts from the States parties to the Convention be set up. The composition of the drafting group should fully embody the principle of equitable and geographical representation. When the drafting group had worked out a draft optional protocol, it should distribute the draft to the States parties to solicit comments from all sides.

Addendum

In accordance with Economic and Social Council resolution 1995/29 of 24 July 1995 on the elaboration of a draft optional protocol to the Convention on the Elimination of All Forms of Discrimination against Women, the Secretary-General prepared a comprehensive report, including a synthesis, on the views expressed in accordance with paragraph 5 of that resolution (E/CN.6/1996/10). After the report was completed, the views of the Government of the United Kingdom were received. They are reported below.

1. The United Kingdom is of the opinion that the introduction of an optional protocol is not appropriate at the present time. The United Kingdom also has concerns about the proposed protocol in its present form. Notwithstanding its concerns, the United Kingdom is prepared to work together with other States parties to ensure that any protocol which may be adopted results in an effective instrument and submits its views in response to the consultation exercise in that spirit.

2. Through its scrutiny of national reports the Committee on the Elimination of Discrimination against Women already has the power to assess progress by States parties in meeting the wide-ranging provisions of the Convention. The United Kingdom recognizes the efforts made by the United Nations to secure the efficient operation of the Committee. However, it believes that at the present time an efficient Committee and the encouragement to all States parties to submit timely periodic reports are the most effective ways of enforcing provisions and reaching those women most in need of support. To proceed with an optional protocol now risks diverting United Nations focus and resources to further scrutiny of those States parties that ratify the optional protocol, in many cases likely to be among the most advanced on equality issues.

3. The United Kingdom believes that an optional protocol would add to the administrative costs of the United Nations and States parties without providing concomitant benefits to those women most in need. It seeks an analysis of the costs of implementation of an optional protocol and clarification on the apportionment of costs between States parties. On a specific point about costs: is it necessary for the optional protocol to stipulate a minimum time period in which the Committee can meet of not less than three weeks? This proposal should be reconsidered.

4. The United Kingdom is also concerned that the proposed protocol appears in some respects to be broader than optional protocols already available under, for ex-

ample, the International Covenant on Civil and Political Rights. The Committee would have power to consider complaints from persons or groups having a sufficient interest in, but not directly affected by, the failure of a State party to comply with its obligations under the Convention; by contrast, the optional protocol to the Covenant permits only individuals who claim to be victims of such a violation to bring a complaint before the Committee. The United Kingdom would be grateful for clarification on this matter and the reasons for the apparently broader approach under the Convention.

5. The United Kingdom is also doubtful whether the obligations in the Convention, some of which are drafted in general terms, can be susceptible to a judicial approach. It seems likely that many of the obligations would be open to wide interpretation, rendering the outcome to any specific complaint unpredictable. The United Kingdom notes that the existing duties and powers of the Committee were those given to it at the time the substantive provisions of the Convention were adopted, and it is doubtful whether those should be extended.

6. Turning to some points of detail, in which the comments of the United Kingdom are without prejudice to its objections in principle: with regard to paragraph 9 (f) of suggestion 7, 1/ the United Kingdom would not

wish to see Committee intervention in issues which had not exhausted domestic remedies and would wish to see the phrase "unless the Committee considered that requirement unreasonable" deleted. Alternatively, the meaning of this phrase should be clarified in the protocol.

7. The United Kingdom also seeks clarification about the responsibility of the State party to redress violations (including the payment of reparations) of the Convention (paras. 7 and 13 of suggestion 7) and would hope to see that responsibility set out in a further draft of the protocol or explanatory note.

8. Finally, on issues of timing, the United Kingdom would hope to see a change in the proposal that acts or omissions before the ratification of or accession to the Convention might also be considered (para. 9 (d)). This is essentially a retrospective measure, which would run contrary to the general principles of legal practice. Furthermore, the draft does not incorporate any time-limit within which complaints must be submitted, which is likely to create a great deal of legal and administrative uncertainty. The United Kingdom would hope to see a reasonable time-limit incorporated in the protocol.

1/ *Official Records of the General Assembly, Fiftieth Session, Supplement No. 38* (A/50/38), chap. I.B.

Document 139

Declarations, reservations, objections and notifications of withdrawal of reservations relating to the Convention on the Elimination of All Forms of Discrimination against Women

CEDAW/SP/1996/2, 8 February 1996

I. Introduction

1. The present document contains the declarations, reservations, objections and notifications of withdrawal of reservations made by States parties with respect to the Convention on the Elimination of All Forms of Discrimination against Women reproduced in *Multilateral Treaties Deposited with the Secretary-General: Status as at 31 December 1994.* 1/ Declarations, reservations, objections and notifications of withdrawal of reservations made from 2 January to 1 August 1995 have been taken from the report of the Secretary-General on the status of the Convention (A/50/346). Accessions reported to the Secretary-General between 1 August 1995 to 2 February 1996 have also been included.

II. Convention on the Elimination of all Forms of Discrimination against Women

A. *General information*

2. The Convention on the Elimination of All Forms of Discrimination against Women was adopted by the General Assembly in its resolution 34/180 of 18 December 1979. It entered into force on 3 September 1981, in accordance with the provisions of its article 27. The status of States parties with respect to the Convention as of 2 February 1996 is shown below.

Status of States parties with respect to the Convention on the Elimination
of All Forms of Discrimination against Women as of 2 February 1996

State	Date of signature	Date of receipt of the instrument of ratification, accession or succession
Afghanistan	14 August 1980	
Albania		11 May 1994 a/
Angola		17 September 1986 a/
Antigua and Barbuda		1 August 1989 a/
Argentina	17 July 1980	15 July 1985 b/
Armenia		13 September 1993 a/
Australia	17 July 1980	28 July 1983 b/
Austria	17 July 1980	31 March 1982 b/
Azerbaijan		10 July 1995 a/
Bahamas		6 October 1993 a/, b/
Bangladesh		6 November 1984 a/, b/
Barbados	24 July 1980	16 October 1980
Belarus	17 July 1980	4 February 1981 c/
Belgium	17 July 1980	10 July 1985 b/
Belize	7 March 1990	16 May 1990
Benin	11 November 1981	12 March 1992
Bhutan	17 July 1980	31 August 1981
Bolivia	30 May 1980	8 June 1990
Bosnia and Herzegovina		1 September 1993 d/
Brazil	31 March 1981 b/	1 February 1984 b/, c/
Bulgaria	17 July 1980	8 February 1982 c/
Burkina Faso		14 October 1987 a/
Burundi	17 July 1980	8 January 1992
Cambodia	17 October 1980	15 October 1992 a/
Cameroon	6 June 1983	23 August 1994 a/
Canada	17 July 1980	10 December 1981 c/
Cape Verde		5 December 1980 a/
Central African Republic		21 June 1991 a/
Chad		9 June 1995 a/
Chile	17 July 1980	7 December 1989 b/
China	17 July 1980 b/	4 November 1980 b/
Colombia	17 July 1980	19 January 1982
Comoros		31 October 1994 a/
Congo	29 July 1980	26 July 1982
Costa Rica	17 July 1980	4 April 1986
Côte d'Ivoire	17 July 1980	18 December 1995 a/
Croatia		9 September 1992 d/
Cuba	6 March 1980	17 July 1980 b/
Cyprus		23 July 1985 a/, b/
Czech Republic e/		22 February 1993 c/, d/
Denmark	17 July 1980	21 April 1983
Dominica	15 September 1980	15 September 1980
Dominican Republic	17 July 1980	2 September 1982

State	Date of signature	Date of receipt of the instrument of ratification, accession or succession
Ecuador	17 July 1980	9 November 1981
Egypt	16 July 1980 b/	18 September 1981 b/
El Salvador	14 November 1980 b/	19 August 1981 b/
Equatorial Guinea		23 October 1984 a/
Eritrea		5 September 1995 a/
Estonia		21 October 1991 a/
Ethiopia	8 July 1980	10 September 1981 b/
Fiji		28 August 1995a/, b/
Finland	17 July 1980	4 September 1986
France	17 July 1980 b/	14 December 1983 b/, c/
Gabon	17 July 1980	21 January 1983
Gambia	29 July 1980	16 April 1993
Georgia		26 October 1994 a/
Germany f/	17 July 1980	10 July 1985 b/
Ghana	17 July 1980	2 January 1986
Greece	2 March 1982	7 June 1983
Grenada	17 July 1980	30 August 1990
Guatemala	8 June 1981	12 August 1982
Guinea	17 July 1980	9 August 1982
Guinea-Bissau	17 July 1980	23 August 1985
Guyana	17 July 1980	17 July 1980
Haiti	17 July 1980	20 July 1981
Honduras	11 June 1980	3 March 1983
Hungary	6 June 1980	22 December 1980 c/
Iceland	24 July 1980	18 June 1985
India	30 July 1980 b/	9 July 1993 b/
Indonesia	29 July 1980	13 September 1984 b/
Iraq		13 August 1986 a/, b/
Ireland		23 December 1985 a/, b/, c/
Israel	17 July 1980	3 October 1991 b/
Italy	17 July 1980 b/	10 June 1985
Jamaica	17 July 1980	19 October 1984 b/, c/
Japan	17 July 1980	25 June 1985
Jordan	3 December 1980 b/	1 July 1992 b/
Kenya		9 March 1984 a/
Kuwait		2 September 1994 a/, b/
Lao People's Democratic Republic	17 July 1980	14 August 1981
Latvia		14 April 1992 a/
Lesotho	17 July 1980	22 August 1995 a/, b/
Liberia		17 July 1984 a/
Libyan Arab Jamahiriya		16 May 1989 a/, b/
Liechtenstein		22 December 1995 a/
Lithuania		18 January 1994 a/
Luxembourg	17 July 1980	2 February 1989 b/

State	Date of signature	Date of receipt of the instrument of ratification, accession or succession
Madagascar	17 July 1980	17 March 1989
Malawi		12 March 1987 a/, c/
Malaysia		5 July 1995 a/, b/
Maldives		1 July 1993 a/, b/
Mali	5 February 1985	10 September 1985
Malta		8 March 1991 a/, b/
Mauritius		9 July 1984 a/, b/
Mexico	17 July 1980 b/	23 March 1981
Mongolia	17 July 1980	20 July 1981 c/
Morocco		21 June 1993 a/, b/
Namibia		23 November 1992 a/
Nepal	5 February 1991	22 April 1991
Netherlands	17 July 1980	23 July 1991
New Zealand	17 July 1980	10 January 1985 b/, c/
Nicaragua	17 July 1980	27 October 1981
Nigeria	23 April 1984	13 June 1985
Norway	17 July 1980	21 May 1981
Panama	26 June 1980	29 October 1981
Papua New Guinea		12 January 1995 a/
Paraguay		6 April 1987 a/
Peru	23 July 1981	13 September 1982
Philippines	15 July 1980	5 August 1981
Poland	29 May 1980	30 July 1980 b/
Portugal	24 April 1980	30 July 1980
Republic of Korea	25 May 1983 b/	27 December 1984 b/, c/
Republic of Moldova		1 July 1994 a/
Romania	4 September 1980 b/	7 January 1982 b/
Russian Federation	17 July 1980	23 January 1981 c/
Rwanda	1 May 1980	2 March 1981
Saint Kitts and Nevis		25 April 1985 a/
Saint Lucia		8 October 1982 a/
Saint Vincent and the Grenadines		4 August 1981 a/
Samoa		25 September 1992 a/
Sao Tome and Principe	31 October 1995	
Senegal	29 July 1980	5 February 1985
Seychelles		5 May 1992 a/
Sierra Leone	21 September 1988	11 November 1988
Singapore		5 October 1995 a/, b/
Slovakia e/		28 May 1993 d/
Slovenia		6 July 1992 d/
South Africa	29 January 1993	15 December 1995 a/
Spain	17 July 1980	5 January 1984 b/
Sri Lanka	17 July 1980	5 October 1981

State	Date of signature	Date of receipt of the instrument of ratification, accession or succession
Suriname		1 March 1993 a/
Sweden	7 March 1980	2 July 1980
Switzerland	23 January 1987	
Tajikistan		26 October 1993 a/
Thailand		9 August 1985 a/, b/, c/
The former Yugoslav Republic of Macedonia		18 January 1994 d/
Togo		26 September 1983 a/
Trinidad and Tobago	27 June 1985 b/	12 January 1990 b/
Tunisia	24 July 1980	20 September 1985 b/
Turkey		20 December 1985 a/, b/
Uganda	30 July 1980	22 July 1985
Ukraine	17 July 1980	12 March 1981 c/
United Kingdom of Great Britain and Northern Ireland	22 July 1981	7 April 1986 b/
United Republic of Tanzania	17 July 1980	20 August 1985
United States of America	17 July 1980	
Uruguay	30 March 1981	9 October 1981
Uzbekistan		19 July 1995 a/
Vanuatu		8 September 1995 a/
Venezuela	17 July 1980	2 May 1983 b/
Viet Nam	29 July 1980	17 February 1982 b/
Yemen g/		30 May 1984 a/, b/
Yugoslavia	17 July 1980	26 February 1982
Zaire	17 July 1980	17 October 1986
Zambia	17 July 1980	21 June 1985
Zimbabwe		13 May 1991 a/

a/ Accession.
b/ Declarations or reservations.
c/ Reservation subsequently withdrawn.
d/ Succession.
e/ Before becoming a separate State on 1 January 1993, the Czech Republic and Slovakia formed part of Czechoslovakia, which had ratified the Convention on 16 February 1982. The Convention entered into force on 18 March 1982.
f/ With effect from 3 October 1990, the German Democratic Republic (which ratified the Convention on 9 July 1980) and the Federal Republic of Germany (which ratified the Convention on 10 July 1985) united to form one sovereign State, which acts in the United Nations under the designation of "Germany".
g/ On 22 May 1990, Democratic Yemen and Yemen merged to form a single State, which acts in the United Nations under the designation of "Yemen".

[Editor's note: As of 15 March 1996, Pakistan became the 152nd State party to the Convention.]

B. Texts of declarations and reservations

Argentina

[Original: Spanish]
[15 July 1985]

Reservation

The Government of Argentina declares that it does not consider itself bound by article 29, paragraph 1, of the Convention on the Elimination of All Forms of Discrimination against Women.

Australia

[Original: English]
[28 July 1983]

Declaration

Australia has a federal constitutional system in which legislative, executive and judicial powers are shared or distributed between the Commonwealth and the Constituent States. The implementation of the Treaty throughout Australia will be effected by the Commonwealth State and Territory Authorities having regard to their respective constitutional powers and arrangements concerning their exercise.

Reservations

The Government of Australia states that maternity leave with pay is provided in respect of most women employed by the Commonwealth Government and the Governments of New South Wales and Victoria. Unpaid maternity leave is provided in respect of all other women employed in the State of New South Wales and elsewhere to women employed under Federal and some State industrial awards. Social security benefits subject to income tests are available to women who are sole parents.

The Government of Australia advises that it is not at present in a position to take the measures required by article 11 (2) (b) to introduce maternity leave with pay or with comparable social benefits throughout Australia.

The Government of Australia advises that it does not accept the application of the Convention in so far as it would require alteration of Defence Force policy which excludes women from combat and combat-related duties. The Government of Australia is reviewing this policy so as to more closely define "combat" and "combat-related duties".

Austria

[Original: English]
[31 March 1982]

Reservation

Austria reserves its right to apply the provision of article 7 (b) as far as service in the armed forces is concerned, and the provision of article 11 as far as night work of women and special protection of working women is concerned, within the limits established by national legislation.

Bahamas

[Original: English]
[6 October 1993]

Reservation

The Government of the Commonwealth of the Bahamas does not consider itself bound by the provisions of article 2 (a), article 9, paragraph 2, article 16, paragraph 1 (h) [and] article 29, paragraph 1, of the Convention.

Bangladesh

[Original: English]
[6 November 1984]

Reservation

The Government of the People's Republic of Bangladesh does not consider as binding upon itself the provisions of articles 2, 13 (a) and 16 (1) (c) and (f) as they conflict with Shariah law based on Holy Qur'an and Sunna.

Belgium

[Original: French]
[3 July 1985]

Reservations

Article 7

The application of article 7 shall not affect the validity of the provisions of the Constitution as laid down in article 60, which reserves for men the exercise of royal powers, and in article 58, which reserves for the sons of the King or, where there are none, for Belgian princes of the branch of the royal family in line to the throne, the function of *ex officio* senators as from the age of 18 years, with entitlement to vote as from the age of 25 years.

Article 15, paragraphs 2 and 3

The application of article 15, paragraphs 2 and 3, shall not affect the validity of the interim provisions enacted for couples married before the entry into force of the Act of 14 July 1976 concerning the reciprocal rights and duties of husbands and wives and their marriage contracts, in cases where, in accordance with the option available to them under the Act, they have declared they are maintaining *in toto* their prior marriage contracts.

Brazil

[Original: English]
[1 February 1984]

Reservation

Brazil does not consider itself bound by article 29, paragraph 1, of the Convention.

China

[Original: Chinese]
[4 November 1980]

Reservation

The People's Republic of China does not consider itself bound by paragraph 1 of article 29 of the Convention.

Cuba

[Original: Spanish]
[17 July 1980]

Reservation

The Government of the Republic of Cuba makes a specific reservation concerning the provisions of article 29 of the Convention inasmuch as it holds that any disputes that may arise between States parties should be resolved by means of direct negotiations through the diplomatic channel.

Cyprus

[Original: English]
[23 July 1985]

Reservation

The Government of the Republic of Cyprus wishes to enter a reservation concerning the granting to women of equal rights with men with respect to the nationality of their children, mentioned in article 9, paragraph 2, of the Convention. This reservation is to be withdrawn upon amendment of the relevant Law.

Egypt

[Original: Arabic]
[18 September 1981]

Reservations

Article 9

Reservation to the text of article 9, paragraph 2, concerning the granting to women of equal rights with men with respect to the nationality of their children, without prejudice to the acquisition by a child born of a marriage of the nationality of his father. This is in order to prevent a child's acquisition of two nationalities, since this may be prejudicial to his future. It is clear that the child's acquisition of his father's nationality is the proce-dure most suitable for the child and that this does not infringe upon the principle of equality between men and women, since it is customary for a woman to agree, upon marrying an alien, that her children shall be of the father's nationality.

Article 16

Reservation to the text of article 16 concerning the equality of men and women in all matters relating to marriage and family relations during the marriage and upon its dissolution, without prejudice to the Islamic Shariah provisions whereby women are accorded rights equivalent to those of their spouses so as to ensure a just balance between them. This is out of respect for the sacrosanct nature of the firm religious beliefs which govern marital relations in Egypt and which may not be called in question and in view of the fact that one of the most important bases of these relations is an equivalency of rights and duties so as to ensure complementarity which guarantees true equality between the spouses, not a quasi-equality that renders the marriage a burden on the wife. The provisions of the Shariah lay down that the husband shall pay bridal money to the wife and maintain her fully and shall also make a payment to her upon divorce, whereas the wife retains full rights over her property and is not obliged to spend anything on her keep. The Shariah therefore restricts the wife's rights to divorce by making it contingent on a judge's ruling, whereas no such restriction is laid down in the case of the husband.

Article 29

The Egyptian delegation maintains the reservation contained in article 29, paragraph 2, concerning the right of a State signatory to the Convention to declare that it does not consider itself bound by paragraph 1 of that article concerning the submission to an arbitral body of any dispute which may arise between States concerning the interpretation or application of the Convention. This is in order to avoid being bound by the system of arbitration in this field.

General reservation to article 2

The Arab Republic of Egypt is willing to comply with the content of this article, provided that such compliance does not run counter to the Islamic Shariah.

El Salvador

[Original: Spanish]
[19 August 1981]

Reservation

The Government of El Salvador made a reservation with regard to the application of the provisions of article 29, paragraph 1, of the Convention.

Ethiopia

[Original: English]
[10 September 1981]

Reservation

Socialist Ethiopia does not consider itself bound by paragraph 1 of article 29 of the Convention.

Fiji

[Original: English]
[28 August 1995]

Reservation

... with reservations on articles 5 (a) and 9 of the Convention.

France

[Original: French]
[14 December 1983]

Declarations

The Government of the French Republic declares that the preamble to the Convention—in particular the eleventh preambular paragraph—contains debatable elements which are definitely out of place in this text.

The Government of the French Republic declares that the term "family education" in article 5 (b) of the Convention must be interpreted as meaning public education concerning the family and that, in any event, article 5 will be applied subject to respect for article 17 of the International Covenant on Civil and Political Rights and article 8 of the European Convention for the Protection of Human Rights and Fundamental Freedoms.

The Government of the French Republic declares that no provision of the Convention must be interpreted as prevailing over provisions of French legislation which are more favourable to women than to men.

Reservations

Article 14

1. The Government of the French Republic declares that article 14, paragraph 2 (c), should be interpreted as guaranteeing that women who fulfil the conditions relating to family or employment required by French legislation for personal participation shall acquire their own rights within the framework of social security.

2. The Government of the French Republic declares that article 14, paragraph 2 (h), of the Convention should not be interpreted as implying the actual provision, free of charge, of the services mentioned in that paragraph.

Article 16

The Government of the French Republic enters a reservation concerning the right to choose a family name

mentioned in article 16, paragraph 1 (g), of the Convention.

Article 29

The Government of the French Republic declares, in pursuance of article 29, paragraph 2, of the Convention, that it will not be bound by the provisions of article 29, paragraph 1.

Germany

[Original: English]
[10 July 1985]

Declaration

The right of peoples to self-determination, as enshrined in the Charter of the United Nations and in the International Covenants of 19 December 1966, applies to all peoples and not only to those living under alien and colonial domination and foreign occupation. All peoples thus have the inalienable right freely to determine their political status and freely to pursue their economic, social and cultural development. The Federal Republic of Germany would be unable to recognize as legally valid an interpretation of the right to self-determination which contradicts the unequivocal wording of the Charter of the United Nations and of the two International Covenants of 19 December 1966 on Civil and Political Rights and on Economic, Social and Cultural Rights. It will interpret the eleventh paragraph of the preamble accordingly.

Reservation

Article 7 (b) will not be applied to the extent that it contradicts the second sentence of article 12 (a) (4) of the Basic Law of the Federal Republic of Germany. Pursuant to this provision of the Constitution, women may on no account render service involving the use of arms.

India

[Original: English]
[9 July 1993]

Declarations

With regard to articles 5 (a) and 16 (1) of the Convention on the Elimination of All Forms of Discrimination against Women, the Government of the Republic of India declares that it shall abide by and ensure these provisions in conformity with its policy of non-interference in the personal affairs of any community without its initiative and consent.

With regard to article 16 (2) of the Convention on the Elimination of All Forms of Discrimination against Women, the Government of the Republic of India declares that, though in principle it fully supports the principle of compulsory registration of marriages, it is not practical in a vast country like India with its variety of customs, religions and level of literacy.

Reservation

With regard to article 29 of the Convention on the Elimination of All Forms of Discrimination against Women, the Government of the Republic of India declares that it does not consider itself bound by paragraph 1 of this article.

Indonesia

[Original: English]
[13 September 1984]

Reservation

The Government of the Republic of Indonesia does not consider itself bound by the provision of article 29, paragraph 1, of this Convention and takes the position that any dispute relating to the interpretation or application of the Convention may only be submitted to arbitration or to the International Court of Justice with the agreement of all the parties to the dispute.

Iraq

[Original: Arabic]
[13 August 1986]

Reservations

1. Approval of and accession to this Convention shall not mean that the Republic of Iraq is bound by the provisions of article 2, subparagraphs (f) and (g), of article 9, paragraphs 1 and 2, or of article 16 of the Convention. The reservations to this last-mentioned article shall be without prejudice to the provisions of the Islamic Shariah according women rights equivalent to the rights of their spouses so as to ensure a just balance between them. Iraq also enters a reservation to article 29, paragraph 1, of this Convention with regard to the principle of international arbitration in connection with the interpretation or application of this Convention.

2. This approval in no way implies recognition of or entry into any relations with Israel.

Ireland

[Original: English]
[23 December 1985]

Reservations

Article 13, subparagraphs (b) and (c)

The question of supplementing the guarantee of equality contained in the Irish Constitution with special legislation governing access to financial credit and other services and recreational activities, where these are pro-

vided by private persons, organizations or enterprises, is under consideration. For the time being, Ireland reserves the right to regard its existing law and measures in this area as appropriate for the attainment in Ireland of the objectives of the Convention.

Article 15

With regard to paragraph 3 of this article, Ireland reserves the right not to supplement the existing provisions in Irish law which accord women a legal capacity identical to that of men with further legislation governing the validity of any contract or other private instrument freely entered into by a woman.

Article 16, paragraphs 1 (d) and (f)

Ireland is of the view that the attainment in Ireland of the objectives of the Convention does not necessitate the extension to men of rights identical to those accorded by law to women in respect of the guardianship, adoption and custody of children born out of wedlock and reserves the right to implement the Convention subject to that understanding.

Israel

[Original: English]
[3 October 1991]

Reservations

The State of Israel hereby expresses its reservation with regard to article 7 (b) of the Convention concerning the appointment of women to serve as judges of religious courts where this is prohibited by the laws of any of the religious communities in Israel. Otherwise, the said article is fully implemented in Israel, in view of the fact that women take a prominent part in all aspects of public life.

The State of Israel hereby expresses its reservation with regard to article 16 of the Convention, in so far as the laws of personal status binding on the several religious communities in Israel do not conform with the provisions of that article.

Declaration

In accordance with paragraph 2 of article 29 of the Convention, the State of Israel hereby declares that it does not consider itself bound by paragraph 1 of that article.

Jamaica

[Original: English]
[19 October 1984]

Reservations

The Government of Jamaica declares that it does not consider itself bound by the provisions of article 29, paragraph 2, of the Convention.

The Government of Jamaica declares that it does not consider itself bound by the provisions of article 29, paragraph 1, of the Convention.

Jordan

[Original: Arabic]
[1 July 1992]

Reservation

Jordan does not consider itself bound by the following provisions:

(a) Article 9, paragraph 2;

(b) Article 15, paragraph 4 (a woman's residence and domicile are with her husband);

(c) Article 16, paragraph 1 (c), relating to the rights arising upon the dissolution of a marriage in connection with maintenance and compensation;

(d) Article 16, paragraphs 1 (d) and (g).

Kuwait

[Original: Arabic]
[2 September 1994]

Reservations

The Government of Kuwait enters a reservation regarding article 7 (a), inasmuch as the provision contained in that paragraph conflicts with the Kuwaiti Electoral Act, under which the right to be eligible for election and to vote is restricted to males.

The Government of Kuwait reserves its right not to implement the provision contained in article 9, paragraph 2, of the Convention, inasmuch as it runs counter to the Kuwaiti Nationality Act, which stipulates that a child's nationality shall be determined by that of his father.

The Government of the State of Kuwait declares that it does not consider itself bound by the provision contained in article 16, paragraph 1 (f), inasmuch as it conflicts with the provisions of the Islamic Shariah, Islam being the official religion of the State.

The Government of Kuwait declares that it is not bound by the provision contained in article 29, paragraph 1.

Lesotho

[Original: English]
[22 August 1995]

Declaration

The Government of the Kingdom of Lesotho declares that it does not consider itself bound by article 2 to the extent that it conflicts with Lesotho's constitutional stipulations relative to succession to the throne of the Kingdom of Lesotho and law relating to succession to chieftainship. The ratification by the Government of Lesotho is subject to the understanding that none of its obligations under the Convention, especially in article 2 (e), shall be treated as extending to the affairs of religious denominations.

Furthermore, the Government of Lesotho declares it shall not take any legislative measures under the Convention where those measures would be incompatible with the Constitution of Lesotho.

Libyan Arab Jamahiriya

[Original: Arabic]
[16 May 1989]

Reservation

Accession is subject to the general reservation that such accession cannot conflict with the laws on personal status derived from the Islamic Shariah.

On 5 July 1995, the Government of the Libyan Arab Jamahiriya notified the Secretary-General of its decision to modify, making it more specific, the general reservation it had made upon accession, to read as follows:

[Original: Arabic]
[5 July 1995]

The Socialist People's Libyan Arab Jamahiriya has declared its accession to the Convention on the Elimination of All Forms of Discrimination against Women, adopted by the General Assembly of the United Nations on 18 December 1979, with the following reservation:

1. Article 2 of the Convention shall be implemented with due regard for the peremptory norms of the Islamic Shariah relating to determination of the inheritance portions of the estate of a deceased person, whether female or male.

2. The implementation of article 16, paragraphs 1 (c) and (d) of the Convention shall be without prejudice to any of the rights guaranteed to women by the Islamic Shariah.

Luxembourg

[Original: French]
[2 February 1989]

Reservations

(a) The application of article 7 shall not affect the validity of the article of our Constitution concerning the hereditary transmission of the crown of the Grand Duchy of Luxembourg, in accordance with the family compact of the House of Nassau of 30 June 1783, maintained by article 71 of the Treaty of Vienna of 9 June 1815 and expressly maintained by article 1 of the Treaty of London of 11 May 1867.

(b) The application of paragraph 1 (g) of article 16

of the Convention shall not affect the right to choose the family name of children.

Malaysia

[Original: English]
[5 July 1995]

Reservation

The Government of Malaysia declares that Malaysia's accession is subject to the understanding that the provisions of the Convention do not conflict with the provisions of the Islamic Shariah law and the Federal Constitution of Malaysia. With regard thereto, further, the Government of Malaysia does not consider itself bound by the provisions of articles 2 (f), 5 (a), 7 (b), 9 and 16 of the aforesaid Convention.

In relation to article 11, Malaysia interprets the provisions of this article as a reference to the prohibition of discrimination on the basis of equality between men and women only.

Maldives

[Original: English]
[1 July 1993]

Reservations

The Government of the Republic of Maldives will comply with the provisions of the Convention, except those which the Government may consider contradictory to the principles of the Islamic Shariah, upon which the laws and traditions of the Maldives are founded.

Furthermore, the Republic of Maldives does not see itself bound by any provision of the Convention which obliges it to change its Constitution and laws in any manner.

Malta

[Original: English]
[8 March 1991]

Reservations

Article 11

The Government of Malta interprets paragraph 1 of article 11, in the light of the provisions of paragraph 2 of article 4, as not precluding prohibitions, restrictions or conditions on the employment of women in certain areas, or the work done by them, where this is considered necessary or desirable to protect the health and safety of women or the human foetus, including such prohibitions, restrictions or conditions imposed in consequence of other international obligations of Malta.

Article 13

(i) The Government of Malta reserves the right, notwithstanding anything in the Convention, to continue to apply its tax legislation, which deems, in certain circumstances, the income of a married woman to be the income of her husband and taxable as such.

(ii) The Government of Malta reserves the right to continue to apply its social security legislation, which in certain circumstances makes certain benefits payable to the head of the household, which is, by such legislation, presumed to be the husband.

Articles 13, 15 and 16

While the Government of Malta is committed to remove, in so far as possible, all aspects of family property law which may be considered as discriminatory to females, it reserves the right to continue to apply present legislation in that regard until such time as the law is reformed and during such transitory period until those laws are completely superseded.

Article 16

The Government of Malta does not consider itself bound by subparagraph (e) of paragraph 1 of article 16, in so far as the same may be interpreted as imposing an obligation on Malta to legalize abortion.

Mauritius

[Original: English]
[9 July 1984]

Reservations

The Government of Mauritius does not consider itself bound by subparagraphs (b) and (d) of paragraph 1 of article 11 and subparagraph (g) of paragraph 1 of article 16.

The Government of Mauritius does not consider itself bound by paragraph 1 of article 29 of the Convention, in pursuance of paragraph 2 of article 29.

Morocco

[Original: French]
[21 June 1993]

Declarations

Article 2

The Government of the Kingdom of Morocco expresses its readiness to apply the provisions of this article provided that:

—They are without prejudice to the constitutional requirements that regulate the rules of succession to the throne of the Kingdom of Morocco;

—They do not conflict with the provisions of the Islamic Shariah. It should be noted that certain of the provisions contained in the Moroccan Code of

Personal Status according women rights that differ from the rights conferred on men may not be infringed upon or abrogated because they derive primarily from the Islamic Shariah, which strives, among its other objectives, to strike a balance between the spouses in order to preserve the coherence of family life.

Article 15, paragraph 4

The Government of the Kingdom of Morocco declares that it can only be bound by the provisions of this paragraph, in particular those relating to the rights of women to choose their residence and domicile, to the extent that they are not incompatible with articles 34 and 36 of the Moroccan Code of Personal Status.

Reservations

Article 9, paragraph 2

The Government of the Kingdom of Morocco makes a reservation with regard to this article in view of the fact that the Law of Moroccan Nationality permits a child to bear the nationality of its mother only in the cases where it is born to an unknown father, regardless of place of birth, or to a stateless father, when born in Morocco, and it does so in order to guarantee to each child its right to a nationality. Further, a child born in Morocco of a Moroccan mother and a foreign father may acquire the nationality of its mother by declaring, within two years of reaching the age of majority, its desire to acquire that nationality, provided that, on making such declaration, its customary and regular residence is in Morocco.

Article 16

The Government of the Kingdom of Morocco makes a reservation with regard to the provisions of this article, particularly those relating to the equality of men and women in respect of rights and responsibilities on entry into and at dissolution of marriage. Equality of this kind is considered incompatible with the Islamic Shariah, which guarantees to each of the spouses the rights and responsibilities within a framework of equilibrium and complementarity in order to preserve the sacred bond of matrimony.

The provisions of the Islamic Shariah oblige the husband to provide a nuptial gift upon marriage and to support his family, while the wife is not required by law to support the family.

Furthermore, at dissolution of marriage, the husband is obliged to pay maintenance. In contrast, the wife enjoys complete freedom of disposition of her property during the marriage and upon its dissolution without supervision by the husband, the husband having no jurisdiction over his wife's property.

For these reasons, the Islamic Shariah confers the right of divorce on a woman only by decision of a Shariah judge.

Article 29

The Government of the Kingdom of Morocco does not consider itself bound by the first paragraph of this article, which provides that "any dispute between two or more States parties concerning the interpretation or application of the present Convention which is not settled by negotiation shall, at the request of one of them, be submitted to arbitration".

The Government of the Kingdom of Morocco is of the view that any dispute of this kind can only be referred to arbitration by agreement of all the parties to the dispute.

New Zealand

[Original: English]
[10 January 1985]

Reservations

The Government of New Zealand, the Government of the Cook Islands and the Government of Niue reserve the right not to apply the provisions of article 11 (2) (b).

The Government of New Zealand, the Government of the Cook Islands and the Government of Niue reserve the right not to apply the provisions of the Convention in so far as they are inconsistent with policies relating to recruitment into or service in:

(a) The armed forces which reflect either directly or indirectly the fact that members of such forces are required to serve on armed forces aircraft or vessels and in situations involving armed combat; or

(b) The law enforcement forces which reflect either directly or indirectly the fact that members of such forces are required to serve in situations involving violence or threat of violence;

The Government of the Cook Islands reserves the right not to apply article 2 (f) and article 5 (a) to the extent that the customs governing the inheritance of certain Cook Islands chief titles may be inconsistent with those provisions.

Poland

[Original: English]
[30 July 1980]

Reservation

The People's Republic of Poland does not consider itself bound by article 29, paragraph 1, of the Convention.

Republic of Korea

[Original: English]
[27 December 1984]

Reservation

The Government of the Republic of Korea, having examined the said Convention, hereby ratifies the Convention considering itself not bound by the provisions of article 9 and subparagraphs [...] (g) of paragraph 1 of article 16 of the Convention.

Romania

[Original: French]
[7 January 1982]

Reservations

The Socialist Republic of Romania states that it does not consider itself bound by the provisions of article 29, paragraph 1, of the Convention, whereby any dispute between two or more States parties concerning the interpretation or application of the Convention which is not settled by negotiation shall, at the request of one of them, be submitted to arbitration.

Romania believes that such disputes may be submitted to arbitration only with the consent of all States parties to the dispute, for each specific case.

Singapore

[Original: English]
[5 October 1995]

Reservation

In the context of Singapore's multi-racial and multi-religious society and the need to respect the freedom of minorities to practise their religious and personal laws, the Republic of Singapore reserves the right not to apply the provisions of articles 2 and 16 where compliance with these provisions would be contrary to their religious or personal laws.

Singapore is geographically one of the smallest independent countries in the world and one of the most densely populated. The Republic of Singapore accordingly reserves the right to apply such laws and conditions governing the entry into, stay in, employment of and departure from its territory of those who do not have the right under the laws of Singapore to enter and remain indefinitely in Singapore, and to the conferment, acquisitions and loss of citizenship of women who have acquired such citizenship by marriage and of children born outside Singapore.

Singapore interprets article 11, paragraph 1, in the light of the provisions of article 4, paragraph 2, as not precluding prohibitions, restrictions or conditions on the employment of women in certain areas, or on work done by them where this is considered necessary or desirable to protect the health and safety of women or the human foetus, including such prohibitions, restrictions or conditions imposed in consequence of other international obligations of Singapore, and considers that legislation in respect of article 11 is unnecessary for the minority of women who do not fall within the ambit of Singapore's employment legislation.

The Republic of Singapore declares, in pursuance of article 29, paragraph 2, of the Convention, that it will not be bound by the provisions of article 29, paragraph 1.

Spain

[Original: Spanish]
[5 January 1984]

Declaration

The ratification of the Convention by Spain shall not affect the constitutional provisions concerning succession to the Spanish crown.

Thailand

[Original: English]
[9 August 1985]

Declaration

The Royal Thai Government wishes to express its understanding that the purposes of the Convention are to eliminate discrimination against women and to accord to every person, men and women alike, equality before the law, and are in accordance with the principles prescribed by the Constitution of the Kingdom of Thailand.

Reservations

1. In all matters which concern national security maintenance of public order and service or employment in the military or paramilitary forces, the Royal Thai Government reserves its right to apply the provisions of the Convention on the Elimination of All Forms of Discrimination against Women, in particular articles 7 and 10, only within the limits established by national laws, regulations and practices.

...

3. The Royal Thai Government does not consider itself bound by the provisions of [...] article 16 and article 29, paragraph 1, of the Convention.

Trinidad and Tobago

[Original: English]
[12 January 1990]

Reservation

The Republic of Trinidad and Tobago declares that it does not consider itself bound by article 29 (1) of the said Convention, relating to the settlement of disputes.

Tunisia

[Original: Arabic]
[20 September 1985]

General declaration

The Tunisian Government declares that it shall not take any organizational or legislative decision in conformity with the requirements of this Convention where such a decision would conflict with the provisions of chapter I of the Tunisian Constitution.

Declaration concerning article 15, paragraph 4

In accordance with the provisions of the Vienna Convention on the Law of Treaties, dated 23 May 1969, the Tunisian Government emphasizes that the requirements of article 15, paragraph 4, of the Convention on the Elimination of All Forms of Discrimination against Women, and particularly that part relating to the right of women to choose their residence and domicile, must not be interpreted in a manner which conflicts with the provisions of the Personal Status Code on this subject, as set forth in chapters 23 and 61 of the Code.

Reservations

Article 9, paragraph 2

The Tunisian Government expresses its reservation with regard to the provisions in article 9, paragraph 2, of the Convention, which must not conflict with the provisions of chapter VI of the Tunisian Nationality Code.

Article 16, paragraphs 1 (c), (d), (f), (g) and (h)

The Tunisian Government considers itself not bound by article 16, paragraphs 1 (c), (d) and (f), of the Convention and declares that paragraphs 1 (g) and (h) of that article must not conflict with the provisions of the Personal Status Code concerning the granting of family names to children and the acquisition of property through inheritance.

Article 29, paragraph 1

The Tunisian Government declares, in conformity with the requirements of article 29, paragraph 2, of the Convention, that it shall not be bound by the provisions of paragraph 1 of that article, which specify that any dispute between two or more States parties concerning the interpretation or application of the present Convention which is not settled by negotiation shall be referred to the International Court of Justice at the request of any one of those parties.

The Tunisian Government considers that such disputes should be submitted for arbitration or consideration by the International Court of Justice only with the consent of all parties to the dispute.

Turkey

[Original: English]
[20 December 1985]

Declaration

Article 9, paragraph 1, of the Convention is not in conflict with the provisions of article 5, paragraph 1, and articles 15 and 17 of the Turkish Law on Nationality, relating to the acquisition of citizenship, since the intent of those provisions regulating acquisition of citizenship through marriage is to prevent statelessness.

Reservations

The Government of the Republic of Turkey [makes reservations] with regard to the articles of the Convention dealing with family relations which are not completely compatible with the provisions of the Turkish Civil Code, in particular, article 15, paragraphs 2 and 4, and article 16, paragraphs 1 (c), (d), (f) and (g), as well as with respect to article 29, paragraph 1. In pursuance of article 29, paragraph 2, of the Convention, the Government of the Republic of Turkey declares that it does not consider itself bound by paragraph1 of this article.

United Kingdom of Great Britain and Northern Ireland

[Original: English]
[7 April 1986]

Declarations and reservations

A. On behalf of the United Kingdom of Great Britain and Northern Ireland

(a) The United Kingdom understands the main purpose of the Convention, in the light of the definition contained in article 1, to be the reduction, in accordance with its terms, of discrimination against women, and does not therefore regard the Convention as imposing any requirement to repeal or modify any existing laws, regulations, customs or practices which provide for women to be treated more favourably than men, whether temporarily or in the longer term; the United Kingdom's undertakings under article 4, paragraph 1, and other provisions of the Convention are to be construed accordingly.

(b) The United Kingdom reserves the right to regard the provisions of the Sex Discrimination Act 1975, the Employment Protection (Consolidation) Act 1978, the Employment Act 1980, the Sex Discrimination (Northern Ireland) Order 1976, the Industrial Relations (No. 2) (Northern Ireland) Order 1976, the Industrial Relations (Northern Ireland) Order 1982, the Equal Pay Act 1970 (as amended) and the Equal Pay Act (Northern Ireland) 1970 (as amended), including the exceptions and exemptions contained in any of these Acts and Orders, as constituting appropriate measures for the practical realization of the objectives of the Convention in the social and economic circumstances of the United Kingdom, and to continue to apply these provisions accordingly; this reservation will apply equally to any future legislation which may modify or replace the above Acts and Orders on the understanding that the terms of such legislation will be compatible with the United Kingdom's obligations under the Convention.

(c) In the light of the definition contained in article 1, the United Kingdom's ratification is subject to the understanding that none of its obligations under the Convention shall be treated as extending to the succession to, or possession and enjoyment of, the Throne, the peerage, titles of honour, social precedence or armorial bearings, or as extending to the affairs of religious denominations or orders or to the admission into or service in the Armed Forces of the Crown.

(d) The United Kingdom reserves the right to continue to apply such immigration legislation governing entry into, stay in and departure from the United Kingdom as it may deem necessary from time to time and, accordingly, its acceptance of article 15 (4) and of the other provisions of the Convention is subject to the provisions of any such legislation as regards persons not at the time having the right under the law of the United Kingdom to enter and remain in the United Kingdom.

Article 1

With reference to the provisions of the Sex Discrimination Act 1975 and other applicable legislation, the United Kingdom's acceptance of article 1 is subject to the reservation that the phrase "irrespective of their marital status" shall not be taken to render discriminatory any difference of treatment accorded to single persons as against married persons, so long as there is equality of treatment as between married men and married women and as between single men and single women.

Article 2

In the light of the substantial progress already achieved in the United Kingdom in promoting the progressive elimination of discrimination against women, the United Kingdom reserves the right, without prejudice to the other reservations made by the United Kingdom, to give effect to subparagraphs (f) and (g) by keeping under review such of its laws and regulations as may still embody significant differences in treatment between men and women with a view to making changes to those laws and regulations when to do so would be compatible with essential and overriding considerations of economic policy. In relation to forms of discrimination more precisely prohibited by other provisions of the Convention, the

obligations under this article must (in the case of the United Kingdom) be read in conjunction with the other reservations and declarations made in respect of those provisions including the declarations and reservations of the United Kingdom contained in paragraphs (a) to (d) above.

With regard to subparagraphs (f) and (g) of this article the United Kingdom reserves the right to continue to apply its law relating to sexual offences and prostitution; this reservation will apply equally to any future law which may modify or replace it.

Article 9

The British Nationality Act 1981, which was brought into force with effect from January 1983, is based on principles which do not allow of any discrimination against women within the meaning of article 1 as regards acquisition, change or retention of their nationality or as regards the nationality of their children. The United Kingdom's acceptance of article 9 shall not, however, be taken to invalidate the continuation of certain temporary or transitional provisions which will continue in force beyond that date.

The United Kingdom reserves the right to take such steps as may be necessary to comply with its obligations under article 2 of the First Protocol to the Convention for the Protection of Human Rights and Fundamental Freedoms signed in Paris on 20 March 1952 and its obligations under paragraph 3 of article 13 of the International Covenant on Economic, Social and Cultural Rights opened for signature in New York on 19 December 1966, to the extent that the said provisions preserve the freedom of parental choice in respect of the education of children; and reserves also the right not to take any measures which may conflict with its obligation under paragraph 4 of article 13 of the said Covenant not to interfere with the liberty of individuals and bodies to establish and direct educational institutions, subject to the observation of certain principles and standards.

Article 10

The United Kingdom can only accept the obligations under subparagraph (c) of article 10 within the limits of the statutory powers of the central Government, in the light of the fact that the teaching curriculum, the provision of textbooks and teaching methods are reserved for local control and are not subject to central Government direction; moreover, the acceptance of the objective of encouraging coeducation is without prejudice to the right of the United Kingdom also to encourage other types of education.

Article 11

The United Kingdom interprets the "right to work"

referred to in paragraph 1 (a) as a reference to the "right to work" as defined in other human rights instruments to which the United Kingdom is a party, notably article 6 of the International Covenant on Economic, Social and Cultural Rights of 19 December 1966.

The United Kingdom interprets paragraph 1 of article 11 in the light of the provisions of paragraph 2 of article 4, as not precluding prohibitions, restrictions or conditions on the employment of women in certain areas, or on the work done by them, where this is considered necessary or desirable to protect the health and safety of women or the human foetus, including such prohibitions, restrictions or conditions imposed in consequence of other international obligations of the United Kingdom [...].

The United Kingdom reserves the right to apply all United Kingdom legislation and the rules of pension schemes affecting retirement pensions, survivors' benefits and other benefits in relation to death or retirement (including retirement on grounds of redundancy), whether or not derived from a social security scheme.

This reservation will apply equally to any future legislation which may modify or replace such legislation, or the rules of pension schemes, on the understanding that the terms of such legislation will be compatible with the United Kingdom's obligations under the Convention.

The United Kingdom reserves the right to apply the following provisions of United Kingdom legislation concerning the benefits specified:

(a) Social security benefits for persons engaged in caring for a severely disabled person under section 37 of the Social Security Act 1975 and section 37 of the Social Security (Northern Ireland) Act 1975;

(b) Increases of benefit for adult dependants under sections 44 to 47, 49 and 66 of the Social Security Act 1975 and under sections 44 to 47, 49 and 66 of the Social Security (Northern Ireland) Act 1975;

(c) Retirement pensions and survivors' benefits under the Social Security Acts 1975 to 1982 and the Social Security (Northern Ireland) Acts 1975 to 1982;

(d) Family income supplements under the Family Income Supplements Act 1970 and the Family Income Supplements Act (Northern Ireland) 1971.

This reservation will apply equally to any future legislation which may modify or replace any of the provisions specified in subparagraphs (a) to (d) above, on the understanding that the terms of such legislation will be compatible with the United Kingdom's obligations under the Convention.

The United Kingdom reserves the right to apply any non-discriminatory requirement for a qualifying period of employment or insurance for the application of the provisions contained in article 11 (2).

Article 13

The United Kingdom reserves the right, notwithstanding the obligations undertaken in article 13, or any other relevant article of the Convention, to continue to apply the income tax and capital gains tax legislation which:

(i) Deems for income tax purposes the income of a married woman living with her husband in a year, or part of a year, of assessment to be her husband's income and not to be her income (subject to the right of the husband and the wife to elect jointly that the wife's earned income shall be charged to income tax as if she were a single woman with no other income); and

(ii) Requires tax in respect of such income and of chargeable gains accruing to such a married woman to be assessed on her husband (subject to the right of either of them to apply for separate assessment) and consequently (if no such application is made) restricts to her husband the right to appeal against any such assessment and to be heard or to be represented at the hearing of any such appeal; and

(iii) Entitles a man who has his wife living with him, or whose wife is wholly maintained by him, during the year of assessment to a deduction from his total income of an amount larger than that to which an individual in any other case is entitled and entitles an individual whose total income includes any earned income of his wife to have that deduction increased by the amount of that earned income or by an amount specified in the legislation whichever is the less.

Article 15

In relation to article 15, paragraph 2, the United Kingdom understands the term "legal capacity" as referring merely to the existence of a separate and distinct legal personality.

In relation to article 15, paragraph 3, the United Kingdom understands the intention of this provision to be that only those terms or elements of a contract or other private instrument which are discriminatory in the sense described are to be deemed null and void, but not necessarily the contract or instrument as a whole.

Article 16

As regards paragraph 1 (f) of article 16, the United Kingdom does not regard the reference to the paramountcy of the interests of the children as being directly relevant to the elimination of discrimination against women, and declares in this connection that the legislation of the United Kingdom regulating adoption, while giving a principal position to the promotion of the children's welfare, does not give to the child's interests the same paramount place as in issues concerning custody over children.

The United Kingdom's acceptance of paragraph 1 of article 16 shall not be treated as either limiting the freedom of a person to dispose of his property as he wishes or as giving a person a right to property the subject of such a limitation.

B. *On behalf of the British Virgin Islands, the Falkland Islands (Malvinas), the Isle of Man, South Georgia and the South Sandwich Islands, and the Turks and Caicos Islands*

[*Same declarations and reservations as those made in respect of the United Kingdom under section A, paragraphs (a), (c) and (d), except that in the case of (d) they apply to the territories and their laws.*]

Article 1

[*Same reservation as the one made in respect of the United Kingdom except with regard to the absence of a reference to United Kingdom legislation.*]

Article 2

[*Same reservation as the one made in respect of the United Kingdom except that reference is made to the laws of the territories, and not to the laws of the United Kingdom.*]

Article 9

[*Same reservation as the one made in respect of the United Kingdom.*]

Article 11

[*Same reservations as those made in respect of the United Kingdom except that reference is made to the laws of the territories, and not to the laws of the United Kingdom.*]

Also, as far as the territories are concerned, the specific benefits listed and which may be applied under the provisions of these territories' legislation are as follows:

(a) Social security benefits for persons engaged in caring for a severely disabled person;

(b) Increases of benefit for adult dependants;

(c) Retirement pensions and survivors' benefits;

(d) Family income supplements.

This reservation will apply equally to any future legislation which may modify or replace any of the provisions specified in subparagraphs (a) to (d) above, on the understanding that the terms of such legislation will be compatible with the United Kingdom's obligations under the Convention.

The United Kingdom reserves the right to apply any non-discriminatory requirement for a qualifying period of employment or insurance for the application of the provisions contained in article 11 (2).

Articles 13, 15 and 16

[*Same reservations as those made in respect of the United Kingdom.*]

Venezuela

[Original: Spanish]
[2 May 1983]

Reservation

Venezuela makes a formal reservation with regard to article 29, paragraph 1, of the Convention, since it does not accept arbitration or the jurisdiction of the International Court of Justice for the settlement of disputes concerning the interpretation or application of this Convention.

Viet Nam

[Original: French]
[17 February 1982]

Reservation

In implementing this Convention, the Socialist Republic of Viet Nam will not be bound by the provisions of paragraph 1 of article 29.

Yemen*

[Original: Arabic]
[30 May 1984]

The Government of the People's Democratic Republic of Yemen declares that it does not consider itself bound by article 29, paragraph 1, of the said Convention, relating to the settlement of disputes which may arise concerning the application or interpretation of the Convention.

C. *Objections to certain declarations and reservations*

Objection by Argentina to the application of the Convention to the Falkland Islands (Malvinas) and South Georgia and the South Sandwich Islands by the United Kingdom, notified upon ratification

[Original: Spanish]
[4 April 1989]

The Republic of Argentina rejects the extension of the territorial application of the Convention on the Elimination of All Forms of Discrimination against Women, adopted by the United Nations General Assembly on 18 December 1979, to the Malvinas (Falkland) Islands, South Georgia and the South Sandwich Islands, notified b y

the*Ratification was effected by the former Democratic Yemen.

Government of the United Kingdom of Great Britain and Northern Ireland upon its ratification of that instrument on 7 April 1986.

The Republic of Argentina reaffirms its sovereignty over the aforementioned archipelagos, which are an integral part of its national territory, and recalls that the General Assembly has adopted resolutions 2065 (XX), 3160 (XXVIII), 31/49, 37/9, 38/12 and 39/6, in which a sovereignty dispute is recognized and the Governments of Argentina and the United Kingdom are urged to resume negotiations in order to find as soon as possible a peaceful and lasting solution to the dispute and their remaining differences relating to this question, through the good offices of the Secretary-General. The General Assembly has also adopted resolutions 40/21, 41/40, 42/19 and 43/25, which reiterate its request to the parties to resume such negotiations.

Communication of the United Kingdom concerning the objection of Argentina

[Original: English]
[27 November 1989]

The Government of the United Kingdom of Great Britain and Northern Ireland rejects the statement made by the Government of Argentina on 4 April 1989 regarding the Falkland Islands and South Georgia and the South Sandwich Islands. The Government of the United Kingdom of Great Britain and Northern Ireland has no doubt as to British sovereignty over the Falkland Islands and South Georgia and the South Sandwich Islands, and its consequent right to extend treaties to those Territories.

Objection by Austria to the reservations made by Maldives upon accession

[Original: English]
[26 October 1994]

The reservation made by the Maldives is incompatible with the object and purpose of the Convention and is therefore inadmissible under article 19 (c) of the Vienna Convention on the Law of Treaties and shall not be permitted, in accordance with article 28 (2) of the Convention on the Elimination of All Forms of Discrimination against Women. Austria therefore states that this reservation cannot alter or modify in any respect the obligations arising from the Convention for any State Party therein.

Objection by Canada to the reservations made by Maldives upon accession

[Original: English]
[25 October 1994]

In the view of the Government of Canada, this reservation is incompatible with the object and purpose of the Convention (article 28, paragraph 2). The Government of Canada therefore enters its formal objection to this reservation. This objection shall not preclude the entry into force of the Convention as between Canada and the Republic of Maldives.

Objection by Finland to the reservations made by Maldives upon accession

[Original: English]
[5 May 1994]

In the view of the Government of Finland, the unlimited and undefined character of the said reservations create serious doubts about the commitment of the reserving State to fulfil its obligations under the Convention. In their extensive formulation, they are clearly contrary to the object and purpose of the Convention. Therefore, the Government of Finland objects to such reservations.

The Government of Finland also recalls that the said reservations are subject to the general principle of treaty interpretation according to which a party may not invoke the provisions of its domestic law as a justification for failure to perform its treaty obligations.

The Government of Finland does not, however, consider that this objection constitutes an obstacle to the entry into force of the Convention between Finland and Maldives.

Objection by Denmark to the reservation made by the Libyan Arab Jamahiriya upon accession

[Original: English]
[3 July 1990]

The Government of Denmark has taken note of the reservation made by the Libyan Arab Jamahiriya when acceding to the Convention on the Elimination of All Forms of Discrimination against Women. In the view of the Government of Denmark this reservation is subject to the general principle of treaty interpretation according to which a party may not invoke the provisions of its internal law as justification for failure to perform a treaty.

Objection by Finland to the reservation made by the Libyan Arab Jamahiriya upon accession

[Original: English]
[8 June 1990]

The Government of Finland has examined the contents of the reservation made by the Libyan Arab Jamahiriya and considers the said reservation as being incompatible with the object and purpose of the Convention. The Government of Finland therefore enters its formal objection to this reservation.

This objection is not an obstacle to the entry into force of the said Convention between Finland and the Libyan Arab Jamahiriya.

*Objections by Germany to the reservations made by
Bangladesh, Iraq, the Libyan Arab Jamahiriya,
Malawi, Mauritius, Thailand and Turkey
upon accession and by Brazil, Egypt, Jamaica,
the Republic of Korea and Tunisia upon ratification*

[Original: English]

[10 July 1985]

The Federal Republic of Germany considers that the reservations made by Egypt regarding article 2, article 9, paragraph 2, and article 16, by Bangladesh regarding article 2, article 13 (a) and article 16, paragraphs 1 (c) and (f), by Brazil regarding article 15, paragraph 4, and article 16, paragraphs 1 (a), (c), (g) and (h), by Jamaica regarding article 9, paragraph 2, by the Republic of Korea regarding article 9 and article 16, paragraphs 1 (c), (d), (f) and (g), and by Mauritius regarding article 11, paragraphs 1 (b) and (d), and article 16, paragraph 1 (g), are incompatible with the object and purpose of the Convention (article 28, paragraph 2) and therefore objects to them. In relation to the Federal Republic of Germany, they may not be invoked in support of a legal practice which does not pay due regard to the legal status afforded to women and children in the Federal Republic of Germany in conformity with the above-mentioned articles of the Convention. This objection shall not preclude the entry into force of the Convention as between Egypt, Bangladesh, Brazil, Jamaica, the Republic of Korea, Mauritius and the Federal Republic of Germany.

Objections of the same nature were also formulated by the Government of the Federal Republic of Germany in regard to reservations made by various States, as follows:

(a) *15 October 1986*: In respect of reservations formulated by the Government of Thailand concerning article 9, paragraph 2, article 10, article 11, paragraph 1 (b), article 15, paragraph 3, and article 16. (The Federal Republic of Germany also holds the view that the reservation made by Thailand regarding article 7 of the Convention is likewise incompatible with the object and purpose of the Convention because for all matters which concern national security it reserves in a general and thus unspecific manner the right of the Royal Thai Government to apply the provisions only within the limits established by national laws, regulations and practices.);

(b) *15 October 1986*: In respect of reservations and some declarations formulated by the Government of Tunisia concerning article 9, paragraph 2, and article 16, as well as the declaration concerning article 15, paragraph 4;

(c) *3 March 1987*: In respect of reservations made by the Government of Turkey to article 15, paragraphs 2 and 4, and article 16, paragraphs 1 (c), (d), (f) and (g);

in respect of reservations made by the Government of Iraq with regard to article 2, subparagraphs (f) and (g), article 9 and article 16;

(d) *7 April 1988*: In respect of the first reservation made by the Government of Malawi;

(e) *20 June 1990*: In respect of the reservation made by the Government of the Libyan Arab Jamahiriya;

(f) *20 October 1994*: In respect of the reservations made by Maldives.

*Objection by Israel to the reservation made by Iraq
upon accession*

[Original: English]

[12 December 1986]

The Government of the State of Israel has noted that the instrument of accession by Iraq to the Convention on the Elimination of All Forms of Discrimination against Women contains a declaration in respect of Israel. In the view of the Government of the State of Israel, such declaration, which is explicitly of a political character, is incompatible with the purposes and objectives of the Convention and cannot in any way affect whatever obligations are binding upon Iraq under general international law or under particular conventions.

The Government of the State of Israel will, in so far as concerns the substance of the matter, adopt towards Iraq an attitude of complete reciprocity.

*Objections by Mexico to the reservations made by
Bangladesh, Cyprus, Iraq, the Libyan Arab
Jamahiriya, Mauritius, Thailand and Turkey
upon accession and by Egypt, Jamaica, New Zealand
and the Republic of Korea upon ratification;
communication regarding Malawi*

[Original: Spanish]

[11 January 1985]

The Government of the United Mexican States has studied the content of the reservations made by Mauritius to article 11, paragraphs 1 (b) and (d), and article 16, paragraph 1 (g), of the Convention and has concluded that they should be considered invalid in the light of article 28, paragraph 2, of the Convention, because they are incompatible with its object and purpose.

Indeed, these reservations, if implemented, would inevitably result in discrimination against women on the basis of sex, which is contrary to all the articles of the Convention. The principles of equal rights of men and women and non-discrimination on the basis of sex, which are embodied in the second preambular paragraph and article 1, paragraph 3, of the Charter of the United Nations, to which Mauritius is a signatory, and in articles 2 and 16 of the Universal Declaration of Human Rights of 1948, were previously accepted by the Government of

Mauritius when it acceded, on 12 December 1973, to the International Covenant on Civil and Political Rights and the International Covenant on Economic, Social and Cultural Rights. The above-mentioned principles were stated in article 2, paragraph 1, and article 3 of the former Covenant and in article 2, paragraph 2, and article 3 of the latter. Consequently, it is inconsistent with these contractual obligations previously assumed by Mauritius for its Government now to claim that it has reservations, on the same subject, about the 1979 Convention.

The objection of the Government of the United Mexican States to the reservations in question should not be interpreted as an impediment to the entry into force of the 1979 Convention between the United Mexican States and Mauritius.

Objections, identical in essence, *mutatis mutandis*, were also formulated by the Government of Mexico in regard to the reservations made by various States, as follows [for the States which were not Parties to the Covenants (marked below with an asterisk), the participation in the Covenants was not invoked by Mexico in its objection with regard to reservations]:

(a) *21 February 1985*: In respect of reservations made by the Government of Bangladesh concerning article 2, article 13, subparagraph (a), and article16, paragraphs 1 (c) and (f);

(b) *21 February 1985*: In respect of the reservation made by the Government of Jamaica concerning article 9, paragraph 2;

(c) *22 May 1985*: In respect of reservations made by the Government of New Zealand (applicable to the Cook Islands) concerning article 2, subparagraph (f), and article 5, subparagraph (a);

(d) *6 June 1985*: In respect of reservations made by the Government of the Republic of Korea concerning article 9 and article 16, paragraphs 1 (c), (d), (e), (f) and (g). In this case, the Government of Mexico stated that the principle of the equal rights of men and women and of non-discrimination on the basis of sex, which are set forth in the Charter of the United Nations as one of its purposes, in the Universal Declaration of Human Rights of 1948 and in various multilateral instruments, have already become general principles of international law which apply to the international community, to which the Republic of Korea belongs;

(e) *29 January 1986*: In respect of the reservation made by the Government of Cyprus to article 9, paragraph 2;

(f) *7 May 1986*: In respect of the reservations made by the Government of Turkey* to paragraphs 2 and 4 of article 15 and paragraphs 1 (c), (d), (f) and (g) of article 16;

(g) *16 July 1986*: In respect of the reservations made by the Government of Egypt to articles 9 and 16;

(h) *16 October 1986*: In respect of the reservations made by Thailand* concerning article 9, paragraph 2, article 15, paragraph 3, and article 16;

(i) *4 December 1986*: In respect of the reservations made by Iraq concerning article 2, subparagraphs (f) and (g), article 9, paragraphs 1 and 2, and article 16;

(j) *23 July 1990*: In respect of the reservation made by the Libyan Arab Jamahiriya.

The Secretary-General received from the Government of Mexico, on the date indicated below, a communication as follows:

Malawi, 5 August 1987: The Government of the United Mexican States hopes that the process of eradication of traditional customs and practices referred to in the first reservation of the Republic of Malawi will not be so protracted as to impair fulfilment of the purpose and intent of the Convention.

Objections by the Netherlands to the reservations made by Bangladesh, Iraq, the Libyan Arab Jamahiriya, Malawi, Maldives, Mauritius, Morocco, Thailand and Turkey upon accession and by Brazil, Egypt, India, Jamaica, the Republic of Korea and Tunisia upon ratification

[Original: English]
[23 July 1990]

The Government of the Kingdom of the Netherlands considers that the reservations made by Bangladesh regarding article 2, article 13, subparagraph (a), and article 16, paragraphs 1 (c) and (f), by Egypt regarding article 2, article 9 and article 16, by Brazil regarding article 15, paragraph 4, and article 16, paragraphs 1 (a), (c), (g) and (h), by Iraq regarding article 2, subparagraphs (f) and (g), article 9 and article 16, by Mauritius regarding article 11, paragraphs 1 (b) and (d), and article 16, paragraph 1 (g), by Jamaica regarding article 9, paragraph 2, by the Republic of Korea regarding article 9 and article 16, paragraphs 1 (c), (d), (f) and (g), by Thailand regarding article 9, paragraph 2, article 15, paragraph 3, and article16, by Tunisia regarding article 9, paragraph 2, article 15, paragraph 4, and article 16, paragraphs 1 (c), (d), (f), (g) and (h), by Turkey regarding article 15, paragraphs 2 and 4, and article 16, paragraphs 1 (c), (d), (f) and (g), by the Libyan Arab Jamahiriya upon accession, and the first paragraph of the reservations made by Malawi upon accession, are incompatible with the object and purpose of the Convention (article 28, paragraph 2).

These objections shall not preclude the entry into force of the Convention as between Bangladesh, Egypt, Brazil, Iraq, Mauritius, Jamaica, the Republic of Korea, Thailand, Tunisia, Turkey, the Libyan Arab Jamahiriya, Malawi and the Kingdom of the Netherlands.

[14 July 1994]

The Government of the Kingdom of the Netherlands considers that the declarations made by India regarding article 5, subparagraph (a), and article 16, paragraph 1, of the Convention are reservations incompatible with the object and purpose of the Convention (article 28, paragraph 2).

The Government of the Kingdom of the Netherlands considers that the declaration made by India regarding article 16, paragraph 2, of the Convention is a reservation incompatible with the object and purpose of the Convention (article 28, paragraph 2).

The Government of the Kingdom of the Netherlands considers that the declaration made by Morocco expressing the readiness of Morocco to apply the provisions of article 2 provided that they do not conflict with the provisions of the Islamic Shariah is a reservation incompatible with the object and purpose of the Convention (article 28, paragraph 2).

The Government of the Kingdom of the Netherlands considers that the declaration made by Morocco regarding article 15, paragraph 4, of the Convention is a reservation incompatible with the object and purpose of the Convention (article 28, paragraph 2).

The Government of the Kingdom of the Netherlands considers that the declaration made by Morocco regarding article 9, paragraph 2, and article 16 of the Convention are reservations incompatible with the object and purpose of the Convention (article 28, paragraph 2).

The Government of the Kingdom of the Netherlands has examined the reservations made by Maldives, by which "the Government of the Republic of Maldives will comply with the provisions of the Convention, except those which the Government may consider contradictory to the principles of the Islamic Shariah, upon which the laws and traditions of the Maldives are founded", and the Republic of Maldives declares that it "does not see itself bound by any provisions of the Convention which obliges it to change its Constitution and laws in any manner". The Government of the Kingdom of the Netherlands considers the said reservations incompatible with the object and purpose of the Convention.

The Government of the Kingdom of the Netherlands objects to the above-mentioned declarations and reservations.

These objections shall not preclude the entry into force of the Convention as between India, Morocco, Maldives and the Kingdom of the Netherlands.

Objections by Norway to the reservations made by Kuwait, the Libyan Arab Jamahiriya and Maldives upon accession

[Original: English]
[16 July 1990]

The Government of Norway has examined the contents of the reservation made by the Libyan Arab Jamahiriya, by which the accession "is subject to the general reservation that such accession cannot conflict with the laws on personal status derived from the Islamic Shariah". The Norwegian Government has come to the conclusion that this reservation is incompatible with the object and purpose of the Convention (art. 28, para. 2). The Government of Norway objects to the reservation.

The Norwegian Government will stress that, by acceding to the Convention, a State commits itself to adopt the measures required for the elimination of discrimination, in all forms and manifestations, against women. A reservation by which a State party limits its responsibilities under the Convention by invoking religious law (Shariah), which is subject to interpretation, modification and selective application in different States adhering to Islamic principles, may create doubts about the commitments of the reserving State to the object and purpose of the Convention. It may also undermine the basis of international treaty law. All States have a common interest in securing that all parties respect the treaties to which they have chosen to become parties.

[25 October 1994]

In the view of the Government of Norway, a reservation by which a State party limits its responsibilities under the Convention by invoking general principles of internal law may create doubts about the commitments of the reserving State to the object and purpose of the Convention and, moreover, contribute to undermine the basis of international treaty law. It is in the common interest of States that treaties to which they have chosen to become parties also are respected, as to their object and purpose, by all parties. Furthermore, under well-established international treaty law, a State is not permitted to invoke internal law as justification for its failure to perform its treaty obligations. For these reasons, the Government of Norway objects to the reservations of Maldives.

The Government of Norway does not consider this objection to constitute an obstacle to the entry into force of the above-stated Convention between the Kingdom of Norway and the Republic of Maldives.

[28 April 1995]

The Government of Norway has examined the content of the reservations made by Kuwait upon accession and stresses that, by acceding to the Convention, a State commits itself to adopt the measures required for the elimination of discrimination, in all its forms and manifestations, against women. A reservation by which a State party limits its responsibilities under the Convention by invoking internal or religious law may create doubts about the commitments of the reserving State to the object and purpose of the Convention. Furthermore, under well-established international treaty law, a State may not invoke the provisions of its internal law as justification for its failure to perform a treaty. It is in the common interest of States that treaties to which they have chosen to become parties also are respected, as to their object and purpose, by all parties. For these reasons, the Government of Norway objects to the Kuwaiti reservation.

The Government of Norway does not consider this objection to preclude the entry into force of the above-stated Convention between the Kingdom of Norway and the State of Kuwait.

Objection by Portugal to the reservation made by Maldives upon accession

[Original: English]
[26 October 1994]

The Government of Portugal considers that the reservations formulated by the Maldives are incompatible with the object and purpose of the Convention and are inadmissible under article 19 (c) of the Vienna Convention on the Law of Treaties.

Furthermore, the Government of Portugal considers that these reservations cannot alter or modify in any respect the obligations arising from the Convention for any State party thereto.

Objections by Sweden to the reservations made by Bangladesh, Iraq, the Libyan Arab Jamahiriya, Malawi, Maldives, Mauritius and Thailand upon accession and by Brazil, Egypt, Jamaica, Jordan, New Zealand, the Republic of Korea and Tunisia upon ratification

[Original: English]
[17 March 1986]

The Government of Sweden considers that [the following reservations] are incompatible with the object and purposes of the Convention (art. 28, para. 2), and therefore objects to them:

— Thailand regarding article 9, paragraph 2, article 15, paragraph 3, and article 16;
— Tunisia regarding article 9, paragraph 2, article 15, paragraph 4, and article 16, paragraphs 1 (c), (d), (f), (g) and (h);
— Bangladesh regarding article 2, article 13, subparagraph (a), and article 16, paragraphs 1 (c) and (f);

— Brazil regarding article 15, paragraph 4, and article 16, paragraphs 1 (a), (c), (g) and (h).

Indeed the reservations in question, if put into practice, would inevitably result in discrimination against women on the basis of sex, which is contrary to everything the Convention stands for. It should also be borne in mind that the principles of equal rights of men and women and of non-discrimination on the basis of sex are set forth in the Charter of the United Nations as one of its purposes, in the Universal Declaration of Human Rights of 1948 and in various multilateral instruments, to which Thailand, Tunisia and Bangladesh are parties.

The Government of Sweden furthermore notes that, as a matter of principle, the same objection could be made to the reservations made by:

— Egypt regarding article 2, article 9, paragraph 2, and article 16;
— Mauritius regarding article 11, paragraphs 1 (b) and (d), and article 16, paragraph 1 (g);
— Jamaica regarding article 9, paragraph 2;
— Republic of Korea regarding article 9 and article 16, paragraphs 1 (c), (d), (f) and (g);
— New Zealand in respect of the Cook Islands regarding article 2, subparagraph (f), and article 5, subparagraph (a).

In this context, the Government of Sweden wishes to take this opportunity to make the observation that the reason why reservations incompatible with the object and purpose of a treaty are not acceptable is precisely that otherwise they would render a basic international obligation of a contractual nature meaningless. Incompatible reservations, made in all forms of discrimination against women, do not only cast doubts on the commitments of the reserving States to the objects and purpose of this Convention, but, moreover, contribute to undermine the basis of international contractual law. It is in the common interest of States that treaties to which they have chosen to become parties also are respected, as to object and purpose, by other parties.

Subsequently, the Secretary-General received from the Government of Sweden, on the dates indicated below, objections of the same nature as the ones above with regard to the reservations made by the following States:

— *12 March 1987*: With regard to the reservations made by Iraq to article 2, subparagraphs (f) and (g), article 9, paragraph 1, and article 16;
— *15 April 1988*: With regard to the first reservation made by Malawi;
— *25 May 1990*: With regard to the reservation made by the Libyan Arab Jamahiriya;
— *5 February 1993*: With regard to the reservations made by Jordan in respect of article 9, paragraph 2,

article 15, paragraph 4, the wording of article 16, paragraphs 1 (c), (d) and (g);

—*26 October 1994*: With regard to the reservations made by Maldives upon accession. The Government of Sweden objects to these reservations and considers that they constitute an obstacle to the entry into force of the Convention between Sweden and the Republic of Maldives.

D. Notifications of withdrawal of certain reservations

Belarus, Ukraine and the Russian Federation

In communications received on 8 March 1989, and 19 and 20 April 1989, respectively, the Governments of the Union of Soviet Socialist Republics, the Byelorussian Soviet Socialist Republic and the Ukrainian Socialist Republic notified the Secretary-General that they had decided to withdraw the reservations made upon their ratification relating to article 29, paragraph 1. The reservations were identical in essence, *mutatis mutandis*, to the reservation made by the Union of Soviet Socialist Republics.

Brazil

On 20 December 1994, the Government of Brazil notified the Secretary-General that it had decided to withdraw the following reservation made upon signature and confirmed upon ratification:

"The Government of the Federative Republic of Brazil hereby expresses its reservations to article 15, paragraph 4, and to article 16, paragraphs 1 (a), (c), (g) and (h) of the Convention on the Elimination of All Forms of Discrimination against Women."

Bulgaria

On 24 June 1992, the Government of Bulgaria notified the Secretary-General of its decision to withdraw the reservation to article 29, paragraph 1, of the Convention, made upon signature and confirmed upon ratification.

Canada

On 28 May 1992, the Government of Canada notified the Secretary-General of its decision to withdraw the declaration relating to article 11, paragraph 1 (d), of the Convention made upon ratification.

France

In a notification received on 26 March 1984, the Government of France informed the Secretary-General of its decision to withdraw the reservation to article 7 of the Convention made upon ratification. The notification specified that the withdrawal was effected because Or-ganic Law No. 83-1096 of 20 December 1983 had abrogated article LO 128 of the electoral code relating to temporary disqualifications of persons who have obtained French nationality.

Subsequently, in a notification received on 21 July 1986, the Government of France informed the Secretary-General that it had decided to withdraw its reservation relating to article 15, paragraphs 2 and 3, and article 16, paragraphs 1 (c), (d) and (h) of the Convention, made upon ratification. The notification specified that the withdrawal was effected because the existing discriminatory provisions against women in the rules governing property rights arising out of a matrimonial relationship and in those concerning the legal administration of the property of children had been abrogated by Act No. 85-1372 of 23 December 1985 concerning equality of spouses in respect of property rights arising out of a matrimonial relationship and equality of parents in respect of the property of minor children, which entered into force on 1 July 1986.

Hungary

In a communication received on 8 December 1989, the Government of Hungary notified the Secretary-General that it had decided to withdraw the reservation in respect of article 29, paragraph 1, made upon ratification.

Ireland

On 19 December 1986, the Government of Ireland notified the Secretary-General of its withdrawal of the reservations made upon accession in respect of article 9, paragraph 1, article 11, paragraph 1, article 13, subparagraph (a), and article 15, paragraph 4.

Jamaica

On 8 September 1995, the Government of Jamaica notified the Secretary-General of its decision to withdraw its reservation with regard to article 9, paragraph 2, of the Convention, which it had made upon ratification of the Convention.

Malawi

On 24 October 1991, the Government of Malawi notified the Secretary-General of its decision to withdraw the following reservations made upon accession:

"Owing to the deep-rooted nature of some traditional customs and practices of Malawians, the Government of the Republic of Malawi shall not, for the time being, consider itself bound by such of the provisions of the Convention as require immediate eradication of such traditional customs and practices.

"While the Government of the Republic of Malawi accepts the principles of article 29, paragraph 2 of the Convention this acceptance should nonetheless be read in conjunction with [its] declaration of 12 December 1966 concerning the recognition, by the Government of the Republic of Malawi, of the jurisdiction of the International Justice, under article 36, paragraph 2, of the Statute of the Court, as compulsory."

Mongolia

In a communication received on 19 July 1990, the Government of Mongolia notified the Secretary-General of its decision to withdraw the reservation made upon ratification with respect to article 29, paragraph 1.

New Zealand

On 13 January 1989, the Secretary-General received from the Government of New Zealand a communication notifying him that, after consultation with the Government of the Cook Islands and the Government of Niue, it had denounced the Convention concerning the employment of women on underground work in mines of all kinds (ILO Convention No. 45) on 23 June 1987 and that in accordance with article 28, paragraph 3, of the Convention on the Elimination of All Forms of Discrimination against Women, it had withdrawn the reservation made upon ratification.

Republic of Korea

On 15 March 1991, the Government of the Republic of Korea notified the Secretary-General of its decision to withdraw the reservation it had made upon ratification of the Convention to the extent that it applied to paragraphs 1 (c), (d) and (f) of article 16.

Thailand

On 25 January 1991, the Government of Thailand notified the Secretary-General of its decision to withdraw the reservation made upon its accession to the Convention, to the extent that it applied to article 11, paragraph 1 (b), and article 15, paragraph 3.

Subsequently, on 26 October 1992, the Government of Thailand notified the Secretary-General of its decision to withdraw one of the reservations made upon accession to the Convention, i.e., that relating to article 9, paragraph 2, which reservation read as follows:

"2. With regard to article 9, paragraph 2, [...], the Royal Thai Government considers that the application of the said provisions shall be subject to the limits and criteria established by national law, regulations and practices."

United Kingdom of Great Britain and Northern Ireland

On 4 January 1995, the Government of the United Kingdom of Great Britain and Northern Ireland notified the Secretary-General of its decision to withdraw the reservation with respect to article 13 as well as the following declaration with respect to article 11 which it had made upon ratification of the Convention. The declaration read as follows:

"... the United Kingdom declares that, in the event of a conflict between obligations under the present Convention and its obligations under the Convention concerning the employment of women on underground work in mines of all kinds (ILO Convention No. 45), the provisions of the last mentioned Convention shall prevail."

1/ *Multilateral Treaties Deposited with the Secretary-General*: Status as at 31 December 1994 (United Nations publication, Sales No. E.95.V.5).

Annex I

Status of declarations, reservations, objections and notifications of withdrawal of reservations by States parties related to articles of the Convention on the Elimination of all Forms af Discrimination against Women

State party	Articles for which declarations or reservations have been made	States parties that have raised objections	Articles for which reservations have been withdrawn
Argentina	29, para. 1		
Australia	11, para. 2 (b)		
Austria	7, para. (b) 11, para. 1 (f)		

State party	Articles for which declarations or reservations have been made	States parties that have raised objections	Articles for which reservations have been withdrawn
Bahamas	2, para. (a) 9, para. 2 16, para. 1 (h) 29, para. 1		
Bangladesh	2	Germany Mexico Netherlands Sweden	
	13, para. (a)	Germany Mexico Netherlands Sweden	
	16, paras. 1 (c) and (f)	Germany Mexico Netherlands Sweden	
Belarus	[29, para. 1]		29, para. 1
Belgium	7		
	15, paras. 2 and 3		
Brazil	[15, para. 4]	Germany Netherlands Sweden	15, para. 4
	[16, paras. 1 (a), (c), (g) and (h)]	Germany Netherlands Sweden	16, paras. 1 (a), (c), (g) and (h)
	29, para. 1		
Bulgaria	[29, para. 1]		29, para. 1
Canada	[11, para. 1 (d)]		11, para 1 (d)
Chile	General declaration		
China	29, para. 1		
Cuba	29, para. 1		
Cyprus	9, para. 2	Mexico	
Egypt	2	Germany Netherlands Sweden	
	9, para. 2	Germany Mexico Netherlands Sweden	
	16	Germany Mexico Netherlands Sweden	

State party	Articles for which declarations or reservations have been made	States parties that have raised objections	Articles for which reservations have been withdrawn
	29, para. 1	Mexico	
El Salvador	29, para. 1		
Ethiopia	29, para. 1		
Fiji	5, para. (a), 9		
France	[7],		7
	14, paras. 2 (c) and (h)]		
	[15, paras. 2 and 3]		15, paras. 2 and 3
	[16, paras. 1 (c), (d) and (h)		16, paras. 1 (c),
	16, para. 1 (g)		(d) and (h)
	29, para. 1		
Germany	General declaration:		
	7, para. (b)		
Hungary	[29, para. 1]		29, para. 1
India	5, para. (a)	Netherlands	
	16, para. 1	Netherlands	
	16, para. 2	Netherlands	
	29, para. 1		
Indonesia	29, para. 1		
Iraq	2, paras. (f) and (g)	Germany	
		Mexico	
		Netherlands	
		Sweden	
	9, para. 1	Sweden	
	9, paras. 1 and 2	Germany	
		Israel	
		Mexico	
		Netherlands	
		Sweden	
	16	Germany	
		Mexico	
		Netherlands	
		Sweden	
	29, para. 1	Sweden	
Ireland	[9, para. 1]		9, para. 1
	[11, para. 1]		11, para. 1
	[13, para. (a)]		13, para. (a)
	13, paras. (b) and (c)		
	15, para. 3		
	[15, para. 4]		15, para. 4
	16, paras. 1 (d) and (f)		
Israel	7, para. (b)		
	16		
	29, para. 1		
Jamaica	[9, para. 2]	Germany	9, para. 2
		Mexico	
		Netherlands	
		Sweden	

State party	Articles for which declarations or reservations have been made	States parties that have raised objections	Articles for which reservations have been withdrawn
	29, para. 1		
Jordan	9, para. 2	Sweden	
	15, para. 4	Sweden	
	16, paras. 1 (c), (d) and (g)	Sweden	
Kuwait	7, para. (a)	Norway	
	9, para. 2	Norway	
	16, para. 1 (f)	Norway	
	29, para. 1	Norway	
Lesotho	2, para. (e)		
Libyan Arab Jamahiriya	General	Denmark	
		Finland	
		Germany	
		Mexico	
		Netherlands	
		Norway	
		Sweden	
	2		
	16, paras. 1 (c) and (d)		
Luxembourg	7		
	16, para. 1 (g)		
Malawi	[5]	Germany	5
		Mexico	
		Netherlands	
		Sweden	
	[29, para. 2]		29, para. 2
Malaysia	2, para. (f)		
	5, para. (a)		
	7, para. (b)		
	9		
	16		
Maldives	2	Austria	
		Canada	
		Finland	
		Germany	
		Netherlands	
		Norway	
		Portugal	
		Sweden	
Malta	11, para. 1		
	13		
	15		
	16, para. 1 (e)		
Mauritius	11, paras. 1 (b) and (d)	Germany	
		Mexico	
		Netherlands	
		Sweden	
	16, para. 1 (g)	Germany	

State party	Articles for which declarations or reservations have been made	States parties that have raised objections	Articles for which reservations have been withdrawn
		Mexico	
		Netherlands	
		Sweden	
	29, para. 1		
Mongolia	[29, para. 1]		29, para. 1
Morocco	2	Netherlands	
	9, para. 2	Netherlands	
	15, para. 4	Netherlands	
	16	Netherlands	
	29		
New Zealand (Cook Islands)	2, para. (f)	Mexico	
		Sweden	
(Cook Islands)	5, para. (a)	Mexico	
		Sweden	
(Cook Islands and Niue)	11, para. 2 (b)		
Poland	29, para. 1		
Republic of Korea	9	Germany	
		Mexico	
		Netherlands	
		Sweden	
	16, paras. 1 [(c), (d) and (f)] (g)	Germany	16, paras. 1 (c), (d) and (f)
		Mexico	
		Netherlands	
		Sweden	
Romania	29, para. 1		
Russian Federation	[29, para. 1]		29, para. 1
Singapore	2		
	16		
	11, para. 1		
	29, para. 1		
Spain	7 (declaration)		
Thailand	7	Germany	
	[9, para. 2]	Germany	9, para. 2
		Mexico	
		Netherlands	
		Sweden	
	10	Germany	
		Mexico	
	[11, para. 1 (b)]	Germany	11, para. 1 (b)
	[15, para. 3]	Germany	15, para. 3
		Mexico	
		Netherlands	

State party	Articles for which declarations or reservations have been made	States parties that have raised objections	Articles for which reservations have been withdrawn
	16	Sweden Germany Mexico Netherlands Sweden	
Trinidad and Tobago	29, para. 1		
Tunisia	29, para. 1		
	9, para. 2	Germany Netherlands Sweden	
	15, para. 4	Germany Netherlands Sweden	
	16, paras. 1 (c), (d), (f), (g) and (h)	Germany Netherlands Sweden	
	29, para. 1		
Turkey	9, para. 1 (declaration)		
	15, paras. 2 and 4	Germany Netherlands	
	16, paras. 1 (c), (d), (f) and (g)	Germany Mexico Netherlands	
	29, para. 1		
Ukraine	[29, para. 1]		29, para. 1
United Kingdom of Great Britain and Northern Ireland	(declarations) 1 2, paras. (f) and (g) 9 10, para. (c) 11, paras. 1 and 2 [13] 15, paras. 2 and 3 16, para. 1	Argentina	11, para. 1 (part) 13
on behalf of: British Virgin Islands, Falkland Islands (Malvinas), Isle of Man, South Georgia and South Sandwich Islands, and Turks and Caicos Islands	(declarations) 1, 2, 9, 11, 13, 15, 16		
Venezuela	29, para. 1		
Viet Nam	29, para. 1		
Yemen	29, para. 1		

Annex II

*Articles of the Convention on the Elimination of all Forms of Discrimination against Women for which
States parties have not yet withdrawn their reservations*

Article	State party
1	United Kingdom and on behalf of: British Virgin Islands, Falkland Islands (Malvinas), South Georgia and South Sandwich Islands, and Turks and Caicos Islands
2	Bangladesh, Egypt, Libyan Arab Jamahiriya, Maldives, Morocco, Singapore, United Kingdom and on behalf of: British Virgin Islands, Falkland Islands (Malvinas), South Georgia and South Sandwich Islands, and Turks and Caicos Islands
2, para. (a)	Bahamas
2, para. (e)	Lesotho
2, para. (f)	Malaysia, New Zealand (Cook Islands)
2, paras. (f) and (g)	Iraq, United Kingdom
5, para. (a)	Fiji, India, Malaysia, New Zealand (Cook Islands)
7	Belgium, Luxembourg, Spain, Thailand
7, para. (a)	Kuwait
7, para. (b)	Austria, Germany, Israel, Malaysia
9	Fiji, Malaysia, Republic of Korea, United Kingdom and on behalf of: British Virgin Islands, Falkland Islands (Malvinas), South Georgia and South Sandwich Islands, and Turks and Caicos Islands
9, paras. 1 and 2	Iraq
9, para. 2	Bahamas, Cyprus, Egypt, Jordan, Kuwait, Morocco, Tunisia
10	Thailand
10, para. (c)	United Kingdom
11	United Kingdom and on behalf of: British Virgin Islands, Falkland Islands (Malvinas), South Georgia and South Sandwich Islands, and Turks and Caicos Islands
11, para. 1	Malta, Singapore
11, paras. 1 (b) and (d)	Mauritius
11, para. 1 (f)	Austria
11, para. 2 (b)	Australia, New Zealand (Cook Islands and Niue)
13	Malta, United Kingdom on behalf of: British Virgin Islands, Falkland Islands (Malvinas), South Georgia and South Sandwich Islands, and Turks and Caicos Islands
13, para. (a)	Bangladesh
13, paras. (b) and (c)	Ireland
14, para. 2 (c)	France
14, para. 2 (h)	France
15	Malta
15, paras. 2 and 3	Belgium, United Kingdom and on behalf of: British Virgin Islands, Falkland Islands (Malvinas), South Georgia and South Sandwich Islands, and Turks and Caicos Islands
15, paras. 2 and 4	Turkey
15, para. 3	Ireland
15, para. 4	Jordan, Morocco, Tunisia
16	Egypt, Iraq, Israel, Malaysia, Malta, Morocco, Singapore, Thailand
16, para. 1	India
16, para. 1 (f)	United Kingdom and on behalf of: British Virgin Islands, Falkland Islands (Malvinas), South Georgia and South Sandwich Islands, and Turks and Caicos Islands
16, paras. 1 (c) and (d)	Libyan Arab Jamahiriya

Article	State party
16, paras. 1 (c), (d), (f) and (g)	Turkey
16, paras. 1 (c), (d), (f), (g) and (h)	Tunisia
16, paras. 1 (c), (d), (g)	Jordan
16, paras. 1 (c) and (f)	Bangladesh
16, paras. 1 (d) and (f)	Ireland
16, para. 1 (f)	Kuwait
16, para. 1 (e)	Malta
16, para. 1 (g)	France, Luxembourg, Mauritius, Republic of Korea
16, para. 1 (h)	Bahamas
16, para. 2	India
29, para. 1	Argentina, Bahamas, Brazil, China, Cuba, Egypt, El Salvador, Ethiopia, France, India, Indonesia, Iraq, Israel, Jamaica, Kuwait, Mauritius, Morocco, Poland, Romania, Singapore, Thailand, Trinidad and Tobago, Tunisia, Turkey, Venezuela, Viet Nam, Yemen

V Subject index to documents

[*This subject index to the documents reproduced in this book should be used in conjunction with the index on pages 840-845. A complete listing of the documents indexed below appears on pages 91-100.*]

Child abuse.
See: Battered women. Crime victims.

Child development.
– Document 130

Child health.
– Document 130

Child needs.
– Document 130

Child nutrition.
– Document 130

Child refugees.
– Documents 103, 105, 108, 116
See also: Women refugees.

Child welfare.
– Document 14
See also: Family welfare. Maternal welfare. Rights of the child.

Children.
– Document 44
See also: Family. Girls. Rights of the child.

Chile—Women's status.
– Documents 45, 70

China.
– Document 105

Civil and political rights.
– Documents 7-8, 12, 19, 21, 35
See also: Right of petition. Right to vote. Women's rights.

Collective self-reliance.
– Document 76
See also: Self-reliance. Technical cooperation among developing countries.

Colonial countries.
– Document 77

Colonialism.
– Documents 48, 50

Compulsory education.
– Document 57
See also: Educational policy. Literacy. School attendance.

Conference and meeting services.
– Documents 68, 94, 111

Conference of the International Women's Year (1975 : Mexico City).
– Document 42

Conferences.
See: International Conference... UN Conference... World Conference... Pledging conferences.

Consensual union.
– Documents 31, 34

Consultations.
– Documents 91, 95, 100, 133

Consultative Committee on the Voluntary Fund for the United Nations Decade for Women.
– Document 80

Convention for the Suppression of the Traffic in Persons and of the Exploitation of the Prostitution of Others (1949).
– Documents 18, 124, 132

Convention on Consent to Marriage, Minimum Age for Marriage and Registration of Marriages (1962).
– Document 31

Convention on the Elimination of All Forms of Discrimination against Women (1979).
– Documents 50, 69, 94, 111, 117-118, 121, 123-124, 139

Convention on the Elimination of All Forms of Discrimination against Women (1979). Protocols, etc. (Draft).
– Document 138

Convention on the Nationality of Married Women (1957).
– Document 29

Convention on the Political Rights of Women (1952).
– Document 26

Convention on the Prevention and Punishment of the Crime of Genocide (1948).
– Document 134

Convention on the Rights of the Child (1989).
– Documents 124, 130

Conventions.
See: Equal Remuneration Convention. International Convention... Treaties.

Cooperation between organizations.
– Document 8
See also: Inter-agency cooperation.

Cooperatives.
– Document 96

Coordination within UN system.
– Documents 8, 23, 55, 81, 85, 90, 93, 110, 129, 133, 135
See also: Inter-agency cooperation. Resident coordinators. Specialized agencies.

Costa Rica.
– Document 64

Crime prevention.
– Documents 132, 134

Crime victims.
– Document 110
See also: Battered women. Rape victims.

Criminal investigation.
– Document 134

D

Data analysis.
– Document 62

Data collection.
– Documents 62, 89, 103, 105, 108, 116
See also: Qustionnaires. Statistical data.

Databases.
– Documents 55, 128

Day care services.
– Documents 84, 116, 136

Debt.
– Document 116
See also: Credit. External debt. Loans.

Decision-making.
– Documents 85, 88, 90-91, 95, 100-103, 105,
  108-109, 116
See also: Policy-making.

Declaration of Mexico on the Equality of Women
and Their Contribution to Development and Peace
(1975).
– Documents 45, 48-49

Declaration of the World Summit for Social
Development (1995).
– Document 122

Declaration on the Elimination of Discrimination
against Women (1967).
– Documents 33, 36

Declaration on the Elimination of Violence against
Women (1993).
– Documents 105, 107-108, 110, 116, 133

Declaration on the Participation of Women in
Promoting International Peace and Cooperation
(1982).
– Document 75

Declaration on the Protection of Women and
Children in Emergency and Armed Conflict (1974).
– Document 44

Declarations.
– Documents 14, 17, 33, 36, 44-45, 48-49, 75,
  105-108, 110, 116, 127, 131, 133

Declarations and reservations.
See: Reservations and declarations.

Denmark.
– Documents 64, 68

Developed market economies.
– Document 120
See also: Economies in transition.

Developing countries.
– Documents 30, 32, 37, 103, 105
See also: Least developed countries. Technical
cooperation among developing countries.

Development.
See: Economic development. Regional development.
Rural development. Social development. Women in
development.

Development assistance.
– Documents 23, 30, 32, 37, 70
See also: International economic relations. Technical
cooperation.

Development planning.
– Documents 53, 76

Disabled women.
– Documents 45, 70, 84, 90-91, 95, 100, 103, 105,
  108, 116

Disarmament.
– Documents 48, 50
See also: International security. Peace.

Discrimination.
See: Age discrimination. Equality. Human rights
violations. Prejudices. Racial discrimination. Sex
discrimination. Tolerance.

Displaced persons.
– Document 134
See also: Humanitarian assistance. Internal
migration. War victims.

Domestic trade.
– Document 86
See also: Illicit traffic.

Domestic violence.
– Documents 70, 93, 102, 110, 115
See also: Battered women. Family.

Drinking water.
– Documents 70, 76

E

Economic development.
– Documents 23, 93
See also: Agricultural development. Industrial development. Rural development. Sustainable development.

Economic growth.
– Document 135

Economic policy.
– Document 125
See also: Resources allocation.

Economic reform.
– Document 120
See also: Structural adjustment.

Economic, social and cultural rights.
– Documents 8, 35
See also: Right to education. Right to health. Rights of the child. Women's rights.

Economic statistics.
– Document 102

Economic surveys.
– Documents 74, 86, 91, 95, 103, 105, 108-109
See also: Social surveys.

Economic trends.
– Document 120

Economies in transition.
– Document 120
See also: Developed market economies.

Education.
– Documents 22, 28, 37, 39, 45, 57, 62, 65, 70, 87, 93, 99, 102-103, 108, 116, 119, 122, 127, 130
See also: Non-formal education. Primary education. Right to education. Secondary education. Technical education. Vocational education.

Education for peace.
– Documents 84, 93
See also: Human rights education. Peace.

Educational assistance.
– Document 57
See also: Fellowships. Scholarships. Training programmes.

Educational policy.
– Document 22
See also: Compulsory education. Right to education.

Educational research.
– Document 99

Educational statistics.
– Document 22

El Salvador—Women's status.
– Document 70

Elections.
See: Right to vote.

Employment.
– Document 122
See also: Promotion. Women's employment.

Employment statistics.
– Document 125

Energy policy.
– Documents 76, 86

Entrepreneurship.
– Document 125

Environment.
– Document 103

Environmental impact assessment.
– Document 116
See also: Sustainable development.

Environmental protection.
– Document 126
See also: Sustainable development.

Equal opportunity.
– Documents 12, 16, 20, 22, 24, 27, 38-40, 45, 49, 52, 57, 62, 70, 75, 84-85, 87, 90-91, 95, 99-100, 103, 105, 108, 113, 116, 122, 125
See also: Recruitment. Sexual harassment. Social justice. Women's employment.

Equal pay.
– Documents 11, 13-15, 41, 87
See also: Racial discrimination. Sex discrimination. Wages. Women's employment.

Equal Remuneration Convention (1951).
– Document 41

Equality.
– Documents 1, 11, 14, 35, 37, 39, 41, 47, 50, 65, 87, 98, 102, 106, 113, 116-117, 122, 130, 135
See also: Social justice.

Ethnic cleansing.
– Document 134
See also: Genocide.

Europe—Women's status.
– Document 93

European Security and Cooperation.
– Document 134

Evaluation.
– Document 135
See also: Programme evaluation.

Human rights.
– Documents 3, 14, 17, 37, 48, 75, 94, 108, 116, 118, 131-132
See also: Civil and political rights. Economic, social and cultural rights. Women's rights. Workers' rights.

Human rights education.
– Document 110
See also: Education for peace.

Human rights in armed conflicts.
– Documents 44, 110, 115, 134
See also: Armed conflicts. Genocide. Law of war. War crimes. War victims.

Human rights violations.
– Documents 108, 110
See also: Genocide. Religious intolerance. Slavery. War crimes. Written communications.

Humanitarian assistance.
– Document 134
See also: Displaced persons. Refugee assistance.

I

Illicit traffic.
– Documents 18, 112, 124, 132
See also: Domestic trade. International trade. Migrant workers. Prostitution. Slavery.

Illiteracy.
– Documents 22, 57, 93, 99
See also: Literacy. Literacy programmes.

ILO.
See: International Labour Organization.

Informal sector.
– Document 102

Information dissemination.
– Documents 45, 49, 55, 58, 62, 68, 70, 76, 84-85, 94-95, 111, 118, 135
See also: Public information.

Information exchange.
– Documents 55, 110

Institution building.
– Documents 5, 87, 95-96, 100, 103, 105, 108, 116, 132, 135
See also: Rural institutions.

Institutional machinery.
– Documents 80, 85, 100, 129, 135
See also: Treaty-monitoring bodies.

Inter-agency cooperation.
– Documents 81, 85, 90-91, 108, 110, 117
See also: Coordination within UN system.

Internal migration.
– Document 120
See also: Displaced persons. Rural-urban migration.

International Committee of the Red Cross.
– Document 134

International Conference on Human Rights (1968 : Tehran).
– Document 37

International Conference on Population and Development (1994 : Cairo).
– Documents 108, 116, 131

International Convention on the Protection of the Rights of All Migrant Workers and Members of Their Families (1990).
– Document 133

International Covenant on Civil and Political Rights (1966).
– Document 35

International Covenant on Economic, Social and Cultural Rights (1966).
– Document 35

International Day for the Abolition of Slavery (2 Dec.).
– Document 132

International days.
– Document 132

International decades.
– Documents 49, 55, 58-60, 62, 64, 70, 72-74, 76, 84, 88, 103, 105, 108

International Drinking Water Supply and Sanitation Decade (1981-1990).
– Documents 70, 76

International economic relations.
– Documents 76, 79
See also: Development assistance.

International financial institutions.
– Document 135

International instruments.
– Documents 21, 37, 45, 50, 55, 57, 112, 115, 124, 127, 132
See also: Declarations. Treaties.

International Labour Organization.
– Documents 15, 23, 57

International Literacy Year (1990).
– Document 99

International migration.
– Document 120

International obligations.
– Document 115
See also: Reservations and declarations. Treaties. Treaty-monitoring bodies.

International security.
– Documents 48, 50, 61
See also: Disarmament. Peace.

International Task Force on Literacy.
– Document 99

International trade.
– Documents 86, 120
See also: Illicit traffic.

International Tribunal for the Prosecution of Persons Responsible for Serious Violations of International Humanitarian Law Committed in the Territory of the Former Yugoslavia Since 1991.
– Document 134

International Women's Day (8 Mar.).
– Document 128

International Women's Year (1975).
– Documents 41-42, 45-47, 49, 59

International years.
– Documents 41-42, 45-47, 49, 59, 99

Interregional Consultation on Women in Public Life (Proposed).
– Documents 100, 103

K

Kenya.
– Documents 77, 82

L

Labour law.
– Documents 23, 112
See also: Trade unions. Wages. Workers' rights.

Land.
– Document 126

Languages.
– Documents 90-91, 95, 100, 103, 105, 108

Latin America—Women's status.
– Document 93

Law of war.
– Document 134
See also: Human rights in armed conflicts.

Laws and regulations.
– Document 37

Least developed countries.
– Documents 68, 103, 105, 108, 116

Lebanon—Women's status.
– Document 70

Legal aid.
– Document 132
See also: Social services.

Legal services.
– Document 133

Literacy.
– Documents 95, 99-100, 103, 108, 116
See also: Compulsory education. Illiteracy.

Literacy programmes.
– Document 99
See also: Illiteracy. Non-formal education.

Loans.
– Document 51
See also: Credit. Debt.

Location of offices.
– Document 73

M

Marriage.
– Documents 31, 34, 102
See also: Consensual union. Family.

Married women.
– Documents 11-12, 17, 29

Maternal and child health.
– Documents 23, 39
See also: Child health. Mothers.

Maternal welfare.
– Documents 14, 45, 70, 84, 87, 116
See also: Child welfare. Family welfare.

Maternity leave.
– Document 84
See also: Salaries and allowances. Women workers. Women's employment.

Migrant workers.
– Document 100
See also: Illicit traffic. Women migrant workers.

Migrant workers' families.
– Document 133
See also: Women migrant workers.

Mothers.
– Documents 14, 84, 87
See also: Maternal and child health. Maternal welfare.

Muslim women.
– Document 45

N

Nairobi Forward-looking Strategies for the Advancement of Women (1985).
– Documents 84-85, 87-91, 93-95, 97-98, 100, 103, 105, 108, 116, 120, 135

Namibia—Women's status.
– Document 70

National liberation movements.
– Documents 42, 48

Nationality.
– Documents 17, 29

Non-formal education.
– Document 52
See also: Basic education. Literacy programmes.

Non-governmental organizations.
– Documents 8, 82, 99, 108, 116

Non-self-governing territories.
– Documents 25, 28
See also: Colonial countries. Trust territories.

Nutrition.
– Documents 23, 70
See also: Child nutrition.

O

Occupational health.
– Document 23
See also: Workers' rights.

Organization for Security and Cooperation in Europe.
– Document 134

Organizational change.
– Document 136

P

Palestinians.
– Documents 45, 66

Participants.
– Documents 42, 63, 68, 74, 105, 108

Peace.
– Documents 48, 50, 61, 75, 84, 93, 127, 129
See also: Disarmament. Education for peace. International security.

Peaceful coexistence.
– Document 48
See also: Regional cooperation.

Periodic reports.
– Documents 85, 94, 108, 111, 118, 135
See also: Reporting procedures.

Personnel management.
– Documents 16, 20, 24, 38, 40, 83, 95, 101, 114, 136
See also: Promotion. Recruitment. Salaries and allowances. Staffing.

Platform for Action of the Fourth World Conference on Women (1995).
– Documents 116-117, 127, 129-130, 135

Pledging conferences.
– Document 59

Policy-making.
– Documents 39-40
See also: Decision-making.

Political participation.
– Documents 2, 21, 26, 50, 58, 87, 90-91, 93, 130
See also: Right to vote. Women in politics.

Popular participation.
– Documents 2, 8, 39, 45, 47, 50, 58, 61, 85, 102, 122, 127, 130
See also: Women in development.

Population.
– Documents 100, 103, 108, 116, 131

Pornography.
– Document 115
See also: Sex crimes.

Poverty.
– Document 109
See also: Social justice. Socially disadvantaged persons.

Poverty mitigation.
– Documents 93, 108, 116-117, 127
See also: Poverty. Social welfare.

Prejudices.
– Document 110
See also: Religious intolerance. Tolerance.

Primary education.
– Document 22

Private law.
– Document 28

Professional staff.
– Documents 24, 38, 40, 85, 90-91, 94-95, 101, 114, 128, 136
See also: General service staff. Geographical distribution of UN staff.

Professional workers.
– Documents 88, 90-91, 95, 108
See also: Lawyers. Teaching personnel.

Programme evaluation.
– Documents 46, 49, 70, 85, 103, 105, 108

Programme implementation.
– Documents 45-46, 49, 58-59, 62, 70-72, 85, 116, 129, 135

Programme of Action for the Second Half of the United Nations Decade for Women: Equality, Development and Peace (1980).
– Documents 62, 70-72

Programme of Action of the International Conference on Population and Development (1994).
– Document 113

Programme planning.
– Document 116

Programme priorities.
– Document 116

Promotion.
– Documents 24, 114, 128, 136
See also: Employment. Personnel management.

Prosecution.
– Document 134

Prostitution.
– Documents 18, 70, 115, 124, 132
See also: Forced prostitution. Sex crimes. Slavery.

Public information.
– Documents 58, 85, 90-91, 100, 103, 105, 108, 116
See also: Information dissemination.

Publications.
– Documents 86, 92, 102-103, 105, 108-109, 119

Q

Questionnaires.
– Document 12
See also: Social research. Social surveys.

R

Racial discrimination.
– Documents 48, 70
See also: Apartheid. Equal pay.

Radio programmes.
– Documents 85, 90-91, 95, 100, 103, 105, 108, 116

Rape.
– Documents 110, 115
See also: Forced prostitution. War crimes.

Rape victims.
– Document 134
See also: Battered women. Sex crimes.

Recruitment.
– Documents 114, 128, 136
See also: Equal opportunity.

Refugee assistance.
– Documents 67, 103
See also: Child refugees. Displaced persons. Humanitarian assistance. Repatriation. Women refugees.

Refugee women.
See: Women refugees.

Regional commissions.
– Document 135

Regional cooperation.
– Documents 85, 135
See also: Peaceful coexistence.

Regional development.
– Document 93

Regional programmes.
– Documents 45, 49, 55

Rehabilitation.
– Documents 132, 134

Religious intolerance.
– Document 110
See also: Human rights violations. Prejudices. Tolerance.

Repatriation.
– Document 132

Reporting procedures.
– Documents 90-91, 94, 118
See also: Periodic reports.

Reproductive freedom.
See: Family planning.

Research institutions.
See: Training and research institutions.

Reservations and declarations.
– Documents 118, 139
See also: International obligations. Signatures, accessions, ratifications.

Resident coordinators.
– Document 135
See also: Coordination within UN system.

Resources allocation.
– Documents 45, 110
See also: Economic policy. Financing. Staffing.

Resources mobilization.
– Documents 100, 103, 130, 135

Right of petition.
– Document 121

Right to education.
– Documents 8, 12
See also: Education. Educational policy.

Right to health.
– Document 108

Right to vote.
– Documents 19, 21, 26
See also: Political participation.

Rights of the child.
– Documents 11, 124, 130
See also: Child welfare. Children.

Roosevelt, Eleanor.
– Document 2

Rules of procedure.
– Document 68

Rural areas.
– Documents 52, 96, 103, 105, 108, 116, 126, 131

Rural development.
– Documents 52, 93, 95-96
See also: Agricultural development. Economic development. Social development.

Rural institutions.
– Document 96
See also: Institution building.

Rural-urban migration.
– Documents 126, 131
See also: Urbanization.

S

Salaries and allowances.
– Documents 20, 24
See also: Maternity leave. Personnel management. Subsistence allowance.

Sanitation.
– Document 76

Scholarships.
– Document 57
See also: Educational assistance. Fellowships.

School attendance.
– Document 99
See also: Compulsory education.

Science and technology.
– Documents 86, 100, 103, 108, 116

Secondary education.
– Document 22

Self-reliance.
– Documents 86, 95, 100, 103, 105, 108
See also: Collective self-reliance.

Seminar on Women and Rural Development, Programmes and Projects (1989 : Vienna).
– Documents 95-96

Sex crimes.
– Documents 110, 115
See also: Pornography. Prostitution. Rape. Rape victims.

Sex discrimination.
– Documents 11, 19, 22, 33, 36, 45, 50, 69-70, 93-94, 102, 110-111, 118, 121, 124, 139
See also: Age discrimination. Equal pay. Women's rights.

Sexual harassment.
– Documents 110, 114-115, 128
See also: Equal opportunity.

Signatures, accessions, ratifications.
– Documents 26, 41, 50, 94, 111, 118, 132-133, 139
See also: Reservations and declarations. Treaties.

Slavery.
– Document 132
See also: Forced prostitution. Prostitution.

Slavery Convention (1926).
– Document 133

Social change.
– Documents 100, 105
See also: Organizational change.

Social development.
– Documents 61, 93, 100, 108, 116, 122, 131
See also: Rural development.

Social indicators.
– Document 133

Social justice.
– Documents 90-91
See also: Equal opportunity. Equality. Poverty.

Social research.
– Document 45
See also: Educational research. Questionnaires.

Social security.
– Documents 23, 45

Social services.
– Documents 93, 100, 103, 105, 108, 112, 116, 133
See also: Day care services. Health services. Legal aid.

Social statistics.
– Documents 93, 105, 108, 116
See also: Educational statistics.

Social surveys.
– Documents 100, 116
See also: Economic surveys. Questionnaires.

Social welfare.
– Document 70
See also: Child welfare. Family welfare. Maternal welfare. Poverty mitigation.

Socially disadvantaged persons.
– Document 99
See also: Poverty.

Socio-economic indicators.
– Document 90
See also: Social indicators.

South Africa—Women's status.
– Document 70

Special rapporteurs.
– Documents 108, 110, 116

Specialized agencies.
– Document 8
See also: Coordination within UN system.

Staffing.
– Documents 103, 135
See also: Personnel management. Resources allocation.

Standards.
– Documents 55, 132

State responsibility.
– Document 115

Statistical data.
– Documents 19-20, 22, 24, 86, 93, 114, 120, 125, 128
See also: Data collection.

Statistical methodology.
– Document 116

Sterility.
See: Fertility.

Strategic Plan of Action for the Improvement of the Status of Women in the Secretariat (1995-2000).
– Document 128

Structural adjustment.
– Document 120
See also: Economic reform.

Subsistence allowance.
– Document 116

Surveys.
See: Economic surveys. Questionnaires. Social surveys.

Sustainable development.
– Documents 102, 104-105, 108, 116, 131, 135
See also: Environmental impact assessment. Environmental protection.

System-wide Medium-term Plan for the Advancement of Women: Equality, Development and Peace, 1996-2001 (Draft).
– Documents 95, 100, 103, 105, 108, 116, 130

System-wide Medium-term Plan for Women and Development, 1990-1995.
– Documents 89, 93

T

Teaching personnel.
– Document 99

Technical cooperation.
– Documents 23, 30, 32, 37, 39, 45, 55, 62, 80-81, 111, 132
See also: Advisory services. Development assistance.

Technical cooperation among developing countries.
– Document 76
See also: Collective self-reliance. Developing countries. Focal points.

Technical education.
– Documents 22, 57
See also: Vocational education.

Tolerance.
– Document 133
See also: Prejudices. Religious intolerance.

Top-echelon staff.
– Documents 40, 100-101, 103, 105, 108

Trade unions.
– Document 133
See also: Labour law.

Traffic in persons.
See: Prostitution. Slavery.

Training and research institutions.
– Documents 39, 45, 49, 54-55, 70, 76, 79

Training programmes.
– Documents 23, 39, 51-52, 58, 76, 79, 96, 110, 114, 118, 128, 132, 136
See also: Educational assistance.

Treaties.
– Documents 18, 26, 29, 31, 35, 37, 41, 57, 69-70, 94, 111-112, 118, 121, 123, 130, 133-134, 138-139
See also: International obligations. Signatures, accessions, ratifications.

Treaty reservations and declarations.
See: Reservations and declarations.

Treaty-monitoring bodies.
– Documents 111, 116
See also: Institutional machinery. International obligations.

Trust Fund for the Fourth World Conference on Women.
– Documents 108, 116

Trust funds.
– Documents 108, 116

Trust territories.
– Documents 25, 28

U

UN—Budget.
– Documents 85, 94, 97, 116, 118, 135

UN—Medium-term plan.
– Documents 90-91, 95

UN—Organizational structure.
– Document 49

UN—Personnel questions.
– Documents 16, 20, 24, 27, 38, 40, 83, 90-91, 95, 101, 103, 105, 108, 114, 128, 136-137

UN—Staff composition.
– Documents 16, 20, 24, 27, 38, 40, 83, 88, 100-101, 103, 105, 108, 114, 116, 128, 136

UN. Ad Hoc Committee on the Restructuring of the Economic and Social Sectors of the United Nations System.
– Document 49

UN. Branch for the Advancement of Women.
– Documents 85, 88, 90-91

UN. Centre for Human Rights.
– Documents 108, 110, 116, 132-133

UN. Centre for Social Development and Humanitarian Affairs.
– Documents 71-72, 88-91, 95, 100, 103, 105, 108

UN. Commission on Crime Prevention and Criminal Justice.
– Document 132

UN. Commission on Human Rights—Establishment.
– Document 3

UN. Commission on Human Rights—Terms of Reference.
– Document 3

UN. Commission on Human Rights. Special Rapporteur on the Human Rights Situation in the Territory of the Former Yugoslavia.
– Document 134

UN. Commission on Human Rights. Special Rapporteur on Violence against Women.
– Documents 110, 124, 133

UN. Commission on Human Rights. Subcommission on the Status of Women—Establishment.
– Document 3

UN. Commission on Human Rights. Subcommission on the Status of Women—Members.
– Document 4

UN. Commission on Human Rights. Subcommission on the Status of Women—Terms of Reference.
– Document 3

UN. Commission on Human Rights. Subcommission on the Status of Women—Chairman.
– Document 5

UN. Commission on Sustainable Development.
– Documents 105, 108, 116

UN. Commission on the Status of Women.
– Documents 10, 37, 39, 46, 50, 61, 70, 81, 85, 88, 91, 94, 100, 103, 105, 108, 110-111, 116-118, 121, 129, 135

UN. Commission on the Status of Women—Establishment.
– Document 6

UN. Commission on the Status of Women—Terms of reference.
– Documents 6, 8-9

UN. Commission on the Status of Women—Work organization.
– Document 90

UN. Commission on the Status of Women—Work programme.
– Documents 89, 97, 135

UN. Commission on the Status of Women—Open-ended Working Group on the Equalization of Opportunities for Disabled Persons.
– Document 103

UN. Commission on the Status of Women (1st sess. : 1947 : Lake Success, New York).
– Document 8

UN. Commission on the Status of Women (2nd sess. : 1948 : Lake Success, New York).
– Document 12

UN. Commission on the Status of Women (3rd sess. : 1949 : Beirut).
– Documents 12, 16, 19, 21

UN. Commission on the Status of Women (8th sess. : 1954 : New York).
– Document 27

UN. Commission on the Status of Women (26th sess. : 1976 : Geneva).
– Document 55

UN. Commission on the Status of Women (29th sess. : 1982 : Vienna).
– Document 72

UN. Commission on the Status of Women (34th sess. : 1990 : Vienna).
– Document 95

UN. Commission on the Status of Women (38th sess. : 1994 : New York).
– Document 108

UN. Commission on the Status of Women (39th sess. : 1995 : New York).
– Document 116

UN. Commission on the Status of Women (1987 sess. : New York).
– Documents 88, 90-91

UN. Committee on the Elimination of Discrimination against Women.
– Documents 99, 103, 105, 110-111, 117, 129, 135

UN. Committee on the Elimination of Discrimination against Women—Work organization.
– Documents 94, 118, 121, 123

UN. Committee on the Elimination of Discrimination against Women (8th sess. : 1989 : Vienna).
– Document 94

UN. Committee on the Elimination of Discrimination against Women (12th sess. : 1993 : Vienna).
– Document 118

UN. Committee on the Elimination of Discrimination against Women (13th sess. : 1994 : New York).
– Document 118

UN. Committee on the Elimination of Discrimination against Women (14th sess. : 1995 : New York).
– Documents 118, 121

UN. Committee on the Elimination of Discrimination against Women (15th sess. : 1996 : New York).
– Document 118

UN. Coordinator for the Improvement of the Status of Women in the Secretariat.
– Documents 85, 90

UN. Department for Policy Coordination and Sustainable Development.
– Document 116

UN. Department of Public Information.
– Documents 90-91, 95, 100, 103, 105, 108, 116

UN. Division for the Advancement of Women.
– Documents 93-94, 108, 110, 116, 129, 133, 135

UN. Economic and Social Council.
– Documents 129, 135

UN. General Assembly.
– Documents 129, 135

UN. General Assembly (30th sess. : 1975)—Agenda.
– Document 42

UN. International Research and Training Institute for the Advancement of Women.
– Documents 45, 55, 59, 70, 72, 79, 88, 90-91, 93, 117, 129, 135

UN. International Research and Training Institute for the Advancement of Women—Budget contributions.
– Document 79

UN. International Research and Training Institute for the Advancement of Women—Establishment.
– Documents 49, 54

UN. International Research and Training Institute for the Advancement of Women—Financing.
– Documents 49, 54

UN. International Research and Training Institute for the Advancement of Women—Organizational structure.
– Document 76

UN. International Research and Training Institute for the Advancement of Women—Terms of reference.
– Documents 78-79

UN. International Research and Training Institute for the Advancement of Women—Work programme.
– Document 76

UN. Office of the Focal Point for Women in the Secretariat.
– Document 128

UN. Preparatory Body for the World Conference to Review and Appraise the Achievements of the United Nations Decade For Women : Equality, Development and Peace.
– Documents 74, 77, 82

UN. Preparatory Committee for the World Conference of the UN Decade for Women : Equality, Development and Peace .
– Documents 60, 68

UN. Preparatory Committee for the World Summit for Social Development.
– Document 117

UN. Secretariat—Staff composition.
– Documents 83, 88, 100-101, 103, 105, 108, 114, 116, 128-129

UN. Secretary-General.
– Documents 19-24, 27, 76, 93, 111-112, 114, 120, 124-126, 128-129, 138

UN. Special Commission on the In-depth Study of the United Nations Intergovernmental Structure and Functions in the Economic and Social Fields.
– Document 90

UN. Statistical Division.
– Document 117

UN. Steering Committee for the Improvement of the Status of Women in the Secretariat.
– Document 128

UN. Subcommission on Prevention of Discrimination and Protection of Minorities.
– Document 110

UN. Subcommission on Prevention of Discrimination and Protection of Minorities. Working Group on Contemporary Forms of Slavery.
– Document 132

UN Conference on Environment and Development (1992 : Rio de Janeiro, Brazil).
– Documents 104-105, 108, 131

UN Conference on Human Settlements (Habitat II) (1996 : Istanbul, Turkey).
– Document 131

UN Decade for Women : Equality, Development and Peace (1976-1985).
– Documents 49, 55, 58-60, 62, 64, 67, 70, 72-74, 76, 84-85, 88, 103, 105, 108

UN Development Fund for Women.
– Documents 88, 90-91, 93, 110, 117, 129, 135

UN High Commissioner for Human Rights.
– Documents 132-133

UN High Commissioner for Refugees.
– Document 134

UN Trust Fund for the International Research and Training Institute for the Advancement of Women.
– Document 79

Unemployment.
See: Employment.

United Nations Development Programme (UNDP).
– Documents 80, 99, 110, 117, 135

United Nations Educational, Scientific and Cultural Organization (UNESCO).
– Documents 22, 57, 99, 130, 134

UNESCO Plan of Action for the Eradication of Illiteracy by the Year 2000 (1989).
– Document 99

United Nations Children's Fund (UNICEF).
– Documents 99, 130, 134

Universal Declaration of Human Rights (1948).
– Documents 14, 17

Universities and colleges.
– Document 22

Urbanization.
– Document 126
See also: Rural-urban migration.

V

Vienna Declaration and Programme of Action (1993).
– Documents 106, 110, 116

Viet Nam—Women's status.
– Document 45

Violence.
– Documents 105, 107, 110, 112, 115, 127, 130, 133-134
See also: Domestic violence.

Vocational education.
– Document 57
See also: Technical education.

Vocational training.
– Documents 23, 45, 70

Voluntary Fund for the United Nations Decade for Women.
– Documents 56, 59, 70, 72-73, 80

W

Wages.
– Documents 23, 102
See also: Equal pay. Labour law.

War crimes.
– Document 134
See also: Genocide. Human rights in armed conflicts. Human rights violations. Rape.

War victims.
– Document 115
See also: Displaced persons. Human rights in armed conflicts.

Western Asia—Women's status.
– Document 93

Western Sahara—Women's status.
– Document 70

WHO.
See: World Health Organization.

Women in agriculture.
– Documents 23, 45, 52, 70, 84, 86, 93, 126

Women in development.
– Documents 23, 30, 32, 37, 39, 41, 45-49, 51-53, 55, 58, 62, 70-72, 74, 76-77, 79, 81-82, 84-93, 95-96, 98-100, 102-105, 108-109, 116-117, 119-120, 125, 127, 131
See also: Popular participation.

Women in politics.
– Documents 2, 19, 21, 26-27, 45, 49, 55, 61, 84, 119
See also: Political participation.

Women managers.
– Documents 84, 101, 103, 105, 108, 116

Women migrant workers.
– Documents 70, 84, 103, 105, 108, 112, 115-116, 133
See also: Migrant workers' families.

Women prisoners.
– Document 115

Women refugees.
– Documents 67, 70, 84, 100, 103, 105, 108, 115-116
See also: Child refugees.

Women workers.
– Documents 13-15, 23, 84, 86, 93, 100, 102,105, 108-109, 116, 119, 125, 127
See also: Maternity leave.

Women's employment.
– Documents 11, 23-24, 38-40, 45, 62, 70, 93, 105, 108-109, 113, 116-117, 120, 125, 127
See also: Equal opportunity. Equal pay. Maternity leave.

Women's health.
– Documents 62, 102, 119, 127

Women's organizations.
– Documents 8, 89, 93, 96, 99

Women's rights.
– Documents 1-2, 7-8, 11-15, 17, 19, 21, 25-26, 28, 35, 37, 41-42, 45, 50, 69, 106-108, 110, 115-116, 122, 124, 127, 133
See also: Civil and political rights. Economic, social and cultural rights. Sex discrimination.

Workers' rights.
– Document 133
See also: Labour law. Occupational health.

Working conditions.
– Documents 20, 24, 128

Working groups.
– Documents 94, 103, 108, 116
See also: Groups of experts.

World Conference of the International Women's Year (1975 : Mexico City).
– Documents 45-47, 49, 59, 76

World Conference of the International Women's Year (1975 : Mexico City). Consultative Committee—Members.
– Document 43

World Conference of the United Nations Decade for Women (1980 : Copenhagen).
– Documents 49, 60-62, 65, 71-72

World Conference of the United Nations Decade for Women (1980 : Copenhagen)—Agenda.
– Documents 63, 66-67, 70

World Conference of the United Nations Decade for Women (1980 : Copenhagen)—Financing.
– Documents 63, 68

World Conference of the United Nations Decade for Women (1980 : Copenhagen)—Participants.
– Documents 63, 68

World Conference of the United Nations Decade for Women (1980 : Copenhagen)—Work organization.
– Documents 63-64

World Conference on Human Rights (1993 : Vienna).
– Documents 105-106, 108, 116, 131

World Conference on Women : Action for Equality, Development and Peace (1995 : Beijing).
– Documents 95, 97, 99-100, 103, 105, 108, 110, 116, 122, 127-129, 131, 135

World Conference to Review and Appraise the Achievements of the United Nations Decade for Women : Equality, Development and Peace (1985 : Nairobi).
– Documents 70-72, 74, 77, 82, 85, 93

World Conference to Review and Appraise the Achievements of the United Nations Decade for Women : Equality, Development and Peace (1985 : Nairobi)—Agenda.
– Document 84

World Food Summit (1996 : Rome).
– Document 131

World Health Organization.
– Documents 23, 130, 134

World Plan of Action for the Implementation of the Objectives of the International Women's Year (1975).
– Documents 45-46, 49, 58-59, 62, 71

World Summit for Social Development (1995 : Copenhagen).
– Documents 108, 116, 122, 131

World Survey on the Role of Women in Development.
– Documents 74, 89, 91-92, 95, 99-100, 103, 105, 108-109, 116

World Trade Organization.
– Document 135

Written communications.
– Documents 8, 10, 121
See also: Human rights violations.

Y

Young women.
– Documents 70, 130
See also: Girls.

Yugoslavia.
See: Former Yugoslavia situation.

VI Index

[The numbers following the entries refer to paragraph numbers in the Introduction.]

Gender equality, 1, 15, 190,
    196-199, 206, 244, 250-261,
    263-267, 274, 280, 288-290,
    293-294, 296, 299
Gender-based violence, 225-233
Genocide, 238
    Convention on (1948), 238
Girls, 70, 79, 84, 87-89, 91, 237,
    252, 264, 270, 276, 282.
    See also Children
Global Tribunal on Violations
    of Women's Rights
    (1993 : Vienna), 246
Grass-roots organizations,
    147-148.
    See also Non-governmental
    organizations
Guidelines on Prevention of and
    Response to Sexual Violence
    against Refugees (1995), 239
Guidelines on the Protection of
    Refugee Women (1991), 239

H

Health, 15, 84, 90, 107, 122, 139,
    141, 146, 174, 190, 194, 197,
    202, 244, 252, 264-265, 268,
    272, 280.
    See also World Health
    Organization
    reproductive health, 263, 268
Human rights, 2, 5-6, 8, 12, 15,
    19, 24, 31, 36, 38-39, 43-44,
    55-58, 75, 85, 91, 101, 103,
    115-120, 145, 150, 164-165,
    168, 171, 198, 213-214,
    221-222, 226-227, 231-258,
    245-249, 259, 264-265, 273,
    282, 296, 299, 302.
    See also UN. Commission on
    Human Rights
Human rights violations, 50, 88, 188,
    221, 231-240, 246, 248-249

I

Illiteracy, 11, 61, 70, 107, 122,
    146, 209.
    See also Education
ILO.
    See International Labour
    Organization
Indigenous women, 192
Infant mortality, 146
Inheritance, 279
INSTRAW.
    See International Research
    and Training Institute for the
    Advancement of Women
Inter-Agency Task Force on the
    Empowerment and
    Advancement of Women, 286
Inter-American Commission of
    Women, 8, 26
International Bill of Human
    Rights, 55
International Conference for the
    Protection of War Victims
    (1993 : Geneva), 232
International Conference on
    Human Rights (1968 :
    Tehran), 118-120
International Conference on
    Population and Development
    (1994 : Cairo), 15, 195,
    250-253, 263
International Convention on the
    Elimination of All Forms of
    Racial Discrimination (1965),
    116
International Covenant on Civil
    and Political Rights (1966),
    50, 58, 116
International Covenant on
    Economic, Social and Cultural
    Rights (1966), 58, 116
International Development
    Strategy for the Second United
    Nations Development Decade
    (1970), 106
International Development
    Strategy for the Third United
    Nations Development Decade
    (1980), 184
International Labour Organization,
    8, 42, 51, 68-69
International Research and Training
    Institute for the Advancement
    of Women, 153-154
International Women's Day
    (8 March), 131, 198, 240
International Women's Year (1975),
    10, 90, 98, 125-130, 138
International Women's Year Tribune
    (1975 : Mexico City), 133-134
International Year for Human
    Rights (1968), 115-116

J

Job creation, 122, 254

L

Land-mines, 278
Latin America and the Caribbean,
    209-210
League of Nations, 26-27, 29-30
Life expectancy, 210
Literacy.
    See Illiteracy

M

Male child preference, 252
Malnutrition, 11, 122, 146.
    See also Nutrition
Marriage.
    See also Divorce
    age, 79-82
    consent, 77-83, 270
    Convention on (1962), 81-83
    dowry, 85, 88
    Recommendation on (1965),
    81-83
Married women, 61, 71-76
Mass media, 140, 275
Maternal mortality, 272
Maternity protection, 107, 220
Migrant women, 139, 182, 192,
    226, 234-235
Migration, 11, 122, 149, 178
Military expenditures, 277
Minority women, 192
Montevideo Convention on the
    Nationality of Married
    Women (1933), 26-27
Mortality, 146, 272

N

Nairobi Forward-looking
    Strategies for the
    Advancement of Women

United Nations publications of related interest

The following UN publications may be obtained from the addresses indicated below, or at your local distributor:

An Agenda for Peace
Second edition, 1995
By Boutros Boutros-Ghali,
Secretary-General of the United Nations
E.95.I.15   92-1-100555-8   155 pp. $7.50

An Agenda for Development
By Boutros Boutros-Ghali,
Secretary-General of the United Nations
E.95.I.16   92-1-100556-6   132 pp. $7.50

Confronting New Challenges, 1995
Annual Report on the Work of the Organization
By Boutros Boutros-Ghali,
Secretary-General of the United Nations
E.95.I.47   92-1-100595-7   380 pp. $7.50

World's Women 1995: Trends and Statistics
Second edition
E.95.XVII.2   92-1-161372-8 $15.95

Women: Challenges to the Year 2000
E.91.I.21   92-1-100458-6 $12.95

Basic Facts About the United Nations
E.95.I.31   92-1-100570-1   341 pp. $7.50

World Economic and Social Survey 1995
E.95.II.C.1   92-1-109130-6   245 pp. $55.00

Yearbook of the United Nations, Vol. 47
E.94.I.1   0-7923-3077-3   1993   1,428 pp. $150.00

Yearbook of the United Nations, Special Edition,
UN Fiftieth Anniversary, 1945-1995
E.95.I.50   0-7923-3112-5   1995   443 pp. $95.00

The United Nations Blue Books Series

The United Nations and Apartheid, 1948-1994
E.95.I.7   92-1-100546-9   565 pp. $29.95

The United Nations and Cambodia, 1991-1995
E.95.I.9   92-1-100548-5   352 pp. $29.95

The United Nations and Nuclear Non-Proliferation
E.95.I.17   92-1-100557-4   199 pp. $29.95

The United Nations and El Salvador, 1990-1995
E.95.I.12   92-1-100552-3   611 pp. $29.95

The United Nations and Mozambique, 1992-1995
E.95.I.20   92-1-100559-0   321 pp. $29.95

The United Nations and Human Rights, 1945-1995
E.95.I.21   92-1-100560-4   536 pp. $29.95

The United Nations and Somalia, 1992-1996
E.96.I.8   92-1-100566-3   516 pp. $29.95

The United Nations and the Iraq-Kuwait Conflict, 1990-1996
E.96.I.3   92-1-100596-5   864 pp. $49.95

United Nations Publications
2 United Nations Plaza, Room DC2-853
New York, NY 10017
United States of America
Tel.: (212) 963-8302; 1 (800) 253-9646
Fax: (212) 963-3489

United Nations Publications
Sales Office and Bookshop
CH-1211 Geneva 10
Switzerland
Tel.: 41 (22) 917-26-13;
        41 (22) 917-26-14
Fax: 41 (22) 917-00-27

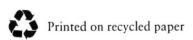 Printed on recycled paper